THE VENETIAN® | THE PALAZZO®

LAS VEGAS

Northern California

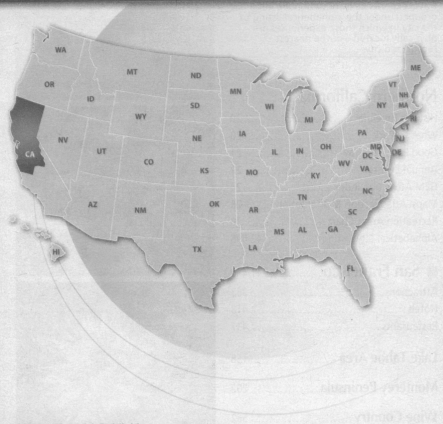

Published by AAA Publishing
1000 AAA Drive, Heathrow, FL 32746-5063
Copyright AAA 2012, All rights reserved

Advertising Rate and Circulation Information: (407) 444-8280

Printed in the USA by Quad/Graphics

This book is printed on paper certified by third-party standards for sustainably managed forestry and production.

Printed on recyclable paper.
Please recycle whenever possible.

Stock #4671

CONTENTS

Attractions, hotels, restaurants and other travel experience information are all grouped under the alphabetical listing of the city in which those experiences are physically located—or the nearest recognized city.

Northern California

Featured Information

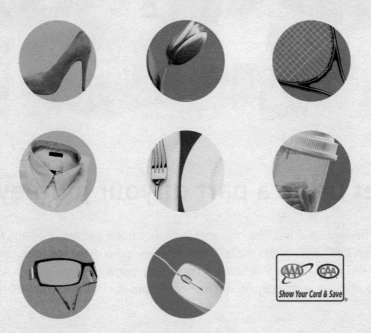

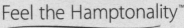

Highlights

Enjoy the trimmer, more colorful, reorganized TourBook® format introduced to make the series richer and easier to use.

Plus, find even more of the visuals, expert recommendations and special extras you value most for reliable travel planning and decision making.

Colorful visuals
- More attraction photos
- *New!* Destination area maps for seven national parks

Travel recommendations
- More *Must Do: AAA Editor's Picks* and *1-Day Itineraries*
- *New!* *Top Picks for Kids* for 19 destination cities

Special extras
- Mass transit information for six metropolitan areas
- *New!* Electric vehicle charging station locations

See for yourself. Travel better with AAA TourBook® guides.

A to Z City Listings

Cities and places are listed alphabetically within each state or province. Attractions, hotels and restaurants are listed once — under the city in which they are physically located.

Cities that are considered part of a larger destination city or area have an expanded city header. The header identifies the larger region and cross-references pages that contain shared trip planning resources:

- Destination map – outline map of the cities that comprise a destination city or area
- Attraction spotting map – regional street map marked with attraction locations
- Hotel/restaurant spotting map and index – regional street map numbered with hotel and restaurant locations identified in an accompanying index

Cities that are not considered part of a larger destination city or area but have a significant number of listings may have these resources within the individual city section:

- Attraction spotting map
- Hotel/restaurant spotting map and index

About Listed Establishments

AAA/CAA Approved attractions, hotels and restaurants are listed on the basis of merit alone after careful evaluation and approval by full-time, professionally trained AAA/CAA inspectors. An establishment's decision to advertise in the TourBook guide has no bearing on its evaluation or rating; nor does inclusion of advertising imply AAA endorsement of products and services.

Information in this guide was believed accurate at the time of publication. However, since changes inevitably occur between annual editions, please contact your AAA travel professional or visit AAA.com to confirm prices and schedules.

Location Abbreviations

Directions are from the center of town unless otherwise specified, using these highway abbreviations:

Bus. Rte.=business route
CR=county road
FM=farm to market

FR=forest road
Hwy.=Canadian highway
I=interstate highway
LR=legislative route
R.R.=rural route
SR/PR=state or provincial route
US=federal highway

Atlas Section

The Atlas Section provides navigable road maps from the AAA Road Atlas series. The overview map displays the entire coverage area. Corresponding, numbered detail maps offer a closer view for route planning and navigation.

Mobile Tags

Look for Microsoft Tags or QR codes throughout the TourBook guide and scan them with your smartphone to access special online offers, menus, videos and more.

To scan Microsoft Tags or QR codes:

- Download AAA's recommended scanning app to your smartphone at http://gettag.mobi.
- Start scanning Tags or QR codes.
- Link to featured content.

Some advertisers may use bar codes other than Microsoft Tags or QR codes. In those cases, please note any accompanying text that indicates where to download the required reader.

Attraction Listings

 GEM SAVE **ATTRACTION NAME,** 3 mi. n. off SR 20A (Main Ave.), consists of 250 acres with Olmsted-designed gardens, a 205-foot marble and coquina bell tower and a Mediterranean-style mansion. One of the state's oldest attractions, the tower and gardens were dedicated to the American people in 1929 by President Calvin Coolidge on behalf of their founder, a Dutch immigrant.

Other features include daily concerts from the 60-bell carillon, a nature observatory and Nature Preserve Trail. The visitor center presents art exhibits, an orientation film and exhibits about the family legacy, the carillon and endangered plants and animals found on the property.

Hours: Gardens daily 8-6. Last admission 1 hour before closing. Visitor center daily 9-5. Estate tours are given at noon and 2. Carillon concerts are given at 1 and 3. Phone ahead to confirm schedule. **Cost:** $10; $3 (ages 5-12). Gardens and estate $16; $8 (ages 5-12). **Phone:** (555) 555-5555.
🔌 🍴 🎋 🚇 Dupont Circle, 13

AAA/CAA inspectors may designate an attraction of exceptional interest and quality as a AAA GEM — a *Great Experience for Members®.* See GEM Attraction Index (listed on CONTENTS page) for complete list of locations.

Adventure Travel

Activities such as air tours, hiking, skiing and white-water rafting are listed to provide member information and do not imply AAA/CAA endorsement. For your safety, be aware of inherent risks and adhere to all safety instructions.

Cost

Prices are quoted without sales tax in the local currency (U.S. or Canadian dollars). Children under the lowest age specified are admitted free when accompanied by an adult. Most establishments accept credit cards, but a small number require cash, so please call ahead to verify.

Icons

SAVE Show Your Card & Save® member discount

🔌 Electric vehicle charging station on premises. Station locations are provided by Department of Energy.

🅐 Camping facilities

🍴 Food on premises

🎾 Recreational activities

🐾 Pets on leash allowed

🎋 Picnicking allowed

In select cities only:

🚇 Mass transit station within 1 mile. Icon is followed by station name and AAA/CAA designated station number within listing.

Information-Only Attraction Listings

Bulleted listings, which include the following categories, are listed for informational purposes as a service to members:

- **Gambling establishments** (even if located in a AAA/CAA Approved hotel)
- **Guided food tours**
- **Participatory recreational activities** (those requiring physical exertion or special skills)
- **Wineries that offer tours and tastings**

Hotel and Restaurant Listings

1 Diamond Rating – AAA/CAA Approved hotels and restaurants are assigned a rating of one to five Diamonds. Red Diamonds distinguish establishments that participate in the AAA/CAA logo licensing program. For details, see p. 11 or AAA.com/Diamonds.

fyi indicates hotels and restaurants that are not AAA/CAA Approved and Diamond Rated but are listed to provide additional choices for members:

- **Hotels** may be unrated if they are: too new to rate, under construction, under major renovation, not evaluated, do not meet all AAA requirements. Hotels that do not meet all AAA requirements may be included if they offer member value or are the only option; details are noted in the listing.

- **Restaurants** may be unrated if they have not yet been evaluated by AAA.

2 Classification or Cuisine Type – Noted after the Diamond Rating.

- **Hotel Classifications** indicate the style of operation, overall concept and service level. Subclassifications may also be added. (See p. 12 list.)

- **Restaurant Cuisine Types** identify the food concept from more than 100 categories. If applicable, a classification may also be added. (See p. 13 list.)

3 Dollar Amounts – Quoted without sales tax in the local currency (U.S. or Canadian dollars), rounded up to the nearest dollar. Most establishments accept credit cards, but a small number require cash, so please call ahead to verify.

- **Hotel Rates** indicate the publicly available two-person rate or rate range for a standard room, applicable all year.

- **Restaurant Prices** represent the minimum and maximum entrée cost per person. Exceptions may include one-of-a-kind or special market priced items.

4 Spotting Symbol – Ovals containing numbers correspond with numbered location markings on hotel and restaurant spotting maps.

5 Parking – Unless otherwise noted, parking is free, on-site self parking.

6 Hotel Value Nationwide – Blue boxes highlight member benefits available at all AAA/CAA Approved locations across a hotel chain. (See Just For Members section for details.)

7 Hotel Unit Limited Availability – Unit types, amenities and room features preceded by "some" are available on a limited basis, potentially as few as one.

8 Hotel Terms – Cancellation and minimum stay policies are listed. Unless otherwise noted, most properties offer a full deposit refund with cancellations received at least 48 hours before standard check-in. Properties that require advance payment may not refund the difference for early departures. "Resort fee" indicates a charge may apply above and beyond the quoted room rate.

9 Hotel Check-in/Check-out – Unless otherwise noted, check-in is after 3 p.m. and check-out is before 10 a.m.

10 Restaurant Dress Code – Unless otherwise noted, dress is casual or dressy casual.

11 Restaurant Menu – Where indicated, menus may be viewed in a secure online environment at AAA.com or, if a mobile tag is provided, via the restaurant's website.

12 Hotel Icons – May be preceded by CALL, FEE and/or SOME UNITS.

Member Information:

SAVE Rate guarantee: discounted standard room rate or lowest public rate available at time of booking for dates of stay.

ECO Eco-certified by government or private organization. Visit AAA.com/eco for details.

Electric vehicle charging station on premises. Station locations are provided by Department of Energy.

X Smoke-free premises

In select cities only:

Mass transit station within 1 mile. Icon is followed by station name and AAA/CAA designated station number within listing.

Services:

Wireless Internet service on premises

Airport transportation

Pets allowed (Call property for restrictions and fees.)

HOTEL LISTING

RESTAURANT LISTING

[↑↓] Restaurant on premises

[↑↓→] Restaurant off premises

Room service for 2 or more meals

Full bar

Child care

BIZ Business services

Accessible features (Call property for available services and amenities.)

Activities:

Full-service casino

Pool

Health club on premises

Health club off premises

In-Room Amenities:

Pay movies

Refrigerator

Microwave

Coffee maker

No air conditioning

No TV

No telephones

13 **Restaurant Icons**

SAVE Show Your Card & Save® member discount

ECO Eco-certified by government or private organization. Visit AAA.com/eco for details.

Electric vehicle charging station on premises. Station locations are provided by Department of Energy.

No air conditioning

Accessible features (Call property for available services and amenities.)

Designated smoking section

[B] Breakfast

[L] Lunch

[D] Dinner

[24] Open 24 hours

[LATE] Open after 11 p.m.

In select cities only:

Mass transit station within 1 mile. Icon is followed by station name and AAA/CAA designated station number within listing.

Just For Members

Understanding the Diamond Ratings

Hotel and restaurant evaluations are unscheduled to ensure our professionally trained inspectors encounter the same experience members do.

- When an establishment is Diamond Rated, it means members can expect a good fit with their needs. The inspector assigns a rating that indicates the type of experience to expect.

- While establishments at high levels must offer increasingly complex personalized services, establishments at every level are subject to the same basic requirements for cleanliness, comfort and hospitality. Learn more at AAA.com/Diamonds.

Hotels

Budget-oriented, offering basic comfort and hospitality.

Affordable, with modestly enhanced facilities, décor and amenities.

Distinguished, multi-faceted with enhanced physical attributes, amenities and guest comforts.

Refined, stylish with upscale physical attributes, extensive amenities and high degree of hospitality, service and attention to detail.

Ultimate luxury, sophistication and comfort with extraordinary physical attributes, meticulous personalized service, extensive amenities and impeccable standards of excellence.

Restaurants

Simple, familiar specialty food at an economical price. Often self-service, basic surroundings.

Familiar, family-oriented experience. Home-style foods and family favorites, often cooked to order, modestly enhanced and reasonably priced. Relaxed service, casual surroundings.

Fine dining, often adult-oriented. Latest cooking trends and/or traditional cuisine, expanded beverage offerings. Professional service staff and comfortable, well-coordinated ambience.

Distinctive fine-dining, typically expensive. Highly creative chefs, imaginative presentations and fresh, top-quality ingredients. Proficient service staff, upscale surroundings. Wine steward may offer menu-specific knowledge.

Luxurious and consistently world-class. Highly acclaimed chefs, artistic and imaginative menu selections using the finest ingredients. Maitre d' and unobtrusive, expert service staff.

What's the difference?

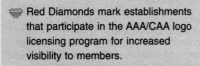 Red Diamonds mark establishments that participate in the AAA/CAA logo licensing program for increased visibility to members.

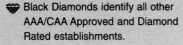 Black Diamonds identify all other AAA/CAA Approved and Diamond Rated establishments.

Hotel Classifications

Quality and comfort are usually consistent across each Diamond Rating level, but décor, facilities and service levels vary by classification.

1884 Paxton House Inn
Thomasville, GA

Bed & Breakfast – Typically small-scale, emphasizing personal touches. Individually decorated units may not include televisions, telephones or private bathrooms. Usually a common room and continental or full, hot breakfast.

Barkwells
Mills River, NC

Cabin – Vacation-oriented, typically small-scale, free-standing units with simple construction and basic décor. Often in wooded, rural or waterfront location. Cleaning supplies, utensils and bath linens provided. Check-in may be off site.

Camelot by the Sea
Myrtle Beach, SC

Condominium – Vacation-oriented, commonly for extended stays. Routinely rented through a management company. Generally one or more bedrooms, living room, full kitchen and eating area. Studio units combine sleeping and living areas. Cleaning supplies, utensils and linens provided. Check-in may be off site.

The Dunes on the Waterfront
Ogunquit, ME

Cottage – Vacation-oriented, typically small-scale, freestanding units with homey design and décor. Often in wooded, rural or waterfront location. Cleaning supplies, utensils and linens provided. Check-in may be off site.

The Lodge at Moosehead
Lake, Greenville, ME

Country Inn – Similar to bed and breakfasts but larger scale with spacious public areas and dining facility that serves, at a minimum, breakfast and dinner.

The Grand America Hotel
Salt Lake City, UT

Hotel – Commonly multistory with interior room entrances. Unit styles vary. Public areas determined by overall theme, location and service level, but may include restaurant, shops, fitness center, spa, business center and meeting rooms.

Best Western Plus Sea Island
Inn, Beaufort, SC

Motel – Commonly one- or two-story with exterior room entrances and drive-up parking. Typically one bedroom with bathroom. Limited public areas and facilities.

Lost Valley Ranch
Deckers, CO

Ranch – Typically a working ranch with rustic, Western theme, equestrian activities and various unit styles.

Indian Creek-Alexander
Holiday Homes
Kissimmee, FL

Vacation Rental House – Commonly for extended stays. Typically large scale, freestanding and of varying design. Routinely rented through a management company. Often two or more bedrooms, living room, full kitchen, dining room and multiple bathrooms. Cleaning supplies, utensils and linens supplied. Check-in may be off site.

Hotel Subclassifications

These additional descriptives may be added to the classification for more information:

- **Boutique** – Often thematic and informal, highly personalized experience. May have fashionable, luxurious or quirky style.
- **Casino** – (Identified by listing icon) Extensive gambling facilities such as blackjack, craps, keno and slot machines.
- **Classic** – Landmark property, older than 50 years, renowned style and ambience.
- **Contemporary** – Design and theme reflective of current mainstream tastes and style.
- **Extended Stay** – Predominantly long-term units with full-service kitchens.
- **Historic** – Typically 75 years or older with historic architecture, design, furnishings, public record or acclaim and at least one of the following: maintains integrity of the historical nature, listed on the National Register of Historic Places, designated a National Historic Landmark or located in a National Register Historic District.
- **Resort** – Recreation-oriented, geared to a specific destination experience. Typically offer travel packages, meal plans, themed entertainment and social and recreational programs. Extensive recreational facilities may include spa treatments, golf, tennis,

skiing, fishing or water sports. Larger resorts may offer a variety of unit types.

- **Retro** – Contemporary design and theme that reinterpret styles of a bygone era.
- **Vacation Rental** – Typically a house, condo, cottage or cabin offering space, value and conveniences such as full kitchens and washers/dryers. Located in a resort or popular destination area near major points of interest. May require reservations and off-site check-in. Limited housekeeping services.
- **Vintage** – Design and theme reflective of a bygone era.

Restaurant Classifications

If applicable, in addition to the cuisine type noted under the Diamond Rating, restaurant listings may also include one or both classifications:

- **Classic** – Renowned and landmark operation in business for 25 plus years; unique style and ambience.
- **Historic** – Meets one of the following: Listed on National Register of Historic Places, designated a National Historic Landmark or located in a National Register Historic District.

Service Animals

Under the Americans with Disabilities Act (ADA), U.S. businesses that serve the public must allow people with disabilities to bring their service animals into all areas of the facility where customers are normally allowed to go.

Businesses may ask if an animal is a service animal and what tasks the animal has been trained to perform. Businesses may not ask about the person's disability, require special identification for the animal or request removal of the animal from the premises except in limited cases that require alternate assistance. Businesses may not charge extra fees for service animals, including standard pet fees, but may charge for damage caused by service animals if guests are normally charged for damage they cause.

Call the U.S. Department of Justice ADA Information Line: (800) 514-0301 or TTY (800) 514-0383, or visit ada.gov. Regulations may differ in Canada.

AAA/CAA Approved Hotels

For members, AAA/CAA Approved means quality assured.

- Only properties that meet basic requirements for cleanliness, comfort and hospitality pass inspection.
- Approved hotels receive a Diamond Rating that tells members the type of experience to expect.

Guest Safety

Inspectors view a sampling of rooms during evaluations and, therefore, AAA/CAA cannot guarantee the presence of working locks and operational fire safety equipment in every guest unit.

Member Rates

AAA/CAA members can generally expect to pay no more than the maximum TourBook listed rate for a standard room. Member discounts apply to rates quoted within the rate range and are applicable at the time of booking. Listed rates are usually based on last standard room availability. Within the range, rates may vary by season and room type. Obtain current AAA/CAA member rates and make reservations at AAA.com.

Exceptions

- Rates for properties operating as concessionaires for the U.S. National Park Service are not guaranteed due to governing regulations.
- Special advertised rates and short-term promotional rates below the rate range are not subject to additional member discounts.
- During special events, hotels may temporarily increase room rates, not recognize discounts or modify pricing policies. Special events may include Mardi Gras, the Kentucky Derby (including pre-Derby events), college football games, holidays, holiday periods and state fairs. Although some special events are listed in the TourBook guides and on AAA.com, it's always wise to check in advance with AAA travel professionals for specific dates.

If you are charged more than the maximum TourBook listed rate, question the additional charge. If an exception is not in effect and management refuses to adhere to the published rate, pay for the room and contact AAA/CAA. The amount paid above the stated maximum will be refunded if our investigation indicates an unjustified charge.

Reservations and Cancellations

When making your reservation, identify yourself as a AAA/CAA member and request written confirmation of your room type, rate, dates of stay, and cancellation and refund policies. At registration, show your membership card.

To cancel, contact the hotel or your AAA/CAA club office, depending on how you booked your reservation. Request a cancellation number or proof of cancellation.

If your room is not as specified and you have written confirmation of your reservation for a specific room type, you should be given the option of choosing a different room or receiving a refund. If management refuses to issue a refund, contact AAA/CAA.

Contacting AAA/CAA About Approved Properties

If your visit to a AAA/CAA Approved attraction, hotel or restaurant doesn't meet your expectations, please tell us about it — *during your visit or within 30 days*. Be sure to save your receipts and other documentation for reference.

Use the easy online form at AAA.com/TourBookComments to send us the details.

Alternatively, you can email your comments to: memberrelations@national.aaa.com or submit them via postal mail to: AAA Member Comments, 1000 AAA Dr., Box 61, Heathrow, FL 32746.

AAA/CAA Preferred Hotels

All AAA/CAA Approved hotels are committed to providing quality, value and member service. In addition, those designated as AAA/CAA Preferred Hotels also offer these extra values at Approved locations nationwide. Valid AAA/CAA membership required.

- **Best AAA/CAA member rates for your dates of stay.**
- **Seasonal promotions and special member offers.** Visit AAA.com to view current offers.
- **Member benefit.** Look for the blue boxes in the TourBook listings to find values offered at AAA/CAA Approved locations nationwide. Chains and offers valid at time of publication may change without notice.

- **Total satisfaction guarantee.** If you book your stay with AAA/CAA Travel and your stay fails to meet your expectations, you can apply for a full refund. Bring the complaint to the hotel's attention during the stay and request resolution; if the complaint is not resolved by the hotel, ask your AAA/CAA travel agent to request resolution through the AAA/CAA Assured Stay program.

Preferred Hotels

Total Satisfaction Guarantee

Best Western, Best Western Plus and Best Western Premier

Conrad Hotels & Resorts, DoubleTree by Hilton, Embassy Suites, Hampton Inns & Suites, Hilton Hotels & Resorts, Hilton Garden Inns, Hilton Grand Vacations, Home2 Suites, Homewood Suites, and Waldorf Astoria

ANdAZ, Grand Hyatt, Hyatt Hotels & Resorts, Hyatt House, Hyatt Place, Hyatt Regency and Park Hyatt

Autograph Collection, Courtyard, EDITION, Fairfield Inn & Suites, JW Marriott, Marriott Hotels & Resorts, Renaissance Hotels, Residence Inn, The Ritz-Carlton, SpringHill Suites and TownePlace Suites

Aloft, Element, Four Points, Le Meridien, Sheraton, St. Regis Hotels & Resorts, The Luxury Collection, Westin and W Hotels

Show Your Card & Save® Member Discounts

Visit AAA.com/Discounts to find local Show Your Card & Save discounts. Your AAA/CAA club may offer even greater discounts on theme park tickets. Amtrak, Gray Line and theme park discounts may be used for up to six tickets; restaurant savings may be used for up to six patrons. Other restrictions may apply. All offers subject to change. For complete restrictions visit your AAA office or AAA.com/restrictions.

ATTRACTIONS

SeaWorld, Busch Gardens, Sesame Place

- Save on admission at the gate, participating AAA/CAA offices or AAA.com/SeaWorld.
- Save 10% on up-close dining; visit Guest Relations for details.

Six Flags

- Save on admission at the gate, participating AAA/CAA offices or AAA.com/SixFlags.
- Save 10% on merchandise of $15 or more at in-park stores.

Universal Orlando Resort and Universal Studios Hollywood

- Save on admission at the gate, participating AAA/CAA offices or AAA.com/Universal.
- Save at select food and merchandise venues in-park and at Universal CityWalk®.

The Entertainment Capital of L.A.

DINING & SHOPPING

Hard Rock Cafe

- Save 10% on food, nonalcoholic beverages and merchandise at all U.S., Canadian and select international locations.

Landry's Seafood House, The Crab House, Chart House, Oceanaire, Saltgrass Steak House, Muer Seafood Restaurants and Aquarium Restaurants

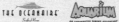

- Save 10% on food and nonalcoholic beverages at all of the above restaurants.
- Save 10% on merchandise at Aquarium and Downtown Aquarium restaurants.
- Location information: AAA.com/Discounts.

Tanger Outlet Centers

- Save up to 20% on total purchase at select merchants with FREE coupon booklet available with registration at AAA/CAA customer service desk.
- Location information: tangeroutlet.com.

TRANSPORTATION & TOURS

Amtrak

- Save 10% on rail fare booked at least 3 days in advance of travel date at AAA.com/Amtrak.

Gray Line

- Save 10% on sightseeing tours of 1 day or less worldwide at AAA.com/GrayLine.

Hertz

- Save on daily, weekend, weekly and monthly rentals at AAA.com/hertz or 1-800-654-3080.

Rolling vineyards of Napa Valley

Northern California

The Golden State's allure must be powerful: Millions of people can't be wrong. Abundant resources and a stunning landscape help explain the attraction. Northern California, from the regal redwoods near the Oregon border to Monterey Peninsula's jagged coastline, is immensely blessed.

Most Americans who have never been west of the Rockies have heard of Yosemite Valley, Big Sur, Lake Tahoe and Wine Country. Thanks to movies and television, California and all its associations—surfing, environmentalists chaining themselves to condemned trees, pollution, earthquakes—have all entered the popular imagination.

When a fad sweeps the country, odds are that it started in California. The sense of style here is often imitated, the cuisine savored around the world.

Besides physical appeal, perhaps nothing epitomizes the "Left Coast" more than the people and their almost mythical lifestyle.

Golden Gate Bridge, San Francisco

Populated by entrepreneurs, visionaries, counterculture radicals, trendsetters and a few eccentrics, the state is fertile ground for innovations and technological breakthroughs. No wonder Americans looking to the future often face west.

The Golden State

Picture a snow-clad mountainside. A man and a woman in ski gear swoosh down an alpine slope. Cut to a sun-washed beach hours later. The same twosome strolls along the shore, water lapping at their feet. Then, at a swank urban bistro that evening the couple sit across from each other savoring a sumptuous dinner.

Although unusually energetic, the duo described above is realistic. It's the setting that seems unreal. Skiing in the mountains within hours of a walk on a picture-postcard beach? Both within reach of a major city? Does such a place really exist?

The place is real. As you've probably guessed, this could only be California.

From that first cry of "Eureka!" at Sutter's Mill to the chaotic tidal wave of the ensuing gold rush and the tragedy of the San Francisco earthquake decades later, drama has been one of the state's most notable traits.

The California landscape itself is dramatic. Breathtaking only begins to describe Big

Sur's rocky, sea-splashed cliffs, the Sierra Nevada's glacier-sculpted peaks or vineyards flourishing in dappled sunlight.

Vistas impossible to truly capture on film abound in Yosemite National Park. It's difficult to comprehend the colossal escarpments and the height of its waterfalls. And what camera could do justice to the grandeur of Half Dome or El Capitan?

Zoom in on the mountains, valleys and shores and you'll find a fascinating array of plants and animals. Off the coast, migrating whales are the stars while sea lions and playful sea otters make their appearances closer to shore. California's signature flora includes giant redwoods and giant sequoias.

The Original Settlers

Even before the flood of gold rush prospectors, Northern California was home to a cast of characters that included Franciscan missionaries, Spanish ranchers and the Native Americans who had lived here for thousands of years. Then the possibility of instant riches created towns almost overnight, and folks have never stopped being drawn to the spectacle of the place.

The results of their labors take myriad forms: centuries-old Spanish missions that dot the coast; the futuristic glass-and-steel skyscrapers of San Francisco; the lovely beach resort of Carmel-by-the-Sea; and the quaint gold rush towns sprinkled along the western slopes of the Sierra Nevadas.

Recreation

The great outdoors truly is great here. Wetsuited surfers flock to Monterey Bay's chilly waters, especially Santa Cruz's Steamer Lane. And the coastline's inlets and coves are perfect for boating.

San Francisco Bay draws wind surfers, with the Presidio's Crissy Field offering amazing urban views and the chance to sail under the Golden Gate Bridge.

Anglers can rent saltwater fishing gear in many coastal towns; salmon is among the most popular catches. Freshwater fishing and boating are plentiful, too. Lake Tahoe and Shasta Lake draw small fleets of pleasure craft on balmy weekends. In addition to being California's second largest freshwater lake, Clear Lake near Kelseyville is one of the nation's finest bass repositories.

April to October is best for white-water rafting on California's rushing rivers. The Lower Klamath or the South Fork of the American River is ideal for families, as the excitement of maneuvering rapids is interspersed with the calm of peaceful floats. The more daring should try the North Fork of the American or the Tuolumne River. A bonus of rafting trips is the chance to see great blue herons, ospreys, bald eagles, river otters and deer.

If hiking or backpacking are your sports, consider the California Coastal Trail or the Pacific Crest Trail, both stretching from Mexico to Canada. Check out Mount Tamalpais and Mount Diablo state parks and the Golden Gate National Recreation Area near San Francisco. Also, Marin County, on the north end of the Golden Gate Bridge, offers mountain biking trails.

Hikers at Lake Tahoe should not miss the views from the Tahoe Rim Trail. Then there's Yosemite, which deserves its reputation for amazing scenery. Don't limit yourself to the valley floor; the park's high country, accessible in summer, offers spectacular vistas.

Many parks and recreation areas are great for camping, too. In fact, Tahoe National Forest claims to have 1,400 camping sites.

California boasts some of the nation's finest golfing. Monterey Peninsula courses offer a choice of windswept ocean views or forested valleys; those near Pebble Beach are probably the best known.

When temperatures drop, Californians head outdoors for great skiing and snowboarding. The Lake Tahoe area alone is sprinkled with more than a dozen ski resorts.

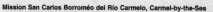

Mission San Carlos Borroméo del Río Carmelo, Carmel-by-the-Sea

Historic Timeline

1769	Fathers Junípero Serra and Fermín Lasuén begin building a chain of 21 missions extending from San Diego to Sonoma.
1848	James Marshall discovers gold at Sutter's Mill; the following year fortune seekers rush into California.
1850	California becomes the 31st state.
1890	Yosemite National Park is established.
1906	An earthquake and resulting fires destroy most of San Francisco.
1945	Representatives of 51 countries meet in San Francisco to sign the charter forming the United Nations.
1962	California becomes the most populous state in the nation.
1989	A 7.1 magnitude earthquake centered 51 miles south of San Francisco causes $6 billion in property damage.
1992	An acquittal verdict in the Rodney King beating trial sparks race riots in Los Angeles.
1994	An earthquake centered 20 miles northwest of Los Angeles leaves 22,000 homeless.
2010	With their state facing a fiscal crisis, voters elect former governor Jerry Brown to another term in office.

What To Pack

Temperature Averages Maximum/Minimum	JANUARY	FEBRUARY	MARCH	APRIL	MAY	JUNE	JULY	AUGUST	SEPTEMBER	OCTOBER	NOVEMBER	DECEMBER
Eureka	55/41	56/42	56/42	57/44	60/48	62/51	63/53	64/53	64/51	61/48	58/44	55/41
Fresno	54/38	61/41	66/45	74/48	83/55	91/61	97/66	95/65	89/60	78/52	63/42	53/37
Mendocino	56/41	57/42	58/42	61/43	62/45	65/48	67/50	67/50	67/49	64/46	59/43	55/40
Mount Shasta	44/26	48/29	52/30	59/33	67/39	76/45	83/49	83/48	76/43	64/37	50/30	44/26
San Francisco	56/43	59/46	61/47	64/48	67/51	70/53	71/55	72/56	73/55	70/52	62/48	56/43
Truckee	40/14	42/17	45/21	52/25	61/31	71/37	79/41	79/41	72/35	62/28	47/21	40/15

From the records of The Weather Channel Interactive, Inc.

Good Facts To Know

ABOUT THE STATE

POPULATION: 37,253,956.
AREA: 158,693 square miles; ranks 3rd.
CAPITAL: Sacramento.
HIGHEST POINT: 14,505 ft., Mount Whitney.
LOWEST POINT: -282 ft., Death Valley.
TIME ZONE(S): Pacific. DST.

GAMBLING

MINIMUM AGE FOR GAMBLING: 18 if alcohol is not available; 21 if alcohol is available.

REGULATIONS

TEEN DRIVING LAWS: Teens who have had a license less than 1 year are not permitted to transport non-family members under 20 unless someone over age 25 is in the front seat. Driving is not permitted 11 p.m.-5 a.m. by licensed teens under 17 (except under special circumstances). The minimum age for an unrestricted license is 17. Phone (800) 777-0133 for more information about California driver's license regulations.

SEAT BELT/CHILD RESTRAINT LAWS: Seat belts are required for the driver and all passengers over 15; passengers ages 8-15 or over 57 inches tall must use an approved child restraint or seat belt. Child restraints are required for children under age 8 or under 57 inches tall and must be in the rear seat if available.

CELLPHONE RESTRICTIONS: All drivers are banned from text messaging and using handheld cellphones. Drivers under 18 are prohibited from all cellphone use.

HELMETS FOR MOTORCYCLISTS: Required.

RADAR DETECTORS: Permitted.

MOVE OVER LAW: Driver is required to slow down and vacate the lane nearest stopped police, fire and rescue vehicles using audible or flashing signals. The law also applies to recovery vehicles, such as tow trucks.

FIREARMS LAWS: Vary by state and/or county. Contact Department of Justice, Firearms Program, P.O. Box 820200, Sacramento, CA 94203-0200; phone (916) 263-4887.

SPECIAL REGULATIONS: The State Department of Food and Agriculture inspects all produce, plant materials and wild animals at the borders to see if they are admissible under current quarantine regulations. For California regulations concerning plants phone (916) 654-0312; for regulations concerning animals phone (916) 654-1447. Dogs older than 4 months must be accompanied by a current rabies vaccination certificate.

HOLIDAYS

HOLIDAYS: Jan. 1 ▪ Martin Luther King Jr. Day, Jan. (3rd Mon.) ▪ Lincoln's Birthday, Feb. 12 ▪ Washington's Birthday/Presidents Day, Feb. (3rd Mon.) ▪ Easter ▪ Memorial Day, May (last Mon.) ▪ July 4 ▪ Labor Day, Sept. (1st Mon.) ▪ Admission Day, Sept. 9 ▪ Columbus Day, Oct. (2nd Mon.) ▪ Veterans Day, Nov. 11 ▪ Thanksgiving, Nov. (4th Thurs.) ▪ Christmas, Dec. 25.

MONEY

TAXES: California's statewide sales tax is 7.25 percent. Additional local taxes of up to 1 percent may be imposed in some counties; more than one tax may be in effect in some locations. A transient occupancy tax may be levied in various counties and cities.

VISITOR INFORMATION

INFORMATION CENTERS: California welcome centers are in Arcata at jct. US 101 and SR 299 ▪ in Anderson off I-5 (Deschutes Road exit) on SR 273 ▪ in Santa Rosa off US 101 (Downtown/Third Street exit) at the end of Fourth Street ▪ in Auburn off I-80 (Foresthill exit) on Lincoln Way ▪ in Truckee at 10065 Donner Pass Rd. ▪ in San Francisco at Pier 39 ▪ in Merced on W. 16th Street ▪ in Pismo Beach on US 101 at Five Cities Drive ▪ in Tulare at 4500 S. Laspina St. ▪ in Barstow off I-15 (Lenwood Road exit) ▪ in Oxnard off US 101 at Town Center Drive ▪ in Yucca Valley on SR 62 ▪ in San Bernardino off I-10 at Hunts Lane ▪ and in Oceanside off I-5 (Coast Highway exit).

ROAD CONDITIONS: Caltrans provides current information about road conditions; phone (800) 427-7623.

FURTHER INFORMATION FOR VISITORS:
California Travel & Tourism Commission
980 9th St., Suite 480
Sacramento, CA 95841
(916) 444-4429
(800) 862-2543

NATIONAL FOREST INFORMATION:
Pacific-Southwest Region
U.S. Forest Service
1323 Club Dr.
Vallejo, CA 94592
(707) 562-8737
(877) 444-6777 (reservations)
TTY (877) 833-6777 (reservations)

FISHING AND HUNTING REGULATIONS:
California Department of Fish and Game
1740 N. Market Blvd.
Sacramento, CA 95834
(916) 928-5805

RECREATION INFORMATION:
California State Park System
Department of Parks and Recreation
P.O. Box 942896
Sacramento, CA 94296-0001
(916) 653-6995
(800) 444-7275 (reservations)
TTY (800) 274-7275 (reservations)

NATIONAL PARKS:
National Park Service
Fort Mason, Bldg. 201
San Francisco, CA 94129
(415) 561-4700
(877) 444-6777 (reservations)
TTY (415) 556-2766

Northern California Annual Events

Please call ahead to confirm event details.

JANUARY

- Sea Lions' Arrival
  San Francisco
  415-705-5500
- Golden Gate Kennel Club
  All-Breed Dog Shows
  San Francisco
  415-819-5773
- New Year's Barrel Bash
  Ferndale
  707-407-6635

FEBRUARY

- AT&T Pebble Beach
  National Pro-Am
  Pebble Beach
  831-649-1533
- Cloverdale Citrus Fair
  Cloverdale
  707-894-3992
- Tulipmania Festival
  San Francisco
  415-705-5500

MARCH

- Dublin's St. Patrick's Day
  Festival / Dublin
  925-556-4500
- SnowFest! of North Lake
  Tahoe and Truckee
  Tahoe City
  916-583-7635
- Contemporary Crafts
  Market / San Francisco
  415-995-4925

APRIL

- Stockton Asparagus
  Festival / Stockton
  209-644-3740
- Northern California Cherry
  Blossom Festival
  San Francisco
  415-922-9300
- Red Bluff Roundup
  Red Bluff
  530-527-5534

MAY

- Calaveras County Fair and
  Jumping Frog Jubilee
  Angels Camp
  209-736-2561
- Sacramento Music Festival
  Sacramento
  916-372-5277
- Stanford Powwow
  Palo Alto
  650-723-4078

JUNE

- The Great Isleton Crawdad
  Festival / Isleton
  916-777-5880
- North Beach Festival
  San Francisco
  415-989-2220
- Valhalla Renaissance Faire
  South Lake Tahoe
  415-897-4555

JULY

- California State Fair
  Sacramento
  877-225-3976
- Gilroy Garlic Festival
  Gilroy
  408-842-1625
- Feast of Lanterns
  Pacific Grove
  831-649-8737

AUGUST

- Rolex Monterey Motorsports
  Reunion / Salinas
  831-648-5111
- Pebble Beach Concours
  d'Elegance / Pebble Beach
  831-659-0663
- Concours d'Elegance
  Wooden Boat Show
  Tahoe City
  530-581-4700

SEPTEMBER

- San Francisco Fringe
  Festival / San Francisco
  415-931-1094
- Valley of the Moon Vintage
  Festival / Sonoma
  707-996-2109
- Gold Rush Days
  Sacramento
  916-264-8142

OCTOBER

- Fleet Week / San Francisco
  650-599-5057
- Sonora Bach Festival
  Sonora
  209-586-5965
- Grand National Rodeo,
  Horse and Livestock Show
  San Francisco
  415-404-4111

NOVEMBER

- Valhalla Holiday Faire
  South Lake Tahoe
  888-632-5859
- Craftsman's Days / Eureka
  707-444-3437
- Harvest Festival Original Art
  and Craft Show
  Sacramento
  800-231-1213

DECEMBER

- Christmas in Coloma
  Coloma
  530-622-3470
- Union Street Holiday
  Festivities / San Francisco
  800-310-6563
- Mendocino Coast
  Candlelight Inn Tours
  Mendocino
  707-964-1228

Julia Pfeiffer Burns State Park, Big Sur

Asian Art Museum of San Francisco

San Francisco Museum of Modern Art

Sequoia National Park

California State Railroad Museum, Sacramento

Index: Great Experience for Members

AAA editor's picks of exceptional note

University of
California Berkeley

Aerospace Museum
of California

Alcatraz Island

Monterey Bay
Aquarium

Golden Gate Park *(See p. 374.)*
Legion of Honor *(See p. 379.)*
Mission San Francisco de Asis *(See p. 379.)*

San Jose (E-9)
Lick Observatory *(See p. 463.)*
Rosicrucian Egyptian Museum *(See p. 464.)*
Winchester Mystery House *(See p. 464.)*

San Juan Bautista (G-3)
Mission San Juan Bautista *(See p. 479.)*
San Juan Bautista State Historic Park *(See p. 479.)*

Santa Clara (E-9)
California's Great America *(See p. 485.)*
Mission Santa Clara de Asis *(See p. 486.)*

Santa Cruz (G-2)
Santa Cruz Beach Boardwalk *(See p. 490.)*

Santa Rosa (B-7)
Safari West *(See p. 502.)*

Sequoia and Kings Canyon National Parks (G-5)
Sequoia and Kings Canyon National Parks *(See p. 514.)*

Shasta (C-2)
Shasta State Historic Park *(See p. 517.)*

Sonoma (B-8)
Sonoma State Historic Park *(See p. 521.)*

Tiburon (C-8)
Angel Island Immigration Station *(See p. 542.)*

Vallejo (C-8)
Six Flags Discovery Kingdom *(See p. 552.)*

Weott (C-1)
Avenue of the Giants *(See p. 556.)*

Yosemite National Park (F-4)
Yosemite National Park *(See p. 578.)*

Atlas
ROAD
2013

Sacramento

Yosemite

Fresno

Monterey

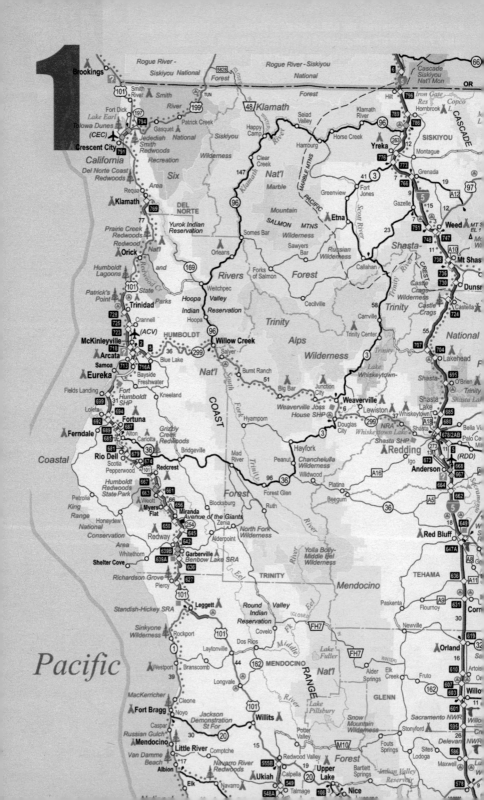

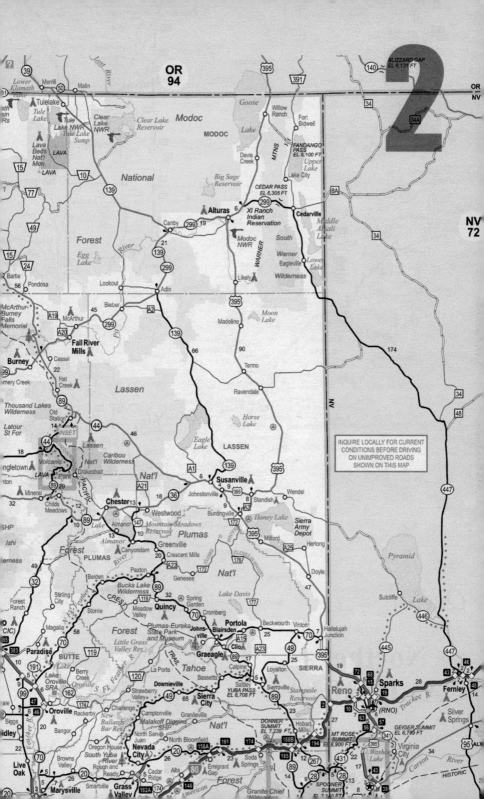

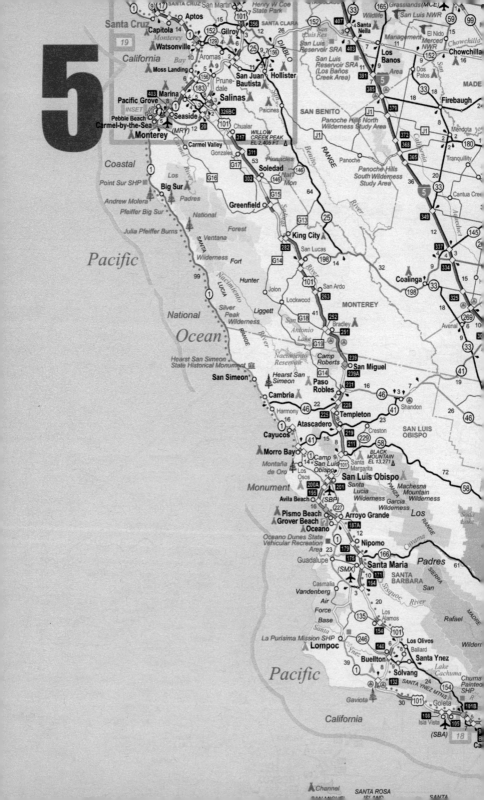

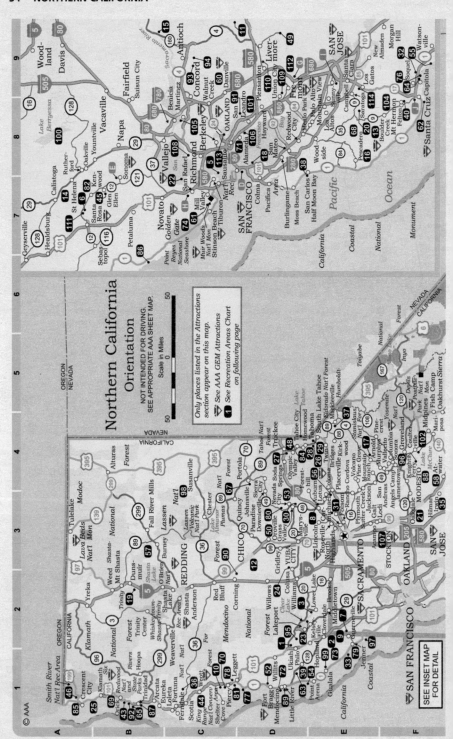

Northern California
Orientation

NOT INTENDED FOR DRIVING.
SEE APPROPRIATE AAA SHEET MAP.

Only places listed in the Attractions section appear on this map.

⬥ See AAA GEM Attractions

1 See Recreation Areas Chart on following page

Scale in Miles
50   0   50

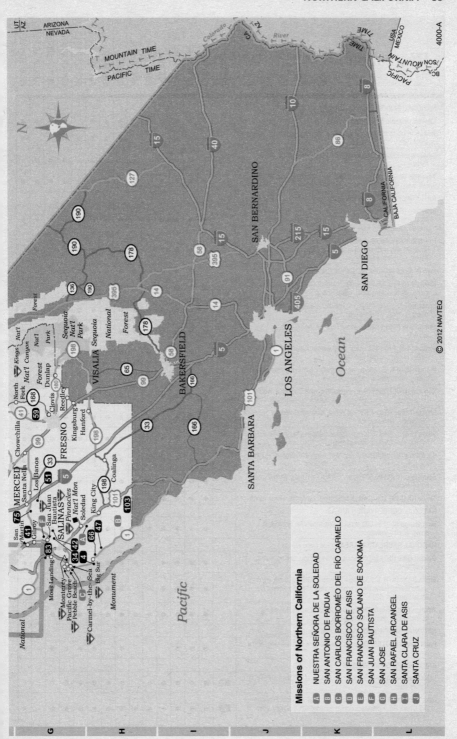

Missions of Northern California

- Ⓐ NUESTRA SEÑORA DE LA SOLEDAD
- Ⓑ SAN ANTONIO DE PADUA
- Ⓒ SAN CARLOS BORROMÉO DEL RÍO CARMELO
- Ⓓ SAN FRANCISCO DE ASIS
- Ⓔ SAN FRANCISCO SOLANO DE SONOMA
- Ⓕ SAN JUAN BAUTISTA
- Ⓖ SAN JOSE
- Ⓗ SAN RAFAEL ARCANGEL
- Ⓘ SANTA CLARA DE ASIS
- Ⓙ SANTA CRUZ

© 2012 NAVTEQ

4000-A

Recreation Areas Chart

The map location numerals in column 2 show an area's location on the preceding map.

	MAP LOCATION	CAMPING	PICNICKING	HIKING TRAILS	BOATING	BOAT RAMP	BOAT RENTAL	FISHING	SWIMMING	PETS ON LEASH	BICYCLE TRAILS	WINTER SPORTS	VISITOR CENTER	LODGE/CABINS	FOOD SERVICE
NATIONAL PARKS *(See place listings.)*															
Lassen Volcanic (C-3) 106,372 acres.		●	●	●				●	●	●		●	●		●
Redwood (B-1) 131,983 acres. Kayaking; horse rental, ranger-led activities.		●	●	●				●	●	●	●	●	●		
Sequoia and Kings Canyon (G-5) 1,351 square miles. Horse rental.		●	●	●				●		●			●	●	●
Yosemite (F-5) 1,189 square miles. Rock climbing; horse rental, raft rental. Motorized vessels prohibited.		●	●	●	●			●	●	●	●	●	●	●	●
NATIONAL FORESTS *(See place listings.)*															
Eldorado (E-4) 676,780 acres. Central California. Bird-watching, equestrian camping, rock climbing, winter sports; off-highway vehicle trails, horse trails.		●	●	●	●	●	●	●	●	●	●	●	●	●	●
Humboldt-Toiyabe (E-5) 6,343,735 acres. Central, western, southern and northern Nevada and eastern California. Horse rental, interpretive trails.		●	●	●	●		●	●	●		●	●	●		●
Inyo (F-5) 1,944,040 acres. Central California. Horse rental.		●	●	●	●		●	●	●	●	●	●	●	●	●
Klamath (A-2) 1,726,000 acres. Northern California. Horseback riding, white-water rafting, winter sports.		●	●	●	●		●	●	●	●	●	●	●	●	●
Lassen (C-3) 1,375,000 acres. Northern California. Horseback riding, hunting, winter sports.		●	●	●	●		●	●	●	●	●	●	●	●	●
Mendocino (D-2) 886,048 acres. Northwestern California. Hunting.		●	●	●	●		●	●	●	●	●	●	●	●	●
Modoc (A-3) 1,654,392 acres. Northeastern California. Horseback riding, hunting, winter sports.		●	●	●	●		●	●	●	●	●	●	●	●	●
Plumas (C-3) 1,162,863 acres. Northern California. White-water rafting; horse rental, motorcycle trails.		●	●	●	●		●	●	●	●	●	●	●	●	●
Sequoia (H-5) 1,139,519 acres. South-central California. Horseback riding, hunting, winter sports; cabins, horse rental.		●	●	●	●		●	●	●	●	●	●	●	●	●
Shasta-Trinity (B-3) 2,129,524 acres. Northern California. Hunting; cabins, horse rental.		●	●	●	●		●	●	●	●	●	●	●	●	●
Sierra (F-5) 1,304,476 acres. Central California. White-water rafting, winter sports; horse rental.		●	●	●	●		●	●	●	●	●	●	●	●	●
Six Rivers (B-1) 990,000 acres. Northwestern California. Hunting, kayaking.		●	●	●	●		●	●	●	●	●	●	●	●	●
Stanislaus (E-4) 898,602 acres. Central California. Winter sports; horse rental.		●	●	●	●		●	●	●	●	●	●	●		●
Tahoe (D-4) 797,205 acres. North-central California. Horse rental.		●	●	●	●		●	●	●	●	●	●	●		
NATIONAL CONSERVATION AREAS															
King Range (C-1) 64,000 acres w. of Garberville. Horseback riding, wildlife viewing.		●	●	●	●			●	●	●	●			●	●
NATIONAL RECREATION AREAS *(See place listings.)*															
Golden Gate (C-7) 74,000 acres. Bird-watching, golfing, sailing; horse rental.		●	●	●	●			●	●	●	●		●		●
Smith River (A-1) 305,337 acres. Historic. Gold panning, hunting, scuba diving; horse trails, scenic byway. *(See Six Rivers National Forest p. 520.)*		●	●	●	●			●	●	●	●		●		
Whiskeytown-Shasta-Trinity (C-1) 246,087 acres. Kayaking, sailing, scuba diving; horse rental.		●	●	●	●		●	●	●	●	●		●	●	
NATIONAL SEASHORES *(See place listings.)*															
Point Reyes (C-7) 65,300 acres. Kayaking, wildlife viewing; horse rental, lighthouse.		●	●	●				●		●			●		●
ARMY CORPS OF ENGINEERS															
Lake Mendocino (D-2) 5,000 acres 5 mi. n.w. of Ukiah on SR 20. Nature trails.	**❶**	●	●	●	●	●	●	●	●	●	●		●		●
Lake Sonoma (E-2) 17,600 acres 26 mi. n.w. of Santa Rosa on Dry Creek Rd. Horseback riding, hunting; fish hatchery, interpretive trails.	**❷**	●	●	●	●	●	●	●	●	●	●		●		●

Recreation Areas Chart

The map location numerals in column 2 show an area's location on the preceding map.

STATE

	MAP LOCATION	CAMPING	PICNICKING	HIKING TRAILS	BOATING	BOAT RAMP	BOAT RENTAL	FISHING	SWIMMING	PETS ON LEASH	BICYCLE TRAILS	WINTER SPORTS	VISITOR CENTER	LODGE/CABINS	FOOD SERVICE
Anderson Marsh (D-2) 1,065 acres .75 mi. n. of Lower Lake on SR 53. Bird-watching; archeological sites, nature trail, tours.	3		•	•	•			•		•			•	•	
Andrew Molera (G-3) 4,800 acres 21 mi. s. of Carmel-by-the-Sea on SR 1. Bird-watching, beachcombing, surfing; horse rental.	4	•	•	•				•	•	•	•				
Angel Island (C-8) 758 acres in San Francisco Bay; ferry from San Francisco or Tiburon. Historic. Beachcombing, kayaking; bicycle rentals, interpretive services, museum, nature trails, tours. *(See Tiburon p. 542.)*	5	•	•	•	•	•	•		•		•		•	•	•
Annadel (A-7) 4,913 acres s.e. of Santa Rosa on Channel Dr. Horse rental, tours.	6		•	•				•		•	•		•		
Armstrong Redwoods (E-2) 752 acres 2 mi. n. of Guerneville on Armstrong Woods Rd. Nature trails.	7		•	•						•			•		
Auburn (E-3) 30,000 acres 1 mi. s. of Auburn on SR 49. Historic. Gold panning, horseback riding, motorcycle trails, rafting, water skiing; farm, marina, pond.	8	•	•	•	•	•	•	•	•	•	•		•		
Austin Creek (E-2) 4,236 acres 2 mi. n. of Guerneville on Armstrong Woods Rd.	9	•	•	•						•					
Benbow Lake (C-1) 1,200 acres 3 mi. s. of Garberville on US 101. Motorboats not permitted. Golfing; tours.	10	•	•	•		•	•	•	•	•			•		
Bethany Reservoir (D-9) 600 acres 7 mi. n. of I-580 via Altamont Pass, Mountain House and Christensen rds. Windsurfing.	11		•		•	•		•							
Bidwell/Sacramento River (D-3) 180 acres 5 mi. w. of Chico on River Rd. Canoeing, kayaking, rafting, tubing.	12	•	•	•	•	•		•							
Big Basin Redwoods (E-8) 18,000 acres 9 mi. n.w. of Boulder Creek on SR 236. Windsurfing; horse rental, nature trails, tours. *(See Boulder Creek p. 58.)*	13	•	•	•				•	•	•	•	•	•	•	•
Bothe-Napa Valley (A-7) 1,916 acres 4 mi. n. of St. Helena on SR 29. Bird-watching; wildlife viewing; horse rental.	14	•	•	•					•	•	•		•		
Brannan Island (C-9) 336 acres 3.25 mi. s. of Rio Vista. Water skiing, windsurfing; nature trails, wildlife habitat.	15	•	•	•	•	•		•	•	•			•		
Butano (E-8) 2,200 acres 7 mi. s. of Pescadero on Cloverdale Rd. Wildlife viewing.	16	•	•	•				•		•					
Calaveras Big Trees (E-4) 6,500 acres 4 mi. e. of Arnold on SR 4. Winter sports; nature trails, tours, wildlife site. *(See Arnold p. 48.)*	17	•	•	•				•	•	•		•	•		
Candlestick Point (D-8) 37 acres in San Francisco e. of US 101 via Candlestick exit. Windsurfing; cultural programs, fishing pier, guided nature walks.	18		•	•				•		•	•		•		
Castle Crags (B-2) 4,350 acres 6 mi. s. of Dunsmuir off I-5 exit 724. Horseback riding, rock climbing; nature trails. *(See Dunsmuir p. 98.)*	19	•	•	•				•		•					
Castle Rock (E-8) 4,350 acres 2 mi. w. of Los Gatos via SRs 9 and 35. Rock climbing, wildlife viewing; horse trails, nature trails.	20	•		•						•	•				
Caswell Memorial (F-3) 258 acres 6 mi. s.w. of Ripon on Austin Rd. Wildlife habitat.	21	•	•	•				•	•	•					
China Camp (C-7) 1,640 acres n. of San Rafael via US 101 and N. San Pedro Rd. Windsurfing; guided tours, horse trails, wildlife site.	22	•	•	•	•			•	•	•	•		•	•	•
Clear Lake (D-2) 565 acres 3.5 mi. n. of Kelseyville on Soda Bay Rd. Water skiing, wildflower viewing; nature trails. *(See Kelseyville p. 153.)*	23	•	•	•	•	•	•	•	•	•	•		•	•	
Colusa-Sacramento River (D-2) 67 acres near downtown Colusa on SR 20. Nature trails.	24	•	•	•	•	•		•		•					
Del Norte Coast Redwoods (B-1) 31,400 acres 7 mi. s. of Crescent City on US 101. Nature trails. *(See Redwood National and State Parks p. 297.)*	25	•	•	•				•		•	•		•	•	
D.L. Bliss (E-4) 1,830 acres on the w. shore of Lake Tahoe on SR 89. Nature trails. *(See South Lake Tahoe p. 524.)*	26	•	•	•				•	•	•			•		
Donner Memorial (D-4) 353 acres 2 mi. w. of Truckee on Donner Pass Rd. Cross-country skiing, windsurfing; nature trails, winter sports. *(See Truckee p. 545.)*	27	•	•	•	•		•	•	•	•			•	•	

Recreation Areas Chart

The map location numerals in column 2 show an area's location on the preceding map.

	Map Location	Camping	Picnicking	Hiking Trails	Boating	Boat Ramp	Boat Rental	Fishing	Swimming	Pets on Leash	Bicycle Trails	Winter Sports	Visitor Center	Lodge/Cabins	Food Service
Ed Z'berg-Sugar Pine Point (E-4) 1,975 acres 10 mi. s. of Tahoe City on SR 89. Historic. Nature trails, cross-country ski trails.	28	•	•	•	•	•		•	•	•	•	•			
Emerald Bay (E-4) 593 acres on the s.w. shore of Lake Tahoe. Boat-in campsites.	29	•	•	•	•	•		•	•	•		•	•		
Empire Mine (D-3) 845 acres in Grass Valley 1 mi. e. of SR 49 on E. Empire St. Guided tours, historic buildings, horse rental. *(See Grass Valley p. 139.)*	30		•	•						•	•	•	•		
Folsom Lake (E-3) 17,718 acres 2 mi. n.w. of Folsom off US 50. Water skiing, windsurfing; horse rental, nature trails.	31	•	•	•	•	•	•	•	•	•	•	•	•		•
Forest of Nisene Marks (F-9) 9,960 acres 4 mi. n. of Aptos on Aptos Creek Rd. Horse trails.	32	•	•	•				•		•	•				
Fort Ross (E-1) 3,386 acres 12 mi. n. of Jenner on SR 1. Scuba diving; historic buildings. *(See Jenner p. 152.)*	33	•	•	•				•		•			•		•
Fremont Peak (G-3) 244 acres 11 mi. s. of San Juan Bautista on San Juan Canyon Rd. Nature trails.	34	•	•	•						•			•		•
George J. Hatfield (F-3) 47 acres 28 mi. w. of Merced on Kelly Rd.	35	•	•		•			•	•	•					
Grizzly Creek Redwoods (C-1) 390 acres 15 mi. e. of Fortuna on SR 36. Nature trails.	36	•	•	•					•	•					
Grover Hot Springs (E-4) 700 acres 4 mi. w. of Markleeville on Hot Springs Rd. Nature trails. *(See Markleeville p. 186.)*	37	•	•	•					•	•		•	•		
Half Moon Bay Beach (D-8) 170 acres .5 mi. w. of US 1 on Kelly Ave. in Half Moon Bay. Horse rental.	38	•	•	•				•		•					
Hendy Woods (D-1) 690 acres 3 mi. w. of Philo off SR 128. Nature and horse trails.	39	•	•	•					•	•					
Henry Cowell Redwoods (F-8) 4,082 acres 3 mi. e. of Felton on Graham Hill Rd. Nature and horse trails. *(See Felton p. 109.)*	40	•	•	•					•	•	•		•		•
Henry W. Coe (G-3) 80,000 acres 14 mi. e. of Morgan Hill on E. Dunne Ave. Nature and horse trails. *(See Morgan Hill p. 227.)*	41	•	•	•					•	•			•		
Hollister Hills (G-3) 6,627 acres 8 mi. s. of Hollister via Cienega Rd. Nature trails, motorcycle trails, trails for four-wheel-drive vehicles.	42	•	•							•	•		•		
Humboldt Lagoons (B-1) 1,886 acres 4 mi. s. of Orick on US 101. Beachcombing, windsurfing. *(See Orick p. 265.)*	43	•	•	•				•	•	•					
Humboldt Redwoods (C-1) 52,000 acres along the Redwoods Hwy. near Weott. Horse rental, nature trails. *(See Weott p. 556.)*	44	•	•	•	•			•	•	•					
Jack London (B-7) 800 acres 1 mi. w. of Glen Ellen on London Ranch Rd. Historic. Horse rental, museum. *(See Glen Ellen p. 137.)*	45		•	•						•			•		•
Jedediah Smith Redwoods (A-1) 10,000 acres 9 mi. n.e. of Crescent City on US 199. Horse rentals, nature trails. *(See Redwood National and State Parks p. 297.)*	46	•	•	•	•			•	•	•	•				
Julia Pfeiffer Burns (H-3) 3,583 acres 37 mi. s. of Carmel-by-the-Sea on SR 1. Scuba diving, whale-watching. *(See Big Sur p. 57.)*	47	•	•	•						•					
Kings Beach (D-4) 8 acres 12 mi. n.e. of Tahoe City on SR 28.	48		•			•	•	•	•	•					
Lake Del Valle (D-9) 4,000 acre park and 750 acre lake on Del Valle Rd. 10 mi. s. of Livermore.	49	•	•	•	•	•	•	•	•	•					
Lake Oroville (D-3) 28,450 acres 6 mi. n.e. of Oroville off SR 70. Water skiing, windsurfing; beach, horse rental, nature trails.	50	•	•	•	•	•	•	•	•	•	•				
Los Baños Creek Reservoir (G-4) 10 mi. s.w. of Los Baños via SR 165, Pioneer and Canyon rds. Horse trails.	51	•	•		•	•		•		•					
MacKerricher (D-1) 2,030 acres 3 mi. n. of Fort Bragg on SR 1. Historic. Bird-watching, scuba diving; nature trails, horse rental.	52	•	•	•				•	•	•	•				
Malakoff Diggins (D-3) 3,000 acres n.e. of Nevada City on N. Bloomfield Rd. Historic. Nature and horseback riding trails. *(See Nevada City p. 243.)*	53	•	•	•					•	•	•	•	•	•	
Manchester (E-1) 760 acres 7 mi. n. of Point Arena on SR 1. Beach.	54	•	•	•				•		•	•				
Manresa Beach (F-9) 83 acres 5 mi. w. of Watsonville off SR 1.	55	•	•					•	•	•					

Recreation Areas Chart

The map location numerals in column 2 show an area's location on the preceding map.

	MAP LOCATION	CAMPING	PICNICKING	HIKING TRAILS	BOATING	BOAT RAMP	BOAT RENTAL	FISHING	SWIMMING	PETS ON LEASH	BICYCLE TRAILS	WINTER SPORTS	VISITOR CENTER	LODGE/CABINS	FOOD SERVICE
Marshall Gold Discovery (E-4) 274 acres in Coloma on SR 49. Historic. Gold panning, nature trails. *(See Coloma p. 83.)*	56	•	•	•				•		•			•	•	•
McArthur-Burney Falls Memorial (B-3) 910 acres. Scenic. Water skiing; nature trails. *(See Burney p. 62.)*	57	•	•	•	•	•	•	•	•	•	•	•	•		•
McConnell (F-4) 74 acres 5 mi. e. of Delhi on the Merced River.	58	•	•		•			•	•	•			•		
Millerton Lake (G-4) 6,553 acres 21 mi. n.e. of Fresno via SR 41. Historic. Water skiing, wildlife viewing, windsurfing; horse trails.	59	•	•	•	•	•	•	•	•	•			•		•
Mount Diablo (C-9) 18,000 acres off I-680 Diablo Rd. exit, then 3 mi. e. to Mount Diablo Scenic Blvd. near Danville. Horse rental, museum. *(See Danville p. 93.)*	60	•	•	•						•	•		•	•	
Mount Tamalpais (C-7) 6,300 acres 6 mi. w. of Mill Valley on Panoramic Hwy. Horse rental, nature trails. *(See Mill Valley p. 196.)*	61	•	•	•					•		•		•	•	•
Natural Bridges State Beach (F-8) 65 acres on West Cliff Dr. in Santa Cruz. Windsurfing; monarch butterfly preserve, nature trails. *(See Santa Cruz p. 490.)*	62		•	•				•	•				•		•
Navarro River Redwoods (D-1) 12 acres 6 mi. w. of Navarro on SR 128. Canoeing, kayaking.	63	•	•		•			•	•	•					
New Brighton Beach (F-9) 94 acres off SR 1 New Brighton/Park Ave. exit in Capitola.	64	•	•	•				•	•				•		
Patrick's Point (B-1) 632 acres 5 mi. n. of Trinidad via US 101. Nature trails. *(See Trinidad p. 544.)*	65	•	•	•				•		•	•	•	•	•	
Pfeiffer Big Sur (H-3) 964 acres s. of the village of Big Sur on SR 101. Nature trails. *(See Big Sur p. 57.)*	66	•	•	•				•	•	•	•		•	•	•
Plumas-Eureka (C-4) 6,749 acres 4 mi. w. of Johnsville on CR A14. Horse rental, nature trails. *(See Johnsville p. 153.)*	67	•	•	•				•		•		•	•		
Portola Redwoods (E-8) 2,010 acres 20 mi. s.w. of Palo Alto off SR 35. Nature trails.	68	•	•	•				•	•	•					
Prairie Creek Redwoods (B-1) 14,000 acres 6 mi. n. of Orick on US 101. Nature trails. *(See Redwood National and State Parks p. 297.)*	69	•	•	•				•		•			•	•	
Richardson Grove (C-1) 1,000 acres 8 mi. s. of Garberville on US 101. Nature trails.	70	•	•	•				•	•	•			•		
Robert W. Crown Memorial State Beach (D-8) 389 acres, including a 2.5-mi. beach, in Alameda at Eighth St. and Otis Dr. Bird sanctuary. *(See Alameda p. 42.)*	71		•	•				•	•	•	•		•		
Russian Gulch (D-1) 1,300 acres 2 mi. n. of Mendocino on US 101. Scuba diving; horse trails.	72	•	•	•				•		•	•		•		
Salt Point (E-1) 5,676 acres 24 mi. n. of Jenner on SR 1. Scuba diving; horse trails.	73	•	•	•	•	•		•		•			•		
Samuel P. Taylor (C-7) 2,708 acres 15 mi. w. of San Rafael on Sir Francis Drake Blvd. Nature and horse trails.	74	•	•	•			•		•	•	•		•		
San Luis Reservoir (G-3) 26,026 acres 12 mi. w. of Los Baños on SR 152. Water skiing, windsurfing; motorbike area. *(See Los Baños p. 180.)*	75	•	•	•	•	•		•	•	•			•		
Seacliff Beach (F-9) 85 acres 5.5 mi. s. of Santa Cruz on SR 1. Fishing pier.	76	•	•	•				•	•	•	•		•	•	•
Sinkyone Wilderness (D-1) 7,302 acres 30 mi. w. of Redway on CR 435 (Briceland Rd.). Horse trails.	77	•	•	•				•		•			•		
Smithe Redwoods (C-1) 665 acres 4 mi. n. of Leggett on US 101.	78		•					•	•	•			•		
Sonoma Coast (E-1) 5,333 acres n. of Bodega Bay on SR 1. Crabbing, surfing; horse rental.	79	•	•					•		•			•		
South Yuba River (D-3) 2,000 acres 8 mi. n.w. of Nevada City on SR 49. Gold panning; nature trail. *(See Nevada City p. 243.)*	80		•	•				•	•				•		
Standish-Hickey (C-1) 1,012 acres 2 mi. n. of Leggett on US 101. Nature trail.	81	•	•	•				•	•	•					
Sugarloaf Ridge (A-7) 2,700 acres 7 mi. e. of Santa Rosa on SR 12. Horse rental, nature trails, observatory.	82	•	•					•	•	•			•		
Sunset Beach (G-3) 324 acres 4 mi. w. of Watsonville via SR 1 and San Andreas Rd.	83	•	•	•				•	•	•			•		

Recreation Areas Chart

The map location numerals in column 2 show an area's location on the preceding map.

	MAP LOCATION	CAMPING	PICNICKING	HIKING TRAILS	BOATING	BOAT RAMP	BOAT RENTAL	FISHING	SWIMMING	PETS ON LEASH	BICYCLE TRAILS	WINTER SPORTS	VISITOR CENTER	LODGE/CABINS	FOOD SERVICE
Tahoe (D-4) 57 acres on Lake Tahoe .25 mi. s. of Tahoe City.	84	•	•	•				•	•	•	•				
Tolowa Dunes (A-1) 5,000 acres n. of Crescent City off US 101. Horse rental.	85	•	•	•	•	•	•	•				•	•		
Tomales Bay (B-7) 2,000 acres 4 mi. n. of Inverness on Pierce Point Rd. Clamming, windsurfing; nature trails.	86	•	•	•	•			•	•	•			•	•	
Trinidad Beach (B-1) 159 acres 19 mi. n. of Eureka on US 101.	87		•	•	•	•	•	•	•	•			•	•	
Turlock Lake (F-4) 408 acres 23 mi. e. of Modesto off SR 132. Water skiing.	88	•	•	•	•	•		•	•	•			•		
Van Damme (D-1) 1,831 acres 3 mi. s. of Mendocino on SR 1. Scuba diving; kayak tours, nature trails.	89	•	•	•				•	•	•	•	•	•		
Woodson Bridge (C-3) 428 acres 6 mi. e. of Corning and I-5. Nature trails.	90	•	•	•	•	•		•		•			•		
OTHER															
Anthony Chabot Regional Park (C-8) 4,500 acres e. of Oakland on Redwood Rd. Horse trails.	91	•	•	•						•	•	•			
Big Lagoon (B-1) 50 acres 7 mi. n. of Trinidad on US 101.	92	•	•	•	•	•		•	•	•					
Black Diamond Mines Regional Preserve (C-9) 6,286 acres 2.5 mi. s. of Antioch off SR 4 Somersville Rd. exit. *(See Antioch p. 45.)*	93	•	•	•						•	•	•			
Contra Loma (C-9) 776 acres 1 mi. s. of Antioch. Sailboarding, windsurfing.	94		•	•	•	•		•	•	•	•				•
Cow Mountain (D-2) 50,000 acres e. of Ukiah on Talmage Rd.	95	•	•	•					•	•			•		
Don Pedro Lake (F-4) 12,960 acres n.e. of La Grange on Bond's Flat Rd.	96	•	•	•	•	•	•	•		•			•	•	•
Doran (E-2) 120 acres on Doran Park Rd. s. of Bodega Bay.	97	•	•	•	•	•		•	•	•					
Eagle Lake (C-3) 22,000 acres 20 mi. n.w. of Susanville. *(See Susanville p. 538.)*	98	•	•	•	•	•	•	•	•	•			•		•
Gualala Point (E-1) 300 acres off SR 1 s. of Gualala.	99	•	•	•				•		•			•		
Lake Berryessa (A-8) 13,000 acres 20 mi. n.w. of Napa on SR 121.	100	•	•	•	•	•	•	•	•	•				•	•
Lake Chabot Marina (D-8) 1,500 acres in Castro Valley off Lake Chabot Rd. Horse trails.	101		•	•	•		•	•		•	•				•
Lake McClure (F-4) 7,100 acres 4 mi. w. of Coulterville on SR 132.	102	•	•	•	•	•	•	•	•	•					•
Lake San Antonio (H-3) 5,000 acres 40 mi. s. of King City off US 101. Bird-watching; horse rental.	103	•	•	•	•	•	•	•	•	•			•	•	•
Loch Lomond (F-8) 2,100 acres n. of Ben Lomond.	104	•	•	•	•		•	•		•					•
Martinez Shoreline (C-8) 343 acres in Martinez. Bird-watching; nature trails.	105		•	•	•			•	•	•	•	•	•		
Martin Luther King Jr. Shoreline (D-8) 1,220 acres in Oakland. Bird-watching; fishing pier.	106		•	•				•		•	•		•		•
Oak Grove Regional Park (F-3) 180 acres off I-5 exit 481 at Eight Mile Rd. in Stockton. Outdoor amphitheater, nature center.	107		•	•				•		•			•	•	
Point Pinole Shoreline (C-8) 2,147 acres n.w. of San Pablo. Fishing pier.	108		•	•				•		•	•				
Quarry Lakes Regional Recreation Area (D-9) 450 acres on three lakes on Isherwood Way in Fremont.	109		•	•	•			•	•	•	•		•		
Shadow Cliffs Regional Recreation Area (D-9) 249 acres at Pleasanton. Waterslides. *(See Pleasanton p. 281.)*	110		•	•	•			•	•	•	•				•
Spring Lake (A-7) 320 acres e. of Santa Rosa at Newanga Ave.	111	•	•	•	•	•	•	•	•	•	•				•
Sunol Wilderness (D-9) 6,858 acres 6 mi. s. of Sunol. Bird-watching; nature trails.	112	•	•	•						•	•		•		
Temescal (C-8) 48 acres in Oakland.	113		•	•				•	•	•	•				•
Vasona Park and Reservoir (E-8) 151 acres near Los Gatos. Motorboats not permitted.	114		•	•	•	•	•	•		•	•	•	•		

ACAMPO (E-3) pop. 341, elev. 52'

WINERIES

- **Woodbridge Winery** is e. off SR 99 exit 268 (Woodbridge Rd.) to 5950 E. Woodbridge Rd. **Hours:** Daily 10:30-4:30. Guided tours are given at 9:30, 1:30 and by appointment. Under 10 are not permitted on tours. Closed Jan. 1, Easter, July 4, Thanksgiving and Christmas. **Phone:** (209) 369-5861 or (209) 365-8139.

AHWAHNEE pop. 2,246

- **Hotels & Restaurants map & index p. 584**
- **Part of Yosemite National Park area — see map p. 578**

THE HOMESTEAD   (559)683-0495   **28**

▼▼▼ Cottage $149-$399 **Address:** 41110 Rd 600 93601 **Location:** Jct SR 41 and 49, 4.5 mi n; 2.5 mi sw of SR 49. Located in a secluded area. **Facility:** Oak-studded acreage surrounds these individual adobe, stone and cedar cottages, which include one studio unit; horse stalls available. 6 cottages. 1-2 stories (no elevator), exterior corridors. **Terms:** check-in 4 pm, 2 night minimum stay - weekends, 7 day cancellation notice. **Amenities:** high-speed Internet. **Activities:** hiking trails. 📶 ✕ ☎ 🖥 🍴 🖥 💻

ALAMEDA (D-8) pop. 73,812, elev. 30'

- **Attractions map p. 250**
- **Hotels & Restaurants map & index p. 254**

Fall and winter in Alameda are the best times to observe such sea birds as loons, grebes and ducks at Robert W. Crown Memorial State Beach. Crab Cove, at the north end of the beach, has been designated a marine reserve. Crab Cove Visitor Center, on McKay near Central, features exhibits about shoreline and undersea life and a saltwater aquarium with live bay creatures; phone (510) 544-3187. *See Recreation Areas Chart.*

Daily ferry service by Harbor Bay Maritime is available between the Ferry Building, at the foot of Clay Street across from The Embarcadero in San Francisco, and Bay Farm Island in Alameda at 2990 Main St.; phone (510) 769-5500 for information, departure times and rates.

The Alameda/Oakland Ferry also departs from 2990 Main St. in Alameda, proceeds to Jack London Square in Oakland and then on to the Ferry Building and Fisherman's Wharf in San Francisco; seasonal service is available to AT&T Park and to Angel Island State Park. Phone (510) 522-3300 for schedule information.

Alameda Chamber of Commerce: 2210-D South Shore Center, Alameda, CA 94501. **Phone:** (510) 522-0414.

ALAMEDA MUSEUM, 2324 Alameda Ave., displays memorabilia associated with the city. There are displays of vintage room vignettes, Native American objects, model ships and trains, toys and unusual bicycles, and exhibits about the fire department and Neptune Beach. Another exhibit is devoted to Phyllis Diller, who was an Alameda housewife in the late 1940s before finding fame as a standup comic; the wacky comedienne with the trademark braying laugh, who died in August 2012 at age 95, had a show business career that spanned more than 50 years. An art gallery features changing exhibits by local groups and children.

Time: Allow 30 minutes minimum. **Hours:** Wed.-Fri. and Sun. 1:30-4, Sat. 11-4, Jan.-Nov.; schedule varies rest of year. Closed major holidays. **Cost:** Donations. **Phone:** (510) 521-1233.

PACIFIC PINBALL MUSEUM is at 1510 Webster St. The museum has a collection of 90 historic pinball machines with games dating from 1936 to the present. All machines are playable and are included with the cost of museum admission. Staff members are available to explain the history and science of pinball, relate stories about the game and provide information about how to play the machines.

Tours: Guided tours are available. **Time:** Allow 1 hour minimum. **Hours:** Tues.-Fri. 2-9 (also Fri. 9 p.m.-midnight), Sat.-Sun. 11-9 (also Sat. 9 p.m.-midnight). Closed Thanksgiving and Christmas. **Cost:** $15; $7.50 (ages 0-11). **Phone:** (510) 769-1349.

USS *HORNET* MUSEUM is docked within the former naval air station at Alameda Point. This aircraft carrier served in World War II and Vietnam and as the prime recovery ship for the Apollo 11 and 12 missions, retrieving astronauts Neil Armstrong and Buzz Aldrin following their splash-down re-entry after walking on the moon. Space artifacts, aircraft, helicopters and restored areas of the ship can be seen on guided tours. Visitors get a feel for life aboard a carrier without having to enlist.

Hours: Daily 10-5. Last admission 1 hour before closing. Closed Jan. 1, Thanksgiving and Christmas. **Cost:** $16; $13 (ages 65+, students with ID and military with ID); $7 (ages 5-17). **Phone:** (510) 521-8448.

HAMPTON INN & SUITES   (510)521-4500   **43**

▼▼▼ Hotel $109-$249 **Address:** 1700 Harbor Bay Pkwy 94502 **Location:** I-880 exit Hegenberger Rd, 1.3 mi e, 2 mi n on Doolittle Dr, then 1.2 mi w. **Facility:** 105 units. 3 stories, interior corridors. **Terms:** 1-7 night minimum stay, cancellation fee imposed. **Amenities:** high-speed Internet. **Pool(s):** heated outdoor. **Activities:** whirlpool, exercise room. **Guest Services:** valet and coin laundry, area transportation-within 3 mi.

AAA Benefit: Members save up to 10%!

🚭 CALL 🏋M 🚐 BIZ 📶 ✕ 💻 / SOME UNITS 🖥 🖥

HAWTHORN SUITES BY
WYNDHAM-OAKLAND/ALAMEDA   (510)522-1000   **42**

▼▼▼ Hotel $100-$160 **Address:** 1628 Webster St 94501 **Location:** I-880 exit Broadway W, through Webster Tube. **Facility:** 50 units. 3 stories, interior corridors. **Amenities:** high-speed Internet. **Activities:** whirlpool, exercise room. **Guest Services:** valet and coin laundry. **Free Special Amenities:** full breakfast and high-speed Internet.

SAVE 🍴 CALL 🏋M BIZ 📶 ✕ 🖥 🖥 💻

(See map & index p. 254.)

MARINA VILLAGE INN

 (510)523-9450 **40**

▼▼▼
Hotel
$64-S179

Address: 1151 Pacific Marina 94501 **Location:** Waterfront. I-880 exit Broadway W, through Webster Tube, s on Atlantic Ave, then just e on Triumph St. **Facility:** 51 units. 2 stories (no elevator), interior/exterior corridors. **Terms:** 3 day cancellation notice-fee imposed. **Amenities:** high-speed Internet, safes. **Pool(s):** outdoor. **Guest Services:** valet and coin laundry. **Free Special Amenities: continental breakfast and high-speed Internet.**

RODEWAY INN-OAKLAND/ALAMEDA

(510)521-8400 **41**

▼▼▼
Motel
$59-$99

Address: 1925 Webster St 94501 **Location:** I-880 exit Webster Tube, W through Webster Tube. **Facility:** 50 units, some kitchens. 2 stories, exterior corridors. **Amenities:** high-speed Internet. **Free Special Amenities: expanded continental breakfast and high-speed Internet.**

WHERE TO EAT

PASTA PELICAN   510/864-7427 **42**

▼▼ Italian. Casual Dining. $10-$21 **AAA Inspector Notes:** A home away from home for scores of residents, this restaurant specializes in Northern Italian cuisine. Dishes are built around fresh seafood from local markets, sandwiches, pizza and pasta. **Bar:** full bar. **Reservations:** suggested. **Address:** 2455 Mariner Square Dr 94501 **Location:** I-880 exit Broadway W through Webster Tube, follow signs for Mariner Square. Lake Merritt, 18.

ROUND TABLE PIZZA   510/748-8600

▼ Pizza. Casual Dining. $7-$28 **AAA Inspector Notes:** This casual, family-oriented pizza place features high-quality ingredients and dough rolled fresh daily. Distinctive specialty pizzas are piled high with toppings. **Bar:** beer & wine. **Address:** 2651 Blanding Ave 94501 **Location:** Just w of Fruitvale Ave. Fruitvale, 19.

ALBION pop. 168
• Part of Wine Country area — see map p. 562

ALBION RIVER INN   707/937-1919

▼▼▼▼ Country Inn. Rates not provided. **Address:** 3790 N SR 1 95410 **Location:** Oceanfront. On SR 1; center. Nestled in 10 cottage-like buildings that curve around a bluff overlooking the Pacific Ocean, the Albion offers a contemporary ambience. 22 units. 1-2 stories (no elevator), exterior corridors. **Dining:** Albion River Inn Restaurant, see separate listing.

FENSALDEN INN   (707)937-4042

▼▼ Bed & Breakfast $149-$253 **Address:** 33810 Navarro Ridge Rd 95410 **Location:** 1.5 mi s on SR 1, 0.5 mi e. **Facility:** 8 units, some kitchens and cottages. 2 stories (no elevator), interior/exterior corridors. **Terms:** closed 12/2-12/20, 2 night minimum stay - weekends, 7 day cancellation notice-fee imposed. **Activities:** horseshoes, volleyball.

WHERE TO EAT

ALBION RIVER INN RESTAURANT   707/937-1919

▼▼▼▼ California. Fine Dining. $15-$33 **AAA Inspector Notes:** On a cliff overlooking the river and ocean, this restaurant offers sophisticated comfort food. The menu changes often. **Bar:** full bar. **Reservations:** suggested. **Address:** 3790 N SR 1 95410 **Location:** On SR 1; center; in Albion River Inn.

ALTURAS (B-4) pop. 2,827, elev. 4,366'
• Restaurants p. 44

Until 1874 Alturas was called Dorris Bridge after the Dorris family, the town's first European settlers. The Dorrises built a simple wooden bridge across the Pit River at the south end of town and later erected a house that served as a stopover for travelers. The county seat, Alturas is a marketing center for ranchers who raise livestock, potatoes and alfalfa.

Alturas Chamber of Commerce: 600 S. Main St., Alturas, CA 96101. **Phone:** (530) 233-4434.

MODOC COUNTY HISTORICAL MUSEUM, 600 S. Main St., documents area development via displays of Native American artifacts and firearms, including pieces dating from the 15th century to World War II. A steam engine once used locally is outside. **Hours:** Mon.-Sat. 10-4, when staff is available. Phone ahead to confirm schedule. **Cost:** $2; free (ages 0-16). **Phone:** (530) 233-2944.

MODOC NATIONAL WILDLIFE REFUGE, .5 mi. s. on US 395, 1 mi. e. on CR 56, then 1.5 mi. s. on CR 115, following signs, serves as a haven for more than 250 species of birds and other wildlife. The refuge's 7,000 acres are popular in spring and fall when large populations of migrating ducks, geese, sandhill cranes and other wetland birds stop to rest and feed. Self-guiding driving tour routes and seasonal fishing, hiking, boating and hunting are available. **Time:** Allow 1 hour minimum. **Hours:** Daily 7 a.m.-dusk. **Cost:** Free. **Phone:** (530) 233-3572.

BEST WESTERN TRAILSIDE INN   (530)233-4111

▼▼▼
Motel
$85-$100

 AAA Benefit: Members save up to 20%, plus 10% bonus points with Best Western Rewards®.

Address: 343 N Main St 96101 **Location:** Just s of jct SR 299/US 395 and Main St; jct W 4th St; center. **Facility:** 38 units. 2 stories (no elevator), exterior corridors. **Pool(s):** heated outdoor. **Free Special Amenities: continental breakfast and high-speed Internet.**

RIM ROCK MOTEL   530/233-5455

▼▼▼
Motel
$58-$75

Address: 22760 US 395 96101 **Location:** Jct SR 299 and US 395, 0.7 mi ne. **Facility:** 33 units, some two bedrooms and kitchens. 1 story, exterior corridors. **Amenities:** Some: high-speed Internet. **Activities:** horseshoes. **Free Special Amenities: local telephone calls and high-speed Internet.**

SUPER 8   (530)233-3545

▼▼▼
Motel
$65-$75

Address: 511 N Main St 96101 **Location:** Jct SR 299 and US 395, 0.4 mi s on US 395; at W 5th St. **Facility:** 47 units. 2 stories (no elevator), exterior corridors. **Amenities:** Some: high-speed Internet. **Free Special Amenities: expanded continental breakfast and high-speed Internet.**

ANTONIO'S CUCINA ITALIANA 530/233-5600

◆◆◆ Traditional Italian. Casual Dining. $7-$22 **AAA Inspector Notes:** This small family restaurant offers original interpretations of traditional Italian fare including pizza, pasta, sandwiches, salads and desserts. Located in the center of downtown, this eatery is within walking distance of hotels. All dishes are prepared to order and cheerfully served by a friendly staff. Pasta dishes are served with soup or salad and warm garlic bread. **Bar:** beer & wine. **Address:** 220 S Main St 96101 **Location:** On US 395; jct W North St; just s of center. [L] [D]

AMADOR CITY pop. 185

IMPERIAL HOTEL RESTAURANT 209/267-9172

◆◆◆ American. Casual Dining. $15-$30 **AAA Inspector Notes:** When visiting Amador's wine country be sure to dine at this restaurant housed in a building dating from 1879. The restaurant features organic, locally-grown produce and an extensive wine list offering selections from local wineries. A charming dining room and a seasonal patio out back are available for dining. Lunch is offered Saturday and Sunday noon-2 p.m. **Bar:** full bar. **Reservations:** suggested. **Address:** 14202 Old Hwy 49 95601 **Location:** Center. [D]

AMERICAN CANYON pop. 19,454
• Part of Wine Country area — see map p. 562

DOUBLETREE BY HILTON HOTEL & SPA NAPA VALLEY-AMERICAN CANYON (707)674-2100

◆◆◆ Hotel $129-$279 **Address:** 3600 Broadway St 94503 **Location:** Off SR 29. **Facility:** 132 units. 3 stories, interior corridors. **Terms:** 1-7 night minimum stay, cancellation fee imposed. **Amenities:** high-speed Internet. **Pool(s):** heated outdoor. **Activities:** whirlpool, exercise room, spa. **Guest Services:** valet laundry.

AAA Benefit: Members save 5% or more!

[ECO] [CALL] [GM] [≈] [?] [X] [?] [?] [?] / SOME UNITS [?]

FAIRFIELD INN & SUITES NAPA AMERICAN CANYON (707)643-3800

◆◆◆ Hotel $132-$289 **Address:** 3800 Broadway St 94503 **Location:** Off SR 29. **Facility:** 80 units. 3 stories, interior corridors. **Amenities:** high-speed Internet. **Pool(s):** heated outdoor. **Activities:** whirlpool, exercise room. **Guest Services:** valet and coin laundry.

AAA Benefit: AAA hotel discounts of 5% or more.

[?] [CALL] [GM] [≈] [?] [X] [?] [?] [?]

HOLIDAY INN EXPRESS & SUITES - NAPA VALLEY AMERICAN CANYON (707)552-8100

◆◆◆ Hotel $119-$259 **Address:** 5001 Main St 94503 **Location:** Off SR 29. **Facility:** 101 units. 3 stories, interior corridors. **Amenities:** high-speed Internet. **Pool(s):** heated outdoor. **Activities:** whirlpool, exercise room. **Guest Services:** valet and coin laundry.

[?] [CALL] [GM] [≈] [?] [X] [?] [?] / SOME UNITS FEE [?] [?] [?]

RISTORANTE LA STRADA 707/226-3027

◆◆◆ Italian. Casual Dining. $11-$22 **AAA Inspector Notes:** The exterior may look like a roadside diner but inside it is Old World Italy. With painted murals on the walls and white tablecloth tables, servers in black vests and pants with crisp, white shirts and aprons serve home-style, well-made dishes ranging from pasta to bistecca. **Bar:** full bar. **Address:** 6240 Broadway St 94503 **Location:** Off SR 29. [L] [D]

ANDERSON (C-2) pop. 9,932, elev. 430'

The railroad arrived in the area near Anderson in 1872. The town was named for Elias Anderson, the owner of the largest land grant in the area at that time. Today part of that grant is Anderson River Park which offers free summer concerts.

Anderson Chamber of Commerce: 2375 North St., P.O. Box 1144, Anderson, CA 96007. **Phone:** (530) 365-8095.

COLEMAN NATIONAL FISH HATCHERY is 10 mi. s.e. via Balls Ferry Rd. to Ashcreek and Gover rds., then continuing on Coleman Fish Hatchery Rd. The largest salmon hatchery in the continental United States, Coleman raises fingerlings in rearing ponds year-round. Salmon and steelhead migrate up the ladders to the hatchery early October to early February during spawning season. The hatchery can be explored on a self-guiding tour. **Hours:** Daily 7:30-dusk. **Cost:** Free. **Phone:** (530) 365-8622. [?]

BEST WESTERN PLUS ANDERSON INN (530)365-2753

◆◆◆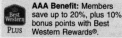

Hotel $85-$150

AAA Benefit: Members save up to 20%, plus 10% bonus points with Best Western Rewards®.

Address: 2688 Gateway Dr 96007 **Location:** I-5 exit 668 (Central Anderson/Lassen Nat'l Park) northbound, just ne on Balls Ferry Rd, then just se; exit southbound, just e, just s on McMurry Dr, then just e. **Facility:** 40 units. 2 stories (no elevator), exterior corridors. **Terms:** cancellation fee imposed. **Amenities:** Some: high-speed Internet. **Pool(s):** outdoor. **Free Special Amenities: full breakfast and high-speed Internet.**

[SAVE] [?] [CALL] [GM] [≈] [BIZ] [?] [?] [?] [?] / SOME UNITS FEE [?]

GAIA HOTEL & SPA SHASTA (530)365-7077

◆◆◆ Hotel $96-$129 **Address:** 4125 Riverside Ave **Location:** I-5 exit 670 (Riverside Ave), just e, then just n. **Facility:** 120 units, some cottages. 2 stories (no elevator), exterior corridors. **Terms:** cancellation fee imposed. **Amenities:** high-speed Internet. **Pool(s):** outdoor. **Activities:** whirlpool, fishing, exercise room, spa. **Fee:** canoes. **Guest Services:** valet laundry.

[ECO] [?] [?] [≈] [BIZ] [?] [X] [?] / SOME UNITS FEE [?] [?] [?]

ANGELS CAMP (F-4) pop. 2,400, elev. 1,379'

Named after shopkeeper Henry Angel, who started a trading post at this site in 1848, Angels Camp was a popular spot for gold miners. Early diggers uncovered riches, and within 1 year approximately 4,000 miners populated the town to try their luck. Angels Camp sits atop numerous tunnels, which proved to be successful mines.

Angels Camp inspired Mark Twain to write his famous short story "The Celebrated Jumping Frog of Calaveras County"—his first published success. The tall tale is remembered each year in May during the ◆ Calaveras County Fair and Jumping Frog Jubilee, held, appropriately enough, at the Frogtown Fairgrounds. Fifty frogs compete in the grand finals in an attempt to break the world record, currently held by Rosie the Ribeter.

Calaveras Visitors Bureau: 1192 S. Main St., P.O. Box 637, Angels Camp, CA 95222-0637. **Phone:** (209) 736-0049 or (800) 225-3764.

Self-guiding tours: A packet that includes walking tour maps and information about the town's historic district, as well as other areas in Calaveras County, is available from the visitors bureau.

ANGELS CAMP MUSEUM, 753 S. Main St., features early mining equipment, wagons, a blacksmith shop with agricultural and logging equipment, minerals and artifacts from the gold rush era and a carriage house with horse-drawn vehicles from gold rush days. **Time:** Allow 1 hour minimum. **Hours:** Thurs.-Mon. 10-4, Mar.-Nov.; Sat.-Sun. 10-4, rest of year. Closed Easter, Thanksgiving and Christmas. **Cost:** $5; $2.50 (ages 5-11). **Phone:** (209) 736-2963. 🎫

RECREATIONAL ACTIVITIES
White-water Rafting

- **O.A.R.S. River Trips** is 1.7 mi. s. on SR 49. **Hours:** Daily Apr.-Oct. **Phone:** (209) 736-4677 or (800) 346-6277.

BEST WESTERN PLUS CEDAR INN & SUITES
(209)736-4000

AAA Benefit: Members save up to 20%, plus 10% bonus points with Best Western Rewards®.

Hotel
$69-$199

Address: 444 S Main St 95222 **Location:** On SR 49; center. **Facility:** 41 units. 2 stories (no elevator), interior/exterior corridors. **Terms:** 3 day cancellation notice. **Pool(s):** outdoor. **Activities:** whirlpool, exercise room. **Guest Services:** coin laundry. **Free Special Amenities:** local telephone calls and high-speed Internet.

JUMPING FROG MOTEL
(209)736-2191

Motel
$70-$165

Address: 330 Murphys Grade Rd 95222 **Location:** Just e of jct SR 49; center. **Facility:** 15 units, some two bedrooms. 1 story, exterior corridors. **Terms:** 2 night minimum stay - weekends, 3 day cancellation notice-fee imposed. **Free Special Amenities:** local telephone calls and high-speed Internet.

TRAVELODGE
(209)736-4242

Hotel $69-$189 **Address:** 600 N Main St 95221 **Location:** On SR 49; north end of town. **Facility:** 55 units. 2 stories (no elevator), exterior corridors. **Terms:** cancellation fee imposed. **Pool(s):** outdoor. **Guest Services:** coin laundry.

WHERE TO EAT

MIKE'S PIZZA OF ANGELS
209/736-9246

Pizza. Quick Serve. $6-$40 **AAA Inspector Notes:** This favorite spot for locals is especially noted for their great pizza. They also offer pasta dishes, ribs and burgers. **Bar:** beer & wine. **Address:** 294 S Main St 95222 **Location:** Jct Murphys Grade Rd, on SR 49; center. L D CALL

ANTIOCH (C-9) pop. 102,372, elev. 43'
• Restaurants p. 46

BLACK DIAMOND MINES REGIONAL PRESERVE is 2.5 mi. s. off SR 4 Somersville Rd. exit. The preserve's 6,286 acres are a haven for hikers, picnickers and those who enjoy nature and a chance to explore the region's mining past. Five coal mining towns prospered here in the late 1800s; in the 1920s underground mining for sand replaced coal mining. A cemetery is virtually all that remains of those communities.

The Greathouse Visitor Center, in a 1920s underground chamber, was the original opening into the sand mine. It now has exhibits about the sand mine and the lives of the coal miners and brochures about the park's facilities and hiking trails. A tour through the Hazel-Atlas Mine lets participants see how the sand was mined to make glass objects. The preserve has 65 miles of trails through grasslands, woodlands and forests. *See Recreation Areas Chart.*

Time: Allow 2 hours minimum. **Hours:** Preserve open daily 8 a.m.-dusk. Sidney Flat Visitor Center Sat.-Sun. 10-4:30, early Mar.-late Nov. Greathouse Visitor Center open Sat.-Sun. 10-4:30, early Mar.-late Nov. Ninety-minute mine tours (reservations required) depart Sat.-Sun. at 11, 1 and 2, Apr.-Nov. Tours on a first-come, first-served basis are given Sat.-Sun. at noon and 3, Mar.-Nov. (arrive at least an hour early to ensure a place on the tour). Closed Thanksgiving and Christmas. Phone ahead to confirm schedule.

Cost: Parking Sat.-Sun. and holidays $5 per private vehicle (when kiosk is attended). Mine tours $5. Fee for dogs $2 (service dogs free). Under 7 are not permitted on mine tours. **Phone:** (510) 544-2750.

COMFORT SUITES ANTIOCH-OAKLEY
(925)755-1222

Hotel $89-$139 **Address:** 5549 Bridgehead Rd 94561 **Location:** In Oakley; just e of SR 160 and 4; just n of Main St. **Facility:** 80 units, some two bedrooms. 3 stories, interior corridors. **Terms:** cancellation fee imposed. **Amenities:** high-speed Internet, safes. **Pool(s):** outdoor. **Activities:** whirlpool, exercise room. **Guest Services:** valet and coin laundry.

DAYS INN & SUITES ANTIOCH
(925)522-0010

Hotel
$55-$79

Address: 1605 Auto Center Dr 94509 **Location:** SR 4 exit Somersville Rd/Auto Center Dr, just n. **Facility:** 46 units. 3 stories, interior corridors. **Pool(s):** outdoor. **Guest Services:** coin laundry. **Free Special Amenities:** expanded continental breakfast and high-speed Internet.

ROUND TABLE PIZZA

▼ Pizza. Casual Dining. $7-$28 **AAA Inspector Notes:** This casual, family-oriented pizza place features high-quality ingredients and dough rolled fresh daily. Distinctive specialty pizzas are piled high with toppings. **Bar:** beer & wine. L D

For additional information, visit AAA.com

LOCATIONS:
Address: 2509 Somersville Rd 94509 **Location:** SR 4 exit Somersville Rd, just s. **Phone:** 925/754-5747
Address: 4504 Deer Valley Rd 94509 **Location:** At Lone Tree Way. **Phone:** 925/776-7777

APTOS pop. 6,220
• Hotels & Restaurants map & index p. 492

BEST WESTERN PLUS SEACLIFF INN
(831)688-7300 45

Hotel
$90-$200

AAA Benefit: Members save up to 20%, plus 10% bonus points with Best Western Rewards®.

Address: 7500 Old Dominion Ct 95003 **Location:** SR 1 exit State Park Dr, just e. **Facility:** 149 units. 2 stories (no elevator), interior/exterior corridors. **Amenities:** high-speed Internet. **Dining:** Severino's Grill, see separate listing, entertainment. **Pool(s):** heated outdoor. **Activities:** whirlpool, exercise room. **Guest Services:** valet and coin laundry. **Free Special Amenities: local telephone calls and high-speed Internet.** *(See ad p. 495.)*

SAVE 🍴 🍽 Y CALL &M 🏊 BIZ 🛜 🛏 💻 / SOME UNITS FEE 🖨

RIO SANDS MOTEL (831)688-3207 46

▼▼ Motel $59-$219 **Address:** 116 Aptos Beach Dr 95003 **Location:** SR 1 exit Rio Del Mar Blvd, 1.5 mi sw. **Facility:** 50 units, some kitchens. 2 stories (no elevator), interior/exterior corridors. **Terms:** 2 night minimum stay - weekends. **Amenities:** high-speed Internet. **Pool(s):** heated outdoor. **Activities:** whirlpool.

CALL &M 🏊 BIZ 🛜 ✕ 🎾 🛏 🖥 💻

SEASCAPE BEACH RESORT (831)688-6800 47

▼▼▼ Resort Hotel $350-$790

Address: One Seascape Resort Dr 95003 **Location:** 1 mi w of SR 1 exit San Andreas Rd, n on Seascape Blvd. **Facility:** On a hillside overlooking the Pacific Ocean, the resort offers condos with gas fireplaces and private patios. 285 units, some two bedrooms, efficiencies and kitchens. 3 stories, exterior corridors. **Terms:** check-in 4 pm, 2-3 night minimum stay - seasonal and/or weekends, 3 day cancellation notice-fee imposed. **Amenities:** video games (fee), high-speed Internet. **Pool(s):** 3 heated outdoor. **Activities:** whirlpools, 11 lighted tennis courts, recreation programs, volleyball. **Fee:** massage. **Guest Services:** complimentary laundry, area transportation-within 5 mi. **Free Special Amenities:** local telephone calls and high-speed Internet. *(See ad p. 496.)*

SAVE FEE 🎁 🍴 🍽 Y CALL &M 🏊 🚴 BIZ 🛜 ✕ 🎾 🐾 🛏 🖥 💻

Visit AAA.com/Travel or CAA.ca/Travel for complete trip planning and reservations

BITTERSWEET CAFE 831/662-9799 24

▼▼ American. Casual Dining. $6-$14 **AAA Inspector Notes:** A great spot for breakfast and lunch, this local favorite offers some traditional favorites as well as some distinctive creations of their own including Southwestern eggs Benedict with carnitas and green chilies with a chipotle Hollandaise, assorted omelets and homemade granola. Lunch offers a variety of salads, sandwiches, panini and wood-fired pizza. Dining is available on the patio, weather permitting. Expect a friendly staff. **Bar:** full bar. **Address:** 787 Rio Del Mar Blvd 95003 **Location:** SR 1 exit Rio Del Mar Blvd, just w.

B L CALL &M

MA MAISON 831/688-5566 23

▼▼▼ French. Fine Dining. $11-$34 **AAA Inspector Notes:** California influences this restaurant's French cuisine, which guests savor in the warm atmosphere of the separate dining rooms, including one with a fireplace. Patio seating is another option at this family-owned-and-operated spot. **Bar:** full bar. **Reservations:** suggested. **Address:** 9051 Soquel Dr 95003 **Location:** SR 1 exit Rio Del Mar Blvd, just n. L D

PALAPAS RESTAURANT & CANTINA 831/662-9000 25

▼▼▼ Mexican. Casual Dining. $10-$25 **AAA Inspector Notes:** Selections, many of which center on seafood, are made from fresh ingredients, including made-on-the-premises sauces. Patio dining offers great views of the Pacific Ocean. **Bar:** full bar. **Reservations:** suggested. **Address:** 21 Seascape Village 95003 **Location:** SR 1 exit San Andreas Rd, 1 mi w, then n on Seascape Blvd.

L D CALL &M

SEVERINO'S GRILL 831/688-8987 22

▼▼▼ American. Casual Dining. $10-$32 **AAA Inspector Notes:** While dining on fresh, locally caught seafood and other specialty entrees, diners can enjoy views of the attractively appointed gardens and koi pond. **Bar:** full bar. **Address:** 7500 Old Dominion Ct 95003 **Location:** SR 1 exit State Park Dr, just e; in BEST WESTERN PLUS Seacliff Inn. *(See ad p. 495.)* B L D CALL &M

ARCATA (B-1) pop. 17,231, elev. 33'
• Restaurants p. 48

Founded in 1858 as a mining supply center, Arcata also was where author Bret Harte once worked as a journalist and miner; he made the town the setting for some of his stories of mining camp life. Arcata also is home to Humboldt State University.

Southwest of town on Humboldt Bay is the 225-acre Arcata Marsh and Wildlife Sanctuary, a former industrial area and county landfill transformed into a breeding ground for more than 250 species of birds. Some 4.5 miles of foot trails wind past seven wetland habitats. The annual spring migration of marbled godwits and other shorebirds is observed during the 🦅 Godwit Days Migratory Bird Festival, a 3-day April event featuring lectures, boat excursions and more than 100 observation field trips.

Arcata Chamber of Commerce: 1635 Heindon Rd., Arcata, CA 95521-5816. **Phone:** (707) 822-3619.

Self-guiding tours: Maps detailing a walking tour of Victorian houses as well as maps of the Humboldt area and of the city-owned Redwood Park within Arcata Community Forest can be obtained at the chamber of commerce.

AZALEA STATE NATURAL RESERVE is 5 mi. n. off US 101 McKinleyville exit, then 2 mi. e. on N. Bank Rd. The 30-acre reserve features western azaleas as well as other plantings common to the area. The reserve is loveliest when the azaleas are in bloom April through May. **Note:** Visitors should stay on designated trails. Dogs are permitted only in the paved parking area. Parking is limited; the reserve is not recommended for trailers. Restroom facilities are not available. **Time:** Allow 30 minutes minimum. **Hours:** Daily dawn-dusk. **Cost:** Free. **Phone:** (707) 677-3570.

HUMBOLDT STATE UNIVERSITY NATURAL HISTORY MUSEUM, 1315 G St. in Wells Fargo Hall, exhibits almost 2,000 animal and plant specimens from around the world, local natural history displays and fossils dating from 500 million years ago.

Exhibits, which change periodically, include a 60-gallon tide pool tank; local salamanders, toads, turtles and snakes; a dire wolf jaw fossil; a 50 million-year-old fish skeleton; bees; birds of the Redwoods; Western minerals and ores; butterflies; and Pacific seashells. **Hours:** Tues.-Sat. 10-5. Phone ahead to confirm schedule. **Cost:** $3; $2 (ages 4-17 and 60+); $10 (family, two adults and up to four children). **Phone:** (707) 826-4479.

ARCATA SUPER 8 (707)822-8888
Hotel $58-$180 **Address:** 4887 Valley West Blvd 95521 **Location:** US 101 exit Giuntoli Ln/Janes Rd, just e, then just s. **Facility:** 60 units. 2 stories (no elevator), interior corridors.

Enjoy exclusive member

discounts and benefits

from Hertz

▼ See AAA listing this page ▼

HOTEL ARCATA
707/826-0217

Historic Hotel. Rates not provided. **Address:** 708 9th St 95521 **Location:** Corner of G St; downtown; in Plaza. **Facility:** All guest rooms at this refurbished 1915 property feature a clawfoot bathtub. 32 units. 3 stories, interior corridors. **Parking:** street only.

 SOME UNITS FEE

HOWARD JOHNSON EXPRESS INN
(707)826-9660

Hotel
$70-$229

Address: 4700 Valley West Blvd 95521 **Location:** US 101 exit Giuntoli Ln/Janes Rd, just e, then just s. **Facility:** 48 units. 2 stories (no elevator), interior corridors. **Amenities:** high-speed Internet, safes. **Pool(s):** heated indoor. **Activities:** whirlpool, exercise room. **Guest Services:** coin laundry. **Free Special Amenities:** expanded continental breakfast and high-speed Internet.

QUALITY INN ARCATA
(707)822-0409

Hotel
$84-$129

Address: 3535 Janes Rd 95521 **Location:** US 101 exit Giuntoli Ln/Janes Rd, just w. **Facility:** 64 units. 2 stories (no elevator), interior corridors. **Amenities:** *Some:* high-speed Internet. **Pool(s):** heated outdoor. **Activities:** whirlpool, tennis court. **Free Special Amenities:** expanded continental breakfast and high-speed Internet.

 SOME UNITS FEE

WHERE TO EAT

ABRUZZI
707/826-2345

Italian. Casual Dining. $12-$29 AAA Inspector Notes: In the Old Town section, this Italian restaurant matches its delicious pasta and fish dishes to selections from its excellent wine list. **Bar:** full bar. **Reservations:** suggested. **Address:** 791 8th St 95521 **Location:** Corner of H St; downtown; ground level of Jacoby's Storehouse. D

FOLIE DOUCE
707/822-1042

California. Casual Dining. $15-$37 AAA Inspector Notes: Translated as sweet madness, this spot is a popular, local favorite and reservations are definitely suggested. The setting at this trendy little bistro is intimate with colorful artwork filling the empty spaces on the bright and vividly-colored walls. The chef makes good use of fresh ingredients from local farmers and vendors to create his nightly specials. The main menu, which changes seasonally, features California cuisine with some Asian and Mediterranean influences. **Bar:** beer & wine. **Reservations:** suggested. **Address:** 1551 G St 95521 **Location:** Between 15th and 16th sts; north town section. D

PLAZA GRILL
707/826-0860

California. Casual Dining. $9-$30 AAA Inspector Notes: On the town square, this restaurant serves California cuisine, including preparations of fresh fish and steak. Produce comes from the local farmer's market. **Bar:** full bar. **Reservations:** suggested. **Address:** 791 8th St 95521 **Location:** Corner of H St; downtown; 3rd floor of Jacoby's Storehouse. **Parking:** street only. D

RITA'S MARGARITA'S & MEXICAN GRILL
707/822-1010

Mexican. Casual Dining. $6-$16 AAA Inspector Notes: This casual eatery attracts local families and university students. **Bar:** full bar. **Address:** 855 8th St 95521 **Location:** Between H and I sts. **Parking:** street only. L D

ARNOLD (E-4) pop. 3,843, elev. 4,000'

The logging industry sustained Arnold until Blagen Mill closed in 1962. Because of the area's proximity to recreational opportunities, a full slate of winter recreation, from snowmobiling to skiing, as well as summer activities in parks, lakes and rivers is available.

CALAVERAS BIG TREES STATE PARK, 4 mi. e. on SR 4, consists of 6,500 acres and contains some of the finest specimens of Sierra redwoods. Hiking trails of various lengths lead through the groves of trees. Interpretive programs are available in summer; snowshoeing and cross-country skiing are available in winter. *See Recreation Areas Chart.* **Hours:** Daily dawn-dusk. **Cost:** Day use fee $8 per private vehicle; $7 (ages 62+ per private vehicle). **Phone:** (209) 795-2334.

SIERRA NEVADA LOGGING MUSEUM is 1 mi. n. off SR 4 on Blagen Rd., then .25 mi. w., following signs. Overlooking White Pines Lake, the museum preserves the logging histories of 18 counties in the Sierra Nevada range, beginning with the 1848 discovery of gold. Indoor displays feature working models of sawmills and lumber camps, photographs, dioramas, tools and a depiction of a family cabin from a 1930s camp.

Outdoors visitors can see historic logging artifacts, including a steam donkey, logging arches, tractors and a grader. **Time:** Allow 1 hour minimum. **Hours:** Thurs.-Sun. noon-4, Apr.-Nov. (weather permitting); by appointment rest of year. **Cost:** Free. **Phone:** (209) 795-6782.

RECREATIONAL ACTIVITIES
White-water Rafting
- **All-Outdoors California Whitewater Rafting** departs from Calaveras Big Trees State Park, 4 mi. e. on SR 4, for trips on the North Fork of the Stanislaus River. **Hours:** Daily Apr.-May. **Phone:** (925) 932-8993 or (800) 247-2387.
- **Beyond Limits Adventures** departs from Calaveras Big Trees State Park, 4 mi. e. on SR 4, for guided rafting trips on the American River. **Hours:** Daily Apr. 1-Labor Day weekend. Guided excursions are dependent on the available water flow; phone ahead to confirm schedule. **Phone:** (209) 526-0027 or (800) 234-7238.

ARNOLD BLACK BEAR INN
209/795-8999

Bed & Breakfast $225-$275 Address: 1343 Oak Cir 95223 **Location:** Off SR 4, just n. **Facility:** Near the national forest, this 4000-square-foot timber-framed lodge, with its ceiling-to-floor windows, is a great place to see nature at its best. 5 units. 1 story, interior corridors. **Terms:** 2 night minimum stay - seasonal and/or weekends, 14 day cancellation notice-fee imposed. **Activities:** whirlpool. *Fee:* massage. CALL

ARNOLD MEADOWMONT LODGE
(209)795-1394

Motel
$84-$175

Address: 2011 Hwy 4 95223 **Location:** On SR 4; west end of town. **Facility:** 19 units. 1 story, exterior corridors. CALL SOME UNITS FEE

WHERE TO EAT

ROUND TABLE PIZZA   209/795-0193
 Pizza. Casual Dining. $7-$28 **AAA Inspector Notes:** This casual, family-oriented pizza place features high-quality ingredients and dough rolled fresh daily. Distinctive specialty pizzas are piled high with toppings. **Bar:** beer & wine. **Address:** 2182 Hwy 4, Suite 300 D 95223 **Location:** On SR 4; at Meadow View Rd; in Meadow Mount Mall; adjacent to Big Trees Market. [L] [D]

ATWATER (F-4) pop. 28,168, elev. 151'

Atwater Chamber of Commerce: 1181 Third St., Atwater, CA 95301. **Phone:** (209) 358-4251.

CASTLE AIR MUSEUM is .5 mi. e. of SR 99 on Buhach Rd., then n. on Santa Fe Dr. Located on 30 acres that include an indoor museum in a remodeled barracks, the complex is named for Brig. Gen. Frederick W. Castle, who earned a posthumous Medal of Honor for his role in a World War II bombing mission over Europe. Photographs, weapons, uniforms and 55 vintage aircraft— including an SR-71 Blackbird, an F-106, a B-36 bomber and an RF8 Crusader—depict the U.S. Air Force's and Navy's development during the World War II, Korean War and Vietnam War eras.

Tours: Guided tours are available. **Time:** Allow 1 hour minimum. **Hours:** Daily 9-5, May-Oct.; 10-4, rest of the year. Closed Jan. 1, Easter, Thanksgiving and Christmas. **Cost:** $10; $8 (ages 6-17 and 60+); free (military with ID). Reservations are required for tours. **Phone:** (209) 723-2178.

AUBURN (E-3) pop. 13,330, elev. 1,255'

Historic Old Auburn, the central section of the city, has many restored mid-1800s buildings, including a firehouse and the oldest continuously used post office in California.

Placer County Visitor Bureau: 1103 High St., Auburn, CA 95603. **Phone:** (530) 887-2111 or (866) 752-2371.

BERNHARD MUSEUM COMPLEX is at 291 Auburn-Folsom Rd. at Fairgate Dr. Guided tours by docents in period garb provide visitors a glimpse into the lifestyle of a hardworking 1890s farm family. Their white, two-story home, built in 1851, was originally a hotel.

The complex also includes a reconstructed carriage house containing such vehicles as a buggy and a mud wagon (a lightweight stagecoach with a canvas top and sides). **Time:** Allow 30 minutes minimum. **Hours:** Tues.-Sun. 11-4. Closed major holidays. **Cost:** Donations. **Phone:** (530) 889-6500.

GOLD COUNTRY MUSEUM, 1273 High St. on the fairgrounds, depicts Placer County's early days through old mining equipment, an exhibit about mining methods, a stamp mill and a period saloon. Visitors can try their luck pannig for gold in a small stream; salted goldbags are provided. **Tours:** Guided tours are available. **Time:** Allow 1 hour

minimum. **Hours:** Tues.-Sun. 11-4. Closed major holidays. **Cost:** Free. Gold panning $3. **Phone:** (530) 889-6500.

PLACER COUNTY MUSEUM & COURTHOUSE, in the courthouse at 101 Maple St., features a Native American habitat with a recorded narration and a 10-minute video presentation about the history of the transcontinental highway that runs through the county. Also inside the 1898 courthouse is a restored sheriff's office circa 1915 and the Pate Collection of American Indian Artifacts. **Time:** Allow 1 hour minimum. **Hours:** Daily 10-4. Closed major holidays. **Cost:** Free. **Phone:** (530) 889-6500.

BEST WESTERN GOLDEN KEY   (530)885-8611

Hotel
$89-$169

AAA Benefit: Members save up to 20%, plus 10% bonus points with Best Western Rewards®.

Address: 13450 Lincoln Way 95603 **Location:** I-80 exit 121 (Foresthill Rd/Auburn Ravine Rd), just e, then n. **Facility:** 68 units. 2 stories (no elevator), exterior corridors. **Amenities:** high-speed Internet. **Pool(s):** heated indoor/outdoor. **Activities:** whirlpool, putting green. **Guest Services:** coin laundry. **Free Special Amenities:** expanded continental breakfast and high-speed Internet.

HOLIDAY INN-AUBURN   (530)887-8787
 Hotel $109-$209 **Address:** 120 Grass Valley Hwy 95603 **Location:** I-80 exit SR 49, just nw. **Facility:** 96 units. 2-3 stories, interior corridors. **Amenities:** video games (fee), high-speed Internet. **Pool(s):** outdoor. **Activities:** whirlpool, exercise room. **Guest Services:** valet and coin laundry.

QUALITY INN GOLD COUNTRY   (530)885-7025

Motel
$55-$75

Address: 13490 Lincoln Way 95603 **Location:** I-80 exit 121 (Foresthill Rd/Auburn Ravine Rd), just e, then n. **Facility:** 75 units, some kitchens. 2 stories, interior/exterior corridors. **Terms:** cancellation fee imposed. **Amenities:** safes (fee). *Some:* high-speed Internet. **Pool(s):** outdoor. **Activities:** whirlpool. **Guest Services:** valet and coin laundry. **Free Special Amenities: expanded continental breakfast and high-speed Internet.**

WHERE TO EAT

AUBURN ALEHOUSE   530/885-2537
American. Casual Dining. $9-$19 **AAA Inspector Notes:** Located in the historic American Block Building in Old Town Auburn, this lively brewpub features fresh, handcrafted beers from the on-site microbrewery and California-style pub fare. Seasonal brew specials are offered. Breakfast is served Saturday and Sunday. Outdoor patio dining is offered in season. Parking can be found in one of the Old Town lots. **Bar:** full bar. **Address:** 289 Washington St 95603 **Location:** I-80 exit Nevada St westbound, just ne, then se on Auburn Folsom Rd, follow signs to Old Town; exit Maple St eastbound, just se on Lincoln Way; jct Sacramento St; across from post office. **Parking:** street only. [L] [D] CALL

AWFUL ANNIE'S
530/888-9857

WV W American. Casual Dining. $7-$13 AAA Inspector Notes: Dine on the porch overlooking old town Auburn or inside the 150-year-old-building where the décor is country. A variety of breakfast treats are offered and include omelets, Awful Annie's waffles and scrambles. Lunch includes salads and gourmet or grilled sandwiches. **Bar:** full bar. **Address:** 160 Sacramento St 95603 **Location:** I-80 exit Nevada St westbound, just ne, then se on Auburn Folsom Rd, follow signs to Old Town; exit Maple St eastbound, just se on Lincoln Way. **Parking:** street only. B L

JOE CARIBE BISTRO & CAFE
530/823-5333

WV WV Caribbean. Casual Dining. $8-$18 AAA Inspector Notes: This bistro is close to shopping and movie theaters. **Bar:** full bar. **Address:** 13470 Lincoln Way 95603 **Location:** I-80 exit 121 (Foresthill Rd/Auburn Ravine Rd), just e, then just n. L D CALL M

LOU LA BONTE'S
530/885-9193

WV WV American. Casual Dining. $9-$27 AAA Inspector Notes: Locals and visitors alike have met at this spot for more than 60 years. The menu features several pasta selections, specialty gourmet burgers, pizza, salads, and American dinner entrées with a Mediterranean flair. Breakfast is served on the weekend. The large pine tree on the outdoor deck provides pleasant shade. **Bar:** full bar. **Reservations:** suggested. **Address:** 13460 Lincoln Way 95603 **Location:** I-80 exit 121 (Foresthill Rd/Auburn Ravine Rd); just e, then just n. L D

MONKEY CAT RESTAURANT & BAR
530/888-8492

WV WV W American. Casual Dining. $9-$29 AAA Inspector Notes: This lively bistro in the Sierra foothills offers a varied menu selection with local produce and products used whenever possible. Lunch is offered Monday through Friday. An outdoor patio is available in season. **Bar:** full bar. **Reservations:** suggested. **Address:** 805 Lincoln Way 95603 **Location:** I-80 exit Elm Ave, just e, then just s; jct Cherry Ave; downtown. **Parking:** street only. D CALL M

BASS LAKE   pop. 527
- Hotels & Restaurants map & index p. 584
- Part of Yosemite National Park area — see map p. 578

THE PINES RESORT CHALETS
559/642-3121   31

WV WV
Cottage
Rates not provided

Address: 54449 Rd 432 93604 **Location:** Waterfront. 6 mi e of SR 41 exit CR 222, e on CR 274, then s on CR 434. Located in Pines Village. **Facility:** 84 cottages. 2 stories (no elevator), exterior corridors. **Terms:** check-in 4 pm. **Amenities:** high-speed Internet. **Dining:** 2 restaurants. **Pool(s):** outdoor. **Activities:** whirlpool, fishing, 2 tennis courts, playground, exercise room. *Fee:* boats, marina, waterskiing, massage. **Guest Services:** coin laundry. **Free Special Amenities:** early check-in/late check-out and high-speed Internet.

 / SOME UNITS FEE

THE PINES RESORT SUITES
559/642-3121   32

WV WV WV
Hotel
Rates not provided

Address: 54449 Rd 432 93604 **Location:** Waterfront. 6 mi e of SR 41 exit CR 222, e on CR 274, then s on CR 434. Located in Pines Village. **Facility:** 20 units. 2 stories, interior corridors. **Terms:** check-in 4 pm. **Amenities:** high-speed Internet. **Dining:** 2 restaurants. **Pool(s):** outdoor. **Activities:** whirlpool, fishing, 2 tennis courts, playground, exercise room. *Fee:* boats, marina, waterskiing, massage. **Guest Services:** coin laundry. **Free Special Amenities:** full breakfast and high-speed Internet.

WHERE TO EAT

DUCEY'S BAR AND GRILL
559/642-3131

fyi Not evaluated. This is a great stop for a casual lunch or dinner with views of the lake. Hearty appetizers can make meals of their own or guests can enjoy one of the tasty burgers, sandwiches, quesadilla or fish and chips. **Address:** 39255 Marina Dr 93604 **Location:** 6 mi e of SR 41 exit CR 222, e on CR 274, then s on CR 434; at Pines Resort.

DUCEY'S ON THE LAKE
559/642-3131

fyi Not evaluated. Enjoy spectacular views of the lake while dining on one of the specialty dishes including hearty salads with organic lettuce, grilled steaks, lamb, fresh salmon or mahi mahi as well as pasta dishes. **Address:** 39255 Marina Dr 93604 **Location:** 6 mi e of SR 41 exit CR 222, e on CR 274, then s on CR 434; at Pines Resort.

BELMONT   pop. 25,835
- Hotels & Restaurants map & index p. 410
- Part of San Francisco area — see map p. 342

HOLIDAY INN EXPRESS HOTEL & SUITES
(650)654-4000   78

WV WV WV
Hotel
$99-$189

Address: 1650 El Camino Real 94002 **Location:** US 101 exit 412 (Ralston Ave), 0.4 mi w to SR 82, then 0.4 mi s. **Facility:** 82 units. 3 stories, interior corridors. **Amenities:** high-speed Internet. **Guest Services:** valet laundry. **Free Special Amenities:** expanded continental breakfast and high-speed Internet.

HOTEL BELMONT
(650)593-3495   77

WV WV WV
Motel
$90-$120

Address: 560 El Camino Real 94002 **Location:** US 101 exit 412 (Ralston Ave/Marine Pkwy), 0.4 mi w on Ralston Ave, then 0.6 mi n. **Facility:** 16 units. 2 stories (no elevator), exterior corridors. **Terms:** cancellation fee imposed. **Free Special Amenities:** local telephone calls and high-speed Internet.

HYATT HOUSE BELMONT/REDWOOD SHORES
(650)591-8600   76

WV WV WV
Extended Stay Hotel
$119-$219

AAA Benefit: Members save 10% or more everyday.

Address: 400 Concourse Dr 94002 **Location:** US 101 exit 412 (Ralston Ave/Belmont), just e, then 0.3 mi n on Island Pkwy. **Facility:** 132 kitchen units, some two bedrooms. 3 stories (no elevator), exterior corridors. **Terms:** cancellation fee imposed. **Amenities:** high-speed Internet. **Pool(s):** heated outdoor. **Activities:** whirlpool, sports court, exercise room. **Guest Services:** valet and coin laundry, area transportation-within 5 mi. **Free Special Amenities:** expanded continental breakfast and high-speed Internet.

/ SOME UNITS FEE

WHERE TO EAT

CAPRINO'S
650/591-4156   56

WV WV WV Italian. Casual Dining. $9-$29 AAA Inspector Notes: At this restaurant, high ceilings are offered with an interesting mural depicting a hole in the ceiling with blue skies and flying cherubs. The dining area is well spaced and comfortable. Food is well-executed with dishes from Italy and New Orleans, including vongole and jambalaya. **Bar:** full bar. **Address:** 1000 6th Ave 94002 **Location:** US 101 exit 412 (Ralston Ave), 0.6 mi w. L

GODFATHER'S BURGER LOUNGE
650/637-9257   58

WV WV Burgers. Casual Dining. $9-$12 AAA Inspector Notes: Aptly named, this small burger joint has an ambience with a bar-lounge vibe. Slides of famed actors and actresses are shown on a flat-screen TV. Gourmet burgers come with such names as Untouchables' burger and Soprano's ultimate burger. Wine from Francis Coppola's winery also are featured. **Bar:** beer & wine. **Address:** 1500 El Camino Real 94002 **Location:** At Harbor Blvd. **Parking:** street only. L D

(See map & index p. 410.)

THE VAN'S RESTAURANT 650/591-6525 (55)

▼▼▼ Continental. Casual Dining. $10-$37 **AAA Inspector Notes:** Built in 1915 as part of the Japanese exhibit for The Panama Pacific Exposition in San Francisco, The Van's is one of only two remaining structures. (The Palace of Fine Arts is the other.) Patrons enjoy panoramic views of the San Francisco Bay as they savor steaks, ribs and seafood. **Bar:** full bar. **Address:** 815 Belmont Ave 94002 **Location:** US 101 exit 412 (Ralston Ave), 0.5 mi w to SR 82, 0.5 mi n to Belmont Ave, then just w. L D

VIVACE RISTORANTE 650/637-0611 (57)

▼▼▼ Italian. Casual Dining. $11-$28 **AAA Inspector Notes:** An elegant skylight brightens the main dining area of this ristorante. Romantic, elegant hanging sconces spotlight booth seats. Osso buco stands out among offerings of Northern Italian fare that emphasizes the regions of Piemonte and Toscana. The wine list is extensive. Complimentary valet parking is available from Thursday through Saturday. **Bar:** full bar. **Address:** 1910 Ralston Ave 94002 **Location:** US 101 exit 412 (Ralston Ave), 1.5 mi w. **Parking:** street only.

L D

BENICIA (C-9) pop. 26,997, elev. 33'

Named after the wife of Mariano Guadalupe Vallejo, one of its founders, Benicia boasts California's oldest standing capitol building. The city supported an Army arsenal and barracks as well as the Pacific Mail Steamship Co. before becoming the state's third capital in 1853. Several well-preserved houses date back to those early years of statehood.

Benicia also boasts the oldest Masonic temple in the state and Saint Paul's Episcopal Church, one of the first Episcopal cathedrals in northern California. Scandinavian shipwrights who worked on the church created a ceiling that resembles an inverted ship's hull, a design similar to those of Norwegian stave churches.

Other historic structures include the four sandstone buildings of the Benicia Camel Barn Museum, built 1853-57. The museum contains exhibits recounting the history of Benicia and the U.S. Army Arsenal. It was at the arsenal that the last of the animals from the Army's camel corps were auctioned off in 1864; the camel corps was a brief attempt at using camels as draft animals in the deserts of the Southwest.

Benicia Chamber of Commerce and Visitor Center: 601 First St., Suite 100, Benicia, CA 94510-3211. **Phone:** (707) 745-2120.

Self-guiding tours: The chamber of commerce distributes a visitors guide that includes information about self-guiding walking tours of historic Benicia.

BENICIA CAPITOL STATE HISTORIC PARK, First and West G sts., preserves the Greek Revival building that served as the third state capitol Feb. 4, 1853-Feb. 25, 1854. The structure is restored and furnished in period. The Fischer-Hanlon House, at 135 West G St. next to the historic park, is a renovated gold rush hotel furnished in period; the house can only be visited on a guided tour.

Time: Allow 30 minutes minimum. **Hours:** Park open Sat.-Sun. 10-5. Closed Jan. 1, Thanksgiving and Christmas. Phone ahead to confirm schedule. **Cost:** $3 (includes Fischer-Hanlon House, when open); $2 (ages 6-17). Reservations are required for guided tours of the capitol and for tours of the Fischer-Hanlon House. **Phone:** (707) 745-3385.

BEST WESTERN PLUS HERITAGE INN (707)746-0401

Hotel
$100-$190

AAA Benefit: Members save up to 20%, plus 10% bonus points with Best Western Rewards®.

PLUS

Address: 1955 E 2nd St 94510 **Location:** I-780 exit Central Benicia/E 2nd St, just e. **Facility:** 97 units. 3 stories, interior/exterior corridors. **Terms:** cancellation fee imposed. **Amenities:** high-speed Internet. **Pool(s):** outdoor. **Activities:** whirlpool. **Guest Services:** valet and coin laundry. **Free Special Amenities:** local telephone calls and high-speed Internet.

    🛜 📠 🖨️ 🖥️ / SOME UNITS FEE 🐾

HOLIDAY INN EXPRESS 707/297-6873

Hotel
Rates not provided

Address: 1375 E Fifth St 94510 **Location:** I-780 exit 6, just s. **Facility:** 49 units. 2 stories, interior corridors. **Bath:** shower only. **Amenities:** high-speed Internet. Some: video games. **Activities:** exercise room. **Guest Services:** valet and coin laundry. **Free Special Amenities:** full breakfast and high-speed Internet.

SAVE 🍴 CALL 📶 🛜 ✖️ 🖨️ 🖥️ 🖲️

WHERE TO EAT

FIRST ST CAFE 707/745-1400

▼▼ American. Casual Dining. $9-$25 **AAA Inspector Notes:** This casual cafe is a definite favorite of the local crowd. Arrive early as tables fill up quickly. The menu offers a selection of favorites including various sandwiches, salads and soups. The dinner menu includes seafood, lamb and pasta dishes. Freshly made pies, crisps, cookies and bread pudding are made on site. **Bar:** beer & wine. **Address:** 440 First St 94510 **Location:** I-780 exit 2nd St/Downtown Benicia W, just n on Military St, then 0.5 mi w. **Parking:** street only.

B L D CALL 📶

ROUND TABLE PIZZA 707/746-7000

▼ Pizza. Casual Dining. $7-$28 **AAA Inspector Notes:** This casual, family-oriented pizza place features high-quality ingredients and dough rolled fresh daily. Distinctive specialty pizzas are piled high with toppings. **Bar:** beer & wine. **Address:** 878 Southampton Rd 94510 **Location:** I-780 exit Southampton Rd N; between Panorama and Chelsea Hills drs. L D

BEN LOMOND pop. 6,234

JAYE'S TIMBERLANE RESORT (831)336-5479

Cottage
$95-$175

Address: 8705 Hwy 9 95005 **Location:** SR 9, 0.5 mi s. **Facility:** 10 cottages. 1 story, exterior corridors. **Bath:** shower only. **Terms:** 2-3 night minimum stay - seasonal and/or weekends, 7 day cancellation notice-fee imposed. **Pool(s):** outdoor. **Free Special Amenities:** preferred room (subject to availability with advance reservations) and high-speed Internet.

SAVE 🏊 🛜 ✖️ 🍴 🎞️ 🖨️ 🖥️

QUALITY INN & SUITES SANTA CRUZ MOUNTAINS (831)336-2292

Motel
$62-$359

Address: 9733 Hwy 9 95005 **Location:** SR 9, 0.3 mi n; on San Lorenzo River. **Facility:** 25 units, some cottages. 2 stories (no elevator), exterior corridors. **Terms:** 3 day cancellation notice-fee imposed. **Amenities:** high-speed Internet. **Pool(s):** outdoor. **Activities:** fishing. **Guest Services:** valet laundry. **Free Special Amenities:** expanded continental breakfast and high-speed Internet. SAVE 🏊 🛜 ✖️ 🖨️ 🖥️ / SOME UNITS 🖨️

BERKELEY (C-8) pop. 112,580, elev. 152'
- Hotels p. 54 • Restaurants p. 55
- Hotels & Restaurants map & index p. 254

Eclectic, inquiring and experimental are all words that apply to Berkeley—and it's no surprise, given the city's reputation as one of the nation's leading academic centers. The University of California Berkeley, with more than 35,000 students, is often in the vanguard of any nationwide campus movement, whether it be political, artistic or philosophic.

The David Brower Center, downtown at 2150 Allston Way, epitomizes this progressive nature. The LEED Platinum mixed-use building utilizes the latest in energy-saving technologies, and more than half of the materials used in its construction were recycled. There are usually thought-provoking art installations on display in the building's public areas.

Like San Francisco, Berkeley spreads over a series of hills that are called, not surprisingly, the Berkeley Hills. Residential neighborhoods cover their western slopes, which overlook the northeast corner of San Francisco Bay. Streets twist and turn according to the contours of the land, and the higher you ascend the more impressive the views become.

And also like San Francisco, Berkeley has a network of pedestrian paths and stairways. Some of these "pathways" are simply steps built into the sidewalk that make it easier to climb a steep section of hill; others are public paths in between houses. And fortunately for walkers and urban explorers, most of them are located in lovely old neighborhoods full of trees, gardens, architecturally diverse homes and frequently glorious vistas.

One of the most picturesque of these stairways is Orchard Lane. (To get to Orchard Lane from the UC campus, walk east on Bancroft Way to the Bancroft Steps, take the Bancroft Steps up to Prospect Street, continue to Panoramic Way, turn right and watch for the sign on the left-hand side of the street.) The formal pedestrian residence to the Panoramic Hill residential neighborhood, it was built in 1909 in the grand classical style, linking houses near and along it with the university and downtown Berkeley. The stone steps, pillars, balustrades and benches all have a weathered beauty, heightened by an overhanging bower of trees. At the top of the stairway you can catch a glimpse of San Francisco Bay in the distance.

Short Cut Path is another attractive stone stairway that begins at a parking lot on the grounds of the Claremont Hotel Club & Spa. This sprawling complex is situated on a hillside and looks every inch the handsomely appointed resort. Built in 1915, the Claremont has long been a favorite honeymoon destination as well as a weekend getaway for well-heeled Bay Area residents. If you're not a guest, you can still stroll around the attractively landscaped grounds.

Many of Berkeley's paths and stairways are hard to find, even if you're a resident, and while they're all named, some of them are not signed. If you intend to do a little exploring, it's well worth obtaining the detailed map produced by the Berkeley Path Wanderers Association. The map can be purchased online or by mail for $8.55; write the Berkeley Path Wanderers Association, 1442A Walnut St., Box 269, Berkeley, CA 94709.

Berkeley Marina, at the foot of University Avenue, serves as a base for a large charter boat fleet. The marina's 3,000-foot public fishing pier is open to the public, and no fishing license is required; phone (510) 981-6740. Boating, model yacht racing and bird-watching are popular on and along the mile-long saltwater lake in Aquatic Park, at the foot of Bancroft Way.

Golden Gate Fields, 1100 Eastshore Hwy., offers horse racing Wednesday through Sunday on a seasonal schedule; for race times and other information phone (510) 559-7300. **Note:** Policies concerning admittance of children to pari-mutuel betting facilities vary. Phone for information.

Visit Berkeley: 2030 Addison St., Suite 102, Berkeley, CA 94704. **Phone:** (510) 549-7040 or (800) 847-4823.

Self-guiding tours: A brochure describing a walking tour of downtown architectural points of interest is available from Visit Berkeley.

BADÈ MUSEUM OF BIBLICAL ARCHAEOLOGY & DOUG ADAMS GALLERY, in the Holbrook Building at the Pacific School of Religion at 1798 Scenic Ave. at jct. Le Conte Ave. and Ridge Rd., displays archeological artifacts from a town in biblical Israel and contemporary art on religious themes.

The museum's collections include ancient artifacts from Tell en-Nasbeh, the biblical site of Mizpah, and permanent displays about themes of everyday life in a biblical city. The Doug Adams gallery, named after a long-time professor at the college, features pieces by artists working in various media and in varied religious and spiritual themes.

Time: Allow 30 minutes minimum. **Hours:** Tues. and Thurs.-Fri. 10-3, June-Apr. Closed major holidays. Phone ahead to confirm schedule. **Cost:** Donations. **Phone:** (510) 849-8286.
🏛 Downtown Berkeley, 11

BERKELEY ROSE GARDEN, Euclid Ave. at Bayview Pl., contains more than 3,000 rose bushes representing 250 varieties of the flower. The main blooming season is May through September; the roses are at their peak in May and June. A terraced amphitheater and arbor overlook the bay and Golden Gate Bridge. Also available are tennis courts and scenic hiking trails. **Hours:** Daily dawn-dusk. The garden may be closed during special occasions; phone ahead. **Cost:** Free. **Phone:** (510) 981-5150. 🏛

GRIZZLY PEAK BOULEVARD, which can be reached from the head of Spruce St. or from other points along the city's n.e. edge, winds along the crest of the hills behind the city at elevations up to

(See map & index p. 254.)

1,600 feet. The scenic drive provides access to attractions within Tilden Regional Park as well as a view of San Francisco Bay.

HABITOT CHILDREN'S MUSEUM is downtown at 2065 Kittredge St.; there are entrances on both Kittredge St. and Shattuck Ave. This hands-on museum geared toward children 7 and under has themed exhibits where infants, toddlers and small children can learn while they play. Kids can dam a stream, get messy in the art studio, shop in a grocery, order and serve food at a cafe, and maneuver through a floor-to-ceiling tunnel-like maze.

Time: Allow 1 hour minimum. **Hours:** Mon.-Thurs. 9:30-12:30, Fri.-Sun. 9:30-4:30, Oct.-Mar.; Mon.-Thurs. 9:30-12:30, Fri.-Sat. 9:30-4:30, rest of year. Closed Jan. 1, Easter, Memorial Day, July 4, Labor Day, Thanksgiving, Christmas Eve and Christmas. **Cost:** $9.75; $8.75 (ages 60+ and the physically impaired); free (ages 0-12 months). **Phone:** (510) 647-1111.
Downtown Berkeley, 11

LACIS MUSEUM OF LACE AND TEXTILES, 2982 Adeline St. at jct. Ashby Ave., exhibits the extensive lace and textile collection of Kaethe and Jules Kliot, an accumulation gathered over a period of 40 years. Examples include pieces from pre-Columbian Peru, 17th-century Europe and laces typical of the 19th-century industrial revolution. **Time:** Allow 1 hour minimum. **Hours:** Mon.-Sat. noon-6. Closed major holidays. **Cost:** Free. **Phone:** (510) 843-7290.
Ashby, 10

TAKARA SAKE USA INC., 708 Addison St., has an exhibit that explains how sake is made as well as a collection of sake artifacts. A video pertaining to the production of Japanese sake and the history of sake making is presented. A variety of samples are available in a tasting room. **Hours:** Daily noon-6. Closed some holidays. **Cost:** $5. **Phone:** (510) 540-8250.

TILDEN REGIONAL PARK is off Grizzly Peak Blvd. on the n.e. edge of Berkeley. Park features include a botanic garden, nature area, golf course and a Herschell Spillman merry-go-round. You can hike and bike the park trails, and go swimming and fishing in Lake Anza. The Environmental Education Center, near Jewel Lake, has an exhibit hall and a farm display complete with livestock and equipment. Miniature steam train rides also are offered.

Hours: Park open daily 5 a.m.-10 p.m. Botanic garden open daily 8:30-5:30, June-Sept.; 8:30-5, rest of year. Environmental Education Center open Tues.-Sun. 10-4:30. Merry-go-round daily 11-5, mid-June through Labor Day; Sat.-Sun. 11-5, rest of year. Train rides Mon.-Fri. 11-5, Sat.-Sun. 11-6, mid-June through Labor Day; Sat.-Sun. 11-6, rest of year. Park closed holidays except July 4 and Labor Day. Environmental center closed major holidays. Phone ahead to confirm schedule.

Cost: Park free. Swimming $3.50; $2.50 (ages 1-15 and 62+). Merry-go-round $2 per ride, or seven rides for $10. Train ride $3; free (ages 0-1); $12 (family, includes five rides). **Phone:** (510) 544-2233 for the Environmental Education Center, (510) 524-6773 for the merry-go-round, (510) 548-6100 for the train, or (888) 327-2757 for the park.

UNIVERSITY OF CALIFORNIA BERKELEY, e. of Oxford St. between Hearst St. and Bancroft Way, occupies a beautiful 1,232-acre campus. South Hall, built in 1873, is California's oldest university building. Regarded as one of the nation's leading public universities, Berkeley is known for its quality undergraduate and graduate programs. Guided 90-minute walking tours of the campus are available.

The University of California Golden Bears football team takes to the gridiron at Memorial Stadium, and the university's men's and women's basketball teams play at Haas Pavilion.

Hours: Guided walking tours depart from the visitor center at 101 Sproul Hall at the corner of Bancroft Way and Telegraph Ave., Mon.-Fri. at 10 and from the clock tower Sat. at 10, Sun. at 1. Reservations are required for tours and can be made online or by phone. **Phone:** (510) 642-5215 for the visitor center, (510) 642-3277 for the athletic department, or (800) 462-3277 for ticket information.
Downtown Berkeley, 11

Campanile, at the center of the University of California Berkeley campus, is 307 feet tall and contains a 61-bell carillon that chimes on the hour and plays music. Also known as Sather Tower, the campus landmark was built in 1914. An elevator and staircase take visitors to the observation deck, from which Oakland, San Francisco and the Golden Gate Bridge can be seen.

Hours: Music is played daily at 7:50 a.m., noon and 6 p.m., during the school year; schedule varies rest of year. Recitals lasting 45 minutes are performed Sun. at 2. Elevator operates Mon.-Fri. 10-3:45, Sat. 10-4:45, Sun. 10-1:30 and 3-5. Closed university holidays. **Cost:** Elevator fee $2; $1 (ages 3-17 and senior citizens). **Phone:** (510) 642-5215.
Downtown Berkeley, 11

Lawrence Hall of Science, Centennial Dr. on the e. side of the University of California Berkeley campus, is a public science center that includes hands-on exhibits, a planetarium and an outdoor science park.

Time: Allow 2 hours minimum. **Hours:** Science hall open daily 10-5. Planetarium shows daily at 1, 2 and 3, mid-June to mid-Aug.; Sat.-Sun. and holidays at 1, 2 and 3, rest of year. Closed Labor Day, Thanksgiving and Christmas. **Cost:** $12; $9 (ages 7-18, ages 62+ and the physically impaired); $6 (ages 3-6). Planetarium shows cost an additional $4; special exhibitions cost an additional $5. **Phone:** (510) 642-5132.

(See map & index p. 254.)

PFA Library & Film Study Center is located inside the UC Berkeley Art Museum and Pacific Film Archive (BAM/PFA) at 2626 Bancroft Way (between College and Telegraph aves.). The library houses a large collection of films and videos from around the world. Public screenings at the PFA Theater, 2575 Bancroft Way, include classic movies, restored silent films and works by renowned directors. **Hours:** Library open Mon.-Wed. 1-5. Films are generally shown Wed.-Sun.; phone for schedule information. **Cost:** Single film feature $9.50; $6.50 (ages 0-17, ages 65+, the physically impaired and non-UC Berkeley students). Additional feature $4 extra. **Phone:** (510) 642-1124, or (510) 642-5249 1 day in advance to order tickets.

Downtown Berkeley, 11

Phoebe A. Hearst Museum of Anthropology is in Kroeber Hall on Bancroft Way (at College Ave.). It has exhibits about ethnology, archeology and anthropology. The nearly 4 million items in the museum's collections include artifacts from California as well as other countries throughout the world. **Note:** The museum is currently closed for renovation and is expected to reopen sometime in 2014. Phone ahead or visit the website for updates. **Hours:** Wed.-Sat. 10-4:30, Sun. noon-4. Closed major holidays. **Cost:** Free. **Phone:** (510) 643-7648.

Downtown Berkeley, 11

UC Berkeley Art Museum and Pacific Film Archive (BAM/PFA) is at 2626 Bancroft Way (between College and Telegraph aves.). It features contemporary and Asian art as well as 18th- and 19th-century paintings. Touring exhibits are presented regularly. **Time:** Allow 1 hour, 30 minutes minimum. **Hours:** Wed.-Sun. 11-5 (also some Fridays 5-9). Phone ahead to confirm schedule. **Cost:** $10; $7 (ages 13-17, ages 65+, the physically impaired, non-UC Berkeley students, and to all on Fridays the museum is open late); free to all first Thurs. of the month (except PFA theater programs). **Phone:** (510) 642-0808. Downtown Berkeley, 11

UC Botanical Garden is at 200 Centennial Dr., about midway between UC Berkeley Memorial Stadium and the Lawrence Hall of Science. This scientific research and display garden has a collection of plants from around the world, grouped according to origin in nine major geographic regions. One of the most interesting sections is New World Desert, which contains a variety of cacti, succulents and other desert dwellers.

Another fascinating collection, Southern Africa, explodes with color in spring when such perennials as Cape cowslips, Cape marigolds and proteas are in bloom. The California collection showcases the state's diversity of native flora, including a redwood forest and such wildflowers as the California poppy (the California state flower), which blooms from February through June.

There's also a garden with rose cultivars from the 19th and early 20th centuries, a Chinese medicinal herb garden, and greenhouses containing cacti, tropicals, orchids, ferns and carnivorous plants. The hillside location, surrounded by woodlands, is serene and lovely.

Time: Allow 1 hour minimum. **Hours:** Daily 9-5. One-hour tours are given Thurs. and Sat.-Sun. at 1:30. Last admission is 30 minutes before closing. Closed Jan. 1, Martin Luther King Jr. Day, Thanksgiving, Christmas Eve, Christmas, Dec. 31 and the first Tues. of the month. **Cost:** $10; $8 (ages 65+ and students with ID); $5 (ages 13-17); $2 (ages 5-12); free (first Thurs. of the month). A fee is charged for parking. **Phone:** (510) 643-2755.

AMERICAS BEST VALUE GOLDEN BEAR INN
(510)525-6770 **18**

Motel
$80-$160

Address: 1620 San Pablo Ave 94702 **Location:** I-80 exit 12 (Gilman St), 0.5 mi e, then just s. North Berkeley, 12. **Facility:** 40 units. 1 story, exterior corridors. **Free Special Amenities:** early check-in/late check-out and high-speed Internet.

CLAREMONT HOTEL CLUB & SPA
(510)843-3000 **25**

Historic Hotel
$189-$499

Address: 41 Tunnel Rd 94705 **Location:** SR 13 and 24 exit SR 24 (Claremont Ave) eastbound, 1 mi n; I-80 exit 11 (University Ave E), just e, then 1.5 mi s on San Pablo Ave, 2.6 mi e on Ashby Ave, then just e. **Facility:** Located in Berkeley Hills, this converted 1915 Victorian castle is a popular spot for honeymooners as well as a weekend getaway for the locals. 279 units. 7 stories, interior corridors. **Parking:** on-site (fee) and valet. **Terms:** check-in 4 pm, cancellation fee imposed, resort fee. **Amenities:** video games (fee), safes. **Dining:** 3 restaurants. **Pool(s):** 3 heated outdoor. **Activities:** saunas, whirlpools, 10 lighted tennis courts, recreation programs, jogging, spa. **Guest Services:** valet laundry. **Free Special Amenities:** newspaper and room upgrade (subject to availability with advance reservations). *(See ad p. 55.)*

DOUBLETREE BY HILTON BERKELEY MARINA
(510)548-7920 **19**

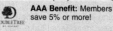
Hotel
$129-$269

AAA Benefit: Members save 5% or more!

Address: 200 Marina Blvd 94710 **Location:** I-80 exit 11 (University Ave), 0.5 mi w; on Berkeley Marina. **Facility:** 378 units. 1-4 stories, interior corridors. **Terms:** 1-7 night minimum stay, cancellation fee imposed. **Amenities:** *Fee:* video games, high-speed Internet. **Pool(s):** 2 heated indoor. **Activities:** sauna, whirlpools, jogging, exercise room. **Guest Services:** valet and coin laundry, area transportation-within 3 mi & BART.

Get more from your membership with an upgrade to Plus or Premier

(See map & index p. 254.)

HOLIDAY INN EXPRESS HOTEL & SUITES
(510)548-1700 **20**

WWW **Hotel** $159-$299 **Address:** 1175 University Ave 94702 **Location:** I-80 exit 11 (University Ave E), 0.7 mi e. North Berkeley, 12. **Facility:** 69 units, some two bedrooms and kitchens. 3 stories, interior corridors. **Amenities:** high-speed Internet, safes. **Activities:** exercise room. **Guest Services:** valet and coin laundry.

【†】 CALL ⅏M BIZ 🛜 ✕ 🗄 🍴 ⊟ 🚗

HOTEL DURANT, A JOIE DE VIVRE HOTEL
510/845-8981 **24**

WWW **Hotel.** Rates not provided. **Address:** 2600 Durant Ave 94704 **Location:** I-80 exit 11 (University Ave E), 0.3 mi s, then 0.5 mi e; jct Bowditch St. Downtown Berkeley, 11. **Facility:** 143 units, some two bedrooms. 6 stories, interior corridors. **Parking:** on-site (fee) and valet. **Amenities:** high-speed Internet, safes. **Guest Services:** valet laundry.

ECO FEE ✕ 【†】 Ⓨ FEE 🛜 ✕ 🖥 / SOME UNITS 🐾 🚗

HOTEL SHATTUCK PLAZA
(510)845-7300 **23**

WWW **Hotel** $139-$450 **Address:** 2086 Allston Way 94704 **Location:** I-80 exit 11 (University Ave E), 2 mi e, just s on Shattuck Ave, then just w. Downtown Berkeley, 11. **Facility:** 199 units. 5 stories, interior corridors. **Parking:** on-site (fee). **Terms:** cancellation fee imposed. **Amenities:** high-speed Internet. **Activities:** exercise room. **Guest Services:** valet laundry.

【†】 Ⓨ CALL ⅏M BIZ 🛜 ✕ / SOME UNITS FEE ⊟ 🍴 🚗

QUALITY INN UNIVERSITY
(510)841-4242 **22**

WWW WW **Motel** $145-$165 **Address:** 1761 University Ave 94703 **Location:** I-80 exit 11 (University Ave E), 1.5 mi e; just e of Grant St. North Berkeley, 12. **Facility:** 28 units. 2 stories (no elevator), exterior corridors. **Terms:** 3 day cancellation notice-fee imposed, resort fee. **Amenities:** high-speed Internet. **Guest Services:** valet laundry.

SAVE 【†】 🛜 ✕ 🗄 🍴 ⊟ 🚗

SUPER 8
(510)841-3844 **21**

WW WW **Motel** $69-$209 **Address:** 1619 University Ave 94703 **Location:** I-80 exit 11 (University Ave E), 1.3 mi e, make U-turn at Jefferson Ave. North Berkeley, 12. **Facility:** 23 units, some two bedrooms. 2 stories (no elevator), exterior corridors. **Bath:** shower only. **Amenities:** high-speed Internet, safes.

CALL ⅏M 🛁 🛜 ✕ 🗄 🍴 ⊟ 🚗

WHERE TO EAT

BISTRO LIAISON
510/849-2155 **18**

WWW
French
Fine Dining
$10-$25

AAA Inspector Notes: Offering such traditional favorites as French onion soup with an Emmental gratinee, escargot and halibut a la Provencal, this French bistro is open early for fresh croissants and hot coffee. The bistro offers French-style decor with an open-grill kitchen. **Bar:** full bar. **Reservations:** suggested. **Address:** 1849 Shattuck Ave 94709 **Location:** I-80 exit 11 (University Ave E), 2 mi e, then just n at Hearst Ave. Downtown Berkeley, 11. **Parking:** street only. *Menu on AAA.com*

Ⓛ Ⓓ 🗡 🚗

CAFE ROUGE RESTAURANT & MEAT MARKET
(510)525-1440 **17**

WWWW **Mediterranean. Casual Dining.** $13-$34 **AAA Inspector Notes:** A pasta market is attached to this cozy, casual bistro. Rustic Mediterranean French and Italian items are prepared with flair and an emphasis on fresh, organic meats and homemade charcuterie. Dry-aged steaks are offered in the meat market and on the daily menu which changes every two weeks. Heated, outside seating is available in season. Upon entering, guests are met with enticing aromas, a trickling water fountain and vibrant décor. **Bar:** full bar. **Reservations:** suggested. **Address:** 1782 4th St 94710 **Location:** I-80 exit 11 (University Ave E) to 6th St, just n, just w on Hearst Ave, then just n; exit 11 northbound, follow signs to 4th St and Frontage Rd; between Hearst Ave and Delaware St. North Berkeley, 12. Ⓛ Ⓓ CALL ⅏M 🗡 🚗

CHEZ PANISSE
510/548-5525 **16**

WWWW **Regional American. Fine Dining.** $20-$80 **AAA Inspector Notes:** California, French and strong Mediterranean influences mingle in this restaurant's intriguing dishes. At the same location, the more casual café serves a full menu for lunch and has a less-restrictive reservation policy. Breakfast is served every morning in the lobby, overlooking the small, relaxing pool area. **Bar:** beer & wine. **Reservations:** required. **Address:** 1517 Shattuck Ave 94709 **Location:** I-80 exit 11 (University Ave E), 1.7 mi e, then 0.5 mi n; jct Cedar St. Downtown Berkeley, 11. **Parking:** street only.

Ⓛ Ⓓ CALL ⅏M 🚗

Get an insider view from AAA/CAA travel experts at AAATravelViews.com

▼ *See AAA listing p. 54* ▼

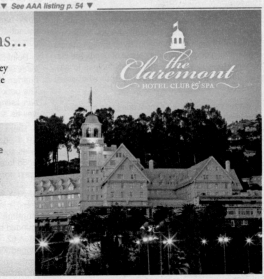

(See map & index p. 254.)

KIRALA RESTAURANT   510/549-3486 ⓴
♥♥♥ Japanese Sushi. Casual Dining. $7-$26 **AAA Inspector
Notes:** A friendly atmosphere prevails at this restaurant where the
menu offers fresh sushi selections daily as well as other traditional
items including tempura, teriyaki, donburi and udon. Come early as
the restaurant fills up quickly. **Bar:** beer & wine. **Address:** 2100 Ward
St 94705 **Location:** I-80 exit Ashby Ave, 1.6 mi e, then 0.3 mi n on
Shattuck Ave. 🖼 Ashby, 10. **Parking:** on-site and street.

Ⓛ Ⓓ 🄺 🄐

SKATES ON THE BAY   510/549-1900 ⓳
♥♥♥ American. Fine Dining. $11-$49 **AAA Inspector Notes:**
Internationally flavored seafood dishes combined with million dollar
views of the Golden Gate Bridge and the San Francisco skyline keep
the locals returning. For an appetizer, try the smoked salmon-
wrapped scallops and, if available, the exotic sounding Barramundi
fish with Thai curry. For dessert, go for the three puddings served in
dainty demitasse cups. **Bar:** full bar. **Reservations:** suggested. **Address:** 100 Seawall Dr 94710 **Location:** I-80 exit 11 (University Ave),
0.3 mi w; on Berkeley Marina. Ⓛ Ⓓ CALL 🄻Ⓜ

BIG SUR (H-3) elev. 155'

The name Big Sur is derived from the Spanish *el
sur grande,* which means "the big south." It's a reference to terrain comprising sheer cliffs that loom
above the ocean; to the foothills of the rugged Santa
Lucia Mountains, rising up less than 10 miles inland;
and to the wooded valleys between them. This entire wilderness region was basically inaccessible
until the opening of SR 1, popularly known as California Highway 1, in 1937. The road paved the way
for tourism.

The village of Big Sur is scenically strung out
along SR 1 south of Andrew Molera State Park *(see
Recreation Areas Chart),* at one of the few points
where the roadway veers inland and tunnels though
a beautiful stand of redwoods. More commonly,
though, Big Sur refers to the magnificently
rugged—and blessedly pristine—90-mile-long
stretch of California coast that runs from Carmel-by-
the-Sea *(see place listing p. 67)* south to San
Simeon.

Two-lane SR 1 snakes along the Big Sur coast in
a seemingly endless series of sinuous S-curves,
rarely out of sight of the ocean. Even though there's
a guardrail along the side, a couple of bends are diz-
zyingly close to a sheer drop-off. Needless to say,
you don't speed on this highway—but who would
want to?

Better yet, there's an almost complete absence of
man-made distractions. There are no billboards. No
strip centers. No fast-food outlets. No gas stations
(just gas pumps at a couple of roadside establishments in Big Sur village). In other words, no visual
blight gets in the way of nature's glory.

Numerous strategically located pull-off parking
areas allow you to stand at the very edge of a cliff
top and position yourself for what is almost guaranteed to be a memorable photo. Just point and click;
nature takes care of the rest. The elevation of the
highway varies from near sea level to nearly 1,000
feet above. But most of the vista points are high
above the Pacific, and the panoramic views of headlands extending for miles along the coastline—

against a backdrop of steel-blue ocean—are simply
breathtaking.

A variety of plants cling for dear life to the cliff
edges. Rocks are carpeted with ice plants, a succulent ground cover with fleshy, deep green leaves
and pink, yellow and white flowers that look like
small daisies. Wildflowers bloom in seasonal bursts
of color. It's nature at its wildest that resembles a
manicured rock garden.

One necessary man-made concession to travel is
the suspension bridge, and there are several of
them along the highway. Shutterbugs can clamber
down an ice plant-covered sand dune to get a shot
of the Rocky Creek Bridge. A bit farther south is the
larger Bixby Bridge, arching above waves crashing
against the rocks far below.

In addition to a wealth of spectacular scenery, Big
Sur has an artsy, quintessentially Californian vibe;
spas, healing centers and art galleries line SR 1 in
the vicinity of Big Sur village. Henry Miller was a
resident for 18 years, Jack Kerouac sang Big Sur's
praises in a novel and Hollywood weighed in with
"The Sandpiper," a 1965 movie starring Richard
Burton and Elizabeth Taylor that featured Taylor
playing a caftan-clad Big Sur artist.

Nepenthe, a combination restaurant, outdoor cafe
(Cafe Kevah) and retail store (Phoenix), totally em-
bodies this bohemian spirit. The three-level complex
perches on a hillside landscaped with pretty gardens; both restaurant and cafe have outdoor ter-
races with umbrella-shaded tables and to-die-for
views of green hills rolling down to the Pacific. Either
one is a perfect spot to just chill for an hour or so.

Phoenix is one of those gift shops that sells things
you don't really need but have to have: Navajo jewelry, wall hangings, meditation tapes, art books,
stone Buddha sculptures and "vertical gardens,"
miniature succulents planted in flat, shallow wood
containers that can be hung on a wall. The shop's
cozy back patio, overlooking the ocean with a
soundtrack of tinkling wind chimes, feels like a little
corner of paradise.

Point Sur State Historic Park faces SR 1 about 19
miles south of Rio Road in Carmel-by-the-Sea and a
quarter mile north of the Point Sur Naval Facility.
The park includes Point Sur Lighthouse *(see attraction listing)* and its seven light-station buildings as
well as an interpretive center.

There are campsites at Limekiln State Park, on
SR 1 56 miles south of Carmel-by-the-Sea and 2
miles south of Lucia. The park, in the midst of a redwood forest, offers breathtaking views of the Big Sur
coast; for information phone (831) 667-2403.

HENRY MILLER LIBRARY is s. on SR 1. The library is in the former home of author Henry Miller's
longtime friend, Emil White, in a meadow surrounded by redwood trees. Miller, a Big Sur resident
1944-62, wrote several works while living along the
rugged Pacific coast. The library staff serve as docents, showing visitors Miller's works, a collection of
his artwork and videos about the writer.

Diverse musical artists from Philip Glass to Arcade Fire and Patti Smith have performed here. A full schedule of workshops and art exhibitions take place on the library's grounds. **Time:** Allow 1 hour minimum. **Hours:** Library Wed.-Mon. 11-6. Phone ahead to confirm concert and special event dates. **Cost:** Donations. **Phone:** (831) 667-2574.

JULIA PFEIFFER BURNS STATE PARK is about 10 mi. s. of Pfeiffer Big Sur State Park on SR 1; watch for the turn-off and prominent entrance sign. Don't confuse Julia Pfeiffer Burns with the similar-sounding park to the north. Named for an early 20th-century pioneer who had an abiding love for the rugged Big Sur backcountry, this 4-square-mile park offers groves of redwood, tan oak and madrone trees as well as dramatic coastal views from the higher elevations of the hiking trails east of SR 1.

The park's unquestionable highlight is McWay Falls. From the parking area, take the signed Waterfall Trail; the approximately quarter-mile path follows McWay Creek, goes through a tunnel that burrows under SR 1 and emerges at a boardwalk that leads to the 80-foot drop, which you'll hear before you see. A slender ribbon of water plunges down to a rocky cove, with an ocean backdrop that is (at least on a sunny day) stunningly turquoise. Since the waterfall is fed by underground springs, it flows year-round. There's no access to the beach below, but the view from the boardwalk's elevated perspective is picture-perfect, and even more so during the spring months when the hillside tumbling down to the cove is blanketed with wildflowers.

The boardwalk continues past the falls for a short distance before ending at the ruins of the Waterfall House, where there's another awesome view—framed by eucalyptus trees—looking north along the Big Sur coastline. Sunsets at this spot are spectacular. In December and January the end of the trail is a good vantage point to spot gray whales migrating south to breeding grounds off the Baja California coast. *See Recreation Areas Chart.*

Time: Allow 2 hours minimum. **Hours:** Park open daily half an hour before sunrise-half an hour after sunset. **Cost:** Day use fee $10 per private vehicle; $9 (ages 62+); free (those arriving on foot or by bicycle). **Phone:** (831) 667-2315. ⊠

PFEIFFER BIG SUR STATE PARK, s. on SR 1, covers 964 acres of coastal redwood and chaparral on the Big Sur River. Visitors can see groves of redwood trees while traversing the hiking trails within the park. Rangers conduct naturalist and campfire programs Memorial Day weekend through Labor Day. Year-round overnight camping is permitted. *See Recreation Areas Chart.*

Note: A major park renovation project, which is scheduled for completion by the end of spring 2013, may cause delays and impact the visitor experience throughout the campground and day-use areas. **Hours:** Park open daily dawn-dusk. **Cost:** Day use

$10 per private vehicle; $9 (ages 62+ per private vehicle). **Phone:** (831) 667-2315.
⛰ 🍴 ⊠ 🐾 🏕

POINT SUR LIGHTSTATION tours meet at the farm gate along the w. side of SR 1, .25 mi. n. of the Point Sur Naval Facility. Docents lead 3-hour walking tours, beginning with a .5-mile uphill walk to the lightstation that includes two stairways. Whale, pelican and eagle sightings are possible on the trek, as are glimpses of spring wildflowers and panoramic views of the Big Sur coast.

Now automated and part of Point Sur State Historic Park, the restored stone lightstation was both home and workplace to lightkeepers and their families 1889-1974. Some of the seven other buildings on the site also have been restored. Visitors can climb to the top of the lighthouse tower to see the light itself and to walk around the tower's catwalk.

Note: Wear comfortable walking shoes and layered clothing; the weather can be quite cold and windy. Strollers are not permitted. **Hours:** Tours are given on a first-come, first-served basis Wed. and Sat. at 10 and 2, Sun. at 10, Apr.-Oct. (also Thurs. at 10, July-Aug.); Wed. at 1, Sat.-Sun. at 10, rest of year. Moonlight tours are offered on select evenings Apr.-Sept. Phone ahead for moonlight tour schedule. **Cost:** Daytime tours $10; $5 (ages 6-17). Moonlight tours $15; $10 (ages 6-17). **Phone:** (831) 625-4419.

VENTANA INN & SPA, A JOIE DE VIVRE HOTEL
(831)667-2331
🏩🏩 🏩🏩 **Hotel** $550-$1800 **Address:** 48123 Hwy 1 93920 **Location:** Off SR 1, 0.3 mi e. **Facility:** This attractive inn is richly appointed yet rustic; expect spectacular views of the Pacific Coast or forest. 60 units. 2 stories, exterior corridors. **Terms:** check-in 4 pm, 2-3 night minimum stay - seasonal and/or weekends, age restrictions may apply, 14 day cancellation notice-fee imposed, resort fee. **Amenities:** high-speed Internet, safes. **Dining:** The Restaurant at Ventana, see separate listing. **Pool(s):** 2 heated outdoor. **Activities:** sauna, whirlpools, hiking trails, jogging, exercise room, spa.
🍴 CALL 📶 ➤ BIZ 📶 ⊠ 🔌 💻 /SOME UNITS 🍽

POST RANCH INN   831/667-2200
ⓕⓨⓘ Not evaluated. **Address:** Hwy 1 93920 **Location:** 30 mi s of Carmel, west side of highway. Facilities, services, and décor characterize an upscale property.

WHERE TO EAT

THE RESTAURANT AT BIG SUR LODGE   831/667-3109
🏩🏩 American. Casual Dining. $12-$27 **AAA Inspector Notes:** This casual and relaxed atmosphere with a creekside setting is great for families. Offered are more upscale dishes including fresh seafood and grilled meats. **Bar:** beer & wine. **Address:** 47225 Hwy 1 93920 **Location:** 26 mi s of Carmel; in Big Sur Lodge.
Ⓑ Ⓛ Ⓓ CALL 📶 🍸

THE RESTAURANT AT VENTANA   831/667-4242
🏩🏩🏩 California. Fine Dining. $14-$38 **AAA Inspector Notes:** California Mediterranean cuisine is prepared on an oak-wood broiler. On a wooded hilltop, the dining room is casually comfortable. **Bar:** full bar. **Reservations:** suggested. **Address:** 48123 Hwy 1 93920 **Location:** Off SR 1, 0.3 mi e; in Ventana Inn & Spa, a Joie de Vivre hotel. Ⓛ Ⓓ CALL 📶

BLAIRSDEN pop. 39

GRIZZLY GRILL 530/836-1300

 American. Casual Dining. $7-$26 **AAA Inspector Notes:** This local restaurant with knotty pine decor offers early-bird specials from 5-6 pm, a small plates menu and a variety of pasta and meat dishes. **Bar:** full bar. **Reservations:** suggested. **Address:** 250 Bonta St 96103 **Location:** Center. **Parking:** street only.

BODEGA BAY pop. 1,077
• Part of Wine Country area — see map p. 562

BODEGA BAY LODGE (707)875-3525

Hotel
$165-$640

Address: 103 Coast Hwy 1 94923 **Location:** 0.5 mi w off SR 1 via Doran Beach Rd. **Facility:** Guest units at this bay-view property feature a balcony or patio, some with ocean and bay views. Many units also include a fireplace. 83 units. 2 stories (no elevator), exterior corridors. **Terms:** check-in 4 pm, 2 night minimum stay - seasonal and/or weekends, 3 day cancellation notice-fee imposed. **Pool(s):** heated outdoor. **Activities:** sauna, whirlpool, exercise room, spa. **Guest Services:** valet laundry. **Free Special Amenities:** high-speed Internet and manager's reception.

/ SOME UNITS

BRANSCOMB'S BODEGA BAY INN (707)875-3388

Motel
$99-$229

Address: 1588 Eastshore Rd 94923 **Location:** SR 1, just w. **Facility:** 7 units. 2 stories (no elevator), interior corridors. **Terms:** 3 day cancellation notice. **Free Special Amenities:** room upgrade (subject to availability with advance reservations) and high-speed Internet.

INN AT THE TIDES (707)875-2751

Hotel
$199-$309

Address: 800 Coast Hwy One 94923 **Location:** Center. **Facility:** 86 units. 2 stories (no elevator), exterior corridors. **Terms:** check-in 4 pm, 3 day cancellation notice-fee imposed. **Dining:** 2 restaurants. **Pool(s):** heated outdoor. **Activities:** sauna, whirlpool, exercise room. **Fee:** massage. **Guest Services:** coin laundry.

SONOMA COAST VILLA & SPA 707/876-9818

(fyi) Not evaluated. **Address:** 16702 Coast Hwy 1 94922 **Location:** On SR 1, 1 mi e. Facilities, services, and décor characterize a midscale property.

LUCAS WHARF RESTAURANT 707/875-3522

Seafood
Casual Dining
$9-$28

AAA Inspector Notes: Diners take in great views of Bodega Bay from this place, which focuses on a variety of dishes. **Bar:** full bar. **Address:** 595 SR 1 94923 **Location:** Center.
Menu on AAA.com

SPUD POINT CRAB COMPANY 707/875-9472

 Seafood. Quick Serve. $4-$11 **AAA Inspector Notes:** This roadside crab shack is known for tasty clam chowder and crab sandwiches. For those who prefer meat there are hot dog and tri-tip sandwiches. Take home some fresh cooked crabs. Limited seating and parking is available. **Address:** 1910 Westshore Rd 94923 **Location:** SR 1 exit Eastshore Rd W, just s on Bay Flat Rd, then 0.6 mi s. **Parking:** street only.

BOULDER CREEK (F-9) pop. 4,923, elev. 493'

BIG BASIN REDWOODS STATE PARK is 9 mi. n.w. on SR 236. Covering more than 18,000 acres, the park was established in 1902 as California's first state park. Some of the trees it protects, including a stand of coast redwoods, have attained a diameter of 18 feet and a height of 330 feet.

Trails for hikers and equestrians, waterfalls and a chance to spot wildlife such as deer, raccoons, egrets and herons draw nature lovers. Among the 80 miles of trails is the Redwood Trail, an easy, half-mile nature hike leading to some of the park's tallest trees; the trail begins near the park headquarters. A natural history museum is on the grounds. Camping supplies and naturalist services are available June through October. *See Recreation Areas Chart.*

Time: Allow 2 hours minimum. **Hours:** Park open daily 6 a.m.-10 p.m. Museum open daily 9-5. **Cost:** Day use $10 per private vehicle; $9 (ages 62+ per private vehicle). **Phone:** (831) 338-8860, or (800) 444-7275 for camping reservations.

MERRYBROOK LODGE 831/338-6813

Cottage
$88-$220

Address: 13420 Big Basin Way 95006 **Location:** Just n on SR 236. **Facility:** 9 cottages. 1 story, exterior corridors. *Bath:* shower only. **Terms:** 2-3 night minimum stay - seasonal and/or weekends, 7 day cancellation notice-fee imposed. **Free Special Amenities:** local telephone calls and high-speed Internet.

/ SOME UNITS

ROUND TABLE PIZZA 831/338-2141

Pizza. Casual Dining. $7-$28 **AAA Inspector Notes:** This casual, family-oriented pizza place features high-quality ingredients and dough rolled fresh daily. Distinctive specialty pizzas are piled high with toppings. **Bar:** beer & wine. **Address:** 13200 Central Ave (Hwy 9), Suite B 95006 **Location:** On SR 9 at Big Basin Way.

BRENTWOOD pop. 51,481

BRENTWOOD HAMPTON INN 925/513-1299

Hotel. Rates not provided. **Address:** 7605 Brentwood Blvd 94513 **Location:** Just s of Sand Creek Rd. **Facility:** 59 units. 3 stories, interior corridors. **Amenities:** high-speed Internet, safes. **Pool(s):** outdoor. **Activities:** whirlpool, exercise room. **Guest Services:** valet and coin laundry.

AAA Benefit: Members save up to 10%!

HOLIDAY INN EXPRESS (925)634-6400

Hotel $110-$159 **Address:** 8820 Brentwood Blvd 94513 **Location:** Just s of Balfour Rd. **Facility:** 50 units. 2 stories (no elevator), interior corridors. **Terms:** 3 day cancellation notice. **Pool(s):** outdoor. **Activities:** exercise room. **Guest Services:** valet laundry.

Be a better driver.
Keep your mind on the road.

WHERE TO EAT

ROUND TABLE PIZZA

 Pizza. Casual Dining. $7-$28 **AAA Inspector Notes:** This casual, family-oriented pizza place features high-quality ingredients and dough rolled fresh daily. Distinctive specialty pizzas are piled high with toppings. **Bar:** beer & wine. L D

For additional information, visit AAA.com

LOCATIONS:

Address: 41 W Sand Creek Rd 94513 **Location:** At Brentwood Blvd. **Phone:** 925/634-1700

Address: 2540 Sand Creek Rd 94513 **Location:** Just e of SR 4. **Phone:** 925/240-8778

BRISBANE pop. 4,282

- **Hotels & Restaurants map & index p. 410**
- **Part of San Francisco area — see map p. 342**

HOMEWOOD SUITES BY HILTON   (650)589-1600   **23**

 Extended Stay Hotel $169-$189 **Address:** 2000 Shoreline Ct 94005 **Location:** US 101 exit Sierra Point Pkwy, just e. **Facility:** 177 units, some two bedrooms and efficiencies. 4 stories, interior corridors. **Terms:** 1-7 night minimum stay, cancellation fee imposed. **Amenities:** high-speed Internet. **Pool(s):** heated indoor. **Activities:** exercise room. **Guest Services:** valet and coin laundry, area transportation-within 5 mi.

AAA Benefit: Contemporary luxury at a special Member rate.

RADISSON HOTEL SAN FRANCISCO AIRPORT AT SIERRA POINT   (415)467-4400   **22**

Hotel $109-$459 **Address:** 5000 Sierra Point Pkwy 94005 **Location:** US 101 exit Sierra Point Pkwy, just e. **Facility:** 210 units. 8 stories, interior corridors. **Terms:** cancellation fee imposed, resort fee. **Amenities:** video games (fee), high-speed Internet, safes. **Pool(s):** heated indoor. **Activities:** whirlpool, exercise room. **Guest Services:** valet and coin laundry, area transportation-within 5 mi.

WHERE TO EAT

7 MILE HOUSE   415/467-2343   **13**

American. Casual Dining. $9-$17 **AAA Inspector Notes:** Call it a dive, a hole in the wall, a honky tonk—this establishment has a long history of offering a respite for travelers and locals since it was built as a stagecoach stop back in 1853, seven miles from the Ferry Building. Located near the PG&E Substation, this spot is popular with Comcast technicians as well as employees of the Radisson and Homewood Suites for lunch. Wednesday night karaoke, local jazz band, reggae, country, R&B and soul are some of the nightly entertainment. **Bar:** full bar. **Address:** 2800 Bayshore Blvd 94005 **Location:** At Geneva Ave. Sunnydale, 110. L D

BROOKS (A-9) elev. 341'

The stretch of SR 16 that runs from Brooks north to where the highway dead-ends at SR 20 at Wilbur Springs is a particularly scenic drive. The road passes beautiful hillsides and follows a creek as it travels through the Capay Valley; driving time is approximately 2 hours.

GAMBLING ESTABLISHMENTS

- **Cache Creek Casino** is at 14455 SR 16. **Hours:** Daily 24 hours. **Phone:** (530) 796-3118, (800) 992-8686, or (800) 452-8181 in Calif.

CACHE CREEK CASINO RESORT   530/796-3118

Resort Hotel
Rates not provided

Address: 14455 State Hwy 16 95606 **Location:** I-505 exit 21 (SR 16/Esparto), 12.4 mi w. **Facility:** The upscale, Mission-style property offers beautiful, sweeping views of the Capay Valley. Cabanas are offered poolside complete with LCD TVs. 200 units. 5 stories, interior corridors. **Parking:** on-site and valet. **Terms:** check-in 4 pm. **Amenities:** high-speed Internet, safes. **Dining:** C2 Steak & Seafood, Canyon Cafe, Chang Shou, Harvest Buffet, see separate listings. **Pool(s):** heated outdoor. **Activities:** whirlpools, exercise room, spa. **Fee:** saunas, steamrooms, golf-18 holes. **Guest Services:** valet laundry, area transportation (fee). **Free Special Amenities:** newspaper and high-speed Internet.

WHERE TO EAT

C2 STEAK & SEAFOOD   530/796-3118

Steak. Casual Dining. $21-$60 **AAA Inspector Notes:** This establishment serves well-prepared, dry-aged USDA Prime steaks and fresh seafood with choices from an extensive wine list. **Bar:** full bar. **Reservations:** suggested. **Address:** 14455 Hwy 16 95606 **Location:** I-505 exit 21 (SR 16/Esparto), 12.4 mi w; in Cache Creek Casino Resort. **Parking:** on-site and valet. D

CANYON CAFE   530/796-3118

American. Casual Dining. $9-$20 **AAA Inspector Notes:** This café serves nicely-prepared American favorites, and a few Filipino selections, all in a casual atmosphere. The wine list includes selections from local wineries. **Bar:** full bar. **Address:** 14455 State Hwy 16 95606 **Location:** I-505 exit 21 (SR 16/Esparto), 12.4 mi w; in Cache Creek Casino Resort. **Parking:** on-site and valet.

B L D 24 CALL

CHANG SHOU   530/796-3118

Asian. Casual Dining. $9-$26 **AAA Inspector Notes:** This restaurant presents a varied menu of dishes from Korea, China (Mandarin, Cantonese and Szechuan) and Vietnam. Seating is offered in contemporary Asia-themed dining areas and on the seasonal bamboo terrace. **Bar:** full bar. **Address:** 14455 Hwy 16 95606 **Location:** I-505 exit 21 (SR 16/Esparto), 12.4 mi w; in Cache Creek Casino Resort. **Parking:** on-site and valet. L D

HARVEST BUFFET   530/796-3118

International. Casual Dining. $14-$25 **AAA Inspector Notes:** A vast array of ethnic specialties is offered among several chef's stations, including American, Asian, Mexican and Italian. A dessert station is lined with several options. Prime rib and seafood are available on Friday and Saturday nights. **Bar:** full bar. **Address:** 14455 State Hwy 16 95606 **Location:** I-505 exit 21 (SR 16/Esparto), 12.4 mi w; in Cache Creek Casino Resort. **Parking:** on-site and valet. L D CALL

BURLINGAME (D-8) pop. 28,806, elev. 39'

- **Hotels p. 60 • Restaurants p. 61**
- **Hotels & Restaurants map & index p. 410**
- **Part of San Francisco area — see map p. 342**

BURLINGAME MUSEUM OF PEZ MEMORABILIA is at 214 California Dr. This small museum, in the back of a retail establishment, exhibits vintage PEZ dispensers as well as what is claimed to be the world's largest dispenser of PEZ candies. Included is a "Star Wars" Princess Leia dispenser autographed by actress Carrie Fisher.

A separate exhibit features a collection of classic toys such as Mr. Potato Head, Lincoln Logs, Tinkertoys, View-Masters and Colorforms. **Time:** Allow 30 minutes minimum. **Hours:** Tues.-Sat. 10-6. Closed major holidays. **Cost:** $3; $1 (ages 4-12 and 65+); free (first Thurs. of the month). **Phone:** (650) 347-2301.

(See map & index p. 410.)

BAY LANDING HOTEL   650/259-9000 **50**

Hotel
Rates not provided

Address: 1550 Bayshore Hwy 94010 **Location:** US 101 exit Broadway-Burlingame, e to Bayshore Hwy, then n. **Facility:** 130 units. 4 stories, interior corridors. **Amenities:** video games (fee), high-speed Internet, safes. **Activities:** jogging, exercise room. **Guest Services:** valet and coin laundry. *(See ad this page.)*

CROWNE PLAZA   (650)342-9200 **53**

Hotel $129-$229 **Address:** 1177 Airport Blvd 94010 **Location:** US 101 exit Broadway-Burlingame or Old Bayshore Hwy, just e. **Facility:** 309 units. 10 stories, interior corridors. **Parking:** on-site (fee). **Terms:** cancellation fee imposed, resort fee. **Amenities:** high-speed Internet (fee). **Pool(s):** heated indoor. **Activities:** whirlpool, exercise room. **Guest Services:** valet laundry.

DOUBLETREE BY HILTON HOTEL SAN FRANCISCO AIRPORT   (650)344-5500 **55**

Hotel $129-$309 **Address:** 835 Airport Blvd 94010 **Location:** US 101 exit Broadway-Burlingame or Anza Blvd, just e. **Facility:** 388 units. 8 stories, interior corridors. **Parking:** on-site (fee).

AAA Benefit:
Members save 5% or more!

Terms: 1-7 night minimum stay, cancellation fee imposed. **Amenities:** *Some:* high-speed Internet (fee). **Activities:** jogging, exercise room. **Guest Services:** valet laundry, area transportation-downtown.

EMBASSY SUITES-SAN FRANCISCO AIRPORT-BURLINGAME   (650)342-4600 **54**

Hotel $150-$350 **Address:** 150 Anza Blvd 94010 **Location:** US 101 exit Broadway-Burlingame, just e. **Facility:** 340 units. 9 stories, interior corridors. **Parking:** on-site (fee). **Terms:** 1-7

AAA Benefit:
Members save 5% or more!

night minimum stay, cancellation fee imposed. **Amenities:** video games (fee). *Some:* high-speed Internet (fee). **Pool(s):** heated indoor. **Activities:** sauna, whirlpools, exercise room. **Guest Services:** valet and coin laundry.

HAMPTON INN & SUITES   650/697-5736 **48**

Hotel. Rates not provided. **Address:** 1755 Bayshore Hwy 94010 **Location:** US 101 exit Millbrae Ave, just e. Millbrae, 45. **Facility:** 77 units. 4 stories, interior corridors. **Amenities:** high-speed Internet. *Some:* safes. **Activities:** exercise room. **Guest Services:** valet and coin laundry.

AAA Benefit:
Members save up to 10%!

HILTON GARDEN INN SAN FRANCISCO AIRPORT/BURLINGAME   650/347-7800 **57**

Hotel. Rates not provided. **Address:** 765 Airport Blvd 94010 **Location:** US 101 exit Broadway-Burlingame or Anza Blvd, just e. **Facility:** 132 units. 6 stories, interior corridors. **Amenities:** video games (fee), high-speed Internet. **Pool(s):** heated indoor. **Activities:** whirlpool, exercise room. **Guest Services:** valet and coin laundry.

AAA Benefit:
Unparalleled hospitality at a special Member rate.

▼ See AAA listing this page ▼

Keep seasonal vehicles travel-ready with a AAA/CAA Battery Tender®

(See map & index p. 410.)

HILTON SAN FRANCISCO AIRPORT BAYFRONT
650/340-8500 **58**

▼▼▼ Hotel
Rates not provided

AAA Benefit: Members save 5% or more!

Hilton

Address: 600 Airport Blvd 94010 **Location:** US 101 exit Broadway-Burlingame or Anza Blvd, 0.3 mi e. **Facility:** 400 units. 15 stories, interior corridors. **Parking:** on-site (fee) and valet. **Amenities:** high-speed Internet (fee), safes. **Pool(s):** heated indoor. **Activities:** whirlpool, exercise room. **Guest Services:** valet laundry. **Free Special Amenities:** airport transportation.

HOLIDAY INN EXPRESS SAN FRANCISCO AIRPORT SOUTH
650/347-2381 **52**

▼▼▼ Hotel. Rates not provided. **Address:** 1250 Bayshore Hwy 94010 **Location:** US 101 exit Broadway-Burlingame or Bayshore Hwy, just e. **Facility:** 146 units. 3 stories, interior corridors. **Pool(s):** outdoor. **Activities:** exercise room. **Guest Services:** valet and coin laundry.

HYATT REGENCY SAN FRANCISCO AIRPORT
(650)347-1234 **51**

▼▼▼ Hotel
$81-$360

HYATT

AAA Benefit: Members save 10% or more everyday.

Address: 1333 Bayshore Hwy 94010 **Location:** US 101 exit Broadway-Burlingame, just e. **Facility:** 789 units. 9 stories, interior corridors. **Parking:** on-site (fee) and valet. **Terms:** cancellation fee imposed. **Amenities:** video games (fee). *Some:* high-speed Internet (fee). **Dining:** 2 restaurants. **Pool(s):** heated outdoor. **Activities:** sauna, whirlpool, exercise room. *Fee:* massage. **Guest Services:** valet laundry, area transportation-Burlingame Trolley. **Free Special Amenities:** early check-in/late check-out and airport transportation.

RED ROOF INN SAN FRANCISCO AIRPORT
(650)342-7772 **56**

▼▼ Motel
$60-$140

Address: 777 Airport Blvd 94010 **Location:** US 101 exit Broadway-Burlingame or E Anza Blvd; just s of airport. **Facility:** 212 units. 5 stories, exterior corridors. **Amenities:** safes. **Dining:** LeAnn's Cafe, see separate listing. **Pool(s):** heated outdoor. **Guest Services:** coin laundry. **Free Special Amenities:** high-speed Internet and airport transportation.

SAN FRANCISCO AIRPORT MARRIOTT WATERFRONT
(650)692-9100 **47**

▼▼▼ Hotel $169-$329 **Address:** 1800 Old Bayshore Hwy 94010 **Location:** US 101 exit Millbrae Ave, just e. Millbrae, 45. **Facility:** 685 units. 11 stories, interior corridors. **Parking:** on-site (fee) and valet. **Amenities:** *Fee:* video games, high-speed Internet. *Some:* safes. **Pool(s):** heated indoor. **Activities:** saunas, whirlpool, exercise room. **Guest Services:** valet and coin laundry.

AAA Benefit: AAA hotel discounts of 5% or more.

VAGABOND INN EXECUTIVE SAN FRANCISCO AIRPORT
(650)692-4040 **49**

▼▼▼ Hotel $69-$199 **Address:** 1640 Bayshore Hwy 94010 **Location:** US 101 exit Millbrae Ave, just e. Millbrae, 45. **Facility:** 90 units. 3 stories, interior/exterior corridors. **Terms:** cancellation fee imposed. **Guest Services:** coin laundry.

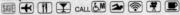

WHERE TO EAT

CAFE FIGARO
650/344-8277 **26**

▼▼ Italian. Casual Dining. $9-$24 **AAA Inspector Notes:** This quaint neighborhood trattoria is a real find. On the menu are plenty of pasta, veal and chicken choices, as well as fine homemade desserts, including tiramisu. **Bar:** full bar. **Address:** 1318 Broadway 94010 **Location:** US 101 exit Broadway, 0.5 mi w. **Parking:** street only. L D

ECCO RESTAURANT
650/342-7355 **28**

▼▼▼ American. Fine Dining. $15-$30 **AAA Inspector Notes:** This well-established restaurant, popular with long-time residents and business folk, offers an elegant, airy ambience with its high ceiling and extravagant flower arrangements. The owner/chef makes the rounds to make sure guests are well served. Try the Moroccan spiced rack of lamb, just a hint of exoticness to lift it from the run of the mill lamb dish. **Bar:** full bar. **Address:** 322 Lorton Ave 94010 **Location:** US 101 exit 419B (Broadway St) southbound, 1 mi s on California Dr, then just w; exit 417B (Peninsula Ave) northbound, 1 mi w, then 0.4 mi n. **Parking:** street only. L D

EL TORITO
650/692-3113

▼▼ Mexican. Family Dining. $8-$18 **AAA Inspector Notes:** Homemade Mexican favorites span from classic preparations to specialties from the country's central regions. Spicy taqueria-style tacos and carnitas Michoacan (marinated pork) are tasty choices. **Bar:** full bar. **Address:** 1590 Old Bayshore Hwy 94010 **Location:** US 101 exit Millbrae Ave, just e, then 0.5 mi s. Millbrae, 45. L D

GULLIVER'S
650/692-6060 **24**

▼▼ American. Casual Dining. $15-$29 **AAA Inspector Notes:** Located in a non-descript building across from San Francisco Airport Marriott Waterfront. Reminiscent of an English Tudor, the servers even sport Colonial attire topped off with a tricorn hat. The prime rib dinner is an excellent choice with such sides as fresh salad, creamed spinach, baked potato and creamed corn as well as Yorkshire pudding. **Bar:** full bar. **Address:** 1699 Old Bayshore Hwy 94010 **Location:** US 101 exit Millbrae Ave, just e. Millbrae, 45. D

LEANN'S CAFE
650/342-8248 **25**

▼▼ American. Casual Dining. $7-$20 **AAA Inspector Notes:** This modest diner offers basic familiar food at economical prices. **Bar:** beer & wine. **Address:** 777 Airport Blvd 94010 **Location:** US 101 exit Broadway-Burlingame or E Anza Blvd; just s of airport; in Red Roof Inn. B L D 24

MINGALABA RESTAURANT
650/343-5130 **30**

▼▼ Burmese. Casual Dining. $10-$16 **AAA Inspector Notes:** A warm, contemporary decor with Burmese accents can be found at this restaurant. Popular with the lunch crowd, there can be a wait for the food but it is worth it. Try the lap pat dok salad (tea leaf salad), a curry and a spicy string bean stir-fry with dry shrimp. **Bar:** beer & wine. **Address:** 1213 Burlingame Ave 94010 **Location:** US 101 exit Broadway, just w, 1 mi s on California Dr, then just w. **Parking:** street only. L D

ROUND TABLE PIZZA
650/343-5676

▼ Pizza. Quick Serve. $7-$28 **AAA Inspector Notes:** This casual, family-oriented pizza place features high-quality ingredients and dough rolled fresh daily. Distinctive specialty pizzas are piled high with toppings. **Bar:** beer & wine. **Address:** 1207 Burlingame Ave 94010 **Location:** US 101 exit Broadway, just w, 1 mi s on California Dr, then just w. **Parking:** street only. L D

(See map & index p. 410.)

SAPORE ITALIANO   650/348-3277   32

♦♦♦ Italian. Casual Dining. $9-$24 **AAA Inspector Notes:** This quaint and often busy restaurant serves well-prepared Italian cuisine, most notably good pasta and seafood. **Bar:** full bar. **Address:** 1447 Burlingame Ave 94010 **Location:** US 101 exit Broadway, just w, 1 mi on California Dr, then 0.5 mi w. **Parking:** street only.
L D CALL M

STEELHEAD BREWING CO.   650/344-6050   27

♦♦ American. Casual Dining. $9-$24 **AAA Inspector Notes:** Hand-crafted microbrews complement wood-fired pizza, steak and pasta dishes. A separate billiards room is in the back. **Bar:** full bar. **Address:** 333 California Dr 94010 **Location:** US 101 exit Broadway, just w, then 1 mi s. **Parking:** street only.   L D CALL M

STRAITS   650/373-7883   29

♦♦♦ Asian. Casual Dining. $12-$40 **AAA Inspector Notes:** A contemporary décor with Asian accents can be found in this fun restaurant. Singaporean cuisine reflects influences from India, China, Malaysia and Indonesia. Among house specialties are origami sea bass with ginger and shiitake mushrooms. Order and share family style to increase the experience. **Bar:** full bar. **Address:** 1100 Burlingame Ave 94010 **Location:** US 101 exit Broadway, just w, then 1 mi s on California Dr. **Parking:** street only.   L D CALL M

TRAPEZE   650/344-4242   31

♦♦♦ Continental. Casual Dining. $12-$32 **AAA Inspector Notes:** Focusing on fine European cuisine, the menu here lists an array of pasta dishes and Mediterranean-inspired choices. This sleek neighborhood restaurant also offers a nice array of California wines. **Bar:** full bar. **Address:** 266 Lorton Ave 94010 **Location:** US 101 exit Broadway, just w, 1 mi s on California Dr, then just w. **Parking:** street only.   L D

BURNEY (B-3) pop. 3,154, elev. 3,173'

Named for an early English settler killed in a Native American raid in 1857, Burney's location between Lassen National Forest and Mount Shasta makes it popular with campers and anglers.

Burney Chamber of Commerce: 36879 Main St., P.O. Box 36, Burney, CA 96013. **Phone:** (530) 335-2111.

McARTHUR-BURNEY FALLS MEMORIAL STATE PARK, 5 mi. e. on SR 299, then 6 mi. n. on SR 89, features a 129-foot spring-fed waterfall that flows down several levels over moss-covered lava rock in a lush forest setting. *See Recreation Areas Chart.* **Hours:** Daily dawn-dusk. **Cost:** Day use $8 per private vehicle; $7 (ages 62+ per private vehicle). **Phone:** (530) 335-2777.

CHARM MOTEL   530/335-3300

♦♦ Motel $65-$185   **Address:** 37363 Main St 96013 **Location:** 0.5 mi ne on SR 299; jct Roff Way. **Facility:** 42 units, some two bedrooms and kitchens. 2 stories (no elevator), exterior corridors. **Terms:** cancellation fee imposed. **Guest Services:** coin laundry. **Free Special Amenities:** local telephone calls and high-speed Internet.
SAVE ⓘ+ CALL M 🛜 ✕ ▤ ▣ ▢ / SOME UNITS FEE 🐾

GREEN GABLES MOTEL   530/335-3300

♦♦ ♦♦ Motel $65-$155   **Address:** 37385 Main St 96013 **Location:** 0.5 mi ne on SR 299; jct Roff Way and SR 299. **Facility:** 27 units, some two bedrooms and kitchens. 1 story, exterior corridors. **Terms:** cancellation fee imposed. **Activities:** horseshoes. **Guest Services:** coin laundry. **Free Special Amenities:** local telephone calls and high-speed Internet.
SAVE ⓘ+ 🛜 ✕ ▤ ▣ ▢ / SOME UNITS FEE 🐾

SHASTA PINES MOTEL   530/335-2201

♦♦ ♦♦ Motel $64-$109   **Address:** 37386 Main St 96013 **Location:** 0.5 mi ne on SR 299; jct Roff Way. **Facility:** 30 units, some efficiencies. 1-2 stories (no elevator), exterior corridors. **Terms:** 4 day cancellation notice-fee imposed. **Free Special Amenities:** local telephone calls and high-speed Internet. SAVE ⓘ+ 🛜 ▤ ▣ ▢

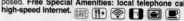
WHERE TO EAT

ART'S OUTPOST   530/335-2835

♦♦ American. Casual Dining. $14-$27 **AAA Inspector Notes:** This rustic, Western-themed eatery offers grilled steaks and seafood. Highlights include the rib-eye and sirloin with the prime rib as the house specialty. Friendly service is offered. **Bar:** full bar. **Address:** 37392 Main St 96013 **Location:** Center.   D

CALIFORNIA COASTAL NATIONAL MONUMENT (D-5, I-2)

Consisting of thousands of islands, rocks, exposed reefs and pinnacles extending up to 12 miles out from the shore off California's entire 1,100-mile coastline, California Coastal National Monument was established to preserve these uninhabited outcroppings.

The diverse geological formations found within the national monument's fragile coastal ecosystem provide feeding and nesting grounds for many sea birds, including gulls; bald eagles; peregrine falcons; pigeon guillemots; common murres; and cormorants. Two threatened species, southern sea otters and Steller sea lions, as well as California sea lions and Guadalupe fur seals are examples of marine mammals that find shelter and breeding habitats within the monument's boundaries. For such birds as brown pelicans, a threatened species, the monument serves as a roosting ground.

Visitor centers for the offshore sanctuaries are being established along the California coast in conjunction with existing marine conservation organizations. The first to open, the Coastal Discovery Center at William Randolph Hearst Memorial State Beach in San Simeon, has interactive exhibits that provide information about the ocean environment. For additional information contact the California Coastal National Monument, 400 Natural Bridges Dr., Santa Cruz, CA 95060; phone (831) 421-9546.

CALISTOGA (A-8) pop. 5,155, elev. 362'

It's obvious that Calistoga, at the Napa Valley's northern end, is all about wine—the tasting rooms of well-respected vintners are within close proximity. However, wellness and water are two other highly regarded Calistoga commodities, a fact that becomes readily apparent as you stroll through this delightful town. Indeed, you may have already sampled the bottled mineral water produced by Calistoga Water Company.

In the late 1800s the railroad transported visitors to Calistoga by the droves to bask in the reputedly therapeutic natural mineral springs, which continue to draw health enthusiasts as well as the curious. Spas dotted along Calistoga's early 1900s main drag, Lincoln Avenue, pipe in the bubbling "medicinal" waters of the hot springs to pamper customers with relaxing treatments—some facilities have outdoor pools. Many establishments post signs out front enticing passersby to take a bath in steaming mud, a concoction prepared from ingredients like mineral water, clay, volcanic ash and peat moss.

If soaking in a tub of mud isn't your thing, explore the Western-influenced downtown's art galleries and funky shops displaying wares that lean toward the artsy and earthy. Or, observe Calistoga's geothermal activity in the form of Old Faithful Geyser (see attraction listing), which reliably erupts about every half-hour. Travel north of town to view an extinct volcano, Mount St. Helena, or hike and bike at Robert Louis Stevenson State Park, 7 miles north on SR 29.

If you prefer, you can head out on a scenic drive. Calistoga is the southern terminus of a 94-mile stretch of SR 128 that heads northwest to the coastal city of Albion. Scenic SR 29 runs 28 miles south to Napa through the valley.

Calistoga Chamber of Commerce and Visitor's Center: 1133 Washington St., Calistoga, CA 94515. **Phone:** (707) 942-6333 or (866) 306-5588.

OLD FAITHFUL GEYSER OF CALIFORNIA, 1 mi. n. on Tubbs Ln. between SRs 29 and 128, is one  of the few regularly erupting geysers in the world. Fed by an underground river, the water heats to 350 degrees Fahrenheit and erupts about every 30 minutes for 1 to 2 minutes on average, spewing 20 to 75 feet into the air. Earthquake activity might disrupt normal eruption patterns. Visitors can take self-guiding geothermal tours. Tennessee fainting goats, llamas and sheep are among the animal residents at a petting zoo.

Hours: Daily 9-6, May-Sept.; 9-5, rest of year. **Cost:** $10; $7 (ages 60+); $3 (ages 6-12). **Phone:** (707) 942-6463. ⊞

PETRIFIED FOREST, 5 mi. w. on Petrified Forest Rd., preserves giant petrified redwoods. The grounds also contain a museum, picnic facilities and a .5-mile self-guiding trail of excavated petrified trees.

Time: Allow 30 minutes minimum. **Hours:** Daily 9-7, Memorial Day-Labor Day; 9-6, day after Labor Day-Oct. 31; 9-5, rest of year. Guided meadow walks are offered Sat.-Sun. at 11; otherwise by appointment (weather permitting). Phone ahead to confirm schedule. **Cost:** $10; $9 (ages 12-17 and 62+); $5 (ages 6-11). Guided tours are an additional $6. **Phone:** (707) 942-6667.

SHARPSTEEN MUSEUM, 1311 Washington St., displays artifacts, photographs and dioramas depicting 19th-century Calistoga; a scale model of Calistoga Hot Springs Resort is included. Attached to the museum is one of the resort's 1860s cottages. In addition to the permanent exhibits, which include an interactive geothermal display, is a rotating exhibit that changes every 3 months. Docents conduct tours on request. **Hours:** Daily 11-4. Closed Thanksgiving and Christmas. **Cost:** Donations. Reservations are required for tours. **Phone:** (707) 942-5911.

RECREATIONAL ACTIVITIES

Hot Air Ballooning

- **Bonaventura Balloons** departs from various locations. **Hours:** Trips depart daily at dawn (weather permitting). **Phone:** (707) 944-2210 or (800) 359-6272.

WINERIES

- **Bennett Lane Winery** is at 3340 SR 128. **Hours:** Tours and tastings daily 10-5:30. **Phone:** (707) 942-6684 or (877) 629-6272.
- **Castello di Amorosa** is 3 mi. s.e. at 4045 N. St. Helena Hwy. **Hours:** Tastings daily 9:30-6, Mar.-Oct.; 9:30-5, rest of year. Tours Mon.-Fri. 9:30-4:30, Sat.-Sun. 9:30-5. Reservations are required for tours. **Phone:** (707) 967-6272.

(See map & index p. 570.)

- **Clos Pegase** is e. off SR 29 at 1060 Dunaweal Ln. **Hours:** Daily 10:30-5. Guided tours are given daily at 11:30 and 2. Closed Christmas. **Phone:** (707) 942-4981.

- **Sterling Vineyards** is between SR 29 and Silverado Tr. at 1111 Dunaweal Ln. **Hours:** Mon.-Fri. 10:30-4:30, Sat.-Sun. 10-5. Closed Jan. 1, Easter, Thanksgiving and Christmas. **Phone:** (707) 942-3344 or (800) 726-6136.

AURORA PARK COTTAGES   (707)942-6733   **9**

 Cottage $229-$289 **Address:** 1807 Foothill Blvd 94515 **Location:** On SR 128, 0.5 mi n of jct SR 29. **Facility:** 6 cottages. 1 story, exterior corridors. **Bath:** shower only. **Terms:** 2 night minimum stay - weekends, 14 day cancellation notice-fee imposed.

CALL

BEST WESTERN PLUS STEVENSON MANOR
(707)942-1112   **4**

Hotel
$129-$285

AAA Benefit: Members save up to 20%, plus 10% bonus points with Best Western Rewards®.

Address: 1830 Lincoln Ave 94515 **Location:** 0.5 mi n on SR 29. **Facility:** 34 units. 2 stories (no elevator), exterior corridors. **Terms:** 2 night minimum stay - seasonal and/or weekends. **Amenities:** high-speed Internet. **Pool(s):** heated outdoor. **Activities:** sauna, whirlpool, steamroom. **Guest Services:** coin laundry. **Free Special Amenities:** local telephone calls and high-speed Internet.

SAVE CALL

BRANNAN COTTAGE INN   (707)942-4200   **7**

Historic Bed & Breakfast
$160-$285

Address: 109 Wapoo Ave 94515 **Location:** At Lincoln Ave. **Facility:** Built in 1860 and still on its original site, the inn is convenient to wineries, spas, biking trails, horseback riding and hot-air balloon rides. 6 units. 1-2 stories (no elevator), exterior corridors. **Terms:** 2 night minimum stay - seasonal and/or weekends, 7 day cancellation notice-fee imposed. **Free Special Amenities:** full breakfast and early check-in/late check-out.

SAVE

CARLIN COUNTRY COTTAGES   707/942-9102   **3**

Cottage $110-$260 **Address:** 1623 Lake St 94515 **Location:** W of SR 29 via Lincoln Ave. **Facility:** 15 units, some kitchens and cottages. 1 story, exterior corridors. **Terms:** 2 night minimum stay - seasonal and/or weekends, 7 day cancellation notice-fee imposed. **Pool(s):** heated outdoor. **Activities:** whirlpool. **Guest Services:** coin laundry.

CALL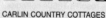

CHELSEA GARDEN INN   (707)942-0948   **8**

Bed & Breakfast
$155-$300

Address: 1443 2nd St 94515 **Location:** Just n of Lincoln Ave. **Facility:** The beautifully landscaped courtyard features lush gardens and a pool area. In the main building there is a common room with a large fireplace, plus a library to curl up in on a rainy day. 5 units, some two bedrooms. 1-2 stories (no elevator), interior/exterior corridors. **Parking:** street only. **Terms:** 2-3 night minimum stay - seasonal and/or weekends, 14 day cancellation notice-fee imposed. **Pool(s):** outdoor. **Free Special Amenities:** full breakfast and high-speed Internet.

SAVE CALL

Learn about inspections and Diamond Ratings at AAA.com/Diamonds

---

CHRISTOPHER'S INN   (707)942-5755   **14**

Bed & Breakfast
$119-$279

Address: 1010 Foothill Blvd 94515 **Location:** On SR 29, just s of jct Lincoln Ave. **Facility:** 21 units. 2 stories (no elevator), interior corridors. **Terms:** 1-2 night minimum stay - seasonal and/or weekends. **Free Special Amenities:** expanded continental breakfast and high-speed Internet.

SAVE CALL

COMFORT INN CALISTOGA, HOT SPRINGS OF THE WEST   (707)942-9400   **1**

Hotel
$99-$289

Address: 1865 Lincoln Ave 94515 **Location:** 0.5 mi n on SR 29. **Facility:** 55 units. 2 stories (no elevator), exterior corridors. **Terms:** cancellation fee imposed. **Amenities:** safes (fee). **Pool(s):** heated outdoor. **Activities:** sauna, whirlpool, steamroom, limited exercise equipment. **Free Special Amenities:** full breakfast and high-speed Internet.

SAVE CALL

COTTAGE GROVE INN   (707)942-8400   **6**

 Cottage $250-$450 **Address:** 1711 Lincoln Ave 94515 **Location:** On SR 29; at Wapoo Ave. **Facility:** These cozy, individually decorated cottages include a fireplace, wet bar and stereo system. 16 cottages. 1 story, exterior corridors. **Terms:** 2 night minimum stay - seasonal and/or weekends, 10 day cancellation notice-fee imposed. **Amenities:** safes. **Activities:** bicycles.

CALL

DR. WILKINSON'S HOT SPRINGS RESORT
(707)942-4102   **10**

Hotel
$139-$329

Address: 1507 Lincoln Ave 94515 **Location:** Center. **Facility:** 42 units, some kitchens and cottages. 2 stories, interior/exterior corridors. **Terms:** 3 day cancellation notice. **Pool(s):** 2 heated outdoor. **Activities:** whirlpool, spa. **Free Special Amenities:** local telephone calls and high-speed Internet.

SAVE

EUROSPA & INN   (707)942-6829   **13**

Motel
$119-$289

Address: 1202 Pine St 94515 **Location:** Just s of Lincoln Ave; at Myrtle St. **Facility:** 13 units. 1 story, exterior corridors. **Terms:** 1-2 night minimum stay - seasonal and/or weekends, 3 day cancellation notice-fee imposed. **Pool(s):** heated outdoor. **Activities:** whirlpool, spa. **Free Special Amenities:** expanded continental breakfast and high-speed Internet.

SAVE CALL

GOLDEN HAVEN SPA RESORT   707/942-8000   **2**

Hotel
$159-$229

Address: 1713 Lake St 94515 **Location:** W of SR 29 via Lincoln Ave. **Facility:** 28 units. 1-2 stories (no elevator), exterior corridors. **Terms:** cancellation fee imposed. **Pool(s):** heated indoor/outdoor. **Activities:** whirlpools, spa. **Free Special Amenities:** high-speed Internet.

SAVE

HIDEAWAY COTTAGES   (707)942-4108   **5**

Cottage
$169-$650

Address: 1412 Fair Way 94515 **Location:** Just n of Lincoln Ave. **Facility:** 15 units, some kitchens and cottages. 1 story, exterior corridors. **Terms:** closed 11/29-2/11, check-in 5 pm, age restrictions may apply, 3 day cancellation notice. **Pool(s):** outdoor. **Activities:** whirlpool. **Free Special Amenities:** continental breakfast and high-speed Internet.

SAVE

(See map & index p. 570.)

MOUNT VIEW HOTEL & SPA (707)942-6877

Historic Hotel
$179-$449

Address: 1457 Lincoln Ave 94515 **Location:** On SR 29; center. **Facility:** A private courtyard and large outdoor pool invite you to relax at this 1917 historic hotel. 31 units, some cottages. 2 stories (no elevator), interior corridors. **Terms:** check-in 4 pm, 2 night minimum stay - seasonal and/or weekends, 7 day cancellation notice-fee imposed. **Pool(s):** heated outdoor. **Activities:** sauna, whirlpool, spa. **Free Special Amenities:** continental breakfast and high-speed Internet.

ROMAN SPA HOT SPRINGS RESORT
707/942-4441

Hotel
$160-$450

Address: 1300 Washington St 94515 **Location:** Just n of Lincoln Ave. **Facility:** 60 units, some kitchens. 2 stories, exterior corridors. **Terms:** 2 night minimum stay - weekends, 3 day cancellation notice-fee imposed. **Pool(s):** heated outdoor. **Activities:** saunas, whirlpool, spa. **Guest Services:** coin laundry. **Free Special Amenities:** local telephone calls and high-speed Internet. (See ad this page.)

WHERE TO EAT

BOSKOS TRATTORIA 707/942-9088
Italian. Casual Dining. $11-$22 **AAA Inspector Notes:** Downtown next to shops, spas and wineries, this friendly, family-owned restaurant specializes in a wide selection of Italian dishes. The menu lists pasta, gourmet pizza and a famous meatball appetizer, made with prepared-in-house marinara sauce. **Bar:** beer & wine. **Address:** 1364 Lincoln Ave 94515 **Location:** On SR 29; center. **Parking:** street only.

BRANNAN'S GRILL 707/942-2233 ③
American. Casual Dining. $11-$40 **AAA Inspector Notes:** The beautiful club-like restaurant has high-beamed ceilings, dyed cement floors and contemporary artwork. **Bar:** full bar. **Reservations:** suggested. **Address:** 1374 Lincoln Ave 94515 **Location:** On SR 29; center. **Parking:** street only.

HYDRO BAR & GRILL 707/942-9777 ①
American. Gastro Pub. $8-$20 **AAA Inspector Notes:** High ceilings and exposed brick walls give this casual bar and grill a nice open ambience. Diners can choose from such selections as burgers, chile rellenos and seafood pasta. The claim to fame is winning the Calistoga Best Burger competition. Live music focusing on jazz and blues is offered on weekends. **Bar:** full bar. **Address:** 1403 Lincoln Ave 94515 **Location:** At Washington St; center. **Parking:** street only.

CAMPBELL (E-9) pop. 39,349, elev. 196'

CAMPBELL HISTORICAL MUSEUM & THE AINSLEY HOUSE are at the corner of N. Central Ave. and Civic Center Dr. at 51 N. Central Ave. Campbell's rich agricultural history is depicted in the museum. Hands-on exhibits focus on the canneries that were the city's lifeblood, home life, and recreation enjoyed during free time. A preliminary 5-minute videotape gives insights into the city's past.

The 1925 Tudor-style Ainsley House, just across the green, is lavishly furnished appropriate to the status of its English-born canning pioneer owner and his wife. Many furnishings are original to the house. A video presentation precedes the guided tour.

Allow 30 minutes minimum each for house and museum. **Hours:** Museum and house Thurs.-Sun. noon-4. Last house tour begins 30 minutes before closing. Closed major holidays. **Cost:** Museum $2; free (ages 0-6). House $6; $4 (ages 55+); $2.50 (ages 7-17). Combination ticket $7; $5 (ages 55+); $4 (ages 7-17). Admission increases for house holiday tours. **Phone:** (408) 866-2119 for the museum, or (408) 866-2118 for the house.

(See map & index p. 468.)

CAMPBELL INN

Hotel
$99-$249

(408)374-4300　**104**

Address: 675 E Campbell Ave 95008 **Location:** SR 17 exit Hamilton Ave E, 0.3 mi to Bascom Ave, 0.3 mi s, then 0.3 mi w. **Facility:** 95 units. 2 stories, exterior corridors. **Pool(s):** heated outdoor.
Activities: whirlpool, lighted tennis court, bicycles, jogging. **Guest Services:** valet laundry. **Free Special Amenities:** full breakfast and high-speed Internet.

CARLYLE HOTEL

408/559-3600　**106**

Hotel. Rates not provided. **Address:** 1300 Camden Ave 95008 **Location:** SR 17 exit Camden Ave E. **Facility:** 38 units. 3 stories, interior corridors.

COURTYARD BY MARRIOTT SAN JOSE/CAMPBELL

(408)626-9590　**102**

Hotel $119-$229 **Address:** 655 Creekside Way 95008 **Location:** SR 17 exit Hamilton Ave, just e. **Facility:** 162 units. 7 stories, interior corridors. **Amenities:** high-speed Internet. **Pool(s):** heated outdoor. **Activities:** whirlpool, exercise room. **Guest Services:** valet and coin laundry.

AAA Benefit: AAA hotel discounts of 5% or more.

LARKSPUR LANDING CAMPBELL

408/364-1514　**101**

Hotel. Rates not provided. **Address:** 550 W Hamilton Ave 95008 **Location:** SR 17 exit Hamilton Ave, 1 mi w. **Facility:** 117 kitchen units. 4 stories, interior corridors. **Amenities:** high-speed Internet. **Activities:** whirlpool, exercise room. **Guest Services:** complimentary laundry.

THE PRUNEYARD PLAZA HOTEL

(408)559-4300　**103**

Hotel $209-$269 **Address:** 1995 S Bascom Ave 95008 **Location:** SR 17 exit Hamilton Ave, 0.3 mi e, then s. **Adjacent to Pruneyard Shopping Center. **Facility:** 171 units, some efficiencies. 3 stories, interior corridors. **Terms:** cancellation fee imposed. **Amenities:** high-speed Internet. **Pool(s):** heated outdoor. **Activities:** whirlpool, exercise room. **Guest Services:** valet laundry.

RESIDENCE INN BY MARRIOTT-SAN JOSE

(408)559-1551　**107**

Extended Stay Hotel $113-$199 **Address:** 2761 S Bascom Ave 95008 **Location:** SR 17 exit Camden Ave E, just n. **Facility:** 80 kitchen units, some two bedrooms. 2 stories (no elevator), exterior corridors. **Amenities:** high-speed Internet. **Pool(s):** heated outdoor. **Activities:** whirlpool, exercise room. **Guest Services:** valet and coin laundry.

AAA Benefit: AAA hotel discounts of 5% or more.

TOWNEPLACE SUITES BY MARRIOTT-SAN JOSE/CAMPBELL

(408)370-4510　**105**

Extended Stay Hotel $129-$249 **Address:** 700 E Campbell Ave 95008 **Location:** SR 17 exit Hamilton Ave E, 0.3 mi to Bascom Ave, 0.3 mi s, then 0.3 mi w. **Facility:** 95 units, some two bedrooms, efficiencies and kitchens. 4 stories, interior corridors. **Amenities:** high-speed Internet. **Activities:** whirlpool, exercise room. **Guest Services:** valet and coin laundry.

AAA Benefit: AAA hotel discounts of 5% or more.

WHERE TO EAT

AL CASTELLO RISTORANTE

408/369-9820　**49**

Italian. Casual Dining. $8-$14 **AAA Inspector Notes:** An Italian menu that will please everyone is offered here. Highlights include assorted panini, pizza, pasta and fresh seafood along with homemade soup, bread sticks and sauces on the pasta dishes. **Bar:** beer & wine. **Address:** 3155 S Bascom Ave, Suite B 95008 **Location:** SR 17 exit Camden Ave, just e.

ROUND TABLE PIZZA

408/374-2640

Pizza. Casual Dining. $7-$28 **AAA Inspector Notes:** This casual, family-oriented pizza place features high-quality ingredients and dough rolled fresh daily. Distinctive specialty pizzas are piled high with toppings. **Bar:** beer & wine. **Address:** 1400 W Campbell Ave 95008 **Location:** Just e of San Tomas Expwy.

CAPITOLA (G-2) pop. 9,918, elev. 50'
• Hotels & Restaurants map & index p. 492

Capitola, a seaside community on the north shore of Monterey Bay, claims to be the state's oldest beach resort. The town, which was founded in 1874, faces New Brighton Beach State Park *(see Recreation Areas Chart)*. The city lies on a scenic stretch of SR 1 that extends from San Francisco to San Luis Obispo.

Capitola-Soquel Chamber of Commerce: 716-G Capitola Ave., Capitola, CA 95010. **Phone:** (831) 475-6522 or (800) 474-6522.

BEST WESTERN PLUS CAPITOLA BY-THE-SEA INN & SUITES
(831)477-0607　**41**

Hotel
$100-$230

AAA Benefit: Members save up to 20%, plus 10% bonus points with Best Western Rewards®.

Address: 1435 41st Ave 95010 **Location:** SR 1 exit 41st Ave, 0.8 mi w. **Facility:** 58 units, some two bedrooms. 3 stories, interior corridors. **Terms:** 2 night minimum stay - seasonal, 3 day cancellation notice. **Amenities:** high-speed Internet. **Pool(s):** heated outdoor. **Activities:** whirlpool, exercise room. **Guest Services:** valet and coin laundry. **Free Special Amenities:** local telephone calls and high-speed Internet.

FAIRFIELD INN & SUITES SANTA CRUZ-CAPITOLA
(831)427-2900　**42**

Hotel $109-$339 **Address:** 1255 41st Ave 95010 **Location:** SR 1 exit 41st Ave, 1 mi w. **Facility:** 84 units. 3 stories, interior corridors. **Amenities:** high-speed Internet. **Pool(s):** heated outdoor. **Activities:** whirlpool, exercise room. **Guest Services:** valet and coin laundry.

AAA Benefit: AAA hotel discounts of 5% or more.

THE INN AT DEPOT HILL
(831)462-3376　**40**

Bed & Breakfast
$279-$389

Address: 250 Monterey Ave 95010 **Location:** SR 1 exit Park Ave, 1 mi w. **Facility:** Occupying a converted former railroad station, the inn has several fireplaces and offers individually decorated accommodations. The property's exterior is surrounded by beautifully landscaped gardens. 12 units. 3 stories (no elevator), interior/exterior corridors. **Terms:** 2 night minimum stay - weekends, 3 day cancellation notice. **Activities:** whirlpool. **Guest Services:** area transportation. **Free Special Amenities:** full breakfast and high-speed Internet.

(See map & index p. 492.)

QUALITY INN & SUITES

(831)462-3004   **39**

♦♦♦♦
Motel
$79-$350

Address: 720 Hill St 95010 **Location:** SR 1 exit Bay Ave, just w. **Facility:** 55 units. 2 stories (no elevator), interior/exterior corridors. **Pool(s):** outdoor. **Guest Services:** coin laundry.

Free Special Amenities: full breakfast.

SAVE CALL ⓈM 🚗 BIZ 📶 ✉ 🛗 🖨 🖥
/ SOME UNITS FEE 🐾

WHERE TO EAT

FRESH CHOICE

831/479-9873

♦♦ American. Cafeteria. $8-$15 **AAA Inspector Notes:** The salad bar of salad bars, the casual restaurant invites patrons to make their own or try one of the already prepared varieties. Other items include freshly baked breads, pizza and soup, as well as make-your-own sundaes for dessert. **Bar:** beer & wine. **Address:** 3555 Clares St 95010 **Location:** SR 1 exit 41st Ave W, just n.

Ⓛ Ⓓ CALL ⓈM

PARADISE BEACH GRILLE

831/476-4900   **19**

♦♦♦♦ Island Fusion. Casual Dining. $10-$34 **AAA Inspector Notes:** Spectacular views of the Pacific Ocean and the Capitola skyline create the perfect setting. The dining room offers a warm Tuscan-style design. The creative menu focuses on island-style cuisine and features wonderful salads, Hawaiian-style seafood, pasta and aged beef. **Bar:** full bar. **Reservations:** suggested. **Address:** 215 Esplanade 95010 **Location:** SR 1 exit Bay St (which becomes Monterey Ave), 1 mi w, n on Capitola Ave, w on Stockton Ave, then just s. **Parking:** street only. Ⓛ Ⓓ CALL ⓈM Ⓚ

SHADOWBROOK RESTAURANT

831/475-1511   **18**

♦♦♦♦ Regional American. Fine Dining. $20-$32 **AAA Inspector Notes:** This rustic setting overlooks a creek and lush, surrounding landscaping. A funicular railway leads down to the dining rooms. Prime rib and fresh, ocean-caught seafood stand out on a menu of seasonal California specialties. Entertainment is lined up on weekends. **Bar:** full bar. **Reservations:** suggested. **Address:** 1750 Wharf Rd 95010 **Location:** 0.5 mi s of SR 1 exit 41st Ave, 0.5 mi e on Capitola Rd. Ⓓ CALL ⓈM Ⓚ

CARMEL-BY-THE-SEA (G-2) pop. 3,722, elev. 20'

- **Hotels p. 69 • Restaurants p. 74**
- **Hotels & Restaurants map & index p. 206**
- **Part of Monterey Peninsula area — see map p. 202**

Carmel-by-the-Sea—just Carmel to its residents and admirers—was established in 1904 by a group of artists and writers as a bucolic retreat. As the settlement grew, its founders fought the encroachment of paved streets, gas, electricity and other modern amenities, and stringent zoning ordinances have preserved Carmel's village flavor and individuality. Even today many locations are indicated by proximity to intersections rather than by numbered street addresses.

To really experience the exceptional beauty of this seaside town up close and personal, you must stroll the length of the very aptly named Scenic Road. Scarcely a mile in length, its name is an almost comic understatement. On one side of the street is a wide expanse of white-sand beach edged by clear turquoise water, picturesque rocks covered with a thick green carpet of ice plants, gracefully arching Monterey pines framing the views. On the other side are homes that collectively comprise some of Monterey Bay's most desirable real estate.

Several sets of steps along the length of Scenic Road lead down to the beach.

Note: The north end of Scenic Road can be accessed via Ocean Avenue west off SR 1. Parking along the street is hard to come by at any time, and all but impossible on weekends. If you're driving, the south end veers left and becomes Carmelo Street; after about half a mile, turn right on Santa Lucia Street, then right again on Rio Street to return to SR 1.

By far the best way to explore Carmel, though, is on foot—an amble along the beach followed by ducking into art galleries, boutiques and antique shops, many of which are secluded behind courtyard walls. There really isn't a prevailing architectural style; Carmel's impossibly charming little bungalows, complete with picture-perfect gardens, do exhibit a degree of Spanish influence but tend to embody the whims of their owners.

The Forest Theater Guild presents a series of summer performances under the stars at the Outdoor Forest Theatre, a block south of Ocean Avenue at Santa Rita Street and Mountain View Avenue. The outdoor theater, founded in 1910, is situated in a lush setting of pine trees in the heart of Carmel. Many theatergoers bring along a bountiful picnic supper. For schedule and ticket information phone (831) 626-1681.

Carmel is located just off the delightfully scenic stretch of SR 1 that extends from San Francisco south to San Luis Obispo. Just north of town is the southern entrance to 17-Mile Drive, yet another beautiful oceanfront route that links Carmel and Pacific Grove *(see Pebble Beach p. 273).*

Downtown parking meter time limits are strictly enforced. If you can find an empty space, a city lot on Third Street at Torres Street offers free, unlimited parking; enter from Third.

Carmel Visitor Center: San Carlos between 5th and 6th streets, P.O. Box 4444, Carmel, CA 93921. **Phone:** (831) 624-2522 or (800) 550-4333.

Self-guiding tours: A brochure describing a walking tour of downtown Carmel and its courtyards is available at the visitor center.

Shopping areas: The compact business center contains unusual shops and galleries that display the work of local artists. The Barnyard, SR 1 and Carmel Valley Road with access from Carmel Rancho Boulevard, is as popular for its garden setting and country atmosphere as for its more than 50 galleries and specialty shops. The Crossroads, east of SR 1 and Father Serra's Carmel Mission on Rio Road, offers nearly 100 boutiques and specialty shops.

(See map & index p. 206.)

INSIDER INFO:
California Missions

To secure its northern territorial claims in the New World, Spain ordered the creation of a series of Franciscan missions in California. Begun under the leadership of Father Junípero Serra, who died in 1784, 21 missions and one asistencia were established 1769-1823, spaced about a day's journey apart along the northern extension of El Camino Real, the Royal Road.

Each mission had its own herd of cattle, fields and vegetable gardens, which were tended by native converts. For furniture, clothing, tools and other implements, the missions traded their surplus of meal, wine, oil, hemp, hides and tallow. Their attempts to "civilize" the indigenous population yielded mixed results: For the thousands of Indians brought under the wing of the church, thousands of others died at the hands of the Spanish or from their diseases. But the missions succeeded in other regards: Around them and their accompanying presidios, or military posts, grew the first permanent settlements in California.

After winning its independence from Spain and during the secularization, Mexico removed control of the missions from the Franciscans and subdivided much of their land among the Mexican soldiers and settlers. During the ensuing years, neglect and earthquakes took their toll; many of the missions were severely damaged or destroyed. Subsequent restoration and reconstruction have revitalized these historic structures, and today US 101 roughly traces the route of the old El Camino Real.

CARMEL WALKS tours meet in the outdoor courtyard of the Pine Inn, Lincoln St. at Ocean Ave. The 2-hour guided walking tours show visitors Carmel's hidden treasures—the town's secluded courtyards, gardens and cottages. A narrative gives the town's history as well as information about the artists, writers and movie stars who call Carmel home. **Time:** Allow 2 hours minimum. **Hours:** Tours depart Tues.-Fri. at 10, Sat. at 10 and 2. **Cost:** $25. Cash only. Reservations are recommended. **Phone:** (831) 642-2700. 🐾

MISSION SAN CARLOS BORROMÉO DEL RÍO CARMELO, at 3080 Rio Rd., is called Carmel Mission. Established by Father Junípero Serra at Monterey in 1770 and moved to its present site the following year, the mission was Father Serra's residence and headquarters until his death in 1784. He is buried beneath the church floor in front of the altar.

Relics of the mission's early days and some of Father Serra's books and documents are displayed. The courtyard gardens and Moorish bell tower are of interest, and a museum contains exhibits about the mission. A fiesta usually is held the last Sunday in September.

Time: Allow 1 hour minimum. **Hours:** Daily 9:30-5. Closed Easter, Easter Monday, Thanksgiving and Dec. 25. **Cost:** $6.50; $4 (ages 62+); $2 (ages 7-17). **Phone:** (831) 624-3600.

POINT LOBOS STATE NATURAL RESERVE, 3 mi. s. on SR 1, is a magnificent example of the central California coast at its grandest: jutting headlands, irregular coves and rolling meadows formed over millions of years through the ceaseless interaction of land and water. The reserve encompasses some 550 acres of rugged seacoast and another 775 acres that are underwater. Pick up a brochure that includes a trail map at the entrance station.

If you don't have a lot of time, the South Shore Trail is an easy, scenic walk. The trail follows the ocean's edge past wave-splashed rocks and cliffs blanketed with ice plants, bluff lettuce and seaside daisy, all of which are adapted to the coastal climate. Toward the southern end of the trail stone steps descend to Hidden Beach, a little cove with pebbly sand where you can sit on a rock and meditate to the soothing sound of the waves. During the month of May wildflowers brighten the meadows and cling to rock walls.

Cypress Grove Trail, which begins at the Sea Lion Point parking area, winds through a spectacular grove of Monterey cypresses. These gnarled trees display the effects of relentless wind and salt spray; they survive by thrusting their roots deep into cracks and crevices of the rocky headlands.

Resident wildlife includes deer, squirrels and rabbits. Harbor seals and sea lions frequent the area around Whalers Cove, where snowy egrets hunt for fish that live in dense growths of kelp. Gray whales can occasionally be spotted offshore, and pelicans and cormorants nest along the coast.

Whalers Cabin, built by Chinese fishermen in the 1850s, and an adjacent museum document the late 19th-century whaling industry at Point Lobos, where an abalone cannery and granite quarry also once operated. Diving in Whalers Cove is permitted by permit only. Guided nature walks are offered; a daily schedule is posted at the entrance station.

Pets are not permitted. **Time:** Allow 2 hours minimum. **Hours:** Daily 8-7, mid-Mar. to early Nov.; 8-5, rest of year. Last admission is 30 minutes before closing. Information station and Whalers Cabin museum open daily 9-4; phone ahead to confirm. **Cost:** $10 per private vehicle; $9 (ages 62+ per private vehicle); $5 (physically impaired per private vehicle). **Phone:** (831) 624-4909, or (831) 624-8413 for diving reservations. 🏕

TOR HOUSE is on Carmel Point at 26304 Ocean View Ave. Perched on a rugged promontory overlooking a dramatic coastline, the 1918 home provided the creative backdrop for poet Robinson Jeffers, who received such guests as Charlie Chaplin, George Gershwin and Edna St. Vincent

(See map & index p. 206.)

Millay. *Tor* is Celtic for an outcropping of rock. Docents guide visitors through the house, the English gardens and Hawk Tower, which Jeffers built himself by transporting stones from the beach.

Time: Allow 1 hour, 30 minutes minimum. **Hours:** Tours are given Fri.-Sat. on the hour 10-3. A maximum of six people is allowed on each tour. **Cost:** $10; $5 (full-time students with ID). Under 12 are not permitted. Cash or checks only. Reservations are required. **Phone:** (831) 624-1813.

WINERIES

• **Chateau Julien Wine Estate** is at 8940 Carmel Valley Rd. **Hours:** Tastings Mon.-Fri. 8-5, Sat.-Sun. 11-5. Tours are given Mon.-Fri. at 10:30 and 2:30, Sat.-Sun. at 12:30 and 2:30. Reservations are required for tours. **Phone:** (831) 624-2600.

ADOBE INN   (831)624-3933

Hotel
$125-$995

Address: Dolores St & 8th Ave 93921 **Location:** Just s off Ocean Ave. **Facility:** 20 units, some two bedrooms. 2 stories, exterior corridors. **Terms:** check-in 4 pm, 2 night minimum stay - seasonal and/or weekends, 5 day cancellation notice, resort fee. **Amenities:** high-speed Internet. **Pool(s):** heated outdoor. **Activities:** sauna. **Guest Services:** valet laundry.

BEST WESTERN CARMEL'S TOWN HOUSE LODGE
(831)624-1261

AAA Benefit: Members save up to 20%, plus 10% bonus points with Best Western Rewards®.

Address: Corner of San Carlos St & 5th Ave 93923 **Location:** 2 blks n off Ocean Ave. **Facility:** 28 units, some two bedrooms. 2 stories, exterior corridors. **Terms:** 3 day cancellation notice-fee imposed. **Amenities:** safes. **Pool(s):** outdoor. **Free Special Amenities: local telephone calls and high-speed Internet.**

BEST WESTERN PLUS CARMEL BAY VIEW INN
(831)624-1831

Hotel
$89-$279

AAA Benefit: Members save up to 20%, plus 10% bonus points with Best Western Rewards®.

Address: Junipero Ave 93923 **Location:** Just n off Ocean Ave; between 5th and 6th aves. **Facility:** 59 units, some two bedrooms. 1-5 stories, exterior corridors. **Amenities:** high-speed Internet. **Pool(s):** outdoor. **Guest Services:** valet laundry. **Free Special Amenities: full breakfast and high-speed Internet.**

BRIARWOOD INN   831/626-9056

Bed & Breakfast
Rates not provided

Address: San Carlos St 93921 **Location:** 3 blks n of Ocean Ave; at 4th Ave. **Facility:** Most rooms have a fireplace and some have a wet bar; a garden beautifies the well-maintained grounds. 12 units, some two bedrooms and kitchens. 1-2 stories (no elevator), exterior corridors.

CANDLE LIGHT INN   (831)624-6451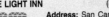

Hotel
$189-$279

Address: San Carlos St 93923 **Location:** 2 blks n of Ocean Ave; between 4th and 5th aves. **Facility:** 20 units, some two bedrooms and kitchens. 2 stories, exterior corridors. **Terms:** 2 night minimum stay - weekends, 3 day cancellation notice. **Free Special Amenities: continental breakfast and high-speed Internet.**

CARMEL-BY-THE-SEA - COMFORT INN
(831)622-7090 106

Hotel
$90-$300

Address: Ocean Ave & Torres St 93921 **Location:** SR 1 exit Ocean Ave W; at Torres St. **Facility:** 19 units. 2 stories (no elevator), exterior corridors. **Parking:** on-site and street. **Terms:** 3 day cancellation notice-fee imposed. **Amenities:** safes. **Free Special Amenities: full breakfast and high-speed Internet.**

CARMEL COUNTRY INN   831/625-3263 87

Bed & Breakfast $275-$425 **Address:** Dolores St & 3rd Ave 93921 **Location:** 4 blks n of Ocean Ave. **Facility:** Well-maintained grounds surround spacious, attractively appointed guest rooms, each with a wet bar and most with a gas fireplace. 12 units, some two bedrooms. 2 stories (no elevator), exterior corridors. **Terms:** 2 night minimum stay - weekends, 7 day cancellation notice-fee imposed.

CARMEL FIREPLACE INN BED & BREAKFAST
831/624-4862 92

Bed & Breakfast
Rates not provided

Address: San Carlos St & 4th Ave 93921 **Location:** 3 blks n of Ocean Ave. **Facility:** Guest rooms vary in size, many have gas-burning fireplaces. Beautiful gardens and mature shade trees surround the inn's walkways. 18 units, some two bedrooms. 2 stories (no elevator), exterior corridors.

CARMEL GARDEN COURT   831/624-6926 95

Bed & Breakfast $150-$245 **Address:** 4th Ave & Torres St 93923 **Location:** 3 blks n of Ocean Ave. **Facility:** Fountains accent the award-winning garden at the property, which offers units with wood-burning fireplaces and some flower-filled private patios. 10 units. 1 story, exterior corridors. **Terms:** check-in 4 pm, 7 day cancellation notice-fee imposed.

CARMEL INN & SUITES   (831)624-1900 99

Hotel
$90-$500

Address: 5th Ave & Junipero Ave 93921 **Location:** 2 blks n of Ocean Ave. **Facility:** 20 units. 2 stories, exterior corridors. **Terms:** 2-5 night minimum stay - seasonal and/or weekends, 7 day cancellation notice-fee imposed. **Pool(s):** outdoor. **Free Special Amenities: expanded continental breakfast and high-speed Internet.**

CARMEL LODGE   831/624-1255 97

Hotel
Rates not provided

Address: San Carlos St & 5th Ave 93921 **Location:** 2 blks n of Ocean Ave. **Facility:** 38 units. 2 stories, interior/exterior corridors. **Parking:** on-site (fee). **Free Special Amenities: continental breakfast and high-speed Internet.**

(See map & index p. 206.)

CARMEL MISSION INN　　　(831)624-1841 **115**

 Hotel $99-$529 **Address:** 3665 Rio Rd 93923 **Location:** 1 mi s on SR 1. **Facility:** 165 units. 4 stories, interior/exterior corridors. **Terms:** check-in 4 pm. **Amenities:** safes. *Some:* high-speed Internet. **Pool(s):** outdoor. **Activities:** whirlpool, limited exercise equipment. **Guest Services:** valet laundry.

CARMEL OAKS INN & SUITES CLARION COLLECTION
　　　　　　　　　　　(831)624-5547 **98**

Hotel
$99-$499

Address: 5th Ave & Mission St 93921 **Location:** 2 blks n of Ocean Ave. **Facility:** 17 units, some efficiencies. 2 stories (no elevator), exterior corridors. **Terms:** 2-4 night minimum stay - seasonal and/or weekends, 7 day cancellation notice-fee imposed, resort fee. **Free Special Amenities:** high-speed Internet.

CARMEL RESORT INN　　　(831)293-8390 **86**

Motel $79-$289 **Address:** Carpenter St & 1st Ave 93923 **Location:** SR 1 exit Carpenter St, 0.5 mi w. **Facility:** 31 units, some two bedrooms and efficiencies. 1 story, exterior corridors. **Terms:** 3 night minimum stay, 3 day cancellation notice-fee imposed. **Activities:** sauna, whirlpool.

CARMEL VILLAGE INN　　　(831)624-3864 **105**

Hotel
$109-$650

Address: Ocean Ave & Junipero Ave 93921 **Location:** At Ocean and Junipero aves. **Facility:** 34 units, some kitchens. 2 stories, exterior corridors. **Terms:** 2 night minimum stay - seasonal and/or weekends, 3 day cancellation notice-fee imposed, resort fee. **Free Special Amenities:** full breakfast and high-speed Internet.

CARRIAGE HOUSE INN　　　(831)625-2585 **112**

Bed & Breakfast
$309-$419

Address: Junipero Ave 93923 **Location:** 2 blks s off Ocean Ave on Junipero Ave; between 7th and 8th aves. **Facility:** Surrounded by mature shade trees and gardens, guest rooms are spacious and individually appointed with a fireplace; some offer distant ocean views. Art galleries and fine dining are steps away. 13 units. 2 stories (no elevator), exterior corridors. **Terms:** 2 night minimum stay - weekends, 3 day cancellation notice. **Amenities:** safes. **Guest Services:** valet laundry. **Free Special Amenities:** expanded continental breakfast and high-speed Internet.

Get an insider view from AAA/CAA travel experts at AAATravelViews.com

▼ See AAA listing p. 71 ▼

Give the gift of security, value and peace of mind: Gift Membership

(See map & index p. 206.)

COACHMAN'S INN
(831)624-6421 **110**

Hotel
$145-$435

Address: San Carlos St at 7th Ave 93921 **Location:** Just s of Ocean Ave on San Carlos St; between 7th and 8th aves. **Facility:** 30 units. 3 stories (no elevator), exterior corridors. **Terms:** 2 night minimum stay - seasonal and/or weekends, 3 day cancellation notice. **Activities:** sauna, whirlpool, limited exercise equipment. **Free Special Amenities: continental breakfast and local telephone calls.** *(See ad p. 70.)*

THE COBBLESTONE INN
(831)625-5222 **113**

Bed & Breakfast
$150-$600

Address: Junipero Ave 93921 **Location:** S of Ocean Ave; between 7th and 8th aves. **Facility:** The inn features a garden and attractive common areas. Gas fireplaces are featured in all guest units. 24 units. 2 stories (no elevator), interior/exterior corridors. **Parking:** street only. **Terms:** check-in 3:30 pm, 7 day cancellation notice-fee imposed. **Free Special Amenities: full breakfast and manager's reception.**

COLONIAL TERRACE INN
(831)624-2741 **114**

Bed & Breakfast
$99-$459

Address: San Antonio Ave & 13th Ave 93921 **Location:** On San Antonio Ave; between 12th and 13th aves. **Facility:** Attractive gardens surround this B&B, which offers guest rooms with gas fireplaces and some units with ocean views. 26 units, some two bedrooms and efficiencies. 2 stories (no elevator), exterior corridors. **Terms:** 7 day cancellation notice-fee imposed. **Guest Services:** valet laundry. **Free Special Amenities: expanded continental breakfast and high-speed Internet.**

Safety tip: Keep a current AAA/CAA Road Atlas in every vehicle

CYPRESS INN
831/624-3871 **108**

Classic Hotel. Rates not provided. **Address:** Lincoln & 7th Ave 93922 **Location:** Just s off Ocean Ave. **Facility:** Built in 1929 in the Spanish Mediterranean style, this inn centers on a garden courtyard. Memorabilia of Doris Day and her movies are displayed throughout the hotel. 44 units. 2 stories, interior/exterior corridors. **Parking:** street only. **Terms:** check-in 4 pm. **Amenities:** *Some:* high-speed Internet. **Activities:** exercise room. **Guest Services:** valet laundry.

DOLPHIN INN
(831)624-5356 **91**

Hotel
$189-$269

Address: 4th Ave & San Carlos St 93923 **Location:** 3 blks n off Ocean Ave. **Facility:** 27 units, some efficiencies. 2 stories (no elevator), exterior corridors. **Terms:** 2 night minimum stay - weekends, 3 day cancellation notice. **Pool(s):** heated outdoor. **Guest Services:** valet laundry. **Free Special Amenities: continental breakfast and high-speed Internet.**

GREEN LANTERN INN BED & BREAKFAST
831/624-4392 **107**

Bed & Breakfast $99-$289 **Address:** Casanova St & 7th Ave 93923 **Location:** Just s of Ocean Ave. **Facility:** 17 units. 2 stories (no elevator), exterior corridors. **Terms:** 2 night minimum stay - seasonal and/or weekends, 3 day cancellation notice-fee imposed.

HOFSAS HOUSE
(831)624-2745 **88**

Hotel
$90-$400

Address: San Carlos St 93921 **Location:** 3 blks n off Ocean Ave; between 3rd and 4th aves. **Facility:** 38 units, some two bedrooms and efficiencies. 4 stories (no elevator), exterior corridors. **Terms:** 2 night minimum stay - seasonal and/or weekends, 3 day cancellation notice-fee imposed. **Pool(s):** heated outdoor. **Activities:** sauna. **Free Special Amenities: continental breakfast.** *(See ad this page.)*

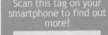

▼ *See AAA listing this page* ▼

Hofsas House
Carmel-by-the-Sea
Casual European Elegance with the Warmth of Family Hospitality

- Ocean views
- Honeymoon or family suites
- Pool heated year-round
- Dry saunas
- Walk to village shops & restaurants
- Off street parking
- Online reservations available
- Wireless internet access

- Family owned & operated
- Pet friendly in some rooms
- Complimentary continental breakfast

Scan this tag on your smartphone to find out more!

Get the free mobile app at http://gettag.mobi

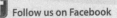
Follow us on Facebook

1-800-221-2548 www.hofsashouse.com
San Carlos and 4th ~ P.O. Box 1195 Carmel-by-the-Sea, CA 93921

(See map & index p. 206.)

HORIZON INN & OCEAN VIEW LODGE
(831)624-5327 **89**

Hotel
$106-$390

Address: 3rd Ave & Junipero Ave 93921 **Location:** 4 blks n off Ocean Ave. **Facility:** 29 units, some efficiencies and kitchens. 2 stories, exterior corridors. **Terms:** 2 night minimum stay - weekends, 3 day cancellation notice-fee imposed. **Activities:** whirlpool. **Guest Services:** coin laundry. **Free Special Amenities: continental breakfast and high-speed Internet.**

HYATT CARMEL HIGHLANDS
(831)620-1234 **116**

Hotel
$319-$1139

HYATT

AAA Benefit:
Members save 10% or more everyday.

Address: 120 Highlands Dr 93923 **Location:** Oceanfront. 4 mi s on SR 1. Located in Carmel Highlands. **Facility:** Located on a cliff with outstanding ocean views, this property offers many units with a wood-burning fireplace and patio; some units are smaller but very tastefully appointed. 48 units, some kitchens. 2-3 stories (no elevator), exterior corridors. **Terms:** check-in 4 pm, 7 day cancellation notice-fee imposed, resort fee. **Amenities:** video games (fee), safes. **Dining:** California Market, Pacific's Edge, see separate listings, entertainment. **Pool(s):** heated outdoor. **Activities:** whirlpools, exercise room. *Fee:* bicycles. **Guest Services:** valet laundry.

LOBOS LODGE
831/624-3874 **103**

Hotel $125-$195 **Address:** Monte Verde St & Ocean Ave 93921 **Location:** Jct Ocean Ave and Monte Verde St. **Facility:** 30 units. 2 stories, exterior corridors. **Terms:** 2 night minimum stay - weekends, 3 day cancellation notice.

NORMANDY INN
(831)624-3825 **102**

Hotel
$98-$399

Address: Monte Verde St & Ocean Ave 93923 **Location:** On Ocean Ave; between Monte Verde and Casanova sts. **Facility:** 48 units, some efficiencies and houses. 2 stories, exterior corridors. **Terms:** 2 night minimum stay - seasonal and/or weekends, 3 day cancellation notice. **Amenities:** high-speed Internet. **Pool(s):** outdoor. **Free Special Amenities: expanded continental breakfast and high-speed Internet.**

PINE INN
(831)624-3851 **104**

Historic Hotel $179-$359 **Address:** Ocean Ave & Monte Verde St 93923 **Location:** Between Lincoln Ln and Monte Verde St. **Facility:** This beautifully restored 1889 turn-of-the-century hotel features elegant furnishings and fabrics in its guest rooms. 49 units. 3 stories (no elevator), interior/exterior corridors. **Terms:** check-in 4 pm, 2 night minimum stay - seasonal and/or weekends, 7 day cancellation notice, resort fee. **Dining:** 2 restaurants, also, Il Fornaio, see separate listing. **Guest Services:** valet laundry. *(See ad this page.)*

SAN ANTONIO HOUSE INN
(831)624-4334 **100**

Bed & Breakfast $180-$245 **Address:** Ocean Ave & San Antonio Ave 93921 **Location:** Just s of Ocean Ave on San Antonio Ave; between Ocean and 7th aves. **Facility:** 5 units, some two bedrooms and kitchens. 2 stories (no elevator), exterior corridors. **Parking:** street only. **Terms:** check-in 4 pm, 7 day cancellation notice-fee imposed.

SVENDSGAARD'S
(831)624-1511 **90**

Hotel
$149-$259

Address: 4th Ave & San Carlos St 93921 **Location:** 3 blks n off Ocean Ave. **Facility:** 35 units, some two bedrooms and efficiencies. 2 stories, exterior corridors. **Terms:** 2 night minimum stay - weekends, 3 day cancellation notice. **Pool(s):** heated outdoor. **Free Special Amenities: continental breakfast and high-speed Internet.**

▼ See AAA listing this page ▼

TICKLE PINK INN
at Carmel Highlands

AAA
Four Diamond
Award

A NAME TO REMEMBER,
a view you will never forget.

Special Features For Our Guests
- Spectacular ocean views from private balconies
- Outdoor hot tub & in-room spas*
- In-room wood burning fireplaces*
- Privacy & personal service
- Private cottage available
- Terrace boardroom
- Pacific Dreams beds & bedding
- 100% Egyptian cotton linens

Pampering Amenities Just For You
- Bottle of champagne upon arrival
- Evening wine & cheese reception
- Terry cloth robes & slippers
- Flat-screen TVs with HD & free movie rentals
- Fresh ground coffee in your room
- Continental breakfast
- Daily newspaper   *Available in select rooms*

RESERVATIONS (866) 611-7465 · WWW.TICKLEPINKINN.COM
155 HIGHLAND DRIVE, CARMEL, CA 93923

(See map & index p. 206.)

TICKLE PINK INN   (831)624-1244 117

▼▼▼▼
Hotel
$231-$599

Address: 155 Highland Dr 93923 **Location:** Oceanfront. 4 mi s on SR 1. Located in Carmel Highlands. **Facility:** Sweeping views are a highlight of this hillside inn offering spacious accommodations, most with a balcony and some with a fireplace. 35 units, some cottages. 2-3 stories (no elevator), exterior corridors. **Terms:** 2-3 night minimum stay - seasonal and/or weekends, 7 day cancellation notice-fee imposed. **Amenities:** safes. **Activities:** whirlpool. **Free Special Amenities:** expanded continental breakfast and high-speed Internet. *(See ad p. 73.)*

WAYSIDE INN   (831)624-5336 109

▼▼▼▼
Hotel
$229-$399

Address: 7th Ave & Mission St 93921 **Location:** 1 blk s off Ocean Ave. **Facility:** 22 units, some two bedrooms and kitchens. 2 stories, exterior corridors. **Terms:** 2 night minimum stay - weekends, 3 day cancellation notice. **Free Special Amenities:** continental breakfast and high-speed Internet.

WHERE TO EAT

ANTON & MICHEL   831/624-2406 51

▼▼▼ Continental. Fine Dining. $14-$36 **AAA Inspector Notes:** Guests who unwind in the romantic solarium setting are treated to attractive courtyard views. Seafood and lamb are specialties on the ambitious menu. Tableside service is traditional. **Bar:** full bar. **Reservations:** suggested. **Address:** Mission St at 7th Ave 93921 **Location:** Just s off Ocean Ave. **Parking:** street only.

AUBERGINE AT L'AUBERGE   831/624-8578 50

▼▼▼ ▼▼▼ European. Fine Dining. $89-$125 **AAA Inspector Notes:** Elegant decor characterizes this intimate 12-table dining room, where patrons savor eight- to 10-course tasting menus. A large wine cellar provides numerous choices and pairings. **Bar:** full bar. **Reservations:** suggested. **Address:** Monte Verde St & 7th Ave 93921 **Location:** Just s of jct Ocean Ave. **Parking:** valet and street only.

BAJA CANTINA   831/625-2252

▼▼▼ Mexican. Casual Dining. $8-$26 **AAA Inspector Notes:** Set in the valley, this eclectic Mexican restaurant boasts gorgeous mountain views. The dining room is filled with colorful signs and pictures, and a large outdoor patio features a fire pit, rose bushes crawling on lattice, numerous potted plants and small white lights hanging from trees. Homemade tortilla chips are a big hit, and Hector's toothpicks—flour tortillas stuffed and rolled with sautéed chicken, onions and cheese—is a great starter. **Bar:** full bar. **Address:** 7166 Carmel Valley Rd 93923 **Location:** Jct SR 1, 3.5 mi e.

CALIFORNIA MARKET   831/622-5450 57

▼▼▼ California. Casual Dining. $12-$20 **AAA Inspector Notes:** Located on a bluff overlooking the Pacific Ocean, this eatery offers guests spectacular views. Patio dining is available, weather permitting. **Bar:** full bar. **Address:** 120 Highlands Dr 93923 **Location:** 4 mi s on SR 1; in Hyatt Carmel Highlands.

CASANOVA   831/625-0501 45

▼▼▼ French. Fine Dining. $14-$52 **AAA Inspector Notes:** A cozy, country atmosphere invites patrons to relax inside or out on the patio. On the menu are Northern Italian and Mediterranean specialties. **Bar:** full bar. **Reservations:** suggested. **Address:** 5th Ave between Mission St & San Carlos St 93922 **Location:** Just n off Ocean Ave. **Parking:** street only.

CHINA DELIGHT   831/625-3367 55

▼▼ Chinese. Casual Dining. $7-$25 **AAA Inspector Notes:** Set in the distinctive shops of Crossroads Village, this Chinese eatery offers a selection of Mandarin and Cantonese favorites. Order individual entrées, or ask for a family dinner to share. **Bar:** beer & wine. **Address:** 145 Crossroads Blvd 93921 **Location:** Jct SR 1 and Rio Rd; in Crossroads Shopping Village.

THE FRENCH POODLE RESTAURANT   831/624-8643 46

▼▼▼▼ French. Fine Dining. $20-$36 **AAA Inspector Notes:** Decorated with lovely paintings, the elegant dining room sustains a warm, charming atmosphere. Dishes are prepared in the classic French tradition. **Bar:** beer & wine. **Reservations:** suggested. **Address:** Junipero Ave & 5th Ave 93921 **Location:** Just n off Ocean Ave; at Junipero and 5th aves. **Parking:** street only.

FROM SCRATCH RESTAURANT   831/625-2448 52

▼▼ American. Casual Dining. $8-$13 **AAA Inspector Notes:** In an upscale shopping center, the restaurant does as its name suggests--prepares homemade food from scratch. The atmosphere is friendly and comfortable. **Bar:** beer & wine. **Address:** 3626 The Barnyard 93923 **Location:** SR 1 exit Carmel Valley Rd, 1 mi s; in Barnyard Shopping Center.

HOG'S BREATH INN CARMEL   831/625-1044 47

▼▼▼
American
Casual Dining
$15-$30

AAA Inspector Notes: This casual spot is noted for memorabilia of Clint Eastwood surrounding the dining room. Guests can enjoy such lunch items as sandwiches, hearty soups, salads and chili or a Dirty Harry burger. Dinner features prime rib, steak, ribs and fresh seafood. Patio dining is available weather permitting. Be sure to stop in at the bar to see the mounted hog heads. **Bar:** full bar. **Address:** San Carlos St between 5th Ave & 6th Ave 93921 **Location:** Just n of Ocean Ave; downtown. **Parking:** street only.

IL FORNAIO   831/622-5100 49

▼▼▼ Italian. Fine Dining. $9-$36 **AAA Inspector Notes:** Accomplished servers begin guests' experiences with crisp, crusty bread hot from the oven. Pasta and flavorful sauces enhance the roasted meats and vegetables. The spacious restaurant thoughtfully replicates the trattorias of Italy. **Bar:** full bar. **Reservations:** suggested. **Address:** Ocean Ave & Monte Verde St 93921 **Location:** Between Lincoln Ln and Monte Verde St; in Pine Inn. **Parking:** street only. *(See ad p. 72.)*

KATY'S PLACE   831/624-0199 48

▼▼ American. Casual Dining. $9-$20 **AAA Inspector Notes:** The specialty, breakfast, is served all day. Popular choices include crab cake eggs Benedict, blintzes with fresh seasonal berries and a wide selection of omelets. Diners can eat inside or on the patio. **Bar:** beer & wine. **Address:** Mission St between 5th Ave & 6th Ave 93921 **Location:** 1 blk n of Ocean Ave. **Parking:** street only.

LUGANO SWISS BISTRO   831/626-3779 53

▼▼ German. Casual Dining. $9-$40 **AAA Inspector Notes:** This quaint dining room displays German heritage memorabilia including muraled walls, traditional German steins and cuckoo clocks all in a casual setting. The friendly staff dishes up traditional German specialties including schnitzel, brats and fondue. Pasta and seafood dishes also are available. Be sure to save room for traditional bread pudding and strudel. **Bar:** beer & wine. **Address:** 3670 The Barnyard 93923 **Location:** Just e of SR 1 via Rio Rd; in Barnyard Shopping Center.

PACIFIC'S EDGE   831/622-5445 56

▼▼▼▼ Regional American. Fine Dining. $24-$49 **AAA Inspector Notes:** The Pacific Ocean views are spectacular from this casually elegant dining room. Light, robustly flavored dishes are made from fresh, local ingredients. **Bar:** full bar. **Reservations:** suggested. **Address:** 120 Highlands Dr 93923 **Location:** 4 mi s on SR 1; in Hyatt Carmel Highlands.

(See map & index p. 206.)

RIO GRILL   831/625-5436   54

▼▼ California. Fine Dining. $10-$37 **AAA Inspector Notes:** The Southwestern atmosphere is upbeat and welcoming, and the California cuisine is creatively prepared with a Western flair. Fresh ingredients are emphasized. **Bar:** full bar. **Reservations:** suggested. **Address:** 101 Crossroads Blvd 93923 **Location:** Just e of SR 1 at Rio Rd; in Crossroads Shopping Center.   L   D   CALL &M

CARMEL VALLEY
- Hotels & Restaurants map & index p. 206
- Part of Monterey Peninsula area — see map p. 202

ACACIA LODGE-COUNTRY GARDEN INNS
    831/659-5361   123

▼▼ ▼▼ Motel. Rates not provided. **Address:** 20 Via Contenta 93924 **Location:** 12.8 mi e of SR 1. Located in a quiet secluded area; in Carmel Valley Village. **Facility:** 19 units. 1 story, exterior corridors. **Pool(s):** outdoor. **Activities:** whirlpool.

🏊 📶 ✕ 🐾 🛄 🖥

BERNARDUS LODGE   (831)658-3400   121

▼▼▼▼   **Address:** 415 W Carmel Valley Rd
Hotel   93924 **Location:** 9.5 mi e of SR 1; just
$315-$2030   e of Los Laureles Grade. **Facility:** Located in the valley surrounded by the Santa Lucia Mountains and grape vineyards, the inn's guest rooms are spacious and feature a limestone fireplace. 57 units. 2 stories (no elevator), exterior corridors. **Parking:** valet only. **Terms:** check-in 4 pm, 2 night minimum stay - weekends, 7 day cancellation notice-fee imposed, resort fee. **Amenities:** high-speed Internet, safes. **Dining:** 2 restaurants, also, Wicket's Bistro, see separate listing. **Pool(s):** heated outdoor. **Activities:** exercise room, spa. **Guest Services:** valet laundry. **Free Special Amenities:** newspaper and high-speed Internet.

SAVE 🍴 🍸 CALL &M 🏊 BIZ 📶 ✕ 🖥
/SOME UNITS FEE 🐾 🛄 🖥

CARMEL VALLEY RANCH   (831)625-9500   120

▼▼ ▼▼ Resort Hotel $300-$1200 **Address:** One Old Ranch Rd 93923 **Location:** 6.3 mi e of SR 1 via Carmel Valley Rd to Robinson Canyon Rd exit, follow signs. **Facility:** Hillside overlooking the Carmel Valley and a golf course, the resort offers spacious units with wood-burning fireplaces. 139 units, some two bedrooms and efficiencies. 1 story, exterior corridors. **Terms:** check-in 4 pm, 7 day cancellation notice-fee imposed, resort fee. **Amenities:** safes. **Dining:** 3 restaurants. **Pool(s):** 3 heated outdoor. **Activities:** saunas, whirlpools, basketball, exercise room, spa. **Fee:** golf-18 holes, 12 tennis courts. **Guest Services:** valet laundry.

🍴 🍸 CALL &M 🏊 BIZ 📶 ✕ 🛄 🖥
/SOME UNITS FEE 🐾 🖥

HIDDEN VALLEY INN-COUNTRY GARDEN INNS
    831/659-5361   122

▼▼ ▼▼ Motel. Rates not provided. **Address:** 102 W Carmel Valley Rd 93924 **Location:** 11 mi e of SR 1. Located in a quiet area. **Facility:** 26 units, some efficiencies. 2 stories, exterior corridors. **Pool(s):** outdoor. 🏊 📶 ✕ 🐾 🖥 /SOME UNITS 🛄

WHERE TO EAT

WICKET'S BISTRO   831/658-3400   60

▼▼▼▼ Regional California. Casual Dining. $15-$35 **AAA Inspector Notes:** A casual setting and well-prepared meals make this an ideal stop for breakfast, lunch or dinner. Diners sit inside the lounge or on the patio overlooking the lodge's beautifully landscaped gardens. Grilled meat and poultry items, fresh local seafood, and locally grown organic greens and herbs add to the overall dining experience. **Bar:** full bar. **Reservations:** suggested. **Address:** 415 Carmel Valley Rd 93924 **Location:** 9.5 mi e of SR 1; just e of Los Laureles Grade; in Bernardus Lodge. **Parking:** valet only.

B   L   D   CALL &M

WILL'S FARGO RESTAURANT   831/659-2774   61

▼▼ Steak. Casual Dining. $20-$40 **AAA Inspector Notes:** The attractive garden setting displays an 1880s decor. Cut-to-order steaks are among selections on the diverse menu. **Bar:** full bar. **Reservations:** suggested. **Address:** 16 E Carmel Valley Rd 93924 **Location:** 12 mi e of SR 1; in village. **Parking:** street only.

D   🐾

CARMICHAEL (E-3) pop. 61,762, elev. 123'
- Hotels & Restaurants map & index p. 314

EFFIE YEAW NATURE CENTER is along the American River in Ancil Hoffman Park at 2850 San Lorenzo Way. In addition to hands-on exhibits, the nature center is home to rescued animals—including birds, snakes and turtles—unable to be reintroduced into the wild. Three nature trails through the center's 77 acres provide opportunities for spotting wildlife such as deer, hawks, woodpeckers, jackrabbits and wild turkeys. Trailheads are at the rear of the center.

Time: Allow 1 hour minimum. **Hours:** Nature center Tues.-Sun. 9-5, mid-Mar. to early Nov.; Thurs.-Sun. 9-4, rest of year. Trails daily dawn-dusk. Closed Jan. 1, Thanksgiving, Christmas Eve and Christmas. Phone ahead to confirm schedule. **Cost:** Nature center free. Park admission $5 per private vehicle. **Phone:** (916) 489-4918. 🏛

AMBIENCE   916/489-8464   97

▼▼▼ New American. Fine Dining. $55-$75 **AAA Inspector Notes:** This sophisticated restaurant offers exquisitely prepared New American and French cuisine with a five-course prix fixe menu and a seven-course tasting menu. Most courses have several options. **Bar:** beer & wine. **Reservations:** suggested. **Address:** 6440 Fair Oaks Blvd 95608 **Location:** I-80 exit Madison Ave, 1.6 mi, 1.6 mi s on Manzanita Ave (which becomes Fair Oaks Blvd), then 1.3 mi s; Business Rt 80 (Capital City Frwy) exit Marconi Ave, 4.6 mi e; just n of jct Marconi Ave. D   CALL &M

FIREBIRD RUSSIAN RESTAURANT & GALLERY
    916/485-7747   96

▼▼ Russian. Casual Dining. $8-$17 **AAA Inspector Notes:** Do not let the exterior fool you. Nicely prepared, authentic Russian cuisine is what diners find at this restaurant with a friendly, caring staff who answer questions. There are a variety of hot and cold appetizers, homemade Russian dumplings and interesting entrées along with a good selection of vodka. Russian artwork adorns the walls. Lunch buffet is offered Tuesday through Saturday and the Sunday brunch buffet is 11 to 4. Dinner is served from 4 to 7 on Sunday. **Bar:** full bar. **Address:** 4715 Manzanita Ave 95608 **Location:** I-80 exit Madison Ave, 1.7 mi e, then 0.8 mi s; just n of jct Winding Way.

L   D   CALL &M

CARNELIAN BAY pop. 524
- Hotels & Restaurants map & index p. 161
- Part of Lake Tahoe Area — see map p. 158

GAR WOODS GRILL & PIER   530/546-3366   21

▼▼▼   **AAA Inspector Notes:** This restaurant
American   offers a varied menu of pasta, fresh sea-
Fine Dining   food and steak items. Patrons can enjoy
$13-$36   views of Tahoe's north shore from the heated, lakefront deck, where menu selections include burgers and fish tacos. Valet boat parking is offered at the 130-foot pier. **Bar:** full bar. **Reservations:** suggested. **Address:** 5000 N Lake Blvd 96140 **Location:** SR 28, 6 mi e of SR 89. *Menu on AAA.com*   L   D   CALL &M 🐾

CASTRO VALLEY pop. 61,388
• Hotels & Restaurants map & index p. 254

CASTRO VALLEY COMFORT SUITES　　(510)889-9300 **62**

Hotel $105-$149 **Address:** 2419 Castro Valley Blvd 94546 **Location:** I-580 exit Castro Valley Blvd, just n. Castro Valley, 27. **Facility:** 54 units. 3 stories, interior corridors. **Terms:** cancellation fee imposed. **Amenities:** high-speed Internet, safes. **Activities:** sauna, whirlpool, exercise room. **Guest Services:** valet and coin laundry. CALL

CASTRO VALLEY INN　　　　(510)538-5757 **63**

Motel
$66-$77

Address: 3954 E Castro Valley Blvd 94552 **Location:** I-580 exit Crow Canyon Rd eastbound; exit Castro Valley Blvd westbound, 0.3 mi e. **Facility:** 49 units. 2 stories (no elevator), exterior corridors. **Terms:** 3 day cancellation notice-fee imposed. **Amenities:** high-speed Internet. **Free Special Amenities: continental breakfast and high-speed Internet.**

SAVE CALL

QUALITY INN　　　　(510)538-9501 **61**

Hotel $79-$189 **Address:** 2532 Castro Valley Blvd 94546 **Location:** I-580 exit Castro Valley Blvd, 0.3 mi n. Castro Valley, 27. **Facility:** 60 units. 3 stories, interior corridors. **Amenities:** high-speed Internet. **Pool(s):** outdoor. **Activities:** exercise room. **Guest Services:** valet laundry.

/SOME UNITS FEE

WHERE TO EAT

ROUND TABLE PIZZA　　　　510/733-9500

Pizza. Quick Serve. $7-$28 **AAA Inspector Notes:** This casual, family-oriented pizza place features high-quality ingredients and dough rolled fresh daily. Distinctive specialty pizzas are piled high with toppings. **Bar:** beer & wine. **Address:** 20920 Redwood Rd 94546 **Location:** I-580 exit Redwood Rd, just n. Castro Valley, 27. [L] [D]

CEDARVILLE pop. 514

SUNRISE MOTEL　　　　530/279-2161

Motel
$69-$79

Address: 62271 Hwy 299 W 96104 **Location:** Jct SR 299 and CR 1, 0.6 mi w on CR 1. Located in a quiet area. **Facility:** 15 units, some houses. 1 story, exterior corridors. **Terms:** 2 night minimum stay - seasonal and/or weekends, 7 day cancellation notice-fee imposed. **Activities:** horseshoes. **Guest Services:** coin laundry. **Free Special Amenities: high-speed Internet and use of on-premises laundry facilities.**

SAVE BIZ /SOME UNITS FEE

CHESTER (C-3) pop. 2,144, elev. 4,528'

Nearby Lake Almanor was formed when a dam was built on the north fork of the Feather River in 1914. When full, the reservoir covers 52 square miles and is a popular recreation area, offering swimming, boating, water skiing, fishing, hiking and camping. Cross-country skiing and snowmobiling draw winter visitors. Resorts, vacation homes and campgrounds nestle among the pines along the shores of the lake.

Lake Almanor Chamber of Commerce and Visitor's Bureau: 162 Main St., P.O. Box 1198, Chester, CA 96020. **Phone:** (530) 258-2426.

CHESTER-LAKE ALMANOR MUSEUM is at 210 First Ave. at jct. Willow St., inside the log building also housing the library. In a rustic 1929 building, the museum features photographs tracing the history of the Lake Almanor basin, with many about dairy farming, logging and gold mining. The museum also has a collection of Maidu Indian basketry. **Hours:** Mon.-Wed. 10-1 and 1:30-5:30, Thurs. noon-5 and 5:30-7 p.m. Closed major holidays. **Cost:** Donations. **Phone:** (530) 258-2742.

BEST WESTERN ROSE QUARTZ INN　　(530)258-2002

Hotel
$116-$151

AAA Benefit: Members save up to 20%, plus 10% bonus points with Best Western Rewards®.

Address: 306 Main St 96020 **Location:** 0.3 mi w of center on SR 36. **Facility:** 50 units. 2 stories, interior corridors. **Activities:** whirlpool, exercise room. **Free Special Amenities: local telephone calls and high-speed Internet.**

SAVE CALL BIZ /SOME UNITS FEE

THE BIDWELL HOUSE　　　　(530)258-3338

Bed & Breakfast
$85-$175

Address: 1 Main St 96020 **Location:** 0.6 mi ne of center on SR 36. **Facility:** This renovated 1901 farmhouse is nestled at the east edge of town near Lake Almanor and offers a fireplace in the living area and wood-burning fireplaces in three guest rooms. 14 units, some cottages. 2 stories (no elevator), interior corridors. **Bath:** some shared. **Terms:** 2 night minimum stay - seasonal and/or weekends, 7 day cancellation notice-fee imposed. **Free Special Amenities: full breakfast and high-speed Internet.**

SAVE BIZ /SOME UNITS

CHICO (D-3) pop. 86,187, elev. 200'
• Restaurants p. 78

Bidwell Park, a 3,618-acre city park spanning an area from downtown to the foothills of the Sierra Nevada, offers hiking and bicycling trails, a pool, a playground and various sports facilities as well as Chico Creek Nature Center *(see attraction listing).* The original acreage was a gift to the city in 1905 from Annie Bidwell, wife of Chico's founder.

Chico Chamber of Commerce & Visitor Bureau: 441 Main St., Suite 150, Chico, CA 95928. **Phone:** (530) 891-5556 or (800) 852-8570.

BIDWELL MANSION STATE HISTORIC PARK, 525 The Esplanade, preserves a three-story, 26-room Victorian residence built 1865-68 for city founder Gen. John Bidwell and his wife Annie. Guests entertained at the brick mansion covered in pink stucco included such well-known figures as Susan B. Anthony, President Rutherford B. Hayes, John Muir and Gen. William Tecumseh Sherman.

Time: Allow 1 hour minimum. **Hours:** Guided tours are given Mon. on the hour noon-4, Sat.-Sun. 11-4. Closed Jan. 1 and Christmas. Phone ahead to confirm schedule. **Cost:** $6; $3 (ages 5-17). **Phone:** (530) 895-6144.

CHICO CREEK NATURE CENTER is n.e. of jct. SRs 32 and 99 at 1968 E. 8th St. in Bidwell Park. The center features nature exhibits; gardens; hiking trails; and a museum with a variety of live birds, reptiles and mammals, including squirrels, tortoises and snakes. **Hours:** Wed.-Sun. 11-4. Closed major holidays. **Cost:** Donations. **Phone:** (530) 891-4671.

CHICO MUSEUM, downtown at 2nd and Salem sts., offers permanent and changing exhibits about regional cultural and natural history. A timeline depicts the history of Chico 1830-2000. **Hours:** Wed.-Sun. noon-4. **Cost:** $3; $2 (ages 50+ and students with ID); free (ages 0-14 with adult). **Phone:** (530) 891-4336 or (530) 892-1525.

NATIONAL YO-YO MUSEUM is at 320 Broadway in the rear of the Bird in Hand store; the entrance is in Diamond Alley. The history of the yo-yo is shown through collections of the toy dating from the 1920s through the golden era of the 1950s. Modern high-tech, machined yo-yos also are exhibited, as are winning yo-yos from national and world contests.

The highlight of the museum is a 50-inch-tall yo-yo weighing in at 256 pounds. Yo-yo lessons are offered on Saturdays. **Time:** Allow 30 minutes minimum. **Hours:** Mon.-Sat. 10-6, Sun. noon-5. Closed major holidays. **Cost:** Free. **Phone:** (530) 893-0545.

SIERRA NEVADA BREWING CO. is w. of SR 99 at 1075 E. 20th St. Thirty- to 40-minute guided tours of the brewery explain how the company's ales and lagers are produced, from their beginnings in the brewhouse, through the fermentation process to the keg or bottle. A series of murals in the brewhouse help define the process. **Hours:** Self-guiding tours Sun.-Thurs. 10-6, Fri.-Sat. 10-7. Guided tours are offered Mon.-Thurs. on the hour 11-4; Fri.-Sat. on the hour at 11 and noon, then every half-hour from 12:30-5; Sun. at 11 and then every hour from noon-4. **Cost:** Free. **Phone:** (530) 893-3520.

BEST WESTERN PLUS HERITAGE INN - CHICO
(530)894-8600

 Hotel $95-$120

AAA Benefit: Members save up to 20%, plus 10% bonus points with Best Western Rewards®.
Address: 25 Heritage Ln 95926 **Location:** Just e of SR 99, via Cohasset Rd. **Facility:** 99 units. 3 stories, interior corridors. **Amenities:** high-speed Internet. **Pool(s):** outdoor. **Activities:** whirlpool. **Free Special Amenities:** expanded continental breakfast and high-speed Internet.

COURTYARD BY MARRIOTT CHICO (530)894-6699
 Hotel $114-$170

AAA Benefit: AAA hotel discounts of 5% or more.
Address: 2481 Carmichael Dr 95928 **Location:** SR 99 exit 383 (Skyway/Park Ave), just w, then just n. **Facility:** 90 units. 3 stories, interior corridors. **Amenities:** Some: high-speed Internet. **Pool(s):** heated indoor. **Activities:** whirlpool, exercise room. **Guest Services:** valet and coin laundry. **Free Special Amenities:** early check-in/late check-out and high-speed Internet.

GOODMAN HOUSE BED & BREAKFAST (530)566-0256
Bed & Breakfast $119-$159 **Address:** 1362 Esplanade 95926 **Location:** SR 99 exit 386 (E 1st Ave), 0.9 mi sw, then just n; jct 4th Ave. **Facility:** Tastefully renovated, this turn-of-the-20th-century Craftsman home features original woodwork and floors, fine antiques and a welcoming front porch. A few guest rooms have an electric fireplace. 5 units. 2 stories (no elevator), interior corridors. **Terms:** 7 day cancellation notice-fee imposed.

HOLIDAY INN CHICO & CONFERENCE CENTER
530/345-2491
Hotel Rates not provided

Address: 685 Manzanita Ct 95926 **Location:** SR 99 exit 387A (Mangrove Ave/Cohasset Rd), follow Mangrove Ave, just sw. **Facility:** 172 units. 5 stories, interior corridors. **Terms:** check-in 4 pm. **Amenities:** video games (fee), high-speed Internet, safes. **Dining:** 2 restaurants. **Pool(s):** outdoor. **Activities:** whirlpool, exercise room. **Guest Services:** valet and coin laundry, area transportation-train & bus stations. **Free Special Amenities:** high-speed Internet and airport transportation.

HOTEL DIAMOND (530)893-3100
Hotel $139-$389

Address: 220 W 4th St 95928 **Location:** SR 99 exit 385 (SR 32), 1.2 mi sw to Salem St, just nw to 4th St, then just ne; jct Broadway; downtown. **Facility:** 43 units. 4 stories, interior corridors. **Terms:** cancellation fee imposed. **Amenities:** high-speed Internet, safes. **Dining:** Johnnie's Restaurant & Lounge, see separate listing. **Guest Services:** valet laundry, area transportation (fee)-within 5 mi.

JOHNSON'S COUNTRY INN (530)345-7829
Bed & Breakfast $105-$145 **Address:** 3935 Morehead Ave 95928 **Location:** From center, 1.5 mi w on W 5th St (which becomes Chico River Rd), 0.7 mi w; look for Morehead Ave sign on telephone pole. **Facility:** Nestled in an almond orchard a few minutes from the downtown area, this Victorian-style farmhouse offers a down-home atmosphere with a wrap-around porch, gazebo and attractive landscaped grounds. 4 units. 2 stories (no elevator), interior corridors. **Terms:** check-in 4 pm, cancellation fee imposed. **Activities:** horseshoes.

OXFORD SUITES (530)899-9090
Hotel $99-$179

Address: 2035 Business Ln 95928 **Location:** SR 99 exit 384 (E 20th St), just e, then just s. **Facility:** 184 units, some two bedrooms, efficiencies and kitchens. 4 stories, interior corridors. **Amenities:** Some: high-speed Internet. **Pool(s):** heated outdoor. **Activities:** sauna, whirlpool, steamroom, exercise room. **Guest Services:** valet and coin laundry, area transportation-train station.

RESIDENCE INN BY MARRIOTT CHICO (530)894-5500

Extended Stay Hotel
$134-$189

AAA Benefit: AAA hotel discounts of 5% or more.

Address: 2485 Carmichael Dr 95928 **Location:** SR 99 exit 383 (Skyway/Park Ave), just w, then just n. **Facility:** 78 units, some two bedrooms, efficiencies and kitchens. 3 stories, interior corridors. **Amenities:** *Some:* high-speed Internet. **Pool(s):** outdoor. **Activities:** whirlpool, sports court, exercise room. **Guest Services:** valet and coin laundry. **Free Special Amenities: full breakfast and high-speed Internet.**

[icons: SAVE, etc.] /SOME UNITS FEE

SUPER 8 (530)345-2533

Hotel
$57-$317

Address: 655 Manzanita Ct 95926 **Location:** SR 99 exit 387A (Mangrove Ave/Cohasset Rd), follow Mangrove Ave, then just se. **Facility:** 51 units. 3 stories (no elevator), interior corridors. **Terms:** cancellation fee imposed. **Pool(s):** outdoor. **Guest Services:** coin laundry. **Free Special Amenities: continental breakfast and high-speed Internet.**

[icons] /SOME UNITS FEE

WHERE TO EAT

5TH STREET STEAKHOUSE 530/891-6328

Steak. Casual Dining. $19-$32 **AAA Inspector Notes:** Old brick walls and antique hardwood floors contribute to the decor of this restaurant, which presents a menu of USDA Prime steaks and fresh seafood. **Bar:** full bar. **Reservations:** suggested. **Address:** 345 W 5th St 95926 **Location:** Just n of SR 32; between Normal Ave and Salem St; downtown. **Parking:** street only. [D]

CASA RAMOS

Mexican. Casual Dining. $9-$15 **AAA Inspector Notes:** A varied Mexican menu is featured in a colorful atmosphere. Mexican favorites include fajitas, enchiladas, burritos and specialty steak and seafood entrees. **Bar:** full bar. [L][D]

For additional information, visit AAA.com

LOCATIONS:

Address: 216C W East Ave 95926 **Location:** SR 99 N exit W East Ave, just w; just w of jct Esplanade; in Chico Town & Country Shopping Center. **Phone:** 530/894-0119

Address: 2490 Fair St 95928 **Location:** SR 99 exit 383 (Skyway/Park Ave), 0.5 mi w. **Phone:** 530/893-5050

HAPPY GARDEN RESTAURANT 530/893-2574

Chinese. Casual Dining. $6-$13 **AAA Inspector Notes:** This restaurant adheres to most people's idea of a Chinese restaurant—a red and gold color scheme and a mural of the Great Wall of China. Traditional dishes from the many regions of China include beef, lamb, chicken, pork and seafood. Lunch, family dinners and chef's specials are offered. **Bar:** beer & wine. **Address:** 180 Cohasset Rd 95926 **Location:** SR 99 exit Cohasset Rd, 1 mi w. [L][D] CALL [&M]

JOHNNIE'S RESTAURANT & LOUNGE 530/895-1515

California. Fine Dining. $8-$30 **AAA Inspector Notes:** Interesting, creative California cuisine preparations are featured at this upscale restaurant that offers an exhibition kitchen. Enter from the alley or through the Hotel Diamond. **Bar:** full bar. **Reservations:** suggested. **Address:** 220 W 4th St 95928 **Location:** SR 99 exit 385 (SR 32), 1.2 mi sw to Salem St, just nw to 4th St, then just ne; jct Broadway; downtown; in Hotel Diamond. **Parking:** street only. [L][D]

Keep seasonal vehicles travel-ready with a AAA/CAA Battery Tender®

NASH'S RESTAURANT 530/896-1147

Regional California. Casual Dining. $9-$24 **AAA Inspector Notes:** The college waitstaff at this established eatery serves up a variety of sandwiches, burgers, salads, daily pasta specials and a few entrée selections. Brunch is offered on Saturday and Sunday from 8 a.m. to 2 p.m. Dinner is served Monday through Saturday. The tin roof, cement floor, plants and miniature twinkle light add to the garden theme. A patio is open in season. **Bar:** full bar. **Reservations:** suggested. **Address:** 1717 Esplanade 95926 **Location:** SR 99 exit 1st Ave, 2 mi sw, then n; jct 7th Ave. [B][L][D]

THE RAWBAR RESTAURANT & SUSHI 530/897-0626

Asian. Casual Dining. $6-$16 **AAA Inspector Notes:** Across the street from the city plaza, this restaurant offers Asian fusion cuisine featuring contemporary and traditional sushi, a wide range of hot and cold appetizers, lunch rice bowls, dinner small plates and tempura. The beverage selection is extensive, too, with a variety of saki, signature saketini drinks and hot teas. Located in a former store, the décor is a contemporary industrial style. Lunch offered daily, except on Sundays. **Bar:** full bar. **Address:** 346 Broadway 95928 **Location:** SR 99 exit 385 (SR 32), w to Main St, n to 3rd St, then s; jct 4th St. [L][D] CALL [&M]

RED TAVERN 530/894-3463

Mediterranean. Casual Dining. $18-$29 **AAA Inspector Notes:** Located in a charming section of town with wide streets and majestic trees, this restaurant is housed in a cream-colored building. The warm colored walls add to the cozy feel of the upscale dining rooms. The attractively landscaped patio has heat lamps, a fire pit, fountain, sail shades and bocce ball. Always perfect for sharing, delectable small and large plates are offered. A monthly menu features California cuisine with Mediterranean influences. Choose from an extensive wine list. **Bar:** full bar. **Reservations:** suggested. **Address:** 1250 Esplanade 95926 **Location:** SR 99 exit 386 (E 1st Ave), 0.9 mi w, then just n; between 2nd and 3rd aves. **Parking:** on-site and street. [D] CALL [&M]

SICILIAN CAFE 530/345-2233

Southern Italian. Casual Dining. $15-$30 **AAA Inspector Notes:** Since 1984, this creekside restaurant has offered Southern Italian cuisine along with an excellent wine list. Recommended is the house specialty, calamari originale, which can be ordered for two to four people. A covered, heated patio is in the back. Lunch is served Tuesday to Friday. **Bar:** beer & wine. **Reservations:** suggested. **Address:** 1020 Main St 95928 **Location:** 2 mi w on SR 32 from jct SR 99, just s; jct Park Ave; downtown. **Parking:** street only. [D] CALL [&M]

SIERRA NEVADA TAP ROOM & RESTAURANT 530/345-2739

American. Casual Dining. $9-$31 **AAA Inspector Notes:** The requisite pub fare shares menu space with wood-fired pizza, burgers (including the house specialty lentil burger), seafood and choice aged beef from the restaurant's own locally raised and hormone- and antibiotic-free herd, which is fed a natural diet with brewer's yeast with beer. Copper brewery kettles, in which fresh, exceptional beers are brewed, can be seen from parts of the dining room or on the brewery tour. The large outdoor patio affords some seating. **Bar:** beer & wine. **Address:** 1075 E 20th St 95928 **Location:** SR 99 exit 384 (E 20th St), 0.5 mi w. [icon][L][D]

TIN ROOF BAKERY & CAFE 530/892-2893

Breads/Pastries. Quick Serve. $5-$10 **AAA Inspector Notes:** An array of artisan breads, scrumptious baked goods and a limited variety of creative sandwiches are served at this popular cafe. Patio seating out front is offered in season. **Address:** 627 Broadway St, Suite 170 95928 **Location:** SR 99 exit 385 (SR 32), 1.1 mi sw to Main St, just nw to 6th St, just w, then just s; jct 7th St. [B][L] CALL [&M]

TRES HOMBRES LONG BAR & GRILL 530/342-0425

Mexican. Casual Dining. $8-$18 **AAA Inspector Notes:** This restaurant features a casual atmosphere, specialty and traditional dishes, quesadillas, burritos and a taco bar with several selections along with lunch specials. More than 160 tequilas are offered along with hand-shaken margaritas. An attractive patio is located in the front of the restaurant. **Bar:** full bar. **Address:** 100 Broadway St 95928 **Location:** SR 99 exit 385 (SR 32), 1.1 mi w, 0.5 mi n on Main St, just w on 1st St; jct w 1st St; downtown. **Parking:** street only. [L][D]

CHOWCHILLA   pop. 18,720, elev. 239'

FOSSIL DISCOVERY CENTER OF MADERA COUNTY is at 19450 Ave. 21 ½. In the early 1990s a landfill worker discovered a mammoth tusk buried in the site's brown clay. Further excavation revealed more than 15,000 bones and fossils from prehistoric animals that lived in California's Central Valley during the last ice age, their bones buried for more than half a million years under sand, silt and clay.

Among the fossils on display are a saber-tooth cat, Columbian mammoth, dire wolf and a giant ground sloth. Children can learn how bones are excavated at a mock digging area. Also on the grounds is a pond landscaped with plants native to the San Joaquin Valley.

Note: The center is located in the midst of fruit and nut orchards; bees are brought in during the spring months to pollinate the trees, so visitors who have an allergic reaction to bee stings should use caution. **Tours:** Guided tours are available. **Time:** Allow 1 hour minimum. **Hours:** Tues.-Sun. 9-4. Closed major holidays. **Cost:** $8; $6 (ages 55+ and military with ID); $4 (ages 4-18). Mock dig program $4. Reservations are recommended. **Phone:** (559) 665-7107.

DAYS INN GATEWAY TO YOSEMITE   (559)665-4821

▼▼ Motel $60-$100 **Address:** 220 E Robertson Blvd 93610 **Location:** SR 99 exit Robertson Blvd, just w. **Facility:** 30 units. 2 stories (no elevator), exterior corridors. **Terms:** cancellation fee imposed. **Amenities:** high-speed Internet. **Pool(s):** outdoor. **Guest Services:** coin laundry.

HOLIDAY INN EXPRESS & SUITES GATEWAY TO YOSEMITE
                (559)665-3300

▼▼▼ Hotel $79-$169 **Address:** 309 Prosperity Blvd 93610 **Location:** SR 99 exit Robertson Blvd, just w. **Facility:** 63 units. 3 stories, interior corridors. **Terms:** cancellation fee imposed. **Amenities:** high-speed Internet. **Pool(s):** outdoor. **Activities:** whirlpool, exercise room. **Guest Services:** valet and coin laundry.

CITRUS HEIGHTS   pop. 83,301
• Hotels & Restaurants map & index p. 314

FRESH CHOICE   916/863-5680

▼ American. Cafeteria. $8-$10 **AAA Inspector Notes:** The salad bar of salad bars, the casual restaurant invites patrons to make their own or try one of the already prepared varieties. Other items include freshly baked breads, pizza and soup, as well as make-your-own sundaes for dessert. **Bar:** beer & wine. **Address:** 5419 Sunrise Blvd 95610 **Location:** I-80 exit 96 (Madison Ave), 4.8 mi w; jct Madison Ave; in Sunrise Village Shopping Center.

THE HABIT BURGER GRILL   916/536-9175 71

▼ Burgers. Quick Serve. $4-$7 **AAA Inspector Notes:** Since 1969, this California chain has been serving quality burgers, char-grilled sandwiches and made-to-order salads. A heated patio is available in winter. **Address:** 5437 Sunrise Blvd 95610 **Location:** I-80 exit 96 (Madison Ave), 4.8 mi w; in Sunrise Village Shopping Center.

CLEARLAKE   pop. 15,250
• Part of Wine Country area — see map p. 562

BEST WESTERN PLUS EL GRANDE INN   (707)994-2000

Hotel $100-$200

AAA Benefit: Members save up to 20%, plus 10% bonus points with Best Western Rewards®.

Address: 15135 Lakeshore Dr 95422 **Location:** SR 53 exit Lakeshore Dr, just w. **Facility:** 68 units. 4 stories, interior corridors. **Amenities:** Some: high-speed Internet. **Pool(s):** heated indoor. **Activities:** whirlpool. **Free Special Amenities:** local telephone calls and high-speed Internet.

CLEAR LAKE COTTAGES AND MARINA   707/995-5253

▼▼ Cottage $119-$209 **Address:** 13885 Lakeshore Dr 95422 **Location:** Waterfront. SR 53 exit Lakeshore Dr, 2.1 mi w. **Facility:** 18 cottages, some kitchens. 1 story, exterior corridors. **Terms:** 2 night minimum stay - seasonal and/or weekends, 14 day cancellation notice-fee imposed. **Pool(s):** outdoor. **Activities:** boat dock. **Guest Services:** coin laundry.

TRAVELODGE CLEARLAKE   (707)994-1499

▼▼ Motel $80-$150 **Address:** 4775 Old Hwy 53 95422 **Location:** SR 53 exit Lakeshore Dr, just w, then just s. **Facility:** 31 units. 2 stories (no elevator), exterior corridors. **Pool(s):** outdoor. **Activities:** whirlpool. **Guest Services:** coin laundry.

CLEARLAKE OAKS   pop. 2,359
• Part of Wine Country area — see map p. 562

LAKE POINT LODGE   (707)998-4350

Motel $79-$199

Address: 13470 E Hwy 20 95423 **Location:** SR 53, 3 mi nw. **Facility:** 40 units. 2 stories (no elevator), exterior corridors. **Terms:** 4 day cancellation notice. **Pool(s):** outdoor. **Activities:** whirlpool. **Guest Services:** coin laundry. **Free Special Amenities:** continental breakfast and high-speed Internet.

CLEMENTS

GRAND OAKS INN   (209)759-3453

▼▼ Bed & Breakfast $115-$175 **Address:** 21941 Buena Vista Rd 95227 **Location:** 1.6 mi e of jct SR 12 and 88; SR 88 exit Buena Vista Rd, 1 mi s. **Facility:** 5 units, some two bedrooms. 2 stories (no elevator), interior corridors. **Terms:** check-in 3:30 pm, 7 day cancellation notice-fee imposed. **Pool(s):** outdoor. **Activities:** whirlpool.

CLIO   pop. 66
• Restaurants p. 80

THE LODGE AT WHITEHAWK RANCH   530/836-4985

fyi Not evaluated. **Address:** 985 Whitehawk Dr 96106 **Location:** 3 mi s of center to Whitehawk Dr, 1.2 mi w. Facilities, services, and décor characterize a mid-scale property.

Plan complete trip routings with
the TripTik® Travel Planner on
AAA.com/CAA.ca

WHERE TO EAT

THE LODGE RESTAURANT AT WHITEHAWK RANCH
530/836-4985

 Seafood Steak. Casual Dining. $18-$29 **AAA Inspector Notes:** This lodge-style restaurant features a floor-to-ceiling rock fireplace and wraparound deck that overlooks the area's premier golf course. Seasonal menu items feature daily fresh fish, hand-cut steaks, peppercorn crusted filet mignon, chicken piccata or pan-seared rack of lamb served with blackberry-white truffle demi-glace. Slow-cooked prime rib infused with rosemary and garlic is served on Sunday. **Bar:** full bar. **Reservations:** suggested. **Address:** 985 Whitehawk Dr 96106 **Location:** 3 mi s of center to Whitehawk Dr, 1.2 mi w. [D] [K]

CLOVERDALE (E-2) pop. 8,618, elev. 335'
- Attractions map p. 567
- Part of Wine Country area — see map p. 562

CLOVERDALE HISTORY CENTER AND HISTORIC GOULD-SHAW HOUSE are at 215 N. Cloverdale Blvd. The 1864 Gothic Revival Gould-Shaw House features Victorian and Craftsman furnishings, period clothing and linens, other items from the late 19th and early 20th centuries, and a Victorian cottage garden. The History Center contains permanent and rotating exhibits, including a "mud wagon" that once carried passengers from Cloverdale to the Geysers Resort.

A research center has photographs, newspaper articles and other historical data about Cloverdale and the surrounding area. **Time:** Allow 1 hour minimum. **Hours:** Thurs. and Sat. 10-4, Fri. 10-2, Sun. noon-4 and by appointment. **Cost:** Donations. **Phone:** (707) 894-2067.

AUBERGE ON THE VINEYARD
(707)894-5956

 Historic Bed & Breakfast $135-$325 **Address:** 29955 River Rd 95425 **Location:** US 101 exit Citrus Fair Dr, just e, 0.5 mi n on Asti Rd, then 0.8 mi e on Crocker Rd. **Facility:** The original 1885 Queen Anne-style Victorian invites guests to sit out on the wraparound porch and savor the picturesque views of the vineyards. 7 units. 2 stories (no elevator), interior corridors. **Terms:** check-in 3:30 pm, 2-3 night minimum stay - seasonal and/or weekends, 7 day cancellation notice-fee imposed.

BEST WESTERN CLOVERDALE INN   (707)894-7500

Hotel
$89-$145

 AAA Benefit: Members save up to 20%, plus 10% bonus points with Best Western Rewards®.

Address: 324 S Cloverdale Blvd 95425 **Location:** US 101 exit Citrus Fair Dr, just w, then just s. **Facility:** 62 units. 2 stories (no elevator), exterior corridors. **Amenities:** high-speed Internet. **Pool(s):** outdoor. **Activities:** whirlpool, steamroom, exercise room. **Guest Services:** coin laundry. **Free Special Amenities:** local telephone calls and high-speed Internet.

OLD CROCKER INN   (707)894-4000

Historic Bed
& Breakfast
$165-$275

Address: 1126 Old Crocker Inn Rd 95425 **Location:** US 101 exit Citrus Fair Dr, just e, 0.5 mi n on Asti Rd, 0.8 mi e on Crocker Rd, 3.8 mi s on River Rd, 1.1 mi e on Asti Ridge Rd, then just n. **Facility:** The property is an attractively restored, historic structure set on five acres in the foothills; all guest rooms include a fireplace. 10 units. 1 story, exterior corridors. **Terms:** check-in 4 pm, 2 night minimum stay - seasonal and/or weekends, 8 day cancellation notice-fee imposed. **Pool(s):** outdoor. **Free Special Amenities:** full breakfast and high-speed Internet.

SUPER 8 CLOVERDALE   (707)894-9288

Hotel
$70-$160

Address: 1147 S Cloverdale Blvd 95425 **Location:** US 101 exit S Cloverdale Blvd, just w at top of off ramp, just n on S Cloverdale Blvd, then just w on Treadway Dr; in shopping center. **Facility:** 43 units. 2 stories (no elevator), interior corridors. **Terms:** cancellation fee imposed. **Amenities:** high-speed Internet. **Pool(s):** heated outdoor. **Activities:** whirlpool, exercise room. **Guest Services:** coin laundry. **Free Special Amenities:** continental breakfast and high-speed Internet.

WHERE TO EAT

LA HACIENDA RESTAURANT   707/894-9365

 Mexican. Casual Dining. $8-$16 **AAA Inspector Notes:** The authentic hacienda decor and festive atmosphere of this restaurant transports diners to south of the border. Some entrée choices include camarones diabla (shrimp in spicy sauce) or chile verde (pork in green chile sauce). Be sure to try the parrillada which comes with prawns, chicken and beef. **Bar:** full bar. **Address:** 134 N Cloverdale Blvd 95425 **Location:** US 101 exit Citrus Fair Dr, 0.3 mi w to N Cloverdale Blvd, then 0.5 mi n. [L] [D]

RUTH MCGOWAN'S BREWPUB   707/894-9610

 American. Casual Dining. $10-$13 **AAA Inspector Notes:** At this casual eatery, locals gather for beers made in house and basic tavern food such as burgers and fish and chips. **Bar:** beer & wine. **Address:** 131 E 1st St 95425 **Location:** At 1st and Main sts; downtown. **Parking:** street only. [D] [K]

CLOVIS (G-4) pop. 95,631, elev. 361'
- Hotels & Restaurants map & index p. 126

The town of Clovis was named after Clovis Cole, the area's largest grain grower, who donated land for a rail station in the late 19th century. The city was incorporated in 1912. Lumbering was the initial economic mainstay, though fruit farming also became important. Many buildings date to the early 1900s, and today the Old Town section of Clovis is a reflection of the city as it was at the turn of the 20th century.

Clovis Tourist Information & Visitors Center: 399 Clovis Ave., Clovis, CA 93612. **Phone:** (559) 324-2084 or (877) 725-6847.

Self-guiding tours: Brochures featuring information about Clovis' antique district and describing walking tours of the historic district are available at the visitors center.

CLOVIS BIG DRY CREEK MUSEUM is at jct. 4th St. and Pollasky Ave. in the Old Town area. The museum displays photographs, documents and memorabilia pertaining to Clovis history. **Time:** Allow 1 hour minimum. **Hours:** Tues.-Sat. 10-2 (also Fri. 6-9 p.m. from mid-May through Sept. 30 when the Farmers Market is operating), and by appointment. Closed major holidays. **Cost:** Donations. **Phone:** (559) 297-8033.

WILD WATER ADVENTURE PARK, 11413 E. Shaw Ave., is a 52-acre water park offering more than 20 water rides and amusements, including waterslides; inner tube rides; a large wave pool; a large swimming pool; three fishing lakes; and the Adventure Bay and Buccaneer Landing children's play areas.

(See map & index p. 126.)

Glass items and alcohol are not permitted. **Hours:** Open Memorial Day weekend-Labor Day. Hours vary throughout the season; phone ahead for hours of operation on specific days. **Cost:** $27.99; $19.99 (age 3 to 48 inches tall); $13.99 (ages 62+). Discounted rates are available after 4 p.m. Single tube rental $5; double tube $7. Life jackets free. A refundable deposit is required for tube and life jacket rentals. **Phone:** (559) 299-9453 or (800) 564-9453.

BEST WESTERN CLOVIS COLE   (559)299-1547 **36**

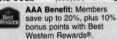

AAA Benefit: Members save up to 20%, plus 10% bonus points with Best Western Rewards®.

Hotel
$95-$165

Address: 415 Clovis Ave 93612 **Location:** SR 168 at 4th St; center. **Facility:** 58 units. 3 stories, interior corridors. **Terms:** 3 day cancellation notice. **Amenities:** high-speed Internet. **Pool(s):** outdoor. **Activities:** sauna, whirlpool, exercise room. **Guest Services:** coin laundry. **Free Special Amenities:** expanded continental breakfast and high-speed Internet.

COMFORT SUITES   (559)299-9992 **35**

Hotel $89-$119 **Address:** 143 Clovis Ave 93612 **Location:** SR 168 exit Herndon Ave E, just s. **Facility:** 54 units. 4 stories, interior corridors. **Terms:** cancellation fee imposed. **Amenities:** high-speed Internet. **Pool(s):** heated outdoor. **Activities:** exercise room. **Guest Services:** valet and coin laundry.

FAIRFIELD INN & SUITES FRESNO CLOVIS
(559)323-8080 **34**

Hotel
$99-$179

AAA Benefit: AAA hotel discounts of 5% or more.

Address: 50 N Clovis Ave 93612 **Location:** SR 168 exit Herndon Ave E, just s. **Facility:** 85 units. 3 stories, interior corridors. **Amenities:** high-speed Internet. **Pool(s):** heated outdoor. **Activities:** whirlpool, exercise room. **Guest Services:** valet and coin laundry. **Free Special Amenities:** expanded continental breakfast and high-speed Internet.

HOLIDAY INN EXPRESS HOTEL & SUITES
(559)297-0555 **37**

Hotel $89-$129 **Address:** 650 W Shaw Ave 93612 **Location:** SR 168 exit Shaw Ave, just e. **Facility:** 91 units. 3 stories, interior corridors. **Amenities:** high-speed Internet. **Pool(s):** outdoor. **Activities:** whirlpool, exercise room. **Guest Services:** valet and coin laundry.

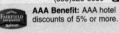

ANDIAMO RISTORANTE ITALIANO   559/298-3196 **18**

Italian. Casual Dining. $7-$20 **AAA Inspector Notes:** A tradition in the valley for many years, this casual restaurant offers a great selection of pizza, sandwiches and pasta. Service is warm and welcoming. **Bar:** full bar. **Address:** 1257 Shaw Ave, Suite 120 93612 **Location:** SR 168 exit Shaw Ave, 2 mi e; in Sierra Pavilions Shopping Center.

Contact us about AAA/CAA Approved properties at AAA.com/TourBookComments

---

COALINGA (H-4) pop. 13,380, elev. 671'

Coalinga began as a loading point for the Southern Pacific Railroad Co., which transported coal from area mines. Eventually "Coaling Station A" grew into a permanent oil-boomer settlement and its name was abbreviated.

Coalinga Area Chamber of Commerce: 380 Coalinga Plaza, Coalinga, CA 93210. **Phone:** (559) 935-2948.

R.C. BAKER MEMORIAL MUSEUM, 297 W. Elm St., preserves area history with displays of fossils, American Indian artifacts, Western ranch hand equipment, early 20th-century household items, a 1924 American La France fire engine, a restored 1930s Richfield service station and a large collection of oil field equipment.

Time: Allow 1 hour minimum. **Hours:** Mon.-Fri. 10-noon and 1-5, Sat. 11-5, Sun. 1-5. Closed major holidays. Phone ahead to confirm schedule. **Cost:** Donations. **Phone:** (559) 935-1914 or (877) 416-5849.

BEST WESTERN BIG COUNTRY INN   559/935-0866

AAA Benefit: Members save up to 20%, plus 10% bonus points with Best Western Rewards®.

Motel
Rates not provided

Address: 25020 W Dorris Ave 93210 **Location:** I-5 exit SR 198/Hanford-Lemoore, just w. **Facility:** 48 units. 1 story, exterior corridors. **Amenities:** safes (fee). **Pool(s):** outdoor. **Guest Services:** coin laundry. **Free Special Amenities:** local telephone calls and high-speed Internet.

THE INN AT HARRIS RANCH   (559)935-0717

Hotel
$159-$350

Address: 24505 W Dorris Ave 93210 **Location:** I-5 exit SR 198/Hanford-Lemoore, just e. **Facility:** 153 units. 2-3 stories, interior/exterior corridors. **Terms:** check-in 4 pm, cancellation fee imposed. **Dining:** Harris Ranch Steak House, Ranch Kitchen, see separate listings. **Pool(s):** heated outdoor. **Activities:** whirlpools, exercise room. **Guest Services:** coin laundry. **Free Special Amenities:** local telephone calls and high-speed Internet.

WHERE TO EAT

HARRIS RANCH STEAK HOUSE   559/935-0717

Steak. Fine Dining. $18-$50 **AAA Inspector Notes:** This dining room evokes an early California elegance and specializes in Harris-raised beef and Harris-grown produce. **Bar:** full bar. **Reservations:** suggested. **Address:** 24505 W Dorris Ave 93210 **Location:** I-5 exit SR 198/Hanford-Lemoore, just e; in The Inn at Harris Ranch.

RANCH KITCHEN   559/935-0717

American. Casual Dining. $10-$32 **AAA Inspector Notes:** Locally-grown produce and Harris Ranch beef have made this family-owned and -operated restaurant a favorite stop of travelers in the central valley. The menu offers everything from salads and burgers to sandwiches and prime rib. **Bar:** full bar. **Address:** 24505 W Dorris Ave 93210 **Location:** I-5 exit SR 198/Hanford-Lemoore, just e; in The Inn at Harris Ranch.

COARSEGOLD   pop. 1,840

• Part of Yosemite National Park area — see map
p. 578

CHUKCHANSI GOLD RESORT & CASINO
(559)692-5200

Hotel
$99-$239

Address: 711 Lucky Ln 93614 **Location:** 5 mi s on SR 41, just e. **Facility:** Located on a hillside overlooking the beautiful foothills, this hotel boasts a relaxing spa and several restaurants. 404 units. 11 stories, interior corridors. **Parking:** on-site and valet. **Terms:** cancellation fee imposed. **Amenities:** video games (fee), high-speed Internet, safes. **Dining:** 6 restaurants, also, Goldfield's Cafe, see separate listing. **Pool(s):** heated outdoor, heated indoor. **Activities:** whirlpools, exercise room, spa. **Guest Services:** valet laundry. **Free Special Amenities:** local telephone calls and high-speed Internet.

SAVE 🎲 🍴 CALL 🖥 🛍 BIZ 🛜 🐾 🔌 💻 / SOME UNITS 📷

WHERE TO EAT

GOLDFIELD'S CAFE   559/692-5200

American. Casual Dining. $8-$25 **AAA Inspector Notes:** A casual and friendly atmosphere can be found at this cafe. The extensive menu offers everything from hearty breakfasts, sandwiches and burgers to pasta, barbecue ribs, chicken-fried steak and seafood. Diners should bring an appetite because the portions are hearty. **Bar:** beer & wine. **Address:** 711 Lucky Ln 93614 **Location:** 5 mi s on SR 41, just e; in Chukchansi Gold Resort & Casino.

B L D 24 CALL 🖥

COLMA   (D-8) pop. 1,792, elev. 190'

• Hotels & Restaurants map & index p. 410
• Part of San Francisco area — see map p. 342

Not many towns can claim that they were founded to serve as a necropolis, a city of the dead—but such is the case with Colma. When San Francisco leaders determined in the late 19th century that land was too valuable to be used for burials, hundreds of thousands of graves were moved to nearby Colma, which came to be known as the "city of souls." Twelve cemeteries, representing various religions and ethnicities, had been established by 1912. That number has since risen to 17, and graveyards now account for approximately three-quarters of the town's total acreage.

Among the notable individuals interred in Colma cemeteries are baseball great Joe DiMaggio, whose grave is in Holy Cross Catholic Cemetery; gunfighter Wyatt Earp, buried with third wife Josephine in Hills of Eternity Memorial Park; and late 19th-century eccentric Emperor Norton (Joshua A. Norton), self-proclaimed "Emperor of the United States and Protector of Mexico," laid to rest in Woodlawn Cemetery.

Daly City-Colma Chamber of Commerce: 355 Gellert Blvd., Suite 138, Daly City, CA 94015. **Phone:** (650) 755-3900.

CYPRESS LAWN MEMORIAL PARK is at 1370 El Camino Real (SR 82). Established in 1892 following San Francisco's edict barring cemeteries within its boundaries, Cypress Lawn is the final resting place of many San Francisco notables, including journalist William Randolph Hearst; Andrew Hallidie, the inventor of the mechanism for operating San Francisco's iconic cable cars; and horticulturist John McLaren, who nurtured the development of Golden Gate Park.

Known as a "garden cemetery," the park-like setting contains many historic and architecturally significant mausoleums, tombstones and sculptures on its landscaped grounds; in fact, the cemetery has been described as an outdoor art gallery. The original community mausoleums feature some of the West's finest stained-glass windows and ceilings. **Time:** Allow 30 minutes minimum. **Hours:** Mon.-Sat. 8-5, Sun. 8:30-5. Guided walking tours are given the third Sat. of the month at 1:30, Apr.-Oct. **Cost:** Free. **Phone:** (650) 755-0580.

🚉 South San Francisco, 42

ESTRADA'S MEXICAN RESTAURANT   650/755-1282 ⑩
Mexican. Casual Dining. $6-$17 **AAA Inspector Notes:** This restaurant has been serving the neighborhood since 1917, offering consistent service and food. On Fridays and Saturdays, the eatery converts to a dance club after 10 pm. **Bar:** full bar. **Address:** 7440 Mission St 94014 **Location:** Between San Pedro Rd and A St. 🚉 Colma, 41. D 🎟 🚉

COLOMA   (E-3) pop. 529, elev. 750'

In January 1848, near Capt. John Sutter's sawmill on the American River, James Marshall discovered the first yellow flecks of metal that launched the great California gold rush. By the summer more than 2,000 miners were sifting for gold along the river near Sutter's mill, and Coloma, the first of the gold rush towns, was born. Finds grew scarce within a few years, and the once thriving city of 10,000 dwindled to the quiet village it is today.

INSIDER INFO:
The Mother Lode

Mexican miners called it "La Veta Madre"—the Mother Lode—a rich vein of gold lacing the western slopes of the Sierra Nevada for 120 miles. The name eventually came to denote the entire band of territory extending roughly from Mariposa to Sierra City, where the gleaming metal was mined during the frenetic years of the California gold rush.

The discovery of gold near Coloma in 1848 lured thousands of prospectors to the Mother Lode. Tales of nuggets littering the hillsides were not entirely unfounded during the early years of the gold rush, and the possibility of unearthing a mammoth find, like the 195-pound nugget found near Carson Hill, stoked the get-rich-quick dreams of many a '49er.

Nearly 550 mining towns proliferated in the Mother Lode; fewer than half remain today. Like the fortunes of many of the miners, the towns rose and fell precipitously and often were simply abandoned when the miners moved on to more profitable stakes. A few, such as Sonora, Placerville, Auburn and Grass Valley, weathered the diminishing reserves to become prosperous small cities. Others survive as little more than intriguing names on a map.

Aptly numbered SR 49 traverses the length of the Mother Lode country. The facades of the surviving buildings, the historical parks along the route and the ghost towns and empty mines scattered throughout the hills still retain a sense of the atmosphere from this colorful period.

MARSHALL GOLD DISCOVERY STATE HISTORIC PARK is on SR 49. The 274-acre park preserves the site where James W. Marshall's discovery of gold began the California gold rush. In partnership with John Sutter to construct a sawmill, Marshall chose a site adjacent to the American River and a stand of pine trees. It was there, on Jan. 24, 1848, that Marshall noticed the glint of gold in the tailrace of the sawmill.

A statue of Marshall, marking his gravesite, points toward the site of his discovery, a half-mile away. The gold rush era and its historical impact are depicted through museum exhibits, mining memorabilia and interpretive programs. Staff provide daily history talks at a replica of Sutter's mill, which stands near the river not far from the site of the original structure. Also part of the park is the 1860 cabin in which Marshall lived. *See Recreation Areas Chart.*

Panning for gold is allowed in designated areas, using hands and pans only, and fishing is permitted in season. **Time:** Allow 1 hour minimum. **Hours:** Park open daily 8-7, Memorial Day-Labor Day; 8-5, rest of year. Museum open daily 10-4, Mar.-Nov.; 10-3, rest of year. Closed Jan. 1, Thanksgiving and Christmas. **Cost:** Day use $8 per private vehicle; $7 (ages 62+ per private vehicle). Museum included in day use fee. Gold panning $7. **Phone:** (530) 622-3470. �🍴 🗙 🏠 🎋

RECREATIONAL ACTIVITIES
White-water Rafting

- **All-Outdoors California Whitewater Rafting** departs from several locations near Coloma. **Hours:** Daily Apr.-Oct. **Phone:** (925) 932-8993 or (800) 247-2387.
- **Beyond Limits Adventures** departs from River Park Resort, off SR 49 at the end of River Park Dr. **Hours:** Daily Apr.-Sept. (depending upon water flow). **Phone:** (209) 526-0027 or (800) 234-7238.
- **Whitewater Connection** departs from Point Pleasant Beach campground, .2 mi. n. of Sutter's Mill on SR 49, for excursions on the south fork of the American River. Guided trips on other rivers also are offered. **Hours:** Trips depart daily Apr.-Sept. (depending upon water flow). **Phone:** (530) 622-6446 or (800) 336-7238.
- **Whitewater Voyages** meets at varying departure points. **Hours:** Daily Apr.-Sept. (depending upon water flow). Reservations office open all year. **Phone:** (510) 222-5994 or (800) 400-7238.

COLUMBIA (F-4) pop. 2,297, elev. 2,143'
• Hotels p. 84

In the foothills of the Sierra Nevada, Columbia was one of the largest and most important mining towns along the Mother Lode. Local placer mines yielded $87 million in gold 1850-70.

Columbia Chamber of Commerce: P.O. Box 1824, Columbia, CA 95310. **Phone:** (209) 536-1672.

COLUMBIA STATE HISTORIC PARK, covering 12 square blocks in the old business district, depicts a typical boomtown of the 1850s. Never completely deserted, the settlement has been partially restored to its appearance in gold rush days. Among the more than 30 restored buildings in the town are a schoolhouse, bank, newspaper building, barbershop, saloons, the Wells Fargo Express Co. building, shops, the Fallon Hotel and the City Hotel, which still houses guests.

A 22-minute DVD presentation weaves information about the original town settlement with how important a permanent source of water was to gold rush towns. The Columbia Diggins 1852, a 4-day living-history event, is held in late May, and plays are presented year-round in the restored Fallon House Theater. Townsite tours, stagecoach rides and gold panning also are available.

Hours: Park, museum and most stores open daily 10-4, Apr. 1 to mid-Oct.; phone to confirm hours rest of year. DVD presentation daily on the half-hour and hour. Townsite tours daily at 11, mid-June through Labor Day; Sat.-Sun. at 11, rest of year. Plays are presented Wed. at 2, Thurs.-Fri. at 7 p.m., Sat. at 8 p.m. (also some Sat. and Sun. at 2 if the production is a musical), except during breaks between one closing and another opening. Stagecoach rides Mon.-Thurs. 10-4, Fri.-Sun. 10-5, Memorial Day-Labor Day; Fri.-Sun. 11-4, Mar. 1-day before Memorial Day and day after Labor Day-Oct. 31; Sat.-Sun. 11-4, rest of year (weather permitting). Phone ahead to confirm stagecoach schedule.

Cost: Park free. Plays $18-$32. Stagecoach fare (inside) $6; $5 (ages 4-12 and 60+). Fare $3 additional to ride on top (minimum age 8). Gold panning $5-$12. **Phone:** (209) 588-9128 for park information, (209) 532-9693 for gold panning information, (209) 532-3120 for play information, (209) 532-3184 for the museum, or (209) 588-0808 for the stagecoach. 🍴

COURTNEY AVIATION, departing from Columbia Airport at 10759 Airport Rd., offers scenic tours. Passengers can choose from various trips that fly over such scenic areas as the Yosemite Valley, Mt. Lyell Glacier, Mammoth Lakes, John Muir Wilderness, Kings Canyon and Sequoia national parks, Mount Whitney and Mono Lake. **Hours:** Flights depart by appointment. **Cost:** Fares range $129-$760 per person based on two or more people. Reservations are required. **Phone:** (209) 532-2345.

COLUMBIA GEM MOTEL
209/532-4508

Motel $99-$159 Address: 22131 Parrotts Ferry Rd 95370 Location: 3 mi n of Sonora; 1 mi from Columbia State Historic Park. Facility: 11 units. 1 story, exterior corridors. Terms: cancellation fee imposed.

HARLAN HOUSE
209/533-4862

Bed & Breakfast $95-$145 Address: 22890 School House St 95310 Location: SR 49 exit Parrotts Ferry Rd, n to Pacific St, then 0.5 mi e. Facility: 5 units. 2 stories (no elevator), interior/exterior corridors. Terms: age restrictions may apply, 5 day cancellation notice-fee imposed.

COLUSA (D-2) pop. 5,971, elev. 61'

More than 4,500 acres of seasonal marsh, permanent ponds, watergrass and uplands west of Colusa shelter large flocks of ducks and geese during fall and winter; the best viewing is during November and mid-January. The Colusa National Wildlife Refuge's 3-mile self-guiding auto tour route and 1-mile walking trail lead through part of the area; phone (530) 934-2801.

CONCORD (C-9) pop. 122,067, elev. 80'
• Restaurants p. 86

Guided tours take visitors onto an active military base to see the Port Chicago Naval Magazine National Memorial, erected to honor the 320 military personnel and civilians (more than 200 of whom were African-Americans) killed on July 17, 1944, in the largest homeland disaster during World War II. The incident, which occurred when a full munitions ship exploded during loading operations, was one of the catalysts that spurred the U.S. military to look into racial justice and equality after World War II. Reservations are required 2 weeks in advance; phone (925) 228-8860 for information.

WATERWORLD CALIFORNIA is .3 mi. e. off I-680 Willow Pass Rd. exit, then n. on Waterworld Pkwy. The water park offers body slides, a lazy river, a wave pool, raft rides, thrill attractions and children's play areas in a lush tropical setting.

Hours: Daily 10:30-6, mid-June to mid Aug.; hours vary Sat.-Sun., mid-May to mid-June and mid-Aug. to late Sept. Cost: $33.99; $24.99 (under 48 inches tall and ages 60+); free (ages 0-2). Parking: $10. Phone: (925) 609-1364.

AMERICAS BEST VALUE INN
(925)682-1601

Motel $65-$100 Address: 3555 Clayton Rd 94519 Location: SR 242 exit Clayton Rd, 2 mi e. Concord, 3. Facility: 43 units. 2 stories (no elevator), interior/exterior corridors. Terms: cancellation fee imposed. Amenities: high-speed Internet. Pool(s): outdoor. Activities: whirlpool. Guest Services: coin laundry. Free Special Amenities: continental breakfast and high-speed Internet.

BEST WESTERN PLUS HERITAGE INN
(925)686-4466

Hotel $87-$90

AAA Benefit: Members save up to 20%, plus 10% bonus points with Best Western Rewards®.

Address: 4600 Clayton Rd 94521 Location: I-680 exit Treat Blvd/Geary Rd, 4.8 mi ne, then 0.4 mi e. Facility: 122 units, some efficiencies. 2 stories, exterior corridors. Terms: cancellation fee imposed. Amenities: Some: high-speed Internet. Pool(s): outdoor. Activities: whirlpool. Guest Services: valet and coin laundry. Free Special Amenities: local telephone calls and high-speed Internet.

CROWNE PLAZA HOTEL CONCORD/WALNUT CREEK
(925)825-7700

Hotel $119-$189

Address: 45 John Glenn Dr 94520 Location: I-680 exit Concord Ave, just e. Facility: 324 units. 3 stories, interior corridors. Dining: Vineyards Chop House-BAR, see separate listing. Pool(s): heated indoor. Activities: whirlpool, putting green, exercise room. Guest Services: valet laundry, area transportation-mall & BART. Free Special Amenities: high-speed Internet and local transportation.

(See ad p. 85.)

DAYS INN CONCORD
(925)674-9400

Hotel $59-$110

Address: 5370 Clayton Rd 94521 Location: 6.5 mi e of jct I-680 and SR 24; I-680 exit SR 242 to Clayton Rd, 5.5 mi e. Facility: 31 units. 2 stories (no elevator), exterior corridors. Activities: whirlpool. Free Special Amenities: continental breakfast and early check-in/late check-out.

HILTON CONCORD
925/827-2000

Hotel Rates not provided

AAA Benefit: Members save 5% or more!

Address: 1970 Diamond Blvd 94520 Location: I-680 exit Willow Pass Rd, just e. Facility: 331 units. 11 stories, interior corridors. Dining: Grissini, see separate listing. Pool(s): outdoor. Activities: whirlpool, exercise room. Guest Services: valet and coin laundry, area transportation-mall & BART. Free Special Amenities: local transportation and use of on-premises laundry facilities.

PREMIER INNS
925/674-0888

Hotel. Rates not provided. Address: 1581 Concord Ave 94520 Location: SR 242 exit Clayton Rd northbound; exit Concord Ave southbound, just e. Concord, 3. Facility: 136 units. 2 stories, exterior corridors. Pool(s): outdoor. Activities: whirlpool. Guest Services: coin laundry.

▼ *See AAA listing p. 84* ▼

WHERE TO EAT

BAMBINO'S CONCORD 925/687-6363
WWW Italian. Casual Dining. $7-$24 **AAA Inspector Notes:** This place will please the Italian lover in all of us. Diners can choose from a great selection of specialty salads, homemade minestrone soup, hearty meatball and Italian sausage sandwiches, pasta dishes and pizza with homemade sauce and dough. **Bar:** beer & wine. **Address:** 1895 Farm Bureau Rd, Suite G 94519 **Location:** SR 242 exit Market St, 1 mi e, just n, then 1.8 mi e on Willow Pass Rd. ⊞ Concord, 3.
L D CALL 🅂🄼 🚇

BUTTERCUP GRILL & BAR 925/521-9224
WWW American. Casual Dining. $7-$20 **AAA Inspector Notes:** Families are welcomed at the casual restaurant, where choices range from burgers and sandwiches to entrees and breakfast items. Peanut butter cup pie is a dessert favorite. **Bar:** full bar. **Address:** 4301 Clayton Rd 94521 **Location:** I-680 exit Treat Blvd/Geary Rd, 4.8 mi ne; in Safeway Shopping Center. B L D CALL 🅂🄼

CLAIM JUMPER 925/798-4300
WWW American. Casual Dining. $10-$36 **AAA Inspector Notes:** Great menu variety makes this place a good stop for parties with diverse tastes. Choices include specialty appetizers, salads, rotisserie chicken and barbecue items, not to mention good comfort foods, such as traditional pot pie. Hearty portions satisfy big appetites. The atmosphere is fun and lively. **Bar:** full bar. **Address:** 1981 Diamond Blvd 94520 **Location:** I-680 exit Willow Pass Rd E, just n; in Willows Shopping Center. L D CALL 🅂🄼

EL TORITO 925/798-7660
WWW Mexican. Casual Dining. $8-$20 **AAA Inspector Notes:** Homemade Mexican favorites span from classic preparations to specialties from the country's central regions. Spicy taqueria-style tacos and carnitas Michoacan (marinated pork) are tasty choices. **Bar:** full bar. **Address:** 1961 Diamond Blvd 94520 **Location:** I-680 exit Willow Pass Rd E, just n; in Willows Shopping Center.
L D CALL 🅂🄼

FRESH CHOICE 925/671-7222
W American. Cafeteria. $8-$15 **AAA Inspector Notes:** The salad bar of salad bars, the casual restaurant invites patrons to make their own or try one of the already prepared varieties. Other items include freshly baked breads, pizza and soup, as well as make-your-own sundaes for dessert. **Bar:** beer & wine. **Address:** 486 Sun Valley Mall Rd 94520 **Location:** I-680 exit Willow Pass Rd W, just n; in Sun Valley Mall. L D

GRISSINI 925/827-2000
WWW Italian. Casual Dining. $13-$30 **AAA Inspector Notes:** Guests can sample an original Italian favorite or one of the specialties prepared in the on-grill kitchen. The staff is warm and welcoming. **Bar:** full bar. **Address:** 1970 Diamond Blvd 94520 **Location:** I-680 exit Willow Pass Rd, just e; in Hilton Concord.
B L D CALL 🅂🄼

ROUND TABLE PIZZA
W Pizza. Casual Dining. $7-$30 **AAA Inspector Notes:** This casual, family-oriented pizza place features high-quality ingredients and dough rolled fresh daily. Distinctive specialty pizzas are piled high with toppings. **Bar:** beer & wine. L D 🚇

For additional information, visit AAA.com
LOCATIONS:
Address: 1743 Willow Pass Rd 94520 **Location:** I-680 exit Willow Pass Rd, just e. ⊞ Walnut Creek, 5. **Phone:** 925/689-8900
Address: 2960 Treat Blvd 94520 **Location:** Just w of Oak Grove Rd. **Phone:** 925/676-1818
Address: 3375 Port Chicago Hwy #57 94520 **Location:** At Olivera Rd. ⊞ North Concord/Martinez, 2. **Phone:** 925/825-1993
Address: 5100-2 Clayton Rd 94521 **Location:** Just w of Ygnacio Valley Rd. **Phone:** 925/676-6565

VINEYARDS CHOP HOUSE-BAR 925/825-7700
WWW Steak. Casual Dining. $12-$30 **AAA Inspector Notes:** This open, airy restaurant features California's own Harris Ranch USDA Prime grade, natural Black Angus beef seared in an 1,800-degree broiler. Pair the meal with an exclusive California wine or a classic cocktail. Happy hour and Sunday brunch are popular here. **Bar:** full bar. **Address:** 45 John Glenn Dr 94520 **Location:** I-680 exit Concord Ave, just e; in Crowne Plaza Hotel Concord/Walnut Creek. **(See ad p. 85.)** B L D CALL 🅂🄼

CORCORAN pop. 24,813

CORCORAN COUNTRY INN (559)992-5724

Motel
$65-$85
Address: 2111 Whitley Ave 93212 **Location:** SR 43 exit Whitley Ave, 1.5 mi w. **Facility:** 20 units. 2 stories, exterior corridors. **Terms:** cancellation fee imposed. **Amenities:** high-speed Internet.
Pool(s): outdoor. **Free Special Amenities:** full breakfast and high-speed Internet.
SAVE 🍴 🏊 BIZ 🛜 ✕ 🅱 📺

CORNING (C-2) pop. 7,663, elev. 279'
• **Restaurants p. 88**

America's "Olive City" is in the northernmost part of the Sacramento Valley. Spanish missionaries introduced olive trees to California in the late 18th century, and Corning's olive connection dates back more than a century. The first olives were planted in the Corning area in the 1890s, and by the start of the 20th century the district emerged as a major producer of olive oil. By the 1920s Corning had seven olive canneries, and the city still claims it packages more than half the nation's olive crop.

Corning Chamber of Commerce: 1110 Solano St., Corning, CA 96021. **Phone:** (530) 824-5550.

GAMBLING ESTABLISHMENTS
• **Rolling Hills Casino** is at 2655 Everett Freeman Way. **Hours:** Daily 24 hours. **Phone:** (530) 528-3500 or (888) 331-6400.

AMERICAN INN 530/824-5103

Motel
$38-$95
Address: 2104 Solano St 96021 **Location:** I-5 exit 631 (Central Corning), 0.3 mi e. **Facility:** 14 units. 1 story, exterior corridors. **Terms:** cancellation fee imposed. **Amenities:** high-speed Internet.
Guest Services: coin laundry. **Free Special Amenities:** continental breakfast and high-speed Internet.
SAVE 🍴 BIZ 🛜 🅱 📺 📺

BEST WESTERN PLUS CORNING INN (530)824-5200

Hotel
$89-$159

AAA Benefit: Members save up to 20%, plus 10% bonus points with Best Western Rewards®.

Address: 910 Hwy 99 W 96021 **Location:** I-5 exit 631 (Central Corning), just e. **Facility:** 58 units. 2 stories (no elevator), interior corridors. **Amenities:** high-speed Internet. **Pool(s):** heated indoor. **Activities:** whirlpool, exercise room. **Free Special Amenities:** full breakfast and high-speed Internet.
SAVE   /SOME UNITS FEE 🐕

DAYS INN
(530)824-2000

Hotel
$54-$135

Address: 3475 Hwy 99 W 96021 **Location:** I-5 exit 630 (South Ave), just e, then just s. **Facility:** 62 units. 2 stories (no elevator), interior corridors. **Amenities:** high-speed Internet. **Pool(s):** outdoor. **Guest Services:** coin laundry. **Free Special Amenities: continental breakfast and high-speed Internet.**

ECONOMY INN
(530)824-4322

Motel
$45-$85

Address: 945 S Hwy 99 W 96021 **Location:** I-5 exit 631 (Central Corning), just e, then just s. **Facility:** 18 units. 1 story, exterior corridors. *Bath:* shower only. **Pool(s):** outdoor. **Free Special Amenities: continental breakfast and high-speed Internet.**

HOLIDAY INN EXPRESS HOTEL & SUITES
(530)824-6400

Hotel $104-$119 **Address:** 3350 Sunrise Way 96021 **Location:** I-5 exit 630 (South Ave), just e, then just s. **Facility:** 78 units. 4 stories, interior corridors. **Terms:** cancellation fee imposed. **Amenities:** high-speed Internet. **Pool(s):** heated outdoor. **Activities:** whirlpool, exercise room. **Guest Services:** valet and coin laundry. *(See ad this page.)*

THE INN AT ROLLING HILLS
(530)824-8300

Hotel
$99-$159

Address: 2645 Everett Freeman Way 96021 **Location:** I-5 exit 628 (Liberal Ave/SR 99), just w, then just s. **Facility:** 51 units. 2 stories, interior corridors. **Amenities:** high-speed Internet. **Pool(s):** heated outdoor. **Activities:** whirlpool, exercise room. **Guest Services:** coin laundry.

THE LODGE, A VAGABOND INN EXECUTIVE
(530)824-3220

Hotel
$104-$169

Address: 2665 Everett Freeman Way 96021 **Location:** I-5 exit 628 (Liberal Ave/SR 99), just w, then just s. Adjacent to Rolling Hills Casino. **Facility:** 60 units. 3 stories, interior corridors. **Amenities:** high-speed Internet, safes. **Pool(s):** heated indoor. **Activities:** whirlpool, limited exercise equipment. *Fee:* game room. **Guest Services:** coin laundry. **Free Special Amenities: full breakfast and high-speed Internet.**

SUPER 8 CORNING
(530)824-2468

Motel
$66-$124

Address: 2165 Solano St 96021 **Location:** I-5 exit 631 (Central Corning), just e. **Facility:** 41 units. 2 stories (no elevator), exterior corridors. **Amenities:** high-speed Internet. **Pool(s):** outdoor. **Free Special Amenities: full breakfast and high-speed Internet.**

Share a New View on Travel at
AAATravelViews.com

Read stories, tips and trends from AAA insiders. Post comments and get your questions answered by our travel experts.

▼ *See AAA listing this page* ▼

CASA RAMOS   530/824-3123

▼▼▼ Mexican. Casual Dining. $8-$16 **AAA Inspector Notes:** A varied Mexican menu is featured in a colorful atmosphere. Mexican favorites include fajitas, enchiladas, burritos and specialty steak and seafood entrees. **Bar:** full bar. **Address:** 636 Edith Ave 96021 **Location:** I-5 exit 631 (Central Corning), just e, then just n; in Olive Tree Plaza. [L] [D] CALL &M

OLIVE PIT CAFE   530/824-4667

▼ American. Quick Serve. $4-$8 **AAA Inspector Notes:** Located in the Olive Pit store which sells everything olive, including an olive tasting bar, this eatery serves sandwiches and a variety of shakes. Open 7-7. **Address:** 2156 Solano St 96021 **Location:** I-5 exit 631 (Corning Rd), just e. [B] [L] [D] CALL &M

CORTE MADERA   pop. 9,253
• Part of San Francisco area — see map p. 342

BEST WESTERN PLUS CORTE MADERA INN
                                                    (415)924-1502

Hotel
$129-$209

AAA Benefit: Members save up to 20%, plus 10% bonus points with Best Western Rewards®.

Address: 56 Madera Blvd 94925 **Location:** US 101 exit Madera Blvd southbound, just w; exit Tamalpais Rd/Paradise Dr northbound, just w, then 0.3 mi n. **Facility:** 110 units. 2 stories (no elevator), exterior corridors. **Terms:** check-in 4 pm, 2-3 night minimum stay - seasonal and/or weekends, cancellation fee imposed. **Amenities:** video games (fee). *Some:* high-speed Internet. **Pool(s):** heated outdoor. **Activities:** whirlpools, putting green, shuffleboard, exercise room. *Fee:* massage. **Guest Services:** valet and coin laundry, area transportation-Larkspur Ferry Terminal & Marin Airporter. **Free Special Amenities:** local telephone calls and high-speed Internet.

SAVE ECO ▯▯ 📶 CALL &M 🐾 🛜 ✕ 📽 ☐
▭ /SOME UNITS 🖼

MARIN SUITES HOTEL   (415)924-3608

Hotel
$109-$280

Address: 45 Tamal Vista Blvd 94925 **Location:** US 101 exit Lucky Dr southbound, just w on Fifer Ave, 0.4 mi s; exit Tamalpais Rd/Paradise Dr northbound, 0.5 mi n on Madera Blvd (which becomes Tamal Vista Blvd). **Facility:** 100 units, some two bedrooms and kitchens. 3 stories, exterior corridors. **Terms:** check-in 4 pm, cancellation fee imposed. **Amenities:** video games (fee), high-speed Internet, safes. **Pool(s):** heated outdoor. **Activities:** sauna, whirlpool, exercise room. **Guest Services:** coin laundry. **Free Special Amenities:** expanded continental breakfast and high-speed Internet. *(See ad this page.)*

SAVE ▯▯ CALL &M 🐾 🛜 ✕ 📽 📽 ☐ 🖼
▭ /SOME UNITS FEE 🐕

BRICK & BOTTLE   415/924-3366

▼▼ California. Casual Dining. $11-$32 **AAA Inspector Notes:** Popular with locals of all ages, a happy, boisterous atmosphere permeates this restaurant. Such California-style comfort food as Margherita pizza to a more exotic duck confit pizza, pan-fried fish with gnocchi, bean soups and burgers are offered. Sweet endings include rum cake and the more sedate butterscotch pudding. **Bar:** full bar. **Address:** 55 Tamal Vista Blvd 94925 **Location:** US 101 southbound exit Lucky Dr; just w on Fifer Ave, 0.4 mi s; exit Tamalpais Rd/Paradise Dr northbound; 0.6 mi n on Madera Blvd (which becomes Tamal Vista Blvd); in Marketplace Shopping Center.
[L] [D] 🅰🅲

COULTERVILLE   (F-4) pop. 201, elev. 1,699'

NORTHERN MARIPOSA COUNTY HISTORY CENTER is at jct. SRs 49 and 132. California's gold rush days, its pioneer families and nearby mining operations are remembered in displays in two historic buildings, one more than 150 years old. The museum also features a model of the original Coulterville Hotel and a barn with a buckboard, a

▼ See AAA listing this page ▼

surrey and a hearse. **Time:** Allow 1 hour minimum. **Hours:** Wed.-Sun. 10-4. A John Muir tour is offered the first Sat. of the month in summer; phone for information. Closed Thanksgiving and Christmas. **Cost:** Donations. **Phone:** (209) 878-3015.

CRESCENT CITY (A-1) pop. 7,643, elev. 44'
• Restaurants p. 91

Founded in 1853 as a gold mining supply center, Crescent City edges a harbor defined by a crescent-shaped beach. Point St. George, just above the harbor, protects the city from strong north winds; it was on Point St. George Reef that the side-wheeler *Brother Jonathan* wrecked on July 30, 1865. Brother Jonathan Cemetery, 9th Street and Pebble Beach Drive, contains the graves of many victims.

Lake Earl Wildlife Area, 5 miles north at the junction of Northcrest Drive and Old Mill Road, is a 6,000-acre wildlife habitat offering wildlife observation, boating, hiking, waterfowl hunting and fishing.

Crescent City is the southern terminus of a scenic 42-mile stretch of US 199 that heads northeast to the Oregon border through Smith River National Recreation Area.

The town's proximity to Jedediah Smith Redwoods and Del Norte Coast Redwoods state parks, both part of Redwood National and State Parks *(see place listing p. 296)*, makes Crescent City a convenient place to stay when visiting them. A visitor center inside the Redwood National and State Parks Headquarters, near the waterfront at 1111 2nd St., supplies maps and brochures describing the parks; phone (707) 464-6101.

Crescent City-Del Norte County Chamber of Commerce: 1001 Front St., Crescent City, CA 95531. **Phone:** (707) 464-3174 or (800) 343-8300.

BATTERY POINT LIGHTHOUSE, on Battery Point Island at the end of A St., is a working 1856 lighthouse that houses a museum, nautical artifacts, antique clocks, and photographs of shipwrecks and American and foreign lighthouses. Guided tours are available (tide permitting). **Time:** Allow 30 minutes minimum. **Hours:** Daily 10-4, Apr.-Sept.; Sat.-Sun. 10-4, rest of year (tide permitting). Phone ahead to confirm schedule. **Cost:** $3; $1 (ages 5-18). **Phone:** (707) 464-3089.

DEL NORTE COUNTY HISTORICAL SOCIETY MUSEUM, 577 H St. at jct. 6th St., is in the building built in 1926 and used until 1963 as the County Hall of Records and the county jail. It features a fine collection of Tolowa and Yurok baskets, musical instruments, logging and mining tools and equipment as well as vintage clothing and furniture. The second floor has some of the jail's original cells, which now house exhibits.

An annex contains the first order Fresnel lens from the St. George Reef Lighthouse and artifacts from an 1856 shipwreck and the 1964 tsunami that destroyed much of the city. **Time:** Allow 1 hour minimum. **Hours:** Mon.-Sat. 10-4, May-Sept.; Mon.

10:30-3, rest of year. Phone ahead to confirm schedule. **Cost:** $3; $1 (ages 5-18). **Phone:** (707) 464-3922.

OCEAN WORLD, 304 US 101S, offers a 40-minute guided tour through a half-million-gallon aquarium featuring the sea life of the northern Pacific coast. Highlights include a touch tide pool, shark petting tank and performances by trained sea lions. **Hours:** Daily 9-8, June-Aug.; 9-6, rest of year. Aquarium tours are available every 20 minutes. Closed Christmas. **Cost:** $9.95; $5.95 (ages 4-11). **Phone:** (707) 464-4900.

AMERICAS BEST VALUE INN   (707)464-4141

Motel
$50-$125

Address: 440 Hwy 101 N 95531 **Location:** Between Cooper and 9th sts; across from Del Norte County Fairground. **Facility:** 61 units. 2 stories (no elevator), exterior corridors. **Terms:** cancellation fee imposed. **Free Special Amenities: continental breakfast and early check-in/late check-out.**

ANCHOR BEACH INN   (707)464-2600

Motel
$56-$158

Address: 880 Hwy US 101 S 95531 **Location:** Oceanfront. At Anchor Way; south end of town. **Facility:** 52 units. 2 stories (no elevator), exterior corridors. **Amenities:** high-speed Internet. **Activities:** whirlpool. **Guest Services:** coin laundry. **Free Special Amenities: expanded continental breakfast and high-speed Internet.**

BAYVIEW INN   (707)465-2050

Motel
$54-$99

Address: 310 Hwy US 101 S 95531 **Location:** On US 101. **Facility:** 67 units. 3 stories (no elevator), interior/exterior corridors. **Guest Services:** coin laundry. **Free Special Amenities: continental breakfast and early check-in/late check-out.**

▼ See AAA listing p. 91 ▼

BEST WESTERN PLUS NORTHWOODS INN
(707)464-9771

Hotel
$89-$225

AAA Benefit: Members save up to 20%, plus 10% bonus points with Best Western Rewards®.

Address: 655 Hwy US 101 S 95531 **Location:** On US 101. Opposite harbor. **Facility:** 89 units. 2 stories (no elevator), interior/exterior corridors. **Terms:** cancellation fee imposed. **Amenities:** safes. *Some:* high-speed Internet. Dining: Northwoods Restaurant & Lounge, see separate listing. **Pool(s):** heated indoor. **Activities:** sauna, whirlpools, exercise room. **Free Special Amenities: local telephone calls and high-speed Internet.** *(See ad p. 90.)*

CRESCENT CITY TRAVELODGE   (707)464-6124

Motel $89-$159 **Address:** 353 L St 95531 **Location:** On US 101; between 3rd and 4th sts; center. **Facility:** 27 units. 2 stories (no elevator), exterior corridors. **Terms:** cancellation fee imposed. **Amenities:** safes. **Activities:** sauna.

CURLY REDWOOD LODGE   707/464-2137

Motel
$58-$110

Address: 701 US Hwy 101 S/Redwood Hwy 95531 **Location:** On US 101. Opposite the harbor. **Facility:** 36 units. 2 stories (no elevator), interior/exterior corridors. **Free Special Amenities: early check-in/late check-out and high-speed Internet.**

ECONO LODGE CRESCENT CITY   (707)464-6106

Motel
$59-$99

Address: 725 Hwy 101 N 95531 **Location:** On US 101, jct Northcrest St. **Facility:** 49 units. 1 story, exterior corridors. **Terms:** 2 night minimum stay - seasonal, 3 day cancellation notice. **Free Special Amenities: expanded continental breakfast and room upgrade (subject to availability with advance reservations).**

HIOUCHI MOTEL   (707)458-3041

Motel $61-$66 **Address:** 2097 Hwy 199 95531 **Location:** On US 199, 5.5 mi e of jct US 101. **Facility:** 17 units. 2 stories (no elevator), exterior corridors. **Terms:** cancellation fee imposed.

LIGHTHOUSE INN   707/464-3993

Hotel
$69-$145

Address: 681 Hwy 101 S 95531 **Location:** On US 101. Opposite the harbor. **Facility:** 65 units. 3 stories, interior corridors. **Guest Services:** coin laundry. **Free Special Amenities: continental breakfast and early check-in/late check-out.**

OCEANFRONT LODGE-CRESCENT CITY   707/465-5400

Hotel
Rates not provided

Address: 100 A St 95531 **Location:** Oceanfront. Jct US 101, 0.7 mi w on Front St. **Facility:** 53 units. 3 stories, interior corridors. **Amenities:** video games (fee), high-speed Internet. **Pool(s):** heated indoor. **Activities:** sauna, whirlpool, exercise room. **Guest Services:** coin laundry. **Free Special Amenities: expanded continental breakfast and early check-in/late check-out.**

PACIFIC INN   707/464-9553

Motel. Rates not provided. **Address:** 220 M St 95531 **Location:** On US 101; between 2nd and 3rd sts; center. **Facility:** 25 units. 1 story, exterior corridors.

SUPER 8   (707)464-4111

Motel
$55-$130

Address: 685 Hwy 101 S/Redwood Hwy 95531 **Location:** On US 101. Opposite the harbor. **Facility:** 49 units. 2 stories (no elevator), exterior corridors. **Terms:** cancellation fee imposed. **Guest Services:** coin laundry. **Free Special Amenities: continental breakfast and high-speed Internet.**

WHERE TO EAT

THE GOOD HARVEST CAFE   707/465-6028

American. Casual Dining. $8-$25 **AAA Inspector Notes:** This family-friendly café take pride in serving fresh, healthy natural foods. There is a bar upstairs with a view of the harbor. **Bar:** full bar. **Address:** 575 Hwy 101 S 95531 **Location:** On US 101; between Thompson and King sts. B L D

HARBOR VIEW GROTTO   707/464-3815

American
Seafood
Casual Dining
$8-$27

AAA Inspector Notes: Surrounding 180-degree windows offer lovely views of the ocean. Great tasting seafood adorn the menu, at affordable prices, and the catch of the day rarely disappoints. **Bar:** full bar. **Reservations:** suggested. **Address:** 150 Starfish Way 95531 **Location:** Just w on Citizens Dock from jct US 101, then just s. L D

NORTHWOODS RESTAURANT & LOUNGE   707/465-5656

American. Casual Dining. $8-$24 **AAA Inspector Notes:** Steak, pasta, seafood and sandwiches are among the varied offerings served in this Northern California town eatery. **Bar:** full bar. **Address:** 675 Hwy 101 S 95531 **Location:** On US 101; in BEST WESTERN PLUS Northwoods Inn. B L D

THAI HOUSE RESTAURANT   707/464-2427

Thai. Casual Dining. $6-$12 **AAA Inspector Notes:** This restaurant offers a casual atmosphere along with an authentic taste of Vietnamese and Thai dishes. Start with crispy Vietnamese rolls or salad rolls. For an entrée, try the panang curry, and for dessert sample the mango and sticky rice. Finish up with a glass of Vietnamese iced coffee to cool the heat. **Bar:** beer & wine. **Address:** 105 N St 95531 **Location:** At Front St; center. L D

WING WAH RESTAURANT   707/465-3935

Chinese. Casual Dining. $7-$13 **AAA Inspector Notes:** Well-appointed décor with efficient friendly service, this restaurant is popular with the locals. For those who like egg dishes, order the egg foo yong with shrimp—a super-sized omelet full of juicy vegetables, bay shrimp and covered with gravy. **Bar:** beer & wine. **Address:** 383 M St 95531 **Location:** On US 101; between 3rd and 4th sts; in shopping center. L D

CROCKETT pop. 3,094

THE DEAD FISH   510/787-3323

Seafood
Casual Dining
$10-$50

AAA Inspector Notes: Savor the spectacular views of the bridge and bay as you arrive at this family-run restaurant that brings in fresh seafood daily. Don't be surprised to find a menu that changes to reflect the best offerings of the sea. Choose from the basic fish and chips, which are incredible, to the delectable crab and lobster entrées. Diners may also choose from a variety of other items including a special prime rib dinner. **Bar:** full bar. **Address:** 20050 San Pablo Ave 94525 **Location:** I-80 exit San Pablo/Pomona, just w. L D

CUPERTINO pop. 58,302
• Hotels & Restaurants map & index p. 468

COURTYARD BY MARRIOTT (408)252-9100 94
◆◆◆ **Hotel** $119-$269 **Address:** 10605 N Wolfe Rd 95014 **Location:** I-280 exit Wolfe Rd N, w on Pruneridge Rd. **Facility:** 149 units. 3 stories, interior corridors. **Amenities:** high-speed Internet. **Pool(s):** heated outdoor. **Activities:** whirlpool, exercise room. **Guest Services:** valet and coin laundry.

AAA Benefit: AAA hotel discounts of 5% or more.

ECO ❘❙ 🛏 CALL &M 🌊 📶 ✕ 🔌 🖥 / SOME UNITS 🛗

CUPERTINO INN 408/996-7700 92
◆◆◆ **Hotel.** Rates not provided. **Address:** 10889 N De Anza Blvd 95014 **Location:** I-280 exit Sunnyvale-Saratoga Rd, just n. **Facility:** 125 units. 4 stories, interior/exterior corridors. **Pool(s):** heated outdoor. **Activities:** whirlpool. **Guest Services:** valet laundry.

✈ ❘❙ 🛏 CALL 🌊 📶 ✕ 🖥 / SOME UNITS 🛗

CYPRESS HOTEL (408)253-8900 95
◆◆◆◆ **Hotel** $84-$319 **Address:** 10050 S De Anza Blvd 95014 **Location:** I-280 exit De Anza Blvd, 0.7 mi s. **Facility:** The hotel is located in the heart of Silicon Valley. The wine-and-cheese reception is a great way to unwind each evening. 224 units. 9 stories, interior corridors. **Terms:** 2-4 night minimum stay - seasonal, cancellation fee imposed. **Amenities:** high-speed Internet, safes. **Dining:** Park Place, see separate listing. **Pool(s):** heated outdoor. **Activities:** exercise room. Fee: massage. **Guest Services:** valet laundry, area transportation-within 5 mi. **Free Special Amenities:** high-speed Internet and manager's reception.

SAVE ECO ✈ ❘❙ 🛏 CALL &M 🌊 BIZ 📶 ✕ 🎥 / SOME UNITS 🐾 🛗

HILTON GARDEN INN (408)777-8787 93
◆◆◆ **Hotel** $94-$227

Hilton Garden Inn

AAA Benefit: Unparalleled hospitality at a special Member rate.

Address: 10741 N Wolfe Rd 95014 **Location:** I-280 exit Wolfe Rd N, w on Pruneridge Rd. **Facility:** 164 units. 5 stories, interior corridors. **Terms:** 1-7 night minimum stay, cancellation fee imposed. **Amenities:** video games (fee), high-speed Internet. **Pool(s):** heated outdoor. **Activities:** whirlpool, exercise room. **Guest Services:** valet and coin laundry, area transportation-within 3 mi. **Free Special Amenities:** newspaper and early check-in/late check-out.

SAVE ✈ ❘❙ CALL &M 🌊 BIZ 📶 🎥 🔌 🖥 🖥

WHERE TO EAT

ALEXANDER'S STEAKHOUSE 408/446-2222 41
◆◆◆◆ Steak Fine Dining $16-$155

AAA Inspector Notes: This casually elegant steakhouse is known for its prime cuts of Certified Angus Beef that is dry aged at the restaurant. A Japanese flair is influenced into the menu items. The open grill kitchen allows guests to watch the chefs prepare their unique creations. Their specialty is wagyu (Japanese beef) from various prefectures such as Miyazaki, Gunma, Kagoshima. The texture and richness is nothing like western beef. **Bar:** full bar. **Reservations:** suggested. **Address:** 10330 N Wolfe Rd 95014 **Location:** I-280 exit Wolfe Rd, just s. L D CALL &M

ARMADILLO WILLY'S BARBECUE 408/252-7427
◆ Barbecue. Casual Dining. $6-$18 **AAA Inspector Notes:** Menu offerings at this eatery include a wide selection of barbecue favorites including ribs, chicken, beef brisket, burgers and salad. The atmosphere here is fun and lively. **Bar:** beer & wine. **Address:** 10100 S De Anza Blvd 95014 **Location:** I-280 exit De Anza Blvd, just s; at Stevens Creek Blvd. L D CALL &M

BLUE PHEASANT RESTAURANT 408/255-3300 39
◆◆ American. Casual Dining. $8-$32 **AAA Inspector Notes:** A longtime tradition in the Silicon Valley, the restaurant's dining room has some tables overlooking the golf course. The menu lists fresh fish selections, including broiled salmon, crab and shrimp, as well as London broil, medallions of pork and pasta primavera. Service is warm and friendly. **Bar:** full bar. **Reservations:** suggested. **Address:** 22100 Stevens Creek Blvd 95014 **Location:** SR 85 exit Stevens Creek Blvd, 0.5 mi w. L D

FONTANA'S ITALIAN RESTAURANT 408/725-0188 40
◆◆ Italian. Fine Dining. $12-$34 **AAA Inspector Notes:** Diners can sit near the cozy fireplace and watch the activity in the display kitchen. The menu boasts varied fresh fish dishes, as well as homemade pasta entrées and sinful desserts. **Bar:** beer & wine. **Reservations:** suggested. **Address:** 20840 Stevens Creek Blvd 95014 **Location:** I-280 exit Sunnyvale-Saratoga Rd, 0.3 mi w. L D CALL &M

FRESH CHOICE 408/253-1605
◆ American. Casual Dining. $9-$16 **AAA Inspector Notes:** The salad bar of salad bars, the casual restaurant invites patrons to make their own or try one of the already prepared varieties. Other items include freshly baked breads, pizza and soup, as well as make-your-own sundaes for dessert. **Bar:** beer & wine. **Address:** 10123 N Wolfe Rd 95014 **Location:** I-280 exit Wolfe Rd S, just n of Stevens Creek; in Cupertino Square Shopping Center. L D

PARK PLACE 408/873-1000 42
◆◆◆ American Casual Dining $10-$30

AAA Inspector Notes: A comfortable, relaxing dining experience awaits guests here. The varied menu includes salads, chicken, beef and fish dishes. **Bar:** full bar. **Address:** 10030 S De Anza Blvd 95014 **Location:** I-280 exit De Anza Blvd, 0.7 mi s; in Cypress Hotel. B L D

DALY CITY pop. 101,123
• Hotels & Restaurants map & index p. 410
• Part of San Francisco area — see map p. 342

BRIDGEPOINT INN 415/467-5600 19
◆◆ Motel. Rates not provided. **Address:** 3255 Geneva Ave 94014 **Location:** US 101 exit Cow Palace/Brisbane, 0.8 mi sw on Bayshore Blvd. Across from PG&E sub-station. 📵 Sunnydale, 110. **Facility:** 35 units. 2 stories, exterior corridors.

❘❙ CALL &M 📶 / SOME UNITS 🔌 🛗

HAMPTON INN (650)755-7500 18
◆◆ **Hotel** $119-$169 **Address:** 2700 Junipero Serra Blvd 94015 **Location:** I-280 exit Eastmoor Ave northbound; exit Junipero Serra Blvd southbound. 📵 Colma, 41. **Facility:** 86 units. 3 stories, interior corridors. **Terms:** 1-7 night minimum stay, cancellation fee imposed. **Amenities:** high-speed Internet. **Pool(s):** heated indoor. **Activities:** exercise room. **Guest Services:** valet and coin laundry.

AAA Benefit: Members save up to 10%!

ECO ❘❙ CALL &M 🌊 BIZ 📶 ✕ 🔌 🖥 / SOME UNITS 🔌 🛗

(See map & index p. 410.)

WHERE TO EAT

KOI PALACE RESTAURANT   650/992-9000 ⑦
♥♥♥♥ Chinese. Casual Dining. $9-$68 **AAA Inspector Notes:**
Enter through the moon-gate entryway to see tanks filled with sea-
food. This popular local restaurant serves top-drawer Cantonese cui-
sine. Lines form out the door for dim sum on Saturday and Sunday.
Bar: full bar. **Address:** 365 Gellert Blvd 94015 **Location:** I-280 exit
Hickey Blvd, just w, then just s. Ⓛ Ⓓ

DANVILLE (D-9) pop. 42,039, elev. 368'
• Hotels p. 94 • Restaurants p. 94
• Hotels & Restaurants map & index p. 254

Historic buildings and tree-lined streets connect
Danville to its Old West past. The symbol of the
town, a massive 300-year-old oak tree, stands on
Diablo Road. Behind the restored Southern Pacific
Railroad Depot is the Iron Horse Trail, a rails-to-
trails conversion that is now a popular jogging,
biking and walking route. The pathway extends almost 25 miles, meandering from Concord to the
county line in San Ramon.

Scenic views of Mount Diablo, visible throughout
Danville, are what brought playwright Eugene
O'Neill to the area. His home in the Las Trampas
foothills can be toured by reservation. Mount Diablo
State Park, popular with hikers and for the views
from its summit, is east on Diablo Road. *(See attraction listings.)*

The parking lot next to The Museum of the San
Ramon Valley at Railroad and W. Prospect avenues
is the location each Saturday morning year-round
for Danville's Certified Farmers' Market, where farm-
fresh fruits and vegetables, flowers and plants,
breads and other food items are available.

Danville Area Chamber of Commerce: 117-E
Town and Country Dr., Danville, CA 94526. **Phone:**
(925) 837-4400.

BLACKHAWK MUSEUM is at 3700 Blackhawk Plaza Cir., at the intersection of Crow
Canyon Rd., Camino Tassajara and Blackhawk Rd.
In an impressive contemporary building, the museum exhibits distinctive automobiles built 1894-
1971. Two large galleries present approximately 90
vehicles dating from the early 1900s, many of which
could be considered works of art.

Included are a 1906 Cadillac Type M, a 1923
Rolls-Royce Silver Ghost and a 1953 Ferrari 250
MM Vignale Spyder. Information about each automobile is provided on stanchions, allowing visitors to
tour at their own pace. A research library containing
books, magazines and reference materials provides
information about automobiles from their earliest
history to the present.

Time: Allow 1 hour minimum. **Hours:** Museum
Wed.-Sun. 10-5. Library open by appointment Wed.-
Sun. 10-5. One-hour guided tours are given Sat.-
Sun. at 2. Closed Jan. 1, Thanksgiving and
Christmas. **Cost:** $10; $7 (ages 65+ and students

with ID); free (ages 0-6 with a paying adult and military with ID). **Phone:** (925) 736-2277 or (925)
736-2280.

EUGENE O'NEILL NATIONAL HISTORIC SITE is
reached by a shuttle from a designated pick-up
point; information is provided when reservations are
made. Guided 2.5-hour tours are given of Tao
House, the Pulitzer- and Nobel Prize-winning playwright's home 1937-44. This sanctuary where
O'Neill wrote his most successful plays—"The
Iceman Cometh," "Long Day's Journey Into Night"
and "A Moon for the Misbegotten." The tour provides insights into O'Neill's life, his marriage to wife
Carlotta and his contributions to American theater.

Time: Allow 2 hours, 30 minutes minimum.
Hours: Guided tours are given Wed.-Fri. and Sun.
at 10 and 2. Self-guiding tours are given Sat.;
shuttles depart from The Museum of the San Ramon
Valley, 205 Railroad Ave., at 10, noon and 2. Closed
Jan. 1, Thanksgiving and Christmas. **Cost:** Free.
Reservations are required 1 to 2 weeks in advance
for guided tours. Reservations are not required for
self-guiding tours. **Phone:** (925) 838-0249.

MOUNT DIABLO STATE PARK is off I-680
Diablo Rd. exit, then 3 mi. e. to Mount Diablo
Scenic Blvd. and the South Gate entrance station.
At 3,849 feet, Mount Diablo isn't all that impressive
from an elevation standpoint. But because this
mountain is surrounded by broad, flat valleys, the
view from its summit is remarkable—under the best
conditions you can see almost 200 miles away, a
40,000-square-mile region that includes the Sacramento Valley, parts of the Sierra Nevada mountain
range and up to 35 California counties. Winter and
early spring, especially after a storm has cleared the
air, are the best times to take it in.

The 8-mile drive to the summit is rewarding. As
you ascend the mountain, pull off the twisty, two-
lane road for panoramic views of rolling hills, some
cloaked in a blanket of tawny grasses and others
dotted with oak trees. Spring (especially April and
May) is the best time to see yellow cow parsnips,
pink shooting stars and other wildflowers that fill the
meadows with color. Resident wildlife includes deer,
rabbits and coyotes.

There are hiking trails throughout the park. Only
the fit should attempt the 6.5-mile Grand Loop Trail,
which encircles the summit and has a 1,700-foot elevation gain. The views from Diablo's rugged upper
reaches are breathtaking. A popular park spot is
Rock City, accessed via South Gate Road (watch for
signs to the parking area). Narrow, crisscrossing
walking paths thread past unusual sandstone formations, many pocked with small caves and meander
through forested meadows.

Other activities include nature photography,
horseback riding and camping. In addition to the
Summit Museum, the Mitchell Canyon Interpretive
Center in nearby Clayton also has informative displays about the park. *See Recreation Areas Chart.*

(See map & index p. 254.)

Note: South Gate Road to the summit has many sharp turns and also is used by cyclists; obey the speed limit and exercise caution. Dogs on leash are permitted except on trails. **Time:** Allow 2 hours minimum. **Hours:** Park open daily 8-dusk. Mitchell Canyon Interpretive Center open Sat.-Sun. and some holidays 8-4, in summer; 10-2, in winter. **Cost:** Day use fee $10 per private vehicle; $9 (ages 62+ per private vehicle). **Phone:** (925) 837-2525 for park information, or (925) 837-6119 for the interpretive center.

Summit Museum, atop Mount Diablo in Mount Diablo State Park, is in a historic 1930s stone building that is also the park's visitor center. Exhibits explain the natural and cultural history of the park, and a rock wall and accompanying video recount geological forces that formed the mountain. A diorama with audio features presents an overview of the park's ecosystems. Key park locations are shown on a model of the mountain. There also are high-quality displays of artwork and photos.

A circular stairway leads to an observation tower with a deck that provides impressive views; marine fossils embedded in the building's sandstone walls can be seen on the way up. **Time:** Allow 1 hour minimum. **Hours:** Daily 10-4. **Cost:** Free. **Phone:** (925) 837-6119.

THE MUSEUM OF THE SAN RAMON VALLEY is at 205 Railroad Ave. at jct. W. Prospect Ave. The museum, in Danville's historic 1891 Southern Pacific depot, documents the history of the San Ramon Valley with displays and artifacts relating to its Native American, farming and pioneer past. A frieze that wraps around the main exhibit room provides scenes from area history. Temporary exhibits complement the museum's historical theme. **Time:** Allow 30 minutes minimum. **Hours:** Tues.-Sat. 10-1, mid-June to mid-Aug.; Tues.-Fri. 1-4, Sat. 10-1, rest of year. Phone ahead to confirm schedule. **Cost:** $3; $2 (students with ID); $1 (ages 0-12); $5 (family, two adults and all children). **Phone:** (925) 837-3750.

BEST WESTERN PLUS DANVILLE SYCAMORE INN
(925)855-8888 **46**

Hotel
$85-S150

Best Western PLUS

AAA Benefit: Members save up to 20%, plus 10% bonus points with Best Western Rewards®.

Address: 803 Camino Ramon 94526 **Location:** I-680 exit Sycamore Valley Rd, just e, then just s. **Facility:** 62 units. 2 stories (no elevator), interior/exterior corridors. **Terms:** check-in 4 pm, 2-4 night minimum stay - seasonal and/or weekends, 3 day cancellation notice. **Amenities:** high-speed Internet. **Pool(s):** outdoor. **Guest Services:** valet laundry. **Free Special Amenities:** local telephone calls and high-speed Internet.

WHERE TO EAT

BLACKHAWK GRILLE 925/736-4295
fyi Regional American Fine Dining $11-$3 Under major renovation, scheduled to be completed June 2012. **Last rated:** AAA Inspector Notes: In an upscale shopping center, this cozy restaurant and its seasonal patio overlook a pond. An emphasis on fresh and local ingredients is evident in menu selections. **Bar:** full bar. **Reservations:** suggested. **Address:** 3540 Blackhawk Plaza Cir 94506 **Location:** Jct Sycamore Valley, Crow Canyon Rd and Camino Tassajara; in Blackhawk Plaza. L D CALL M

EL NIDO MEXICAN RESTAURANT 925/820-5330 **45**
Mexican. Casual Dining. $8-$18 AAA Inspector Notes: Family owned and operated for more than 20 years, this city tradition specializes in Mexican preparations. Patio seating is an option during nice weather. **Bar:** full bar. **Address:** 107 A Town and Country Dr 94526 **Location:** I-680 exit Sycamore Valley Rd W, n on San Ramon Valley Blvd, then just w; in The Village Shopping Center, 2nd Floor. L D CALL M

DAVIS (E-3) pop. 65,622, elev. 50'
• Restaurants p. 96

This progressive city has made a commitment to preserve native habitats. The 400-acre City of Davis Wetlands is unusual in that it depends on storm water and treated wastewater runoff as its source of water. The wetlands environment draws more than 80 species of wildlife, including migrating waterfowl and songbirds, and also provides a recreational outlet for Davis residents, who utilize the open spaces for wildlife viewing, hiking and biking. The site is off CR 28H, about a mile past the Davis Wastewater Pollution Control Plant; phone (530) 757-5686.

Another wetland habitat that serves a dual purpose is the 16,000-acre Yolo Bypass Wildlife Area, at the east end of CR 32B. Wildlife share the area with walkers and visitors enjoying a driving loop; phone (530) 757-2461.

As a result of its foresight and commitment to conservation, Davis has received several energy conservation awards. In addition, the city offers more than 100 miles of bicycle paths; in fact, it claims to have as many bikes as people. Residents also take advantage of more than 500 acres of parks, scenic greenbelts and open space for recreation.

The city's focal point, though, is the University of California Davis, with 30,000 students. You can see the campus courtesy of free guided 90-minute walking tours; reservations are required and should be made at least 1 week in advance. Tours, given weekdays at 10 and 2 and Saturday at 11:30, depart from the Walter A. Buehler Alumni and Visitors Center; phone (530) 752-8111.

The university's art museum, Richard L. Nelson Gallery & The Fine Art Collection, with more than 4,000 pieces in various media, focuses on changing exhibits of contemporary and historical American and California works. The gallery is in the UC Davis Art Building at One Shields Ave.; phone (530) 752-8500.

Students and residents alike congregate at the Davis Farmers Market, held Saturday mornings 8-1 year-round. On Wednesdays from 4:30-8:30, late March through late October, a festival atmosphere prevails at "Picnic in the Park." The event features international food vendors, a wine and beer garden, live performances from local musicians, a carousel, a portable fountain and play areas for children. To get to the market from I-80, take the Downtown Davis exit to Richards Boulevard, turn left on 1st Street, then turn right on C Street; the market is between 4th and 5th streets.

Davis Chamber of Commerce: 604 Third St., Davis, CA 95616. **Phone:** (530) 756-5160.

C.N. GORMAN MUSEUM is on the UC Davis campus at 1316 Hart Hall, One Shields Ave. The museum exhibits contemporary fine art by Native American and indigenous artists. Founded in 1973, the museum is named in honor of retired faculty member Carl Nelson Gorman, who was a Navajo artist, World War II code-talker, cultural historian and advocate for Native peoples. **Hours:** Mon.-Fri. noon-5, Sun. 2-5. Closed major holidays. **Cost:** Free. **Phone:** (530) 752-6567.

PENCE GALLERY is at 212 D St. at jct. 3rd St. The gallery's changing exhibitions feature contemporary works of art by local and regional artists. **Time:** Allow 30 minutes minimum. **Hours:** Tues.-Sun. 11:30-5 (also second Fri. of the month 6-9 p.m.). Closed major holidays. **Cost:** Free. **Phone:** (530) 758-3370.

UC DAVIS ARBORETUM is off I-80 exit 71 (UC Davis), then n. to the central campus. The arboretum headquarters is on LaRue Rd. just w. of California Ave.; the gardens also can be accessed from several campus locations.

The 100-acre arboretum has bridges connecting both sides of a creek. Collections focus on plants adapted to a Mediterranean climate and include gardens with native California plants; with only white flowers; with plantings indigenous to the Mediterranean basin; a home demonstration garden; a garden with heat- and drought-resistant plants; and oak and redwood groves. The arboretum also has plantings indigenous to Australia, Mexico and South Africa. A map of the arboretum is available at the headquarters building.

Hours: Gardens daily 24 hours. Headquarters open Mon.-Fri. 8-5. Guided tours are given most weekends; phone ahead for hours. **Cost:** Free. **Parking:** $7 (Mon.-Fri.); free (Sat.-Sun.). **Phone:** (530) 752-4880.

T. Elliot Weier Redwood Grove is within the UC Davis Arboretum along Putah Creek; Lot 5 is the closest visitor parking to the redwood grove. The redwood grove consists of about 150 trees named after the botany professor at the university who helped create the arboretum in 1936.

The grove, one of the largest collections of coast redwoods outside their native range, was planted by students and faculty beginning in 1941. Many of the trees, still in their infancy, are 60 to 70 feet tall. Interpretive placards explain the history of the grove and the redwood trees. **Time:** Allow 15 minutes minimum. **Hours:** Daily 24 hours. **Cost:** Free. **Parking:** $7 (Mon.-Fri.); free (Sat.-Sun.). **Phone:** (530) 752-4880.

AGGIE, AN ASCEND COLLECTION HOTEL
(530)756-0352

Hotel
$99-S189

Address: 245 1st St 95616 **Location:** I-80 exit 72B (Richards Blvd) westbound, just nw, then just w; exit 72 eastbound, just nw. **Facility:** 33 units, some kitchens and cottages. 2 stories (no elevator), interior/exterior corridors. **Amenities:** Some: high-speed Internet. **Activities:** limited exercise equipment. **Free Special Amenities: continental breakfast and high-speed Internet.**

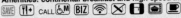

BEST WESTERN PLUS PALM COURT HOTEL
(530)753-7100

Hotel
$149-S259

AAA Benefit: Members save up to 20%, plus 10% bonus points with Best Western Rewards®.

Address: 234 D St 95616 **Location:** I-80 exit 72B (Richards Blvd) westbound, just nw, w on 1st St, then just n; exit 72 (Richards Blvd) eastbound; corner of 3rd and D sts; downtown. **Facility:** 27 units. 3 stories, interior corridors. **Amenities:** high-speed Internet. **Activities:** sauna, whirlpool, exercise room. **Free Special Amenities: local telephone calls and high-speed Internet.**

BEST WESTERN UNIVERSITY LODGE (530)756-7890

Motel
$99-S120

AAA Benefit: Members save up to 20%, plus 10% bonus points with Best Western Rewards®.

Address: 123 B St 95616 **Location:** I-80 exit 72B (Richards Blvd) westbound, just nw to 1st St, just w to B St, then just n; exit 72 (Richards Blvd) eastbound, just nw to 1st St, just w to B St, then just n; at 2nd and B sts. **Facility:** 52 units, some two bedrooms and kitchens. 2 stories (no elevator), exterior corridors. **Amenities:** high-speed Internet. **Activities:** whirlpool, bicycles, exercise room. **Free Special Amenities: local telephone calls and high-speed Internet.**

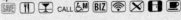

COMFORT SUITES - UC DAVIS (530)297-1500

Hotel $129-$149 **Address:** 1640 Research Park Dr 95618 **Location:** I-80 exit 72A (Richards Blvd) westbound, just se, then just n. **Facility:** 71 units, some two bedrooms. 3 stories, interior corridors. **Terms:** cancellation fee imposed. **Amenities:** high-speed Internet. **Pool(s):** heated outdoor. **Activities:** whirlpool. **Guest Services:** valet and coin laundry.

HYATT PLACE UC DAVIS (530)756-9500

Hotel
$129-S249

HYATT PLACE **AAA Benefit:** Members save 10% or more everyday.

Address: 173 Old Davis Rd Ext 95616 **Location:** I-80 exit 71 (UC Davis), 0.6 mi ne; just n of jct Alumni Ln; follow signs for Mondavi Center. **Facility:** 75 units. 4 stories, interior corridors. **Terms:** cancellation fee imposed. **Amenities:** video games (fee), high-speed Internet. **Pool(s):** heated outdoor. **Activities:** bicycles, exercise room. **Guest Services:** valet laundry, area transportation-within 5 mi & downtown. **Free Special Amenities: expanded continental breakfast and high-speed Internet.**

LA QUINTA INN & SUITES DAVIS (530)758-2600

Hotel
$84-$233

Address: 1771 Research Park Dr 95616 **Location:** I-80 exit 72A (Richards Blvd) westbound, just se, then just n; exit 72 (Richards Blvd) eastbound. **Facility:** 51 units. 3 stories, interior corridors. **Pool(s):** heated outdoor. **Activities:** whirlpool. **Guest Services:** valet and coin laundry. **Free Special Amenities: expanded continental breakfast and high-speed Internet.**

UNIVERSITY PARK INN & SUITES (530)756-0910

Hotel
$88-$199

Address: 1111 Richards Blvd 95616 **Location:** I-80 exit 72B (Richards Blvd) westbound; exit 72 (Richards Blvd) eastbound, just nw. **Facility:** 43 units, some efficiencies. 2 stories (no elevator), exterior corridors. **Terms:** cancellation fee imposed. **Amenities:** high-speed Internet. **Pool(s):** outdoor. **Free Special Amenities: expanded continental breakfast and high-speed Internet.**

ECONO LODGE 530/756-1040

[fyi] Not evaluated. **Address:** 221 D St 95616 **Location:** I-80 exit 72A (Richards Blvd) westbound, just nw, w on 1st St, then just n; exit 72 (Richards Blvd) eastbound; downtown. Facilities, services, and décor characterize an economy property.

WHERE TO EAT

BLACK BEAR DINER 530/756-4190

American. Family Dining. $6-$15 **AAA Inspector Notes:** A homey atmosphere characterizes this family-oriented restaurant. Familiar comfort foods, such as meatloaf with mashed potatoes, are at the heart of the menu and are served in generous portions. **Bar:** beer & wine. **Address:** 255 2nd St 95616 **Location:** I-80 exit 72B (Richards Blvd) westbound; exit 72 (Richards Blvd) eastbound, just nw to 1st St, just w to B St, then just n. B L D CALL M

CAFFE ITALIA 530/758-7200

Italian. Casual Dining. $6-$22 **AAA Inspector Notes:** For more than 30 years, guests have enjoyed this Italian, garden-style restaurant with lots of greenery, pine booths, hanging garlic and wine bottles. Choose from pizza, calzones, Italian sandwiches and a good choice of pasta dishes and steaks. Half orders are available for some items and lunch specials are offered Monday through Friday. Take a seat on the seasonal patio. **Bar:** beer & wine. **Address:** 1121 Richards Blvd 95616 **Location:** I-80 exit 72B (Richards Blvd) westbound; exit 72 (Richards Blvd) eastbound, just w. B L D CALL M

LITTLE PRAGUE BOHEMIAN RESTAURANT 530/756-1107

Czechoslovakian. Casual Dining. $8-$22 **AAA Inspector Notes:** This European-style restaurant with Old World charm offers hearty Bohemian fare, including delicious sausages, schnitzel and distinctive Czech drinks and beers. The desserts are baked in-house. Saturday and Sunday brunch is offered 9 a.m. to 2 p.m. Inviting fire pits are located on the terrace. Closed for lunch on Monday. **Bar:** full bar. **Address:** 330 G St 95616 **Location:** I-80 exit 72B (Richards Blvd) westbound; exit 72 (Richards Blvd) eastbound, just nw to 1st St, just e to G St, then just n. **Parking:** street only. L D CALL M

MIKUNI JAPANESE RESTAURANT & SUSHI BAR
530/756-2111

Japanese. Casual Dining. $10-$20 **AAA Inspector Notes:** This casual, contemporary eatery offers small and large plates, nigiri, sashimi and a variety of maki rolls. Guests can sit at the sushi bar and watch the chefs prepare the sushi. Lunch is served Monday through Friday and lunch specials are offered. A heated patio is a cozy place to dine. **Bar:** full bar. **Address:** 500 1st St, Suite 11 95616 **Location:** I-80 exit 72B (Richards Blvd) westbound; exit 72 (Richards Blvd) eastbound, just nw to 1st St, then just w; in Davis Commons Shopping Center. L D CALL M

PAESANOS 530/758-8646

Italian Pizza. Casual Dining. $8-$12 **AAA Inspector Notes:** Salads, sandwiches and a variety of pizza and pasta in tasty combinations are offered at this eatery with a small, inviting heated patio area. Gluten-free pizza dough is available. **Bar:** full bar. **Address:** 139 G St 95616 **Location:** I-80 exit 72B (Richards Blvd) westbound; exit 72 (Richards Blvd) eastbound, just nw to 1st St, just e, then just n. **Parking:** street only. L D CALL M

SEASONS RESTAURANT 530/750-1801

New American. Casual Dining. $8-$26 **AAA Inspector Notes:** This contemporary restaurant is wildly popular and features an interesting menu of new American cuisine utilizing the freshest ingredients. Seasonal menus change every three months. The extensive wine selection offers local wines and makers whose wines are produced by University of California-Davis alumni. **Bar:** full bar. **Reservations:** suggested. **Address:** 102 F St 95616 **Location:** I-80 exit 72B (Richards Blvd) westbound; exit 72 (Richards Blvd) eastbound, just nw to 1st St, then just e; jct 1st St. L D CALL M

DEVILS POSTPILE NATIONAL MONUMENT (F-5)

Near Mammoth Lakes and surrounded by Inyo National Forest, Devils Postpile National Monument lies at an elevation of 7,560 feet in the eastern Sierra Nevada. The highlight of this 800-acre monument is a sheer wall of symmetrical basaltic columns more than 60 feet high. The formation is a remnant of a basalt flow worn smooth on top by glacial action. A trail leads to the top where the surface resembles a tile inlay.

The Middle Fork of the San Joaquin River drops more than 100 feet at Rainbow Falls, 2 miles by trail from the Devils Postpile formation. Fishing is permitted; anyone over 15 must have a California license. Hunting is prohibited.

The monument is reached via SR 203, which leads west from US 395 and Mammoth Visitor Center to the Mammoth Mountain Ski Area parking lot, then by shuttle bus to the Postpile ranger station. The shuttle, which runs 7 a.m.-7 p.m., also departs from the Mammoth Mountain Adventure Center in Mammoth Lakes. A half-mile trail leads to the Postpile. Except for vehicles with camping permits, the physically impaired, overnight resort guests or trailers carrying horses or other livestock, private vehicles are not allowed beyond Minaret Vista (just beyond the ski area parking lot) during the day, mid-June to late September.

Rangers conduct interpretive walks and campfire programs early July through Labor Day (weather permitting). Leashed pets are permitted. Monument open May-Oct. (weather permitting). Ranger station open daily 9-5, July 1-Labor Day. Daily access fee $7; $4 (ages 3-15). Three-day pass $14; $8 (ages 3-15). Shuttle bus free with access fee. The Federal Recreation Pass is not valid at this site. Phone (760) 934-2289.

DIXON pop. 18,351

BEST WESTERN PLUS INN DIXON   (707)678-1400

Hotel
$89-$155

 AAA Benefit: Members save up to 20%, plus 10% bonus points with Best Western Rewards®.

Address: 1345 Commercial Way 95620 **Location:** I-80 exit 64 (Pitt School Rd), just s, then just e. **Facility:** 103 units. 2 stories (no elevator), interior/exterior corridors. **Terms:** 2 night minimum stay - seasonal and/or weekends, 3 day cancellation notice. **Amenities:** high-speed Internet. **Pool(s):** outdoor. **Activities:** sauna, whirlpool, steamroom, exercise room. **Guest Services:** valet and coin laundry. **Free Special Amenities: local telephone calls and high-speed Internet.**

COMFORT SUITES - WEST OF UC DAVIS   (707)676-5000

Hotel $75-$250 **Address:** 155 Dorset Dr 95620 **Location:** I-80 exit 66A (Currey Rd) westbound, follow SR 113 S; exit 66 (Currey Rd) eastbound, just s on SR 113. **Facility:** 80 units. 3 stories, interior corridors. **Terms:** cancellation fee imposed. **Amenities:** high-speed Internet. **Pool(s):** heated outdoor. **Activities:** limited exercise equipment. **Guest Services:** valet and coin laundry.

WHERE TO EAT

CATTLEMENS   707/678-5518

Steak. Casual Dining. $14-$32 **AAA Inspector Notes:** Western decor, beamed ceilings and a mix of booths and tables set the stage for excellent hand-cut steaks and all-you-can-eat salad. **Bar:** full bar. **Reservations:** suggested. **Address:** 250 Dorset Ct 95620 **Location:** I-80 exit 63 (Curry Rd) eastbound; exit Dixon Hwy (SR 113) westbound, just sw. **D**

DORRIS pop. 939

GOLDEN EAGLE MOTEL   (530)397-3114

Motel
$39-$99

Address: 100 W 1st St 96023 **Location:** US 97; center. **Facility:** 19 units. 1 story, exterior corridors. **Terms:** cancellation fee imposed. **Free Special Amenities: continental breakfast and high-speed Internet.**

DOUGLAS CITY pop. 713

INDIAN CREEK LODGE   530/623-6294

Motel
$69-$89

Address: 59741 Hwy 299 W 96024 **Location:** On SR 299, 1.5 mi w of jct SR 299 and CR 3. **Facility:** 16 units, some efficiencies and kitchens. 2 stories (no elevator), exterior corridors. **Terms:** 3 day cancellation notice-fee imposed. **Pool(s):** outdoor. **Activities:** boat ramp, fishing, horseshoes, volleyball. **Free Special Amenities: early check-in/late check-out and children's activities.**

Download eTourBook guides for top destinations at AAA.com/ebooks

DOWNIEVILLE (D-3) pop. 282, elev. 2,899'

Once the center of enormously rich gold diggings, Downieville retains much of its early atmosphere. Old brick and stone buildings with picturesque iron doors and shutters flank narrow, tree-lined Main Street, where some sections of sidewalk are still made of planks. Amateur prospectors can try their luck panning for gold in the Yuba River where it flows through the center of town.

Downieville's status as the county seat of Sierra County and location at the confluence of the Downie River and the North Fork of the Yuba River ensured its survival once gold rush days were over. It's a popular stopping point for mountain bikers and a convenient base if you're embarking on a nearby hiking, fishing or kayaking excursion.

DOWNIEVILLE MUSEUM, Main St., was built in 1852 and features eclectic exhibitions including collections of antique bottles, horse snowshoes, mining implements and photographs. The stone structure once was a Chinese store and gambling house and contains period artifacts and clothing.

Hours: Daily 11-4, Memorial Day to mid-Oct.; Sat.-Sun. 11-4 (weather permitting), mid-Apr. through day before Memorial Day. Phone ahead to confirm schedule. **Cost:** Donations. **Phone:** (530) 289-3580.

RECREATIONAL ACTIVITIES
White-water Rafting

- **Beyond Limits Adventures** departs from Convict Flat Picnic Area, 8 mi. w. on SR 49, for guided excursions on the American River. **Hours:** Daily Apr.-Sept. (depending upon water flow). **Phone:** (209) 526-0027 or (800) 234-7238.

- **Whitewater Voyages** meets at varying departure points. **Hours:** Daily Apr.-Sept. (depending upon water flow). Reservations office open all year. **Phone:** (510) 222-5994 or (800) 400-7238.

RIVERSIDE INN   530/289-1000

Motel $88-$180 **Address:** 206 Commercial St (SR 49) 95936 **Location:** On SR 49; center. **Facility:** 11 units, some two bedrooms and kitchens. 2 stories (no elevator), exterior corridors. **Terms:** 2 night minimum stay - seasonal and/or weekends, 3 day cancellation notice-fee imposed.

DUBLIN pop. 46,036
- **Restaurants p. 98**

HOLIDAY INN DUBLIN   (925)828-7750

Hotel $69-$149 **Address:** 6680 Regional St 94568 **Location:** At northwest quadrant of I-580 and 680. West Dublin/Pleasanton, 28. **Facility:** 222 units. 3 stories, interior corridors. **Terms:** resort fee. **Dining:** Ballybunion Bar & Grille, see separate listing. **Pool(s):** heated indoor. **Activities:** whirlpool, exercise room, spa. **Guest Services:** valet and coin laundry.

HYATT PLACE DUBLIN/PLEASANTON   (925)828-9006

▼▼▼ ▼
Hotel
$89-$179

▦HYATT PLACE· **AAA Benefit:** Members save 10% or more everyday.

Address: 4950 Hacienda Dr 94568 **Location:** I-580 exit Hacienda Dr, then n. ▦ Dublin-Pleasanton, 29. **Facility:** 127 units. 6 stories, interior corridors. **Terms:** cancellation fee imposed. **Amenities:** *Some:* high-speed Internet. **Pool(s):** heated outdoor. **Activities:** exercise room. **Guest Services:** valet laundry. **Free Special Amenities: expanded continental breakfast and high-speed Internet.**

〔SAVE〕 〔📶〕 CALL 〔&M〕 🏊 〔📶〕 ✖ 🅱 💻 🚗

LA QUINTA INN & SUITES DUBLIN - PLEASANTON
(925)828-9393

▼▼▼ **Hotel $60-$210 Address:** 6275 Dublin Blvd 94568 **Location:** I-580 exit Hopyard/Dougherty Rd, just n. ▦ Dublin-Pleasanton, 29. **Facility:** 91 units. 3 stories, interior corridors. **Amenities:** video games (fee), high-speed Internet. **Pool(s):** heated outdoor. **Activities:** whirlpool, exercise room. **Guest Services:** valet and coin laundry.

〔📶〕 CALL 〔&M〕 🏊 〔📶〕 📹 🅱 💻 💻 / SOME UNITS 〔📶〕 🚗

WHERE TO EAT

ARMADILLO WILLY'S BARBECUE   925/833-0400

▼ Barbecue. Quick Serve. $8-$22 **AAA Inspector Notes:** Menu offerings at this eatery include a wide selection of barbecue favorites including ribs, chicken, beef brisket, burgers and salad. The atmosphere here is fun and lively. **Bar:** beer & wine. **Address:** 4480 Tassajara Rd 94568 **Location:** I-580 exit Santa Rita Rd, just n.

〔L〕 〔D〕 CALL 〔&M〕

BALLYBUNION BAR & GRILLE   925/828-7750

▼▼ American. Casual Dining. $12-$25 **AAA Inspector Notes:** Off the lobby of the Holiday Inn Dublin, this bistro presents a menu of varied pasta and chicken dishes, as well as barbecue ribs and burgers. The adjacent lounge is a great place to meet friends around the fireplace. **Bar:** full bar. **Address:** 6680 Regional St 94568 **Location:** At northwest quadrant of I-580 and 680; in Holiday Inn Dublin. ▦ West Dublin/Pleasanton, 28. 〔B〕 〔D〕 CALL 〔&M〕 🚗

CASA OROZCO   925/828-5464

▼ Mexican. Casual Dining. $8-$20 **AAA Inspector Notes:** This distinctively designed restaurant with its wall murals and memorabilia gives the feel of dining in Mexico. Family owned and operated, many of the items on the menu are from old family recipes. Traditional favorites are offered, but the carnitas are a favorite. Portions are hearty so bring an appetite. This is an extremely popular spot with the locals. **Bar:** full bar. **Address:** 7995 Amador Valley Blvd 94568 **Location:** I-580 exit San Ramon Rd, just n. ▦ West Dublin/Pleasanton, 28. 〔L〕 〔D〕 CALL 〔&M〕 🚗

ROUND TABLE PIZZA   925/828-6680

▼ Pizza. Casual Dining. $7-$28 **AAA Inspector Notes:** This casual, family-oriented pizza place features high-quality ingredients and dough rolled fresh daily. Distinctive specialty pizzas are piled high with toppings. **Bar:** beer & wine. **Address:** 7841 Amador Valley Blvd 94568 **Location:** I-580 exit San Ramon Rd/Foothill Rd N, then just e. ▦ West Dublin/Pleasanton, 28. 〔L〕 〔D〕 🚗

YANAGI SUSHI & GRILL   925/556-9575

▼▼ Japanese Sushi. Casual Dining. $10-$30 **AAA Inspector Notes:** Guests can dine at the sushi bar to watch the chefs prepare the many varieties of house special rolls and sashimi made from albacore, lobster, salmon and octopus. Or they can choose to sit at a table where the meal is prepared right there on an open flame. A third option would be to sit in the dining room. There is something sure to please everyone on the extensive menu. In addition to homemade sushi, there also are rice bowls, udon, boat combinations and the teriyaki selections. **Bar:** beer & wine. **Address:** 6599 Dublin Blvd 94568 **Location:** I-580 exit Hopyard/Dougherty Rd, just n, then just w; in Tralee Village Center. ▦ Dublin-Pleasanton, 29.

〔L〕 〔D〕 CALL 〔&M〕 🚗

DUNLAP (G-5) elev. 1,914'

PROJECT SURVIVAL'S CAT HAVEN is on SR 180 at 38257 E. Kings Canyon Rd. A quarter-mile guided tour of this wild animal park devoted to big cats provides an up-close look at tigers, lions and several types of leopards in natural settings.

Time: Allow 1 hour, 30 minutes minimum. **Hours:** Wed.-Mon. 10-5, May-Sept.; Mon. and Thurs.-Sat. 10-4, Sun. noon-4, rest of year. Last tour departs 1 hour before closing. Closed Jan. 1, Easter, Thanksgiving and Christmas. **Cost:** $9; $7.50 (ages 62+); $6 (ages 5-12). **Phone:** (559) 338-1336 or (559) 338-3216. 🅰

DUNSMUIR (B-2) pop. 1,650, elev. 2,289'

Dunsmuir is an old railroad town just south of Mount Shasta. The Sacramento River, which runs through town, offers excellent fly fishing. Other recreational opportunities in the area include camping, hiking and skiing.

Dunsmuir Chamber of Commerce and Visitor's Center: 5915 Dunsmuir Ave., Suite 100, P.O. Box 122, Dunsmuir, CA 96025. **Phone:** (530) 235-2177 or (800) 386-7684.

CASTLE CRAGS STATE PARK lies 6 mi. s. off I-5 exit 724. The granite crags tower more than 4,000 feet over the nearby Sacramento River. In addition to its own 28 miles of hiking trails, the Pacific Crest Trail also passes through the park. *See Recreation Areas Chart.*

Pets must be leashed and are not allowed on trails. **Hours:** Daily 24 hours. Phone ahead to confirm. **Cost:** Day use $8 per private vehicle; $7 (ages 62+ per private vehicle). **Phone:** (530) 235-2684.

DUNSMUIR INN & SUITES   (530)235-4395

▼▼▼
Motel
$69-$150

Address: 5400 Dunsmuir Ave 96025 **Location:** I-5 exit 730 (Central Dunsmuir), just w. **Facility:** 16 units. 2 stories (no elevator), exterior corridors. **Terms:** cancellation fee imposed. **Free Special Amenities: continental breakfast and high-speed Internet.**

〔SAVE〕 〔📶〕 〔📶〕 🅱 💻 💻

OAK TREE INN   530/235-4100

▼▼ Hotel. Rates not provided. **Address:** 4000 Siskiyou Ave 96025 **Location:** I-5 exit 732 (Siskiyou Ave), just e. **Facility:** 21 units. 2 stories (no elevator), interior corridors. **Parking:** street only. **Terms:** check-in 4 pm. **Activities:** exercise room. **Guest Services:** coin laundry.

〔📶〕 〔📶〕 ✖ 🅱 💻 / SOME UNITS FEE 🐾 💻

CABOOSE MOTEL-RAILROAD PARK RESORT   530/235-4440

〔fyi〕 Not evaluated. **Address:** 100 Railroad Park Rd 96025 **Location:** I-5 exit 728 (Railroad Park Rd), just nw. Facilities, services, and décor characterize a mid-scale property.

WHERE TO EAT

CORNERSTONE BAKERY & CAFE   530/235-4677

▼▼ American. Casual Dining. $6-$13 **AAA Inspector Notes:** Tasty food, including fresh vegetarian sandwiches, salads, soups and burgers, is what diners can find at this eatery with an original tin ceiling and cheery décor. **Address:** 5759 Dunsmuir Ave 96025 **Location:** I-5 exit 730 (Central Dunsmuir), just se. **Parking:** street only.

〔B〕 〔L〕

RAILROAD PARK DINNER HOUSE & LOUNGE   530/235-4611

WWWW American. Casual Dining. $13-$24 **AAA Inspector Notes:** Diners can sit in restored railroad cars more than 100 years old while tasting good steaks and fish. **Bar:** full bar. **Reservations:** suggested. **Address:** 100 Railroad Park Rd 96025 **Location:** I-5 exit 728 (Railroad Park Rd), just nw; in Caboose Motel-Railroad Park Resort. D

CAFE MADDALENA   530/235-2725

fyi Not evaluated. Located in the historic district, this bistro serves fresh Mediterranean cuisine in a rustic, wood-paneled dining room. In season, dine al fresco in a garden setting under a grape arbor. **Address:** 5801 Sacramento Ave 96025 **Location:** Jct Pine St; center.

EAST PALO ALTO   pop. 28,155

FOUR SEASONS HOTEL SILICON VALLEY AT EAST PALO ALTO   (650)566-1200

WWW WWW Hotel $525-$645 **Address:** 2050 University Ave 94303 **Location:** US 101 exit University Ave. **Facility:** This is a splendid hotel with a shimmering curved glass facade and Douglas fir and African cherry wood millwork on display in the public areas. 200 units. 10 stories, interior corridors. **Parking:** on-site (fee) and valet. **Terms:** cancellation fee imposed. **Amenities:** safes. *Fee:* video games, high-speed Internet. **Dining:** Quattro Restaurant & Bar, see separate listing. **Pool(s):** heated outdoor. **Activities:** whirlpool, steamrooms, exercise room, spa. **Guest Services:** valet laundry, area transportation-within 3 mi.

WHERE TO EAT

QUATTRO RESTAURANT & BAR   650/470-2889

WWWW WWWW Italian. Fine Dining. $12-$38 **AAA Inspector Notes:** This smart, sophisticated restaurant is set inside a modernly luxurious hotel. One distinctive feature to the dining room is the large back-lit display case with life-size concave sculptures of three individuals. As guests walk past each figure, and the angle of view changes, the sculptures are seen wearing clothing from all four seasons of the year. The menu is modern Italian with fresh, organically grown items and many exotic items. **Bar:** full bar. **Reservations:** suggested. **Address:** 2050 University Ave 94303 **Location:** US 101 exit University Ave; in Four Seasons Hotel Silicon Valley at East Palo Alto. **Parking:** valet only. B L D CALL &M

EL CERRITO   pop. 23,549

SUPER 8-EL CERRITO   (510)232-0900

WWW WWW Hotel $75-$155 **Address:** 6009 Potrero Ave 94530 **Location:** I-80 exit Potrero Ave eastbound; exit Cutting Blvd westbound, just e, just s on San Pablo Ave, then just w. El Cerrito del Norte, 14. **Facility:** 48 units. 3 stories, interior corridors. **Amenities:** high-speed Internet. **Free Special Amenities: continental breakfast and high-speed Internet.**

WHERE TO EAT

PASTA POMODORO   510/225-0128

WWWW WWWW Italian. Casual Dining. $8-$18 **AAA Inspector Notes:** Families are welcomed at this laid-back restaurant, which brings in plenty of loyal locals who enjoy its varied Italian favorites, including tempting pasta and chicken dishes. **Bar:** beer & wine. **Address:** 5040 El Cerrito Plaza, Suite E1 94530 **Location:** I-80 exit Central Ave/El Cerrito, 0.5 mi e, then just s on Liberty St. El Cerrito Plaza, 13. L D CALL &M

Learn about inspections and Diamond Ratings at AAA.com/Diamonds

EL DORADO HILLS   pop. 42,108

• **Hotels & Restaurants map & index p. 314**

HOLIDAY INN EXPRESS HOTEL & SUITES   (916)358-3100   53

WWWW Hotel $109-$189 **Address:** 4360 Town Center Blvd 95762 **Location:** US 50 exit 30A (Latrobe Rd) eastbound, just s; exit 30 westbound; in Town Center Shopping Center. **Facility:** 93 units. 4 stories, interior corridors. **Amenities:** high-speed Internet, safes. **Pool(s):** heated outdoor. **Activities:** whirlpool, exercise room. **Guest Services:** valet and coin laundry. **Free Special Amenities: expanded continental breakfast and manager's reception.**

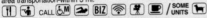

WHERE TO EAT

BAMIYAN AFGHAN RESTAURANT   916/941-8787   75

WWWW Afghan. Casual Dining. $9-$29 **AAA Inspector Notes:** Beautiful Afghani carpets adorn the walls at this restaurant which offers a distinctive cuisine where each dish is seasoned with a small portion of herbs and spices. Traditional Afghan dishes, shish kebabs, seafood and vegetarian entrées make up the menu. Patio dining is an option in season. **Bar:** full bar. **Address:** 1121 White Rock Rd 95762 **Location:** US 50 exit 30A (Latrobe Rd) eastbound, 0.5 mi s, then just e; exit 30 westbound. L D CALL &M

CHANTARA THAI CUISINE   916/939-0389   74

WWWW Thai. Casual Dining. $8-$16 **AAA Inspector Notes:** Tasty Thai cuisine is served here, including soups, salads, noodle dishes, curries and lunch specials. There is a patio overlooking the lake and fountain. **Bar:** full bar. **Address:** 4361 Town Center Blvd, Suite 110 95762 **Location:** US 50 exit 30A (Latrobe Rd) eastbound, just s, then just e; exit 30 westbound; in Town Center Shopping Center. L D CALL &M

ELDORADO NATIONAL FOREST   (E-4)

Elevations in the forest range from 3,382 ft. in the foothills to 9,983 ft. at Pyramid Peak. Refer to AAA maps for additional elevation information.

Bounded on the west by the Mother Lode Country and on the east by Lake Tahoe, Eldorado National Forest encompasses 676,780 acres in the rugged, lake-strewn Sierra Nevada. US 50 and SR 88 provide access to most of the forest's recreational facilities. Carson Pass Highway (SR 88) is a 58-mile scenic route through the forest.

Although the forest is most popular in spring and summer, three downhill ski areas and trails for cross-country skiing and snowmobiling attract winter visitors as well. Segments of the Pacific Crest National Scenic Trail pass through the forest; snow renders some sections impassable until mid-June or July. Hikers wishing to camp on the trail should obtain campfire permits. Permits also are required for day use and overnight stays in the Desolation Wilderness and Mokelumne Wilderness.

Maps for off-road vehicle use are available at national forest offices; for information phone (530) 644-2349. For additional information contact the Forest Supervisor, Eldorado National Forest, 100 Forni Rd., Placerville, CA 95667; phone (530) 622-5061. *See Recreation Areas Chart.*

ELK

• Part of Wine Country area — see map p. 562

ELK COVE INN & SPA   (707)877-3321

▼▼▼ **Country Inn** $100-$395 **Address:** 6300 S Hwy 1 95432 **Location:** Oceanfront. SR 1, 6.3 mi s of jct SR 128; just s of center. **Facility:** Built in the late 1800s, this property, a former lumber baron's estate, is nestled in peaceful seclusion atop a bluff on the Mendocino coast. 15 units. 2 stories (no elevator), interior/exterior corridors. **Terms:** 2 night minimum stay - seasonal and/or weekends, 14 day cancellation notice-fee imposed. **Activities:** spa.

(icons)

ELK GROVE pop. 153,015

EXTENDED STAYAMERICA-SACRAMENTO-ELK GROVE
(916)683-3753

▼▼▼ **Extended Stay Hotel** $79-$94 **Address:** 2201 Longport Ct 95758 **Location:** I-5 exit 508 (Laguna Blvd), 0.5 mi e, just s on Harbour Point Dr, then just w. **Facility:** 92 efficiencies. 3 stories, interior corridors. **Guest Services:** coin laundry.

(icons) CALL / SOME UNITS FEE

FAIRFIELD INN & SUITES BY MARRIOTT SACRAMENTO ELK GROVE   (916)681-5400

▼▼▼
Hotel
$99-$159

AAA Benefit: AAA hotel discounts of 5% or more.

Address: 8058 Orchard Loop Ln 95624 **Location:** SR 99 exit 289 (Cosumnes River Blvd/Calvine Rd), then just s. **Facility:** 76 units. 3 stories, interior corridors. **Amenities:** high-speed Internet. **Pool(s):** heated indoor. **Activities:** whirlpool, exercise room. **Guest Services:** complimentary and valet laundry.

(icons) CALL / SOME UNITS FEE

HAMPTON INN & SUITES SACRAMENTO/ELK GROVE
(916)683-9545

▼▼▼ **Hotel** $99-$209 **Address:** 2305 Longport Ct 95758 **Location:** I-5 exit 508 (Laguna Blvd), 0.5 mi e, then just s on Harbour Point Dr. **Facility:** 110 units. 4 stories, interior corridors. **Terms:**

AAA Benefit: Members save up to 10%!

1-7 night minimum stay, cancellation fee imposed. **Amenities:** video games (fee), high-speed Internet. **Pool(s):** heated outdoor. **Activities:** whirlpool, exercise room. **Guest Services:** valet and coin laundry.

(icons) CALL / SOME UNITS

HILTON GARDEN INN SACRAMENTO/ELK GROVE
(916)691-1900

▼▼▼
Hotel
$99-$149

Hilton Garden Inn **AAA Benefit:** Unparalleled hospitality at a special Member rate.

Address: 9241 Laguna Springs Dr 95757 **Location:** SR 99 exit 287 (Laguna Blvd), just w, then just s. Located at Laguna Pointe Business Park. **Facility:** 116 units. 4 stories, interior corridors. **Terms:** 1-7 night minimum stay, cancellation fee imposed. **Amenities:** high-speed Internet. **Pool(s):** heated outdoor. **Activities:** whirlpool, exercise room. **Guest Services:** valet and coin laundry. **Free Special Amenities:** local telephone calls and high-speed Internet.

(icons) CALL

Keep seasonal vehicles travel-ready
with a AAA/CAA Battery Tender®

HOLIDAY INN EXPRESS & SUITES   (916)478-4000

▼▼▼ **Hotel** $89-$120 **Address:** 2460 Maritime Dr 95758 **Location:** I-5 exit 506 (Elk Grove Blvd), just e to Harbour Point Dr, just n, then just w; SR 99 exit Elk Grove Blvd, 5 mi w, just n on Harbour Point Dr, then just w. **Facility:** 65 units. 3 stories, interior corridors. **Terms:** cancellation fee imposed. **Amenities:** high-speed Internet. **Pool(s):** heated outdoor. **Activities:** whirlpool, exercise room. **Guest Services:** valet and coin laundry.

(icons) CALL / SOME UNITS FEE

HOLIDAY INN EXPRESS HOTEL & SUITES
(916)478-9000

▼▼▼
Hotel
$116-$152

Address: 9175 W Stockton Blvd 95758 **Location:** SR 99 exit 287 (Laguna Blvd), just w, then just n; in Laguna Gateway Shopping Center. **Facility:** 116 units. 3 stories, interior corridors. **Amenities:** video games (fee), high-speed Internet. **Pool(s):** outdoor. **Activities:** whirlpool, exercise room. **Guest Services:** valet and coin laundry. **Free Special Amenities:** full breakfast and high-speed Internet.

(icons) CALL / SOME UNITS FEE

WHERE TO EAT

BOULEVARD BISTRO   916/685-2220

▼▼▼ American. Casual Dining. $18-$34 **AAA Inspector Notes:** This bistro, set in an attractive turn-of-the century bungalow, features well-prepared menu items with seasonal inspirations, along with a good selection of local California wines. Dining on the porch is an option. **Bar:** beer & wine. **Address:** 8941 Elk Grove Blvd 95624 **Location:** SR 99 exit Elk Grove Blvd, just e; jct 3rd St.

D CALL

BRICK HOUSE RESTAURANT & LOUNGE   916/714-0840

▼▼ Italian. Casual Dining. $11-$35 **AAA Inspector Notes:** Located in historic Elk Grove, this restaurant with exposed brick walls serves entrée salads and pasta dishes a la carte or family style with soup and salad. The garlic butter served is a garlic lover's dream. Dine in the back or in the lively lounge—both offer a welcoming atmosphere with good service. **Bar:** full bar. **Address:** 9027 Elk Grove Blvd, Suite 100 95624 **Location:** SR 99 exit Elk Grove Blvd, 1.3 mi e; jct Walnut St; in historic downtown. L D CALL

HABIT BURGER GRILL   916/683-3551

▼ Burgers. Quick Serve. $3-$7 **AAA Inspector Notes:** Tucked away in the corner of a shopping center, this California chain has been serving quality burgers, grilled sandwiches and salads since 1969. Patio area seating is available in season. **Address:** 7400 Laguna Blvd 95758 **Location:** SR 99 exit 287 (Laguna Blvd), 1.2 mi w; jct Bruceville Rd; in Laguna Pavilion Shopping Center.

L D CALL

MIKUNI JAPANESE RESTAURANT & SUSHI BAR
916/714-2112

▼▼ Japanese. Casual Dining. $10-$23 **AAA Inspector Notes:** This popular, contemporary Japanese restaurant offers the freshest seafood and sushi, including various rolls, seafood plates, boxes, lunch combinations and dinner entrées. Sit at the sushi bar or dine on the patio in season. Choose from an extensive sake selection. Without a reservation, expect a wait during busy times. **Bar:** full bar. **Reservations:** suggested. **Address:** 8525 Bond Rd 95624 **Location:** SR 99 exit Laguna Blvd/Bond Rd, just e; jct Elk Crest Dr; in Elk Grove Marketplace. L D LATE CALL

ORIGINAL PETE'S PIZZA PASTA GRILL   916/683-5757

▼▼ Italian. Casual Dining. $8-$22 **AAA Inspector Notes:** Easily accessible from the freeway, this restaurant serves pizza, pasta dishes, salads, sandwiches, wraps and burgers. A simple décor is offered along with an open kitchen and sidewalk seating out front. **Bar:** beer & wine. **Address:** 2475 Elk Grove Blvd, Suite 100 95758 **Location:** I-5 exit 506 (Elk Grove Blvd), just e; in Harbor Palms Shopping Center. L D CALL

THAI CHILI 916/714-3519

▼▼ Thai. Casual Dining. $6-$13 AAA Inspector Notes: An extensive selection of delicious Thai cuisine is offered at this restaurant tucked away in a shopping center. Friendly and efficient service can be expected. Lunch specials are featured. Bar: beer & wine. Address: 8696 Elk Grove Blvd, Suite 5 95624 Location: SR 99 exit 286 (Elk Grove Blvd) northbound, just ne to Elk Grove Blvd, then just e; exit southbound, just e; jct Elk Ridge Way. [L] [D]

TODO UN POCO 916/684-7774

▼▼ International. Casual Dining. $9-$18 AAA Inspector Notes: This neighborhood bistro features Mexican and Italian cuisine with some interesting combinations as well as specialty pizza. Bar: full bar. Address: 9080 Laguna Main St, Suite 1A 95758 Location: I-5 exit Laguna Blvd, 0.7 mi e; SR 99 exit Laguna Blvd W, 4.8 mi; adjacent to Bank of America; in Main St Plaza Shopping Center. [L] [D] CALL 🅼

EL PORTAL pop. 474
- **Hotels & Restaurants map & index p. 584**
- **Part of Yosemite National Park area — see map p. 578**

CEDAR LODGE (209)379-2612 **12**

Hotel
$95-$700

Address: 9966 Hwy 140 95318 Location: 6 mi w of Yosemite National Park West Gate. Facility: 209 units, some three bedrooms, efficiencies and kitchens. 2 stories (no elevator), exterior corridors. Terms: 2 night minimum stay - seasonal, 14 day cancellation notice-fee imposed, resort fee. Pool(s): outdoor, heated indoor. Activities: whirlpool. (See ad p. 589.)

SAVE [items] / SOME UNITS

YOSEMITE VIEW LODGE (209)379-2681 **11**

Hotel
$95-$499

Address: 11136 Hwy 140 95318 Location: Just w of Yosemite National Park West Gate. Facility: 336 units, some two bedrooms, efficiencies and kitchens. 1-3 stories, exterior corridors. Terms: 7 day cancellation notice-fee imposed. Dining: 2 restaurants. Pool(s): 3 outdoor, heated indoor. Activities: whirlpools, fishing, hiking trails. Guest Services: coin laundry. Free Special Amenities: use of on-premises laundry facilities. (See ad p. 589.)

SAVE [items] / SOME UNITS FEE 🐾

EMERYVILLE pop. 10,080
- **Hotels & Restaurants map & index p. 254**

COURTYARD BY MARRIOTT EMERYVILLE

(510)652-8777 **31**

▼▼▼ Hotel $149-$249 Address: 5555 Shellmound St 94608 Location: I-80 exit Powell St, just e. Facility: 296 units. 11 stories, interior corridors. Parking: on-site (fee). Amenities: Some: high-speed Internet. Pool(s): heated indoor. Activities: whirlpool, exercise room. Guest Services: valet and coin laundry.

AAA Benefit: AAA hotel discounts of 5% or more.

ECO [items] / SOME UNITS

FOUR POINTS BY SHERATON-SAN FRANCISCO BAY BRIDGE (510)547-7888 **30**

FOUR POINTS BY SHERATON
Hotel
$109-$249

AAA Benefit: Members get up to 20% off, plus Starwood Preferred Guest® bonuses.

Address: 1603 Powell St 94608 Location: I-80 exit Powell St westbound; exit Shellmound St eastbound, just e. Facility: 153 units. 7 stories, interior corridors. Terms: cancellation fee imposed. Amenities: video games (fee), high-speed Internet. Pool(s): outdoor. Activities: whirlpool, exercise room. Guest Services: valet laundry. Free Special Amenities: newspaper and high-speed Internet.

SAVE ECO [items] CALL 🅼 [items]

HILTON GARDEN INN (510)658-9300 **28**

Hilton Garden Inn
Hotel
$189-$259

AAA Benefit: Unparalleled hospitality at a special Member rate.

Address: 1800 Powell St 94608 Location: I-80 exit Powell St, just w. Facility: 278 units. 12 stories, interior corridors. Parking: on-site (fee). Terms: 1-7 night minimum stay, cancellation fee imposed. Amenities: video games (fee), high-speed Internet. Activities: whirlpool, exercise room. Guest Services: valet and coin laundry, area transportation-within 3 mi. Free Special Amenities: local telephone calls and high-speed Internet.

SAVE ECO FEE [items] CALL 🅼 BIZ [items]

HYATT HOUSE EMERYVILLE/SAN FRANCISCO BAY AREA (510)601-5880 **29**

HYATT house
Extended Stay Hotel
$139-$259

AAA Benefit: Members save 10% or more everyday.

Address: 5800 Shellmound St 94608 Location: I-80 exit Powell St, just e. Facility: 234 units, some kitchens. 12 stories, interior corridors. Terms: cancellation fee imposed. Amenities: Some: high-speed Internet, safes. Pool(s): heated outdoor. Activities: whirlpool, exercise room. Guest Services: valet and coin laundry. Free Special Amenities: expanded continental breakfast and high-speed Internet.

SAVE [items] CALL 🅼 BIZ [items] / SOME UNITS FEE 🐾

WHERE TO EAT

PASTA POMODORO 510/923-1173

▼▼ Italian. Casual Dining. $8-$18 AAA Inspector Notes: Families are welcomed at this laid-back restaurant, which brings in plenty of loyal locals who enjoy its varied Italian favorites, including tempting pasta and chicken dishes. Bar: beer & wine. Address: 5614 Shellmound St, Suite 236 94608 Location: I-80 exit Powell St, just e, then just s on Christie Ave. [L] [D] CALL 🅼

P.F. CHANG'S CHINA BISTRO 510/879-0990 **23**

▼▼▼ Chinese. Casual Dining. $8-$22 AAA Inspector Notes: Trendy, upscale decor provides a pleasant backdrop for New Age Chinese dining. Appetizers, soups and salads are a meal by themselves. Vegetarian plates and sides, noodles, meins, chicken and meat dishes are created from exotic, fresh ingredients. Bar: full bar. Address: 5633 Bay St 94608 Location: I-80 exit Powell St, just e, then s on Shellmound St. [L] [D] CALL 🅼

EUREKA (B-1) pop. 27,191, elev. 44'
• Restaurants p. 107

The chief port between San Francisco and the Columbia River, Eureka is a lumbering, industrial and commercial city on Humboldt Bay. Ornate Victorian dwellings like the Carson Mansion at 2nd and M streets (not open to the public) reflect the days when lumber barons prospered. Old Town Eureka, running the length of First, Second and Third streets between C and M streets, is a historic district of renovated 19th-century buildings housing specialty shops, restaurants and art galleries.

Humboldt Bay yields catches of crab, salmon, shrimp, albacore and bottom fish. Fishing fleets dock just across the Samoa Bridge at Woodley Island Marina, where a copper-clad redwood statue of a fisherman commemorates fishermen lost at sea. Humboldt Bay Maritime Museum, adjacent to the Samoa Cookhouse, displays marine artifacts and early photographs of the area; phone (707) 444-9440.

Hundreds of pieces of folk art crafted from wood by Italian immigrant Romano Gabriel, a carpenter and gardener by trade, are on view in the Romano Gabriel Garden. The "garden" can be seen behind a windowed wall at 315 Second St. Gabriel spent nearly 3 decades during the mid-20th century fashioning the whimsical art, which was originally displayed in his front yard. The brightly painted pieces were made by hand from vegetable crates. Some of the art can be viewed as social commentary reflecting Gabriel's beliefs and attitudes.

Established in the late 1800s as a large lumber camp chowhouse, the Samoa Cookhouse Museum, 79 Cookhouse Ln., displays equipment, utensils and memorabilia from the lumber and logging industry in the restaurant's museum and dining rooms; phone (707) 442-1659.

Native grasslands, a Douglas fir reserve and a Mediterranean *allée* are among the gardens and themed areas at the Humboldt Botanical Garden, 7351 Tompkins Hill Rd. (on the College of the Redwoods campus); phone (707) 442-5139.

Humboldt County Convention and Visitors Bureau: 1034 Second St., Eureka, CA 95501. **Phone:** (707) 443-5097 or (800) 346-3482.

Self-guiding tours: Information about 100 vintage residences is available from the Greater Eureka Chamber of Commerce, 2112 Broadway, Eureka, CA 95501-2189; phone (707) 442-3738 or (800) 356-6381.

BLUE OX MILLWORKS SCHOOL AND HISTORIC PARK is at 1 X St., 4 blks. n. of US 101. In this Victorian millwork shop visitors can learn about the craftsmanship of the Victorian era as they watch products being made on 19th-century equipment. The tour includes a full-production wood shop, a blacksmith shop, ceramics studio, print shop, recreated logging skid camp, rose garden, aviary and farm.

Visitors may watch the artisans at work via a 60- to 90-minute self-guiding tour. Casual dress and low-heeled shoes are advised. **Hours:** Mon.-Fri. 9-5, Sat. 9-1, May-Nov.; Mon.-Fri. 9-5, rest of year. **Cost:** $7.50; $6.50 (ages 65+); $3.50 (ages 6-12). **Phone:** (707) 444-3437 or (800) 248-4259.

CLARKE HISTORICAL MUSEUM, 240 E St., displays Native American artifacts, antique weapons and exhibits about regional and natural history. The museum also has a significant collection of northwestern California Native American basketry, ceremonial regalia and stone artifacts from the Yurok, Karuk, Hupa and Wiyot tribes. **Time:** Allow 1 hour minimum. **Hours:** Wed.-Sat. 11-4. Closed Jan. 1, Thanksgiving and Christmas. **Cost:** $3; $5 (family). **Phone:** (707) 443-1947.

DISCOVERY MUSEUM is at 501 Third St. at jct. F St. This children's museum features hands-on exhibits designed to promote an understanding of science, art and technological and cultural concepts. A weather station, a 20-foot-tall ship, a child-sized grocery store and an animation station are some of the themed areas. **Time:** Allow 30 minutes minimum. **Hours:** Tues.-Sat. 10-4, Sun. noon-4. **Cost:** $4; free (ages 0-24 months). **Phone:** (707) 443-9694.

FORT HUMBOLDT STATE HISTORIC PARK is off US 101 via Highland Ave. to 3431 Fort Ave. This site on a bluff preserves what remains of 1853 Fort Humboldt. Of the fort's original 14 structures, only the clapboard hospital is left. A museum inside describes the fort's history and North Coast Indian culture. Ulysses S. Grant was stationed at the fort 1853-54.

An adjacent museum displays the massive equipment required to move redwood logs, including locomotives and large winches called steam donkeys. **Tours:** Guided tours are available. **Time:** Allow 30 minutes minimum. **Hours:** Park daily 8-5. Museum daily 8-4:30. Phone ahead to confirm schedule. **Cost:** Free. **Phone:** (707) 445-6567.

HUMBOLDT BAY HARBOR CRUISE departs from the foot of C St. The MV *Madaket,* an original 1910 ferry, takes visitors on a 75-minute narrated history cruise around Humboldt Bay. Bring a sweater or jacket. Cocktail cruises also are available. **Hours:** Harbor cruise departs Wed.-Sat. at 1, 2:30 and 4, Sun.-Tues. at 1 and 2:30, May-Oct. **Cost:** Harbor cruise $18; $16 (ages 13-17 and 55+); $10 (ages 5-12). **Phone:** (707) 445-1910.

THE MORRIS GRAVES MUSEUM OF ART is at 636 F St. Named for noted 20th-century Northwest artist and Humboldt County resident Morris Graves, the museum features many of Graves' works in its seven galleries. Also included are a sculpture garden and changing exhibits. **Hours:** Wed.-Sun. noon-5. Closed major holidays. **Cost:** $4. **Phone:** (707) 442-0278.

SEQUOIA PARK ZOO is at 3414 W St. In addition to the zoo's bear grotto, walk-through aviary and barnyard petting zoo, the park contains a 52-acre grove of redwoods more than a century old, a formal flower garden, an interpretive center, a duck pond and a playground.

Hours: Park open daily 10-5, Memorial Day-Labor Day; Tues.-Sun. 10-5, rest of year. **Cost:** $6; $5 (ages 60+ and military with ID); $4 (ages 3-12). Admission is discounted on Wed. **Phone:** (707) 441-4263.

ABIGAIL'S ELEGANT VICTORIAN MANSION HISTORIC LODGING   707/444-3144

 Historic Hotel $89-$125 **Address:** 1406 C St 95501 **Location:** 0.5 mi e of jct US 101; at 14th St. Located in a quiet residential area. **Facility:** An 1878 national landmark, this symbol of opulence, grace and grandeur is breathtakingly authentic with all the nostalgic trimmings of a century ago. 4 units. 2 stories (no elevator), interior corridors. **Parking:** on-site and street. **Terms:** 10 day cancellation notice-fee imposed. **Guest Services:** complimentary laundry.

AMERICAS BEST VALUE INN & SUITES   (707)443-9751

Motel
$55-$150

Address: 129 4th St 95501 **Location:** On US 101 southbound; corner of C St. **Facility:** 25 units. 2 stories (no elevator), exterior corridors. **Terms:** 2 night minimum stay, cancellation fee imposed.
Free Special Amenities: continental breakfast and local telephone calls.

▼ *See AAA listing p. 105* ▼

BEST WESTERN PLUS BAYSHORE INN
(707)268-8005

Hotel
$80-$230

Best Western PLUS

AAA Benefit: Members save up to 20%, plus 10% bonus points with Best Western Rewards®.

Address: 3500 Broadway 95503 **Location:** US 101; south end of town. Adjacent to Bayshore Mall. **Facility:** 129 units, some two bedrooms and kitchens. 3 stories, exterior corridors. **Amenities:** video games (fee). *Some:* high-speed Internet. **Dining:** 2 restaurants. **Pool(s):** heated indoor/outdoor. **Activities:** sauna, whirlpool, exercise room. **Guest Services:** valet and coin laundry. **Free Special Amenities:** full breakfast and high-speed Internet. *(See ad p. 104.)*

BEST WESTERN PLUS HUMBOLDT BAY INN
(707)443-2234

Motel
$85-$205

Best Western PLUS

AAA Benefit: Members save up to 20%, plus 10% bonus points with Best Western Rewards®.

Address: 232 W 5th St 95501 **Location:** On US 101. **Facility:** 108 units. 2 stories (no elevator), exterior corridors. **Amenities:** *Some:* high-speed Internet, safes. **Pool(s):** heated indoor/outdoor. **Activities:** whirlpool, exercise room. **Guest Services:** valet and coin laundry, area transportation-local restaurants. **Free Special Amenities:** expanded continental breakfast and high-speed Internet. *(See ad p. 106.)*

CARTER HOUSE INNS
(707)444-8062

 Country Inn $159-$595 **Address:** 301 L St 95501 **Location:** Just w of US 101 S. **Facility:** Guest units are located in the main inn as well as in a separate five-unit house and three-unit cottage; a one-unit cottage is across the street. 32 units. 3 stories, interior corridors. **Terms:** 3 day cancellation notice-fee imposed. **Dining:** 301 At Carter House Inns, see separate listing. **Activities:** *Fee:* massage. **Guest Services:** valet laundry.

CLARION HOTEL
(707)442-3261

Hotel
$100-$160

Address: 2223 4th St 95501 **Location:** US 101 exit V St northbound; exit W St southbound. **Facility:** 65 units. 2-3 stories, interior/exterior corridors. **Terms:** cancellation fee imposed. **Amenities:** safes. **Pool(s):** heated indoor. **Activities:** exercise room. **Guest Services:** valet and coin laundry. **Free Special Amenities:** expanded continental breakfast and high-speed Internet.

COMFORT INN EUREKA
(707)444-2019

Hotel
$99-$199

Address: 4260 Broadway 95503 **Location:** On US 101; south end of town. **Facility:** 48 units. 2 stories (no elevator), interior corridors. **Amenities:** high-speed Internet. **Pool(s):** heated indoor. **Activities:** whirlpool, exercise room. **Free Special Amenities:** full breakfast and high-speed Internet.

CORNELIUS DALY INN BED & BREAKFAST
(707)445-3638

Historic Bed & Breakfast $130-$225 **Address:** 1125 H St 95501 **Location:** 0.3 mi e of jct US 101; between 11th and 12th sts. Located in a residential area. **Facility:** This exquisite Colonial Revival mansion was built in 1905 and features lovely Victorian gardens and a unique, third-floor Christmas ballroom. Please call or e-mail the property for room availability. 5 units. 2 stories (no elevator), interior corridors. *Bath:* some shared. **Parking:** on-site and street. **Terms:** check-in 4 pm, 7 day cancellation notice-fee imposed.

EUREKA SUPER 8
(707)443-3193

Motel
$65-$189

Address: 1304 4th St 95501 **Location:** On US 101 southbound; at N St. **Facility:** 50 units, some two bedrooms and kitchens. 2 stories (no elevator), interior/exterior corridors. **Pool(s):** heated indoor. **Activities:** sauna, whirlpool. **Free Special Amenities:** continental breakfast and high-speed Internet.

EUREKA TOWN HOUSE MOTEL
(707)443-4536

Motel
$55-$150

Address: 933 4th St 95501 **Location:** On US 101 southbound; corner of K St. **Facility:** 20 units. 2 stories (no elevator), exterior corridors. **Amenities:** high-speed Internet. **Free Special Amenities:** local telephone calls and high-speed Internet.

EUREKA TRAVELODGE
(707)443-6345

Motel $80-$130 **Address:** 4 4th St 95501 **Location:** On US 101; corner of 4th and B sts. **Facility:** 44 units. 2 stories (no elevator), exterior corridors.

QUALITY INN EUREKA
707/443-1601

Motel
Rates not provided

Address: 1209 4th St 95501 **Location:** On US 101 southbound; between M and N sts. **Facility:** 59 units. 2 stories (no elevator), exterior corridors. **Amenities:** *Some:* high-speed Internet. **Pool(s):** heated outdoor. **Activities:** sauna, whirlpool. **Free Special Amenities:** expanded continental breakfast and high-speed Internet.

RED LION HOTEL EUREKA
(707)445-0844

Hotel
$99-$189

Address: 1929 4th St 95501 **Location:** On US 101 southbound; between T and V sts. **Facility:** 175 units. 3 stories, interior corridors. **Terms:** cancellation fee imposed. **Pool(s):** heated outdoor. **Activities:** whirlpool, exercise room. **Guest Services:** valet laundry. **Free Special Amenities:** local telephone calls and high-speed Internet.

RODEWAY INN EUREKA
(707)444-0401

Motel
$70-$200

Address: 2014 4th St 95501 **Location:** On US 101 southbound; corner of V St. **Facility:** 30 units. 2 stories (no elevator), exterior corridors. **Terms:** check-in 4 pm, cancellation fee imposed.

SCOTTFEILD EXECUTIVE HOTELS
707/443-2206

Hotel
Rates not provided

Address: 270 5th St 95501 **Location:** Between C and D sts. **Facility:** 41 units. 2 stories, interior corridors. **Guest Services:** coin laundry. **Free Special Amenities:** expanded continental breakfast and high-speed Internet.

▼ See AAA listing p. 105 ▼

EUREKA

Best Western

PLUS

HumboldtBayInn

Eureka's FUN place to stay...

Ride to dinner in our stretch Limousine...for free!

~108 Beautiful Guest Rooms and Suites
~All Rooms have 42" LCD T.V.'s
~Restaurant with Room Service
~Deluxe Continental Breakfast
~Area's Finest Fitness/Cardio Center
~In/Outdoor 85° Pool, Spa & Rec. Area
~Free Limousine Ride 6pm-10pm (Mon-Fri)
~Guest Laundry/Valet
~Free! WI-FI Internet

BEST WESTERN PLUS

HumboldtBayInn
707.443.2234   800.521.6996

232 W. 5th. St. Eureka, CA 95501
5th St. @ Broadway (U.S. 101)
www.humboldtbayinn.com

WHERE TO EAT

301 AT CARTER HOUSE INNS   707/444-8062

▼▼▼ American. Fine Dining. $24-$35 **AAA Inspector Notes:** The intimate corner location of this quaint inn offers large windows to watch the passing action. Seasonal specials show creativity. **Bar:** full bar. **Reservations:** suggested. **Address:** 301 L St 95501 **Location:** Just w of US 101 S; in Carter House Inns. **Parking:** street only.

[D] [⚡]

THE BANANA HUT HAWAIIAN BBQ   707/444-3447

▼▼ Hawaiian. Casual Dining. $7-$18 **AAA Inspector Notes:** The sky always is blue and the sun always shining with a slight breeze in the air at this casual spot reminiscent of Hawaii. Hawaiian music plays in the background while servers in aloha outfits serve pina coladas and home-style dishes. Try their ribs, Kahlua pork and teriyaki chicken. The owner always is around making sure the island hospitality is flowing. **Bar:** beer & wine. **Address:** 621 5th St 95501 **Location:** Between G and H sts. **Parking:** street only.

[L] [D] [⚡]

CAFE MARINA   707/443-2233

▼▼▼▼
▼▼
Seafood
Casual Dining
$9-$20

AAA Inspector Notes: The menu is built around fresh local seafood. The casual dining room, as well as the seasonal patio, overlooks the marina. **Bar:** full bar. **Address:** 601 Startare Dr 95501 **Location:** On Woodley Island; w on SR 255 from jct US 101.

[B] [L] [D] CALL [♿M] [⚡]

CAFE NOONER   707/443-4663

▼▼ International. Casual Dining. $7-$17 **AAA Inspector Notes:** This modest little restaurant serves an interesting marriage of Louisiana- and Greek-flavored dishes. Diners get big flavors for reasonable prices. For dessert, try the homemade pecan baklava topped with whipped cream—it is crunchy and chewy. **Bar:** beer & wine. **Address:** 409 Opera Alley 95501 **Location:** Just w of jct US 101; in Old Town. **Parking:** street only. [L] [⚡]

LOST COAST BREWERY AND CAFE   707/445-4480

▼▼ American. Casual Dining. $6-$23 **AAA Inspector Notes:** To locate this one, just look for the bright yellow building and watch out for the spider upon entering. Casual eatery with great housemade beers, this café specializes in basic foods such as pasta, sandwiches, burgers, salads and appetizers. **Bar:** beer & wine. **Address:** 617 4th St 95501 **Location:** US 101 exit 4th St; between H and G sts; downtown. [L] [D] [⚡]

PORTER STREET BBQ   707/443-1700

▼ Barbecue. Casual Dining. $4-$18 **AAA Inspector Notes:** This casual joint offers hearty servings of such barbecue specialties as tri-tip, pork ribs or pulled pork. If making a decision on what to order is hard, ask for a taste or get the combo plate. There is a large warmer full of barbecue sauce at the condiment table. **Address:** 605 Broadway St 95501 **Location:** At W 6th St. [L] [D] [⚡]

RITA'S MARGARITAS & MEXICAN GRILL   707/268-0700

▼▼ Mexican. Casual Dining. $4-$12 **AAA Inspector Notes:** Hearty servings ensure you will not leave hungry. **Bar:** beer & wine. **Address:** 107 Wabash Ave 95501 **Location:** Between B and C sts.

[L] [D] [⚡]

THE SEA GRILL   707/443-7187

▼▼ Seafood. Casual Dining. $7-$29 **AAA Inspector Notes:** In the main downtown area, this established favorite specializes in seafood, steak and pasta. **Bar:** full bar. **Reservations:** suggested. **Address:** 316 E St 95501 **Location:** Just w of jct US 101; in Old Town. [L] [⚡]

STARRS HAMBURGERS   707/445-2061

▼ American. Quick Serve. $4-$7 **AAA Inspector Notes:** Grass-fed, hormone-free beef burgers are juicy, with good beef flavor, and their fresh-cut onion rings have just the right amount of batter. Also on the menu are curry chicken sandwich and salad. **Address:** 2009 Harrison Ave 95501 **Location:** Between Munson and 23rd sts. **Parking:** street only. [L] [⚡]

FAIRFAX   pop. 7,441
• Part of San Francisco area — see map p. 342

CAFE LOTUS   415/457-7836

▼▼ ▼▼ Indian. Casual Dining. $6-$17 **AAA Inspector Notes:** This casual, laid-back cafe serves organic Indian food. Bhel puri is addictive with tasty morsels of puffed rice, yogurt and spices. Try the not-too-spicy bengan bharta (eggplant in tomatoes and onion) and the crunchy and chewy naan (leavened bread). **Bar:** beer & wine. **Address:** 1912 Sir Francis Drake Blvd 94930 **Location:** US 101 exit 450B (Sir Francis Drake Blvd), toward town. **Parking:** street only.

[L] [D]

FAIRFIELD   (B-9) pop. 105,321, elev. 15'
• Hotels p. 108 • Restaurants p. 108

Fairfield, founded in 1903, is located southeast of the Vaca Mountains. The Jimmy Doolittle Air and Space Museum at Travis Air Force Base features aircraft, photographs, uniforms and memorabilia pertaining to the base's history and its role in providing troop airlift to the Pacific region. Public access to the base is limited due to security restrictions; phone (707) 424-5605 in advance for information about base access for visitors.

Fairfield-Suisun Chamber of Commerce: 1111 Webster St., Fairfield, CA 94533. **Phone:** (707) 425-4625.

Shopping areas: JCPenney, Macy's and Sears are the anchor stores at Westfield Solano, off I-80 exit 45 at Travis Boulevard and Pennsylvania Avenue.

ANHEUSER-BUSCH FAIRFIELD BREWERY TOUR, 3101 Busch Dr., details the brewing process via a 1-hour guided tour of the brewery. Two-hour behind-the-scenes Beermaster tours also are available.

Note: Closed-toed shoes are required for Beermaster tours. **Hours:** General tours are given Mon.-Sat. on the hour 10-4, June-Aug.; Tues.-Sat. on the hour 10-4, rest of year. Beermaster tours are given Mon.-Fri. at 10 and 2, Sat. at 10, noon and 2, June-Aug.; Tues.-Sat. at 10 and 2, rest of year.

Cost: General tours free. Beermaster tours $25; $10 (ages 13-20). Under 21 are not permitted to schedule Beermaster tours or purchase beer. Reservations are required for Beermaster tours. **Phone:** (707) 429-7595.

JELLY BELLY FACTORY TOUR is offered at the Jelly Belly Candy Company at 1 Jelly Belly Ln., off N. Watney Way. The company offers 40-minute guided tours of its jelly bean-making facilities. Visitors can see the process, which includes pouring and curing the jelly bean centers, coating the centers with a candy shell, and polishing and seasoning the jelly beans before they are packaged.

Time: Allow 30 minutes minimum. **Hours:** Tours are given daily 9-4. Since production takes place Mon.-Fri., tours on Sat.-Sun. include a video presentation. Phone ahead to confirm special events. Closed Jan. 1, Easter, Thanksgiving and Christmas. **Cost:** Free. **Phone:** (707) 428-2838 or (800) 953-5592.

BEST WESTERN CORDELIA INN
(707)864-2029

Hotel
$79-$99

AAA Benefit: Members save up to 20%, plus 10% bonus points with Best Western Rewards®.

Address: 4373 Central Pl 94534 **Location:** I-80 exit 41 (Suisun Valley Rd), just e. Located in a quiet area. **Facility:** 60 units. 2 stories (no elevator), exterior corridors. **Amenities:** high-speed Internet. **Pool(s):** outdoor. **Activities:** whirlpool. **Guest Services:** coin laundry. **Free Special Amenities: local telephone calls and high-speed Internet.**

COMFORT INN
(707)864-1446

Hotel
$59-$179

Address: 4441 Central Pl 94534 **Location:** I-80 exit 41 (Suisun Valley Rd), just e. **Facility:** 57 units. 3 stories, interior/exterior corridors. **Terms:** check-in 4 pm, cancellation fee imposed. **Pool(s):** heated outdoor. **Activities:** exercise room. **Guest Services:** valet and coin laundry. **Free Special Amenities: expanded continental breakfast and high-speed Internet.**

/SOME UNITS FEE 🛏 FEE 🐾

COURTYARD BY MARRIOTT FAIRFIELD NAPA VALLEY AREA
(707)422-4111

Hotel
$89-$169

AAA Benefit: AAA hotel discounts of 5% or more.

Address: 1350 Holiday Ln 94534 **Location:** I-80 exit Travis Blvd W, 0.3 mi nw. **Facility:** 137 units. 4 stories, interior corridors. **Pool(s):** heated outdoor. **Activities:** exercise room, spa. **Guest Services:** valet and coin laundry. **Free Special Amenities: early check-in/late check-out and manager's reception.**

EXTENDED STAYAMERICA-FAIRFIELD-NAPA VALLEY
(707)438-0932

Extended Stay Hotel $94-$109 **Address:** 1019 Oliver Rd 94534 **Location:** I-80 exit Texas St, just w. **Facility:** 104 efficiencies. 3 stories, interior corridors. **Amenities:** high-speed Internet (fee). **Guest Services:** coin laundry.

CALL 🅜 🤟 🏠 🛏 🖼 🖳 /SOME UNITS FEE 🐾

FAIRFIELD INN & SUITES NAPA VALLEY AREA
(707)864-6672

Hotel $89-$109 **Address:** 315 Pittman Rd 94534 **Location:** I-80 exit 41 (Suisun Valley Rd), just e. **Facility:** 67 units. 4 stories, interior corridors. **Amenities:** high-speed Internet. **Pool(s):** heated indoor. **Activities:** whirlpool, exercise room. **Guest Services:** valet and coin laundry.

AAA Benefit: AAA hotel discounts of 5% or more.

HILTON GARDEN INN FAIRFIELD
(707)426-6900

Hotel $139-$199 **Address:** 2200 Gateway Ct 94533 **Location:** I-80 exit Travis Blvd, just e. **Facility:** 150 units. 4 stories, interior corridors. **Terms:** 1-7 night minimum stay, cancellation fee imposed. **Amenities:** high-speed Internet. **Pool(s):** heated outdoor. **Activities:** whirlpool, exercise room. **Guest Services:** valet and coin laundry.

AAA Benefit: Unparalleled hospitality at a special Member rate.

HOMEWOOD SUITES FAIRFIELD-NAPA VALLEY AREA
(707)863-0300

Extended Stay Hotel $129-$189 **Address:** 4755 Business Center Dr 94534 **Location:** I-80 exit Green Valley Rd/Suisun Valley Rd, n on Green Valley Rd, then just e. **Facility:** 85 efficiencies, some two bedrooms. 4 stories, interior corridors. **Terms:** check-in 4 pm, 1-7 night minimum stay, cancellation fee imposed. **Amenities:** high-speed Internet. **Pool(s):** heated indoor. **Activities:** whirlpool, sports court, exercise room. **Guest Services:** complimentary and valet laundry.

AAA Benefit: Contemporary luxury at a special Member rate.

CALL 🅜 🤟 BIZ 🏠 🖼 🛏 🖳 /SOME UNITS FEE 🐾

QUALITY INN & SUITES
(707)864-3797

Hotel
$69-$149

Address: 316 Pittman Rd 94534 **Location:** I-80 exit 41 (Suisun Valley Rd), just e. **Facility:** 60 units. 3 stories, interior corridors. **Amenities:** high-speed Internet. **Pool(s):** heated outdoor. **Activities:** whirlpool, exercise room. **Guest Services:** valet laundry. *(See ad p. 239.)*

STAYBRIDGE SUITES FAIRFIELD-NAPA VALLEY AREA
707/863-0900

Extended Stay Hotel. Rates not provided. **Address:** 4775 Business Center Dr 94534 **Location:** I-80 exit Green Valley Rd/Suisun Valley Rd, n on Green Valley Rd, then just e. **Facility:** 82 efficiencies, some two bedrooms. 3 stories, interior corridors. **Terms:** check-in 4 pm. **Amenities:** high-speed Internet. **Pool(s):** heated indoor. **Activities:** whirlpool, exercise room. **Guest Services:** valet and coin laundry.

CALL 🅜 🤟 BIZ 🏠 🖼 🛏 🖳 /SOME UNITS FEE 🐾

TOWN HOUSE INN
(707)422-1333

Motel
$55-$85

Address: 2170 N Texas St 94533 **Location:** I-80 exit Air Base Pkwy, 1.2 mi e, then 0.3 mi s. **Facility:** 44 units. 2 stories, exterior corridors. **Pool(s):** outdoor. **Guest Services:** coin laundry. **Free Special Amenities: local telephone calls and high-speed Internet.**

WHERE TO EAT

FRESH CHOICE
707/429-2560

American. Cafeteria. $9-$16 **AAA Inspector Notes:** The salad bar of salad bars, the casual restaurant invites patrons to make their own or try one of the already prepared varieties. Other items include freshly baked breads, pizza and soup, as well as make-your-own sundaes for dessert. **Bar:** beer & wine. **Address:** 1501 Travis Blvd 94533 **Location:** I-80 exit Travis Blvd, just e; in Westfield Mall.

ROUND TABLE PIZZA

Pizza. Casual Dining. $7-$28 **AAA Inspector Notes:** This casual, family-oriented pizza place features high-quality ingredients and dough rolled fresh daily. Distinctive specialty pizzas are piled high with toppings. **Bar:** beer & wine.

For additional information, visit AAA.com

LOCATIONS:
Address: 5085 Business Center Dr, Suite 102 94534 **Location:** I-80 exit Green Valley Rd N, just n. **Phone:** 707/207-0378

Address: 3336-M N Texas St 94533 **Location:** I-80 exit N Texas St, just e. **Phone:** 707/426-6202

FAIR OAKS pop. 30,912
• Hotels & Restaurants map & index p. 314

FINS MARKET & GRILL   916/967-0954 (78)

W W Seafood. Casual Dining. $8-$22 **AAA Inspector Notes:** A variety of simply prepared charbroiled seafood entrées and seafood sandwiches are offered at this neighborhood favorite located in the corner of the shopping center. **Bar:** beer & wine. **Address:** 8525 Madison Ave 95628 **Location:** I-80 exit Madison Ave, 6.1 mi e; jct Kenneth Ave; in Fair Oaks Pointe Shopping Center.

L D CALL M

MIKUNI JAPANESE RESTAURANT & SUSHI BAR
                                   916/961-2112

W W Japanese Sushi. Casual Dining. $10-$19 **AAA Inspector Notes:** Sit at the large sushi bar and watch the many variety of rolls being prepared at this busy restaurant-the original Mikuni's. Lunch combinations, Mikuni boxes, seafood plates, sushi and sashimi entrées also are offered. **Bar:** full bar. **Address:** 4323 Hazel Ave 95628 **Location:** US 50 exit Hazel Ave, 0.9 mi n; just s of jct Winding Way; in Hazel Ridge Plaza. D CALL M

FALL RIVER MILLS (B-3) pop. 573, elev. 3,291'

FORT CROOK MUSEUM, Fort Crook Ave., features Native American artifacts, photographs and items from the late 1800s to the early 1900s, a dugout canoe and a 360-degree view. Adjacent are a turn-of-the-20th-century schoolhouse, a barn housing a 1911 Wichita Flat-Bed Motorstage, an 1860 log cabin, a jailhouse, a working blacksmith shop, a historical round barn, the Fort Crook cabin and the James Showcase building. Genealogical records are available. **Time:** Allow 30 minutes minimum. **Hours:** Tues.-Sun. noon-4, May-Oct. **Cost:** Donations. **Phone:** (530) 336-5110.

HI-MONT MOTEL   530/336-5541

Motel
$69-$104

Address: 43021 Bridge St 96028 **Location:** 0.4 mi sw on SR 299; jct SR 299 E and Bridge St. Across from Fort Crook Museum. **Facility:** 31 units, some kitchens. 2 stories (no elevator), exterior corridors. **Terms:** cancellation fee imposed. **Free Special Amenities:** local telephone calls and high-speed Internet.

SAVE ⓘ 🛜 ✕ 🅗 📷 💻 / SOME UNITS FEE 🐾

FELTON (G-2) pop. 4,057, elev. 286'
• Hotels & Restaurants map & index p. 492

One of the tallest covered bridges in the United States—and the only one made of redwood—can be found in Felton. The city lies on a scenic stretch of SR 9 that extends from Los Gatos to Santa Cruz.

Just east of the city on SR 9 is Henry Cowell Redwoods State Park (see Recreation Areas Chart), where an easy .75-mile hike along Redwood Grove Trail takes visitors around a group of these giant trees. The trail can be accessed from the park's nature center. Phone the park at (831) 335-4598 for additional information.

In addition to its standard excursions, Roaring Camp Railroads (see attraction listing) also offers seasonal trips, including the 🚂 Children's Ghost Train. This evening journey through a forest, held just before Halloween, includes a narration of Washington Irving's classic short story "The Legend of Sleepy Hollow."

ROARING CAMP STEAM TRAIN, .5 mi. s.e. on Graham Hill Rd., runs south from Roaring Camp Station through the redwoods of the Santa Cruz Mountains. Late 19th- and early 20th-century steam locomotives pull open-air and covered passenger cars along a 6-mile, 75-minute round-trip route as the conductor recounts area history. A barbecue lunch is offered on summer weekends.

Hours: Departures daily at 11, 12:30 and 2 (also Sat.-Sun. at 3:30), mid-June to mid-Aug.; Mon.-Fri. at 11, Sat.-Sun. at 11, 12:30 and 2, Apr. 1 to mid-June and mid-Aug. through Oct. 31; schedule varies rest of year. Closed Christmas. Phone ahead to confirm schedule. **Cost:** $24; $17 (ages 2-12); free (ages 0-1 on parent's lap). **Parking:** $8 per private vehicle. **Phone:** (831) 335-4400 for recorded information or (831) 335-4484.

Santa Cruz Beach Train departs Roaring Camp Station for a 3-hour round-trip excursion to the Santa Cruz Beach Boardwalk (see attraction listing in Santa Cruz p. 490). Vintage passenger coaches and open-air excursion cars travel through Henry Cowell Redwoods State Park and along the San Lorenzo River gorge. Conductors point out scenic highlights and provide information about the history of the railway line, which was established in 1875.

Hours: Departures daily at 10:15 and 2:15, mid-June to mid-Aug.; Sat.-Sun. at 10:15 and 2:15, late May to mid-June and mid-Aug. to late Sept. Phone ahead to confirm schedule. **Cost:** $26; $20 (ages 2-12); free (ages 0-1 on parent's lap). **Parking:** $8 per private vehicle. **Phone:** (831) 335-4400 for recorded information or (831) 335-4484.

FERN RIVER RESORT   831/335-4412 (33)

Cottage
$69-$198

Address: 5250 Hwy 9 95018 **Location:** On SR 9, 1 mi s; across river from Henry Cowell State Park. **Facility:** 14 cottages. 1 story, exterior corridors. Bath: shower only. **Terms:** 2-4 night minimum stay - seasonal and/or weekends, 30 day cancellation notice-fee imposed. **Activities:** whirlpool, fishing, hiking trails, playground, horseshoes. **Free Special Amenities:** high-speed Internet and children's activities.

SAVE ⓘ 🛜 ✕ 🅺 🅩 🅗 📷 💻

WHERE TO EAT

ROUND TABLE PIZZA   831/335-5344

W Pizza. Casual Dining. $7-$28 **AAA Inspector Notes:** This casual, family-oriented pizza place features high-quality ingredients and dough rolled fresh daily. Distinctive specialty pizzas are piled high with toppings. **Bar:** beer & wine. **Address:** 6267 Graham Hill Rd 95018 **Location:** Just e of Mt Hermon Rd. L D CALL M

FERNDALE (C-1) pop. 1,371, elev. 30'

Ferndale, in the lower Eel River Valley along the northern California coast, was settled in 1852 by Vermonters Seth and Stephen Shaw, but it was Danish pioneers who established the town's dairying industry in the 1870s, producing the butter that Ferndale has been identified with ever since.

The ornate Victorian houses known as "butterfat palaces," built by Danish and Portuguese dairymen, reflect the town's past and present. In fact, due to preservation efforts the entire town is designated a state historical landmark. Fern Cottage, 3 miles west on Ocean Avenue, is an 1866 farmhouse containing 19th-century items; phone (707) 786-4835.

South of town via Bluff Street is Russ Park, which features 3 miles of nature trails looping through a 110-acre tract of coastal forest. The park is a popular spot for bird-watchers.

The Ferndale Repertory Theatre, 447 Main St., offers several productions each year, including contemporary American, musical and classic plays; phone (707) 786-5483 for schedule information, (800) 838-3006 for the box office.

Ferndale Chamber of Commerce: P.O. Box 325, Ferndale, CA 95536-0325. **Phone:** (707) 786-4477.

Self-guiding tours: A souvenir newspaper with information about attractions, events, and walking and driving tours can be obtained at various shops on Main Street.

FERNDALE MUSEUM, Third and Shaw sts., features Victorian room settings; a smithy; a working seismograph; farm, dairy and logging equipment; microfilmed newspapers dating from 1878; and cemetery records. Genealogy information also is available. **Hours:** Tues.-Sat. 11-4, Sun. 1-4, June-Sept.; Wed.-Sat. 11-4, Sun. 1-4, Feb.-May and Oct.-Dec. **Cost:** $1; 50c (ages 6-16). **Phone:** (707) 786-4466.

SHAW HOUSE INN
707/786-9958

▼▼▼▼ Historic Bed & Breakfast $125-$275 **Address:** 703 Main St 95536 **Location:** Center. **Facility:** Said to have once been the residence of the city's founder, this 1854 Carpenter Gothic house is situated on an acre of landscaped grounds. 8 units. 2 stories (no elevator), interior/exterior corridors. **Terms:** check-in 4 pm, 15 day cancellation notice-fee imposed. **Activities:** horseshoes.

VICTORIAN INN
(707)786-4949

▼▼▼▼ Historic Country Inn $115-$295

Address: 400 Ocean Ave 95536 **Location:** Corner of Main St; center. **Facility:** This lovely historic inn is located in downtown Ferndale. 13 units, some kitchens. 2 stories (no elevator), interior corridors. **Parking:** street only. **Terms:** 7 day cancellation notice. **Dining:** VI Restaurant, see separate listing. **Free Special Amenities:** full breakfast and high-speed Internet.

VI RESTAURANT
707/786-4950

▼▼ ▼ American. Casual Dining. $10-$36 **AAA Inspector Notes:** Housed in a Victorian inn, this restaurant's 20-foot ceilings offer an elegant touch. Guests will think they are on a tropical island while sipping one of the fun cocktails, yet local wines paired with contemporary American foods lend a decidedly Northern California touch. Try the braised antelope short ribs served with pappardelle. Servers are friendly and knowledgeable. **Bar:** full bar. **Address:** 400 Ocean Ave 95536 **Location:** Corner of Main St; center; in Victorian Inn. **Parking:** street only. B L D

FIREBAUGH pop. 7,549

BEST WESTERN APRICOT INN
(559)659-1444

▼▼▼ Motel $80-$110

AAA Benefit: Members save up to 20%, plus 10% bonus points with Best Western Rewards®.

Address: 46290 W Panoche Rd 93622 **Location:** I-5 exit W Panoche Rd, just w. **Facility:** 74 units. 2 stories (no elevator), exterior corridors. **Terms:** 2 night minimum stay - seasonal and/or weekends. **Amenities:** high-speed Internet, safes (fee). **Pool(s):** outdoor. **Guest Services:** coin laundry. **Free Special Amenities:** local telephone calls and high-speed Internet.

FISH CAMP (F-4) pop. 59, elev. 4,990'

- Attractions map p. 581
- Hotels & Restaurants map & index p. 584
- Part of Yosemite National Park area — see map p. 578

YOSEMITE MOUNTAIN SUGAR PINE RAILROAD is 2 mi. s. on SR 41. The scenic narrow-gauge railroad offers a 1-hour narrated tour through the Sierra National Forest aboard railcars pulled by restored vintage Shay steam locomotives or gas-powered Jenny railcars. The Moonlight Special excursion features a barbecue dinner and entertainment.

Hours: The Logger Steam Train runs daily mid-Apr. through Oct. 31 and some fall and winter holidays (weather permitting); departure times vary. Jenny railcars operate daily every half-hour 9:30-3:30, May-Aug.; 9:30-3, in Sept.; 9:30-2:30, in Apr.; 10-2:30, late Mar.-Mar. 31; 10-2, in Oct.; phone for limited winter schedule. Jenny railcar schedule varies when steam train is in operation. Moonlight Special runs Wed. and Sat. evenings during the summer.

Cost: Steam train $19; $9.50 (ages 3-12). Railcars $16; $8 (ages 3-12). Moonlight Special $49; $24.50 (ages 3-12). Reservations are recommended for the Moonlight Special. **Phone:** (559) 683-7273.

THE COTTAGES AT TENAYA LODGE
(559)683-6555 [15]

▼▼▼▼ Hotel $149-$425

Address: 1122 Hwy 41 93623 **Location:** 2 mi from Yosemite National Park South Gate. **Facility:** 53 units. 2 stories, exterior corridors. **Terms:** 7 day cancellation notice-fee imposed. **Amenities:** video games (fee), safes. **Pool(s):** heated indoor. **Activities:** whirlpool, racquetball court, cross country skiing, hiking trails. **Guest Services:** coin laundry. **Free Special Amenities:** full breakfast and newspaper.

(See map & index p. 584.)

THE NARROW GAUGE INN   (559)683-7720   **17**
Hotel $79-$250 **Address:** 48571 Hwy 41 93623 **Location:** 4 mi from Yosemite National Park South Gate. **Facility:** 26 units. 2 stories (no elevator), exterior corridors. **Terms:** 2 night minimum stay - seasonal and/or weekends, 4 day cancellation notice-fee imposed. **Dining:** restaurant, see separate listing. **Pool(s):** outdoor. **Activities:** whirlpool, hiking trails.

TENAYA LODGE AT YOSEMITE   (559)683-6555   **16**
Hotel
$129-$425
Address: 1122 Hwy 41 93623 **Location:** 2 mi from Yosemite National Park South Gate. **Facility:** On landscaped grounds surrounded by a national forest, the lodge is convenient to many seasonal activity areas. A comprehensive "green" program is adopted here. 244 units. 3-4 stories, interior corridors. **Terms:** 7 day cancellation notice-fee imposed. **Amenities:** video games (fee), safes. **Dining:** 4 restaurants, also, Jackalope's Bar & Grill, Sierra Restaurant, see separate listings. **Pool(s):** outdoor, heated indoor. **Activities:** saunas, whirlpools, steamrooms, recreation programs, hiking trails, spa. **Fee:** downhill & cross country skiing, ice skating, bicycles, horseback riding, game room. **Guest Services:** valet and coin laundry. **Free Special Amenities:** full breakfast and newspaper. *(See ad p. 588.)*

WHERE TO EAT

JACKALOPE'S BAR & GRILL   559/683-6555   **9**
American. Casual Dining. $10-$14 **AAA Inspector Notes:** The menu at this grill offers traditional pub-style favorites and fresh sandwiches and salads. Gaze out the floor-to-ceiling windows offering mountain views or relax by the bar to watch sports on TV. Expect the service to be warm and friendly. **Bar:** full bar. **Address:** 1122 Hwy 41 93623 **Location:** 2 mi from Yosemite National Park South Gate; in Tenaya Lodge at Yosemite. **Parking:** on-site and valet.

THE NARROW GAUGE INN RESTAURANT
559/683-6446   **10**
American
Fine Dining
$17-$36
AAA Inspector Notes: Experience fine dining in a lodge setting with mountain views. Well-known for game meats such as venison and elk, this inn features white linens, oil lamps and fireplaces to create a memorable evening. Patio dining is available during the summer months. Open mid-April to the end of October. **Bar:** full bar. **Reservations:** suggested. **Address:** 48571 Hwy 41 93623 **Location:** 4 mi from Yosemite National Park South Gate.

SIERRA RESTAURANT   559/683-6555   **8**
 American. Fine Dining. $21-$35 **AAA Inspector Notes:** A comfortable setting with a fireplace in the center of the dining room can be found at this fine dining location. The menu offers traditional favorites in the morning including Denver omelets, eggs Benedict and the extensive buffet. Dinner is more elegant, yet still casual, with fresh seafood items including crab cakes, scallops, lobster and salmon, as well as filet mignon, grilled pork chops and chicken piccata. Service is friendly and attentive. **Bar:** full bar. **Address:** 1122 Hwy 41 93623 **Location:** 2 mi from Yosemite National Park South Gate; in Tenaya Lodge at Yosemite. **Parking:** on-site and valet.

Give the gift of security, value and peace of mind: Gift Membership

FOLSOM (E-3) pop. 72,203, elev. 218'
- Hotels p. 112 • Restaurants p. 112
- Hotels & Restaurants map & index p. 314

A gold-mining town dating from the 1860s, Folsom retains much of its historic character. Many restored houses and buildings of that era line Sutter Street; they include the Wells Fargo Office—the terminus of the Pony Express.

The old Southern Pacific Depot, 200 Wool St., now houses the chamber of commerce. A Southern Pacific railcar, boxcar and caboose are displayed. Alongside the cars is the 1868 Ashland Freight Depot, said to be the oldest standing station west of the Mississippi River.

A self-guiding tour at Gekkeikan Sake provides visitors with an understanding of the steps taken in the sake brewing process. The facility, at 1136 Sibley St., also has a koi pond and a small Japanese garden in addition to offering tastings of its products; phone (916) 985-3111 for information.

Two miles north of town is the massive granite Folsom State Prison. A museum contains displays of photographs and other items that describe the prison's history. Folsom City Park and Zoo, behind the city hall complex on Natoma Street, has picnic facilities, a children's play area, a railway and a small zoo.

Recreational pursuits can be enjoyed along the 32-mile-long Jedediah Smith Memorial Trail. Also known as the American River Bike Trail, this is a paved path that parallels the American River between Folsom and Sacramento *(see place listing p. 305)*. Picnicking, bicycling, inline skating, fishing, boating and rafting can be enjoyed along the corridor, which was named for the 19th-century fur trapper; there are access points along US 50.

Folsom Chamber of Commerce: 200 Wool St., Folsom, CA 95630. **Phone:** (916) 985-2698.

Shopping areas: Folsom Premium Outlets, 13000 Folsom Blvd., has more than 80 factory-direct and specialty stores.

FOLSOM HISTORY MUSEUM, downtown at 823 Sutter St., is in a reconstruction of the former Wells Fargo & Co. assay office and bank. The museum features exhibits about the gold rush, mining camps, the area's Native Americans and Chinese immigrants, the railroad, Folsom Prison and the Folsom Powerhouse. Changing exhibits also are scheduled throughout the year. **Hours:** Tues.-Sun. 11-4. **Cost:** $4; $2 (ages 12-17). **Phone:** (916) 985-2707.

FOLSOM POWERHOUSE STATE HISTORIC PARK, on the American River at the foot of Riley St., performed the first long-distance transmission of hydroelectric power to Sacramento in 1895. Now a national landmark as well as a state historic park, it is part of Folsom Lake State Recreation Area *(see Recreation Areas Chart)*. Guided tours of the dam are available. **Hours:** Wed.-Sun. noon-4. Closed major holidays. **Cost:** Tours free. **Parking:** $5. **Phone:** (916) 985-4843.

(See map & index p. 314.)

COURTYARD BY MARRIOTT SACRAMENTO-FOLSOM
(916)984-7624 **59**

▼▼▼ **Hotel** $109-$169 **Address:** 2575 Iron Point Rd 95630 **Location:** US 50 exit E Bidwell St, just n, then just w. **Facility:** 125 units. 4 stories, interior corridors. **Pool(s):** heated indoor. **Activities:** whirlpool, exercise room. **Guest Services:** valet and coin laundry.

AAA Benefit: AAA hotel discounts of 5% or more.

HAMPTON INN & SUITES
(916)235-7744 **61**

▼▼▼ Hotel $89-$169

AAA Benefit: Members save up to 10%!

Address: 155 Placerville Rd 95630 **Location:** US 50 exit East Bidwell St/Scott Rd, just n on East Bidwell St, then just se. **Facility:** 147 units. 4 stories, interior corridors. **Terms:** 1-7 night minimum stay, cancellation fee imposed. **Amenities:** high-speed Internet. **Pool(s):** heated indoor. **Activities:** whirlpool, exercise room. **Guest Services:** complimentary and valet laundry, area transportation-within 5 mi. **Free Special Amenities:** expanded continental breakfast and local transportation.

HILTON GARDEN INN
(916)353-1717 **58**

▼▼▼ **Hotel** $89-$209 **Address:** 221 Iron Point Rd 95630 **Location:** US 50 exit Folsom Blvd, 0.5 mi n to Iron Point Rd, then 0.3 mi e. **Facility:** 100 units. 4 stories, interior corridors. **Terms:** 1-7 night minimum stay, cancellation fee imposed. **Amenities:** high-speed Internet. **Pool(s):** heated outdoor. **Activities:** whirlpool, exercise room. **Guest Services:** complimentary and valet laundry.

AAA Benefit: Unparalleled hospitality at a special Member rate.

LAKE NATOMA INN HOTEL & CONFERENCE CENTER
(916)351-1500 **56**

▼▼▼ Hotel $89-$169

Address: 702 Gold Lake Dr 95630 **Location:** US 50 exit Folsom Blvd, 3 mi n, then 0.5 mi e on Riley St; behind The Lakes Specialty Shopping Center. Adjacent to Lake Natoma. **Facility:** 138 units. 4 stories, interior corridors. **Terms:** cancellation fee imposed. **Amenities:** video games (fee). **Pool(s):** heated outdoor. **Activities:** saunas, whirlpool, fishing, hiking trails, jogging, exercise room. **Fee:** bicycles. **Guest Services:** valet laundry. **Free Special Amenities:** local telephone calls and high-speed Internet.

LARKSPUR LANDING HOME SUITE HOTELS FOLSOM
(916)355-1616 **57**

▼▼▼ **Hotel.** Rates not provided. **Address:** 121 Iron Point Rd 95630 **Location:** US 50 exit Folsom Blvd, 0.5 mi n to Iron Point Rd, then 0.3 mi e. **Facility:** 84 efficiency kitchen units. 4 stories, interior corridors. **Amenities:** high-speed Internet. **Activities:** whirlpool, exercise room. **Guest Services:** complimentary and valet laundry.

RESIDENCE INN BY MARRIOTT
(916)983-7289 **60**

▼▼▼ **Extended Stay Hotel** $119-$179 **Address:** 2555 Iron Point Rd 95630 **Location:** US 50 exit E Bidwell St, just n, then just w. **Facility:** 107 units, some two bedrooms, efficiencies and kitchens. 3 stories, interior corridors. **Pool(s):** heated indoor. **Activities:** whirlpool, putting green, sports court, exercise room. **Guest Services:** valet and coin laundry.

AAA Benefit: AAA hotel discounts of 5% or more.

WHERE TO EAT

BIDWELL STREET BISTRO
916/984-7500 **87**

▼▼▼ American. Fine Dining. $12-$26 **AAA Inspector Notes:** This upscale bistro features a variety of well-prepared dishes with seasonal inspirations that can be paired with a fine selection of wine. Grab a seat on the small patio and enjoy innovative sandwiches at lunch. Closed on Sunday and Monday in summer. **Reservations:** suggested. **Address:** 1004 E Bidwell St, Suite 100 95630 **Location:** US 50 exit E Bidwell St, 3 mi nw, then just n on Montrose Dr; in Willow Creek Town Center. [L] [D] CALL

BLUE NAMI
916/983-3388 **92**

▼▼ Sushi. Casual Dining. $9-$25 **AAA Inspector Notes:** Across from a cinema, this restaurant prepares fresh sashimi and an extensive variety of creative sushi rolls. Diners can watch the chef prepare the sushi at the sushi bar. A sake menu is available. **Bar:** beer & wine. **Address:** 330 Palladio Pkwy, Suite 2045 95630 **Location:** US 50 exit E Bidwell St/Scott Rd, just nw, then just w on Via Felice; jct Via Solo; in Palladio at Broadstone Shopping Center. [L] [D] [LATE] CALL

CHICAGO FIRE
916/353-0140 **85**

▼▼ Pizza. Casual Dining. $8-$27 **AAA Inspector Notes:** Authentic Chicago-style pizza, including thin crust (sliced in squares), deep dish and stuffed pizza, are prepared with quality ingredients at this casual spot. Open for lunch Saturday and Sunday. Patio seating is available. **Bar:** full bar. **Address:** 614 Sutter St, Suite C 95630 **Location:** US 50 exit Folsom Blvd, 3 mi n; follow signs to historic downtown; jct Riley St. [D] CALL

CHICAGO FIRE
916/984-0140 **91**

▼▼ Pizza. Casual Dining. $8-$27 **AAA Inspector Notes:** Authentic Chicago-style pizza, including thin crust (sliced in squares), deep dish and stuffed, is offered at this upscale, casual spot. Salads and sandwiches round out the menu. On the weekend arrive early (before 4:30 p.m.) otherwise expect a long wait. Patio dining is an option in season. **Bar:** full bar. **Address:** 310 Palladio Pkwy 95630 **Location:** US 50 exit East Bidwell St/Scott Rd, just nw; jct Via Felice. **Parking:** street only. [L] [D] CALL

FAT'S ASIA BISTRO & DIM SUM BAR
916/983-1133 **93**

▼▼▼ Asian. Fine Dining. $9-$21 **AAA Inspector Notes:** The contemporary restaurant décor is inspired by the ancient temples of Asia and features palm trees and a large Buddha. Asian fusion cuisine is tastefully prepared. A few semi-private dining tables are available. **Bar:** full bar. **Reservations:** suggested. **Address:** 2585 Iron Point Rd 95630 **Location:** US 50 exit E Bidwell St, just n. [L] [D] CALL

ICING ON THE CUPCAKE
916/984-9300 **90**

▼ American. Quick Serve. $3 **AAA Inspector Notes:** Made fresh, the creative cupcake menu offerings at this spot change daily. It is best to arrive earlier in the day to avoid disappointment in case a favorite flavor is sold out. **Address:** 2779 E Bidwell St, Suite 200 95630 **Location:** US 50 exit E Bidwell St/Scott Rd, just n; jct Power Center Dr; in Broadstone Plaza Shopping Center. [L] CALL

(See map & index p. 314.)

KAREN'S BAKERY CAFE & CATERING   916/985-2665   84

ᵂᵂ ᵂᵂ Breads/Pastries. Quick Serve. $9-$15 **AAA Inspector Notes:** Delicious salads and specialty sandwiches, tempting bakery items and a dizzying array of sinful desserts are offered at this café with a delightful outdoor patio. Daily menu specials and breakfast also are featured. **Bar:** beer & wine. **Address:** 705 Gold Lake Dr, Suite 340 95630 **Location:** Jct Leidesdorf St; downtown; near American River Bridge. **Parking:** on-site and street.

B   L   CALL 🅂🄼

LAND OCEAN NEW AMERICAN STEAKHOUSE
916/983-7000   89

ᵂᵂᵂ Steak Seafood. Casual Dining. $11-$28 **AAA Inspector Notes:** This upscale, casual restaurant offers salads, tempting burgers, steaks and a few seafood entrées, along with wood-fired rotisserie menu items. Relax in an inviting, club-like atmosphere with subdued amber lighting. **Bar:** full bar. **Address:** 2720 E Bidwell St 95630 **Location:** US 50 exit E Bidwell St/Scott Rd, 1.3 mi nw; jct Power Center Dr; in Broadstone Marketplace.

L   D   CALL 🅂🄼

MEXQUITE MEXICAN CUISINE & TEQUILA LOUNGE
916/984-8607   82

ᵂᵂ Mexican. Casual Dining. $8-$16 **AAA Inspector Notes:** Burritos, salads, quesadillas and a variety of chicken, beef and seafood dishes are served here as well as regional Mexican plates. Relax on the patio in the summer. Breakfast is offered Saturday and Sunday 9 a.m. to 2 p.m. **Bar:** full bar. **Address:** 25095 Blue Ravine Rd 95630 **Location:** Jct E Natoma St; in Parkway Shopping Center near Raley's.   L   D   CALL 🅂🄼

SCOTT'S SEAFOOD GRILL & BAR   916/989-6711   81

ᵂᵂ Seafood. Casual Dining. $12-$32 **AAA Inspector Notes:** A variety of seafood and steak selections are offered at this contemporary establishment. Oyster specials are featured on Thursday in the bar. A few tables afford views of the town in the distance. A patio is open in season. **Bar:** full bar. **Reservations:** suggested. **Address:** 9611 Greenback Ln 95630 **Location:** Just ne from jct Madison Ave; in River Rock Plaza.   L   D   CALL 🅂🄼

SUTTER STREET STEAKHOUSE   916/351-9100   83

ᵂᵂᵂ Steak. Fine Dining. $19-$37 **AAA Inspector Notes:** This new restaurant, offering views of the surrounding area, features an enhanced high-heat broiler to prepare the certified black Angus or USDA Prime cuts of beef. Diners also can choose from fresh fish entrées. A wine tower room and an extensive wine list complement the menu. A parking garage and lot are adjacent to the restaurant. **Bar:** full bar. **Reservations:** suggested. **Address:** 604 Sutter St 95630 **Location:** US 50 exit Folsom Blvd, 3 mi n, 0.5 mi e on Riley St, then just ne; jct Scott St; follow signs to historic downtown.

D   CALL 🅂🄼

VISCONTI'S RISTORANTE   916/983-5181   86

ᵂᵂ Italian. Casual Dining. $8-$24 **AAA Inspector Notes:** This family-friendly restaurant serves a variety of tempting pasta, chicken and veal dinners, along with pizza and calzones. At lunch sandwiches are offered along with some specials. Lunch is not served on Sunday. Take advantage of the heated outdoor patio when it is chilly outside. **Bar:** full bar. **Reservations:** suggested. **Address:** 2700 E Bidwell St, Suite 700 95630 **Location:** SR 50 exit E Bidwell St/Scott Rd, 1.3 mi w; jct Power Center Dr; in Broadstone Marketplace.

L   D   CALL 🅂🄼

SUDWERK RIVERSIDE   916/989-9243

fyi Not evaluated. The outdoor deck of this eatery offers one of the best views of the American River. Sandwiches, burgers and entrée selections are offered as well as several fresh beer selections. **Address:** 9900 Greenback Ln 95630 **Location:** US 50 exit Folsom Blvd, 3 mi ne.

FORESTHILL   (E-3) pop. 1,483, elev. 3,225'

RECREATIONAL ACTIVITIES
White-water Rafting
- **All-Outdoors California Whitewater Rafting** departs from the Foresthill Community Center. **Hours:** Daily Apr.-Oct. **Phone:** (925) 932-8993 or (800) 247-2387.

FORESTVILLE   pop. 3,293
- **Part of Wine Country area — see map p. 562**

FARMHOUSE INN & RESTAURANT   (707)887-3300

ᵂᵂ ᵂᵂ **Historic Country Inn** $395-$845 **Address:** 7871 River Rd 95436 **Location:** US 101 exit River Rd, 7.2 mi w. **Facility:** At this property you can peruse the attractively landscaped grounds and chef's garden, roast marshmallows at the outdoor fire pit or relax in the private sauna or steam shower found in the room. 18 units. 2 stories (no elevator), interior/exterior corridors. **Terms:** 2 night minimum stay - seasonal and/or weekends, 14 day cancellation notice-fee imposed. **Dining:** Farmhouse Restaurant, see separate listing. **Pool(s):** heated outdoor. **Activities:** spa. **Guest Services:** complimentary laundry.

🍴 CALL 🅂🄼 ⊃ 📶 ✕ 🛄 💻

WHERE TO EAT

FARMHOUSE RESTAURANT   707/887-3300

ᵂᵂ ᵂᵂ New American. Fine Dining. $69-$84 **AAA Inspector Notes:** Set in the inn of the same name, this is truly an excellent and upscale dining experience. The service staff is highly knowledgeable and polished. The food is the freshest and utilizes local and regional favorites such as tartar of Wagyu beef, wild Alaskan halibut and roasted Berkshire pork tenderloin. **Bar:** beer & wine. **Reservations:** suggested. **Address:** 7871 River Rd 95436 **Location:** US 101 exit River Rd, 7.2 mi w; in Farmhouse Inn & Restaurant.   D   CALL 🅂🄼

FORT BRAGG   (D-1) pop. 7,273, elev. 80'
- **Hotels p. 114** • **Restaurants p. 119**
- **Attractions map p. 566**
- **Part of Wine Country area — see map p. 562**

Fort Bragg, on a scenic stretch of SR 1 that extends from Leggett to Sausalito, was established in 1857 to oversee the Mendocino Indian Reservation. When the reservation was moved, the fort was abandoned and Fort Bragg subsequently became a lumber and port town. Noyo Harbor, at the south end of town, is a small commercial fishing port; fishing and whale-watching cruises are available.

Just north of town is MacKerricher State Park, home to tidal flats, sand dunes, headlands and a lagoon. The park offers horseback riding, bicycling, picnicking, fishing and hiking and camping opportunities. Harbor seals and migrating gray whales can be seen from overlooks. *See Recreation Areas Chart.*

Fort Bragg-Mendocino Coast Chamber of Commerce: 217 S. Main St., P.O. Box 1141, Fort Bragg, CA 95437. **Phone:** (707) 961-6300 or (800) 726-2780.

THE GUEST HOUSE MUSEUM, 343 N. Main St., is the 1892 three-story Victorian home built by the city's first mayor, who also was the founder of the Union Lumber Co. It became the company's "guest house" in 1912. Local history is depicted inside, while outside are locomotives and steam donkeys, a type of engine used in the logging industry. The nearby Fort Building is the only structure remaining from the town's 1857-64 military post; it contains a model of the original structure and historical artifacts.

Hours: Mon. 1-3, Tues.-Fri. 11-2, Sat.-Sun. 10-4, June-Oct.; Thurs.-Sun. 11-2, rest of year. Closed Jan. 1, Labor Day, Thanksgiving and Christmas. Phone ahead to confirm schedule. **Cost:** Donations. **Phone:** (707) 964-4251.

 MENDOCINO COAST BOTANICAL GARDENS, 1 mi. s. on SR 1, encompasses 47 acres of gardens featuring numerous varieties of camellias, dahlias, lilies, hydrangeas, fuchsias, heathers, Pacifica irises, roses and rhododendrons. Some of the rhododendrons reach a height of 20 feet. Two creeks wind through a lush native forest filled with ferns and pines, and perennials and succulents are planted in beds along grass trails.

Paths lead from a nursery to scenic ocean bluffs adorned with wildflowers. Three miles of trails meander through the gardens, leading to the ocean. A vegetable garden, a meadow and picnic areas flank the trails. Free electric carts are available.

Time: Allow 1 hour minimum. **Hours:** Daily 9-5, Mar.-Oct.; 9-4, rest of year. Closed first Sat. in Aug., Sat. after Labor Day, Thanksgiving and Christmas. **Cost:** $14; $10 (ages 65+); $5 (ages 5-17). **Phone:** (707) 964-4352. 🐾

SKUNK TRAIN, departing from the Skunk Depot on Laurel St. w. off SR 1, travels round-trip to Northspur. The 40-mile, 3.5-hour trip crosses 30 bridges, navigates the Noyo River Canyon, and passes through redwood groves and the 1,000-foot Tunnel #1. The train's unusual name is derived from the smelly gas engines used in the 1920s; while the vintage equipment no longer uses the bad-smelling fuel, the name has continued. A 4.5-hour barbecue dinner trip is available in summer. A second Skunk Train operates from Willits *(see attraction listing in Willits p. 559).*

Hours: Sightseeing trips depart daily from Fort Bragg at 10, and barbecue dinner trips depart Tues.-Sat. at 3:30, Memorial Day-Labor Day. **Cost:** Sightseeing trip $49; $24 (ages 2-12). Barbecue dinner trip $70; $40 (ages 2-12). Reservations are recommended. **Phone:** (707) 964-6371, or (866) 457-5865 for reservations. *(See ad p. 118.)*

RECREATIONAL ACTIVITIES
Horseback Riding

• **Ricochet Ridge Ranch** is 2 mi. n. of Pudding Creek Bridge at 24201 SR 1. **Hours:** Rides are offered daily at 10, noon, 2 and 4 by appointment. **Phone:** (707) 964-7669 or (888) 873-5777.

BEACHCOMBER MOTEL   (707)964-2402

Motel
$119-$269

Address: 1111 N Main St 95437 **Location:** 1 mi n on SR 1. **Facility:** 72 units, some efficiencies. 2 stories (no elevator), exterior corridors. **Terms:** 3 day cancellation notice. **Activities:** exercise room, spa. **Guest Services:** coin laundry. **Free Special Amenities: continental breakfast and high-speed Internet.** *(See ad p. 115.)*

 / SOME UNITS FEE

BEACH HOUSE INN   707/961-1700

Motel
$69-$250

Address: 100 Pudding Creek Rd 95437 **Location:** 0.7 mi n on SR 1. **Facility:** 30 units. 2 stories (no elevator), interior corridors. **Terms:** 2 night minimum stay - weekends, cancellation fee imposed. **Free Special Amenities: continental breakfast and high-speed Internet.**

/ SOME UNITS FEE

BEST WESTERN VISTA MANOR LODGE   (707)964-4776

Motel
$90-$160

Best Western

AAA Benefit: Members save up to 20%, plus 10% bonus points with Best Western Rewards®.

Address: 1100 N Main St 95437 **Location:** 1 mi n on SR 1. **Facility:** 55 units, some cottages. 2 stories (no elevator), exterior corridors. **Terms:** 2 night minimum stay - weekends, cancellation fee imposed. **Pool(s):** heated indoor. **Activities:** volleyball. **Free Special Amenities: local telephone calls and high-speed Internet.**

COAST INN AND SPA   (707)964-2852

Motel $80-$390 **Address:** 18661 N Hwy 1 95437 **Location:** 0.3 mi s of SR 20. **Facility:** 28 units, some efficiencies and kitchens. 1 story, exterior corridors. **Terms:** 3 day cancellation notice-fee imposed. **Activities:** spa. **Guest Services:** coin laundry.

/ SOME UNITS FEE

COUNTRY INN BED & BREAKFAST   (707)964-3737

Bed & Breakfast $65-$145 **Address:** 632 N Main St 95437 **Location:** On SR 1; between Fir and Bush sts. **Facility:** 8 units. 2 stories (no elevator), interior corridors. **Terms:** 7 day cancellation notice-fee imposed. **Activities:** whirlpool.

EBB TIDE LODGE   (707)964-5321

Motel $60-$251 **Address:** 250 S Main St 95437 **Location:** Just s on SR 1; at Maple St. **Facility:** 31 units. 2 stories (no elevator), exterior corridors. **Terms:** 2 night minimum stay - seasonal and/or weekends, 3 day cancellation notice-fee imposed.

EMERALD DOLPHIN INN & MINI GOLF   (707)964-6699

Hotel
$65-$185

Address: 1211 S Main St 95437 **Location:** On SR 1; at Harbor View Dr. **Facility:** 43 units. 2 stories (no elevator), exterior corridors. **Terms:** 2 night minimum stay - seasonal and/or weekends, 7 day cancellation notice. **Amenities:** safes. **Activities:** fishing, hiking trails, game room. *Fee:* miniature golf, massage. **Free Special Amenities: continental breakfast and high-speed Internet.**

CALL / SOME UNITS FEE

HARBOR LITE LODGE   (707)964-0221

Motel
$89-$189

Address: 120 N Harbor Dr 95437 **Location:** SR 1 (S Main St); at north end of Noyo River Bridge. **Facility:** 79 units. 2 stories (no elevator), exterior corridors. **Terms:** check-in 4 pm, 2 night minimum stay - seasonal and/or weekends, cancellation fee imposed, resort fee. **Activities:** sauna. **Free Special Amenities:** expanded continental breakfast and high-speed Internet.

HOLIDAY INN EXPRESS   (707)964-1100

Hotel
$119-$199

Address: 250 Hwy 20 95437 **Location:** On SR 20, just e of jct SR 1. **Facility:** 54 units. 3 stories, interior/exterior corridors. **Terms:** cancellation fee imposed. **Pool(s):** heated indoor. **Activities:** whirlpool, exercise room. **Free Special Amenities:** full breakfast and high-speed Internet.

NORTH CLIFF HOTEL   707/962-2500

Motel
$99-$295

Address: 1005 S Main St 95437 **Location:** At Noyo Point Rd; north end of Noyo River Bridge. **Facility:** 39 units. 3 stories (no elevator), exterior corridors. **Terms:** check-in 4 pm, 2 night minimum stay - seasonal and/or weekends, cancellation fee imposed. **Amenities:** safes. **Free Special Amenities:** continental breakfast and high-speed Internet.

OCEAN VIEW LODGE   (707)964-1951

Hotel
$109-$265

Address: 1141 N Main St 95437 **Location:** 1 mi n on SR 1. **Facility:** 30 units. 2 stories (no elevator), exterior corridors. **Terms:** 2 night minimum stay - seasonal and/or weekends, 3 day cancellation notice-fee imposed. **Amenities:** safes (fee). **Free Special Amenities:** local telephone calls and high-speed Internet. *(See ad p. 116.)*

SEABIRD LODGE   (707)964-4731

Motel
$75-$150

Address: 191 South St 95437 **Location:** 0.8 mi n of Noyo River Bridge; 1 blk e off SR 1. **Facility:** 65 units. 2 stories (no elevator), exterior corridors. **Pool(s):** heated indoor. **Activities:** whirlpool. **Guest Services:** coin laundry. **Free Special Amenities:** expanded continental breakfast and high-speed Internet.

Find thousands of places to show your card and save at AAA.com/discounts

▼ See AAA listing p. 114 ▼

SHORELINE COTTAGES   (707)964-2977

◈◈ **Cottage** $95-$160 **Address:** 18725 N Hwy 1 95437 **Location:** On SR 1, 0.3 mi s of SR 20. **Facility:** 11 units, some kitchens and cottages. 1 story, exterior corridors. **Terms:** 3 day cancellation notice-fee imposed. **Activities:** whirlpool.

SUPER 8   (707)964-4003

◈◈ **Motel** $82-$199 **Address:** 888 S Main St 95437 **Location:** 0.5 mi s on SR 1; north end of Noyo River Bridge. **Facility:** 53 units. 2 stories (no elevator), exterior corridors. **Terms:** cancellation fee imposed.

SURF & SAND LODGE   (707)964-9383

◈◈◈ Hotel $109-$349

Address: 1131 N Main St 95437 **Location:** 1 mi n on SR 1. **Facility:** 30 units. 2 stories (no elevator), interior corridors. **Terms:** 3 day cancellation notice. **Free Special Amenities:** local telephone calls and high-speed Internet. *(See ad p. 117.)*

▼ See AAA listing p. 115 ▼

COMING TO THE OCEAN...

Ocean **View** Lodge

Fort Bragg

...STAY ON THE OCEAN
ROOM (*spacious*)...VIEW (*awesome*)...ON TEN MILE OCEAN TRAIL
(*secluded beaches, tidepools, spouting whales, etc.*)
www.oceanviewlodging.com   800-643-5482

SURF MOTEL & GARDENS   707/964-5361

Motel
$59-$275

Address: 1220 S Main St 95437 **Location:** At Oceanview Dr. **Facility:** 54 units, some kitchens. 1 story, exterior corridors. **Terms:** 3 day cancellation notice-fee imposed. **Activities:** horseback riding. **Guest Services:** area transportation-within 15 mi. **Free Special Amenities: continental breakfast and high-speed Internet.** *(See ad p. 118.)*

WELLER HOUSE INN   707/964-4415

Historic Bed & Breakfast. Rates not provided. **Address:** 524 Stewart St 95437 **Location:** Just w of SR 1 via Pine St, just n. **Facility:** Described as being in the Renaissance style with an Italian flair, this property, built in the late 1800s, has been renovated into an elegant B&B. 9 units. 3 stories (no elevator), interior corridors.

Plan complete trip routings with the TripTik®
Travel Planner on AAA.com/CAA.ca

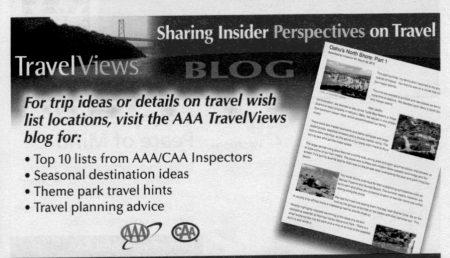

▼ See AAA listing p. 116 ▼

WHERE TO EAT

CLIFF HOUSE RESTAURANT OF FORT BRAGG
707/961-0255

◆◆◆ American Casual Dining $16-$33

AAA Inspector Notes: Panoramic view of the coast can be had at this restaurant with green and pink leather booths and green metal frame chairs. Offerings of seafood, steak, pasta, crab cakes and crème brûlée are offered. **Bar:** full bar. **Address:** 1011 S Main St 95437 **Location:** South end of Noyo River Bridge.

D CALL &M 𝒦

Ocean view. Open daily at 4 PM. Full bar. FREE WIFI.

EGGHEADS RESTAURANT
707/964-5005

◆◆ American. Casual Dining. $8-$20 **AAA Inspector Notes:** This modest little family run restaurant plays homage to the Wizard of Oz with pictures adorning the walls and some menu items named after the characters. Follow the yellow brick road to the Emerald City, which is actually a bathroom shack painted green. Lines are long on the weekends so arrive early. **Address:** 326 N Main St 95437 **Location:** On SR 1, between Laurel and Redwood sts; center. **Parking:** on-site (fee). B L 𝒦

MENDO BISTRO
707/964-4974

◆◆◆ American. Casual Dining. $13-$29 **AAA Inspector Notes:** Owner/chef Nicholas Petti has succeeded in offering creative dining at affordable prices. His cooking style is simple and the focus is on the ingredients. Fresh pasta, bread and desserts are made in-house daily. **Bar:** beer & wine. **Address:** 301 N Main St 95437 **Location:** Corner of Redwood St; center. **Parking:** on-site and street. D 𝒦

NORTH COAST BREWING CO. TAPROOM & GRILL
707/964-3400

◆◆ American. Casual Dining. $11-$30 **AAA Inspector Notes:** This restaurant offers all the North Coast specialty brews, such as Red Seal and Old Rasputin. Seafood is a favorite, and the catch of the day always is fresh off the boat. **Bar:** beer & wine. **Address:** 455 N Main St 95437 **Location:** On SR 1; corner of Pine St; center. L D 𝒦

THE RESTAURANT
707/964-9800

◆◆ American. Casual Dining. $17-$32 **AAA Inspector Notes:** This longtime, family-owned restaurant is known for its well-prepared dishes. **Bar:** beer & wine. **Reservations:** suggested. **Address:** 418 N Main St 95437 **Location:** On SR 1; between Laurel and Pine sts; center. **Parking:** street only. D CALL &M 𝒦

SILVER'S AT THE WHARF
707/964-5049

◆◆ Seafood. Casual Dining. $10-$39 **AAA Inspector Notes:** Situated on the wharf of the Noyo River, this family-style restaurant offers a surprising ninety-degree view of the inlet, including boaters, fisherman and a pair of sea lions, all for the entertainment of the diner. **Bar:** full bar. **Reservations:** suggested. **Address:** 32260 N Harbor Dr 95437 **Location:** SR 1 exit N Harbor Dr, 1.5 mi e. L D 𝒦

Plan complete trip routings with the TripTik® Travel Planner on AAA.com/CAA.ca

FORTUNA (C-1) pop. 11,926, elev. 51'

Established in 1875 and named Springville after the numerous springs in the surrounding hills, Fortuna was renamed Slide and finally, Fortuna by its "fortunate" citizens. Fortuna is within the Redwood Empire, a name referring to the string of majestically scenic coastal counties extending from San Francisco Bay north to the Oregon border.

Fortuna Chamber of Commerce: 735 14th St., P.O. Box 797, Fortuna, CA 95540. **Phone:** (707) 725-3959 or (800) 426-8166.

CHAPMAN'S GEM AND MINERAL SHOP AND MUSEUM, 4 mi. s. off US 101, has displays of fossils, gems, minerals, petrified wood and Native American artifacts. **Time:** Allow 30 minutes minimum. **Hours:** Daily 10-5. Closed Jan. 1, Easter, Thanksgiving and Christmas. **Cost:** Donations. **Phone:** (707) 725-2714.

THE FORTUNA DEPOT MUSEUM, e. of US 101 in Rohner Park, presents local history exhibits in a restored 1893 Northwestern-Pacific depot. Included are displays about fishing, logging, railroading and barbed wire. **Time:** Allow 30 minutes minimum. **Hours:** Daily noon-4:30, June-Aug.; Thurs.-Sun. noon-4:30, rest of year. Closed major holidays. **Cost:** Free. **Phone:** (707) 725-7645.

Plan complete trip routings with the TripTik® Travel Planner on AAA.com/CAA.ca

---

BEST WESTERN COUNTRY INN   (707)725-6822

Motel
$70-$139

AAA Benefit: Members save up to 20%, plus 10% bonus points with Best Western Rewards®.

Address: 2025 Riverwalk Dr 95540 **Location:** US 101 exit 687 (Kenmar Rd), just w. **Facility:** 66 units, some two bedrooms. 2 stories (no elevator), exterior corridors. **Amenities:** *Some:* high-speed Internet. **Pool(s):** heated indoor/outdoor. **Activities:** whirlpool. **Guest Services:** coin laundry. **Free Special Amenities: full breakfast and local telephone calls.** (See ad this page.)

COMFORT INN & SUITES   707/725-7025

Hotel
Rates not provided

Address: 1583 Riverwalk Dr 95540 **Location:** US 101 exit 687 (Kenmar Rd), 0.4 mi w. **Facility:** 51 units, some two bedrooms. 3 stories, interior corridors. **Amenities:** high-speed Internet. **Pool(s):** heated indoor. **Activities:** whirlpool, exercise room. **Guest Services:** coin laundry. **Free Special Amenities: expanded continental breakfast.**

FORTUNA SUPER 8   (707)725-2888

Motel
$80-$230

Address: 1805 Alamar Way 95540 **Location:** US 101 exit 687 (Kenmar Rd), 0.3 mi w on Riverwalk Dr. **Facility:** 46 units. 2 stories (no elevator), exterior corridors. **Amenities:** high-speed Internet. **Guest Services:** coin laundry. **Free Special Amenities: continental breakfast and high-speed Internet.**

▼ See AAA listing this page ▼

Contact us about AAA/CAA Approved properties
at AAA.com/TourBookComments

HOLIDAY INN EXPRESS   707/725-5500

▼▼▼ **Hotel.** Rates not provided. **Address:** 1859 Alamar Way 95540 **Location:** US 101 exit 687 (Kenmar Rd), 0.3 mi w on River-walk Dr. **Facility:** 46 units. 2 stories (no elevator), exterior corridors. **Amenities:** high-speed Internet. **Pool(s):** heated indoor. **Activities:** whirlpool. **Guest Services:** valet and coin laundry.

/ SOME UNITS FEE 🐾

WHERE TO EAT

EEL RIVER BREWING COMPANY   707/725-2739

▼▼▼ American. Casual Dining. $12-$30 **AAA Inspector Notes:** Claimed to be America's first certified organic brewery, this restaurant's well-flavored, hearty entrées are prepared with organic, locally sourced ingredients, when possible. Since this spot is popular with the locals and tourists alike, there might be a wait. **Bar:** beer & wine. **Address:** 1777 Alamar Way 95540 **Location:** US 101 exit 687 (Kenmar Rd), 0.3 mi w on Riverwalk Dr. Ⓛ Ⓓ Ⓚ

TACO LOCO   707/725-5546

▼ Mexican. Quick Serve. $3-$12 **AAA Inspector Notes:** This small eatery is popular with the locals looking for a quick, hearty meal. **Bar:** beer only. **Address:** 955 Main St 95540 **Location:** Between 9th and 10th sts. **Parking:** street only.

Ⓛ Ⓓ Ⓚ

FOSTER CITY pop. 30,567
- **Hotels & Restaurants map & index p. 410**
- **Part of San Francisco area — see map p. 342**

COURTYARD BY MARRIOTT   (650)377-0600 62

◆◆◆◆
Hotel
$116-$126

AAA Benefit: AAA hotel discounts of 5% or more.

Address: 550 Shell Blvd 94404 **Location:** SR 92 exit Foster City Blvd S; se of jct US 101 and SR 92. **Facility:** 147 units. 3 stories, interior corridors. **Amenities:** high-speed Internet. **Pool(s):** heated indoor. **Activities:** whirlpool, exercise room. **Guest Services:** valet and coin laundry.

SAVE ECO 🍴 CALL 📶 🏊 📶 ✕ 🖥 💻
/ SOME UNITS 🖥

CROWNE PLAZA HOTEL FOSTER CITY-SAN MATEO
                                    650/570-5700 61

▼▼▼ **Hotel.** Rates not provided. **Address:** 1221 Chess Dr 94404 **Location:** Jct US 101 and SR 92, 1 mi e to exit SR 92 (Foster City Blvd), then 0.3 mi n. **Facility:** 350 units. 6 stories, interior corridors. **Amenities:** high-speed Internet. *Some:* safes. **Dining:** 3 restaurants. **Pool(s):** heated indoor/outdoor. **Activities:** whirlpool, exercise room. **Guest Services:** valet and coin laundry, area transportation-Hillsdale Shopping Center.

✈ 🍴 CALL 📶 🏊 BIZ 📶 🎥 💻
/ SOME UNITS 🖥 🖥

WHERE TO EAT

ABC SEAFOOD RESTAURANT   650/328-2288 35

▼▼ Cantonese. Casual Dining. $10-$35 **AAA Inspector Notes:** The main dining room is enclosed in glass, giving the room an airy and spacious feel. Cloth-covered tables give the room a classy feel. Popular with the lunch crowd, this spot serves appropriately-sized dim sum unlike the super-sized monstrosities served in some restaurants. **Bar:** beer & wine. **Address:** 973 E Hillsdale Blvd 94404 **Location:** SR 92 exit Foster City Blvd S, just sw on Metro Center Blvd, just s on Shell Blvd, then just w.

Ⓛ Ⓓ CALL 📶

EL TORITO   650/574-6844

▼▼ Mexican. Family Dining. $7-$18 **AAA Inspector Notes:** Homemade Mexican favorites span from classic preparations to specialties from the country's central regions. Spicy taqueria-style tacos and carnitas Michoacan (marinated pork) are tasty choices. **Bar:** full bar. **Address:** 388 Vintage Park Dr 94404 **Location:** SR 92 exit Foster City Blvd, 0.3 mi n, then 0.3 mi w on Chess Dr.

Ⓛ Ⓓ

FREMONT (D-9) pop. 214,089, elev. 53'
- **Hotels p. 122** • **Restaurants p. 123**

Spanish priests and native Ohlone Indians founded a mission in the Fremont area in 1797. Pioneer John Fremont, for whom the city is named, was apparently so taken with the mission that he offered to buy the adjacent property on which to build his house. The gold rush transformed the mission-based trade and agricultural outpost into a boisterous supply stop for miners, and the use of salt to extract silver from the Comstock Lode led to the development of salt production facilities along San Francisco Bay.

The presence of artesian springs spurred the development of resort facilities. Essanay Studio began a 4-year production stint in 1912, and Charlie Chaplin filmed "The Tramp" here in 1915. Traces of the past provide a backdrop for the futuristic-looking Fremont City Hall building at 3300 Capitol Ave. (between Hastings and Liberty streets), overlooking Lake Elizabeth and Central Park.

Fremont Chamber of Commerce: 39488 Stevenson Pl., Suite 100, Fremont, CA 94539. **Phone:** (510) 795-2244.

ARDENWOOD HISTORIC FARM is at 34600 Ardenwood Blvd., .2 mi. n. of SR 84. This 205-acre living-history park depicts farm life from the 1870s to the 1920s. The complex includes the Victorian-style Patterson house, a farmyard with resident animals, gardens and a picnic area. Horse-drawn railcar rides, a blacksmith demonstration and 40-minute guided house tours are available from April 1 to mid-November. The house is open for Christmas tours in early December.

Hours: Tues.-Sun. 10-4. Last admission is 1 hour before closing. Closed Thanksgiving and Christmas. **Cost:** $6 Thurs.-Fri. and Sun., Apr. 1 to mid-Nov. (includes grounds, house tour, blacksmith demonstration and train); $5 (ages 4-17 and 62+). Grounds only Tues.-Wed. and Sat. $3, Apr. 1 to mid-Nov.; $2 (ages 4-17). The house can be toured Sat. for an additional $3; $2 (ages 4-17). Admission rest of year (grounds only) $2; $1 (ages 4-17). Additional admission is charged during special events. **Phone:** (510) 544-2797, (510) 791-4196 for information about house tours, or (510) 327-2757 for picnic reservations.

CENTRAL PARK AT LAKE ELIZABETH, 40000 Paseo Padre Pkwy., includes a waterfowl refuge where ducks and Canada geese congregate; a lake; bicycling and jogging trails; a skate park; play structures; small and large dog parks; the Aqua Adventure water park; and two basketball courts. A visitor center has displays of live and mounted animals. Sailboat, kayak and paddleboat rentals are available on weekends. A golf driving range, sand volleyball courts, softball and soccer fields, and tennis courts also are available.

Hours: Park open daily dawn-10 p.m., early Apr. to mid-Aug.; closing times vary rest of year. Visitor center open daily 10-7. Lake access is permitted daily noon-5, early Apr. to mid-Aug. Phone ahead to confirm schedule. **Cost:** Park free. Nonmotorized boat launch fee $7. **Phone:** (510) 790-5541. Fremont, 26

COYOTE HILLS REGIONAL PARK is at 8000 Patterson Ranch Rd. The park is a 977-acre wildlife sanctuary containing 2,000-year-old Native American shell mounds and a reconstructed Indian village. The park also has more than 40 miles of hiking, bicycling and jogging trails, a museum, a visitor center, a butterfly garden and a boardwalk through a freshwater marsh habitat. Nature programs are conducted on weekends.

Hours: Park open daily 8-8, Apr.-Oct.; 8-6, rest of year. Visitor center and museum open Wed.-Sun. 10-4 (also Mon. holidays, Memorial Day-Labor Day). Closed Thanksgiving and Christmas. **Cost:** Day`use $5 per private vehicle, $4 per trailered vehicle. Leashed dogs are permitted in some areas; fee $2. **Phone:** (888) 327-2757 option 3, ext. 4519.

DON EDWARDS SAN FRANCISCO BAY NATIONAL WILDLIFE REFUGE, on Marshlands Rd., was the country's first urban national wildlife refuge. Its 30,000 acres around the south San Francisco Bay area offer a sanctuary for the bay's endangered species and for the migratory shorebirds and waterfowl using the Pacific Flyway. More than 280 bird species take advantage of the shelter provided by the refuge's bay, mudflat, salt marsh, salt pond and vernal pool habitats.

From the refuge's visitor center near the Dumbarton Bridge there are views of tidal sloughs and salt marshes. You can learn about the refuge's residents from wildlife exhibits inside the center and explore the animals' environment outdoors on self-guiding trails. Two of the more popular trails are the Tidelands Trail and the LaRiviere Marsh Trail. The best time to spot wildlife is October through April.

Naturalists conduct programs and walks on weekends. A schedule is available at the visitor center, where you also can find information and regulations about fishing, hunting and boating in the refuge. The refuge was named for a congressman who spearheaded efforts to preserve the bay's wetlands. **Hours:** Trails daily 7 a.m.-8 p.m., Apr.-Oct.; 7-6, rest of year. Visitor center open Tues.-Sun 10-5. Closed federal holidays. **Cost:** Free. **Phone:** (510) 745-0222.

MISSION SAN JOSE CHAPEL AND MU-SEUM, 43300 Mission Blvd., was founded in 1797 by Father Fermín Francisco de Lasuén. The original adobe structure was destroyed by an 1868 earthquake. The interior of the reconstructed church, based on church inventories from the 1830s, is unusually elegant, containing crystal chandeliers, murals, religious paintings and a gold leaf altar. Several statues, the baptismal font and the mission bells remain from the original structure.

The mission contains a small museum, which displays old paintings, photographs, mission period artifacts and exhibits about the Ohlone Indians and the mission restoration. **Hours:** Daily 10-5. Closed Jan. 1, Easter, Thanksgiving and Christmas. **Cost:** $3; $2 (students with ID). **Phone:** (510) 657-1797.

BEST WESTERN PLUS GARDEN COURT INN
(510)792-4300

Hotel
$110-$130

AAA Benefit: Members save up to 20%, plus 10% bonus points with Best Western Rewards®.

Address: 5400 Mowry Ave 94538 **Location:** I-880 exit Mowry Ave, just e. **Facility:** 123 units. 3 stories, interior corridors. **Terms:** cancellation fee imposed. **Amenities:** Some: high-speed Internet. **Pool(s):** outdoor. **Activities:** whirlpool. **Guest Services:** valet laundry. **Free Special Amenities: expanded continental breakfast and high-speed Internet.**

COMFORT INN BY CHOICE HOTELS   (510)490-2900
Hotel $69-$169 **Address:** 47031 Kato Rd 94538 **Location:** I-880 exit Warren Ave/Mission Blvd E, just e. **Facility:** 113 units. 3 stories, interior corridors. **Terms:** cancellation fee imposed. **Amenities:** high-speed Internet. **Pool(s):** outdoor. **Activities:** whirlpool, exercise room. **Guest Services:** valet and coin laundry.

COURTYARD BY MARRIOTT   (510)656-1800
Hotel $99-$209 **Address:** 47000 Lakeview Blvd 94538 **Location:** I-880 exit Fremont Blvd W, e on Warren Ave, then just s. **Facility:** 146 units. 3 stories, interior corridors. **Amenities:** high-speed Internet. **Pool(s):** heated indoor. **Activities:** whirlpool, exercise room. **Guest Services:** valet and coin laundry.

AAA Benefit: AAA hotel discounts of 5% or more.

GOOD NITE INN   510/656-9307
Hotel. Rates not provided. **Address:** 4135 Cushing Pkwy 94538 **Location:** I-880 exit Fremont Blvd/Cushing Pkwy, just w. **Facility:** 120 units. 3 stories, exterior corridors. **Pool(s):** outdoor. **Activities:** whirlpool. **Guest Services:** coin laundry.

HAMPTON INN   510/498-1900
Hotel. Rates not provided. **Address:** 46500 Landing Pkwy 94538 **Location:** I-880 exit Warren Ave, just w. **Facility:** 100 units. 3 stories, interior corridors. **Amenities:** high-speed Internet. **Pool(s):** outdoor. **Activities:** exercise room. **Guest Services:** valet and coin laundry.

AAA Benefit: Members save up to 10%!

Contact us about AAA/CAA Approved properties at AAA.com/TourBookComments

HOLIDAY INN EXPRESS & SUITES FREMONT MILPITAS
(510)651-7373

▼▼▼▼ **Hotel** $119-$169 **Address:** 42200 Albrae St 94538 **Location:** I-880 exit Auto Mall Pkwy, just w, n on Christy St, then e. **Facility:** 126 units. 4 stories, interior corridors. **Terms:** cancellation fee imposed. **Amenities:** video games (fee), high-speed Internet. **Pool(s):** outdoor. **Activities:** whirlpool, exercise room. **Guest Services:** valet and coin laundry.

HYATT PLACE FREMONT/SILICON VALLEY
(510)623-6000

▼▼▼ Hotel $89-$159

HYATT PLACE **AAA Benefit:** Members save 10% or more everyday.

Address: 3101 W Warren Ave 94538 **Location:** I-880 exit Warren Ave, just w. **Facility:** 151 units. 7 stories, interior corridors. **Terms:** cancellation fee imposed. **Amenities:** high-speed Internet. **Pool(s):** heated outdoor. **Activities:** exercise room. **Guest Services:** valet laundry, area transportation-within 5 mi. **Free Special Amenities:** expanded continental breakfast and high-speed Internet.

LA QUINTA INN & SUITES FREMONT
(510)445-0808

▼▼▼ **Hotel** $66-$184 **Address:** 46200 Landing Pkwy 94538 **Location:** I-880 exit Fremont Blvd/Cushing Pkwy, just w. **Facility:** 146 units. 5 stories, interior corridors. **Amenities:** Some: high-speed Internet. **Pool(s):** outdoor. **Activities:** whirlpool, exercise room. **Guest Services:** valet and coin laundry.

MARRIOTT FREMONT SILICON VALLEY
(510)413-3700

▼▼▼ Hotel $219-$239

Marriott **AAA Benefit:** AAA hotel discounts of 5% or more.

Address: 46100 Landing Pkwy 94538 **Location:** I-880 exit Fremont Blvd/Cushing Pkwy, then w. **Facility:** 357 units. 10 stories, interior corridors. **Amenities:** high-speed Internet (fee). **Dining:** the Greatroom, see separate listing. **Pool(s):** heated outdoor. **Activities:** whirlpool, exercise room. **Guest Services:** valet and coin laundry, area transportation-within 5 mi. **Free Special Amenities:** newspaper and high-speed Internet.

RESIDENCE INN BY MARRIOTT
(510)794-5900

▼▼▼ **Extended Stay Hotel** $89-$149 **Address:** 5400 Farwell Pl 94536 **Location:** I-880 exit Mowry Ave, just e. **Facility:** 80 units, some two bedrooms, efficiencies and kitchens. 2 stories, exterior corridors. **Pool(s):** heated outdoor. **Activities:** whirlpool, sports court, exercise room. **Guest Services:** valet and coin laundry, area transportation-within 5 mi.

AAA Benefit: AAA hotel discounts of 5% or more.

WHERE TO EAT

BRONCO BILLY'S PIZZA
510/792-1070

▼ Pizza. Casual Dining. $5-$26 **AAA Inspector Notes:** Located in the historic downtown area, this local favorite offers varied pizza, sandwiches, burgers, salads and hot wings in a fun and lively atmosphere. **Bar:** beer & wine. **Address:** 37651 Niles Blvd 94536 **Location:** I-880 exit Mowry Ave, 3.6 mi e, just n on Mission Blvd (SR 238), then just w; between I and J sts. **Parking:** street only.
L D

CICI'S ITALIAN RISTORANTE
510/574-0560

▼▼ Italian. Casual Dining. $7-$20 **AAA Inspector Notes:** Located in the historic downtown area, this casual eatery offers friendly service. Traditional Italian favorites include fettuccine Alfredo, homemade cannelloni, lasagna, lobster ravioli and grilled salmon in a butter and caper sauce. **Bar:** beer & wine. **Address:** 37378 Niles Blvd 94536 **Location:** I-880 exit Mowry Ave, 3.4 mi e, 0.3 mi n on Mission Blvd, then 0.4 mi w. **Parking:** street only. L D

CLAIM JUMPER
510/445-1850

▼▼ American. Casual Dining. $10-$24 **AAA Inspector Notes:** Great menu variety makes this place a good stop for parties with diverse tastes. Choices include specialty appetizers, salads, rotisserie chicken and barbecue items, not to mention good comfort foods, such as traditional pot pie. Hearty portions satisfy big appetites. The atmosphere is fun and lively. **Bar:** full bar. **Address:** 43330 Pacific Commons Blvd 94538 **Location:** I-880 exit Auto Mall Pkwy, just w; in Pacific Commons Shopping Center. L D CALL

CLASSIC DINER
510/651-7241

▼ American. Casual Dining. $5-$10 **AAA Inspector Notes:** This 1950s-style diner serves up traditional favorites from breakfast through dinner. Hearty breakfasts, great hamburgers, sandwiches, ice cream malts and milk shakes are all great selections. **Bar:** beer & wine. **Address:** 39403 Fremont Blvd 94538 **Location:** I-880 exit Mowry Ave, 1.4 mi e, then 0.4 mi s; between Walnut Ave and Sundale Dr; adjacent to Fremont Hub Shopping Center. Fremont, 26. B L D CALL

COUNTRY WAY
510/797-3188

▼▼ American. Casual Dining. $7-$10 **AAA Inspector Notes:** This long-time local favorite is a great stop for families as they offer traditional home-style cuisine. Breakfast is the specialty here and is served all day long. Portions are hearty, so come hungry. **Bar:** beer & wine. **Address:** 5325 Mowry Ave 94536 **Location:** I-880 exit Mowry Ave, just e. B L D CALL

FALAFEL, ETC.
510/795-7170

▼ Middle Eastern. Quick Serve. $6-$13 **AAA Inspector Notes:** This family- owned and -operated restaurant serves up traditional Middle Eastern favorites including falafel and plates of lamb and chicken in a special Shawarma seasoning from Israel. Dine inside or out on the patio. **Bar:** beer & wine. **Address:** 39200 Fremont Blvd 94538 **Location:** I-880 exit Mowry Ave, 1.5 mi e, then just s at Beacon Ave; in Gas Light Square. Fremont, 26. L D CALL

FREMONT MARKET BROILER
510/791-8675

▼▼▼ Seafood. Casual Dining. $10-$32 **AAA Inspector Notes:** The menu here offers an extensive variety of fresh seafood, pasta, poultry and steak. A fish market is on the premises. **Bar:** full bar. **Address:** 43406 Christy St 94538 **Location:** I-880 exit Auto Mall Pkwy, just w; in Pacific Commons Shopping Center. L D CALL

THE GREATROOM
510/413-3700

▼▼▼ California. Casual Dining. $10-$28 **AAA Inspector Notes:** Patrons are treated to a comfortable and relaxing dining experience at this restaurant. The menu lists varied entrées. **Bar:** full bar. **Address:** 46100 Landing Pkwy 94538 **Location:** I-880 exit Fremont Blvd/Cushing Pkwy, then w; in Marriott Fremont Silicon Valley. B L D CALL

KAENYAMA RESTAURANT & BAR
510/683-8800

▼▼▼ Japanese. Fine Dining. $9-$39 **AAA Inspector Notes:** This Asian fusion restaurant, a favorite among the local crowd, offers a wide selection of homemade sushi including those with fresh vegetables, crab, lobster, tuna and eel. In addition to the sushi, they also offer teriyaki, tempura and donburi. **Bar:** full bar. **Address:** 43785 Boscell Rd 94538 **Location:** I-880 exit Auto Mall Pkwy, 0.4 mi w, then 0.3 mi s. L D CALL

MINERVA'S RESTAURANT & CATERING
510/793-9602

▼▼ American. Casual Dining. $7-$12 **AAA Inspector Notes:** Homemade breads, pastries and cookies are freshly baked throughout the day at this casual spot. The menu offers a wide selection of sandwiches served in pita pocket breads. Pizza and pasta also are available in this relaxed, friendly atmosphere. **Address:** 37463 Fremont Blvd 94536 **Location:** I-880 exit Thornton Ave, 1 mi e, then 0.4 mi s. B L D

P.F. CHANG'S CHINA BISTRO   510/657-1400
♥♥♥♥ Chinese. Fine Dining. $10-$20 AAA Inspector Notes:
Trendy, upscale decor provides a pleasant backdrop for New Age
Chinese dining. Appetizers, soups and salads are a meal by them-
selves. Vegetarian plates and sides, noodles, meins, chicken and
meat dishes are created from exotic, fresh ingredients. **Bar:** full bar.
Address: 43316 Christy St 94538 **Location:** I-880 exit Auto Mall
Pkwy, just w. L D CALL M

ROUND TABLE PIZZA
♥ Pizza. Casual Dining. $7-$28 AAA Inspector Notes: This casual, family-oriented pizza place features high-quality ingredients and
dough rolled fresh daily. Distinctive specialty pizzas are piled high
with toppings. **Bar:** beer & wine. L D

For additional information, visit AAA.com
LOCATIONS:
Address: 37480 Fremont Blvd 94536 **Location:** Just w of Central
Ave. **Phone:** 510/793-9393
Address: 40831 Fremont Blvd 94538 **Location:** Just e of Grimmer
Blvd. **Phone:** 510/651-2111

SPIN-A-YARN STEAKHOUSE AND SEAFOOD   510/656-9141
♥♥♥♥ American. Fine Dining. $10-$36 AAA Inspector Notes:
A city tradition since 1951, this restaurant employs a warm, gracious
staff. Included on the diverse menu is the house specialty osso buco.
Bar: full bar. **Reservations:** suggested. **Address:** 45915 Warm
Springs Blvd 94539 **Location:** I-880 exit Mission northbound; exit
Warren southbound, just e, then just n. L D CALL M

SUSHI HARBOR   510/792-8800
♥♥ ♥♥ Japanese. Casual Dining. $8-$15 AAA Inspector Notes:
This quaint eatery features a large selection of assorted sushi and
sashimi rolls that are hand-rolled daily with fresh salmon, tuna, eel,
squid and crab. For those who prefer other Japanese favorites, the
menu offers teriyaki chicken, beef and salmon as well as tempura
shrimp and vegetables. **Bar:** beer & wine. **Address:** 81 Fremont Hub
Courtyard 94538 **Location:** I-880 exit Mowry Ave, 1.3 mi e; in Fremont Hub Shopping Center; adjacent to Bed, Bath & Beyond.
▣ Fremont, 26. L D CALL M 🚲

WORLD GOURMET BUFFET RESTAURANT   510/490-6888
♥ Chinese. Casual Dining. $9-$18 AAA Inspector Notes: This
buffet-style restaurant features more than 200 selections of Asian entrées including Chinese, Korean and Vietnamese. Traditional favorites include egg flower soup, hot and sour soup, fried rice, beef and
broccoli, and General Tso's chicken, crab and shrimp as well as a
Mongolian bbq and Hawaiian barbecue. **Bar:** beer & wine. **Address:**
6010 Stevenson Blvd 94538 **Location:** I-880 exit Stevenson Blvd,
just w. L D

FRESNO (G-4) pop. 494,665, elev. 294'
• **Hotels p. 128** • **Restaurants p. 131**
• **Hotels & Restaurants map & index p. 126**

More than a million acres in the San Joaquin
Valley are irrigated; on this land grow the grapes, or-
anges and cotton that make Fresno County one of
the nation's agricultural leaders. More turkeys are
raised in this area than anywhere else in the
country.

Guided tours of Kearney Mansion Museum, 7160
W. Kearney Blvd. in Kearney Park, are offered
Friday through Sunday and feature many original
furnishings and wall coverings; phone (559)
441-0862. Also of historical interest is the 1889
Meux Home Museum, 1007 R St. at Tulare Street,
where guided tours are also offered Friday through
Sunday; phone (559) 233-8007.

Within Woodward Park, on N. Friant Road along
the San Joaquin River, is the Shinzen Friendship
Garden *(see attraction listing)*. The park also has an
equestrian trail, an amphitheater, children's playgrounds, picnic areas, a lake and ponds, and 5
miles of multi-purpose trails that offer good opportunities for bird-watching.

Fresno/Clovis Convention & Visitors Bureau:
1550 E. Shaw Ave., Suite 101, Fresno, CA 93710.
Phone: (559) 981-5500 or (800) 788-0836.

Self-guiding tours: Blossom Trail is a scenic 63-
mile self-guiding tour encompassing vineyards, orchards and historical points of interest. The best
time to drive the route is from late February through
March, when almond, apricot, peach, plum and nec-
tarine trees are covered with a profusion of blos-
soms. A map is available from the convention and
visitors bureau.

Shopping areas: Fashion Fair Mall, 1 block east of
SR 41 on Shaw Avenue between Fresno and First
streets, has JCPenney and Macy's as well as more
than 140 specialty stores. Fig Garden Village, at
Palm and Shaw avenues, features about 40 spe-
cialty shops including Banana Republic, Chico's,
Coldwater Creek, Pottery Barn and Williams-
Sonoma as well as more than a dozen eateries.

River Park, N. Blackstone Avenue near SR 41
(Yosemite Freeway), is a shopping village with
stores, restaurants and entertainment in three sections, all centered around a landscaped courtyard.
Shops include Ann Taylor Loft, buybuy Baby, Macy's
and REI.

FORESTIERE UNDERGROUND GARDENS is .3
mi. e. off SR 99 exit 140 (Shaw Ave.) at 5021 W.
Shaw Ave. It took Sicilian immigrant Baldassare Forestiere 40 years to create this underground retreat
by hand, beginning in the early 1900s. Subterranean
rooms, passageways, gardens, patios and courtyards with fruit trees are connected by tunnels and
lit by skylights. The arches and stonework resemble
the catacombs in Rome, Italy. The underground
complex also contains a home and a chapel.

Time: Allow 1 hour minimum. **Hours:** Guided
tours are given Wed.-Sun. on the hour 10-4, Memorial Day-Labor Day (weather permitting); schedule
varies rest of year. Phone ahead to confirm
schedule. **Cost:** $14; $12 (ages 60+); $7 (ages
5-17). **Phone:** (559) 271-0734.

FRESNO ART MUSEUM, 2233 N. First St. next to
Radio Park, offers changing exhibits of national and
international artists in eight galleries. Bonner Auditorium screens films and features lectures by guest
artists. **Time:** Allow 1 hour minimum. **Hours:** Thurs.-
Sun. 11-5. Closed Jan. 1, July 4, Thanksgiving and
Christmas. **Cost:** $5; free (ages 0-5). **Phone:** (559)
441-4221.

ISLAND WATERPARK is w. off SR 99 Shaw Ave.
exit at 6099 W. Barstow Ave. The park has waterslides, including a three-story drop slide; a lazy river;
a wave pool; and a children's area. Locker, tube and
cabana rentals are available.

Time: Allow 1 hour minimum. **Hours:** Park opens
Sun.-Fri. at 11, Sat. at 10, mid-June to late Aug.;
schedule varies mid-May to mid-June and late Aug.

(See map & index p. 126.)

to mid-Sept. Closing times vary; phone ahead. Phone ahead to confirm schedule. **Cost:** $27.99; $19.99 (under 48 inches tall); $16.99 (after 3 p.m.); $14.99 (ages 55+). **Parking:** $3-$5. **Phone:** (559) 277-6800. ⓘ

ROEDING PARK is e. of SR 99 via the Olive Ave. or Belmont Ave. exits. In addition to recreational facilities, it contains the Fresno Chaffee Zoo, the Rotary Storyland and Playland, and the Japanese-American War Memorial. **Time:** Allow 1 hour, 30 minutes minimum. **Hours:** Daily 6 a.m.-10 p.m., Apr.-Oct.; 6 a.m.-7 p.m., rest of year. **Cost:** $5 per private vehicle. **Phone:** (559) 621-2900.

Fresno Chaffee Zoo, on Belmont Ave. in Roeding Park, houses mammals, birds and reptiles in a setting of dense vegetation and winding pathways. The computerized Reptile House modifies temperature, humidity and light cycles to mimic the native environment of each species. South American plants and animals share the Rain Forest habitat.

Hours: Daily 9-6, Mar.-Oct.; 9-4, rest of the year. Closed Christmas. **Cost:** $7; $3.50 (ages 2-11 and 62+). Park admission $5 per private vehicle. Under 16 must be with an adult. **Phone:** (559) 498-5910. ⓘ

Rotary Storyland and Playland, 890 W. Belmont Ave. in Roeding Park, features a fairy-tale theme with its castle, carousel, rides and miniature railway.

Hours: Playland open Wed.-Sun. 10-6, Storyland 9-4, mid-June to mid-Aug.; Playland Sat.-Sun. 10-6, Storyland 9-4, Presidents Day weekend to mid-June and mid-Aug. to mid-Nov. Phone ahead to confirm schedule. **Cost:** Storyland $5; $4 (ages 55+); $3.50 (ages 2-11). Playland free; ride tickets 50c each (three to six tickets are required per ride). Train tickets $3. Combination tickets also are available. **Parking:** $5. **Phone:** (559) 486-2124.

SHINZEN FRIENDSHIP GARDEN is in Woodward Park, which is bordered by SR 41 (Yosemite Frwy.), N. Friant Rd. and E. Audubon Dr. The park entrance is on Audubon Dr., just off Friant Rd. The serene

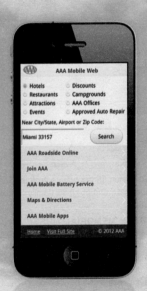

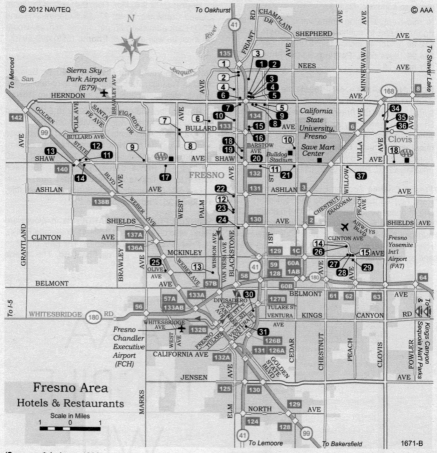

© 2012 NAVTEQ

Fresno Area
Hotels & Restaurants
Scale in Miles
1 0 1

1671-B

(See map & index p. 126.)

5-acre garden was established to honor Fresno's sister city of Kochi, Japan.

Divided into sectors according to the four seasons, the garden has plantings representative of each time of year. The gardens feature a thatched-roof teahouse; stream beds with waterfalls; bridges; a koi pond; and paved pathways from which visitors can appreciate the azaleas, camellias, crab apples, flowering cherries, tulip trees, pines and evergreens.

Tours: Guided tours are available. **Time:** Allow 1 hour minimum. **Hours:** Mon.-Fri. 5 p.m.-dusk, Sat.-Sun. and holidays 10 a.m.-dusk, May-Sept.; Sat.-Sun. and holidays 10 a.m.-dusk, rest of year. **Cost:**

Park admission $5 per private vehicle. Gardens $3; 50c (ages 4-14 and 55+); $5 (family). **Phone:** (559) 621-2900.

VETERANS MEMORIAL MUSEUM: HOME OF THE LEGION OF VALOR is near downtown at 2425 Fresno St. (at O St.). It honors those who have received the nation's highest military honors—the Medal of Honor, the Distinguished Service Cross, the Navy Cross and the Air Force Cross. Uniforms, weapons, war memorabilia dating as far back as the Civil War and military equipment also are exhibited. **Time:** Allow 30 minutes minimum. **Hours:** Mon.-Sat. 10-3. Closed Jan. 1, Thanksgiving and Christmas. **Cost:** Free. **Phone:** (559) 498-0510.

Fresno Area

This index helps you "spot" where approved hotels and restaurants are located on the corresponding detailed maps. Hotel daily rate range is for comparison only. Restaurant price range is a combination of lunch and/or dinner. Turn to the listing page for more detailed rate and price information and consult display ads for special promotions.

FRESNO

Map Page	Hotels	Diamond Rated	Rate Range	Page
1 p. 126	Extended StayAmerica Fresno-North	◈◈	$79-$94	129
2 p. 126	TownePlace Suites by Marriott	◈◈◈	$89-$169	131
3 p. 126	Holiday Inn Express - River Park	◈◈◈	$89-$109	129
4 p. 126	**La Quinta Inn & Suites Fresno Riverpark**	◈◈◈	$119-$188 SAVE	130
5 p. 126	Hampton Inn & Suites	◈◈◈	$115-$159	129
6 p. 126	**Comfort Suites**	◈◈◈	$99-$149	128
7 p. 126	Rodeway Inn	◈◈	Rates not provided	130
8 p. 126	SpringHill Suites by Marriott	◈◈◈	$113-$169	130
9 p. 126	Homewood Suites by Hilton	◈◈◈	$132-$176	129
10 p. 126	**Summerfield Inn**	◈◈	$60-$80 SAVE	130
11 p. 126	**La Quinta Inn & Suites Fresno Northwest**	◈◈◈	$89-$166 SAVE	129
12 p. 126	Motel 6 Fresno #4390	◈◈	$50-$80	130
13 p. 126	**Comfort Inn**	◈◈	$69-$89 SAVE	128
14 p. 126	Garden Inn & Suites	◈◈◈	$110-$159	129
15 p. 126	Country Inn & Suites By Carlson North	◈◈◈	Rates not provided	128
16 p. 126	**Quality Inn**	◈◈	$70-$100 SAVE	130
17 p. 126	Piccadilly Inn-Shaw	◈◈◈	$109-$189	130
18 p. 126	Residence Inn by Marriott	◈◈◈	$98-$149	130
19 p. 126	Courtyard by Marriott-Shaw Ave	◈◈◈	$89-$149	129
20 p. 126	**BEST WESTERN PLUS Fresno Inn**	◈◈◈	$90-$160 SAVE	128
21 p. 126	**University Square Hotel**	◈◈◈	$79-$149 SAVE	131
22 p. 126	Red Roof Inn Fresno-Yosemite Gateway	◈◈	$69-$99	130
23 p. 126	**Park Inn by Radisson Fresno**	◈◈◈	$120-$185 SAVE	130
24 p. 126	**BEST WESTERN PLUS Village Inn**	◈◈◈	Rates not provided SAVE	128
25 p. 126	**Ambassador Inn & Suites**	◈◈	$55-$80 SAVE	128
26 p. 126	Holiday Inn Fresno Airport	◈◈◈	$99-$149	129
27 p. 126	Piccadilly Inn Express	◈◈	Rates not provided	130
28 p. 126	**Piccadilly Inn-Airport**	◈◈◈	$94-$119 SAVE	130
29 p. 126	Courtyard by Marriott-Fresno Airport	◈◈◈	$169-$186	128
30 p. 126	La Quinta Inn Fresno Yosemite	◈◈	$63-$133	130
31 p. 126	**Radisson Hotel**	◈◈◈	$89-$189 SAVE	130

Map Page	Restaurants	Diamond Rated	Cuisine	Price Range	Page
① p. 126	P.F. Chang's China Bistro	◈◈◈	Chinese	$10-$20	131
② p. 126	Ruth's Chris Steak House	◈◈◈	Steak	$23-$70	132
③ p. 126	Sal's Mexican Restaurant	◈◈	Mexican	$7-$13	132
④ p. 126	Toledo's Mexican Restaurant	◈◈	Mexican	$7-$20	132

Map Page	Restaurants (cont'd)	Diamond Rated	Cuisine	Price Range	Page
⑤ p. 126	Thai Royal Orchid	▼▼	Thai	$8-$25	132
⑥ p. 126	Veni Vidi Vici	▼▼▼	American	$21-$32	132
⑦ p. 126	Max's Bistro and Bar	▼▼▼	California	$11-$39	131
⑧ p. 126	Manhattan Steakhouse and Bar	▼▼▼	American	$24-$50	131
⑨ p. 126	Diana's Armenian Cuisine	▼▼	Armenian	$8-$12	131
⑩ p. 126	**Tacos Marquitos**	▼	Mexican	$5-$10	132
⑪ p. 126	The Cheesecake Factory	▼▼	American	$15-$30	131
⑫ p. 126	Smuggler's Restaurant	▼▼	California	$10-$29	132
⑬ p. 126	Rousseau	▼▼	Italian	$11-$28	132
⑭ p. 126	Skyline Cafe	▼▼	American	$8-$22	132
⑮ p. 126	Steak & Anchor	▼▼▼	Steak	$14-$26	132

CLOVIS

Map Page	Hotels	Diamond Rated	Rate Range	Page
34 p. 126	**Fairfield Inn & Suites Fresno Clovis**	▼▼▼	$99-$179 SAVE	81
35 p. 126	Comfort Suites	▼▼▼	$89-$119	81
36 p. 126	**BEST WESTERN Clovis Cole**	▼▼	$95-$165 SAVE	81
37 p. 126	Holiday Inn Express Hotel & Suites	▼▼▼	$89-$129	81

Map Page	Restaurant	Diamond Rated	Cuisine	Price Range	Page
18 p. 126	Andiamo Ristorante Italiano	▼▼	Italian	$7-$20	81

AMBASSADOR INN & SUITES (559)442-1082 **25**

▼▼▼ Motel $55-$80

Address: 1804 W Olive Ave 93728 **Location:** SR 99 exit Olive Ave, just w. **Facility:** 54 units. 2 stories (no elevator), exterior corridors. **Pool(s):** outdoor. **Guest Services:** coin laundry. **Free Special Amenities:** continental breakfast and high-speed Internet.

BEST WESTERN PLUS FRESNO INN (559)229-5811 **20**

▼▼▼ Hotel $90-$160

AAA Benefit: Members save up to 20%, plus 10% bonus points with Best Western Rewards®.

Address: 480 E Shaw Ave 93710 **Location:** SR 41 exit Shaw Ave, just e. **Facility:** 55 units. 3 stories, interior corridors. **Amenities:** Some: high-speed Internet. **Pool(s):** outdoor. **Activities:** whirlpool, exercise room. **Guest Services:** valet and coin laundry. **Free Special Amenities:** local telephone calls and high-speed Internet.

BEST WESTERN PLUS VILLAGE INN 559/226-2110 **24**

▼▼▼ Hotel Rates not provided

AAA Benefit: Members save up to 20%, plus 10% bonus points with Best Western Rewards®.

Address: 3110 N Blackstone Ave 93703 **Location:** SR 41 exit Shields Ave, 0.3 mi w. **Facility:** 151 units. 2 stories (no elevator), interior corridors. **Pool(s):** outdoor. **Activities:** whirlpool. **Free Special Amenities:** local telephone calls and high-speed Internet.

COMFORT INN (559)275-2374 **13**

▼▼▼ Hotel $69-$89

Address: 5455 W Shaw Ave 93722 **Location:** SR 99 exit Shaw Ave, just w. **Facility:** 69 units. 2 stories, interior corridors. **Terms:** cancellation fee imposed. **Amenities:** safes (fee). Some: high-speed Internet. **Pool(s):** outdoor. **Activities:** whirlpool, exercise room. **Guest Services:** valet laundry. **Free Special Amenities:** full breakfast and high-speed Internet.

COMFORT SUITES (559)435-5650 **6**

▼▼▼ Hotel $99-$149

Address: 102 E Herndon Ave 93720 **Location:** SR 41 exit Herndon Ave, just w. **Facility:** 70 units. 3 stories, interior corridors. **Terms:** cancellation fee imposed. **Amenities:** high-speed Internet. **Pool(s):** heated indoor. **Activities:** whirlpool, exercise room. **Guest Services:** valet and coin laundry. **Free Special Amenities:** full breakfast and high-speed Internet.

COUNTRY INN & SUITES BY CARLSON NORTH **15**

▼▼▼ Hotel. Rates not provided. **Address:** 6065 N Thesta Ave 93710 **Location:** SR 41 exit Bullard Ave, just e. **Facility:** 60 units. 3 stories, interior corridors. **Pool(s):** heated indoor. **Activities:** whirlpool, exercise room. **Guest Services:** valet and coin laundry.

COURTYARD BY MARRIOTT-FRESNO AIRPORT (559)251-5200 **29**

▼▼▼ Hotel $169-$186 **Address:** 1551 W Shaw Ave 93727 **Location:** SR 180 exit Peach Ave, 0.8 mi n. **Facility:** 116 units. 4 stories, interior corridors. **Amenities:** high-speed Internet. **Pool(s):** outdoor. **Activities:** whirlpool, exercise room. **Guest Services:** valet and coin laundry.

AAA Benefit: AAA hotel discounts of 5% or more.

(See map & index p. 126.)

COURTYARD BY MARRIOTT-SHAW AVE   (559)221-6000   **19**
▼▼▼ **Hotel $89-$149 Address:** 140 E Shaw Ave 93710 **Location:** SR 41 exit Shaw Ave W, just n. **Facility:** 146 units. 3 stories, interior corridors. **Amenities:** high-speed Internet. **Pool(s):** heated outdoor. **Activities:** whirlpool, exercise room. **Guest Services:** valet and coin laundry.

AAA Benefit: AAA hotel discounts of 5% or more.

EXTENDED STAYAMERICA FRESNO-NORTH
(559)438-7105   **1**
▼▼ **Extended Stay Hotel $79-$94 Address:** 7135 N Fresno St 93710 **Location:** SR 41 exit Herndon Ave E, just n. **Facility:** 120 kitchen units. 3 stories, exterior corridors. **Guest Services:** coin laundry.

GARDEN INN & SUITES   (559)277-3888   **14**
▼▼▼ **Hotel $110-$159 Address:** 4949 N Forestiere Ave 93722 **Location:** SR 99 exit Shaw Ave, just e. **Facility:** 40 units, some two bedrooms. 2 stories (no elevator), exterior corridors. **Terms:** cancellation fee imposed. **Amenities:** high-speed Internet. *Some:* safes. **Pool(s):** outdoor. **Activities:** whirlpool. **Guest Services:** valet and coin laundry.

HAMPTON INN & SUITES   (559)447-5900   **5**
▼▼▼ **Hotel $115-$159 Address:** 327 E Fir Ave 93720 **Location:** SR 41 exit Herndon Ave, just e. **Facility:** 85 units. 4 stories, interior corridors. **Terms:** 1-7 night minimum stay, cancellation fee imposed. **Amenities:** high-speed Internet. **Pool(s):** heated outdoor. **Activities:** whirlpool, exercise room. **Guest Services:** valet and coin laundry.

AAA Benefit: Members save up to 10%!

HOLIDAY INN EXPRESS - RIVER PARK   (559)577-1350   **3**
▼▼▼ **Hotel $89-$109 Address:** 7115 N Howard St 93720 **Location:** SR 41 exit Herndon Ave E, then just n. **Facility:** 86 units. 4 stories, interior corridors. **Amenities:** high-speed Internet. **Pool(s):** outdoor. **Activities:** whirlpool, exercise room. **Guest Services:** valet and coin laundry.

HOLIDAY INN FRESNO AIRPORT   (559)252-3611   **26**
▼▼▼ **Hotel $99-$149 Address:** 5090 E Clinton Ave 93727 **Location:** SR 180 exit Peach Ave, 1.4 mi n. **Facility:** 210 units. 2 stories (no elevator), interior corridors. **Dining:** Skyline Cafe, see separate listing. **Pool(s):** outdoor, heated indoor. **Activities:** whirlpool, exercise room. **Guest Services:** valet and coin laundry, area transportation-within 5 mi.

HOMEWOOD SUITES BY HILTON   (559)440-0801   **9**
▼▼▼ **Extended Stay Hotel $132-$176 Address:** 6820 N Fresno St 93710 **Location:** SR 41 exit Herndon Ave, just e. **Facility:** 119 efficiencies, some two bedrooms. 3 stories, interior corridors. **Terms:** 1-7 night minimum stay, cancellation fee imposed. **Amenities:** video games (fee), high-speed Internet. **Pool(s):** heated outdoor. **Activities:** whirlpool, basketball, exercise room. **Guest Services:** valet and coin laundry.

AAA Benefit: Contemporary luxury at a special Member rate.

LA QUINTA INN & SUITES FRESNO NORTHWEST
(559)275-3700   **11**
▼▼▼ **Hotel $89-$166**
Address: 5077 N Cornelia Ave 93722 **Location:** SR 99 exit Shaw Ave E, just n. **Facility:** 72 units. 3 stories, interior corridors. **Amenities:** high-speed Internet. **Pool(s):** heated outdoor. **Activities:** whirlpool, exercise room. **Guest Services:** coin laundry. **Free Special Amenities:** expanded continental breakfast and high-speed Internet.

Trust your vehicle to AAA/CAA Approved Auto Repair facilities

(See map & index p. 126.)

LA QUINTA INN & SUITES FRESNO RIVERPARK
(559)449-0928 **4**

Hotel
$119-$188

Address: 330 E Fir Ave 93720 **Location:** SR 41 exit Herndon Ave, just e. **Facility:** 56 units. 4 stories, interior corridors. **Amenities:** high-speed Internet. **Pool(s):** outdoor. **Activities:** whirlpool, exercise room. **Guest Services:** coin laundry. **Free Special Amenities:** expanded continental breakfast and use of on-premises laundry facilities.

LA QUINTA INN FRESNO YOSEMITE
(559)442-1110 **30**

Hotel $63-$133 **Address:** 2926 Tulare St 93721 **Location:** SR 99 exit Fresno St, 1 mi e to R St, then s, then just e. **Facility:** 128 units. 3 stories, interior/exterior corridors. **Amenities:** Some: high-speed Internet. **Pool(s):** outdoor. **Activities:** exercise room.

MOTEL 6 FRESNO #4390
(559)276-1910 **12**

Motel $50-$80 **Address:** 5021 N Barcus Ave 93722 **Location:** SR 99 exit Shaw Ave, just e. **Facility:** 86 units. 2 stories (no elevator), exterior corridors. **Terms:** 14 day cancellation notice-fee imposed. **Amenities:** safes. **Pool(s):** outdoor.

PARK INN BY RADISSON FRESNO
(559)226-2200 **23**

Hotel
$120-$185

Address: 3737 N Blackstone Ave 93726 **Location:** SR 41 exit Shields Ave, 0.3 mi w, then just e. **Facility:** 204 units. 2 stories (no elevator), interior corridors. **Amenities:** video games (fee), high-speed Internet. **Dining:** Smuggler's Restaurant, see separate listing. **Pool(s):** outdoor. **Activities:** whirlpool, exercise room. **Guest Services:** valet and coin laundry, area transportation-bus & train stations. **Free Special Amenities:** high-speed Internet and airport transportation.

PICCADILLY INN-AIRPORT
(559)375-7760 **28**

Hotel
$94-$119

Address: 5115 E McKinley Ave 93727 **Location:** SR 180 exit Peach Ave, 1 mi n. **Facility:** 185 units. 2 stories (no elevator), interior corridors. **Terms:** cancellation fee imposed. **Dining:** Steak & Anchor, see separate listing. **Pool(s):** outdoor. **Activities:** whirlpool, exercise room. **Guest Services:** valet and coin laundry, area transportation-bus & train stations.

PICCADILLY INN EXPRESS
559/375-7720 **27**

Hotel. Rates not provided. **Address:** 5113 E McKinley Ave 93727 **Location:** SR 180 exit Peach Ave, 1 mi n, then just w. **Facility:** 78 units. 2 stories (no elevator), interior corridors. **Pool(s):** outdoor.

PICCADILLY INN-SHAW
(559)348-5520 **17**

Hotel $109-$189 **Address:** 2305 W Shaw Ave 93711 **Location:** SR 99 exit Shaw Ave, 3 mi e. **Facility:** 194 units. 2 stories (no elevator), interior/exterior corridors. **Terms:** cancellation fee imposed. **Pool(s):** outdoor. **Activities:** whirlpool, putting green, exercise room. **Guest Services:** coin laundry.

QUALITY INN
(559)435-6593 **16**

Hotel
$70-$100

Address: 6051 N Thesta Ave 93710 **Location:** SR 41 exit Bullard Ave, just e. **Facility:** 56 units. 2 stories (no elevator), exterior corridors. **Pool(s):** outdoor. **Guest Services:** valet laundry. **Free Special Amenities:** expanded continental breakfast and high-speed Internet.

RADISSON HOTEL
(559)268-1000 **31**

Hotel
$89-$189

Address: 2233 Ventura St 93721 **Location:** SR 99 exit Ventura St, 0.5 mi e. Adjacent to convention center. **Facility:** 321 units. 8 stories, interior corridors. **Terms:** check-in 3:30 pm, cancellation fee imposed. **Amenities:** Some: safes. **Pool(s):** heated outdoor. **Activities:** saunas, whirlpool, exercise room. **Guest Services:** valet laundry, area transportation-bus & train stations. **Free Special Amenities:** high-speed Internet and airport transportation.

RED ROOF INN FRESNO-YOSEMITE GATEWAY
(559)222-4445 **22**

Hotel $69-$99 **Address:** 4141 N Blackstone Ave 93726 **Location:** SR 41 exit Ashlan Ave, 0.3 mi w. **Facility:** 134 units. 2 stories (no elevator), interior corridors. **Terms:** cancellation fee imposed. **Pool(s):** outdoor.

RESIDENCE INN BY MARRIOTT
(559)222-8900 **18**

Extended Stay Hotel $98-$149 **Address:** 5322 N Diana St 93710 **Location:** SR 41 exit Shaw Ave, 0.3 mi w, n on Blackstone Ave, then e on Barstow Ave. **Facility:** 120 kitchen units, some two bedrooms. 3 stories, interior corridors. **Amenities:** high-speed Internet. **Pool(s):** heated outdoor. **Activities:** whirlpool, sports court, exercise room. **Guest Services:** valet and coin laundry.

AAA Benefit:
AAA hotel discounts of 5% or more.

RODEWAY INN
559/431-3557 **7**

Hotel. Rates not provided. **Address:** 6730 N Blackstone Ave 93710 **Location:** SR 41 exit Herndon Ave W, then s. **Facility:** 137 units. 3 stories, exterior corridors. **Pool(s):** heated outdoor. **Activities:** whirlpool. **Guest Services:** coin laundry.

SPRINGHILL SUITES BY MARRIOTT
(559)431-0004 **8**

Hotel $113-$169 **Address:** 6844 N Fresno St 93710 **Location:** SR 41 exit Herndon Ave, just e. **Facility:** 118 units. 4 stories, interior corridors. **Amenities:** high-speed Internet. **Pool(s):** heated outdoor. **Activities:** whirlpool, exercise room. **Guest Services:** valet and coin laundry.

AAA Benefit:
AAA hotel discounts of 5% or more.

SUMMERFIELD INN
(559)439-0320 **10**

Motel
$60-$80

Address: 6309 N Blackstone Ave 93710 **Location:** SR 41 exit Bullard Ave W, just n. **Facility:** 35 units. 1 story, exterior corridors. **Terms:** cancellation fee imposed. **Amenities:** high-speed Internet. **Pool(s):** outdoor. **Guest Services:** coin laundry. **Free Special Amenities:** continental breakfast and high-speed Internet.

(See map & index p. 126.)

TOWNEPLACE SUITES BY MARRIOTT   (559)435-4600 **2**

▼▼▼▼ **Extended Stay Hotel**
$89-$169 **Address:** 7127 N Fresno St
93720 **Location:** SR 41 exit Herndon
Ave E, then just n. **Facility:** 92 kitchen
units, some two bedrooms. 3 stories, in-
terior corridors. **Amenities:** high-speed Internet. **Pool(s):** outdoor.
Activities: whirlpool, exercise room. **Guest Services:** valet and coin
laundry.

AAA Benefit:
AAA hotel discounts
of 5% or more.

[icons] SOME UNITS FEE

UNIVERSITY SQUARE HOTEL   (559)224-4200 **21**

▼▼▼
Hotel
$79-$149

Address: 4961 N Cedar Ave 93726 **Location:** SR 41 exit Shaw Ave, 1.5 mi e.
Facility: 190 units. 3 stories, interior corridors. **Terms:** cancellation fee imposed.
Pool(s): outdoor. **Activities:** whirlpool,
exercise room. **Guest Services:** valet and coin laundry, area
transportation-bus & train stations. **Free Special Amenities:** expanded continental breakfast and airport transportation.

[icons] SOME UNITS

WHERE TO EAT

THE CHEESECAKE FACTORY   559/228-1400 **11**

▼▼▼▼ American. Casual Dining. $15-$30 **AAA Inspector
Notes:** A display case of mouthwatering cheesecakes is the first thing
visitors see as they walk through the door. The extensive menu incor-
porates many types of cuisine, including Asian, Italian, Greek and
Spanish. **Bar:** full bar. **Address:** 639 E Shaw Ave 91301 **Location:**
SR 41 exit Shaw Ave, just e; in Fashion Fair Mall.

[L] [D] CALL

DIANA'S ARMENIAN CUISINE   559/277-9500 **9**

▼▼ Armenian. Casual Dining. $8-$12 **AAA Inspector Notes:**
Classic Armenian and Mediterranean cuisine, especially kebabs,
make up the menu at this conveniently located restaurant. Everything, including the baklava pastries for dessert, is made on the property. The staff is friendly and attentive. **Bar:** beer & wine. **Address:**
3050 W Shaw Ave, Suite 106 93711 **Location:** Just w of N Marks
Ave; in Target Shopping Center. [L] [D] CALL

MANHATTAN STEAKHOUSE AND BAR   559/449-1731 **8**

▼▼▼▼ American. Fine Dining. $24-$50 **AAA Inspector Notes:**
This restaurant offers a nice combination of fine dining and friendly,
professional service. The relaxed atmosphere shows a backdrop of
the famous New York skyline. **Bar:** full bar. **Reservations:** suggested. **Address:** 1731 W Bullard Ave 93711 **Location:** SR 99 exit
Bullard Ave, 5 mi e; at N West St. [D]

MAX'S BISTRO AND BAR   559/439-6900 **7**

▼▼▼▼ California. Fine Dining. $11-$39 **AAA Inspector Notes:**
This bistro has been a favorite in the area since 1997. The menu, offering California cuisine inspired by French preparations, changes to
reflect the freshest of ingredients. A great start to the meal is truffle
fries or seared scallops. Salads are meals in their own while entrées
include salmon served with cauliflower and eggplant hash or filet mignon in a brandy and peppercorn sauce. Be sure to save room for
one of their special desserts. **Bar:** full bar. **Reservations:** suggested.
Address: 1784 W Bullard Ave 93711 **Location:** At N West Ave.
[L] [D] CALL

P.F. CHANG'S CHINA BISTRO   559/438-0814 **1**

▼▼▼▼ Chinese. Casual Dining. $10-$20 **AAA Inspector
Notes:** Trendy, upscale decor provides a pleasant backdrop for New
Age Chinese dining. Appetizers, soups and salads are a meal by
themselves. Vegetarian plates and sides, noodles, meins, chicken
and meat dishes are created from exotic, fresh ingredients. **Bar:** full
bar. **Address:** 7894 N Blackstone Ave 93720 **Location:** SR 41 exit
Nees Ave, just w; in River Park Shopping Center.
[L] [D] CALL

ROUND TABLE PIZZA

▼ Pizza. Casual Dining. $7-$30 **AAA Inspector Notes:** This casual, family-oriented pizza place features high-quality ingredients and
dough rolled fresh daily. Distinctive specialty pizzas are piled high
with toppings. **Bar:** beer & wine. [L] [D]

For additional information, visit AAA.com
LOCATIONS:
Address: 7010 N Marks Ave, Suite 102 93711 **Location:** At W
Herndon Ave. **Phone:** 559/261-0778
Address: 3710 W Shields Ave 93722 **Location:** SR 99 exit Shields
Ave, just w. **Phone:** 559/271-7575
Address: 3262 E Tulare St 93702 **Location:** SR 41 exit E Tulare St,
just e. **Phone:** 559/485-7878
Address: 5040 N West Ave 93705 **Location:** Just n of W Shaw Ave.
Phone: 559/438-7676
Address: 5763 N First St 93710 **Location:** SR 41 exit E Bullard Ave
E, just s. **Phone:** 559/449-7676
Address: 7775 N First St 93710 **Location:** SR 41 exit Nees Ave,
just e. **Phone:** 559/435-7474

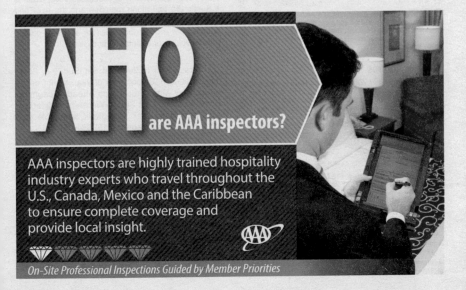

(See map & index p. 126.)

ROUSSEAU 559/445-1536 13
♦♦ Italian. Casual Dining. $11-$28 **AAA Inspector Notes:** Located in the downtown's Tower District, this creative Italian eatery offers a variety of specialty pasta dishes including ravioli with either lobster, artichoke, goat cheese or pumpkin. Meat dishes may include pork tenderloin with port wine, veal saltimbocca or grilled lamb chops. Service is warm and friendly. **Bar:** full bar. **Reservations:** suggested. **Address:** 568 E Olive Ave 93728 **Location:** SR 99 exit Olive Ave, 1.5 mi e, at Echo; in Tower District. **Parking:** street only.
L D

RUTH'S CHRIS STEAK HOUSE 559/490-0358 2
♦♦ Steak. Fine Dining. $23-$70 **AAA Inspector Notes:** The main fare is steak, which is prepared from several cuts of prime beef and cooked to perfection, but the menu also lists lamb, chicken and seafood dishes. Guests should come hungry because the side dishes, which are among the a la carte offerings, could make a meal in themselves. **Bar:** full bar. **Address:** 7844 N Blackstone Ave 93720 **Location:** SR 41 exit Blackstone Ave, just e. D CALL M

SAL'S MEXICAN RESTAURANT 559/438-3030 3
♦♦ Mexican. Casual Dining. $7-$13 **AAA Inspector Notes:** A tradition in the central valley for many years, this family-operated eatery serves up traditional favorites. Try one of Sal's special dishes such as incredible short ribs, chile verde or prawn fajitas. Bring an appetite as portions are hearty. **Bar:** full bar. **Address:** 7476 N Fresno St 93720 **Location:** SR 41 exit Herndon, 0.5 mi e on Fresno St; in Northgate Shopping Center. L D

SKYLINE CAFE 559/252-3611 14
♦♦ American. Casual Dining. $8-$22 **AAA Inspector Notes:** Near the airport, this cafe is a nice place for a quick yet relaxing meal. The salad bar is among popular choices at this breakfast, lunch and dinner spot. **Bar:** full bar. **Address:** 5090 E Clinton Ave 93727 **Location:** SR 180 exit Peach Ave, 1.4 mi n; in Holiday Inn Fresno Airport. B L D

SMUGGLER'S RESTAURANT 559/230-8450 12
♦♦ California. Casual Dining. $10-$29 **AAA Inspector Notes:** A city landmark for more than 30 years, this restaurant employs a friendly staff. The adjacent lounge is popular with tourists, businesspeople and locals alike. **Bar:** full bar. **Reservations:** suggested. **Address:** 3787 N Blackstone Ave 93726 **Location:** SR 41 exit Shields Ave, 0.3 mi w, then just n; in Park Inn by Radisson Fresno.
B D

STEAK & ANCHOR 559/251-6000 15
♦♦♦ Steak. Fine Dining. $14-$26 **AAA Inspector Notes:** A nice selection of beef, seafood and pasta dishes are available at this warm and welcoming restaurant. **Bar:** full bar. **Address:** 5115 E McKinley Ave 93727 **Location:** SR 180 exit Peach Ave, 1 mi n; in Piccadilly Inn-Airport. L D CALL M

TACOS MARQUITOS 559/447-5569 10
♦
Mexican
Quick Serve
$5-$10
AAA Inspector Notes: This favorite spot of students and the local crowd offers traditional Mexican favorites made with homemade tortillas. **Address:** 1772 E Barstow Ave 93710 **Location:** At Cedar Ave; adjacent to CSU Fresno; in Barstow Plaza. *Menu on AAA.com*
L D

TAHOE JOE'S FAMOUS STEAKHOUSE
♦♦ Steak. Casual Dining. $12-$28 **AAA Inspector Notes:** At this ski lodge-themed spot, aged steaks are grilled over an almond fire and slow roasted prime rib are top picks. Other menu selections include railroad camp shrimp and Joe's bowls (salads and burgers). **Bar:** full bar. L D CALL M
For additional information, visit AAA.com
LOCATIONS:
Address: 7006 N Cedar Ave 93720 **Location:** SR 41 exit Herndon Ave E. **Phone:** 559/299-9740
Address: 2700 W Shaw Ave 93711 **Location:** SR 99 exit Shaw Ave; at N Marks Ave. **Phone:** 559/277-8028

THAI ROYAL ORCHID 559/431-0132 5
♦♦ Thai. Casual Dining. $8-$25 **AAA Inspector Notes:** The aberrantly appointed dining rooms at this restaurant set the scene for a meal of Asian cuisine. The menu offers both Thai and Chinese specialties including rice and noodle dishes, seafood, poultry and pork. **Bar:** beer & wine. **Address:** 6735 N First St 93710 **Location:** SR 41 exit Herndon Ave E, just s. L D

TOLEDO'S MEXICAN RESTAURANT 559/438-5944 4
♦♦ Mexican. Casual Dining. $7-$20 **AAA Inspector Notes:** Long an area tradition, this restaurant offers a cozy dining room and there is live music on Sunday. The menu features a large selection of traditional Mexican dishes and there also are many specialty Margaritas offered. Most people prefer eating on the covered patio. **Bar:** full bar. **Address:** 7315 N Blackstone Ave 93710 **Location:** SR 41 exit Herndon Ave, just w, then just n. B L D

VENI VIDI VICI 559/266-5510 6
♦♦♦ American. Fine Dining. $21-$32 **AAA Inspector Notes:** Located in the historic area of the Tower District, this local favorite is creative in both the décor and menu. A brick wall is filled with paintings from local artists. The menu offers fresh ingredients in its preparations including shrimp and pasta, portobello ravioli, salmon with horseradish aioli and New York steak in red wine tomatillo demi glaze. **Bar:** full bar. **Address:** 1116 N Fulton St 93728 **Location:** SR 99 exit Olive Ave, 1.5 mi e, then just s. **Parking:** street only. D

GALT (E-3) pop. 23,647, elev. 52'

COSUMNES RIVER PRESERVE is 2.4 mi. n. on SR 99, 7 mi. w. off exit 277 on SR 104 (Twin Cities Rd.), then 1.8 mi. s. to the visitor center at 13501 Franklin Blvd. The preserve protects more than 46,000 acres. A sampling of the habitats can be appreciated by two brief walks, a paddle trip on the Cosumnes River or a self-guiding driving tour.

The visitor center has interpretive displays and information about habitats and native wildlife. From here visitors can access the paved, 1-mile Lost Slough Wetlands Walk, a boardwalk that leads to an observation platform. The Cosumnes River Walk is a 3-mile dirt trail along marshes and the river and through forested areas. Non-gas-powered boats can launch from a boat dock. Visitors also can participate in volunteer restoration activities.

Hours: Visitor center open Sat.-Sun. 9-5, Sept.-June; Sat.-Sun. 8-noon, rest of year. Visitor center hours vary Mon.-Fri.; phone ahead. Cosumnes River Walk and Lost Slough Wetlands Walk accessible daily dawn-dusk. Boardwalk accessible daily 10-4. **Cost:** Free. **Phone:** (916) 684-2816.

BEST WESTERN GALT INN (209)745-9500
♦♦♦
Hotel
$66-$70

AAA Benefit: Members save up to 20%, plus 10% bonus points with Best Western Rewards®.
Address: 620 N Lincoln Way 95632 **Location:** SR 99 exit 275A (Simmerhorn Rd) northbound, just e, then just nw; exit 275B (Pringle Ave) southbound, just sw. **Facility:** 44 units. 2 stories (no elevator), interior corridors. **Terms:** cancellation fee imposed. **Amenities:** high-speed Internet. **Pool(s):** outdoor. **Activities:** whirlpool, exercise room. **Guest Services:** valet and coin laundry. **Free Special Amenities:** local telephone calls and high-speed Internet.
  CALL M  BIZ

COMFORT INN & SUITES   (209)744-7800

Hotel
$79-$229

Address: 10380 Twin Cities Rd 95632 **Location:** SR 99 exit 277 (SR 104/Jackson) to Twin Cities Rd, then just e; in Raley's Shopping Center. **Facility:** 70 units. 3 stories, interior corridors.
Terms: cancellation fee imposed. **Amenities:** high-speed Internet. **Pool(s):** heated indoor. **Activities:** whirlpool, exercise room. **Guest Services:** coin laundry. **Free Special Amenities: expanded continental breakfast and high-speed Internet.**

SAVE ⓘ CALL ⓖM 🏊 BIZ 🛜 🔌 🍴 🖥

WHOLEY RAVIOLI ITALIAN RISTORANTE   209/745-5109

🔷🔷 Italian. Casual Dining. $7-$21 **AAA Inspector Notes:** Tucked away in a shopping center, this restaurant serves giant, hand-made ravioli and other traditional Italian fare from home-style recipes. Lunch specials and complete four-course dinners are available. **Bar:** beer & wine. **Address:** 1067 C St, Suite 132 95632 **Location:** SR 99 exit 274B (Central Galt), just s on Fairway Dr, then just w; southeast corner of Galt Plaza Shopping Center. ⓛ ⓓ CALL ⓖM

Learn the local driving laws at DrivingLaws.AAA.com

GARBERVILLE pop. 913

BENBOW INN
(707)923-2124

Historic Hotel
$110-$595

Address: 445 Lake Benbow Dr 95542
Location: US 101 exit Benbow Lake Rd, just w; 2 mi s of downtown. **Facility:** A spot of tea with scones is an afternoon tradition at this English Tudor-style inn. Guest rooms are furnished in period pieces and include complimentary sherry. 57 units. 3 stories (no elevator), interior corridors. **Terms:** 5 day cancellation notice-fee imposed. **Dining:** Benbow Inn Restaurant, see separate listing. **Pool(s):** heated outdoor. **Activities:** whirlpool, bicycles, hiking trails, jogging, horseshoes, shuffleboard. **Fee:** golf-9 holes, game room. **Guest Services:** valet and coin laundry. **Free Special Amenities:** room upgrade (subject to availability with advance reservations) and high-speed Internet.

BEST WESTERN PLUS HUMBOLDT HOUSE INN
(707)923-2771

Motel
$110-$140

AAA Benefit: Members save up to 20%, plus 10% bonus points with Best Western Rewards®.

Address: 701 Redwood Dr 95542 **Location:** US 101 exit Garberville, just e. **Facility:** 76 units, some two bedrooms and kitchens. 2-3 stories (no elevator), exterior corridors. **Amenities:** *Some:* high-speed Internet. **Pool(s):** heated outdoor. **Activities:** whirlpool. **Guest Services:** coin laundry. **Free Special Amenities:** full breakfast and high-speed Internet.

(See ad this page.)

Visit your AAA/CAA Travel office to book a AAA Vacations® Disney package

HUMBOLDT REDWOODS INN
(707)923-2451

Motel
$65-$115

Address: 987 Redwood Dr 95542 **Location:** On US 101 business route. **Facility:** 20 units, some two bedrooms. 1 story, exterior corridors. **Terms:** check-in 4 pm. **Free Special Amenities:** high-speed Internet.

▼ See AAA listing this page ▼

WHERE TO EAT

BENBOW INN RESTAURANT   707/923-2124

Regional California Fine Dining
$22-$45

AAA Inspector Notes: *Historic.* Listed as a national historic landmark, the restaurant is an oasis for pleasant dining and good food made from fresh ingredients. The patio is a great spot for relaxing. The wine selection is plentiful. **Bar:** full bar. **Reservations:** suggested. **Address:** 445 Lake Benbow Dr 95542 **Location:** US 101 exit Benbow Lake Rd, just w; 2 mi s of downtown; in Benbow Inn. B D JC

CECIL'S NEW ORLEANS BISTRO   707/923-7007

Creole. Casual Dining. $20-$36 **AAA Inspector Notes:** With the ceiling fan spinning lazily and blues music playing in the background, this modest restaurant offers up Californian Cajun food. Try the wild boar and okra gumbo, the crawfish pasta or the home-made pecan pie with bananas Foster and ice cream. Live music at the bar gets the place hopping on Thursdays and Fridays. **Bar:** full bar. **Address:** 773 Redwood Dr 95542 **Location:** Downtown; in Jacob Garber Square on 2nd Floor. **Parking:** street only. D

GEYSERVILLE (A-7) pop. 862, elev. 209'
- **Attractions map p. 567**
- **Part of Wine Country area — see map p. 562**

Despite the name, there aren't any geysers in the vicinity of Geyserville—steaming hot springs and fumaroles were discovered in the area in the mid-19th century, and these natural phenomena were mistaken for geysers.

"Downtown," along Geyserville Avenue, the main thoroughfare, earns such overused adjectives as quaint and rustic due to a scattering of eclectic shops and eateries as well as Locals (21023 Geyserville Ave.), a popular tasting room featuring the award-winning products of 11 regional wineries. A handful of cozy Victorian-style bed and breakfast inns make convenient home bases for exploring some of the approximately 50 wineries in the nearby Alexander and Dry Creek valleys.

Outdoor enthusiasts head to nearby Lake Sonoma for kayaking, fishing and canoeing. Bike tours travel the Alexander Valley's rolling hills, passing bucolic pasturelands laced with grapevines. And although visitors usually venture to "big city" neighbor Healdsburg for provisions, it's always fun to stop by the Jimtown Store (6706 SR 128). This quintessential country store, decorated with vintage Americana, offers a heaping helping of nostalgia along with plenty of fixings for a gourmet picnic lunch.

LAKE SONOMA MILT BRANDT VISITOR CENTER, 3333 Skaggs Springs Rd., displays Pomo Indian baskets and arrowheads and has exhibits about local flora and fauna. It also provides information about recreational activities in the Lake Sonoma/Warm Springs Dam area. Steelhead are raised at the Congressman Don Clausen Fish Hatchery, behind the visitor center. There's a designated swimming area at Yorty Creek.

Note: The visitor center and hatchery are currently closed for renovations and are tentatively scheduled to reopen Apr. 15, 2013. Phone ahead for updated information. **Cost:** Free. **Phone:** (707) 431-4533.

WINERIES

- **Clos du Bois** is at 19410 Geyserville Ave. **Hours:** Tastings daily 10-4:30. Marlstone Experience (includes tour and tasting) daily at 12:30, May.-Nov. Reservation required for Marlstone Experience. Closed major holidays. **Phone:** (800) 222-3189.

- **Francis Ford Coppola Winery** is w. off US 101 Independence Ln. exit to 300 Via Archimedes. **Hours:** Tastings daily 11-6. A variety of tours are offered daily; phone ahead for schedule. **Phone:** (707) 857-1400 or (877) 590-3329.

GEYSERVILLE INN   (707)857-4343

Hotel
$115-$499

Address: 21714 Geyserville Ave 95441 **Location:** US 101 exit E Canyon Rd, just s. **Facility:** 41 units. 2 stories (no elevator), interior corridors. **Terms:** 2 night minimum stay - seasonal and/or weekends, 3 day cancellation notice. **Amenities:** high-speed Internet. **Pool(s):** outdoor. **Activities:** whirlpool. **Free Special Amenities:** local telephone calls and high-speed Internet.

HOPE-MERRILL HOUSE   707/857-3356

Historic Bed & Breakfast. Rates not provided. **Address:** 21253 Geyserville Ave 95441 **Location:** US 101 exit Geyserville Ave/SR 128 E, 1.3 mi ne. **Facility:** The Hope-Merrill House is a late-1800s Victorian; four units are also available at the Hope-Bosworth House across the street. 12 units. 2 stories (no elevator), interior corridors. **Terms:** check-in 3:30 pm. **Pool(s):** heated outdoor.

WHERE TO EAT

DIAVOLA PIZZERIA   707/814-0111

Pizza. Casual Dining. $14-$25 **AAA Inspector Notes:** If author/chef Anthony Bourdain ate at this contemporary pizzeria/salumeria, he would go for the ox tongue salad followed by pork belly pizza. To wash it down, he would order a nice red wine and finish off with panna cotta and an espresso. **Bar:** full bar. **Address:** 21021 Geyserville Ave 95441 **Location:** US 101 exit Geyserville Ave/SR 128, 0.5 mi s. **Parking:** street only. L D

GILROY (G-3) pop. 48,821, elev. 194'
- **Hotels p. 136 • Restaurants p. 136**

Garlic was first commercially grown in Gilroy by immigrant Japanese farmers following World War I, and today this town a little more than an hour's drive south of San Francisco is the world's largest garlic processor. The darling of cooks and bane of vampires is a $100-million-a-year industry in the self-proclaimed "Garlic Capital of the World." During the annual Garlic Festival in July, this distinctively fragrant relative of the onion is showcased in every imaginable edible form.

Among nearly 50 historic buildings, many of them along Monterey Street downtown, are the 1897 I.O.O.F. Children's Home for California and the 1906 City Hall. The 1910 Carnegie Library building on the corner of Fifth and Church streets now houses the Gilroy Historical Museum, which displays historical photographs and regional artifacts; phone (408) 846-0446.

Gilroy Welcome Center: 8155 Arroyo Cir., Suite 6, Gilroy, CA 95020. **Phone:** (408) 842-6436.

Self-guiding tours: The welcome center and the Gilroy Historical Museum both offer a walking tour pamphlet of Gilroy's historic district for $1. Oenophiles can follow the Gilroy Wine Trail to approximately a dozen wineries; for more information write P.O. Box 48764, Los Angeles, CA 90048.

Shopping areas: Gilroy Premium Outlets, 681 Leavesley Rd., has more than 145 stores, including Ann Taylor, Banana Republic, Eddie Bauer, Gap, Levi's, Polo Ralph Lauren and Tommy Hilfiger. Browse for antiques in historic downtown Gilroy along a five-block stretch of Monterey Street.

GILROY GARDENS FAMILY THEME PARK is w. on SR 152 (Hecker Pass Hwy. W.) to just past Burchell Rd., following signs. This 28-acre theme park is centered around trees and horticulture but also has more than 40 rides and attractions geared to families with young children. For kids there are several roller coasters, a monorail, a rock maze, a 1927 carousel, antique car rides, and pitch and win games. Adults can admire the extensive themed gardens and pick up gardening tips. Be sure to check out the "circus trees," topiaries that have been grafted together to form interesting shapes.

Hours: Park open Mon.-Fri. 11-5, Sat.-Sun. 10-6, early June-late Aug. (also spring break week in mid-Apr.); Sat.-Sun. 10-6 (also some Mon. and Fri. holidays), early Apr.-early June and late Aug.-Nov. 30. Phone ahead to confirm schedule. **Cost:** $44.99; $34.99 (ages 3-10 and 62+). **Parking:** $10. **Phone:** (408) 840-7100.

BEST WESTERN PLUS FOREST PARK INN
(408)848-5144

Hotel
$109-$239

AAA Benefit: Members save up to 20%, plus 10% bonus points with Best Western Rewards®.

Address: 375 Leavesley Rd 95020 **Location:** US 101 exit Leavesley Rd, just w. **Facility:** 122 units, some two bedrooms. 3 stories, interior corridors. **Amenities:** video games (fee). *Some:* high-speed Internet. **Pool(s):** heated outdoor. **Activities:** sauna, whirlpool, tennis court, exercise room. **Guest Services:** valet and coin laundry. **Free Special Amenities:** local telephone calls and high-speed Internet.

GILROY INN
408/847-0688

Motel
Rates not provided

Address: 611 Leavesley Rd 95020 **Location:** US 101 exit Leavesley Rd, just e. **Facility:** 44 units. 2 stories (no elevator), exterior corridors. **Guest Services:** coin laundry.

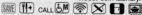

HILTON GARDEN INN GILROY (408)840-7000

Hotel $119-$209 **Address:** 6070 Monterey Rd 95020 **Location:** US 101 exit Monterey Rd, just w. **Facility:** 137 units. 4 stories, interior corridors. **Terms:** 1-7 night minimum stay, cancellation fee imposed. **Amenities:** *Some:* high-speed Internet. **Pool(s):** heated outdoor. **Activities:** whirlpool, exercise room. **Guest Services:** valet and coin laundry.

AAA Benefit: Unparalleled hospitality at a special Member rate.

QUALITY INN & SUITES (408)847-5500

Hotel
$79-$249

Address: 8430 Murray Ave 95020 **Location:** US 101 exit Leavesley Rd, just w. **Facility:** 47 units. 2 stories (no elevator), exterior corridors. **Terms:** cancellation fee imposed. **Pool(s):** outdoor. **Activities:** whirlpool. **Guest Services:** coin laundry. **Free Special Amenities:** full breakfast and high-speed Internet.

WHERE TO EAT

BLACK BEAR DINER 408/842-9901

American. Casual Dining. $7-$16 **AAA Inspector Notes:** A homey atmosphere characterizes this family-oriented restaurant. Familiar comfort foods, such as meatloaf with mashed potatoes, are at the heart of the menu and are served in generous portions. **Bar:** beer & wine. **Address:** 395 Leavesley Rd 95020 **Location:** US 101 exit Leavesley Rd, just w. B L D CALL

CIELITO LINDO RESTAURANT 408/842-7724

Mexican. Casual Dining. $6-$15 **AAA Inspector Notes:** Located in the historic downtown area, this favorite spot of the locals offers traditional Mexican favorites including burritos, tacos, tamales and chimichangas. **Bar:** beer & wine. **Address:** 7460 Monterey Rd 95020 **Location:** US 101 exit Monterey Rd, 1.5 mi nw; just n of 6th St. **Parking:** street only. B L D

FRESH CHOICE 408/842-6919

American. Cafeteria. $8-$15 **AAA Inspector Notes:** The salad bar of salad bars, the casual restaurant invites patrons to make their own or try one of the already prepared varieties. Other items include freshly baked breads, pizza and soup, as well as make-your-own sundaes for dessert. **Bar:** beer & wine. **Address:** 8697 San Ysidro Ave 95020 **Location:** US 101 exit Leavesley Rd, just e, then just n; in outlet center. L D

ROUND TABLE PIZZA 408/842-0321

Pizza. Casual Dining. $7-$28 **AAA Inspector Notes:** This casual, family-oriented pizza place features high-quality ingredients and dough rolled fresh daily. Distinctive specialty pizzas are piled high with toppings. **Bar:** beer & wine. **Address:** 815 First St 95020 **Location:** At Wren Ave. L D

GLEN ELLEN (B-8) pop. 784, elev. 230'

- Attractions map p. 568
- Hotels & Restaurants map & index p. 570
- Part of Wine Country area — see map p. 562

It's refreshing that Glen Ellen hasn't changed that much since the early 20th century, when author Jack London settled here to build his dream ranch and estate. "Sonoma" is the term Native Americans used to describe the sight of the moon rising from a backdrop of rolling hills, a vista that inspired missionary Father Jose Altimira to give it the name "Valley of the Moon." London also penned a novel by the same name.

(See map & index p. 570.)

Today's travelers head to this charming enclave's trendy eateries that specialize in gourmet fare paired with local wines. Glen Ellen makes a convenient base from which to explore Sonoma's most popular wineries; some offer concerts, food pairings and other activities in addition to the usual tastings. You can view fine art at the Imagery Estate Winery (14335 SR 12), learn about organic farming at the Benziger Family Winery, and check out Doobie Brothers memorabilia or attend an olive curing workshop at the B.R. Cohn Winery.

Sample the delectable cheeses at Raymond & Co., then head next door for a taste of the divine Zinfandel-flavored ganache at Wine Country Chocolates. Pick up items for a savory picnic lunch at the Village Market (13751 Arnold Dr.) and take your portable feast to one of the area wineries with picnic facilities. Another delightful spot for a picnic is Sonoma Valley Regional Park, 13630 Sonoma Hwy. It's particularly lovely when colorful wildflowers bloom in the spring. Jack London State Historic Park *(see attraction listing)* also is a favorite picnicking and hiking spot.

JACK LONDON STATE HISTORIC PARK, 1 mi. w. on London Ranch Rd., contains 800 acres and encompasses the author's ranch, house and grave. The two-story museum house contains his papers, personal belongings and mementos of his travels, including South Pacific art objects. The burnt ruins of Wolf House, the 26-room mansion he built but never lived in, are nearby. The original cottage, where London died in 1916, contains period furnishings. *See Recreation Areas Chart.*

Off-road vehicles are not permitted. Leashed dogs are permitted in historic area only. **Time:** Allow 1 hour, 30 minutes minimum. **Hours:** Park and museum open Thurs.-Mon. 9:30-5. Cottage open Thurs.-Mon. noon-4. Closed Jan. 1, Thanksgiving and Christmas. Phone ahead to confirm schedule. **Cost:** Day use $10 per private vehicle; $9 (ages 62+ per private vehicle). **Phone:** (707) 938-5216. 🎯 🏕

QUARRYHILL BOTANICAL GARDEN is at 12841 Sonoma Hwy. (SR 12). This Asian-inspired public garden, set above vineyards on 25 acres of rocky, steep hillsides, is dedicated to preserving biodiversity. To accomplish this goal, seed-collecting trips to Asia each year have resulted in the oaks, maples, dogwoods, lilies and roses that form the basis of the garden. Ponds and waterfalls add beauty to the site.

Hours: Daily 9-4. Last admission 1 hour before closing. Guided 90-minute tours are given the third Sat. of the month at 10, Mar.-Oct. Closed major holidays. **Cost:** $10; $5 (students with ID); free (ages 65+ on Tues.). Guided tour $15; $10 (students with ID). **Phone:** (707) 996-3166, or (707) 996-6027 for reservations. 🏕

WINERIES
- **Benziger Family Winery** is at 1883 London Ranch Rd. **Hours:** Daily 10-5. Tram tours are given daily on the half-hour 11-noon and 1-3:30. Behind-the-scenes tours with tastings are offered daily at 11:15, 12:45 and 2:15. Closed Jan. 1, Easter, Thanksgiving and Christmas. **Phone:** (888) 490-2739. ◾

- **B.R. Cohn Winery** is at 15000 Sonoma Hwy. **Hours:** Tastings and self-guiding tours daily 10-5. Closed Thanksgiving and Christmas. **Phone:** (707) 938-4064 or (800) 330-4064.

JACK LONDON LODGE   707/938-8510 **41**

♦♦ **Hotel.** Rates not provided. **Address:** 13740 Arnold Dr 95442 **Location:** SR 12 exit Arnold Dr, 1 mi w; downtown. **Facility:** 22 units. 2 stories (no elevator), exterior corridors. **Dining:** Wolf House, see separate listing. **Pool(s):** outdoor. **Activities:** whirlpool.

🍽 🍷 🛤 🛜 ⊠ 🛢 ▭

GAIGE HOUSE, A JOIE DE VIVRE HOTEL   707/935-0237

fyi Not evaluated. **Address:** 13540 Arnold Dr 95442 **Location:** SR 12 exit Arnold Dr, 0.5 mi w. Facilities, services, and décor characterize a mid-scale property.

WHERE TO EAT

WOLF HOUSE   707/996-4401 **23**

♦♦ American. Gastro Pub. $11-$27 **AAA Inspector Notes:** This classic pub was reputed to be Jack London's hangout whenever he had writer's block. Movie posters and old photographs line the walls. Locals favorites include fried calamari and burgers. **Bar:** full bar. **Address:** 13740 Arnold Dr 95442 **Location:** SR 12 exit Arnold Dr, 1 mi w; downtown; in Jack London Lodge.

Ⓛ Ⓓ 🍴

GOLDEN GATE NATIONAL RECREATION AREA (C-7)
- **Part of San Francisco area — see map p. 342**

Encompassing both the rolling coastal hill country north of the Golden Gate Bridge and the diverse urban parklands strung around San Francisco's northern and western edges, Golden Gate National Recreation Area covers approximately 74,000 acres of land and water.

The Marin Headlands across the Golden Gate Bridge contrast dramatically with the densely packed city to the south. Smooth, grassy ridges slope down through valleys to a craggy shoreline scalloped with sandy coves. Abandoned gun emplacements stud the hillsides above the Golden Gate and offer good vantage points for viewing the bridge and the city.

Northward from the Marin Headlands are Mount Tamalpais State Park *(see Mill Valley p. 196)* and Muir Woods National Monument *(see place listing p. 233).* Beyond the state park, the Olema Valley section of the recreation area abuts Point Reyes National Seashore *(see place listing p. 284).*

About 100 miles of hiking and riding trails traverse the pastoral countryside between Point Reyes and the Golden Gate. Hikers should stay on the trails, as the hillsides are often laced with poison oak. Dress in layers so you can adapt to the changeable weather (cool ocean winds and frequent fog). Swimming is permitted at Stinson Beach, China Beach, Muir Beach and Aquatic Park. Back-country campsites require reservations. Fishing spots and picnic facilities are scattered throughout these parklands.

The Marine Mammal Center, in the Marin Headlands at 2000 Bunker Rd., rescues and rehabilitates marine animals native to this section of California coast; phone (415) 289-7325 for information regarding hours of operation. *See attraction listing in Sausalito p. 511.*

Fort Baker, across the bay from San Francisco, was once filled with artillery fortifications. It is now a popular recreational area offering hiking, bicycling, fishing and picnicking as well as splendid views of the bay and Angel Island. To reach Fort Baker, follow signs after taking the Alexander Avenue exit across the Golden Gate Bridge; phone (415) 331-1540 for additional information.

The southern extreme of the recreation area is Fort Funston, where hang gliders launch themselves from the cliffs. The long, windswept strand of Ocean Beach links Fort Funston with the Cliff House, the adjacent Sutro Baths and Lands End *(see attraction listing in San Francisco p. .377)*, the city's northwestern corner. The Coastal Trail follows Lands End to China and Baker beaches and the abandoned coastal batteries just south of the Golden Gate Bridge.

The Golden Gate Promenade extends 3.5 miles along the shore of San Francisco Bay and connects Fort Point, below the Golden Gate Bridge, with Crissy Field and Fort Mason. Alcatraz Island *(see attraction listing in San Francisco p. .363)* also is part of the recreation area. The information center at Fort Mason is open Mon.-Fri. 9:30-4:30. For further information write the Information Center, Golden Gate National Recreation Area, Building 201, Fort Mason, San Francisco, CA 94123; phone (415) 561-4700. *See Recreation Areas Chart.*

BAY AREA DISCOVERY MUSEUM is off US 101 at 557 McReynolds Rd. in Golden Gate National Recreation Area at the n. end of Golden Gate Bridge. The hands-on children's museum features both indoor exhibitions and outdoor activities. Crawling through an underwater sea tunnel, creating natural art and fishing off a boat or pier are some of the activities offered. Tot Spot is an animal habitat environment for ages 1-3.

Hours: Tues.-Fri. 9-4, Sat.-Sun. 10-5. Closed major holidays and the last 2 weeks in Sept. **Cost:** $11; free (ages 0-5 months). **Phone:** (415) 339-3900. ⓉⒾ

FORT POINT NATIONAL HISTORIC SITE is at the s. end of the Golden Gate Bridge, off Long Ave. at the end of Marine Dr. Built by the U.S. Army between 1853 and 1861, Fort Point is similar in design to Fort Sumter, S.C. Although it once was the principal defense bastion on the West Coast, no battle ever occurred at Fort Point.

Practically beneath Golden Gate Bridge, this vantage point affords expansive views of Angel and Alcatraz islands and San Francisco Bay. The fishing pier across from the Warming Hut, at the western end of Crissy Field, offers a prime view of the Golden Gate Bridge.

To reach the bridge from Fort Point, walk along Marine Drive until you see the sign for the steps that lead up a hill to the bridge's southeast side visitor parking lot. The climb is steep but fairly short (fourtenths of a mile), and there's an up-close perspective of the bridge that you won't get anywhere else.

The Warming Hut has a selection of books and eco-friendly gifts as well as a cafe. You also can watch video presentations about the history of the fort and the construction of the Golden Gate Bridge. There are restrooms in the building behind the Warming Hut. Free guided 30-minute tours of the site as well as cannon-loading demonstrations are offered. **Note:** During security alerts the fort may be closed. **Hours:** Daily 10-5. Closed Jan. 1 and Christmas. Phone ahead to confirm schedule. **Cost:** Free. **Phone:** (415) 556-1693.

PRESIDIO OF SAN FRANCISCO, in the n.w. section of the city, was an active military garrison almost continuously for 218 years; it closed as an Army post in 1994. Within the 1,480-acre site are historic military barracks as well as wooded areas, beaches, and expansive bay and ocean vistas.

The Presidio's boundaries encompass Fort Point, San Francisco National Cemetery, Fort Winfield Scott, Crissy Field, The Walt Disney Family Museum and film and animation giant Lucasfilm Ltd. Maps outlining 11 miles of hiking and bicycling trails are available at the visitor center in Building 150 on Montgomery Street, near the corner of Lincoln Boulevard.

Note: A new, permanent visitor center is being built and is scheduled to open sometime in 2014; phone for updated information. **Tours:** Guided tours are available. **Hours:** Visitor center open Thurs.-Sun. 10-5. Closed Jan. 1, Thanksgiving and Christmas. **Cost:** Park and guided tours free. **Phone:** (415) 561-4323 or TTY (415) 561-4314.

◆ⒼⒺⓂ ⓈⒶⓋⒺ **The Walt Disney Family Museum** is at 104 Montgomery St. in the Presidio of San Francisco. The inspirational story of Walt Disney, from his beginnings on a Marceline, Mo., farm to his rise to the pinnacle of the entertainment world, is told in 10 galleries on the site of this former military base.

Walls of family photographs include some photos that are actually video screens showing Disney family home movies. Listening stations, interactive displays and more than 200 video monitors show the progression of Disney's achievements in animation, the development of the Disney theme parks and improvements in technology. Mickey Mouse's evolution over the years is depicted, and visitors have an opportunity to try their hand at animation.

Many original artworks from the Disney archives and trophies, such as Oscars, can be seen. The Oscar for "Snow White and the Seven Dwarfs," which was made specially for Disney, features one large and seven small figures. A model of Disneyland is so intricate it even shows the details of the tea cup ride.

Time: Allow 2 hours minimum. **Hours:** Wed.-Mon. 10-6. Last admission is 1 hour, 15 minutes before closing. Closed Jan. 1, Thanksgiving and Christmas. **Cost:** $20; $15 (ages 66+ and students with ID); $12 (ages 6-17). Admission is by a timed-entry ticket; tickets can be purchased at the door or online. Last ticket is sold at 4:45. **Phone:** (415) 345-6800. ⑪

GRAEAGLE pop. 737

CHALET VIEW LODGE   (530)832-5528
▼▼▼▼ Boutique Hotel $89-$315 **Address:** 72056 Hwy 70 96103 **Location:** Jct SR 70 and 89, 5.7 mi e on SR 70. **Facility:** This distinctive hotel features upscale appointments in its public spaces and luxurious rooms, terrace suites, villas and private cabins. Most units feature loft bedrooms. 49 units, some two bedrooms, cabins and cottages. 1 story, exterior corridors. **Terms:** 7 day cancellation notice-fee imposed. **Pool(s):** outdoor. **Activities:** whirlpool, fishing, snowmobiling, playground, basketball, horseshoes, volleyball, spa. *Fee:* golf-9 holes.

⑪ ▼ 🛎 FEE 🛗 BIZ 🛜 ✕ 🖥
/ SOME UNITS FEE 🐾 🎿 🛁 📠

GRAEAGLE MEADOWS   530/836-1100
🔘 fyi Not evaluated. **Address:** 6934 SR 89 96103 **Location:** Jct SR 70 and 89, 1.7 mi se. Facilities, services, and décor characterize a mid-scale property.

WHERE TO EAT

GRAEAGLE MILL WORKS CAFE   530/836-2828
▼▼ Sandwiches Soup. Casual Dining. $5-$9 **AAA Inspector Notes:** This cozy cafe serves home-style soups and chowder, sandwiches, pastries and seasonal pies and desserts. Gourmet coffee is presented in an assortment of coffee mugs while tea is served in old-fashioned teapots. Picnic lunches are available for any occasion. The seasonal outdoor patio has a play area for pets. **Address:** 115 Hwy 89 96103 **Location:** 0.5 mi s of jct SR 70 and 89. B L

GRANITE BAY pop. 20,402
• Hotels & Restaurants map & index p. 314

THE HABIT BURGER GRILL   916/791-6790 65
▼ Burgers. Quick Serve. $4-$7 **AAA Inspector Notes:** Since 1969, this California chain has been serving quality burgers, char-grilled sandwiches and made-to-order salads. Sidewalk seating is available in season. **Address:** 4060 Douglas Blvd, Suite 109 95746 **Location:** I-80 exit Douglas Blvd, 2.5 mi e; located in Sierra Oaks Plaza Center. L D CALL ⑤M

HAWKS RESTAURANT   916/791-6200 66
▼▼▼ American. Fine Dining. $8-$38 **AAA Inspector Notes:** Modern American cuisine with an emphasis on fresh local ingredients is served at this casually upscale restaurant with some tables and the patio overlooking the Quarry Ponds. Lunch is served Tuesday through Friday and brunch is offered the second Sunday of every month. **Bar:** full bar. **Reservations:** suggested. **Address:** 5530 Douglas Blvd, Suite 110 95746 **Location:** I-80 exit Douglas Blvd, 3.7 mi e; in Quarry Ponds Town Center. D CALL ⑤M

PETE'S BREWHOUSE & RESTAURANT   916/797-4992 68
▼▼ American. Casual Dining. $9-$22 **AAA Inspector Notes:** Pizza, pasta, burgers, sandwiches, wraps and salads, along with a few of Pete's favorite entrées, are offered at this casual restaurant with friendly servers. Crafted beers are an option. An attractive patio overlooks Quarry Ponds. **Bar:** beer & wine. **Address:** 5540 Douglas Blvd 95746 **Location:** I-80 exit Douglas Blvd, 3.7 mi e; in Quarry Ponds Town Center. L D CALL ⑤M

SOURCE GLOBAL TAPAS RESTAURANT 916/772-3900 67
▼▼ International Small Plates. Casual Dining. $4-$13 **AAA Inspector Notes:** A variety of tasty tapas, perfect for sharing, are served at this restaurant overlooking Quarry Ponds. Wednesday and Thursday live music is played from 6 to 9 p.m. Brunch on Saturday and Sunday is from 8 a.m. to 1:30 p.m. Covered patio dining is available in season. **Bar:** full bar. **Reservations:** required. **Address:** 5540 Douglas Blvd, Suite 110 95746 **Location:** I-80 exit Douglas Blvd, 3.7 mi e; in Quarry Ponds Town Center. L D LATE CALL ⑤M

GRASS VALLEY (D-3) pop. 12,860,
elev. 2,420'
• Hotels p. 140 • Restaurants p. 140

In 1850 George Knight stubbed his toe on a piece of quartz laced with gold and put Grass Valley on the map. Aided by advanced mining techniques that first were developed and used in this region, Grass Valley ultimately became the richest gold-mining town in California. Unlike most gold rush towns, Grass Valley survived its mining heyday; today high-tech manufacturing and tourism anchor the economy.

Grass Valley-Nevada County Chamber of Commerce: 422 Henderson St., P.O. Box 1107, Grass Valley, CA 95945. **Phone:** (530) 273-4667 or (800) 655-4667.

EMPIRE MINE STATE HISTORIC PARK, 1 mi. e. of SR 49 at 10791 E. Empire St., produced nearly 6 million ounces of gold during its operation. The park has 10 miles of hiking trails and a mine with 367 miles of passageways. Restored buildings include the owner's cottage, clubhouse, a smithy, hoist and compression houses and a machine shop. Living-history tours, with guides in period garb; a scale model of the underground workings of the mine; and guided tours of the cottage and the mine yard are offered. *See Recreation Areas Chart.*

Picnic facilities are in the parking area; food is not permitted inside the park. **Time:** Allow 30 minutes minimum. **Hours:** Park open daily 10-5. Cottage and mine yard tours are given daily Mar.-Dec.; Sat.-Sun., rest of year (weather permitting). Living-history tours are given Sat.-Sun. in summer. Closed Jan. 1, Thanksgiving and Christmas. Phone ahead to confirm schedule. **Cost:** $7; $3 (ages 6-16). Most tours free; cottage tours $2 additional. **Phone:** (530) 273-8522. 🎫 ⛲

NORTH STAR MINING MUSEUM, on Allison Ranch Rd. at the s. end of Mill St., houses the three-story Pelton wheel, a type of water wheel used for hydro-pneumatic power; an assay room; a smithy; a stamp mill; and a dynamite-packing machine. The museum features one of the few operating Cornish pumps in the country. A collection of gold samples also is shown. **Hours:** Tues.-Sun. 10-4, May-Oct. **Cost:** Donations. **Phone:** (530) 273-4255. ⛲

Visit AAA.com/Travel or
CAA.ca/Travel for complete
trip planning and reservations

ANNIE HORAN'S BED & BREAKFAST   (530)272-1516

Historic Bed & Breakfast $99-$140 Address: 415 W Main St 95945 Location: SR 49 exit 182A (SR 174/Colfax Ave/Central Grass Valley) northbound, just n on S Auburn St, then just w; exit 182B (E Main St/Grass Valley) southbound, just n to E Main St, then 0.6 mi w. Facility: The 120-year-old Queen Anne Victorian home, with a tranquil pond out back, is perfectly situated for strolling to the shops, restaurants, theater and wine tasting of the historic downtown area. 4 units. 2 stories (no elevator), interior corridors. Terms: 2 night minimum stay - weekends, 7 day cancellation notice-fee imposed.

BEST WESTERN GOLD COUNTRY INN   (530)273-1393

Motel
$89-$189

AAA Benefit: Members save up to 20%, plus 10% bonus points with Best Western Rewards®.

Address: 972 Sutton Way 95945 Location: SR 20 and 49 exit 183 (Brunswick Rd), just e, then just n; midway between Grass Valley and Nevada City. Facility: 84 units, some two bedrooms. 1-2 stories (no elevator), exterior corridors. Amenities: Some: high-speed Internet. Pool(s): outdoor. Activities: whirlpool, exercise room. Guest Services: coin laundry. Free Special Amenities: local telephone calls and high-speed Internet.

ELAM BIGGS BED AND BREAKFAST   (530)477-0906

Bed & Breakfast $85-$120 Address: 220 Colfax Ave 95945 Location: Just e of jct SR 49 and 174 (Colfax Ave). Facility: Merchant Elam Biggs, owner of a local hardware store during the Gold Rush era, built this charming Victorian home. 4 units. 2 stories (no elevator), interior corridors. Terms: 2 night minimum stay - seasonal and/or weekends, 7 day cancellation notice-fee imposed.

THE GOLD MINERS INN HOLIDAY INN EXPRESS & SUITES
(530)477-1700

Hotel $109-$199 Address: 121 Bank St 95945 Location: SR 49 exit 182A (SR 174/Colfax Ave) northbound, just n on Auburn St, then just e; exit 182B (SR 174/Colfax Ave) southbound, just n on Auburn St, then just e. Facility: 80 units. 3 stories, interior corridors. Terms: cancellation fee imposed. Amenities: high-speed Internet. Guest Services: valet laundry.

GRASS VALLEY COURTYARD SUITES SPA & CONFERENCE CENTER   (530)272-7696

Hotel
$160-$360

Address: 210 N Auburn St 95945 Location: SR 49 exit 182A (SR 174) northbound, just w to S Auburn St, then just n; exit 182B (E Main St/Grass Valley) southbound, just n to E Main St, just w to S Auburn St, then just n; just n of jct Richardson St. Located in a quiet residential area. Facility: 36 units, some two bedrooms and kitchens. 2 stories (no elevator), exterior corridors. Terms: 2 night minimum stay - seasonal and/or weekends, 3 day cancellation notice-fee imposed. Amenities: high-speed Internet, safes. Pool(s): outdoor. Activities: sauna, whirlpool, exercise room, spa. Guest Services: valet and coin laundry. Free Special Amenities: continental breakfast and high-speed Internet.

VICTORIAN LADY BED & BREAKFAST INN   530/477-8181

Bed & Breakfast. Rates not provided. Address: 304 S Church St 95945 Location: SR 49 exit 182A (SR 174/Colfax Ave/Central Grass Valley) northbound, just n on S Auburn St, just nw on Neal St, then just sw; exit 182 southbound, just nw on Neal St, then just sw; jct Walsh St. Located in a quiet residential area. Facility: 4 units, some two bedrooms. 2 stories (no elevator), interior corridors. Pool(s): outdoor. Activities: whirlpool.

WHERE TO EAT

CIRINO'S AT MAIN STREET   530/477-6000

Mediterranean. Casual Dining. $10-$26 AAA Inspector Notes: Sicilian influences flavor some preparations of classic Mediterranean cuisine. Among choices are risotto, pasta and polenta dishes, in addition to panini sandwiches. Bar: full bar. Reservations: suggested. Address: 213 W Main St 95945 Location: SR 49 exit 182E (E Main St/Grass Valley) southbound; exit 182A (SR 174/Colfax Ave) northbound; in historic downtown. Parking: street only.

DIEGOS RESTAURANT   530/477-1460

Latin American. Casual Dining. $9-$19 AAA Inspector Notes: Latin flavors from Central and South America influence the menu at this neighborhood cafe with eclectic decor and a charming patio in season. Arrive early to sign in for a table, unless you do not mind waiting. Bar: beer & wine. Address: 217 Colfax Ave 95945 Location: Just e of jct SR 49 and 174 (Colfax Ave). Parking: street only.

MARSHALL'S PASTIES   530/272-2844

English. Quick Serve. $4-$6 AAA Inspector Notes: This eatery offers a baked delicacy from yesteryear—several varieties of Cornish pasties (pronounced past-e) are offered in two sizes, including beef, sausage, chicken, turkey, ham and cheese, vegetable and apple. The pasties are prepared and rolled by hand. This traditional food was originally brought to the California mines by the early Cornish settlers from Cornwall, England. Address: 203 Mill St 95945 Location: SR 49 exit 182A (SR 174/Colfax Ave/Central Grass Valley) northbound, just n on S Auburn St, then just w on Neal St; exit 182B southbound (E Main St/Grass Valley), just n to E Main St, 0.4 mi w, then just s. Parking: street only.

NEVADA COUNTY GRILL   530/273-1353

American. Casual Dining. $9-$24 AAA Inspector Notes: Patrons can opt to sit in the inviting dining room or outside in the attractive courtyard to enjoy this restaurant's delicious salads, sandwiches and entrées. Bar: full bar. Reservations: suggested. Address: 212 W Main St 95945 Location: SR 49 exit 182A (SR 174/Colfax Ave/Central Grass Valley) northbound, just n on S Auburn St, then just w; exit 182B (E Main St/Grass Valley) southbound, just n to E Main St, then 0.4 mi w; in Holbrooke Hotel.

PAULETTE'S COUNTRY KITCHEN   530/273-4008

American. Family Dining. $6-$12 AAA Inspector Notes: This family restaurant, located in a shopping center, has served burgers, hot and cold sandwiches, salads and low-fat items since 1989. Breakfast is served all day. Most items made from scratch daily. Expect prompt service. Bar: beer & wine. Reservations: suggested. Address: 875 Sutton Way 95945 Location: Jct SR 49 and 20 exit Brunswick Rd, just e, then just n.

SOUTH PINE CAFE   530/274-0261

California. Casual Dining. $9-$13 AAA Inspector Notes: This small restaurant focuses on natural, organic food, which patrons can enjoy with natural juices and microbrewed beers. A variety of breakfast items include eggs Benedict, scrambled eggs and sandwiches. The plain, simple dining room features hardwood floors. Bar: beer & wine. Address: 102 Richardson St 95945 Location: SR 49 exit Colfax Ave (SR 174), just n on S Auburn St, then just e; jct N Auburn St. Parking: street only.

VILLA VENEZIA RISTORANTE   530/273-3555

Italian. Casual Dining. $7-$18 AAA Inspector Notes: This restaurant serves a variety of pasta, chicken and meat dishes in a charming Victorian period home. Lunch is served only on Friday. A garden patio is open in season. Bar: beer & wine. Address: 124 Bank St 95945 Location: SR 49 exit 182A (SR 174/Colfax Ave) northbound, just n on Auburn St, then just e; exit 182B (SR 174/Colfax Ave) southbound, just n on Auburn St, then just e.

TOFANELLI'S GOLD COUNTRY BISTRO   530/272-1468

Not evaluated. An extensive breakfast menu, including 101 omelet options, is offered at this bistro. Daily fresh fish specials and prime rib is featured on Tuesday. Charming outdoor patio dining is an option. Parking is behind the building. Address: 302 W Main St 95945 Location: SR 49 exit 182A (SR 174/Colfax/Central Grass Valley) northbound, just n to S Auburn St, then just w; exit 182B (E Main St/Grass Valley) southbound, just n to E Main St, then 0.4 mi w; center.

GREENFIELD pop. 16,330

CHEEZER'S GOURMET PIZZA   831/385-4914

🛇 Pizza. Quick Serve. $7-$23 **AAA Inspector Notes:** In addition to pizza, this restaurant offers hot sandwiches, pasta and salads all served in a casual atmosphere. **Bar:** beer & wine. **Address:** 670 Walnut Ave 93927 **Location:** US 101 exit Walnut Ave, just w; in Santa Lucia Shopping Center. ⒧ ⒟

GRIDLEY (D-3) pop. 6,584, elev. 91'

GRAY LODGE WILDLIFE AREA, w. on Gridley-Colusa Hwy., then s. on Pennington Rd., comprises 9,200 acres. Gray Lodge is a significant breeding ground for California wetland wildlife, including orioles, river otters, waterfowl, turtles, hawks and herons. Viewing is best in the late spring and early summer, as the young begin to emerge. In addition, this is an important Pacific Flyway stopover for wintering waterfowl. The peak season for waterfowl viewing is the third week of November through the end of December.

More than 200 bird species use the wildlife area through the year. Walking trails and observation areas are available for wildlife watchers year-round. An auto route traverses the area; fishing and hunting are permitted in season.

Hours: Daily dawn-dusk (certain areas may be closed during hunting season). **Cost:** Wildlife watching $4; free (ages 0-16 and holders of a current California hunting, trapping or fishing license). **Phone:** (530) 846-7500, or (530) 846-7505 for information about tours.

BLACK BEAR DINER   530/846-3043

🛇 🛇 American. Casual Dining. $7-$14 **AAA Inspector Notes:** A homey atmosphere characterizes this family-oriented restaurant. Familiar comfort foods, such as meatloaf with mashed potatoes, are at the heart of the menu and are served in generous portions. **Bar:** beer & wine. **Address:** 1586 Hwy 99 E 95948 **Location:** On SR 99 E; center. ⒝ ⒧ ⒟

CASA LUPE   530/846-5152

🛇 🛇 Mexican. Casual Dining. $7-$19 **AAA Inspector Notes:** Adjacent to the market, this restaurant offers traditional Mexican favorites and décor. Breakfast is served all day and lunch specials are offered daily. Carnitas are served on Saturday and Sunday. **Bar:** full bar. **Address:** 130 Magnolia St 95948 **Location:** SR 99; center. ⒝ ⒧ ⒟ CALL 🖬

GROVELAND (F-4) pop. 601, elev. 2,846'

• **Hotels & Restaurants map & index p. 584**
• **Part of Yosemite National Park area — see map p. 578**

This gold rush-era boom town went through a pair of menacing-sounding names—Savage's Diggings and Garrote—before citizens agreed on a more benign moniker.

GROVELAND YOSEMITE GATEWAY MUSEUM is at 18990 Main St. (SR 120), next to Mary Lavaroni Park in the same building as the county library. Displays depict area history from the 1849 gold rush era to the early space age, as well as flora and fauna native to the Sierra foothills. A theater features DVD programs about local history and pioneer families as well as Yosemite National Park. **Time:** Allow

1 hour minimum. **Hours:** Sun.-Thurs. 1-4:30; Fri.-Sat. 10-4:30. Closed Jan. 1, Easter, Thanksgiving, Christmas Eve, Christmas and Dec. 31. Phone ahead to confirm hours Nov.-Mar. **Cost:** Free. **Phone:** (209) 962-0300.

RECREATIONAL ACTIVITIES

White-water Rafting

• **All-Outdoors California Whitewater Rafting** departs from 8 mi. e. on SR 120. **Hours:** Daily Apr.-Sept. **Phone:** (925) 932-8993 or (800) 247-2387.

• **ARTA River Trips** has departure points on several rivers. **Hours:** Daily Apr.-Sept. **Phone:** (209) 962-7873 or (800) 323-2782.

• **Whitewater Voyages** meets at varying departure points. **Hours:** Daily Apr.-Oct. (depending upon water flow). Reservations office open all year. **Phone:** (510) 222-5994 or (800) 400-7238.

AMERICAS BEST VALUE INN-YOSEMITE WESTGATE LODGE   (209)962-5281 ⑧

🛇🛇🛇
Hotel
$79-$459

Address: 7633 Hwy 120 95321 **Location:** On SR 120, 12 mi e; at Buck Meadows. **Facility:** 45 units. 1-2 stories (no elevator), exterior corridors. **Terms:** 3 day cancellation notice-fee imposed.

Pool(s): outdoor. **Activities:** whirlpool, playground. **Guest Services:** coin laundry. **Free Special Amenities:** high-speed Internet.

SAVE 🛏 CALL 🖬 ⊿ 🛜 ✕ 🖪 🖵 🖵

GROVELAND HOTEL AT YOSEMITE NATIONAL PARK
                                         (209)962-4000 ⑥

🛇🛇🛇
Historic
Country Inn
$145-$345

Address: 18767 Main St 95321 **Location:** Center. **Facility:** The eclectic property includes an 1849 adobe and a 1914 Queen Anne home believed to be modeled after the first American mansion. 17 units. 2 stories (no elevator), interior corridors. **Terms:** cancellation fee imposed, resort fee. **Dining:** Cellar Door Restaurant, see separate listing. **Free Special Amenities:** full breakfast and high-speed Internet.

SAVE 🔼 🍴 🛜 ✕ 🖵 /SOME UNITS FEE 🐾

YOSEMITE ROSE BED & BREAKFAST   209/962-6548 ⑦

🛇🛇🛇 Bed & Breakfast $155-$275 **Address:** 22830 Ferretti Rd 95321 **Location:** On SR 120, 7.5 mi e, then 2.7 mi n. **Facility:** The inn is a great place to stay at night while you explore nature's majesty in Yosemite National Park during the day. The B&B is located in a secluded area surrounded by mature pine and oak trees. 7 units, some cottages. 2 stories (no elevator), interior/exterior corridors. **Terms:** 2 night minimum stay - seasonal and/or weekends, 14 day cancellation notice-fee imposed. **Activities:** fishing, hiking trails. **Fee:** horseback riding, massage. **Guest Services:** complimentary laundry. 🛜 ✕ 🕮 /SOME UNITS 🖪 🖵 🖵

WHERE TO EAT

BUCK MEADOWS RESTAURANT   209/962-5181 ⑤

🛇🛇 American. Casual Dining. $8-$23 **AAA Inspector Notes:** Open mid-March through the end of November, this restaurant serves up traditional family favorites in hearty portions. All items are prepared on site including a selection of fresh fruit and cream pies for dessert. This is a great place to stop on the way to or from Yosemite National Park. **Bar:** full bar. **Address:** 7647 SR 120 95321 **Location:** 12 mi e on SR 120; at Buck Meadows. ⒝ ⒧ ⒟ CALL 🖬

(See map & index p. 584.)

CELLAR DOOR RESTAURANT 209/962-4000 ④

California
Fine Dining
$12-$25

AAA Inspector Notes: This casually elegant restaurant presents a menu of well-prepared beef, pork, chicken and seafood dishes as well as an extensive wine list. The staff is friendly and attentive. **Bar:** full bar. **Reservations:** suggested. **Address:** 18767 Main St 95321 **Location:** Center; in Groveland Hotel at Yosemite National Park.

Ⓑ Ⓓ

GUALALA (E-1) elev. 67'
• Part of Wine Country area — see map p. 562

Originally settled by Pomo Indians, Gualala (wa-LA-la) means "where the water meets," due to its location above the mouth of the Gualala River and the Pacific Ocean. Formerly sustained by redwood logging and milling, the town is now a popular weekend retreat known for its redwoods, fishing, abalone diving, kayaking and vibrant artists' community.

Redwood Coast Chamber of Commerce/Visitor's Center: 39150 S. Hwy. 1, Gualala, CA 95445. **Phone:** (707) 884-1080 or (800) 778-5252.

RECREATIONAL ACTIVITIES
Kayaking

• **Adventure Rents Canoes & Kayaks** is on the Gualala River at Mill Bend. **Hours:** Daily mid-June through Labor Day; by appointment, day after Labor Day-Oct. 31. **Phone:** (707) 884-4386 or (888) 881-4386.

GUALALA COUNTRY INN (707)884-4343

Motel
$77-$190

Address: 47975 Center St 95445 **Location:** South end of town; just n of Old State Hwy. **Facility:** 20 units. 2 stories (no elevator), interior/exterior corridors. **Terms:** 3 day cancellation notice. **Amenities:** high-speed Internet. **Free Special Amenities: expanded continental breakfast and high-speed Internet.**

NORTH COAST COUNTRY INN (707)884-4537

▼▼▼▼ **Bed & Breakfast** $195-$225 **Address:** 34591 S Hwy 1 95445 **Location:** On SR 1, 4.5 mi n. **Facility:** Nestled on a hillside overlooking the Pacific Ocean, the inn features antique furnishings and handmade quilts. 6 units, some efficiencies. 1-2 stories (no elevator), exterior corridors. **Terms:** 2 night minimum stay - seasonal and/or weekends, 3 day cancellation notice-fee imposed.

SURF MOTEL (707)884-3571

Motel
$89-$209

Address: 39170 S SR 1 95445 **Location:** Oceanfront. Center. **Facility:** 20 units, some kitchens. 1 story, interior/exterior corridors. **Terms:** 3 day cancellation notice-fee imposed. **Free Special Amenities: full breakfast and high-speed Internet.**

BREAKERS INN 707/884-3200

fyi Not evaluated. **Address:** 39300 S SR 1 95445 **Location:** Oceanfront. Center. Facilities, services, and décor characterize a mid-scale property.

BONES ROADHOUSE 707/884-1188

▼▼ ▼▼ American. Casual Dining. $6-$24 **AAA Inspector Notes:** A classic barbecue roadhouse ambience with a panoramic view of the coast, this spot offers house-cut potato chips sliced just thick enough to taste the fresh sweetness not found in a bag. If turf is not your style, there is surf too-from fish and chips to house-smoked salmon. **Bar:** full bar. **Address:** 39080 S Hwy 1 95445 **Location:** Center. Ⓑ Ⓛ Ⓓ

ST ORRES 707/884-3335

▼▼▼ California. Fine Dining. $45-$50 **AAA Inspector Notes:** Representative of the distinctive Russian architecture is this three-story domed dining room. Three-course dinners include a choice of several entrées. Daily specials often center on wild game. Fresh appetizers and desserts are delicious. **Bar:** beer & wine. **Reservations:** suggested. **Address:** 36601 S SR 1 95445 **Location:** On SR 1, 2.3 mi n. Ⓓ 🅺

GUERNEVILLE (B-7) pop. 4,534, elev. 56'
• Attractions map p. 567
• Part of Wine Country area — see map p. 562

Lumber mills flourished during Guerneville's early years. Railroads were built to ship wood from the town, and agricultural endeavors were undertaken on the cleared land.

The Russian River Chamber of Commerce and Visitor Information Center: 16209 First St., P.O. Box 331, Guerneville, CA 95446. **Phone:** (707) 869-9000.

WINERIES

• **Korbel Champagne Cellars** is at 13250 River Rd. **Hours:** Tastings daily 10-5, May-Sept.; 10-4:30, rest of year. Tours are given daily 11-3:45, May-Sept.; 11-3, rest of year. Garden tours Tues.-Sun. at 1 and 3, mid-Apr. to mid-Oct. **Phone:** (707) 824-7000.

APPLEWOOD INN, RESTAURANT & SPA (707)869-9093

▼▼▼▼
Country Inn
$195-$375

Address: 13555 Hwy 116 95446 **Location:** 0.5 mi s of River Rd. **Facility:** Sheltered by towering redwoods and surrounded by fruit orchards and gardens, this inn is located on a knoll in the Russian River Valley. 19 units. 2 stories (no elevator), exterior corridors. **Terms:** 2 night minimum stay - weekends, age restrictions may apply, 14 day cancellation notice-fee imposed. **Dining:** restaurant, see separate listing. **Pool(s):** heated outdoor. **Activities:** whirlpool. **Fee:** massage. **Free Special Amenities: full breakfast and early check-in/late check-out.**

COTTAGES ON RIVER ROAD (707)869-3848

▼▼ ▼▼ Cottage $80-$250 **Address:** 14880 River Rd 95446 **Location:** 1.6 mi ne of jct SR 116. **Facility:** 17 cottages, some kitchens. 1 story, exterior corridors. **Terms:** 2-3 night minimum stay - seasonal and/or weekends, 3 day cancellation notice. **Pool(s):** outdoor. **Activities:** **Fee:** massage.

FERNGROVE COTTAGES (707)869-8105

▼▼▼ ▼▼
Cottage
$89-$269

Address: 16650 Hwy 116 95446 **Location:** Just w of downtown. **Facility:** 21 units, some kitchens and cottages. 1 story, exterior corridors. **Terms:** 2 night minimum stay - seasonal and/or weekends, 3 day cancellation notice-fee imposed. **Pool(s):** heated outdoor. **Activities:** hiking trails, jogging. **Free Special Amenities: expanded continental breakfast and high-speed Internet.**

WEST SONOMA INN & SPA   707/869-2470
Motel $109-$299 Address: 14100 Brookside Ln 95446 Location: Just n of SR 116; on west end of downtown. Facility: 36 units, some efficiencies and cottages. 1-2 stories (no elevator), exterior corridors. Terms: check-in 4 pm, 2-3 night minimum stay - seasonal and/or weekends, 14 day cancellation notice-fee imposed, resort fee. Pool(s): outdoor. Activities: spa.

WHERE TO EAT

APPLEWOOD INN, RESTAURANT & SPA   707/869-9093
California. Fine Dining. $24-$40 AAA Inspector Notes: This restaurant is known for its Sonoma Wine Country cuisine with Mediterranean influences. Built in the style of a French country barn, the restaurant's menu is seasonal and locally sourced. Its wine program is Russian River-centric. Bar: full bar. Reservations: suggested. Address: 13555 Hwy 116 95446 Location: 0.5 mi s of River Rd.

HALF MOON BAY (E-8) pop. 11,324, elev. 69'

- Restaurants p. 144
- Hotels & Restaurants map & index p. 410
- Part of San Francisco area — see map p. 342

Half Moon Bay lies on a scenic stretch of SR 1 that extends from San Francisco south to San Luis Obispo. The rugged coastline is bordered by sandy beaches perfect for walking and beachcombing. This is a popular launching spot for sightseeing, fishing and whale-watching cruises. Contact Bait and Switch Sport Fishing for information about excursions; phone (650) 726-7133. Visitors flock to Half Moon Bay's Flower Market, held the third Saturday of the month (except October) at Kelly and Main streets.

Half Moon Bay Coastside Chamber of Commerce and Visitors Bureau: 235 Main St., Half Moon Bay, CA 94019. Phone: (650) 726-8380.

BEACH HOUSE HOTEL   (650)712-0220 **103**
Hotel $195-$425 Address: 4100 N Cabrillo Hwy 94019 Location: On SR 1, 3 mi n of jct SR 92 and 1. Facility: 54 units. 3 stories, interior corridors. Terms: check-in 4 pm, 3 day cancellation notice-fee imposed. Amenities: safes. Pool(s): heated outdoor. Activities: whirlpool, exercise room. Fee: massage. Guest Services: valet laundry.

BEST WESTERN PLUS HALF MOON BAY LODGE
(650)726-9000 **111**
Hotel $149-$239
AAA Benefit: Members save up to 20%, plus 10% bonus points with Best Western Rewards®.
Address: 2400 Cabrillo Hwy S 94019 Location: 2.5 mi s of jct SR 92 and 1, just w. Facility: 80 units. 2 stories (no elevator), exterior corridors. Terms: check-in 4 pm, 2 night minimum stay - seasonal and/or weekends, cancellation fee imposed. Amenities: video games (fee). Some: high-speed Internet. Pool(s): heated outdoor. Activities: sauna, whirlpool, exercise room. Guest Services: valet laundry. Free Special Amenities: full breakfast and high-speed Internet.

COASTSIDE INN HALF MOON BAY
(650)726-3400 **107**
Hotel $89-$239
Address: 230 S Cabrillo Hwy 94019 Location: On SR 1, just s of SR 92. Facility: 52 units. 2 stories (no elevator), exterior corridors. Free Special Amenities: expanded continental breakfast and high-speed Internet.

COMFORT INN HALF MOON BAY   (650)712-1999 **106**
Hotel $100-$230
Address: 2930 Cabrillo Hwy N 94019 Location: On SR 1, 2 mi n of jct SR 92 and 1. Facility: 54 units, some kitchens. 2 stories (no elevator), exterior corridors. Terms: cancellation fee imposed. Activities: exercise room. Free Special Amenities: expanded continental breakfast and high-speed Internet.

CYPRESS INN ON MIRAMAR BEACH
(650)726-6002 **105**
Bed & Breakfast $199-$399
Address: 407 Mirada Rd 94019 Location: Oceanfront. 3 mi n of jct SR 1 and 92 to Mirada Rd, then just w. Facility: 18 units. 3 stories (no elevator), interior/exterior corridors. Terms: 2 night minimum stay - weekends, 3 day cancellation notice. Activities: limited beach access, bicycles, hiking trails, jogging. Fee: massage. Free Special Amenities: full breakfast and high-speed Internet.

HARBOR VIEW INN   (650)726-2329 **101**
Motel $79-$249
Address: 51 Ave Alhambra 94018 Location: On SR 1 exit Capistrano Ave; just e; 4 mi n of jct SR 92. Located in El Granada. Facility: 17 units. 2 stories (no elevator), exterior corridors. Bath: shower only. Terms: 27 night minimum stay. Free Special Amenities: continental breakfast and high-speed Internet.

LANDIS SHORES OCEANFRONT INN   (650)726-6642 **104**
Bed & Breakfast $225-$345 Address: 211 Mirada Rd 94019 Location: Oceanfront. 3 mi n of jct SR 1 and 92 to Medio Ave, just w, then just n. Facility: Heated stone floors are among the special touches at this contemporary property. Each room is decorated around a wine region theme and feature a gas fireplace, private deck and an ocean view. 8 units. 3 stories, interior corridors. Terms: 2 night minimum stay - weekends, 7 day cancellation notice-fee imposed. Amenities: safes. Some: high-speed Internet. Activities: limited beach access, hiking trails, jogging, limited exercise equipment. Fee: massage.

MILL ROSE INN   (650)726-8750 **108**
Bed & Breakfast $175-$360
Address: 615 Mill St 94019 Location: Just e of jct SR 1 and 92, just s on Main St, then just w on Mill St; north end of downtown. Facility: Manicured, landscaped gardens surround this English inn while beautifully appointed suites, fireplaces and claw-foot tubs enhance the ambiance inside. This is a nice alternative for the business traveler. 6 units. 2 stories (no elevator), exterior corridors. Terms: 21 day cancellation notice-fee imposed. Activities: whirlpool. Fee: massage. Guest Services: valet laundry. Free Special Amenities: full breakfast and high-speed Internet.

(See map & index p. 410.)

OCEANO HOTEL & SPA 650/726-5400 `102`

▼▼▼▼ **Hotel.** Rates not provided. **Address:** 280 Capistrano Rd 94019 **Location:** Oceanfront. From jct SR 92, 3.7 mi nw on Cabrillo Hwy to Capistrano Rd, then just sw. Across from Half Moon Bay Harbor. **Facility:** 106 units, some two bedrooms, kitchens and condominiums. 3 stories, interior corridors. **Amenities:** safes. *Some:* high-speed Internet. **Activities:** limited beach access, bicycles, hiking trails, exercise room, spa. *Fee:* sailboats, marina. **Guest Services:** valet and coin laundry.

[icons] / SOME UNITS

OLD THYME INN (650)726-1616 `109`

▼▼▼ **Bed & Breakfast** $159-$349 **Address:** 779 Main St 94019 **Location:** At Filbert and Main sts; south end of downtown. **Facility:** Feather beds and two-person whirlpools are among the guest room amenities enhancing this 1899 Queen Anne Victorian. The darling enclosed outdoor garden is perfect for relaxation. 7 units. 2 stories (no elevator), interior corridors. **Terms:** 2 night minimum stay - seasonal and/or weekends, 7 day cancellation notice.

[icons] FEE [icons] / SOME UNITS

THE RITZ-CARLTON, HALF MOON BAY

(650)712-7000 `110`

▼▼▼▼▼
Resort Hotel
$355-$4050

THE RITZ-CARLTON® **AAA Benefit:** Unequaled service at Special Member Savings.

Address: 1 Miramontes Point Rd 94019 **Location:** Oceanfront. 2.5 mi s of jct SR 1 (Cabrillo Hwy S) and 92, 0.8 mi w. **Facility:** On a high bluff that juts into the Pacific Ocean, this seaside resort is surrounded by gorgeous golf courses. 261 units. 6 stories, interior/exterior corridors. **Parking:** valet only. **Terms:** check-in 4 pm, cancellation fee imposed, resort fee. **Amenities:** high-speed Internet, safes. **Dining:** 2 restaurants, also, Navio, see separate listing. **Pool(s):** heated indoor. **Activities:** saunas, whirlpools, steamrooms, 6 lighted tennis courts, bicycles, hiking trails, spa. *Fee:* golf-36 holes. **Guest Services:** valet laundry, area transportation-within 5 mi. **Free Special Amenities:** local telephone calls and newspaper.

SAVE [icons] CALL [icons] BIZ [icons]
[icons] / SOME UNITS FEE [icons]

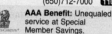
WHERE TO EAT

CAFFE MEZZA LUNA 650/560-0137 `76`

▼ Italian Sandwiches Desserts. Quick Serve. $5-$10 **AAA Inspector Notes:** Comfortable and low key, this cafe offers simple hot entrées made to order. Make room for a slice of mousse cake or gelato--all desserts are made on site. **Bar:** beer & wine. **Address:** 240 Capistrano Rd 94019 **Location:** SR 1, 4 mi n of jct SR 92; in Harbor Village. [B] [L] [D] [icon]

CETRELLA 650/726-4090 `80`

▼▼▼ Mediterranean. Fine Dining. $17-$27 **AAA Inspector Notes:** This European bistro serves a variety of creative and artistic Mediterranean dishes. Huge fireplaces warm the dining area on cool nights. **Bar:** full bar. **Address:** 845 Main St 94019 **Location:** 1 mi s of jct SR 1 and 92; downtown. [D]

HALF MOON BAY BREWING COMPANY 650/728-2739 `75`

▼▼ American. Casual Dining. $13-$27 **AAA Inspector Notes:** Coastsiders and visitors alike patronize the friendly restaurant/brewpub. Microbrews complement menu offerings of seafood right off the dock, as well as pasta, steak and salad. Seating is offered indoors in front of the fireplace or outside on the patio, weather permitting. **Bar:** full bar. **Address:** 390 Capistrano Rd 94018 **Location:** SR 1, just w. [L] [D] [icon]

MEZZALUNA ITALIAN RESTAURANT 650/728-8108 `74`

▼▼ Italian. Casual Dining. $11-$26 **AAA Inspector Notes:** A fine restaurant situated near Pillar Point Harbor, a mi familia ambience prevails here. Neighbors are regulars, on a first name basis with the staff. The menu reflects the ambience-unpretentious classic Italian fare. **Bar:** full bar. **Address:** 459 Prospect Way 94019 **Location:** SR 1, 4 mi n of jct SR 92. [L] [D] [icon]

MIRAMAR BEACH RESTAURANT 650/726-9053 `78`

▼▼▼ ◆◆
California
Casual Dining
$11-$35

AAA Inspector Notes: Inside this restaurant, guests' attention is drawn to the spectacular view of the ocean and many surrounding photographs of the 1920s era. Fresh seafood, fine steak and their infamous seafood chowder are featured. **Bar:** full bar. **Reservations:** suggested. **Address:** 131 Mirada Rd 94019 **Location:** 2.7 mi n of jct SR 92 and 1, then w. [L] [D] [icon]

NAVIO 650/712-7040 `81`

▼▼▼▼ ◆◆◆◆ Northern California. Fine Dining. $28-$38 **AAA Inspector Notes:** This upscale restaurant features an open-grill kitchen and tables with views of the bluffs and the Pacific Ocean. The menu offers local fresh ingredients prepared in Northern California-style cuisine. Brunch is served on Sunday with two seatings. **Reservations:** required. **Address:** 1 Miramontes Point Rd 94019 **Location:** 2.5 mi s of jct SR 1 (Cabrillo Hwy S) and 92, 0.8 mi w; in The Ritz-Carlton, Half Moon Bay. **Parking:** valet only. [B] [D]

PASTA MOON RISTORANTE 650/726-5125 `79`

▼▼▼
Italian
Casual Dining
$12-$26

AAA Inspector Notes: Daily specials and homemade soups are among selections at this restaurant that emphasizes fresh ingredients and unusual preparation. A large orchid plant serves as both decor and a serving table. The pasta is made fresh daily. Try the squid ink pasta with calamari, fava beans and tomatoes. **Bar:** full bar. **Reservations:** suggested. **Address:** 315 Main St 94019 **Location:** Just s of SR 92; e of SR 1. **Parking:** street only. [L] [D] [icon]

SAM'S CHOWDER HOUSE 650/712-0245 `77`

▼▼▼
Seafood
Casual Dining
$12-$35

AAA Inspector Notes: Serving traditional seafood dishes and New England clam chowder, this eatery is situated on a small hill, the dining room and lounge have panoramic views of Half Moon Bay, and outdoor dining is available in season. The lobster roll has received acclaim as a top sandwich. **Bar:** full bar. **Address:** 4210 N Cabrillo Hwy 94019 **Location:** 3.5 mi n of jct SR 92. [L] [D]

HANFORD (H-4) pop. 53,967, elev. 248'

Founded in 1882 in the San Joaquin Valley, Hanford was named for a Southern Pacific Railroad paymaster who became a power in the community. He paid millions of dollars of workers' wages in gold.

Hanford once claimed one of the largest Chinese communities in California. In China Alley, a remnant of that community, are a Taoist temple and a landmark restaurant operated by the descendants of the family who started the business in 1883. Courthouse Square, the center of historic Hanford, includes a renovated carousel and many specialty shops.

Hanford Visitor Agency: 113 Court St., Suite 306, Hanford, CA 93230. **Phone:** (559) 582-5024.

Self-guiding tours: Maps for tours of historic Hanford are available from the visitor agency.

THE CLARK CENTER FOR JAPANESE ART AND CULTURE is 6 mi. s. of SR 198 at 15770 10th Ave. In a rural setting, the museum presents changing exhibits of Japanese paintings, sculpture and decorative arts, with works dating from the 8th to the 21st centuries.

Highlights include Buddhist sculptures and paintings from the Kamakura period (1185-1333), paintings from the Edo period (1615-1868) and an impressive collection of folding screens and ceramics. **Time:** Allow 1 hour minimum. **Hours:** Tues.-Sat. 12:30-5, Sept.-July. Guided tours are given Sat. at 1. Closed major holidays. **Cost:** $5; $3 (students and military with ID); free (ages 0-12). **Phone:** (559) 582-4915.

HANFORD CARNEGIE MUSEUM, 109 E. Eighth St., is in a Romanesque-style library built in 1905. Among items depicting Hanford and Kings County history are clothes (including a dress that belonged to Amelia Earhart), furniture and photographs. A large collection of military memorabilia from World War I and World War II also is on display. There is a rose garden on the museum grounds. Guided tours are available by appointment. **Time:** Allow 1 hour minimum. **Hours:** Tues.-Sat. 11-4. Phone ahead to confirm schedule. **Cost:** $3; $1 (ages 0-17 and 55+). **Phone:** (559) 584-1367.

KINGS ART CENTER is at 605 N. Douty St. The 10 gallery shows mounted each year feature media such as photography, water colors, prints, oil paintings, pottery, sculpture and textiles. **Time:** Allow 1 hour minimum. **Hours:** Wed.-Fri. 11-4, Sat.-Sun. noon-3. Closed major holidays. **Cost:** Donations. **Phone:** (559) 584-1065.

BEST WESTERN HANFORD INN   (559)583-7300

Motel
$85-$150

AAA Benefit: Members save up to 20%, plus 10% bonus points with Best Western Rewards®.

Address: 755 Cadillac Ln 93230 **Location:** SR 198 exit 11th Ave eastbound; exit Redington St westbound, just s. **Facility:** 40 units. 2 stories, exterior corridors. **Amenities:** Some: high-speed Internet. **Pool(s):** outdoor. **Guest Services:** coin laundry. **Free Special Amenities: continental breakfast and high-speed Internet.**

COMFORT INN   (559)584-9300

Hotel
$90-$165

Address: 10 N Irwin St 93230 **Location:** SR 198 exit Redington St westbound; exit Douty Rd eastbound. **Facility:** 65 units. 3 stories, interior corridors. **Terms:** cancellation fee imposed. **Amenities:** high-speed Internet, safes (fee). **Pool(s):** outdoor. **Activities:** whirlpool. **Guest Services:** valet and coin laundry. **Free Special Amenities: expanded continental breakfast.**

SEQUOIA INN   (559)582-0338

Hotel
$81-$89

Address: 1655 Mall Dr 93230 **Location:** SR 198 exit 12th Ave N, just e. **Facility:** 56 units. 3 stories, interior corridors. **Terms:** check-in 4 pm, cancellation fee imposed. **Amenities:** high-speed Internet. **Pool(s):** outdoor. **Activities:** whirlpool, limited exercise equipment. **Guest Services:** coin laundry. **Free Special Amenities: continental breakfast and high-speed Internet.**

/ SOME UNITS FEE

WHERE TO EAT

BLACK BEAR DINER   559/584-8278

American. Casual Dining. $8-$16 **AAA Inspector Notes:** A homey atmosphere characterizes this family-oriented restaurant. Familiar comfort foods, such as meatloaf with mashed potatoes, are at the heart of the menu and are served in generous portions. **Bar:** beer & wine. **Address:** 1790 W Lacey Blvd 93230 **Location:** SR 198 exit 12th Ave, 0.6 mi n, then just w. B L D CALL

NASHVILLE'S BAR & GRILL   559/583-8424

Barbecue. Casual Dining. $7-$25 **AAA Inspector Notes:** This is a great stop for families as a variety of barbecue favorites are available including ribs, chicken, steak, burgers and a selection of wraps and salads. Expect friendly service. **Bar:** full bar. **Reservations:** suggested. **Address:** 2601 N 11th Ave, Suite 105 93230 **Location:** SR 198 exit 11th Ave eastbound; exit Redington St westbound, 2.4 mi n; at Fargo Rd. L D CALL

HAYWARD (D-9) pop. 144,186, elev. 111'
- **Restaurants p. 146**
- **Hotels & Restaurants map & index p. 254**

HAYWARD AREA HISTORICAL SOCIETY MUSEUM, 22701 Main St., features exhibits pertaining to Hayward, Castro Valley and San Lorenzo history. Tours of historic homes and sites also are offered. **Note:** The museum is relocating to a new home on Foothill Boulevard and is scheduled to reopen sometime in spring 2013; phone ahead for updates. **Time:** Allow 1 hour minimum. **Cost:** Free. **Phone:** (510) 581-0223. Hayward, 23

JAPANESE GARDENS, 22325 N. Third St. off Crescent Ave., encompasses 3.3 acres of trees native to Japan and California, along with stones and plants arranged in traditional Japanese style. A small pond contains koi and goldfish, and there's also a gazebo. **Hours:** Daily 8-4. **Cost:** Free. **Phone:** (510) 881-6700. Castro Valley, 27

BEST WESTERN PLUS INN OF HAYWARD   (510)785-8700

Hotel
$100-$130

AAA Benefit: Members save up to 20%, plus 10% bonus points with Best Western Rewards®.

Address: 360 West A St 94541 **Location:** I-880 exit A St, just e. **Facility:** 91 units, some kitchens. 3 stories, interior/exterior corridors. **Amenities:** Some: high-speed Internet. **Pool(s):** outdoor. **Activities:** whirlpool. **Guest Services:** valet laundry. **Free Special Amenities: local telephone calls and high-speed Internet.**

COMFORT INN   (510)538-4466

Hotel $70-$130 **Address:** 24997 Mission Blvd 94544 **Location:** 1.8 mi e of I-880 exit SR 92 (Jackson St), 0.5 mi s on SR 238 (Mission Blvd). **Facility:** 62 units. 2 stories, exterior corridors. **Terms:** cancellation fee imposed. **Amenities:** high-speed Internet. **Activities:** sauna. **Guest Services:** valet and coin laundry.

DAYS INN AIRPORT   (510)670-0555

Motel $85-$99 **Address:** 450 West A St 94541 **Location:** I-880 exit A St, just w. **Facility:** 32 units. 3 stories, exterior corridors. **Terms:** 3 night minimum stay - seasonal and/or weekends, cancellation fee imposed.

(See map & index p. 254.)

FAIRFIELD INN & SUITES OAKLAND HAYWARD
(510)782-5000

WWWW Hotel $149-$179 **Address:** 25921 Industrial Blvd 94545 **Location:** SR 92 exit Industrial Blvd, just n. **Facility:** 84 units. 3 stories, interior corridors. **Amenities:** high-speed Internet. **Activities:** sauna, whirlpool, exercise room. **Guest Services:** valet and coin laundry.

AAA Benefit:
AAA hotel discounts of 5% or more.

CALL BIZ

HAMPTON INN-HAYWARD
(510)247-1555

WWWW Hotel $84-$199 **Address:** 24137 Mission Blvd 94544 **Location:** 1.8 mi e of I-880 exit SR 92 (Jackson St), just s on SR 238 (Mission Blvd). Hayward, 23. **Facility:** 70 units. 3 stories, interior corridors. **Terms:** 1-7 night minimum stay, cancellation fee imposed. **Pool(s):** heated outdoor. **Activities:** exercise room. **Guest Services:** valet and coin laundry.

AAA Benefit:
Members save up to 10%!

CALL BIZ

LA QUINTA INN & SUITES HAYWARD OAKLAND AIRPORT
(510)732-6300

WWWW Hotel $83-$188 **Address:** 20777 Hesperian Blvd 94541 **Location:** I-880 exit A St, 0.5 mi w. **Facility:** 145 units. 3 stories, interior corridors. **Amenities:** high-speed Internet. **Pool(s):** heated outdoor. **Activities:** whirlpool, exercise room. **Guest Services:** valet and coin laundry. **Free Special Amenities:** expanded continental breakfast and high-speed Internet.

SAVE CALL BIZ / SOME UNITS FEE

WHERE TO EAT

BUFFALO BILL'S BREWERY
510/886-9823 61

WW American. Casual Dining. $8-$20 **AAA Inspector Notes:** Located in the historic downtown area, this fun and lively atmosphere offers traditional pub favorites including specialty sandwiches, grilled meats, specialty salads and pizza. Beer is brewed on site. **Bar:** beer & wine. **Address:** 1082 B St 94541 **Location:** I-880 exit A St, 1.5 mi e, just s on Foothill Blvd, then just w. Hayward, 23. **Parking:** street only. L D CALL

ROUND TABLE PIZZA

W Pizza. Casual Dining. $7-$30 **AAA Inspector Notes:** This casual, family-oriented pizza place features high-quality ingredients and dough rolled fresh daily. Distinctive specialty pizzas are piled high with toppings. **Bar:** beer & wine. L D

For additional information, visit AAA.com
LOCATIONS:
Address: 157 Harder Rd 94544 **Location:** Between Huntwood Ave and Mission Blvd. **Phone:** 510/581-7777
Address: 20906 Mission Blvd 94541 **Location:** I-238 exit SR 238 (Mission Blvd), just s. Bay Fair, 22. **Phone:** 510/278-3228
Address: 22457 Foothill Blvd 94541 **Location:** At Redwood Rd. Hayward, 23. **Phone:** 510/581-7777

HEALDSBURG (A-7) pop. 11,254, elev. 106'
• Attractions map p. 567
• Part of Wine Country area — see map p. 562

Healdsburg is one of those northern California towns that just radiates charm. for one thing it's a shopper's delight, packed with trendy boutiques, art galleries and antique shops. The compact downtown area is perfect for strolling, dog walking, people watching at an outdoor cafe or partaking of the libations at any number of coffee houses and wine bars. During the weekend, shady Healdsburg

Plaza is usually the center of activity, and you're quite likely to come across an art show, free concert or antique sale.

Those in search of culinary excellence make the trek to experience such upscale restaurants as Dry Creek Kitchen and Spoonbar. Sample the vintages of the neighboring Dry Creek, Alexander and Russian River valleys at one of the tasting rooms bordering the plaza. Or get out and explore some of these renowned vineyards, many of which are open to visitors for tastings and tours. Access Westside Road, just off Healdsburg Avenue, and head west—the winding route is exceptionally scenic, passing rolling hills and gorgeous countryside.

The Russian River flows through town, providing invigorating recreation for canoeists and kayakers as well as an excuse to relax for the casual daytripper. Healdsburg Veterans Memorial Beach, 13839 Healdsburg Ave., has picnic facilities as well as a man-made swimming beach along the river. Biking through the surrounding wine country is a perfect way to combine exercise and bucolic scenery.

The Raven Performing Arts Theater, 115 North St., presents everything from plays and musical and comedy acts to fashion shows. For schedule information phone (707) 433-6335.

Healdsburg Chamber of Commerce and Visitors Bureau: 217 Healdsburg Ave., Healdsburg, CA 95448. **Phone:** (707) 433-6935, or (800) 648-9922 in Calif.

Self-guiding tours: Maps outlining tours of local historic buildings as well as a winery map are available at the chamber of commerce and visitors bureau.

THE HEALDSBURG MUSEUM is 2 blks. e. of the downtown plaza at 221 Matheson St. Housed in the former Carnegie Library, the landmark museum collects, protects, preserves and presents artifacts, documents and photographs that trace the history of Healdsburg and the surrounding area. Items displayed include 19th-century weapons, tools, textiles and crafts along with Pomo Indian basketry and other artifacts. Rotating exhibits also are featured.

Time: Allow 30 minutes minimum. **Hours:** Museum Wed.-Sun. 11-4. Research center Thurs.-Sat. 11-4 by appointment. Closed major holidays and between exhibitions. Phone ahead to confirm schedule. **Cost:** Free. **Phone:** (707) 431-3325.

WINERIES
• **Foppiano Vineyards** is just s. at 12707 Old Redwood Hwy. **Hours:** Tastings and self-guiding tours daily 11-5. Phone ahead to confirm schedule. **Phone:** (707) 433-7272.
• **Manzanita Creek Winery** is e. off US 101 (Dry Creek Road exit) to Grove St. **Note:** This working facility has a different atmosphere than many other wineries, since there are no vineyards on site. **Hours:** Tastings Wed.-Sat. 10-4, Sun.-Tues.

by appointment. Tours of the facility are by appointment only; advance reservations are required. Closed major holidays. **Cost:** Free. **Phone:** (707) 433-4052.

- **Rodney Strong Vineyards** is 3 mi. s. off US 101 at 11455 Old Redwood Hwy. **Hours:** Daily 10-5. Tours are given daily at 11 and 3, except during concerts (weather and staff permitting). Closed Thanksgiving and Christmas. Phone ahead to confirm schedule. **Phone:** (707) 431-1533 or (800) 678-4763.

- **Simi Winery** is off US 101 Dry Creek Rd. exit, e. to Healdsburg Ave., then 1 mi. n. to 16275 Healdsburg Ave. **Hours:** Daily 10-5. Guided tours are given at 11 and 2. Closed Jan. 1, Easter, Thanksgiving, Christmas Eve and Christmas. **Phone:** (707) 433-6981 or (800) 746-4880.

AMERICAS BEST VALUE INN & SUITES   707/433-5548

▼▼ **Motel.** Rates not provided. **Address:** 74 Healdsburg Ave 95448 **Location:** US 101 exit Central Healdsburg, just se. **Facility:** 38 units. 2 stories (no elevator), exterior corridors. **Amenities:** high-speed Internet. **Pool(s):** outdoor. **Activities:** whirlpool.

BELLA VILLA MESSINA   707/433-6655

▼▼▼ **Bed & Breakfast** $220-$390 **Address:** 316 Burgundy Rd 95448 **Location:** US 101 exit Dry Creek Rd, just e to Grove St, 0.5 mi n to Chiquita Rd, then 0.5 mi w. **Facility:** This elegant Italian-style villa features a 360-degree panoramic view overlooking the Alexander, Dry Creek and Russian River valleys. 5 units. 2 stories (no elevator), interior corridors. **Terms:** 2 night minimum stay - weekends, 7 day cancellation notice-fee imposed.

BEST WESTERN PLUS DRY CREEK INN   (707)433-0300

▼▼▼
Hotel
$99-$299

AAA Benefit: Members save up to 20%, plus 10% bonus points with Best Western Rewards®.

Address: 198 Dry Creek Rd 95448 **Location:** US 101 exit Dry Creek Rd, just se. **Facility:** 163 units. 3 stories, exterior corridors. **Terms:** 2 night minimum stay - seasonal and/or weekends, resort fee. **Amenities:** safes. *Some:* high-speed Internet. **Pool(s):** 2 heated outdoor. **Activities:** sauna, whirlpools, steamroom, exercise room. **Guest Services:** complimentary laundry. **Free Special Amenities: continental breakfast and high-speed Internet.**

HEALDSBURG INN ON THE PLAZA   (707)433-6991

▼▼▼▼ **Hotel** $310-$425 **Address:** 112 Matheson St 95448 **Location:** On the Plaza; downtown. **Facility:** 12 units, some kitchens. 2 stories, interior corridors. **Parking:** street only. **Terms:** 7 day cancellation notice-fee imposed.

HONOR MANSION A RESORT INN   707/433-4277

▼▼▼▼
Historic Bed & Breakfast
$250-$600

Address: 891 Grove St 95448 **Location:** US 101 exit Dry Creek Rd, just e. then 0.4 mi s. **Facility:** Decks and a koi pond provide interest as you step out of this 1883 Italianate Victorian mansion to explore the manicured grounds, rose garden and small vineyard. 13 units. 2 stories (no elevator), interior/exterior corridors. **Terms:** check-in 4 pm, 2-4 night minimum stay - seasonal and/or weekends, age restrictions may apply, 30 day cancellation notice-fee imposed. **Amenities:** high-speed Internet. *Some:* safes. **Pool(s):** heated outdoor. **Activities:** putting green, tennis court, jogging, basketball. *Fee:* massage. **Free Special Amenities: full breakfast and high-speed Internet.**

MADRONA MANOR WINE COUNTRY INN & RESTAURANT   (707)433-4231

▼▼▼▼ **Historic Country Inn** $220-$625 **Address:** 1001 Westside Rd 95448 **Location:** US 101 exit Central Healdsburg, 0.7 mi w. **Facility:** In the hills above the Dry Creek Valley of Sonoma County, this Victorian estate is surrounded by eight acres of wooded and landscaped grounds. 22 units. 3 stories (no elevator), interior/exterior corridors. **Terms:** 2 night minimum stay - weekends, age restrictions may apply, 7 day cancellation notice-fee imposed. **Amenities:** *Some:* safes. **Dining:** restaurant, see separate listing. **Pool(s):** heated outdoor. **Activities:** *Fee:* massage.

WINE COUNTRY TRAVELODGE   (707)433-0101

▼▼ **Hotel** $79-$299 **Address:** 178 Dry Creek Rd 95448 **Location:** US 101 exit Dry Creek Rd, just e. **Facility:** 23 units. 3 stories (no elevator), interior corridors. **Terms:** 2 night minimum stay - weekends, 3 day cancellation notice-fee imposed. **Amenities:** safes. **Activities:** sauna, whirlpool.

DUCHAMP   707/431-1300

fyi Not evaluated. **Address:** 421 Foss St 95448 **Location:** US 101 exit Central Healdsburg. Facilities, services, and décor characterize a mid-scale property.

LES MARS HOTEL   707/433-4211

fyi Not evaluated. **Address:** 27 North St 95448 **Location:** Jct Healdsburg Ave; downtown. Facilities, services, and décor characterize an upscale property.

WHERE TO EAT

BEAR REPUBLIC BREWING CO   707/433-2337

▼▼ American. Casual Dining. $10-$17 **AAA Inspector Notes:** Serving more than just the bear necessities, this restaurant makes a name for itself with brewed beers and homemade root beer floats, as well as good bar-type appetizers, salads, burgers, sandwiches and seafood dishes. On a lazy afternoon, it is hard to beat the shaded outdoor seats, which are removed from the hustle of Healdsburg Avenue. **Bar:** beer & wine. **Address:** 345 Healdsburg Ave 95448 **Location:** Downtown.

BISTRO RALPH   707/433-1380

▼▼▼ California. Fine Dining. $12-$36 **AAA Inspector Notes:** On a quiet side street, this bistro has a couple of outdoor tables along with an indoor dining room where friends gather to sample wines from an extensive list and dine on grilled sirloin, duck confit and Hawaiian albacore. **Bar:** beer & wine. **Address:** 109 Plaza St 95448 **Location:** Downtown. **Parking:** street only.

BOVOLO   707/431-2962

▼▼ Italian. Quick Serve. $11-$14 **AAA Inspector Notes:** The food raises this counter service eatery to the next level. The theme here is slow food fast. The chef cures his own meats, ingredients are locally sourced and all menu items are made in-house. Try their seasonal bacon/asparagus/egg pizza-add truffle oil for a richer version. Order a glass of wine to wash it down and finish with a scoop of the gelato-like mint julep. **Bar:** beer & wine. **Address:** 106 Matheson St 95448 **Location:** Downtown; in Healdsburg Plaza, in Copperfield's Books. **Parking:** street only.

DRY CREEK KITCHEN   707/431-0330

▼▼▼
California Fine Dining
$25-$38

AAA Inspector Notes: Renowned chef Charlie Palmer utilizes local ingredients in creating an innovative menu at this fine dining establishment. Located right across from The Plaza, patio dining affords park-like views and the bustling energy of the street. Inside dining tends to be more serene and peaceful, with views of the kitchen through frosted glass. **Bar:** full bar. **Reservations:** suggested. **Address:** 317 Healdsburg Ave 95448 **Location:** Downtown; in Hotel Healdsburg.

MADRONA MANOR WINE COUNTRY INN & RESTAURANT
707/433-4231

❤❤❤ ❤❤❤ Regional American. Fine Dining. $85-$119 **AAA Inspector Notes:** This elegant manor atop a hill is surrounded by vibrant roses and an extensive cultivated garden. Patrons enjoy sophisticated dining while savoring items prepared with locally and globally sourced ingredients. A fun way to satisfy the sweet tooth is with a bowl of ice cream, prepared tableside by a hand-churned process using nitrogen. After the meal, diners can enjoy a stroll through the gardens to enjoy the fragrant lemon and orange trees. **Bar:** full bar. **Reservations:** suggested. **Address:** 1001 Westside Rd 95448 **Location:** US 101 exit Central Healdsburg, 0.7 mi w.

Ⓓ CALL 🅖Ⓜ

SPOONBAR
707/433-7222

❤❤❤ Mediterranean. Casual Dining. $9-$19 **AAA Inspector Notes:** See and be seen through this spot's glass walls overlooking a casually, trendy decor with a touch of retro. Menu items are visually vibrant, bold in taste and full of texture. Start with one of the handmade pasta dishes, followed by any of the main plates and if it is on the menu, the beignets with lemon curd cream and blueberries and quinoa are a must. Instead of pairing dishes with wine, try pairing them with a cocktail. **Bar:** full bar. **Address:** 219 Healdsburg Ave 95448 **Location:** Between Matheson and Mill sts; in H2 Hotel. **Parking:** street only. Ⓛ Ⓓ

HILMAR-IRWIN (F-3) pop. 5,197, elev. 95'

HILMAR CHEESE CO. is at 9001 N. Lander Ave. (SR 165). The company's visitor center has viewing windows through which guests can watch the cheese-making and packaging process. More than a million pounds of cheddar and Monterey Jack cheese are produced here each day.

Hands-on exhibits allow young visitors to dress like a cheesemaker, mix a cow's meal and learn about nutrition. The film "Lights, Camera, Cheese" provides additional information. Guided tours are available, including a special tour that concludes with a make-your-own-ice cream activity. Complimentary cheese samples are provided.

Time: Allow 30 minutes minimum. **Hours:** Visitor center open Mon.-Sat. 7-7, Sun. 7-5. Guided visitor center tours are given Mon.-Fri. at 11 and 1, Sat.-Sun. at 10 and 11, mid-June through Aug. 31; Sat.-Sun. at 10 and 11, rest of year. Make-your-own-ice cream activity is added to the Mon.-Fri. 11 a.m. tour, mid-June to late Aug. Closed major holidays. **Cost:** Free. Make-your-own-ice cream tour $3; reservations are recommended. **Phone:** (209) 656-1196 or (800) 577-5772. 🍽 🪧

HOLLISTER pop. 34,928

BEST WESTERN SAN BENITO INN
831/637-9248

❤❤❤ ❤❤
Hotel
Rates not provided

AAA Benefit: Members save up to 20%, plus 10% bonus points with Best Western Rewards®.

Address: 660 San Felipe Rd 95023 **Location:** 1.5 mi n on SR 25 and 156. **Facility:** 42 units. 2 stories (no elevator), exterior corridors. **Amenities:** high-speed Internet. **Pool(s):** outdoor. **Free Special Amenities:** local telephone calls and high-speed Internet.

🆂🅰🆅🅴 CALL 🅖Ⓜ 🍽 🛜 🔲 🔲 🔲

Be a better driver.
Keep your mind on the road.

The Peacock Inn at Casa de Fruta
408/842-9316

❤❤❤ ❤❤ **Hotel** $99-$159 **Address:** 10031 Pacheco Pass Hwy 95023 **Location:** Just s of SR 152 at Casa de Fruta. **Facility:** 14 units. 1 story, exterior corridors. **Dining:** 2 restaurants. **Pool(s):** outdoor. **Activities:** playground. **Guest Services:** coin laundry.

🍽 CALL 🅖Ⓜ 🍽 🛜 ❌

WHERE TO EAT

CASA DE FRUTA-CASA DE COFFEE
408/842-7282

❤❤ American. Casual Dining. $7-$18 **AAA Inspector Notes:** The coffee shop is a favorite stop of travelers on their way to the Monterey Peninsula. Shops and fruit and produce markets are nearby. **Bar:** beer & wine. **Address:** 10031 Pacheco Pass Hwy 95023 **Location:** Just s of SR 152.

Ⓑ Ⓛ Ⓓ ㉔ CALL 🅖Ⓜ

ROUND TABLE PIZZA
831/637-7444

❤ Pizza. Casual Dining. $7-$28 **AAA Inspector Notes:** This casual, family-oriented pizza place features high-quality ingredients and dough rolled fresh daily. Distinctive specialty pizzas are piled high with toppings. **Bar:** beer & wine. **Address:** 496 Tres Pinos Rd 95023 **Location:** Just w of Airline Hwy. Ⓛ Ⓓ

HOMEWOOD (D-4) elev. 6,234'
• Part of Lake Tahoe Area — see map p. 158

TAHOE MARITIME MUSEUM is at 5205 W. Lake Blvd. at jct. Fawn St. The boating history of Lake Tahoe is presented at this museum, which showcases watercraft and maritime artifacts from the lake's past. The museum features several vessels in its permanent exhibit and many more in a museum annex that can be viewed twice a month during summer open houses; some vessels date to the late 19th century. A collection of outboard motors mounted on the wall, photographs and a children's area also are available.

Tours: Guided tours are available. **Time:** Allow 30 minutes minimum. **Hours:** Thurs.-Tues. 10-5, Memorial Day-Sept. 30; Fri.-Sun. 10-5, rest of year. Phone ahead to confirm holiday schedule. **Cost:** $5; free (ages 0-12). **Phone:** (530) 525-9253.

HOOPA (B-1) elev. 300'

HOOPA TRIBAL MUSEUM, on SR 96 in the Hoopa Shopping Center, displays baskets, jewelry, tools, a redwood canoe, hats and ceremonial clothing still used during Hoopa tribal events. Tours to the ceremonial grounds and villages can be arranged by appointment. **Time:** Allow 1 hour minimum. **Hours:** Mon.-Fri. 9-5, May-Sept. Closed major holidays. **Cost:** Museum by donation. Tours $10. **Phone:** (530) 625-4110.

HOPLAND (E-2) pop. 756, elev. 488'
• Attractions map p. 566
• Part of Wine Country area — see map p. 562

REAL GOODS SOLAR LIVING CENTER, 13771 US 101S, encompasses 12 acres of outdoor displays about energy conservation, recycling and solar power. Highlights include permaculture gardens, unusual living structures, solar timepieces and a building constructed of rice straw bales. **Hours:** Mon.-Sat. 10-7, Sun. 10-6, Memorial Day-Labor

Day; Mon.-Sat. 10-6, Sun. 10-5, rest of year. Guided tours are given Fri.-Sun. at 11 and 3. Closed Jan. 1, Thanksgiving and Christmas. **Cost:** Center free. Guided tours by donation. **Phone:** (707) 472-2400.

WINERIES
- **Milano Family Winery** is at 14594 S. US 101. **Hours:** Tours and tastings daily 10-5. Closed Jan. 1, Thanksgiving and Christmas. **Phone:** (707) 744-1396.

HUMBOLDT-TOIYABE NATIONAL FOREST (E-5)

Elevations in the forest range from 100 ft. below sea level at Death Valley in Calif. to 12,374 ft. at Castle Peak. Refer to AAA maps for additional elevation information.

Scattered across divisions in central, northern, western and southern Nevada and in eastern California, Humboldt-Toiyabe National Forest is the second largest national forest in the country, totaling 6,343,735 acres. Ranges in north-central Nevada include the Independence, Santa Rosa, Ruby, White Pine, Jarbidge, Schell Creek and Quinn Canyon. Part of the forest lies along the rugged Monitor, Toquima, Toiyabe, Shoshone and Paradise ranges of central Nevada and along the eastern slopes of the Sierra Nevada and the Spring Mountains near Las Vegas.

Jarbidge Wilderness is north of Elko, Nev.; no motorized vehicles are allowed, but six trails suitable for hiking and horseback riding traverse the area. The Ruby Mountains Wilderness, southeast of Elko, offers backpacking and other recreational opportunities within 90,000 acres of alpine lakes, glaciated canyons and rugged mountains. Other wilderness areas include Currant Mountain, East Humboldt, Grant Range, Mount Moriah, Quinn Canyon and Santa Rosa-Paradise Peak.

Three national hiking trails are within the forest. The Pacific Crest National Scenic Trail traverses 74 miles of forest land; the Toiyabe Crest National Recreation Trail runs 67 miles along the Toiyabe Range; and the Mount Charleston National Recreation Trail ascends the 11,918-foot summit of Charleston Peak. Due to unpredictable weather conditions, hiking on these trails should only be attempted June through October; high elevations can receive snow during any month of the year.

Recreational activities within the forest include backpacking and hiking on nearly 900 miles of trails, as well as fishing, hunting, camping and picnicking. Several mountain biking trails have been developed near Austin in central Nevada. Winter sports areas are at Heavenly Valley, Lee Canyon and Mount Rose. Winter sports such as heli-skiing, snowmobiling and cross-country skiing are popular. Other areas noted for visual and recreational appeal are Lake Tahoe, the Sierra Nevada near Bridgeport, Calif., and Mount Rose.

For further information contact the Forest Supervisor, Humboldt-Toiyabe National Forest, 1200

Franklin Way, Sparks, NV 89431; phone (775) 331-6444. *See Recreation Areas Chart.*

LAMOILLE CANYON SCENIC AREA is in Humboldt-Toiyabe National Forest, 20 mi. s.e. of Elko, Nev., via SR 227. A paved, two-lane scenic drive, overshadowed by towering cliffs, winds 12 miles along the canyon. Several overlooks with posted information enable visitors to observe the effects of glacial activity. Wildflowers bloom abundantly in spring throughout the canyon's meadows. Rest areas are available. ▲ ⊞

INVERNESS pop. 1,304

MOTEL INVERNESS	415/236-1967

Motel
Rates not provided
Address: 12718 Sir Francis Drake Blvd 94937 **Location:** 3 mi w of SR 1. **Facility:** 7 units, some two bedrooms, efficiencies and kitchens. 1 story, exterior corridors. **Free Special Amenities:** early check-in/late check-out and room upgrade (subject to availability with advance reservations).
[SAVE] CALL [&M] [📶] [✕] [🐾] [✖] [▣] / SOME UNITS [♿]

TOMALES BAY RESORT & MARINA	415/669-1389

[fyi] Not evaluated. **Address:** 12938 Sir Francis Drake Blvd 94937 **Location:** 5 mi w of SR 1. Facilities, services, and décor characterize an economy property.

WHERE TO EAT

BLACKBIRD	415/669-7195

🐦 Breads/Pastries. Quick Serve. $2-$7 **AAA Inspector Notes:** This favorite serves pastries and bagels from Bovine Bakery and breads from Brickmaids along with premium coffee and tea. Located next to Inverness Post Office, there is a piano onsite and sometimes someone would be playing classics to contemporary music. Free Wi-Fi is offered. **Address:** 12781 Sir Francis Drake Blvd 94937 **Location:** 3.8 mi w of SR 1. [B] [L] [D] [🐾]

INYO NATIONAL FOREST (F-5)

Elevations in the forest range from 3,700 ft. in Owens Valley to 14,505 ft. at the summit of Mount Whitney. Refer to AAA maps for additional elevation information.

Inyo National Forest parallels US 6 and US 395 for 165 miles between the eastern California towns of Inyokern and Lee Vining. The forest contains Mount Whitney—at 14,505 feet, the highest point in the contiguous United States—as well as portions of the Pacific Crest Trail and the John Muir Trail. Inyo National Forest shares in managing nine wilderness areas, including the Ansel Adams and John Muir wildernesses. Between US 6 and the Nevada border, the White Mountains rise to 14,246 feet and hold the Ancient Bristlecone Pine Forest, with the oldest living trees on the planet; the Bristlecone visitor center is open to the public from mid-June through Labor Day. Most of the Sierra's highest peaks are visible to the west from US 395.

Vehicle travel is restricted in Devils Postpile National Monument and the Reds Meadow area of the forest: Only vehicles with camping permits are allowed beyond the Minaret Vista turnoff between 7:30 a.m. and 5:30 p.m., mid-June through Sept. 30.

All others are required to use a shuttle bus that operates during the restricted times.

The 2-hour round trip makes 10 stops, including the Devils Postpile ranger station, where trails lead to recreation areas. Shuttles depart the Mammoth Mountain Adventure Center every 20-30 minutes beginning at 7:15 a.m. The last return shuttle departs Reds Meadow at 7 p.m. Shuttle fare is $7; $4 (ages 3-15); phone (800) 922-1930. Permits are required for overnight access to the Ansel Adams and John Muir wildernesses and are available by reservation.

Mammoth and June mountains have ski areas that are popular in winter, while mountain biking, hiking, camping, fishing and backpacking are the main summertime diversions. Gondola rides to the top of Mammoth Mountain provide outstanding views and access to hiking and mountain biking trails. Rides are available daily 9-4:30, mid-June through Sept. 30 (weather and wind permitting). Fare $24; $19 (ages 13-18 and 65-79); free (ages 0-12 with paying adult and ages 80+). Phone (760) 934-2571 or (800) 626-6684.

Minaret Vista, at 9,175 feet, offers a sweeping view of the Ritter Range. A store and cafe, as well as saddle and pack horses, are available at Reds Meadow. An interagency welcome center on Main Street in Mammoth Lakes is open year-round; phone (760) 924-5500.

Roads throughout the remainder of the forest provide scenic drives. An interagency visitor center is south of Lone Pine at the junction of US 395 and SR 136. Phone (760) 876-6222 or TTY (760) 876-6228. For additional information contact the Superintendent, Inyo National Forest, 351 Pacu Ln., Suite 200, Bishop, CA 93514; phone (760) 873-2400 or TTY (760) 873-2538. For wilderness information phone (760) 873-2483. Campground and wilderness permit reservations can be obtained online through www.recreation.gov. *See Recreation Areas Chart.*

INSIDER INFO:
High-Altitude Health

Temples throbbing, gasping for breath and nauseated, you barely notice the scudding clouds or the spectacular view.

You might be suffering from Acute Mountain Sickness (AMS). Usually striking at around 8,000 feet (2,450 m) in altitude, AMS is your body's way of coping with the reduced oxygen and humidity of high altitudes. Among the symptoms are headaches, shortness of breath, loss of appetite, insomnia and lethargy. Some people complain of temporary weight gain or swelling in the face, hands and feet.

You can reduce the effect of high altitude by being in top condition. If you smoke or suffer from heart or lung ailments, consult your physician before your trip. Certain drugs will intensify the symptoms. To avoid Acute Mountain Sickness, adjust to elevations slowly; a gradual ascent with a couple days of acclimatization is best if you have time. For example, if you are planning a trip to the Rocky Mountains of Colorado, you might want to spend the first night in a lower altitude city such as Denver as opposed to heading directly to an environment with extreme elevations.

On the way up, eat light, nutritious meals and stay hydrated by drinking a large amount of water, taking care to avoid caffeine, alcohol and salt. In addition, your doctor may be able to prescribe medication that can offset the effects of high-altitude.

If you develop AMS, you should stop ascending; you will recover in a few days. If the AMS is mild, a quick descent will end the suffering immediately.

Other high-altitude health problems include sunburn and hypothermia. Dress in layers to protect yourself from the intense sun and wide fluctuations in temperature.

Finally, after you lounge in the sauna or whirlpool bath at your lodgings, remember to stand up carefully, for the heat has relaxed your blood vessels and lowered your blood pressure.

BISHOP CREEK CANYON is 16 mi. w. of Bishop, Calif., on SR 168. Lined by 1,000-foot granite cliffs, the canyon is a popular fishing area late April to mid-November. Fishing areas include North Lake, South Lake, Lake Sabrina, Intake II and Bishop Creek. Developed hiking trails are available. **Hours:** Daily 24 hours. **Cost:** Free. **Phone:** (760) 873-8405 for the chamber or (888) 395-3952.

JACKSON (E-3) pop. 4,651, elev. 1,200'

Jackson's downtown and vintage Victorian homes are reminders of its gold rush heritage; it was founded in 1848. North of town are several mine headframes; one shaft is approximately 6,000 feet deep. Kennedy Gold Mine Tours allows visitors to view buildings and other structures associated with a mining site that closed in 1942. The tours are offered on weekends from March through October; for additional information phone (209) 223-9542.

Amador County Chamber of Commerce: 115 Main St., P.O. Box 596, Jackson, CA 95642. **Phone:** (209) 223-0350 or (800) 649-4988.

BEST WESTERN AMADOR INN   (209)223-0211

AAA Benefit: Members save up to 20%, plus 10% bonus points with Best Western Rewards®.

Address: 200 S Hwy 49 95642 **Location:** Just se of jct SR 49 and 88. **Facility:** 118 units, some kitchens. 2 stories (no elevator), interior corridors. **Terms:** cancellation fee imposed. **Amenities:** *Some:* high-speed Internet. **Pool(s):** heated outdoor. **Guest Services:** valet laundry, area transportation-casino. **Free Special Amenities:** expanded continental breakfast and high-speed Internet.

EL CAMPO CASA RESORT MOTEL   209/223-0100

Vintage Motel $48-$98 **Address:** 12548 Kennedy Flat Rd 95642 **Location:** 1.5 mi w of town; jct SR 49 and 88 on Frontage Rd; approach off SR 88. **Facility:** The grounds surrounding this charming gem include an attractively landscaped garden area. Reservations are required for Monday through Wednesday. 15 units. 2 stories (no elevator), exterior corridors. **Bath:** shower only. **Terms:** closed 1/1-1/31, cancellation fee imposed. **Pool(s):** outdoor. **Activities:** playground.

HOLIDAY INN EXPRESS HOTEL & SUITES
(209)257-1500

Hotel
$99-$160

Address: 101 Clinton Rd 95642 **Location:** 0.7 mi se of jct SR 49 and 88; jct SR 49 and Clinton Rd. Adjacent to Jackson Cinemas. **Facility:** 51 units. 2 stories, interior corridors. **Terms:** cancellation fee imposed. **Amenities:** high-speed Internet. **Activities:** exercise room. **Guest Services:** coin laundry. **Free Special Amenities:** expanded continental breakfast and high-speed Internet.

THE JACKSON LODGE   (209)223-0486

Motel
$65-$135

Address: 850 N Hwy 49 95642 **Location:** On SR 49 and 88, 0.5 mi w. **Facility:** 36 units, some cabins. 1-2 stories (no elevator), exterior corridors. **Terms:** cancellation fee imposed. **Amenities:** Some: safes. **Pool(s):** heated outdoor. **Guest Services:** coin laundry.

JACKSON RANCHERIA CASINO & HOTEL
209/223-1677

Hotel
$89-$399

Address: 12222 New York Ranch Rd 95642 **Location:** 2.5 mi e of jct SR 49 and 88, 1.8 mi n on Dalton Rd. **Facility:** This modern hotel offers full gaming activities and a spacious lobby with a fireplace. Most of the guest rooms are recently renovated. 86 units. 1-4 stories, interior corridors. **Parking:** on-site and valet. **Terms:** cancellation fee imposed. **Amenities:** high-speed Internet (fee), safes. **Dining:** 5 restaurants. **Pool(s):** heated outdoor. **Activities:** whirlpools, spa. **Fee:** game room. **Guest Services:** area transportation-casino. **Free Special Amenities:** local telephone calls and high-speed Internet.

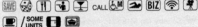
WHERE TO EAT

JOSE'S MEXICAN RESTAURANT   209/223-3886

Mexican. Casual Dining. $6-$14 AAA Inspector Notes: Since 1983, this family-friendly restaurant has been serving traditional Mexican fare and some specialty items including a few Mexican breakfast items such as machaca (mildly spiced shredded beef) with scrambled eggs. **Bar:** full bar. **Address:** 609 Hwy 49 95642 **Location:** 0.6 mi se of jct SR 49 and 88; just n of jct Clinton Rd; in Mother Lode Plaza. L D CALL

STRINGS ITALIAN CAFE   209/223-7874

Italian. Casual Dining. $8-$15 AAA Inspector Notes: The local chain offers pasta, chicken and seafood dishes, pizza and calzones. All-you-can-eat pasta night is on Wednesday after 4 p.m. Nightly specials are available. **Bar:** beer & wine. **Address:** 11976 SR 88 95642 **Location:** Jct SR 49 and 88, 0.5 mi w; in Amador Plaza Shopping Center. L D CALL

THOMI'S CAFE & BAKERY   209/257-0800

American. Casual Dining. $8-$18 AAA Inspector Notes: A nice selection of salads, sandwiches and breakfast items are featured at this café. At dinner, traditional American food such as meatloaf and St. Louis-style ribs are offered. Order at the counter first before taking a seat. **Bar:** beer & wine. **Address:** 627 S Hwy 49 95642 **Location:** 0.6 mi se of jct SR 49 and 88; just n of jct Clinton Rd; in Mother Lode Plaza. B L D

MEL & FAYE'S DINER   209/223-0853

fyi Not evaluated. Since 1956, this diner has been serving breakfast fare, burgers, sandwiches and shakes. Deck dining is available in season. **Address:** 31 SR 49 95642 **Location:** Just nw of jct SR 88.

JAMESTOWN (F-4) pop. 3,433, elev. 1,405'
• Hotels p. 152 • Restaurants p. 152

The first gold discovery in Tuolumne County was made near Jamestown in 1848. "Jimtown," as it once was called, has served as a backdrop for such movies as "High Noon" and "Butch Cassidy and the Sundance Kid." Several buildings in town date to the 1870s. Many of the balconied buildings in the town's business district, which date from the 1860s and '70s, now house galleries, boutiques and shops.

GOLD PROSPECTING ADVENTURES, 18170 Main St., is a living-history re-creation of a mining camp. Among the camp's buildings along Woods Creek is a re-creation of a cabin said to be once inhabited by Mark Twain. Gold panning and other classes are available. **Time:** Allow 1 hour minimum. **Hours:** Daily 9-5, Memorial Day-Labor Day; 10-5, rest of year. Closed Christmas. Phone ahead to confirm schedule. **Cost:** Camp free. Gold panning $20-$300. **Phone:** (209) 984-4653 or (800) 596-0009.

JAMESTOWN GOLD PANNING is .5 mi. s. on SR 49/108, then .5 mi. w. to 17712 Harvard Mine Rd. Gold panning and sluicing on Woods Creek in the historic Harvard Mine District are taught by seasoned prospectors who relate the history and stories of the gold mining camp. Participants can see what the early miners experienced back in the 1800s.

A change of clothing is recommended for children. **Tours:** Guided tours are available. **Time:** Allow 2 hours minimum. **Hours:** Daily 9-5. Closed Christmas. **Cost:** Two hours of panning and sluicing with an instructor $50; $75 (one adult and one child); $100 (family rate, two adults and two children). Three hours $70; $90 (one adult and one child); $120 (family, two adults and two children). One hour of panning only with instructor $25; $35 (one adult and one child); $55 (family, two adults and two children). Two hours $30; $40 (one adult and one child); $65 (family, two adults and two children). Additional children ages 13-17, $10; $5 (additional children ages 0-12). Other packages also are available. Reservations are required. **Phone:** (209) 984-4038.

RAILTOWN 1897 STATE HISTORIC PARK is at 11855 5th Ave. Within the park are an interpretive center, a roundhouse, station, trains and yard facilities. Sierra Railway Co. began operating from Jamestown in 1897, carrying passengers and freight throughout the region's gold-mining area. Visitors can observe the maintenance and restoration of railroad equipment.

A video presentation and seasonal train excursions are available. Self-guiding and guided tours (when a guide is available) are offered. Steam train excursions on the historic Sierra #3 also are offered; phone ahead for information.

Hours: Park open Thurs.-Mon. 10-3. Phone ahead for hours of roundhouse and shop tours. Train rides are given Sat.-Sun. and holidays, Apr.-Oct., and on select weekends the rest of the year. Closed Jan. 1, Thanksgiving and Christmas. Phone ahead to confirm schedule. **Cost:** $5; $3 (ages 6-17). Train (includes park admission) $13; $6 (ages 6-17). **Phone:** (209) 984-3953.

1859 HISTORIC NATIONAL HOTEL, A COUNTRY INN

(209)984-3446

Historic Boutique
Country Inn
$140-$160

Address: 18183 Main St 95327 **Location:** In historic downtown. **Facility:** You will find beautifully appointed period décor in this historic hotel built in 1859. The staff is warm and gracious. 9 units. 2 stories (no elevator), interior corridors. *Bath:* shower only. **Parking:** street only. **Terms:** 3 day cancellation notice. **Dining:** National Hotel Restaurant, see separate listing. **Free Special Amenities:** full breakfast and high-speed Internet.

 / SOME UNITS FEE

COUNTRY INN SONORA (209)984-0315

Motel $59-$289 **Address:** 18730 Hwy 108 95327 **Location:** SR 108 and 49, 1 mi e of town. **Facility:** 61 units. 3 stories (no elevator), exterior corridors. **Terms:** cancellation fee imposed. **Amenities:** high-speed Internet. **Pool(s):** outdoor. **Guest Services:** valet laundry.

/ SOME UNITS FEE

JAMESTOWN RAILTOWN MOTEL 209/984-3332

Motel
Rates not provided

Address: 10301 Willow St 95327 **Location:** Center. **Facility:** 20 units. 2 stories (no elevator), exterior corridors. **Pool(s):** outdoor.

/ SOME UNITS FEE

VICTORIAN GOLD BED & BREAKFAST (209)984-3429

Historic Bed & Breakfast $115-$185 **Address:** 10382 Willow St 95327 **Location:** Center; in historic downtown. **Facility:** Themes such as stained glass and Victorian décor dress the guest rooms at this quaint, two-story B&B. 8 units. 2 stories (no elevator), interior corridors. **Terms:** 5 day cancellation notice-fee imposed.

/ SOME UNITS FEE

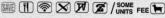
WHERE TO EAT

KAMM'S CHINESE RESTAURANT 209/984-3105

Chinese. Casual Dining. $8-$11 **AAA Inspector Notes:** For three generations, this family-owned restaurant has served up traditional favorites of chow mein, fried rice, Mongolian beef, beef and broccoli, kung pao chicken and sweet and sour pork. The small dining room fills up quickly as this is a favorite stop for the local crowd. **Bar:** beer & wine. **Address:** 18208 Main St 95327 **Location:** Center; in historic downtown area. **Parking:** street only. L D

NATIONAL HOTEL RESTAURANT 209/984-3446

Continental
Casual Dining
$8-$29

AAA Inspector Notes: Casual elegance marks this restaurant, occupying a restored landmark established in 1859. **Bar:** full bar. **Reservations:** suggested. **Address:** 18183 Main St 95327 **Location:** In historic downtown; in 1859 Historic National Hotel, A Country Inn.

Parking: street only. L D

JENNER (E-2) pop. 136, elev. 12'
• **Part of Wine Country area — see map p. 562**

FORT ROSS STATE HISTORIC PARK, 12 mi. n. on SR 1, was the site of an 1812 trading post and fort established by Russians to protect their claim against the Spanish. Restored or reconstructed buildings within the stockade include the chapel, officers' barracks, commandant's house and blockhouses; the visitor center has a museum. Cultural Heritage Day is the last Saturday in July. Russian Orthodox services are held Memorial Day, July 4 and the last Saturday in July. *See Recreation Areas Chart.*

Time: Allow 1 hour minimum. **Hours:** Grounds Fri.-Sun. dawn-dusk. Visitor center Fri.-Sun. 10-4:30. Guided tours are given when staff is available; phone ahead for tour times. Closed Jan. 1, Thanksgiving and Christmas. Phone ahead to confirm schedule. **Cost:** $8 per private vehicle; $7 (ages 62+ per private vehicle). Phone for Cultural Heritage Day admission. **Phone:** (707) 847-3286 for information, or (707) 847-3437 for the museum.

KRUSE RHODODENDRON STATE NATURAL RESERVE is 20 mi. n. on SR 1, then .5 mi. e. on Kruse Ranch Rd. The period of peak bloom for these rhododendrons—some up to 14 feet tall—is late April to early June. The lush understory growth includes mosses, ferns and sorrel. Four miles of hiking trails wind through the reserve's 317 acres. **Note:** The road to the reserve is rough and should be driven with caution. The reserve is not suitable for vehicles larger than a van or pickup truck; trailers are not permitted. **Time:** Allow 1 hour minimum. **Hours:** Daily dawn-dusk. **Cost:** Free. **Phone:** (707) 847-3221.

JENNER INN & COTTAGES (707)865-2377

Country Inn $118-$348 **Address:** 10400 Hwy 1 95450 **Location:** On SR 1, 1 mi n of SR 116. **Facility:** 21 units, some kitchens, houses and cottages. 2 stories (no elevator), exterior corridors. **Terms:** 2 night minimum stay - weekends, 10 day cancellation notice-fee imposed. **Activities:** sauna, whirlpools, horseshoes, volleyball.

CALL / SOME UNITS FEE

WHERE TO EAT

RIVER'S END 707/865-2484

California. Casual Dining. $10-$43 **AAA Inspector Notes:** Perched above the beach with a panorama of the coast, this elegant little restaurant is the place to enjoy the sunset while dining on fresh local fares. Start with the oysters for an appetizer. For an entrée, the duck two ways is a good choice. Finish with crème brûlée. Enjoy a glass of champagne after dinner on the deck and enjoy the view. **Bar:** full bar. **Reservations:** suggested. **Address:** 11048 Hwy 1 95450 **Location:** On SR 1, 1.6 mi n of SR 116. L D

JOHNSVILLE (D-4) pop. 20

Johnsville was established in 1872 at the base of Eureka Peak. Ski racing, which relies on speed rather than negotiating a serpentine course, is one of the area's popular winter sports thrills.

PLUMAS-EUREKA STATE PARK AND MUSEUM is 4 mi. w. on CR A14 at 310 Johnsville Rd. The museum, originally a building miners' bunkhouse, has a collection of photographs, tools and memorabilia of mining days. A partially restored stamp mill is featured. Recreational activities available include hiking, fishing and skiing. *See Recreation Areas Chart.*

Time: Allow 30 minutes minimum. **Hours:** Park open daily 24 hours, Memorial Day-Sept. 30 (weather permitting). Museum open daily 9-5, Memorial Day-Sept. 30; schedule varies rest of year according to staff availability. Closed Jan. 1, Thanksgiving and Christmas. Phone ahead to confirm schedule. **Cost:** Park admission free. Museum by donation. **Phone:** (530) 836-2380, or (800) 444-7275 for camping reservations through ReserveAmerica.

THE IRON DOOR   530/836-2376
American. Casual Dining. $20-$39 **AAA Inspector Notes:** Housed in a building dating from 1907 with knotty pine decor, this restaurant serves American-style cuisine including steak, seafood and pasta. An enclosed porch offers alternative seating. **Bar:** full bar. **Reservations:** suggested. **Address:** 5417 Main St 96103 **Location:** 5 mi w of Graeagle on CR A14 (Graeagle-Johnsville Rd).

KELSEYVILLE (E-2) pop. 3,353, elev. 1,386'
• Part of Wine Country area — see map p. 562

Known as the "Bartlett Pear Capital of the World," Kelseyville is the agricultural center of Lake County. Pear and walnut orchards share the surrounding valley with vineyards.

CLEAR LAKE STATE PARK is 3 mi. n.e. at 5300 Soda Bay Rd. The lake, California's largest freshwater body of water, is a popular spot for all forms of water-based recreation. Fishing, for bass in particular, is particularly good, and a nature trail passes through the site of a former Pomo Indian village. The visitor center has wildlife dioramas and exhibits depicting the lake environment both on land and in water. A theater presents videos, films and demonstrations. *See Recreation Areas Chart.*

Time: Allow 1 hour minimum. **Hours:** State park daily dawn-dusk. Visitor center open Sat. 10-4, Sun. 10-1, Memorial Day-Labor Day. Phone ahead to

confirm visitor center schedule. **Cost:** Park $8 per private vehicle; $7 (ages 62+ per private vehicle). **Phone:** (707) 279-4293.

KENWOOD (B-8) pop. 1,028, elev. 415'
• Attractions map p. 568
• Hotels & Restaurants map & index p. 570
• Part of Wine Country area — see map p. 562

WINERIES
• **Kunde Family Estate** is at 9825 Sonoma Hwy. (SR 12). **Tours:** Guided tours are available. **Hours:** Tastings daily 10:30-5. Closed Jan. 1, Easter, Thanksgiving and Christmas. **Phone:** (707) 833-5501.

BIRMINGHAM BED & BREAKFAST   707/833-6996   **31**
Historic Bed & Breakfast. Rates not provided. **Address:** 8790 Hwy 12 95452 **Location:** SR 12, just n of town. **Facility:** Located in a tranquil setting and lovingly restored by the current owners, this historic landmark, built in 1912, offers a cozy, comfortable respite from your hectic days. 5 units, some cottages. 2 stories (no elevator), interior corridors.

WHERE TO EAT

KENWOOD RESTAURANT   707/833-6326   **14**
Continental. Casual Dining. $13-$27 **AAA Inspector Notes:** The light and airy dining room of this casual restaurant overlooks the hills and vineyards of Sonoma County. Menu items include roasted duck and escargots. **Bar:** full bar. **Address:** 9900 Hwy 12 95452 **Location:** On SR 12; between Santa Rosa and Sonoma.

THE VINEYARDS INN BAR & GRILL   707/833-4500   **13**
Spanish. Casual Dining. $10-$29 **AAA Inspector Notes:** Popular with the locals, this casual family-run bar and grill serves everything tapas style, from pork to grilled artichokes, salsa and fries. Excellent entrée choices include adobo or the polo abuela for a taste of Basque cuisine. **Bar:** full bar. **Address:** 8445 Sonoma Hwy 95452 **Location:** On SR 12, just n of Golf Rd; between Sonoma and Santa Rosa.

KETTLEMAN CITY pop. 1,439

BEST WESTERN KETTLEMAN INN & SUITES
                                          (559)386-0804

Motel
$108-$160

AAA Benefit: Members save up to 20%, plus 10% bonus points with Best Western Rewards®.

Address: 33410 Powers Dr 93239 **Location:** E of and adjacent to I-5 exit SR 41 N, 0.3 mi to Bernard Dr, then 0.3 mi n. **Facility:** 72 units, some two bedrooms. 2 stories (no elevator), exterior corridors. **Terms:** cancellation fee imposed. **Amenities:** *Some:* high-speed Internet. **Pool(s):** outdoor. **Activities:** whirlpool. **Guest Services:** coin laundry. **Free Special Amenities:** expanded continental breakfast and use of on-premises laundry facilities.

SUPER 8   (559)386-9530
Motel
$69-$75

Address: 33415 Powers Dr 93239 **Location:** E of and adjacent to I-5 exit SR 41 N, 0.3 mi to Bernard Dr, then 0.3 mi n. **Facility:** 60 units. 2 stories, exterior corridors. **Pool(s):** outdoor. **Free Special Amenities:** continental breakfast and high-speed Internet.

KING CITY (H-3) pop. 12,874, elev. 330'

King City takes its name from pioneer Charles H. King, who bought 13,000 acres of land in 1884 and founded King Ranch. The town was incorporated in 1911. Crops grown in the surrounding region range from broccoli, lettuce and wine grapes to barley and beans.

King City Chamber of Commerce & Agriculture: 200 Broadway St., Suite 40, King City, CA 93930. **Phone:** (831) 385-3814.

MISSION SAN ANTONIO DE PADUA is 23 mi. s.w. via Jolon Rd., surrounded by Fort Hunter Liggett. The mission was founded by Father Junípero Serra on July 14, 1771. Abandoned 1882-1928, partially because of its remote location, the mission has been restored to resemble its 1813 appearance. Original remains include the well, gristmill, tannery and parts of the aqueduct system. A museum exhibits Native American artifacts. The mission's annual fiesta is held the second Sunday in June.

Note: A valid ID, vehicle registration and proof of insurance are required to enter the fort. Guided tours are available by appointment. **Hours:** Daily 10-4. Closed Easter, Thanksgiving and Christmas. Phone ahead to confirm schedule. **Cost:** $5; $3 (ages 3-11). **Phone:** (831) 385-4478.

MONTEREY COUNTY AGRICULTURAL AND RURAL LIFE MUSEUM, in San Lorenzo County Park at 1160 Broadway, features a museum complex and an exhibit barn. Displays in the barn trace the evolution of agriculture in Monterey County. Historic buildings include the restored 1898 Spreckels farmhouse, a blacksmith shop, an 1887 schoolhouse and the original 1903 King City train depot. The History of Irrigation Museum also is part of the complex. An outdoor exhibit displays farm equipment from the 1800s to the 1940s.

Time: Allow 30 minutes minimum. **Hours:** Exhibit barn open Tues.-Fri. 10-4. Other buildings open Fri. noon-4, Sat.-Sun. 11-4. Guided tours are available Fri.-Sun. Closed Jan. 1, Thanksgiving, day after Thanksgiving, and Dec. 24-25 and 31. **Cost:** Park admission Mon.-Fri. (includes parking) $6; free (ages 62+ and walk-ins). Park admission Sat.-Sun. and holidays $8; free (ages 62+ and walk-ins). Museum free. **Phone:** (831) 385-8020.

DAYS INN   (831)385-5921

Motel
$55-$110

Address: 1130 Broadway St 93930 **Location:** US 101 exit Broadway St, just e. **Facility:** 46 units, some efficiencies. 2 stories (no elevator), exterior corridors. **Terms:** cancellation fee imposed. **Amenities:** high-speed Internet. **Pool(s):** outdoor. **Guest Services:** coin laundry. **Free Special Amenities:** expanded continental breakfast and high-speed Internet.

KEEFER'S INN   (831)385-4843

Motel
$59-$199

Address: 615 Canal St 93930 **Location:** US 101 exit Canal St, just w. **Facility:** 47 units. 2 stories (no elevator), interior/exterior corridors. **Terms:** cancellation fee imposed. **Amenities:** high-speed Internet. **Pool(s):** outdoor. **Activities:** whirlpool. **Guest Services:** coin laundry. **Free Special Amenities:** continental breakfast and high-speed Internet.

QUALITY INN   (831)385-6733

Hotel $79-$180 **Address:** 1190 Broadway St 93930 **Location:** US 101 exit Broadway St, just e. **Facility:** 47 units. 2 stories (no elevator), exterior corridors. **Amenities:** safes. *Some:* high-speed Internet. **Pool(s):** outdoor.

KINGS BEACH pop. 3,796

- Hotels & Restaurants map & index p. 161
- Part of Lake Tahoe Area — see map p. 158

FERRARI'S CROWN RESORT   (530)546-3388

Motel
$69-$250

Address: 8200 N Lake Blvd 96143 **Location:** SR 28, 0.3 mi e of SR 267. Located near lakefront. **Facility:** 71 units, some two bedrooms and efficiencies. 2 stories (no elevator), exterior corridors. **Terms:** 2 night minimum stay - seasonal, 7 day cancellation notice. **Amenities:** high-speed Internet. **Pool(s):** 2 outdoor. **Activities:** whirlpool, beach access. **Free Special Amenities:** continental breakfast and high-speed Internet.

WHERE TO EAT

LANZA'S ITALIAN RESTAURANT   530/546-2434 30

Italian. Casual Dining. $14-$22 **AAA Inspector Notes:** Red-checkered tablecloths drape the tables at this Italian restaurant with knotty pine decor. A wine menu, as well as choices from the full bar, complements the pasta, veal, chicken and pizza choices. The house favorite is stuffed lumaconi. **Bar:** full bar. **Address:** 7739 N Lake Blvd 96143 **Location:** SR 28, 0.5 mi w of SR 267.

STEAMERS BEACH SIDE BAR AND OVEN   530/546-2218 31

American. Casual Dining. $10-$24 **AAA Inspector Notes:** This restaurant's name indicates its best offering: steamers. Pizza and oven-baked sandwiches also share space on the menu. Rustic decor characterizes the storefront restaurant, which treats guests to views of the lake via picture windows. A seasonal patio with picnic tables offers additional seating options. **Bar:** full bar. **Address:** 8290 N Lake Blvd 96143 **Location:** SR 28, 0.3 mi e of SR 267.

KINGSBURG (G-5) pop. 11,382, elev. 297'

Kingsburg was established in 1875 by the Southern Pacific Railroad. A wave of Swedish emigrants in the late 19th century influenced the local architecture; a number of restored buildings date back to the early 1900s and feature steep, wood-shingled roofs, dormer windows and half-timbers.

Raisin grapes and other fruits are grown in the San Joaquin Valley's fertile soil; both Sun-Maid Growers and Del Monte maintain processing facilities in Kingsburg. In keeping with its heritage, the town water tower takes the shape of a giant coffee pot, colorfully decorated in a traditional Swedish motif. This local landmark is illuminated at night.

Kingsburg District Chamber of Commerce: 1475 Draper St., Kingsburg, CA 93631. **Phone:** (559) 897-1111.

FAIRFIELD INN & SUITES BY MARRIOTT KINGSBURG
(559)897-8840

Hotel
$119-$159

 AAA Benefit: AAA hotel discounts of 5% or more.

Address: 216 Ventura Ct 93631 **Location:** SR 99 exit SR 201 W (Sierra St/Conejo Ave) w, n on Morgan Dr, then just e. **Facility:** 86 units. 3 stories, interior corridors. **Amenities:** high-speed Internet. **Pool(s):** heated outdoor. **Activities:** whirlpool, exercise room. **Guest Services:** valet and coin laundry. **Free Special Amenities: continental breakfast and high-speed Internet.**

 CALL

KIRKWOOD   (E-4) pop. 158, elev. 7,690'

RECREATIONAL ACTIVITIES
Skiing
- **Kirkwood Mountain Resort** is 1 mi. s. off SR 88 on Kirkwood Meadows Dr. **Hours:** Daily 9-4, mid-Nov. to late Apr. **Phone:** (209) 258-6000.

KIT CARSON

KIT CARSON LODGE   209/258-8500

fyi Not evaluated. **Address:** 32161 Kit Carson Rd 95644 **Location:** 0.3 mi off SR 88; on Silver Lake. Facilities, services, and décor characterize an economy property.

WHERE TO EAT

KIT CARSON RESTAURANT   209/258-8500

Continental. Casual Dining. $14-$36 **AAA Inspector Notes:** This restaurant offers a varied menu utilizing fresh ingredients and housemade sauces. Views of Silver Lake enhance the inviting casual ambience that includes knotty pine walls and deck dining. A Continental breakfast and Sunday barbecue are featured. The restaurant opens the third week of June and closes the second weekend in October. **Bar:** beer & wine. **Reservations:** suggested. **Address:** 32161 Kit Carson Rd 95644 **Location:** 0.3 mi off SR 88; on Silver Lake; in Kit Carson Lodge. B L D

KLAMATH   (B-1) pop. 779, elev. 29'
- **Restaurants p. 156**

Above the Klamath River on aptly named Bear Bridge, two golden bear statues welcome visitors to the city. Originally painted gray, the bears were repainted gold in the early 1960s by a group of residents intending to give them a face-lift. State government officials had the bears painted gray again, assuming the new color was the work of vandals; when they realized that well-meaning citizens were responsible, the bears went back to gold.

Klamath Chamber of Commerce: P.O. Box 476, Klamath, CA 95548. **Phone:** (800) 200-2335.

KLAMATH RIVER JET BOAT TOURS departs from 17635 US 101S. Two-hour, 45-mile round-trip narrated jet boat excursions on the Klamath River provide an opportunity to see bears, deer, ospreys,

eagles and other wildlife in their natural habitat as well as learn about the history of the river. The captain makes several stops to allow for photographs.

Time: Allow 2 hours minimum. **Hours:** Departures require a minimum of 10 adults. Tours depart daily at 10, 1 and 4, May 1-early Oct. (weather permitting). Phone ahead to confirm schedule. **Cost:** $42; $38 (ages 60+ and military with ID); $32 (ages 12-17); $22 (ages 4-11). Reservations are recommended. **Phone:** (707) 482-7775 or (800) 887-5387.

TREES OF MYSTERY is 4 mi. n. on US 101. A .8-mile, groomed interpretive trail leads through a magnificent redwood forest, showcasing a number oddly formed trees, some nearly 2,000 years old and 300 feet tall. A section of the trail called the Trail of Tall Tales features chainsaw-carved redwood sculptures depicting the legend of Paul Bunyan.

The End of the Trail Museum displays crafts, beadwork and shell ornaments made by members of the Yurok, Karok and Tolowa tribes of northern California. The museum's six rooms also contain kachina dolls, objects made from cedar wood and exhibits focusing on Native American history. The SkyTrail, a six-passenger gondola, transports visitors through the forest canopy.

Hours: Complex open daily 8-7, June-Aug.; 9-5, rest of year. Museum opens half an hour later and closes half an hour earlier. Last admission 1 hour, 30 minutes before closing. Closed Christmas. Phone ahead to confirm schedule. **Cost:** $15; $11 (ages 60+); $8 (ages 7-12). Museum free. **Phone:** (707) 482-2251 or (800) 638-3389.

MOTEL TREES
(707)482-3152

Motel
$70-$145

 Address: 15495 Hwy 101 N 95548 **Location:** On US 101, 4.5 mi n of Klamath. Opposite Trees of Mystery. **Facility:** 23 units, some two bedrooms. 1 story, exterior corridors. **Bath:** shower only. **Activities:** tennis court, hiking trails.

RAVENWOOD MOTEL
707/482-5911

Motel
$75-$150

Address: 151 Klamath Blvd 95548 **Location:** Jct US 101, just e on Ehlers Ave, then just s. **Facility:** 15 units, some kitchens. 1 story, exterior corridors. **Terms:** 4 day cancellation notice-fee imposed. **Activities:** hiking trails. **Guest Services:** coin laundry.

FOREST CAFE   707/482-5585

fyi Not evaluated. With a giant statue of Paul Bunyan towering across the highway, visitors should not be surprised at the decor of this casual eatery. A giant statue of a black bear stands guard with a bald eagle in flight overhead. Half of the ceiling is covered with faux vines and flowers like a rainforest while the other half contains replicas of duck feet and tails as if you are underwater looking up. Tabletops are beautifully sealed redwood. Lunch offerings are simple sandwiches with grilled salmon at night. **Address:** 15499 US Hwy 101 N 95548 **Location:** On US 101, 4.5 mi n of Klamath; opposite Trees of Mystery.

KLAMATH NATIONAL FOREST (A-2)

Elevations in the forest range from 523 ft. at Somes Bar to 8,563 ft. at Caribou Mountain. Refer to AAA maps for additional elevation information.

Covering about 1,726,000 acres in northern California with a small segment also extending into Oregon, Klamath National Forest is characterized by rugged forested ridges, rushing rivers and high mountain lakes and streams. Much of this scenic area is included in the Marble Mountain Wilderness and Trinity Alps Wilderness, which are accessible only by trail. Vehicular traffic is prohibited in wilderness areas. Hunting, fishing and white-water rafting opportunities are available.

Good fishing spots abound, and the forest is a prime location for anglers in search of steelhead and salmon. Trout fishing is popular in creeks and high mountain lakes. Outdoor enthusiasts also can camp, hike, horseback ride, ski and snowmobile.

Klamath River Highway and forest roads and trails provide access to the region. For information contact the Forest Supervisor, Klamath National Forest, 1711 S. Main St., Yreka, CA 96097-9549; phone (530) 842-6131. *See Recreation Areas Chart.*

RECREATIONAL ACTIVITIES
White-water Rafting

- **Marble Mountain Guest Ranch** trips depart from various points. Other activities are available. **Hours:** Daily Apr.-Nov. **Phone:** (530) 469-3322 or (800) 552-6284.

- **Rogue Klamath River Adventures** offers pick-up service at Yreka area hotels; passengers also can meet n. of Yreka at the Collier Rest Area, SR 96 and I-5. **Hours:** Full-day trips on the Class III Lower Klamath River depart daily May 1-Oct. 1. Full-day trips on the Class V Scott and Cal Salmon rivers and Class III-V Smith River depart daily Apr. 1-June 15. **Phone:** (541) 779-3708 or (800) 231-0769.

KNIGHTS FERRY (F-4) elev. 200'

A 330-foot-long covered bridge dating from gold rush days crosses the Stanislaus River north of Knights Ferry. Said to be the longest covered bridge west of the Mississippi River, it was completed in 1863 and replaced an earlier bridge that was destroyed by a flood; it is open to foot traffic only.

RECREATIONAL ACTIVITIES
White-water Rafting

- **Beyond Limits Adventures** departs from Stanislaus River Park, 14842 Orange Blossom Rd., for guided excursions on the south fork of the American River. **Hours:** Daily Apr.-Sept. (depending on available water flow). **Phone:** (209) 526-0027 or (800) 234-7238.

LAFAYETTE pop. 23,893
- **Hotels & Restaurants map & index p. 254**

LAFAYETTE PARK HOTEL & SPA   (925)283-3700 **34**

Hotel
$199-$289

Address: 3287 Mt. Diablo Blvd 94549 **Location:** SR 24 exit Pleasant Hill Rd S, just w. **Facility:** Featuring flower gardens and a courtyard with a fountain, the property offers elegant surroundings and spacious, well-appointed guest rooms. 138 units. 3 stories, interior corridors. **Parking:** on-site (fee) and valet. **Terms:** cancellation fee imposed. **Amenities:** *Fee:* video games, high-speed Internet. **Dining:** The Duck Club Restaurant, see separate listing. **Pool(s):** heated outdoor. **Activities:** sauna, whirlpool, exercise room, spa. **Guest Services:** valet laundry. **Free Special Amenities:** newspaper and local transportation.

BO'S BARBECUE & CATERING RESTAURANT
                                        925/283-7133 **28**

Barbecue. Casual Dining. $10-$23 **AAA Inspector Notes:** A local favorite for barbecue beef, chicken and ribs, this spot nurtures a casual atmosphere inside and out on the patio under the shade trees. Credit cards are not accepted. **Bar:** beer & wine. **Address:** 3422 Mt. Diablo Blvd 94549 **Location:** SR 24 exit Pleasant Hill Rd S, then e. Lafayette, 6.

THE DUCK CLUB RESTAURANT   925/283-7108 **26**

American. Fine Dining. $12-$40 **AAA Inspector Notes:** Artistic, light fare exhibits a Continental influence at this restaurant. The menu changes to reflect the freshest of ingredients. Be sure to try their award-winning French onion soup. Entrées may include grilled salmon, braised short ribs or roast duck. The surroundings are comfortable and attractive. **Bar:** full bar. **Reservations:** suggested. **Address:** 3287 Mt. Diablo Blvd 94549 **Location:** SR 24 exit Pleasant Hill Rd, just s; in Lafayette Park Hotel & Spa. **Parking:** on-site and valet.

MOUNTAIN MIKE'S PIZZA   925/283-6363 **27**

Pizza. Casual Dining. $6-$37 **AAA Inspector Notes:** Customers can design their own or select from one of the specialty pizzas at this great spot for families. Sandwiches and a salad bar are available. **Bar:** beer & wine. **Address:** 3614 Mt. Diablo Blvd 94549 **Location:** SR 24 exit Central Lafayette/Moraga, just nw on Deer Hill Rd, just s on Oak Hill Rd, then just w. Lafayette, 6.

ROUND TABLE PIZZA   925/283-0404

Pizza. Casual Dining. $7-$30 **AAA Inspector Notes:** This casual, family-oriented pizza place features high-quality ingredients and dough rolled fresh daily. Distinctive specialty pizzas are piled high with toppings. **Bar:** beer & wine. **Address:** 3637 Mt. Diablo Blvd 94549 **Location:** At Happy Valley Rd. Lafayette, 6.

AAA/CAA travel information:
Available in print, online
and on the go!

LAKEPORT (D-2) pop. 4,753, elev. 1,343'
• Part of Wine Country area — see map p. 562

On the western shore of Clear Lake (see Recreation Areas Chart), one of California's largest, Lakeport is known for excellent fishing (especially bass) and water recreation.

Lake County Chamber of Commerce: 875 Lakeport Blvd., P.O. Box 295, Lakeport, CA 95453. **Phone:** (707) 263-5092 or (866) 525-3767.

LAKE COUNTY HISTORIC COURTHOUSE MUSEUM, 255 N. Main St., contains displays of items depicting Pomo Indian culture, period rooms of the late 1800s and early 1900s, a restored courtroom and a gem and mineral collection. Changing exhibits also are featured. **Time:** Allow 30 minutes minimum. **Hours:** Wed.-Sat. 10-4, Sun. noon-4. **Cost:** Donations. **Phone:** (707) 263-4555.

FORBESTOWN INN   707/263-7858

▼▼▼ **Bed & Breakfast.** Rates not provided. **Address:** 825 N Forbes St 95453 **Location:** SR 29 exit 103 (11th St), 0.8 mi e, then just s. **Facility:** This 1860 residential home, with a lovely outdoor pool and landscaped patios, is two stories and offers ample homelike comforts. 4 units. 2 stories (no elevator), interior corridors. **Pool(s):** outdoor.

KONOCTI VISTA CASINO RESORT & MARINA   707/262-1900

▼▼ **Motel** $79-$89 **Address:** 2755 Mission Rancheria Rd 95453 **Location:** Jct SR 175, 1.7 mi se on Soda Bay Rd, then 0.4 mi n. **Facility:** Set on the shores of a peaceful lake, the motel offers nice accommodations within a short stroll of the adjoining casino. 79 units. 2 stories (no elevator), exterior corridors. **Terms:** cancellation fee imposed, resort fee. **Amenities:** Some: safes. **Pool(s):** heated outdoor. **Activities:** marina. **Guest Services:** coin laundry.

LAKEPORT ENGLISH INN   707/263-4317

▼▼▼
Bed & Breakfast
$165-$195

Address: 675 N Main St 95453 **Location:** SR 29 exit 103 (11th St); between 6th and 7th sts. **Facility:** Comprised of two historical Victorian homes and a cottage surrounding an English village garden, the inn's charming small-town setting is enhanced by the state's largest lake. 10 units, some cottages. 2 stories (no elevator), interior corridors. **Parking:** street only. **Terms:** 4 day cancellation notice-fee imposed. **Amenities:** high-speed Internet. **Activities:** game room. **Free Special Amenities:** full breakfast and room upgrade (subject to availability with advance reservations).

SKYLARK SHORES RESORT   (707)263-6151

▼▼▼
Motel
$59-$199

Address: 1120 N Main St 95453 **Location:** SR 29 exit 103 (11th St), 0.8 mi e, then just n. **Facility:** 45 units, some two bedrooms, kitchens and cabins. 1-2 stories (no elevator), exterior corridors. **Terms:** cancellation fee imposed. **Pool(s):** heated outdoor. **Activities:** boat dock, fishing, playground, horseshoes, volleyball. **Guest Services:** coin laundry. **Free Special Amenities:** high-speed Internet and children's activities.

LAKE TAHOE AREA

Lake Tahoe, which holds enough water to cover the entire state of California to a depth of 14 inches, was named "big water" by the Washoe Indians. According to Washoe legend, Lake Tahoe was created when an Evil Spirit was in pursuit of an innocent Native American. Attempting to aid the pursued, the Great Spirit gave him a branch of leaves with the assurance that each leaf dropped would produce a body of water the Evil Spirit would have to circumvent. But during the chase the whole branch was dropped in fright, creating Lake Tahoe.

It is said that the water in Lake Tahoe is 97 percent pure, nearly the same as distilled water. Remarkably clear and deep blue, the lake is 22 miles long and 12 miles wide; about one-third lies in Nevada. Its average depth is 989 feet; the deepest point is 1,645 feet, making Tahoe the third deepest lake in North America. The first 12 feet below the surface can warm to 68 F in summer, while depths below 700 feet remain a constant 39 F.

This "lake in the sky," at an elevation of 6,229 feet, lies in a valley between the main Sierra Nevada and an eastern offshoot, the Carson Range. The mountains, which are snowcapped except in late summer, rise more than 4,000 feet above the resort-lined shore. Most of the surrounding area is within the Eldorado, Humboldt-Toiyabe and Tahoe national forests.

Immigrants and miners were lured to the rugged Sierras by tales of fortunes made during the California gold rush. The discovery of the Comstock Lode increased traffic and depleted the Tahoe Basin's natural resources to a dangerously low level. Between 1860 and 1890 lumber was needed for fuel and to support the web of mines constructed beneath Virginia City. The decline of the Comstock Lode was likely the saving grace for Tahoe's forests.

By the early 1900s the picturesque lake had become a retreat for the rich. Elaborate hotels began dotting the shores. Roads were paved during the 1920s and '30s, and Lake Tahoe no longer was an enclave only for the wealthy. Development continued in the 1950s and roads were plowed during the winter, enabling year-round residence. In 1968 the Tahoe Regional Planning Agency was established, ensuring environmentally responsible development for years to come.

In winter snow covers the entire landscape. An average of 125 inches falls along the lake's shores, but snow depth in the mountains can reach 300-500 inches. Snow skiing and snowboarding enthusiasts flock to Lake Tahoe each year to enjoy their favorite winter sports. Well-known Tahoe ski areas include

This map shows cities in the Lake Tahoe Area where you will find attractions, hotels and restaurants. Cities are listed alphabetically in this book on the following pages.

Lake Tahoe Area

6065-A

Alpine Meadows, Diamond Peak, Heavenly and Squaw Valley. Despite the cold winters, though, the lake never freezes due to the constant exchange of water from the bottom to the surface.

In summer, when the snow melts and the weather becomes warmer, popular recreational activities include mountain biking, hiking, fishing, golfing, kayaking, windsurfing, canoeing, horseback riding, snorkeling, water skiing, boating and swimming.

The Tahoe Rim Trail, a 165-mile loop running along the ridges and peaks surrounding Lake Tahoe, offers a splendid panorama of the lake, California's High Sierra and Nevada's Great Basin as well as a route used in summer by hikers and horseback riders and in winter for snowshoeing. Mountain biking is allowed in certain areas. For additional information contact the Tahoe Rim Trail Association; phone (775) 298-0012.

The headquarters of the U.S. Forest Service-Lake Tahoe Basin Management Unit provides year-round information about wilderness permits and forest activities, including camping and hiking in summer and cross-country skiing in winter. The headquarters is open Mon.-Fri. 8-4:30 (weather permitting). For information contact Lake Tahoe Basin Management Unit, 35 College Dr., South Lake Tahoe, CA 96150; phone (530) 543-2600, or TTY (530) 543-0956.

The Taylor Creek Visitor Center (see attraction listing p. 526), on SR 89 between Camp Richardson and Emerald Bay in South Lake Tahoe, Calif., is operated by the U.S. Forest Service; phone (530) 543-2694.

The lake has two main approaches: the North Shore via I-80 and the South Shore via US 50. The North Shore, roughly the 14 miles between Tahoe City, Calif., and Incline Village, Nev., has a more rural atmosphere and smaller lakeside towns, while South Shore destinations like South Lake Tahoe and Stateline, Nev., are more bustling and tourist-oriented, offering lots of casinos, shopping and restaurants.

Both roads that encompass the lake are two-lane highways providing excellent views and interesting drives. A drive completely around the lake covers 72 miles. Scenic overlooks off the loop road, such as Inspiration Point near Vikingsholm (see attraction listing p. 526), offer expansive lake and mountain vistas. SR 89 on the west side around Emerald Bay occasionally is closed during heavy snowfalls. Road information is available from the California Department of Transportation (Caltrans); phone (800) 427-7623.

Safety tip: Keep a current AAA/CAA Road Atlas in every vehicle

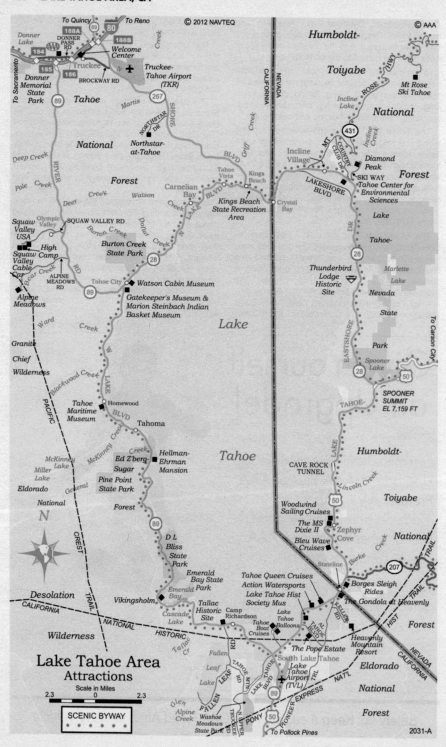

© 2012 NAVTEQ

© AAA

To Quincy   To Reno

Humboldt-

Toiyabe

Donner Lake

188A

80

Donner Pass Rd

188B

Welcome Center

184

Truckee

185

186

BROCKWAY RD

Truckee-Tahoe Airport (TKR)

Mt Rose Ski Tahoe

To Sacramento

Donner Memorial State Park

89

Tahoe

267

Martis

Incline Lake

ROSE HWY

National

NORTHSTAR DR

Northstar-at-Tahoe

Deep Creek

RIVER

Pole Creek

Deer

Creek

Forest

Watson

Carnelian Bay

Tahoe Vista

Kings Beach

BLVD

Incline Village

431

Incline Creek

MT COUNTRY CLUB DR

Diamond Peak

SKI WAY

National

Forest

Creek

Griff

Kings Beach State Recreation Area

Crystal Bay

LAKESHORE BLVD

Tahoe Center for Environmental Sciences

Squaw Valley USA

Olympic Valley

SQUAW VALLEY RD

High Camp

Squaw Valley Cable Car

ALPINE MEADOWS RD

Burton Creek

Dollar Creek

Burton Creek State Park

28

Lake

Tahoe-

28

Lake

DR

EASTSHORE

Thunderbird Lodge Historic Site

Marlette Lake

Nevada

State

Alpine Meadows

Bear Creek

Tahoe City

Watson Cabin Museum

Gatekeeper's Museum & Marion Steinbach Indian Basket Museum

Lake

Park

Spooner Lake

Ward Creek

Granite Chief Wilderness

89

W

Blackwood Creek

Tahoe

28

50

Homewood

Tahoe Maritime Museum

BLVD

Tahoma

LAKE

McKinney Creek

Tahoe

SPOONER SUMMIT EL 7,159 FT

TAHOE-

Humboldt-

McKinney Lake

Miller Lake

Eldorado

National

General

Creek

Ed Z'berg-Sugar Pine Point State Park

Hellman-Ehrman Mansion

Forest

89

CAVE ROCK TUNNEL

Lincoln Creek

50

Toiyabe

N

PACIFIC

CREST

TRAIL

D L Bliss State Park

Woodwind Sailing Cruises

The MS Dixie II

Bleu Wave Cruises

Zephyr Cove

National

Burke

Creek

207

Desolation

CALIFORNIA

Vikingsholm

Emerald Bay

Emerald Bay State Park

Cascade Lake

Tallac Historic Site

Camp Richardson

Stateline

Tahoe Queen Cruises
Action Watersports
Lake Tahoe Hist Society Mus

Lake Tahoe Balloons

Borges Sleigh Rides

The Gondola at Heavenly

KELLER RD

Forest

Wilderness

NATIONAL

HISTORIC

Tallac Cr

RD

Tahoe Boat Cruises

AL TAHOE BLVD

The Pope Estate

South Lake Tahoe

Heavenly Mountain Resort

NEVADA

CALIFORNIA

Lake Tahoe Area
Attractions

Scale in Miles
2.3   0   2.3

SCENIC BYWAY

Fallen Leaf Lake

LEAF

FALLEN

RD

TAHOE MTN RD

LAKE TAHOE BLVD

89

Lake Tahoe Airport (TVL)

TRL

Eldorado

National

PIONEER EXPRESS

PONY

Glen Alpine Creek

Washoe Meadows State Park

N UPPER TRUCKEE

50

Forest

To Pollock Pines

2031-A

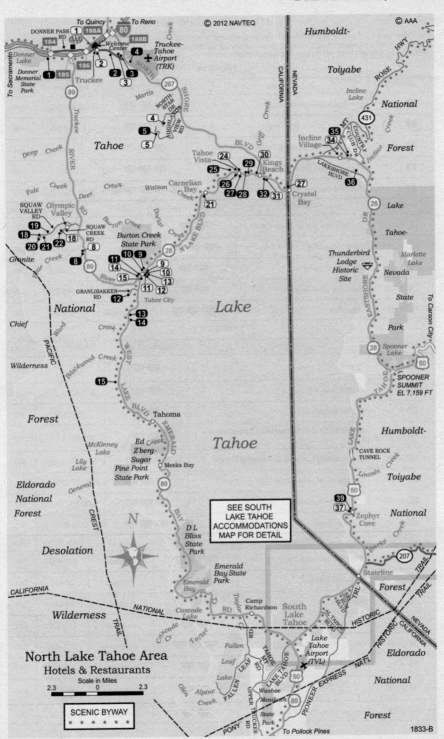

North Lake Tahoe Area
Hotels & Restaurants

Scale in Miles

2.3   0   2.3

SCENIC BYWAY

North Lake Tahoe Area

This index helps you "spot" where approved hotels and restaurants are located on the corresponding detailed maps. Hotel daily rate range is for comparison only. Restaurant price range is a combination of lunch and/or dinner. Turn to the listing page for more detailed rate and price information and consult display ads for special promotions.

TRUCKEE

Map Page	Hotels	Diamond Rated	Rate Range	Page
❶ p. 161	The Truckee Donner Lodge	▽▽▽	$109-$219 SAVE	546
❷ p. 161	The Cedar House Sport Hotel	▽▽▽	$170-$390	546
❸ p. 161	Larkspur Hotel Truckee-Tahoe	▽▽▽	$136-$212 SAVE	546
❹ p. 161	Hampton Inn & Suites Tahoe-Truckee	▽▽▽	$149-$399	546
❺ p. 161	The Ritz-Carlton, Lake Tahoe	▽▽▽▽▽	$249-$899 SAVE	546

Map Page	Restaurants	Diamond Rated	Cuisine	Price Range	Page
① p. 161	Pacific Crest Grill at Bar of America	▽▽	American	$13-$29	546
② p. 161	Cottonwood Restaurant & Bar	▽▽▽	American	$12-$35	546
③ p. 161	Fifty Fifty Brewing Co.	▽▽	American	$9-$29	546
④ p. 161	Rubicon Pizza Company	▽▽	Italian	$13-$25	546
⑤ p. 161	Manzanita	▽▽▽	California	$12-$40	546

TAHOE CITY

Map Page	Hotels	Diamond Rated	Rate Range	Page
❽ p. 161	River Ranch Lodge	▽▽	Rates not provided	540
❾ p. 161	Pepper Tree Inn	▽▽	$75-$225 SAVE	540
❿ p. 161	Mother Nature's Inn	▽▽	$65-$149	540
⓫ p. 161	Americas Best Value Inn Lake Tahoe/Tahoe City	▽▽	$70-$215 SAVE	540
⓬ p. 161	Granlibakken Lodge & Conference Center	▽▽▽	$143-$236 SAVE	540
⓭ p. 161	Cottage Inn at Lake Tahoe	▽▽▽	$160-$340	540
⓮ p. 161	Sunnyside Steakhouse & Lodge	▽▽▽	$135-$380	540
⓯ p. 161	Chaney House	▽▽▽	$180-$275	540

Map Page	Restaurants	Diamond Rated	Cuisine	Price Range	Page
⑧ p. 161	River Ranch Lodge Restaurant	▽▽▽	American	$20-$32	541
⑨ p. 161	Jake's on the Lake	▽▽	Seafood	$9-$32	541
⑩ p. 161	Wolfdale's	▽▽▽	Fusion	$8-$40	541
⑪ p. 161	Rosie's Cafe	▽▽	American	$10-$20	541
⑫ p. 161	Christy Hill Restaurant	▽▽▽	American	$12-$30	541
⑬ p. 161	Dockside 700 Wine Bar & Grill	▽▽	American	$5-$30	541
⑭ p. 161	The Blue Agave Mexican Restaurant & Cantina	▽▽	Mexican	$8-$26	540
⑮ p. 161	Bridge Tender Tavern & Grill	▽▽	American	$5-$13	541

OLYMPIC VALLEY

Map Page	Hotels	Diamond Rated	Rate Range	Page
⑱ p. 161	PlumpJack Squaw Valley Inn	◆◆◆	Rates not provided	264
⑲ p. 161	The Village at Squaw Valley	◆◆◆	$99-$999	264
⑳ p. 161	Squaw Valley Lodge	◆◆◆	$184-$1099	264
㉑ p. 161	Red Wolf Lodge at Squaw Valley	◆◆◆	$139-$419	264
㉒ p. 161	**Resort at Squaw Creek**	◆◆◆◆	$159-$499 SAVE	264

Map Page	Restaurant	Diamond Rated	Cuisine	Price Range	Page
⑱ p. 161	Six Peaks Grill	◆◆◆	American	$16-$32	264

TAHOE VISTA

Map Page	Hotels	Diamond Rated	Rate Range	Page
㉕ p. 161	Cedar Glen Lodge	◆◆	$99-$216	541
㉖ p. 161	**Mourelatos Lakeshore Resort**	◆◆◆	$130-$375 SAVE	542
㉗ p. 161	Franciscan Lakeside Lodge	◆◆	Rates not provided	542
㉘ p. 161	The Shore House at Lake Tahoe	◆◆◆	$149-$325	542
㉙ p. 161	Holiday House	◆◆	$125-$225	542

Map Page	Restaurant	Diamond Rated	Cuisine	Price Range	Page
㉔ p. 161	Spindleshanks American Bistro	◆◆	American	$13-$36	542

KINGS BEACH

Map Page	Hotel	Diamond Rated	Rate Range	Page
㉜ p. 161	**Ferrari's Crown Resort**	◆◆	$69-$250 SAVE	154

Map Page	Restaurants	Diamond Rated	Cuisine	Price Range	Page
㉚ p. 161	Lanza's Italian Restaurant	◆◆	Italian	$14-$22	154
㉛ p. 161	Steamers Beach Side Bar and Oven	◆◆	American	$10-$24	154

INCLINE VILLAGE, NV

Map Page	Hotels	Diamond Rated	Rate Range	Page
㉟ p. 161	Club Tahoe Resort	◆◆	Rates not provided	168
㊱ p. 161	**Hyatt Regency Lake Tahoe Resort, Spa and Casino**	◆◆◆◆	$108-$450 SAVE	168

Map Page	Restaurant	Diamond Rated	Cuisine	Price Range	Page
㉞ p. 161	Azzara's Italian Restaurant	◆◆	Italian	$15-$30	168

ZEPHYR COVE, NV

Map Page	Hotel	Diamond Rated	Rate Range	Page
㊴ p. 161	Zephyr Cove Resort	◆◆	Rates not provided	170

Map Page	Restaurant	Diamond Rated	Cuisine	Price Range	Page
㊲ p. 161	Zephyr Cove Lodge Restaurant	◆◆	American	$10-$23	170

CARNELIAN BAY

Map Page	Restaurant	Diamond Rated	Cuisine	Price Range	Page
㉑ p. 161	**Gar Woods Grill & Pier**	◆◆◆	American	$13-$36	75

CRYSTAL BAY, NV

Map Page	Restaurant	Diamond Rated	Cuisine	Price Range	Page
㉗ p. 161	Crystal Bay Steak & Lobster House	◆◆◆	Steak	$11-$60	167

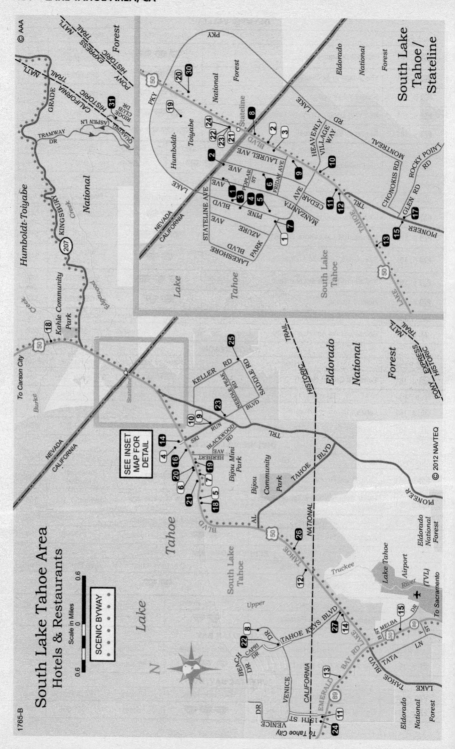

South Lake Tahoe Area
Hotels & Restaurants

South Lake Tahoe/
Stateline

South Lake Tahoe Area

This index helps you "spot" where approved hotels and restaurants are located on the corresponding detailed maps. Hotel daily rate range is for comparison only. Restaurant price range is a combination of lunch and/or dinner. Turn to the listing page for more detailed rate and price information and consult display ads for special promotions.

SOUTH LAKE TAHOE

Map Page	Hotels	Diamond Rated	Rate Range	Page
1 p. 164	Lake Tahoe Ambassador Lodge	◆	$95-$145	527
2 p. 164	**Capri Motel**	◆	$40-$300 SAVE	527
3 p. 164	**Rodeway Inn Casino Center**	◆◆	$49-$249 SAVE	528
4 p. 164	**Americas Best Value Inn**	◆◆	$49-$159 SAVE	526
5 p. 164	Alpenrose Inn	◆◆	$69-$199	526
6 p. 164	Big Pines Mountain House of Tahoe	◆◆	$55-$65	527
7 p. 164	**BEST WESTERN PLUS Station House Inn**	◆◆◆	$129-$169 SAVE	526
8 p. 164	Embassy Suites Lake Tahoe-Hotel & Ski Resort	◆◆◆	Rates not provided	527
9 p. 164	**Stardust Lodge**	◆◆	$100-$370 SAVE	528
10 p. 164	Park Tahoe Inn	◆◆	Rates not provided	528
11 p. 164	Highland Inn	◆◆	$69-$299	527
12 p. 164	**Holiday Inn Express**	◆◆◆	$125-$185 SAVE	527
13 p. 164	**Tahoe Chalet Inn-The Theme Inn**	◆◆	Rates not provided SAVE	528
14 p. 164	Lake Tahoe Vacation Resort - A Diamond Resort	◆◆◆	Rates not provided	528
15 p. 164	**Americana Village**	◆◆	$89-$200 SAVE	526
16 p. 164	**Tahoe Beach & Ski Club**	◆◆◆	$144-$309 SAVE	528
17 p. 164	**The Lodge at Lake Tahoe**	◆◆	$120-$170 SAVE	528
18 p. 164	**Inn By The Lake**	◆◆◆	$130-$680 SAVE	527
19 p. 164	Days Inn South Lake Tahoe	◆◆	$39-$300	527
20 p. 164	Howard Johnson Inn	◆	$49-$229	527
21 p. 164	**BEST WESTERN PLUS Timber Cove Lodge**	◆◆	$139-$269 SAVE	527
22 p. 164	**Tahoe Keys Resort** *(See ad p. 529.)*	◆◆◆	$112-$1700 SAVE	530
23 p. 164	Heavenly Valley Lodge	◆◆	$125-$290	527
24 p. 164	**Fireside Lodge - An All Inclusive Premier Bed & Breakfast**	◆◆◆	$119-$325 SAVE	527
25 p. 164	**Tahoe Seasons Resort**	◆◆◆	$122-$180 SAVE	530
26 p. 164	Econo Lodge	◆	$55-$65	527
27 p. 164	**Tahoe Valley Lodge**	◆◆	$125-$495 SAVE	530

Map Page	Restaurants	Diamond Rated	Cuisine	Price Range	Page
① p. 164	**LewMarNel's Steaks & Spirits**	◆◆◆	Steak	$17-$40	531
② p. 164	Echo Restaurant & Lounge	◆◆	American	$9-$27	530
③ p. 164	McP's Pub Tahoe	◆	American	$9-$18	531
④ p. 164	Riva Grill	◆◆◆	Seafood	$14-$39	531
⑤ p. 164	Freshies Restaurant & Bar	◆◆	Hawaiian	$10-$28	530
⑥ p. 164	Heidi's Pancake House	◆◆	American	$8-$13	530
⑦ p. 164	**Tep's Villa Roma**	◆◆	Italian	$10-$20	531
⑧ p. 164	The Fresh Ketch	◆◆◆	Seafood	$15-$39	530

Map Page	Restaurants (cont'd)	Diamond Rated	Cuisine	Price Range	Page
⑨ p. 164	Cafe Fiore Ristorante Italiano	▽▽▽	Italian	$16-$35	530
⑩ p. 164	Nepheles	▽▽▽	California	$23-$34	531
⑪ p. 164	Evans American Gourmet Cafe	▽▽▽	American	$24-$35	530
⑫ p. 164	**Swiss Chalet Restaurant**	▽▽▽	Continental	$19-$32	531
⑬ p. 164	Cantina Bar & Grill	▽▽	Mexican	$8-$17	530
⑭ p. 164	Artemis Mediterranean Grill	▽▽	Mediterranean	$7-$19	530
⑮ p. 164	Passaretti's Italian Restaurant	▽▽	Italian	$9-$24	531

STATELINE, NV

Map Page	Hotels	Diamond Rated	Rate Range	Page
㉚ p. 164	**MontBleu Resort Casino & Spa**	▽▽▽	$59-$300 SAVE	168
㉛ p. 164	**The Ridge Tahoe**	▽▽▽	$135-$405 SAVE	169

Map Page	Restaurants	Diamond Rated	Cuisine	Price Range	Page
⑱ p. 164	Friday's Station Steak & Seafood Grill	▽▽▽	Steak	$34-$60	170
⑲ p. 164	Four Seasons Restaurant	▽▽	American	$7-$25	170
⑳ p. 164	**Ciera Steak & Chop House**	▽▽▽▽	Steak	$26-$60	169
㉑ p. 164	Cabo Wabo Cantina	▽▽	Mexican	$7-$25	169
㉒ p. 164	19 Kitchen Bar	▽▽▽	Continental	$16-$55	169
㉓ p. 164	Hard Rock Cafe	▽▽	American	$9-$23 SAVE	170
㉔ p. 164	Sage Room Steak House	▽▽▽	Steak	$30-$51	170

Nearby Nevada

CRYSTAL BAY pop. 305

- **Hotels & Restaurants map & index p. 161**
- **Part of Lake Tahoe Area — see map p. 158**

CRYSTAL BAY STEAK & LOBSTER HOUSE

775/833-6333 (27)

▼▼▼ Steak. Fine Dining. $11-$60 **AAA Inspector Notes:** Known for an elegant dining room and great service, this steakhouse offers a wide range of steak and seafood dishes. Guests can choose from an extensive wine list. **Bar:** full bar. **Reservations:** suggested. **Address:** 14 State Route 28 89402 **Location:** Jct SR 431 and 28, 0.9 mi w; in Crystal Bay Club & Casino. (D)

INCLINE VILLAGE pop. 8,777, elev. 6,404'

- **Hotels p. 168 • Restaurants p. 168**
- **Hotels & Restaurants map & index p. 161**
- **Part of Lake Tahoe Area — see map p. 158**

Incline Village, the second largest community on Lake Tahoe and the largest on the Nevada shore, spreads back toward the mountains from the lake's northeastern corner. The town takes its name from the Great Incline Tramway, built in 1874 to transport logs to the crest of the Carson Range; from there a flume sluiced them down to the Washoe Valley.

This was Tahoe's quietest corner before development took off in the 1960s; today it's a popular resort town. Lakeshore Drive, a 3-mile stretch that parallels Tahoe Boulevard (SR 28), runs along the lake past pricey-looking homes and condo developments shaded by lush growths of pines and conifers. Businesses and restaurants line busy Tahoe Boulevard.

Perhaps the most spectacularly scenic way to enter Incline Village is via SR 431, better known as the Mount Rose Highway. From downtown Reno, access US 395 South and get off at exit 59 (Damonte Ranch Parkway), following the directional signs to the beginning of this designated scenic route. The road immediately narrows from four lanes to two, and the flat Washoe Valley is left behind for the gently rolling, sagebrush-dotted Sierra Nevada foothills once the climb into the mountains begins.

The Mount Rose Highway doesn't actually ascend Mount Rose; it negotiates the rugged Carson Range of the Sierras, and Mount Rose, at 10,776 feet, is one of several impressively lofty mountain peaks in this wilderness region. The road quickly gains elevation in a series of serpentine bends, with designated pull-offs offering dizzying views of the valley far below.

A different vista reveals itself around each curve. Snow often covers the mountainsides—at this elevation, July and August are just about the only snow-free months of the year. The layer of white glints under the brilliant blue sky like diamonds, adding a fairy-tale beauty to the scene.

Mount Rose Summit, at an elevation of just over 8,900 feet, is the point where the highway crests the Sierras. After that the descent toward Incline Village and Lake Tahoe begins via another series of hairpin curves. The initial view of Lake Tahoe, a distant, sapphire-blue mirage framed by tall pine trees, is a stunner. The highway ends at SR 28; turn left to head into Incline Village.

A right turn on Village Boulevard will take you down to Lakeshore Drive; turn left and watch for the entrance to Incline Beach (967 Lakeshore Dr.), a little park right along the shore. The pebbly beach here is often delightfully uncrowded, and the aromatic scent of pine fills the air. The water is calm—only the slightest ripple of a wave breaking at the shoreline—and amazingly clear. The reason? Nearly half of the precipitation falling on the Lake Tahoe Basin lands directly on the lake; the remaining rain and snowfall drains through soils of decomposed granite, which creates a filtering system. This magnificent outdoor setting is a lovely place to spend a peaceful hour.

South of town SR 28 runs through Lake Tahoe-Nevada State Park, which extends from the lake to the summit of the Carson Range. Hidden Beach and Sand Harbor State Park are popular spots known for their large, rounded boulder formations. The highway then climbs above the lake, offering sweeping views westward.

Incline Village/Crystal Bay Visitor Information Center: 969 Tahoe Blvd., Incline Village, NV 89451. **Phone:** (775) 832-1606 or (800) 468-2463.

TAHOE CENTER FOR ENVIRONMENTAL SCIENCES is at 291 Country Club Dr. on the Sierra Nevada College campus. The center, in an environmentally friendly, LEED-certified building, educates visitors and provides information about energy and water efficiency, green materials used in construction, the creation of a green indoor environment and sustainable landscaping.

The Thomas J. Long Foundation Education Center features interactive science exhibits, including one about the Lake Tahoe Basin. Visitors can enter a virtual research vehicle to see how water quality is studied; check out a virtual lab with microscopic zooplankton; and explore a 3-D visualization lab with models of Lake Tahoe and Earth.

Time: Allow 1 hour, 15 minutes minimum. **Hours:** Tues.-Sat. 1-5, Memorial Day-Labor Day; Tues.-Fri. 1-5, rest of year. Guided tours are available; phone ahead for schedule. Closed Thanksgiving and Christmas. **Cost:** Free. **Phone:** (775) 881-7560.

◤GEM◢ **THUNDERBIRD LODGE HISTORIC SITE** tours depart from the Incline Village/Crystal Bay Visitor Information Center at 969 Tahoe Blvd. (SR 28). A shuttle bus takes visitors to this magnificent estate built in 1936 by George Whittell, an eccentric San Francisco millionaire. The prominent family's fortune was accumulated from gold rush-era banking, real estate and railroads. The somewhat reclusive Whittell developed a fancy for exotic animals and frequently brought his pet lion Bill and Mingo the elephant to his summer retreat.

A picturesque example of the "old Tahoe" style of architecture, the stone lodge was designed to blend into its secluded setting overlooking the lake. The

(See map & index p. 161.)

heavily forested site on the eastern shore of Lake Tahoe affords amazing views. In addition to the Tudor Revival lodge, the 6-acre property encompasses a gatehouse, three cottages, a card house, a boathouse, three garages, a lighthouse, and a barn for Whittell's elephant.

The 75-minute guided tour includes the lighthouse room; the old lodge; the servants' quarters; and a 600-foot tunnel leading to the boathouse, home to Whittell's 1939, 55-foot mahogany-hulled yacht *Thunderbird*. After hearing a few card house poker stories, visitors enjoy the gardens and fountains. Exceptional iron, stone and woodwork can be seen throughout the estate.

Note: The tour requires being able to walk on uneven ground and climb steps. **Time:** Allow 1 hour, 30 minutes minimum. **Hours:** Tours are given Tues.-Fri. at 10, 11:30, 1 and 2:30, Sat. at 10, 11:30 and 1, July 1 to mid-Sept.; Tues.-Sat. at 11:30 and 1, in June and mid-Sept. through Oct. 31. Phone ahead to confirm schedule. Guests should arrive at the visitor center 30 minutes prior to departure.

Cost: $39; $19 (ages 6-12). Under 6 are not permitted. Reservations are required. **Phone:** (775) 832-8752, (888) 867-6394 for tours by water from the south shore area, or (800) 468-2463 for reservations from the north shore area.

RECREATIONAL ACTIVITIES
Skiing
• **Diamond Peak** is 2.8 mi. n.e. **Hours:** Daily 9-4, Dec.-Apr. (weather permitting). **Phone:** (775) 832-1177, or (775) 831-3211 for snow updates.

CLUB TAHOE RESORT   775/831-5750 **35**
▼▼▼ **Vacation Rental Condominium.** Rates not provided. **Address:** 914 Northwood Blvd 89451 **Location:** SR 28 at N Village Blvd, 0.3 mi e. Located in North Lake Tahoe area. **Facility:** This lodge-style property is perfect for large groups and families due to the many activities offered. Pine trees surround many rooms. 92 condominiums. 2 stories (no elevator), exterior corridors. **Terms:** check-in 4 pm. **Pool(s):** heated outdoor. **Activities:** sauna, whirlpool, 2 lighted tennis courts, racquetball courts, horseshoes. *Fee:* game room. **Guest Services:** complimentary laundry.

HYATT REGENCY LAKE TAHOE RESORT, SPA AND CASINO   (775)832-1234 **36**
▼▼▼▼ **HYATT** **AAA Benefit:** Members save 10% or more everyday.
Resort Hotel
$108-$450
Address: 111 Country Club Dr at Lakeshore 89450 **Location:** 0.4 mi w of SR 28, toward lake via Country Club Dr; 2 mi s of Mt. Rose Hwy. **Facility:** Nestled in the pines, this resort offers extensive recreational facilities and manicured grounds. Some rooms front a private Lake Tahoe beach, others overlook the pools. 422 units, some cottages. 3-12 stories, interior corridors. **Parking:** on-site and valet. **Terms:** check-in 4 pm, 3 day cancellation notice-fee imposed, resort fee. **Amenities:** high-speed Internet (fee), safes. **Dining:** 4 restaurants, entertainment. **Pool(s):** heated indoor/outdoor. **Activities:** whirlpools, recreation programs, rental bicycles, volleyball, spa. *Fee:* game room. **Guest Services:** valet laundry. **Free Special Amenities:** high-speed Internet and local transportation.

WHERE TO EAT

AZZARA'S ITALIAN RESTAURANT   775/831-0346 **34**
▼▼ Italian. Casual Dining. $15-$30 **AAA Inspector Notes:** European decor gives the dining room a charming feel. Pasta, veal and chicken dishes are prominent on the varied menu, along with a few seafood selections. **Bar:** full bar. **Address:** 930 Tahoe Blvd 89450 **Location:** On SR 28. **D**

THE WILDFLOWER CAFE   775/831-8072
fyi Not evaluated. Cinnamon/orange French toast is one of the popular breakfast items at this casual diner, where locals congregate for coffee and large portions of old-fashioned comfort food. **Address:** 869 Tahoe Blvd 89451

STATELINE pop. 842, elev. 6,283'
• Hotels & Restaurants map & index p. 161, 164
• Part of Lake Tahoe Area — see map p. 158

Lake Tahoe South Shore Chamber of Commerce: 169 US 50, 3rd floor, P.O. Box 7139, Stateline, NV 89449. **Phone:** (775) 588-1728.

BORGES SLEIGH RIDES is at 50 US 50, next to the MontBleu Resort Casino & Spa. A handmade sleigh, pulled by a team of blond Belgian horses, makes its way through a wooded, wintry landscape that ends with a scenic view of Lake Tahoe. Elevation prevents the horses from going very fast or very far. The sleigh driver narrates the tour, pointing out local landmarks. Once the snow melts (typically April or May) the mode of conveyance is an antique European-style carriage.

Hours: Thirty-minute and 1-hour sleigh rides daily 10-dusk (weather permitting), in winter; dinner sleigh rides also are available. Thirty-minute and 1-hour carriage rides daily noon-dusk, in summer (weather permitting). Private dinner carriage rides also are available. **Cost:** Sleigh or carriage ride $20; $10 (ages 2-10). Reservations are recommended. **Phone:** (775) 588-2953 or (800) 726-7433. **T**

MONTBLEU RESORT CASINO & SPA   (775)588-3515 **30**
▼▼▼ Hotel **Address:** 55 Lake Tahoe Blvd (US 50) 89449 **Location:** 0.4 mi sw of jct SR 207. **Facility:** A casino, shops and restaurants are featured on site. Many guest rooms have ski mountain and golf course views. 437 units. 15 stories, interior corridors. **Parking:** on-site and valet. **Terms:** check-in 4 pm, 2 night minimum stay - weekends, cancellation fee imposed. **Amenities:** safes. **Dining:** 2 restaurants, also, Ciera Steak & Chop House, see separate listing, nightclub, name entertainment. **Pool(s):** heated indoor. **Activities:** saunas, whirlpool, spa. *Fee:* game room. **Guest Services:** valet laundry.
$59-$300

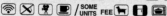

(See maps & indexes p. 161, 164.)

THE RIDGE TAHOE   (775)588-3553 **31**

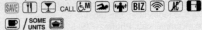

Vacation Rental
Condominium
$135-$405

Address: 400 Ridge Club Dr 89449 **Location:** 3 mi e of US 50 via SR 207 (Kingsbury Grade), 0.8 mi s via Tramway Dr, then 1.3 mi e on Quaking Aspen Ln. **Facility:** Perched at 7,600 feet above sea level, the property has a gondola to the ski lift and offers a range of accommodations, including some units with a kitchen and fireplace. 539 condominiums. 4-11 stories, interior/exterior corridors. **Terms:** check-in 4 pm, 3 day cancellation notice-fee imposed. **Amenities:** safes. **Dining:** 2 restaurants. **Pool(s):** heated outdoor, heated indoor/outdoor. **Activities:** saunas, whirlpools, putting green, 4 tennis courts (1 indoor, 2 lighted), racquetball courts, recreation programs, hiking trails, playground, shuffleboard. *Fee:* downhill skiing, game room, massage. **Guest Services:** complimentary laundry, area transportation-casino area.

HARRAH'S LAKE TAHOE   775/588-6611

fyi Not evaluated. **Address:** 15 US 50 89449 **Location:** US 50; south end of town. Facilities, services, and décor characterize a mid-scale property.

HARVEYS HOTEL, CASINO & RESORT   775/588-2411

fyi Not evaluated. **Address:** 18 US 50 89449 **Location:** Jct US 50 and Stateline Ave. Facilities, services, and décor characterize a mid-scale property.

WHERE TO EAT

19 KITCHEN BAR   775/588-2411 **22**

Continental. Fine Dining. $16-$55 **AAA Inspector Notes:** Elegant surroundings befit this refined restaurant, where diners take in spectacular views of Lake Tahoe and the mountains from the 19th floor of Harveys Hotel. A smaller bistro menu is served during the week and the full menu is only served on Friday and Saturday. **Bar:** full bar. **Reservations:** suggested. **Address:** 18 US 50 89449 **Location:** Jct US 50 and Stateline Ave; in Harveys Hotel, Casino & Resort. **D**

CABO WABO CANTINA   775/588-2411 **21**

Mexican. Casual Dining. $7-$25 **AAA Inspector Notes:** After a day at the lake or mountains, guests can enjoy dinner in the comfortable dining room or in the lounge, where they can watch the big-screen TV. Good-size portions and friendly service await. **Bar:** full bar. **Address:** 18 US 50 89449 **Location:** Jct US 50 and Stateline Ave; in Harveys Hotel, Casino & Resort. **Parking:** on-site and valet. **D**

CIERA STEAK & CHOP HOUSE   775/588-3515 **20**

Steak
Fine Dining
$26-$60

AAA Inspector Notes: High-grade steaks and seafood are prepared in an upscale setting that is elegant, yet comfortable. Rich wood accents and private, expansive booths add to the appeal of the dining room. Desserts are delicious, and an extensive wine list has many enticing options. **Bar:** full bar. **Reservations:** suggested. **Address:** 55 Lake Tahoe Blvd (US 50) 89449 **Location:** 0.4 mi sw of jct SR 207; in MontBleu Resort Casino & Spa. **Parking:** on-site and valet. **D**

Find thousands of places to show your card
and save at AAA.com/discounts

(See maps & indexes p. 161, 164.)

FOUR SEASONS RESTAURANT   775/588-6211   (19)
▼▼▼ American. Casual Dining. $7-$25 AAA Inspector Notes:
Set away from the noise of the casino, this casual restaurant is
popular with the locals and tourists and covers all four seasons with
a menu that lists something for everyone. Bar: full bar. Address: 50
Hwy 50 89449 Location: On US 50; in casino area; in Horizon Casino Resort. Parking: on-site and valet. (B) (L) (D)

FRIDAY'S STATION STEAK & SEAFOOD GRILL
                                 775/588-6611   (18)
▼▼▼ Steak. Casual Dining. $34-$60 AAA Inspector Notes:
Named after a famous Pony Express stop, this steakhouse sits on
the top floor of the Harrah's Hotel tower and offers wonderful views of
the Lake Tahoe area. Good food and service complement the beau-
tiful scenery. The menu offers fresh seafood and a variety of cuts of
Prime beef. Bar: full bar. Reservations: suggested. Address: 15
Hwy 50 89449 Location: US 50; south end of town; in Harrah's Lake
Tahoe. Parking: on-site and valet. (D)

HARD ROCK CAFE   775/588-6200   (23)
▼▼ American. Casual Dining. $9-$23 AAA Inspector Notes:
Rock 'n' roll memorabilia decorates the walls of the popular theme
restaurant. Live music on the weekends contributes to the bustling atmosphere. On the menu is a wide variety of American cuisine--from
burgers and sandwiches to seafood, steaks and pasta. Bar: full bar.
Address: 18 US 50 89449 Location: Jct US 50 and Stateline Ave;
in Harveys Hotel, Casino & Resort. Parking: on-site and valet.
(SAVE) (L) (D) CALL (&M)

SAGE ROOM STEAK HOUSE   775/588-2411   (24)
▼▼▼ Steak. Casual Dining. $30-$51 AAA Inspector Notes:
Since 1947, this rustic-style restaurant has offered an extensive selection of classic steak dishes, punctuated by tableside flambé service for such classic dishes as steak Diane and for dessert, bananas
Foster. Western artwork adorns the walls in the subdued, upscale atmosphere. Bar: full bar. Reservations: suggested. Address: 18 US
50 89449 Location: Jct US 50 and Stateline Ave; in Harveys Hotel,
Casino & Resort. Parking: on-site and valet. (D) CALL (&M)

ZEPHYR COVE pop. 565, elev. 6,348'
• Hotels & Restaurants map & index p. 161
• Part of Lake Tahoe Area — see map p. 158

BLEU WAVE CRUISES departs from Round Hill
Pines Beach and Marina at 325 US 50. Two-hour
sightseeing cruises to Emerald Bay on Lake Tahoe's
west shore offer stunning views of the lake, 3,000-
foot-high mountains and Vikingsholm castle. While
aboard the classic 77-foot, 49-passenger yacht you
might spot wildlife, including ospreys nesting around
Emerald Bay. Other cruises also are available.

Time: Allow 2 hours minimum. Hours: Lunch
cruises depart daily at 11, sightseeing cruises depart
daily at 2, June-Sept. Cost: Lunch cruise $65.
Sightseeing cruise $55; $25 (ages 4-11). Phone:
(775) 588-9283 or (866) 413-0985.

THE MS DIXIE II departs from the Zephyr Cove Resort on US 50; a shuttle bus is available by reservation. This 400-passenger paddlewheeler offers
2-hour narrated sightseeing cruises of Emerald Bay
and Lake Tahoe. Other cruises, including sunset
dinner dance cruises, also are available.

Time: Allow 2 hours, 30 minutes minimum.
Hours: Emerald Bay sightseeing cruises depart
daily at noon and 3, June-Sept.; schedule varies
rest of year. Cost: Emerald Bay sightseeing cruise
$47; $10 (ages 3-11). Reservations are required.
Parking: $8. Phone: (775) 589-4906 or (800)
238-2463.

WOODWIND SAILING CRUISES departs from the
Zephyr Cove Resort on US 50. Sightseeing cruises
aboard the 55-foot, glass-bottom catamaran Woodwind II take visitors along the Nevada shoreline of
Lake Tahoe, featuring views of the Cave Rock geological formation and the Sierra Nevada mountains.
The boat offers both indoor and outdoor seating.
Happy Hour and Sunset Celebration cruises also
are offered.

Time: Allow 2 hours minimum. Hours: Sightseeing cruise departs daily at 11:30, 1:30, 3:30, 5:30
and 7 (weather permitting), early Apr.-Oct. 31.
Phone ahead for Happy Hour and Sunset Celebration schedules and fares. Cost: Sightseeing cruise
$39; $35 (ages 60+); $15 (ages 2-12). Reservations
are recommended. Phone: (775) 588-3000 or (888)
867-6394.

ZEPHYR COVE RESORT   775/589-4907   (39)
▼▼ Cabin. Rates not provided. Address: 760 Hwy 50 89449
Location: 4 mi n of Stateline, NV. Facility: 33 units, some cabins.
1-2 stories, interior/exterior corridors. Dining: Zephyr Cove Lodge
Restaurant, see separate listing. Activities: beach access, waterskiing, fishing, volleyball. Fee: boats, canoes, paddleboats, boat
dock, snowmobiling, horseback riding. Guest Services: coin
laundry.
(❚❙) (Y) (📶) (✕) (🔒) (🖨) (💻) / SOME UNITS FEE (🐾) (🎿)

WHERE TO EAT

ZEPHYR COVE LODGE RESTAURANT   775/589-4968   (37)
▼▼ American. Family Dining. $10-$23 AAA Inspector Notes:
Friendly staff serves up three squares a day with a good selection of
American food. Located at Lake Tahoe. Bar: full bar. Address: 760
Hwy 50 89448 Location: 4 mi n of Stateline, NV; in Zephyr Cove
Resort. (B) (L) (D)

This ends the Lake Tahoe Area section and
resumes the alphabetical city listings
for Northern California.

LARKSPUR pop. 11,926
• Part of San Francisco area — see map p. 342

COURTYARD BY MARRIOTT   (415)925-1800
▼▼▼ Hotel $119-$239 Address:
2500 Larkspur Landing Cir 94939 Loca-   AAA Benefit:
tion: US 101 exit E Sir Francis Drake   AAA hotel discounts
Blvd, 0.3 mi e. Facility: 146 units. 3 sto-   of 5% or more.
ries, interior corridors. Amenities: high-
speed Internet. Pool(s): heated outdoor. Activities: whirlpool,
exercise room. Guest Services: valet and coin laundry.
(ECO) (❚❙) CALL (&M) (🛏) (BIZ) (📶) (✕) (🔒) (💻)
/ SOME UNITS (🖨)

WHERE TO EAT

FUKUSUKE   415/924-8848
▼▼ Japanese. Casual Dining. $14-$26 AAA Inspector Notes:
Located in a strip mall, this unassuming restaurant belies a warm,
airy interior. Regulars call the owner mama-san. Serving home-style
Japanese dishes, dinner set comes with miso soup, rice and
sunomono. Expect casual and friendly service. Bar: beer & wine. Address: 578 Magnolia Ave 94939 Location: US 101 exit Lucky Dr, just
sw, then 1.2 mi w on Doherty Dr. (D) CALL (&M)

LEFT BANK   415/927-3331

▼▼▼ French. Casual Dining. $10-$23 **AAA Inspector Notes:** Chef Roland Passot refers to the menu as cuisine grand-mere, which translates to grandma's cooking. Dishes center on rustic and farm-fresh country French ingredients. **Bar:** full bar. **Address:** 507 Magnolia Ave 94939 **Location:** At Ward St; downtown. **Parking:** street only. L D

PIZZERIA PICCO   415/945-8900

▼▼ Pizza. Casual Dining. $10-$18 **AAA Inspector Notes:** A Larkspur favorite, this tiny pizzeria is packed from the moment it opens the doors. Try the beet salad with burrata and the pizza of the day. Finish with their soft-serve ice cream drizzled with olive oil and sea salt. **Bar:** beer & wine. **Address:** 316 Magnolia Ave 94939 **Location:** At King St; downtown. **Parking:** street only. D K

THE TAVERN AT LARK CREEK   415/924-7766

▼▼▼ American. Casual Dining. $13-$29 **AAA Inspector Notes:** Built in 1888, the restored Victorian home occupies a pleasant garden setting. Smoking is not permitted. **Bar:** full bar. **Address:** 234 Magnolia Ave 94939 **Location:** US 101 exit Tamalpais Dr, 1.3 mi w. **Parking:** valet and street only. D K

LASSEN NATIONAL FOREST (C-3)

Elevations in the forest range from 800 ft. near Butte Meadows to 8,172 ft. at West Prospect Peak. Refer to AAA maps for additional elevation information.

Covering approximately 1,375,000 acres surrounding Lassen Volcanic National Park, Lassen National Forest includes numerous lakes formed by ancient volcanic action.

Several highways, forest roads and trails afford access to the region. The Caribou, Thousand Lakes and Ishi wilderness areas allow backpacking. Campfire permits are required, except in campgrounds with developed facilities. Obtain permits in person at any Forest Service, Bureau of Land Management or California Department of Forestry Office. Hunting, fishing, cross-country skiing and snowmobiling are permitted.

Lake Almanor, one of the largest man-made bodies of water in California, and Eagle Lake, the second largest natural lake in California, offer fishing, sailing, water skiing and swimming. Eagle Lake and Hat Creek offer trout fishing. Recreation sites usually are open mid-May to mid-October (weather permitting); the season is shorter at higher elevations. For more information contact the Supervisor's Office, Lassen National Forest, 2550 Riverside Dr., Susanville, CA 96130; phone (530) 257-2151. *See Recreation Areas Chart.*

SUBWAY CAVE is off SR 89 about .1 mi. n. of SR 44. This lava tube winds 1,300 feet through a lava flow that covered the Hat Creek Valley nearly 20,000 years ago. Carry a jacket and a reliable lantern or flashlight while exploring the .3-mile self-guiding interpretive trail through this cave. The temperature in the cave is 46 degrees Fahrenheit year-round. **Hours:** Open daily dawn-dusk. The gate to the cave is closed Nov. 1-late May, but the site is accessible year-round. **Cost:** Free. **Phone:** (530) 336-5521 or (530) 335-7517.

⬥ LASSEN VOLCANIC NATIONAL PARK (C-3)
• Hotels p. 172

Elevations in the park range from 5,650 ft. at Warner Valley to 10,457 ft. at Lassen Peak. Refer to AAA maps for additional elevation information.

Accessible via SR 36, 9 miles east of Mineral, Lassen Volcanic National Park covers 106,372 acres in northeastern California where the Cascades join the Sierra Nevada. In addition to Lassen Peak (10,457 ft.) and Cinder Cone (6,907 ft.), the park boasts Prospect Peak (8,338 ft.) and Mount Harkness (8,048 ft.), two shield volcanoes topped by cinder cones with trails leading to their summits. Other features include smaller volcanoes and lava flows, fumaroles, boiling springs, boiling lakes and mudpots.

For a period of several thousand years Lassen Peak was quiescent; then in the spring of 1914 a series of relatively small eruptions began. After reaching its peak in 1915, the activity continued until about 1921.

A plug dome volcano, Lassen Peak once protruded from the north flank of ancestral Mount Tehama. This great stratovolcano was destroyed by glaciers, hydrothermal activity and erosion by Mill Creek and other water. Main Park Road winds around Lassen Peak, affording views of the volcano and evidence of its destructive might.

In the southern half of the park gurgling mudpots and roaring fumaroles contribute to the unusual atmosphere. The eastern sector encompasses a splendid chain of lakes, extending from Juniper Lake at the northern base of Mount Harkness to Butte Lake near the eastern base of Prospect Peak.

SRs 36, 44 and 89 border the park and provide scenic forest and mountain views. The main park road traverses the park 30 miles from north to south.

General Information and Activities

Although the park is open all year, heavy snows render most sections inaccessible from late October to mid-June. Winter roads are maintained from the northern gate to the district ranger's office (about 1 mile) and from the southern gate to the southwest area. Although this is a backcountry experience with no ski lift, cross-country skiing is usually possible from early December to late spring. Mountain bikes are not permitted on trails in the park.

Some of the park's many lakes and streams contain trout. A state fishing license is required, and catch limits and regulations are posted. Wilderness permits issued by the park are required for backcountry camping; phone the park headquarters for information. Gates are open 24 hours daily, but the hours they are attended vary. Motorists entering the park when the stations are unattended must self-register their entrance.

Park headquarters is 1 mile west of Mineral on SR 36. Maps, information and bulletins can be obtained at the visitor center or at Loomis Museum. Interpretive and evening programs, guided nature walks and self-guiding trails are available during the summer; snowshoe walks are offered in winter.

Kohm Yah-mah-nee Visitor Center, the park's main visitor facility, is on SR 89 near the southwest entrance. Kohm Yah-mah-nee, the Mountain Maidu name for Lassen Peak, translates as "Snow Mountain." A 21-minute film provides an overview about the park, and exhibit panels focus on its geology and natural and cultural history. The visitor center is open daily 9-6, June 1-Labor Day; 9-5, day after Labor Day-Oct. 31; 9-4, rest of year. Phone (530) 595-4480. The park headquarters in Mineral is open Mon.-Fri. 8-4:30; closed holidays. *See Recreation Areas Chart.*

Note: Stay on established trails at all times in boiling springs and thermal areas; small children should be kept under strict control. Ground crusts that appear safe can be dangerously thin.

ADMISSION to the park is $10 per private vehicle, or $5 per person arriving by other means. Entrance fees are good for 7 days, with a receipt.

PETS are permitted in the park only if they are on a leash, crated or otherwise physically restrained at all times. Pets are not allowed on trails or in buildings.

ADDRESS inquiries to the Superintendent, Lassen Volcanic National Park, Box 100, Mineral, CA 96063-0100. Phone (530) 595-4444.

BUMPASS HELL TRAIL, about .5 mi. beyond Emerald Lake, leads 1.5 mi. off the main park road to Bumpass Hell, a large area of spectacular boiling springs, mudpots, boiling pools and other types of hydrothermal activity. Boardwalks lead to up-close views of these features.

BUTTE LAKE is 6 mi. off SR 44 in the n.e. corner of the park. A marked trail with wayside exhibits leads to the Cinder Cone summit; interpretive leaflets are available. The trail is 2 miles one way.

CINDER CONE is accessible from a trail beginning at Butte Lake. The Cinder Cone volcano is known for its lava flow, called the Fantastic Lava Beds, and multicolored volcanic ash and cinders. It is possible that some lava flows occurred as recently as 1650.

LASSEN PEAK TRAIL leaves the main park road less than 1 mi. beyond Lake Helen and travels 2.5 miles to the top of the volcano. The round trip requires 4 to 5 hours.

MAIN PARK ROAD, between the s. entrance and Manzanita Lake in the n.w. region, is a 30-mile drive. A road guide to points of interest along the route is available for a fee at the park's contact stations. Due to heavy snowfall, most of the road is impassable late Oct. to mid-June.

Chaos Crags and Chaos Jumbles are 2 mi. s. from the n.w. boundary. The Chaos Crags are lava plugs believed to have been pushed up more than 1,000 years ago; subsequent falling rocks formed the Chaos Jumbles. The small coniferous trees in the Chaos Jumbles—some more than 300 years old—constitute the Dwarf Forest.

Devastated Area begins about 2.5 mi. n. of Summit Lake. It was stripped of all vegetation by hot blasts, avalanches and mudflows from the May 1915 eruptions of Lassen Peak. Natural reforestation is taking place. Another eruption remnant is Hot Rock, a large black lava rock near the north end of the area.

Diamond Peak is reached by the main park road, which, from 2 mi. n. of the Sulphur Works, winds up the remains of old Mount Tehama. The road, which encompasses Diamond Peak, offers a glimpse of steam vents across the canyon in Little Hot Springs Valley.

Kings Creek Meadows (7,400 ft.) are 4.5 mi. n. from the summit. A trail leads 1.2 miles to beautiful Kings Creek Falls. Both the cascades and falls are visible from the left side of the creek downstream.

Loomis Museum, .5 mi. beyond the n.w. entrance station, is named for B.F. Loomis, who photographed the early 20th-century eruptions and was a proponent of the park's establishment. The museum has a contact station where park information, exhibits, books and wilderness maps can be obtained and visitor assistance is available. **Hours:** Daily 9-5, late May-Oct. 31. Closed major holidays. Phone ahead to confirm schedule. **Cost:** Free. **Phone:** (530) 595-6140.

Sulphur Works Thermal Area, about 1 mi. n. of the s.w. entrance station, has steam vents and mudpots. Stay on the trails in these areas at all times. Ground that appears safe might be dangerously thin.

Summit Lake, 5 mi. n.e. of Kings Creek Meadows, has two lakeside campgrounds. They are convenient to hiking, fishing and points of interest.

WARNER VALLEY, in the s. part of the park, is reached by road from Chester or by trail from Summit Lake to Drakesbad. Marked trails lead to Boiling Springs Lake and Devils Kitchen, a large area of boiling pools and other volcanic features.

DRAKESBAD GUEST RANCH

fyi Not evaluated. **Address:** End of Warner Valley Rd 96020 **Location:** Jct SR 147 and Feather River Rd in Chester (at fire house), 0.7 mi w on Feather River Rd to Warner Valley Rd, then 16 mi nw on Warner Valley Rd to end; signage is limited; pavement ends 3.2 mi before arrival. Facilities, services, and décor characterize an economy property.

Plan complete trip routings with the TripTik® Travel Planner on AAA.com/CAA.ca

LATHROP pop. 18,023

COMFORT INN (209)983-1177

▼▼▼ Hotel $90-$170 **Address:** 14730 S Harlan Rd 95330 **Location:** I-5 exit Lathrop Rd, just e. **Facility:** 41 units. 3 stories, interior corridors. **Terms:** cancellation fee imposed. **Amenities:** high-speed Internet. **Pool(s):** heated indoor/outdoor. **Activities:** sauna, whirlpool, exercise room. **Guest Services:** valet and coin laundry.

DAYS INN (209)982-1959

▼▼ Hotel $55-$90 **Address:** 14750 S Harlan Rd 95330 **Location:** I-5 exit Lathrop Rd, just e. **Facility:** 40 units. 2 stories, interior corridors. **Amenities:** high-speed Internet. **Pool(s):** outdoor. **Activities:** sauna. **Guest Services:** coin laundry.

HAMPTON INN & SUITES (209)982-5070

▼▼▼ Hotel $79-$169 **Address:** 103 E Louise Ave 95330 **Location:** I-5 exit Louise Rd, just e. **Facility:** 76 units. 3 stories, interior corridors. **Terms:** 1-7 night minimum stay, cancellation fee imposed. **Amenities:** high-speed Internet. **Pool(s):** heated indoor. **Activities:** whirlpool, exercise room. **Guest Services:** valet and coin laundry.

> **AAA Benefit:**
> Members save up to 10%!

QUALITY INN & SUITES (209)858-1234

▼▼▼ Hotel $70-$100 **Address:** 16855 Harlan Rd 95330 **Location:** I-5 exit Louise Ave, just e. **Facility:** 65 units. 2 stories, exterior corridors. **Terms:** cancellation fee imposed. **Amenities:** high-speed Internet. **Pool(s):** outdoor. **Activities:** whirlpool, exercise room. **Guest Services:** valet and coin laundry.

WHERE TO EAT

CK GRILL & BAR 209/983-8881

▼ American. Casual Dining. $8-$15 **AAA Inspector Notes:** Traditional home favorites are served in a country-style atmosphere. Portions are hearty so bring an appetite. **Bar:** full bar. **Address:** 14725 S Harlan Rd 95330 **Location:** I-5 exit Lathrop Rd, just e.

LAVA BEDS NATIONAL MONUMENT (B-3)

In northeastern California, Lava Beds National Monument is reachable from SR 139, following the brown highway signs from Tulelake (the southern entrance road to the monument is paved but in poor repair). Lava Beds National Monument was created from molten lava spewed centuries ago from Medicine Lake volcano. When the lava cooled, the monument's rugged terrain was formed. The 46,500-acre area is characterized by cinder cones, deep chasms and more than 450 lava tube caves of various sizes.

Some of the caves contain permanent ice. The Modoc Indians used the volcanic formations as fortifications 1872-73 during the only major Indian war fought in California. Visitors can explore a lava tube cave on their own or on a ranger-guided tour offered during the summer. Mushpot, a lighted cave, is accessible from the visitor center parking lot. Free-use flashlights for cave exploration are available at the visitor center. Campfire programs are presented in summer.

Hiking trails, some as short as .75 mile in length, lead to other caves, pictographs and petroglyphs, the fire lookout, crater rims, overlooks and battlefield sites. The visitor center has trail brochures.

Camping is allowed, but no lodgings, supplies, gas or oil are available. Pets on leash are permitted in certain areas of the park, but not on the trails. The monument is open all year, and although there are no specified visiting hours, those planning to camp should arrive before 5 p.m. The geology and history of the area are interpreted at a visitor center.

Daily 8-6, Fri. before Memorial Day-Labor Day; 8:30-5, rest of year. Closed Christmas. Admission $10 per private vehicle; $5 per person arriving by other means. For more information contact the Superintendent's Office, Lava Beds National Monument, 1 Indian Well Headquarters, P.O. Box 1240, Tulelake, CA 96134; phone (530) 667-2282.

LEGGETT (D-1) pop. 122
• Part of Wine Country area — see map p. 562

Leggett is at the crossroads of Redwood Highway (US 101) and scenic SR 1. The scenic location is near the ocean and also blessed with stands of redwoods.

CHANDELIER TREE, in Drive-Thru Tree Park off US 101, towers 315 feet into the air and is 21 feet in diameter. Visitors can drive a full-size automobile through the hand-hewn opening at the base of the tree. **Hours:** Daily 8:30-dusk. Phone to confirm opening time in winter. Closed Thanksgiving and Christmas. **Cost:** $5 per private vehicle; $3 (those arriving on foot, bicycle or motorcycle). **Phone:** (707) 925-6363.

REDWOODS RIVER RESORT 707/925-6249

Cabin
$75-$175

Address: 75000 Hwy 101 95585 **Location:** 6.5 mi n of jct SR 1. **Facility:** 15 units, some two bedrooms, efficiencies and cabins. 1-2 stories (no elevator), exterior corridors. **Terms:** 2-3 night minimum stay - seasonal and/or weekends, 7 day cancellation notice-fee imposed. **Pool(s):** heated outdoor. **Activities:** fishing, hiking trails, playground, basketball, horseshoes, shuffleboard, volleyball. **Guest Services:** coin laundry. **Free Special Amenities:** children's activities and use of on-premises laundry facilities.

STONEGATE VILLAS 707/925-6226

▼ Motel $62-$125 **Address:** 65260 Drive Thru Tree Rd 95585 **Location:** US 101 exit S Leggett/Drive Thru Tree Rd, 0.4 mi e on SR 271, then 0.5 mi e. Located in a quiet area. **Facility:** 9 units, some two bedrooms and kitchens. 1 story, exterior corridors. **Terms:** 5 day cancellation notice.

**Contact us about AAA/CAA
Approved properties at
AAA.com/TourBookComments**

LEMOORE pop. 24,531

BEST WESTERN PLUS INN & SUITES LEMOORE
(559)924-3200

Hotel
$105

AAA Benefit: Members save up to 20%, plus 10% bonus points with Best Western Rewards®.

Address: 820 E Bush St 93245 **Location:** SR 198 exit Houston St eastbound; D St westbound; 0.8 mi nw. **Facility:** 100 units. 2 stories (no elevator), exterior corridors. **Amenities:** high-speed Internet. **Pool(s):** outdoor. **Activities:** whirlpool, exercise room. **Guest Services:** valet and coin laundry. **Free Special Amenities: full breakfast and high-speed Internet.**

WHERE TO EAT

THE VINEYARD RESTAURANT   559/924-1988

American. Casual Dining. $8-$16 **AAA Inspector Notes:** This family-owned and -operated eatery serves up traditional favorites in hearty portions. Breakfast is served all day and lunch offers a variety of specialty salads, burgers and sandwiches including salmon Caesar salad, prime rib sandwich, chicken portobello melt and turkey cranberry melt with cornbread stuffing. Dinner favorites include chicken-fried steak, roast turkey with all the trimmings, meat loaf with mashed potatoes and pasta dishes. Save room for one the homemade pies. **Bar:** full bar. **Address:** 819 E Bush St 93245 **Location:** SR 198 exit Houston St eastbound; D St westbound, 0.8 mi nw.

LINCOLN pop. 42,819, elev. 167'

GAMBLING ESTABLISHMENTS

• **Thunder Valley Casino** is at 1200 Athens Ave. **Hours:** Daily 24 hours. **Phone:** (916) 408-7777 or (877) 468-8777. *(See ad on insert, p. 435, p. 331.)*

HOLIDAY INN EXPRESS HOTEL & SUITES   (916)644-3440

Hotel $109-$159 **Address:** 155 Ferrari Ranch Rd 95648 **Location:** SR 65 exit Ferrari Ranch Rd, 0.9 mi sw, then just s on Groveland Ln. **Facility:** 87 units. 3 stories, interior corridors. **Terms:** 2 night minimum stay - seasonal and/or weekends, resort fee. **Amenities:** high-speed Internet. **Pool(s):** heated indoor. **Activities:** sauna, whirlpool, exercise room. **Guest Services:** complimentary and valet laundry, area transportation-Thunder Valley Casino.

/SOME UNITS FEE

THUNDER VALLEY CASINO RESORT   (916)408-7777

Resort Hotel
$100-$460

Address: 1200 Athens Ave 95648 **Location:** SR 65 exit Sunset Blvd, just w, just nw on Placer Corp Dr, 1.3 mi n on Industrial Ave, then just w. **Facility:** This new upscale lodging features a large gaming area and several restaurants. Spacious suites are available as well as shuttle service from several cities (call hotel for the current schedule). 297 units, some two bedrooms. 17 stories, interior corridors. **Parking:** on-site and valet. **Terms:** check-in 4 pm, 3 day cancellation notice-fee imposed, resort fee. **Amenities:** high-speed Internet, safes. **Dining:** 9 restaurants, also, High Steaks Steakhouse, Red Lantern, Thunder Cafe, see separate listings. **Activities:** whirlpool, lifeguard on duty, exercise room, spa. *Fee:* saunas, steamrooms. **Guest Services:** valet laundry, area transportation-Sacramento. *(See ads on insert p. 435, p. 331.)*

/SOME UNITS

WHERE TO EAT

CASA RAMOS   916/409-0766

Mexican. Casual Dining. $7-$17 **AAA Inspector Notes:** Guests will find all of the Mexican favorites here-enchiladas, burritos and fajitas-along with chicken, seafood and meat dishes prepared in a variety of ways and most are large portions. Lunch and dinner combinations and a lite menu are offered. There are mariachi's on Wednesday evenings. **Bar:** full bar. **Address:** 925 S SR 65 95648 **Location:** Just s of Joiner Pkwy; jct Sterling Pkwy.

HIGH STEAKS STEAKHOUSE   916/408-8327

Steak
Fine Dining
$28-$52

AAA Inspector Notes: This upscale restaurant serves dry-aged, hand-cut Prime steaks with sauces to complement the steak and several seafood selections. Live entertainment is presented on Friday and Saturday nights. **Bar:** full bar. **Reservations:** suggested. **Address:** 1200 Athens Ave 95648 **Location:** SR 65 exit Sunset Blvd, just w, just nw on Placer Corp Dr, 1.3 mi n on Industrial Ave, then just w; in Thunder Valley Casino Resort. **Parking:** on-site and valet.

ORCHID THAI CUISINE   916/543-9988

Thai. Casual Dining. $7-$16 **AAA Inspector Notes:** Tasty Thai food and friendly service can be found at this restaurant with an outdoor patio. Be sure to specify mild, medium or hot when ordering. Daily chef specials are offered, along with several choices of curries, seafood and stir-fried dishes. **Bar:** full bar. **Reservations:** suggested. **Address:** 835 Twelve Bridges Dr, Suite 100 95648 **Location:** SR 65 exit Twelve Bridges Dr, just e.

RED LANTERN   916/408-8315

Chinese. Casual Dining. $9-$40 **AAA Inspector Notes:** A modern Chinese décor permeates throughout this restaurant where a fireplace roars. The extensive menu offers an interesting selection of items not typically found at the usual Chinese restaurant. A noodle bar menu is featured and a dim sum lunch is served daily. **Bar:** full bar. **Reservations:** suggested. **Address:** 1200 Athens Ave 95648 **Location:** SR 65 exit Sunset Blvd, just w, just nw on Placer Corp Dr, 1.3 mi n on Industrial Ave, then just w; in Thunder Valley Casino Resort. **Parking:** on-site and valet.

THUNDER CAFE   916/408-8328

American. Casual Dining. $8-$17 **AAA Inspector Notes:** Hot and cold sandwiches, char-grilled burgers, pizza and a few entrées round out the menu at this café. Early bird and late night specials as well as a healthy choice menu are available, too. Tempting dessert choices are displayed in the bakery cases. **Bar:** full bar. **Address:** 1200 Athens Ave 95648 **Location:** SR 65 exit Sunset Blvd, just w, just nw on Placer Corp Dr, 1.3 mi n on Industrial Ave, then just w; in Thunder Valley Casino Resort. **Parking:** on-site and valet.

LITTLE RIVER (D-1) pop. 117, elev. 90'

• **Attractions map p. 566**
• **Part of Wine Country area — see map p. 562**

Founded as a lumber and shipbuilding town in the mid-19th century, Little River boasts architecture to reflect its settlers' New England heritage. The town is a popular spot for divers. Little River lies on a scenic stretch of SR 1 on the north coast that runs from Leggett southward to Sausalito and the San Francisco Bay.

PYGMY FOREST, s on SR 1, then 3 mi. e. on Little River Airport Rd., is thought to be the result of acidic soil. Even though they are decades old, some of the rare pygmy pine and pygmy cypress trees are only 2 feet high.

DENNEN'S VICTORIAN FARMHOUSE   707/937-0697

▼▼▼ **Bed & Breakfast** $145-$295 **Address:** 7001 N SR 1 95456 **Location:** SR 1, 0.8 mi s of Van Damme State Park entrance. **Facility:** On grounds graced by gardens and a creek, this 1877 farmhouse is said to have been used as a model by artist Thomas Kinkade. Room service is the norm. 11 units, some cottages. 1-2 stories (no elevator), interior/exterior corridors. **Terms:** 2 night minimum stay - seasonal and/or weekends, age restrictions may apply, 15 day cancellation notice-fee imposed. **Activities:** *Fee:* massage.

GLENDEVEN INN   707/937-0083

▼▼▼ **Bed & Breakfast.** Rates not provided. **Address:** 8205 N SR 1 95456 **Location:** SR 1, 0.3 mi n of Van Damme State Park entrance. **Facility:** A New England Federalist-style farmhouse, built in 1867, serves as the core of this appealing country inn. Contemporary décor incorporates pieces of antique furniture. 14 units, some houses. 2-3 stories (no elevator), interior/exterior corridors. **Terms:** age restrictions may apply. **Activities:** hiking trails.

THE INN AT SCHOOLHOUSE CREEK   707/937-5525

▼▼▼ **Country Inn.** Rates not provided. **Address:** 7051 N SR 1 95456 **Location:** SR 1, 0.8 mi s of Van Damme State Park entrance. **Facility:** Situated around the main building, a farmhouse dating from 1862, are rustic cabins, cottages and a yurt. 20 units, some efficiencies, kitchens, houses, cottages and condominiums. 1-2 stories (no elevator), exterior corridors. **Activities:** sauna, whirlpool, hiking trails. *Fee:* massage.

LITTLE RIVER INN   (707)937-5942

▼▼▼ **Country Inn** $130-$365 **Address:** 7901 N SR 1 95456 **Location:** On SR 1, just s of Van Damme State Park entrance. **Facility:** This hillside property, originally built in the 1850s, offers the feel of a classic seaside resort. Guests select from a variety of room types. 66 units, some cottages. 1-2 stories (no elevator), interior/exterior corridors. **Terms:** check-in 4 pm, 2 night minimum stay - weekends, 5 day cancellation notice-fee imposed. **Dining:** restaurant, see separate listing. **Activities:** fishing, hiking trails, jogging, spa. *Fee:* golf-9 holes.

STEVENSWOOD SPA RESORT   (707)937-2810

◆◆◆◆
Country Inn
$159-$399

Address: 8211 N Hwy 1 95456 **Location:** On SR 1, 0.4 mi n of Van Damme State Park entrance. Located in a quiet area. **Facility:** In a forest setting, this lodge features a private hot tub and a casually elegant restaurant. Guest rooms have eco-logs to burn in the fireplace and bamboo floors. 10 units. 2 stories (no elevator), interior corridors. **Terms:** 2 night minimum stay - seasonal and/or weekends, 99 day cancellation notice-fee imposed. **Amenities:** safes. **Dining:** The Restaurant at Stevenswood, see separate listing. **Activities:** sauna, whirlpools, hiking trails, exercise room, spa. **Guest Services:** valet laundry. **Free Special Amenities:** full breakfast and high-speed Internet.

WHERE TO EAT

LITTLE RIVER INN RESTAURANT   707/937-5942

▼▼▼ California. Casual Dining. $13-$31 **AAA Inspector Notes:** This restaurant, which occupies a charming 1853 Victorian inn, offers panoramic view of the bay as well as the lovely garden. The menu features dishes that combine familiarity with modern twists. The staff is known to be friendly and hospitable. **Bar:** full bar. **Reservations:** suggested. **Address:** 7901 N SR 1 95456 **Location:** On SR 1, just s of Van Damme State Park entrance; in Little River Inn. [B] [L] [D]

THE RESTAURANT AT STEVENSWOOD   707/937-2810

▼▼▼ Western California. Fine Dining. $11-$31 **AAA Inspector Notes:** Upon entering this tasteful, sophisticated dining room, guests catch sight of large French doors flanked by big bay windows that lead to the beautiful gardens. Adding to the visual appeal are a rustic fireplace, candles in artfully designed holders, soft lighting and linen-draped tables. An extensive wine list complements the Mediterranean-influenced dishes. **Bar:** beer & wine. **Reservations:** suggested. **Address:** 8211 N Hwy 1 95460 **Location:** On SR 1, 0.4 mi n of Van Damme State Park entrance; in Stevenswood Spa Resort. [B] [D] [X]

LIVE OAK   pop. 8,392

PASQUINI'S FINE ITALIAN FOOD   530/695-3384

▼▼ Italian. Casual Dining. $12-$28 **AAA Inspector Notes:** This Italian bistro is housed in an adobe-style, cream-colored building with a stone fireplace. Pasta specialties, steaks and chops round out the menu. Nightly specials are offered. **Reservations:** suggested. **Address:** 6241 SR 99 Hwy 95953 **Location:** On SR 99, 4 mi s of town; just n of jct Live Oak Blvd/Encinal Rd. [D]

LIVERMORE   (F-3) pop. 80,968, elev. 486'
• Hotels p. 176 • Restaurants p. 177

Livermore is located in the scenic Livermore Valley, an area characterized by vineyards and cattle ranches. Sycamore trees—some more than 2 centuries old—grow along the banks of the Arroyo del Valle.

Livermore Chamber of Commerce: 2157 First St., Livermore, CA 94550-4543. **Phone:** (925) 447-1606.

LAWRENCE LIVERMORE NATIONAL LABORATORY'S DISCOVERY CENTER, off Greenville Rd. about 2.2 mi. s. of I-580 at East Gate entrance, presents a broad-based display of the scientific technology developed at the laboratory and highlights the lab's research in defense, homeland security, biotechnology and new energy sources. Guided tours of the main site last 3 hours. Tours of Site 300, a 7,000-acre experimental test facility south of Tracy, also are available.

Time: Allow 30 minutes minimum. **Hours:** Tues.-Fri. 1-4, Sat. 10-2. Guided tours of the main site are given Tues. at 8:30. Site 300 tours are given by appointment when staff is available. Tour reservations must be made at least 2 weeks in advance and are subject to availability. Closed major holidays. **Cost:** Free. Under 18 are not permitted on Tues. or on Site 300 tours. **Phone:** (925) 423-3272 for the discovery center, or (925) 424-4175 for tour reservations.

AAA.com/TourBook Comments

Tell Us How We're Doing

If your visit to a TourBook-listed property doesn't meet your expectations, tell us about it.

AAA.com/TourBookComments

WINERIES

- **Concannon Vineyard** is at 4590 Tesla Rd. The winery, particularly noted for its Petite Sirah wine, has a tasting room surrounded by beautiful vineyards and views of surrounding mountains. **Hours:** Tastings are available daily 11-4:30. Tours are given Sat.-Sun. at 12:30 and 2; phone ahead to confirm holiday schedule. Closed Jan. 1, July 4 and Christmas. **Cost:** Tastings $5. **Phone:** (925) 456-2505 or (800) 258-9866.

- **Wente Vineyards** is 3 mi. s. off the I-580 Vasco Rd. exit, then w. to 5565 Tesla Rd. **Hours:** Daily 11-4:30. Tours are given at 11 and 2. **Phone:** (925) 456-2305.

BEST WESTERN PLUS VINEYARD INN (925)456-5422

Hotel
$89-$129

AAA Benefit: Members save up to 20%, plus 10% bonus points with Best Western Rewards®.

Address: 7600 Southfront Rd 94551 **Location:** I-580 exit N Greenville Rd, just s. **Facility:** 66 units, 3 stories, interior corridors. **Terms:** 2 night minimum stay - seasonal. **Amenities:** high-speed Internet. **Pool(s):** outdoor. **Activities:** exercise room. **Guest Services:** valet and coin laundry. **Free Special Amenities: expanded continental breakfast and high-speed Internet.**

COMFORT INN (925)606-6200

Hotel
$79-$139

Address: 2625 Constitution Dr 94551 **Location:** I-580 exit Airway Blvd/Collier Canyon Rd, just n. **Facility:** 60 units. 2 stories, exterior corridors. **Terms:** cancellation fee imposed. **Amenities:** high-speed Internet. **Pool(s):** outdoor. **Activities:** exercise room. **Free Special Amenities: expanded continental breakfast and high-speed Internet.**

COURTYARD BY MARRIOTT-LIVERMORE (925)243-1000

 Hotel $99-$169 **Address:** 2929 Constitution Dr 94551 **Location:** I-580 exit Airway Blvd/Collier Canyon Rd, just n. **Facility:** 121 units. 3 stories, interior corridors. **Pool(s):** heated indoor.

AAA Benefit: AAA hotel discounts of 5% or more.

Activities: whirlpool, exercise room. **Guest Services:** valet and coin laundry.

DOUBLETREE BY HILTON HOTEL LIVERMORE (925)443-4950

Hotel
$85-$130

DOUBLETREE

AAA Benefit: Members save 5% or more!

Address: 720 Las Flores Rd 94551 **Location:** I-580 exit Springtown Blvd, just s. **Facility:** 125 units. 4 stories, interior corridors. **Terms:** 1-7 night minimum stay, cancellation fee imposed. **Amenities:** high-speed Internet. **Pool(s):** outdoor. **Activities:** exercise room. **Guest Services:** valet and coin laundry. **Free Special Amenities: local telephone calls and newspaper.**

Visit AAA.com/Travel or CAA.ca/Travel for complete trip planning and reservations

HAMPTON INN 925/606-6400

 Hotel. Rates not provided. **Address:** 2850 Constitution Dr 94551 **Location:** I-580 exit N Airway Blvd/Collier Canyon Rd, just n. **Facility:** 79 units. 2 stories, interior corridors. **Amenities:** high-speed Internet. **Pool(s):** heated outdoor. **Activities:** exercise room. **Guest Services:** valet laundry, area transportation-within 5 mi.

AAA Benefit: Members save up to 10%!

HAWTHORN SUITES BY WYNDHAM (925)606-6060

Hotel $85-$190 **Address:** 1700 N Livermore Ave 94551 **Location:** I-580 exit N Livermore Ave, just s. **Facility:** 62 units, some efficiencies. 3 stories, interior corridors. **Terms:** cancellation fee imposed. **Amenities:** high-speed Internet. **Pool(s):** outdoor. **Activities:** whirlpool, exercise room. **Guest Services:** valet and coin laundry.

HILTON GARDEN INN LIVERMORE (925)292-2000

Hotel
$84-$229

Hilton Garden Inn

AAA Benefit: Unparalleled hospitality at a special Member rate.

Address: 2801 Constitution Dr 94551 **Location:** I-580 exit Airway Blvd/Collier Canyon Rd, just n. **Facility:** 97 units. 2 stories, interior corridors. **Terms:** 1-7 night minimum stay, cancellation fee imposed. **Amenities:** high-speed Internet. **Pool(s):** heated indoor. **Activities:** sauna, whirlpool, exercise room. **Guest Services:** valet and coin laundry. **Free Special Amenities: full breakfast and high-speed Internet.**

HOLIDAY INN EXPRESS HOTEL & SUITES-LIVERMORE (925)961-9600

Hotel $99-$139 **Address:** 3000 Constitution Dr 94551 **Location:** I-580 exit Airway Blvd/Collier Canyon Rd, just n. **Facility:** 92 units. 3 stories, interior corridors. **Terms:** resort fee. **Amenities:** high-speed Internet. **Pool(s):** outdoor. **Activities:** exercise room. **Guest Services:** valet and coin laundry.

LA QUINTA INN LIVERMORE (925)373-9600

Hotel $65-$155 **Address:** 7700 Southfront Rd 94551 **Location:** I-580 exit Greenville Rd, just s. **Facility:** 58 units. 3 stories, interior corridors. **Amenities:** high-speed Internet. **Pool(s):** heated indoor. **Activities:** sauna, whirlpool, exercise room. **Guest Services:** coin laundry.

QUALITY INN LIVERMORE 925/606-7171

Hotel. Rates not provided. **Address:** 5959 Preston Ave 94551 **Location:** I-580 exit Vasco Rd, just s. **Facility:** 37 units. 3 stories, exterior corridors. **Amenities:** high-speed Internet. **Activities:** whirlpool, exercise room. **Guest Services:** valet laundry.

RESIDENCE INN BY MARRIOTT (925)373-1800

Extended Stay Hotel $94-$208 **Address:** 1000 Airway Blvd 94551 **Location:** I-580 exit Airway Blvd/Collier Canyon Rd, just n. **Facility:** 96 kitchen units, some two bedrooms. 2 stories (no elevator), exterior corridors. **Amenities:** high-speed Internet. **Pool(s):** outdoor. **Activities:** whirlpool, sports court, exercise room. **Guest Services:** valet and coin laundry.

AAA Benefit: AAA hotel discounts of 5% or more.

WHERE TO EAT

CAMPO DI BOCCE OF LIVERMORE   925/249-9800

▼▼▼ Italian. Casual Dining. $10-$26 **AAA Inspector Notes:** This truly distinctive dining experience combines bocce ball and dining. Specialties at this family-owned and -operated eatery include calamari, pancetta-wrapped prawns, gnocchi, pasta, chicken Marsala, lamb shanks and fresh seafood. Great pizza also is an option. Before or after a good meal, be sure to check out the bocce courts. **Bar:** full bar. **Address:** 175 E Vineyard Ave 94550 **Location:** I-580 exit SR 84/Isabel Ave, 3 mi s, then just e.

L D CALL M

CASA OROZCO   925/449-3045

▼▼ Mexican. Casual Dining. $8-$20 **AAA Inspector Notes:** This family-owned and -operated restaurant offers an incredible selection of menu items. The traditional favorites include tacos and burritos, but be sure to try the house specialty carnitas or chile verde. The distinctive décor gives the feeling of dining in Mexico. **Bar:** full bar. **Address:** 325 S L St 94550 **Location:** At 3rd St; downtown.

L D CALL M

CATTLEMENS   925/447-1224

▼▼ Steak. Casual Dining. $17-$32 **AAA Inspector Notes:** This casual Western-theme restaurant specializes in aged, hand-cut steaks. Be sure to bring an appetite because portions are hearty. **Bar:** full bar. **Address:** 2882 Kitty Hawk Rd 94551 **Location:** I-580 exit Airway Blvd eastbound, continue straight over Airway Blvd; exit westbound, just s, then just e. D

THE RESTAURANT AT WENTE VINEYARDS   925/456-2450

▼▼▼ American. Fine Dining. $17-$39 **AAA Inspector Notes:** In the middle of Wente Vineyards, this relaxed restaurant looks out over the surrounding valley. Fresh herb gardens produce outstanding seasonings for the delicious cuisine. All items are freshly prepared as the menu changes daily. **Bar:** full bar. **Reservations:** suggested. **Address:** 5050 Arroyo Rd 94550 **Location:** I-580 exit N Livermore Ave, 1.2 mi s to 1st St, 0.8 mi w to L St, then 4.5 mi s via L St and Arroyo Rd. **Parking:** on-site and valet. L D CALL M

THE RIATA DINER AND TAVERN   925/294-9170

▼▼ American. Casual Dining. $9-$23 **AAA Inspector Notes:** A fun and lively atmosphere prevails at the tavern, a place that celebrates the area's ranching traditions and a favorite haunt of the downtown crowd. **Bar:** full bar. **Address:** 190 S J St 94550 **Location:** Just s of 1st St; downtown. **Parking:** street only.

B L D

ROUND TABLE PIZZA

▼ Pizza. Casual Dining. $7-$30 **AAA Inspector Notes:** This casual, family-oriented pizza place features high-quality ingredients and dough rolled fresh daily. Distinctive specialty pizzas are piled high with toppings. **Bar:** beer & wine. L D

For additional information, visit AAA.com
LOCATIONS:
Address: 1024 E Stanley Blvd 94550 **Location:** At Fenton St.
Phone: 925/455-1345
Address: 4098 East Ave 94550 **Location:** At Hayes Ave.
Phone: 925/443-2700

LOCKEFORD pop. 3,233

THE INN AT LOCKE HOUSE   209/727-5715

▼▼▼ Historic Bed & Breakfast $150-$245 **Address:** 19960 N Elliott Rd 95237 **Location:** SR 99 exit SR 12 E, 9 mi e to Elliott Rd, then just n. **Facility:** The inn is named for the doctor said to have built it between 1865 and 1882. Guest rooms are decorated with antique furnishings. 5 units. 2 stories (no elevator), interior corridors. **Terms:** check-in 3:30 pm, 8 day cancellation notice-fee imposed.

BIZ 🛜 ✕ / SOME UNITS 🅿

Save on theme park tickets
at AAA.com/discounts

LODI (F-3) pop. 62,134, elev. 52'
• Restaurants p. 179

With more than 80 wineries nearby, Lodi is an important wine-producing center. Nearby Lodi Lake Park offers water skiing, boating, swimming and hiking. Hill House Museum, 826 S. Church St., occupies one of the city's few Victorian houses. The museum is open Sunday and by appointment; phone (209) 369-6073.

A trip in autumn provides an opportunity to witness the yearly arrival of approximately 7,000 sandhill cranes as they complete their journey south from Alaska along the Pacific Flyway. The birds spend the winter months at the Isenberg Sandhill Crane Reserve; they can be observed from lookout points along Woodbridge Road, which traverses the reserve's south site. Guided tours are given several times a month from October through February; for schedule information phone (209) 948-7708.

Visit Lodi Conference & Visitor's Bureau: 115 S. School St., Suite 9, Lodi, CA 95240. **Phone:** (209) 365-1195 or (800) 798-1810.

MICKE GROVE REGIONAL PARK is at 11793 N. Micke Grove Rd. Within the park are amusement rides, a Japanese garden, a zoo and the San Joaquin Valley Historical Museum.

Hours: Park open daily 8-dusk. Zoo open Mon.-Fri. 10-5, Sat.-Sun. and holidays 10-6, Memorial Day-Labor Day; daily 10-5, rest of year. Japanese garden open Mon.-Thurs. 9-2, Fri.-Sun. and holidays 9-1. Closed Christmas. **Cost:** Park admission $5 (per private vehicle). Leashed pets $1. Zoo $4; $2 (ages 3-17). Japanese garden free. **Phone:** (209) 331-7400 for the park, or (209) 331-7270 for the zoo. 🐾 🏕

San Joaquin County Historical Museum, in Micke Grove Regional Park, has exhibits about local history, agriculture, earth moving and Native American culture. The Weber Gallery displays furnishings belonging to Capt. Charles Weber, the founder of the city of Stockton.

Time: Allow 2 hours minimum. **Hours:** Wed.-Sun. 10-4, Wed. after Memorial Day-first Sun. in Nov.; Wed.-Sun. 11-4, rest of year. Closed major holidays. **Cost:** Museum (in addition to park admission) $5; $4 (ages 13-17 and 65+); $2 (ages 6-12). An additional fee may be charged for special events. **Phone:** (209) 331-2055.

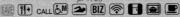

BEST WESTERN ROYAL HOST INN (209)369-8484

Hotel
$90-$120

AAA Benefit: Members save up to 20%, plus 10% bonus points with Best Western Rewards®.

Address: 710 S Cherokee Ln 95240 **Location:** 0.8 mi s on SR 99 business route. **Facility:** 48 units, some two bedrooms. 2 stories (no elevator), exterior corridors. **Terms:** cancellation fee imposed. **Amenities:** high-speed Internet. **Pool(s):** outdoor. **Activities:** exercise room. **Guest Services:** coin laundry. **Free Special Amenities:** full breakfast and high-speed Internet.

HAMPTON INN & SUITES (209)369-2700

Hotel
$109-$189

AAA Benefit: Members save up to 10%!

Address: 1337 S Beckman Rd 95240 **Location:** SR 99 exit Kettleman Ln E. **Facility:** 101 units. 4 stories, interior corridors. **Terms:** 1-7 night minimum stay, cancellation fee imposed. **Amenities:** high-speed Internet. **Pool(s):** outdoor. **Activities:** whirlpool, exercise room. **Guest Services:** valet and coin laundry. **Free Special Amenities:** expanded continental breakfast and high-speed Internet.

HOLIDAY INN EXPRESS (209)210-0150

Hotel $109-$199 **Address:** 1337 E Kettleman Ln 95240 **Location:** SR 99 exit Kettleman Ln, 0.4 mi e. **Facility:** 89 units. 3 stories, interior corridors. **Amenities:** high-speed Internet. **Pool(s):** heated indoor. **Activities:** whirlpool, exercise room. **Guest Services:** valet and coin laundry.

MICROTEL INN & SUITES BY WYNDHAM (209)367-9700

Hotel
$69-$79

Address: 6428 W Banner St 95242 **Location:** I-5 exit SR 12, just e. **Facility:** 51 units. 3 stories, interior corridors. **Terms:** cancellation fee imposed. **Pool(s):** outdoor. **Guest Services:** coin laundry.

MOTEL 6 LODI 209/334-6422

Hotel. Rates not provided. **Address:** 1140 S Cherokee Ln 95240 **Location:** SR 99 exit Kettleman Ln W, just n. **Facility:** 93 units. 2 stories, exterior corridors. **Amenities:** video games (fee). **Pool(s):** outdoor. **Activities:** whirlpool, exercise room. **Guest Services:** coin laundry.

WINE & ROSES HOTEL SPA AND RESTAURANT (209)334-6988

Country Inn $239-$495 **Address:** 2505 W Turner Rd 95242 **Location:** I-5 exit Turner Rd, 5 mi e; SR 99 exit Turner Rd, 2.4 mi w. **Facility:** Seven acres of landscaped botanical gardens surround this 1902 estate. A few guest rooms include a fireplace. Many upscale features and amenities are found throughout. 80 units. 2 stories, exterior corridors. **Terms:** cancellation fee imposed, resort fee. **Amenities:** Some: high-speed Internet. **Dining:** entertainment. **Pool(s):** outdoor. **Activities:** whirlpool, exercise room, spa. Fee: steamroom. **Guest Services:** valet laundry.

Trust your vehicle to AAA/CAA
Approved Auto Repair facilities

▼ See AAA listing p. 177 ▼

Learn the local driving laws at DrivingLaws.AAA.com

WHERE TO EAT

ANDRE'S CAFE & CATERING   209/367-5411

♦ American. Casual Dining. $5-$14 **AAA Inspector Notes:** Among the traditional favorites at this small hole in the wall are great hamburgers. Diners receive friendly, relaxed service. **Address:** 722 W Lodi Ave 95240 **Location:** Just e of Crescent Ave. **Parking:** street only. [L] [D] CALL [M]

DEE DEE'S FAMILY DINING   209/368-8313

♦♦ American. Family Dining. $6-$12 **AAA Inspector Notes:** The laid-back restaurant whips up a selection of family favorites. **Address:** 1170 S Cherokee Ln 95240 **Location:** SR 99 exit Kettleman Ln W, just n. [B] [L] CALL [M]

EL ROSAL AUTHENTIC MEXICAN RESTAURANT
                                     209/369-4989

♦♦ Mexican. Casual Dining. $7-$16 **AAA Inspector Notes:** Prepare to come to this Mexican restaurant hungry because portions are hearty. Choose from a great selection of traditional favorites with homemade sauces including an incredible verde sauce served over their well-known super burrito. **Bar:** full bar. **Address:** 728 W Kettleman Ln 95240 **Location:** SR 99 exit Kettleman Ln, 1.3 mi w; in Vineyard Shopping Center. [B] [L] [D] CALL [M]

PIETRO'S TRATTORIA   209/368-0613

♦♦♦ Italian. Casual Dining. $9-$30 **AAA Inspector Notes:** Come on in and enjoy the taste and feel of Italy with Italian-style decor featuring a three-dimensional wall mural which gives diners the impression they are dining along one of the streets of Italy. A variety of homemade pasta, fresh seafood and poultry dishes are at the top of the menu. Freshly-made pizza, calzones and salads also are available. Come early as this is a favorite stop for both locals and visitors alike. **Bar:** full bar. **Address:** 317 E Kettleman Ln 95240 **Location:** SR 99 exit Kettleman Ln, 0.4 mi w. [L] [D] CALL [M]

ROUND TABLE PIZZA   209/368-8600

♦ Pizza. Casual Dining. $7-$28 **AAA Inspector Notes:** This casual, family-oriented pizza place features high-quality ingredients and dough rolled fresh daily. Distinctive specialty pizzas are piled high with toppings. **Bar:** beer & wine. **Address:** 2715 W Kettleman Ln, Suite 204 95242 **Location:** SR 99 exit Kettleman Ln, 3 mi w. [L] [D] CALL [M]

LOLETA (C-1) pop. 783, elev. 46'

LOLETA CHEESE FACTORY is at 252 Loleta Dr. This small, family-owned company makes award-winning natural cheeses. Visitors can watch the cheese being made through large viewing windows and enjoy samples of the finished products. **Hours:** Daily 9-5. Closed Jan. 1, Easter, July 4, Thanksgiving and Christmas. **Cost:** Free. **Phone:** (707) 733-5470 or (800) 995-0453.

LOOMIS pop. 6,430
• Hotels & Restaurants map & index p. 314

FLOWER FARM INN   916/652-4200

[fyi] Not evaluated. **Address:** 4150 Auburn Folsom Rd 95650 **Location:** I-80 exit Horseshoe Bar Rd, 0.5 mi e, then 3.2 mi on Horseshoe Bar Rd. Facilities, services, and décor characterize a mid-scale property.

WHERE TO EAT

HIGH HAND CONSERVATORY   916/652-2064

♦♦♦ American. Casual Dining. $7-$28 **AAA Inspector Notes:** Dine inside the conservatory or out on the patio, then stroll through the gardens/nursery at this attractive spot. Fresh salads, wood-oven baked pizza and a nice selection of entrées round out the menu. Fresh produce from the garden is served. Dinner is offered only on Friday and Saturday from 5:30 p.m. with live music. Saturday and Sunday brunch is from 9 a.m. to 3 p.m. **Bar:** beer & wine. **Reservations:** suggested. **Address:** 3790 Taylor Rd 95650 **Location:** I-80 exit Loomis/Horseshoe Bar Rd, just w, then just s. [L] CALL [M]

TSUDA'S FLOWER FARM CAFE   916/652-5661 (37)

♦ American. Quick Serve. $6-$10 **AAA Inspector Notes:** This delightful spot serves light breakfast, sandwiches, salads and fresh baked goods. Save room for the homemade pie. Patio seating is available or a few tables beside the pond are a good choice. Stroll through the attractive nursery grounds after lunch. **Address:** 4150 Auburn Folsom Rd 95650 **Location:** I-80 exit Loomis/Horseshoe Bar Rd, 0.5 mi se, then 3.2 mi ne on Horseshoe Bar Rd. [B] [L] CALL [M]

LOS ALTOS (E-9) pop. 28,976, elev. 165'
• Hotels p. 180 • Restaurants p. 180

The Los Altos area was on the route of a 1775-76 expedition led by Spanish commander Juan Bautista de Anza from Mexico into Alta (Upper) California. The purpose of this overland journey was to establish a Spanish presence, including a presidio and mission, near the Bay of San Francisco. In the early 20th century the city became a railroad link between Palo Alto and Los Gatos, which spurred development.

Each July the city celebrates the ♦ Los Altos Arts and Wine Festival. The 2-day juried event, held downtown, features arts and crafts created by more than 400 artisans, concerts, children's activities, and booths offering food and wine from local merchants and vineyards.

Los Altos Chamber of Commerce: 321 University Ave., Los Altos, CA 94022. **Phone:** (650) 948-1455.

LOS ALTOS HISTORY MUSEUM is at 51 S. San Antonio Rd., in the Civic Center complex behind the Los Altos Main Library. The museum's permanent exhibit surveys area development from the days when Ohlone Indians occupied the land to the present. Recorded sounds add realism to the displays, which include information about early ranchos, the apricot orchards prevalent in the early 20th century and an animated model train setup that depicts the city during the 1930s. Changing exhibits also are featured.

Time: Allow 30 minutes minimum. **Hours:** Thurs.-Sun. noon-4. Closed Jan. 1, Easter, July 4, Thanksgiving and Christmas. **Cost:** Free. **Phone:** (650) 948-9427. [⊞]

COURTYARD BY MARRIOTT-PALO ALTO/LOS ALTOS
(650)941-9900

▼▼▼ **Hotel** $139-$299 **Address:**
4320 El Camino Real 94022 **Location:**
US 101 exit San Antonio Rd, 2 mi w to
SR 82, then just n. **Facility:** 190 units. 3
stories, interior corridors. **Amenities:**
video games (fee), high-speed Internet. **Pool(s):** heated outdoor. **Activities:** whirlpools, exercise room. **Guest Services:** valet and coin
laundry.

AAA Benefit:
AAA hotel discounts
of 5% or more.

RESIDENCE INN-PALO ALTO/LOS ALTOS   (650)559-7890

▼▼▼ **Extended Stay Hotel**
$149-$289 **Address:** 4460 El Camino
Real 94022 **Location:** US 101 exit San
Antonio Rd, 2 mi w to SR 82, then just n.
Facility: 156 units, some two bedrooms,
efficiencies and kitchens. 3 stories, interior corridors. **Amenities:**
video games (fee), high-speed Internet. **Pool(s):** heated outdoor. **Activities:** whirlpool, sports court, exercise room. **Guest Services:** valet
and coin laundry.

AAA Benefit:
AAA hotel discounts
of 5% or more.

WHERE TO EAT

ARMADILLO WILLY'S BARBECUE   650/941-2922

▼ Barbecue. Quick Serve. $6-$22 **AAA Inspector Notes:** Menu
offerings at this eatery include a wide selection of barbecue favorites
including ribs, chicken, beef brisket, burgers and salad. The atmosphere here is fun and lively. **Bar:** beer & wine. **Address:** 1031 N San
Antonio Rd 94022 **Location:** Just s of W El Camino Real.

MURACCI'S 2 JAPANESE CURRY & GRILL   650/917-1101

▼▼ Japanese. Casual Dining. $9-$17 **AAA Inspector Notes:**
This small restaurant is reminiscent of the restaurants in Japan
serving everything from teishoku (a set menu) to tonkatsu (pork) curry
and grilled salmon. Famous for their Japanese-style curry sauce
(which takes two days to prepare), visitors have a choice of spiciness
from mild to super spicy. **Bar:** beer & wine. **Address:** 244 State St
94022 **Location:** Between 2nd and 3rd sts; downtown. **Parking:**
street only.

SUMIKA   650/917-1822

▼▼ Japanese. Casual Dining. $3-$32 **AAA Inspector Notes:**
Kushiyaki, or skewered-grilling, is this restaurant's specialty. They import Binchoutan charcoal for grilling the skewered items. The simplicity of the dish (bite-size meats) requires top-notch ingredients and
they do not disappoint. Organic chicken from Petaluma Farms and
Kobe beef are used as well as imported sea salt from Hokkaido in
Japan. Nabe (hot pot) and donburi are some of the more substantial
offerings. To end the meal on a sweet note, try the sesame panna
cotta or frozen custard. **Bar:** beer & wine. **Address:** 236 Central
Plaza 94022 **Location:** Between 2nd and 3rd sts; downtown.
Parking: street only.

LOS BAÑOS (G-3) pop. 35,972, elev. 120'

Los Baños is named for Los Baños Creek, once
a popular bathing spot for missionaries. Cotton, rice
and alfalfa were introduced in the mid-19th century,
and agriculture remains the leading industry.

Los Baños Chamber of Commerce: 503 J St., Los
Baños, CA 93635. **Phone:** (209) 826-2495, or (800)
336-6354 in most states.

**SAN LUIS RESERVOIR STATE RECREATION
AREA,** 12 mi. w. on SR 152, is an important link in
the Central Valley Project and the California Water
Project. Swimming, windsurfing, boating, camping
and picnicking are permitted at the recreation area,
which includes San Luis Creek, Los Baños Detention Dam and O'Neill Forebay. Romero Visitors
Center has a video program, telescopes and information about the water projects. **Note:** All boats
must be inspected for the presence of zebra mussels. *See Recreation Areas Chart.*

Hours: Park open daily dawn-dusk (weather permitting). Visitor center open daily 9-5. Closed Jan. 1,
Thanksgiving and Christmas. Phone ahead to confirm schedule. **Cost:** Day use $10 per private vehicle; $9 (ages 62+ per private vehicle). Boating fee
$6. **Phone:** (209) 826-1196 for park information, or
(209)   827-5353   for   the   visitor   center.

AMERICAS BEST VALUE INN   (209)826-5002

▼▼▼ Motel $62-$82

Address: 330 W Pacheco Blvd 93635
Location: On SR 152; center. **Facility:**
25 units. 2 stories (no elevator), exterior
corridors. **Terms:** cancellation fee imposed. **Pool(s):** outdoor. **Free Special**
Amenities: continental breakfast and high-speed Internet.

BEST WESTERN EXECUTIVE INN   (209)827-0954

▼▼▼ Hotel $78-$99

AAA Benefit: Members
save up to 20%, plus 10%
bonus points with Best
Western Rewards®.

Address: 301 W Pacheco Blvd 93635 **Location:** On SR 152;
center. **Facility:** 56 units. 3 stories, interior corridors. **Amenities:**
Some: high-speed Internet. **Pool(s):** outdoor. **Activities:** whirlpool, exercise room. **Guest Services:** coin laundry. **Free Special Amenities: local telephone calls and high-speed Internet.**

VAGABOND INN EXECUTIVE   209/827-4677

▼▼▼ Hotel
Rates not provided

Address: 20 W Pacheco Blvd 93635
Location: On SR 152; center. **Facility:**
43 units. 2 stories (no elevator), interior
corridors. **Pool(s):** heated indoor. **Activities:** whirlpool, exercise room. **Guest**
Services: coin laundry. **Free Special Amenities: expanded**
continental breakfast and high-speed Internet.

WHERE TO EAT

RYAN'S PLACE   209/826-2616

▼▼ American Comfort Food. Casual Dining. $8-$15 **AAA Inspector Notes:** A long time tradition in the area, this place has a
strong local following. Hearty portions of comfort foods are offered as
well as daily specials. Be sure to save room for a slice of freshly
baked pie. **Bar:** beer & wine. **Address:** 955 W Pacheco Blvd 93635
Location: On SR 152; west end of town.

LOS GATOS (E-9) pop. 29,413, elev. 385'
• Hotels & Restaurants map & index p. 468

Los Gatos is guarded by two mountain ridges, El Sombroso (the shadowing one) and El Sereno (the night watchman). The town was founded in the late1860s on a portion of an 1840 Spanish land grant. The original grant was known as *La Rinconada de los Gatos* (corner of the cats), a name derived from the many mountain lions and wildcats that then inhabited the nearby hills.

By the early 1900s Los Gatos was a rural community supporting mostly orchards. Urbanization arrived with the onset of World War II. The History Museum of Los Gatos at 75 Church St. has exhibits about local and regional history; phone (408) 395-7375.

The Los Gatos Creek Trail is a popular multi-use pathway that runs for 9 miles from Los Gatos through Campbell *(see place listing p. 65)* and on to San Jose *(see place listing p. 461)*. The trail, which follows Los Gatos Creek, is enjoyed by walkers, runners, hikers, bicyclists and nature lovers. Los Gatos is the northern terminus of a scenic 38-mile stretch of SR 17 to Santa Cruz.

Los Gatos Chamber of Commerce: 10 Station Way, Los Gatos, CA 95030. **Phone:** (408) 354-9300.

Self-guiding tours: Maps for a self-guiding walking tour of historic sites in Los Gatos are available at the chamber of commerce.

Shopping areas: Old Town, on University Avenue, has about a dozen chain retailers and a couple of restaurants in an attractively landscaped setting of Spanish-style architecture and topiary trees.

ART MUSEUM OF LOS GATOS is at 4 Tait Ave. at W. Main St. In an adobe-style building, the museum features changing exhibits by area artists. **Time:** Allow 30 minutes minimum. **Hours:** Wed.-Sun. 11-5, when staff is available. Closed major holidays. Phone ahead to confirm schedule. **Cost:** Donations. **Phone:** (408) 354-7386.

HISTORY MUSEUM OF LOS GATOS, just e. of Main St. at 75 Church St., is in the remains of a gold rush-era flour mill. The museum presents exhibits chronicling the history of the mill and the Los Gatos area. **Time:** Allow 1 hour minimum. **Hours:** Wed.-Sun. 11-5. Closed major holidays. Phone ahead to confirm schedule. **Cost:** Donations. **Phone:** (408) 395-7375.

OAK MEADOW PARK/VASONA PARK are at University Ave. and Blossom Hill Rd. Oak Meadow Park has a playground, sports field, a 1910 English carousel and a lake stocked for fishing. Vasona Lake County Park has a playground and fishing, picnicking and boating facilities; boat rentals are available *(see Recreation Areas Chart).*

Hours: Daily 8 a.m.-half an hour after sunset. **Cost:** Free. Carousel $2 per ride; free (ages 0-2).

Parking: $6. **Phone:** (408) 399-5770 for Oak Meadow Park, or (408) 356-2729 for Vasona Park.

Billy Jones Wildcat Railroad, in Oak Meadow Park, is a restored 1905 steam train, although a diesel train occasionally is featured. The scenic 1-mile trip passes over Los Gatos Creek and proceeds through Vasona Park. **Hours:** Train departs daily 10:30-4:30, mid-June through Labor Day; Sat.-Sun. 10:30-4:30, mid-Mar. to mid-June and day after Labor Day-Oct. 31; Sat.-Sun. 11-3, rest of year (weather permitting). **Cost:** $2 per ride; free (physically impaired individuals and ages 0-2 with paying adult). **Phone:** (408) 395-7433.

LOS GATOS LODGE   (408)354-3300 **111**

Hotel
$109-$229

Address: 50 Los Gatos Saratoga Rd 95032 **Location:** SR 17 exit E Los Gatos, just e. **Facility:** 129 units, some efficiencies. 2 stories, interior/exterior corridors. **Terms:** cancellation fee imposed. **Pool(s):** outdoor. **Activities:** exercise room. **Guest Services:** valet and coin laundry.

LOS GATOS MOTOR INN   (408)356-9191 **110**

Motel
$120-$200

Address: 55 Los Gatos Saratoga Rd 95032 **Location:** SR 17 exit E Los Gatos, just e. Located in a quiet area. **Facility:** 50 units. 2 stories (no elevator), exterior corridors. **Terms:** cancellation fee imposed. **Free Special Amenities:** high-speed Internet and use of on-premises laundry facilities.

TOLL HOUSE, A LARKSPUR COLLECTION HOTEL
                                   408/395-7070

fyi Not evaluated. **Address:** 140 S Santa Cruz Ave 95030 **Location:** SR 17 exit SR 9, 0.5 mi w. Facilities, services, and décor characterize a mid-scale property.

WHERE TO EAT

MANRESA   408/354-4330 **53**

French. Fine Dining. $95-$160 **AAA Inspector Notes:** Situated along the quaint streets of Los Gatos, this little eatery offers a creative and artistic menu centered around French influences. Fresh dishes from the often-changing menu may include rack of veal, spring lamb or Monterey Bay abalone. **Bar:** full bar. **Reservations:** suggested. **Address:** 320 Village Ln 95030 **Location:** SR 17 exit Downtown Los Gatos (SR 9), just w, just s on N Santa Cruz Ave, then just e on Bachman Ave into city parking lot (parking lot is behind the restaurant). D CALL

PEDRO'S RESTAURANT & CANTINA   408/354-7570 **52**

Mexican. Casual Dining. $10-$22 **AAA Inspector Notes:** Mexican specialties make up the menu at the downtown spot, which is amid shops and businesses. The interior design gives the impression of dining in a Mexican cantina. **Bar:** full bar. **Address:** 316 N Santa Cruz Ave 95030 **Location:** SR 17 exit Saratoga Los Gatos Rd W, just s. **Parking:** street only. L D

ROUND TABLE PIZZA

Pizza. Casual Dining. $7-$30 **AAA Inspector Notes:** This casual, family-oriented pizza place features high-quality ingredients and dough rolled fresh daily. Distinctive specialty pizzas are piled high with toppings. **Bar:** beer & wine. L D

For additional information, visit AAA.com

LOCATIONS:
Address: 1472 Pollard Rd 95032 **Location:** At La Corona Ct. **Phone:** 408/379-4691
Address: 57 N Santa Cruz Ave 95030 **Location:** At Elm St; downtown. **Phone:** 408/354-7520

LOTUS (E-3) elev. 722'

RECREATIONAL ACTIVITIES
White-water Rafting

- **Action Whitewater Adventures** departs from Gold Rush Campground, 6260 SR 49. **Hours:** Trips depart Thurs.-Tues., Apr.-Sept. (depending upon water flow). **Phone:** (888) 922-8466.

- **Beyond Limits Adventures** departs from River Park Resort, off SR 49 at the end of River Park Dr. **Hours:** Daily Apr.-Sept. (depending upon water flow). **Phone:** (209) 526-0027 or (800) 234-7238.

CAFE MAHJAIC   530/622-9587

fyi Not evaluated. Housed in a historic building, this restaurant serves new American cuisine with ethnic influences and fresh ingredients are used whenever possible. Seasonal specials are featured. Reservations are recommended. **Address:** 1006 Lotus Rd 95651 **Location:** Center.

LOWER LAKE pop. 1,294, elev. 1,440'
- Part of Wine Country area — see map p. 562

LOWER LAKE HISTORIC SCHOOLHOUSE MUSEUM is at 16435 Morgan Valley Rd. (Main St.). This 1877 brick schoolhouse served as the city's grammar school until 1935. An excellent, well-organized collection features a map showing the trail that pioneers followed to California, a model of a nearby dam, displays of late 19th- and early 20th-century clothing, Native American artifacts, a re-created classroom and a re-created Victorian parlor. The upstairs auditorium is a venue for art shows and theatrical productions. **Time:** Allow 30 minutes minimum. **Hours:** Wed.-Sat. 11-4. Closed Jan. 1, Easter, July 4, Thanksgiving, day after Thanksgiving, Christmas Eve and Christmas. **Cost:** Donations. Cash or check only. **Phone:** (707) 995-3565.

MADERA pop. 61,416

HOLIDAY INN EXPRESS & SUITES   (559)661-7400

Hotel
$101-$113

Address: 2290 Market Place Dr 93637 **Location:** SR 99 exit Ave 16/Gateway Dr, just w. **Facility:** 62 units. 3 stories, interior corridors. **Amenities:** high-speed Internet. **Pool(s):** heated outdoor. **Activities:** whirlpool, exercise room. **Guest Services:** valet and coin laundry. **Free Special Amenities:** full breakfast and high-speed Internet.

MADERA VALLEY INN   (559)664-0100

Hotel $59-$169 **Address:** 317 North G St 93637 **Location:** SR 99 exit Central Madera, just e. **Facility:** 93 units. 5 stories, interior corridors. **Terms:** cancellation fee imposed. **Amenities:** high-speed Internet. **Dining:** restaurant, see separate listing. **Pool(s):** outdoor. **Activities:** limited exercise equipment. **Guest Services:** valet laundry.

SPRINGHILL SUITES BY MARRIOTT   (559)664-9800

Hotel
$104-$151

AAA Benefit: AAA hotel discounts of 5% or more.

Address: 1219 E Almond Ave 93637 **Location:** SR 99 exit Almond Ave, just w. **Facility:** 88 units. 3 stories, interior corridors. **Amenities:** high-speed Internet. **Pool(s):** heated outdoor. **Activities:** whirlpool, exercise room. **Guest Services:** valet and coin laundry. **Free Special Amenities:** full breakfast and high-speed Internet.

WHERE TO EAT

BLACK BEAR DINER   559/675-1332

American. Casual Dining. $8-$18 **AAA Inspector Notes:** A homey atmosphere characterizes this family-oriented restaurant. Familiar comfort foods, such as meatloaf with mashed potatoes, are at the heart of the menu and are served in generous portions. **Bar:** beer & wine. **Address:** 1209 E Almond Ave 93637 **Location:** SR 99 exit Almond Ave southbound, exit Gateway northbound, U turn, just w.

MADERA VALLEY INN CAFE 559/661-4977

♦♦ American. Casual Dining. $8-$18 **AAA Inspector Notes:** Centrally located, a good selection of dishes are offered at this café including sandwiches, burgers and some Italian and Mexican dishes. Expect a very friendly staff. **Bar:** full bar. **Address:** 317 N G St 93637 **Location:** SR 99 exit Central Madera, just e; in Madera Valley Inn.

B L D

ROUND TABLE PIZZA 559/673-7043

♦ Pizza. Casual Dining. $7-$28 **AAA Inspector Notes:** This casual, family-oriented pizza place features high-quality ingredients and dough rolled fresh daily. Distinctive specialty pizzas are piled high with toppings. **Bar:** beer & wine. **Address:** 1930 Howard Rd, Suite 101 93637 **Location:** Just e of Schnoor Ave. L D

THE VINEYARD RESTAURANT 559/674-0923

American
Casual Dining
$8-$37

AAA Inspector Notes: Conveniently located off the freeway, this casual, relaxed eatery offers a menu with a wide selection to please everyone. The menu lists great sandwiches, beef, poultry, fish and pasta dishes. Lasagna with homemade Italian sausage is a specialty worth trying. **Bar:** full bar. **Address:** 605 S I St 93637 **Location:** SR 99 exit 153 (SR 145/Kerman), just w. L D CALL

MANTECA pop. 67,096

BEST WESTERN PLUS EXECUTIVE INN & SUITES (209)825-1415

Hotel
$79-$99

PLUS

AAA Benefit: Members save up to 20%, plus 10% bonus points with Best Western Rewards®.

Address: 1415 E Yosemite Ave 95336 **Location:** Jct SR 99 and 120 exit E Yosemite Ave, just w. **Facility:** 101 units. 3 stories, exterior corridors. **Terms:** cancellation fee imposed. **Amenities:** safes. **Pool(s):** outdoor. **Activities:** whirlpool. **Guest Services:** coin laundry. **Free Special Amenities: local telephone calls and high-speed Internet.**

SAVE ⊺↕ CALL &M ➔ FEE 🐾 BIZ 🛜 🛏 ▦ 🖥 / SOME UNITS FEE 🐕

HAMPTON INN & SUITES (209)823-1926

♦♦♦ Hotel $89-$139 **Address:** 1461 Bass Pro Dr 95336 **Location:** SR 120 exit Union Rd S, 0.4 mi e on Atherton Dr. **Facility:** 101 units. 4 stories, interior corridors. **Terms:** 1-7 night minimum stay, cancellation fee imposed. **Amenities:** high-speed Internet. **Pool(s):** outdoor. **Activities:** whirlpool, exercise room. **Guest Services:** valet and coin laundry.

AAA Benefit: Members save up to 10%!

⊺↕ CALL &M ➔ BIZ 🛜 🛏 ▦ 🖥

HOLIDAY INN EXPRESS HOTEL & SUITES (209)239-5600

♦♦♦
Hotel
$129-$149

Address: 179 Commerce Ave 95336 **Location:** Jct SR 99 and 120 exit Yosemite Ave, just w. **Facility:** 72 units. 3 stories, interior corridors. **Terms:** 2 night minimum stay - seasonal and/or weekends, 3 day cancellation notice-fee imposed. **Amenities:** high-speed Internet. **Pool(s):** outdoor. **Activities:** whirlpool, exercise room. **Guest Services:** valet and coin laundry. **Free Special Amenities: full breakfast and high-speed Internet.**

SAVE ⊺↕ CALL &M ➔ BIZ 🛜 🛏 ▦ 🖥

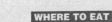
WHERE TO EAT

DE VEGA BROTHERS 209/823-0947

♦ Italian. Casual Dining. $8-$27 **AAA Inspector Notes:** A favorite in the Manteca area for many years this spot is family owned and operated. A warm and friendly staff dishes up a variety Italian specialties. Come early as this place fills up quickly. **Bar:** beer & wine. **Address:** 515 N Main St 95336 **Location:** SR 120 exit Main St, 1.3 mi n at Alameda St. L D

KELLEY BROTHERS BREWING COMPANY 209/825-1727

♦♦ American. Gastro Pub. $8-$20 **AAA Inspector Notes:** A traditional pub-style atmosphere prevails at the fun, lively spot, where guests appreciate friendly service and great food along the lines of varied appetizers, sandwiches, salads and grilled meats. **Bar:** full bar. **Address:** 112 E Yosemite Ave 95336 **Location:** SR 120 exit Main St N, just e. **Parking:** on-site and street. L D CALL &M

ROUND TABLE PIZZA 209/824-7500

♦ Pizza. Casual Dining. $7-$28 **AAA Inspector Notes:** This casual, family-oriented pizza place features high-quality ingredients and dough rolled fresh daily. Distinctive specialty pizzas are piled high with toppings. **Bar:** beer & wine. **Address:** 2120 Daniels St 95337 **Location:** SR 120 exit Airport Way, just n. L D CALL &M

MARINA pop. 19,718

• Part of Monterey Peninsula area — see map p. 202

BEST WESTERN BEACH DUNES INN (831)883-0300

♦♦♦
Hotel
$80-$450

AAA Benefit: Members save up to 20%, plus 10% bonus points with Best Western Rewards®.

Address: 3290 Dunes Dr 93933 **Location:** SR 1 exit Reservation Rd, just w. **Facility:** 84 units. 2 stories (no elevator), exterior corridors. **Terms:** 2-4 night minimum stay - seasonal and/or weekends, cancellation fee imposed. **Activities:** whirlpool, playground. **Guest Services:** coin laundry. **Free Special Amenities: local telephone calls and high-speed Internet.**

SAVE CALL &M BIZ 🛜 ✕ 🖥 / SOME UNITS 🛏 ▦

HOLIDAY INN EXPRESS MONTEREY-MARINA 831/884-2500

♦♦♦ Hotel. Rates not provided. **Address:** 189 Seaside Cir 93933 **Location:** SR 1 exit Reservation Rd, 0.5 mi e, then just s. **Facility:** 80 units. 3 stories, interior corridors. **Amenities:** video games (fee), high-speed Internet. **Activities:** sauna, whirlpool, exercise room. **Guest Services:** valet and coin laundry.

CALL &M BIZ 🛜 ✕ 📹 🛏 ▦ 🖥

RAMADA (831)582-9100

♦♦♦
Hotel
$60-$370

Address: 323 Reservation Rd 93933 **Location:** SR 1 exit Reservation Rd, 1.2 mi e. **Facility:** 43 units. 3 stories, interior corridors. **Terms:** cancellation fee imposed. **Amenities:** high-speed Internet, safes. **Activities:** exercise room. **Guest Services:** valet laundry. **Free Special Amenities: continental breakfast and early check-in/late check-out.**

SAVE ⊺↕ CALL &M BIZ 🛜 ✕ 🛏 ▦ 🖥

THE SANCTUARY BEACH RESORT (831)883-9478

♦♦♦ Hotel $169-$550 **Address:** 3295 Dunes Dr 93933 **Location:** SR 1 exit Reservation Rd, just w. **Facility:** 60 units. 2 stories (no elevator), exterior corridors. **Terms:** check-in 4 pm, 2 night minimum stay - seasonal and/or weekends, 3 day cancellation notice-fee imposed. **Amenities:** safes. **Pool(s):** outdoor. **Activities:** whirlpool, spa. **Guest Services:** valet laundry.

⊺↕ CALL &M ➔ BIZ 🛜 ✕ 🔪 🛏 🖥 / SOME UNITS FEE 🐕 ▦

WHERE TO EAT

DISHES BISTRO & GRILL 831/883-1207

♦♦ Mediterranean. Casual Dining. $15-$20 **AAA Inspector Notes:** California and Mediterranean influences merge to create a distinctive menu at this casual and relaxed eatery. **Bar:** full bar. **Reservations:** suggested. **Address:** 330 Reservation Rd 93933 **Location:** SR 1 exit Reservation Rd, 1.2 mi e; just e of Crescent Ave.

L D CALL &M 🔪

KULA RANCH ISLAND STEAKHOUSE AND SUSHI BAR
831/883-9479

♦♦ ♦♦ Steak Sushi. Casual Dining. $9-$25 **AAA Inspector Notes:** Guests should come hungry and ready to eat, as the courses just keep coming. Traditional Western fare--grilled steaks, barbecue ribs, beans and garlic bread--shares menu space with some fresh fish entrees. Some tables offer views of the Pacific Ocean. **Bar:** full bar. **Address:** 3295 Dunes Rd 93933 **Location:** SR 1 exit Reservation Rd W, just n. L D CALL M AC

ROUND TABLE PIZZA
831/384-7227

♦ Pizza. Casual Dining. $7-$28 **AAA Inspector Notes:** This casual, family-oriented pizza place features high-quality ingredients and dough rolled fresh daily. Distinctive specialty pizzas are piled high with toppings. **Bar:** beer & wine. **Address:** 3120 Del Monte Blvd 93933 **Location:** SR 1 exit Del Monte Blvd/Marina, just n.

L D

MARIPOSA (F-4) pop. 2,173, elev. 1,953'
- **Restaurants p. 186**
- **Hotels & Restaurants map & index p. 584**
- **Part of Yosemite National Park area — see map p. 578**

An old mining town, Mariposa is at the southern end of the Mother Lode country, a gold mining district that covered the lower western edge of the Sierra Nevada from Sierra City in the north to Mariposa in the south. SR 49 now traces this route.

Originally called Logtown, Mariposa was renamed after the Spanish word for butterfly. Gold mining has been supplanted by the scenic riches of nearby Yosemite Valley, which draw thousands of visitors each year.

Yosemite/Mariposa County Tourism Bureau: 5158 Hwy. 140, P.O. Box 425, Mariposa, CA 95338. **Phone:** (209) 966-7081 or (866) 425-3366.

CALIFORNIA STATE MINING AND MINERAL MUSEUM, 1.8 mi. s. on SR 49 at the county fairgrounds, contains a collection of minerals, gold, diamonds and other gems, including examples of benitoite, the California state gemstone. A highlight is the Frisco Nugget, a nearly 14-pound chunk of crystalline gold discovered in the American River in 1864. Other exhibits include models of an assay office and stamp mill (a machine that crushed quartz) and a full-scale replica of a mine. The museum also presents rotating exhibitions of gem and mineral specimens from other institutions and private collections.

Time: Allow 1 hour minimum. **Hours:** Thurs.-Sun. 10-5, May-Sept.; 10-4, rest of year. Closed Jan. 1, Thanksgiving and Christmas. Phone ahead to confirm schedule. **Cost:** $4; free (ages 0-12). **Phone:** (209) 742-7625.

MARIPOSA COUNTY HISTORICAL COURTHOUSE, 5088 Bullion St., was built in 1854 and is the oldest courthouse in the state still in use. Wooden pegs were used in the construction of the two-story white pine building; the second floor contains original furnishings. The old clock in the square clock tower, which was added in 1866, was brought by way of Cape Horn, at the southern tip of South America. **Hours:** Mon.-Fri. 8:30-3. Guided tours are given Sat.-Sun. 10-2, Memorial Day-Labor Day; by appointment rest of year. Phone ahead to confirm tour schedule. **Cost:** Donations. **Phone:** (209) 966-7081.

MARIPOSA MUSEUM AND HISTORY CENTER INC., SR 140 at 12th and Jessie sts., contains a re-created 1850s street, including a five-stamp mill, horse-drawn vehicles and mining and printing equipment. Featured are replicas of a schoolroom, a Native American village, a miner's cabin, a print shop, a sheriff's office, a saloon and an apothecary as well as the restored house of the 1860s county treasurer.

Time: Allow 1 hour minimum. **Hours:** Daily 10-4. Closed Jan.1, first Tues. in Jan., Thanksgiving, Christmas Eve, Christmas and Dec. 31. **Cost:** $4; free (ages 0-17). **Phone:** (209) 966-2924.

BEST WESTERN YOSEMITE WAY STATION MOTEL
(209)966-7545 24

 Hotel $59-$229   **AAA Benefit:** Members save up to 20%, plus 10% bonus points with Best Western Rewards®.

Address: 4999 Hwy 140 95338 **Location:** SR 140 at SR 49 S. **Facility:** 78 units. 2-3 stories (no elevator), exterior corridors. **Pool(s):** outdoor. **Activities:** whirlpool, exercise room. Free **Special Amenities:** local telephone calls and high-speed Internet.

SAVE ❘↑❘ CALL M ➰ BIZ 🛜 ✕ 🛏 🖥 ▣ / SOME UNITS FEE 🐾

(See map & index p. 584.)

COMFORT INN YOSEMITE VALLEY GATEWAY
(209)966-4344   23

Hotel
S90-$170

Address: 4994 Bullion St 95338 **Location:** Jct SR 140 and 49 S, just e. **Facility:** 59 units, some kitchens. 2-3 stories (no elevator), exterior corridors. **Terms:** check-in 4 pm. **Pool(s):** outdoor. **Activities:** whirlpool. **Free Special Amenities:** full breakfast and high-speed Internet. *(See ad this page.)*

THE MARIPOSA LODGE
(209)966-3607   22

Hotel
S69-$159

Address: 5052 Hwy 140 95338 **Location:** Center. **Facility:** 44 units. 2 stories (no elevator), exterior corridors. **Pool(s):** outdoor. **Activities:** whirlpool. **Free Special Amenities:** local telephone calls and high-speed Internet. *(See ad p. 590.)*

LITTLE VALLEY INN
(209)742-6204   25

Bed & Breakfast
$140-$200

Address: 3483 Brooks Rd 95338 **Location:** SR 49, 7 mi s. **Facility:** 6 units, some kitchens. 1 story, exterior corridors. **Terms:** 2 night minimum stay - weekends, 14 day cancellation notice-fee imposed. **Free Special Amenities:** expanded continental breakfast and high-speed Internet.

Learn about inspections
and Diamond Ratings
at AAA.com/Diamonds

▼ See AAA listing this page ▼

Learn about inspections and Diamond
Ratings at AAA.com/Diamonds

(See map & index p. 584.)

MINERS INN MOTEL (209)742-7777 21

Motel
$69-$249

Address: 5181 Hwy 49 N 95338 **Location:** On SR 49, n at SR 140. **Facility:** 78 units, some efficiencies. 2 stories (no elevator), interior/exterior corridors. **Terms:** cancellation fee imposed. **Dining:** Miners Inn Restaurant, see separate listing. **Pool(s):** outdoor. **Activities:** whirlpool. *(See ad this page, p. 588.)*

SAVE ⍥ 🏊 BIZ 🛜 ✕
🕹 📷 💻 / SOME UNITS FEE 🐾

YOSEMITE INN (209)742-6800 20

Motel $50-$250 **Address:** 5180 Jones St 95338 **Location:** Jct SR 49 and 140 N. **Facility:** 27 units. 2 stories (no elevator), exterior corridors. **Terms:** cancellation fee imposed. **Pool(s):** outdoor. **Activities:** whirlpool.

⍥+ 🏊 BIZ 🛜 ✕ 🕹 📷

WHERE TO EAT

CASTILLO'S MEXICAN RESTAURANT 209/742-4413 15
Mexican. Casual Dining. $8-$16 **AAA Inspector Notes:** Just off Main Street, the casual restaurant lets patrons request seats in the small dining room or on the patio. Well-prepared favorites make up the menu. **Bar:** beer & wine. **Address:** 4995 5th St 95338 **Location:** Just e of SR 49; center. **Parking:** street only. L D

MINERS INN RESTAURANT 209/966-2444 13
American. Casual Dining. $8-$19 **AAA Inspector Notes:** On the way to or from Yosemite National Park, this popular eatery is a great stop for breakfast, lunch or dinner. Menu highlights include traditional favorites and homemade pies and cobblers. **Bar:** full bar. **Address:** 5159 Hwy 140 95338 **Location:** On SR 49, n at SR 140; in Miners Inn Motel. B L D CALL 🔊M

SAVOURY'S 209/966-7677 14
American. Fine Dining. $15-$30 **AAA Inspector Notes:** Guests can take a seat by the window and watch small-town-style hustle and bustle. On the way to scenic Yosemite National Park, this dinner-only dining room has lots of charm and good food. **Bar:** full bar. **Address:** 5034 Hwy 140 95338 **Location:** At 6th St; center. **Parking:** street only. D

MARKLEEVILLE (E-4) pop. 210, elev. 5,525'

ALPINE COUNTY MUSEUM COMPLEX, .2 mi. w. of SR 89 at School and Montgomery sts., includes an 1882 schoolhouse and a jail that have been restored and furnished in period. A museum contains exhibits about mining, the history and culture of the Washoe Indians and the history of a *vaquero* (cowboy herder) camp. **Hours:** Fri.-Sun. 11-4, Memorial Day weekend-Oct. 31. **Cost:** Donations. **Phone:** (530) 694-2317.

GROVER HOT SPRINGS STATE PARK is 4 mi. w. at the end of Hot Springs Rd. Known for its pool filled with natural hot springs water, the 700-acre park also offers another pool, hiking and mountain biking trails and camping as well as cross-country skiing and snowshoeing in winter. One pool is kept at 102-104 F, the other at 75-85 F (depending on the season). *See Recreation Areas Chart.*

Hours: Park hours daily dawn-dusk; closed Thanksgiving, Dec. 25 and for maintenance 2 weeks in late Sept. Pool operation varies; phone ahead for schedule. **Cost:** Park $8 per private vehicle; $7 (ages 62+ per private vehicle). Pool $7; $5 (ages 0-16). **Phone:** (530) 694-2248 for the park, or (530) 694-2249 for the pool. 🏕 ✕ 🐾 🎣

Visit AAA.com/Travel or CAA.ca/Travel for complete trip planning and reservations

---

▼ See AAA listing this page ▼

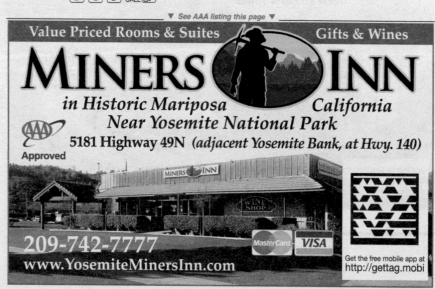

MARSHALL

NICK'S COVE & COTTAGE   415/663-1033

California
Casual Dining
$14-$29

AAA Inspector Notes: Overlooking Tomales Bay, this elegantly casual fish shack offers a warm, cozy ambience with panoramic views. Seating is available inside at white cloth-covered tables or out on the enclosed patio. The food is simply sophisticated. An excellent choice is the barbecue oysters or steelhead trout if it is on the menu. Although there is a slight wait for the baked-to-order chocolate soufflé cake, it is well worth the time. **Bar:** full bar. **Address:** 23240 Hwy One 94940 **Location:** Between Inverness and Tomales Bay.

L D CALL 🖬M 🅰️

MARTINEZ (C-9) pop. 35,824, elev. 23'

JOHN MUIR NATIONAL HISTORIC SITE, 4202 Alhambra Ave., was the residence of the conservationist and founder of the Sierra Club. His crusade for wilderness preservation aided in the establishment of national parks and forests. The 1882 house has original furnishings. Visitors may tour the 17-room mansion and the surrounding orchards. A videotape provides information about Muir's life and the site. The two-story Martinez Adobe, built in 1848, also can be seen.

Time: Allow 1 hour, 30 minutes minimum. **Hours:** Daily 10-5. Half-hour guided tours of the first level of the Muir home are given Mon.-Fri. at 2, Sat.-Sun. at 2 and 3. Closed Jan. 1, Thanksgiving and Christmas. Phone ahead to confirm schedule. **Cost:** Free. **Phone:** (925) 228-8860. 🏧

BEST WESTERN PLUS JOHN MUIR INN   (925)229-1010

Hotel
$112-$116

Best
Western
PLUS

AAA Benefit: Members save up to 20%, plus 10% bonus points with Best Western Rewards®.

Address: 445 Muir Station Rd 94553 **Location:** Jct I-680 and SR 4, 2.3 mi w on SR 4 to Pine/Center Ave exit, then just s. **Facility:** 115 units, some efficiencies and kitchens. 3 stories, interior corridors. **Amenities:** video games (fee). **Pool(s):** outdoor. **Activities:** whirlpool. **Guest Services:** valet laundry. **Free Special Amenities:** local telephone calls and high-speed Internet.

SAVE 🍴 CALL 🖬M 🏊 BIZ 🛜 🎦 🛗 🖼 💻
/SOME UNITS FEE 🐾

MUIR LODGE MOTEL   (925)228-3308

Motel
$75-$110

Address: 3930 Alhambra Ave 94553 **Location:** SR 4 exit Alhambra Ave, 0.3 mi n. **Facility:** 20 units. 1 story, exterior corridors. **Terms:** cancellation fee imposed. **Amenities:** high-speed Internet.

Pool(s): outdoor. **Free Special Amenities:** continental breakfast and high-speed Internet.

SAVE 🏊 🛜 🛗 🖼 💻

ROUND TABLE PIZZA

🛡️ Pizza. Casual Dining. $7-$28 **AAA Inspector Notes:** This casual, family-oriented pizza place features high-quality ingredients and dough rolled fresh daily. Distinctive specialty pizzas are piled high with toppings. **Bar:** beer & wine. L D

For additional information, visit AAA.com
LOCATIONS:
Address: 504 Center Ave 94553 **Location:** SR 4 exit Pine St/Center Ave, just s. **Phone:** 925/370-0626
Address: 6648 Alhambra Ave 94553 **Location:** Between Blue Ridge and Virginia Hills drs. **Phone:** 925/934-6996

MARYSVILLE (D-3) pop. 12,072, elev. 63'

Marysville was named for Mary Murphy Covillaud, an early settler and Donner party survivor. Central to Marysville is Ellis Lake, named for W.T. Ellis, a prosperous town merchant in the early 1900s. John McLaren, the designer of San Francisco's Golden Gate Park, converted a swampy area into this popular recreational outlet. The boulevard along the shore testifies to the merchant's efforts to beautify the lake. Paddleboats are available seasonally.

Riverfront Park, along the Feather River, is beneath the 5th and 10th street bridges, which link Marysville and Yuba City. Recreational facilities include a boat-launching dock, picnic area, playgrounds, soccer fields, baseball fields and motorbike trails. The park also has a concert bowl with grassy slopes for seating.

The Sleep Train Amphitheatre, on Forty Mile Road, features name entertainment during the summer; phone (530) 743-5200 for information.

COMFORT SUITES   (530)742-9200

Hotel
$77-$144

Address: 1034 N Beale Rd 95901 **Location:** SR 70 exit 20A (Feather River Blvd/Yuba College) northbound, just e, then just n; exit 20B (N Beale Rd) southbound, just e, then just s. **Facility:** 65 units, some two bedrooms. 3 stories, interior corridors. **Terms:** cancellation fee imposed. **Amenities:** high-speed Internet. **Pool(s):** heated indoor. **Activities:** exercise room. **Guest Services:** coin laundry.

SAVE 🍴 CALL 🖬M 🏊 BIZ 🛜 🎦 🛗 🖼 💻
/SOME UNITS FEE 🐾

MOTEL 6 (SOUTH)   (530)742-2700

Hotel
$89-$109

Address: 1111 N Beale Rd 95901 **Location:** SR 70 exit 20A (Feather River Blvd/Yuba College) northbound, just e; exit 20B (N Beale Rd) southbound, just e, just s, then just e; jct Feather River Blvd. **Facility:** 62 units. 2 stories (no elevator), interior corridors. **Amenities:** high-speed Internet. **Pool(s):** heated indoor. **Activities:** whirlpool, exercise room. **Guest Services:** coin laundry.

SAVE 🍴 🏊 BIZ 🛜 💻 /SOME UNITS FEE 🐾 🛗 🖼

PREGAME BAR & GRILL   530/742-6363

🛡️🛡️ American. Casual Dining. $8-$13 **AAA Inspector Notes:** Situated on Ellis Lake, this sports bar offers burgers, salads and a few pasta entrées. Patio seating overlooks the lake. **Bar:** full bar. **Address:** 900 B St, Suite A 95901 **Location:** Jct 9th St; near jct SR 20/70; in Watermarke at Ellis Lake Shopping Center.

L D CALL 🖬M

McCLOUD   pop. 1,101, elev. 3,281'

MCCLOUD DANCE COUNTRY RV RESORT   530/964-2252

▼▼ **Cabin.** Rates not provided. **Address:** 480 Hwy 89 96057 **Location:** Jct SR 89 and Squaw Valley Rd, just s; behind big red barn. **Facility:** 7 cabins, some efficiencies and kitchens. 2 stories (no elevator), exterior corridors. *Bath:* shower only. **Activities:** horseshoes, volleyball. **Guest Services:** coin laundry.

📶➕ CALL ᴸⓂ 📶 🅿 🍽 🖥 📺 / SOME UNITS FEE 🐾

MCCLOUD GUEST HOUSE   530/964-3160

▼▼▼▼ **Historic Bed & Breakfast.** Rates not provided. **Address:** 606 W Colombero Dr 96057 **Location:** Jct SR 89 and W Minnesota Ave, 0.3 mi se on W Minnesota Ave to Main St, just n on Main St to Colombero Dr, then just nw. **Facility:** This large stand-alone Victorian home (circa 1907) features a wrap-around veranda and sits on seven acres of manicured lawns with graceful oaks. 7 units, some cottages. 2 stories (no elevator), interior corridors. **Terms:** check-in 4 pm. 📶 ⊠ 🕸 🅩

MCCLOUD HOTEL   (530)964-2822

Historic Bed
& Breakfast
$125-$215

Address: 408 Main St 96057 **Location:** I-5 exit 736 (SR 89/McCloud), 9 mi e; jct SR 89 and W Minnesota Ave, 0.3 mi se on W Minnesota to Main St, then just n. Located in historic district. **Facility:** The historic property and town centerpiece offers spacious communal parlors and a fieldstone fireplace, which adds character to the 1916 hotel. There also is a nice patio garden area. 16 units. 2 stories (no elevator), interior corridors. **Terms:** 10 day cancellation notice-fee imposed. **Activities:** bicycles. **Free Special Amenities: full breakfast and high-speed Internet.**

SAVE 📶➕ CALL ᴸⓂ BIZ 📶 ⊠ 🕸 🅩
/ SOME UNITS FEE 🐾

MCCLOUD MERCANTILE HOTEL   530/964-2330

▼▼▼ **Hotel.** Rates not provided. **Address:** 241 Main St 96057 **Location:** I-5 exit 736 (SR 89/McCloud), 9 mi e; jct SR 89 and W Minnesota Ave, 0.3 mi se on W Minnesota Ave to Main St, just n. **Facility:** 12 units. 2 stories, interior corridors. **Parking:** street only. **Dining:** 2 restaurants. **Activities:** *Fee:* massage.

🍴 📶 ⊠ 🅩 / SOME UNITS 🐾

MCCLOUD RIVER INN BED & BREAKFAST
(530)964-2130

Historic Bed
& Breakfast
$99-$199

Address: 325 Lawndale Ct 96057 **Location:** I-5 exit 736 (SR 89/McCloud), 9 mi e; jct SR 89 and W Minnesota Ave, 0.3 mi se on W Minnesota Ave to Main St, just n to Lawndale Ct, then just w. Located in historic district. **Facility:** Once the headquarters of the McCloud River Lumber company and McCloud's first bank, the two-story historic 1903 Victorian home is just off the town's main thoroughfare. 5 units, some two bedrooms. 2 stories (no elevator), interior corridors. **Terms:** 7 day cancellation notice-fee imposed. **Activities:** *Fee:* massage. **Free Special Amenities: full breakfast and high-speed Internet.**

SAVE 📶➕ 📶 ⊠ 🕸 🅩

WHERE TO EAT

WHITE MOUNTAIN CAFE   530/964-2005

fyi Not evaluated. Located in the historic Mercantile Building, this restaurant is known for offering good breakfast and sandwiches. Closed for lunch on Monday and Tuesday. **Address:** 245 Main St 96057 **Location:** Jct SR 89 and W Minnesota Ave, 0.3 mi se on W Minnesota Ave to Main St, then just n.

McKINLEYVILLE   pop. 15,177

HOLIDAY INN EXPRESS HOTEL & SUITES   (707)840-9305

▼▼▼ **Hotel.** $109-$179 **Address:** 3107 Concord Dr 95519 **Location:** US 101 exit 722 (Arcata Airport Rd), just e, then just s on Boeing Dr. **Facility:** 84 units. 2 stories, interior corridors. **Amenities:** high-speed Internet. **Pool(s):** heated indoor. **Activities:** whirlpool, exercise room. **Guest Services:** coin laundry.

➕ 🚐 📶 ⊠ 🏃 🍽 🖥 📺

WHERE TO EAT

DON JUAN'S   707/839-2460

▼▼ Mexican. Casual Dining. $7-$18 **AAA Inspector Notes:** This spacious eatery serves hearty portions in a casual setting. **Bar:** beer & wine. **Address:** 1738 Central Ave 95519 **Location:** Between Sutter Rd and Nursery Way. Ⓛ Ⓓ

MENDOCINO   (D-1) pop. 894, elev. 90'
• Restaurants p. 191
• Attractions map p. 566
• Part of Wine Country area — see map p. 562

Beguilingly picturesque Mendocino—unlike Carmel-by-the-Sea, Monterey, Santa Cruz and other coastal communities—is definitely off the beaten path, which gives it some under-the-radar cachet. The natural setting, on headlands overlooking the ocean, is glorious. Architecturally speaking, Mendocino's well-preserved 19th-century buildings and houses reflect the New England roots of early settlers, who initially settled in the region because of the surrounding countryside's rich timber resources.

Despite relative inaccessibility—or perhaps because of it—the beauty began attracting artists in the 1950s, and Mendocino remains a haven for those with a creative bent. The Mendocino Art Center, 45200 Little Lake St., is a highly regarded educational institution that offers more than 200 retreat-style workshops each year. The center's galleries feature changing monthly exhibitions spotlighting local and national artists; phone (707) 937-5818 or (800) 653-3328.

This is perhaps the most popular travel destination on the northern California coast, especially for San Francisco Bay Area residents on summer weekends. As a result Mendocino has many bed-and-breakfast properties, most of them of the delightfully charming variety. And if everything looks vaguely familiar there's a reason; Mendocino stood in for fictional Cabot Cove, Maine, in the long-running TV show "Murder She Wrote."

If you're visiting during the off-season months of December through February, head to the beach or a rocky outcropping for an opportunity to spot gray whales during their winter migration between Alaska and Mexico's Baja Peninsula. The big creatures make their return trip north between February and April. Nearby Anderson Valley (southeast of town near Boonville) is peppered with wineries.

A 60-mile driving tour along the coastline via SR 1, the Pacific Coast Highway, offers scenic riches in return for the knuckle-whitening aspects of negotiating this serpentine roadway. Begin the journey at the small town of Gualala *(see place listing p. 142)*; originally a lumber settlement, it offers browsing potential in the form of art galleries and boutiques housed in a mix of 19th-century and contemporary buildings. North of Gualala is Point Arena *(see place listing p. 284)*, one of the better spots along the coast from which to observe migrating gray whales during the winter months.

At Elk there's a cliff-top cluster of country inns, restaurants and shops that feature the work of local artisans. Albion, the next town up the coast, is the site of the last wooden bridge constructed along the Pacific Coast Highway, in 1944. Like neighboring Mendocino, the architectural legacy in Little River *(see place listing p. 174)* reflects the heritage of the town's original mid-19th-century New England settlers.

Fort Bragg *(see place listing p. 113)* is larger than its neighbors but still a small town at heart. North of Westport, the northernmost town on the Mendocino coast, SR 1 veers inland in deference to a spectacularly rugged coastline. The Pacific Coast Highway ends at the junction with US 101 (also known as the Redwood Highway) and Leggett *(see place listing p. 173)*, which is enviably close to three natural attractions: the ocean, the redwoods and the California wine country.

KELLEY HOUSE MUSEUM, 45007 Albion St., is in a restored dwelling dating from 1861. It contains photographs and brief histories of many historic buildings and houses in the area, as well as genealogy records. Guided walking tours are offered. **Hours:** Thurs.-Tues. 11-3, June-Sept.; Fri.-Mon. 11-3, rest of year. **Cost:** Donations. **Phone:** (707) 937-5791.

MENDOCINO HEADLANDS STATE PARK surrounds Mendocino on three sides. A rugged promontory offers panoramic ocean views and the opportunity to spot gray whales during early winter and early spring migrations to and from Mexico's Baja California Peninsula. Three miles of walking trails, fishing and a beach for picnicking and sunbathing are popular day-use options. **Time:** Allow 1 hour minimum. **Hours:** Daily 6 a.m.-10 p.m. **Cost:** Free. **Phone:** (707) 937-5804.

Ford House Visitor Center and Museum is at 735 Main St. The Ford House was built in 1854 for the bride of one of the city's founders. Jerome B. Ford also was the superintendent of the town's first sawmill.

The house is now the visitor center for Mendocino Headlands State Park as well as a museum where exhibits depict the mid-19th-century era when this coastal area was settled. A focal point is a scale model of the town as it appeared in 1890. Docents conduct guided walks along the headlands. **Time:** Allow 30 minutes minimum. **Hours:** Sun.-Thurs. 11-4, Fri.-Sat. 11-5, Memorial Day-Labor Day; daily 11-4, rest of year. **Cost:** Donations. **Phone:** (707) 937-5397.

POINT CABRILLO LIGHT STATION STATE HISTORIC PARK is 2 mi. n. on SR 1, then 1.3 mi. w. on Point Cabrillo Rd., following signs. This 300-acre preserve, which can be reached by a .5-mile walk from the parking lot, consists of the 1909 lighthouse, three restored outbuildings and 3.5 miles of hiking trails. The lighthouse has an original Third Order Fresnel lens and an exhibit about the 1850 shipwreck of the San Francisco-bound *Frolic*. The restored lightkeeper's home is now a museum. Guided preserve walks are available seasonally.

Time: Allow 1 hour minimum. **Hours:** Preserve open daily dawn-dusk. Lighthouse and museum open daily 10-5, May-Sept.; 11-4, rest of year. Guided walks depart from the upper parking lot Sun. at 11, June-Sept. Phone ahead to confirm schedule. **Cost:** Donations. **Phone:** (707) 937-6122.

RECREATIONAL ACTIVITIES

Canoeing

- **Catch a Canoe & Bicycles, Too!** is at SR 1 and Comptche-Ukiah Rd., at the Stanford Inn by the Sea. **Hours:** Daily 9-5. **Phone:** (707) 937-0273.

AGATE COVE INN   707/937-0551

◆◆◆◆ **Cottage** $189-$349 **Address:** 11201 N Lansing St 95460 **Location:** Just w on Little Lake Rd from jct SR 1, then 0.6 mi n. **Facility:** Consisting of a simply styled 1860s farmhouse and a cluster of cottages, the inn is on a bluff overlooking the Pacific Ocean. These well-appointed rooms have fireplaces. 10 cottages. 1 story, exterior corridors. **Terms:** 2 night minimum stay - seasonal and/or weekends, age restrictions may apply, 14 day cancellation notice-fee imposed. **Activities:** whirlpool. *Fee:* massage.

 / SOME UNITS FEE

BLACKBERRY INN   707/937-5281

◆◆◆◆
Motel
$100-$225

Address: 44951 Larkin Rd 95460 **Location:** 0.5 mi n on SR 1, then just e. **Facility:** 17 units, some efficiencies and cottages. 1 story, exterior corridors. **Terms:** 2 night minimum stay - seasonal and/or weekends, 7 day cancellation notice-fee imposed. **Free Special Amenities:** early check-in/late check-out and high-speed Internet.

 / SOME UNITS FEE

BREWERY GULCH INN   (707)937-4752

◆◆◆◆
Bed & Breakfast
$235-$495

Address: 9401 N Hwy 1 95460 **Location:** 1.3 mi s to Mendocino Village, then just e. **Facility:** Vintage redwood was salvaged for use in the construction of this Craftsman-style inn situated on a bluff with distant views of Smuggler's Cove. Lush gardens and dense foliage give it a retreat-like ambiance. 10 units. 2 stories (no elevator), interior corridors. **Terms:** 2 night minimum stay - weekends, age restrictions may apply, 14 day cancellation notice-fee imposed. **Activities:** hiking trails. *Fee:* massage. **Free Special Amenities:** full breakfast and high-speed Internet.

SAVE CALL / SOME UNITS

HEADLANDS INN BED & BREAKFAST   (707)937-4431

◆◆◆ **Historic Bed & Breakfast** $99-$249 **Address:** 10453 Howard St 95460 **Location:** Just e of Lansing St; corner of Albion St; center. **Facility:** This 1868 Victorian saltbox with an English garden is located in the Mendocino village. A few rooms feature a fireplace or a deck, all with feather beds and breakfast delivered to your room. 7 units, some cottages. 1-3 stories (no elevator), interior/exterior corridors. **Parking:** street only. **Terms:** 2 night minimum stay - weekends, age restrictions may apply, 14 day cancellation notice-fee imposed.

/ SOME UNITS

HILL HOUSE INN   (707)937-0554

◆◆◆
Hotel
$203-$309

Address: 10701 Pallette Dr 95460 **Location:** Just w on Little Lake St from jct SR 1, then just n on Lansing St. **Facility:** 44 units. 2 stories (no elevator), exterior corridors. **Terms:** cancellation fee imposed. **Activities:** *Fee:* massage. **Free Special Amenities:** continental breakfast and high-speed Internet.

 / SOME UNITS FEE FEE

JOHN DOUGHERTY HOUSE
707/937-5266

▼▼▼ **Historic Bed & Breakfast.** Rates not provided. **Address:** 571 Ukiah St 95460 **Location:** Just w of Lansing St; between Kasten and William sts. **Facility:** Styled like a New England saltbox, the John Dougherty House was built in 1867. Also on the grounds are cottages, a water tower and English gardens. 8 units. 2 stories (no elevator), interior/exterior corridors. **Terms:** age restrictions may apply.

MENDOCINO HOTEL & GARDEN SUITES
707/937-0511

▼▼ **Historic Hotel.** Rates not provided. **Address:** 45080 Main St 95460 **Location:** 0.4 mi w on Main St from jct SR 1. **Facility:** Built in 1878, this restored Victorian hotel has a few small rooms with a European-style shared bath and others with a private bath. 51 units. 2-3 stories (no elevator), interior/exterior corridors. *Bath:* some shared. **Parking:** on-site and street. **Terms:** check-in 4 pm, age restrictions may apply. **Dining:** 2 restaurants, restaurant, see separate listing. **Activities:** *Fee:* massage.

MENDOCINO SEASIDE COTTAGE
707/485-0239

▼▼▼
Cottage
$187-$299

Address: 10940 Lansing St 95460 **Location:** Just w on Little Lake Rd from jct SR 1, 0.3 mi n. **Facility:** This replica Victorian seaside cottage houses units with unobstructed views of the ocean and Headlands State Park. 5 cottages, some kitchens. 2 stories (no elevator), interior/exterior corridors. **Terms:** 2 night minimum stay - seasonal and/or weekends, 7 day cancellation notice-fee imposed. **Free Special Amenities:** local telephone calls and high-speed Internet.

NICHOLSON HOUSE INN
(707)937-0934

▼▼ **Bed & Breakfast** $99-$239 **Address:** 951 Ukiah St 95460 **Location:** Just e of Lansing St; center. **Facility:** 6 units, some kitchens. 2 stories (no elevator), interior/exterior corridors. **Parking:** on-site and street. **Terms:** 2 night minimum stay - seasonal and/or weekends, 3 day cancellation notice-fee imposed.

PACKARD HOUSE
707/937-2677

▼▼▼ **Historic Bed & Breakfast.** Rates not provided. **Address:** 45170 Little Lake St 95460 **Location:** Just w of Lansing St; center. **Facility:** One of four landmark homes on executive row, this B&B offers sophisticated luxury and modern elegance in the heart of Mendocino village. An upscale reception area greets guests. 6 units, some cottages. 2 stories (no elevator), interior/exterior corridors. **Parking:** street only. **Terms:** age restrictions may apply.

SEA ROCK BED & BREAKFAST INN
(707)937-0926

▼▼▼ **Cottage** $179-$399 **Address:** 11101 Lansing St 95460 **Location:** Just w on Little Lake Rd from jct SR 1, 0.5 mi n. **Facility:** The property offers a range of accommodations, including suites and individual cottages. All units include a fireplace and deck with ocean or garden views. 14 units, some efficiencies, kitchens and cottages. 1-2 stories (no elevator), exterior corridors. **Terms:** 2 night minimum stay - weekends, 14 day cancellation notice-fee imposed. **Activities:** sauna, spa.

STANFORD INN BY THE SEA ECO-LODGE
(707)937-5615

▼▼▼ ▼▼▼
Country Inn
$199-$460

Address: 44850 Comptche-Ukiah Rd 95460 **Location:** SR 1 exit Comptche-Ukiah Rd, just e. **Facility:** Spacious grounds, a rustic setting and many rooms with ocean views and fireplaces are appealing; llamas and an organic farm share the grounds. 41 units, some cottages. 2-3 stories (no elevator), exterior corridors. **Terms:** check-in 4 pm, 2 night minimum stay - seasonal and/or weekends, 7 day cancellation notice-fee imposed. **Dining:** The Ravens', see separate listing. **Pool(s):** heated indoor. **Activities:** sauna, whirlpool, rental canoes, bicycles, hiking trails, exercise room, spa. **Free Special Amenities:** full breakfast and local telephone calls. *(See ad this page.)*

BLUE DOOR INN
707/937-4892

fyi Not evaluated. **Address:** 10481 Howard St 95460 **Location:** Just e of Lansing St; corner of Albion St; center. Facilities, services, and décor characterize a mid-scale property.

▼ *See AAA listing this page* ▼

CAFE BEAUJOLAIS   707/937-5614
♦♦♦ California. Casual Dining. $11-$34 **AAA Inspector Notes:** This bungalow cottage restaurant features wood floors and whitewashed walls. The cuisine is fresh organic with a hint of French. Service is impeccable. **Bar:** beer & wine. **Reservations:** suggested. **Address:** 961 Ukiah St 95460 **Location:** Just e of Lansing St; center. **Parking:** street only. L D Ⓚ

MACCALLUM HOUSE RESTAURANT AND GREY WHALE BAR & CAFE   707/937-6759
♦♦♦ California. Fine Dining. $25-$42 **AAA Inspector Notes:** This casual restaurant occupies the main floor of the historic bed and breakfast. If scallops, papaya salad and shrimp toast are on the seasonal menu, go for it. Do not forget to order the soufflé for dessert. **Bar:** full bar. **Reservations:** suggested. **Address:** 45020 Albion St 95460 **Location:** Just w of Lansing St; center; in MacCallum House Inn. **Parking:** street only. B D Ⓚ

MENDOCINO HOTEL AND RESTAURANTS   707/937-0511
♦♦ Continental. Casual Dining. $11-$35 **AAA Inspector Notes:** Diners can enjoy breakfast and lunch in the glass-enclosed courtyard, where skylights provide an outdoor feel and protection from winter rains. Dinner is served either at the casual lobby bar, with its stained-glass dome ceiling, or in a more intimate dining room, furnished in the Victorian style. A menu offers seasonal California cuisine with sustainable organic produce and meats. **Bar:** full bar. **Reservations:** suggested. **Address:** 45080 Main St 95460 **Location:** 0.4 mi w on Main St from jct SR 1; in Mendocino Hotel & Garden Suites. **Parking:** street only. B L D Ⓚ

THE RAVENS'   707/937-5615
♦♦♦
Vegetarian
Casual Dining
$16-$25
AAA Inspector Notes: Known for its delectable hearty cuisine and monthly changing vegetarian and vegan menu, this restaurant gets most of its produce from its own private gardens. **Bar:** full bar. **Reservations:** suggested. **Address:** 44850 Comptche-Ukiah Rd 95460 **Location:** SR 1 exit Comptche-Ukiah Rd, just e; in Stanford Inn by the Sea Eco-Lodge. B D Ⓚ

MENDOCINO NATIONAL FOREST (D-2)

Elevations in the forest range from 1,000 ft. at Elk Creek to 8,110 ft. at the summit of Mount Linn. Refer to AAA maps for additional elevation information.

In the North Coast Mountain Range north of San Francisco, Mendocino National Forest encompasses nearly 886,048 acres. Hang gliding and motorcycling areas are available. Roads and trails afford access to scenic points. Many roads within the forest are unsurfaced; driving can be hazardous, especially in the dusty, dry months.

Yolla Bolly-Middle Eel Wilderness at the north end of the forest and Snow Mountain Wilderness in the south provide peaceful settings for horseback riding and hiking. Wilderness entry permits are not required, but users should sign the registry at trailheads.

The Red Bluff Recreation Area, 488 acres adjacent to the Sacramento River 2 miles from Red Bluff (see place listing p. 288), has such diverse habitats as forests, wetlands and woodlands. In addition to hiking trails and summer fishing, the area also is known for its bird-watching opportunities. The Sacramento River Discovery Center, 1000 Sale Ln. in Red Bluff, has interpretive displays about the river's watershed; phone (530) 527-1196.

Campfire permits are required in some areas; check with the Forest Supervisor, Mendocino National Forest, 825 N. Humboldt Ave., Willows, CA 95988, or a district office. For information phone (530) 934-3316, or TTY (530) 934-7724. *See Recreation Areas Chart.*

MENLO PARK (E-9) pop. 32,026, elev. 70'
• Restaurants p. 192
• Hotels & Restaurants map & index p. 410

ALLIED ARTS GUILD, off SR 82 at the end of Cambridge Ave. on Arbor Rd., is on 3.5 acres of land originally granted by the King of Spain to the Commandant of the Presidio de San Francisco in the early 19th century. The complex of buildings, courtyards, gardens, fountains, murals and frescoes has a Spanish architectural flavor, a simpatico backdrop for the working artists in residence. **Hours:** Mon.-Sat. 10-5 (also Sun. noon-5, Nov.-Dec.). **Cost:** Free. **Phone:** (650) 322-2405.

SUNSET PUBLISHING CORP., 80 Willow Rd. at Middlefield Rd., is the publishing headquarters of *Sunset* magazine. Visitors can take a self-guiding walking tour of the company's gardens. Divided into areas representing various Western habitats, they exhibit more than 300 varieties of trees, shrubs, vines, ground covers, annuals and perennials. **Time:** Allow 30 minutes minimum. **Hours:** Mon.-Fri. 9-4. Closed major holidays. **Cost:** Free. **Phone:** (650) 321-3600.

BEST WESTERN PLUS RIVIERA   (650)321-8772 117
♦♦♦
Motel
$119-$269
Best Western PLUS
AAA Benefit: Members save up to 20%, plus 10% bonus points with Best Western Rewards®.
Address: 15 El Camino Real 94025 **Location:** On SR 82. Adjacent to Stanford University. **Facility:** 37 units, some efficiencies and kitchens. 3 stories, exterior corridors. **Amenities:** high-speed Internet. **Pool(s):** outdoor. **Activities:** sauna, whirlpool, exercise room. **Guest Services:** coin laundry. **Free Special Amenities:** continental breakfast and high-speed Internet.
SAVE ❗ CALL ☾M ➤ 🛰 ✕ 🍴 🖥 ▭

(See map & index p. 410.)

MENLO PARK INN
(650)326-7530

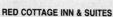
Motel
$109-$249

Address: 1315 El Camino Real 94025 **Location:** US 101 exit 406 (Marsh Rd), 0.4 mi s on Middlefield Willow Rd, 0.6 mi w on Watkins Ave, then 0.6 mi s. **Facility:** 30 units. 2 stories (no elevator), exterior corridors. **Terms:** cancellation fee imposed. **Amenities:** high-speed Internet. **Activities:** exercise room. **Guest Services:** valet laundry. **Free Special Amenities:** continental breakfast and high-speed Internet. *(See ad this page.)*

RED COTTAGE INN & SUITES
(650)326-9010

Motel
$129-$219

Address: 1704 El Camino Real 94025 **Location:** US 101 exit 406 (Marsh Rd), 0.4 mi s on Middlefield Rd, 0.6 mi w on Encinal Rd, then just n. **Facility:** 28 units, some efficiencies. 2 stories (no elevator), exterior corridors. **Terms:** cancellation fee imposed. **Amenities:** high-speed Internet. **Pool(s):** heated outdoor. **Activities:** exercise room. **Guest Services:** valet laundry. **Free Special Amenities:** expanded continental breakfast and high-speed Internet.

/ SOME UNITS FEE

STANFORD PARK HOTEL
(650)322-1234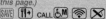

Boutique Hotel
$199-$705

Address: 100 El Camino Real 94025 **Location:** On SR 82, 0.5 mi ne of Stanford University. **Facility:** Fireplaces are featured in some guest rooms at this elegantly appointed hotel surrounded by manicured grounds. 163 units. 4 stories, interior corridors. **Parking:** on-site (fee) and valet. **Terms:** 2-4 night minimum stay - seasonal and/or weekends, cancellation fee imposed, resort fee. **Amenities:** high-speed Internet, safes. **Pool(s):** heated outdoor. **Activities:** sauna, whirlpool, exercise room. *Fee:* massage. **Guest Services:** valet laundry, area transportation-within 3 mi. **Free Special Amenities:** local telephone calls and newspaper.

WHERE TO EAT

CARPACCIO
650/322-1211

Italian. Casual Dining. $12-$23 **AAA Inspector Notes:** A warm Tuscan atmosphere envelops this longstanding restaurant, where pizza and pasta are at the heart of the enticing menu. **Bar:** full bar. **Address:** 1120 Crane St 94025 **Location:** SR 82, 0.3 mi w on Santa Cruz Ave, then just n.

LEFT BANK
650/473-6543

French. Casual Dining. $11-$27 **AAA Inspector Notes:** Casually elegant as only a French brasserie can be, the dining room is accented by polished wood and vintage French posters. With outdoor seating, it is a bit of Paris in Menlo Park. Such expertly done, classic French dishes as salade Lyonnaise and crème brûlée are part of the chef's repertoire. **Bar:** full bar. **Address:** 635 Santa Cruz Ave 94025 **Location:** Just w of SR 82; downtown. **Parking:** street only.

MERCED (F-4) pop. 78,958, elev. 167'

Merced, in the agricultural San Joaquin Valley, is the principal western gateway to Yosemite National Park for travelers from the north.

Merced National Wildlife Refuge is 16 miles southwest. Water sports are offered 7 miles northeast at Lake Yosemite. Sparky the alpaca is one of

▼ See AAA listing this page ▼

the animal residents at Applegate Park Zoo, 25th and R streets, which also has children's rides; phone (209) 725-3337.

Merced Visitor Services: 710 W. 16th St., Merced, CA 95340. **Phone:** (209) 724-8104 or (800) 446-5353.

Self-guiding tours: The conference and visitors bureau distributes a guide to historic Merced as well as a blossom guide.

MERCED COUNTY COURTHOUSE MUSEUM, 21st and N sts., is in the Old County Courthouse, one of the oldest buildings in the state. The 1875 three-story Italianate structure, which resembles the state Capitol building, houses exhibits about Merced County history and the Central Valley pioneers who settled the area. Permanent exhibits include a turn-of-the-20th-century classroom, a courtroom and a blacksmith shop. **Time:** Allow 2 hours minimum. **Hours:** Wed.-Sun. 1-4. Closed major holidays. **Cost:** Free. **Phone:** (209) 723-2401.

BEST WESTERN PLUS INN   (209)723-2163

Hotel
$86-$95

AAA Benefit: Members save up to 20%, plus 10% bonus points with Best Western Rewards®.

Address: 1033 Motel Dr 95341 **Location:** SR 99 exit E Childs Ave or SR 140, just e. **Facility:** 42 units. 2 stories (no elevator), exterior corridors. **Amenities:** high-speed Internet. **Pool(s):** outdoor. **Activities:** exercise room. **Guest Services:** coin laundry. **Free Special Amenities: local telephone calls and high-speed Internet.**

COMFORT INN MERCED   (209)383-0333

Hotel
$69-$79

Address: 730 Motel Dr 95341 **Location:** SR 99 exit SR 140, just e. **Facility:** 65 units. 3 stories, exterior corridors. **Terms:** cancellation fee imposed. **Pool(s):** outdoor. **Activities:** sauna, whirlpool. **Guest Services:** valet laundry. **Free Special Amenities: full breakfast and high-speed Internet.**

COURTYARD BY MARRIOTT   (209)725-1221

Hotel $94-$124 **Address:** 750 Motel Dr 95340 **Location:** SR 99 exit SR 140, just e. **Facility:** 90 units. 3 stories, interior corridors. **Amenities:** high-speed Internet. **Pool(s):** heated indoor. **Activities:** whirlpool, exercise room. **Guest Services:** valet and coin laundry.

AAA Benefit: AAA hotel discounts of 5% or more.

HAMPTON INN & SUITES-MERCED   (209)386-1210

Hotel
$109-$129

AAA Benefit: Members save up to 10%!

Address: 225 S Parsons Ave 95340 **Location:** SR 99 exit E Childs Ave, e to Parsons Ave. **Facility:** 83 units. 3 stories, interior corridors. **Terms:** 1-7 night minimum stay, cancellation fee imposed. **Amenities:** video games (fee), high-speed Internet. **Pool(s):** outdoor. **Activities:** whirlpool, exercise room. **Guest Services:** coin laundry. **Free Special Amenities: full breakfast and high-speed Internet.**

HOLIDAY INN EXPRESS HOTEL & SUITES   (209)384-3700

Hotel $89-$139 **Address:** 151 S Parsons Ave 95341 **Location:** SR 99 exit E Childs Ave, just e. **Facility:** 91 units. 3 stories, interior corridors. **Amenities:** high-speed Internet. **Pool(s):** heated outdoor. **Activities:** whirlpool, exercise room. **Guest Services:** valet and coin laundry.

RAMADA INN   (209)723-3121

Hotel $79-$99 **Address:** 2010 E Childs Ave 95340 **Location:** SR 99 exit E Childs Ave, just e. **Facility:** 110 units. 2 stories (no elevator), interior/exterior corridors. **Amenities:** high-speed Internet. **Pool(s):** outdoor.

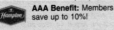 **WHERE TO EAT**

BLACK BEAR DINER   209/383-9600

American. Casual Dining. $7-$16 **AAA Inspector Notes:** A homey atmosphere characterizes this family-oriented restaurant. Familiar comfort foods, such as meatloaf with mashed potatoes, are at the heart of the menu and are served in generous portions. **Bar:** full bar. **Address:** 1435 V St 95340 **Location:** SR 99 exit R St E, 0.4 mi n on W 14th St, then just e.

THE BRANDING IRON   209/722-1822

Steak. Casual Dining. $10-$28 **AAA Inspector Notes:** A casual Western decor gives the dining room a homey feel. Quality food is served in ample portions. Grilled steak, ribs and rack of lamb are available in addition to fresh seafood including lobster, crab and scallops. Service is prompt and friendly. Patio seating is a seasonal option. **Bar:** full bar. **Address:** 640 W 16th St 95340 **Location:** 0.5 mi e of SR 99; between M and N sts.

NEW ASIA CHINESE FOOD   209/383-3953

Chinese. Casual Dining. $7-$32 **AAA Inspector Notes:** Although the overall décor here is nothing fancy, the food definitely makes up for it. Highly recommended by the locals, great lunch specials include an entrée with soup and appetizer of the day. **Bar:** beer & wine. **Address:** 1513 W Main St 95340 **Location:** SR 99 exit R St E, 0.3 mi n.

TREVINO'S MEXICAN RESTAURANT   209/723-5610

Mexican. Casual Dining. $10-$16 **AAA Inspector Notes:** A casual atmosphere, friendly service and an extensive menu can all be found at this favorite of locals and tourists. Family owned and operated for more than 20 years, homemade tortillas are this restaurant's specialty. Choices divert from the traditional fajitas and tacos, to authentic Mexican dishes. **Bar:** full bar. **Address:** 408 W Main St 95340 **Location:** At K St; downtown.

MIDDLETOWN (A-8) pop. 1,323, elev. 1,105'

• Hotels p. 194
• Attractions map p. 567
• Part of Wine Country area — see map p. 562

CALPINE GEOTHERMAL VISITOR CENTER is just w. of SR 29 at 15500 Central Park Rd. Calpine is a leader in the production of renewable energy and geothermal power—naturally occurring underground steam that is harnessed to spin turbine-generators to make electricity. Hands-on displays and exhibits and a videotape presentation in the visitor center explain the process. Guided bus tours, which include a visit to a nearby power plant, are offered once a month; phone for details.

Time: Allow 30 minutes minimum. **Hours:** Visitor center Wed.-Sat. 10-4. Closed major holidays. **Cost:** Free. **Phone:** (707) 987-4270 or (866) 439-7377.

WINERIES

- **Langtry Estate & Vineyards** is at 21000 Butts Canyon Rd. **Hours:** Tastings and self-guiding tours daily 11-5. **Phone:** (707) 987-9127.

BACKYARD GARDEN OASIS BED AND BREAKFAST INN
(707)987-0505

▼▼▼▼ **Bed & Breakfast** $139-$159 **Address:** 24019 Hilderbrand Dr 95461 **Location:** 3.9 mi s on SR 29, just e. **Facility:** Located in a natural setting with opportunity for observing birds and wildlife, the inn offers the ideal setting for a relaxing getaway. 4 units, some cottages. 1 story, interior/exterior corridors. **Terms:** 5 day cancellation notice-fee imposed. **Activities:** whirlpool. *Fee:* massage.

🛜 ✕ 🖥 💻 / SOME UNITS FEE 🐾

TWIN PINE CASINO & HOTEL   707/987-0197

▼▼▼▼
Hotel
$160

Address: 22223 Hwy 29 at Rancheria Rd 95461 **Location:** Jct SR 175, 1.6 mi s on SR 29. **Facility:** This property offers contemporary accommodations and numerous gaming options. 60 units. 3 stories, interior corridors. **Terms:** cancellation fee imposed. **Amenities:** safes. **Free Special Amenities:** local telephone calls and high-speed Internet.

🆂🅰🆅🅴 🤸 🍽 🛎 CALL 🅶🅼 🛜 📷 🖥 💻 / SOME UNITS 🖨

MIDPINES (F-4) pop. 1,204, elev. 2,575'

RECREATIONAL ACTIVITIES

White-water Rafting

- **All-Outdoors California Whitewater Rafting** departs from the Midpines Country Store on SR 140. **Hours:** Excursions depart daily, Apr. 1 to mid-July. **Phone:** (925) 932-8993 or (800) 247-2387.

MILLBRAE pop. 21,532

- Hotels & Restaurants map & index p. 410
- Part of San Francisco area — see map p. 342

BEST WESTERN PLUS EL RANCHO INN & SUITES
(650)588-8500 **41**

▼▼▼▼
Hotel
$109-$199

Best Western PLUS

AAA Benefit: Members save up to 20%, plus 10% bonus points with Best Western Rewards®.

Address: 1100 El Camino Real 94030 **Location:** US 101 exit Millbrae Ave, 0.3 mi sw, then 0.8 mi n on SR 82. ⓜ San Francisco International Airport, 44. **Facility:** 306 units, some two bedrooms and kitchens. 2 stories, exterior corridors. **Terms:** cancellation fee imposed. **Amenities:** high-speed Internet. **Dining:** Terrace Cafe, see separate listing. **Pool(s):** 2 heated outdoor. **Activities:** whirlpools, exercise room. **Guest Services:** valet and coin laundry. **Free Special Amenities:** high-speed Internet and airport transportation. *(See ad p. 195.)*

🆂🅰🆅🅴 🔧 🍽 CALL 🅶🅼 🏊 🛜 ✕ 📷 💻 / SOME UNITS 🖥 🖨 🖨

THE DYLAN AT SFO   650/697-7373 **44**

▼▼ **Hotel.** Rates not provided. **Address:** 110 S El Camino Real 94030 **Location:** US 101 exit Millbrae Ave, just s on SR 82 (El Camino Real). ⓜ Millbrae, 45. **Facility:** 58 units. 3 stories, interior/exterior corridors. **Amenities:** safes (fee).

🔧 🍽 CALL 🅶🅼 🛜 ✕ / SOME UNITS 🖥 🖨 🖨

FAIRFIELD INN & SUITES SAN FRANCISCO AIRPORT/ MILLBRAE   (650)259-0400 **42**

▼▼▼ **Hotel** $119-$269 **Address:** 250 El Camino Real 94030 **Location:** US 101 exit Millbrae Ave, 0.3 mi w, then 0.3 mi n. ⓜ Millbrae, 45. **Facility:** 86 units. 4 stories, interior corridors. **Parking:** on-site (fee). **Amenities:** *Some:* high-speed Internet. **Activities:** whirlpool, exercise room. **Guest Services:** valet and coin laundry.

AAA Benefit: AAA hotel discounts of 5% or more.

🅴🅲🅾 🔧 🍽 CALL 🅶🅼 🛜 ✕ 🖥 🖨 💻 🖨

MILLWOOD INN & SUITES   (650)583-3935 **40**

▼▼▼▼
Motel
$97-$280

Address: 1375 El Camino Real 94030 **Location:** 0.3 mi sw of US 101 exit Millbrae Ave, 1 mi n on SR 82. ⓜ San Francisco International Airport, 44. **Facility:** 34 units, some two bedrooms. 1-2 stories (no elevator), exterior corridors. **Amenities:** high-speed Internet. **Activities:** exercise room. **Guest Services:** valet and coin laundry.

🆂🅰🆅🅴 🔧 🍽 CALL 🅶🅼 🛜 ✕ 🖥 🖨 💻 🖨

THE WESTIN SAN FRANCISCO AIRPORT
(650)692-3500 **43**

▼▼▼
Hotel
$129-$409

WESTIN HOTELS & RESORTS

AAA Benefit: Enjoy up to 20% off your next stay, plus Starwood Preferred Guest® bonuses.

Address: 1 Old Bayshore Hwy 94030 **Location:** Just e of US 101 exit Millbrae Ave. Located in a busy commercial area. ⓜ Millbrae, 45. **Facility:** 397 units. 7 stories, interior corridors. **Parking:** on-site (fee) and valet. **Terms:** cancellation fee imposed. **Amenities:** high-speed Internet (fee), safes. **Pool(s):** heated indoor. **Activities:** whirlpool, hiking trails, exercise room. **Guest Services:** valet laundry. **Free Special Amenities:** newspaper and airport transportation.

🆂🅰🆅🅴 🅴🅲🅾 🍽 🔧 🍽 🤸 🍸 CALL 🅶🅼 🛟 🅱🅸🆉 🛜 ✕ 📷 💻 / SOME UNITS 🖨 🖨

WHERE TO EAT

HONG KONG FLOWER LOUNGE RESTAURANT
650/878-8108 **21**

▼▼▼ Chinese. Casual Dining. $10-$58 **AAA Inspector Notes:** This large, multi-level restaurant serves dim sum and classic Chinese dishes. **Bar:** full bar. **Address:** 51 Millbrae Ave 94030 **Location:** US 101 exit Millbrae Ave, 0.3 mi w. ⓜ Millbrae, 45.

🇱 🇩 CALL 🅶🅼 🖨

LA COLLINA RISTORANTE   650/652-9655 **20**

▼▼▼ Italian. Casual Dining. $14-$23 **AAA Inspector Notes:** Traditional Italian fare is served in large portions at this casual eatery. The warm atmosphere makes guests feel welcomed. Excellent desserts merit a splurge. **Bar:** full bar. **Address:** 355 El Camino Real 94030 **Location:** US 101 exit Millbrae Ave, 0.3 mi w, then 0.4 mi n. ⓜ Millbrae, 45. **Parking:** street only. 🇩 🖨

TERRACE CAFE   650/742-5588 **19**

▼▼▼ American. Casual Dining. $9-$20 **AAA Inspector Notes:** The exterior of this casual cafe is mission style with palm trees and a pool, while the dining room is comfortably urban. **Reservations:** suggested. **Address:** 1100 El Camino Real 94030 **Location:** US 101 exit Millbrae Ave, 0.3 mi sw, then 0.8 mi n on SR 82; in BEST WESTERN PLUS El Rancho Inn & Suites. ⓜ San Francisco International Airport, 44. *(See ad p. 195.)*

🇧 🇱 🇩 🖨

▼ See AAA listing p. 194 ▼

MILL VALLEY (C-8) pop. 13,903, elev. 70'
• Part of San Francisco area — see map p. 342

Mill Valley is a residential community at the base of Mount Tamalpais. The heavy redwood frame of the sawmill for which the town was named still stands in Old Mill Park on Throckmorton Avenue. Hikers can follow a nearby trail up the mountain.

Mill Valley Chamber of Commerce: 85 Throckmorton Ave., Mill Valley, CA 94941. **Phone:** (415) 388-9700.

MOUNT TAMALPAIS STATE PARK, 6 mi. w. on Panoramic Hwy., encompasses 6,300 acres of picturesque coastal hill country dominated by triple-peaked Mount Tamalpais; the mountain's profile from the south is said to resemble a sleeping Native American girl. Hiking and bicycling trails and a winding road lead to spectacular vistas at the summit, where there is a visitor center.

Theatrical productions known as the Mountain Play are presented in the Sidney B. Cushing Memorial Amphitheatre, 801 Panoramic Hwy., also known as the Mountain Theater. It was constructed out of rock by the Civilian Conservation Corps in the 1930s, although performances have taken place in the amphitheater since 1913. *See Recreation Areas Chart.*

Hours: Park open daily 7-dusk. Visitor center open Sat.-Sun. and holidays, Apr.-Oct.; hours vary. Visitor center schedule varies rest of year. Ranger station open daily 8-5, Mar.-Aug.; hours vary rest of year. Plays are presented mid-May to mid-June. Phone ahead to confirm schedule. **Cost:** Day use $8 per private vehicle; $7 (ages 62+ per private vehicle). **Phone:** (415) 388-2070 for the state park, or (415) 383-1100 for play and amphitheater information.

ACQUA HOTEL   415/380-0400
▼▼▼ **Hotel.** Rates not provided. **Address:** 555 Redwood Hwy 94941 **Location:** US 101 exit Seminary Dr. **Facility:** 49 units. 3 stories, interior/exterior corridors. **Amenities:** high-speed Internet. **Activities:** hiking trails. **Guest Services:** valet laundry.

LARKSPUR HOTEL MILL VALLEY   (415)332-5700
▼▼▼ **Hotel** $139-$229 **Address:** 160 Shoreline Hwy 94941 **Location:** US 101 exit Stinson Beach southbound, just nw; exit Mill Valley/SR 1/Stinson Beach northbound, 0.4 mi nw. **Facility:** 100 units. 2 stories (no elevator), interior corridors. **Terms:** cancellation fee imposed. **Pool(s):** heated outdoor. **Activities:** whirlpool, bicycles, exercise room. **Guest Services:** valet laundry.

MILL VALLEY INN   (415)389-6608
▼▼▼ **Hotel** $159-$439 **Address:** 165 Throckmorton Ave 94941 **Location:** Center. **Facility:** 25 units. 3 stories, interior/exterior corridors. **Terms:** check-in 4 pm, 2-3 night minimum stay - seasonal and/or weekends, 7 day cancellation notice-fee imposed. **Guest Services:** valet laundry.

MILL VALLEY/SAUSALITO TRAVELODGE   (415)383-0340

▼▼ ▼▼
Motel
$70-$125

Address: 707 Redwood Hwy 94941 **Location:** US 101 exit Seminary Dr. **Facility:** 48 units. 2 stories, exterior corridors. **Terms:** check-in 4 pm, 2-3 night minimum stay - seasonal and/or weekends, 3 day cancellation notice-fee imposed. **Amenities:** safes. **Free Special Amenities: continental breakfast and high-speed Internet.**

WHERE TO EAT

THE BUCKEYE ROADHOUSE   415/331-2600
▼▼▼ American. Casual Dining. $14-$33 **AAA Inspector Notes:** Comfortable and welcoming, this elegant roadhouse serves comfort food with a touch of California. Start with raw oyster or oysters Rockefeller, followed by scallops with piquillo pepper risotto. Finish it all off with a slice of lemon pudding cake with huckleberry lemon sauce. **Bar:** full bar. **Address:** 15 Shoreline Hwy 94941 **Location:** US 101 exit 445B (Mill Valley/Stinson Beach), just w. **Parking:** valet only. L D

EL PASEO HOUSE OF CHOPS   415/388-0741
▼▼▼ Steak. Casual Dining. $17-$40 **AAA Inspector Notes:** This casual restaurant's dining areas used to be a complex of stores, courtyards and gardens connected by a private pathway. It has a feel of a Shakespearean tavern meets Carmel-by-the-Sea. Menu items are what one would expect at a chophouse, yet with just enough creativity to keep it comfortable but exciting enough to be a neighborhood dining destination. The loaded baked potato is an inside out dish—mashed potato and baked potato skin that is crunchy and soft at the same time. **Bar:** full bar. **Address:** 17 Throckmorton Ave 94941 **Location:** Center. **Parking:** street only. D ✗

PEARL'S PHAT BURGERS   415/381-6010
▼ Burgers. Quick Serve. $5-$12 **AAA Inspector Notes:** This no-frills, tiny burger joint offers standard (half pound) and mini (quarter pound) sizes. Diners request how they want it cooked and out comes a burger, oozing delicious juices. Besides burgers, there are other items on the menu—veggie, chicken and buffalo burgers along with hot dogs and salads. The hardest part is choosing which special burger to order. Check out the teriyaki burger (with just enough sweetness to kick it to the next level), the bomb or the bula burger. **Address:** 8 E Blithedale Ave 94941 **Location:** Center. **Parking:** street only. L D ✗

MILPITAS pop. 66,790
• Restaurants p. 198
• Hotels & Restaurants map & index p. 468

BEST WESTERN PLUS BROOKSIDE INN   (408)263-5566 [33]

▼▼▼
Hotel
$99-$169

Best Western PLUS

AAA Benefit: Members save up to 20%, plus 10% bonus points with Best Western Rewards®.

Address: 400 Valley Way 95035 **Location:** I-880 exit Calaveras Blvd (SR 237), just e. **Facility:** 78 units. 2 stories (no elevator), interior/exterior corridors. **Terms:** cancellation fee imposed. **Amenities:** high-speed Internet. **Pool(s):** heated outdoor. **Activities:** sauna, steamroom, exercise room. **Guest Services:** valet and coin laundry. **Free Special Amenities: local telephone calls and high-speed Internet.**

Visit AAA.com/Travel or
CAA.ca/Travel for complete
trip planning and reservations

(See map & index p. 468.)

BEVERLY HERITAGE HOTEL   (408)943-9080 🖩

Hotel
$69-$239

Address: 1820 Barber Ln 95035 **Location:** Northwest quadrant of I-880 and Montague Expwy. **Facility:** 236 units. 3 stories, interior corridors. **Terms:** cancellation fee imposed. **Amenities:** video games (fee), high-speed Internet. **Dining:** Brandon's, see separate listing. **Pool(s):** outdoor. **Activities:** whirlpool, jogging, exercise room. **Guest Services:** valet laundry, area transportation-within 5 mi. *(See ad this page.)*

SAVE 🚐 🍴 CALL 🛗 🚲
BIZ 🛜 ✕ 🎦 🍳
/ SOME UNITS FEE 🐾 🎛 🖼

EMBASSY SUITES MILPITAS/SILICON VALLEY
(408)942-0400 🖩

Hotel $109-$259 **Address:** 901 E Calaveras Blvd 95035 **Location:** I-680 exit Calaveras Blvd (SR 237), just w. **Facility:** 266 units. 8 stories, interior corridors. **Terms:** 1-7 night minimum stay, cancellation fee imposed. **Amenities:** *Fee:* video games, high-speed Internet. **Dining:** Swan Court Cafe, see separate listing. **Pool(s):** heated indoor. **Activities:** whirlpool, exercise room. **Guest Services:** valet and coin laundry.

AAA Benefit:
Members save 5% or more!

ECO 🍴 CALL 🛗 🚲 BIZ 🛜 🎦 🎛 🖼 🖥

HILTON GARDEN INN-SAN JOSE/MILPITAS
(408)719-1313 🖩

Hotel $94-$329 **Address:** 30 Ranch Dr 95035 **Location:** SR 237 exit McCarthy Blvd, just n. **Facility:** 161 units. 4 stories, interior corridors. **Terms:** 1-7 night minimum stay, cancellation fee imposed. **Amenities:** high-speed Internet. **Pool(s):** outdoor. **Activities:** whirlpool, exercise room. **Guest Services:** valet and coin laundry, area transportation-within 5 mi.

AAA Benefit:
Unparalleled hospitality at a special Member rate.

🚐 🍴 CALL 🛗 🚲 BIZ 🛜 🎛 🖼 🖥

LARKSPUR LANDING MILPITAS/SAN JOSE
(408)719-1212 🖩

Hotel $99-$269 **Address:** 40 Ranch Dr 95035 **Location:** SR 237 exit McCarthy Blvd, just n. **Facility:** 124 units, some efficiencies. 4 stories, interior corridors. **Terms:** cancellation fee imposed. **Amenities:** high-speed Internet. **Activities:** whirlpool, exercise room. **Guest Services:** complimentary laundry, area transportation-within 5 mi.

ECO 🚐 🍴 CALL 🛗 BIZ 🛜 ✕ 🎛 🖼 🖥
/ SOME UNITS FEE 🐾

MILPITAS COURTYARD BY MARRIOTT   (408)719-1966 🖩

Hotel $109-$249 **Address:** 1480 Falcon Dr 95035 **Location:** I-680 exit Montague Expwy W, then just n. **Facility:** 155 units. 3 stories, interior corridors. **Amenities:** high-speed Internet. **Pool(s):** heated outdoor. **Activities:** whirlpool, exercise room. **Guest Services:** valet and coin laundry.

AAA Benefit:
AAA hotel discounts of 5% or more.

ECO 🍴 CALL 🛗 🚲 BIZ 🛜 ✕ 🎛 🖼 🖥
/ SOME UNITS 🖼

RESIDENCE INN BY MARRIOTT   (408)941-9222 🖩

Extended Stay Hotel $109-$249 **Address:** 1501 California Cir 95035 **Location:** I-880 exit Dixon Landing Rd E, just s. **Facility:** 120 units, some two bedrooms and kitchens. 3 stories, interior corridors. **Amenities:** high-speed Internet. **Pool(s):** heated outdoor. **Activities:** whirlpool, sports court, exercise room. **Guest Services:** valet and coin laundry.

AAA Benefit:
AAA hotel discounts of 5% or more.

CALL 🛗 🚲 BIZ 🛜 ✕ 🎛 🖼 🖥
/ SOME UNITS FEE 🐾

Be a better driver.
Keep your mind on the road.

▼ *See AAA listing this page* ▼

(See map & index p. 468.)

SHERATON SAN JOSE HOTEL   (408)943-0600

Hotel
$99-$269

 Sheraton
HOTELS & RESORTS

AAA Benefit: Members get up to 20% off, plus Starwood Preferred Guest® bonuses.

Address: 1801 Barber Ln 95035 **Location:** 4 mi n of San Jose International Airport; 0.3 mi nw of I-880 and Montague Expwy. **Facility:** 229 units. 2-9 stories, interior/exterior corridors. **Terms:** cancellation fee imposed. **Amenities:** Fee: video games, high-speed Internet. **Pool(s):** outdoor. **Activities:** whirlpool, jogging, exercise room. **Guest Services:** valet laundry. **Free Special Amenities:** airport transportation.

TOWNEPLACE SUITES BY MARRIOTT   (408)719-1959 35

Extended Stay Hotel
$109-$249 **Address:** 1428 Falcon Dr 95035 **Location:** I-680 exit Montague Expwy W, then just n. **Facility:** 143 units, some two bedrooms, efficiencies and kitchens. 4 stories, interior corridors. **Amenities:** high-speed Internet. **Pool(s):** heated outdoor. **Activities:** exercise room. **Guest Services:** valet and coin laundry.

AAA Benefit: AAA hotel discounts of 5% or more.

WHERE TO EAT

BLACK BEAR DINER   408/946-2327
Comfort Food. Casual Dining. $7-$16 **AAA Inspector Notes:** A homey atmosphere characterizes this family-oriented restaurant. Familiar comfort foods, such as meatloaf with mashed potatoes, are at the heart of the menu and are served in generous portions. **Bar:** beer & wine. **Address:** 174 W Calaveras Blvd 95035 **Location:** I-880 exit SR 237 (Calaveras Blvd), 0.3 mi e.

BRANDON'S   408/570-5470 17

California
Fine Dining
$10-$35

AAA Inspector Notes: Fresh seafood, assorted pasta dishes and grilled beef and lamb are at the heart of the menu at this fine dining spot where views of the outside courtyard offer a peaceful setting. **Bar:** full bar. **Reservations:** suggested, for lunch. **Address:** 1800 Barber Ln 95035 **Location:** Northwest quadrant of I-880 and Montague Expwy; in Beverly Heritage Hotel. (See ad p. 197.)

CHEZ CHRISTINA   408/263-2220 14
Vietnamese. Casual Dining. $8-$20 **AAA Inspector Notes:** The specialty of the house at this friendly, family-owned-and-operated eatery is the grilled New York steak served with mushrooms on a sizzling metal plate, but the menu offers a wide selection of Vietnamese entrées and a few French dishes as well. **Bar:** beer & wine. **Address:** 1339 Jacklin Rd 95035 **Location:** I-680 exit Jacklin Rd, just e.

EL TORITO   408/946-8012
Mexican. Casual Dining. $8-$20 **AAA Inspector Notes:** Homemade Mexican favorites span from classic preparations to specialties from the country's central regions. Spicy taqueria-style tacos and carnitas Michoacan (marinated pork) are tasty choices. **Bar:** full bar. **Address:** 477 E Calaveras Blvd (SR 237), just w; in Town Center Shopping Center.

Get more from your membership with an upgrade to Plus or Premier

---

FRESH CHOICE   408/934-9090
American. Cafeteria. $9-$15 **AAA Inspector Notes:** The salad bar of salad bars, the casual restaurant invites patrons to make their own or try one of the already prepared varieties. Other items include freshly baked breads, pizza and soup, as well as make-your-own sundaes for dessert. **Bar:** beer & wine. **Address:** 248 Great Mall Dr 95035 **Location:** I-880 exit Montague Expwy/Great Mall Pkwy, just e; in Great Mall.

ON THE BORDER MEXICAN GRILL & CANTINA   408/935-6070 15
Mexican. Casual Dining. $10-$20 **AAA Inspector Notes:** In addition to traditional Mexican dishes, the restaurant prepares some specialties of its own. The setting is lively and fun. **Bar:** full bar. **Address:** 260 Ranch Dr 95035 **Location:** SR 237 exit McCarthy, just n; in McCarthy Ranch Shopping Center.

PASTA POMODORO   408/582-0160
Italian. Casual Dining. $7-$16 **AAA Inspector Notes:** Families are welcomed at this laid-back restaurant, which brings in plenty of loyal locals who enjoy its varied Italian favorites, including tempting pasta and chicken dishes. **Bar:** beer & wine. **Address:** 181 Ranch Dr 95035 **Location:** SR 237 exit McCarthy, just n; in McCarthy Ranch Shopping Center.

SWAN COURT CAFE   408/942-0400 16
American. Casual Dining. $10-$25 **AAA Inspector Notes:** On the main floor of the hotel, this casual cafe surrounds its tables with a koi pond and an abundance of greenery. Offerings include varied sandwiches, salads and entrées. **Bar:** full bar. **Address:** 901 E Calaveras Blvd 95035 **Location:** I-680 exit Calaveras Blvd (SR 237), just w; in Embassy Suites Milpitas/Silicon Valley.

MIRANDA pop. 520

MIRANDA GARDENS RESORT   (707)943-3011

Cottage
$105-$265

Address: 6766 Ave of the Giants 95553 **Location:** US 101 exit 650, 0.3 mi s on Maple Hills Rd, then 1.5 mi e. Located in quiet village area. **Facility:** 16 units, some kitchens and cottages. 1 story, exterior corridors. **Terms:** closed 1/1-3/31, 7 day cancellation notice-fee imposed, resort fee. **Pool(s):** heated outdoor. **Activities:** playground, basketball. **Free Special Amenities:** continental breakfast.

MI-WUK VILLAGE pop. 941

CHRISTMAS TREE INN   (209)586-1005

Hotel
$89-$129

Address: 24685 Hwy 108 95346 **Location:** On SR 108, 15 mi e of Sonora. **Facility:** 16 units. 2 stories (no elevator), exterior corridors. **Terms:** 2 night minimum stay - seasonal and/or weekends, 3 day cancellation notice-fee imposed. **Pool(s):** outdoor. **Activities:** whirlpool. **Free Special Amenities:** local telephone calls and high-speed Internet.

MODESTO (F-3) pop. 201,165, elev. 88'
• Restaurants p. 200

In the northern San Joaquin Valley on the Tuolumne River, Modesto is near the geographic center of the state. When the Central Pacific Railroad brought about the city's founding in 1870, its proponents wanted to name it after a San Francisco banker. When the banker rejected the idea, his modesty was commemorated in the chosen name. From

Modesto there is access to Sonora Pass in Stanislaus National Forest, the Mother Lode Country and the Big Oak Flat route to Yosemite.

Great Valley Museum of Natural History, 1100 Stoddard Ave., features exhibits about Central Valley ecosystems; phone (209) 575-6196.

George Lucas Plaza, at Downey Street, McHenry Avenue and 17th and J streets, salutes native son and filmmaker George Lucas, whose 1973 film "American Graffiti" was an evocative, music-filled reverie recalling the times he spent cruising the streets of his hometown in the early 1960s. A statue in the plaza depicts two teenagers leaning against a '57 Chevrolet.

Modesto Convention and Visitors Bureau: 1150 9th St., Suite C, Modesto, CA 95354. **Phone:** (209) 526-5588 or (888) 640-8467.

Shopping areas: Off SR 99 Standiford/Beckwith exit between Sisk and Dale roads, Vintage Faire Mall offers JCPenney, Macy's, Sears and 125 other stores to tempt shoppers.

BLUE DIAMOND GROWERS, 4800 Sisk Rd., offers a videotape presentation about the growing and harvesting of almonds. Samples are available. **Hours:** Mon.-Fri. 9-5, Sat. 10-4. Last video presentation is 1 hour before closing. Closed major holidays. **Cost:** Free. **Phone:** (209) 545-6230.

McHENRY MANSION is at the jct. of 15th and I sts. Built in 1883 by a prominent local rancher and banker, the Victorian Italianate mansion is decorated in period to look as it did while occupied by Robert McHenry and his wife Matilda. Three rooms on the second floor reflect turn-of-the-20th-century style, a time when their son lived in the mansion. Guided tours begin at the visitors center with a DVD introduction. **Time:** Allow 1 hour minimum. **Hours:** Sun.-Fri. 12:30-4. Closed major holidays. **Cost:** Donations. **Phone:** (209) 577-5344.

McHENRY MUSEUM is at 1402 I St. Exhibits about the history of Modesto and Stanislaus County focus on the Yokut Indians, the gold rush, the founding of Modesto, agriculture and irrigation, local baseball and that old teenage rite of passage, automobile cruising. Re-created period settings include a barbershop, general store, school and county assessor's office. Changing exhibits also are featured. **Tours:** Guided tours are available. **Hours:** Tues.-Sun. noon-4. Closed major holidays. **Cost:** Donations. Reservations are required for guided tours. **Phone:** (209) 577-5366.

BEST WESTERN TOWN HOUSE LODGE (209)524-7261

Hotel
$70-$81

AAA Benefit: Members save up to 20%, plus 10% bonus points with Best Western Rewards®.

Address: 909 16th St 95354 **Location:** SR 99 exit Central Modesto, 1 mi e; at I St. **Facility:** 55 units. 2 stories (no elevator), exterior corridors. **Pool(s):** outdoor. **Activities:** whirlpool. **Free Special Amenities:** local telephone calls and high-speed Internet.

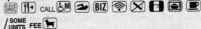

COMFORT INN (209)544-2000

Hotel
$69-$82

Address: 2025 W Orangeburg Ave 95350 **Location:** SR 99 exit Briggsmore Ave E, then just s. **Facility:** 77 units. 3 stories, interior corridors. **Terms:** cancellation fee imposed. **Pool(s):** outdoor. **Guest Services:** valet laundry. **Free Special Amenities:** expanded continental breakfast and high-speed Internet.

COURTYARD BY MARRIOTT (209)577-3825

Hotel
$104-$114

AAA Benefit: AAA hotel discounts of 5% or more.

Address: 1720 Sisk Rd 95350 **Location:** SR 99 exit Briggsmore Ave, 0.3 mi n. **Facility:** 125 units. 2 stories, interior corridors. **Activities:** whirlpool, exercise room. **Guest Services:** valet and coin laundry. **Free Special Amenities:** continental breakfast and high-speed Internet.

DOUBLETREE BY HILTON HOTEL MODESTO
 (209)526-6000

Hotel
$99-$259

AAA Benefit: Members save 5% or more!

Address: 1150 9th St 95354 **Location:** SR 99 exit Central Modesto northbound; exit Maze Blvd southbound, just e. Located at Convention Center Plaza. **Facility:** 258 units. 15 stories, interior corridors. **Parking:** on-site (fee). **Terms:** 1-7 night minimum stay, cancellation fee imposed. **Amenities:** high-speed Internet. **Dining:** Maxi's, see separate listing. **Pool(s):** outdoor. **Activities:** whirlpool. **Guest Services:** valet laundry.

HOLIDAY INN EXPRESS HOTEL & SUITES 209/543-9009

Hotel. Rates not provided. **Address:** 4300 Bangs Ave 95356 **Location:** SR 99 exit Pelandale Ave E, 0.4 mi n on Sisk Rd, then just e. **Facility:** 95 units, some two bedrooms. 3 stories, interior corridors. **Amenities:** high-speed Internet, safes. **Pool(s):** heated outdoor. **Activities:** whirlpool, exercise room. **Guest Services:** valet and coin laundry.

MICROTEL INN & SUITES BY WYNDHAM
 (209)538-6466

Hotel
$65-$89

Address: 1760 Herndon Rd 95307 **Location:** SR 99 exit Hatch Rd E, just s. **Facility:** 59 units. 3 stories, interior corridors. **Amenities:** high-speed Internet, safes. **Pool(s):** outdoor. **Activities:** whirlpool, limited exercise equipment. **Guest Services:** coin laundry. **Free Special Amenities:** expanded continental breakfast and high-speed Internet.

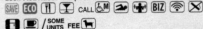
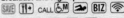

QUALITY INN
(209)578-5400

◆◆◆ Hotel
$55-$105

Address: 500 Kansas Ave 95351 **Location:** SR 99 exit Kansas Ave, just e. **Facility:** 67 units. 3 stories, interior corridors. **Terms:** cancellation fee imposed. **Pool(s):** outdoor. **Guest Services:** valet and coin laundry. **Free Special Amenities:** expanded continental breakfast and high-speed Internet.

SAVE / SOME UNITS FEE

SPRINGHILL SUITES BY MARRIOTT MODESTO
(209)526-2157

◆◆◆ Hotel
$109-$139

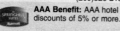

AAA Benefit: AAA hotel discounts of 5% or more.

Address: 1901 W Orangeburg Ave 95350 **Location:** SR 99 exit Briggsmore Ave E, just s. **Facility:** 111 units. 3 stories, interior corridors. **Amenities:** high-speed Internet. **Pool(s):** heated outdoor. **Activities:** whirlpool, exercise room. **Guest Services:** valet and coin laundry. **Free Special Amenities:** expanded continental breakfast and high-speed Internet.

WHERE TO EAT

BELLA ITALIA RISTORANTE & PIZZERIA
209/577-1094

◆◆◆ Italian. Casual Dining. $8-$25 **AAA Inspector Notes:** A warm, Tuscan-style design with distinctive artwork decorates this restaurant. The menu has something for everyone from the more casual pizza and calzones to the homemade pasta, veal, poultry and seafood. Service is warm and friendly at this favorite spot for locals. **Bar:** beer & wine. **Address:** 2625 Coffee Rd, Suite K 95355 **Location:** SR 99 exit Briggsmore Ave, 3.3 mi e, then 0.8 mi n, just n of Floyd Ave.

BLACK BEAR DINER
209/529-1440

◆◆ American. Casual Dining. $8-$16 **AAA Inspector Notes:** A homey atmosphere characterizes this family-oriented restaurant. Familiar comfort foods, such as meatloaf with mashed potatoes, are at the heart of the menu and are served in generous portions. **Bar:** beer & wine. **Address:** 2200 Plaza Pkwy 95350 **Location:** SR 99 exit Briggsmore Ave E, then just n.

DAMIAN'S AUTHENTIC MEXICAN FOOD AND BAR
209/526-3800

◆ Mexican. Casual Dining. $5-$16 **AAA Inspector Notes:** A fun and lively ambience prevails at this casual cantina where a sunset is painted on the ceiling. Guests can choose from traditional Mexican specialties including fajitas, tacos and burritos made with homemade sauce. **Bar:** full bar. **Address:** 2075 W Orangeburg Ave 95350 **Location:** SR 99 exit Briggsmore Ave E, just s.

EL ROSAL
209/543-0898

◆◆ Mexican. Casual Dining. $6-$14 **AAA Inspector Notes:** The menu here serves up traditional favorites including tacos, burritos and enchiladas. Some of the specialty items include carnitas and chile verde. The service is warm and friendly. **Bar:** beer & wine. **Address:** 3900 Pelandale Ave, Suite 155 95356 **Location:** SR 99 exit Pelandale Ave, just e.

FRESH CHOICE
209/523-8875

◆ American. Casual Dining. $8-$15 **AAA Inspector Notes:** The salad bar of salad bars, the casual restaurant invites patrons to make their own or try one of the already prepared varieties. Other items include freshly baked breads, pizza and soup, as well as make-your-own sundaes for dessert. **Bar:** beer & wine. **Address:** 2225 Plaza Pkwy, Suite C-1 95350 **Location:** SR 99 exit Briggsmore Ave/Carpenter Rd E, just n; in Walmart Shopping Center.

JACOB'S ART OF FINE DINING
209/529-2829

◆◆◆ California. Fine Dining. $12-$35 **AAA Inspector Notes:** This casually elegant restaurant offers up a great menu starting with such appetizers as bruschetta with sun-dried tomato, roasted garlic and fresh basil leaves. Entrée salads include blackened chicken and a wedge salad served with New York steak. Other highlights include grilled meat, pasta dishes and seafood items including calamari and filet of sole. **Bar:** full bar. **Reservations:** suggested. **Address:** 2501 McHenry Ave, Suite C & D 95350 **Location:** Just n of Briggsmore Ave; at Floyd Ave.

MAXI'S
209/525-3075

◆◆◆ American. Casual Dining. $8-$25 **AAA Inspector Notes:** Located just off the main lobby, this casually elegant restaurant offers great specialty salads, panini, sandwiches, fresh seafood, pasta dishes, beef and poultry. A casual and friendly atmosphere prevails both inside and outside where a lounge area is available for a cocktail. **Bar:** full bar. **Address:** 1150 9th St 95354 **Location:** SR 99 exit Central Modesto northbound; exit Maze Blvd southbound, just e; in DoubleTree by Hilton Hotel Modesto. **Parking:** on-site (fee) and valet.

MEXICALI GRILL
209/526-9999

◆ Mexican. Quick Serve. $8-$12 **AAA Inspector Notes:** Although this place is ultra-casual and service is limited, all items, including specialty burritos and other Mexican dishes, are freshly prepared. **Bar:** beer & wine. **Address:** 1700 McHenry Ave, Suite 138 95350 **Location:** At Briggsmore Ave; in McHenry Village Shopping Center.

MIKE'S ROADHOUSE BAR & GRILL
209/529-6453

◆◆ American. Gastro Pub. $9-$23 **AAA Inspector Notes:** A fun and lively atmosphere prevails at this bar, which displays memorabilia of many sports teams. Diners explore a wide range of choices, from start your engine appetizers to finish line desserts. **Bar:** full bar. **Address:** 3250 Dale Rd 95356 **Location:** SR 99 exit Standiford Ave E, just n; across from Vintage Faire Mall.

ROUND TABLE PIZZA

◆ Pizza. Casual Dining. $7-$28 **AAA Inspector Notes:** This casual, family-oriented pizza place features high-quality ingredients and dough rolled fresh daily. Distinctive specialty pizzas are piled high with toppings. **Bar:** beer & wine.

For additional information, visit AAA.com

LOCATIONS:
Address: 3848 McHenry Ave, Suite 145 95356 **Location:** Between Pelandale and Standiford aves. **Phone:** 209/526-9904
Address: 2401 E Orangeburg Ave 95355 **Location:** Just e of Oakdale Rd. **Phone:** 209/522-7213

TAHOE JOE'S FAMOUS STEAKHOUSE
209/545-6885

◆◆◆ Steak. Casual Dining. $12-$40 **AAA Inspector Notes:** At this ski lodge-themed spot, aged steaks are grilled over an almond fire and slow roasted prime rib are top picks. Other menu selections include railroad camp shrimp and Joe's bowls (salads and burgers). **Bar:** full bar. **Reservations:** suggested. **Address:** 3801 Pelandale Ave 95356 **Location:** SR 99 exit Pelandale Ave, just e.

MODOC NATIONAL FOREST (A-3)

Elevations in the forest range from 4,500 ft. at Devils Gardens to 9,892 ft. at Eagle Peak. Refer to AAA maps for additional elevation information.

Encompassing much of the state's remote northeastern corner, Modoc National Forest's 1,654,392 acres were covered millions of years ago by an immense lava flow. Although geologically the area is known as the Modoc Plateau, it doesn't look like a plateau. The region is distinguished by basins, mountains, lakes and meadows. And despite the relatively dry climate, the plateau supports some of the country's most significant wetlands.

The forest is home to more than 300 species of wildlife, including Rocky Mountain mule deer, pronghorn antelopes, bald and golden eagles and wild horses. The Pacific Flyway for migratory birds crosses directly over the forest.

Volcanism has left many marks on the forest's terrain, and some of the most dramatic examples are in the Medicine Lake highlands. There are such unusual features as Glass Mountain, a huge flow of obsidian, and the Burnt Lava Flow, which is a jumble of black lava interspersed with islands of timber. Medicine Lake itself fills an old volcanic crater and is popular for boating and swimming.

On the forest's eastern boundary, the Warner Mountains are a rolling upland that drops steeply on its eastern edge. Most of the range is above 5,000 feet, and some of the peaks reach an altitude over 9,000 feet in the 70,385-acre South Warner Wilderness, which includes Modoc's highest mountain, Eagle Peak. The forest has 118 miles of trails, accessible by eight trailheads, suited for hikers and

horseback riders. Carrying a topography map is advised. Fishing is prime in many reservoirs. Cross-country skiing is a popular wintertime diversion.

Maps, brochures and information about recreational opportunities are available at the district ranger stations and the forest headquarters in Alturas. For more information write the Forest Supervisor, Modoc National Forest, 800 W. 12th St., Alturas, CA 96101; phone (530) 233-5811, or TDD (530) 233-8708. *See Recreation Areas Chart.*

MONTARA pop. 2,909
• Part of San Francisco area — see map p. 342

GOOSE & TURRETS BED & BREAKFAST INN   (650)728-5451
♥♥ **Bed & Breakfast** $145-$190 **Address:** 835 George St 94037 **Location:** 7.5 mi n of jct SR 92 and 1; SR 1 exit 2nd St E, s on Main St, then 0.5 mi e on 3rd St. Located in a quiet residential area. **Facility:** 5 units. 1 story, interior corridors. **Terms:** check-in 4 pm, 3 day cancellation notice-fee imposed.

MONTEREY PENINSULA

Although Spanish explorer Juan Rodriguez Cabrillo, the first European to enter Monterey Bay, came within sight of the bay's pine forest-edged beaches in 1542, he was unable to reach land due to high seas. It would be another 60 years before Sebastián Vizcaíno explored the bay and named it for the Count of Monte Rey, viceroy of Mexico. Vizcaíno also named a nearby valley after his patron saint, Our Lady of Carmel.

The remote area was officially claimed for Spain but was not settled until Franciscan priest Junípero Serra and Spanish governor Gaspar de Portolá arrived in 1770 to build a mission and establish a seat of government, respectively. Fishing and whaling provided livelihoods, but by the 1880s tourism began developing. The ocean beckoned once again, however, when sardine harvesting led to the birth of Monterey's Cannery Row during the 1920s.

The peninsula's striking natural beauty restored tourism to the economic forefront after the collapse of the sardine industry. In addition to the obvious attractions of dramatic coastline, beaches and Pacific surf, the Monterey Peninsula also is blessed with gently rolling hills, streams and lush woodlands. It's a mecca for golf aficionados; the 🏌 AT&T Pebble Beach National Pro-Am, held in early February, is one of the highlights of the professional circuit. And it is offering increasing competition to the Napa and Sonoma valleys courtesy of vineyards, wineries and tasting rooms that offer samples of award-winning products.

Those seeking more active pursuits should check out the Monterey Peninsula Recreational Trail, a walking, jogging and biking path that runs along the coast for 18 miles from Pacific Grove to Castroville. Following the Southern Pacific Railroad line, it passes Monterey's famed Cannery Row and Fisherman's Wharf and the impressive sand dunes at Monterey State Beach while offering myriad scenic vistas of the rocky Pacific shoreline.

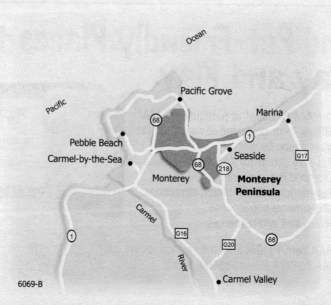

6069-B

This map shows cities in the Monterey Peninsula where you will find attractions, hotels and restaurants. Cities are listed alphabetically in this book on the following pages.

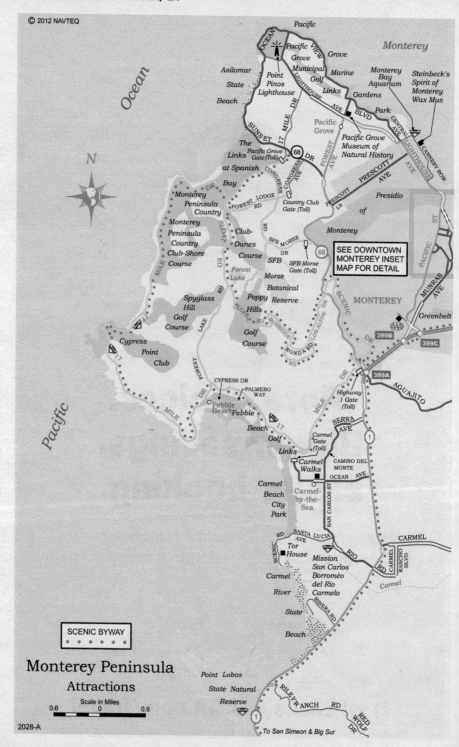

Pacific

Monterey

Ocean

Pacific View
Grove
Grove

Pacific
Ocean

Asilomar
State
Beach

Point
Pinos
Lighthouse

Pacific View DR

Pacific Grove
Municipal
Golf
Links

Marine
Gardens

LIGHTHOUSE AVE

Monterey
Bay
Aquarium

Monterey

Steinbeck's
Spirit of
Monterey
Wax Mus

Pacific Grove

SUNSET DR

17 MILE DR

Pacific
Grove

FOREST AVE

CENTRAL AVE

LIGHTHOUSE

CANNERY ROW

The
Links
at Spanish
Bay

Pacific Grove
Gate (Toll)

68

DR

Pacific Grove
Museum of
Natural History

PRESCOTT AVE

PACIFIC ST

CONGRESS AVE

Presidio

Monterey
Peninsula
Country
Club

FOREST LODGE RD

Country Club
Gate (Toll)

PRESCOTT LN

of

Monterey

MUNRAS AVE

17 MILE DR

SLOAT RD

Monterey
Peninsula
Country
Club-Shore
Course

Club-
Dunes
Course

SFB MORSE DR

SFB
Morse

SFB Morse
Gate (Toll)

68

SEE DOWNTOWN
MONTEREY INSET
MAP FOR DETAIL

SCENIC DR

MONTEREY

Forest
Lake

LAKE RD

Spyglass
Hill
Golf
Course

Botanical
Reserve

Poppy
Hills
Golf
Course

LOPEZ RD

SUNRIDGE RD

RONDA RD

LOS ALTOS DR

399B

Greenbelt

399C

Cypress
Point
Club

17

FOREST DR

17 MILE DR

CYPRESS DR

PALMERO
WAY

17 MILE DR

399A

Highway
1 Gate
(Toll)

AGUAJITO

Pacific

Pebble
Beach

Pebble
Beach
Golf
Links

Carmel
Gate
(Toll)

SERRA AVE

1

Carmel
Walks

CAMINO DEL
MONTE

Carmel
Beach
City
Park

Carmel-
by-the-
Sea

SAN CARLOS ST

OCEAN AVE

CARMEL

Tor
House

SANTA LUCIA AVE

SCENIC RD

Mission
San Carlos
Borroméo
del Rio
Carmelo

RIO RD

CARMEL RD

RANCHO BLVD

Carmel

Carmel
River

RIBERA RD

State
Beach

Point Lobos
State Natural
Reserve

1

RILEY RANCH RD

RED WOLF DR

To San Simeon & Big Sur

SCENIC BYWAY
• • • • • •

Monterey Peninsula
Attractions

Scale in Miles
0.6   0   0.6

2028-A

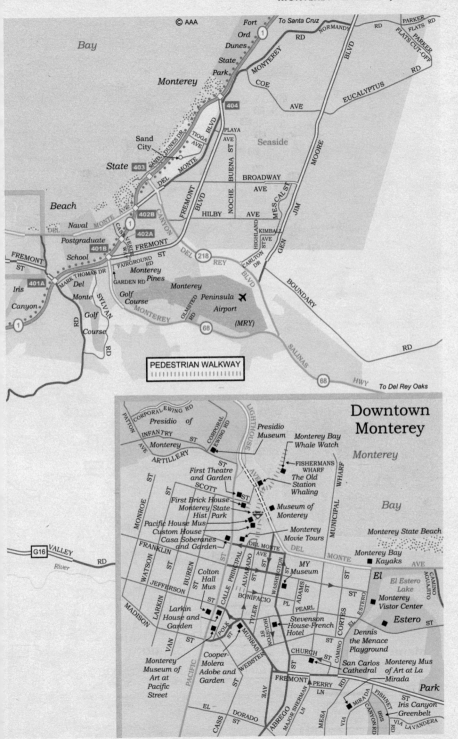

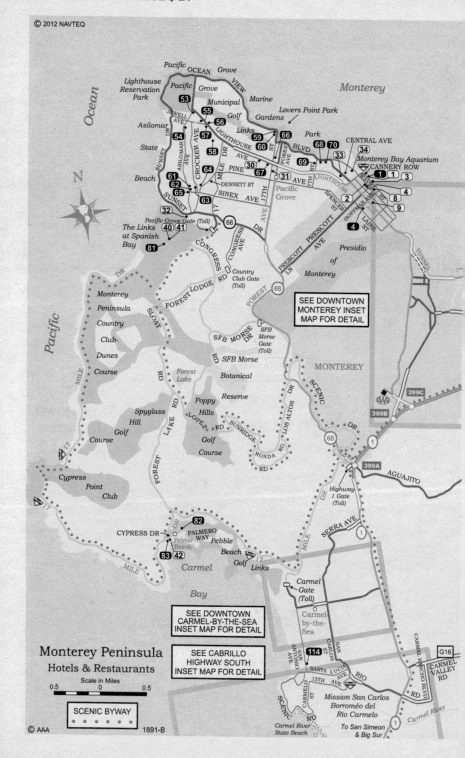

© 2012 NAVTEQ

Ocean

Pacific OCEAN Grove VIEW

Monterey

Lighthouse
Reservation
Park

Pacific Grove 53

Grove Marine
Gardens

Municipal 55

Lovers Point Park

JEWELL AVE 56

Golf
Links

Park

Asilomar 54 57

59 66

CENTRAL AVE

State 58

60 68 70 34

Beach 61 64 30 67 69 33

Monterey Bay Aquarium
CANNERY ROW

62 DENNETT ST 31 1 1

65 SINEX AVE 2 4

63 8

32 9

The Links
at Spanish
Bay 81

Pacific Grove Gate (Toll) 40 41 68

Congress
Ave

4

Pacific
Grove

N

Pacific

Monterey
Peninsula
Country
Club-
Dunes
Course

Country
Club Gate
(Toll)

FOREST LODGE RD

FOREST

68

SEE DOWNTOWN
MONTEREY INSET
MAP FOR DETAIL

SLOAT

SFB MORSE DR

SFB
Morse
Gate
(Toll)

MONTEREY

Forest
Lake

SFB Morse

RD

SCENIC DR

LOS ALTOS RD

399C

Spyglass
Hill
Golf
Course

Botanical
Reserve

Poppy
Hills
Golf
Course

LOPEZ RD

SUNRIDGE

RONDA

RD

399B

17

FOREST LAKE RD

DR

68

399A

AGUAJITO

Cypress
Point
Club

17

Highway
1 Gate
(Toll)

1

82

CYPRESS DR

PALMERO WAY

Pebble

SERRA AVE

83 42

Pebble
Beach
Golf
Links

17

Carmel
Gate
(Toll)

Carmel

Bay

Carmel-
by-the-
Sea

CARMEL RANCHO BLVD

G16

Monterey Peninsula
Hotels & Restaurants

SEE DOWNTOWN
CARMEL-BY-THE-SEA
INSET MAP FOR DETAIL

114

SAN CARLOS ST

SAN

RIO

CARMEL VALLEY RD

0.5   0   0.5
Scale in Miles

SEE CABRILLO
HIGHWAY SOUTH
INSET MAP FOR DETAIL

SANTA LUCIA AVE

15TH AVE

SCENIC RD

CARMELO ST

Mission San Carlos
Borroméo del
Rio Carmelo

RD

SCENIC BYWAY

© AAA

1891-B

Carmel River
State Beach

To San Simeon
& Big Sur

1

Carmel River

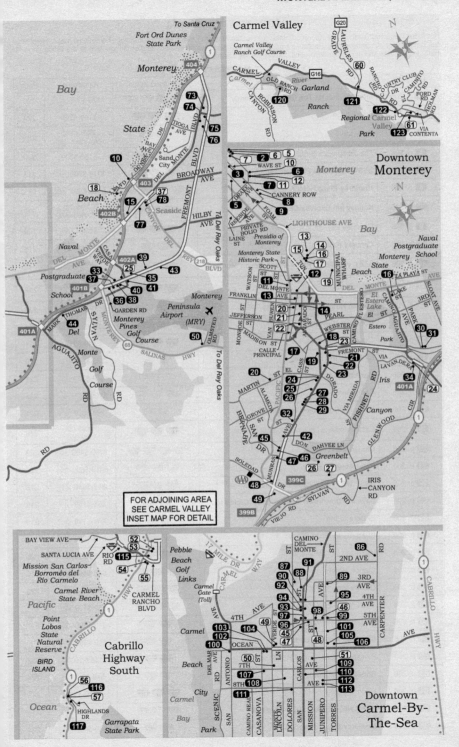

Monterey Peninsula

This index helps you "spot" where approved hotels and restaurants are located on the corresponding detailed maps. Hotel daily rate range is for comparison only. Restaurant price range is a combination of lunch and/or dinner. Turn to the listing page for more detailed rate and price information and consult display ads for special promotions.

MONTEREY

Map Page	Hotels	Diamond Rated	Rate Range	Page
1 p. 206	**InterContinental The Clement Monterey**	◈◈◈◈	$179-$399 SAVE	220
2 p. 206	Spindrift Inn	◈◈◈	$169-$700	224
3 p. 206	Otter Inn	◈◈	Rates not provided SAVE	223
4 p. 206	The Jabberwock Bed & Breakfast Inn	◈◈◈	$169-$309	220
5 p. 206	**BEST WESTERN PLUS Victorian Inn**	◈◈◈	$119-$700 SAVE	218
6 p. 206	**Monterey Plaza Hotel & Spa**	◈◈◈◈	$179-$995 SAVE	223
7 p. 206	Holiday Inn Express-Cannery	◈◈◈	Rates not provided SAVE	219
8 p. 206	Monterey Bay Inn	◈◈◈	$169-$700	220
9 p. 206	**Cannery Row Inn**	◈◈	$89-$699 SAVE	218
10 p. 206	**BEST WESTERN PLUS Beach Resort Monterey**	◈◈◈	Rates not provided SAVE	217
11 p. 206	Hotel Pacific	◈◈◈	Rates not provided	219
12 p. 206	**Portola Hotel & Spa** (See ad p. 224.)	◈◈◈◈	$179-$525 SAVE	223
13 p. 206	**Monterey Marriott**	◈◈◈◈	$189-$599 SAVE	221
14 p. 206	The Monterey Hotel	◈◈◈	$99-$319	221
15 p. 206	**La Quinta Inn Monterey**	◈◈	$83-$353 SAVE	220
16 p. 206	**Monterey Bay Lodge** (See ad p. 222.)	◈◈◈	$79-$349 SAVE	221
17 p. 206	**Colton Inn**	◈◈◈	$109-$209 SAVE	218
18 p. 206	**Monterey Downtown Travelodge**	◈◈	$99-$399 SAVE	221
19 p. 206	Casa Munras, A Larkspur Collection Hotel	◈◈◈	Rates not provided	218
20 p. 206	**Old Monterey Inn**	◈◈◈◈	$199-$499 SAVE	223
21 p. 206	**Hotel Abrego** (See ad p. 220.)	◈◈◈	$119-$600 SAVE	219
22 p. 206	**BEST WESTERN PLUS Monterey Inn**	◈◈◈	$89-$349 SAVE	218
23 p. 206	**Days Inn-Downtown Monterey/San Carlos Inn**	◈◈	$55-$259 SAVE	219
24 p. 206	**El Dorado Inn**	◈◈	$49-$199 SAVE	219
25 p. 206	**El Adobe Inn**	◈◈	$49-$299 SAVE	219
26 p. 206	Vagabond Inn - Monterey	◈◈	$59-$399	225
27 p. 206	**Clarion Hotel**	◈◈◈	$60-$400 SAVE	218
28 p. 206	**Quality Inn**	◈◈◈	$60-$400 SAVE	223
29 p. 206	**BEST WESTERN Park Crest Inn**	◈◈◈	$59-$199 SAVE	217
30 p. 206	**Americas Best Value Inn Stage Coach Lodge**	◈◈	$49-$399 SAVE	217
31 p. 206	**Monterey Fireside Lodge**	◈◈	$69-$599 SAVE	221
32 p. 206	Ramada Limited-Carmel Hill-Monterey	◈◈	$63-$600	223
33 p. 206	**Rodeway Inn Monterey**	◈◈	$46-$86 SAVE	224
34 p. 206	Hilton Garden Inn-Monterey	◈◈◈	$119-$329	219
35 p. 206	**BEST WESTERN PLUS De Anza Inn**	◈◈◈	$90-$286 SAVE	218
36 p. 206	**Monterey Bay Travelodge**	◈◈	$89-$499 SAVE	221

MONTEREY (cont'd)

Map Page	Hotels (cont'd)	Diamond Rated	Rate Range	Page
37 p. 206	**Econo Lodge Monterey Fairground**	◆◆	$46-$86 [SAVE]	219
38 p. 206	**Comfort Inn-Monterey Bay**	◆◆	$59-$189 [SAVE]	218
39 p. 206	**Lone Oak Lodge**	◆◆	$60-$124 [SAVE]	220
40 p. 206	Ramada Limited-Monterey	◆◆	$63-$600	224
41 p. 206	**El Castell Motel**	◆◆	Rates not provided [SAVE]	219
42 p. 206	**Comfort Inn-Monterey by the Sea**	◆◆	$65-$189 [SAVE]	218
43 p. 206	**BEST WESTERN Ramona Inn**	◆◆	$59-$300 [SAVE]	218
44 p. 206	**Hyatt Regency Monterey Hotel & Spa**	◆◆◆	$99-$450 [SAVE]	220
45 p. 206	**Padre Oaks**	◆◆	$39-$299 [SAVE]	223
46 p. 206	**Days Inn-Monterey**	◆◆	$55-$259 [SAVE]	219
47 p. 206	Super 8	◆◆	$55-$1050	224
48 p. 206	Mariposa Inn & Suites	◆◆◆	Rates not provided	220
49 p. 206	**Bay Park Hotel** (See ad p. 217.)	◆◆◆	$99-$350 [SAVE]	217
50 p. 206	**Comfort Inn Monterey Peninsula Airport**	◆◆◆	Rates not provided [SAVE]	218

Map Page	Restaurants	Diamond Rated	Cuisine	Price Range	Page
① p. 206	The C Restaurant + Bar	◆◆◆	California	$14-$45	225
② p. 206	**Whaling Station Prime Steaks & Seafood**	◆◆◆	Steak	$20-$55	227
③ p. 206	**The Fish Hopper**	◆◆	Seafood	$10-$33	225
④ p. 206	**Sardine Factory**	◆◆◆◆	Seafood	$22-$70	226
⑤ p. 206	Louie Linguini's	◆◆	Seafood	$10-$29	226
⑥ p. 206	**Paradiso Trattoria**	◆◆◆	Italian	$10-$35	226
⑦ p. 206	Captain Bullwacker's Restaurant & Patio Pub	◆◆	American	$9-$27	225
⑧ p. 206	Jose's Mexican Restaurant	◆◆	Mexican	$7-$17	226
⑨ p. 206	Loose Noodle Pasta House	◆◆◆	Italian	$8-$20	226
⑩ p. 206	Chart House	◆◆◆	Seafood	$20-$47 [SAVE]	225
⑪ p. 206	The Duck Club	◆◆◆◆	American	$20-$40	225
⑫ p. 206	**Schooners Coastal Kitchen & Bar**	◆◆◆	American	$12-$38	226
⑬ p. 206	Isabella's on the Wharf	◆◆◆	Seafood	$15-$30	225
⑭ p. 206	Abalonetti Seafood	◆◆	Seafood	$13-$20	225
⑮ p. 206	**Cafe Fina**	◆◆◆	Seafood	$12-$30	225
⑯ p. 206	**Domenico's on The Wharf**	◆◆◆	Seafood	$11-$35	225
⑰ p. 206	Gilbert's Red Snapper Restaurant & Bar	◆◆	Seafood	$14-$30	225
⑱ p. 206	Cafe Beach	◆◆	American	$10-$26	225
⑲ p. 206	Sandbar & Grill	◆◆	Seafood	$10-$25	226
⑳ p. 206	Montrio Bistro	◆◆◆	Regional California	$17-$33	226
㉑ p. 206	**Rosine's**	◆	American	$9-$20	226
㉒ p. 206	Lallapalooza Restaurant	◆◆◆	American	$12-$44	226
㉓ p. 206	El Palomar	◆◆	Mexican	$10-$25	225

Map Page	Restaurants (cont'd)	Diamond Rated	Cuisine	Price Range	Page
24 p. 206	Pacific Grille	◆◆	American	$10-$27	226
25 p. 206	Caruso's Corner Restaurant	◆◆	Italian	$10-$30	225
26 p. 206	P.F. Chang's China Bistro	◆◆◆	Chinese	$10-$20	226
27 p. 206	Lalla Grill	◆◆◆	California	$8-$20	226

PACIFIC GROVE

Map Page	Hotels	Diamond Rated	Rate Range	Page
53 p. 206	Lighthouse Lodge & Cottages	◆◆◆	$99-$895	268
54 p. 206	Bide-A-Wee Inn & Cottages	◆◆	$79-$429 SAVE	267
55 p. 206	Monarch Resort	◆◆	$60-$300 SAVE	268
56 p. 206	Sea Breeze Inn and Cottages	◆◆◆	$79-$499	268
57 p. 206	Sea Breeze Lodge	◆◆	$79-$499	268
58 p. 206	Butterfly Grove Inn	◆◆	$79-$359 SAVE	267
59 p. 206	Borg's Ocean Front Motel	◆	$69-$185 SAVE	267
60 p. 206	Lovers Point Inn (See ad p. 221.)	◆◆	$89-$499 SAVE	268
61 p. 206	Pacific Gardens Inn	◆◆◆	$99-$203	268
62 p. 206	Rosedale Inn	◆◆◆	Rates not provided SAVE	268
63 p. 206	Deer Haven Inn	◆◆	$59-$249	267
64 p. 206	Howard Johnson Inn & Suites	◆◆	$100-$400 SAVE	268
65 p. 206	Asilomar Conference Grounds	◆◆	$145-$285 SAVE	267
66 p. 206	The Centrella Bed & Breakfast Inn	◆◆◆	$119-$299	267
67 p. 206	Gosby House Inn	◆◆◆	$135-$310	268
68 p. 206	Green Gables Inn	◆◆◆	$155-$325	268
69 p. 206	Old St. Angela Inn	◆◆◆	$149-$285	268
70 p. 206	Martine Inn	◆◆◆	$199-$499	268

Map Page	Restaurants	Diamond Rated	Cuisine	Price Range	Page
30 p. 206	Passionfish	◆◆◆	California	$16-$28	269
31 p. 206	Fandango	◆◆◆	Mediterranean	$10-$36	268
32 p. 206	Fish Wife	◆◆◆	Seafood	$10-$20	269
33 p. 206	Tillie Gort's	◆◆	Vegetarian	$8-$14	269
34 p. 206	First Awakenings	◆◆	American	$6-$11	268

SEASIDE

Map Page	Hotels	Diamond Rated	Rate Range	Page
73 p. 206	Seaside Inn	◆◆	$59-$249 SAVE	513
74 p. 206	Sandcastle Inn	◆◆	$59-$299 SAVE	512
75 p. 206	Thunderbird Motel	◆◆	$39-$249 SAVE	513
76 p. 206	Magic Carpet Lodge	◆◆	$50-$199 SAVE	512
77 p. 206	Holiday Inn Express at Monterey Bay	◆◆◆	$119-$299 SAVE	512
78 p. 206	Embassy Suites Hotel & Conference Center	◆◆◆	$159-$459	512

Map Page	Restaurant	Diamond Rated	Cuisine	Price Range	Page
37 p. 206	Pacifica Cafe	◆◆	American	$10-$30	513

PEBBLE BEACH

Map Page	Hotels	Diamond Rated	Rate Range	Page
81 p. 206	The Inn at Spanish Bay	◆◆◆◆	Rates not provided	274
82 p. 206	Casa Palmero	◆◆◆◆	Rates not provided	274
83 p. 206	The Lodge at Pebble Beach	◆◆◆◆	Rates not provided	274

Map Page	Restaurants	Diamond Rated	Cuisine	Price Range	Page
40 p. 206	Roy's	◆◆◆	Pacific Rim	$15-$35	274
41 p. 206	Peppoli at Pebble Beach	◆◆◆	Italian	$20-$44	274
42 p. 206	Stillwater Bar and Grill	◆◆◆	Regional American	$15-$65	274

CARMEL-BY-THE-SEA

Map Page	Hotels	Diamond Rated	Rate Range	Page
86 p. 206	Carmel Resort Inn	◆◆	$79-$289	70
87 p. 206	Carmel Country Inn	◆◆◆	$275-$425	69
88 p. 206	Hofsas House *(See ad p. 71.)*	◆◆	$90-$400 SAVE	71
89 p. 206	Horizon Inn & Ocean View Lodge	◆◆◆	$106-$390 SAVE	72
90 p. 206	Svendsgaard's	◆◆◆	$149-$259 SAVE	72
91 p. 206	Dolphin Inn	◆◆◆	$189-$269 SAVE	71
92 p. 206	Carmel Fireplace Inn Bed & Breakfast	◆◆◆	Rates not provided SAVE	69
93 p. 206	Candle Light Inn	◆◆	$189-$279 SAVE	69
94 p. 206	Briarwood Inn	◆◆◆	Rates not provided SAVE	69
95 p. 206	Carmel Garden Court	◆◆◆	$150-$245	69
96 p. 206	BEST WESTERN Carmel's Town House Lodge	◆◆◆	$89-$499 SAVE	69
97 p. 206	Carmel Lodge	◆◆◆	Rates not provided SAVE	69
98 p. 206	Carmel Oaks Inn & Suites Clarion Collection	◆◆◆	$99-$499 SAVE	70
99 p. 206	Carmel Inn & Suites	◆◆◆	$90-$500 SAVE	69
100 p. 206	San Antonio House Inn	◆◆	$180-$245	72
101 p. 206	BEST WESTERN PLUS Carmel Bay View Inn	◆◆◆	$89-$279 SAVE	69
102 p. 206	Normandy Inn	◆◆◆	$98-$399 SAVE	72
103 p. 206	Lobos Lodge	◆◆◆	$125-$195	72
104 p. 206	Pine Inn *(See ad p. 72.)*	◆◆◆	$179-$359	72
105 p. 206	Carmel Village Inn	◆◆	$109-$650 SAVE	70
106 p. 206	Carmel-By-The-Sea - Comfort Inn	◆◆◆	$90-$300 SAVE	69
107 p. 206	Green Lantern Inn Bed & Breakfast	◆◆	$99-$289	71
108 p. 206	Cypress Inn	◆◆◆	Rates not provided	71
109 p. 206	Wayside Inn	◆◆◆	$229-$399 SAVE	74
110 p. 206	Coachman's Inn *(See ad p. 70.)*	◆◆◆	$145-$435 SAVE	71
111 p. 206	Adobe Inn	◆◆◆	$125-$995 SAVE	69
112 p. 206	Carriage House Inn	◆◆◆	$309-$419 SAVE	70
113 p. 206	The Cobblestone Inn	◆◆◆	$150-$600 SAVE	71
114 p. 206	Colonial Terrace Inn	◆◆◆	$99-$459 SAVE	71

CARMEL-BY-THE-SEA (cont'd)

Map Page	Hotels (cont'd)	Diamond Rated	Rate Range	Page
115 p. 206	Carmel Mission Inn	◆◆◆	$99-$529	70
116 p. 206	**Hyatt Carmel Highlands**	◆◆◆◆	$319-$1139 [SAVE]	72
117 p. 206	**Tickle Pink Inn** (See ad p. 73.)	◆◆◆◆	$231-$599 [SAVE]	74

Map Page	Restaurants	Diamond Rated	Cuisine	Price Range	Page
45 p. 206	Casanova	◆◆◆	French	$14-$52	74
46 p. 206	The French Poodle Restaurant	◆◆◆◆	French	$20-$36	74
47 p. 206	**Hog's Breath Inn Carmel**	◆	American	$15-$30	74
48 p. 206	Katy's Place	◆	American	$9-$20	74
49 p. 206	Il Fornaio (See ad p. 72.)	◆◆	Italian	$9-$36	74
50 p. 206	Aubergine at L'Auberge	◆◆◆◆	European	$89-$125	74
51 p. 206	Anton & Michel	◆◆◆	Continental	$14-$36	74
52 p. 206	From Scratch Restaurant	◆◆	American	$8-$13	74
53 p. 206	Lugano Swiss Bistro	◆◆	German	$9-$40	74
54 p. 206	Rio Grill	◆◆◆	California	$10-$37	75
55 p. 206	China Delight	◆◆	Chinese	$7-$25	74
56 p. 206	Pacific's Edge	◆◆◆◆	Regional American	$24-$49	74
57 p. 206	California Market	◆◆◆	California	$12-$20	74

CARMEL VALLEY

Map Page	Hotels	Diamond Rated	Rate Range	Page
120 p. 206	Carmel Valley Ranch	◆◆◆◆	$300-$1200	75
121 p. 206	**Bernardus Lodge**	◆◆◆◆	$315-$2030 [SAVE]	75
122 p. 206	Hidden Valley Inn-Country Garden Inns	◆◆	Rates not provided	75
123 p. 206	Acacia Lodge-Country Garden Inns	◆◆	Rates not provided	75

Map Page	Restaurants	Diamond Rated	Cuisine	Price Range	Page
60 p. 206	Wicket's Bistro	◆◆◆	Regional California	$15-$35	75
61 p. 206	Will's Fargo Restaurant	◆◆	Steak	$20-$40	75

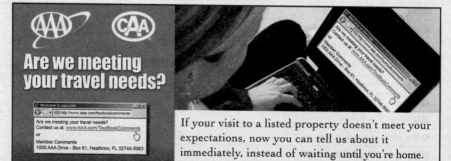

MONTEREY (G-3) pop. 27,810, elev. 60'

The capital of Alta California under the Spanish, Mexican and American flags, Monterey lies on the Monterey Peninsula and ranges in altitude from sea level to 360 feet. The peninsula is a popular year-round playground boasting a dozen public and resort golf courses. South of Monterey SR 1 winds through redwood forests and comes perilously close to the cliff edges of the spectacular Big Sur coast.

On Cannery Row, the colorfully boisterous locale of John Steinbeck's novels "Cannery Row" and "Sweet Thursday," trendy art galleries, boutiques and restaurants long ago replaced sardine canneries. Similarly, whale-watching cruises, handicraft shops and the Wharf Theater at another touristy hangout, Fisherman's Wharf, have taken the place of Monterey's early 20th-century commercial fishing industry.

Tourists and locals alike flock to the Old Monterey Farmers Market, which sets up along three blocks of Alvarado Street between Del Monte Avenue and Pearl Street. The market is a cornucopia of organic fruit and vegetable stands featuring the bounty of agricultural areas like Watsonville and the Salinas and Sacramento valleys. Baker's Alley features luscious pastries, cookies, muffins and European breads, and prepared food vendors whip up everything from Korean barbecue to naan curry wraps. Arts and crafts vendors sell trinkets and treasures from all over the world. Local musicians add a lively touch to what is a real community event. The market is open Tuesdays 4-8 p.m. from mid-May through August, 4-7 the rest of the year; phone (831) 655-2607.

The Monterey Presidio, a block from the Wharf Theater on Pacific Street, was founded in 1770 by Capt. Gaspar de Portolá, assisted by fathers Junípero Serra and Juan Crespi. The presidio is now the site of the Defense Language Institute Foreign Language Center, which trains military interpreters for the Department of Defense. Lower Presidio Historic Park, off Lighthouse Avenue below the Sloat Monument, is open to the public.

Vintage race and sports cars are the focus of the Rolex Monterey Motorsports Reunion, part of an entire August weekend devoted to classic cars. Held at the Mazda Raceway Laguna Seca, the event draws close to 400 participants competing in 14 races. A highlight of the event is the paddock area, where visitors can speak with the drivers and get an up-close look at the cars.

Music lovers flock to Monterey the third weekend in September for the Monterey Jazz Festival, where masters and newcomers share the stage for 3 days of performances. Dizzy Gillespie and Billie Holiday were among the performers at the first festival in 1958, and it consistently draws the world's best jazz musicians. The festival takes place at the Monterey County Fairgrounds, 2000 Fairground Rd.; for

schedule and ticket information phone (831) 373-3366 or (888) 248-6499.

Monterey County Convention and Visitors Bureau: 401 Camino El Estero, Monterey, CA 93940. **Phone:** (888) 221-1010.

Self-guiding tours: Maps of the 2-mile Monterey Path of History walking tour, which includes gardens, adobe buildings and historic sites, are available from the visitor center at Camino el Estero (between Del Monte Avenue and Fremont Street) and at Monterey State Historic Park *(see attraction listing p. 215).*

Shopping areas: About 85 shops and restaurants, including anchor store Macy's, comprise the open-air Del Monte Center at SR 1 and Munras Avenue.

 17-MILE DRIVE—see Pebble Beach p. 273.

COLTON HALL MUSEUM, in the civic center on Pacific St. facing Friendly Plaza, is in the building where the first Constitution of California was written in 1849. The building is now a museum dedicated to that constitutional convention. Adjoining Colton Hall, which was completed in 1849, is the Old Monterey Jail, built in 1854. **Time:** Allow 30 minutes minimum. **Hours:** Daily 10-4. Closed Jan. 1, Thanksgiving and Christmas. **Cost:** Donations. **Phone:** (831) 646-5640.

DENNIS THE MENACE PLAYGROUND is in the park on Lake El Estero. Hank Ketcham, creator of the cartoon strip "Dennis the Menace," aided in its development. The playground contains climbing structures, slides, a balancing bridge, a maze, a railroad switch engine and a lion-shaped drinking fountain. **Hours:** Daily 10-dusk, June-Aug.; Wed.-Mon. 10-dusk, rest of year. **Cost:** Free. **Phone:** (831) 646-3866.

MONTEREY BAY AQUARIUM is at 886 Cannery Row. This acclaimed facility houses more than 35,000 animals and plants representing 550 species of marine life. Nearly 200 galleries and exhibits display such marine creatures as jellyfish, sunfish, mahi-mahi, tuna, sharks and sea turtles. The Open Sea exhibit explores the mysteries of the open ocean.

The Ocean's Edge galleries introduce visitors to the central California coast's varied shoreline habitats. The impressive features include a three-story living kelp forest, octopuses, a walk-through aviary inhabited by shore birds, touch pools, rockfish, sand dollars, wharf pilings and an indoor/outdoor coastal stream.

Splash Zone galleries depict a coral reef and the reef and rocky shore habitats of almost 60 species of marine life, including blackfooted penguins. The Secret Lives of Seahorses special exhibition presents more than 15 varieties of these elusive fishes— yes, they're fishes—and provides information about

(See map & index p. 206.)

their vulnerable habitats and surprising life cycle (males, not females, get pregnant).

A new special exhibition, The Jellies Experience, introduces visitors to these free-swimming marine animals found in every one of the world's oceans. Characterized by an umbrella-shaped, pulsating gelatinous bell and long, trailing tentacles, they have an otherworldly beauty. Elsewhere in the aquarium are life-size models of whales and other marine animals as well as historical displays. Feeding demonstrations take place daily at the sea otter, kelp forest and penguin exhibits.

Aquarium Adventures programs, which require an additional fee, include a surface SCUBA experience for kids, day and sunset sailing expeditions, behind-the-scenes tours and family programs.

Note: The sea otter exhibit is closed for renovations and is scheduled to reopen in spring 2013. **Time:** Allow 3 hours minimum. **Hours:** Mon.-Fri. 9:30-6, Sat.-Sun. 9:30-8, Memorial Day weekend-Labor Day and holidays; daily 10-5, rest of year. Closed Christmas. **Cost:** $34.95; $31.95 (ages 65+ and college students with ID); $21.95 (ages 3-12 and the physically impaired). Rates are seasonal and can vary; phone ahead to confirm. **Phone:** (831) 648-4800, or (866) 963-9645 for advance tickets. *(See ad p. 362, this page.)* 🍴

MONTEREY BAY WHALE WATCH departs from 84 Fisherman's Wharf. A marine biologist/naturalist is on board to describe the behavior of various marine animals seen on the trip. Depending on the season, visitors have the opportunity to spot gray, humpback, blue and killer whales as well as dolphins, porpoises, sea otters, seals, sea lions and sea birds.

Visitors are advised to dress warmly and bring sunscreen. Photography is permitted. Allow a half-day minimum. **Hours:** Four- to 5-hour morning trips depart daily at 9, mid-Apr. to mid-Dec. Three- to 4-hour afternoon trips depart daily at 2, mid-Apr. through Nov. 30; Sat.-Sun. at 2, Dec. 1 to mid-Dec. Three-hour winter and spring trips depart daily at 10 and 1:30 (also some weekends and holidays at 7 a.m.), mid-Dec. to mid.-Apr. Closed Thanksgiving and Christmas. Phone ahead to confirm schedule.

Cost: Four- to 5-hour morning trips $49; $39 (ages 4-12). Three- to 4-hour afternoon trips $41; $29 (ages 4-12). Three-hour winter and spring trips $40; $27 (ages 4-12). Guests should arrive 30 minutes prior to departure. Reservations are required. **Phone:** (831) 375-4658.

SAVE **MONTEREY MOVIE TOURS** departs from in front of the Monterey Conference Center downtown at One Portola Plaza; pickups also are made at some local lodgings. The 3-hour scenic motor-coach tour of the Monterey Peninsula showcases the history and beauty of the area and is augmented by showing scenes from movies such as

▼ See AAA listing p. 213 ▼

(See map & index p. 206.)

"Play Misty for Me," "Star Trek IV-The Voyage Home," "A Summer Place" and "National Velvet" at the locations where they were filmed.

The guide provides narration about the filming passengers view the scenes on overhead monitors. The tour includes three photo stops along nearby 17-Mile Drive in Pebble Beach. **Time:** Allow 3 hours minimum. **Hours:** Tours depart daily at 1 (boarding begins at 12:30). Closed Thanksgiving and Christmas. **Cost:** $55; $50 (ages 65+); $35 (ages 3-15). Reservations are required. **Phone:** (831) 372-6278 or (800) 343-6437.

MONTEREY MUSEUM OF ART AT LA MIRADA is at 720 Via Mirada (off Fremont St.). The permanent collection includes works by Pablo Picasso, Ansel Adams and Andy Warhol as well as contemporary emerging artists. Modern galleries complement the Old World elegance of this historic former estate, where international celebrities once congregated. Rose and rhododendron gardens are on the grounds.

Hours: Wed.-Sat. 11-5, Sun. 1-4. Closed major holidays. **Cost:** $10; $5 (military and students with ID); free (ages 0-12). Includes admission to Monterey Museum of Art at Pacific Street. **Phone:** (831) 372-3689.

MONTEREY MUSEUM OF ART AT PACIFIC STREET, 559 Pacific St., presents permanent and changing exhibitions of early California and American paintings, photography, prints and contemporary work of the region. Works by Ansel Adams, Armin Hansen and Edward Weston often can be seen.

Time: Allow 1 hour minimum. **Hours:** Wed.-Sat. 11-5, Sun. 1-4. Closed major holidays. **Cost:** $10; $5 (military and students with ID); free (ages 0-12). Includes admission to Monterey Museum of Art at La Mirada. **Phone:** (831) 372-5477.

MONTEREY STATE HISTORIC PARK, 20 Custom House Plaza, is a 7-acre site that preserves the historical and architectural heritage of old Monterey. Nearby is the original 1602 landing site of Sebastián Vizcaíno and—167 years later— Father Junípero Serra.

Monterey served as California's capital under Spanish and Mexican rule and was where the U.S. flag was first officially raised in the state on July 7, 1846. The park's buildings and sites, many restored and with period furnishings, are scattered throughout the city.

Guided 45-minute walking tours, departing from the Pacific House Museum on Custom House Plaza, allow visitors to see the park and buildings and residences from early California history. Tours of some of the individual historic houses also are available on a first-come, first-served basis *(see attraction listings)*. Gardens, some with fountains or arbors, can be seen on self-guiding and guided tours.

Hours: Gardens open daily 9-5, May-Sept.; 10-4, rest of year. Walking tours are given Fri.-Sun. at 10:30, noon and 2. Tour times are subject to change; phone ahead to confirm. Closed Jan. 1, Thanksgiving and Christmas. **Cost:** Park and gardens free. Guided tours $5; free (ages 0-12). **Phone:** (831) 649-7118.

Casa Soberanes and Garden, jct. Pacific St. and Del Monte Ave., was built in 1842 and occupied by members of the Soberanes family from 1860 to 1922. Known for its blue entrance gate and garden walkways, this well-preserved adobe house contains period antiques from New England and China as well as Mexican folk art. **Hours:** Open for private tours by appointment only. **Phone:** (831) 649-7118.

Cooper-Molera Adobe and Garden, jct. Polk and Alvarado sts. and Munras Ave., is the restored Victorian home of a Yankee sea captain, rancher and adventurer who married the sister of Gen. Mariano Vallejo. Also on the grounds are a barn, vegetable and fruit gardens, farm animals and a history display. **Hours:** Guided 45-minute tours are given Fri.-Sun. at 10:30 and 1:30 on a first-come, first-served basis. Phone ahead to confirm schedule. **Cost:** Tour $5; free (ages 0-6). **Phone:** (831) 649-7118.

Custom House, on Custom House Plaza at Fisherman's Wharf, is the oldest standing government building in California; its north section was constructed around 1827. When Commodore John Drake Sloat raised the American flag over the building in 1846, approximately 600,000 square miles became part of the United States. Inside are displays of replica trade goods from the 1840s.

A cactus garden is on the grounds, which also offer scenic views of Monterey harbor. **Hours:** Fri.-Sun. 10-4. Phone ahead to confirm schedule. **Cost:** $3 (includes Pacific House Museum). **Phone:** (831) 649-7118.

First Brick House is adjacent to the Old Whaling Station. The structure, built by settler Gallant Dickenson in 1847, marks one of the first uses in California of fired clay bricks for building purposes; the new material was stronger, more durable and more water-repellent than traditional sun-dried mud bricks. Dickenson left for the Sierra foothills in search gold rush riches before finishing his home. Inside are displays about Monterey history. **Hours:** Fri.-Sun. 10-4. **Cost:** Free. **Phone:** (831) 649-7118.

First Theatre and Garden, Pacific and Scott sts., once was a lodging house for sailors as well as the first venue in Monterey to charge admission for a theatrical performance. The 1846 building contains early California historical artifacts. Succulents and cypress trees grace the garden.

Note: The theater is closed while undergoing renovations; phone ahead for information regarding a possible reopening. The garden remains open. **Hours:** Garden daily 9-5, May-Sept.; 10-4, rest of year. Phone ahead to confirm schedule. **Phone:** (831) 649-7118.

(See map & index p. 206.)

Larkin House and Garden is at Pacific and Jefferson sts. The house's combination of Mexican Colonial and New England architectural features reflects the New England origins of its builder, merchant Thomas Oliver Larkin. The 1835 two-story adobe house served as the American consulate 1843-46. The rooms contain early 19th-century antiques from many parts of the world. The garden was planted by Larkin's granddaughter. Tours include the adjacent Sherman Quarters.

Hours: Guided 45-minute tours are given Fri.-Sun. at noon and 3 on a first-come, first-served basis. Phone ahead to confirm schedule. **Cost:** Tour $5; free (ages 0-6). **Phone:** (831) 649-7118.

The Old Whaling Station is in Heritage Harbour, adjacent to the pedestrian bridge. This adobe was built in 1847 by Scottish adventurer David Wight for his family, and was later the headquarters of the Old Monterey Whaling Co. Whale vertebrae were used to create the pathway in front of the building, one of only a few such pathways in the U.S. A garden is at the rear of the property. **Hours:** Tues.-Fri. 10-2. Garden open daily. Phone ahead to confirm schedule. **Phone:** (831) 375-5356.

Pacific House Museum is on Custom House Plaza. The 1847 adobe building, built as a U.S. Army storage facility, is a museum with interactive displays depicting the history of Monterey during its days as the capital of Spanish and Mexican California. On the second floor, the Museum of the American Indian features Native American baskets and pottery. Behind the building is an attractive courtyard called the Memory Garden. **Hours:** Fri.-Sun. 10-4. Phone ahead to confirm schedule. **Cost:** $3 (includes Custom House). **Phone:** (831) 649-7118.

Stevenson House-French Hotel is at 530 Houston St. Robert Louis Stevenson spent the fall of 1879 in this two-story former rooming house, then known as the French Hotel. Several rooms in the 19th-century adobe house contain Stevenson's personal belongings. **Hours:** House open Sat. (also fourth Sun. of the month) 1-4. Phone ahead to confirm schedule. **Cost:** Free. **Phone:** (831) 649-7118.

MUSEUM OF MONTEREY is at 5 Custom House Plaza in Stanton Center. Among other collections, it displays artifacts amassed by seaman Allen Knight, who built a stone ship next to his home as a repository for his treasures. A nearly 10,000-pound Fresnel lens from Point Sur Lighthouse illuminates the museum's historical exhibits, which include navigational instruments, ship models, photos and maritime charts. There also are displays of California art, costumes and textiles, and decorative arts.

Time: Allow 1 hour minimum. **Hours:** Tues.-Sat. 10-5 (also first Tues. of the month 5-7), Sun. noon-5. Closed Jan. 1, Thanksgiving and Christmas. **Cost:** $10; $5 (ages 55+ and students and military with ID); free (first Tues. of the month 3-7). **Phone:** (831) 372-2608.

MY MUSEUM is at 425 Washington St., just e. of Fisherman's Wharf. It offers a variety of hands-on exhibits for children. Young visitors can create sandcastles with special "sandcastle" blocks at the MY Day at the Beach exhibit (3 and under only); strengthen hand-eye coordination at MY Go-Fore Golf; or help a nurse administer a shot in MY Hospital. They also can visit MY Healthy Farm or dress up and pretend at MY Theater.

Time: Allow 1 hour minimum. **Hours:** Tues.-Sat. 10-5, Sun. noon-5. Closed major holidays. **Cost:** $7; free (ages 0-2). **Phone:** (831) 649-6444.

 NATIONAL STEINBECK CENTER—see attraction listing in Salinas p. 337.

PRESIDIO MUSEUM is in Lower Presidio Historic Park on Corporal Ewing Rd., Bldg. 113 (just off Artillery St.). It traces the history of this site from its habitation by Native Americans through a rich military past that began with the mission and presidio that founded Monterey in 1770. Exhibits depict such events as a pirate attack on Monterey in 1818, as well as the presidio's development from the first military base in California to a U.S. Army training base.

Several monuments are within walking distance, including the Sloat Monument, honoring the commander of the American forces that captured Monterey in 1846. **Time:** Allow 30 minutes minimum. **Hours:** Thurs.-Sat. 10-4, Sun. 1-4, Mon. 10-1. Closed Jan. 1, Thanksgiving and Christmas. **Cost:** Free. **Phone:** (831) 646-3456.

SAN CARLOS CATHEDRAL, at 500 Church St., also is known as Royal Presidio Chapel. Founded in 1770 to be the mission church of the port, San Carlos Cathedral became the church for the Spanish colonists and soldiers instead, as the mission moved to Carmel the following year. The present church has been in continuous use since 1795. A museum has historical and church-related items.

Tours: Guided tours are available. **Hours:** Cathedral open Mon.-Sat. 7-4, Sun. 7 until after the last mass. Museum open Wed. 10-noon, Fri. 10-3, Sat. 10-2, Sun. 1-3 (also second and fourth Mon. of the month 10-noon and 1:15-3:15). Phone ahead to confirm schedule. **Cost:** Donations. **Phone:** (831) 373-2628.

STEINBECK'S SPIRIT OF MONTEREY WAX MUSEUM, 700 Cannery Row in the Monterey Cannery Building, displays more than 100 wax figures from Monterey's turbulent history. **Time:** Allow 30 minutes minimum. **Hours:** Daily 9-9. **Cost:** $8.95; $7.95 (ages 13-17); $6.95 (ages 60+); $5.95 (ages 6-12). **Phone:** (831) 655-7743.

(See map & index p. 206.)

RECREATIONAL ACTIVITIES

Kayaking

- **Monterey Bay Kayaks** is at 693 Del Monte Ave. **Hours:** Daily 9-7, Memorial Day weekend-Labor Day weekend; 9-5, rest of year. Closed Thanksgiving and Christmas. Phone ahead to confirm schedule. **Phone:** (831) 373-5357 or (800) 649-5357.

AMERICAS BEST VALUE INN STAGE COACH LODGE

(831)373-3632

Motel
$49-$399

Address: 1111 10th St 93940 **Location:** SR 1 exit Aguajito Rd or Monterey, just w. **Facility:** 25 units. 2 stories (no elevator), exterior corridors. **Terms:** 3 day cancellation notice-fee imposed. **Amenities:** safes. **Pool(s):** outdoor. **Guest Services:** coin laundry. **Free Special Amenities: continental breakfast and high-speed Internet.**

BAY PARK HOTEL

(831)649-1020

Hotel
$99-$350

Address: 1425 Munras Ave 93940 **Location:** SR 1 exit Soledad Dr/Munras Ave, just w. Across from Del Monte Shopping Center. **Facility:** 80 units. 3 stories, interior corridors. **Terms:** cancellation fee imposed. **Amenities:** high-speed Internet. **Pool(s):** outdoor. **Activities:** whirlpool, exercise room. **Guest Services:** valet laundry. **Free Special Amenities: early check-in/late check-out and high-speed Internet.** *(See ad this page.)*

BEST WESTERN PARK CREST INN

(831)372-4576

Hotel
$59-$199

AAA Benefit: Members save up to 20%, plus 10% bonus points with Best Western Rewards®.

Address: 1100 Munras Ave 93940 **Location:** SR 1 exit Soledad Dr/Munras Ave, 0.5 mi w. **Facility:** 53 units. 2 stories (no elevator), exterior corridors. **Terms:** 3 day cancellation notice-fee imposed. **Pool(s):** outdoor. **Activities:** whirlpool. **Free Special Amenities: expanded continental breakfast and high-speed Internet.**

BEST WESTERN PLUS BEACH RESORT MONTEREY

831/394-3321

Hotel
Rates not provided

AAA Benefit: Members save up to 20%, plus 10% bonus points with Best Western Rewards®.

Address: 2600 Sand Dunes Dr 93940 **Location:** Oceanfront. SR 1 exit Del Rey Oaks, just w. **Facility:** 196 units. 4 stories, exterior corridors. **Parking:** on-site (fee). **Terms:** check-in 4 pm. **Amenities:** safes. **Dining:** Cafe Beach, see separate listing, entertainment. **Pool(s):** outdoor. **Activities:** whirlpool, exercise room. **Guest Services:** valet laundry. **Free Special Amenities: local telephone calls and high-speed Internet.**

AAA/CAA travel information:

Available in print, online

and on the go!

▼ *See AAA listing this page* ▼

- Free Wi-Fi & Parking
- 32" LCD TV / DVD player
- Restaurant & Lounge
- Fitness & Business Center
- Heated Pool & Spa
- Pet Friendly Hotel

Bay Park Hotel

Reservations 1-800-338-3564

1425 Munras Ave. Monterey, CA 93940 | www.bayparkhotel.com

Give the gift of security, value and peace of mind: Gift Membership

(See map & index p. 206.)

BEST WESTERN PLUS DE ANZA INN
(831)646-8300

Hotel
$90-$286

AAA Benefit: Members save up to 20%, plus 10% bonus points with Best Western Rewards®.

Address: 2141 N Fremont St 93940 **Location:** SR 1 exit Casa Verde Way or Fremont St, 0.4 mi e. **Facility:** 43 units, some two bedrooms. 3 stories, interior corridors. **Terms:** 2-4 night minimum stay - seasonal and/or weekends. **Amenities:** safes. **Pool(s):** outdoor. **Activities:** whirlpool. **Guest Services:** valet laundry. **Free Special Amenities:** local telephone calls and high-speed Internet.

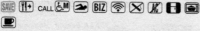

BEST WESTERN PLUS MONTEREY INN
(831)373-5345

Hotel
$89-$349

AAA Benefit: Members save up to 20%, plus 10% bonus points with Best Western Rewards®.

Address: 825 Abrego St 93940 **Location:** SR 1 exit Soledad Dr/Munras Ave, 0.7 mi w. **Facility:** 80 units, some two bedrooms. 3 stories, interior corridors. **Terms:** 2 night minimum stay - seasonal and/or weekends. **Amenities:** high-speed Internet. **Pool(s):** outdoor. **Activities:** whirlpool. **Guest Services:** valet laundry. **Free Special Amenities:** full breakfast and high-speed Internet.

BEST WESTERN PLUS VICTORIAN INN
(831)373-8000

Hotel
$119-$700

AAA Benefit: Members save up to 20%, plus 10% bonus points with Best Western Rewards®.

Address: 487 Foam St 93940 **Location:** SR 1 exit Monterey, 3.4 mi w. **Facility:** 70 units. 3 stories, interior/exterior corridors. **Parking:** on-site (fee). **Terms:** check-in 4 pm, 2-4 night minimum stay - seasonal and/or weekends, 3 day cancellation notice-fee imposed, resort fee. **Amenities:** safes. **Activities:** whirlpool. **Guest Services:** valet laundry. **Free Special Amenities:** local telephone calls and high-speed Internet.

BEST WESTERN RAMONA INN
(831)373-2445

Motel
$59-$300

AAA Benefit: Members save up to 20%, plus 10% bonus points with Best Western Rewards®.

Address: 2332 Fremont St 93940 **Location:** SR 1 exit Del Rey Oaks or Fremont St, 0.7 mi e. **Facility:** 34 units. 2 stories (no elevator), exterior corridors. **Terms:** 2 night minimum stay - seasonal. **Free Special Amenities:** local telephone calls and high-speed Internet.

CANNERY ROW INN
(831)649-8580

Hotel
$89-$699

Address: 200 Foam St 93940 **Location:** SR 1 exit Monterey, 3 mi w. Located in Cannery Row area. **Facility:** 32 units, some two bedrooms. 3 stories, interior corridors. **Terms:** 2 night minimum stay - seasonal, 3 day cancellation notice-fee imposed, resort fee. **Free Special Amenities:** expanded continental breakfast and high-speed Internet.

CASA MUNRAS, A LARKSPUR COLLECTION HOTEL
831)375-2411

Hotel. Rates not provided. **Address:** 700 Munras Ave 93940 **Location:** SR 1 exit Soledad Dr/Munras Ave, 0.8 mi w. **Facility:** 171 units. 1-2 stories (no elevator), interior/exterior corridors. **Terms:** check-in 4 pm. **Pool(s):** heated outdoor. **Activities:** exercise room, spa. **Guest Services:** valet laundry.

CLARION HOTEL
(831)373-1337

Hotel
$60-$400

Address: 1046 Munras Ave 93940 **Location:** SR 1 exit Soledad Dr/Munras Ave, 0.5 mi w. **Facility:** 52 units, some two bedrooms and kitchens. 2 stories (no elevator), exterior corridors. **Terms:** cancellation fee imposed. **Amenities:** high-speed Internet. **Pool(s):** heated indoor. **Activities:** whirlpool. **Free Special Amenities:** full breakfast and high-speed Internet.

COLTON INN
(831)649-6500

Hotel
$109-$209

Address: 707 Pacific St 93940 **Location:** In Old Monterey. **Facility:** 50 units. 3 stories, exterior corridors. **Terms:** 3 day cancellation notice. **Activities:** sauna. **Free Special Amenities:** continental breakfast and high-speed Internet.

COMFORT INN-MONTEREY BAY
(831)373-3081

Hotel
$59-$189

Address: 2050 N Fremont St 93940 **Location:** SR 1 exit Fremont St or Casa Verde Way, 0.3 mi e. Across from fairgrounds. **Facility:** 47 units. 2 stories (no elevator), exterior corridors. **Terms:** cancellation fee imposed. **Amenities:** safes. **Activities:** sauna, whirlpools. **Free Special Amenities:** expanded continental breakfast and high-speed Internet.

COMFORT INN-MONTEREY BY THE SEA
(831)372-2908

Hotel
$65-$189

Address: 1252 Munras Ave 93940 **Location:** SR 1 exit Soledad Dr/Munras Ave, just s. **Facility:** 67 units. 2 stories, exterior corridors. **Terms:** cancellation fee imposed. **Amenities:** safes. **Pool(s):** heated outdoor. **Activities:** exercise room. **Free Special Amenities:** expanded continental breakfast and high-speed Internet.

COMFORT INN MONTEREY PENINSULA AIRPORT
831)372-2945

Hotel
Rates not provided

Address: 1200 Olmstead Rd 93940 **Location:** SR 1 exit Airport-Salinas, 1.5 mi e on SR 68. Across from airport. **Facility:** 46 units. 2 stories (no elevator), exterior corridors. **Guest Services:** valet laundry. **Free Special Amenities:** full breakfast and early check-in/late check-out.

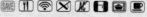

Safety tip: Keep a current AAA/CAA
Road Atlas in every vehicle

(See map & index p. 206.)

DAYS INN-DOWNTOWN MONTEREY/SAN CARLOS INN
(831)649-6332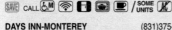

Hotel
$55-$259

Address: 850 Abrego St 93940 **Location:** SR 1 exit Fremont St or Soledad Dr/Munras Ave, 0.8 mi w. **Facility:** 55 units. 2-4 stories, exterior corridors. **Terms:** 2 night minimum stay - seasonal and/or weekends, 3 day cancellation notice-fee imposed. **Activities:** whirlpool. **Free Special Amenities:** expanded continental breakfast and high-speed Internet.

DAYS INN-MONTEREY
(831)375-2168

Motel
$55-$259

Address: 1288 Munras Ave 93940 **Location:** SR 1 exit Soledad Dr/Munras Ave, just w. **Facility:** 35 units. 1-2 stories (no elevator), exterior corridors. **Terms:** 2 night minimum stay - seasonal and/or weekends, cancellation fee imposed. **Free Special Amenities:** expanded continental breakfast and high-speed Internet.

ECONO LODGE MONTEREY FAIRGROUND
(831)372-5851

Hotel
$46-$86

Address: 2042 Fremont St 93940 **Location:** SR 1 exit Fremont St or Casa Verde Way, just e. **Facility:** 47 units, some efficiencies. 1-2 stories (no elevator), exterior corridors. **Terms:** 3 day cancellation notice-fee imposed. **Pool(s):** outdoor. **Activities:** whirlpool. **Guest Services:** coin laundry. **Free Special Amenities:** continental breakfast.

EL ADOBE INN
831/372-5409

Motel
$49-$299

Address: 936 Munras Ave 93940 **Location:** SR 1 exit Soledad Dr/Munras Ave, 0.6 mi w. **Facility:** 26 units. 2 stories (no elevator), exterior corridors. **Terms:** 3 day cancellation notice-fee imposed. **Free Special Amenities:** continental breakfast and high-speed Internet.

EL CASTELL MOTEL
831/372-8176

Motel
Rates not provided

Address: 2102 N Fremont St 93940 **Location:** SR 1 exit Fremont St or Casa Verde Way, 0.5 mi e. **Facility:** 55 units, some two bedrooms and kitchens. 1-2 stories (no elevator), exterior corridors. **Amenities:** high-speed Internet. **Pool(s):** indoor. **Guest Services:** coin laundry. **Free Special Amenities:** continental breakfast and high-speed Internet.

EL DORADO INN
831/373-2921

Motel
$49-$199

Address: 900 Munras Ave 93940 **Location:** SR 1 exit Soledad Dr/Munras Ave, 0.6 mi w. **Facility:** 15 units. 3 stories (no elevator), exterior corridors. **Bath:** shower only. **Terms:** 3 day cancellation notice-fee imposed. **Free Special Amenities:** continental breakfast and high-speed Internet.

HILTON GARDEN INN-MONTEREY
(831)373-6141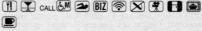

Hotel $119-$329 Address: 1000 Aguajito Rd 93940 **Location:** SR 1 exit Aguajito Rd or Fisherman's Wharf, just w. **Facility:** 204 units. 3 stories, interior corridors. **Terms:** check-in 4 pm, 1-7 night minimum stay, cancellation fee imposed. **Amenities:** video games (fee), high-speed Internet. **Dining:** Pacific Grille, see separate listing. **Pool(s):** heated outdoor. **Activities:** whirlpool, exercise room. **Guest Services:** valet and coin laundry.

> **AAA Benefit:** Unparalleled hospitality at a special Member rate.

HOLIDAY INN EXPRESS-CANNERY
831/372-1800 **7**

Hotel
Rates not provided

Address: 443 Wave St 93940 **Location:** SR 1 exit Monterey, 3 mi w. **Facility:** 43 units. 3 stories, interior/exterior corridors. **Amenities:** high-speed Internet, safes. **Guest Services:** valet laundry. **Free Special Amenities:** high-speed Internet and manager's reception.

HOTEL ABREGO
(831)372-7551 **21**

Hotel
$119-$600

Address: 755 Abrego St 93940 **Location:** SR 1 exit Fremont St, 0.8 mi w. **Facility:** 93 units. 3 stories, interior/exterior corridors. **Terms:** check-in 4 pm, 3 day cancellation notice-fee imposed. **Amenities:** safes. **Pool(s):** heated outdoor. **Activities:** whirlpool. **Guest Services:** valet and coin laundry. **Free Special Amenities:** local telephone calls and high-speed Internet. *(See ad p. 220.)*

Boutique hotel located in downtown Monterey within walking distance of Fisherman's Wharf and beaches.

HOTEL PACIFIC
831/373-5700 **11**

Hotel. Rates not provided. Address: 300 Pacific St 93940 **Location:** SR 1 exit Del Monte Ave, 2.2 mi w. Located near conference center. **Facility:** 105 units, some two bedrooms. 4 stories, interior/exterior corridors. **Parking:** on-site (fee). **Terms:** check-in 4 pm. **Amenities:** high-speed Internet (fee), safes. **Activities:** whirlpools. **Guest Services:** valet laundry.

(See map & index p. 206.)

HYATT REGENCY MONTEREY HOTEL & SPA
(831)372-1234 **44**

Hotel
$99-$450

  AAA Benefit:
Members save 10%
or more everyday.

Address: 1 Old Golf Course Rd 93940 **Location:** SR 1 exit Aguajito Rd northbound; exit Monterey southbound, just e. **Facility:** 550 units. 2-4 stories, interior corridors. **Terms:** check-in 4 pm, 3 day cancellation notice-fee imposed, resort fee. **Amenities:** video games (fee), safes. **Dining:** 3 restaurants. **Pool(s):** 2 heated outdoor. **Activities:** whirlpools, rental bicycles, jogging, shuffleboard, volleyball, spa. *Fee:* golf-18 holes, 6 tennis courts (2 lighted). **Guest Services:** valet laundry.

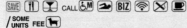

INTERCONTINENTAL THE CLEMENT MONTEREY
(831)375-4500 **1**

Hotel
$179-$399

Address: 750 Cannery Row 93940 **Location:** Between Prescott and David aves. **Facility:** On Cannery Row surrounded by several shops and restaurants and near the Monterey Bay Aquarium, this waterfront property overlooks Monterey Bay and the Pacific Ocean. 208 units. 4 stories, interior corridors. **Parking:** on-site (fee) and valet. **Terms:** check-in 4 pm. **Amenities:** high-speed Internet (fee), safes. **Dining:** The C Restaurant + Bar, see separate listing. **Pool(s):** heated outdoor. **Activities:** whirlpool, exercise room, spa. **Guest Services:** valet laundry. **Free Special Amenities: local telephone calls and newspaper.**

THE JABBERWOCK BED & BREAKFAST INN
(831)372-4777 **4**

 Bed & Breakfast $169-$309 **Address:** 598 Laine St 93940 **Location:** In New Monterey; at Hoffman Ave; close to Cannery Row. **Facility:** Surrounded by beautifully landscaped gardens, this attractively appointed inn follows the theme of Jabberwocky, Lewis Carroll's poem. 7 units. 3 stories (no elevator), interior corridors. **Terms:** 2 night minimum stay - weekends, age restrictions may apply, 7 day cancellation notice-fee imposed.

LA QUINTA INN MONTEREY
(831)373-7100 **15**

Hotel
$83-$353

Address: 2401 Del Monte Ave 93940 **Location:** SR 1 exit Del Rey Oaks, just e. **Facility:** 48 units. 3 stories, interior corridors.

LONE OAK LODGE
(831)372-4924 **39**

Motel
$60-$124

Address: 2221 N Fremont St 93940 **Location:** SR 1 exit Del Rey Oaks or Fremont St, 0.6 mi e. **Facility:** 46 units, some two bedrooms and kitchens. 1 story, exterior corridors. **Activities:** sauna, whirlpool, exercise room. **Free Special Amenities: local telephone calls and high-speed Internet.**

MARIPOSA INN & SUITES
831/649-1414 **48**

Hotel. Rates not provided. **Address:** 1386 Munras Ave 93940 **Location:** SR 1 exit Soledad Dr/Munras Ave, just w. **Facility:** 50 units. 3-4 stories, interior/exterior corridors. **Amenities:** high-speed Internet, safes. **Pool(s):** heated outdoor. **Activities:** whirlpool.

MONTEREY BAY INN
(831)373-6242 **8**

Hotel $169-$700 **Address:** 242 Cannery Row 93940 **Location:** SR 1 exit Monterey, 3.5 mi w. **Facility:** 49 units. 4 stories, interior/exterior corridors. **Parking:** on-site (fee). **Terms:** check-in 4 pm, 2 night minimum stay - seasonal and/or weekends, 3 day cancellation notice-fee imposed, resort fee. **Amenities:** safes. **Activities:** sauna, whirlpools, spa. **Guest Services:** valet laundry.

Get pet travel tips and enter the photo
contest at AAA.com/PetBook

▼ *See AAA listing p. 219* ▼

(See map & index p. 206.)

MONTEREY BAY LODGE   (831)372-8057 16

Hotel
$79-S349

Address: 55 Camino Aguajito 93940 **Location:** SR 1 exit Aguajito Rd, just w. Across from El Estero Lagoon and Park. **Facility:** 46 units, some two bedrooms. 2 stories (no elevator), exterior corridors. **Amenities:** safes. **Pool(s):** heated outdoor. **Activities:** whirlpool. **Guest Services:** valet laundry. **Free Special Amenities:** early check-in/late check-out and high-speed Internet. (See ad p. 222.)

[SAVE] [TI] CALL [&M] [≈] [BIZ] [≈] [X] [†] [≈] [≡] / SOME UNITS FEE [🐾] [AC]

MONTEREY BAY TRAVELODGE   (831)373-3381 36

Hotel
$89-S499

Address: 2030 Fremont St 93940 **Location:** Jct SR 1 and Fremont St, at SR 68. **Facility:** 104 units, some two bedrooms. 2 stories (no elevator), interior/exterior corridors. **Terms:** 3 day cancellation notice-fee imposed. **Amenities:** safes (fee). **Pool(s):** outdoor. **Activities:** exercise room. **Guest Services:** coin laundry. **Free Special Amenities:** expanded continental breakfast and high-speed Internet.

[SAVE] [TI] CALL [&M] [≈] [BIZ] [≈] [AC] [†] [≈] [≡] / SOME UNITS FEE [🐾]

MONTEREY DOWNTOWN TRAVELODGE
                                      (831)373-1876 18

Motel
$99-S399

Address: 675 Munras Ave 93940 **Location:** SR 1 exit Fremont St or Soledad Dr/Munras Ave, 0.7 mi w. **Facility:** 51 units. 3 stories, exterior corridors. **Amenities:** safes (fee). **Pool(s):** outdoor. **Free Special Amenities:** continental breakfast and high-speed Internet.

[SAVE] [ECO] [TI+] [≈] [BIZ] [≈] [X] [≡] / SOME UNITS [†]

MONTEREY FIRESIDE LODGE   (831)373-4172 31

Motel
$69-$599

Address: 1131 10th St 93940 **Location:** SR 1 exit Aguajito Rd or Monterey, just w. **Facility:** 27 units. 2 stories (no elevator), exterior corridors. **Terms:** 3 day cancellation notice-fee imposed, resort fee. **Guest Services:** coin laundry. **Free Special Amenities:** high-speed Internet and use of on-premises laundry facilities. [SAVE] [≈] [AC] [†] [≈] [≡] / SOME UNITS FEE [🐾]

THE MONTEREY HOTEL   (831)375-3184 14

Historic Hotel $99-$319 **Address:** 406 Alvarado St 93940 **Location:** At Franklin St; downtown. **Facility:** Built in 1904, this Victorian hotel has some small rooms, a few featuring a gas fireplace and wet bar. Its location makes it accessible to the convention center, Fisherman's Wharf and historic downtown area. 45 units. 4 stories (no elevator), interior corridors. **Parking:** valet only. **Terms:** 2-3 night minimum stay - seasonal and/or weekends, 3 day cancellation notice-fee imposed. **Activities:** spa. **Guest Services:** valet laundry. [BIZ] [≈] [X] [AC] / SOME UNITS [†] [≡]

MONTEREY MARRIOTT   (831)649-4234 13

Hotel
$189-$599

AAA Benefit: AAA hotel discounts of 5% or more.

Address: 350 Calle Principal 93940 **Location:** SR 1 exit Del Monte Ave or Soledad Dr/Munras Ave, 2 mi w. Opposite conference center. **Facility:** The hotel is adjacent to Fisherman's Wharf, the convention center and the historic downtown area. Many units afford views of Monterey Bay. 341 units. 10 stories, interior corridors. **Parking:** valet only. **Terms:** check-in 4 pm. **Amenities:** Fee: video games, high-speed Internet. **Dining:** 2 restaurants, entertainment. **Pool(s):** heated outdoor. **Activities:** whirlpool, exercise room, spa. **Guest Services:** valet and coin laundry.

[SAVE] [ECO] [TI] [🍽] [👤] [TV] CALL [&M] [≈] [BIZ] [≈] [X] [📷] [≡] / SOME UNITS [†] [≡]

Find thousands of places to show your card and save at AAA.com/discounts

▼ See AAA listing p. 268 ▼

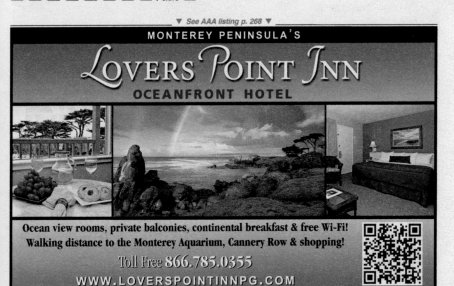

MONTEREY PENINSULA'S

LOVERS POINT INN
OCEANFRONT HOTEL

Ocean view rooms, private balconies, continental breakfast & free Wi-Fi!
Walking distance to the Monterey Aquarium, Cannery Row & shopping!

Toll Free 866.785.0355
WWW.LOVERSPOINTINNPG.COM

▼ See AAA listing p. 221 ▼

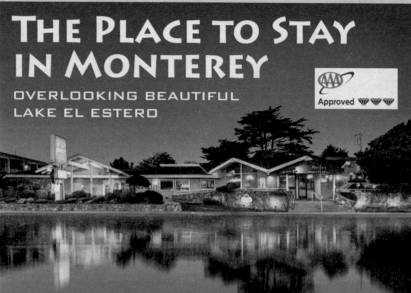

(See map & index p. 206.)

MONTEREY PLAZA HOTEL & SPA (831)646-1700

Hotel
$179-$995

Address: 400 Cannery Row 93940 **Location:** SR 1 exit Del Monte Ave or Soledad Dr/Munras Ave, 3 mi w. **Facility:** On historic Cannery Row overlooking Monterey Bay and the Pacific Ocean, this property offers many units with balconies and bay views. The hotel is beautifully appointed in rich wood tones throughout. 291 units. 3-5 stories, interior corridors. **Parking:** valet only. **Terms:** check-in 4 pm, 2-4 night minimum stay - seasonal and/or weekends, cancellation fee imposed, resort fee. **Amenities:** high-speed Internet (fee), safes. **Dining:** The Duck Club, Schooners Coastal Kitchen & Bar, see separate listings. **Activities:** exercise room, spa. **Guest Services:** valet laundry. **Free Special Amenities:** newspaper and local transportation.

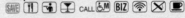

OLD MONTEREY INN 831/375-8284

Bed & Breakfast
$199-$499

Address: 500 Martin St 93940 **Location:** SR 1 exit Soledad Dr/Munras Ave, 1 mi w; from Fisherman's Wharf, 1 mi s on Pacific St to Martin St, 2 blks w. **Facility:** This 1929 Tudor-style home is on a wooded hillside and features individually decorated rooms, most with feather beds and some with a fireplace. Beautiful gardens surround the inn's exterior. 10 units. 1-3 stories (no elevator), interior/exterior corridors. **Terms:** 2 night minimum stay - weekends, 14 day cancellation notice-fee imposed. **Amenities:** high-speed Internet, safes. **Activities:** Fee: massage. **Free Special Amenities:** full breakfast and high-speed Internet.

OTTER INN 831/375-2299

Hotel
Rates not provided

Address: 571 Wave St 93940 **Location:** SR 1 exit Monterey, 3.5 mi w. Located in Cannery Row area. **Facility:** 33 units. 4 stories, exterior corridors. **Amenities:** high-speed Internet. **Activities:** whirlpool. **Free Special Amenities:** early check-in/late check-out and high-speed Internet.

PADRE OAKS (831)373-3741

Motel
$39-$299

Address: 1278 Munras Ave 93940 **Location:** SR 1 exit Soledad Dr/Munras Ave, 0.3 mi w. **Facility:** 20 units. 1 story, exterior corridors. *Bath:* shower only. **Terms:** 3 day cancellation notice-fee imposed. **Free Special Amenities:** continental breakfast and high-speed Internet.

PORTOLA HOTEL & SPA (831)649-4511

Hotel
$179-$525

Address: 2 Portola Plaza 93940 **Location:** 2 mi w of SR 1 exit Del Monte or Munras aves; near Fisherman's Wharf; downtown. **Facility:** The property is located adjacent to Fisherman's Wharf, the convention center and the historic downtown area. Enjoy spectacular vista views of Monterey Bay and an on-site full-service spa. 379 units. 1-7 stories, interior corridors. **Parking:** on-site (fee). **Terms:** cancellation fee imposed. **Amenities:** safes. *Fee:* video games, high-speed Internet. **Dining:** 2 restaurants. **Pool(s):** outdoor. **Activities:** whirlpool, exercise room, spa. **Guest Services:** valet laundry.
(See ad p. 224.)

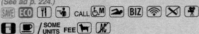

QUALITY INN (831)372-3381

Hotel
$60-$400

Address: 1058 Munras Ave 93940 **Location:** SR 1 exit Munras Ave, 0.5 mi w. **Facility:** 55 units. 2 stories (no elevator), exterior corridors. **Terms:** cancellation fee imposed. **Amenities:** high-speed Internet. **Free Special Amenities:** full breakfast and high-speed Internet.

RAMADA LIMITED-CARMEL HILL-MONTEREY
(831)375-2679

Motel $63-$600 **Address:** 1182 Cass St 93940 **Location:** SR 1 exit Soledad Dr/Munras Ave, 0.5 mi w. **Facility:** 19 units, some two bedrooms. 2 stories (no elevator), exterior corridors. **Terms:** cancellation fee imposed. **Pool(s):** outdoor.

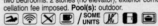

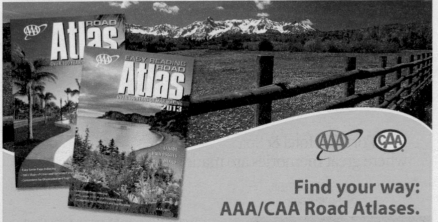

(See map & index p. 206.)

RAMADA LIMITED-MONTEREY (831)375-9511 **40**
Hotel $63-$600 **Address:** 2058 N Fremont St 93940 **Location:** SR 1 exit Fremont St or Casa Verde Way, 0.3 mi e. **Facility:** 48 units. 1-2 stories, exterior corridors. **Terms:** cancellation fee imposed. **Pool(s):** outdoor. **Activities:** whirlpool. **Guest Services:** valet laundry.

RODEWAY INN MONTEREY (831)373-2911 **33**
Motel
$46-$86
Address: 2041 N Fremont St 93940 **Location:** SR 1 exit Fremont St or Casa Verde Way, 0.3 mi e. **Facility:** 22 units. 2 stories (no elevator), exterior corridors. **Terms:** 3 day cancellation notice. **Free Special Amenities: continental breakfast.**

SPINDRIFT INN (831)646-8900 **2**
Hotel $169-$700 **Address:** 652 Cannery Row 93940 **Location:** SR 1 exit Monterey, 3.7 mi w. **Facility:** 45 units. 4 stories, interior corridors. **Parking:** valet only. **Terms:** check-in 4 pm, 2 night minimum stay - seasonal and/or weekends, 3 day cancellation notice-fee imposed, resort fee. **Amenities:** high-speed Internet, safes. **Guest Services:** valet laundry.

SUPER 8 (831)373-3203 **47**
Motel $55-$1050 **Address:** 1300 Munras Ave 93940 **Location:** SR 1 exit Soledad Dr/Munras Ave, just w. **Facility:** 34 units. 2 stories (no elevator), exterior corridors. **Terms:** cancellation fee imposed. **Amenities:** high-speed Internet. **Pool(s):** outdoor.

▼ See AAA listing p. 223 ▼

(See map & index p. 206.)

VAGABOND INN - MONTEREY (831)646-9696  26

⬦⬦ **Hotel** $59-$399 **Address:** 1010 Munras Ave 93940 **Location:** SR 1 exit Soledad Dr/Munras Ave, 0.7 mi w. **Facility:** 29 units. 2 stories (no elevator), interior corridors.

WHERE TO EAT

ABALONETTI SEAFOOD 831/373-1851 14

⬦⬦ Seafood. Casual Dining. $13-$20 **AAA Inspector Notes:** Calamari is a specialty among the many listed appetizers at this eatery. Fresh seafood comes in from the restaurant's own boat. **Bar:** full bar. **Address:** 57 Fisherman's Wharf 93940 **Location:** On Fisherman's Wharf. **Parking:** on-site (fee). L D

BLACK BEAR DINER 831/645-9700

⬦⬦ American. Casual Dining. $7-$16 **AAA Inspector Notes:** A homey atmosphere characterizes this family-oriented restaurant. Familiar comfort foods, such as meatloaf with mashed potatoes, are at the heart of the menu and are served in generous portions. **Bar:** beer & wine. **Address:** 2450 N Fremont St 93940 **Location:** SR 1 exit Seaside/Del Rey Oaks E, just s. B L D CALL

CAFE BEACH 831/394-3321 18

⬦⬦ American. Casual Dining. $10-$26 **AAA Inspector Notes:** Most tables at this relaxed spot afford views of the Pacific Ocean and Monterey skyline. At lunch, offerings center on sandwiches and salads including fresh locally caught seafood, while dinner skews more toward upscale preparations. **Bar:** full bar. **Address:** 2600 Sand Dunes Dr 93940 **Location:** SR 1 exit Del Rey Oaks, just w; in BEST WESTERN PLUS Beach Resort Monterey. **Parking:** on-site (fee). B L D CALL

CAFE FINA 831/372-5200 15

⬦⬦⬦ Seafood Fine Dining $12-$30

AAA Inspector Notes: Mesquite-broiled seafood, brick-oven pizza and homemade pasta dishes are foremost on the menu at this café. The neat, small dining area includes a few tables on the second level. **Bar:** full bar. **Reservations:** suggested. **Address:** 47 Fisherman's Wharf 93940 **Location:** On Fisherman's Wharf. **Parking:** on-site (fee). *Menu on AAA.com* L D

CAPTAIN BULLWACKER'S RESTAURANT & PATIO PUB 831/373-1353 7

⬦⬦ American. Casual Dining. $9-$27 **AAA Inspector Notes:** Located on Cannery Row, this is a favorite among tourists and locals alike. The specialty of the house is fish and chips. Outside patio dining is available, weather permitting. **Bar:** full bar. **Address:** 653 Cannery Row 93940 **Location:** On Cannery Row. **Parking:** street only. L D CALL

CARUSO'S CORNER RESTAURANT 831/375-5014 25

⬦⬦ Italian. Casual Dining. $10-$30 **AAA Inspector Notes:** Small and quaint, this family-owned restaurant is a long time tradition in Monterey. The menu offers a great selection of Italian sandwiches, pasta and pizza in addition to some seafood specialties. A salad bar or traditional minestrone soup is offered with entrée selections. Come hungry because portions are hearty. **Bar:** full bar. **Address:** 2101 N Fremont St 93940 **Location:** SR 1 exit Casa Verde Way, just e. D

CHART HOUSE 831/372-3362 10

⬦⬦ Seafood. Fine Dining. $20-$47 **AAA Inspector Notes:** Examples of the fabulous food include prime rib, filet mignon, tomato-basil chicken and varied fresh fish and seafood dishes. **Bar:** full bar. **Reservations:** suggested. **Address:** 444 Cannery Row 93940 **Location:** On Cannery Row at Hoffman Ave. **Parking:** street only. SAVE D CALL

THE C RESTAURANT + BAR 831/375-4800 1

⬦⬦⬦⬦ California. Casual Dining. $14-$45 **AAA Inspector Notes:** Sit back and enjoy spectacular views of Monterey Bay at this restaurant while enjoying the influences of California cuisine. Fresh seafood is the specialty accompanied by organically grown produce. **Bar:** full bar. **Address:** 750 Cannery Row 93940 **Location:** Between Prescott and David aves; in InterContinental The Clement Monterey. **Parking:** valet only. L D CALL

DOMENICO'S ON THE WHARF 831/372-3655 16

⬦⬦⬦ Seafood Fine Dining $11-$35

AAA Inspector Notes: This restaurant overlooks the marina and Monterey Bay. Mesquite-grilled seafood and pasta dishes emphasize fresh, local ingredients. **Bar:** full bar. **Reservations:** suggested. **Address:** 50 Fisherman's Wharf 93940 **Location:** On Fisherman's Wharf. **Parking:** on-site (fee). *Menu on AAA.com* L D

THE DUCK CLUB 831/646-1706 11

⬦⬦⬦ American. Fine Dining. $20-$40 **AAA Inspector Notes:** Seats in the sophisticated dining room afford beautiful views of Monterey Bay. Imaginative California specialties center on grilled steak and fresh fish. **Bar:** full bar. **Reservations:** suggested. **Address:** 400 Cannery Row 93940 **Location:** SR 1 exit Del Monte Ave or Soledad Dr/Munras Ave, 3 mi w; in Monterey Plaza Hotel & Spa. **Parking:** valet only. B D CALL

EL PALOMAR 831/372-1032 23

⬦⬦ Mexican. Casual Dining. $10-$25 **AAA Inspector Notes:** Locals frequent this restaurant for its traditional Mexican cuisine, as well as a few signature specialties. **Bar:** full bar. **Address:** 724 Abrego St 93940 **Location:** SR 1 exit Monterey; just s of Fremont St; in Cypress Plaza. L D CALL

EL TORITO 831/373-0611

⬦⬦ Mexican. Casual Dining. $8-$20 **AAA Inspector Notes:** Homemade Mexican favorites span from classic preparations to specialties from the country's central regions. Spicy taqueria-style tacos and carnitas Michoacan (marinated pork) are tasty choices. **Bar:** full bar. **Address:** 600 Cannery Row 93940 **Location:** On Cannery Row, between Hoffman and Prescott aves; 2 blks n of Monterey Bay Aquarium. L D CALL

THE FISH HOPPER 831/372-8543 3

⬦⬦ Seafood Casual Dining $10-$33

AAA Inspector Notes: Over the water on Monterey Bay and Cannery Row, the restaurant features a cozy dining deck. **Bar:** full bar. **Reservations:** suggested. **Address:** 700 Cannery Row 93940 **Location:** On Cannery Row. **Parking:** street only. *Menu on AAA.com* L D CALL

GILBERT'S RED SNAPPER RESTAURANT & BAR 831/375-3113 17

⬦⬦ Seafood. Casual Dining. $14-$30 **AAA Inspector Notes:** Located on Fisherman's Wharf, this restaurant offers a wide selection of fresh fish entrées served in a casual setting. This is a great spot for families as a child's menu is offered. Most tables boast views of Monterey Bay. **Bar:** full bar. **Address:** 30 Fisherman's Wharf 93940 **Location:** On Fisherman's Wharf. **Parking:** on-site (fee). L D CALL

ISABELLA'S ON THE WHARF 831/375-3956 13

⬦⬦⬦ Seafood. Fine Dining. $15-$30 **AAA Inspector Notes:** Located on Fisherman's Wharf, this restaurant's floor-to-ceiling windows offer spectacular views of Monterey Bay and the Pacific Ocean. Fresh, locally-caught seafood is a specialty. **Bar:** full bar. **Reservations:** suggested. **Address:** 60 Fisherman's Wharf 93940 **Location:** On Fisherman's Wharf. **Parking:** on-site (fee). L D

(See map & index p. 206.)

JOSE'S MEXICAN RESTAURANT   831/655-4419   8

Mexican. Casual Dining. $7-$17 **AAA Inspector Notes:** Located in a converted home one block from Cannery Row, this Mexican restaurant serves up a wide selection of favorites with a few specialties of their own including chile verde and carnitas. The staff is friendly and welcoming. **Bar:** full bar. **Address:** 638 Wave St 93940 **Location:** Between Hoffman and Prescott aves; on Cannery Row. **Parking:** street only. L D CALL M

LALLA GRILL   831/324-4632   27

California. Casual Dining. $8-$20 **AAA Inspector Notes:** Casual elegance awaits at this trendy restaurant where the atmosphere is bustling from the time diners arrive through their departure. The menu offers everything from street tacos to specialty burgers and sandwiches. Entrées include Korean beef short ribs, mushroom-stuffed chicken, fresh salmon and filet mignon made with oyster mushrooms and cauliflower puree. **Bar:** full bar. **Address:** 1400 Del Monte Shopping Center 93940 **Location:** SR 1 exit Munras Ave W; adjacent to Century Theater. B L D CALL M

LALLAPALOOZA RESTAURANT   831/645-9036   22

American. Casual Dining. $12-$44 **AAA Inspector Notes:** This contemporary yet casual restaurant boasts high ceilings, colorful artwork and an open kitchen design. Candles and fresh flowers decorate the tables. Great-tasting pizzas from the brick oven are always a great choice, as are the fresh fish specialties. **Bar:** full bar. **Address:** 474 Alvarado St 93940 **Location:** SR 1 exit Monterey, 1.1 mi nw on Munras Ave, then just n. **Parking:** street only. D

LOOSE NOODLE PASTA HOUSE   831/641-0130   9

Italian. Casual Dining. $8-$20 **AAA Inspector Notes:** This locally favorite Italian eatery is sure to please anyone as it offers traditional and house specialty pasta dishes. The extensive menu offers vegetarian, seafood and meat dishes as well as some house favorites including shrimp scampi, homemade lasagna and ravioli, cioppino and chicken parmigiana. Service is warm and friendly. **Bar:** beer & wine. **Address:** 538 Lighthouse Ave 93940 **Location:** Between McClellan and Hoffman aves; in New Monterey/Cannery Row area. **Parking:** street only. L D CALL M

LOUIE LINGUINI'S   831/648-8500   5

Seafood. Casual Dining. $10-$29 **AAA Inspector Notes:** Located upstairs on Cannery Row, this eatery overlooks the Pacific Ocean and Monterey coast line. Selections of fresh seafood and pasta make this a favorite for all. **Bar:** full bar. **Address:** 660 Cannery Row 93940 **Location:** On Cannery Row. **Parking:** street only. L D

MONTRIO BISTRO   831/648-8880   20

Regional California. Fine Dining. $17-$33 **AAA Inspector Notes:** This charming bistro channels influences from Italy, France and America. The open kitchen features a wood-burning rotisserie. Some of the specialties include braised short ribs, pesto-rubbed sirloin with prawns and roast duck with a cornbread stuffing. **Bar:** full bar. **Reservations:** suggested. **Address:** 414 Calle Principal 93940 **Location:** Between Franklin and Jefferson sts; downtown. **Parking:** street only. D

PACIFIC GRILLE   831/373-6141   24

American. Casual Dining. $10-$27 **AAA Inspector Notes:** Patrons of this casual restaurant can enjoy everything from sandwiches to complete dinners. Fresh seafood is caught locally. **Bar:** full bar. **Address:** 1000 Aguajito Rd 93940 **Location:** SR 1 exit Aguajito Rd or Fisherman's Wharf, just w; in Hilton Garden Inn-Monterey. B D CALL M

PARADISO TRATTORIA   831/375-4155   6

Italian Casual Dining $10-$35

AAA Inspector Notes: Overlooking Monterey Bay from its Cannery Row location, this restaurant prepares a variety of Italian specialties, including homemade pasta dishes, pizza and fresh, locally caught seafood. The dining room has a comfortable, laid-back feel with friendly staff. **Bar:** full bar. **Reservations:** suggested. **Address:** 654 Cannery Row 93940 **Location:** On Cannery Row; adjacent to Spindrift Inn. **Parking:** street only. *Menu on AAA.com* L D CALL M

P.F. CHANG'S CHINA BISTRO   831/375-0143   26

Chinese. Fine Dining. $10-$20 **AAA Inspector Notes:** Trendy, upscale decor provides a pleasant backdrop for New Age Chinese dining. Vegetarian plates and sides, noodles, meins, chicken and meat dishes are created from exotic, fresh ingredients. **Bar:** full bar. **Address:** 1200 Del Monte Center 93940 **Location:** SR 1 exit Soledad Dr W; in Del Monte Center. L D CALL M

ROSINE'S   831/375-1400   21

American Casual Dining $9-$20

AAA Inspector Notes: Breakfast is a specialty at the family-owned and -operated restaurant, a favorite of the local and downtown crowd for many years. Desserts, particularly the cakes and pies, also are popular. **Address:** 434 Alvarado St 93940 **Location:** At Bonifacio St; downtown. **Parking:** street only. B L D CALL M

ROUND TABLE PIZZA   831/373-1351

Pizza. Casual Dining. $7-$28 **AAA Inspector Notes:** This casual, family-oriented pizza place features high-quality ingredients and dough rolled fresh daily. Distinctive specialty pizzas are piled high with toppings. **Bar:** beer & wine. **Address:** 375 Alvarado St 93940 **Location:** At W Franklin St; downtown. L D

SANDBAR & GRILL   831/373-2818   19

Seafood. Casual Dining. $10-$25 **AAA Inspector Notes:** Overlooking the marina and Monterey Bay, this cozy restaurant presents a menu of pasta, steak and rib choices. **Bar:** full bar. **Address:** Wharf #2, Suite 16 93940 **Location:** Just n of Fisherman's Wharf. **Parking:** on-site (fee). L D M

SARDINE FACTORY   831/373-3775   4

Seafood Fine Dining $22-$70

AAA Inspector Notes: The menu comprises preparations of fresh seafood, steaks and pasta dishes. Diners can sit in one of four individually decorated dining rooms, from the casual, glass-domed conservatory to the refined captain's room. **Bar:** full bar. **Reservations:** suggested. **Address:** 701 Wave St 93940 **Location:** At Prescott Ave; in Cannery Row area. *Menu on AAA.com* D CALL M

SCHOONERS COASTAL KITCHEN & BAR   831/372-2628   12

American Casual Dining $12-$38

AAA Inspector Notes: Situated on the water, this downstairs pub-style bistro affords beautiful views of the Pacific Ocean and Monterey Bay and carries on this appreciation for the sea in its offerings of fresh fish. The atmosphere is friendly and upbeat. **Bar:** full bar. **Address:** 400 Cannery Row 93940 **Location:** SR 1 exit Del Monte Ave or Soledad Dr/Munras Ave, 3 mi w; in Monterey Plaza Hotel & Spa. **Parking:** on-site (fee) and street. L D CALL M

TARPY'S ROADHOUSE   831/647-1444

Regional American. Fine Dining. $9-$47 **AAA Inspector Notes:** Distinctive dining rooms and intimate garden patios contribute to the attractive, relaxed setting of this roadhouse. Menu items are prepared over a wood-burning grill. Prime cuts of meat and fresh, locally-caught seafood are available. **Reservations:** suggested. **Address:** 2999 Monterey Salinas Hwy 93940 **Location:** On SR 68, 2.5 mi e of jct SR 1. L D CALL M

Contact us about AAA/CAA
Approved properties at
AAA.com/TourBookComments

(See map & index p. 206.)

WHALING STATION PRIME STEAKS & SEAFOOD

831/373-3778

Steak
Fine Dining
$20–$55

AAA Inspector Notes: Tuscan decor gives this dining room an upscale feel. Prime beef and fresh seafood are prepared over a mesquite-wood broiler. The menu also lists a variety of pasta dishes with special homemade sauces as well as wonderful steaks. A complimentary plate of steamed artichoke leaves with aioli and mayonnaise are offered. Try the pineapple carpaccio for dessert-translucent pieces with brown sugar sprinkled on top are torched, then topped with a scoop of ice cream. **Bar:** full bar. **Reservations:** suggested. **Address:** 763 Wave St 93940 **Location:** In Cannery Row area; between Irving and Prescott aves.
Menu on AAA.com D

MONTE RIO pop. 1,152
• Part of Wine Country area — see map p. 562

NORTHWOOD LODGE & RESORT 707/865-1655

Motel
$109–$289

Address: 19455 SR 116 95462 **Location:** 0.8 mi ne. **Facility:** 26 units, some cottages. 1 story, exterior corridors. **Terms:** 2 night minimum stay - seasonal and/or weekends, 7 day cancellation notice-fee imposed. **Pool(s):** heated outdoor. **Guest Services:** coin laundry. **Free Special Amenities:** early check-in/late check-out and high-speed Internet.

RIO VILLA BEACH RESORT 707/865-1143

Motel $100–$300 **Address:** 20292 Hwy 116 95462 **Location:** Center. **Facility:** 11 units, some two bedrooms and kitchens. 1 story, exterior corridors. **Terms:** 2 night minimum stay - seasonal and/or weekends, 7 day cancellation notice-fee imposed.

MORAGA pop. 16,016
• Hotels & Restaurants map & index p. 254

RISTORANTE AMOROMA 925/377-7662 31

Italian. Fine Dining. $14–$26 **AAA Inspector Notes:** The restaurant features a quaint and comfortable atmosphere. A varied selection of Italian entrées include fresh pasta, chicken and seafood. **Bar:** full bar. **Reservations:** suggested. **Address:** 360 Park St 94556 **Location:** Just w of Center St; downtown. L D

ROUND TABLE PIZZA 925/376-1411

Pizza. Casual Dining. $7–$28 **AAA Inspector Notes:** This casual, family-oriented pizza place features high-quality ingredients and dough rolled fresh daily. Distinctive specialty pizzas are piled high with toppings. **Bar:** beer & wine. **Address:** 361 Rheem Blvd 94556 **Location:** Just w of Moraga Rd. L D

MORGAN HILL (G-3) pop. 37,882, elev. 345'
• Restaurants p. 228

Before the arrival of Spanish soldiers and priests in 1776, this area was home to the peaceful Costanoan Indians. The first English-speaking community sprang up around a prosperous estate known as Morgan Hill's Ranch in 1845 and was incorporated in 1906. Morgan Hill is at the southern end of the agriculturally rich Santa Clara Valley, where the French prune was developed.

About 14 miles east of the city via E. Dunne Avenue is Henry W. Coe State Park, its 80,000 acres encompassing a varied terrain of ridges and canyons. Once the home of Ohlone Indians, the park has more than 250 miles of trails to hike and a variety of indigenous plants and animals, including the elusive mountain lion. Within the park are the headwaters of Coyote Creek; recreational activities include camping, picnicking , fishing, mountain biking and horseback riding. *See Recreation Areas Chart.*

Morgan Hill Chamber of Commerce: 17485 Monterey Rd., Suite 105, P.O. Box 786, Morgan Hill, CA 95037-0786. **Phone:** (408) 779-9444.

COMFORT INN & SUITES (408)778-3400

Hotel
$89–$120

Address: 16225 Condit Rd 95037 **Location:** US 101 exit Tennant Ave, then just n. **Facility:** 53 units. 3 stories, interior corridors. **Terms:** cancellation fee imposed. **Amenities:** high-speed Internet. **Pool(s):** outdoor. **Activities:** sauna, whirlpool, exercise room. **Guest Services:** coin laundry. **Free Special Amenities:** expanded continental breakfast and high-speed Internet.

COURTYARD BY MARRIOTT (408)782-6034

Hotel $99–$249 **Address:** 18610 Madrone Pkwy 95037 **Location:** US 101 exit Cochrane W, then n. **Facility:** 90 units. 3 stories, interior corridors. **Amenities:** *Some:* high-speed Internet. **Pool(s):** heated indoor. **Activities:** whirlpool, exercise room. **Guest Services:** valet and coin laundry.

AAA Benefit:
AAA hotel discounts of 5% or more.

HAMPTON INN SAN JOSE SOUTH-MORGAN HILL (408)779-7666

Hotel $119-$159 **Address:** 16115 Condit Rd 95037 **Location:** US 101 exit Tennant Ave, just e. **Facility:** 101 units, some efficiencies. 3 stories, interior corridors. **Terms:** 1-7 night minimum stay, cancellation fee imposed. **Amenities:** video games (fee). **Pool(s):** outdoor. **Activities:** whirlpool, exercise room. **Guest Services:** valet and coin laundry.

AAA Benefit:
Members save up to 10%!

HOLIDAY INN EXPRESS HOTEL & SUITES (408)776-7676

Hotel $115-$145 **Address:** 17035 Condit Rd 95037 **Location:** US 101 exit Dunne Ave, then e. **Facility:** 85 units. 3 stories, interior corridors. **Amenities:** high-speed Internet. **Pool(s):** heated indoor. **Activities:** sauna, whirlpool, exercise room. **Guest Services:** complimentary laundry.

MORGAN HILL INN (408)779-1900

Motel
$50–$99

Address: 16250 Monterey Hwy 95037 **Location:** US 101 exit Dunne Ave, 1 mi w, then 0.5 mi s. **Facility:** 24 units. 2 stories (no elevator), exterior corridors. **Free Special Amenities:** early check-in/late check-out and high-speed Internet.

RESIDENCE INN BY MARRIOTT (408)782-8311

Extended Stay Hotel $109-$259 **Address:** 18620 Madrone Pkwy 95037 **Location:** US 101 exit Cochrane W, just n. **Facility:** 90 units, some two bedrooms and kitchens. 3 stories, interior corridors. **Amenities:** *Some:* high-speed Internet. **Pool(s):** heated indoor. **Activities:** whirlpool, exercise room. **Guest Services:** valet and coin laundry.

AAA Benefit:
AAA hotel discounts of 5% or more.

LADERA GRILL   408/201-9200

♦♦♦♦ American. Fine Dining. $14-$45 **AAA Inspector Notes:** Located in the historic downtown area, this casually elegant restaurant has become a favorite of the local crowd. The menu is very diverse and offers varied pasta dishes, beef, poultry and a nice selection of seafood. **Bar:** full bar. **Address:** 17305 Monterey Rd, Suite 110 95037 **Location:** US 101 exit Dunne Ave, 1.3 mi w, then just n; at 3rd St. **Parking:** on-site and street. L D CALL M

LAS PALMAS FINE MEXICAN DINING   408/779-7400

♦♦♦ Mexican. Casual Dining. $9-$18 **AAA Inspector Notes:** In addition to the traditional selections of Mexican entrées, this restaurant serves up some specialties of their own including a few fresh fish selections. An outdoor miniature golf course is a great start or end to a good meal. **Bar:** full bar. **Address:** 16825 Condit Rd 95037 **Location:** US 101 exit E Dunne Ave, just s. L D CALL M

ROUND TABLE PIZZA   408/779-6300

♦ Pizza. Casual Dining. $7-$30 **AAA Inspector Notes:** This casual, family-oriented pizza place features high-quality ingredients and dough rolled fresh daily. Distinctive specialty pizzas are piled high with toppings. **Bar:** beer & wine. **Address:** 16740 Monterey Hwy 95037 **Location:** Just s of E Dunne Ave. L D

SINALOA CAFE   408/779-9740

♦♦ Mexican. Casual Dining. $5-$16 **AAA Inspector Notes:** A longtime Morgan Hill tradition, the family-owned-and-operated restaurant treats the local clientele to traditional Mexican favorites. The atmosphere is relaxed and friendly. **Bar:** full bar. **Address:** 17535 Monterey Rd 95037 **Location:** US 101 exit E Dunne Ave, 1 mi w, then 0.5 mi n; at Main Ave. **Parking:** on-site and street.

L D

MOSS BEACH (E-8) pop. 3,103, elev. 80'
• Part of San Francisco area — see map p. 342

JAMES V. FITZGERALD MARINE RESERVE, w. off SR 1 via California Ave., preserves marine life in one of the state's most diverse intertidal regions. The reserve is within the Montara State Marine Reserve. Marine life typically visible includes crabs, snails, mussels, sea stars, sea slugs and harbor seals. Low tide is the best time to explore; consult a local tide chart or phone the reserve for information.

Note: No buckets or containers are allowed on the beach. Collecting shells, rocks and plants is strictly prohibited. Dogs and other pets are not permitted. **Hours:** Daily dawn-dusk. **Cost:** Free. **Phone:** (650) 728-3584.

SEAL COVE INN   (650)728-4114

♦♦♦ ♦♦♦ Bed & Breakfast $245-$360 **Address:** 221 Cypress Ave 94038 **Location:** 6.5 mi n of jct SR 1 and 92 to Cypress Ave, then just w. Located in Moss Beach; adjacent to Fitzgerald Marine Reserve. **Facility:** Bordered by wildflowers, a county park and ocean views, a Cypress tree-lined road leads to this inn. Guest rooms feature a towel warmer, balcony or terrace and some log-burning fireplaces. 10 units. 2 stories (no elevator), interior corridors. **Terms:** 7 day cancellation notice-fee imposed. **Activities:** beach access, bicycle trails, hiking trails.

 / SOME UNITS FEE

MOSS BEACH DISTILLERY   650/728-5595

Seafood
Casual Dining
$11-$35

SR 92. L D

AAA Inspector Notes: The resident ghost, Blue Lady, occupies this restaurant situated on a bluff overlooking the Pacific. Sunset views are spectacular. **Bar:** full bar. **Reservations:** suggested. **Address:** 140 Beach Way 94038 **Location:** SR 1 exit Cypress St, 6 mi n of jct

MOSS LANDING (G-3) pop. 204, elev. 10'

ELKHORN SLOUGH SAFARI NATURE BOAT TOURS departs from the Moss Landing Harbor, w. off SR 1 onto Moss Landing Rd., n. onto Sandholdt Rd., then e. into the harbor parking lot. Two-hour cruises on a 27-foot pontoon boat explore the 7-mile Elkhorn Slough estuary. Led by a naturalist, the tours provide opportunities for sighting sea otters, harbor seals, terns, grebes and other species of waterfowl and shorebirds. The captain and naturalist provide information about slough ecology and natural history; photographs circulated during the trip help identify wildlife.

Time: Allow 2 hours, 30 minutes minimum. **Hours:** Departures daily; times vary depending on the tide and the migration of species. Closed Thanksgiving and Christmas. Phone ahead to confirm schedule. **Cost:** $35; $32 (ages 65+); $26 (ages 3-12). Under 3 not permitted on tours. Reservations are required at least 1-2 weeks in advance and can be made online or by phone. **Parking:** $3. **Phone:** (831) 633-5555.

SANCTUARY CRUISES departs from "A" dock in Moss Landing Harbor; go 1 blk. w. off SR 1 on Moss Landing Rd., n. onto Sandholdt Rd., then e. into the main harbor parking lot. Four- to 5-hour whale-watching cruises led by knowledgeable captains and naturalists offer opportunities to spot and learn about humpbacks, orcas, gray whales, dolphins, blue whales, sea otters, sea lions, harbor seals and other creatures (depending on the season) in Monterey Bay.

Time: Allow 4 hours minimum. **Hours:** Trips depart daily at 10. Schedule may vary; phone ahead. Closed Christmas. **Cost:** $50; $40 (ages 3-12); $10 (ages 0-2). Reservations are recommended. **Parking:** $3 in harbor lot. **Phone:** (831) 917-1042.

CAPTAIN'S INN AT MOSS LANDING   (831)633-5550

♦♦♦ ♦♦♦
Bed & Breakfast
$149-$295

Address: 8122 Moss Landing Rd 95039 **Location:** Just w of SR 1. **Facility:** Nautically appointed, the inn is located along the Pacific Ocean. Guests enjoy viewing a variety of marine wildlife and birds. 10 units. 2 stories (no elevator), interior/exterior corridors. **Terms:** check-in 4 pm, 2 night minimum stay - weekends, 7 day cancellation notice-fee imposed. **Amenities:** high-speed Internet. **Free Special Amenities:** full breakfast and high-speed Internet.

SAVE CALL M

MOUNTAIN RANCH (E-4) pop. 1,628, elev. 2,117'

CALIFORNIA CAVERN is e. on Mountain Ranch Rd., then about 2.8 mi. s.e. on Michel and Cave City rds., following signs. Chambers and passageways contain glittering formations ranging from fragile soda straws on the ceiling to colossal stalagmites rising from the floor. Discovered in 1850, the cavern offers gemstone mining and a nature trail in addition to a variety of cave trips.

A 60- to 80-minute guided walking tour provides information about area history as well as the history and geology of the cave. Depending on water levels in the cave, the trip includes a visit to the Jungle Room, named for the crystalline vines that cover its ceiling. For the more adventurous, two more physically demanding spelunking trips are available by reservation.

Hours: Walking tour departs (weather permitting) daily on the hour 10-5, May-Oct.; phone for schedule rest of year. **Cost:** Walking tour $14.95; $7.95 (ages 3-12). **Phone:** (209) 736-2708 or (866) 762-2837.

MOUNTAIN VIEW (E-9) pop. 74,066, elev. 97'
• Hotels p. 230 • Restaurants p. 231
• Hotels & Restaurants map & index p. 468

Located as it is in the heart of Silicon Valley, Mountain View is a center of high-tech industry. On a more natural note is Shoreline Park, a regional recreation area off the US 101 Shoreline Boulevard exit near San Francisco Bay. In addition to being a sanctuary for wildlife and more than 150 species of birds (including many migratory birds that pass through from October through February on their way south), the park offers 7 miles of jogging, hiking and bicycling trails, a saltwater lake for windsurfing and sailing, level expanses for kite flying and an 18-hole golf course. Major music stars appear at the Shoreline Amphitheatre.

Mountain View Chamber of Commerce: 580 Castro St., Mountain View, CA 94041. **Phone:** (650) 968-8378.

COMPUTER HISTORY MUSEUM is just n. off US 101 Shoreline Blvd. exit at 1401 N. Shoreline Blvd. Appropriately located in Silicon Valley, the museum is dedicated to the preservation and celebration of computing history.

Revolution: The First 2000 Years of Computing, chronicles the evolution and impact of modern computing from the abacus to the smart phone. This multimedia experience includes computer hardware, software, documentation, ephemera, photographs and moving images. **Time:** Allow 1 hour minimum. **Hours:** Wed.-Sun. 10-5. **Cost:** $15; $12 (ages 65+ and students and military with ID); free (ages 0-12). **Phone:** (650) 810-1010.

MOFFETT FIELD MUSEUM is off US 101 Moffett Field exit. Enter at the main gate's far left lane and proceed via S. Akron Dr. to Severyns Ave.; the museum is on Severyns Ave. in Building 126, adjacent to Hangar One. Originally a home for Navy airships, Moffett Field was an Army Air Corps training base in 1940. Blimps returned to the base during World War II, when it became a Naval Air Station.

Exhibits include dioramas, memorabilia and airship replicas as well as artifacts pertaining to the field's history. Visitors can see Hangar One, the huge structure that housed the blimps.

Note: Photo ID is required. **Time:** Allow 1 hour, 30 minutes minimum. **Hours:** Wed.-Sat. 10-2. Closed Jan. 1, Thanksgiving and Christmas. **Cost:** $8; $5 (ages 65+ and the physically impaired); $3 (ages 13-17); free (military with ID). **Phone:** (650) 964-4024.

(See map & index p. 468.)

NASA AMES RESEARCH CENTER is off US 101 (Moffett Field exit). This NASA field center conducts research on information technology, astrobiology and aeronautics. The Ames Exploration Center features a moon rock, a Mercury spacecraft, space suits and interactive displays highlighting a variety of NASA missions to the moon and Mars. Also displayed is a mock-up of a laboratory aboard the International Space Station. The Immersive Theater's 14-foot-tall, 36-foot-wide screen features high-definition videos showing Mars missions and simulated flights through the Milky Way galaxy and beyond, as well as numerous scientific contributions made by NASA Ames researchers. **Hours:** Exploration Center open Tues.-Fri. 10-4, Sat.-Sun. noon-4. Closed major holidays. **Cost:** Free. **Phone:** (650) 604-6274.

THE RENGSTORFF HOUSE is off US 101 (N. Shoreline Blvd. exit) in Shoreline Park, at 3070 N. Shoreline Blvd. German immigrant Henry Rengstorff, who came to California in 1850 to seek his fortune, arrived too late to take advantage of the gold rush; instead, he accumulated acreage in the Santa Clara Valley and built this 12-room, two-story Victorian Italianate home in 1867. It has four fireplaces, a large dining room, a staircase with a handcrafted newel post, and parlors decorated with period wallpaper. Docents in period attire conduct guided tours. **Time:** Allow 30 minutes minimum. **Hours:** Tues.-Wed. and Sun. 11-5. **Cost:** Free. **Phone:** (650) 903-6392.

BEST WESTERN PLUS MOUNTAIN VIEW INN
(650)962-9912

Hotel
$99-$199

AAA Benefit: Members save up to 20%, plus 10% bonus points with Best Western Rewards®.

Address: 2300 W El Camino Real 94040 **Location:** US 101 exit Rengstorff Rd, 1.3 mi s. **Facility:** 71 units, some efficiencies and kitchens. 2-3 stories (no elevator), exterior corridors. **Terms:** cancellation fee imposed. **Amenities:** high-speed Internet. **Pool(s):** outdoor. **Activities:** sauna, whirlpool, exercise room. **Guest Services:** valet and coin laundry. **Free Special Amenities: expanded continental breakfast and high-speed Internet.**

COMFORT INN-MOUNTAIN VIEW   (650)967-7888
Hotel $115-$209 **Address:** 1561 W El Camino Real 94040 **Location:** US 101 exit Shoreline Blvd, 2 mi to SR 82, then just n. **Facility:** 44 units. 3 stories, interior corridors. **Terms:** cancellation fee imposed. **Amenities:** high-speed Internet. **Guest Services:** valet laundry.

COUNTY INN   (650)961-1131   43
Hotel $79-$169 **Address:** 850 Leong Dr 94043 **Location:** US 101 exit Moffett Blvd, just s. Located in a quiet residential area. **Facility:** 53 units, some two bedrooms and kitchens. 2 stories, exterior corridors. **Terms:** cancellation fee imposed. **Amenities:** high-speed Internet. *Some:* safes. **Pool(s):** heated outdoor. **Activities:** exercise room. **Guest Services:** valet and coin laundry.

EXTENDED STAYAMERICA-SAN JOSE, MOUNTAIN VIEW
(650)962-1500   46
Extended Stay Hotel $119-$134 **Address:** 190 E El Camino Real 94040 **Location:** SR 82, just w of SR 85. **Facility:** 133 efficiencies. 2 stories (no elevator), exterior corridors. **Amenities:** high-speed Internet (fee). **Guest Services:** coin laundry.

HAMPTON INN & SUITES   (650)988-0300   44
Hotel $169-$219 **Address:** 390 Moffett Blvd 94043 **Location:** US 101 exit Moffett Blvd, 0.8 mi w. **Facility:** 88 units. 3 stories, interior corridors. **Terms:** 1-7 night minimum stay, cancellation fee imposed. **Amenities:** high-speed Internet, safes. **Activities:** whirlpool, exercise room. **Guest Services:** valet laundry.

AAA Benefit: Members save up to 10%!

THE HOTEL ARIA   650/559-9115
Hotel. Rates not provided. **Address:** 2700 W El Camino Real 94040 **Location:** US 101 exit San Antonio Rd W, 0.5 mi n on SR 82. **Facility:** 98 units. 2-3 stories, interior corridors. **Amenities:** high-speed Internet. **Pool(s):** heated outdoor. **Activities:** whirlpool, exercise room. **Guest Services:** valet and coin laundry.

HOTEL AVANTE, A JOIE DE VIVRE HOTEL
(650)940-1000   48
Hotel $89-$499 **Address:** 860 E El Camino Real 94040 **Location:** US 101 exit 398B (SR 85/Cupertino); exit SR 82 S (Sunnyvale), 0.5 mi e. **Facility:** 91 units. 4 stories, interior corridors. **Terms:** cancellation fee imposed. **Amenities:** high-speed Internet. **Pool(s):** heated outdoor. **Activities:** whirlpool, exercise room. **Guest Services:** valet laundry.

HOTEL STRATA - MOUNTAIN VIEW TOWN CENTER
(650)967-6957   45
Motel $130-$280 **Address:** 93 W El Camino Real 94040 **Location:** US 101 exit SR 237 northbound, 3 mi w, then just n on SR 82; exit SR 85 southbound, 0.5 mi s to Grant Rd exit, then just n on SR 82. **Facility:** 58 units, some efficiencies and kitchens. 2 stories (no elevator), exterior corridors. **Terms:** cancellation fee imposed. **Amenities:** high-speed Internet, safes. **Pool(s):** outdoor. **Activities:** exercise room. **Guest Services:** valet and coin laundry.

(See map & index p. 468.)

HOTEL ZICO

650/969-8200

Contemporary Hotel

Rates not provided

Address: 200 E El Camino Real 94040 **Location:** On SR 82, just w of SR 85. **Facility:** 58 units. 2 stories, interior corridors. **Amenities:** high-speed Internet. **Activities:** exercise room. **Guest Services:** valet and coin laundry. **Free Special Amenities: full breakfast and high-speed Internet.** *(See ad this page.)*

QUALITY INN & SUITES AT NASA AMES

(650)934-0155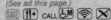

Hotel
$100-$200

Address: 5 Fairchild Dr 94043 **Location:** US 101 exit Moffett Blvd, 0.3 mi e on Leong Dr (which becomes Fairchild Dr). **Facility:** 70 units. 2 stories, interior corridors. **Terms:** cancellation fee imposed. **Amenities:** high-speed Internet. **Activities:** limited exercise equipment. **Guest Services:** valet and coin laundry. **Free Special Amenities: full breakfast and high-speed Internet.**

RAMADA LIMITED

(650)967-6856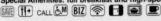

Hotel $99-$159 **Address:** 55 Fairchild Dr 94043 **Location:** US 101 exit Moffett Blvd, 0.3 mi e on Leong Dr (which becomes Fairchild Dr). **Facility:** 50 units. 2 stories (no elevator), exterior corridors. **Terms:** off-site registration. **Amenities:** high-speed Internet. **Pool(s):** outdoor. **Activities:** whirlpool, exercise room. **Guest Services:** coin laundry.

Save on theme park tickets at AAA.com/discounts

RESIDENCE INN BY MARRIOTT - PALO ALTO/MOUNTAIN VIEW

(650)940-1300

Extended Stay Hotel $119-$289 **Address:** 1854 W El Camino Real 94040 **Location:** US 101 exit 399 (Shoreline Blvd/Mountain View), 2 mi to SR 82, then 0.5 mi n. **Facility:** 112 kitchen units, some two bedrooms. 2 stories (no elevator), exterior corridors. **Amenities:** high-speed Internet. **Pool(s):** heated outdoor. **Activities:** whirlpool, sports court, exercise room. **Guest Services:** valet and coin laundry.

AAA Benefit: AAA hotel discounts of 5% or more.

/SOME UNITS FEE

SUPER 8

(650)969-9641

Motel
$80-$129

Address: 1665 W El Camino Real 94040 **Location:** US 101 exit Shoreline Blvd, 2 mi to SR 82, then just n. **Facility:** 31 units. 2 stories (no elevator), exterior corridors. **Terms:** cancellation fee imposed. **Amenities:** high-speed Internet. **Free Special Amenities: continental breakfast and high-speed Internet.**

HILTON GARDEN INN

650/964-1700

fyi Not evaluated. **Address:** 840 E El Camino Real 94040 **Location:** US 101 exit SR 85 to exit SR 82 S, 0.5 mi e. Facilities, services, and décor characterize a mid-scale property.

AAA Benefit: Unparalleled hospitality at a special Member rate.

WHERE TO EAT

THE CANTANKEROUS FISH

650/966-8124

American. Casual Dining. $10-$27 **AAA Inspector Notes:** Diners settle down in a relaxed contemporary atmosphere to savor entrées of fresh seafood, including favorites of sea bass and ginger-glazed salmon. **Bar:** full bar. **Address:** 420 Castro St 94041 **Location:** Downtown. **Parking:** street only. L D CALL

▼ *See AAA listing this page* ▼

Trust your vehicle to AAA/CAA Approved Auto Repair facilities

CASCAL   650/940-9500

▼▼▼ Latin American Small Plates. Casual Dining. $13-$27 **AAA Inspector Notes:** Known primarily for its tapas menu, which comprises small appetizer-size dishes, this restaurant also serves seviche, paellas and other preparations of Latin cuisine. **Bar:** full bar. **Address:** 400 Castro St 94041 **Location:** Corner of Castro and California sts; downtown. ⓛ ⓓ

HONG KONG BISTRO   650/968-8938

▼▼ Chinese. Casual Dining. $6-$17 **AAA Inspector Notes:** This casual eatery offers Hong Kong-style fusion food ranging from macaroni soup noodles to Portuguese-baked pork chop and rice. Pair your meal with Hong Kong milk tea with or without bubbles or yin yang tea (coffee and tea mixed). Note that a minimum charge applies for credit card usage. **Bar:** beer & wine. **Address:** 147 Castro St 94041 **Location:** Between Evelyn and Villa sts. ⓛ ⓓ

RISTORANTE DON GIOVANNI   650/961-9749

▼▼▼ Italian. Casual Dining. $10-$27 **AAA Inspector Notes:** Fresh pasta and risotto dishes share menu space with veal and steak entrees. **Bar:** full bar. **Address:** 235 Castro St 94041 **Location:** US 101 exit Moffett Blvd, 1 mi w. **Parking:** street only. ⓛ ⓓ

SCRATCH   650/237-3132

▼▼▼ American. Casual Dining. $11-$29 **AAA Inspector Notes:** This spacious restaurant with contemporary decor has various sitting areas to suit your mood. For intimate dining, request the booth area. If you want to be part of the action, dine at the bar. Feeling casual? Go for the tables. If you want to dine alone, sit at the raw bar/kitchen area. Cuisine is American comfort food brought up a notch from crab cakes to BBQ ribs. **Bar:** full bar. **Address:** 401 Castro St 94041 **Location:** At California St; downtown. **Parking:** street only. ⓛ ⓓ

SHALALA   650/965-8001

▼▼ Japanese. Casual Dining. $8-$12 **AAA Inspector Notes:** This unassuming restaurant specializes in richly-flavored ramen with a choice of size and spiciness. There also are classic izakaya dishes from gyoza and yaki onigiri to tuna poke. If ramen is not on the radar, there also are donburis (rice bowls). **Bar:** beer only. **Address:** 698 W Dana St 94041 **Location:** At Hope St; downtown. **Parking:** street only. ⓛ ⓓ 🄰🄲

SHIVA'S   650/960-3802

▼▼▼ Indian. Casual Dining. $12-$24 **AAA Inspector Notes:** Enjoy dinner in this elegant dining room with a touch of contemporary Indian motifs. Kebabs and curries are prepared in a large wok, which enhances the full flavor of the spices. Buffet-style lunches are offered. **Bar:** full bar. **Address:** 800 California St 94041 **Location:** Corner of Castro St; downtown. **Parking:** street only. ⓛ ⓓ CALL 🄶Ⓜ

TIED HOUSE BREWERY   650/965-2739

▼▼ American. Casual Dining. $6-$18 **AAA Inspector Notes:** This popular brewpub prepares such dishes as steaks, smoked salmon and trout as well as other seafood. **Bar:** full bar. **Address:** 954 Villa St 94041 **Location:** Between Castro St and Shoreline Blvd; downtown. ⓛ ⓓ CALL 🄶Ⓜ

ZUCCA RISTORANTE   650/864-9940

▼▼ Mediterranean. Casual Dining. $9-$23 **AAA Inspector Notes:** Many foods and flavors infuse the chef's flair-filled preparations, making this restaurant popular with the locals. **Bar:** full bar. **Reservations:** suggested. **Address:** 186 Castro St 94041 **Location:** US 101 exit Moffett Blvd, 1 mi w. **Parking:** street only. ⓛ ⓓ

MOUNT HERMON (G-2) pop. 1,037, elev. 400'

RECREATIONAL ACTIVITIES

Ziplines

• **Redwood Canopy Tours** staging area is at the Fieldhouse at 17 Conference Dr. **Hours:** Two-hour canopy tours depart approximately every half-hour daily 9:30-5, May-Aug.; Thurs.-Mon., Sept.-Feb.; Wed.-Mon., rest of year. Reservations are required. **Phone:** (831) 430-4357.

MOUNT SHASTA (B-2) pop. 3,394, elev. 3,554'

A small city named for a tall mountain, Mount Shasta is the northern gateway via scenic SR 89 to Whiskeytown-Shasta-Trinity National Recreation Area *(see place listing p. 557)*, Shasta-Trinity National Forests *(see place listing p. 518)*, and nearby Lake Siskiyou.

Mount Shasta Visitors Bureau: 300 Pine St., Mount Shasta, CA 96067. **Phone:** (530) 926-4865 or (800) 926-4865.

MOUNT SHASTA STATE FISH HATCHERY AND SISSON MUSEUM, .5 mi. w. of I-5 exit 738 (Central Mount Shasta) at 1 N. Old Stage Rd., produces 3 to 5 million trout annually to stock the streams and lakes of northern California. The museum has exhibits pertaining to the region's geological and human history and the unusual lenticular clouds that form over Mount Shasta. There also is a display of Native American basketry.

Time: Allow 1 hour minimum. **Hours:** Hatchery open daily 8 a.m.-dusk. Museum open daily 10-4, Memorial Day-Labor Day; daily 1-4, day after Labor Day-Sept. 30; Fri.-Sun. 1-4, Oct. 1-early Dec. and early Apr.-day before Memorial Day. Closed Thanksgiving. Phone ahead to confirm schedule. **Cost:** Hatchery free. Museum by donation. **Phone:** (530) 926-2215 for the hatchery, or (530) 926-5508 for the museum.

BEST WESTERN PLUS TREE HOUSE   (530)926-3101

▼▼▼ Hotel $99-$199

AAA Benefit: Members save up to 20%, plus 10% bonus points with Best Western Rewards®.

Address: 111 Morgan Way 96067 **Location:** I-5 exit 738 (Central Mount Shasta), just e. **Facility:** 98 units. 2-3 stories, interior/exterior corridors. **Amenities:** high-speed Internet. **Dining:** Tree House Restaurant, see separate listing. **Pool(s):** heated indoor. **Activities:** whirlpool, exercise room. **Guest Services:** coin laundry. **Free Special Amenities:** full breakfast and room upgrade (subject to availability with advance reservations).

SAVE 🍴 🍸 🏊 BIZ 🛜 ✕ 🖥 🖼 🖵 / SOME UNITS FEE 🐾

COLD CREEK INN   530/926-9851

▼ Motel $69-$155

Address: 724 N Mount Shasta Blvd 96067 **Location:** I-5 exit 738 (Central Mount Shasta), 0.5 mi ne on W Lake St, then 0.5 mi nw. **Facility:** 19 units, some two bedrooms and kitchens. 1 story, exterior corridors. **Terms:** cancellation fee imposed. **Free Special Amenities:** continental breakfast and high-speed Internet.

SAVE 🛜 ✕ 🖥 🖼 🖵 / SOME UNITS FEE 🐾

EVERGREEN LODGE   (530)926-2143

▼ Motel $59-$129

Address: 1312 S Mount Shasta Blvd 96067 **Location:** I-5 exit 737 (Mount Shasta City), 0.9 mi n. **Facility:** 20 units, some kitchens. 1 story, exterior corridors. **Terms:** 3 day cancellation notice-fee imposed. **Pool(s):** outdoor. **Activities:** whirlpool. **Free Special Amenities:** local telephone calls.

SAVE 🏊 🛜 / SOME UNITS 🖥 🖼

MOUNT SHASTA INN & SUITES

530/918-9292

Motel
$59-$189

Address: 710 S Mount Shasta Blvd 96067 **Location:** I-5 exit 738 (Central Mount Shasta), 0.5 mi e, then 0.5 mi s. **Facility:** 30 units. 2 stories (no elevator), exterior corridors. **Terms:** cancellation fee imposed. **Free Special Amenities: continental breakfast and high-speed Internet.**

MOUNT SHASTA RESORT

(530)926-3030

Cottage $99-$319 **Address:** 1000 Siskiyou Lake Blvd 96067 **Location:** I-5 exit 738 (Central Mount Shasta), 0.4 mi w on Lake St (which becomes Hatchery Ln), just s on S Old Stage Rd, at the split follow sign, 1.4 mi s on W A Barr Rd, then just ne. **Facility:** This lodge offers well-appointed hotel rooms as part of a cozy triplex in a secluded setting or inviting chalets featuring a private deck, a skylight and a gas fireplace. 65 cottages, some two bedrooms and kitchens. 1 story, exterior corridors. **Terms:** off-site registration, check-in 4 pm, 2 night minimum stay - seasonal and/or weekends, 14 day cancellation notice-fee imposed, resort fee. **Dining:** Highland House Restaurant, see separate listing. **Activities:** fishing, 4 tennis courts, bicycle trails, hiking trails, jogging, spa. *Fee:* golf-18 holes. **Guest Services:** coin laundry.

WHERE TO EAT

BLACK BEAR DINER

530/926-4669

American. Casual Dining. $7-$16 **AAA Inspector Notes:** A homey atmosphere characterizes this family-oriented restaurant. Familiar comfort foods, such as meatloaf with mashed potatoes, are at the heart of the menu and are served in generous portions. **Address:** 401 W Lake St 96067 **Location:** I-5 exit 738 (Central Mount Shasta E), just e. B L D

CASA RAMOS

530/926-0250

Mexican. Casual Dining. $7-$15 **AAA Inspector Notes:** A varied Mexican menu is featured in a colorful atmosphere. Mexican favorites include fajitas, enchiladas, burritos and specialty steak and seafood entrees. **Bar:** full bar. **Address:** 1136 S Mount Shasta Blvd 96067 **Location:** I-5 exit 737 (Mount Shasta City), 0.9 mi n. **Parking:** street only. L D

HIGHLAND HOUSE RESTAURANT

530/926-3030

American. Casual Dining. $8-$29 **AAA Inspector Notes:** Enjoy the panoramic view of Mt. Shasta as you dine on such classics as shrimp cocktail, New York steak and a chocolate raspberry bombe. **Bar:** full bar. **Address:** 1000 Siskiyou Lake Blvd 96067 **Location:** I-5 exit 738 (Central Mount Shasta), 0.4 mi w on Lake St (which becomes Hatchery Ln), just s on S Old Stage Rd, at the split follow sign, 1.4 mi s on W A Barr Rd, then just ne; in Mount Shasta Resort. **Parking:** street only. B L D

LILYS

530/926-3372

California
Casual Dining
$10-$27

AAA Inspector Notes: Located in a quaint cottage, the pleasant surroundings enhance the nice selection of seafood, pasta, salads, Mexican and vegetarian specialties which make this restaurant a popular stop. Specials are featured daily. Patio or deck dining is offered in season. **Bar:** full bar. **Address:** 1013 S Mount Shasta Blvd 96067 **Location:** I-5 exit 737 (Mount Shasta City), 1.3 mi n. **Parking:** on-site and street. *Menu on AAA.com*

B L D

TREE HOUSE RESTAURANT

530/926-3101

American. Casual Dining. $10-$25 **AAA Inspector Notes:** Adding to the charmingly rustic decor is a fireplace, open to both the restaurant and lobby. Some seats afford a view of spectacular Mount Shasta. Diners can savor pasta, steak or prime rib. **Bar:** full bar. **Address:** 111 Morgan Way 96067 **Location:** I-5 exit 738 (Central Mount Shasta), just e; in BEST WESTERN PLUS Tree House Motor Inn.

B D

MUIR WOODS NATIONAL MONUMENT (D-7)

• Part of San Francisco area — see map p. 342

Muir Woods National Monument, 12 miles north of the Golden Gate Bridge on the southwestern slope of Mount Tamalpais, can be reached via US 101 and SR 1. Named for Scottish-born American conservationist and Sierra Club founder John Muir, 560-acre Muir Woods preserves a stand of Sequoia sempervirens, or coast redwoods—trees that once blanketed coastal valleys in much of northern California. A very tall evergreen (some specimens reach more than 250 feet in height), the coast redwood also can live to be more than 1,000 years old.

Muir Woods is a world unto itself. Situated along a canyon floor—part of a coastal valley traversed by Redwood Creek—it's a refuge of cool dampness and deep shade. Animals and birds are elusive (environmental conditions contribute to a lack of food), and there's a serene silence. This region never experienced the depredations of logging, so living redwoods of all ages thrive among dead giants still standing, rotting logs and an exuberant undergrowth of trees, ferns and other plants adapted to the moist, low-light conditions.

Although coast redwoods dominate, Douglas fir, maple, oak and bay laurel also thrive. Paved trails for hiking and exploring range from a half-mile to 2 miles long. One loop trail is divided into half-hour, 1-hour and 90-minute segments, all providing plenty of opportunities to marvel at the giant redwoods. If you don't feel like going on a long hike, Cathedral Grove, a short walk from the entrance, has some particularly large trees and a hushed quiet that seems to envelop the forest. Longer trails cross over into adjoining Mount Tamalpais State Park, near Mill Valley.

Picnicking and camping are not permitted, and pets are not allowed. Vehicles longer than 35 feet are not permitted on steep, winding SR 1. Adverse weather conditions can cause delays on roads leading to Muir Woods. Various companies offer Muir Woods sightseeing tours that include transportation. Marin Transit provides shuttle service from Marin City to Muir Woods Sat.-Sun. and holidays, Memorial Day-Labor Day; Sat.-Sun., early May-day before Memorial Day and day after Labor Day-late Sept. Round-trip fare $3; $1 (ages 6-18, ages 65+ and the physically impaired). For additional information phone (415) 526-3239.

Food is available. Walking trails open daily 8-dusk. Visitor center open daily 9-7:30, mid-Mar. to mid.-Sept.; hours vary, rest of year. To avoid summer crowds, plan to arrive before 10 or after 3. Rainy weather is a possibility from November through May. Admission $7; free (ages 0-15). For additional information contact the Site Supervisor, Muir Woods National Monument, Mill Valley, CA 94941-2696; phone (415) 388-2595, or TTY (415) 556-2766.

MURPHYS (F-4) pop. 2,213, elev. 2,171'

MERCER CAVERNS, 1.5 mi. n. via Sheep Ranch Rd., has been open since 1885. Guided tours lasting 45 to 50 minutes visit 10 rooms with various crystalline formations. **Hours:** Tours are given daily 9:30-5, Memorial Day weekend-Labor Day; 10:30-4:30, rest of year. Phone ahead for winter hours. Closed Christmas. **Cost:** $13.95; $7.95 (ages 3-12). **Phone:** (209) 728-2101.

WINERIES

• **Ironstone Vineyards** is 1 mi. s. at 1894 Six Mile Rd. **Hours:** Tastings daily 10-5. Tours are given daily; phone for schedule. **Phone:** (209) 728-1251.

DUNBAR HOUSE 1880   209/728-2897

Bed & Breakfast
$199-$275

Address: 271 Jones St 95247 **Location:** In historic downtown. **Facility:** Featuring a wrap-around porch, private patio areas and guest rooms with elegant style, this property is walking distance to unique gift, food and wine shops as well as wine tasting rooms in the downtown area. 5 units. 2 stories (no elevator), interior corridors. **Terms:** 2 night minimum stay - weekends, 10 day cancellation notice-fee imposed. **Free Special Amenities: full breakfast and high-speed Internet.**

MURPHYS INN MOTEL   (209)728-1818
🏨 Hotel $85-$159 **Address:** 76 Main St 95247 **Location:** Jct SR 4 and Main St. **Facility:** 37 units. 2 stories (no elevator), interior corridors. **Terms:** cancellation fee imposed. **Pool(s):** outdoor. **Activities:** limited exercise equipment. **Guest Services:** coin laundry.

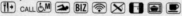

MURPHYS SUITES   (209)728-2121
🏨 Hotel $119-$209 **Address:** 134 Hwy 4 95247 **Location:** On SR 4; just s of business district. **Facility:** 70 units. 2 stories, interior corridors. **Terms:** cancellation fee imposed. **Pool(s):** outdoor. **Activities:** sauna, whirlpool, exercise room. **Guest Services:** coin laundry.

WHERE TO EAT

EL JARDIN   209/728-8300
🍷🍷 Mexican. Casual Dining. $7-$20 **AAA Inspector Notes:** A long time tradition in this area, this family-owned and -operated restaurant offers a great selection of traditional favorites as well as incorporating favorite family recipes. **Bar:** beer & wine. **Address:** 484 E Hwy 4 95247 **Location:** Just e on SR 4. L D CALL

GROUNDS RESTAURANT   209/728-8663
🍷🍷 American. Casual Dining. $8-$26 **AAA Inspector Notes:** Located among the historic shops and sites of the downtown area, this favorite eatery of both locals and visitors offers breakfasts consisting of omelets, Belgian waffles and homemade granola. Lunch brings out the sandwiches served on homemade breads and homemade soups. The dinner menu offers such items as crab cakes, cioppino (fish, shellfish and tomato stew), steak with mushrooms and pasta dishes. The staff is warm and friendly. **Bar:** wine only. **Address:** 402 Main St 95247 **Location:** Between Algiers St and Surrey Ln; in historic downtown. **Parking:** street only. B L D CALL

MYERS FLAT pop. 146

MYERS INN   (707)943-3259
🍷🍷🍷
Bed & Breakfast
$161-$203

Address: 12913 Ave of the Giants 95554 **Location:** US 101 exit Myers Flat, just w. **Facility:** Rooms with white wicker furnishings and second-floor decks occupy the building, which served as a stagecoach stop in 1867. A hiking trail is nearby. 10 units. 2 stories (no elevator), interior corridors. **Terms:** check-in 4 pm, 14 day cancellation notice-fee imposed. **Activities:** whirlpool. **Free Special Amenities: full breakfast and early check-in/late check-out.**

NAPA (B-8) pop. 76,915, elev. 17'
• **Hotels p. 236** • **Restaurants p. 243**
• **Attractions map p. 568**
• **Hotels & Restaurants map & index p. 570**
• **Part of Wine Country area — see map p. 562**

Napa is nestled in one of California's most famous wine-producing regions, the Napa Valley. This area was a center of gold rush activity in the 1850s. Grapevine cuttings supplied by priests from the missions at Sonoma and San Rafael were the start of what grew into a major industry, and today Napa Valley is a leader in the production of American table wines.

Napa is at the southern end of a scenic 28-mile stretch of SR 29, which heads northwest through the valley to Calistoga. The two-lane road passes acres of vineyards and more than 40 wineries. The Silverado Trail, running parallel to SR 29 to the east, provides stunning views of the valley and the Napa River. There are additional wineries along this less-traveled route.

Downtown Napa is filled with turn-of-the-20th-century houses and buildings in architectural styles from Art Deco, Classic Revival and Italianate to Spanish Colonial and Victorian Gothic. Some 2,500 of these buildings are on the National Historical Registry. The restored Napa Valley Opera House, built in 1880, is a local landmark at 1030 Main St. It features two theaters; phone (707) 226-7372 for information and schedules.

TravelBrains' "Napa Valley Tour Guide" features a 150-page illustrated guidebook with profiles of more than 60 wineries, a wine journal and descriptions of the valley's winery towns. Included are a CD-ROM and a self-guiding audio (CD) tour of 11 wineries and five historic locations with background information about Napa's wine heritage and history. The guide is available for $34.95; phone (888) 458-6475.

Napa Valley Welcome Center: 600 Main St., Napa, CA 94559. **Phone:** (707) 251-5895.

Self-guiding tours: Maps of wineries and the historic downtown area are available from the welcome center.

Shopping areas: Napa Premium Outlets, west of SR 29 at 629 Factory Stores Dr., has 50 stores, including Ann Taylor, Barneys New York, Calvin Klein and Kenneth Cole.

(See map & index p. 570.)

INSIDER INFO:
Wine Country

Spotlight's Wine Country Guide, a 100-page brochure providing maps and detailed information about towns, events, wineries, attractions, accommodations and retail establishments in Lake, Lower Mendocino, Napa and Sonoma counties is available free at the concierge desk of most Bay Area hotels, at most retail establishments in Wine Country and at select northern California AAA offices in the Wine Country region. The brochure's 4-month calendar of events is updated monthly.

The brochure is available from the publisher for $3.50 to cover postage and handling. Write *Spotlight's Wine Country Guide*, 5 Kenilworth Ct., Novato, CA 94945-2622; phone (415) 898-7908.

DI ROSA is at 5200 Sonoma Hwy. (SR 12/121). Surrounded by vineyards, olive trees and a lake, the 217-acre preserve features three gallery buildings and a sculpture meadow exhibiting nearly 2,000 pieces of contemporary Bay Area art. The Gatehouse Gallery features changing exhibitions and works from the permanent collection. One- and 2-hour guided tours cover the other galleries and the grounds. The 2.5-hour Art & Meadow Tour includes the main gallery and the sculpture meadow. Nature hikes also are offered; reservations are required.

Time: Allow 2 hours minimum. **Hours:** Gatehouse Gallery open Wed.-Sun. 10-6, May-Oct.; Wed.-Sun. 10-4, rest of year. One- and 2-hour guided tours of the other two galleries are given Wed.-Sun. at 10, 11, and 1 (also Sat.-Sun. at 4), May-Oct.; phone for tour schedule, rest of year. Art & Meadow Tour given Sun. at 10, May-Sept. Closed major holidays.

Cost: Gatehouse Gallery by donation. Guided tours $12-$15; $9-$12 (ages 65+, students with ID and the physically impaired); free (ages 0-11). Reservations are recommended for both 1- and 2-hour tours, especially on weekends. **Phone:** (707) 226-5991.

NAPA RIVER ADVENTURES departs from the Kennedy Park Dock just s. of downtown; take Streblow Dr. w. off SR 128 (Soscol Ave.) to the riverfront. Two-hour cruises on the *Napa Queen*, an 11-passenger electric motor launch with wraparound windows, take passengers along the Napa River while the captain provides information about the town's history, the levees and wetlands, the microclimates that aid in the production of Napa Valley wines, and the region's indigenous wildlife, which includes many species of birds. A cheese platter, wine and soft drinks are provided.

Guests also may bring their own beverages and snacks. There are no restrooms on board. **Time:**

(See map & index p. 570.)

Allow 2 hours, 30 minutes minimum. **Hours:** Cruises depart daily at 3 and 6 p.m. Times may vary based on tide conditions; phone ahead. Closed Jan. 1, Thanksgiving and Christmas. **Cost:** $50 (minimum of four passengers); $25 (ages 0-12). Two-person rate $95 per passenger. Reservations are required. **Phone:** (707) 224-9080.

NAPA VALLEY WINE TRAIN, 1275 McKinstry St., is a 36-mile, 3-hour journey that winds through the heart of Napa Valley wine country. Lunch and dinner—cooked to order on board—are offered in elegantly restored Pullman dining, lounge and Vista Dome cars. Winery tours and other specialty excursions also are available.

Time: Allow 3 hours minimum. **Hours:** Departures daily; times vary. **Cost:** Fares, which include lunch or dinner, start at $99. Prepayment is required. Reservations are recommended. **Phone:** (707) 253-2111 or (800) 427-4124. *(See ad this page.)*

SKYLINE WILDERNESS PARK is 1.4 mi. e. of Soscol Ave. on Imola Ave. This 900-acre tract of Napa Valley land offers hiking, biking and horseback riding trails, camping, picnicking, bird-watching and wildlife viewing, an archery range, a disc golf course and—last but not least—an abundance of scenic views. Wild turkeys and deer are among the animal residents. The 2.5-acre Martha Walker Native Habitat Garden features plants found in the Napa Valley and the surrounding region.

Time: Allow 2 hours minimum. **Hours:** Daily 8-7, mid-Mar through Sept. 30; 8-6, in Oct.; 8-5, rest of year. Closed Christmas. **Cost:** $5 per private vehicle (up to four people) plus $1 for each additional passenger; free (those arriving on foot, bicycle or on horseback). Fees apply for some activities. **Phone:** (707) 252-0481. 🅰 🆇 🅰

RECREATIONAL ACTIVITIES

Hot Air Ballooning

- **Balloons Above the Valley** trips depart from the Napa Valley Marriott at 3425 Solano Ave. **Hours:** Trips depart daily at sunrise (weather permitting). **Phone:** (707) 253-2222 or (800) 464-6824.
- **Napa Valley Balloons** departs from Domain Chandon at 1 California Dr. **Hours:** Trips depart daily at dawn (weather permitting). **Phone:** (707) 944-0228 or (800) 253-2224.

WINERIES

- **Artesa Vineyards & Winery** is at 1345 Henry Rd. **Hours:** Daily 10-5. Last pour is 30 minutes before closing. Guided tours are given daily at 11 and 2. **Phone:** (707) 224-1668 for general information, or (707) 254-2140 for the tasting room.
- **Domaine Carneros** is 4 mi. s.w. just off SR 121/12 (Carneros Hwy.) at 1240 Duhig Rd. **Hours:** Daily 10-6. Tours are given daily at 11, 1 and 3. Closed Jan. 1, Thanksgiving and Christmas. **Phone:** (707) 257-0101, ext. 108 or (800) 716-2788.
- **Pine Ridge Vineyards** is at 5901 Silverado Tr. **Hours:** Tasting room daily 10:30-4:30. Guided tours are given by appointment daily at 10, noon and 2. Closed major holidays. **Phone:** (707) 257-4720 or (800) 575-9777.

THE 1801 INN (707)224-3739 **61**

◆◆◆ **Historic Bed & Breakfast** $225-$495 **Address:** 1801 1st St 94559 **Location:** SR 29 exit 1st St, 0.5 mi e to Jefferson St, then just n. **Facility:** Occupying a restored 1903 Queen Anne Victorian, the inn also includes cottages with private patios and colorful flower gardens. 8 units, some cottages. 2 stories (no elevator), interior/exterior corridors. **Terms:** 2-3 night minimum stay - seasonal and/or weekends, age restrictions may apply, cancellation fee imposed. **Activities:** Fee: massage. **Guest Services:** valet laundry.
🍽 CALL 🅼 📶 ✉ /SOME UNITS 🔧 💲

(See map & index p. 570.)

ANDAZ NAPA
(707)224-3900 **63**

Hotel
$169-$799

ANDAZ **AAA Benefit:** The latest in style, High-tech innovation, Special Member Rates.

Address: 1450 First St 94559 **Location:** 0.3 mi w of Soscol Ave; in historic downtown. **Facility:** This intimate, contemporary lodging is located in Napa's historic downtown area and sits adjacent to many shops and restaurants. 141 units. 5 stories, interior corridors. **Parking:** on-site and valet. **Terms:** check-in 4 pm, 3 day cancellation notice-fee imposed. **Amenities:** high-speed Internet, safes. **Activities:** Fee: massage. **Guest Services:** valet laundry. **Free Special Amenities:** high-speed Internet.

BEL ABRI
(707)253-2100 **58**

Bed & Breakfast
$129-$310

Address: 837 California Blvd 94559 **Location:** SR 29 exit 1st St, just e. **Facility:** Centered in Napa Valley, this B&B offers spacious and attractively appointed guest units. 15 units. 3 stories, interior corridors. **Terms:** 7 day cancellation notice-fee imposed. **Free Special Amenities:** expanded continental breakfast and high-speed Internet.

BEST WESTERN PLUS ELM HOUSE INN
(707)255-1831 **59**

Hotel
$109-$329

 AAA Benefit: Members save up to 20%, plus 10% bonus points with Best Western Rewards®.

Address: 800 California Blvd 94559 **Location:** SR 29 exit 1st St, 1 1/2 blks s. Located in a residential area. **Facility:** 22 units. 3 stories, interior/exterior corridors. **Terms:** 2 night minimum stay - seasonal and/or weekends. **Amenities:** high-speed Internet. **Activities:** whirlpool. **Guest Services:** valet and coin laundry. **Free Special Amenities:** local telephone calls and high-speed Internet.

Learn the local driving laws
at DrivingLaws.AAA.com

▼ See AAA listing p. 238 ▼

Share a New View on Travel at
AAATravelViews.com
Read stories, tips and trends from AAA insiders.
Post comments and get your questions answered by our travel experts.

(See map & index p. 570.)

BEST WESTERN PLUS INN AT THE VINES
(707)257-1930 **69**

Hotel
$110-$260

AAA Benefit: Members save up to 20%, plus 10% bonus points with Best Western Rewards®.

Address: 100 Soscol Ave 94559 **Location:** Jct SR 121 and Soscol Ave. **Facility:** 69 units. 2-3 stories, interior/exterior corridors. **Terms:** check-in 4 pm, 2-3 night minimum stay - seasonal and/or weekends. **Amenities:** *Some:* high-speed Internet. **Pool(s):** heated outdoor. **Activities:** whirlpool. **Guest Services:** valet laundry. **Free Special Amenities: full breakfast and high-speed Internet.** *(See ad p. 237.)*

BEST WESTERN PREMIER IVY HOTEL NAPA
(707)253-9300 **47**

Hotel
$159-$299

AAA Benefit: Members save up to 20%, plus 10% bonus points with Best Western Rewards®.

Address: 4195 Solano Ave 94558 **Location:** W of and adjacent to SR 29; at Wine Country Ave. **Facility:** 115 units. 2 stories, interior corridors. **Terms:** 2 night minimum stay - seasonal, cancellation fee imposed. **Amenities:** safes. **Pool(s):** heated outdoor. **Activities:** whirlpool, exercise room. **Guest Services:** valet and coin laundry. **Free Special Amenities: local telephone calls and high-speed Internet.**

BLACKBIRD INN (707)226-2450 **62**
Bed & Breakfast $195-$310 **Address:** 1755 1st St 94559 **Location:** SR 29 exit 1st St, 0.5 mi e to Jefferson St, then just n. **Facility:** A spacious front porch, huge stone fireplace and liberal use of fine woods help the inn stand out as an example of early-20th-century craftsmanship. 8 units. 2 stories (no elevator), interior corridors. **Terms:** 7 day cancellation notice-fee imposed.

CEDAR GABLES INN 707/224-7969 **66**
Historic Bed & Breakfast $199-$359 **Address:** 486 Coombs St 94559 **Location:** Just s of downtown. **Facility:** The inn occupies a historic building designed by English architect Ernest Coxhead and constructed in 1892. The property is closed for the week of Thanksgiving and Christmas. 9 units. 4 stories (no elevator), interior corridors. **Terms:** 2 night minimum stay - seasonal and/or weekends, age restrictions may apply, 14 day cancellation notice-fee imposed.

THE CHABLIS INN (707)257-1944 **51**
Motel $79-$179 **Address:** 3360 Solano Ave 94558 **Location:** Just w off SR 29 via Redwood Rd, then just s. **Facility:** 34 units. 2 stories (no elevator), exterior corridors. **Terms:** 2 night minimum stay - seasonal and/or weekends, 3 day cancellation notice-fee imposed. **Pool(s):** outdoor. **Activities:** whirlpool.

EMBASSY SUITES NAPA VALLEY (707)253-9540 **54**
Hotel $179-$399 **Address:** 1075 California Blvd 94559 **Location:** SR 29 exit 1st St E. **Facility:** 205 units. 3 stories, interior/exterior corridors. **Terms:** check-in 4 pm, 1-7 night minimum stay, cancellation fee imposed. **Amenities:** *Fee:* video games, high-speed Internet. **Pool(s):** outdoor, heated indoor. **Activities:** sauna, whirlpool. *Fee:* bicycles. **Guest Services:** valet laundry.

AAA Benefit: Members save 5% or more!

HAWTHORN SUITES BY WYNDHAM
(707)226-1878 **67**

Hotel
$105-$249

Address: 314 Soscol Ave 94559 **Location:** SR 29 exit Imola Ave, 1 mi e, then 0.5 mi n. **Facility:** 60 units. 3 stories, exterior corridors. **Terms:** cancellation fee imposed. **Amenities:** high-speed Internet. **Pool(s):** heated indoor. **Activities:** whirlpool, limited exercise equipment. **Guest Services:** valet laundry. **Free Special Amenities: expanded continental breakfast and high-speed Internet.** *(See ad p. 239.)*

HILTON GARDEN INN-NAPA (707)252-0444 **49**
Hotel $129-$349 **Address:** 3585 Solano Ave 94558 **Location:** SR 29 exit Redwood Rd, just n. **Facility:** 80 units. 3 stories, interior corridors. **Terms:** 1-7 night minimum stay, cancellation fee imposed. **Amenities:** high-speed Internet. **Pool(s):** heated outdoor. **Activities:** whirlpool, exercise room. **Guest Services:** valet and coin laundry.

AAA Benefit: Unparalleled hospitality at a special Member rate.

THE INN ON FIRST 707/253-1331 **60**
Bed & Breakfast $199-$425 **Address:** 1938 1st St 94559 **Location:** SR 29 exit 1st St, just e via Clay St. **Facility:** This four-square craftsman home with upscale touches is near downtown. Every room has a fireplace and whirlpool tub. 10 units. 2 stories (no elevator), interior/exterior corridors. **Terms:** check-in 3:30 pm, 2 night minimum stay - seasonal and/or weekends, age restrictions may apply, 30 day cancellation notice-fee imposed. **Amenities:** *Some:* high-speed Internet. **Free Special Amenities: full breakfast and high-speed Internet.**

THE MERITAGE RESORT AND SPA 707/251-1900 **70**
Resort Hotel Rates not provided **Address:** 875 Bordeaux Way 94558 **Location:** 0.5 mi n of jct SR 29 and 121; SR 121 N, follow Downtown Napa/Lake Berryessa, w on Napa Valley Corporate Way, then just s. **Facility:** Surrounded by acres of grape vineyards and a gazebo, this resort is beautifully appointed in rich warm colors. Two fireplaces, one inside and another outside near the pool, offer perfect spots to relax. 154 units, some kitchens. 3 stories, interior corridors. **Terms:** check-in 4 pm. **Amenities:** high-speed Internet, safes. **Pool(s):** heated outdoor. **Activities:** whirlpool, exercise room, spa. *Fee:* bicycles. **Guest Services:** valet laundry, area transportation-within 5 mi. **Free Special Amenities: preferred room (subject to availability with advance reservations).**

THE NAPA INN (707)257-1444 **57**
Historic Bed & Breakfast $149-$295 **Address:** 1137 Warren St 94559 **Location:** SR 29 exit 1st St, 0.5 mi e, then 0.3 mi n. **Facility:** This turn-of-the-century Queen Anne home retains the romantic aura of the Victorian era. Guests like to relax in the quiet gardens or in front of the fireplace. 14 units. 2-3 stories (no elevator), interior corridors. **Terms:** 2 night minimum stay - seasonal and/or weekends, 10 day cancellation notice-fee imposed. **Activities:** *Fee:* massage. **Free Special Amenities: full breakfast and preferred room (subject to availability with advance reservations).**

(See map & index p. 570.)

NAPA OLD WORLD INN   707/257-0112   56

▼▼▼ **Historic Bed & Breakfast.** Rates not provided. **Address:** 1301 Jefferson St 94559 **Location:** SR 29 exit Lincoln Ave E, 0.5 mi e to Jefferson St, then 0.5 mi s. **Facility:** Conveniently located within walking distance to downtown Napa, this historic B&B consists of six buildings, some with off-site registration. 35 units. 2 stories (no elevator), interior corridors. CALL 🔲M 🛜 ✕ ⚷

NAPA RIVER INN   (707)251-8500   65

▼▼▼ **Historic Hotel** $209-$599 **Address:** 500 Main St 94559 **Location:** Downtown. **Facility:** The property is on the Napa River and in the area of the historic Napa Mill, a National Registered Landmark. Restaurants, art galleries, specialty shops and a spa are within walking distance. 66 units. 2-3 stories, interior corridors. **Terms:** check-in 4 pm, 2-4 night minimum stay - seasonal and/or weekends, cancellation fee imposed. **Amenities:** high-speed Internet. *Some:* video games (fee), safes. **Activities:** exercise room. **Guest Services:** valet laundry.

🍴⁺ CALL 🔲M 🛜 ✕ 🎥 🔲 ▯ / SOME UNITS FEE 🐾

NAPA VALLEY HOTEL & SUITES/A 3 PALMS HOTEL & RESORT AT THE NAPA RIVER   (707)226-1871   64

▼▼▼
Hotel
$129-$249

Address: 853 Coombs St 94559 **Location:** At 2nd and Coombs sts. Across from courthouse. **Facility:** 47 units. 3 stories, exterior corridors. **Terms:** 7 day cancellation notice-fee imposed. **Amenities:** high-speed Internet, safes. **Pool(s):** outdoor. **Free Special Amenities:** local telephone calls and high-speed Internet.

SAVE CALL 🔲M 🛌 FEE🍴⁺ 🛜 ✕ ▯

Located by Uptown Theater, Oxbow Market, Opera House, Napa Riverwalk in Historic Old Town, Free Internet

Napa Valley Hotel & Suites AT THE NAPA RIVER A 3 Palms Boutique Hotel & Resort

NAPA VALLEY MARRIOTT HOTEL & SPA   (707)253-8600   50

▼▼▼ **Hotel** $155-$379 **Address:** 3425 Solano Ave 94558 **Location:** 1 blk w off SR 29 via Redwood Rd, 0.5 blk n. **Facility:** 274 units. 2 stories, interior corridors. **Terms:** check-in 4 pm. **Amenities:** high-speed Internet (fee), safes.

AAA Benefit: AAA hotel discounts of 5% or more.

Pool(s): heated outdoor. **Activities:** whirlpool, exercise room, spa. **Guest Services:** valet and coin laundry.

🍴 🍷 CALL 🔲M 🛌 🛜 ✕ 🎥 🔲 ▯

NAPA VALLEY RESORTS AT SILVERADO   707/255-0199   45

▼▼▼ **Condominium.** Rates not provided. **Address:** 100 Fairways Dr 94558 **Location:** Silverado Tr exit Hardman Ave, 0.8 mi e, 1 mi n on Atlas Peak Rd, 0.4 mi e on Westgate Dr, then just s. **Facility:** The pleasing setting right on Silverado Country Club will allow renters to enjoy all that the area has to offer. The spacious units are all well furnished and comfortable. 16 condominiums. 1 story, exterior corridors. **Parking:** on-site (fee). **Terms:** check-in 4 pm. **Amenities:** high-speed Internet. **Pool(s):** heated outdoor. **Guest Services:** coin laundry. 🛌 🛜 ✕ 🎥 🔲 ▯ ▯

OAK KNOLL INN   (707)255-2200   44

▼▼▼ **Bed & Breakfast** $350-$750 **Address:** 2200 E Oak Knoll Ave 94558 **Location:** Just w of Silverado Tr. **Facility:** Located just outside the city limits, this attractively appointed inn is surrounded by vineyards. 4 units. 1 story, exterior corridors. **Terms:** 2-5 night minimum stay - seasonal and/or weekends, 14 day cancellation notice-fee imposed. **Pool(s):** outdoor. **Activities:** whirlpool. **Guest Services:** valet laundry.

🛌 💈 🛜 ✕ 🎥 🔲 ▯

QUALITY INN NAPA WINERY INN   (707)257-7220   48

▼▼▼

Hotel
$149-$399

Address: 1998 Trower Ave 94558 **Location:** SR 29 exit E Trower Ave. **Facility:** 59 units, some efficiencies. 3 stories, interior corridors. **Terms:** 2 night minimum stay - seasonal and/or weekends, 3 day cancellation notice-fee imposed. **Pool(s):** outdoor. **Activities:** whirlpool. **Guest Services:** valet laundry. **Free Special Amenities:** expanded continental breakfast and high-speed Internet.

SAVE 🍴⁺ CALL 🔲M 🛌 🛜 ✕ 🔲 ▯ / SOME UNITS FEE 🐾 ▯

RIVER TERRACE INN   (707)320-9000   53

▼▼▼ **Hotel** $149-$699 **Address:** 1600 Soscol Ave 94559 **Location:** 0.5 mi ne of downtown. Adjacent to Napa River. **Facility:** 106 units. 3 stories, interior corridors. **Parking:** on-site and valet. **Terms:** 2-5 night minimum stay - weekends, 3 day cancellation notice-fee imposed. **Amenities:** high-speed Internet, safes. **Pool(s):** heated outdoor. **Activities:** exercise room. **Fee:** massage. **Guest Services:** valet laundry.

🍴 🍷 CALL 🔲M 🛌 🛜 ✕ 🎥 🔲 ▯

SILVERADO RESORT AND SPA   (707)257-0200   46

▼▼▼▼
Resort Hotel
$179-$559

Address: 1600 Atlas Peak Rd 94558 **Location:** 5.8 mi e of town via SR 121. **Facility:** This sprawling complex has its own golf course and spa where you can indulge, relax and rejuvenate. 415 units, some two bedrooms, three bedrooms, efficiencies and kitchens. 2 stories, exterior corridors. **Parking:** on-site (fee) and valet. **Terms:** check-in 4 pm, 2 night minimum stay - seasonal and/or weekends, 7 day cancellation notice-fee imposed, resort fee. **Amenities:** *Some:* safes. **Dining:** 2 restaurants. **Pool(s):** 8 outdoor, heated outdoor. **Activities:** whirlpool, 14 tennis courts (3 lighted), spa. **Fee:** golf-36 holes, bicycles. **Guest Services:** valet and coin laundry. **Free Special Amenities:** newspaper.

SAVE 🍴 💈 🍷 CALL 🔲M 🛌 FEE🍴⁺ BIZ 🛜 ✕ 🎥 🔲 / SOME UNITS 🔲 ▯

SPRINGHILL SUITES NAPA VALLEY   (707)253-1900

▼▼▼ **Hotel** $199-$329 **Address:** 101 Gateway Rd E 94558 **Location:** SR 29 exit Airport Blvd, just w, just n on Devlin Rd, then just e. **Facility:** 100 units. 3 stories, interior corridors. **Amenities:** high-speed Internet. **Pool(s):** heated outdoor. **Activities:** whirlpool, exercise room. **Guest Services:** valet laundry.

AAA Benefit: AAA hotel discounts of 5% or more.

🍴⁺ CALL 🔲M 🛌 🛜 ✕ 🔲 ▯ ▯

STAHLECKER HOUSE   (707)257-1588   52

▼▼▼ **Bed & Breakfast** $112-$339 **Address:** 1042 Easum Dr 94558 **Location:** SR 29 exit 1st St, 0.5 mi w. **Facility:** Nestled beside a creek and surrounded by attractively landscaped grounds, the B&B offers some units with a fireplace. 5 units. 1 story, interior corridors. **Terms:** 2 night minimum stay - seasonal and/or weekends, 14 day cancellation notice-fee imposed.

CALL 🔲M 🛜 ✕ ⚷

▼ See AAA listing p. 336 ▼

⊶ VINEYARD COUNTRY INN ⊷

In the Napa Valley Wine Country

 An all-suite bed and breakfast inspired by the gentle beauty of the French countryside ▣ All suites with old-world brick fireplaces ▣ Heated pool and jacuzzi ▣ Generous morning meal ▣ All suites non-smoking ▣ Free DSL and wireless internet access

201 Main Street St. Helena, CA 94574
TEL (707) 963-1000   FAX (707) 963-1794
www.VineyardCountryInn.com

(See map & index p. 570.)

THE WESTIN VERASA, NAPA (707)257-1800 [55]

Hotel
$159-$699

WESTIN
HOTELS & RESORTS
AAA Benefit: Enjoy up to 20% off your next stay, plus Starwood Preferred Guest® bonuses.

Address: 1314 McKinstry St 94559 **Location:** Jct Soscol Ave. **Facility:** An outdoor heated saltwater pool and whirlpool are some of the more unusual amenities found at this beautiful, California-contemporary and upscale property. 180 units, some efficiencies and kitchens. 3 stories, interior corridors. **Parking:** valet only. **Terms:** 2 night minimum stay - seasonal and/or weekends, 3 day cancellation notice-fee imposed, resort fee. **Amenities:** video games, high-speed Internet, safes. **Dining:** 2 restaurants. **Pool(s):** heated outdoor. **Activities:** whirlpool, exercise room. *Fee:* massage. **Guest Services:** valet laundry. **Free Special Amenities:** local telephone calls and manager's reception. *(See ad this page.)*

WINE VALLEY LODGE (707)224-7911 [68]

Motel
$79-$225

Address: 200 S Coombs St 94559 **Location:** SR 29 exit Imola Ave (SR 121), 0.5 mi e to S Coombs St, then just n. **Facility:** 54 units, some two bedrooms. 1 story, exterior corridors. *Bath:* shower only. **Terms:** cancellation fee imposed. **Pool(s):** outdoor. **Free Special Amenities:** continental breakfast and high-speed Internet.

LA RESIDENCE COUNTRY INN 707/253-0337

[fyi] Not evaluated. **Address:** 4066 Howard Ln 94558. Facilities, services, and décor characterize a mid-scale property.

RIVERPOINTE NAPA VALLEY RESORT 707/252-4200

[fyi] Vacation Rental Cabin Did not meet all AAA rating requirements for locking devices in some guest rooms at time of last evaluation on 04/23/2012. **Address:** 500 Lincoln Ave 94558 **Location:** Between SR 29 and Silverado Trail. Facilities, services, and décor characterize a mid-scale property.

Download eTourBook guides for top destinations at AAA.com/ebooks

▼ See AAA listing this page ▼

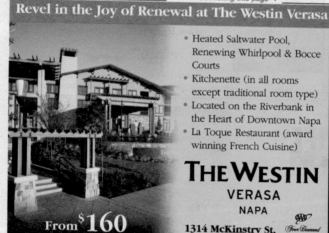

Revel in the Joy of Renewal at The Westin Verasa

- Heated Saltwater Pool, Renewing Whirlpool & Bocce Courts
- Kitchenette (in all rooms except traditional room type)
- Located on the Riverbank in the Heart of Downtown Napa
- La Toque Restaurant (award winning French Cuisine)

THE WESTIN
VERASA
NAPA

From $160
Single/Double
Limited availability. Taxes not included.

1314 McKinstry St.
Napa, CA 94559

Four Diamond Award

www.westinnapa.com

707-257-1800

(See map & index p. 570.)

WHERE TO EAT

BISTRO DON GIOVANNI 707-224-3300 **26**

▼▼▼ Italian. Casual Dining. $13-$38 **AAA Inspector Notes:** An enormous sculpture of a wine opener points the way to the entrance of this casual spot where the decor is a little Napa, a little Italian and a whole lot of ambience. An airy feel can be found in the dining room with its high ceilings and fireplace. Patio dining offers a panoramic view of the Napa hills, along with a lovely fountain and statuettes. Start with a classic frito misto. If choosing a pasta is difficult, order a tasting of two or three. Finish with the seasonal lemony dessert. **Bar:** full bar. **Reservations:** suggested. **Address:** 4110 Howard Ln 94558 **Location:** 6.4 mi n from jct SR 121 N and 29 N. L D

BLACK BEAR DINER 707/255-2345

▼▼ American. Casual Dining. $8-$18 **AAA Inspector Notes:** A homey atmosphere characterizes this family-oriented restaurant. Familiar comfort foods, such as meatloaf with mashed potatoes, are at the heart of the menu and are served in generous portions. **Bar:** beer & wine. **Address:** 303 Soscol Ave 94559 **Location:** Just n of Imola Ave. B L D CALL 🄢

CELADON 707/254-9690 **33**

▼▼ American. Fine Dining. $13-$35 **AAA Inspector Notes:** A wonderful combination of laid back and glamorous, this restaurant offers comfort food in either the dining room or a relaxed patio. **Bar:** full bar. **Reservations:** suggested. **Address:** 500 Main St, Suite G 94559 **Location:** Downtown. L D

COLE'S CHOP HOUSE 707/224-6328 **31**

▼▼▼ Steak. Casual Dining. $15-$69 **AAA Inspector Notes:** This eatery is a classic American steakhouse located in historic downtown. **Bar:** full bar. **Reservations:** suggested. **Address:** 1122 Main St 94559 **Location:** Just w of Soscol Ave; between Pearl and 1st sts; downtown. D

THE FOOD MILL 707/256-3663 **27**

▼ American. Quick Serve. $6-$23 **AAA Inspector Notes:** This eatery is a great stop for a quick lunch. Deli-style sandwiches are freshly made. Other menu options include pizza and burgers. Dine in or take out is available. **Bar:** full bar. **Address:** 704 Trancas St 94558 **Location:** Just w of Soscol Ave. L D

HOG ISLAND OYSTER BAR NAPA 707/251-8113 **30**

▼▼ Seafood. Casual Dining. $12-$24 **AAA Inspector Notes:** Exceptionally fresh oysters come in at least six varieties and share menu space with clam chowder, salads and a yummy grilled cheese sandwich that blends three Cowgirl Creamery cheeses. Beverages include local beer and a nice choice of wines. Go early—it is packed by 5 p.m. **Bar:** beer & wine. **Address:** 610 1st St 94559 **Location:** Jct SR 29; in Oxbow Market. L D 🄚

NAPA VALLEY WINE TRAIN 707/253-2111 **29**

▼▼▼

Continental Casual Dining

$99-$139

AAA Inspector Notes: Diners sit back in restored turn-of-the-20th-century Pullman cars for a three-hour, 36-mile excursion through scenic wine country. Prix fixe menus list three entrée choices. **Bar:** wine only. **Reservations:** required. **Address:** 1275 McKinstry St 94559 **Location:** SR 29 exit 1st St, 0.8 mi e, then 4 blks n on Soscol Ave. *(See ad p. 236.)* L D

OENOTRI 707/252-1022 **32**

▼▼▼ Italian. Casual Dining. $10-$29 **AAA Inspector Notes:** An industrial décor softened by warm earthy tones, potted olive saplings on tables and an open kitchen with an imported pizza oven invite guests to linger. The food is made with care, flavored with the best ingredients—Italian oregano and fragrant olive oil. Salumi and pasta is made in house. **Bar:** full bar. **Address:** 1425 1st St 94559 **Location:** 0.3 mi w of Soscol Ave; in historic downtown. **Parking:** street only. L D

ROUND TABLE PIZZA 707/253-1211

▼ Pizza. Casual Dining. $7-$28 **AAA Inspector Notes:** This casual, family-oriented pizza place features high-quality ingredients and dough rolled fresh daily. Distinctive specialty pizzas are piled high with toppings. **Bar:** beer & wine. **Address:** 701 Lincoln Ave 94558 **Location:** At Soscol Ave. L D

ZINSVALLEY RESTAURANT 707/224-0695 **28**

▼▼▼ New American. Fine Dining. $13-$28 **AAA Inspector Notes:** This eatery with solid service is a California contemporary. Order a glass of the signature Zinfandel wine and enjoy the yellow curry-it has been on the menu for ten years. **Bar:** full bar. **Address:** 1106 1st St 94559 **Location:** Downtown. **Parking:** street only. L D LATE

NEVADA CITY (D-3) pop. 3,068, elev. 2,525'
• Hotels p. 244 • Restaurants p. 244

In the foothills of the High Sierras, Nevada City has been a gold-mining center since the mid-19th century. It also is the seat of Nevada County; during the gold rush era the county's lode and placer mines yielded more than half of California's production of gold. The Nevada Theatre, 401 Broad St., opened in July 1865 and is said to be the state's oldest theater. It presents movies as well as live performances; for schedule information phone (530) 265-6161.

The Nevada County Narrow Gauge Railroad Museum, 5 Kidder Ct., has exhibits about local transportation, including a steam automobile and artifacts related to the area's narrow gauge railroad, which operated 1876-1942. Railroad memorabilia, the narrow gauge line's Engine 5 and rolling stock can be seen; phone (530) 470-0902.

Firehouse No. 1 Museum, 214 Main St., displays pioneer relics, Native American and Donner party artifacts and a collection of Chinese artifacts that includes an altar from an 1870s Chinese joss house as well as a Quan Yin altar, named after the goddess of compassion and mercy; phone (530) 265-5468.

Numerous hiking and mountain biking trails in the surrounding area cater to all experience levels, including trails along the South Yuba River Canyon and others that wind past streams, historic sites and scenic views.

About 8 miles northwest on SR 49 is South Yuba River State Park, a 2,000-acre scenic corridor noted for spring wildflowers, kayaking and a 251-foot, single-span covered bridge (off Pleasant Valley Road near Bridgeport). *See Recreation Areas Chart.*

Nevada City Chamber of Commerce: 132 Main St., Nevada City, CA 95959. **Phone:** (530) 265-2692 or (800) 655-6569.

Self-guiding tours: Thirteen points of interest in Nevada City's downtown historic district are described in a walking tour brochure provided by the chamber of commerce.

MALAKOFF DIGGINS STATE HISTORIC PARK is 26 mi. n.e. Take SR 49 n. 11 mi., then e. onto Tyler-Foote Crossing Rd. (the road changes names several times; the last mile is unpaved). This was the world's largest hydraulic gold mine before it ceased operation in 1884.

The park museum has exhibits and a 20-minute videotape explaining hydraulic mining methods and describing the miners' way of life. Highlights include a restored church, 1860s general store, drugstore, barber shop, livery stable and house. The home-coming celebration is held in mid-June. *See Recreation Areas Chart.*

Dogs are not permitted in buildings or on some trails. **Time:** Allow 1 hour minimum. **Hours:** Historic park daily dawn-dusk. Museum daily 10-5, mid-June through Labor Day; Sat.-Sun. 10-4, rest of year. Tours of the townsite are available at 1:30 when the museum is open. Phone ahead to confirm schedule. **Cost:** $8 per private vehicle; $7 (ages 62+ per private vehicle). Reservations for camping are required. **Phone:** (530) 265-2740 for information and cabin reservations, or (800) 444-7275 for camping reservations through ReserveAmerica.

MINERS FOUNDRY CULTURAL CENTER, 325 Spring St., was built in 1856 for industrial metal working and metal casting. This cultural center has performing arts facilities, a hall built of native stone and displays mining equipment. Special programs are scheduled throughout the year. Guided tours are available by appointment. **Hours:** Mon.-Fri. 10-3. Phone ahead to confirm schedule. **Cost:** Free. **Phone:** (530) 265-5040 for information about programs.

DEER CREEK INN   (530)264-7038
◆◆◆◆ Historic Bed & Breakfast $160-$199 **Address:** 116 Nevada St 95959 **Location:** SR 49 exit 186 (Broad St), just e; in historic district. **Facility:** Overlooking historic Deer Creek, this Victorian Bed and Breakfast was restored to its original splendor in 2011. 5 units. 3 stories (no elevator), interior corridors. **Terms:** 2 night minimum stay - weekends, 10 day cancellation notice-fee imposed.

EMMA NEVADA HOUSE   530/265-4415
◆◆◆ Historic Bed & Breakfast $159-$259 **Address:** 528 E Broad St 95959 **Location:** SR 49 exit 186 (Broad St), 0.4 mi w; in historic district. Located in a quiet residential area. **Facility:** This delightful B&B features a front porch, a spacious deck with a fountain feature and a sunny garden room for breakfast. The fireplace warms the living room of this restored 1856 house. 7 units. 2 stories (no elevator), interior corridors. **Terms:** 2 night minimum stay - weekends, 14 day cancellation notice-fee imposed. **Activities:** *Fee:* massage.

PIETY HILL COTTAGES MOTEL AND B&B   (530)265-2245
◆◆ Cottage $80-$195 **Address:** 523 Sacramento St 95959 **Location:** SR 20 and 49 exit 185B (Sacramento St) northbound; exit Coyote St southbound, just e on Broad St, then 0.6 mi w; jct Zion and Sacramento sts. **Facility:** 9 cottages, some kitchens. 1 story, exterior corridors. **Terms:** 2 night minimum stay - seasonal and/or weekends, 7 day cancellation notice-fee imposed.

WHERE TO EAT

CIRINO'S BAR & GRILL   530/265-2246
◆◆ Italian. Casual Dining. $8-$25 **AAA Inspector Notes:** This family business, housed in an historic building, has been satisfying patrons from the same location for more than 50 years. Photographs of the city line the walls. On the menu are pasta, chicken, fish, risotto and steak preparations. On Wednesday and Sunday evenings wood-fired pizza is offered and reservations are strongly recommended, otherwise expect a wait. Lunch is offered Friday through Sunday. **Bar:** full bar. **Reservations:** suggested. **Address:** 309 Broad St 95959 **Location:** SR 49 exit 186 (Broad St), just w; in historic district. **Parking:** street only. D

SOUTH PINE CAFE   530/265-0260
◆ American Breakfast. Casual Dining. $9-$13 **AAA Inspector Notes:** Popular with the local crowd, this eatery serves a variety of breakfast items (all day), sandwiches, burgers and salads sometimes with a Mexican flair. Fresh-squeezed juices are offered. **Bar:** beer & wine. **Address:** 110 S Pine St 95959 **Location:** SR 49 exit 186 (Broad St), just w, then just s; center. **Parking:** street only. B L

NEW ALMADEN (G-3) elev. 440'

NEW ALMADEN QUICKSILVER MINING MUSEUM is 2.5 mi. w. off Almaden Expwy. (CR G8) at 21350 Almaden Rd., in New Almaden Quicksilver County Park. The museum is housed in La Casa Grande, an 1854 brick residence that was home to the New Almaden Quicksilver Mine manager and his family.

Exhibits depict the mercury mining operations that began in New Almaden in 1845 and explain the process of extracting mercury from the cinnabar ore found in the area. Mining family artifacts are displayed, and a diorama replicates the interior of a mine shaft. One room is restored to resemble the mine manager's office. **Time:** Allow 30 minutes minimum. **Hours:** Fri. noon-4, Sat.-Sun. 10-4. Closed major holidays. **Cost:** Free. **Phone:** (408) 323-1107.

NEWARK pop. 42,573

CHASE SUITE HOTEL   510/795-1200
◆◆◆ Hotel. Rates not provided. **Address:** 39150 Cedar Blvd 94560 **Location:** I-880 exit Mowry Ave, just w, then 0.3 mi s. **Facility:** 148 kitchen units, some two bedrooms. 2 stories, exterior corridors. **Pool(s):** heated outdoor. **Activities:** whirlpool. **Guest Services:** valet and coin laundry, area transportation-within 5 mi.
/ SOME UNITS FEE

COMFORT INN & SUITES   (510)795-7995
◆◆◆ Hotel $89-$109 **Address:** 5977 Mowry Ave 94560 **Location:** I-880 exit Mowry Ave, 0.5 mi w. **Facility:** 98 units. 4 stories, interior corridors. **Amenities:** video games (fee). **Pool(s):** outdoor. **Activities:** exercise room. **Guest Services:** valet laundry.

COURTYARD BY MARRIOTT NEWARK/SILICON VALLEY
(510)792-5200

Hotel
$85-$219

AAA Benefit: AAA hotel discounts of 5% or more.

Address: 34905 Newark Blvd 94560 **Location:** SR 84 exit Newark Blvd, just s. **Facility:** 181 units. 6 stories, interior corridors. **Amenities:** high-speed Internet. **Pool(s):** heated outdoor. **Activities:** whirlpool, exercise room. **Guest Services:** valet and coin laundry, area transportation-within 5 mi. **Free Special Amenities: high-speed Internet.**

HILTON NEWARK/FREMONT
(510)490-8390

Hotel $109-$209 Address: 39900 Balentine Dr 94560 **Location:** I-880 exit Stevenson Blvd, just w. **Facility:** 313 units. 2-7 stories, interior corridors. **Terms:** 1-7 night minimum stay, cancellation fee imposed. **Dining:** Ginger's Bar and Grill, see separate listing. **Pool(s):** outdoor. **Activities:** whirlpool, exercise room. **Guest Services:** valet laundry.

AAA Benefit: Members save 5% or more!

HOMEWOOD SUITES BY HILTON
(510)791-7700

Extended Stay Hotel $109-$169 Address: 39270 Cedar Blvd 94560 **Location:** I-880 exit Mowry Ave, w to Cedar Blvd, then 0.3 mi s. **Facility:** 192 units, some two bedrooms and kitchens. 4 stories, interior corridors. **Terms:** 1-7 night minimum stay, cancellation fee imposed. **Amenities:** video games (fee). **Pool(s):** heated outdoor. **Activities:** whirlpool, sports court, exercise room. **Guest Services:** valet and coin laundry.

AAA Benefit: Contemporary luxury at a special Member rate.

RESIDENCE INN BY MARRIOTT NEWARK/SILICON VALLEY
(510)739-6000

Extended Stay Hotel
$85-$299

AAA Benefit: AAA hotel discounts of 5% or more.

Address: 35466 Dumbarton Ct 94560 **Location:** SR 84 exit Newark Blvd, just s. **Facility:** 168 kitchen units, some two bedrooms. 6 stories, interior corridors. **Amenities:** high-speed Internet. **Pool(s):** heated outdoor. **Activities:** whirlpool, sports court, exercise room. **Guest Services:** valet and coin laundry, area transportation-within 5 mi.

W SILICON VALLEY
510/494-8800

Hotel. Rates not provided. **Address:** 8200 Gateway Blvd 94560 **Location:** SR 84 exit Thornton Ave, just s. **Facility:** 172 units. 5 stories, interior corridors. **Amenities:** high-speed Internet (fee), safes. **Pool(s):** heated outdoor. **Activities:** whirlpool, exercise room. **Guest Services:** valet and coin laundry, area transportation-within 5 mi.

Learn about inspections and Diamond Ratings at AAA.com/Diamonds

---

• Part of Wine Country area — see map p. 562

WHERE TO EAT

CAMPANELLA MODERN ITALIAN CUISINE   510/794-9900

Italian. Casual Dining. $10-$25 AAA Inspector Notes: Family owned and operated, this Italian eatery offers an extensive menu with entrée salads, panini sandwiches and wonderful pasta dishes. The open-grill kitchen allows diners to watch the chef as he prepares the meals. **Bar:** wine only. **Address:** 34903 Newark Blvd 94560 **Location:** SR 84 exit Newark Blvd, just s.

GINGER'S BAR AND GRILL   510/490-8390

California. Fine Dining. $10-$26 AAA Inspector Notes: Just off the main hotel lobby and overlooking the piano bar, the restaurant is a favorite among visitors. In addition to the traditional menu, an abundant salad bar is offered during the lunch hours. **Bar:** full bar. **Address:** 39900 Balentine Dr 94560 **Location:** I-880 exit Stevenson Blvd, just w; in Hilton Newark/Fremont.

ROUND TABLE PIZZA   510/796-4040

Pizza. Casual Dining. $7-$28 AAA Inspector Notes: This casual, family-oriented pizza place features high-quality ingredients and dough rolled fresh daily. Distinctive specialty pizzas are piled high with toppings. **Bar:** beer & wine. **Address:** 5544 Thornton Ave 94560 **Location:** I-880 exit Thornton Ave W; at Cedar Blvd.

NICE pop. 2,731
• Part of Wine Country area — see map p. 562

FEATHERBED RAILROAD CO.   (707)274-8378

Bed & Breakfast $99-$220 Address: 2870 Lakeshore Blvd 95464 **Location:** 0.5 mi s of SR 20. **Facility:** These authentically restored caboose cars, each in a different decor theme, share a tree-shaded, park-like setting. 9 units. 1 story, exterior corridors. **Terms:** 2 night minimum stay - seasonal and/or weekends, 3 day cancellation notice-fee imposed, resort fee. **Pool(s):** heated outdoor. **Activities:** boat dock, fishing, bicycles.

ROBINSON RANCHERIA RESORT & CASINO   (707)262-3700

Hotel $79-$225 Address: 1545 E Hwy 20 95464 **Location:** On SR 20, north of town. **Facility:** Located near the north shore of Clear Lake, this property offers modern accommodations and numerous gaming opportunities. 48 units. 3 stories, interior corridors. **Amenities:** high-speed Internet, safes. **Activities:** exercise room. *Fee:* game room. **Guest Services:** coin laundry.

NORTH FORK (G-5) elev. 2,629'

SIERRA MONO MUSEUM, 33103 CR 228 at jct. CRs 225 and 228, displays artifacts and items important to Mono Indian culture. Central to the museum's exhibits is an extensive collection of Mono Indian baskets. Other highlights include natural dioramas featuring wildlife such as bears, mountain lions and wolves; tools; historic information; and traditional and contemporary beadwork.

Guided tours are available by appointment. **Hours:** Mon.-Sat. 10-3:30 or by appointment. Phone ahead to confirm holiday schedule. **Cost:** Donations. **Phone:** (559) 877-2115.

NORTH HIGHLANDS (E-3) pop. 42,694, elev. 100'

The former McClellan Air Force Base, now repurposed as McClellan Business Park, is the site of two area attractions, the Aerospace Museum of California and The California Foundry History Museum, in the Technikon facility at 5301 Price Ave. It traces California's foundry history from its beginnings during the gold rush era. Displays provide information about the casting process through photographs, equipment and related items and explain the importance of casting to industries such as transportation, recycling and defense; phone (916) 929-8001.

Antelope-Highlands Chamber of Commerce: P.O. Box 20, North Highlands, CA 95660. **Phone:** (916) 725-5652.

 AEROSPACE MUSEUM OF CALIFORNIA is w. off Watt Ave. at 3200 Freedom Park Dr., in McClellan Business Park. On display are 40 iconic military and civilian aircraft and 15 restored engines. The museum also features a number of cutting-edge interactive educational programs. Visitors get an up-close look at aircraft ranging from a fully restored 1932 Curtiss-Wright "speed wing" biplane to an A-10 Warthog. Engines on display include a few models built prior to World War I, the first jet engine and the J-58 jet engine that powered the SR-71 Blackbird to three times the speed of sound. Non-motion flight simulators and a motion ride simulator offer some nerve-tingling thrills.

Time: Allow 1 hour, 30 minutes minimum. **Hours:** Tues.-Sat. 9-5, Sun. 10-5. Closed Jan. 1, Easter, Thanksgiving and Christmas. **Cost:** $8; $6 (ages 13-17 and 65+); $5 (ages 6-12); free (military with ID). Additional admission may apply for special exhibits. **Phone:** (916) 643-3192.

NOVATO (C-8) pop. 51,904, elev. 18'

North of San Francisco on US 101, Novato has one foot in the past and one in the present: It was named for a chief of the Coast Miwok Indians and also is a leading producer of CD-ROMs. The Novato History Museum, 815 DeLong Ave., occupies the house of the town's first postmaster. Exhibits include vintage photographs and historical artifacts related to the city's early days; artifacts depicting life in Novato from its earliest days; phone (415) 897-4320.

Novato Chamber of Commerce: 807 DeLong Ave., Novato, CA 94945. **Phone:** (415) 897-1164.

MARIN MUSEUM OF THE AMERICAN INDIAN, 2200 Novato Blvd. in Miwok Park, displays Native American art. The museum also has changing exhibits that highlight various cultures. Original and replicated artifacts including stone tools and tule, or reeds used to build boats, are in a hands-on room especially for children. There is also a diorama of a Miwok village.

Time: Allow 30 minutes minimum. **Hours:** Tues.-Fri. noon-5, Sat.-Sun. noon-4. Museum may close during exhibit changes. Closed Jan. 1, Easter, July 4, Thanksgiving and Christmas. **Cost:** $5; $3 (ages 6-17 and 65+); $10 (family, up to five people). **Phone:** (415) 897-4064.

OLOMPALI STATE HISTORIC PARK, 2.5 mi. n. on US 101 (southbound only), is a 700-acre park featuring several historic buildings including the ruins of the 1913 Burdell Mansion, which consists of three older structures built 1830-66. A traditional Victorian garden surrounds the ruins and an 1870s frame house stands nearby. Also within the park is a reconstruction of a Coast Miwok village.

Time: Allow 30 minutes minimum. **Hours:** Sat.-Sun. 10-5. Visitor center open only when staff is available. Phone ahead to confirm schedule. **Cost:** $8 per private vehicle; $7 (ages 62+ per private vehicle). **Phone:** (415) 892-3383.

BEST WESTERN PLUS NOVATO OAKS INN

(415)883-4400

 Hotel $119-$169

AAA Benefit: Members save up to 20%, plus 10% bonus points with Best Western Rewards®.

Address: 215 Alameda Del Prado 94949 **Location:** US 101 exit Alameda Del Prado southbound; exit Hamilton Field northbound. **Facility:** 107 units. 3 stories, interior corridors. **Amenities:** Some: high-speed Internet. **Dining:** Wild Fox Restaurant, see separate listing. **Pool(s):** heated outdoor. **Activities:** whirlpool, exercise room. **Guest Services:** valet and coin laundry, area transportation-within 5 mi. **Free Special Amenities:** expanded continental breakfast and high-speed Internet.

COURTYARD BY MARRIOTT

(415)883-8950

Hotel $159-$199 **Address:** 1400 N Hamilton Pkwy 94949 **Location:** US 101 exit Bel Marin Keys Blvd/Ignacio Blvd northbound, just w, just s on Nave Dr, then just e; exit Ignacio Blvd/Entrada Dr southbound, just w, just s on Enfrente Rd, just e on Ignacio Blvd, 0.5 mi s on Nave Dr, then just e. **Facility:** 136 units. 4 stories, interior corridors. **Amenities:** high-speed Internet. **Pool(s):** heated outdoor. **Activities:** whirlpool, exercise room. **Guest Services:** valet and coin laundry.

AAA Benefit: AAA hotel discounts of 5% or more.

INN MARIN

(415)883-5952

Motel $119-$329

Address: 250 Entrada Dr 94949 **Location:** US 101 exit Ignacio Blvd, just w, just n on Enfrente Rd, then just e. **Facility:** 70 units. 1 story, exterior corridors. **Terms:** 2 night minimum stay - seasonal and/or weekends. **Amenities:** high-speed Internet. **Dining:** Rickey's, see separate listing. **Pool(s):** heated outdoor. **Activities:** whirlpool, exercise room. **Guest Services:** valet and coin laundry. **Free Special Amenities:** expanded continental breakfast and early check-in/late check-out.

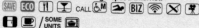 WHERE TO EAT

ANOKHA

415/892-3440

Indian. Casual Dining. $9-$24 **AAA Inspector Notes:** Contemporary and cozy, this restaurant serves solid Northern Indian cuisine. Buffet lunches are served Monday through Saturday. **Bar:** beer & wine. **Address:** 811 Grant Ave 94945 **Location:** US 101 exit De Long Ave; in Old Town Novato. **Parking:** street only.

L D

BOCA PIZZERIA   415/883-2302

▼▼ ▼▼ Italian. Casual Dining. $7-$18 **AAA Inspector Notes:** Rustic, contemporary casual décor can be found at this pizzeria with reused wood, high ceilings, industrial lighting and tall wall windows that are left open on sunny days. An open kitchen reveals the pizza-making process where piping hot Neapolitan-style pizza is baked in a 900-degree wood burning oven. Other well-executed menu offerings include pecorino flan, portabello and porcini ravioli in lemon black truffle cream sauce and house-brined pork chops. **Bar:** beer & wine. **Address:** 454 Ignacio Blvd 94949 **Location:** US 101 exit Ignacio Blvd, 0.3 mi w. [L] [D] [X]

DRAGON CAFE   415/883-4595

▼▼ ▼▼ Chinese. Casual Dining. $7-$13 **AAA Inspector Notes:** This modest, family-run cafe offers cooked-to-order meals with reasonable prices. **Bar:** beer & wine. **Address:** 528 Alameda Del Prado 94949 **Location:** US 101 exit Ignacio Blvd, just w on Alameda Del Prado; in Del Prado Square. [L] [D]

MOYLAN'S BREWERY & RESTAURANT   415/898-4677

▼▼ ▼▼ American. Casual Dining. $10-$20 **AAA Inspector Notes:** The handful of hand-crafted beer varieties go down easy with pizza made in a wood-fired oven and such standards as steak, pasta, fish, sandwiches and burgers. On sunny days, some outdoor seats can be had. **Bar:** beer & wine. **Address:** 15 Rowland Way 94945 **Location:** US 101 exit Rowland Way, just e. [L] [D] CALL [&M]

RICKEY'S   415/883-9477

▼▼▼ ▼▼▼ American. Fine Dining. $12-$24 **AAA Inspector Notes:** Patrons can savor American favorites in this warm and comfortable atmosphere. Seating ranges from a more formal dining area to casual poolside dining. **Bar:** full bar. **Address:** 250 Entrada Dr 94949 **Location:** US 101 exit Ignacio Blvd, just w, just n on Enfrente Rd, then just e; in Inn Marin. [⊖] [D] CALL [&M]

TOAST RESTAURANT   415/382-1144

▼▼ ▼▼ American. Casual Dining. $10-$20 **AAA Inspector Notes:** This contemporary eatery is organic with cork walls and pressed bamboo chairs. Popular with families at night, the cavernous restaurant offers everything from homey meatloaf and pizza to sophisticated duck breast salad with a NorCal touch. Start with baked oysters, then move on to grilled salmon with purple Peruvian potatoes and finish with the brioche bread pudding with spiced ice cream. **Bar:** beer & wine. **Address:** 5800 Nave Dr 94949 **Location:** US 101 exit Ignacio Blvd/Bel Marin Keys Blvd northbound; exit Ignacio Blvd/Entrada Dr southbound; in Hamilton Marketplace. **Parking:** street only.

[B] [L] [D]

WILD FOX RESTAURANT   415/883-9125

▼▼ ▼▼ American. Casual Dining. $12-$48 **AAA Inspector Notes:** The varied menu at this casual spot lists not only mesquite-grilled steaks and chops but also pasta and seafood selections. **Bar:** full bar. **Address:** 225 Alameda Del Prado 94949 **Location:** US 101 exit W Alameda Del Prado. [L] [D] CALL [&M]

OAKDALE (F-3) pop. 20,675, elev. 155'

Located in a region known for its Western heritage as well as a number of ranches, Oakdale bills itself—with tongue slightly in cheek—as "The Cowboy Capital of the World." Just east of town, Woodward Reservoir offers both local wranglers and visitors a chance to unwind; swimming, fishing, sailing, water skiing, camping and picnicking can be enjoyed.

At Oakdale Cheese & Specialties, 10040 SR 120, observe employees making Gouda cheese several days a week; at other times the process can be seen via a video presentation. Phone (209) 848-3139.

Oakdale Chamber of Commerce & Visitors Bureau: 590 N. Yosemite Ave., Oakdale, CA 95361. **Phone:** (209) 847-2244.

OAKDALE COWBOY MUSEUM is at 355 E. F St., just off SR 120. Located in a former Southern Pacific train depot, the museum displays Oakdale's Western culture and ranching heritage through rodeo memorabilia, items belonging to local cowboys enshrined in halls of fame, saddles, photographs, awards, branding irons and different types of barbed wire. **Time:** Allow 30 minutes minimum. **Hours:** Mon.-Sat. 10-2. **Cost:** $1. **Phone:** (209) 847-5163.

BEST WESTERN PLUS RAMA INN   (209)845-2500

▼▼ ▼▼
Hotel
$90-$170

AAA Benefit: Members save up to 20%, plus 10% bonus points with Best Western Rewards®.

Address: 1450 East F St 95361 **Location:** 1 mi e of jct SR 108 and 120. **Facility:** 47 units. 3 stories, interior corridors. **Amenities:** high-speed Internet. **Pool(s):** heated indoor. **Activities:** sauna, whirlpool, exercise room. **Guest Services:** valet and coin laundry. **Free Special Amenities: expanded continental breakfast and newspaper.**

[SAVE] [¶→] CALL [&M] [⇌] [BIZ] [�] [✕] [🖥] [📷] [💻]

HOLIDAY INN EXPRESS   (209)847-9121

▼▼▼ ▼▼▼
Hotel
$84-$149

Address: 828 East F St 95361 **Location:** 0.8 mi e on SR 108 and 120. **Facility:** 50 units. 2 stories (no elevator), interior/exterior corridors. **Terms:** cancellation fee imposed. **Amenities:** high-speed Internet. **Pool(s):** outdoor. **Activities:** exercise room. **Guest Services:** valet and coin laundry. **Free Special Amenities: expanded continental breakfast and high-speed Internet.**

[SAVE] [¶→] CALL [&M] [⇌] [BIZ] [ç] [🖥] [📷] [💻]

WHERE TO EAT

ROUND TABLE PIZZA   209/847-2296

▼ Pizza. Casual Dining. $7-$28 **AAA Inspector Notes:** This casual, family-oriented pizza place features high-quality ingredients and dough rolled fresh daily. Distinctive specialty pizzas are piled high with toppings. **Bar:** beer & wine. **Address:** 1449 East F St 95361 **Location:** On SR 108, east end of town; just w of Maag Ave. [L] [D]

OAKHURST (F-4) pop. 2,829, elev. 2,289'

- **Hotels p. 248 • Restaurants p. 248**
- **Hotels & Restaurants map & index p. 584**
- **Part of Yosemite National Park area — see map p. 578**

CHILDREN'S MUSEUM OF THE SIERRA is e. off SR 41 (Southern Yosemite Hwy.) on SR 426 (Crane Valley Rd.), then just n. to 49269 Golden Oak Dr., Suite 104. This hands-on museum has a natural history area where kids can "dig" for bones; a bank with a teller's window, play money and an old-fashioned typewriter; a theater for role-playing; and an emergency services area with a child-sized fire truck and ambulance, a brass sliding pole and a 911 console simulator. Children can dress in hospital scrubs, study X-rays and listen to hearts in the Teddy Bear Hospital.

Time: Allow 2 hours minimum. **Hours:** Tues.-Sat. 10-4, Sun. 1-4, mid-Sept. to mid-June; Tues.-Sat. 10-5, rest of year. **Cost:** $4; $3 (ages 60+); free (ages 0-1). **Phone:** (559) 658-5656.

(See map & index p. 584.)

FRESNO FLATS HISTORICAL PARK is e. on SR 426 to SR 427 (School Rd.), then n. .75 mi. to the museum. On the grounds are a museum and a collection of historic buildings typical of those that would have been found in a local late 19th-century community. Highlights include the Taylor Log House, the collection of antiques in the Laramore House, a smithy, a logging exhibit, an agricultural barn, a schoolhouse, and a collection of wagons and stagecoaches. Visitors also can use the research library.

Hours: Park open daily dawn-dusk, Mar.-Dec. Museum open Mon, Wed. and Fri. 9-3, Mar.-Dec. Guided tours of the museum are offered when staff is available. Research library open by appointment only. Closed Thanksgiving and Christmas. **Cost:** Park and guided tours by donation. **Phone:** (559) 683-6570.

TOUR YOSEMITE AND BEYOND picks up passengers at area hotels for all-day narrated tours of Yosemite National Park and other area sights. Visitors will see such attractions as Yosemite Valley, the Mariposa Grove of giant sequoias and Glacier Point.

Time: Allow 5 hours minimum. **Hours:** Daily 8-5. Pickup times vary depending on hotel location and the season. **Cost:** Fees begin at $90; $85 (ages 62+); $50 (ages 13-17); $30 (ages 6-12). Reservations are required. **Phone:** (559) 641-6789.

BEST WESTERN PLUS YOSEMITE GATEWAY INN
(559)683-2378 **38**

Hotel
$85-$199

Best Western PLUS

AAA Benefit: Members save up to 20%, plus 10% bonus points with Best Western Rewards®.

Address: 40530 Hwy 41 93644 **Location:** SR 49, 0.8 mi n. **Facility:** 121 units, some two bedrooms and kitchens. 2 stories (no elevator), exterior corridors. **Amenities:** *Some:* high-speed Internet. **Dining:** Yosemite Gateway Restaurant, see separate listing. **Pool(s):** outdoor, heated indoor. **Activities:** whirlpools, playground, exercise room. **Guest Services:** coin laundry. **Free Special Amenities: local telephone calls and high-speed Internet.**

CHÂTEAU DU SUREAU
(559)683-6860 **40**

Country Inn
$385-$585

Address: 48688 Victoria Ln 93644 **Location:** Just w of jct SR 41 and 49. **Facility:** Seven acres of terraced gardens give this castle-like property an atmosphere of Provence; rooms are individually appointed with antiques and art pieces. 13 units, some houses. 1-2 stories (no elevator), interior/exterior corridors. **Parking:** valet only. **Terms:** 2 night minimum stay - seasonal and/or weekends, 14 day cancellation notice-fee imposed, resort fee. **Dining:** Erna's Elderberry House Restaurant, see separate listing. **Pool(s):** outdoor. **Activities:** hiking trails, spa. **Guest Services:** valet laundry. **Free Special Amenities: room upgrade (subject to availability with advance reservations) and high-speed Internet.**

COMFORT INN YOSEMITE AREA
(559)683-8282 **39**

Hotel
$70-$200

Address: 40489 Hwy 41 93644 **Location:** SR 49, 0.5 mi n. **Facility:** 117 units, some two bedrooms. 2 stories (no elevator), exterior corridors. **Terms:** cancellation fee imposed. **Amenities:** high-speed Internet. **Pool(s):** outdoor. **Activities:** whirlpool. **Free Special Amenities: full breakfast and high-speed Internet.**

DAYS INN
(559)642-2525 **36**

Motel
$80-$259

Address: 40662 Hwy 41 93644 **Location:** SR 49, 0.8 mi n. **Facility:** 42 units. 4 stories (no elevator), exterior corridors. **Pool(s):** outdoor. **Free Special Amenities: continental breakfast and high-speed Internet.**

HOUNDS TOOTH INN
(559)642-6600 **35**

Bed & Breakfast $95-$235 **Address:** 42071 Hwy 41 93644 **Location:** North end of town. **Facility:** Fireplaces are featured in some accommodations at this inn, which is convenient to the national park. 13 units. 2 stories (no elevator), interior/exterior corridors. **Terms:** 3 day cancellation notice.

CALL

YOSEMITE SOUTHGATE HOTEL & SUITES
(559)683-3555 **37**

Hotel $79-$300 **Address:** 40644 Hwy 41 93644 **Location:** SR 49, 0.8 mi n. **Facility:** 80 units. 4 stories, interior corridors. **Terms:** check-in 4 pm, cancellation fee imposed, resort fee. **Pool(s):** outdoor. **Activities:** sauna, whirlpool, steamroom, exercise room. **Guest Services:** coin laundry.

CALL

WHERE TO EAT

CRAB CAKES
559/641-7667 **19**

Seafood
Casual Dining
$7-$40

AAA Inspector Notes: In addition to the fun, family seafood for which it is known, this restaurant also prepares beef and chicken dishes. Come early for dinner and take advantage of the frequent specials. **Bar:** beer & wine. **Reservations:** suggested. **Address:** 40278 Stagecoach Rd, Suite 7 93644 **Location:** Just off SR 41; center.
Menu on AAA.com L D

EL CID
559/683-6668 **18**

Mexican. Casual Dining. $8-$20 **AAA Inspector Notes:** This restaurant is a favorite for those coming home from a well-spent day in Yosemite National Park. Diners can enjoy a great view on the deck overlooking the High Sierras as they await their meal of well-prepared Mexican food. **Bar:** full bar. **Address:** 41939 Hwy 41 93644 **Location:** Jct SR 49, 2.3 mi n. B L D

ERNA'S ELDERBERRY HOUSE RESTAURANT
559/683-6800 **23**

French
Fine Dining
$45-$95

AAA Inspector Notes: Elegant décor and the finest table settings are among special touches that enable the dining room to exude warm country French ambience. European influences punctuate inventive preparations of French cuisine. The menu changes daily, based on the freshest local ingredients available. Cigars are welcomed in the sophisticated smoking garden. Service is impeccable. Semi-formal attire. **Bar:** full bar. **Reservations:** suggested. **Address:** 48688 Victoria Ln 93644 **Location:** Just w of jct SR 41 and 49; in Château du Sureau. D

(See map & index p. 584.)

OL'KETTLE RESTAURANT   559/683-7505 (20)
♦♦♦ American. Casual Dining. $8-$18 AAA Inspector Notes:
Noted for its good down-home cooking, this restaurant serves breakfast all day. Family owned and operated, this spot has been a long
time tradition in this area. Bar: beer & wine. Address: 40650 Hwy 41
93644 Location: Center. [B] [L] [D]

ROUND TABLE PIZZA   559/683-7472
♦ Pizza. Casual Dining. $7-$28 AAA Inspector Notes: This casual, family-oriented pizza place features high-quality ingredients and
dough rolled fresh daily. Distinctive specialty pizzas are piled high
with toppings. Bar: beer & wine. Address: 40034 Hwy 49, Suite A-2
93644 Location: Just w of jct SR 41. [L] [D]

WOODY'S NEW ORLEANS WEST   559/683-4414 (21)
♦♦ Cajun. Casual Dining. $13-$26 AAA Inspector Notes: A
taste of the South has come to the foothills with traditional favorites
including red beans and rice and jambalaya. Start off the meal with
fried dill pickle appetizer and be sure to save room for the homemade
pecan pie. Bar: beer & wine. Address: 40291 Junction Dr, Suite 103
Dr 93644 Location: Just n of jct SR 41 and 49. [D]

YOSEMITE GATEWAY RESTAURANT   559/683-2378 (22)
♦♦♦ American. Casual Dining. $8-$27 AAA Inspector Notes:
This family-friendly restaurant offers a great selection of sandwiches,
burgers, pasta dishes, beef and seafood. A buffet breakfast is fea-
tured in the morning. Expect service to be friendly and welcoming.
Bar: full bar. Address: 40530 Hwy 41 93644 Location: SR 49, 0.8
mi n; in BEST WESTERN PLUS Yosemite Gateway Inn.
[B] [D] CALL [&M]

OAKLAND (F-2) pop. 390,724, elev. 42'
• Hotels p. 260 • Restaurants p. 262
• Attractions map p. 250
• Hotels & Restaurants map & index p. 254

Oakland, a major West Coast port and manufacturing center stretching along the mainland side of
San Francisco Bay, varies in elevation from sea
level to 1,500 feet. The San Francisco-Oakland Bay
Bridge, commonly referred to as simply the Bay
Bridge, links the city with San Francisco; a westbound toll of $2.50-$6 is charged.

Nine regional parks adjoin the city, offering rolling
hills, scenic vistas and forested areas laced with
trails, plus plenty of opportunities for picnicking,
hiking, fishing, swimming and horseback riding. The
parks are Anthony Chabot (see Recreation Areas
Chart), Claremont Canyon Regional Preserve,
Huckleberry Botanic Regional Preserve, Martin Luther King Jr. Shoreline (see Recreation Areas
Chart), Miller/Knox, Redwood, Robert Sibley Volcanic Regional Preserve, Temescal (see Recreation
Areas Chart) and Tilden (see Berkeley p. 53). Facilities vary from park to park; for more information
phone (510) 238-7275 (Office of Parks &
Recreation).

Woodminster Amphitheater, on Joaquin Miller
Road in Joaquin Miller Park, is an open-air theater
built by the federal WPA program during the mid-
20th century. Performances, mostly Broadway musicals, are scheduled from early July to early
September; for event and schedule information
phone (510) 531-9597.

Bret Harte Boardwalk, on 5th Street between Jefferson and Clay streets, is next to the site of the author's boyhood home. A block of renovated Victorian
houses and barns house shops and restaurants.

Visitor information centers are located at 11th Street
and Broadway and at Jack London Square,
Broadway and Embarcadero.

Daily round-trip ferries provide a transportation link
between Jack London Square (see attraction listing) in
Oakland and San Francisco. The Alameda-Oakland
Ferry transports passengers to the Ferry Building, at
the foot of Market Street on The Embarcadero, Pier 39
and AT&T Park in San Francisco, as well as to Angel
Island in the summer. For schedule and fare information phone (510) 522-3300.

O.co Coliseum and Oracle Arena, both off I-880
at the 66th Avenue or Hegenberger Road exits, are
where the city's three professional sports teams
play. O.co Coliseum is the home of the Oakland A's
(baseball) and the Oakland Raiders (football). The
Golden State Warriors (basketball) play at Oracle
Arena, adjacent to the stadium; the arena also is utilized for concerts, wrestling events and circus performances. Phone (510) 569-2121 for either facility.

Oakland Convention & Visitors Bureau: 463 11th
St., Oakland, CA 94607. Phone: (510) 839-9000.

AFRICAN AMERICAN MUSEUM & LIBRARY AT
OAKLAND, 659 14th St. at Martin Luther King Jr.
Way, displays items depicting the historical and cultural legacy of African-Americans who lived in California and the American West. There also are art
exhibitions and a reference library and archives with
diaries, newspapers and an oral history collection.
Time: Allow 1 hour minimum. Hours: Tues.-Sat.
noon-5:30. Closed major holidays. Phone ahead to
confirm schedule. Cost: Free. Phone: (510)
637-0200. 12th St.
📮 12th St. Oakland City Center, 17

CHABOT SPACE & SCIENCE CENTER, 10000
Skyline Blvd. in Joaquin Miller Park, is a hands-on
science center with an emphasis on astronomy and
space exploration. The center has a digital full-dome
planetarium that presents both live and recorded
shows, large-format films in a domed theater and interactive exhibits. Telescopes are available for free
public viewing.

Hours: Exhibits, planetarium and theater Sun.
and Tues.-Thurs. (also Mon. holidays) 10-5, Fri.-Sat.
10-10, mid-June through Labor Day; Sun. and
Wed.-Thurs. (also Mon. holidays) 10-5, Fri.-Sat.
10-10, rest of year. Observatory open Fri.-Sat. dusk-
10:30 p.m., Apr.-Oct.; 7:30-10:30 p.m., rest of year
(weather permitting). Phone ahead for daytime
viewing schedule. Closed July 4, Thanksgiving,
Christmas Eve and Christmas. Cost: $15.95 (in-
cludes exhibits, observatory and planetarium show);
$12.95 (ages 13-18, ages 65+ and college students
with ID); $11.95 (ages 3-12). Phone: (510)
336-7300. [†1]

GREEK ORTHODOX CATHEDRAL OF THE AS-
CENSION, 4700 Lincoln Ave., overlooks downtown
Oakland and the bay. Designed in the Byzantine

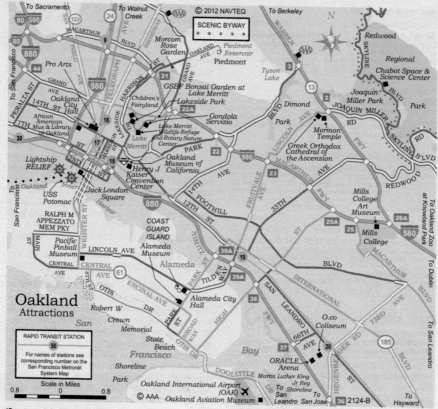

To Sacramento · To Walnut Creek · To Berkeley · © 2012 NAVTEQ

SCENIC BYWAY ••••••

N

To San Francisco

Pro Arts

Morcom Rose Garden

Piedmont Reservoir

Piedmont

Redwood

Regional

Chabot Space & Science Center

GSBF Bonsai Garden at Lake Merritt

Oakland City Hall

Children's Fairyland

Lakeside Park

Tyson Lake

Joaquin Miller Park

JOAQUIN MILLER

Park

African American Mus & Library at Oakland

Gondola Servizio

Lake Merritt Wildlife Refuge and Rotary Nature Center

Dimond Park

Mormon Temple

Greek Orthodox Cathedral of the Ascension

Lightship RELIEF

Oakland Museum of California

To Oakland

USS Potomac

Jack London Square

RALPH M APPEZZATO MEM PKY

Henry J Kaiser Convention Center

Harbor

COAST GUARD ISLAND

Mills College Art Museum

Mills College

To Oakland Zoo at Knowland Park

To Dublin

Pacific Pinball Museum

CENTRAL AVE

LINCOLN AVE

Alameda Museum

Alameda

To San Leandro

Oakland Attractions

Robert W Crown Memorial State Beach

Alameda City Hall

San Francisco Bay

Shoreline Park

O.co Coliseum

ORACLE Arena

To San Leandro

To Hayward

RAPID TRANSIT STATION
50
For names of stations see corresponding number on the San Francisco Metrorail System Map

Scale in Miles
0.8   0   0.8

Oakland International Airport (OAK)
© AAA Oakland Aviation Museum

Martin Luther King Jr Reg Shoreline

To San Leandro · To San Jose

2124-B

(See map & index p. 254.)

style, the copper-domed church houses colorful mosaics and icons of Christ and the disciples. It is crowned with a 12-foot cross set with light-catching Baccarat crystals. A 3-day Greek festival is held in mid-May. **Time:** Allow 1 hour minimum. **Hours:** Mon.-Fri. 9-noon and 1-4. Closed major holidays. **Cost:** Free. **Phone:** (510) 531-3400.

JACK LONDON SQUARE, bounded by Clay St., Alice St., the Embarcadero and the Oakland estuary, is a lively waterfront area with shopping and dining options. A statue of the author, who worked at the port's docks, stands on the wharf. Heinolds' First and Last Chance Saloon, built in 1880 and a favorite haunt of the author, is at the foot of Webster Street.

Fresh produce, baked goods, flowers and more are sold at the Jack London Square Farmers Market, held Sundays 9-2. The area also has an Amtrak station and is the site of several museums. **Phone:** (510) 645-9292 for information about special events and activities at the square. 12th St. 12th St. Oakland City Center, 17

LAKESIDE PARK is along the n. shore of Lake Merritt, a saltwater tidal lake in the center of the city. Boat rentals, sailing lessons and bowling greens are

available. A tour boat also cruises the lake. The Camron-Stanford House, an 1876 Victorian, was home to several prominent Oakland families and also housed the Oakland Museum. Preserved as a house museum, it can be toured several times a month.

Cost: Free. A fee is charged for tours of the Camron-Stanford House. **Parking:** $2-$10 (after 1 p.m. Mon.-Fri.); $5 (Sat.-Sun. and holidays). **Phone:** (510) 238-2196 for tour boat information and reservations, or (510) 444-1876 for the Camron-Stanford House. 19th Street/Oakland, 16

Children's Fairyland, jct. Grand and Bellevue aves., depicts fairy tales and nursery rhymes and has children's rides. Puppet shows also are given.

Time: Allow 2 hours minimum. **Hours:** Mon.-Fri. 10-4, Sat.-Sun. 10-5, mid-June through Labor Day; Wed.-Sun. 10-4, Apr. 1 to mid-June and day after Labor Day-late Oct.; Fri.-Sun. 10-4, rest of year. Puppet shows are presented at 11, 2 and 4. Closed Jan. 1 and Christmas. **Cost:** $8; free (ages 0-1). **Parking:** $2-$10 (Mon.-Fri.); $5 (Sat.-Sun. and holidays). **Phone:** (510) 238-6876 or (510) 452-2259. 19th Street/Oakland, 16

(See map & index p. 254.)

Gondola Servizio, at the Lake Merritt Boating Center within Lakeside Park, offers 30- and 55-minute cruises in handmade Venetian gondolas. **Hours:** Daily 5 p.m.-midnight, June-Sept.; Wed.-Sun. 5 p.m.-midnight, rest of year. **Cost:** Fare $40-$225 per couple. Reservations are required. **Phone:** (866) 737-8494. 🚇 19th Street/Oakland, 16

GSBF Bonsai Garden at Lake Merritt is in Lakeside Park on Bellevue Ave. near the Lakeside Park Demonstration Garden. The Golden State Bonsai Federation displays the intricate art of bonsai. A curved pathway leads visitors to approximately 50 plantings and viewing stones (suiseki), a tradition of Japanese culture. Docents can provide background information.

   Time: Allow 1 hour minimum. **Hours:** Wed.-Fri. (also second and fourth Tues. of the month) 11-3, Sat. 10-4, Sun. noon-4 (weather permitting). Closed Jan. 1, Thanksgiving and Christmas. Phone ahead to confirm schedule. **Cost:** Donations. **Phone:** (510) 763-8409. 🚇 19th Street/Oakland, 16

Lake Merritt Wildlife Refuge and Rotary Nature Center, Bellevue Ave. and Perkins St., has seasonal displays of birds, mammals and reptiles. During migratory seasons hundreds of wild geese, herons, egrets and ducks pass through the wildlife refuge outside the museum; founded in 1870, this is said to be the first established refuge in North America. The nature center also contains a native plant garden. **Time:** Allow 30 minutes minimum. **Hours:** Tues.-Sun. 9-3. **Cost:** Free. **Phone:** (510) 238-3739. 🚇 19th Street/Oakland, 16

Lakeside Park Demonstration Gardens, 666 Bellevue Ave., has a variety of displays, including Japanese, Polynesian, cactus, dahlia, palm, fuchsia, firescape, chrysanthemum, herb and fragrance gardens. Seasonal flower shows also are presented. **Time:** Allow 2 hours minimum. **Hours:** Daily 10-4, Nov.-Apr.; Mon.-Fri. 10-5, rest of year. **Cost:** Free. **Parking:** $2-$10 (Mon.-Fri.); $5 (Sat.-Sun. and holidays). **Phone:** (510) 238-2197.
🚇 19th Street/Oakland, 16

(See map & index p. 254.)

LIGHTSHIP *RELIEF* is on the waterfront at Jack London Square, berthed next to the USS *Potomac*. Lightships served as floating lighthouses where construction of a permanent structure was impractical. Lightship *RELIEF*, formerly Coast Guard Lightship (WLV 605), is one of a group of ships that relieved regularly stationed lightships when the latter returned to port for maintenance. All U.S. lightships are now retired.

A guided tour covers the crew's living quarters and explains the workings of the ship's anchor. **Time:** Allow 1 hour minimum. **Hours:** Guided tours are given Sat.-Sun. 11-4. **Cost:** Free. **Phone:** (510) 520-6852. 12th St.

Ⓣ 12th St. Oakland City Center, 17

MILLS COLLEGE ART MUSEUM, on campus at 5000 MacArthur Blvd., offers changing exhibits by contemporary artists and senior art students. **Time:** Allow 1 hour, 30 minutes minimum. **Hours:** Tues.-Sun. 11-4 (also Wed. 4-7:30). Closed major holidays. Phone ahead to confirm schedule. **Cost:** Free. **Phone:** (510) 430-2164.

MORCOM ROSE GARDEN is 1 blk. w. of Grand Ave. at 700 Jean St.; additional street parking is available on Olive Ave. It features 8 acres of gardens, reflecting pools and trees, with various varieties in bloom from May through November; the peak season is May through September. **Hours:** Daily dawn-dusk. The garden may be closed for weddings on weekends, May-Oct. Phone ahead to confirm schedule. **Cost:** Free. **Phone:** (510) 238-3187.

MORMON TEMPLE, 4770 Lincoln Ave., is a magnificent example of religious architecture and offers a scenic vista of Oakland as well as San Francisco across the bay. Guided 25-minute tours of the gardens and visitor center include a 12-minute video presentation about the temple. A family history center is located below the visitor center. Nonmembers of the church are not permitted to enter the temple interior.

Time: Allow 1 hour minimum. **Hours:** Grounds open 8 a.m.-10 p.m. Visitor center open daily 9-9. Last tour departs 30 minutes before closing. **Cost:** Free. **Phone:** (510) 531-3200, or (510) 531-1475 for the visitor center. Ⓣ

OAKLAND AVIATION MUSEUM is at 8252 Earhart Rd., across the street from Hangar 6 (Alaska Airlines) in Building 621 at Oakland Airport's North Field. Housed in a 1940 hangar, it presents a collection of unusual aircraft as well as exhibits about the history of aviation and aviators. **Hours:** Wed.-Sun. 10-4. Closed Jan. 1, Thanksgiving and Christmas. **Cost:** $9; $8 (ages 55+); $7 (ages 13-18, students and active military with ID); $5 (ages 6-12). **Phone:** (510) 638-7100.

OAKLAND MUSEUM OF CALIFORNIA (OMCA), 10th and Oak sts., brings art, historical and natural science collections under one roof to tell the story of California's cultural heritage and environmental successes and challenges. Many of the exhibits draw on first-person accounts by people who have helped shape the Golden State's legacy.

The Natural Sciences Gallery depicts California ecology through an interactive walk across the state from ocean to mountains to desert, with native plants and animals shown in realistic settings. The Cowell Hall of California History preserves the state's past from its pre-Spanish period to the present, with an emphasis on such events as earthquakes, the 1960s counterculture, the computer chip and the diverse groups of people that have collectively influenced the state's development.

The Gallery of California Art features paintings, sculpture, photography, decorative arts and conceptual media works. Highlights include mid- and late 19th-century California landscape paintings, gold rush-era daguerreotypes, furniture and California ceramics.

Time: Allow 1 hour minimum. **Hours:** Wed.-Sun. 11-5 (also last Fri. of the month 5-9, Apr.-Oct.). Closed Jan. 1, July 4, Thanksgiving and Christmas. **Cost:** $12; $9 (ages 65+ and students with ID); $6 (ages 9-17); free (first Sun. of the month). An additional fee may be charged for special exhibitions. **Parking:** $1 per hour. **Phone:** (510) 318-8400.

Ⓣ Lake Merritt, 18

OAKLAND ZOO AT KNOWLAND PARK, off I-580 at 9777 Golf Links Rd., offers picnic facilities, playgrounds, amusement rides, a train and more than 400 exotic and native animals in naturalistic habitats. An aerial tram affords a bird's-eye view of the area. A children's zoo lets kids visit a bug house as well as see sheep, goats, snakes, turtles, fruit bats and lemurs.

Time: Allow 1 hour minimum. **Hours:** Zoo open Mon.-Fri. 10-4, Sat.-Sun. and holidays 10-5:30, Memorial Day-Labor Day; daily 10-4, rest of year. Ride area, train and sky ride open daily at 11. Park open daily 9-5. Closed Thanksgiving and Christmas. **Cost:** Zoo $13.75; $11 (military with ID and military children ages 15+); $9.75 (ages 2-14 and 65-79); $8.25 (military children ages 2-14 and military ages 65-79 with ID). Rides $1.50-$3. **Parking:** $7. **Phone:** (510) 632-9525. Ⓣ

PERALTA HACIENDA HISTORICAL PARK is at 2465 34th Ave., at jct. Coolidge Ave. and Hyde St. The 6-acre site was the headquarters of the vast Rancho San Antonio, given as a land grant to Antonio Peralta in 1820. Tours offer insight into Peralta's life as he migrated north from Mexico, and docents provide information about the cattle ranch, its upheaval during the gold rush and the vibrant Fruitvale neighborhood that grew up in its place.

Time: Allow 1 hour minimum. **Hours:** Wed.-Sat. 2:30-5:30. Guided 45-minute tours are given at 2:30 and 4. **Cost:** $5; free (ages 0-10). Reservations are

(See map & index p. 254.)

recommended for guided tours. **Phone:** (510) 532-9142.

PRO ARTS is at 150 Frank Ogawa Plaza, across from Oakland City Hall between Broadway and Clay sts. This regional arts center presents some 15 exhibitions annually that showcase the work of more than 500 Oakland and East Bay artists.

Time: Allow 30 minutes minimum. **Hours:** Tues.-Fri. 10-5, Sat. 11-4. Closed major holidays. Phone ahead to confirm schedule. **Cost:** Free. **Phone:** (510) 763-4361. 12th St.
12th St. Oakland City Center, 17

SKYLINE BOULEVARD follows the rim of the Oakland Hills through the upscale Montclair neighborhood and a series of parklands. Architecturally distinctive homes perch on steep hillsides, and on clear days the East Bay vistas are spectacular. **Hours:** Daily 24 hours. **Cost:** Free.

USS POTOMAC is at 540 Water St. in Jack London Square, berthed next to the Lightship *Relief*. Dockside tours of President Franklin Delano Roosevelt's "floating White House" last 45 minutes and allow visitors to see the restored 165-foot vessel—modified to accommodate FDR's physical limitations—that once hosted European heads of state. Two-hour history cruises on the presidential yacht travel into San Francisco Bay. Both tours are preceded by a 15-minute video presentation in the visitor center.

Allow 1 hour minimum for dockside tours; 2 hours, 30 minutes minimum for history cruises. **Hours:** Dockside tours given Wed., Fri. and Sun. 11-3. History cruises depart on the first Thurs. and fourth Sat. of the month, May-Nov.; phone for departure times. **Cost:** Dockside tours $10; $8 (ages 60+); free (ages 0-12). History cruise $45; $40 (ages 60+); $25 (ages 6-12). Reservations are recommended for history cruises. **Phone:** (510) 627-1215, or (866) 468-3399 for history cruise reservations. 12th St. 12th St. Oakland City Center, 17

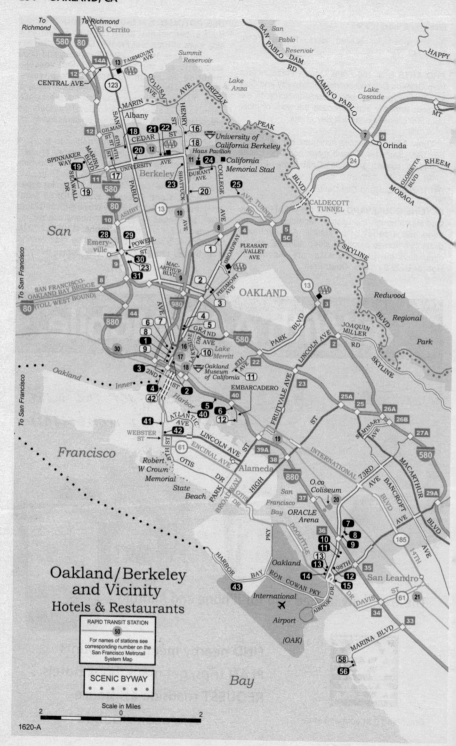

Oakland/Berkeley and Vicinity
Hotels & Restaurants

RAPID TRANSIT STATION

50

For names of stations see corresponding number on the San Francisco Metrorail System Map

SCENIC BYWAY

Scale in Miles

1620-A

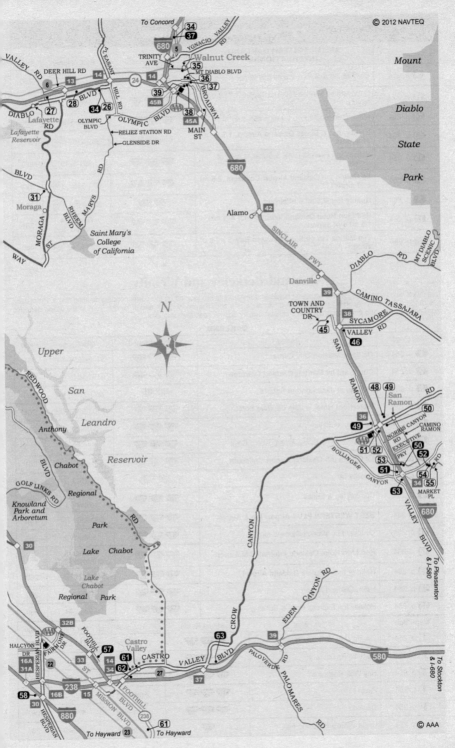

✈ Airport Accommodations

Map Page	METROPOLITAN OAKLAND INTERNATIONAL	Diamond Rated	Rate Range	Page
9 p. 254	Comfort Inn & Suites, 2.3 mi e of airport	◈◈◈	Rates not provided	260
11 p. 254	Courtyard by Marriott-Oakland Airport, 1.7 mi e of airport	◈◈◈	$98-$170	260
14 p. 254	Hilton Oakland Airport, 1.3 mi e of airport	◈◈◈	$129-$199	260
13 p. 254	Holiday Inn & Suites Oakland Airport, 1.5 mi e of airport	◈◈◈	$89-$159 SAVE	260
15 p. 254	Holiday Inn Express Hotel & Suites, 1 mi e of airport	◈◈◈	$99-$249	260
7 p. 254	La Quinta Inn Oakland Airport Coliseum, 2.5 mi e of airport	◈◈◈	$71-$155 SAVE	261
8 p. 254	Quality Inn, 2.5 mi e of airport	◈◈	$69-$149 SAVE	261
12 p. 254	Red Lion Hotel Oakland International Airport, 1.5 mi e of airport	◈◈◈	Rates not provided SAVE	261
56 p. 254	The Marina Inn on San Francisco Bay, 3 mi s of airport	◈◈◈	$109-$149 SAVE	480

Oakland/Berkeley and Vicinity

This index helps you "spot" where approved hotels and restaurants are located on the corresponding detailed maps. Hotel daily rate range is for comparison only. Restaurant price range is a combination of lunch and/or dinner. Turn to the listing page for more detailed rate and price information and consult display ads for special promotions.

OAKLAND

Map Page	Hotels	Diamond Rated	Rate Range	Page
1 p. 254	**Oakland Marriott City Center**	◈◈◈	$142-$256 SAVE	261
2 p. 254	**Courtyard by Marriott Oakland Downtown**	◈◈◈	$132-$246 SAVE	260
3 p. 254	**The Inn at Jack London Square**	◈◈	$89-$159 SAVE	260
4 p. 254	**Waterfront Hotel, a Joie de Vivre hotel**	◈◈◈	$105-$279 SAVE	261
5 p. 254	Homewood Suites	◈◈◈	$129-$219	260
6 p. 254	Executive Inn & Suites Embarcadero Cove	◈◈◈	$99-$229	260
7 p. 254	La Quinta Inn Oakland Airport Coliseum	◈◈◈	$71-$155 SAVE	261
8 p. 254	Quality Inn	◈◈	$69-$149 SAVE	261
9 p. 254	Comfort Inn & Suites	◈◈◈	Rates not provided	260
10 p. 254	**BEST WESTERN PLUS Airport Inn & Suites**	◈◈◈	$80-$300 SAVE	260
11 p. 254	Courtyard by Marriott-Oakland Airport	◈◈◈	$98-$170	260
12 p. 254	**Red Lion Hotel Oakland International Airport**	◈◈◈	Rates not provided SAVE	261
13 p. 254	**Holiday Inn & Suites Oakland Airport**	◈◈◈	$89-$159 SAVE	260
14 p. 254	Hilton Oakland Airport	◈◈◈	$129-$199	260
15 p. 254	Holiday Inn Express Hotel & Suites	◈◈◈	$99-$249	260

Map Page	Restaurants	Diamond Rated	Cuisine	Price Range	Page
① p. 254	Oliveto Cafe & Restaurant	◈◈◈	Italian	$14-$35	262
② p. 254	Commis Restaurant	◈◈◈	American	$68	262
③ p. 254	Bay Wolf Restaurant	◈◈◈	California	$10-$25	262
④ p. 254	Pican	◈◈◈	American	$12-$32	262
⑤ p. 254	Ozumo	◈◈◈	Japanese	$7-$21	262
⑥ p. 254	Uncle Willie's BBQ and Fish	◈	Barbecue	$6-$22	263

Map Page	Restaurants (cont'd)	Diamond Rated	Cuisine	Price Range	Page
⑦ p. 254	475 Cafe	◆	American	$4-$7	262
⑧ p. 254	Max's Diner and Bar	◆◆	American	$10-$18	262
⑨ p. 254	The Go Sports Bar & Grill	◆	American	$7-$16	262
⑩ p. 254	Lake Chalet Seafood Bar & Grill	◆◆◆	American	$12-$28	262
⑪ p. 254	Champa Garden	◆◆	Thai	$6-$11	262
⑫ p. 254	Quinn's Lighthouse Restaurant & Pub	◆◆	American	$10-$23	262
⑬ p. 254	Francesco's	◆◆	Italian	$8-$31	262

BERKELEY

Map Page	Hotels	Diamond Rated	Rate Range	Page
18 p. 254	**Americas Best Value Golden Bear Inn**	◆	$80-$160 (SAVE)	54
19 p. 254	**DoubleTree by Hilton Berkeley Marina**	◆◆◆	$129-$269 (SAVE)	54
20 p. 254	Holiday Inn Express Hotel & Suites	◆◆◆	$159-$299	55
21 p. 254	Super 8	◆◆	$69-$209	55
22 p. 254	**Quality Inn University**	◆◆	$145-$165 (SAVE)	55
23 p. 254	Hotel Shattuck Plaza	◆◆◆	$139-$450	55
24 p. 254	Hotel Durant, a Joie de Vivre hotel	◆◆◆	Rates not provided	55
25 p. 254	**Claremont Hotel Club & Spa** (See ad p. 55.)	◆◆◆◆	$189-$499 (SAVE)	54

Map Page	Restaurants	Diamond Rated	Cuisine	Price Range	Page
⑯ p. 254	Chez Panisse	◆◆◆	Regional American	$20-$80	55
⑰ p. 254	Cafe Rouge Restaurant & Meat Market	◆◆◆	Mediterranean	$13-$34	55
⑱ p. 254	**Bistro Liaison**	◆◆◆	French	$10-$25	55
⑲ p. 254	Skates on the Bay	◆◆◆	American	$11-$49	56
⑳ p. 254	Kirala Restaurant	◆◆	Japanese	$7-$26	56

EMERYVILLE

Map Page	Hotels	Diamond Rated	Rate Range	Page
28 p. 254	**Hilton Garden Inn**	◆◆◆	$189-$259 (SAVE)	101
29 p. 254	**Hyatt house Emeryville/San Francisco Bay Area**	◆◆◆	$139-$259 (SAVE)	101
30 p. 254	**Four Points by Sheraton-San Francisco Bay Bridge**	◆◆◆	$109-$249 (SAVE)	101
31 p. 254	Courtyard by Marriott Emeryville	◆◆◆	$149-$249	101

Map Page	Restaurant	Diamond Rated	Cuisine	Price Range	Page
㉓ p. 254	P.F. Chang's China Bistro	◆◆◆	Chinese	$8-$22	101

LAFAYETTE

Map Page	Hotel	Diamond Rated	Rate Range	Page
34 p. 254	**Lafayette Park Hotel & Spa**	◆◆◆◆	$199-$289 (SAVE)	156

Map Page	Restaurants	Diamond Rated	Cuisine	Price Range	Page
㉖ p. 254	The Duck Club Restaurant	◆◆◆◆	American	$12-$40	156
㉗ p. 254	Mountain Mike's Pizza	◆	Pizza	$6-$37	156
㉘ p. 254	Bo's Barbecue & Catering Restaurant	◆	Barbecue	$10-$23	156

WALNUT CREEK

Map Page	Hotel	Diamond Rated	Rate Range	Page
37 p. 254	Walnut Creek Marriott	◆◆◆	$132-$256	554

Map Page	Restaurants	Diamond Rated	Cuisine	Price Range	Page
34 p. 254	Atriu	◆◆◆	American	$10-$24	554
35 p. 254	Massimo Ristorante	◆◆◆	Northern Italian	$10-$35	554
36 p. 254	Il Fornaio	◆◆◆	Italian	$9-$36	554
37 p. 254	P.F. Chang's China Bistro	◆◆◆	Chinese	$10-$20	554
38 p. 254	Ruth's Chris Steak House	◆◆◆	Steak	$23-$70	554
39 p. 254	The Cheesecake Factory	◆◆◆	American	$6-$28	554

ALAMEDA

Map Page	Hotels	Diamond Rated	Rate Range	Page
40 p. 254	Marina Village Inn	◆◆	$64-$179 [SAVE]	43
41 p. 254	Rodeway Inn-Oakland/Alameda	◆◆	$59-$99 [SAVE]	43
42 p. 254	Hawthorn Suites by Wyndham-Oakland/Alameda	◆◆◆	$100-$160 [SAVE]	42
43 p. 254	Hampton Inn & Suites	◆◆◆	$109-$249	42

Map Page	Restaurant	Diamond Rated	Cuisine	Price Range	Page
42 p. 254	Pasta Pelican	◆◆	Italian	$10-$21	43

DANVILLE

Map Page	Hotel	Diamond Rated	Rate Range	Page
46 p. 254	BEST WESTERN PLUS Danville Sycamore Inn	◆◆◆	$85-$150 [SAVE]	94

Map Page	Restaurant	Diamond Rated	Cuisine	Price Range	Page
45 p. 254	El Nido Mexican Restaurant	◆◆	Mexican	$8-$18	94

SAN RAMON

Map Page	Hotels	Diamond Rated	Rate Range	Page
49 p. 254	Hyatt house San Ramon	◆◆◆	$79-$249 [SAVE]	484
50 p. 254	San Ramon Marriott at Bishop Ranch	◆◆◆	$109-$299	484
51 p. 254	Extended StayAmerica-San Ramon-Bishop Ranch-West	◆◆	$94-$109	484
52 p. 254	Residence Inn by Marriott	◆◆◆	$123-$224	484
53 p. 254	Courtyard by Marriott	◆◆◆	$99-$209	484

Map Page	Restaurants	Diamond Rated	Cuisine	Price Range	Page
48 p. 254	Max's Restaurant & Bar	◆◆	American	$8-$24	485
49 p. 254	Uncle Yu's	◆◆◆	Szechuan	$8-$30	485
50 p. 254	Zachary's Chicago Pizza	◆◆	Pizza	$15-$30	485
51 p. 254	Levy's Bagels & Co	◆	Deli	$4-$8	485
52 p. 254	New York Pizza	◆	Pizza	$12-$28	485
53 p. 254	Stixx & Steaks	◆◆◆	Pacific Rim	$10-$36	485
54 p. 254	Kilohana Grill	◆	Hawaiian	$5-$12	485
55 p. 254	The Hopyard American Alehouse & Grill	◆◆	American	$8-$18	484

SAN LEANDRO

Map Page	Hotels	Diamond Rated	Rate Range	Page
56 p. 254	The Marina Inn on San Francisco Bay	◆◆◆	$109-$149 [SAVE]	480
57 p. 254	Budget Inn	◆◆	$60-$95 [SAVE]	479

SAN LEANDRO (cont'd)

Map Page	Hotels (cont'd)	Diamond Rated		Rate Range	Page
58 p. 254	Hilton Garden Inn	❖❖❖		$139-$169	479

Map Page	Restaurant	Diamond Rated	Cuisine	Price Range	Page
58 p. 254	Horatio's	❖❖❖	American	$8-$46	480

CASTRO VALLEY

Map Page	Hotels	Diamond Rated		Rate Range	Page
61 p. 254	Quality Inn	❖❖❖		$79-$189	76
62 p. 254	Castro Valley Comfort Suites	❖❖❖		$105-$149	76
63 p. 254	**Castro Valley Inn**	❖❖		$66-$77 [SAVE]	76

MORAGA

Map Page	Restaurant	Diamond Rated	Cuisine	Price Range	Page
31 p. 254	Ristorante Amoroma	❖❖❖	Italian	$14-$26	227

HAYWARD

Map Page	Restaurant	Diamond Rated	Cuisine	Price Range	Page
61 p. 254	Buffalo Bill's Brewery	❖❖	American	$8-$20	146

BEST WESTERN PLUS AIRPORT INN & SUITES
(510)633-0500   **10**

Hotel
$80-$300

Best Western PLUS

AAA Benefit: Members save up to 20%, plus 10% bonus points with Best Western Rewards®.

Address: 170 Hegenberger Loop 94621 **Location:** I-880 exit Hegenberger Rd W, just s. **Facility:** 76 units. 3 stories, interior corridors. **Terms:** resort fee. **Amenities:** high-speed Internet. **Pool(s):** heated indoor. **Activities:** whirlpool, exercise room. **Guest Services:** coin laundry. **Free Special Amenities: local telephone calls and high-speed Internet.**

COMFORT INN & SUITES
510/568-1500   **9**

Hotel. Rates not provided. **Address:** 8452 Edes Ave 94621 **Location:** I-880 exit Hegenberger Rd, just e. Coliseum/Oakland Airport, 20. 3 stories, interior corridors. **Amenities:** video games (fee), high-speed Internet. **Activities:** sauna, whirlpool, steamroom, exercise room. **Guest Services:** valet and coin laundry.

COURTYARD BY MARRIOTT-OAKLAND AIRPORT
(510)568-7600   **11**

Hotel $98-$170 **Address:** 350 Hegenberger Rd 94621 **Location:** I-880 exit Hegenberger Rd, just w. **Facility:** 156 units. 3 stories, interior corridors. **Amenities:** high-speed Internet. **Pool(s):** outdoor. **Activities:** whirlpool, exercise room. **Guest Services:** valet and coin laundry, area transportation-BART.

AAA Benefit: AAA hotel discounts of 5% or more.

COURTYARD BY MARRIOTT OAKLAND DOWNTOWN
(510)625-8282   **2**

Hotel
$132-$246

AAA Benefit: AAA hotel discounts of 5% or more.

Address: 988 Broadway 94607 **Location:** I-880 exit Broadway E, at 9th St. 12th St. Oakland City Center, 17. **Facility:** 162 units. 5 stories, interior corridors. **Parking:** valet only. **Amenities:** high-speed Internet. **Pool(s):** heated outdoor. **Activities:** whirlpool, exercise room. **Guest Services:** valet and coin laundry. **Free Special Amenities: high-speed Internet.**

EXECUTIVE INN & SUITES EMBARCADERO COVE
(510)536-6633   **6**

Hotel $99-$229 **Address:** 1755 Embarcadero 94606 **Location:** I-880 exit 16th Ave/Embarcadero southbound, just w; exit 5th Ave/Embarcadero northbound. **Facility:** 224 units. 3 stories, interior corridors. **Amenities:** high-speed Internet. *Some:* safes. **Pool(s):** heated outdoor. **Activities:** whirlpool, fishing, exercise room. **Guest Services:** valet and coin laundry, area transportation-within 3 mi.

HILTON OAKLAND AIRPORT
(510)635-5000   **14**

Hotel $129-$199 **Address:** 1 Hegenberger Rd 94621 **Location:** I-880 exit Hegenberger Rd, 1 mi w; 1.3 mi e of Metropolitan Oakland International Airport. **Facility:** 363 units. 3 stories, interior corridors. **Parking:** on-site (fee). **Terms:** 1-7 night minimum stay, cancellation fee imposed. **Amenities:** *Fee:* video games, high-speed Internet. **Dining:** 2 restaurants. **Pool(s):** heated outdoor. **Activities:** exercise room. **Guest Services:** valet laundry, area transportation-BART.

AAA Benefit: Members save 5% or more!

HOLIDAY INN & SUITES OAKLAND AIRPORT
(510)638-7777   **13**

Hotel
$89-$159

Address: 77 Hegenberger Rd 94621 **Location:** I-880 exit Hegenberger Rd, 0.5 mi w. **Facility:** 145 units. 4 stories, interior corridors. **Terms:** cancellation fee imposed. **Amenities:** high-speed Internet. **Pool(s):** heated outdoor. **Activities:** exercise room. **Guest Services:** valet and coin laundry, area transportation-within 1 mi. **Free Special Amenities: high-speed Internet and airport transportation.**

HOLIDAY INN EXPRESS HOTEL & SUITES
(510)569-4400   **15**

Hotel $99-$249 **Address:** 66 Airport Access Rd 94603 **Location:** I-880 exit Hegenberger Rd W; jct Doolittle Dr and Airport Access Rd. **Facility:** 95 units, some kitchens. 3 stories, interior corridors. **Terms:** cancellation fee imposed. **Amenities:** high-speed Internet. **Activities:** whirlpool, exercise room. **Guest Services:** valet and coin laundry, area transportation-within 3 mi.

HOMEWOOD SUITES
(510)663-2700   **5**

Extended Stay Hotel $129-$219 **Address:** 1103 Embarcadero 94606 **Location:** I-880 exit 16th Ave/Embarcadero southbound; exit 5th Ave/Embarcadero northbound, just w. Lake Merritt, 18. **Facility:** 132 units, some two bedrooms and efficiencies. 3 stories, interior corridors. **Terms:** 1-7 night minimum stay, cancellation fee imposed. **Amenities:** video games (fee), high-speed Internet. **Pool(s):** outdoor. **Activities:** whirlpool, limited exercise equipment. **Guest Services:** valet and coin laundry, area transportation-within 2 mi.

AAA Benefit: Contemporary luxury at a special Member rate.

THE INN AT JACK LONDON SQUARE
(510)452-4565   **3**

Hotel
$89-$159

Address: 233 Broadway 94607 **Location:** I-880 exit Broadway, 0.3 mi w. Located at entrance to Jack London Square. 12th St. Oakland City Center, 17. **Facility:** 100 units. 3 stories, interior/exterior corridors. **Terms:** cancellation fee imposed. **Pool(s):** outdoor. **Activities:** exercise room. **Guest Services:** valet and coin laundry. **Free Special Amenities: newspaper and high-speed Internet.**

LA QUINTA INN OAKLAND AIRPORT COLISEUM
(510)632-8900

Hotel
$71-$155

Address: 8465 Enterprise Way 94621 **Location:** I-880 exit Hegenberger Rd, just e. Coliseum/Oakland Airport, 20. **Facility:** 148 units. 3 stories, interior corridors. **Amenities:** video games (fee). **Pool(s):** outdoor. **Activities:** whirlpool, limited exercise equipment. **Guest Services:** valet and coin laundry, area transportation-within 2 mi. **Free Special Amenities:** expanded continental breakfast and high-speed Internet.

OAKLAND MARRIOTT CITY CENTER
(510)451-4000

Hotel
$142-$256

 **Marriott** HOTELS & RESORTS

AAA Benefit: AAA hotel discounts of 5% or more.

Address: 1001 Broadway 94607 **Location:** I-880 exit Broadway, just e; at 10th St. 12th St. Oakland City Center, 17. **Facility:** 489 units. 21 stories, interior corridors. **Parking:** onsite (fee) and valet. **Pool(s):** heated outdoor. **Activities:** exercise room. **Guest Services:** valet and coin laundry.

QUALITY INN
(510)562-4888

Hotel
$69-$149

Address: 8471 Enterprise Way 94621 **Location:** I-880 exit Hegenberger Rd, just e. Coliseum/Oakland Airport, 20. **Facility:** 98 units. 3 stories, exterior corridors. **Terms:** cancellation fee imposed. **Pool(s):** outdoor. **Activities:** whirlpool. **Free Special Amenities:** expanded continental breakfast and airport transportation.

RED LION HOTEL OAKLAND INTERNATIONAL AIRPORT
510/635-5300

Hotel
Rates not provided

Address: 150 Hegenberger Rd 94621 **Location:** I-880 exit Hegenberger Rd, 0.8 mi w. **Facility:** 189 units. 2-6 stories, interior corridors. **Amenities:** video games (fee). **Pool(s):** outdoor. **Activities:** exercise room. **Guest Services:** valet and coin laundry, area transportation (fee)-BART. **Free Special Amenities:** high-speed Internet and airport transportation.

WATERFRONT HOTEL, A JOIE DE VIVRE HOTEL
(510)836-3800

Hotel
$105-$279

Address: Ten Washington St 94607 **Location:** I-880 exit Broadway, 0.5 mi w. Located in Jack London Square. 12th St. Oakland City Center, 17. **Facility:** 145 units. 5 stories, interior corridors. **Parking:** valet only. **Terms:** cancellation fee imposed. **Amenities:** safes. **Pool(s):** heated outdoor. **Activities:** sauna, exercise room. **Guest Services:** valet laundry, area transportation-within 4 mi. **Free Special Amenities:** high-speed Internet and manager's reception.

WHERE TO EAT

475 CAFE 510/451-5959 (7)

American. Quick Serve. $4-$7 **AAA Inspector Notes:** Conveniently located downtown adjacent to City Hall and the Convention Center, this small café serves up a quick breakfast or lunch featuring pastries, omelets, freshly-squeezed juices, fruit plates, sandwiches and salads. Daily hot lunch specials include meatloaf with mashed potatoes, spaghetti and meatballs or roast chicken. This is a favorite of the local clientèle, so come early. **Address:** 475 14th St, Suite 110 94612 **Location:** I-880 exit Broadway E; adjacent to City Hall. 12th St. Oakland City Center, 17. **Parking:** on-site (fee).

B L

BAY WOLF RESTAURANT 510/655-6004 (3)

California. Fine Dining. $10-$25 **AAA Inspector Notes:** This pretty, converted house invites diners to sample California cuisine with Mediterranean influences. The menu changes to reflect the freshest ingredients available. **Bar:** beer & wine. **Reservations:** suggested. **Address:** 3853 Piedmont Ave 94611 **Location:** I-580 exit Oakland Ave, 2 blks e on Piedmont Ave, then 0.3 mi n on MacArthur Blvd. MacArthur, 9. **Parking:** street only.

D

BUTTERCUP GRILL & BAR

American. Casual Dining. $10-$20 **AAA Inspector Notes:** Extensive choices of traditional comfort foods-including great sandwiches, hamburgers, soups and desserts-are served in hearty portions. The staff is warm and friendly. **Bar:** full bar.

B L D CALL

For additional information, visit AAA.com

LOCATIONS:

Address: 229 Broadway 94607 **Location:** I-880 exit Broadway, just w. 12th St. Oakland City Center, 17. **Phone:** 510/444-2976

Address: 1000 Cotton St 94606 **Location:** I-880 exit 23rd Ave northbound, just w; southbound, U-turn on 23rd Ave, 0.3 mi s, w on E 7th St, 0.3 mi n on Kennedy St, then just w. Fruitvale, 19.
Phone: 510/535-1640

CHAMPA GARDEN 510/238-8819 (11)

Thai. Casual Dining. $6-$11 **AAA Inspector Notes:** This popular neighborhood diner offers a mix of Asian-style cuisines including Thai, Vietnamese and Laotian. **Bar:** beer & wine. **Address:** 2102 8th Ave 94606 **Location:** I-580 exit 14th Ave/Park Blvd, 1 mi s, then 0.4 mi w; at E 21st St. **Parking:** street only. L D

COMMIS RESTAURANT 510/653-3902 (2)

American. Fine Dining. $68 **AAA Inspector Notes:** Food is the star at this petite restaurant. The young/owner chef is known for creative cuisine utilizing locally-grown ingredients. Diners can sit at the bar and watch the chefs perform. **Bar:** full bar. **Address:** 3859 Piedmont Ave 94611 **Location:** I-580 exit MacArthur Blvd, just nw, then just n; between Rio Vista Ave and Montell St. MacArthur, 9. **Parking:** street only. D CALL

FRANCESCO'S 510/569-0653 (13)

Italian. Casual Dining. $8-$31 **AAA Inspector Notes:** A tradition in this area for more than 40 years, this family-owned and -operated Italian eatery offers up favorites including spaghetti, ravioli, veal scallopini, chicken parmigiana and fresh seafood. Service is friendly and welcoming at this local favorite. **Bar:** full bar. **Address:** 8520 Pardee Dr 94621 **Location:** I-580 exit Hegenberger Rd, 0.7 mi w, then just n. L D CALL

THE GO SPORTS BAR & GRILL 510/452-1258 (9)

American. Casual Dining. $7-$16 **AAA Inspector Notes:** This is a great stop for a quick bite or an after-hours evening of fun while watching the big game. Homemade soups, sandwiches and entrées are offered along with great hamburgers. A friendly staff can be expected. **Bar:** full bar. **Address:** 736 Washington St 94607 **Location:** I-880 exit Broadway E, just n on Washington St; at 8th St. 12th St. Oakland City Center, 17. **Parking:** street only. L D

LAKE CHALET SEAFOOD BAR & GRILL 510/208-5253 (10)

American. Fine Dining. $12-$28 **AAA Inspector Notes:** Overlooking Lake Merritt, this restaurant offers a nice selection of beef, poultry and seafood items. Also available is an oyster bar. Service is warm and welcoming. **Bar:** full bar. **Reservations:** suggested. **Address:** 1520 Lakeside Dr 94612 **Location:** I-880 exit Oak St/Lakeside Dr, 0.5 mi e. Lake Merritt, 18. **Parking:** valet and street only. L D CALL

MAX'S DINER AND BAR 510/451-6297 (8)

American. Casual Dining. $10-$18 **AAA Inspector Notes:** This is a great stop for sandwiches, burgers, seafood and pasta. Be sure to bring an appetite because portions are hearty. Remember to save room for dessert. **Bar:** full bar. **Address:** 500 12th St 94607 **Location:** I-880 exit Broadway, just e; between Broadway and Clay St; in Broadway Plaza. 12th St. Oakland City Center, 17. **Parking:** on-site (fee). L D CALL

OLIVETO CAFE & RESTAURANT 510/547-5356 (1)

Italian. Fine Dining. $14-$35 **AAA Inspector Notes:** Fresh seasonal ingredients are prepared in the Italian tradition with a flair for style in the restaurant; while the cafe is trattoria style for casual dining. **Bar:** full bar. **Reservations:** suggested. **Address:** 5655 College Ave 94618 **Location:** Opposite Rockridge BART station; in Market Hall Building. Rockridge, 8. **Parking:** street only.

B L D

OZUMO 510/286-9866 (5)

Japanese. Fine Dining. $7-$21 **AAA Inspector Notes:** An innovative menu with a nice selection of Japanese favorites including tempura, kushi, donburi, noodles, bento boxes and home-made sushi and sashimi are served in this restaurant with an open-grill kitchen. Service is friendly. **Bar:** full bar. **Reservations:** suggested. **Address:** 2251 Broadway Ave 94612 **Location:** I-980 exit 27th St/W Grand Ave, 0.4 mi e, then just s at Grand Ave. 19th Street/Oakland, 16. **Parking:** street only. L D

PASTA POMODORO 510/923-0900

Italian. Casual Dining. $8-$18 **AAA Inspector Notes:** Families are welcomed at this laid-back restaurant, which brings in plenty of loyal locals who enjoy its varied Italian favorites, including tempting pasta and chicken dishes. **Bar:** beer & wine. **Address:** 5500 College Ave 94611 **Location:** SR 24 exit College Ave, 0.3 mi s; at Lawton Ave. Rockridge, 8. **Parking:** street only.

L D CALL

PICAN 510/834-1000 (4)

American. Casual Dining. $12-$32 **AAA Inspector Notes:** Southern cuisine meets California cuisine at this upscale restaurant. Traditional Southern favorites include fried chicken (soaked in a buttermilk brine for 3 days before fried to perfection) accompanied by Gouda macaroni and cheese-be sure to try it with truffle honey drizzled onto the chicken tableside. Other menu items include pan-roasted sea scallops, braised short ribs, duck with Southern sauerkraut, Mississippi catfish and the house specialty Berkshire pork chop with Amish-raised pork. **Bar:** full bar. **Reservations:** suggested. **Address:** 2295 Broadway 94612 **Location:** I-980 exit Downtown Oakland/27th St, 0.4 mi e on 27th St, then just s at 23rd St. 19th Street/Oakland, 16. **Parking:** street only.

L D CALL

QUINN'S LIGHTHOUSE RESTAURANT & PUB
510/536-2050 (12)

American Seafood. Casual Dining. $10-$23 **AAA Inspector Notes:** In a historic 1890 lighthouse, the restaurant presents a menu of contemporary fare, including preparations of seafood, pasta and chicken. The upstairs deck is a beautiful lookout. **Bar:** full bar. **Reservations:** suggested. **Address:** 1951 Embarcadero Cove Marina, Embarcadero E 94606 **Location:** I-880 exit 16th Ave/Embarcadero southbound; exit 5th Ave/Embarcadero northbound, just w, then 0.3 mi s. **Parking:** street only.

L D CALL

ROUND TABLE PIZZA 510/336-3333

Pizza. Casual Dining. $7-$28 **AAA Inspector Notes:** This casual, family-oriented pizza place features high-quality ingredients and dough rolled fresh daily. Distinctive specialty pizzas are piled high with toppings. **Bar:** beer & wine. **Address:** 2854 Mountain Blvd 94602 **Location:** SR 13 exit Joaquin Miller Rd E. L D

UNCLE WILLIE'S BBQ AND FISH   510/465-9200 [6]

[W] Barbecue. Quick Serve. $6-$22 AAA Inspector Notes: This small hole-in-the-wall restaurant downtown near the courthouse offers a variety of barbecue favorites including ribs and chicken along with a choice of mild, medium or spicy sauce. Fish and chips and other seafood items also are available. Address: 614 14th St 94612 Location: I-880 exit Broadway, 0.4 mi e, then just n; at Jefferson St. [回] 12th St. Oakland City Center, 17. Parking: street only.

[L] [D] [回]

SIAM BAY   510/452-1499

[fyi] Not evaluated. The menu at this restaurant offers traditional Thai favorites. Address: 1009 Clay St 94607 Location: I-880 exit Broadway E, then just n at 10th St. [回] 12th St. Oakland City Center, 17.

OAKLEY pop. 35,432

BLACK BEAR DINER   925/625-3555

[W][W] American Comfort Food. Casual Dining. $6-$18 AAA Inspector Notes: A homey atmosphere characterizes this family-oriented restaurant. Familiar comfort foods, such as meatloaf with mashed potatoes, are at the heart of the menu and are served in generous portions. Bar: beer & wine. Address: 3201 Main St 94561 Location: 2 mi e of jct SR 160 and 4. [B] [L] [D] CALL [&M]

OAKVILLE (B-8) pop. 71, elev. 155'
- Attractions map p. 568
- Part of Wine Country area — see map p. 562

Oakville, named for the area's dense oak groves, started out as a sleepy little railroad stop that replenished steam trains with water in the 1860s. These days the Napa Valley Wine Train chugs through town on the same stretch (see attraction listing in Napa p. 236).

In addition to the railroad, the 1860s also brought the first vineyard to Oakville when settler H.W. Crabb purchased acreage near the Napa River. Battling pests and diseases, Crabb prevailed. Today, the University of California at Davis owns a vineyard in town called Oakville Station, used to conduct experiments in ongoing efforts to refine viticultural practices.

Connoisseurs make the pilgrimage to this laid-back hamlet to indulge their taste buds with some of the world's finest cabernet; a warm, sunny climate and rich soil results in ideal growing conditions for this grape. Wineries start cropping up as you travel along SR 29 (St. Helena Highway). You're really in the thick of things, though, once you reach the junction with the Oakville Crossroad, a couple of miles south of Oakville. The Oakville Grocery (7856 St. Helena Hwy.), a long-established gourmet food market in the heart of the Napa Valley, is a favorite with both locals and visitors. It's the perfect place to pick up picnic goodies, sample local food specialties from nearby farms and indulge in a caffeinated concoction from the espresso bar.

Take the Oakville Crossroad east until it runs into the Silverado Trail, where there are more wineries within the Oakville appellation; along the way you'll see the white water tower of Silver Oak Cellars looming over expansive vineyards. Take Oakville Grade Road west and you'll enter the Oakville Grade linking the Napa and Sonoma valleys. This winding mountain drive offers spectacular panoramas, but requires caution and should only be driven during daylight hours.

WINERIES
- Robert Mondavi Winery is .5 mi. n. on SR 29. Hours: Tastings daily 10-5. Various tours are offered daily; phone ahead for details. Closed Jan. 1, Easter, Thanksgiving and Christmas. Phone: (888) 766-6328.

O'BRIEN (B-2)

LAKE SHASTA CAVERNS/NATIONAL NATURAL LANDMARK is reached from Shasta Caverns Rd., 1.5 mi. e. of I-5. Columns, stalactites, stalagmites and flowstone deposits can be seen on 2-hour tours; more than 600 steps are included. The caverns remain a constant temperature of 58 F. Round-trip boat and bus transportation to the cave entrance are provided.

Time: Allow 2 hours minimum. Hours: Tours depart daily every half-hour 9-4, Memorial Day weekend-Labor Day; every hour 9-3, Apr. 1-day before Memorial Day weekend and day after Labor Day-Sept. 30; at 10, noon and 2, rest of year (weather permitting). Closed Thanksgiving and Christmas. Cost: $24; $14 (ages 3-15). Phone: (530) 238-2341 or (800) 795-2283. [T]

OCCIDENTAL pop. 1,115
- Part of Wine Country area — see map p. 562

INN AT OCCIDENTAL   (707)874-1047

[W][W][W] Bed & Breakfast $199-$379 Address: 3657 Church St 95465 Location: Town center. Facility: Covered porches and wicker furnishings enhance the exterior of this elegantly restored 1860 Victorian; most rooms have a fireplace. If you must, in-room televisions are available upon request. 17 units, some houses. 3 stories (no elevator), interior/exterior corridors. Terms: 2 night minimum stay - seasonal and/or weekends, 10 day cancellation notice-fee imposed.

[T↑→] CALL [&M] [BIZ] [⊚] [✕] [W] / SOME UNITS FEE [🐾] [▤]

OCCIDENTAL HOTEL   (707)874-3623

[W][W] Motel $95-$180 Address: 3610 Bohemian Hwy 95465 Location: In the village. Facility: 27 units, some two bedrooms. 2 stories (no elevator), exterior corridors. Terms: 2 night minimum stay - seasonal and/or weekends, 3 day cancellation notice-fee imposed. Pool(s): outdoor.

[T↑→] CALL [&M] [☀] [⊚] [✕] [▤] [▤] [▤] / SOME UNITS FEE [🐾]

OLEMA

POINT REYES SEASHORE LODGE AND RESTAURANT
                                           415/663-9000

[W][W] Motel $145-$295 Address: 10021 SR 1 94950 Location: Center. Adjacent to Point Reyes Seashore National Park. Facility: 24 units, some kitchens and cottages. 2-3 stories (no elevator), interior/exterior corridors. Terms: 2 night minimum stay - weekends, 7 day cancellation notice-fee imposed. Activities: Fee: massage.

[T] [Y] CALL [&M] [⊚] [✕] [W] [W] / SOME UNITS [▤] [▤] [▤]

Be a better driver.
Keep your mind on the road.

OLYMPIC VALLEY (D-4) elev. 6,079'

- **Hotels & Restaurants map & index p. 161**
- **Part of Lake Tahoe Area — see map p. 158**

SQUAW VALLEY CABLE CAR is 2.1 mi. w. to Squaw Valley USA's base village. The cable car provides a full aerial view of Lake Tahoe and Squaw Valley, site of the 1960 Winter Olympics and a year-round recreation area, as it ascends to High Camp, the trailhead of the Pacific Crest Trail and the site of activities such as ice-skating and swimming. A museum at the summit commemorates those games. Activities packages are available.

Hours: Sun.-Thurs. 10:40-5, Fri.-Sat. 10:40-6, early June-late Sept.; schedule varies in ski season. Phone ahead to confirm schedule. **Cost:** Cable car $29; $22 (ages 13-18 and 65+); $10 (ages 5-12); free (ages 0-4 and active military with ID). A fee is charged for activities. Prices may vary. **Phone:** (530) 583-6985. ⟨T⟩

High Camp, at the upper terminus of the Squaw Valley Cable Car, boasts panoramic views of Lake Tahoe and the High Sierra and is where many beginner runs start. After riding the tram up the mountain to an elevation of 8,200 feet, visitors can take advantage of several recreational options, including swimming and roller skating. In addition, the Olympic Museum offers memorabilia and video presentations from the 1960 Winter Olympics.

Time: Allow 3 hours minimum. **Hours:** High Camp open Sun.-Thurs. 11-5, Fri.-Sat. 11-6, early June-late Sept. Museum open daily; phone ahead for schedule. **Cost:** Cable car (includes Olympic Museum) $29; $22 (ages 13-18 and 65+); $10 (ages 5-12); free (ages 0-4 and active military with ID). Swimming only $18; $8 (ages 0-12). Roller skating only $12; $6 (ages 5-12). An all-access pass and combination tickets also are available; phone ahead for prices and age restrictions. **Phone:** (530) 583-6985. ⟨T⟩ ⟨X⟩

RECREATIONAL ACTIVITIES

Skiing

- **Squaw Valley USA** is 2.1 mi. w. to Squaw Valley USA's base village. **Hours:** Mon.-Fri. 9-4, Sat.-Sun. and holidays 8:30-4, mid-Nov. through Memorial Day (also 4-9, mid-Dec. to mid-Apr.), weather permitting. **Phone:** (530) 583-6985, or (530) 583-6955 for 24-hour information.

PLUMPJACK SQUAW VALLEY INN   530/583-1576 18
▼▼▼▼ **Boutique Contemporary Hotel.** Rates not provided. **Address:** 1920 Squaw Valley Rd 96146 **Location:** I-80 exit SR 89, 8.3 mi s, then 2.2 mi sw. **Facility:** This boutique-style hotel offers unique furnishings in its comfortable rooms and a great location within walking distance to many shops, restaurants and ski lifts. 56 units, some kitchens. 3 stories (no elevator), interior corridors. **Parking:** on-site and valet. **Terms:** check-in 4 pm. **Pool(s):** outdoor. **Activities:** whirlpools, hiking trails, basketball, exercise room.
⟨T+⟩ ⟨Y⟩ CALL ⟨&M⟩ ⟨⟩ ⟨BIZ⟩ ⟨⟩ ⟨X⟩ ⟨K⟩ ⟨⟩ ⟨▣⟩
/ SOME UNITS FEE ⟨🐕⟩ ⟨▯⟩ ⟨▣⟩

RED WOLF LODGE AT SQUAW VALLEY (530)583-7226 21
▼▼▼▼ Hotel $139-$419 **Address:** 2000 Squaw Loop Rd 96146 **Location:** I-80 exit SR 89, 8.3 mi s, 2 mi sw on Squaw Valley Rd, then just s; in Olympic Valley. Located at Squaw Valley Ski area. **Facility:** 32 kitchen units, some two bedrooms. 3 stories, interior corridors. **Terms:** check-in 4 pm, 7 day cancellation notice-fee imposed. **Activities:** sauna, whirlpools, bicycles, hiking trails, game room, exercise room. **Fee:** downhill & cross country skiing. **Guest Services:** complimentary and valet laundry.
⟨T+⟩ CALL ⟨&M⟩ ⟨⟩ ⟨X⟩ ⟨▯⟩ ⟨▣⟩ ⟨▣⟩

RESORT AT SQUAW CREEK   (530)583-6300 22
▼▼▼▼
Resort Hotel
$159-$499
Address: 400 Squaw Creek Rd 96146 **Location:** I-80 exit SR 89, 8.3 mi s, 0.6 mi on Squaw Valley Rd, then just w; in Olympic Valley. Located at Squaw Valley Ski area. **Facility:** In a spectacular mountain setting, the property's extensive recreational activities are available in both summer and winter, including the resort's 18-hole golf course. 348 units, some two bedrooms and efficiencies. 9 stories, interior corridors. **Parking:** on-site and valet. **Terms:** check-in 4 pm, 2 night minimum stay - seasonal and/or weekends, 14 day cancellation notice-fee imposed, resort fee. **Amenities:** video games (fee). **Dining:** 4 restaurants, also, Six Peaks Grill, see separate listing. **Pool(s):** 2 outdoor, heated outdoor. **Activities:** saunas, whirlpools, steamrooms, waterslide, 2 tennis courts, ice skating, tobogganing, recreation programs, rental bicycles, hiking trails, basketball, spa. **Fee:** golf-18 holes, downhill & cross country skiing, game room. **Guest Services:** valet and coin laundry, area transportation-The Village. **Free Special Amenities:** local telephone calls and high-speed Internet.
⟨SAVE⟩ ⟨T⟩ ⟨Y⟩ ⟨⟩ ⟨↔⟩ ⟨BIZ⟩ ⟨⟩ ⟨X⟩ ⟨⟩ ⟨▯⟩ ⟨▣⟩
/ SOME UNITS ⟨▣⟩

SQUAW VALLEY LODGE   (530)583-5500 20
▼▼▼ **Resort Condominium** $184-$1099 **Address:** 201 Squaw Peak Rd 96146 **Location:** I-80 exit SR 89, 8.3 mi s, then 2.2 mi sw on Squaw Valley Rd. Located at Squaw Valley Ski area. **Facility:** At the foot of the ski slopes, 150 feet from the cable car, this ski-in/ski-out lodge features views of the mountain or valley from most rooms. Varied decor and loft-style units are available. 136 condominiums. 2-3 stories, interior corridors. **Terms:** check-in 4 pm, 1-2 night minimum stay - weekends, 14 day cancellation notice-fee imposed. **Pool(s):** outdoor. **Activities:** sauna, whirlpools, steamroom, 2 tennis courts. **Fee:** downhill skiing, massage. **Guest Services:** coin laundry.
⟨T+⟩ CALL ⟨&M⟩ ⟨⟩ ⟨↔⟩ ⟨BIZ⟩ ⟨⟩ ⟨X⟩ ⟨K⟩ ⟨▯⟩ ⟨▣⟩
⟨▣⟩

THE VILLAGE AT SQUAW VALLEY   (530)584-1000 19
▼▼▼ **Resort Condominium** $99-$999 **Address:** 1750 Village East Rd 96146 **Location:** I-80 exit SR 89, 8.3 mi s, then 2 mi sw on Squaw Valley Rd; in Olympic Valley; at Squaw Valley ski area. **Facility:** Accommodations at this resort are located among five buildings with a variety of shops and restaurants nearby. 184 condominiums. 4 stories, interior corridors. **Terms:** check-in 4 pm, 2-3 night minimum stay - seasonal and/or weekends, 5 day cancellation notice-fee imposed. **Amenities:** high-speed Internet. **Activities:** saunas, whirlpools, hiking trails, jogging, exercise room. **Fee:** downhill & cross country skiing, snowmobiling, ice skating, massage. **Guest Services:** coin laundry, area transportation-Resort at Squaw Creek and Alpine Meadows.
⟨T+⟩ CALL ⟨&M⟩ ⟨BIZ⟩ ⟨⟩ ⟨X⟩ ⟨K⟩ ⟨▣⟩ / SOME UNITS ⟨▯⟩ ⟨▣⟩

WHERE TO EAT

SIX PEAKS GRILL   530/583-6300 18
▼▼▼ American. Casual Dining. $16-$32 **AAA Inspector Notes:** Patrons are treated to panoramic mountains and valley views through floor-to-ceiling windows at this grill. When available, local fresh produce combines with the restaurant's creative regional preparations of wild game, steak and seafood. An inviting fire pit enhances the outdoor seating area. **Bar:** full bar. **Reservations:** suggested. **Address:** 400 Squaw Creek Rd 96146 **Location:** I-80 exit SR 89, 8.3 mi s, 0.6 mi on Squaw Valley Rd, then just w; in Olympic Valley; in Resort at Squaw Creek. **Parking:** on-site and valet.
⟨B⟩ ⟨D⟩

(See map & index p. 161.)

POOLSIDE CAFE 530/452-7278

[fyi] Not evaluated. Ride the cable car to High Camp (elevation 8,200') and enjoy spectacular views of the upper peaks of Squaw Valley USA and beyond. Located overlooking the pool and spa, this café offers sandwiches, burgers and a few entrée items. Deck dining also is available. The prices tend to be high and should be overlooked due to the wonderful views. Sunset dinner packages are available Friday and Saturday evenings which can be purchased at the base of the cable car. Opens in mid-June. **Address:** 1960 Squaw Valley Rd 96146 **Location:** I-80 exit SR 89, 8.3 mi s, then 2.3 mi sw on Squaw Valley Rd to cable car; at High Camp.

ORICK (B-1) pop. 357, elev. 34'

HUMBOLDT LAGOONS STATE PARK, 4 mi. s. on US 101, contains 1,886 acres. The park has a sandy marshland with more than 200 bird species, a lagoon and rocky headlands. Wild azaleas and lilacs bloom in June. *See Recreation Areas Chart.* **Hours:** Park open daily dawn-dusk. Visitor center open when staff is available. **Cost:** Free. **Phone:** (707) 488-2169.

ELK MEADOW CABINS 707/488-2222

Vacation Rental Cabin
$200-$300

Address: 7 Valley Green Camp Rd 95555 **Location:** US 101, milepost 124. **Facility:** Inviting cabins offer all the modern comforts of home. Elk roam freely throughout the property giving guests up close views of the region's wildlife. 6 cabins, some efficiencies and kitchens. 1 story, exterior corridors. **Terms:** 21 day cancellation notice-fee imposed, resort fee. **Activities:** whirlpool, hiking trails, basketball. *Fee:* bicycles. **Guest Services:** complimentary laundry. **Free Special Amenities:** high-speed Internet.

ORLAND pop. 7,291

ORLAND INN (530)865-7632

Motel
$59-$89

Address: 1052 South St 95963 **Location:** I-5 exit 618 (CR 16/South St), just ne; in Stony Creek Shopping Center. **Facility:** 40 units. 2 stories, exterior corridors. **Pool(s):** outdoor. **Free Special Amenities:** local telephone calls and early check-in/late check-out.

WHERE TO EAT

FARWOOD BAR & GRILL 530/865-9900

American. Casual Dining. $8-$25 **AAA Inspector Notes:** Housed in a 1916 building, the lunch buffet at this grill is offered Monday through Friday 11 a.m. to 2 p.m., along with lunch specials, sandwiches and burgers. Be sure to start with the delicious clam chowder. Grilled steaks, seafood and a few pasta dishes round out the dinner menu nicely. Patio dining is available and live music is offered on Saturday nights. **Bar:** full bar. **Address:** 705 5th St 95963 **Location:** I-5 exit 619 (SR 32), 0.7 mi e; jct 5th St and SR 32; center. [L] [D]

OROVILLE (D-3) pop. 15,546, elev. 174'
• Hotels p. 266 • Restaurants p. 266

Cherokee Indians migrated to Oroville from Georgia in the 1850s to work in gold mines north of town. In 1870 alone, hydraulic mining operations at the site yielded $5 million in gold. Later diamonds were discovered; the Cherokee Diamond Mine opened in 1873 and went on to produce some 300 diamonds of industrial quality.

The diamond reserves were soon depleted, however, and the nearby town of Cherokee—like so many other mining towns in California—was forgotten. Ruins of brick stores and foundations identified by markers are all that remain in this ghost town on Cherokee Road, 10 miles north of Oroville via SR 70, the Feather River Scenic Byway.

One of the largest collections of hand tools in the country—more than 5,000 hand-crafted and production implements dating as far back as the 1820s—can be seen at Bolt's Antique Tool Museum, 1650 Broderick St.; phone (530) 538-2528.

A good time to explore the Oroville area is from late March through mid-May, when wildflowers—particularly poppies and lupine—are in glorious bloom on Table Mountain, just north of the city. Recreational activities at Lake Oroville *(see Recreation Areas Chart)* include sailing, jet skiing, water skiing, camping and houseboating, while the Feather River is popular with kayakers, canoers and anglers in search of salmon, sturgeon, bass and steelhead.

Oroville Area Chamber of Commerce: 1789 Montgomery St., Oroville, CA 95965. **Phone:** (530) 538-2542 or (800) 655-4653.

BUTTE COUNTY MEMORIAL PIONEER MUSEUM, 2332 Montgomery St., has a room resembling an 1849 cabin, a replica of a Victorian parlor and varied collections ranging from Native American artifacts to early home furnishings. **Hours:** Fri.-Sun. noon-4, Feb. 1 to mid-Dec. **Cost:** $3; free (ages 0-11). **Phone:** (530) 538-2529, or (530) 538-2497 for tour information.

CHINESE TEMPLE is at 1500 Broderick St. This 1863 temple contains furnishings donated by the Emperor of China. A self-guiding tour includes three chapels devoted to Confucianism, Taoism and Buddhism, a courtyard garden and collections of puppets, costumes and tapestries. **Time:** Allow 1 hour minimum. **Hours:** Daily noon-4, Feb. 1 to mid-Dec. **Cost:** $3; free (ages 0-11). **Phone:** (530) 538-2496.

FEATHER RIVER HATCHERY, 5 Table Mountain Blvd., releases more than 10 million salmon and steelhead yearlings into the Feather River each year. The best time to visit the hatchery is during the spawning season, mid-September to mid-November. A Salmon Festival is held the first Saturday in September. **Time:** Allow 30 minutes minimum. **Hours:** Daily dawn-dusk. **Cost:** Free. **Phone:** (530) 538-2222.

LAKE OROVILLE VISITOR CENTER is 7 mi. n.e. of SR 162 to Kelly Ridge, then 1.5 mi. n. The center, overlooking Lake Oroville and Oroville Dam, displays exhibits depicting wildlife, the gold rush era, state water projects, the Beckwourth Trail across the Sierra Nevada and the Maidu Indians. Videos about the area are shown on request. **Time:** Allow 1 hour minimum. **Hours:** Daily 9-5. Closed Jan. 1, Thanksgiving and Christmas. **Cost:** Free. **Phone:** (530) 538-2219.

LOTT HOME MUSEUM is between 3rd and 4th aves. at 1067 Montgomery St., in Sank Park. This 1856 house, built by a prominent lawyer for his bride, is furnished in period. The park grounds include a Victorian garden. **Tours:** Guided tours are available. **Hours:** House open Sun.-Mon. and Fri. 11:30-3:30 and by appointment, Feb. 1 to mid-Dec. Park grounds Mon.-Sat. 9-9, Sun. 9-8:30. **Cost:** House $3; free (ages 0-11). Park free. **Phone:** (530) 538-2497. 🅿️

AMERICAS BEST VALUE INN & SUITES (530)533-7070

Motel
$65-$95
Address: 580 Oro Dam Blvd 95965 **Location:** SR 70 exit SR 162 (Oro Dam Blvd), 0.3 mi e. **Facility:** 69 units. 1 story, exterior corridors. **Terms:** cancellation fee imposed. **Amenities:** high-speed Internet. **Guest Services:** coin laundry. **Free Special Amenities: continental breakfast and early check-in/late check-out.**

GOLD COUNTRY CASINO & HOTEL 530/538-4560
🔹🔹🔹 **Hotel** $89-$199 **Address:** 4020 Olive Hwy 95966 **Location:** SR 70 exit SR 162 (Oroville Dam Blvd), 0.9 mi e to Olive Hwy (SR 162), then 2.1 mi e. **Facility:** Top entertainers have performed at this hotel, which features spacious guest rooms, some with valley views, deep soaking tubs or whirlpool tubs. A few units include a private balcony. 87 units. 6 stories, interior corridors. **Parking:** on-site and valet. **Terms:** cancellation fee imposed. **Amenities:** high-speed Internet. **Dining:** 3 restaurants, also, The Steakhouse, see separate listing. **Activities:** *Fee:* game room. **Guest Services:** complimentary laundry.

HOLIDAY INN EXPRESS & SUITES-LAKE OROVILLE (530)534-5566
🔹🔹🔹 **Hotel** $99-$250 **Address:** 550 Oro Dam Blvd 95966 **Location:** SR 70 exit SR 162 (Oroville Dam Blvd), 0.3 mi e. **Facility:** 66 units. 3 stories, interior corridors. **Amenities:** high-speed Internet. **Pool(s):** heated indoor. **Activities:** whirlpool, exercise room. **Guest Services:** valet and coin laundry.

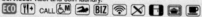

THE LODGE AT FEATHER FALLS CASINO (530)533-3885
🔹🔹🔹 Hotel $89-$195
Address: 4 Alverda Dr 95966 **Location:** SR 70 exit Ophir Rd, 3.1 mi e. **Facility:** This tastefully decorated property with upscale enhancements offers a fireplace in the lobby and easy access to the adjacent casino. A few guest rooms include a wet bar. 84 units. 3 stories, interior corridors. **Terms:** check-in 4 pm. **Amenities:** video games (fee), high-speed Internet. *Some:* safes. **Dining:** 2 restaurants. **Pool(s):** heated indoor/outdoor. **Activities:** sauna, whirlpool, exercise room. **Guest Services:** area transportation-Feather Falls Casino. **Free Special Amenities: local telephone calls and high-speed Internet.**

SUPER 8 OROVILLE (530)533-9673
🔹🔹 **Hotel** $70-$90 **Address:** 1470 Feather River Blvd 95965 **Location:** SR 70 exit 47 (Montgomery St), just ne, then s. **Facility:** 54 units. 3 stories, interior corridors. **Terms:** cancellation fee imposed. **Amenities:** high-speed Internet. **Pool(s):** outdoor. **Activities:** sauna, whirlpool, exercise room. **Guest Services:** coin laundry.

WHERE TO EAT

THE STEAKHOUSE 530/538-4560
🔹🔹🔹 Steak. Casual Dining. $17-$38 **AAA Inspector Notes:** Hand-cut, USDA Choice grade beef and well-prepared seafood selections are hallmarks of this steakhouse. Its seventh floor location affords nice views. **Bar:** full bar. **Reservations:** suggested. **Address:** 4020 Olive Hwy 95966 **Location:** SR 70 exit SR 162 (Oroville Dam Blvd), 0.9 mi e to Olive Hwy (SR 162), then 2.1 mi e; in Gold Country Casino & Hotel. **Parking:** on-site and valet. 🅳 CALL 📠

PACIFICA (D-8) pop. 37,234, elev. 60'
• Hotels & Restaurants map & index p. 410
• Part of San Francisco area — see map p. 342

One of California's newest towns, Pacifica was formed in 1957. Its history, however, goes back to 1769, when Gaspar de Portolá first sighted San Francisco Bay from Discovery Point in the mountains behind present-day Pacifica. Francisco Sanchez, an alcalde of San Francisco under the Spanish government, later was awarded the land in return for his service to Mexico. His adobe was built 1842-46. The two-story house, a half-mile east of SR 1 at 1000 Linda Mar Blvd., is preserved as Sanchez Adobe Historic Site and is decorated with period furniture, objects, implements and clothing.

A popular beach resort area for more than a century, Pacifica still draws visitors eager to enjoy surfing, hiking, mountain biking and fishing.

Pacifica Chamber of Commerce and Visitors Center: 225 Rockaway Beach Ave., Suite 1, Pacifica, CA 94044. **Phone:** (650) 355-4122.

AMERICAS BEST VALUE INN 650/359-9494 **35**
🔹🔹 Hotel. Rates not provided. **Address:** 2160 Francisco Blvd 94044 **Location:** SR 1 exit 505B (Oceana Blvd) northbound; exit 506 (Francisco Blvd) southbound. **Facility:** 25 units, some kitchens. 3 stories, interior corridors. **Amenities:** high-speed Internet. **Guest Services:** coin laundry.

BEST WESTERN PLUS LIGHTHOUSE HOTEL (650)355-6300 **36**
🔹🔹🔹 Hotel $139-$209

AAA Benefit: Members save up to 20%, plus 10% bonus points with Best Western Rewards®.
Address: 105 Rockaway Beach Ave 94044 **Location:** SR 1 exit Rockaway Beach Ave, just w. **Facility:** 97 units. 4 stories, interior corridors. **Terms:** check-in 4 pm. **Amenities:** video games (fee). **Pool(s):** heated outdoor. **Activities:** whirlpool, beach access, exercise room. **Guest Services:** valet laundry. **Free Special Amenities: local telephone calls and high-speed Internet.**

HOLIDAY INN EXPRESS HOTEL & SUITES (650)355-5000 **37**
🔹🔹🔹 Hotel $149-$399
Address: 519 Nick Gust Way 94044 **Location:** W of SR 1 exit Rockaway Beach. **Facility:** 38 units. 2 stories, interior corridors. **Amenities:** high-speed Internet. **Guest Services:** coin laundry.
Free Special Amenities: expanded continental breakfast and high-speed Internet.

(See map & index p. 410.)

PACIFICA BEACH RESORT   650/355-9999

fyi Not evaluated. **Address:** 525 Crespi Dr 94044. Facilities, services, and décor characterize a mid-scale property.

PACIFIC GROVE (G-2) pop. 15,041, elev. 55'

- **Restaurants p. 268**
- **Hotels & Restaurants map & index p. 206**
- **Part of Monterey Peninsula area — see map p. 202**

In 1875 this delightfully picturesque community strung along the shore of Monterey Bay was a Methodist summer camp, with tents set up under the Monterey pines. As the retreat grew in popularity the tents gave way to more permanent residences. Pacific Grove's last chautauqua was held in 1926, but more than 1,200 historic buildings remain, and the residential neighborhoods are full of well-preserved Victorian houses.

Pacific Grove adjoins Monterey and also is the northern starting point for the popular and breathtaking 17-Mile Drive *(see Pebble Beach p. 273).* Another way of experiencing the town's scenic waterfront is by hiking or biking the Monterey Peninsula Recreational Trail, which runs from Pacific Grove to Castroville. The trail passes such area landmarks as Point Pinos Lighthouse and Del Monte Beach.

Within the Monarch Grove Sanctuary, 1 block west of Lighthouse Avenue and 17-Mile Drive on Ridge Road, is an area where visitors have the opportunity to view orange-and-black monarch butterflies that gather here from early October through February. The sanctuary is on the butterflies' seasonal migration route; phone (831) 648-5716.

Pacific Grove Chamber of Commerce Information Center: 584 Central Ave., Pacific Grove, CA 93950. **Phone:** (831) 373-3304 or (800) 656-6650.

Self-guiding tours: Walking tour brochures with information about Pacific Grove's Victorian homes and historic buildings are available at the information center.

Shopping areas: American Tin Cannery Premium Outlets, 125 Ocean View Blvd., includes factory-direct and specialty stores.

PACIFIC GROVE MUSEUM OF NATURAL HISTORY, 165 Forest Ave., spotlights the natural history of Monterey County through exhibits about birds and wildlife, plants, geology and the cultural richness of California's central coast. **Time:** Allow 1 hour minimum. **Hours:** Tues.-Sun. 10-5. Closed major holidays. **Cost:** Free. **Phone:** (831) 648-5716.

POINT PINOS LIGHTHOUSE is at 98 Asilomar Blvd., off Lighthouse Ave. Standing at the northern tip of the Monterey Peninsula, it is said to be the oldest continuously operating lighthouse on the Pacific Coast and has been guiding ships since 1855.

The brick lighthouse tower is part of a stone, Cape Cod-style lightkeeper's house; the different

levels are connected by a spiral staircase. Displays focus on buoys, shipwrecks and Fresnel lenses. **Time:** Allow 1 hour minimum. **Hours:** Thurs.-Mon. 1-4. **Cost:** Donations. **Phone:** (831) 648-3176.

ASILOMAR CONFERENCE GROUNDS
(831)372-8016 **65**

Historic Hotel
$145-$285

Address: 800 Asilomar Ave 93950 **Location:** Just n of SR 68. Located at Asilomar State Beach and Conference grounds. **Facility:** Beautiful views of the Pacific Ocean as well as glimpses of wandering deer and squirrels can be enjoyed at this property, where the ocean meets the forest. 312 units. 1-2 stories, interior/exterior corridors. **Terms:** check-in 4 pm, 2-3 night minimum stay - seasonal and/or weekends, 3 day cancellation notice-fee imposed, resort fee. **Pool(s):** outdoor. **Activities:** rental bicycles, hiking trails, volleyball. **Guest Services:** valet laundry. **Free Special Amenities: preferred room (subject to availability with advance reservations) and high-speed Internet.**

BIDE-A-WEE INN & COTTAGES
(831)372-2330 **54**

Motel
$79-$429

Address: 221 Asilomar Ave 93950 **Location:** 1 mi n of SR 68. **Facility:** 20 units, some two bedrooms and efficiencies. 1-2 stories (no elevator), exterior corridors. **Terms:** 2 night minimum stay - seasonal and/or weekends, 3 day cancellation notice-fee imposed, resort fee. **Free Special Amenities: continental breakfast and high-speed Internet.**

BORG'S OCEAN FRONT MOTEL
831/375-2406 **59**

Motel
$69-$185

Address: 635 Ocean View Blvd 93950 **Location:** Oceanfront. At Lover's Point. **Facility:** 60 units, some two bedrooms. 2 stories, exterior corridors. **Terms:** 3 day cancellation notice. **Free Special Amenities:** local telephone calls and high-speed Internet.

BUTTERFLY GROVE INN
(831)373-4921 **58**

Motel
$79-$359

Address: 1073 Lighthouse Ave 93950 **Location:** Just w of Seventeen Mile Dr. **Facility:** 30 units, some two bedrooms and efficiencies. 2 stories, exterior corridors. **Terms:** 2-4 night minimum stay - weekends, 3 day cancellation notice-fee imposed. **Pool(s):** outdoor. **Activities:** whirlpool. **Free Special Amenities: continental breakfast and high-speed Internet.**

THE CENTRELLA BED & BREAKFAST INN
(831)372-3372 **66**

Bed & Breakfast $119-$299 **Address:** 612 Central Ave 93950 **Location:** At 17th St; center. **Facility:** Accommodations, some with a gas fireplace, are offered in a restored 1890s Victorian home and five cottages. 25 units. 3 stories (no elevator), interior/exterior corridors. **Parking:** street only. **Terms:** 2 night minimum stay - seasonal and/or weekends, 7 day cancellation notice-fee imposed.

DEER HAVEN INN
(831)373-7784 **63**

Motel $59-$249 **Address:** 750 Crocker Ave 93950 **Location:** Just e of SR 68 via Sinex Ave. **Facility:** 26 units. 2 stories, exterior corridors. **Terms:** 3 day cancellation notice-fee imposed. **Guest Services:** valet laundry.

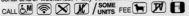

(See map & index p. 206.)

GOSBY HOUSE INN   (831)375-1287   67

◆◆◆ **Bed & Breakfast** $135-$310 **Address:** 643 Lighthouse Ave 93950 **Location:** Downtown. **Facility:** Whether in the main house or in one of the structures adjacent to the gardens, each room at this handsomely restored inn is uniquely decorated. 22 units. 2 stories (no elevator), interior/exterior corridors. **Parking:** street only. **Terms:** 7 day cancellation notice-fee imposed.

[𝖸𝖨⚬] [BIZ] 📶 ⊠ 𝒜𝒞 /SOME UNITS FEE 🐾 🕅 🕮 📺

GREEN GABLES INN   (831)375-2095   68

◆◆◆◆ **Bed & Breakfast** $155-$325 **Address:** 301 Ocean View Blvd 93950 **Location:** Oceanfront. At 5th St. **Facility:** The inn, across from the bay, offers spacious, elegantly appointed public areas and some units with ocean views. 11 units. 2-3 stories (no elevator), interior/exterior corridors. **Bath:** some shared. **Terms:** 7 day cancellation notice-fee imposed.

[BIZ] 📶 ⊠ 𝒜𝒞 🕮 /SOME UNITS FEE 🐾 🕅

HOWARD JOHNSON INN & SUITES (831)373-8777   64

◆◆◆
Hotel
$100-$400

Address: 660 Dennett St 93950 **Location:** Just e of SR 68 via Sinex Ave. Located in a quiet area. **Facility:** 30 units, some two bedrooms and kitchens. 2 stories, exterior corridors. **Terms:** cancellation fee imposed. **Amenities:** high-speed Internet, safes. **Guest Services:** coin laundry. **Free Special Amenities:** expanded continental breakfast and high-speed Internet.

[SAVE] CALL 𝖫𝖬 [BIZ] 📶 ⊠ 𝒜𝒞 🕮 🕮 📺

LIGHTHOUSE LODGE & COTTAGES   (831)655-2111   53

◆◆◆ **Hotel** $99-$895 **Address:** 1150 Lighthouse Ave 93950 **Location:** 0.5 mi w of Seventeen Mile Dr. **Facility:** 95 units. 1-2 stories, exterior corridors. **Terms:** check-in 4 pm, 2 night minimum stay - weekends, 3 day cancellation notice-fee imposed. **Amenities:** video games (fee). **Pool(s):** outdoor. **Activities:** whirlpool.

CALL 𝖫𝖬 🛥 [BIZ] ⊠ 𝒜𝒞 🕮 🕮 📺 /SOME UNITS FEE 🐾

MARTINE INN   (831)373-3388   70

◆◆◆◆ **Bed & Breakfast** $199-$499 **Address:** 255 Ocean View Blvd 93950 **Location:** Oceanfront. At 4th St. **Facility:** Spectacular views of Monterey Bay can be enjoyed from many areas of the inn; guest rooms are decorated with antiques, and some have claw-foot tubs. 25 units, some two bedrooms. 3 stories (no elevator), interior/exterior corridors. **Terms:** 3 day cancellation notice-fee imposed. **Guest Services:** valet laundry.

[BIZ] 📶 ⊠ 𝒜𝒞 𝖶 🕮

MONARCH RESORT   (831)646-8885   55

◆◆◆
Motel
$60-$300

Address: 1111 Lighthouse Ave 93950 **Location:** Just w of Seventeen Mile Dr. **Facility:** 50 units, some efficiencies. 2 stories, interior corridors. **Terms:** check-in 4 pm, 2 night minimum stay - seasonal and/or weekends, 3 day cancellation notice-fee imposed, resort fee. **Amenities:** high-speed Internet. **Pool(s):** outdoor. **Activities:** sauna, whirlpool. **Guest Services:** valet laundry.

[SAVE] CALL 𝖫𝖬 🛥 📶 📺 /SOME UNITS 𝒜𝒞 🕮 🕮

OLD ST. ANGELA INN   831/372-3246   69

◆◆◆ **Bed & Breakfast** $149-$285 **Address:** 321 Central Ave 93950 **Location:** At Forest Ave; center. **Facility:** A country elegance characterizes the rooms at this handsomely restored 1910 Cape Cod nestled on well-landscaped grounds. 9 units. 2 stories (no elevator), interior/exterior corridors. **Terms:** 3 day cancellation notice-fee imposed.

[𝖸𝖨⚬] 📶 ⊠ 𝒜𝒞 𝖶

PACIFIC GARDENS INN   831/646-9414   61

◆◆◆ **Hotel** $99-$203 **Address:** 701 Asilomar Blvd 93950 **Location:** Just n of SR 68. Across from conference grounds. **Facility:** 28 units, some two bedrooms and kitchens. 2 stories, exterior corridors. **Terms:** 2 day cancellation notice. **Activities:** whirlpools. **Guest Services:** valet and coin laundry, area transportation-within 10 mi.

FEE [𝖸𝖨⚬] [BIZ] 📶 ⊠ 𝒜𝒞 🕮 🕮 📺 /SOME UNITS 🐾 🕮

ROSEDALE INN   831/655-1000   62

◆◆◆
Hotel
Rates not provided

Address: 775 Asilomar Blvd 93950 **Location:** Just n of SR 68. Across from conference grounds. **Facility:** 19 units. 1 story, exterior corridors. **Guest Services:** valet laundry. **Free Special Amenities:** expanded continental breakfast and high-speed Internet.

[SAVE] CALL 𝖫𝖬 📶 ⊠ 𝒜𝒞 🕮 🕮 📺

SEA BREEZE INN AND COTTAGES   (831)372-7771   56

◆◆◆ **Hotel** $79-$499 **Address:** 1100 Lighthouse Ave 93950 **Location:** Just w of Seventeen Mile Dr; jct Lighthouse and Grove Acre aves. **Facility:** 37 units, some kitchens. 2 stories (no elevator), interior/exterior corridors. **Terms:** 2 night minimum stay - weekends.

[𝖸𝖨⚬] 📶 ⊠ 𝒜𝒞 🕮 /SOME UNITS FEE 🐾 🕮 🕮

SEA BREEZE LODGE   (831)372-3431   57

◆◆ **Motel** $79-$499 **Address:** 1101 Lighthouse Ave 93950 **Location:** Just w of Seventeen Mile Dr. **Facility:** 30 units, some kitchens. 1 story, exterior corridors. **Terms:** 2 night minimum stay - weekends. **Pool(s):** outdoor. **Activities:** whirlpool.

[𝖸𝖨⚬] 🛥 [BIZ] 📶 ⊠ 𝒜𝒞 🕮 🕮 /SOME UNITS FEE 🐾 🕮

WHERE TO EAT

FANDANGO   831/372-3456   31

◆◆◆
Mediterranean
Fine Dining
$10-$36

AAA Inspector Notes: Mesquite-grilled seafood and meat are at the heart of the menu of European specialties at this eatery, including the specialty osso buco. The individually appointed dining rooms evoke a Mediterranean feel. The staff is very warm and welcoming. **Bar:** full bar. **Reservations:** suggested. **Address:** 223 17th St 93950 **Location:** Center. [L] [D] 𝒜𝒞

FIRST AWAKENINGS   831/372-1125   34

◆◆ **American. Casual Dining.** $6-$11 **AAA Inspector Notes:** Located within the former American Tin Cannery building and just a short walk from the Monterey Aquarium, this popular café offers delicious breakfast dishes that feature many fresh local fruits and vegetables as main ingredients. The restaurant is nicely decorated with green plants hanging from the vaulted ceilings and along oversized windows, while an outdoor patio features a fire pit amid umbrella-topped tables. **Address:** 125 Oceanview Blvd, Suite 105 93950 **Location:** At Eardley Ave; in The American Tin Cannery Outlet Center. **Parking:** on-site (fee). [B] [L] 𝒜𝒞

(See map & index p. 206.)

FISH WIFE   831/375-7107 **32**
▼▼▼ Seafood. Fine Dining. $10-$20 **AAA Inspector Notes:** A great selection of fresh seafood is prepared here with California and Caribbean accents. Whether it's served with pasta, freshly grilled or sautéed, there is something sure to please everyone. Be sure to try the crab tostaditas appetizer and save room the Key lime pie for dessert—a favorite of the locals for many years. **Bar:** full bar. **Reservations:** suggested. **Address:** 1996 1/2 Sunset Dr 93950 **Location:** At Asilomar Ave. **Parking:** street only. [L] [D] CALL [M] [K]

PASSIONFISH   831/655-3311 **30**
▼▼▼ California Seafood. Fine Dining. $16-$28 **AAA Inspector Notes:** In the heart of downtown, this restaurant uses fresh local fish and organic produce in its menu preparations. The menu changes daily to reflect the freshest ingredients. **Bar:** beer & wine. **Reservations:** suggested. **Address:** 701 Lighthouse Ave 93950 **Location:** Between Congress and Cypress aves; center. **Parking:** street only. [D] CALL [M] [K]

TILLIE GORT'S   831/373-0335 **33**
▼▼ Vegetarian. Casual Dining. $8-$14 **AAA Inspector Notes:** Established in 1969, this small hole in the wall serves up an abundance of vegan, vegetarian and some meat items. Dishes are freshly prepared and feature influences of Italian, Greek, Indian and American. This local favorite offers very friendly service. **Bar:** beer & wine. **Address:** 111 Central Ave 93950 **Location:** Just w of Eardley Ave. **Parking:** street only. [B] [L] [D] CALL [M] [K]

PALO ALTO (E-9) pop. 64,403, elev. 23'
- **Hotels p. 270 • Restaurants p. 271**
- **Hotels & Restaurants map & index p. 410**

Palo Alto (Spanish for "tall tree") is at the southeastern end of a scenic 31-mile stretch of I-280 heading northwest to San Francisco. It was named for a double-trunked redwood tree, a landmark used by travelers and explorers as early as 1769. A likeness of the tree appears on the seal of Stanford University. The opening of the university in 1891 provided the impetus for Palo Alto's growth, and the livelihoods of both city and university have remained closely intertwined.

Stanford's SLAC National Accelerator Laboratory is on Sand Hill Road. The research facility, which includes what is said to be the world's longest building, is a U.S. Department of Energy national laboratory. Ninety-minute guided tours of the lab include a visit to the 2-mile linear accelerator. Tours are offered on the first and third Friday of the month (the schedule may vary) and must be made online in advance; phone (650) 926-4931 for information.

The Eucalyptus Grove at Stanford is the site each Mother's Day weekend of the ▼ Stanford Powwow, a 3-day celebration of Native American culture. Clad in colorful costumes, tribal members perform exhibition dances and compete in dance contests.

Palo Alto Chamber of Commerce: 400 Mitchell Ln., Palo Alto, CA 94301. **Phone:** (650) 324-3121.

Shopping areas: Bloomingdale's, Macy's, Neiman Marcus and Nordstrom are the anchor stores at Stanford Shopping Center, on Sand Hill Road adjacent to Stanford University. This upscale, open-air mall includes some 140 retailers, restaurants and services in a setting beautified by lots of blooming plants, ornamental shrubs and whimsical sculptures.

MUSEUM OF AMERICAN HERITAGE, downtown at 351 Homer Ave., is housed in a 1907 residence designed by architect Ernest Coxhead. Permanent exhibits showcase the history of technological innovation in the 19th and early 20th centuries. Two exhibits change annually. There also are historic gardens on the grounds. **Hours:** Fri.-Sun. 11-4. **Cost:** Free. **Phone:** (650) 321-1004.

STANFORD UNIVERSITY is about 1 mi. w. off Sand Hill Rd. The campus sprawls on 8,200-acre Stanford Farm, a former estate. Frederick Law Olmstead created the general concept for the grounds, dotted with oak and eucalyptus trees, and the unifying architectural theme: Romanesque sandstone buildings with arched arcades and red-tiled roofs.

One-hour walking tours of the campus depart from the visitor center at 295 Galvez St. **Hours:** Tours are given daily at 11 and 3:15, except some holidays and during winter break. Phone ahead to confirm schedule. **Cost:** Free. **Phone:** (650) 723-2560. ▣

◆ **Cantor Arts Center at Stanford University** is just off Palm Dr. at Lomita Dr. and Museum Way. The center's 24 galleries display art from around the world, from Africa to the Americas to Asia and from classical to contemporary. Works from ancient Egypt, China and Greece as well as the 21st century span 5,000 years of art history and a diversity of cultures.

Three galleries are dedicated to sculpture by Auguste Rodin; his famous "The Thinker," "Age of Bronze" and "The Kiss" are crowd-pleasers. The outdoor Rodin Sculpture Garden displays larger-than-life-size bronze figures. Adam and Eve flank "The Gates of Hell," the artist's greatest masterpiece, which also includes many smaller figures.

Other highlights are works by Ansel Adams, Albert Bierstadt, Andy Goldsworthy, Georgia O'Keeffe, Pablo Picasso and Richard Serra. Stanford family memorabilia and changing exhibits also are featured.

Time: Allow 2 hours minimum. **Hours:** Wed.-Sun. 11-5 (also Thurs. 5-8). Various guided tours are offered daily; phone for schedule. The introductory Cantor Arts Center tour is given Sat.-Sun. at 1. Closed Thanksgiving and Christmas. **Cost:** Free. **Parking:** Parking is metered; free after 4 p.m. and all day on weekends. **Phone:** (650) 723-4177 or TTY (650) 723-1216. [†]

Hoover Tower, on Serra Mall, houses the Hoover Institution on War, Revolution and Peace, a public policy research center devoted to the study of world conflict. The institution was founded in 1919 by Herbert Hoover, a member of the university's first class, who would later become the nation's 31st president.

The 285-foot-tall tower is topped by a 48-bell carillon. The building and an observation platform can be visited. **Time:** Allow 30 minutes minimum. **Hours:** Open daily 10-4. Closed major holidays, examination weeks and during school breaks. Phone ahead to confirm schedule. **Cost:** $2; $1 (ages 0-12 and 65+). **Phone:** (650) 723-2053.

(See map & index p. 410.)

AMERICAS BEST VALUE INN - SKY RANCH INN
(650)493-7221

Motel
$99-$175

Address: 4234 El Camino Real 94306 **Location:** US 101 exit San Antonio Rd, 2 mi w to SR 82, then 1 mi n. **Facility:** 29 units. 1-2 stories (no elevator), exterior corridors. **Terms:** cancellation fee imposed. **Amenities:** high-speed Internet. **Guest Services:** coin laundry. **Free Special Amenities:** early check-in/late check-out and high-speed Internet. *(See ad this page.)*

COMFORT INN PALO ALTO/STANFORD AREA
(650)493-3141

Motel
$85-$280

Address: 3945 El Camino Real 94306 **Location:** US 101 exit Oregon Expwy/Page Mill Rd, 1 mi s. **Facility:** 69 units. 2 stories (no elevator), exterior corridors. Terms: cancellation fee imposed. **Guest Services:** valet laundry. **Free Special Amenities:** full breakfast and high-speed Internet.

COUNTRY INN MOTEL
650/948-9154

Motel
$76-$120

Address: 4345 El Camino Real 94306 **Location:** US 101 exit San Antonio Rd, 2 mi w to SR 82, then just n. **Facility:** 27 units, some kitchens. 1-2 stories (no elevator), exterior corridors. *Bath:* shower only. **Terms:** cancellation fee imposed, resort fee. **Pool(s):** heated outdoor. **Free Special Amenities:** continental breakfast and high-speed Internet.

CREEKSIDE INN
(650)493-2411

Hotel
$168-$239

Address: 3400 El Camino Real 94306 **Location:** On SR 82, 0.3 mi s of Oregon Expwy/Page Mill Rd. **Facility:** 136 units, some efficiencies, interior/exterior corridors. **Terms:** 2-3 night minimum stay - seasonal, cancellation fee imposed, resort fee. **Amenities:** high-speed Internet, safes. **Pool(s):** heated outdoor. **Activities:** exercise room. **Guest Services:** valet and coin laundry, area transportation-within 5 mi. **Free Special Amenities:** newspaper and high-speed Internet.

CROWNE PLAZA CABANA HOTEL
(650)857-0787

Hotel
$109-$529

Address: 4290 El Camino Real 94306 **Location:** US 101 exit San Antonio Rd, 0.4 mi n. **Facility:** 194 units. 2-8 stories, interior/exterior corridors. **Terms:** cancellation fee imposed. **Amenities:** high-speed Internet. **Pool(s):** heated outdoor. **Activities:** whirlpool, exercise room. **Guest Services:** valet laundry, area transportation-within 5 mi. **Free Special Amenities:** high-speed Internet and local transportation.

DAYS INN STANFORD UNIVERSITY
(650)493-4222

Motel
$69-$290

Address: 4238 El Camino Real 94306 **Location:** US 101 exit San Antonio Rd, 2 mi w to SR 82, then 1 mi n. **Facility:** 23 units. 2 stories, exterior corridors. **Terms:** cancellation fee imposed. **Amenities:** high-speed Internet. **Guest Services:** coin laundry. **Free Special Amenities:** local telephone calls and high-speed Internet.

▼ See AAA listing this page ▼

Keep seasonal vehicles travel-ready with a AAA/CAA Battery Tender®

(See map & index p. 410.)

DINAH'S GARDEN HOTEL   (650)493-2844

Hotel
$99-$750

Address: 4261 El Camino Real 94306 **Location:** US 101 exit San Antonio Rd S, 0.4 mi n on SR 82. **Facility:** 129 units. some two bedrooms, efficiencies and kitchens. 1-3 stories, interior/exterior corridors. **Amenities:** high-speed Internet, safes. **Dining:** 2 restaurants. **Pool(s):** heated outdoor. **Activities:** exercise room. **Guest Services:** valet laundry. **Free Special Amenities: high-speed Internet.**

HOTEL KEEN   (650)327-2775   120

 Hotel $119-$309 **Address:** 425 High St 94301 **Location:** US 101 exit 404B (Willow Rd W), 0.4 mi w, 0.4 mi s on Middlefield Rd, 0.5 mi w on Lytton Ave, just s. **Facility:** 42 units. 3 stories, interior corridors. *Bath:* shower only. **Parking:** street only. **Terms:** cancellation fee imposed. **Amenities:** high-speed Internet. **Guest Services:** valet laundry.

PALO ALTO LODGE   650/493-2521

 Motel. Rates not provided. **Address:** 3339 El Camino Real 94306 **Location:** US 101 exit 402 (Embarcadero Rd/Oregon Expwy), 1.7 mi w on Oregon Expwy, then 0.5 mi s. **Facility:** 18 units. 1 story, exterior corridors. *Bath:* shower only.

QUALITY INN PALO ALTO/STANFORD AREA   (650)493-2760

Motel
$85-$280

Address: 3901 El Camino Real 94306 **Location:** US 101 exit Oregon Expwy/Page Mill Rd, 2 mi w to SR 82, then se to Ventura Ave. **Facility:** 54 units. 1-2 stories (no elevator), exterior corridors. **Terms:** cancellation fee imposed. **Guest Services:** valet laundry. **Free Special Amenities: full breakfast and high-speed Internet.**

SHERATON PALO ALTO HOTEL   (650)328-2800   121

Hotel
$109-$509

(S) Sheraton
AAA Benefit: Members get up to 20% off, plus Starwood Preferred Guest® bonuses.

Address: 625 El Camino Real 94301 **Location:** US 101 exit 402 (Embarcadero Rd/Oregon Expwy), 1.8 mi w, then just n on SR 82. Opposite Stanford University. **Facility:** 346 units. 4 stories, interior corridors. **Parking:** on-site (fee) and valet. **Terms:** 3 day cancellation notice-fee imposed. **Amenities:** *Fee:* video games, high-speed Internet. **Pool(s):** heated outdoor. **Activities:** exercise room. **Guest Services:** valet and coin laundry.

STANFORD TERRACE INN   650/857-0333

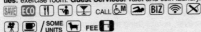 **Hotel.** Rates not provided. **Address:** 531 Stanford Ave 94306 **Location:** US 101 exit Oregon Expwy, 0.4 mi n on SR 82, then just w. Adjacent to Stanford University. **Facility:** 80 units, some efficiencies. 3 stories, exterior corridors. **Amenities:** video games (fee), high-speed Internet. **Pool(s):** heated outdoor. **Activities:** exercise room. **Guest Services:** valet and coin laundry, area transportation-within 5 mi.

Get more from your membership with an upgrade to Plus or Premier

SUPER 8 PALO ALTO   (650)493-9085

Motel
$89-$159

Address: 3200 El Camino Real 94306 **Location:** 0.3 mi s of Oregon Expwy. Located in a commercial area. **Facility:** 36 units. 2 stories, exterior corridors. **Terms:** cancellation fee imposed. **Amenities:** high-speed Internet.

THE WESTIN PALO ALTO   (650)321-4422   122

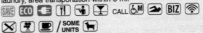
Hotel
$129-$559

WESTIN HOTELS & RESORTS
AAA Benefit: Enjoy up to 20% off your next stay, plus Starwood Preferred Guest® bonuses.

Address: 675 El Camino Real 94301 **Location:** US 101 exit 402 (Embarcadero Rd), 1.8 mi w, then just n on SR 82. **Facility:** The cool and calming color palette is a welcoming oasis after a long day of work or play; bathrooms are spacious with a separate shower and bath. 184 units. 5 stories, interior corridors. **Parking:** on-site (fee) and valet. **Amenities:** safes. *Fee:* video games, high-speed Internet. **Pool(s):** heated outdoor. **Activities:** whirlpool, bicycles, exercise room. *Fee:* massage. **Guest Services:** valet laundry, area transportation-within 3 mi.

THE ZEN HOTEL   (650)493-4492

Motel
$109-$209

Address: 4164 El Camino Real 94306 **Location:** US 101 exit Oregon Expwy/Page Mill Rd, 2 mi w to SR 82; at Maybell Ave. **Facility:** 37 units, some two bedrooms, efficiencies and kitchens. 1-2 stories, exterior corridors. **Terms:** cancellation fee imposed. **Activities:** whirlpool, exercise room. **Guest Services:** valet and coin laundry. **Free Special Amenities: full breakfast and high-speed Internet.**

WHERE TO EAT

CALIFORNIA CAFE   650/325-2233

Regional American. Casual Dining. $12-$32 **AAA Inspector Notes:** Contemporary California cuisine is prepared with a decidedly Continental flair at this fine dining café. **Bar:** full bar. **Reservations:** suggested. **Address:** 700 Welch Rd 94304 **Location:** SR 82 exit Palm Dr, s to Arboretum Rd, then w to Quarry Rd; at Stanford Barn. L D

THE CHEESECAKE FACTORY   650/473-9622

American. Casual Dining. $6-$28 **AAA Inspector Notes:** A display case of mouthwatering cheesecakes is the first thing visitors see as they walk through the door. The extensive menu incorporates many types of cuisine, including Asian, Italian, Greek and Spanish. **Bar:** full bar. **Address:** 375 University Ave 94304 **Location:** Between Waverley and Bryant sts. L D CALL

EVVIA ESTIATORIO   650/326-0983   90

Greek. Casual Dining. $15-$37 **AAA Inspector Notes:** This upscale, rustic restaurant, with an open kitchen and a rotisserie pit, serves contemporary Hellenic cuisine prepared with the freshest ingredients. **Bar:** full bar. **Address:** 420 Emerson St 94301 **Location:** US 101 exit 404B (Willow Rd W), 1.3 mi e, 0.5 mi s on Middlefield Rd, 0.5 mi w on University Ave, then just n. **Parking:** valet and street only. L D

THE FISH MARKET & TOP OF THE MARKET   650/493-9188

American. Casual Dining. $11-$44 **AAA Inspector Notes:** This small regional chain combines a seafood market and a restaurant. Seafood dominates on the extensive menu. **Bar:** full bar. **Address:** 3150 El Camino Real 94306 **Location:** Just s of jct Page Mill Rd. L D

(See map & index p. 410.)

HOWIE'S ARTISAN PIZZA 650/327-4992
▼▼ ▼ Pizza. Casual Dining. $7-$19 **AAA Inspector Notes:** Conveniently located in a shopping center, this bright, modern pizzeria specializes in thin-crust pizza made with locally sourced artisanal ingredients. **Bar:** beer & wine. **Address:** 855 El Camino Real, Suite 60 94301 **Location:** US 101 exit Embarcadero Rd, 2 mi w; in Town & Country Village. L D 🎟

LA STRADA 650/324-8300
▼▼▼ Italian. Casual Dining. $10-$25 **AAA Inspector Notes:** This eatery prepares traditional Italian favorites employing some distinctive twists and blended ingredients to create dishes ranging from local to global. Risottos are excellent. The contemporary décor incorporates earth tones. **Bar:** full bar. **Address:** 335 University Ave 94301 **Location:** Downtown. **Parking:** street only. L D

LAVANDA RESTAURANT & WINE BAR 650/321-3514 92
▼▼▼ Mediterranean. Casual Dining. $12-$38 **AAA Inspector Notes:** Located in trendy, downtown Palo Alto, the upscale restaurant features a menu of small plates as well as main courses. **Bar:** full bar. **Address:** 185 University Ave 94301 **Location:** At Emerson Ave. **Parking:** valet and street only. L D

MANDARIN GOURMET 650/328-8898 88
▼▼▼ Chinese. Casual Dining. $10-$33 **AAA Inspector Notes:** Modern and attractive, this restaurant tempts diners with well-prepared traditional dishes. Try the Changsha chicken garnished with julienned bits of raw ginger which adds a refreshing heat to each bite. **Bar:** full bar. **Reservations:** suggested. **Address:** 420 Ramona St 94301 **Location:** Between University and Lytton aves. **Parking:** street only. L D

MING'S RESTAURANT 650/856-7700
▼▼ ▼ Regional Chinese. Casual Dining. $8-$36 **AAA Inspector Notes:** Among choices are dim sum on carts, fresh seafood, Chinese barbecue and Cantonese favorites. Seating is comfortable. **Bar:** full bar. **Reservations:** suggested. **Address:** 1700 Embarcadero Rd 94303 **Location:** US 101 exit 402 (Embarcadero Rd/Oregon Expwy), just e. L D

PARIS BAGUETTE 650/838-0404
▼ Breads/Pastries Desserts. Quick Serve. $2-$7 **AAA Inspector Notes:** Soaring ceiling and a contemporary décor with a sophisticated touch of French, this bakery café serves Korean-French pastries and desserts. Highlights include a Korean version of sesame balls (minus the sesame) of croquette-stuffed japchae (sweet potato noodles) as well as sandwiches made with multi-grain breads and croissants. **Address:** 383 University Ave 94301 **Location:** US 101 exit University Ave, 1.4 mi w; between Waverley and Bryant sts. **Parking:** street only. B L D 🎟

P.F. CHANG'S CHINA BISTRO 650/330-1782 91
▼▼▼▼ Chinese. Casual Dining. $10-$21 **AAA Inspector Notes:** Trendy, upscale decor provides a pleasant backdrop for New Age Chinese dining. Appetizers, soups and salads are a meal by themselves. Vegetarian plates and sides, noodles, meins, chicken and meat dishes are created from exotic, fresh ingredients. **Bar:** full bar. **Address:** 900 Stanford Shopping Center, Bldg W 94304 **Location:** Just w of El Camino Real; in Stanford Shopping Center. L D CALL ♿M

SCOTT'S SEAFOOD 650/323-1555
▼▼▼ Seafood. Casual Dining. $11-$36 **AAA Inspector Notes:** This dining room nurtures a casual, New England atmosphere. On the menu are pasta, chicken and Prime steak dishes. **Bar:** full bar. **Address:** 855 El Camino Real, Bldg 1 94301 **Location:** US 101 exit Embarcadero Rd, 2 mi w; in Town & Country Village. B L D

STRAITS CAFE 650/494-7168
▼▼▼ Asian. Casual Dining. $10-$37 **AAA Inspector Notes:** Authentic Singaporean cuisine created by Christopher Yeo who blends flavors and cooking styles of Thai, Chinese, Malay and Indian to create exciting and wonderful foods. **Bar:** full bar. **Reservations:** suggested. **Address:** 3295 El Camino Real 94306 **Location:** On SR 82, just s of Oregon Expwy. L D

SUNDANCE THE STEAKHOUSE 650/321-6798
▼▼▼ American. Casual Dining. $13-$45 **AAA Inspector Notes:** Steak, prime rib and seafood specials line this comfortable and modern restaurant's menu. Soft lighting, mahogany paneling and light jazz music mingle to create an intimate dining experience. The wine list is lengthy. **Bar:** full bar. **Reservations:** suggested. **Address:** 1921 El Camino Real 94306 **Location:** US 101 exit 402 (Embarcadero Rd E/Oregon Expwy), 1.7 mi w on Oregon Expwy, then 0.5 mi n; between Stanford Ave and Serra St. L D

TAMARINE RESTAURANT 650/325-8500
▼▼▼ Vietnamese. Casual Dining. $15-$27 **AAA Inspector Notes:** This contemporary restaurant serves light yet very flavorful Vietnamese cuisine. **Bar:** full bar. **Reservations:** suggested. **Address:** 546 University Ave 94301 **Location:** Downtown. L D

THREE SEASONS RESTAURANT 650/838-0353
▼▼▼ Vietnamese. Casual Dining. $12-$28 **AAA Inspector Notes:** On Ramona Plaza, this contemporary restaurant and its comfortable outdoor patio are particularly popular at lunchtime and during happy hour. Representative of Asian fusion cuisine are such choices as fresh green papaya salad with shrimp. **Bar:** full bar. **Address:** 518 Bryant St 94301 **Location:** At University Ave; entrance from Ramona Plaza. **Parking:** street only. L D

TRADER VIC'S 650/849-9800
▼▼▼ Polynesian. Casual Dining. $17-$36 **AAA Inspector Notes:** A distinctive, exotic menu features a diversity of tastes: European, Chinese and Polynesian cuisines. The decor is a mix of refinement and fun. **Bar:** full bar. **Reservations:** suggested. **Address:** 4269 El Camino Real 94306 **Location:** US 101 exit San Antonio Rd, 0.5 mi n on SR 82; adjacent to Dinah's Garden Hotel. D CALL ♿M

UNIVERSITY CAFE 650/322-5301 89
▼▼▼ American. Casual Dining. $9-$21 **AAA Inspector Notes:** In trendy downtown Palo Alto, this sidewalk cafe serves healthy California cuisine and features a coffee and juice bar. The coffee is roasted here and the desserts are made on site. Menu offerings range from burgers and wraps to noodle soup and paella. **Bar:** beer & wine. **Address:** 271 University Ave 94301 **Location:** At Bryant St. **Parking:** street only. B L D

BAUME 650/328-8899
(fyi) Not evaluated. Fascinating menu combines classic French cuisine with modern gastronomical cooking techniques. **Address:** 201 California Ave 94306

PARADISE (D-3) pop. 26,218, elev. 1,708'

It was gold that brought prospectors in search of their fortunes to this area in the foothills of the Sierra Nevada during California's gold rush. Although a 54-pound nugget was found nearby, the frenzy for gold eventually died down. Many of the miners stayed, however, establishing the farms, orchards, sawmills and shops that became the community of Paradise.

Visitors to Paradise today enjoy a variety of outdoor activities such as hiking, walking on nature trails, boating, bicycling, fishing, gold panning and taking backroad adventures to old mining sites.

Paradise Ridge Chamber of Commerce and Visitors Bureau: 5550 Skyway 1, Paradise, CA 95969. **Phone:** (530) 877-9356 or (888) 845-2769.

GOLD NUGGET MUSEUM, 502 Pearson Rd., exhibits a miner's cabin, smithy, general store and a replica of a gold mine. Also displayed are exhibits depicting the history of Paradise and Magalia Ridge. A research library is on the premises. Several weekend events celebrating Native American and pioneer cultures are held spring through fall. **Time:** Allow 1 hour minimum. **Hours:** Wed.-Sun. noon-4. Closed major holidays. **Cost:** Donations. **Phone:** (530) 872-8722.

COMFORT INN
(530)876-0191

Hotel
$80-$120

Address: 5475 Clark Rd 95969 **Location:** SR 191 (Skyway Rd), 1.1 mi e on Pearson Rd, 0.3 mi s. **Facility:** 62 units. 3 stories, interior corridors. **Amenities:** high-speed Internet. **Pool(s):** heated outdoor. **Activities:** whirlpool, exercise room. **Guest Services:** coin laundry. **Free Special Amenities:** local telephone calls and high-speed Internet.

SAVE 🛏️ CALL 🅜 🛎️ BIZ 🛜 ❌ 🅷 🖥️ 📠 / SOME UNITS FEE 🐕

LANTERN INN
530/877-5553

Motel
$55-$82

Address: 5799 Wildwood Ln 95969 **Location:** Just n of jct Pearson and Skyway rds, then 1 blk w off Skyway Rd. Located in a quiet area. **Facility:** 16 units. 1 story, exterior corridors. *Bath:* shower only. **Pool(s):** outdoor. **Free Special Amenities:** early check-in/late check-out and high-speed Internet.

SAVE 🛏️ 🛎️ 🛜 🅷 🖥️ 📠 / SOME UNITS FEE 🐕

PONDEROSA GARDENS MOTEL
530/872-9094

🔻 **Motel** $89-$139 **Address:** 7010 Skyway 95969 **Location:** 2 blks e; center. Located in a secluded area. **Facility:** 48 units, some kitchens. 1 story, exterior corridors. **Terms:** cancellation fee imposed. **Pool(s):** outdoor. **Activities:** whirlpool. **Guest Services:** coin laundry.

🛏️ CALL 🅜 🛎️ FEE 🐕 🛜 🅷 🖥️ 📠 / SOME UNITS FEE 🐕

WHERE TO EAT

COME BACK DINER
530/877-9466

🔻 American. Casual Dining. $4-$16 **AAA Inspector Notes:** Lending to the retro 1950s look are red and white accents, a bing cherry wall border, chrome tables and chairs and a jukebox. Traditional breakfast fare is served at all times. The lunch menu lists burgers, sandwiches, wraps, salads and homemade pies while dinner rolls out pasta, steaks and seafood dishes. **Bar:** beer & wine. **Address:** 6053 Clark Rd 95969 **Location:** SR 191, 0.5 mi n of Pearson Rd; just n of jct Elliott Rd. B L D CALL 🅜

SMOKIE MOUNTAIN STEAKHOUSE & LOUNGE
530/872-3323

🔻🔻 American. Casual Dining. $16-$33 **AAA Inspector Notes:** Known for their prime rib, this restaurant also serves a nice selection of steaks and seafood, as well as a few pasta and chicken dishes. Recommended is the clam chowder, if available. Early bird specials are offered from 5-6 pm. **Bar:** full bar. **Reservations:** suggested. **Address:** 7039 Skyway Rd 95969 **Location:** SR 99 exit Skyway Rd S. D CALL 🅜 🍽️

PATTERSON pop. 20,413

BEST WESTERN PLUS VILLA DEL LAGO INN
(209)892-5300

Hotel
$80-$140

AAA Benefit: Members save up to 20%, plus 10% bonus points with Best Western Rewards®.

Address: 2959 Speno Dr 95363 **Location:** I-5 exit Sperry Rd, just e. **Facility:** 82 units. 3 stories, interior corridors. **Pool(s):** outdoor. **Activities:** sauna, whirlpool, exercise room. **Guest Services:** coin laundry. **Free Special Amenities:** newspaper and high-speed Internet.

SAVE 📶 🛏️ CALL 🅜 🛎️ BIZ 🛜 🅷 🖥️ / SOME UNITS FEE 🐕 📷

WHERE TO EAT

EL ROSAL
209/895-6132

🔻🔻 Mexican. Casual Dining. $7-$20 **AAA Inspector Notes:** The menu at this casual spot offers traditional Mexican favorites plus some specialties of their own. Be sure to try the homemade green sauce on the super burrito, it's incredible. Portions are hearty so bring an appetite. **Bar:** full bar. **Address:** 2985 Renzo Ln, Suite A 95363 **Location:** I-5 exit Sperry Rd, just e. B L D CALL 🅜

PEBBLE BEACH (G-2) elev. 12'
• Hotels p. 274 • Restaurants p. 274
• Hotels & Restaurants map & index p. 206
• Part of Monterey Peninsula area — see map p. 202

17-MILE DRIVE can be entered through several gates off SRs 1 and 68; the Pacific Grove gate at Sunset Dr. and SR 68 and the Carmel gate on San Antonio Ave. are the n. and s. entrances, respectively. This winding road hugs the Monterey Peninsula coast as it traverses the private gated community of Pebble Beach. Grandly scenic, it has plenty of places to pull off, park and admire the panoramic ocean views up close.

Point Joe, where early seafarers often ran aground due to the erroneous belief that it was the entrance to Monterey Bay, is a good spot to take in the beauty of the rocky shoreline. Another good photo op is Bird Rock; just offshore, it's a favored gathering place for sea gulls and shore birds and also is occasionally visited by harbor seals and California sea lions.

The route's most famous landmark is the Lone Cypress. This solitary Monterey cypress, estimated to be more than 250 years old, stands atop a rocky outcrop that juts into the ocean. Monterey cypresses once had a much wider range but now grow in the wild at only two sheltered seaside locations—here and within Point Lobos State Natural Reserve *(see attraction listing p. 68)*. A bit farther on is Pescadero Point, where there are thick green carpets of fleshy-leaved ice plants, rounded rocks and lovely views of deep blue water.

Well-known golf courses along the route include The Links at Spanish Bay, Spyglass Hill and the Pebble Beach Golf Links, scene of the final round of the AT&T Pebble Beach National Pro-Am, played in early February.

Bicycles are permitted during daylight hours when no major sporting event is scheduled; no motorcycles or motorbikes are allowed. Bicyclists must enter through the Pacific Grove gate on weekends, holidays and during events. **Time:** Allow 2 hours minimum. **Hours:** Road open to visitors daily dawn-30 minutes before dusk. **Cost:** Toll fee $9.75 per car (includes a map showing points of interest along the route). The fee is subtracted if visitors eat at a Pebble Beach restaurant and provide the toll receipt; the bill must total more than $25. Cash only. **Phone:** (800) 654-9300.

(See map & index p. 206.)

CASA PALMERO
831/622-6650 **82**

▼▼▼ ▼▼▼ **Resort Hotel.** Rates not provided. **Address:** 1518 Cypress Dr 93953 **Location:** Off SR 1, on Seventeen Mile Dr. **Facility:** Adjacent to Pebble Beach Resort, the property features elegantly appointed guest rooms, welcoming public areas and extensive spa facilities. 24 units. 2 stories, exterior corridors. **Amenities:** video games (fee), high-speed Internet, safes. **Pool(s):** 2 heated outdoor. **Activities:** sauna, whirlpool, rental bicycles, hiking trails, jogging, exercise room, spa. **Fee:** golf-18 holes, 12 tennis courts, horseback riding. **Guest Services:** valet laundry. Affiliated with A Preferred Hotel.

THE INN AT SPANISH BAY
831/647-7500 **81**

▼▼▼ ▼▼▼ **Resort Hotel.** Rates not provided. **Address:** 2700 Seventeen Mile Dr 93953 **Location:** Oceanfront. 3.5 mi w of SR 1 exit SR 68, follow signs. **Facility:** Bordered by a golf course, the property offers rooms with bay or forest views and a gas-burning fireplace; many units include a balcony or patio. 269 units. 3-5 stories, interior corridors. **Amenities:** video games (fee), high-speed Internet, safes. **Dining:** 3 restaurants, also, Peppoli at Pebble Beach, Roy's, see separate listings. **Pool(s):** heated outdoor. **Activities:** saunas, whirlpool, recreation programs, rental bicycles, hiking trails, jogging. **Fee:** golf-18 holes, 8 tennis courts (2 lighted), horseback riding, massage. **Guest Services:** valet laundry, area transportation (fee). Affiliated with A Preferred Hotel.

THE LODGE AT PEBBLE BEACH
831/624-3811 **83**

▼▼▼ ▼▼▼ **Resort Hotel.** Rates not provided. **Address:** 1700 Seventeen Mile Dr 93953 **Location:** Oceanfront. Off SR 1. **Facility:** Notable for its sweeping views of Monterey Bay, the lodge features spacious guest rooms, many with a wood-burning fireplace. 161 units. 2-3 stories, interior/exterior corridors. **Terms:** check-in 4 pm. **Amenities:** video games (fee), high-speed Internet, safes. **Dining:** 5 restaurants, also, Stillwater Bar and Grill, see separate listing, entertainment. **Pool(s):** 2 heated outdoor. **Activities:** sauna, whirlpool, rental bicycles, jogging, spa. **Fee:** golf-18 holes, 12 tennis courts, horseback riding. **Guest Services:** valet laundry, area transportation (fee). Affiliated with A Preferred Hotel.

PEPPOLI AT PEBBLE BEACH
831/647-7433 **41**

▼▼▼ ▼▼▼ Italian. Fine Dining. $20-$44 **AAA Inspector Notes:** Rich in Italian flavor, dishes offer a taste of Tuscany. Guests can sample lasagna tradizionale and carbonara or veal piccata while enjoying a glass from the restaurant's extensive wine list and taking in gorgeous views: Tables overlook the Links at Spanish Bay and the Pacific Ocean. **Bar:** full bar. **Reservations:** suggested. **Address:** 2700 Seventeen Mile Dr 93953 **Location:** 3.5 mi w of SR 1 exit SR 68, follow signs; in The Inn at Spanish Bay.

ROY'S
831/647-7423 **40**

▼▼▼ ▼▼▼ Pacific Rim. Fine Dining. $15-$35 **AAA Inspector Notes:** Enjoy fusion of fresh Pacific seafood, French sauces and Asian seasonings. The ever-changing menu has many entrées such as, grilled salmon and barbecue lamb rack, and the signature dessert, chocolate soufflé. **Bar:** full bar. **Reservations:** suggested. **Address:** 2700 Seventeen Mile Dr 93953 **Location:** 3.5 mi w of SR 1 exit SR 68, follow signs; in The Inn at Spanish Bay.

STILLWATER BAR AND GRILL
831/625-8524 **42**

▼▼▼ ▼▼▼ Regional American. Fine Dining. $15-$65 **AAA Inspector Notes:** This casual, yet upscale, restaurant offers diners views of the golf course and Monterey Bay. Fresh seafood is locally caught and prepared. **Bar:** full bar. **Reservations:** suggested. **Address:** 1700 Seventeen Mile Dr 93953 **Location:** Off SR 1; in The Lodge at Pebble Beach.

PESCADERO (E-8) pop. 643, elev. 30'

On SR 1 south of Bean Hollow State Beach is Pigeon Point Light Station State Historic Park. Built in 1872, the 115-foot lighthouse is one of the nation's tallest. Although the lighthouse is closed for renovation, the grounds are open daily. Docents periodically offer 30-minute history walks of the grounds on weekends (when staff is available and weather permits); for more information phone (650) 879-2120. The lighthouse keeper's home has been restored and operates as a hostel.

AÑO NUEVO STATE PARK, 13 mi. s. on SR 1, is known for its colony of northern elephant seals,

which come ashore to give birth, breed and molt. Guided 3-mile, 2.5-hour walks are conducted from mid-December through March, the best viewing months; tickets must be bought in advance (up to 56 days ahead) either online or by phone through ReserveAmerica. Visitors can take a self-guiding hike to see the seals April through November; permits are required and are available at the entrance station or visitor center.

Layered clothing and sturdy shoes are recommended. Pets are not allowed. **Hours:** Park open daily 8-dusk, year-round; the wildlife protection area has some seasonal restrictions. Guided walks depart daily every quarter-hour 8:30-3:30, mid-Dec. through Mar. 31. Walks take place regardless of weather; no refunds are issued. Permits the rest of the year are available on a first-come, first-served basis daily 8:30-3:30, Apr.-Aug.; 8:30-3, Sept. 1 to mid-Dec. The seal viewing area closes at 4. Closed Jan. 1, Thanksgiving and Christmas. **Cost:** Guided walk tickets $7 per person. **Parking:** $10 per private vehicle; $9 (ages 62+ per private vehicle). **Phone:** (650) 879-0227, (650) 879-2025, or (800) 444-4445 for ReserveAmerica.

COSTANOA COASTAL LODGE AND CAMP   (650)879-1100

Hotel $89-$379 **Address:** 2001 Rossi Rd 94060 **Location:** 11 mi s on SR 1, 0.5 mi e; just n of jct Whitehorse Canyon Rd; 3 mi s of Pigeon Point Lighthouse. **Facility:** 39 units. 2 stories (no elevator), interior corridors. **Terms:** check-in 4 pm, 2 night minimum stay - seasonal and/or weekends, 3 day cancellation notice-fee imposed, resort fee. **Activities:** whirlpool, horseback riding, playground. *Fee:* bicycles, massage. **Guest Services:** coin laundry.

PESCADERO CREEK INN BED & BREAKFAST   (650)879-1898

Bed & Breakfast $175-$255 **Address:** 393 Stage Rd 94060 **Location:** Jct SR 1, 2 mi e on Pescadero Rd to Stage Rd, then just n. Located in a quiet residential area on edge of town. **Facility:** 4 units, some cottages. 1 story, interior/exterior corridors. **Terms:** check-in 4 pm, 7 day cancellation notice-fee imposed.

WHERE TO EAT

DUARTE'S TAVERN   650/879-0464

American. Casual Dining. $6-$40 **AAA Inspector Notes:** Family run since 1894, each generation has added their own dishes to the menu. Known for artichoke soup and olallieberry pie as well as such classics as cioppino. This historic tavern was awarded the 2003 James Beard Foundation Coca-Cola America's Classics Awards. **Bar:** full bar. **Address:** 202 Stage Rd 94060 **Location:** Jct SR 1, 2 mi e on Pescadero Rd to Stage Rd, then just n.

PETALUMA (B-8) pop. 57,941, elev. 12'
- **Hotels p. 277** • **Restaurants p. 277**
- **Attractions map p. 568**
- **Part of Wine Country area — see map p. 562**

Petaluma boasts three of California's oldest and best-preserved historic districts. The Oakhill-Brewster Historic District, north and west of downtown, and the "A" Street Historic District, south and east of downtown, contain many carefully preserved 19th-century Victorian homes. The Petaluma Historic Commercial District, encompassing much of downtown, includes well-known landmarks like the Philip Sweed House (301 Keokuk St.), the United States Post Office (4th and D streets) and the Phoenix Theatre (201 Washington St.). The Petaluma Adobe in Petaluma Adobe State Historic Park *(see attraction listing)* is said to be one of the oldest adobe buildings in the country.

Experience this architectural legacy by taking one of the free, 1-hour guided walking tours organized by the Petaluma Historical Museum and led by a docent dressed in Victorian-era garb. The tours are conducted on most Saturdays from May through October; for more information phone (707) 778-4398.

Farms, artisan food producers and wineries in this rich agricultural region offer a variety of tours, tastings and activities, from picking your own organic apples and tomatoes to bakery tours and garden walks. For information about area ranches and farm trails contact the Petaluma Visitor Center.

Petaluma and vicinity have appeared in such movies as "American Graffiti," "Peggy Sue Got Married" and "Mumford." Just 32 miles north of the Golden Gate Bridge, the city makes a convenient

base for exploring Sonoma County's wineries, towering redwoods, dramatic Pacific coastline and Point Reyes National Seashore.

Stroll through Shollenberger Park, just off the S. McDowell Boulevard extension along the Petaluma River; many species of birds, animals, fish and plants reside in this wetlands preserve. The visitor center has a brochure as well as a list of birds that can be seen.

Petaluma Visitor Center: 210 Lakeville St., Petaluma, CA 94952. **Phone:** (707) 769-0429 or (877) 273-8258.

Self-guiding tours: Maps and brochures detailing a driving tour; a self-guiding walking tour of historic residential and commercial areas; film sites; heritage trees; and wetland preserve areas can be obtained at the visitor center.

Shopping areas: Banana Republic, Gap, Nike, Saks Fifth Avenue OFF 5th, Tommy Hilfiger and Van Heusen are some of the 60 outlet stores to be found at Petaluma Village Premium Outlets, 2200 Petaluma Blvd. N.

GARDEN VALLEY RANCH is at 498 Pepper Rd. Self-guiding tours of this 10-acre ranch, which specializes in roses, include such areas of interest as the Fragrance Garden, Pond Garden, Shade Garden and flower borders. Rose arbors and a koi pond accent the property.

Time: Allow 1 hour minimum. **Hours:** Wed.-Sun. 10-4, mid-Jan. through Oct. 31. **Cost:** $5; free (ages 0-15). **Phone:** (707) 795-0919.

MARIN FRENCH CHEESE, 9 mi. s.w. at 7500 Red Hill Rd. (Petaluma-Point Reyes Rd.), offers tours of its cheesemaking operation. Visitors also can purchase cheese and sample the company's products. Situated in a coastal valley, the grounds are lovely and offer spectacular views, making them perfect for a relaxed stroll. **Note:** Tours have been temporarily suspended due to remodeling; phone ahead for updated information. **Time:** Allow 30 minutes minimum. **Hours:** Store open daily 8:30-5. Closed Jan. 1, Easter, Thanksgiving and Christmas. **Cost:** Free. **Phone:** (707) 762-6001 or (800) 292-6001. 🍴 🎪

MRS. GROSSMAN'S TOURS is at 3810 Cypress Dr. at jct. S. McDowell Blvd. A 5-minute video presentation precedes the tour and explains how Mrs. Grossman began her decorative sticker company. During a 45-minute walking tour of the manufacturing plant, visitors can see the presses at work and how laser-cut stickers are produced. Hands-on demonstrations are available at each station. A sticker art class where guests create their own masterpiece follows the tour. Sticker samples are provided.

Time: Allow 1 hour minimum. **Hours:** Guided tours are given Mon.-Thurs. at 10, 11, 1 and 2. Closed Jan. 1, Presidents Day, Memorial Day, July 4, Labor Day, Thanksgiving and Christmas week. **Cost:** $7; $5 (ages 3-11). Reservations are required. **Phone:** (800) 429-4549.

PETALUMA ADOBE STATE HISTORIC PARK, .7 mi. e. on Adobe Rd., preserves the large adobe ranch headquarters built by General Mariano Vallejo about 1836. Exhibits include furnished rooms, weaving tools, outdoor ovens, live animals and interpretive displays.

Time: Allow 1 hour minimum. **Hours:** Sat.-Sun. 10-5. Closed Jan. 1, Thanksgiving and Christmas. Phone ahead to confirm schedule. **Cost:** $3 (includes house); $2 (ages 5-16). **Phone:** (707) 762-4871.

PETALUMA HISTORICAL MUSEUM/LIBRARY, 20 4th St., houses permanent and rotating exhibits,

▼ *See AAA listing p. 277* ▼

many reflecting life in early 19th-century Petaluma. Philanthropist Andrew Carnegie awarded the town $12,500 toward the building's construction in 1903. A highlight is the free-standing stained-glass dome. Exhibits include historic photographs and items pertaining to the poultry industry.

Time: Allow 30 minutes minimum. **Hours:** Museum Thurs.-Sat. 10-4, Sun. noon-3. Library staffed Mon. and Thurs. 1-4. **Cost:** Donations; a $3-$5 fee may be charged for special exhibitions. **Phone:** (707) 778-4398.

BEST WESTERN PETALUMA INN (707)763-0994

Hotel
$80-$190

AAA Benefit: Members save up to 20%, plus 10% bonus points with Best Western Rewards®.

Address: 200 S McDowell Blvd 94954 **Location:** US 101 exit Washington St, just e. **Facility:** 73 units. 2 stories (no elevator), exterior corridors. **Amenities:** *Some:* high-speed Internet. **Pool(s):** heated outdoor. **Guest Services:** coin laundry. **Free Special Amenities:** local telephone calls and high-speed Internet. *(See ad p. 276.)*

QUALITY INN-PETALUMA (707)664-1155

Hotel
$69-$289

Address: 5100 Montero Way 94954 **Location:** US 101 exit Old Redwood Hwy-Penngrove northbound; exit Petaluma Blvd N-Penngrove southbound (east side), just n on N McDowell Blvd, then just e. **Facility:** 108 units. 2 stories (no elevator), interior/exterior corridors. **Amenities:** safes. **Pool(s):** heated outdoor. **Activities:** sauna, whirlpool, exercise room. **Guest Services:** valet and coin laundry.

SHERATON SONOMA COUNTY-PETALUMA
(707)283-2888

Hotel
$119-$339

AAA Benefit: Members get up to 20% off, plus Starwood Preferred Guest® bonuses.

Address: 745 Baywood Dr 94954 **Location:** US 101 exit SR 116 (Lakeville Hwy), just se. **Facility:** 183 units. 4 stories, interior corridors. **Terms:** 2 night minimum stay - seasonal and/or weekends, 3 day cancellation notice-fee imposed. **Amenities:** video games (fee), high-speed Internet, safes. **Dining:** Tolay, see separate listing. **Pool(s):** heated outdoor. **Activities:** saunas, whirlpool, exercise room. *Fee:* massage. **Guest Services:** valet and coin laundry. **Free Special Amenities:** room upgrade (subject to availability with advance reservations) and high-speed Internet. *(See ad this page.)*

WHERE TO EAT

BEYOND THE GLORY SPORTS BAR & GRILL 707/775-3775

American. Casual Dining. $8-$18 **AAA Inspector Notes:** This family-friendly sports bar offers a small video arcade to keep the kids happy while the parents enjoy sports on big screen TVs. **Bar:** full bar. **Address:** 1371 McDowell Blvd 94954 **Location:** US 101 exit Old Redwood Hwy/Penngrove northbound, just s; US 101 exit Petaluma Blvd N/Penngrove southbound, just e on Old Redwood Hwy, then just s; at Kohl's Shopping Center. L D

CUCINA PARADISO 707/782-1130

Italian. Casual Dining. $6-$23 **AAA Inspector Notes:** An extensive array of Sonoma and Italian wines complements fine Italian cuisine prepared from scratch, including pasta and grilled meats. The atmosphere is warm and friendly. **Bar:** full bar. **Address:** 114 Petaluma Blvd N 94952 **Location:** US 101 exit Washington St, just s. **Parking:** street only. L D CALL

▼ See AAA listing this page ▼

DEMPSEY'S RESTAURANT & BREWERY 707-765-9694

American
Casual Dining
$10-$22

AAA Inspector Notes: The restaurant is a bit hard to find, but upon arrival diners can relax on the tranquil patio and watch people stroll past and boats float by on the gently flowing Petaluma River. Award-winning, hand-crafted beers complement the organic foods gathered daily from Red Rooster Ranch. Many entrées are cooked or finished in a wood-burning oven. Among good choices are pizza, pork chops and flatbread sandwiches, not to mention the outrageous desserts. **Bar:** beer & wine. **Address:** 50 E Washington St 94952 **Location:** US 101 exit SR 116 (Lakeville Hwy), 1 mi w on Lakeville St, then just s; in Golden Eagle Shopping Center.

L D

GRAFFITI 707/765-4567

California. Casual Dining. $11-$33 **AAA Inspector Notes:** The bustling contemporary restaurant presents an eclectic menu. The highlight is "graffiti," an array of small plates that enable guests to sample several of the wonderful kitchen staff's creations. Spacious outdoor seating is a great option. **Bar:** full bar. **Address:** 101 2nd St, Suite 190 94952 **Location:** At B St; downtown. **Parking:** street only. L D

GRAZIANO'S RISTORANTE 707/762-5997

Italian. Casual Dining. $13-$40 **AAA Inspector Notes:** In the historic Wickersham Building, which once was a Prohibition-era speakeasy, this restaurant prepares such dishes as veal, gnocchi and pork tenderloin. Attractive murals decorate the walls. Patrons wanting to sample over 70 premium vodkas may head to the lounge, where the temperature is maintained at -28 degrees. Faux fur coats are available on loan. **Bar:** full bar. **Address:** 170 Petaluma Blvd N 94952 **Location:** Downtown. **Parking:** on-site and valet. D

PEPPER'S RESTAURANT 707/775-4296

American. Casual Dining. $10-$18 **AAA Inspector Notes:** This cheery and bright diner offers breakfast all day, burgers your way and various dinner options-Italian three ways offers creamy fettuccine Alfredo, lasagna and chicken parmigiana. If it is on the menu, finish with a generous slice of yellow cake with pink lemonade frosting. **Bar:** beer & wine. **Address:** 335 S McDowell Blvd 94954 **Location:** US 101 exit Washington St, just e. **Parking:** street only. B L D

SUGO 707/782-9298

Italian. Casual Dining. $9-$23 **AAA Inspector Notes:** In addition to fresh pasta, this restaurant treats patrons to varied chicken and meat entrées. **Bar:** beer & wine. **Address:** 5 Petaluma Blvd S 94952 **Location:** Jct B St; downtown. L D CALL M

TOLAY 707/283-2900

California. Casual Dining. $8-$29 **AAA Inspector Notes:** Enjoy views of the hotel's pool and local marina. Experience an explosive fusion of flavors complemented by a global wine list. **Bar:** full bar. **Address:** 745 Baywood Dr 94954 **Location:** US 101 exit SR 116 (Lakeville Hwy), just se; in Sheraton Sonoma County-Petaluma. B L D CALL M

PHILO (D-1) pop. 349, elev. 331'
• Attractions map p. 566
• Part of Wine Country area — see map p. 562

WINERIES
• **Navarro Vineyards** is at 5601 SR 128. **Hours:** Tastings daily 9-6, Apr.-Oct.; 9-5, rest of year. Tours are given daily at 10:30 and 3. **Phone:** (707) 895-3686 or (800) 537-9463.

PIERCY (C-1) elev. 622'
• Part of Wine Country area — see map p. 562

CAMPBELL BROS. CONFUSION HILL, 3 mi. s. on US 101, is an experience in contradictory optical and physical sensations in an apparently confused gravitational or magnetic field. In addition to the gravity house, a 1.25-mile, 30-minute miniature mountain train ride meanders (weather permitting) through a redwood forest to a hilltop and back, with the engineer providing information about the unique characteristics of coastal redwoods and pointing out historical logging artifacts along the way.

Time: Allow 1 hour minimum. **Hours:** Gravity house open daily 9-6, May-Sept.; 9-5, rest of year. Train departures require a minimum of four passengers. Train operates daily 10-5, Memorial Day weekend-Labor Day; Sat.-Sun. 10-5, day after Labor Day-Oct. 31 (weather permitting). **Cost:** Gravity house $5; $4 (ages 4-12). Train ride $8.50; $6.50 (ages 4-12). **Phone:** (707) 925-6456.

PINECREST (E-4) elev. 5,679'

RECREATIONAL ACTIVITIES
Skiing
• **Dodge Ridge Winter Sports Area** is 3.5 mi. s.e. on Dodge Ridge Rd. **Hours:** Daily 9-4, Nov.-Apr. **Phone:** (209) 536-5300 or (209) 965-3474.

PINECREST LAKE RESORT 209/965-3411

Motel
$85-$280

Address: 421 Pinecrest Lake Rd 95364 **Location:** Center. **Facility:** 27 units, some cabins and cottages. 1 story, exterior corridors. **Terms:** 7 night minimum stay - seasonal, 60 day cancellation notice-fee imposed. **Activities:** boating, canoeing, paddleboats, sailboats, windsurfing, boat dock, 2 tennis courts, rental bicycles, hiking trails. **Fee:** downhill & cross country skiing.

SAVE / SOME UNITS

PINE GROVE (E-4) pop. 2,219, elev. 2,500'

INDIAN GRINDING ROCK STATE HISTORIC PARK, e. on SR 88/104, then 1.4 mi. n. to 14881 Pine Grove-Volcano Rd., is a 135-acre park where Miwok Indians once chiseled out of rock mortar cups in which they pulverized acorns and other seeds for food. On the grounds are a ceremonial roundhouse and a re-created village. Chaw Se' Regional Indian Museum includes artifacts, presentations, exhibits and video presentations about 10 Sierra Nevada Indian tribes.

Hours: Park open daily dawn-dusk. Museum open Fri.-Mon. 11-2:30. Closed Jan. 1 and Christmas. **Cost:** $8 per private vehicle; $7 (ages 62+ per private vehicle). **Phone:** (209) 296-7488 during museum hours.

PINNACLES NATIONAL MONUMENT (G-3)

Entered from the east via SR 146, 35 miles south of Hollister via SR 25, or 35 miles north of King City via CR G13, the monument also can be approached from the west via SR 146, off US 101 in Soledad. Pinnacles National Monument embraces about 24,000 acres of precipitous bluffs, spires and crags of colorful volcanic rock and a series of caves underneath the formations. The forces of heat, cold, water and wind have worn the contours of the rocky terrain.

The east entrance to the park is open daily 24 hours. The Pinnacles Visitor Center, in the campground at the east entrance to the park, is open daily 9:30-5, with extended hours Fri.-Sat. in spring and summer; phone (831) 389-4485. The Bear Gulch Nature Center, accessible by car from the east entrance, is open Sat.-Sun. 9-5, late Mar. to mid-Nov. The west entrance, open 7:30 a.m.-8 p.m., has a ranger station; the entrance road is winding and narrow. Trailers and motor homes are advised to use the east entrance. No roads connect the east and west districts.

Pinnacles is strictly a hiking park, although some major formations can be seen from the roadway into the monument. The best viewing by car is from the west side. Hiking trails range from easy 1-mile treks to strenuous hikes of more than 10 miles. It also is popular with rock climbers, whose favorite spots include the Balconies and High Peaks.

The monument is bisected from north to south by a 1,000-foot-high ridge. Most of the spire-shaped formations, some more than 600 feet high, are located on or alongside the ridge. This central backbone has been cut in two places by streams; huge fragments of rock have fallen into the resulting deep clefts, creating caves. Bear Gulch Cave and Balconies Cave require visitors to carry flashlights. Bear Gulch Cave is generally closed mid-May to mid-July and may be partially closed at other times; phone ahead for schedule.

Note: Neither pets nor bicycles are permitted on the trails. In parking lots, roads and picnic areas, pets must be kept leashed and under physical control; they cannot be left unattended in vehicles. Beware of poison oak.

In addition to geological and scenic interest, the monument has an abundant deer and bird population as well as a vibrant display of spring wildflowers. The plant and animal species are characteristic of a coast range chaparral ecosystem. Picnic facilities are available. Admission is $5 per private vehicle or $3 per person for walk-in visitors (both fees are valid for 7 days). Parking areas fill up early on weekends and during spring, the busiest season. Phone (831) 389-4486.

PINOLE pop. 18,390

DAYS INN-SF/PINOLE   (510)222-9400

Motel $59-$99 **Address:** 2600 Appian Way 94564 **Location:** I-80 exit Appian Way, 0.3 mi s. **Facility:** 50 units. 2 stories (no elevator), exterior corridors. **Activities:** whirlpool, exercise room. **Guest Services:** coin laundry.

WHERE TO EAT

ROUND TABLE PIZZA   510/222-9988

Pizza. Casual Dining. $7-$28 **AAA Inspector Notes:** This casual, family-oriented pizza place features high-quality ingredients and dough rolled fresh daily. Distinctive specialty pizzas are piled high with toppings. **Bar:** beer & wine. **Address:** 1409 Fitzgerald Dr 94564 **Location:** I-80 exit Richmond Pkwy/Fitzgerald Dr E.

PITTSBURG pop. 63,264

HAMPTON INN & SUITES   (925)473-1300

Hotel $99-$119 **Address:** 1201 California Ave 94565 **Location:** SR 4 exit Loveridge Rd N, then just w. **Facility:** 95 units. 4 stories, interior corridors. **Terms:** 1-7 night minimum stay, cancellation fee imposed. **Amenities:** high-speed Internet, safes. **Pool(s):** outdoor. **Activities:** whirlpool, exercise room. **Guest Services:** valet and coin laundry.

AAA Benefit: Members save up to 10%!

WHERE TO EAT

ROUND TABLE PIZZA

Pizza. Casual Dining. $7-$28 **AAA Inspector Notes:** This casual, family-oriented pizza place features high-quality ingredients and dough rolled fresh daily. Distinctive specialty pizzas are piled high with toppings. **Bar:** beer & wine.

For additional information, visit AAA.com

LOCATIONS:

Address: 408 Bailey Rd 94565 **Location:** SR 4 exit Bailey Rd, just s. Pittsburg/Bay Point, 1. **Phone:** 925/458-2244

Address: 1331 Buchanan Rd 94565 **Location:** Just e of Loveridge Rd. **Phone:** 925/432-1000

PLACERVILLE (E-3) pop. 10,389, elev. 1,860'
• Hotels p. 280 • Restaurants p. 280

Originally called Dry Diggin's, Placerville became so prosperous—and lawless—that criminals were hanged in pairs. This practice gave rise to a new name for the rough-and-tumble settlement, Hangtown. Located less than 10 miles from the site of the first gold discovery in California, Placerville's past is still evident in the restored late 19th-century architecture along downtown's Main Street.

The Fountain Tallman Museum, 524 Main St., is in a building dating from 1852, the oldest in Placerville. It originally served as the settlement's soda works, providing bottled water to gold rush miners. Exhibits depict Placerville's early history as a mining outpost; phone (530) 626-0773.

El Dorado County Chamber of Commerce: 542 Main St., Placerville, CA 95667. **Phone:** (530) 621-5885 or (800) 457-6279.

EL DORADO COUNTY HISTORICAL MUSEUM is just n. of US 50 at 104 Placerville Dr., within the El Dorado County Fairgrounds. Exhibits feature ranching, logging, farming and mining equipment, a re-created country store, Studebaker wagons, a Shay locomotive and other railroad rolling stock. Changing exhibits also are presented, and a research library is on site.

Time: Allow 1 hour minimum. **Hours:** Wed.-Sat. 10-4, Sun. noon-4. Research library open Tues. 9-3 or by appointment. Closed Jan. 1, Thanksgiving, Christmas Eve and Christmas. **Cost:** Donations. **Phone:** (530) 621-5865.

HANGTOWN'S GOLD BUG PARK & MINE is 1 mi. n. off the US 50 Bedford Ave. exit, within Gold Bug Park. On the east side of the Mother Lode vein, the

Gold Bug mine has wood floors and a 352-foot horizontal drift. Also in the 62-acre park are Hattie's Museum, which displays mining equipment, and the Hendy Stamp Mill and Museum, which shows how gold was extracted from quartz. Visitors can take a self-guiding tour using an audio wand, go hiking and pan for gemstones.

Tours: Guided tours are available. **Time:** Allow 30 minutes minimum. **Hours:** Mine, museum and stamp mill open daily 10-4, Apr.-Oct.; Sat.-Sun. noon-4, rest of year. **Cost:** $5; $3 (ages 10-17); $2 (ages 3-9). Under 18 must be with an adult. Gem panning $2 per hour. Reservations are required for guided tours. **Phone:** (530) 642-5207. 🍴

ALBERT SHAFSKY HOUSE BED & BREAKFAST
(530)642-2776

💎💎 **Bed & Breakfast** $135-$195 **Address:** 2942 Coloma St 95667 **Location:** US 50 exit Spring St (SR 49), just n; corner of Coloma and Spring (SR 49) sts. **Facility:** 3 units. 2 stories (no elevator), interior corridors. **Terms:** check-in 4 pm, 2 night minimum stay - weekends, 14 day cancellation notice-fee imposed.

BEST WESTERN PLUS PLACERVILLE INN
530/622-9100

Hotel
Rates not provided

 AAA Benefit: Members save up to 20%, plus 10% bonus points with Best Western Rewards®.

Address: 6850 Green Leaf Dr 95667 **Location:** US 50 exit 44A (Missouri Flat Rd S), just e. **Facility:** 107 units. 3 stories (no elevator), interior corridors. **Amenities:** high-speed Internet. *Fee:* video games, safes. **Pool(s):** outdoor. **Activities:** whirlpool, exercise room. **Guest Services:** valet and coin laundry. **Free Special Amenities:** full breakfast and high-speed Internet.

NATIONAL 9 INN
530/622-3884

💎 Motel
Rates not provided

Address: 1500 Broadway 95667 **Location:** US 50 exit 48 (Schnell School Rd), just e. **Facility:** 24 units. 2 stories (no elevator), exterior corridors. **Free Special Amenities:** continental breakfast and high-speed Internet.

EDEN VALE INN
530/621-0901

[fyi] Not evaluated. **Address:** 1780 Springvale Rd 95667 **Location:** US 50 exit 37 (Ponderosa Rd), just n. 6.5 mi ne on N Shingle Springs Rd (which becomes Green Valley Rd/Lotus Rd), then just nw; from SR 49, 4.7 mi sw on Lotus Rd, just nw. Facilities, services, and décor characterize an upscale property.

 WHERE TO EAT

CASA RAMOS
530/622-2303

💎💎 Mexican. Casual Dining. $7-$16 **AAA Inspector Notes:** A varied Mexican menu is featured in a colorful atmosphere. Mexican favorites include fajitas, enchiladas, burritos and specialty steak and seafood entrees. **Bar:** full bar. **Address:** 6840 Green Leaf Dr 95667 **Location:** US 50 exit 44A (Missouri Flat Rd S), just e.

PLEASANT HILL pop. 33,152

COURTYARD BY MARRIOTT-PLEASANT HILL
(925)691-1444

💎💎💎 Hotel $86-$220 **Address:** 2250 Contra Costa Blvd 94523 **Location:** I-680 exit Gregory Ln southbound, just w; exit Contra Costa Blvd/Pleasant Hill northbound. **Facility:** 135 units. 4 stories, interior corridors. **Amenities:** high-speed Internet. **Pool(s):** heated indoor. **Activities:** whirlpool, exercise room. **Guest Services:** valet and coin laundry.

AAA Benefit: AAA hotel discounts of 5% or more.

EXTENDED STAYAMERICA-PLEASANT HILL-BUSKIRK AVE
(925)945-6788

💎💎 Extended Stay Hotel $99-$114 **Address:** 3220 Buskirk Ave 94523 **Location:** I-680 exit Treat Blvd/Geary Rd E, just n. 🏢 Pleasant Hill/Contra Costa Centre, 4. **Facility:** 122 efficiencies. 3 stories, interior corridors. **Guest Services:** coin laundry.

HYATT HOUSE PLEASANT HILL
(925)934-3343

💎💎💎 Extended Stay Hotel $99-$219

AAA Benefit: Members save 10% or more everyday.

Address: 2611 Contra Costa Blvd 94523 **Location:** I-680 exit Contra Costa Blvd, then w. **Facility:** 142 units, some two bedrooms and efficiencies. 4 stories, interior corridors. **Terms:** cancellation fee imposed. **Amenities:** high-speed Internet. **Pool(s):** heated outdoor. **Activities:** whirlpool, sports court, exercise room. **Guest Services:** valet and coin laundry. **Free Special Amenities:** expanded continental breakfast and high-speed Internet.

RESIDENCE INN BY MARRIOTT-PLEASANT HILL
(925)689-1010

💎💎💎 Extended Stay Hotel $109-$259 **Address:** 700 Ellinwood Way 94523 **Location:** I-680 exit Willow Pass Rd W to S Contra Costa Blvd, e on Ellinwood Dr, then n. **Facility:** 126 kitchen units, some two bedrooms. 2 stories (no elevator), interior/exterior corridors. **Amenities:** high-speed Internet. **Pool(s):** heated outdoor. **Activities:** whirlpool, sports court, exercise room. **Guest Services:** valet and coin laundry, area transportation-within 5 mi.

AAA Benefit: AAA hotel discounts of 5% or more.

WHERE TO EAT

PASTA POMODORO
925/363-9641

💎💎 Italian. Casual Dining. $8-$18 **AAA Inspector Notes:** Families are welcomed at this laid-back restaurant, which brings in plenty of loyal locals who enjoy its varied Italian favorites, including tempting pasta and chicken dishes. **Bar:** beer & wine. **Address:** 45 Crescent Dr 94523 **Location:** I-680 exit Monument Blvd, just w, then just n on Contra Costa Blvd.

ROUND TABLE PIZZA

💎 Pizza. Casual Dining. $7-$28 **AAA Inspector Notes:** This casual, family-oriented pizza place uses high-quality ingredients and dough rolled fresh daily. Distinctive specialty pizzas are piled high with toppings. **Bar:** beer & wine.

For additional information, visit AAA.com

LOCATIONS:
Address: 85 Chilpancingo Pkwy 94523 **Location:** I-680 exit Concord Ave, just w. **Phone:** 925/798-3355
Address: 1938 Oak Park Blvd 94523 **Location:** I-680 exit Treat Blvd/Geary Rd, just w, n on Putnam Blvd, then just w. **Phone:** 925/930-9004

TAHOE JOE'S FAMOUS STEAKHOUSE   925/687-8096

 Steak. Casual Dining. $10-$27 **AAA Inspector Notes:** At this ski lodge-themed spot, aged steaks are grilled over an almond fire and slow roasted prime rib are top picks. Other menu selections include railroad camp shrimp and Joe's bowls (salads and burgers). **Bar:** full bar. **Address:** 999 Contra Costa Blvd 94523 **Location:** I-680 exit Willow Pass Rd, 0.3 mi w, then just n. [L] [D]

PLEASANTON (D-9) pop. 70,285, elev. 352'
• Restaurants p. 282

Downtown Pleasanton has a number of restored old buildings and houses. Stop by the Museum on Main at 603 Main St. for a crash course in regional history; phone (925) 462-2766. One of the nation's oldest racetracks is at the Alameda County Fairgrounds, off Pleasanton Avenue; it was built in 1858 by the sons of a Spanish don, Augustin Bernal. The presence of limestone in the soil is credited with making this an exceptionally fine track. For upcoming events information phone the events hotline at (925) 426-7559.

Shadow Cliffs Regional Recreation Area, on the outskirts of town, was developed from an abandoned gravel quarry. A lake in the park offers swimming, boating and fishing. *See Recreation Areas Chart.*

Pleasanton Chamber of Commerce: 777 Peters Ave., Pleasanton, CA 94566. **Phone:** (925) 846-5858.

AAA/CAA travel information:
Available in print, online
and on the go!

BEST WESTERN PLUS PLEASANTON INN
(925)463-1300

 Hotel $110-$130   **AAA Benefit:** Members save up to 20%, plus 10% bonus points with Best Western Rewards®.

Address: 5375 Owens Ct 94588 **Location:** I-580 exit Hopyard Rd, just s. 📶 Dublin-Pleasanton, 29. **Facility:** 100 units. 3 stories, exterior corridors. **Terms:** cancellation fee imposed. **Amenities:** *Some:* high-speed Internet. **Pool(s):** outdoor. **Activities:** whirlpool. **Guest Services:** valet laundry. **Free Special Amenities: expanded continental breakfast and high-speed Internet.**

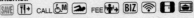

COURTYARD BY MARRIOTT   (925)463-1414

 Hotel $89-$259 **Address:** 5059 Hopyard Rd 94588 **Location:** I-580 exit Hopyard Rd, 0.5 mi s. 📶 Dublin-Pleasanton, 29. **Facility:** 145 units. 2-3 stories, interior corridors. **Pool(s):** outdoor. **Activities:** whirlpool, exercise room. **Guest Services:** valet and coin laundry.

AAA Benefit: AAA hotel discounts of 5% or more.

FOUR POINTS BY SHERATON   (925)460-8800

 Hotel $119-$275   FOUR POINTS BY SHERATON   **AAA Benefit:** Members get up to 20% off, plus Starwood Preferred Guest® bonuses.

Address: 5115 Hopyard Rd 94588 **Location:** 0.5 mi e of jct I-680 and 580 exit I-580 at Hopyard Rd, 0.5 mi s. 📶 Dublin-Pleasanton, 29. **Facility:** 214 units. 2 stories, interior corridors. **Terms:** cancellation fee imposed, resort fee. **Amenities:** *Some:* high-speed Internet. **Pool(s):** outdoor. **Activities:** whirlpool, exercise room. **Guest Services:** valet laundry, area transportation-within 7 mi. **Free Special Amenities: newspaper and high-speed Internet.**

HILTON PLEASANTON AT THE CLUB
(925)463-8000

▼▼▼▼ **Hotel** $109-$249 **Address:** 7050 Johnson Dr 94588 **Location:** In southeast quadrant of jct I-580 and 680. Ⓟ West Dublin/Pleasanton, 28. **Facility:** 294 units. 5 stories, interior corridors. **Terms:** 1-7 night minimum stay, cancellation fee imposed. **Amenities:** Fee: video games, high-speed Internet. **Dining:** Players Restaurant at the Club, see separate listing. **Pool(s):** 4 heated outdoor. **Activities:** whirlpools. Fee: 18 tennis courts (14 indoor, 4 lighted), racquetball courts. **Guest Services:** valet laundry, area transportation-within 6 mi.

AAA Benefit: Members save 5% or more!

HYATT HOUSE PLEASANTON
(925)730-0070

▼▼▼▼ Extended Stay Hotel $89-S219

H HYATT house®

AAA Benefit: Members save 10% or more everyday.

Address: 4545 Chabot Dr 94588 **Location:** I-580 exit Hopyard Rd, 1 mi s, e on Stoneridge Dr, then s. Located in a business park. Ⓟ Dublin-Pleasanton, 29. **Facility:** 128 kitchen units, some two bedrooms. 3 stories (no elevator), exterior corridors. **Terms:** cancellation fee imposed. **Amenities:** high-speed Internet. **Pool(s):** heated outdoor. **Activities:** whirlpool, sports court, exercise room. **Guest Services:** valet and coin laundry. **Free Special Amenities:** expanded continental breakfast and high-speed Internet.

LARKSPUR LANDING PLEASANTON
925/463-1212

▼▼▼ **Hotel.** Rates not provided. **Address:** 5535 Johnson Dr 94588 **Location:** I-580 exit Hopyard Rd S, w on Owen. Ⓟ Dublin-Pleasanton, 29. **Facility:** 124 units, some efficiencies. 4 stories, interior corridors. **Amenities:** high-speed Internet. **Activities:** whirlpool, exercise room. **Guest Services:** complimentary laundry, area transportation-within 5 mi.

PLEASANTON MARRIOTT
(925)847-6000

▼▼▼▼ Hotel $99-S359

Marriott HOTELS & RESORTS

AAA Benefit: AAA hotel discounts of 5% or more.

Address: 11950 Dublin Canyon Rd 94588 **Location:** I-580 exit Foothill Rd, 0.3 mi s. Ⓟ West Dublin/Pleasanton, 28. **Facility:** 242 units. 6 stories, interior corridors. **Amenities:** Some: high-speed Internet (fee). **Pool(s):** outdoor. **Activities:** whirlpool, exercise room. **Guest Services:** valet and coin laundry, area transportation-within 6 mi. **Free Special Amenities:** local transportation.

RESIDENCE INN BY MARRIOTT
(925)227-0500

▼▼▼ Extended Stay Hotel $89-$189 **Address:** 11920 Dublin Canyon Rd 94588 **Location:** I-580 exit Foothill Rd S, then w. Ⓟ West Dublin/Pleasanton, 28. **Facility:** 135 kitchen units, some two bedrooms. 3 stories, interior corridors. **Amenities:** video games (fee), high-speed Internet. **Pool(s):** heated outdoor. **Activities:** whirlpool, sports court, exercise room. **Guest Services:** valet and coin laundry.

AAA Benefit: AAA hotel discounts of 5% or more.

THE ROSE HOTEL
(925)846-8802

▼▼▼ **Hotel** $240-$260 **Address:** 807 Main St 94566 **Location:** I-580 exit Santa Rita, 3 mi s. **Facility:** 34 units. 3 stories, interior corridors. **Terms:** cancellation fee imposed. **Amenities:** high-speed Internet, safes. **Activities:** exercise room. **Guest Services:** valet laundry.

SHERATON PLEASANTON HOTEL
(925)463-3330

▼▼▼ Hotel $89-S219

Ⓢ Sheraton HOTELS & RESORTS

AAA Benefit: Members get up to 20% off, plus Starwood Preferred Guest® bonuses.

Address: 5990 Stoneridge Mall Rd 94588 **Location:** Jct I-580 and 680, 0.5 mi sw; I-580 exit Foothill Rd, 0.3 mi s, then 0.3 mi e on Canyon Way. Opposite Stoneridge Mall. Ⓟ West Dublin/Pleasanton, 28. **Facility:** 170 units. 6 stories, interior corridors. **Terms:** 2-3 night minimum stay - seasonal and/or weekends, cancellation fee imposed. **Amenities:** Some: high-speed Internet. **Dining:** Garden Terrace, see separate listing. **Pool(s):** heated outdoor. **Activities:** whirlpool, exercise room. **Guest Services:** valet laundry. **Free Special Amenities:** newspaper and high-speed Internet.

WHERE TO EAT

BLUE AGAVE CLUB
925/417-1224

▼▼▼ Mexican. Casual Dining. $9-$31 **AAA Inspector Notes:** This is a great spot for those who enjoy Mexican food that is more than just the typical tacos and burritos. The family-owned restaurant incorporates family recipes into the menu, some of which are 100 years old and from the different regions in Mexico including carnitas from Michoacan, carne asada from Chihuahua and a great grand mother's recipe of enjococado (chicken breast in a sour cream sauce with roasted chiles and herbs). Patio seating is available, weather permitting. **Bar:** full bar. **Address:** 625 Main St 94566 **Location:** I-580 exit Santa Rita Rd, 3 mi s; between Mary and Division sts. **Parking:** street only.

THE CHEESECAKE FACTORY
925/463-1311

▼▼▼ American. Casual Dining. $8-$28 **AAA Inspector Notes:** A display case of mouthwatering cheesecakes is the first thing visitors see as they walk through the door. The extensive menu incorporates many types of cuisine, including Asian, Italian, Greek and Spanish. **Bar:** full bar. **Address:** 1350 Stoneridge Mall Rd 94588 **Location:** I-580 exit San Ramon Rd, just s; in Stoneridge Mall. Ⓟ West Dublin/Pleasanton, 28.

FAZ
925/460-0444

▼▼▼ Mediterranean. Fine Dining. $10-$28 **AAA Inspector Notes:** The attractive dining area looks out onto the exterior gardens and hotel pool area. On the menu are creative, freshly grilled meats and pasta specialties. **Bar:** full bar. **Reservations:** suggested. **Address:** 5121 Hopyard Rd 94588 **Location:** I-580 exit Hopyard Rd, just s. Ⓟ Dublin-Pleasanton, 29.

FERNANDO'S MEXICAN RESTAURANT
925/846-5740

▼▼ Mexican. Casual Dining. $9-$20 **AAA Inspector Notes:** In the heart of the historic district, the convenient downtown spot entices guests with a wide selection of Mexican favorites. **Bar:** full bar. **Address:** 348 St. Mary St 94566 **Location:** Just w of Main St; in historic downtown. **Parking:** street only.

FONTINA RISTORANTE
925/462-9299

▼▼▼ Italian. Casual Dining. $18-$36 **AAA Inspector Notes:** In the historic downtown area, the restaurant presents a seasonally changing menu of Italian specialties that burst with fresh flavors. Patio seating is an option. **Bar:** full bar. **Reservations:** suggested. **Address:** 349 Main St, Suite 150 94566 **Location:** Between W Angela and Abbie sts; downtown. **Parking:** street only.

FRESH CHOICE 925/734-8186

American. Cafeteria. $9-$15 **AAA Inspector Notes:** The salad bar of salad bars, the casual restaurant invites patrons to make their own or try one of the already prepared varieties. Other items include freshly baked breads, pizza and soup, as well as make-your-own sundaes for dessert. **Bar:** beer & wine. **Address:** 2453 Stoneridge Mall Rd 94588 **Location:** I-580 exit Foothill Rd, 0.3 mi s, then 0.3 mi e on Canyon Way; in Stoneridge Mall. West Dublin/Pleasanton, 28. L D CALL M

GARDEN TERRACE 925/463-3330

American. Casual Dining. $12-$20 **AAA Inspector Notes:** Located just off the lobby, dine in a casual and relaxed atmosphere. Menu offerings include traditional favorites such as specialty salads, burgers, steaks and pasta dishes. **Bar:** full bar. **Address:** 5990 Stoneridge Mall Rd 94588 **Location:** Jct I-580 and 680, 0.5 mi sw; I-580 exit Foothill Rd, 0.3 mi s, then 0.3 mi e on Canyon Way; in Sheraton Pleasanton Hotel. West Dublin/Pleasanton, 28.

D CALL M

THE HOPYARD AMERICAN ALEHOUSE & GRILL
925/426-9600

American. Casual Dining. $8-$20 **AAA Inspector Notes:** The traditional sports bar and grill has a friendly and inviting atmosphere. A wide selection of beers on tap is offered. **Bar:** full bar. **Address:** 3015-H Hopyard Rd 94588 **Location:** I-680 exit Stoneridge Dr, 1.5 mi e, then 1.2 mi s; at Valley Ave. L D CALL M

THE HUNAN CHEF CHINESE RESTAURANT 925/484-0480

Chinese. Casual Dining. $7-$14 **AAA Inspector Notes:** A tradition in the area since the early 1980s, this spot offers diners a seat around a distinctive water fountain in the center of the dining room. Serving up a great selection of Chinese favorites in hearty portions, lunch specials include an appetizer. The famous hot and sour soup and entrée are offered at a great price. **Bar:** beer & wine. **Address:** 4285 Valley Ave 94566 **Location:** I-580 exit Santa Rita Rd, 2 mi s; in Valley Plaza Shopping Center. L D CALL M

P.F. CHANG'S CHINA BISTRO 925/224-9916

Chinese. Fine Dining. $10-$20 **AAA Inspector Notes:** Trendy, upscale decor provides a pleasant backdrop for New Age Chinese dining. Appetizers, soups and salads are a meal by themselves. Vegetarian plates and sides, noodles, meins, chicken and meat dishes are created from exotic, fresh ingredients. **Bar:** full bar. **Address:** 1330 Stoneridge Mall Rd 94588 **Location:** I-580 exit San Ramon Rd, just s; in Stoneridge Mall. West Dublin/Pleasanton, 28. L D CALL M

PLAYERS RESTAURANT AT THE CLUB 925/463-8000

American. Casual Dining. $10-$24 **AAA Inspector Notes:** The classy restaurant's casual atmosphere has made it a local favorite for many years. Diners are treated to views of the outside pool and patio. **Bar:** full bar. **Address:** 7050 Johnson Dr 94588 **Location:** In southeast quadrant of jct I-580 and 680; in Hilton Pleasanton at the Club. West Dublin/Pleasanton, 28.

B L D CALL M

ROUND TABLE PIZZA

Pizza. Casual Dining. $7-$28 **AAA Inspector Notes:** This casual, family-oriented pizza place features high-quality ingredients and dough rolled fresh daily. Distinctive specialty pizzas are piled high with toppings. **Bar:** beer & wine. L D

For additional information, visit AAA.com
LOCATIONS:
Address: 4855 Hopyard Rd, Suite C-1 94588 **Location:** Just n of Stoneridge Dr; in Gateway Shopping Center. Dublin-Pleasanton, 29. **Phone:** 925/847-0750
Address: 530 Main St 94566 **Location:** At W Neal St; downtown.
Phone: 925/461-0140

SENRO SUSHI 925/600-8040

Japanese Sushi. Casual Dining. $8-$22 **AAA Inspector Notes:** The menu here offers a variety of authentic Japanese cuisine. More than 60 specialty rolls are made while guests watch. Expect a friendly and casual atmosphere. **Bar:** beer & wine. **Address:** 30 W Neal St 94566 **Location:** I-580 exit Santa Rita Rd/Tassajara Rd, 3 mi s, then just e; in downtown area. L D CALL M

SOZO SUSHI 925/484-5588

Japanese Sushi. Casual Dining. $10-$17 **AAA Inspector Notes:** This popular restaurant serves up a great selection of udon, tempura and donburi. The sozo rolls offer the freshest seafood and are created by the sushi staff. **Bar:** beer & wine. **Address:** 2835 Hopyard Rd 94588 **Location:** I-580 exit Hopyard Rd, 2 mi s, at Valley Ave; in Rite Aid Shopping Center. L D CALL M

STRIZZI'S 925/484-9600

Italian. Casual Dining. $10-$16 **AAA Inspector Notes:** This spot is an area tradition for great Italian food served in a casual, relaxed atmosphere. Seafood and meat items are prepared on a wood fire grill and many specialty pasta dishes also are available. **Bar:** full bar. **Address:** 649 Main St 94566 **Location:** I-580 exit Santa Rita Rd, 3 mi s, at St. Mary St; in historic downtown. **Parking:** street only. L D CALL M

PLUMAS NATIONAL FOREST (C-3)

Elevations in the forest range from 1,000 ft. at Feather River Canyon to 8,372 ft. at the summit of Mount Ingalls. Refer to AAA maps for additional elevation information.

Plumas National Forest covers 1,162,863 acres in northern California, straddling the transition zone between two of the West's great mountain ranges, the Sierra Nevada and the Cascades. Although the Sierra block disappears under the younger volcanic rock of the Cascades on the forest's northern boundary near Lake Almanor, it is difficult to tell where one range ends and the other begins.

The mountains of the northern Sierra Nevada, which make up most of the forest lands, are neither as high nor as spectacular as those south of Lake Tahoe. Yet within these mountains are a history of hidden treasure and a wealth of scenery.

The forest's principal gem is the Feather River watershed. The Feather River has carved numerous canyons and ravines full of cascades and white water. Portions of the Middle Fork of the river and three of its tributaries have been designated Feather Falls Scenic Area. The centerpiece of this 15,000-acre scenic area is 640-foot Feather Falls, which is just above Lake Oroville and is the highest of the numerous waterfalls on the 93-mile-long Middle Fork of the Feather River—a designated wild and scenic river. Water from this forest creates the headwaters for the California state water system.

Because of the rugged terrain and dangerous rapids, canoeing and tubing are recommended only in the recreation zone. Hiking trails and campgrounds are located along the river. Near the headwaters of the South Fork is Little Grass Valley Lake Recreation Area, which offers swimming, fishing and camping.

An extensive network of roads crisscrosses the national forest. Routes such as the Feather River National Scenic Byway, which crosses the lowest pass in the Sierra Nevada, are a legacy of the gold rush era when towns like Rich Bar, Pulga and La Porte were flourishing mining camps. Anglers and hikers have replaced miners, frequenting such popular areas as Bucks Lake, Lake Davis, Frenchman Lake and Antelope Lake. Seventy-one miles of the Pacific Crest Trail run through the national forest.

Information about campgrounds and recreational opportunities is available at the District Ranger stations and the Forest Headquarters in Quincy. Maps and guides to the Pacific Crest Trail and the Feather Falls Scenic Area also are available at the headquarters. For more information contact Plumas National Forest, 159 Lawrence St., P.O. Box 11500, Quincy, CA 95971; phone (530) 283-2050 or TTY (530) 534-7984. *See Recreation Areas Chart.*

PLYMOUTH (E-3) pop. 1,005, elev. 1,086'

AMADOR FLOWER FARM is at 22001 Shenandoah School Rd. More than 1,000 varieties of day lilies are featured among the farm's 14 acres of gardens, which include landscaped demonstration gardens and a nursery. Fall is celebrated each October with a pumpkin patch and a corn maze. **Hours:** Daily 9-4, Mar.-Nov.; Thurs.-Sun. 9-4, rest of year. Closed Jan. 1, Thanksgiving and Christmas. **Cost:** Free. **Phone:** (209) 245-6660.

WINERIES

• **Sobon Estate** is 7.5 mi. n.e. of SR 49 at 14430 Shenandoah Rd. **Hours:** Daily 9:30-5, Apr.-Oct.; 9:30-4:30, rest of year. Closed Jan. 1, Easter, Thanksgiving and Christmas. **Phone:** (209) 245-6554.

• **Terra d'Oro Winery** is 1.6 mi. n.e. on Shenandoah Rd., then 2 mi. s.e. on Shenandoah School Rd. **Hours:** Tastings daily 10-4:30. Tours are given Fri.-Sun. at noon and 2. Closed Easter and Christmas. **Phone:** (209) 245-6942.

SHENANDOAH INN   (209)245-4491

Hotel
$99-$149

Address: 17674 Village Dr 95669 **Location:** On SR 49, south end of town. **Facility:** 46 units. 2 stories (no elevator), exterior corridors. **Terms:** check-in 4 pm, 3 day cancellation notice. **Pool(s):** outdoor. **Activities:** whirlpool, exercise room.

POINT ARENA (E-1) pop. 449, elev. 220'

• **Attractions map p. 566**
• **Part of Wine Country area — see map p. 562**

POINT ARENA LIGHTHOUSE AND MUSEUM are 1 mi. n.w. on SR 1, then 2.4 mi. w. on Lighthouse Rd. The 115-foot-tall, steel-reinforced concrete lighthouse opened in 1908 to replace the 1870 structure that was destroyed by the 1906 earthquake; guided tours are available. The point is a popular spot from which to watch migrating whales. Historical items are displayed in the adjacent maritime museum. **Hours:** Daily 10-4:30, Memorial Day weekend-Labor Day; 10-3:30, rest of year. Closed Thanksgiving and Christmas. **Cost:** $7.50; $1 (ages 6-12); $25 (per car, maximum of eight people). **Phone:** (707) 882-2777 or (877) 725-4448.

WHARF MASTER'S INN   (707)882-3171

Hotel $105-$395 **Address:** 785 Port Rd 95468 **Location:** 1 mi w on Iversen Ave from jct SR 1; at wharf. **Facility:** 26 units, some houses. 2-3 stories (no elevator), exterior corridors. **Terms:** 2 night minimum stay - seasonal and/or weekends, 3 day cancellation notice-fee imposed.

POINT REYES NATIONAL SEASHORE (C-7)
• Part of San Francisco area — see map p. 342

Twenty-two miles north of San Francisco along SR 1, the blunt headlands of Point Reyes National Seashore jut into the sea. Grass-tufted dunes lie along miles of secluded beaches. Inland are rolling hills, freshwater lakes and Inverness Ridge, where the Douglas fir, typical of the northern California coastal ranges, and the Bishop pine of the southern forest areas merge. More than 350 species of birds and 72 species of mammals inhabit Point Reyes National Seashore's 65,300 acres. Fragile tide pool life can be observed at several locations.

Park headquarters is at Bear Valley, .25 miles west of Olema on Bear Valley Road. The headquarters is adjacent to the seashore's main visitor center, Bear Valley Visitor Center, which provides information about facilities and nature trails and has exhibits dealing with the park's natural and cultural heritage. The visitor center is open Mon.-Fri. 9-5, Sat.-Sun. 8-5. Closed Christmas.

Kenneth C. Patrick Visitor Center, off Sir Frances Drake Boulevard at Drakes Beach, is open Sat.-Sun. 10-5. Closed Christmas. Exhibits at this visitor center provide information about maritime exploration and marine environments; phone (415) 669-1250.

Lighthouse Visitor Center, at the end of Sir Frances Drake Boulevard, is open Thurs.-Mon. 10-4:30. Closed Christmas. The visitor center, which has exhibits about wildflowers, whales and lighthouses, is a .4-mile, mostly uphill, walk from the parking lot; phone (415) 669-1534.

Point Reyes Lighthouse shares the rocky headland with the Lighthouse Visitor Center. Hours of operation are the same (weather permitting). Visitors must descend 300 narrow steps from an observation deck to reach the oceanfront beacon, built in 1870. The lens room is open 2:30-4. The stairs to the lighthouse are closed if sustained winds reach 40 mph or greater.

Near the park headquarters are the Morgan Horse Ranch, a working ranch with exhibits about the breed; Kule Loklo, a replica of a Coast Miwok Indian village; the Pierce Ranch, a former dairy ranch with self-guiding trail exhibits; and the Earthquake Trail. At the end of Mesa Road is the Point Reyes Bird Observatory. Bird-banding demonstrations are given Saturday and Sunday mornings.

Popular activities include hiking, bird-watching, beachcombing, kayaking, bicycling, picnicking and swimming. Two of the more accessible beaches are Drakes Beach, near the Drakes Beach Visitor

Center, and Limantour Beach, at the end of Limantour Road, where shorebirds and harbor seals frequently can be seen. Panoramic views are available at many observation spots and overlooks; from some locations it is possible to spot harbor seals, sea lions and migrating gray whales.

More than 140 miles of hiking and horseback riding trails fan out from the Bear Valley trailhead. Some 35 miles of trails are open to bicyclists; trail maps are available at the visitor centers. Hikers and campers should carry a canteen, since the stream water is not potable. Pets are barred from all trails and campgrounds, but may be taken to North and South beaches and a portion of Limantour Beach if leashed.

Point Reyes National Seashore lies along a scenic stretch of SR 1 that extends from Leggett south to Sausalito. Varied programs are conducted, and the park has four hike-in campgrounds. The required permits can be obtained at Bear Valley Visitor Center; phone (877) 444-6777 for camping reservations. Camping is $20 per night for up to six people; reservations are highly recommended on weekends and in summer. The park is open all year. All sites are closed Christmas. Admission to the national seashore is free. For additional information contact the Superintendent, Point Reyes National Seashore, 1 Bear Valley Rd., Point Reyes, CA 94956; phone (415) 464-5137. *See Recreation Areas Chart.*

POLLOCK PINES pop. 6,871

BEST WESTERN STAGECOACH INN   (530)644-2029

Motel
$99-$139

AAA Benefit: Members save up to 20%, plus 10% bonus points with Best Western Rewards®.

Address: 5940 Pony Express Tr 95726 **Location:** US 50 exit 57 (Pollock Pines) eastbound, just n, then 1 mi e; exit Sly Park Rd westbound, just n, then 1 mi w. **Facility:** 26 units. 2 stories (no elevator), exterior corridors. **Terms:** 2 night minimum stay - seasonal. **Amenities:** high-speed Internet. **Pool(s):** heated outdoor. **Free Special Amenities:** expanded continental breakfast and high-speed Internet.

 CALL 🛏 BIZ 🛎 📶 🍴 🖥 / SOME UNITS FEE 🐾

PORTOLA (D-4) pop. 2,104, elev. 4,850'

Portola is intersected by the Union Pacific Railroad and the Middle Fork of the Feather River. Nearby Lake Davis is a favorite trout-fishing spot.

WESTERN PACIFIC RAILROAD MUSEUM is .6 mi. s. of SR 70 on CR A15 (Gulling St.), then w. to 700 Western Pacific Way. Housed in a former Western Pacific diesel shop, it displays more than 140 locomotives and railcars, including a 1950 streamline diesel and a Union Pacific Centennial, billed as the world's largest diesel locomotive. Railroad artifacts also can be seen. Train rides are offered. For an additional fee, the Run-A-Locomotive program offers rail fans the opportunity to operate a locomotive.

Time: Allow 1 hour minimum. **Hours:** Daily 10-5, early Apr.-early Nov.; open weather permitting rest of year. Phone ahead to confirm winter hours. Caboose train rides Sat.-Sun. 11-4, Memorial Day weekend-Labor Day; phone to confirm train schedule. **Cost:** $8; $4 (ages 4-18); $20 (family, two adults and children). All-day train ride $4; $10 (family, two adults and children). Run-A-Locomotive $150-$275; advance reservations are required. **Phone:** (530) 832-4131. 🚇

PULLMAN INN   (530)832-0107

Bed & Breakfast $55-$90 **Address:** 256 Commercial St 96112 **Location:** Just s of SR 70 via Gulling St (CR A15), then just w. **Facility:** 6 units. 2 stories (no elevator), interior corridors. **Terms:** closed 12/15-4/15, age restrictions may apply, cancellation fee imposed. 🖨 🍴 📶 ✕ 🖥

SLEEPY PINES MOTEL   530/832-4291

Vintage Motel $67-$140 **Address:** 74631 Hwy 70 96122 **Location:** 1 mi w of center on SR 70. **Facility:** This vintage roadside motel features basic, compact accommodations. The owners have a very large collection of bird houses displayed throughout the property. 15 units. 1 story, exterior corridors. **Terms:** 3 day cancellation notice. **Activities:** basketball. 📶 🛏 🖥 🖥 / SOME UNITS FEE 🐾 🎾

QUINCY (C-3) pop. 1,728, elev. 3,432'
• Restaurants p. 286

Quincy is nestled against the western slope of the Sierra Nevada range, at the top of the scenic Feather River Canyon. Settlement began in the mid-19th century, and Main Street is lined with restored buildings dating from the late 19th and early 20th centuries, many of them decorated with colorful murals depicting local history.

Quincy Chamber of Commerce: 464 W. Main St., Quincy, CA 95971. **Phone:** (530) 283-0188.

Self-guiding tours: A walking tour of Quincy's preserved and renovated downtown begins at the Plumas County Museum, which also has a brochure and map describing historic sites along the way.

PLUMAS COUNTY MUSEUM, 500 Jackson St., displays historical documents and photographs; permanent and rotating exhibits; cultural and natural history displays that illustrate area history since the 1850s; mining, logging and railroad exhibits; and woven baskets and artifacts from the native Maidu Indians. The restored 1878 Victorian Coburn-Variel House next to the museum is furnished to depict a middle-class lifestyle representative of the era. **Time:** Allow 30 minutes minimum. **Hours:** Tues.-Sat. 10-4. Phone for Coburn-Variel House schedule. Closed major holidays. **Cost:** $2; $1 (ages 12-17). **Phone:** (530) 283-6320.

THE FEATHERBED   530/283-0102

Bed & Breakfast
$110-$175

Address: 542 Jackson St 95971 **Location:** Just s of Blue Lakes Rd and SR 70; corner of Court and Jackson sts; downtown. Located behind the courthouse. **Facility:** Located on the town's square, this Queen Anne-style home features a large, Greco-Roman-influenced veranda that's perfect for relaxing and people-watching. 7 units, some cottages. 2 stories (no elevator), interior/exterior corridors. **Terms:** 14 day cancellation notice. **Activities:** bicycles. **Free Special Amenities:** full breakfast and room upgrade (subject to availability with advance reservations). 🖨 🍴 📶 ✕ / SOME UNITS 🅦 🖥

HASKINS VALLEY INN
530-283-9667

Bed & Breakfast
$129-$159

Address: 16788 Bucks Lake Rd 95971 **Location:** 16 mi sw of center. **Facility:** Built specifically as a B&B, this four-season inn in the snow country features gourmet meals and close proximity to a matrix of snowmobile passes. 6 units. 2 stories (no elevator), interior corridors. **Terms:** age restrictions may apply, 14 day cancellation notice-fee imposed. **Free Special Amenities:** full breakfast and high-speed Internet.

LARIAT LODGE
530-283-1000

Motel
$65-$98

Address: 2370 E Main St 95971 **Location:** 3 mi e of center on SR 70/89. **Facility:** 19 units, some two bedrooms. 1 story, exterior corridors. **Terms:** 3 day cancellation notice-fee imposed, resort fee. **Pool(s):** outdoor. **Free Special Amenities:** newspaper and high-speed Internet.

WHERE TO EAT

PANGEA CAFE & PUB
530/283-0426

Natural/Organic. Casual Dining. $4-$12 **AAA Inspector Notes:** This café offers a little something for everyone. A large selection of vegan and vegetarian options, burritos, sandwiches and salads are featured. A majority of the menu items are made from organic, fresh and local ingredients. In addition to the great food, they also take pride in offering patrons an ever changing selection of draft beer and wine. **Bar:** beer & wine. **Address:** 461 W Main St 95971 **Location:** Downtown. **Parking:** street only. L D CALL M

RANCHO CORDOVA (E-3) pop. 64,776, elev. 90'
• Restaurants p. 287
• Hotels & Restaurants map & index p. 314

NIMBUS FISH HATCHERY is .7 mi. n. of US 50 on Hazel Ave., then w. on Gold Country Blvd. to 2001 Nimbus Rd. On the American River, the hatchery raises chinook salmon and steelhead trout for release into the Sacramento River system. Visitors can see the raceway ponds where the fish are raised, the fish ladder used during spawning season, and a visitor center with a videotape presentation and exhibits about the fish, ecology and conservation. A .25-mile trail runs downstream from the fish ladder.

Time: Allow 1 hour minimum. **Hours:** Fish ladder daily 7:30-3 when salmon are running (generally Nov.-Feb.). Visitor center open Mon.-Fri. 8-3, Sat.-Sun. 9-3. Closed Christmas. Phone ahead to confirm schedule. **Cost:** Free. **Phone:** (916) 358-2884.

SACRAMENTO CHILDREN'S MUSEUM is at 2701 Prospect Park Dr. next to Rancho Cordova's city hall. Geared to children up to age 8, the museum provides hands-on learning activities and exploration opportunities. Waterways is an area where kids can get wet as they experiment with the flow of water with toy boats. In My Neighborhood they can enjoy storytelling and have fun role playing, and in Airways and Raceways see what friction, gravity and acceleration are all about.

Time: Allow 30 minutes minimum. **Hours:** Tues.-Sat. and Mon. holidays 9-5, Sun. noon-5. **Cost:** $7; $6 (ages 60+ and military with ID); free (under 1). **Phone:** (916) 638-7225.

COURTYARD BY MARRIOTT
(916)638-3800 **81**

Hotel
$62-$139

AAA Benefit: AAA hotel discounts of 5% or more.

Address: 10683 White Rock Rd 95670 **Location:** US 50 exit Zinfandel Dr, just s, then just w. **Facility:** 145 units. 3 stories, interior corridors. **Pool(s):** heated outdoor. **Activities:** whirlpool, exercise room. **Guest Services:** valet and coin laundry. **Free Special Amenities:** newspaper and high-speed Internet.

(See map & index p. 314.)

EXTENDED STAYAMERICA-SACRAMENTO-WHITE ROCK RD
(916)635-2363 **79**

Extended Stay Hotel $69-$84 **Address:** 10721 White Rock Rd 95670 **Location:** US 50 exit Zinfandel Dr, just s. **Facility:** 132 efficiencies. 3 stories, exterior corridors. **Guest Services:** coin laundry.

FAIRFIELD INN & SUITES BY MARRIOTT (916)858-8680 **77**

Hotel $69-$139 **Address:** 10745 Gold Center Dr 95670 **Location:** US 50 exit Zinfandel Dr, just s to White Rock Rd, just e, then just n; jct Gold Center Dr. **Facility:** 104 units. 4 stories, interior corridors. **Amenities:** high-speed Internet, safes. **Pool(s):** outdoor. **Activities:** whirlpool, exercise room. **Guest Services:** valet and coin laundry.

AAA Benefit: AAA hotel discounts of 5% or more.

HAMPTON INN BY HILTON (916)638-4800 **76**

Hotel $99-$159 **Address:** 10755 Gold Center Dr 95670 **Location:** US 50 exit Zinfandel Dr, just s to White Rock Rd, just e, then just n. **Facility:** 86 units. **Terms:**

AAA Benefit: Members save up to 10%!

1-7 night minimum stay, cancellation fee imposed. **Pool(s):** heated indoor. **Activities:** whirlpool, exercise room. **Guest Services:** valet laundry.

HOLIDAY INN RANCHO CORDOVA (916)635-4040 **71**

Hotel $99-$149 **Address:** 11269 Point East Dr 95742 **Location:** US 50 exit Sunrise Blvd S, e on Folsom Blvd, then just n. Located near light rail. **Facility:** 122 units, some two bedrooms. 3 stories, interior corridors. **Terms:** cancellation fee imposed, resort fee. **Amenities:** high-speed Internet. **Pool(s):** outdoor. **Activities:** sauna, whirlpool, exercise room. **Guest Services:** complimentary and valet laundry.

HYATT HOUSE SACRAMENTO/RANCHO CORDOVA
(916)638-4141 **72**

Hotel
$79-$169

AAA Benefit: Members save 10% or more everyday.

Address: 11260 Point East Dr 95742 **Location:** US 50 exit Sunrise Blvd S, e on Folsom Blvd, then just n. Located near light rail. **Facility:** 156 units, some two bedrooms and kitchens. 3 stories, interior corridors. **Terms:** cancellation fee imposed. **Amenities:** high-speed Internet. **Pool(s):** heated outdoor. **Activities:** whirlpool. **Guest Services:** valet and coin laundry, area transportation-within 5 mi. **Free Special Amenities:** expanded continental breakfast and high-speed Internet.

HYATT PLACE SACRAMENTO/RANCHO CORDOVA
(916)635-4799 **78**

Hotel
$89-$219

HYATT PLACE

AAA Benefit: Members save 10% or more everyday.

Address: 10744 Gold Center Dr 95670 **Location:** U5 50 exit Zinfandel Dr, just s on Zinfandel Dr, just e on White Rock Rd, just n on Prospect Park Dr, then just w. **Facility:** 127 units. 6 stories, interior corridors. **Terms:** cancellation fee imposed. **Amenities:** Some: high-speed Internet. **Pool(s):** heated outdoor. **Activities:** exercise room. **Guest Services:** valet laundry, area transportation-within 5 mi. **Free Special Amenities:** expanded continental breakfast and high-speed Internet.

LA QUINTA INN & SUITES SACRAMENTO RANCHO CORDOVA (916)638-1111 **74**

Hotel $59-$151 **Address:** 11131 Folsom Blvd 95670 **Location:** US 50 exit Sunrise Blvd, just s, then just w. **Facility:** 131 units. 5 stories, interior corridors. **Amenities:** video games (fee), high-speed Internet. **Pool(s):** outdoor. **Activities:** whirlpool, exercise room. **Guest Services:** coin laundry.

RED LION INN 916/631-7500 **80**

Hotel. Rates not provided. **Address:** 10713 White Rock Rd 95670 **Location:** US 50 exit Zinfandel Dr, just s, then just w. **Facility:** 109 units. 3 stories, interior/exterior corridors. **Amenities:** high-speed Internet. **Pool(s):** heated outdoor. **Activities:** exercise room. **Guest Services:** valet and coin laundry.

RESIDENCE INN BY MARRIOTT (916)851-1550 **75**

Extended Stay Hotel $90-$250 **Address:** 2779 Prospect Park Dr 95670 **Location:** US 50 exit Zinfandel Dr, just s to White Rock Rd, just e, then just n; jct Gold Center Dr. **Facility:** 90 units, some two bedrooms, efficiencies and kitchens. 3 stories, interior corridors. **Pool(s):** heated indoor. **Activities:** whirlpool, sports court, exercise room. **Guest Services:** valet and coin laundry.

AAA Benefit: AAA hotel discounts of 5% or more.

SACRAMENTO MARRIOTT RANCHO CORDOVA
(916)638-1100 **73**

Hotel
$99-$229

Marriott
HOTELS & RESORTS

AAA Benefit: AAA hotel discounts of 5% or more.

Address: 11211 Point East Dr 95742 **Location:** US 50 exit Sunrise Blvd, just s, then just e. **Facility:** This property offers attractively appointed and spacious guest units. The pool is surrounded by a well-tended garden and a water feature. 264 units. 11 stories, interior corridors. **Amenities:** video games, high-speed Internet (fee). **Pool(s):** heated outdoor. **Activities:** whirlpool, exercise room. **Guest Services:** complimentary and valet laundry, area transportation-within 5 mi. **Free Special Amenities:** use of on-premises laundry facilities.

WHERE TO EAT

ANDY NGUYEN'S 2 916/362-2270 **106**

Vietnamese Vegetarian. Casual Dining. $9-$14 **AAA Inspector Notes:** Since 1984, this restaurant has been serving Vietnamese and vegetarian foods. Complete Vietnamese dinners and house specials are featured. **Bar:** beer & wine. **Address:** 10145 Folsom Blvd 95670 **Location:** US 50 exit 15 (Mather Field Rd), just n, then just sw; jct La Loma Dr.

Plan.
Map.
Go.
TripTik® Travel Planner
AAA.com and CAA.ca

(See map & index p. 314.)

BROOKFIELDS   916/638-2046 (104)
♥♥ American. Casual Dining. $8-$16 **AAA Inspector Notes:**
Since 1981, this family-friendly restaurant has been serving burgers,
sandwiches, salads, a few south-of-the-border favorites and a good
selection of entrées and fresh-baked pies. Breakfast is served all day.
An awning-covered patio is available in season. Servers are polite
and friendly. **Bar:** beer & wine. **Address:** 11135 Folsom Blvd 95670
Location: US 50 exit Sunrise Blvd, just s, then just w.

[B] [L] [D] CALL &M

CATTLEMENS   916/985-3030
♥♥ American. Casual Dining. $13-$32 **AAA Inspector Notes:**
The Western décor enhances the experience of dining on Harris
Ranch corn-fed natural beef. Aged, hand-cut, tender steaks are the
main feature here. A few seafood and chicken dishes round out the
menu. Each entrée includes an all-you-can-eat salad. Weeknight
specials are offered. **Bar:** full bar. **Address:** 12409 Folsom Blvd
95670 **Location:** US 50 exit Hazel Ave, just s to Folsom Blvd, then
just e; in Nimbus Winery Complex. [D]

CORDOVA RESTAURANT CASINO   916/293-7470 (105)
♥♥ American. Casual Dining. $8-$26 **AAA Inspector Notes:**
This distinctive restaurant, with a contemporary lodge décor which includes a stone fireplace, features dining on one side and table games
on the other; food also can be brought to the gaming tables. Aged
beef, seafood, pasta, and burgers are served. Ninety-
nine beers are offered. Breakfast anytime. The nonsmoking casino is
open 24 hours. Patio dining is offered in season. **Bar:** full bar. **Address:** 2801 Prospect Park Dr 95670 **Location:** SR 50 exit Zinfandel
Dr, just s, just e on White Rock Rd, then just n. [D]

[B] [L] [D] [LATE] CALL &M

SHEEPHERDER BAR & GRILLE   916/638-4584 (103)
♥♥ American. Casual Dining. $9-$25 **AAA Inspector Notes:**
Originally built in 1913 as the Citrus Inn, this spot is the oldest existing
building in Rancho Cordova. Restored and nicely decorated, a cozy
fireplaces completes the ambience. A variety of entrées and more ca-
sual fare is served, including pasta, fish, sandwiches and salads.
Bar: full bar. **Reservations:** suggested. **Address:** 11275 Folsom
Blvd 95742 **Location:** SR 50 exit Sunrise Blvd, just s, then just e.

[L] [D] CALL &M

RED BLUFF (C-2) pop. 14,076, elev. 304'
• Restaurants p. 290

Named for the colored sand and gravel cliffs characteristic of the surrounding area, Red Bluff is a
gateway to Lassen Volcanic National Park *(see
place listing p. 171).*

The area's Western heritage is remembered each
April at the ♥♥ Red Bluff Roundup. In addition to a
traditional rodeo, attendees can enjoy a parade, wild
horse races, a chili cook-off and live entertainment.

**Red Bluff-Tehama County Chamber of Com-
merce:** 100 Main St., P.O. Box 850, Red Bluff, CA
96080. **Phone:** (530) 527-6220.

GAUMER'S JEWELRY AND MUSEUM is off I-5 exit
649 (SR 36W) at 78 Belle Mill Rd. This jewelry shop
features a wide variety of gems in unique settings,
many made by Gaumer's jewelers.

The museum has displays of gems, minerals,
crystals, fossils and Native American artifacts. A reproduction of a mine entrance—with an ore car used
by the owner's grandfather as well as tracks and
mining equipment—also can be seen. **Hours:** Mon.-
Fri. 9-5 (also Sat. 10-5, Dec. 1-Christmas). Closed
major holidays. **Cost:** Free. **Phone:** (530) 527-6166.

SALMON VIEWING PLAZA, .1 mi. e. of I-5 exit 649
on SR 36, then 2 mi. s. on Sale Ln., is at Diversion
Dam on the Sacramento River. Underwater television cameras monitor the fish ladders. There is no
viewing mid-September to mid-May. The plaza has
exhibits about salmon as well as camping, picnicking and boat-launching facilities.

Hours: Viewing plaza open daily 6 a.m.-8 p.m.,
mid-May to mid-Sept. River ramp closed in Aug.
Cost: Free. **Phone:** (530) 527-3043, (530)
527-2813 for camping information, or (530)
527-1196 for the Discovery Center. [▲] [⚎]

WILLIAM B. IDE ADOBE STATE HISTORIC PARK,
1 mi. n. on Adobe Rd., has an 1850 adobe that is a
memorial to the founder and president of the short-
lived California Republic. In 1846 rumors that
Mexican authorities were about to expel American
settlers compelled Ide to join a band of settlers in
the Bear Flag Revolt. Subsequently, California became an independent country with Ide as its president for 24 days until the Mexican War began and
the area was occupied by U.S. troops.

Hours: Park open daily dawn-dusk. Visitor center
open Thurs.-Sun. 10-4 when staff is available.
Phone ahead to confirm schedule. **Cost:** Day use
$6 per private vehicle; $5 (ages 62+ per private vehicle). **Phone:** (530) 529-8599. [⚎]

BEST WESTERN PLUS ANTELOPE INN

(530)527-8882

Hotel
$92-$150

AAA Benefit: Members save up to 20%, plus 10% bonus points with Best Western Rewards®.

Address: 203 Antelope Blvd 96080 **Location:** I-5 exit 649 (SR 36), just e. **Facility:** 67 units. 2 stories (no elevator), interior corridors. **Amenities:** Some: high-speed Internet. **Pool(s):** outdoor. **Guest Services:** coin laundry. **Free Special Amenities:** full breakfast and high-speed Internet. (See ad this page.)

/SOME UNITS FEE

COMFORT INN

(530)529-7060

Hotel
$80-$155

Address: 90 Sale Ln 96080 **Location:** I-5 exit 649 (SR 36), 0.3 mi e. **Facility:** 67 units. 3 stories, interior corridors. **Terms:** cancellation fee imposed. **Amenities:** high-speed Internet, safes (fee). **Pool(s):** outdoor. **Activities:** whirlpool, exercise room. **Guest Services:** coin laundry.

/SOME UNITS FEE

HAMPTON INN & SUITES

(530)529-9916

Hotel
$99-$109

AAA Benefit: Members save up to 10%!

Address: 520 Adobe Rd 96080 **Location:** I-5 exit 650 (Adobe Rd), then w. **Facility:** 97 units. 3 stories, interior corridors. **Terms:** 1-7 night minimum stay, cancellation fee imposed. **Amenities:** high-speed Internet. **Pool(s):** heated outdoor. **Activities:** exercise room. **Guest Services:** valet and coin laundry. **Free Special Amenities:** full breakfast and high-speed Internet.

SPORTSMAN LODGE

(530)527-2888

Motel
$55-$150

Address: 768 Antelope Blvd 96080 **Location:** I-5 exit 649 (SR 36), 1.5 mi e. Located near fairgrounds. **Facility:** 19 units. 1 story, exterior corridors. Bath: shower only. **Terms:** 1-3 night minimum stay, 3 day cancellation notice-fee imposed. **Pool(s):** outdoor. **Free Special Amenities:** local telephone calls and high-speed Internet.

SUPER 8 RED BLUFF

(530)529-2028

Motel
$55-$135

Address: 30 Gilmore Rd 96080 **Location:** I-5 exit 649 (SR 36), just w, then just s. **Facility:** 57 units. 2 stories (no elevator), exterior corridors. **Pool(s):** outdoor. **Guest Services:** coin laundry. **Free Special Amenities:** continental breakfast and high-speed Internet.

/SOME UNITS FEE

Give the gift of security, value and peace of mind: Gift Membership

▼ See AAA listing this page ▼

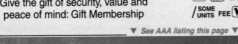

Antelope Inn
203 Antelope Blvd.
Red Bluff, CA. 96080
Ph.530-527-8882

Microwave - Refrigerator
Coffee/Tea maker I-pod Clock
Iron/Ironing Board - Pillow Top mattress
37" LED/LCD T.V. with 4 HBO,ESPN & CNN
High Speed internet Access

Outdoor Pool - Guest Laundry
Fax/Photo copy Services
Free RV/Truck Parking
Wake Up Calls
24 Hour Front Desk
Ice/Vending Machines

PETS WELCOME

1-800-WESTERN
www.bestwesternredbluff.com
From I-5, Take Antelope Blvd. Exit. # 649
Located Behind McDonald's

Each Best Western Branded Hotel is independently owned and operated

AAA MOBILE WEB
EVERYTHING AAA 24/7
From your smartphone: AAA.mobi • CAA.mobi

WHERE TO EAT

CASA RAMOS   530/527-2684

 Mexican. Casual Dining. $8-$17 **AAA Inspector Notes:** A varied Mexican menu is featured in a colorful atmosphere. Mexican favorites include fajitas, enchiladas, burritos and specialty steak and seafood entrees. **Bar:** full bar. **Address:** 2001 N Main St 96080 **Location:** I-5 exit 650 (Adobe Rd), just w, then just s.

L D CALL M

GREEN BARN STEAKHOUSE   530/527-3161

Steak. Casual Dining. $10-$29 **AAA Inspector Notes:** This restaurant emphasizes steak on a menu that also lists pasta and chicken dishes. Prime rib is served after 5 pm on Fridays and Saturdays. Courteous servers circulate through the dining room and around the patio. **Bar:** full bar. **Reservations:** suggested. **Address:** 5 Chestnut Ave 96080 **Location:** I-5 exit 649 (SR 36), 1 mi e.

L D

M & M RANCH HOUSE   530/527-1420

Steak. Casual Dining. $7-$25 **AAA Inspector Notes:** In addition to the wide variety of steaks, this restaurant brings in patrons on Friday and Saturday night for the prime rib offering. **Bar:** beer & wine. **Address:** 645 Antelope Blvd, Suite 1 96080 **Location:** I-5 exit 649 (SR 36), 1.3 mi e; in Frontier Village.   B L D

REDCREST pop. 89

REDCREST RESORT   (707)722-4208

Cabin
$80-$275

Address: 26459 Ave of the Giants 95569 **Location:** US 101 exit Redcrest southbound; exit Redcrest/Holmes northbound, just e, then just n. **Facility:** 11 cabins. 1 story, exterior corridors. **Bath:** shower only. **Terms:** 14 day cancellation notice-fee imposed. **Activities:** whirlpool, hiking trails, horseshoes, volleyball.

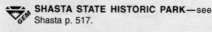

 / SOME UNITS FEE

REDDING (C-2) pop. 89,861, elev. 560'

• Hotels p. 291 • Restaurants p. 294

Redding, in the center of a year-round recreation area, provides scenic access via I-5 to the surrounding Shasta-Trinity National Forests *(see place listing p. 518)* and Whiskeytown-Shasta-Trinity National Recreation Area *(see place listing p. 557)*.

The Sundial Bridge at Turtle Bay *(see attraction listing)*, which crosses the Sacramento River in the center of town, serves as both a local landmark and as a connector to hiking and bicycling trails, including the Sacramento River National Recreation Trail, a 10-mile path that runs along both sides of the Sacramento River. There are scenic views of the river from benches along the shady trail. Trail users might catch a glimpse of beavers, otters, turtles and deer.

Redding Convention & Visitors Bureau: 777 Auditorium Dr., Redding, CA 96001. **Phone:** (530) 225-4100 or (800) 874-7562.

SHASTA DAM—see Shasta Lake p. 518.

SHASTA STATE HISTORIC PARK—see Shasta p. 517.

TURTLE BAY EXPLORATION PARK is off SR 44W (Sundial Bridge Dr.) to Auditorium Dr. (exit 1), then n. to the park entrance. This 300-acre interpretive park explores the region's people,

cultures and natural resources. Within the complex are the Turtle Bay Museum, with regional history, art and natural science exhibits; Paul Bunyan's Forest Camp, a children's area with a logging theme; an arboretum and garden; and Parrot Playhouse, a walk-through aviary where the resident lorikeets will eat nectar right out of a cup. The glass-decked Sundial Bridge connects the park's two campuses.

Also featured are railroad and changing exhibits, a visitor center and a boardwalk. On site is the Monolith, the remains of the aggregate plant that processed gravel used to make concrete for the construction of nearby Shasta Dam in the early 1940s. Segway tours of the park are offered.

Hours: Complex open Mon.-Sat. 9-5, Sun. 10-5, early Apr. to mid.-Sept.; Wed.-Sat. 9-4, Sun. 10-4, rest of year. Parrot Playhouse open daily 9:30-11:45 and 1-5. Closed Jan. 1, Thanksgiving and Christmas. Phone ahead to confirm schedule. **Cost:** $14 (includes arboretum and garden, forest camp and museum); $10 (ages 4-12 and 65+). An additional fee may be charged for special exhibits. **Phone:** (530) 243-8850 or (800) 887-8532.

McConnell Arboretum & Botanical Gardens is accessible from Turtle Bay Exploration Park's east entrance at the north plaza of the Sundial Bridge and from the west entrance of the park off Arboretum Dr. The 200-acre arboretum features 1.5 miles of trails through an oak savannah and a riparian forest, while the 20-acre botanical gardens consist of 12 areas, including gardens representing the Mediterranean basin, California, Australia, South Africa and Chile.

Among the other gardens are an area specially for children and one devoted to medicinal plants. **Hours:** Daily 7-7. Closed Jan. 1, Thanksgiving and Christmas. **Cost:** Included with Turtle Bay Exploration Park fee. Arboretum and gardens only $4; free (ages 0-3).

Parrot Playhouse is in the Paul Bunyan's Forest section of Turtle Bay Exploration Park. This walk-through aviary is inhabited by Australian lorikeets so tame they'll perch on your arms, head and hand in exchange for a sip from a cup of nectar. An attendant is on hand to answer questions about these colorful, playful members of the parrot family and will also provide a towel for clean-up if you happen to get hit by droppings launched from one of the free-flying birds.

Hours: Daily 9:30-11:45 and 1-5. Closed Jan. 1, Thanksgiving, Christmas and Mon. and Tues. during the winter months. **Cost:** $1 (in addition to Turtle Bay Park admission). Aviary admission includes one cup of nectar; additional cups $1 each. **Phone:** (530) 243-8850.

Paul Bunyan's Forest Camp, in Turtle Bay Exploration Park, has a working model of the Sacramento River, play equipment for children, ecology and logging displays, a maze and a forest trail. Wings of Summer Butterflies! features hundreds of free-flying butterflies within a tranquil enclosed garden. **Hours:** Mon.-Sat. 9-5, Sun. 10-5, early Apr. to mid-Sept.; Wed.-Sat. 9-4, Sun. 10-4, rest of year. Butterfly house open Mon.-Sat. 9:30-3:30, Sun. 10:30-3:30. Closed Jan. 1, Thanksgiving and Christmas. **Cost:** Included with Turtle Bay Exploration Park admission.

Shasta Glide 'n Ride is at 844 Auditorium Dr. in Turtle Bay Exploration Park, following signs. Segway transportation devices are the means of conveyance for a 1-hour, 2.25-mile guided Arboretum Glide that takes participants over the park's Sundial Bridge and along a section of the Sacramento River Trail around the McConnell Arboretum. Other tours also are offered, including one in the evening. A brief training session precedes the tour. Helmets and a communications system are provided.

Note: Height and weight restrictions apply. The company plans to relocate to the new hotel under construction in Turtle Bay Exploration Park; phone ahead to confirm location. **Time:** Allow 1 hour, 15 minutes minimum. **Hours:** Departures require a minimum of two people. Tours depart Wed.-Mon. Closed Jan. 1 and Christmas. **Cost:** Tours range from $25 to $65. Arboretum Glide $35. Under 14 years are not permitted. Under 18 must be accompanied by a parent or guardian. Advance reservations are required. **Phone:** (530) 242-1150 or (866) 466-4111.

Sundial Bridge at Turtle Bay spans the Sacramento River, linking Turtle Bay Exploration Park's two campuses. Designed by noted Spanish architect and engineer Santiago Calatrava, the artistic sundial design features a glass deck that is illuminated at night. The steel, glass and granite suspension bridge, 700 feet long, transports only foot traffic and features public plazas at each end. The bridge's pylon and cables create changing shapes, shadows and angles depending on the viewpoint. **Hours:** Daily 24 hours. **Cost:** Free.

Turtle Bay Museum, in Turtle Bay Exploration Park, has exhibits that examine the relationship between man and nature. At the Visible River visitors can view native fish species from an underwater perspective. Historical dioramas, Native American displays, science experiments and art exhibits also explore the man/nature theme.

Hours: Mon.-Sat. 9-5, Sun. 10-5, early Apr. to mid-Sept.; Wed.-Sat. 9-4, Sun. 10-4, rest of year. Closed Jan. 1, Thanksgiving and Christmas. Phone ahead to confirm schedule. **Cost:** Included with Turtle Bay Exploration Park admission.

WATERWORKS PARK, 151 N. Boulder Dr., has three flume rides, thrill rides like the Cyclone and the Awesome Avalanche, the Raging River inner tube ride, an activity pool and a children's pool with slides and a fountain. A new enclosed flume slide, the Dragon, is expected to open sometime in 2013.

Lockers and dressing rooms are available. **Hours:** Daily 10-6 (also Tues. 6-8 p.m.), Memorial Day weekend-Labor Day. Hours may be reduced in early June and late Aug. Phone ahead to confirm schedule. **Cost:** $19; $15 (under 48 inches tall); $5 (ages 63+); free (ages 0-2). Reduced admission rates apply beginning 3 hours before closing. **Phone:** (530) 246-9550.

BAYMONT INN & SUITES REDDING (530)722-9100

Hotel
$84-$140

Address: 2600 Larkspur Ln 96002 **Location:** I-5 exit 677 (Cypress Ave), just e, then just s. **Facility:** 84 units. 2 stories, interior corridors. **Amenities:** high-speed Internet. **Pool(s):** heated indoor. **Activities:** whirlpool, limited exercise equipment. **Free Special Amenities: expanded continental breakfast and high-speed Internet.**

BEST WESTERN PLUS HILLTOP INN (530)221-6100

Hotel
$129-$169

Best Western PLUS

AAA Benefit: Members save up to 20%, plus 10% bonus points with Best Western Rewards®.

Address: 2300 Hilltop Dr 96002 **Location:** I-5 exit 677 (Cypress Ave), just e, then just n. **Facility:** 114 units. 2 stories (no elevator), exterior corridors. **Terms:** cancellation fee imposed, resort fee. **Dining:** C.R. Gibbs American Grill, see separate listing. **Pool(s):** heated outdoor. **Activities:** whirlpool, exercise room. **Guest Services:** valet and coin laundry. **Free Special Amenities: local telephone calls and high-speed Internet.**

BEST WESTERN PLUS TWIN VIEW INN & SUITES
(530)241-5500

Hotel
$89-$149

Best Western PLUS

AAA Benefit: Members save up to 20%, plus 10% bonus points with Best Western Rewards®.

Address: 1080 Twin View Blvd 96003 **Location:** I-5 exit 681 (Twin View Blvd), just w. **Facility:** 79 units. 2 stories, interior corridors. **Amenities:** *Some:* high-speed Internet. **Pool(s):** outdoor. **Activities:** whirlpool, exercise room. **Guest Services:** valet and coin laundry. **Free Special Amenities: expanded continental breakfast and high-speed Internet.**

BRIDGE BAY RESORT (530)275-3021

Motel
$85-$190

Address: 10300 Bridge Bay Rd 96003 **Location:** I-5 exit 690, just w. Located on Shasta Lake. **Facility:** 40 units, some kitchens. 2 stories (no elevator), exterior corridors. **Terms:** 3 day cancellation notice. **Pool(s):** outdoor. **Activities:** rental boats, fishing. **Fee:** marina, waterskiing.

COMFORT INN (530)221-4472

Hotel
$90-$145

Address: 850 Mistletoe Ln 96002 **Location:** I-5 exit 677 (Cypress Ave), 0.8 mi n on Hilltop Dr. then just e. **Facility:** 70 units. 3 stories, interior corridors. **Terms:** cancellation fee imposed. **Amenities:** high-speed Internet. **Pool(s):** outdoor. **Activities:** whirlpool, exercise room. **Guest Services:** coin laundry.

FAIRFIELD INN & SUITES BY MARRIOTT   (530)243-3200

 Contemporary Hotel
$109-$159 **Address:** 5164 Caterpillar Rd 96003 **Location:** I-5 exit 681 (Twin View Blvd) northbound; exit 681B southbound, just w, then just n. **Facility:** 72 units. 3 stories, interior corridors. **Amenities:** high-speed Internet. **Pool(s):** heated outdoor. **Activities:** whirlpool, exercise room. **Guest Services:** valet and coin laundry.

AAA Benefit: AAA hotel discounts of 5% or more.

⟦ⁱ↑⟧ CALL ⟦&M⟧ ⟦≈⟧ ⟦BIZ⟧ ⟦🛜⟧ ⟦✕⟧ ⟦▣⟧ / SOME UNITS FEE ⟦🐾⟧ ⟦🛗⟧ ⟦🖼⟧

FAWNDALE LODGE & RV RESORT   530/275-8000

 Motel. Rates not provided. **Address:** 15215 Fawndale Rd 96003 **Location:** I-5 exit 689 (Fawndale Rd), just e, then 0.3 mi s; 10 mi n of town; 1 mi s of Shasta Lake. **Facility:** 7 units, some two bedrooms and kitchens. 1 story, exterior corridors. *Bath:* shower only. **Pool(s):** heated outdoor. **Activities:** whirlpool, game room, horseshoes, volleyball. **Guest Services:** coin laundry.

⟦≈⟧ ⟦🛜⟧ ⟦✕⟧ ⟦🛗⟧ ⟦🖼⟧ ⟦▣⟧ / SOME UNITS FEE ⟦🐾⟧

HAMPTON INN & SUITES   (530)224-1001

Hotel
$139-$189

 AAA Benefit: Members save up to 10%!

Address: 2160 Larkspur Ln 96002 **Location:** I-5 exit 677 (Cypress Ave), just e, then just n. **Facility:** 80 units. 3 stories, interior corridors. **Terms:** 1-7 night minimum stay, cancellation fee imposed. **Amenities:** high-speed Internet. **Pool(s):** heated outdoor. **Activities:** whirlpool, exercise room. **Guest Services:** valet and coin laundry.

⟦SAVE⟧ ⟦ⁱ↑⟧ CALL ⟦&M⟧ ⟦≈⟧ ⟦BIZ⟧ ⟦🛜⟧ ⟦🛗⟧ ⟦🖼⟧ ⟦▣⟧

Safety tip:
Keep a current AAA/CAA
Road Atlas in every vehicle

HILTON GARDEN INN REDDING   (530)226-5111

 Hotel
$129-$149

 **AAA Benefit:** Unparalleled hospitality at a special Member rate.

Address: 5050 Bechelli Ln 96002 **Location:** I-5 exit 675 (Bechelli Ln/Bonnyview Rd/Churn Creek), just w. **Facility:** 93 units. 3 stories, interior corridors. **Terms:** 1-7 night minimum stay, cancellation fee imposed. **Amenities:** high-speed Internet. **Pool(s):** heated outdoor. **Activities:** whirlpool, exercise room. **Guest Services:** valet and coin laundry, area transportation-casino & River Tasalmi Golf Course. **Free Special Amenities:** high-speed Internet and airport transportation. *(See ad this page.)*

⟦SAVE⟧ ⟦✈⟧ ⟦ⁱ↑⟧ ⟦Y⟧ ⟦≈⟧ ⟦BIZ⟧ ⟦🛜⟧ ⟦🛗⟧ ⟦🖼⟧ ⟦▣⟧

HOLIDAY INN   (530)221-7500

 Hotel
$115-$185

Address: 1900 Hilltop Dr 96002 **Location:** I-5 exit 677 (Cypress Ave), just e, then 0.8 mi n. **Facility:** 125 units. 2 stories, interior corridors. **Amenities:** high-speed Internet. **Pool(s):** outdoor. **Activities:** whirlpool, exercise room. **Guest Services:** valet and coin laundry. **Free Special Amenities:** newspaper and high-speed Internet.

⟦SAVE⟧ ⟦✈⟧ ⟦ⁱ↑⟧ ⟦Y⟧ ⟦≈⟧ ⟦BIZ⟧ ⟦🛜⟧ ⟦🛗⟧ ⟦▣⟧ / SOME UNITS FEE ⟦🐾⟧ ⟦🖼⟧

OXFORD SUITES   (530)221-0100

 Hotel
$99-$159

Address: 1967 Hilltop Dr 96002 **Location:** I-5 exit 677 (Cypress Ave), just e, then just n. **Facility:** 139 units, some two bedrooms. 3-4 stories, interior/exterior corridors. **Terms:** cancellation fee imposed. **Amenities:** high-speed Internet. **Pool(s):** heated outdoor. **Activities:** whirlpool, exercise room. **Guest Services:** valet and coin laundry, area transportation-within 5 mi.

⟦SAVE⟧ ⟦✈⟧ ⟦ⁱ↑⟧ CALL ⟦&M⟧ ⟦≈⟧ ⟦BIZ⟧ ⟦🛜⟧ ⟦✕⟧ ⟦🛗⟧ ⟦🖼⟧ ⟦▣⟧ / SOME UNITS FEE ⟦🐾⟧

▼ See AAA listing this page ▼

QUALITY INN

(530)221-6530

Motel

$73-$76

Address: 2059 Hilltop Dr 96002 **Location:** I-5 exit 677 (Cypress Ave), just e, then 0.4 mi n. **Facility:** 90 units. 2-3 stories (no elevator), exterior corridors. **Terms:** cancellation fee imposed. **Pool(s):** outdoor. **Free Special Amenities:** expanded continental breakfast and high-speed Internet.

Get pet travel tips and enter the photo contest at AAA.com/PetBook

▼ See AAA listing p. 294 ▼

Travelodge

AAA Approved Lodging

Shasta County's only

Travelodge
in Redding, CA

FEATURES
- Pillow-top Queen & King Beds
- FREE sit-down BREAKFAST
- Outdoor Pool open all year
- Indoor Spa/Fitness Room
- Non-smoking (all rooms)
- Fridges & Microwaves (all rooms)

AMENITIES
- FREE Hi-Speed Internet
- In-room Coffee
- Free local calls
- Express Check-in/out
- Enhanced cable & HBO
- Guest Laundry
- AAA/Senior Discounts

Get the free mobile app at
http://gettag.mobi

1-800-243-1106

"Redding's Best Kept Lodging Secret"

540 North Market Street - Redding, Ca. 96003
530-243-5291 - 800-243-1106 Reservations • www.reddingtravelodge.com

Find thousands of places to show your

card and save at AAA.com/discounts

REDDING TRAVELODGE   (530)243-5291

Hotel
$85-$209

Address: 540 N Market St 96003 **Location:** I-5 exit 680 (Lake Blvd) northbound, 0.5 mi w to Market St, then 0.5 mi s; exit Market St southbound, 2 mi s. **Facility:** 42 units, some two bedrooms and kitchens. 2 stories (no elevator), exterior corridors. **Pool(s):** heated outdoor. **Activities:** whirlpool, exercise room. **Guest Services:** coin laundry. **Free Special Amenities:** full breakfast and high-speed Internet. *(See ad p. 293.)*

SAVE 🛗 CALL 🗲M 🛄 BIZ
📶 🚪 📺 ▭
/ SOME UNITS FEE 🐾

RED LION HOTEL REDDING   (530)221-8700

Hotel $109-$189 **Address:** 1830 Hilltop Dr 96002 **Location:** I-5 exit SR 44 (Hilltop Dr) southbound, just e, then just s; exit 677 (Cypress Ave) northbound, just e, then 0.6 mi n. **Facility:** 192 units. 2 stories (no elevator), interior corridors. **Terms:** cancellation fee imposed. **Amenities:** Some: high-speed Internet. **Pool(s):** outdoor. **Activities:** whirlpool, exercise room. **Guest Services:** valet laundry, area transportation-bus & train stations.

✈ 🛗 🍽 CALL 🗲M 🛄 📶 ✕ ▭
/ SOME UNITS FEE 🐾 🚪 📺

TIFFANY HOUSE BED & BREAKFAST   (530)244-3225

Bed & Breakfast $125-$170 **Address:** 1510 Barbara Rd 96003 **Location:** I-5 exit 680 (Lake Blvd), 0.5 mi w to Market St, 0.7 mi s, just w on Benton Dr, then just n; jct Nancy Ct. Located in a residential neighborhood. **Facility:** A canopy of aged oaks adds a tranquil ambiance to this 1930s home offering a pool and views of Lassen Peak from its hilltop location. The Victorian Parlor features 19th-century antiques. 4 units, some cottages. 2 stories (no elevator), interior/exterior corridors. **Terms:** check-in 4 pm, 5 day cancellation notice-fee imposed. **Pool(s):** outdoor.

🛗 🛄 📶 ✕ 🎦 📷

TOWNEPLACE SUITES   530/223-0690

[fyi] **Extended Stay Hotel.** Rates not provided. Too new to rate, opening scheduled for December 2012. **Address:** 2180 Larkspur Ln 96002 **Location:** I-5 exit 677 (Cypress Ave).
Amenities: 101 units, pets, coffeemakers, microwaves, refrigerators, pool, exercise facility.

AAA Benefit: AAA hotel discounts of 5% or more.

WHERE TO EAT

BLACK BEAR DINER   530/221-7600

American. Casual Dining. $7-$15 **AAA Inspector Notes:** A homey atmosphere characterizes this family-oriented restaurant. Familiar comfort foods, such as meatloaf with mashed potatoes, are at the heart of the menu and are served in generous portions. **Bar:** beer & wine. **Address:** 2605 Hilltop Dr 96002 **Location:** I-5 exit 677 (Cypress Ave E), just e. B L D

BUZ'S CRAB RESTAURANT & SEAFOOD MARKET   530/243-2120

Seafood. Casual Dining. $5-$80 **AAA Inspector Notes:** Since 1968, this casual eatery has been serving up a variety of seafood prepared in several different ways. Seafood baskets, salads, burgers, hot sandwiches and charbroiled seafood entrées are offered. **Bar:** beer & wine. **Address:** 2159 East St 96001 **Location:** I-5 exit SR 44, 1.4 mi w, then 0.6 mi s. L D CALL 🗲M

CASA RAMOS   530/224-7223

Mexican. Casual Dining. $8-$17 **AAA Inspector Notes:** A varied Mexican menu is featured in a colorful atmosphere. Mexican favorites include fajitas, enchiladas, burritos and specialty steak and seafood entrees. **Bar:** full bar. **Address:** 995 Hilltop Dr 96003 **Location:** I-5 exit 677 (Cypress Ave), just e, then 1.3 mi n; jct Browning St. L D

CATTLEMENS   530/221-6295

Steak. Casual Dining. $13-$30 **AAA Inspector Notes:** Since 1968, this Western-style California restaurant chain has been serving aged and hand-cut Harris corn-fed natural beef. Ribs, chicken and a few seafood items also are available. Each entrée includes all-you-can-eat salad, ranch-style beans and choice of potato. Friendly servers can be expected. **Bar:** full bar. **Reservations:** suggested. **Address:** 2184 Hilltop Dr 96002 **Location:** I-5 exit 677 (Cypress Ave), just e, then just n. D

C.R. GIBBS AMERICAN GRILL   530/221-2335

American
Casual Dining
$9-$29

AAA Inspector Notes: Servers deliver tasty entrées, brick oven pizza, sandwiches and a few lighter items at this restaurant. Two can share the chocolate wedge, a delicious dessert that comes highly recommended. Patio dining is a nice option in season. Sunday brunch is offered from 10-2. **Bar:** full bar. **Reservations:** suggested. **Address:** 2300 Hilltop Dr 96002 **Location:** I-5 exit 677 (Cypress Ave), just e, then just n; in BEST WESTERN PLUS Hilltop Inn. L D CALL 🗲M

GIRONDA'S CHICAGO STYLE RESTAURANT & BAR   530/244-7663

Italian
Casual Dining
$12-$20

AAA Inspector Notes: Veal, family-style salads, pasta and ravioli, beef, chicken, thin and deep dish pizza and stuffed pizza pies are served, along with fresh bread and a savory dipping oil. A good selection of California and Italian wines are offered. Dine in, take-out, or delivery all are available. **Bar:** full bar. **Address:** 1100 Center St 96001 **Location:** Corner of Trinity and Center sts; downtown; just n of Eureka Way overpass (SR 299) and Center St. L D

MARITIME SEAFOOD & GRILL   530/229-0700

Seafood. Fine Dining. $19-$36 **AAA Inspector Notes:** The casual and elegant setting at this restaurant blends well with the French and California inspired menu which offers such items as duck paté, oysters, grilled salmon steak, pork tenderloin and delicious seasonal desserts. **Bar:** full bar. **Address:** 1600 California St 96001 **Location:** At Placer and California sts; downtown. **Parking:** street only. D CALL 🗲M

NELLO'S PLACE   530/223-1636

Italian. Casual Dining. $15-$34 **AAA Inspector Notes:** Since 1980, this establishment has been offering authentic Italian cuisine-including seafood, veal and chicken dishes-all served in a dark and cozy romantic ambience. The service is attentive and a few menu items are prepared tableside. **Bar:** full bar. **Reservations:** suggested. **Address:** 3055 Bechelli Ln 96002 **Location:** I-5 exit 677 (Cypress Ave), just w, then just s; just s of jct Hartnell Ave. D CALL 🗲M

PUERTO VALLARTA   530/244-2941

Mexican. Casual Dining. $7-$17 **AAA Inspector Notes:** A tropical ambience and an extensive menu is offered at this eatery. **Bar:** full bar. **Address:** 2315 Eureka Way 96001 **Location:** From SR 273, 0.7 mi w on SR 299 (Eureka Way); at Orange and Eureka ways. L D

REDWOOD CITY (E-8) pop. 76,815, elev. 15'

- Restaurants p. 296
- Hotels & Restaurants map & index p. 410

Lathrop House, in the county government center at 627 Hamilton St., was moved to its present site in 1905 and survived the earthquakes of 1906 and 1989. The restored 1863 house, built by Benjamin Lathrop, is an example of early Gothic Revival architecture and is furnished in period. Two floors feature period clothing and changing exhibits. Phone (650) 365-5564 for information about house tours.

Redwood City-San Mateo County Chamber of Commerce: 1450 Veterans Blvd., Suite 125, Redwood City, CA 94063. **Phone:** (650) 364-1722.

SAN MATEO COUNTY HISTORY MUSEUM is at 2200 Broadway. Housed in a 1910 building that was formerly a courthouse, the museum's permanent exhibits depict the history of the San Francisco Peninsula beginning with the Ohlone Indians. Nature's Bounty explains the utilization of the area's natural resources. A courtroom, in use until 1998, retains the witness stand, judge's bench and jury box. Other exhibits include a 40-foot virtual wave known as Maverick's Waverider and History Making Entrepreneurs, which surveys companies like Electronic Arts and Intel.

Time: Allow 1 hour minimum. **Hours:** Tues.-Sun. 10-4. Closed Jan. 1, Easter, Thanksgiving and Christmas. **Cost:** $5; $3 (ages 62+ and students with ID). **Phone:** (650) 299-0104.

AMERICA'S BEST INN & SUITES   (650)369-1731 90

Motel
$79-$100

Address: 1090 El Camino Real 94063 **Location:** US 101 exit 409 (Whipple Ave), just s on Veterans Blvd, 0.4 mi w on Whipple Ave, then 0.7 mi s. **Facility:** 39 units. 2 stories (no elevator), exterior corridors. **Terms:** cancellation fee imposed. **Pool(s):** outdoor. **Free Special Amenities:** continental breakfast and high-speed Internet.

  CALL   FEE

ATHERTON INN   (650)474-2777 96

 Bed & Breakfast $139-$259 **Address:** 1201 W Selby Ln 94061 **Location:** US 101, 2 mi w on Woodside Rd (SR 84), 0.3 mi s on Nimitz Ave to W Selby Ln, then just w. Located in a residential neighborhood. **Facility:** A replica of a French chateau on the Brittany coast, this inn is conveniently located one block from Atherton. 5 units. 2 stories, interior corridors. **Terms:** age restrictions may apply, 3 day cancellation notice. **Amenities:** high-speed Internet. **Guest Services:** complimentary laundry.

BEST WESTERN PLUS EXECUTIVE SUITES   (650)366-5794 95

Motel
$89-$179

AAA Benefit: Members save up to 20%, plus 10% bonus points with Best Western Rewards®.

Address: 25 5th Ave 94063 **Location:** US 101 exit SR 84, 1 mi w, 1.5 mi s on SR 82, then just e. **Facility:** 29 units. 2 stories (no elevator), exterior corridors. **Amenities:** high-speed Internet. **Activities:** sauna, whirlpool, steamroom, exercise room. **Guest Services:** valet and coin laundry. **Free Special Amenities:** local telephone calls and high-speed Internet.

BEST WESTERN PLUS INN   (650)366-3808 89

Motel
$105-$165

AAA Benefit: Members save up to 20%, plus 10% bonus points with Best Western Rewards®.

Address: 316 El Camino Real 94062 **Location:** US 101 exit Whipple Ave, 0.5 mi w to SR 82, then 0.3 mi n. **Facility:** 31 units. 2 stories (no elevator), exterior corridors. **Amenities:** *Some:* high-speed Internet. **Pool(s):** outdoor. **Guest Services:** valet laundry. **Free Special Amenities:** expanded continental breakfast and high-speed Internet.

  CALL

COMFORT INN BY CHOICE HOTELS   (650)599-9636 91

Hotel
$130-$160

Address: 1818 El Camino Real 94063 **Location:** US 101 exit Whipple Ave, 0.5 mi w to SR 82, then 1 mi s. **Facility:** 51 units, some efficiencies. 2 stories, interior corridors. **Terms:** cancellation fee imposed. **Pool(s):** heated outdoor. **Activities:** sauna. **Guest Services:** valet laundry. **Free Special Amenities:** continental breakfast and high-speed Internet.

  CALL

HOLIDAY INN EXPRESS REDWOOD CITY CENTRAL   (650)299-0909 92

Hotel $159-$209 **Address:** 1836 El Camino Real 94063 **Location:** US 101 N exit Woodside Rd W; US 101 S exit Whipple Ave, w to El Camino Real, then 1.5 mi s. **Facility:** 62 units. 2 stories, interior corridors. **Amenities:** high-speed Internet. **Activities:** exercise room. **Guest Services:** valet and coin laundry.

HOLIDAY INN EXPRESS REDWOOD CITY/MENLO PARK   650/366-2000 94

Hotel. Rates not provided. **Address:** 2834 El Camino Real 94061 **Location:** US 101 exit SR 84, 1 mi w, then 1 mi s on SR 82. **Facility:** 38 units. 2 stories (no elevator), exterior corridors. **Amenities:** high-speed Internet, safes. **Activities:** sauna, steamroom, exercise room. **Guest Services:** valet and coin laundry.

PACIFIC INN REDWOOD CITY   (650)368-1495 93

Motel
$79-$169

Address: 2610 El Camino Real 94061 **Location:** US 101 exit 408 (Woodside Rd/SR 84/Seaport Blvd), 1 mi w on Woodside Rd, then 0.4 mi s. **Facility:** 73 units, some two bedrooms, efficiencies and kitchens. 1-2 stories (no elevator), interior/exterior corridors. **Terms:** cancellation fee imposed. **Guest Services:** coin laundry. **Free Special Amenities:** full breakfast and use of on-premises laundry facilities.

SOFITEL SAN FRANCISCO BAY   (650)598-9000 87

Hotel
$110-$315

Address: 223 Twin Dolphin Dr 94065 **Location:** US 101 exit Marine Pkwy E, 0.5 mi s. **Facility:** The hotel's handsome lobby includes a restaurant and lounge; some units overlook a lagoon and bay. 421 units. 8 stories, interior corridors. **Parking:** on-site and valet. **Terms:** 7 day cancellation notice-fee imposed. **Amenities:** *Fee:* video games, high-speed Internet. *Some:* safes. **Pool(s):** heated outdoor. **Activities:** exercise room. *Fee:* massage. **Guest Services:** valet laundry, area transportation-within 5 mi.

 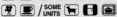

(See map & index p. 410.)

TOWNEPLACE SUITES BY MARRIOTT   (650)593-4100 88

▼▼▼▼ **Extended Stay Hotel**
$149-$249 **Address:** 1000 Twin Dolphin
Dr 94065 **Location:** US 101 exit Redwood Shores Pkwy, 0.3 mi e, then just s.
Facility: 95 kitchen units, some two bed-
rooms. 4 stories, interior corridors. **Amenities:** high-speed Internet.
Activities: whirlpool, exercise room. **Guest Services:** valet and coin
laundry.

AAA Benefit:
AAA hotel discounts
of 5% or more.

CALL ⓂⓂ 🛜 ☒ 🅱 🖨 🖥 / SOME UNITS FEE 🐾

WHERE TO EAT

HARRY'S HOFBRAU   650/366-3733 70

▼ American. Cafeteria. $5-$18 **AAA Inspector Notes:** This spacious, popular neighborhood restaurant offers well-made food at reasonable prices. Take a look at the mouth-watering comfort food and
choose before getting in line. Braised short ribs, chicken pot pie, ham
hocks and a carved turkey sandwich are all good choices. **Bar:** full
bar. **Address:** 1909 El Camino Real 94063 **Location:** US 101 N exit
Woodside Rd W; southbound exit Whipple Ave, w to El Camino Real,
then 1.5 mi s. L D

MILAGROS CANTINA RESTAURANT   650/369-4730 69

▼▼ Mexican. Casual Dining. $9-$20 **AAA Inspector Notes:** A
festive atmosphere at this restaurant with authentic Mexican decor
makes guests want to linger indoors amid numerous imported
Mexican art pieces or out on the patio. The menu specializes in entrées from various regions of Mexico. Try the tacos al pastor (roasted
adobo and pineapple marinated pork)-a bit tropical, a bit fiery and a
bit sweet. For dessert, the Mexican flan is rich and silky. **Bar:** full bar.
Address: 1099 Middlefield Rd 94061 **Location:** US 101 exit Whipple
Ave, 0.5 mi s on Veterans Blvd, then 0.5 mi w on Main St. **Parking:**
street only. L D

NEW KAPADOKIA   650/368-5500 68

▼▼ Turkish. Casual Dining. $8-$24 **AAA Inspector Notes:**
This bright and airy little restaurant specializes in home-style Turkish
dishes, including entrées that come with a choice of soup or salad. If
it is on the menu, try cevizli ezme, an appetizer made from pureed
red pepper paste, garlic and walnuts that goes well with the bread.
Service is casual and friendly. **Bar:** beer & wine. **Address:** 2399
Broadway St 94063 **Location:** US 101 exit 409, 0.7 mi se on Veterans Blvd, 0.3 mi s on Jefferson, then just w. **Parking:** street only.

 L D CALL ⓂⓂ

◆ REDWOOD NATIONAL AND
GEM STATE PARKS (B-1)

Elevations in the park range from sea level at
Crescent City to 3,262 ft. at an unnamed
peak. Refer to AAA maps for additional
elevation information.

Along the northern California coast between Crescent City and Orick, 302 miles north of San Francisco
on US 101, Redwood National and State Parks encompasses 131,983 acres. Within its boundaries are
the 55,400 combined acres of Del Norte Coast, Jedediah Smith and Prairie Creek Redwoods state parks
(see Recreation Areas Chart). In addition to dense forests of coast redwoods, the park embraces marshland, beaches, rugged coastline, rivers, streams,
prairies and oak woodlands.

General Information and Activities

The beaches are open all year, but visitors should
use caution when swimming or surfing. The coastline in Northern California is a dangerous combination of steeply descending beaches, heavy
undertows, very cold water and jagged, rocky
shoals. Visitors walking along the beaches should
be aware of the time of high tide and keep an eye
out for the unusually large, strong waves known as
"sneaker waves."

Coastal Drive, reached from US 101 exit 768
(Klamath Beach Road), is an 8-mile parade of spectacular coastal scenery. Lost Man Creek Road
passes through a beautiful redwood forest and offers access to .75-mile Lost Man Creek Trail. Both of
these scenic byways are not suitable for RV or
trailer travel.

Paved scenic routes include Requa Road, which
leads 4 miles up a steep grade from US 101 to the
Klamath River Overlook, 600 feet above the Pacific
Ocean. Enderts Beach Road connects US 101 near
Crescent City with the dramatic vistas of Crescent
Beach Overlook (see attraction listing). Both overlooks provide particularly good opportunities for
whale-watching. Newton B. Drury Scenic Parkway
(see attraction listing) through Prairie Creek Redwood State Park is a scenic alternate to US 101.

Some public roads also serve adjoining private
forest lands; logging truck traffic and other private
activities take place along some of the routes.

Trails traverse some 37 miles of wild and un-
touched coastline along rock promontories that protrude into the ocean, offering vistas of sea lion
colonies and migrating whales. Birds inhabit bluffs,
lagoons and offshore rocks; bird-watching is particularly rewarding during waterfowl migrations. More
than 170 miles of trails provide access to magnificent redwood groves.

The Coastal Trail extends 25 miles, nearly the entire length of the parks, through a variety of spectacular landscapes. Hikers will navigate bluffs and
pass through grasslands and along deserted
beaches, with frequent stretches descending into
dim glades created by coast redwood forests. The
trail can be accessed at various places within the
park, including the Crescent Beach Overlook at the
end of Enderts Beach Road; from Damnation Creek
Trail in Del Norte Coast Redwoods State Park; and
from near Fern Canyon, at the end of Davison Road
in Prairie Creek Redwoods State Park.

The park also contains 41 miles of horseback
riding trails and 33 miles of bicycle trails. Park staff
conduct free guided walks, evening programs and
other activities from mid-June through Labor Day.

Developed campgrounds are within the state
parks and along US 101 (the Redwood Highway).
Reservations are recommended in summer; phone
ReserveAmerica at (800) 444-7275. There also are
five primitive walk-in campsites in the national park,
although space is limited. Freshwater and surf
fishing are permitted; a California fishing license is
required. See Recreation Areas Chart.

The Crescent City Information Center is located
at Redwood National and State Parks Headquarters, 1111 2nd St. near the Crescent City waterfront;
phone (707) 465-7306.

ADMISSION to the national park is free. The state parks charge day use and overnight fees for developed picnicking and camping areas.

PETS must be kept under physical restraint while in the park and are prohibited on most trails. Campers are required to have proof of rabies shots for pets.

ADDRESS inquiries to the Superintendents, Redwood National and State Parks, 1111 2nd St., Crescent City, CA 95531-4198. Phone (707) 465-7765 or (707) 465-7335.

CRESCENT BEACH OVERLOOK is within Redwood National Park about 5 mi. s. of Crescent City via US 101 and Enderts Beach Rd. The overlook provides a stunning vantage point high above the Pacific. A half-mile-long trail leads down the bluffs to sandy Enderts Beach and also connects to the Coastal Trail. **Hours:** Daily 24 hours. **Cost:** Free.

DEL NORTE COAST REDWOODS STATE PARK, 7 mi. s. of Crescent City on US 101, contains 15 memorial redwood groves within its 31,400 acres. The growths extend down steep slopes almost to the ocean shore at Damnation Creek. Wildlife can be seen. Accessible from a turnout on US 101 at mile marker 16, Damnation Creek Trail descends 1,000 feet via switchbacks through primeval redwood forest to a starkly beautiful rocky beach. *See Recreation Areas Chart.*

Hours: Daily dawn-dusk. Phone ahead to confirm schedule. **Cost:** Day use $8 (per private vehicle); $7 (ages 62+ per private vehicle). **Phone:** (707) 465-2146, or (800) 444-7275 for camping reservations through ReserveAmerica. 🅰 ⊠ 🏠 ⛩

ELK MEADOW DAY USE AREA is in Redwood National Park 2 mi. n. of Orick, just off US 101 on Davison Rd. Named for the Roosevelt elk frequently seen grazing here, this area was allowed to return to a more natural state after being the site of a logging company. The 2.5-mile-long Trillium Falls Loop provides access to small but picturesque Trillium Falls. Beyond the day use area, Davison Road enters Prairie Creek Redwoods State Park and is unpaved; trailers are prohibited along this section. **Hours:** Daily 24 hours. **Cost:** Free.

JEDEDIAH SMITH REDWOODS STATE PARK is 9 mi. e. of Crescent City on US 199. Named for 19th-century fur trapper Jedediah Strong Smith, the state park includes a section of the lovely Smith River in addition to preserving thousands of acres of ancient redwoods. Trails accessible from turnouts on US 199 include the Hiouchi Trail and Hatton Loop.

Visitors can reach Stout Memorial Grove via Howland Hill Road, an unimproved stage route not suitable for RVs or trailers. *See Recreation Areas Chart.* **Hours:** Daily dawn-dusk. **Cost:** Day use $8 per private vehicle at developed parking lots; $7 (ages 62+ per private vehicle). **Phone:** (707) 465-7335. 🅰 ⊠ 🏠 ⛩

Hiouchi Information Center is on US 199 just outside the eastern entrance to Jedediah Smith Redwoods State Park. The center features exhibits about area wildlife and the coast redwood forest. **Hours:** Daily 9-6, mid-June to early Sept. **Phone:** (707) 458-3294.

Jedediah Smith Visitor Center is off US 199 just inside the eastern entrance to Jedediah Smith Redwoods State Park. Within the Jedediah Smith Campground, on the opposite side of US 199 from the Hiouchi Information Center, this center offers a few displays about the area's flora and fauna. Trails lead from the center to the Smith River, and in summer hikers can cross the seasonal footbridge and follow trails along Mill Creek and into Stout Memorial Grove. **Hours:** Daily 9-5. **Cost:** Free. **Phone:** (707) 458-3496.

LADY BIRD JOHNSON GROVE is 1 mi. n. of Orick, then 3 mi. e. on Bald Hills Rd. following signs. The grove features a 1-mile, self-guiding loop trail through a mature grove of coastal redwoods that passes a plaque marking the site where Lady Bird Johnson dedicated the park in 1968. A lush understory of rhododendrons and sword ferns grows here. **Note:** Bald Hills Road has many sharp turns; motor homes and trailers are not recommended. **Time:** Allow 1 hour minimum. **Hours:** Daily 24 hours. **Cost:** Free.

PRAIRIE CREEK REDWOODS STATE PARK is 6 mi. n. of Orick on US 101. A coastal redwood park consisting of 14,000 acres, it protects one of the last wild herds of native Roosevelt elks. Davison Road, off US 101, is a narrow, unpaved route between the base of Gold Bluffs and Gold Bluffs Beach; elk are frequently seen along the road, which leads to picturesque Fern Canyon.

The beach was the site of gold-mining operations in the 1850s. Guided nature hikes and campfire programs are conducted June 1-Labor Day. *See Recreation Areas Chart.* **Hours:** Daily 24 hours. **Cost:** Day use $8 per private vehicle; $7 (ages 62+ per private vehicle). **Phone:** (707) 465-7347. 🅰 ⊠ ⛩

Fern Canyon is off US 101 at the end of Davison Rd. in Prairie Creek Redwoods State Park. This gorge features 30-foot-high walls covered with delicate five-fingered and sword ferns. Water seeping from the walls keeps the luxuriant foliage moist and green throughout the year. A loop trail leads along one side and down into the canyon, although runoff sometimes floods the chasm's floor. The 4.5-mile James Irvine Trail connects Fern Canyon to the Prairie Creek Visitor Center.

Note: Trailers are prohibited on the narrow, unpaved road to the canyon. **Hours:** Daily dawn-dusk. **Cost:** Included in Prairie Creek Redwoods State Park admission. **Phone:** (707) 465-7347.

Newton B. Drury Scenic Parkway is off US 101 6 mi. n. of Orick in Prairie Creek Redwoods State

Park. The parkway, connected to US 101 at either end via interchanges, offers a beautifully scenic, 10-mile drive through an old-growth redwood forest, with huge trees often abutting the pavement. Several hiking trails as well as the Prairie Creek Visitor Center can be accessed from the parkway. From Big Tree Wayside, a short trail leads to a coast redwood more than 300 feet tall and estimated to be 1,500 years old. **Hours:** Daily 24 hours. **Cost:** Free.

Prairie Creek Visitor Center is off US 101 exit 753 near the southern end of Newton B. Drury Scenic Pkwy. Natural history exhibits focus on the coastal redwood environment. Several trailheads are located behind the center, including those for the James Irvine Trail to Fern Canyon and the Prairie Creek Trail to the Big Tree Wayside. **Hours:** Daily 9-5. Closed Jan. 1, Thanksgiving and Christmas. Phone ahead to confirm schedule. **Cost:** Free. **Phone:** (707) 488-2039.

THOMAS H. KUCHEL VISITOR CENTER is on US 101 w. of Orick, near the southern end of Redwood National Park. The center features displays about the national park, including one describing the restoration of land that has been extensively logged. A small theater shows videos about the coast redwoods, and a short interpretive trail leads through wetlands to the beach. **Hours:** Daily 9-5. Closed Jan. 1, Thanksgiving and Christmas. **Cost:** Free. **Phone:** (707) 465-7765.

REEDLEY (G-5) pop. 24,194, elev. 348'

KOREAN HERITAGE PAVILION is at 196 N. Reed Ave. The pavilion consists of a replica of the Korean Independence Gate (Dongnimmun) in Seoul, Korea, and 10 monuments honoring prominent Central California individuals who made important contributions to the Korean community. The Reedley area is considered to be the site of the first settlement of Korean-Americans in the U.S. mainland. **Time:** Allow 30 minutes minimum. **Hours:** Daily dawn-dusk. **Cost:** Free.

EDGEWATER INN (559)637-7777

Motel
$75-$79

Address: 1977 W Manning Ave 93654 **Location:** 12 mi e of SR 99 via Manning Ave. **Facility:** 48 units, some two bedrooms. 2 stories, exterior corridors. **Terms:** cancellation fee imposed. **Pool(s):** outdoor. **Activities:** whirlpool. **Free Special Amenities:** continental breakfast and high-speed Internet.

 SAVE · · · · · / SOME UNITS FEE

WHERE TO EAT

JON'S BEAR CLUB 559/638-2396

American. Casual Dining. $10-$24 **AAA Inspector Notes:** A good selection of steak, seafood and chicken dishes are served at this friendly restaurant where a relaxed setting adds to a nice overall dining experience. **Bar:** full bar. **Address:** 1695 E Manning Ave 93654 **Location:** Center. L D

RICHMOND (C-8) pop. 103,701

SS RED OAK VICTORY is 1.5 mi. s. off I-580 Canal Blvd. exit, following signs to 1337 Canal Blvd., Berth 6A. (**Note:** This is an active port area with heavy industrial equipment; the speed limit is 5 mph.) Launched in 1944 at the Kaiser Shipyards, the 455-foot-long cargo ship is the only one of the 747 vessels built at the shipyard that is being restored. The ship served in World War II, the Korean War and in Vietnam.

A reminder of the tremendous war effort provided by the Kaiser Shipyards in Richmond, the ship serves as a maritime museum depicting the wartime efforts of Richmond citizens and the shipbuilding skill of Henry J. Kaiser. The site is part of the Rosie the Riveter/WWII Home Front National Historical Park.

Docent-led tours provide access to the main deck, officer's mess hall, captain's office and stateroom, chart room, the engine and boiler chamber and the inside hold.

Note: Ship access requires being able to walk up a steep ramp and climb stairs. **Time:** Allow 1 hour minimum. **Hours:** Guided tours are given Tues., Thurs. and Sat.-Sun. 10-3. Last tour departs 1 hour before closing. Closed major holidays. Phone ahead to confirm schedule. **Cost:** $5; $2 (ages 0-4). **Phone:** (510) 237-2933.

COURTYARD BY MARRIOTT (510)262-0700

Hotel $149-$275 **Address:** 3150 Garrity Way 94806 **Location:** I-80 exit Hilltop Mall, just w on Hilltop Dr, just n on Blume Dr, then just w. Located near Hilltop Mall. **Facility:** 149 units. 5 stories, interior corridors. **Amenities:** high-speed Internet. **Pool(s):** heated outdoor. **Activities:** whirlpool, exercise room. **Guest Services:** valet laundry.

AAA Benefit: AAA hotel discounts of 5% or more.

HOTEL MAC 510/235-0010

Hotel $135-$195 **Address:** 10 Cottage Ave 94801 **Location:** I-580 exit Pt. Richmond/Richmond Pkwy via Castro St, just e on Tewksbury Ave to Washington Ave. **Facility:** 10 units. 3 stories, interior corridors. **Terms:** cancellation fee imposed. **Amenities:** safes. **Dining:** restaurant, see separate listing.

WHERE TO EAT

HOTEL MAC RESTAURANT 510/233-0576

Continental. Fine Dining. $13-$29 **AAA Inspector Notes:** In a nicely restored building downtown, this sophisticated restaurant presents a diverse menu including a crab melt sandwich, chicken club, braised short ribs, lamb and prime rib. **Bar:** full bar. **Reservations:** suggested. **Address:** 50 Washington Ave 94801 **Location:** I-580 exit Pt. Richmond/Richmond Pkwy via Castro St, just e on Tewksbury Ave to Washington Ave; in Hotel Mac. **Parking:** on-site and street. L D

SALUTE E VITA RISTORANTE AT MARINA BAY   510/215-0803

WWW Italian. Fine Dining. $12-$21 **AAA Inspector Notes:** Seats in this charming 100-year-old Cape Cod Victorian's attractive dining rooms look out over the marina. The menu blends traditional and modern dishes, each creatively prepared with fresh ingredients. A dining deck is an option in season. **Bar:** full bar. **Reservations:** suggested. **Address:** 1900 Esplanade Dr 94804 **Location:** I-580 exit Marina Bay Pkwy, 0.3 mi s to Regatta Blvd, just w to Melville Square, then just w; I-80 exit Cutting Blvd, 1.5 mi w, 1 mi s on 23rd St (which becomes Marina Bay Pkwy), just w on Regatta Blvd to Melville Square, then just w. [L] [D] CALL [&M]

RIO DELL pop. 3,368

HUMBOLDT GABLES MOTEL   (707)764-5609

WWW
Motel
$60-$135

Address: 40 W Davis St 95562 **Location:** US 101 exit Wildwood Ave, 0.5 mi w. **Facility:** 16 units. 1 story, exterior corridors. **Amenities:** high-speed Internet. **Guest Services:** coin laundry. **Free Special Amenities:** local telephone calls and high-speed Internet.

/ SOME UNITS FEE

RIO VISTA pop. 7,360

THE POINT WATERFRONT RESTAURANT   707/374-5400

WWW
Seafood
Casual Dining
$10-$30

AAA Inspector Notes: On the river, this restaurant offers docking facilities for guests who arrive by boat. The glassed-in garden room on the deck is ideal for brunch or lunch. The menu offers a nice selection of fresh seafood, broiled steaks and pasta. **Bar:** full bar. **Address:** 120 Marina Dr 94571 **Location:** 0.5 mi s of SR 12; adjacent to Sacramento River. [L] [D]

RIPON pop. 14,297

LA QUINTA INN & SUITES MANTECA - RIPON
(209)599-8999

WWW
Hotel
$83-$150

Address: 1524 Colony Rd 95366 **Location:** SR 99 exit Jack Tone Rd, just e. **Facility:** 60 units. 3 stories, interior corridors. **Amenities:** high-speed Internet. **Pool(s):** outdoor. **Activities:** whirlpool, exercise room. **Guest Services:** coin laundry. **Free Special Amenities:** full breakfast and high-speed Internet.

/ SOME UNITS

WHERE TO EAT

THE BARNWOOD RESTAURANT & CATERING   209/599-4324

WW American. Casual Dining. $8-$20 **AAA Inspector Notes:** This favorite stop of the local crowd offers a casual and relaxed atmosphere with a friendly staff. Menu selections that are sure to please everyone include grilled steak, burgers, pasta, fish, fried chicken and entrée salads. Specialty sandwiches include an Italian meatball sandwich. Be sure to save room for one of the homemade desserts. **Bar:** beer & wine. **Address:** 338 Main St 95366 **Location:** SR 99 exit Main St, just e. [B] [L] [D] CALL [&M]

ROCKLIN pop. 56,974
• Hotels & Restaurants map & index p. 314

DAYS INN - ROCKLIN   (916)632-0101 31

WW Hotel $55-$95 **Address:** 4515 Granite Dr 95677 **Location:** I-80 exit Rocklin Rd, just w, then just n. **Facility:** 65 units. 2 stories, exterior corridors. **Pool(s):** outdoor. **Activities:** sauna, whirlpool, limited exercise equipment. **Guest Services:** coin laundry.

HERITAGE INN EXPRESS, ROCKLIN   (916)632-3366 33

WWW Hotel $65-$75 **Address:** 4480 Rocklin Rd 95677 **Location:** I-80 exit Rocklin Rd, just w, then just s. **Facility:** 102 units. 3 stories, interior corridors. **Terms:** cancellation fee imposed, resort fee. **Amenities:** high-speed Internet. **Pool(s):** outdoor. **Activities:** whirlpool. **Guest Services:** coin laundry.

HOWARD JOHNSON HOTEL   (916)624-4500 32

WWW Hotel $59-$119 **Address:** 4420 Rocklin Rd 95677 **Location:** I-80 exit Rocklin Rd, just w, then just s. **Facility:** 124 units. 3 stories, interior corridors. **Amenities:** safes (fee). Some: high-speed Internet. **Pool(s):** heated outdoor. **Activities:** whirlpool, exercise room. **Guest Services:** coin laundry.

STAYBRIDGE SUITES   (916)781-7500 30

WWWW Extended Stay Hotel $99-$159 **Address:** 6664 Lonetree Blvd 95765 **Location:** SR 65 exit Blue Oaks Blvd, just e, just n to Redwood Dr, then just w; behind Blue Oaks Town Center (directly behind Petco). **Facility:** 98 efficiencies, some two bedrooms. 4 stories, interior corridors. **Terms:** cancellation fee imposed. **Amenities:** high-speed Internet. **Pool(s):** heated indoor. **Activities:** whirlpool, exercise room. **Guest Services:** complimentary and valet laundry.

WHERE TO EAT

ANATOLIAN TABLE TURKISH CUISINE & PATISSERIE
916/772-3020 29

WWW Turkish. Casual Dining. $9-$23 **AAA Inspector Notes:** Fresh, authentic and nicely prepared Turkish cuisine includes hot and cold appetizers that are great for sharing and sampling, in addition to pide (Turkish pizza), beverages from Turkey and the requisite kebabs. Made-in-house yogurt sauces enhance many dishes. Recommended for dessert is kunefe-shredded phyllo dough filled with unsalted cheese and topped with a house syrup. Belly dancing on Saturday nights from 6:30-8 pm. **Bar:** beer & wine. **Reservations:** suggested, for dinner Fri & Sat. **Address:** 6815 Lonetree Blvd, Suite 105 95765 **Location:** SR 65 exit Blue Oaks Blvd, just e, then just n; in Blue Oaks Marketplace. [L] [D] CALL [&M]

THE CHEF'S TABLE   916/771-5656 30

WWW American. Casual Dining. $10-$20 **AAA Inspector Notes:** Tucked away in a shopping center, this bistro and wine bar feature a creative, seasonally changing, small and large plate menu, as well as microbrews and distinctive wines. Sit at the wine bar and watch the food being prepared in the open kitchen. Reservations are suggested due to the limited number of tables, otherwise plan on dining at the bar. Lunch is served Tuesday through Friday. **Bar:** beer & wine. **Reservations:** suggested. **Address:** 6843 Lonetree Blvd, Suite 103 95765 **Location:** SR 65 exit Blue Oaks Blvd, just e, then just n; in Blue Oaks Marketplace. [L] [D] CALL [&M]

CRAZY SUSHI   916/771-4300 28

WWW Japanese Sushi. Casual Dining. $9-$25 **AAA Inspector Notes:** Tucked away in a shopping center, this restaurant offers a variety of appetizers, special rolls, sushi bar-style lunches and dinners and bento boxes. Arrive early on the weekends to avoid the nearby theater crowd. A patio is available in season. **Bar:** beer & wine. **Address:** 6696 Lonetree Blvd, Suite 700 95765 **Location:** SR 65 exit Blue Oaks Blvd, just e, then just n; in Blue Oaks Town Center. [L] [D] CALL [&M]

ICING ON THE CUPCAKE   916/315-9500 34

W American. Quick Serve. $3 **AAA Inspector Notes:** Made-from-scratch cupcakes are served at this busy spot and the creative cupcake menu offerings change daily. Enjoy your treat on the outside patio. **Address:** 5065 Pacific St 95677 **Location:** I-80 exit Rocklin Rd, 0.7 mi w, then just ne; jct Oak St. [L]

(See map & index p. 314.)

LUCILLE'S SMOKEHOUSE BAR-B-QUE & CATERING
916/780-7427 (26)

 Barbecue. Casual Dining. $11-$29 **AAA Inspector Notes:** Start the meal off at this popular California chain with complimentary, warm buttermilk biscuits with apple butter. Most meats are smoked for several hours over hickory wood and then slathered with barbecue sauce. Southern folk art adorns the walls. Live blues is offered on Saturday nights. A heated patio area is available. **Bar:** full bar. **Address:** 6628 Lonetree Blvd 95765 **Location:** SR 65 exit Blue Oaks Blvd, just e, then just n; in Blue Oaks Town Center. (L) (D)

POTTERY WORLD CAFE
916/624-8080 (32)

American. Casual Dining. $10-$16 **AAA Inspector Notes:** This local favorite is decorated with the charming décor from the adjacent store. Tasty preparations of soup, sandwiches and salads are offered. Tempting desserts are on display to tempt those with a sweet tooth. An attractive patio area has misters in season. Breakfast is served on the weekend starting at 9 a.m. while high tea is offered the first and third Thursday of each month. **Address:** 4419 Granite Dr 95677 **Location:** I-80 exit Rocklin Rd, just w, then just 0.9 mi n; in Pottery World. (L)

RUBINO'S RISTORANTE
916/624-3401 (33)

Italian. Casual Dining. $8-$27 **AAA Inspector Notes:** Located downtown, this local favorite offers delicious house specialties which include veal prepared several ways, seafood, steaks and traditional classic pasta dishes. A lunch buffet is offered Tuesday through Friday, along with the regular lunch menu. Early bird specials take place Sunday from 2 p.m. to 6 p.m. and Monday through Thursday 4 p.m. to 6 p.m. Enjoy Sunday brunch from 9:30 a.m. to 2 p.m. Prime rib is featured on Friday and Saturday evenings. Patio dining is a nice touch. **Bar:** full bar. **Reservations:** suggested. **Address:** 5015 Pacific St 95677 **Location:** I-80 exit Rocklin Rd, 0.6 mi w, then just n. (L) (D) CALL (&M)

SKIPOLINI'S PIZZA & PASTA
916/789-1818 (27)

Italian. Casual Dining. $7-$26 **AAA Inspector Notes:** This casual restaurant serves panini sandwiches, salads, pizza and pasta entrée selections. Save room for gelato that can be found in the gelato room inside the restaurant. An attractive outdoor patio houses an oversize TV and fireplace. **Bar:** beer & wine. **Address:** 6600 Lonetree Blvd 95765 **Location:** SR 65 exit Blue Oaks Blvd, just e, then just n; jct Grand Canyon Dr; in Blue Oaks Town Center. (L) (D) CALL (&M)

VENITA RHEA'S CAFE
916/624-2697 (31)

American. Casual Dining. $7-$15 **AAA Inspector Notes:** For more than 36 years, this Rocklin landmark cafe with a French countryside decor, has been dishing up tasty breakfasts, burgers, sandwiches and salads. The portions are large, so come hungry. Food is prepared with zero trans fat. **Address:** 4415 Granite Dr 95677 **Location:** I-80 exit Rocklin Rd, just w, then 0.7 mi n. (B) (L) CALL (&M)

ROHNERT PARK pop. 40,971

• Part of Wine Country area — see map p. 562

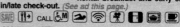

BEST WESTERN INN   (707)584-7435

Motel
$95-$104

AAA Benefit: Members save up to 20%, plus 10% bonus points with Best Western Rewards®.

Address: 6500 Redwood Dr 94928 **Location:** US 101 exit Rohnert Park Expwy, just w. **Facility:** 142 units. 2 stories (no elevator), exterior corridors. **Amenities:** *Some:* high-speed Internet. **Pool(s):** heated outdoor. **Activities:** whirlpool, exercise room. **Guest Services:** coin laundry. **Free Special Amenities:** expanded continental breakfast and early check-in/late check-out. *(See ad this page.)*

▼ See AAA listing this page ▼

DOUBLETREE BY HILTON SONOMA WINE COUNTRY
(707)584-5466

Hotel $129-$349 **Address:** One Doubletree Dr 94928 **Location:** US 101 exit Golf Course Dr; 3 mi s of Santa Rosa. **Facility:** 245 units. 3 stories, interior corridors. **Terms:** 1-7 night minimum stay, cancellation fee imposed. **Amenities:** high-speed Internet (fee). **Dining:** Bacchus Restaurant & Wine Bar, see separate listing. **Pool(s):** heated outdoor. **Activities:** whirlpool, sports court, exercise room. **Guest Services:** valet and coin laundry, area transportation-within 2 mi.

AAA Benefit:
Members save 5% or more!

GOOD NITE INN   707/584-8180

Motel. Rates not provided. **Address:** 5040 Redwood Dr 94928 **Location:** US 101 exit Golf Course Dr, just w. **Facility:** 123 units. 3 stories, exterior corridors. **Pool(s):** heated outdoor. **Activities:** whirlpool. **Guest Services:** coin laundry.

HAMPTON INN & SUITES   707/586-8700

Hotel. Rates not provided. **Address:** 6248 Redwood Dr 94928 **Location:** US 101 exit W Rohnert Park Expwy, just n. **Facility:** 102 units. 4 stories, interior corridors. **Amenities:** video games (fee), high-speed Internet. **Pool(s):** heated outdoor. **Activities:** exercise room. **Guest Services:** valet and coin laundry.

AAA Benefit:
Members save up to 10%!

RODEWAY INN   707/584-1600

Motel. Rates not provided. **Address:** 6288 Redwood Dr 94928 **Location:** US 101 exit W Rohnert Park Expwy, just n. **Facility:** 120 units. 2 stories (no elevator), exterior corridors. **Pool(s):** outdoor.

WHERE TO EAT

BACCHUS RESTAURANT & WINE BAR   707/586-4679

California. Casual Dining. $10-$30 **AAA Inspector Notes:** Named for the god of wine, this restaurant does its name justice with its extensive wine list. Fresh Sonoma-grown ingredients come together in preparations of northern Californian cuisine. **Bar:** full bar. **Address:** One Doubletree Dr 94928 **Location:** US 101 exit Golf Course Dr; 3 mi s of Santa Rosa; in DoubleTree by Hilton Hotel Sonoma Wine Country.

HANA JAPANESE RESTAURANT   707/586-0270

Japanese. Casual Dining. $12-$28 **AAA Inspector Notes:** Traditional Japanese cuisine can be enjoyed here with a number of sakes, while fresh choices tempt from the sushi bar. Sashimi is top notch and sourced locally as well as globally, including many from Tsukiji Market. **Bar:** beer & wine. **Address:** 101 Golf Course Dr 94928 **Location:** US 101 exit Golf Course Dr, just e.

ROSEVILLE (E-3) pop. 118,788, elev. 160'

- **Restaurants p. 303**
- **Hotels & Restaurants map & index p. 314**

GOLFLAND SUNSPLASH is e. off I-80 Atlantic St./Eureka Rd. exit, then just s. to 1893 Taylor Rd. The water park is part of a larger complex that also includes miniature golf, laser tag, go-carts and an arcade with more than 200 video games.

The water park includes 10 slides in addition to a wave pool, a lazy river and a children's area. Among park favorites are The Vortex, The Dark Holes, The Stealth, Master Blaster Water Coaster, Thunder Bay Wavepool and Bermuda Triangle. Lockers and cabanas can be rented.

Note: Height and weight requirements may apply for some slides. **Time:** Allow 4 hours minimum. **Hours:** Water park daily 11-6:30, early June to mid-Aug.; Sat.-Sun. 11-6:30, Memorial Day weekend-early June and mid-Aug. through Labor Day. Nite Slides 5-10:30 p.m., mid-June through Labor Day. Hours for other attractions vary. Phone ahead to confirm schedule. **Cost:** Waterpark $27.99; $21.99 (age 3-47 inches tall and ages 60+); $19.99 (twilight admission after 3 p.m. and for Nite Slides); $1 (ages 0-2). **Phone:** (916) 784-1273.

MAIDU MUSEUM & HISTORIC SITE is at 1970 Johnson Ranch Dr. The museum, designed to resemble a Native American roundhouse, has exhibits about Maidu Indian culture and artifacts and displays about California tribes.

A nature trail winds through the site, which was a Nisenan Maidu village for thousands of years until the mid-1800s. Along the trail visitors can see native plants; a midden; sandstone outcroppings carved with petroglyphs; and areas where the rocky ground is pitted with mortar holes, indentations created in order to process food. An art gallery features contemporary Maidu art.

Tours: Guided tours are available. **Time:** Allow 2 hours minimum. **Hours:** Mon.-Fri. 9-4, Sat. 9-1 (also third Sat. of the month 6:30-8:30 p.m.). Guided tours are given Sat. at 10 a.m. **Cost:** $4.50; $4 (ages 3-12 and 55+); $2 (Mon.-Fri. 2-4); $16 (family, up to four people); free (third Sat. of the month 6:30-8:30 p.m.). **Phone:** (916) 774-5934.

BEST WESTERN PLUS ROSEVILLE INN
916/782-4434 **48**

Hotel Rates not provided	Best Western PLUS	AAA Benefit: Members save up to 20%, plus 10% bonus points with Best Western Rewards®.

Address: 220 Harding Blvd 95678 **Location:** I-80 exit 103 westbound; exit 103B eastbound, just w, then just n. **Facility:** 126 units, some kitchens. 2 stories (no elevator), exterior corridors. **Amenities:** Some: high-speed Internet. **Pool(s):** outdoor. **Guest Services:** valet and coin laundry. **Free Special Amenities:** continental breakfast and high-speed Internet.

COURTYARD BY MARRIOTT   (916)772-5555 **43**

Hotel $89-$129 **Address:** 1920 Taylor Rd 95661 **Location:** I-80 exit 105A (Atlantic St/Eureka Rd), just n. **Facility:** 90 units. 3 stories, interior corridors. **Amenities:** high-speed Internet. **Pool(s):** heated indoor. **Activities:** whirlpool, exercise room. **Guest Services:** valet and coin laundry.

AAA Benefit:
AAA hotel discounts of 5% or more.

Trust your vehicle to AAA/CAA
Approved Auto Repair facilities

(See map & index p. 314.)

COURTYARD BY MARRIOTT GALLERIA (916)772-3404 **40**

▼▼▼ **Hotel** $89-$129 **Address:** 301 Creekside Ridge Ct 95678 **Location:** I-80 exit SR 65, 1 mi w to Stanford Ranch Rd/Galleria Blvd exit, 0.5 mi s to Antelope Creek Rd, just e, then just ne. **Facility:** 125 units. 4 stories, interior corridors. **Amenities:** *Some:* high-speed Internet. **Pool(s):** heated indoor. **Activities:** whirlpool, exercise room. **Guest Services:** valet and coin laundry.

AAA Benefit:
AAA hotel discounts of 5% or more.

EXTENDED STAYAMERICA-SACRAMENTO-ROSEVILLE (916)781-9001 **47**

▼▼ **Extended Stay Hotel** $84-$99 **Address:** 1000 Lead Hill Blvd 95678 **Location:** I-80 Douglas Blvd w exit 103B (eastbound), just w, then 0.6 mi on Harding Blvd, just e; exit 103 Douglas Blvd/Sunrise Ave (westbound), just w, then 0.6 mi n on Harding Blvd, just e. **Facility:** 122 efficiencies. 3 stories, interior corridors. **Guest Services:** coin laundry.

FAIRFIELD INN BY MARRIOTT (916)772-3500 **45**

▼▼▼ **Hotel** $79-$109 **Address:** 1910 Taylor Rd 95661 **Location:** I-80 exit 105A (Atlantic St/Eureka Rd), just e on Eureka Rd, then 0.4 mi n. **Facility:** 82 units. 3 stories, interior corridors. **Pool(s):** heated indoor. **Activities:** whirlpool. **Guest Services:** valet laundry.

AAA Benefit:
AAA hotel discounts of 5% or more.

HAMPTON INN & SUITES ROSEVILLE (916)772-9900 **50**

Hotel
$109-$149

AAA Benefit: Members save up to 10%!

Address: 110 N Sunrise Ave 95661 **Location:** I-80 Douglas Blvd exit 103A eastbound, just e, then just n; exit 103 westbound, just e, then just n; entrance on N Sunrise Ave. **Facility:** 85 units. 4 stories, interior corridors. **Terms:** 1-7 night minimum stay, cancellation fee imposed. **Amenities:** high-speed Internet. **Pool(s):** heated outdoor. **Activities:** whirlpool, exercise room. **Guest Services:** valet laundry. **Free Special Amenities: full breakfast and high-speed Internet.**

HILTON GARDEN INN ROSEVILLE (916)773-7171 **42**

▼▼▼ **Hotel** $89-$189 **Address:** 1951 Taylor Rd 95661 **Location:** I-80 exit 105A (Atlantic St/Eureka Rd), just e on Eureka Rd, then 0.4 mi n. **Facility:** 131 units. 3 stories, interior corridors. **Terms:** 1-7 night minimum stay, cancellation fee imposed. **Amenities:** high-speed Internet. **Pool(s):** heated outdoor. **Activities:** whirlpool, exercise room. **Guest Services:** valet and coin laundry.

AAA Benefit:
Unparalleled hospitality at a special Member rate.

HOLIDAY INN EXPRESS & SUITES-ROSEVILLE GALLERIA (916)774-6060 **46**

▼▼▼ Hotel $99-$119

Address: 1398 E Roseville Pkwy 95661 **Location:** I-80 exit 105A (Atlantic St/Eureka Rd), just e, then n on Sunrise Ave. Located near Golfland/Sunsplash. **Facility:** 83 units. 3 stories, interior corridors. **Terms:** 3 day cancellation notice. **Amenities:** high-speed Internet. **Pool(s):** outdoor. **Activities:** exercise room. **Guest Services:** complimentary and valet laundry. **Free Special Amenities: full breakfast and high-speed Internet.**

HOMEWOOD SUITES BY HILTON (916)783-7455 **39**

▼▼▼ **Extended Stay Hotel** $109-$179 **Address:** 401 Creekside Ridge Ct 95678 **Location:** I-80 exit SR 65, 1 mi w to Galleria Blvd, 0.5 mi s to Antelope Creek Rd, then just e. **Facility:** 111 efficiencies, some two bedrooms. 4 stories, interior corridors. **Terms:** 1-7 night minimum stay, cancellation fee imposed. **Pool(s):** heated outdoor. **Activities:** whirlpool, exercise room. **Guest Services:** valet and coin laundry.

AAA Benefit:
Contemporary luxury at a special Member rate.

HYATT PLACE SACRAMENTO/ROSEVILLE (916)781-6400 **38**

Hotel
$89-$169

■ HYATT PLACE **AAA Benefit:** Members save 10% or more everyday.

Address: 220 Conference Center Dr 95678 **Location:** I-80 exit 105A (Atlantic St/Eureka Rd), just e on Eureka Rd, 0.4 mi ne on Taylor Rd, 1.1 mi w on E Roseville Pkwy, just n on Gibson Dr, then just e. Adjacent to Westfield Galleria. **Facility:** 151 units. 6 stories, interior corridors. **Terms:** cancellation fee imposed. **Amenities:** *Some:* high-speed Internet, safes. **Pool(s):** heated outdoor. **Activities:** whirlpool, exercise room. **Guest Services:** valet laundry. **Free Special Amenities: expanded continental breakfast and high-speed Internet.**

LARKSPUR LANDING ROSEVILLE (916)773-1717 **44**

▼▼▼ **Extended Stay Hotel** $89-$219 **Address:** 1931 Taylor Rd 95661 **Location:** I-80 exit 105A (Atlantic St/Eureka Rd), just e on Eureka Rd, then 0.4 mi n. **Facility:** 90 efficiencies. 3 stories, interior corridors. **Terms:** cancellation fee imposed. **Amenities:** high-speed Internet. **Activities:** whirlpool, exercise room. **Guest Services:** complimentary and valet laundry, area transportation-within 7 mi.

ORCHID SUITES ROSEVILLE (916)784-2222 **49**

▼▼▼ Hotel $80-$199

Address: 130 N Sunrise Ave 95661 **Location:** I-80 exit Douglas Blvd, just e, then 0.3 mi n. **Facility:** 178 units, some two bedrooms. 3 stories, interior/exterior corridors. **Terms:** resort fee. **Amenities:** high-speed Internet. **Pool(s):** heated outdoor. **Activities:** whirlpool, putting green, exercise room. **Guest Services:** valet and coin laundry, area transportation-within 5 mi & casino. **Free Special Amenities: full breakfast and high-speed Internet.**

RESIDENCE INN BY MARRIOTT (916)772-5500 **41**

▼▼▼ **Extended Stay Hotel** $109-$149 **Address:** 1930 Taylor Rd 95661 **Location:** I-80 exit 105A (Atlantic St/Eureka Rd), just n. **Facility:** 90 units, some two bedrooms and kitchens. 3 stories, interior corridors. **Pool(s):** heated indoor. **Activities:** whirlpool, sports court, exercise room. **Guest Services:** valet and coin laundry.

AAA Benefit:
AAA hotel discounts of 5% or more.

SPRINGHILL SUITES BY MARRIOTT ROSEVILLE (916)782-2989 **36**

▼▼▼ **Extended Stay Hotel** $109-$129 **Address:** 10593 Fairway Dr 95678 **Location:** SR 65 exit Blue Oaks Blvd, just e. **Facility:** 124 units. 4 stories, interior corridors. **Pool(s):** heated indoor. **Activities:** whirlpool, exercise room. **Guest Services:** valet and coin laundry.

AAA Benefit:
AAA hotel discounts of 5% or more.

(See map & index p. 314.)

TOWNEPLACE SUITES BY MARRIOTT ROSEVILLE
(916)782-2232 **37**

▽▽▽ **Extended Stay Hotel** | **AAA Benefit:**
$99-$169 **Address:** 10569 Fairway Dr | AAA hotel discounts
95678 **Location:** SR 65 exit Blue Oaks | of 5% or more.
Blvd, just e. **Facility:** 115 units, some
two bedrooms, efficiencies and kitchens.
4 stories, interior corridors. **Pool(s):** heated indoor. **Activities:** whirlpool, exercise room. **Guest Services:** valet and coin laundry.

🛗 CALL 🕭M 🛄 BIZ 🛜 ✕ 🛏 🖻 🖵
/ SOME UNITS FEE 🐕

WHERE TO EAT

BLUE NAMI TASTE OF JAPAN   916/787-1177 **54**

▽▽ Japanese. Casual Dining. $9-$25 **AAA Inspector Notes:**
This popular restaurant serves an extensive offering of artistic and
creative rolls along with bento boxes and dinner combinations. A
soothing water feature is on one side of the dining room while a large
screen TV dominates the noisier side of the room. **Bar:** wine only.
Reservations: suggested. **Address:** 1465 Eureka Rd, Suite 120
95661 **Location:** I-80 exit 105A (Atlantic St/Eureka Rd), 0.4 mi e; e
of Sunrise Ave; in Stone Point Center. L D CALL 🕭M

BOUDIN BAKERY & CAFE   916/782-1849

▽ Sandwiches. Casual Dining. $8-$12 **AAA Inspector Notes:**
This popular eatery is a spin-off of the famous San Francisco Boudin
Bakery. The signature sourdough clam chowder bread bowl is served
here in addition to various salads and sandwiches. The line forms
early at lunch, so expect to wait. Sidewalk patio seating is available.
Address: 1017 Galleria Blvd, Suite 100 95678 **Location:** I-80 exit
105A (Atlantic St/Eureka Rd), 0.4 mi n on Taylor Rd, 0.7 mi nw on
Roseville Pkwy, then just n; in Fountains Shopping Center.

B L D CALL 🕭M

BROOKFIELDS   916/784-3399 **49**

▽▽ American. Casual Dining. $7-$16 **AAA Inspector Notes:**
Efficient, polite servers deliver breakfast all day as well as daily soups
and nightly dinner specials. Burgers, sandwiches and a few south-of-
the-border favorites are staples at this family-friendly restaurant. **Bar:**
beer & wine. **Address:** 1817 Taylor Rd 95661 **Location:** I-80 exit
105A (Atlantic St/Eureka Rd), just e, then just n; behind Shell gas
station. B L D

CATTLEMENS   916/782-5587

▽▽ American. Casual Dining. $14-$33 **AAA Inspector Notes:**
An all-you-can-eat salad complements the main menu offering-aged
and hand-cut steaks as well as chicken and seafood entrées. Defining the Western decor are beamed ceilings and your choice of a
booth or table seating. **Bar:** full bar. **Reservations:** suggested. **Address:** 2000 Taylor Rd 95678 **Location:** I-80 exit Taylor Pacific Rd
eastbound; exit Eureka Rd/Taylor Rd westbound, follow signs for
Rocklin-Taylor Rd, then 0.4 mi s. D CALL 🕭M

CHICAGO FIRE   916/771-2020 **50**

▽▽ Italian Pizza. Casual Dining. $9-$27 **AAA Inspector
Notes:** Authentic Chicago-style pizza at this upscale, casual spot includes thin crust (sliced in squares), deep dish and stuffed. Plan to
arrive early on weekend nights to avoid the adjacent movie theater
crowd. **Bar:** full bar. **Address:** 500 N Sunrise Ave 95661 **Location:**
I-80 exit 105A (Atlantic St/Eureka Rd), just e; jct Eureka Rd.

L D CALL 🕭M

CLAIM JUMPER   916/788-1705

▽▽ American. Casual Dining. $9-$30 **AAA Inspector Notes:**
Great menu variety makes this place a good stop for parties with diverse tastes. Choices include specialty appetizers, salads, rotisserie
chicken and barbecue items, not to mention good comfort foods,
such as traditional pot pie. Hearty portions satisfy big appetites. The
atmosphere is fun and lively. **Bar:** full bar. **Address:** 250 Harding
Blvd 95661 **Location:** I-80 exit Douglas Blvd W, just n.

L D CALL 🕭M

COSTA VIDA FRESH MEXICAN GRILL   916/773-9283 **61**

▽ Mexican. Quick Serve. $5-$8 **AAA Inspector Notes:** Burritos,
tacos, enchiladas and quesadillas are served with hand-made corn,
wheat or flour tortillas that can be seen being made while ordering at
the counter. Nachos and salads are available, too. Patio seating is
available in season. **Address:** 1745 Eureka Rd, Suite 100 95661 **Location:** I-80 exit 105A (Atlantic St/Eureka Rd), 0.4 mi e, then just e of
Sunrise Ave; in Stone Point Center. L D CALL 🕭M

THE COUNTER   916/773-2333 **48**

▽▽ American. Casual Dining. $6-$13 **AAA Inspector Notes:**
This eatery near the fountain offers a trendy, industrial décor. Guests
can build their own burger (beef, chicken or turkey) as they choose
from an extensive variety of toppings and sauces or they can try one
of the signature burgers. A heated sidewalk patio provides outdoor
seating. **Bar:** beer & wine. **Address:** 1005 Galleria Blvd, Suite 150
95678 **Location:** I-80 exit 105A (Atlantic St/Eureka Rd), 0.4 mi n on
Taylor Rd, 0.7 mi nw on Roseville Pkwy, then just n; in Fountains
Shopping Center. L D CALL 🕭M

CRUSH 29   916/773-2929 **56**

▽▽▽ American. Casual Dining. $12-$26 **AAA Inspector
Notes:** Influenced by Napa Valley, this casually elegant restaurant offers a palate-pleasing menu, rustic contemporary decor and an extensive list of California wines. **Bar:** full bar. **Reservations:**
suggested. **Address:** 1480 Eureka Rd 95661 **Location:** I-80 exit
105A (Atlantic St/Eureka Rd), 0.6 mi e; jct Rocky Ridge Rd; in Eureka
Ridge Plaza. L D CALL 🕭M ✒

FAT'S ASIA BISTRO & DIM SUM BAR   916/787-3287 **57**

▽▽▽ Chinese. Casual Dining. $9-$22 **AAA Inspector Notes:**
This well-established, trendy restaurant offers Chinese cuisine with
influences from a variety of Asian areas. **Bar:** full bar. **Reservations:**
suggested. **Address:** 1500 Eureka Rd 95661 **Location:** I-80 exit Eureka Rd, just e. L D

FINS MARKET & GRILL   916/783-5200 **62**

▽▽ Seafood. Casual Dining. $8-$22 **AAA Inspector Notes:**
Tucked in the corner of a shopping center, this casual eatery serves
a variety of simply-prepared fresh seafood, including appetizers,
salads, sandwiches and entrées. The seafood is flown in daily. Recommended are the fish tacos. **Bar:** beer & wine. **Address:** 8680
Sierra College Blvd 95661 **Location:** I-80 exit Douglas Blvd, 1.5 mi
e, then just s; in Renaissance Creek Shopping Center.

L D CALL 🕭M

FRESH CHOICE   916/783-5886

▽ American. Cafeteria. $8-$10 **AAA Inspector Notes:** The salad
bar of salad bars, the casual restaurant invites patrons to make their
own or try one of the already prepared varieties. Other items include
freshly baked breads, pizza and soup, as well as make-your-own
sundaes for dessert. **Bar:** beer & wine. **Address:** 2030 Douglas Blvd,
Suite 28 95661 **Location:** I-80 exit Douglas Blvd, 0.8 mi e; jct Rocky
Ridge Dr; in Rocky Ridge Town Center. L D

THE HABIT BURGER GRILL   916/791-5292 **42**

▽ American. Quick Serve. $4-$7 **AAA Inspector Notes:** This
California chain has been serving quality char-grilled burgers, grilled
sandwiches and salads since 1969. **Address:** 933 Pleasant Grove
Blvd 95678 **Location:** SR 65 exit Pleasant Grove Blvd, just s; jct
Highland Pointe, in Pleasant Pointe Shopping Center.

L D CALL 🕭M

IL FORNAIO   916/788-1200 **45**

▽▽▽ Italian. Fine Dining. $9-$35 **AAA Inspector Notes:** Accomplished servers begin guests' experiences with crisp, crusty
bread hot from the oven. Pasta and flavorful sauces enhance the
roasted meats and vegetables. The spacious restaurant thoughtfully
replicates the trattorias of Italy. **Bar:** full bar. **Reservations:** suggested. **Address:** 1179 Galleria Blvd 95678 **Location:** I-80 exit SR
65 N, 1.1 mi nw to Stanford Ranch Rd exit, 0.6 mi s, then just w on
Roseville Pkwy; at Roseville Galleria in the Promenade. **Parking:** on-
site and valet. L D

(See map & index p. 314.)

JOHNNY GARLIC'S   916/789-2000 (41)

▼▼▼ American. Casual Dining. $9-$29 **AAA Inspector Notes:** This upbeat, contemporary casual restaurant offers tasty food. Hand-tossed, thin-crust pizza baked in a wood-fired oven is available as well as pasta, burgers, sandwiches, salads, premium steak and seafood. Diners can sit at the counter and watch the food being prepared. Breakfast fare is served on the weekend. **Bar:** full bar. **Address:** 10505 Fairway Dr 95661 **Location:** SR 65 exit Blue Oaks Blvd, just e, then just s. L D CALL &M

JOHN'S INCREDIBLE PIZZA CO.   916/772-1111 (52)

▼ Pizza. Cafeteria. $7-$10 **AAA Inspector Notes:** Great for families with children this eatery offers an all-you-can-eat salad, pizza, pasta and dessert buffet and an extensive game room for the children. Theme dining rooms are kid friendly and include Toon Time which has continuously-running cartoons. **Bar:** beer & wine. **Address:** 384 N Sunrise Ave 95661 **Location:** I-80 exit 105A (Atlantic St/Eureka Rd), just e on Eureka Rd, then just n. L D CALL &M

LA PROVENCE RESTAURANT & TERRACE
    916/789-2002 (40)

▼▼▼ Regional French. Casual Dining. $9-$33 **AAA Inspector Notes:** The seasonal menus at this restaurant reflect a fusion of French cuisine prepared California-style. French country elegance includes a dual-sided fireplace and creekside terrace patio seating. Sunday brunch is offered 9:30 a.m. to 1:30 p.m. **Bar:** full bar. **Reservations:** suggested. **Address:** 110 Diamond Creek Pl 95747 **Location:** SR 65 exit Blue Oaks Blvd, 2 mi w, then just n. L D CALL &M

MAS COCINA MEXICANA   916/773-3778 (59)

▼▼▼ Mexican. Casual Dining. $7-$17 **AAA Inspector Notes:** Contemporary renditions of Mexican food are prepared at this restaurant that rocks to a Latin/Mexican beat. Mariachi Fridays are offered from 6 to 8:30 p.m. and monthly tequila tastings also take place. Breakfast is served on Saturday and Sunday 9 a.m. to 3 p.m. Guests can dine on the enclosed patio. **Bar:** full bar. **Reservations:** suggested. **Address:** 1563 Eureka Rd 95661 **Location:** I-80 exit Eureka Rd, just e; jct Lead Hill Blvd. L D CALL &M

MCCORMICK & SCHMICK'S   916/960-4875 (47)

▼▼▼ Seafood. Casual Dining. $12-$35 **AAA Inspector Notes:** This place is all about seafood, which is imported from all over the world. Among good choices are Washington state oysters, Maine clams, delicate Hawaiian escolar and tuna from Ecuador. The club-like decor is cozy and the staff is attentive. **Bar:** full bar. **Reservations:** suggested. **Address:** 1194 Roseville Pkwy 95678 **Location:** I-80 exit 105A (Atlantic St/Eureka Rd), just e on Eureka Rd, 0.4 mi n on Taylor Rd, then 1.5 mi nw; in Fountains at Roseville Shopping Center. L D CALL &M

MIKUNI JAPANESE RESTAURANT & SUSHI BAR
    916/797-2112

▼▼ Japanese Sushi. Casual Dining. $10-$21 **AAA Inspector Notes:** This popular local chain serves an extensive variety of rolls along with sashimi, box combinations and seafood plates. Dine at the sushi bar and watch the chefs prepare the sushi offerings. Plan to arrive early to avoid a long wait at dinner. **Bar:** full bar. **Address:** 1565 Eureka Rd 95661 **Location:** I-80 exit 105A (Atlantic St/Eureka Rd), 0.5 mi e, then just e of Sunrise Ave. L D

MIKUNI KAIZEN   916/780-2119

▼▼ Japanese Sushi. Casual Dining. $7-$15 **AAA Inspector Notes:** This restaurant features an extensive variety of creative sushi rolls, seafood, vegetarian and Japanese tapas—all great for sharing in a contemporary, high-energy setting. Lunch is offered daily, except on Sunday. **Bar:** full bar. **Address:** 1017 Galleria Blvd, Suite 160 95678 **Location:** I-80 exit 105A (Atlantic St/Eureka Rd), 0.4 mi n on Taylor Rd, 0.7 mi nw on Roseville Pkwy, then just n; in Fountains Shopping Center. D CALL &M

PASTA POMODORO   916/773-4027

▼▼ Italian. Casual Dining. $8-$19 **AAA Inspector Notes:** Families are welcomed at this laid-back restaurant, which brings in plenty of loyal locals who enjoy its varied Italian favorites, including tempting pasta and chicken dishes. **Bar:** beer & wine. **Address:** 3984 Douglas Blvd, Suite 110 95661 **Location:** I-80 exit 103 (Douglas Blvd), 2.5 mi e; jct Sierra College Blvd; in Renaissance Creek Shopping Center. L D CALL &M

PAUL MARTIN'S AMERICAN BISTRO   916/783-3600 (53)

▼▼▼ American. Casual Dining. $12-$30 **AAA Inspector Notes:** This popular, upscale bistro serves well-prepared food in a contemporary ambience that includes oversized, circular lighting and polished cement floors. The varied menu features fresh local ingredients and organic produce. More than 80 bottles of California wines line the wine list. The patio area is inviting. **Bar:** full bar. **Reservations:** suggested. **Address:** 1455 Eureka Rd, Suite 100 95661 **Location:** I-80 exit 105A (Atlantic St/Eureka Rd), 0.4 mi e, just e of Sunrise Ave; in Stone Point Center. L D CALL &M

P.F. CHANG'S CHINA BISTRO   916/788-2800 (43)

▼▼▼ Chinese. Casual Dining. $10-$25 **AAA Inspector Notes:** Trendy, upscale decor provides a pleasant backdrop for New Age Chinese dining. Appetizers, soups and salads are a meal by themselves. Vegetarian plates and sides, noodles, meins, chicken and meat dishes are created from exotic, fresh ingredients. **Bar:** full bar. **Address:** 1180 Galleria Blvd 95678 **Location:** I-80 exit SR 65, 1 mi w to Galleria Blvd, then 0.5 mi s to Antelope Creek Rd. L D CALL &M

RUEN THAI   916/774-1499 (55)

▼▼ Thai. Casual Dining. $8-$15 **AAA Inspector Notes:** The varied menu here offers flavorful Thai dishes such as curries, stir fries and seafood and noodle dishes. Generous portions and affordable lunch specials are featured. Choose the degree of spiciness to suit preferences. A good selection of beer, including Thai, is available. **Bar:** beer & wine. **Address:** 1470 Eureka Rd 95661 **Location:** I-80 exit 105A (Atlantic St/Eureka Rd), 0.6 mi e; jct Rocky Ridge Rd; in Eureka Ridge Plaza. L D CALL &M

RUTH'S CHRIS STEAK HOUSE   916/780-6910 (44)

▼▼▼ Steak. Fine Dining. $8-$48 **AAA Inspector Notes:** The main fare is steak, which is prepared from several cuts of prime beef and cooked to perfection, but the menu also lists lamb, chicken and seafood dishes. Guests should come hungry because the side dishes, which are among the a la carte offerings, could make a meal in themselves. **Bar:** full bar. **Reservations:** suggested. **Address:** 1185 Galleria Blvd 95678 **Location:** I-80 exit SR 65 N, 1.1 mi nw to Stanford Ranch Rd exit, 0.6 mi s, then just w on Roseville Pkwy; at Roseville Galleria in Promenade. **Parking:** on-site and valet. D CALL &M

SQUEEZE INN   916/783-2874 (58)

▼ Burgers. Quick Serve. $2-$5 **AAA Inspector Notes:** Come hungry to this basic eatery—a local favorite known for cheese skirt burgers (cheddar cheese bubbling off all sides) and the toothpicks hanging from the ceiling. Also offered are hot dogs, steak sandwiches, veggie burgers and milk shakes. **Address:** 106 N Sunrise Ave, Suite C1 95661 **Location:** I-80 exit Douglas Blvd, just e, then just n. L D CALL &M

SUEDE BLUE   916/782-5525 (51)

▼▼▼ Steak Seafood. Fine Dining. $12-$46 **AAA Inspector Notes:** Warm and inviting, this upscale restaurant offers well-prepared steaks accompanied with savory sauces, if desired. Prime rib, chicken and fresh seafood entrées, also are available. A patio area is an option for seating. **Bar:** full bar. **Reservations:** suggested. **Address:** 1400 Eureka Rd 95661 **Location:** I-80 exit Eureka Rd/Taylor Rd, just se. L D CALL &M

TAHOE JOE'S FAMOUS STEAKHOUSE   916/797-9220

▼▼ American. Casual Dining. $9-$28 **AAA Inspector Notes:** At this ski lodge-themed spot, aged steaks are grilled over an almond fire and slow roasted prime rib are top picks. Other menu selections include railroad camp shrimp and Joe's bowls (salads and burgers). **Bar:** full bar. **Address:** 1905 Taylor Rd 95661 **Location:** I-80 exit 105A (Atlantic St/Eureka Rd), just e on Eureka Rd, then 0.4 mi n; jct Roseville Pkwy. L D

THAI BASIL RESTAURANT   916/782-8424 (60)

▼▼ Thai. Casual Dining. $9-$17 **AAA Inspector Notes:** Tucked in the back of a shopping center, this restaurant offers tasty salads, grilled items, curries and noodle plates. **Bar:** beer & wine. **Address:** 1613 Douglas Blvd 95661 **Location:** I-80 exit Douglas Blvd, just e; jct Sunrise Blvd; near Office Depot. L D

(See map & index p. 314.)

YARD HOUSE   916/780-9273   46

▼▼ American. Casual Dining. $10-$31 **AAA Inspector Notes:** This popular, high energy (loud) restaurant offers burgers, sandwiches, pizza, salads and seafood entrées with a slight touch of the Hawaiian islands. More than 100 beers and a good selection of martini's are part of the extensive beverage list. The outdoor patio features a tree in the center. At busy times, expect long waits. Call ahead seating is available 15 minutes before arrival. **Bar:** full bar. **Address:** 1166 Roseville Pkwy, Bldg E 95678 **Location:** I-80 exit 105A (Atlantic St/Eureka Rd), just e on Eureka Rd, 0.4 mi n on Taylor Rd, then 1.5 mi nw; in Fountains at Roseville Shopping Center.

L   D   LATE   CALL 丘M

RUTHERFORD (B-8) pop. 164, elev. 170'
• **Attractions map p. 568**
• **Hotels & Restaurants map & index p. 570**
• **Part of Wine Country area — see map p. 562**

RECREATIONAL ACTIVITIES

Hot Air Ballooning

• **Bonaventura Balloons of Napa Valley** departs from Rancho Caymus Inn, 1140 SR 128 (Rutherford Rd.). **Hours:** Trips depart daily shortly after dawn (weather permitting). **Phone:** (707) 944-2210 or (800) 359-6272.

WINERIES

• **Beaulieu Vineyard** is off SR 29 at 1960 St. Helena Hwy. **Hours:** Daily 10-5. A variety of tours are available; reservations are required. Closed major holidays. Phone ahead to confirm schedule. **Phone:** (707) 967-5232 or (800) 264-6918, ext. 5232.

• **Inglenook** is off SR 29 at 1991 St. Helena Hwy. **Hours:** Tastings daily 10-5. A variety of tours are offered daily. Reservations are required for most tours; phone ahead for information. Closed Thanksgiving and Christmas. **Phone:** (707) 968-1161 or (800) 782-4266.

• **Mumm Napa Valley Winery** is at 8445 Silverado Tr. **Hours:** Daily 10-5. The last seating is 15 minutes before closing. Guided tours are given daily at 10 (complimentary) and at 11, 1 and 3 (for a fee). Closed major holidays. **Phone:** (707) 967-7700 or (800) 686-6272.

• **Peju Province Winery** is at 8466 St. Helena Hwy. (SR 29). **Hours:** Tastings and self-guiding tours daily 10-6. Closed Thanksgiving and Christmas. **Phone:** (707) 963-3600 or (800) 446-7358.

• **Rutherford Hill Winery** is e. off Silverado Tr. at the end of Rutherford Hill Rd. **Hours:** Tastings daily 10-5. Guided tours are given daily at 11:30, 1:30 and 3:30. Closed Jan. 1, Easter, Thanksgiving and Christmas. **Phone:** (707) 963-1871.

• **St. Supéry Vineyards and Winery** is off SR 29 at 8440 St. Helena Hwy. **Hours:** Tastings and self-guiding tours daily 10-5. A variety of guided tours are available. Phone ahead for holiday schedule. **Phone:** (707) 963-4507 or (800) 942-0809.

Learn the local driving laws
at DrivingLaws.AAA.com

RANCHO CAYMUS   (707)963-1777   28

▼▼▼ Hotel $149-$499 **Address:** 1140 Rutherford Rd 94573 **Location:** Just e of SR 29 and 128; 4 mi s of St. Helena. **Facility:** 26 units, some efficiencies. 2 stories (no elevator), exterior corridors. **Terms:** 2 night minimum stay - weekends, 3 day cancellation notice. **Guest Services:** valet laundry.

📶 CALL 丘M 🛜 ✕ 🔒 🖥 / SOME UNITS FEE 🐾 🖨

SACRAMENTO (E-3) pop. 466,488, elev. 30'
• **Hotels p. 320** • **Restaurants p. 324**
• **Attractions map p. 307**
• **Hotels & Restaurants map & index p. 311, 314**

It was 1839 when Capt. John Sutter, a Swiss emigrant, settled at the confluence of the American and Sacramento rivers, the beneficiary of a 50,000-acre land grant from the Mexican government. Sacramento was platted on Sutter's property in 1848—the same year that James Marshall's discovery of gold near the South Fork of the American River inaugurated the great California gold rush.

Sacramento quickly became a major supply center for the northern Mother Lode country. But right off the bat there were challenges—two floods and two fires in the early 1850s that leveled some two-thirds of the new settlement. It was nevertheless chosen as the state capital in 1854 and retained that status despite subsequent challenges by Berkeley, San Jose and Monterey.

In 1856 the first railroad in California connected Sacramento with Folsom, and in 1860 it became the western terminus of the Pony Express line from St. Joseph, Mo. The transcontinental railroad was completed in 1869. Once agriculture was established in the fertile Sacramento Valley, continued prosperity was assured. A deepwater channel to San Francisco Bay was completed in 1963, making the city a major inland port in addition to an important highway, rail and river hub.

A landmark in the heart of downtown, the Cathedral of the Blessed Sacrament, 1017 11th St. (at K Street) is part of a complex of historic buildings. Built in the Italian Renaissance style in 1886, it was the largest Roman Catholic church west of the Mississippi River until 1966. The cathedral's 218-foot bell tower and stained-glass windows are noteworthy. Mass takes place on weekdays at 12:10 and 5:10; phone (916) 444-3071.

The Wells Fargo History Museum, in the lobby of the Wells Fargo Center at 400 Capitol Mall, has exhibits illustrating the development of the company. Topics covered include the gold rush, the Pony Express and early banking. Visitors can see a re-creation of an agent's office, a telegraph key, gold scales, a restored Concord stagecoach, quartz specimens flecked with gold, a fool's gold display, photographs and a postage stamp collection; phone (916) 440-4161.

History is also the topic at the Donald and June Salvatori California Pharmacy Museum, 4030 Lennane Dr. at the headquarters of the Pharmacy Foundation of California. Four rooms depict different eras of the state's pharmacy history. The room representing the 1890s has a pressed tin ceiling, a collection of glass bottles and period pharmaceutical

(See maps & indexes p. 311, 314.)

items; a re-created 1940s pharmacy includes a sampling of vintage over-the-counter medications and other remedies. It is open by appointment; phone (916) 779-1410.

The Sacramento-San Joaquin River Delta, bounded by the cities of Sacramento, Stockton, Tracy and Pittsburg, was reclaimed in the 19th century thanks to Chinese laborers. Known for its laid-back lifestyle, this area is one of northern California's premier water recreation destinations. A series of waterways, dotted with hundreds of islands, winds throughout this region of rich agricultural land. There are historic towns to explore, and a favorite way to get around is by houseboat. Marinas and resorts are plentiful; popular activities include fishing, camping and picnicking.

Sleep Train Arena, at One Sports Pkwy. near the intersection of I-5 and I-80, is the home of the Sacramento Kings professional basketball team. Many other events and performances take place at the arena; phone (916) 928-6900 for information.

The 4-day ▼ Sacramento Music Festival over the long Memorial Day weekend is one heck of a street party. The music—played by bands on outdoor stages in the Old Sacramento historic district and in the ballrooms of surrounding hotels—ranges from jazz to big band swing, blues to zydeco and rockabilly to bluegrass. Other activities include a Saturday morning parade and a salute to servicemen and women on Memorial Day. For schedule and ticket information phone (916) 444-2004.

Close to a million people make their way to the Cal Expo fairgrounds in July for the 14-day ▼ California State Fair. In addition to traditional midway rides and games of chance, the fair also boasts big-name entertainment on three stages, competitions in everything from fine arts to livestock, a Kids Park, horse racing, extreme sports, wildlife exhibits, monster truck rides and more. The fairgrounds are off SR 99/Capital City Freeway (Cal Expo exit); for schedule, ticket and parking information phone (916) 263-3247 or (877) 225-3976.

Horse-drawn wagons? The Pony Express? Wild West shootouts? Sacramento relives the past—at least for the 4 days leading up to Labor Day—during the ▼ Gold Rush Days festival. Some 200 tons of trucked-in dirt add a little 19th-century authenticity to Old Sacramento streets. Costumed interpreters give shooting and cooking demonstrations, and street musicians enliven the atmosphere. The diverse cultures that settled the Sacramento Valley are spotlighted at the Ethnic Village. For festival information phone (916) 808-7777.

Downtown Sacramento is the end point of the 32-mile Jedediah Smith Memorial Trail, which winds its way west from Folsom (see place listing p. 111). Also known as the American River Bike Trail, the pathway is used by hikers, bikers, inline skaters and those just out for a stroll. Sacramento also is the northern point of a scenic 33-mile stretch of SR 160

that proceeds south to Isleton, following the Sacramento River.

Sacramento Convention and Visitors Bureau: 1608 I St., Sacramento, CA 95814. **Phone:** (916) 808-7777 or (800) 292-2334.

Self-guiding tours: Maps and brochures detailing walking tours of Old Sacramento are available at the Old Sacramento Visitor Center, 1002 2nd St.; phone (916) 442-7644.

Shopping areas: Regional malls include Arden Fair, I-80 and Arden Way, and Westfield Galleria at Roseville, off I-80 (SR 65 exit); anchor stores at both are JCPenney, Macy's, Nordstrom and Sears. The anchors at Sunrise Mall, Sunrise Boulevard and Greenback Lane, are JCPenney, Macy's and Sears. Macy's is the anchor store at Sacramento Downtown Plaza, an open-air complex on K Street between 4th and 7th streets.

▼ **AEROSPACE MUSEUM OF CALIFORNIA**—see North Highlands p. 246.

BLUE DIAMOND GROWERS, 1701 C St., presents a 20-minute video about almond growing and processing and also offers product tastings. **Time:** Allow 1 hour minimum. **Hours:** Mon.-Fri. 9:30-5, Sat. 9:30-4. **Cost:** Free. **Phone:** (916) 446-8438.

CALIFORNIA AUTOMOBILE MUSEUM, 2200 Front St., displays more than 150 vintage automobiles. The development of the automobile is depicted via representations of varied models and makes, from the primitive vehicles of the early 20th century to cosmetic adaptations (tail fins), styles (muscle and race cars) and the future (alternative-power vehicles). Car-related memorabilia and artifacts also are displayed.

Tours: Guided tours are available. **Time:** Allow 30 minutes minimum. **Hours:** Daily 10-6 (also third Thurs. of the month 6-9 p.m.). Last tour begins 1 hour before closing. Closed Jan. 1, Thanksgiving and Christmas. **Cost:** $8; $7 (ages 65+); $4 (students with ID); free (ages 0-4). **Phone:** (916) 442-6802.

[SAVE] **THE CALIFORNIA MUSEUM** is at 1020 O St. in Archives Plaza, 1 blk. s. of the State Capitol. Permanent exhibits showcase California's history, especially the state's influence on ideas, arts and culture worldwide. California's Remarkable Women chronicles the impact women from various walks of life have made on the state. California Indians: Making a Difference represents more than 150 tribes, while Uprooted! Japanese Americans During WWII addresses civil rights, internment and redress. The California Hall of Fame exhibit changes to showcase personal items pertaining to the year's inductees as well as their significant contributions to history.

Time: Allow 1 hour, 30 minutes minimum. **Hours:** Tues.-Sat. 10-5, Sun. noon-5. Last admission is 15 minutes before closing. Closed Jan. 1, Thanksgiving

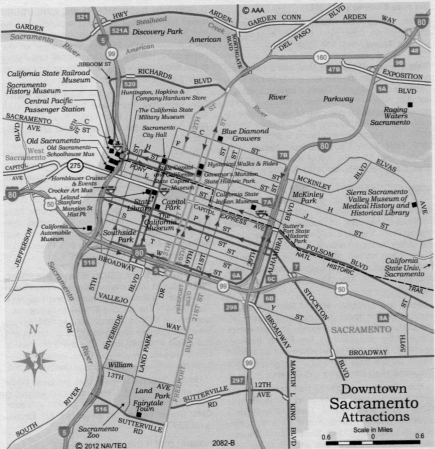

Downtown
Sacramento
Attractions

Scale in Miles
0.6   0   0.6

© 2012 NAVTEQ   2082-B

(See maps & indexes p. 311, 314.)

and Christmas. **Cost:** $8.50; $7 (ages 65+ and college students with ID); $6 (ages 6-13). **Phone:** (916) 653-7524.

CALIFORNIA STATE CAPITOL MUSEUM is
bounded by 10th, 15th, L and N sts. This "museum," a 12-block expanse in downtown Sacramento, encompasses not just the building where the state's legislature meets, but also the gardens, monuments and statues in Capitol Park and the adjacent State Library. **Hours:** Daily 9-5. Closed Jan. 1, Thanksgiving and Christmas. **Cost:** Free. **Phone:** (916) 324-0333.

Capitol Park is bounded by 10th, 15th, L and N sts. This 40-acre park surrounding the State Capitol has gardens, including the World Peace Rose Garden, and trees and plantings from around the world. Memorials and statues commemorating significant events in state history include a statue of Father Junípero Serra, the Civil War Memorial Grove, the California Veterans Memorial, California Vietnam Veterans Memorial and the Firefighters Memorial.

A brochure describing a walking tour of the park is available at the State Capitol. Phone for information about guided tours of the park. **Hours:** Open daily dawn-dusk. **Cost:** Free. **Phone:** (916) 324-0333.

State Capitol, on 10th St. between L and N sts., was built 1860-74 in an architectural style similar to that of the United States Capitol. The main building contains art exhibits, murals and statuary. Marble floors and the rotunda dome are highlights; murals depicting important events in California's history are at the base of the rotunda.

One-hour guided tours cover the renovated main building; the legislative chambers, where representatives' desks date from the 1860s; and several offices of state officials, including a 1906 re-creation of the governor's office suite. Limited gallery seating is available on a first-come, first-served basis when the legislature is in session. A 10-minute video presentation is shown in the basement theater.

Time: Allow 1 hour minimum. **Hours:** Guided tour offered daily on the hour 9-4. The legislature is in session from early Jan. to mid-Sept. in odd-numbered years and from early Jan.-Nov. 30 in

(See maps & indexes p. 311, 314.)

even-numbered years. Closed Jan. 1, Thanksgiving and Christmas. **Cost:** Free. Children must be with an adult. **Phone:** (916) 324-0333.

State Library, 914 Capitol Mall, has a handsome neoclassic granite exterior with a 100-foot mural by California artist Maynard Dixon. A second building at 900 N St. houses the state history section, which includes an interesting collection of early state newspapers. **Note:** The building at 914 Capitol Mall is closed for renovation; reopening is scheduled for 2013. **Time:** Allow 1 hour minimum. **Hours:** N St. building open Mon.-Fri. 9:30-4. Closed major holidays. **Cost:** Free. **Phone:** (916) 654-0261.

GEM **CROCKER ART MUSEUM** is off I-5 (J St. exit), s. on 3rd St., then just w. to 216 O St. It was founded in 1885 and is said to be the longest continuously operating art museum west of the Mississippi River. The 1872 building originally served as the gallery for the art collections of Judge Edwin B. Crocker and his wife Margaret. The museum exhibits paintings, drawings, sculpture and decorative arts from Europe, Asia, Africa, Oceania and California.

Asian and European art and international ceramics are the focal displays in the original, Italianate-style gallery building. The expansive wings of the contemporary Teel Family Pavilion, opened in 2010, feature American and Californian artists, several halls presenting changing exhibits and works of art from Africa and Oceania.

Note: Backpacks and baby back carriers are not permitted; a parcel check is available. **Tours:** Guided tours are available. **Time:** Allow 2 hours minimum. **Hours:** Tues.-Sun. and some Mon. holidays 10-5 (also Thurs. 5-9). Closed Jan. 1, Thanksgiving and Christmas. **Cost:** $10; $8 (ages 65+, military and college students with ID); $5 (ages 7-17); donations (third Sun. of the month). **Phone:** (916) 808-7000, or (916) 808-1182 for tour reservations.

DISCOVERY MUSEUM SCIENCE & SPACE CENTER, 3615 Auburn Blvd., has rotating, hands-on exhibits about animals, reptiles, insects, space, the human body, dinosaurs and geology. Student-oriented planetarium shows are geared to different grade levels. The Robotics Lab teaches kids how to build and program robots. A wildlife pond is on the center's grounds.

Time: Allow 30 minutes minimum. **Hours:** Daily 10-4:30, July-Aug.; Tues.-Fri. noon-4:30, Sat.-Sun. 10-4:30, rest of year. Planetarium shows Sat.-Sun. at 1 and 3. Live animal presentations Sat.-Sun. at noon and 2. Science Discovery Weekend activities take place Sat.-Sun. noon-4. Under age 4 are not permitted in planetarium shows. **Cost:** Admission Mon.-Fri. $6; $5 (ages 13-17 and 60+); $4 (ages 4-12). Admission Sat.-Sun. and holidays $8; $7 (ages 13-17 and 60+); $6 (ages 4-12). **Phone:** (916) 808-3942.

DOWNTOWN SACRAMENTO WALKING TOURS depart from different locations, depending on the tour selected. Led by knowledgeable guides, the tours provide insight into the city's history, art and architecture. This is a great way for first-time visitors to get acquainted with Sacramento or for locals to explore a different aspect of their city.

Currently offered tours are Tales of the Central City; Yesterday, Today and Tomorrow; Art is All Around Us; Rock 'n Roll History Tour; The Art of Terra Cotta; and the Old Sacramento Speak Easy Tour.

Guests must be able to walk for approximately 90 minutes without a rest break. Some stair climbing is involved. Most tours are accessible, and guides can make special accommodations. Some tours are limited to participants over 21 years of age. **Time:** Allow 1 hour, 30 minutes minimum. **Hours:** Tours are offered daily. Schedules vary depending upon the tour; phone ahead for specific days and times. No tours on Mon. holidays. **Cost:** $10. Reservations are required. **Phone:** (916) 442-8575.

GOVERNOR'S MANSION STATE HISTORIC PARK, 1526 H St., contains the governor's mansion that served 13 California governors and their families 1903-67. The Second Empire Italianate mansion, built in 1877 for a hardware merchant, reflects the evolving tastes and styles of the governors and first ladies who lived there. The mansion grounds contain flowers, shrubs and trees, including some trees planted the year the mansion was constructed.

Hours: Guided 45-minute tours are given Wed.-Sun. on the hour 10-4. Closed Jan. 1, Thanksgiving and Christmas. Phone ahead to confirm schedule. **Cost:** Guided tour fee $5; $3 (ages 6-17). **Phone:** (916) 323-3047.

HORNBLOWER CRUISES & EVENTS is at 1206 Front St. A 1-hour narrated cruise on the Sacramento River provides information about Sacramento's history from gold rush days to the present. Dinner dance, evening and champagne brunch cruises also are available.

Time: Allow 1 hour minimum. **Hours:** One-hour river cruise departs Fri.-Sat. at 1:30, 3 and 5:30, Thurs. at 1:30 and 3, Sun. at 11 and 3, May-Sept.; Fri.-Sat. at noon, 1:30 and 3, Sun. at 11 and 3, Oct.-Dec. Schedule varies rest of year. Phone ahead to confirm schedule. **Cost:** River cruise $20; $18 (ages 65+ and military with ID); $12 (ages 4-12). Reservations are recommended. **Phone:** (916) 446-1185 or (888) 467-6256.

HYSTERICAL WALKS & RIDES Segway tours depart from the parking lot of the Clarion Hotel Mansion Inn at 700 16th St. (at H St.). A brief training session prior to departure teaches participants how to operate their Segway Personal Transporter. The 2-hour tours provide a city orientation as well as historical background information.

Sights seen along the way include the Crocker Art Museum, Leland Stanford Mansion State Historic

(See maps & indexes p. 311, 314.)

Park, Capitol Park and the State Capitol, the Governor's Mansion and the city's Chinatown. There are photo stops at the American River and the State Capitol. Two-hour Sunset River Segway tours and 1-hour History & Ghost walking tours also are available.

Time: Allow 2 hours, 30 minutes minimum. **Hours:** Downtown Segway tours depart daily at 9 and 1. Phone for other tour schedules. Phone ahead to confirm schedule. **Cost:** Segway tours $80-$120. Ages 14-17 must be with a guardian. Under 14 are not permitted. Reservations are required. **Phone:** (916) 441-2527.

LELAND STANFORD MANSION STATE HISTORIC PARK is at 800 N St. Built in 1856 and recently restored, the house served three governors during the 1860s. As a pro-Union Civil War governor and president of the Central Pacific Railroad, Leland Stanford negotiated deals to help complete the transcontinental railroad.

Stanford had the mansard-roofed mansion expanded in 1872. He died in 1893, and the house was used as an orphanage and a home for girls from the turn of the 20th century until 1986. It now serves a dual purpose: as a museum recalling an elegant 19th-century past and as a site for state meetings and receptions.

Time: Allow 1 hour minimum. **Hours:** Guided tours are given Wed.-Sun. on the hour 10-4. Tour times may be limited when the legislature is in session; phone ahead to confirm schedule. Closed Jan. 1, Thanksgiving and Christmas. **Cost:** $5; $3 (ages 6-17). **Phone:** (916) 324-0575 or (800) 777-0369.

OLD SACRAMENTO is a four-block, 28-acre section of downtown delineated by the Capitol Mall, I St., 2nd St. and the Sacramento River. This was the city's commercial district during the gold rush era. Cobblestone streets and wood sidewalks lend a touch of yesteryear to this vibrant commercial district, which includes Old Sacramento State Historic Park as well as museums, shops and restaurants.

The 1853 B.F. Hastings Building at 2nd and I streets once housed a Wells, Fargo & Co. office, marked the western end of the Pony Express route and, for a time, housed California's Supreme Court; today it's a visitor and interpretive center. The Wells Fargo History Museum within the building displays a Wells Fargo agent's office, a scale model of a Wells Fargo stagecoach, a 19th-century copy machine, a working telegraph and a scale used for weighing gold.

Hours: Guided walking tours of the historic park are offered Mar.-Sept.; by appointment rest of year. Wells Fargo History Museum open daily 10-5. **Cost:** Wells Fargo History Museum free. **Phone:** (916) 442-7644 for the visitor center, or (916) 440-4263 for the Wells Fargo History Museum.

The California State Military Museum, 1119 2nd St., honors Californians who served and protected their state and country in times of war, peace and natural disaster. Exhibits include weapons, uniforms, battle flags, photographs, medals and documents pertaining to the Spanish explorers through the Civil War, World Wars I and II, Korea, Vietnam, Desert Storm and current conflicts, as well as earthquakes. A research center covers all branches of the military.

Time: Allow 1 hour minimum. **Hours:** Sun. and Tues.-Thurs. 10-5, Fri.-Sat. 10-6, Memorial Day-late Sept.; Sun. and Tues.-Thurs. 10-4, Fri.-Sat. 10-5, rest of year. Phone ahead to confirm winter schedule. Closed Jan. 1, Easter, Thanksgiving and Christmas. **Cost:** $5; $3 (ages 6-17 and 55+); free (military and veterans with ID). **Phone:** (916) 854-1900.

California State Railroad Museum is at 2nd and I sts. The three-level building houses 21 restored locomotives and train cars. More than 40 interpretive exhibits, dioramas, pictures, murals and a 20-minute film presentation document the history of American railroading 1860-1960. The building's striking thematic design and gleaming exhibits are impressive.

Sacramento Southern Railroad steam trains transport visitors on a 6-mile sightseeing journey weekends from April through September. Trains depart from the freight depot in Old Sacramento at Front and K streets.

Tours: Guided tours are available. **Time:** Allow 2 hours minimum. **Hours:** Museum open daily 10-5. Last admission 30 minutes before closing. Trains operate Sat.-Sun. on the hour 11-5, Apr.-Sept. Closed Jan. 1, Thanksgiving and Christmas. **Cost:** Museum $9; $4 (ages 6-17). Train fare $10; $5 (ages 6-17). **Phone:** (916) 445-6645.

Huntington, Hopkins & Company Hardware Store is at street level in the Big Four Building at 111 I St. This representation of a small-town 19th-century hardware store has such period items as lanterns hanging from the ceiling, crates stacked on the floor, and an assortment of vintage tools and implements. Docents provide historical information and explain how some of the older tools were used. A back room displays additional tools and machinery.

The store also has a retail operation that sells hard-to-find items like oil lamps and old-fashioned toys. **Time:** Allow 30 minutes minimum. **Hours:** Thurs.-Sun. 11-4. Closed Jan. 1, Thanksgiving and Christmas. Phone ahead to confirm schedule. **Cost:** Free. **Phone:** (916) 323-7234.

Old Sacramento Schoolhouse Museum is at 1200 Front St. at jct. L St. Designed to resemble an 1884 one-room schoolhouse that served students in Yolo County, the exhibits include a potbellied stove and both original and replica furniture and fixtures. **Hours:** Mon.-Sat. 10-4, Sun. noon-4. Closed Jan. 1,

(See maps & indexes p. 311, 314.)

Easter, Thanksgiving and Christmas. Phone ahead to confirm schedule. **Cost:** Free. **Phone:** (916) 483-8818.

Old Sacramento Underground Tours departs from the Sacramento History Museum at 101 I St. Sacramento's streets were raised in the 1860s and '70s to guard against flooding. As a result, participants on these 1-hour, partially underground walking tours will see disappearing windows and doors, alleyways and retaining walls. In addition to historic buildings and excavated building foundations, historic photos and items excavated from beneath the buildings are shown.

Note: Participants should arrive 10-15 minutes before the start of the tour to pick up their tickets. Wear comfortable walking shoes. The tour includes walking over uneven surfaces and in areas with low ceilings and small spaces. Photography is not allowed underground. **Time:** Allow 1 hour, 15 minutes minimum. **Hours:** Tours depart Thurs.-Sun. every half-hour 10:30-3, June-Aug.; Sat.-Sun. (also some Thursdays and Fridays) every half-hour 10:30-3, Sept.-Nov. **Cost:** $15; $10 (ages 6-17). Reservations are recommended. **Phone:** (916) 808-7059.

Sacramento History Museum, 101 I St., occupies a structure designed to resemble the 1854 City Hall & Waterworks Building. The museum documents Sacramento history, beginning with the lobby exhibit Gold, Greed & Speculation: The Beginnings of Sacramento City. City founders, rivers, the gold rush and agriculture are among the topics covered. Original artifacts and interactive exhibits include a historic print shop, gold troughs, agricultural machinery and a Wells Fargo delivery wagon.

Time: Allow 30 minutes minimum. **Hours:** Daily 10-5. Last admission 30 minutes before closing. Closed Jan. 1, Thanksgiving, Christmas Eve and Christmas. **Cost:** $6; $4 (ages 6-17). **Phone:** (916) 808-7059.

SAVE **RAGING WATERS SACRAMENTO** is .3 mi. e. off I-80 Bus. Rte./Capital City Frwy. (Exposition Blvd. exit), on the Cal Expo Fairgrounds. More than 25 rides and slides include Dragon's Den, a twisting tube ride through darkness; Honolulu Halfpipe, a four-story, near-vertical plunge; CliffHanger's dual speed-racing slides; a tranquil lazy river ride; Hook's Lagoon, an interactive, family-oriented play structure; wading and wave pools; waterslides; a river tube ride; and the in-line water luge Shark Attack.

Lockers and inner tubes are available for rent. **Time:** Allow 4 hours minimum. **Hours:** Mon.-Fri. 11-6, Sat.-Sun. 11-7, mid-June to mid-Aug.; hours vary Sat.-Sun. (also Memorial Day and Labor Day), mid-May to mid-June and mid-Aug. to mid-Sept. Park also open during the California State Fair in the last half of July; phone ahead for schedule. **Cost:** $30.99; $21.99 (under 48 inches tall and ages 60+);

free (ages 0-2). **Parking:** $10. **Phone:** (916) 924-3747.

SACRAMENTO CHILDREN'S MUSEUM—see Rancho Cordova p. 286.

SACRAMENTO ZOO is off I-5 exit 516 (Sutterville Rd.) to 3930 West Land Park Dr., at jct. 16th Ave. This attractively landscaped zoo exhibits a variety of animals, including giraffes, chimpanzees, orangutans, lions, Sumatran tigers, jaguars, snow leopards, Grevy's zebras, spotted hyenas and giant anteaters. Gila monsters, ball pythons and eyelash vipers are among the residents in the Reptile House.

Asian Forest includes a red panda exhibit. Among the resident bird species are hornbills and flamingos. Giraffes can be viewed from a platform deck, and twice-daily giraffe encounters allow visitors to feed these gentle giants. There's also a carousel that features 32 hand-crafted animals. A small train traverses the grounds. "Zoo Backyard" has picnic facilities and a children's play area.

Note: There is no parking on site; it's best to go early in the day (especially on weekends), when the animals are more active and it's easier to find a parking space. **Time:** Allow 2 hours minimum. **Hours:** Daily 9-5, Feb.-Oct.; 10-5, rest of year. Last admission 1 hour before closing. Closed Thanksgiving and Christmas. **Cost:** $11.25; $10.50 (ages 65+); $7.25 (ages 2-11). Carousel ride $2, accompanying adults free. Train ride $3; free (ages 0-1). Giraffe encounter $3. Combination ticket with Fairytale Town Mon.-Fri. $15; $14.50 (ages 65+); $11 (ages 2-11). Combination ticket Sat.-Sun. $16; $15.50 (ages 65+); $12 (ages 2-11). **Phone:** (916) 808-5888, or (916) 808-5885 (after-hours information hotline). ⊓⊔

SIERRA SACRAMENTO VALLEY MUSEUM OF MEDICAL HISTORY AND HISTORICAL LIBRARY is at 5380 Elvas Ave. The museum contains journals dating to the 1700s as well as displays of medical artifacts, including an iron lung. Collections include items from the fields of surgery, clinical diagnosis, radiology, Chinese medicine, infectious disease, obstetrics and gynecology and medical quackery. Guided tours are available by appointment. **Hours:** Museum Mon.-Fri. 9-4. Library by appointment. Closed major holidays. **Cost:** Free. **Phone:** (916) 456-3152.

GEM **SUTTER'S FORT STATE HISTORIC PARK**, 27th and L sts., was the first European outpost in the interior of California. Established by Swiss immigrant John Sutter after the receipt of a 48,000-acre land grant from the Mexican government, the fort's walls were 2.5 feet thick and between 15 and 18 feet tall. The settlement was initially known as New Helvetia (New Switzerland).

After the discovery of gold, Sutter's lands were virtually taken over by prospectors and he eventually left California. The restored, 1839 adobe fort contains pioneer and gold rush artifacts. **Time:** Allow

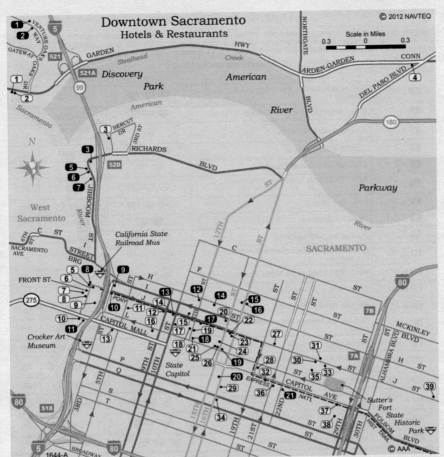

Downtown Sacramento
Hotels & Restaurants

© 2012 NAVTEQ

(See maps & indexes p. 311, 314.)

1 hour minimum. **Hours:** Tues.-Sun. 10-5. Hours may vary during special events; phone ahead. Closed Jan. 1, Thanksgiving and Christmas. **Cost:** $5; $3 (ages 6-17). Admission may increase during special events. **Phone:** (916) 445-4422.

California State Indian Museum is at 2618 K St., on the grounds of Sutter's Fort. It focuses on California's Native American cultures through displays of feather baskets, jewelry, clothing and art. **Hours:** Wed.-Sun. 10-5. Closed Jan. 1, Thanksgiving and Christmas. **Cost:** $3; $2 (ages 6-17). **Phone:** (916) 324-0971.

WILLIAM LAND PARK, bounded by Freeport and Riverside blvds., 13th Ave. and Sutterville Rd., encompasses 600 acres, including picnic facilities, a public golf course and a grove of cherry trees. **Phone:** (916) 277-1207 for golf information.

Fairytale Town is at 3901 Land Park Dr., across from the Sacramento Zoo. The park has play sets based on themes from popular children's nursery rhymes and fairy tales. Kids also can pet farm animals. Arts and crafts activities are conducted seasonally.

Hours: Daily 9-5, Mar.-Oct.; Thurs.-Sun. 10-4 (also Martin Luther King Jr. Day, Presidents Day and Veterans Day), rest of year (weather permitting). Last admission 1 hour before closing. Closed Jan. 1, Thanksgiving and Christmas. **Cost:** Admission Mon.-Fri. $4; free (ages 0-1). Admission Sat.-Sun. and holidays $5; free (ages 0-1). Combination ticket with Sacramento Zoo Mon.-Fri. $15; $14.50 (ages 65+); $11 (ages 2-12). Combination ticket Sat.-Sun. $16; $15.50 (ages 65+); $12 (ages 2-12). Adults must be accompanied by a child. **Phone:** (916) 808-7462 for activities and price information.

Downtown Sacramento

This index helps you "spot" where approved hotels and restaurants are located on the corresponding detailed maps. Hotel daily rate range is for comparison only. Restaurant price range is a combination of lunch and/or dinner. Turn to the listing page for more detailed rate and price information and consult display ads for special promotions.

DOWNTOWN SACRAMENTO

Map Page	Hotels	Diamond Rated	Rate Range	Page
1 p. 311	SpringHill Suites by Marriott-Sacramento Airport Natomas	◈◈◈	$89-$189	322
2 p. 311	Hilton Garden Inn Sacramento/South Natomas	◈◈◈	$99-$209	321
3 p. 311	**Americas Best Value Inn**	◈	Rates not provided (SAVE)	320
5 p. 311	Comfort Suites-Downtown	◈◈◈	$94-$114	321
6 p. 311	**Days Inn-Sacramento Downtown**	◈◈	$55-$109 (SAVE)	321
7 p. 311	**BEST WESTERN Sandman Motel** *(See ad p. 320.)*	◈◈◈	$69-$100 (SAVE)	320
8 p. 311	Delta King Hotel	◈◈◈	$101-$201	321
9 p. 311	Vagabond Executive Inn Old Town	◈◈	$79-$150	324
10 p. 311	**Holiday Inn Capitol Plaza**	◈◈◈	$99-$185 (SAVE)	321
11 p. 311	**Embassy Suites Sacramento-Riverfront Promenade**	◈◈◈	$149-$349 (SAVE)	321
12 p. 311	**BEST WESTERN PLUS Sutter House**	◈◈◈	$129-$200 (SAVE)	320
13 p. 311	The Citizen, a Joie de Vivre hotel	◈◈◈	$139-$299	321
14 p. 311	**Sterling Hotel Sacramento**	◈◈◈	$99-$199 (SAVE)	324
15 p. 311	**Holiday Inn Express Sacramento Convention Center**	◈◈◈	$89-$199 (SAVE)	321
16 p. 311	**Econo Lodge**	◈	$49-$99 (SAVE)	321
17 p. 311	**Sheraton Grand Sacramento Hotel** *(See ad p. 322.)*	◈◈◈	$119-$359 (SAVE)	322
18 p. 311	**Hyatt Regency Sacramento**	◈◈◈	$99-$369 (SAVE)	321
19 p. 311	**Residence Inn by Marriott- Sacramento at Capitol Park**	◈◈◈	$118-$313 (SAVE)	322
20 p. 311	**Inn Off Capitol Park, an Ascend Collection hotel**	◈◈◈	$99-$159 (SAVE)	321
21 p. 311	**Amber House Bed & Breakfast Inn**	◈◈◈◈	$179-$289 (SAVE)	320

Map Page	Restaurants	Diamond Rated	Cuisine	Price Range	Page
1 p. 311	Pearl on the River	◈◈◈	American	$12-$35	325
2 p. 311	Crawdad's River Cantina	◈◈	Cajun	$9-$19	324
3 p. 311	Monterey Bay Canners	◈◈	Seafood	$9-$30	325
4 p. 311	Enotria Restaurant & Wine Bar	◈◈◈	California	$20-$30	324
5 p. 311	Pilothouse Restaurant Aboard the Delta King	◈◈◈	Continental	$9-$24	326
6 p. 311	**Fat City Bar & Cafe**	◈◈	American	$10-$27	324
7 p. 311	Suspects Mystery Comedy Dinner Theater	◈◈	American	$40	326
8 p. 311	Rio City Cafe	◈◈	California	$9-$23	326
9 p. 311	The Firehouse	◈◈◈◈	Continental	$12-$45	324
10 p. 311	Tower Bridge Bistro	◈◈	American	$10-$38	326
11 p. 311	River City Brewing Company	◈◈	American	$9-$18	326
12 p. 311	Temple Coffee & Tea	◈	Coffee/Tea	$2-$5	326
13 p. 311	Il Fornaio	◈◈◈	Italian	$10-$35	325
14 p. 311	Grange Restaurant & Bar	◈◈◈	American	$12-$38	325
15 p. 311	McCormick & Schmick's	◈◈◈	Seafood	$10-$32	325

Map Page	Restaurants (cont'd)	Diamond Rated	Cuisine	Price Range	Page
16 p. 311	**Frank Fat's**	▽▽▽	Chinese	$9-$26	325
17 p. 311	Pizza Rock	▽▽	Pizza	$11-$30	326
18 p. 311	Ella Dining Room & Bar	▽▽▽	American	$12-$32	324
19 p. 311	The Broiler	▽▽	Steak	$14-$39	324
20 p. 311	Zen Sushi	▽▽	Japanese	$8-$19	326
21 p. 311	Dawson's	▽▽▽	American	$26-$37	324
22 p. 311	Mikuni japanese restaurant & sushi bar	▽▽	Japanese	$10-$19	325
23 p. 311	P.F. Chang's China Bistro	▽▽▽	Chinese	$10-$21	326
24 p. 311	Cafeteria 15L	▽▽	American	$11-$22	324
25 p. 311	Spataro Restaurant and Bar	▽▽▽	Italian	$10-$23	326
26 p. 311	Ma Jong's Asian Diner	▽	Asian	$9-$11	325
27 p. 311	Pete's Restaurant & Brewhouse	▽▽	Italian	$7-$20	325
28 p. 311	Mulvaney's Building & Loan	▽▽▽	American	$11-$34	325
29 p. 311	Paesanos Pronto	▽▽	Italian	$7-$10	325
30 p. 311	Chicago Fire	▽▽	Pizza	$9-$22	324
31 p. 311	Thai Basil	▽▽	Thai	$8-$14	326
32 p. 311	The Waterboy Restaurant	▽▽▽	French	$17-$25	326
33 p. 311	Kru	▽▽	Japanese	$7-$35	325
34 p. 311	Hot Italian	▽▽	Italian	$9-$16	325
35 p. 311	Tres Hermanas	▽	Mexican	$10-$14	326
36 p. 311	Bombay Bar and Grill	▽▽	Indian	$9-$19	324
37 p. 311	Cafe Bernardo Midtown/Monkey Bar	▽	Regional American	$6-$15	324
38 p. 311	Paragary's Bar and Oven	▽▽▽	Mediterranean	$11-$24	325
39 p. 311	La Trattoria Bohemia	▽▽	Czechoslovakian	$10-$18	325

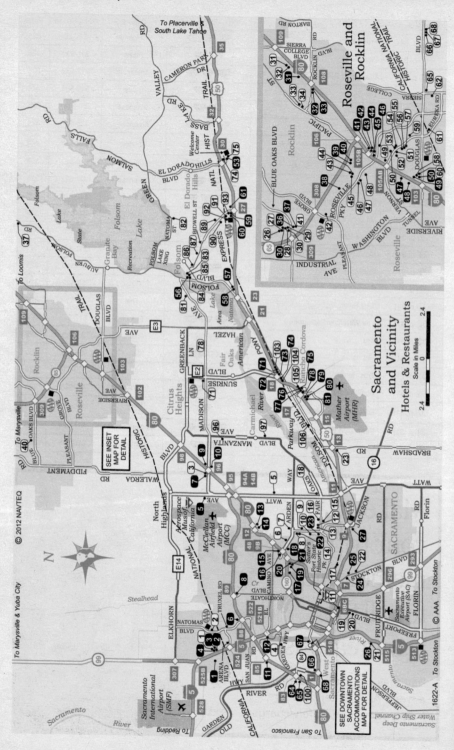

✈ Airport Accommodations

Map Page	SACRAMENTO INTERNATIONAL	Diamond Rated	Rate Range	Page
1 p. 314	Four Points by Sheraton Sacramento International Airport, 6.1 mi se of terminal	▽▽▽	$169-$369 SAVE	327
4 p. 314	Hampton Inn & Suites Sac-Airport/Natomas, 5.8 mi se of terminal	▽▽▽	$109-$199 SAVE	329
3 p. 314	Holiday Inn Express & Suites-Sacramento Airport/Natomas, 5.8 mi se of terminal	▽▽▽	$129-$199 SAVE	329
2 p. 314	Homewood Suites by Hilton Sacramento Airport, 5.8 mi se of terminal	▽▽▽	$109-$300 SAVE	330

Sacramento and Vicinity

This index helps you "spot" where approved hotels and restaurants are located on the corresponding detailed maps. Hotel daily rate range is for comparison only. Restaurant price range is a combination of lunch and/or dinner. Turn to the listing page for more detailed rate and price information and consult display ads for special promotions.

SACRAMENTO

Map Page	Hotels	Diamond Rated	Rate Range	Page
1 p. 314	Four Points by Sheraton Sacramento International Airport	▽▽▽	$169-$369 SAVE	327
2 p. 314	Homewood Suites by Hilton Sacramento Airport	▽▽▽	$109-$300 SAVE	330
3 p. 314	Holiday Inn Express & Suites-Sacramento Airport/Natomas	▽▽▽	$129-$199 SAVE	329
4 p. 314	Hampton Inn & Suites Sac-Airport/Natomas	▽▽▽	$109-$199 SAVE	329
5 p. 314	Lions Gate Hotel & Conference Center	▽▽▽	$99-$109 SAVE	330
6 p. 314	Staybridge Suites Sacramento Airport/Natomas	◆◆◆	$99-$159	332
7 p. 314	Super 8 Sacramento	◆◆	$65-$79	332
8 p. 314	Quality Inn Natomas	◆	$55-$90 SAVE	330
9 p. 314	Crowne Plaza Sacramento	◆◆◆	$75-$95	327
10 p. 314	La Quinta Inn Sacramento North	◆◆◆	$71-$133	330
11 p. 314	Fairfield Inn & Suites Sacramento Airport Natomas	▽▽▽	$76-$160 SAVE	327
12 p. 314	Residence Inn by Marriott-Sacramento Airport Natomas	▽▽▽	$189-$199 SAVE	330
13 p. 314	Hampton Inn & Suites	◆◆◆	$99-$149	327
14 p. 314	Holiday Inn Express & Suites Sacramento Cal Expo	▽▽▽	$99-$139	330
15 p. 314	Hilton Sacramento Arden West	▽▽▽	$89-$239 SAVE	329
16 p. 314	Extended StayAmerica-Sacramento-Arden Way	◆◆	$76-$91	327
17 p. 314	Red Lion Hotel Woodlake Conference Center Sacramento	▽▽▽	$89-$209 SAVE	330
18 p. 314	DoubleTree by Hilton Hotel Sacramento	▽▽▽	$89-$229 SAVE	327
19 p. 314	Fairfield Inn by Marriott Sacramento Cal Expo	▽▽▽	$69-$134 SAVE	327
20 p. 314	TownePlace Suites by Marriott Sacramento Cal Expo	▽▽▽	$79-$159 SAVE	332
21 p. 314	Courtyard Sacramento Cal Expo	▽▽▽	$79-$144 SAVE	327
22 p. 314	Quality Inn & Suites	▽▽	Rates not provided SAVE	330
23 p. 314	Larkspur Landing Sacramento	▽▽▽	$109-$189	330
24 p. 314	Hotel Med Park, Sacramento	▽▽▽	$129-$149 SAVE	330
25 p. 314	Courtyard by Marriott Midtown Sacramento	▽▽▽	$169-$189	327

SACRAMENTO (cont'd)

Map Page	Hotels (cont'd)	Diamond Rated	Rate Range	Page
26 p. 314	Le Rivage Hotel, A Preferred Hotel	▼▼▼▼	$129-$799	330
27 p. 314	**Comfort Inn & Suites**	▼▼▼	$90-$250 SAVE	327

Map Page	Restaurants	Diamond Rated	Cuisine	Price Range	Page
1 p. 314	Malabar	▼▼	American	$10-$25	333
2 p. 314	Tuk Tuk Restaurant	▼▼	Thai	$7-$16	334
3 p. 314	Brookfields Restaurant	▼▼	American	$8-$16	332
4 p. 314	The Virgin Sturgeon Restaurant-Marina	▼▼	American	$8-$18	334
5 p. 314	Sam's Hof Brau	▼	Comfort Food	$5-$12	334
6 p. 314	Taro's by Mikuni	▼▼	Japanese	$9-$19	334
7 p. 314	Tex Wasabi's	▼▼	Japanese	$11-$29	334
8 p. 314	The Habit Burger Grill	▼	Burgers	$4-$7	333
9 p. 314	**The Kitchen Restaurant**	▼▼▼▼▼	American	$125	333
10 p. 314	Lemon Grass Asian Grill & Noodle Bar	▼	Asian	$7-$10	333
11 p. 314	Andy Nguyen's Vegetarian Restaurant	▼▼	Vegetarian	$9-$15	332
12 p. 314	Piatti Ristorante & Bar	▼▼▼	Italian	$12-$28	334
13 p. 314	Ruth's Chris Steak House	▼▼▼	American	$21-$48	334
14 p. 314	Selland's Market - Cafe	▼▼	American	$5-$23	334
15 p. 314	Ettore's European Bakery & Restaurant	▼▼	American	$8-$18	333
16 p. 314	Boudin SF	▼	American	$6-$10	332
17 p. 314	OneSpeed	▼▼	Pizza	$9-$18	334
18 p. 314	Cafe Vinoteca	▼▼	Italian	$9-$28	332
19 p. 314	Taylors Market	▼	Sandwiches	$6-$8	334
20 p. 314	Freeport Bakery	▼	Breads/Pastries	$2-$10	333
21 p. 314	Scott's Seafood Grill & Bar	▼▼▼	Seafood	$11-$41	334
22 p. 314	Louie's Restaurant & Catering	▼▼	Chinese	$8-$18	333
23 p. 314	Perko's Cafe & Grill	▼▼	American	$8-$16	334

ROCKLIN

Map Page	Hotels	Diamond Rated	Rate Range	Page
30 p. 314	Staybridge Suites	▼▼▼	$99-$159	299
31 p. 314	Days Inn - Rocklin	▼▼	$55-$95	299
32 p. 314	Howard Johnson Hotel	▼▼	$59-$119	299
33 p. 314	Heritage Inn Express, Rocklin	▼▼	$65-$75	299

Map Page	Restaurants	Diamond Rated	Cuisine	Price Range	Page
26 p. 314	Lucille's Smokehouse Bar-B-Que & Catering	▼▼	Barbecue	$11-$29	300
27 p. 314	Skipolini's Pizza & Pasta	▼▼	Italian	$7-$26	300
28 p. 314	Crazy Sushi	▼▼	Japanese	$9-$25	299
29 p. 314	Anatolian Table Turkish Cuisine & Patisserie	▼▼	Turkish	$9-$23	299
30 p. 314	The Chef's Table	▼▼	American	$10-$20	299

Map Page	Restaurants (cont'd)	Diamond Rated	Cuisine	Price Range	Page
㉛ p. 314	Venita Rhea's Cafe	◆◆	American	$7-$15	300
㉜ p. 314	Pottery World Cafe	◆◆	American	$10-$16	300
㉝ p. 314	Rubino's Ristorante	◆◆	Italian	$8-$27	300
㉞ p. 314	Icing on the Cupcake	◆	American	$3	299

ROSEVILLE

Map Page	Hotels	Diamond Rated	Rate Range	Page
㊱ p. 314	SpringHill Suites by Marriott Roseville	◆◆◆	$109-$129	302
㊲ p. 314	TownePlace Suites by Marriott Roseville	◆◆◆	$99-$169	303
㊳ p. 314	**Hyatt Place Sacramento/Roseville**	◆◆◆	$89-$169 SAVE	302
㊴ p. 314	Homewood Suites by Hilton	◆◆◆	$109-$179	302
㊵ p. 314	Courtyard by Marriott Galleria	◆◆◆	$89-$129	302
㊶ p. 314	Residence Inn by Marriott	◆◆◆	$109-$149	302
㊷ p. 314	Hilton Garden Inn Roseville	◆◆◆	$89-$189	302
㊸ p. 314	Courtyard by Marriott	◆◆◆	$89-$129	301
㊹ p. 314	Larkspur Landing Roseville	◆◆◆	$89-$219	302
㊺ p. 314	Fairfield Inn by Marriott	◆◆◆	$79-$109	302
㊻ p. 314	**Holiday Inn Express & Suites-Roseville Galleria**	◆◆◆	$99-$119 SAVE	302
㊼ p. 314	Extended StayAmerica-Sacramento-Roseville	◆◆	$84-$99	302
㊽ p. 314	**BEST WESTERN PLUS Roseville Inn**	◆◆◆	Rates not provided SAVE	301
㊾ p. 314	**Orchid Suites Roseville**	◆◆	$80-$199 SAVE	302
㊿ p. 314	**Hampton Inn & Suites Roseville**	◆◆◆	$109-$149 SAVE	302

Map Page	Restaurants	Diamond Rated	Cuisine	Price Range	Page
㊵ p. 314	La Provence Restaurant & Terrace	◆◆◆	Regional French	$9-$33	304
㊶ p. 314	Johnny Garlic's	◆◆	American	$9-$29	304
㊷ p. 314	The Habit Burger Grill	◆	American	$4-$7	303
㊸ p. 314	P.F. Chang's China Bistro	◆◆◆	Chinese	$10-$25	304
㊹ p. 314	Ruth's Chris Steak House	◆◆◆	Steak	$8-$48	304
㊺ p. 314	Il Fornaio	◆◆◆	Italian	$9-$35	303
㊻ p. 314	Yard House	◆◆	American	$10-$31	305
㊼ p. 314	McCormick & Schmick's	◆◆◆	Seafood	$12-$35	304
㊽ p. 314	The Counter	◆◆	American	$6-$13	303
㊾ p. 314	Brookfields	◆◆	American	$7-$16	303
㊿ p. 314	Chicago Fire	◆◆	Italian	$9-$27	303
(51) p. 314	Suede blue	◆◆◆	Steak	$12-$46	304
(52) p. 314	John's Incredible Pizza Co.	◆	Pizza	$7-$10	304
(53) p. 314	Paul Martin's American Bistro	◆◆◆	American	$12-$30	304
(54) p. 314	Blue Nami Taste of Japan	◆◆	Japanese	$9-$25	303
(55) p. 314	Ruen Thai	◆◆	Thai	$8-$15	304
(56) p. 314	Crush 29	◆◆◆	American	$12-$26	303

Map Page	Restaurants (cont'd)	Diamond Rated	Cuisine	Price Range	Page
57 p. 314	Fat's Asia Bistro & Dim Sum Bar	◆◆◆	Chinese	$9-$22	303
58 p. 314	Squeeze Inn	◆	Burgers	$2-$5	304
59 p. 314	Mas Cocina Mexicana	◆◆◆	Mexican	$7-$17	304
60 p. 314	Thai Basil Restaurant	◆◆	Thai	$9-$17	304
61 p. 314	Costa Vida Fresh Mexican Grill	◆	Mexican	$5-$8	303
62 p. 314	Fins Market & Grill	◆◆	Seafood	$8-$22	303

EL DORADO HILLS

Map Page	Hotel	Diamond Rated	Rate Range	Page
53 p. 314	**Holiday Inn Express Hotel & Suites**	◆◆◆	$109-$189 SAVE	99

Map Page	Restaurants	Diamond Rated	Cuisine	Price Range	Page
74 p. 314	Chantara Thai Cuisine	◆◆	Thai	$8-$16	99
75 p. 314	Bamiyan Afghan Restaurant	◆◆◆	Afghan	$9-$29	99

FOLSOM

Map Page	Hotels	Diamond Rated	Rate Range	Page
56 p. 314	**Lake Natoma Inn Hotel & Conference Center**	◆◆◆	$89-$169 SAVE	112
57 p. 314	Larkspur Landing Home Suite Hotels Folsom	◆◆◆	Rates not provided	112
58 p. 314	Hilton Garden Inn	◆◆◆	$89-$209	112
59 p. 314	Courtyard by Marriott Sacramento-Folsom	◆◆◆	$109-$169	112
60 p. 314	Residence Inn by Marriott	◆◆◆	$119-$179	112
61 p. 314	**Hampton Inn & Suites**	◆◆◆	$89-$169 SAVE	112

Map Page	Restaurants	Diamond Rated	Cuisine	Price Range	Page
81 p. 314	Scott's Seafood Grill & Bar	◆◆◆	Seafood	$12-$32	113
82 p. 314	Mexquite Mexican Cuisine & Tequila Lounge	◆◆	Mexican	$8-$16	113
83 p. 314	Sutter Street Steakhouse	◆◆◆	Steak	$19-$37	113
84 p. 314	Karen's Bakery Cafe & Catering	◆◆	Breads/Pastries	$9-$15	113
85 p. 314	Chicago Fire	◆◆	Pizza	$8-$27	112
86 p. 314	Visconti's Ristorante	◆◆	Italian	$8-$24	113
87 p. 314	Bidwell Street Bistro	◆◆◆	American	$12-$26	112
89 p. 314	Land Ocean New American Steakhouse	◆◆◆	Steak	$11-$28	113
90 p. 314	Icing on the Cupcake	◆	American	$3	112
91 p. 314	Chicago Fire	◆◆	Pizza	$8-$27	112
92 p. 314	Blue Nami	◆◆	Sushi	$9-$25	112
93 p. 314	Fat's Asia Bistro & Dim Sum Bar	◆◆◆	Asian	$9-$21	112

WEST SACRAMENTO

Map Page	Hotels	Diamond Rated	Rate Range	Page
64 p. 314	Extended StayAmerica-Sacramento-West Sacramento	◆◆	$84-$99	557
65 p. 314	Hampton Inn & Suites-West Sacramento	◆◆◆	$99-$179	557
66 p. 314	**Holiday Inn Express - West Sacramento**	◆◆◆	Rates not provided SAVE	557

WEST SACRAMENTO (cont'd)

Map Page	Hotels (cont'd)	Diamond Rated	Rate Range	Page
67 p. 314	**Rodeway Inn Capitol**	▽	$50-$70 SAVE	557
68 p. 314	Ramada Inn & Plaza Harbor Conference Center	▽▽▽	$69-$104	557

Map Page	Restaurant	Diamond Rated	Cuisine	Price Range	Page
100 p. 314	IKEA Restaurant	▽	Swedish	$3-$7	557

RANCHO CORDOVA

Map Page	Hotels	Diamond Rated	Rate Range	Page
71 p. 314	Holiday Inn Rancho Cordova	▽▽▽	$99-$149	287
72 p. 314	**Hyatt house Sacramento/Rancho Cordova**	▽▽▽	$79-$169 SAVE	287
73 p. 314	**Sacramento Marriott Rancho Cordova**	▽▽▽	$99-$229 SAVE	287
74 p. 314	La Quinta Inn & Suites Sacramento Rancho Cordova	▽▽▽	$59-$151	287
75 p. 314	Residence Inn by Marriott	▽▽▽	$90-$250	287
76 p. 314	Hampton Inn by Hilton	▽▽▽	$99-$159	287
77 p. 314	Fairfield Inn & Suites by Marriott	▽▽▽	$69-$139	287
78 p. 314	**Hyatt Place Sacramento/Rancho Cordova**	▽▽▽	$89-$219 SAVE	287
79 p. 314	Extended StayAmerica-Sacramento-White Rock Rd	▽▽	$69-$84	287
80 p. 314	Red Lion Inn	▽▽	Rates not provided	287
81 p. 314	**Courtyard by Marriott**	▽▽▽	$62-$139 SAVE	286

Map Page	Restaurants	Diamond Rated	Cuisine	Price Range	Page
103 p. 314	Sheepherder Bar & Grille	▽▽	American	$9-$25	288
104 p. 314	Brookfields	▽▽	American	$8-$16	288
105 p. 314	Cordova Restaurant Casino	▽▽	American	$8-$26	288
106 p. 314	Andy Nguyen's 2	▽▽	Vietnamese	$9-$14	287

LOOMIS

Map Page	Restaurant	Diamond Rated	Cuisine	Price Range	Page
37 p. 314	Tsuda's Flower Farm Cafe	▽	American	$6-$10	179

GRANITE BAY

Map Page	Restaurants	Diamond Rated	Cuisine	Price Range	Page
65 p. 314	The Habit Burger Grill	▽	Burgers	$4-$7	139
66 p. 314	Hawks Restaurant	▽▽▽	American	$8-$38	139
67 p. 314	Source Global Tapas Restaurant	▽▽	International	$4-$13	139
68 p. 314	Pete's Brewhouse & Restaurant	▽▽	American	$9-$22	139

CITRUS HEIGHTS

Map Page	Restaurant	Diamond Rated	Cuisine	Price Range	Page
71 p. 314	The Habit Burger Grill	▽	Burgers	$4-$7	79

FAIR OAKS

Map Page	Restaurant	Diamond Rated	Cuisine	Price Range	Page
78 p. 314	Fins Market & Grill	▽▽	Seafood	$8-$22	109

CARMICHAEL

Map Page	Restaurants	Diamond Rated	Cuisine	Price Range	Page
96 p. 314	Firebird Russian Restaurant & Gallery	▽▽	Russian	$8-$17	75
97 p. 314	Ambience	▽▽▽	New American	$55-$75	75

DOWNTOWN SACRAMENTO

- Restaurants p. 324
- Hotels & Restaurants map & index p. 311

AMBER HOUSE BED & BREAKFAST INN

(916)444-8085

Bed & Breakfast
$179-$289

Address: 1315 22nd St 95816 **Location:** Between Capitol and N sts; midtown. **Facility:** Two restored craftsman-style mansions make up this residential-area, historic inn; rooms feature upscale amenities, like an LCD television and private garden. 10 units. 2 stories (no elevator), interior corridors. **Terms:** check-in 4 pm, 7 day cancellation notice-fee imposed. **Guest Services:** valet laundry. **Free Special Amenities:** full breakfast and high-speed Internet. SAVE 🛏️ FEE 🐾 📶

AMERICAS BEST VALUE INN

916/442-7777 🟢

Motel
Rates not provided

Address: 221 Jibboom St 95811 **Location:** I-5 exit Richards Blvd, just w. **Facility:** 28 units. 2 stories (no elevator), exterior corridors. **Free Special Amenities:** continental breakfast and high-speed Internet. SAVE 🛏️ CALL 🛜 📶 🔲 🔲 / SOME UNITS 🔲

Download eTourBook
guides for top destinations
at AAA.com/ebooks

BEST WESTERN PLUS SUTTER HOUSE

(916)441-1314

Hotel
$129-$200

AAA Benefit: Members save up to 20%, plus 10% bonus points with Best Western Rewards®.

Address: 1100 H St 95814 **Location:** 4 blks from state capitol; between 11th and 12th sts. **Facility:** 95 units. 3 stories, interior/exterior corridors. **Amenities:** high-speed Internet. **Pool(s):** outdoor. **Guest Services:** valet laundry. **Free Special Amenities:** local telephone calls and high-speed Internet. SAVE 🛏️ 🍽️ CALL 🛜 🐾 FEE 🐾 BIZ 📶 ❌ 🔲

BEST WESTERN SANDMAN MOTEL

(916)443-6515 🟢

Hotel
$69-$100

AAA Benefit: Members save up to 20%, plus 10% bonus points with Best Western Rewards®.

Address: 236 Jibboom St 95811 **Location:** I-5 exit Richards Blvd, just w. **Facility:** 109 units. 2 stories (no elevator), exterior corridors. **Terms:** check-in 4 pm. **Amenities:** Some: high-speed Internet. **Pool(s):** heated outdoor. **Activities:** whirlpool, exercise room. **Guest Services:** valet and coin laundry, area transportation-Amtrak station. **Free Special Amenities:** expanded continental breakfast and high-speed Internet. *(See ad this page.)* SAVE ➡️ 🛏️ CALL 🛜 🐾 BIZ 📶 🔲 🔲 🔲 / SOME UNITS FEE 🐾

▼ See AAA listing this page ▼

(See map & index p. 311.)

THE CITIZEN, A JOIE DE VIVRE HOTEL   (916)447-2700   13

▼▼▼▼ **Boutique Hotel** $139-$299 **Address:** 926 J St 95814 **Location:** I-5 exit J St (Old Sacramento), 0.6 mi e; jct 10th St. **Facility:** The historic 1926 hotel, featuring luxury accommodations, is close to the state capitol and convention center. Guest room televisions offer the capitol channels. Some units include a wet bar or balcony. 196 units. 13 stories, interior corridors. **Terms:** cancellation fee imposed. **Amenities:** high-speed Internet (fee), safes. **Dining:** Grange Restaurant & Bar, see separate listing. **Activities:** exercise room. **Guest Services:** valet laundry.

[ECO] [ⓘ] [🍴] [♿] [CALL] [&M] [BIZ] [📶] [✕] [💻] / SOME UNITS [🐾] FEE [🎒]

COMFORT SUITES-DOWNTOWN   (916)446-9400   5

▼▼▼ **Hotel** $94-$114 **Address:** 226 Jibboom St 95811 **Location:** I-5 exit Richards Blvd, just w. **Facility:** 53 units. 3 stories, interior corridors. **Terms:** cancellation fee imposed. **Amenities:** high-speed Internet. **Pool(s):** outdoor. **Activities:** whirlpool. **Guest Services:** valet and coin laundry.

[ⓘ] [CALL] [&M] [♨] [📶] [✕] [🅿] [🖨] [💻]

DAYS INN-SACRAMENTO DOWNTOWN   (916)443-4811   6

▼▼▼ Hotel $55-$109
Address: 228 Jibboom St 95814 **Location:** I-5 exit Richards Blvd, just w. **Facility:** 69 units. 2 stories (no elevator), interior corridors. **Amenities:** high-speed Internet. **Pool(s):** outdoor. **Guest Services:** valet and coin laundry. **Free Special Amenities:** expanded continental breakfast and high-speed Internet.

[SAVE] [✈] [ⓘ] [CALL] [&M] [♨] [BIZ] [📶] [🅿] [🖨] [💻] / SOME UNITS FEE [🎒]

DELTA KING HOTEL   (916)444-5464   8

▼▼▼▼ Hotel $101-$201 **Address:** 1000 Front St 95814 **Location:** I-5 exit J St (Old Sacramento), just s on 3rd St, just n. Located on the Sacramento River. **Facility:** 44 units. 5 stories, interior/exterior corridors. **Parking:** valet only. **Terms:** check-in 4 pm, cancellation fee imposed. **Dining:** Pilothouse Restaurant Aboard the Delta King, Suspects Mystery Comedy Dinner Theater, see separate listings. **Guest Services:** valet laundry.

[ⓘ] [CALL] [&M] FEE [♨] [BIZ] [📶] [✕] [💻]

ECONO LODGE   (916)443-6631   16

▼▼▼ Motel $49-$99
Address: 711 16th St 95814 **Location:** Business Rt I-80 exit SR 160, 3.5 mi sw to N 12th St, 0.5 mi s to H St, just se, then just n; I-5 exit J St (Old Sacramento), 1 mi e, then just n. **Facility:** 40 units, some two bedrooms. 3 stories, exterior corridors. **Terms:** cancellation fee imposed. **Free Special Amenities:** continental breakfast and local telephone calls.

[SAVE] [ⓘ] [CALL] [&M] [📶] [🅿] / SOME UNITS FEE [🎒] [🖨]

EMBASSY SUITES SACRAMENTO-RIVERFRONT PROMENADE   (916)326-5000   11

▼▼▼ Hotel $149-$349   [E] EMBASSY SUITES HOTELS*
AAA Benefit: Members save 5% or more!

Address: 100 Capitol Mall 95814 **Location:** I-5 exit J St (Old Sacramento), just s on 3rd St, then just w. Located on the Sacramento River; adjacent to Old Sacramento. **Facility:** 242 units. 8 stories, interior corridors. **Parking:** valet only. **Terms:** check-in 4 pm, 1-7 night minimum stay, cancellation fee imposed. **Amenities:** safes. **Fee:** video games, high-speed Internet. **Dining:** 2 restaurants, also, Tower Bridge Bistro, see separate listing. **Pool(s):** heated indoor. **Activities:** whirlpool, exercise room. **Guest Services:** valet and coin laundry, area transportation-within 2 mi.

[SAVE] [ECO] [✈] [ⓘ] [Y] [CALL] [&M] [♨] [BIZ] [📶] [📹] [🅿] [🖨] [💻]

HILTON GARDEN INN SACRAMENTO/SOUTH NATOMAS   (916)568-5400   2

▼▼▼ Hotel $99-$209 **Address:** 2540 Venture Oaks Way 95833 **Location:** I-5 exit 521 (Garden Hwy), 0.3 mi w, just n to Gateway Oaks Dr, then 0.3 mi ne. **Facility:** 154 units. 3 stories, interior corridors. **Terms:** 1-7 night minimum stay, cancellation fee imposed. **Amenities:** high-speed Internet. **Pool(s):** heated outdoor. **Activities:** whirlpool, exercise room. **Guest Services:** valet and coin laundry.

AAA Benefit: Unparalleled hospitality at a special Member rate.

[✈] [ⓘ] [🍴] [CALL] [&M] [♨] [BIZ] [📶] [🅿] [🖨] [💻]

HOLIDAY INN CAPITOL PLAZA   (916)446-0100   10

▼▼▼ Hotel $99-$185
Address: 300 J St 95814 **Location:** I-5 exit J St (Old Sacramento); adjacent to Downtown Westfield Plaza Shopping Mall. **Facility:** 359 units. 16 stories, interior corridors. **Parking:** on-site (fee) valet. **Amenities:** high-speed Internet. **Pool(s):** heated outdoor. **Activities:** exercise room. **Guest Services:** complimentary and valet laundry.

[SAVE] [ECO] [ⓘ] [♿] [Y] [CALL] [&M] [♨] [BIZ] [📶] [💻] / SOME UNITS [🅿] [🖨]

HOLIDAY INN EXPRESS SACRAMENTO CONVENTION CENTER   (916)444-4436   15

▼▼▼ Hotel $89-$199
Address: 728 16th St 95814 **Location:** Jct H and 16th sts. Across from Wells Fargo Pavilion/Sacramento Theatre. **Facility:** 132 units. 4 stories, interior corridors. **Terms:** cancellation fee imposed. **Activities:** exercise room. **Guest Services:** valet laundry. **Free Special Amenities:** expanded continental breakfast and high-speed Internet.

[SAVE] [ECO] FEE [✈] [ⓘ] [CALL] [&M] [BIZ] [📶] [✕] [🅿] [💻] / SOME UNITS FEE [🎒] [🖨]

HYATT REGENCY SACRAMENTO   (916)443-1234   18

▼▼▼▼ Hotel $99-$369   HYATT*
AAA Benefit: Members save 10% or more everyday.

Address: 1209 L St 95814 **Location:** 1/2 blk from state capitol; jct 12th and L sts. Located near convention center. **Facility:** Upscale appointments adorn the spacious lobby and common areas of this centrally located hotel. An attractive patio area features several outdoor fireplaces with seating areas. 503 units. 15 stories, interior corridors. **Parking:** on-site (fee) and valet. **Terms:** cancellation fee imposed. **Amenities:** video games (fee), safes. **Dining:** 2 restaurants, also, Dawson's, see separate listing. **Pool(s):** heated outdoor. **Activities:** whirlpool, exercise room. **Fee:** massage. **Guest Services:** valet laundry.

[SAVE] [ECO] [ⓘ] [♿] [Y] [CALL] [&M] [♨] [BIZ] [📶] [✕] [💻] / SOME UNITS FEE [🎒]

INN OFF CAPITOL PARK, AN ASCEND COLLECTION HOTEL   (916)447-8100   20

▼▼▼ Hotel $99-$159
Address: 1530 N St 95814 **Location:** 0.3 mi e of state capitol; jct 16th and N sts; midtown. **Facility:** 37 units. 3 stories, interior corridors. **Terms:** cancellation fee imposed. **Amenities:** high-speed Internet. **Activities:** limited exercise equipment. **Free Special Amenities:** continental breakfast and high-speed Internet.

[SAVE] [ⓘ] [CALL] [&M] [BIZ] [📶] [✕] [🅿] [🖨] [💻]

Learn about inspections and Diamond Ratings at AAA.com/Diamonds

(See map & index p. 311.)

RESIDENCE INN BY MARRIOTT- SACRAMENTO AT CAPITOL PARK
(916)443-0500

Extended Stay Hotel
$118-$313

AAA Benefit: AAA hotel discounts of 5% or more.

Address: 1121 15th St 95814 **Location:** Jct 15th and L sts; just e of state capitol. **Facility:** 235 units, some two bedrooms, efficiencies and kitchens. 15 stories, interior corridors. **Parking:** on-site (fee). **Terms:** check-in 4 pm. **Amenities:** high-speed Internet. **Pool(s):** heated outdoor. **Activities:** whirlpool, rental bicycles, exercise room. **Guest Services:** valet and coin laundry. **Free Special Amenities: full breakfast and high-speed Internet.**

Visit AAA.com/Travel
or CAA.ca/Travel for
complete trip planning
and reservations

SHERATON GRAND SACRAMENTO HOTEL
(916)447-1700

Hotel
$119-$359

AAA Benefit: Members get up to 20% off, plus Starwood Preferred Guest® bonuses.

Address: 1230 J St 95814 **Location:** I-5 exit J St (Old Sacramento), 1 mi e; jct 12th St. Adjacent to Sacramento Convention Center. **Facility:** Located in the beautifully restored historic Public Market Building, the hotel is steps away from the convention center and the state capitol. 503 units. 27 stories, interior corridors. **Parking:** on-site (fee) and valet. **Terms:** cancellation fee imposed. **Amenities:** Fee: video games, high-speed Internet. **Dining:** 2 restaurants. **Pool(s):** heated outdoor. **Activities:** exercise room. **Guest Services:** valet laundry. **Free Special Amenities:** newspaper. (See ad this page.)

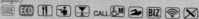

SPRINGHILL SUITES BY MARRIOTT-SACRAMENTO AIRPORT NATOMAS
(916)925-2280

Hotel $89-$189 **Address:** 2555 Venture Oaks Way 95833 **Location:** I-5 exit Garden Hwy, 0.3 mi w, just n on Gateway Oaks Dr, then 0.3 mi ne. **Facility:** 95 units. 4 stories, interior corridors. **Amenities:** high-speed Internet. **Pool(s):** heated indoor. **Activities:** whirlpool, exercise room. **Guest Services:** valet and coin laundry, area transportation-within 5 mi.

AAA Benefit: AAA hotel discounts of 5% or more.

▼ See AAA listing this page ▼

(See map & index p. 311.)

STERLING HOTEL SACRAMENTO (916)448-1300 **14**

Hotel
$99-$199

Address: 1300 H St 95814 **Location:** 4 blks n of state capitol; jct 13th St. **Facility:** 16 units. 3 stories, interior corridors. **Parking:** on-site (fee) and street. **Terms:** cancellation fee imposed. **Guest Services:** valet laundry. **Free Special Amenities: continental breakfast and high-speed Internet.**

[SAVE] [icons] CALL [icons] FEE [icons] [BIZ] [icons] [icons] [icons]
/ SOME UNITS [icon]

VAGABOND EXECUTIVE INN OLD TOWN
(916)446-1481 **9**

Hotel $79-$150 **Address:** 909 3rd St 95814 **Location:** I-5 exit J St (Old Sacramento); 8 blks w of state capitol; jct J and 3rd sts. Adjacent to Chinese Cultural Center and Old Sacramento. **Facility:** 108 units. 3 stories, exterior corridors. **Pool(s):** heated outdoor. **Activities:** whirlpool, exercise room. **Guest Services:** area transportation-bus & train stations.

[icons] CALL [icons] [icons] [BIZ] [icons] [icons] [icons] [icons]
/ SOME UNITS FEE [icon]

WHERE TO EAT

BOMBAY BAR AND GRILL 916/441-7100 **36**

Indian. Casual Dining. $9-$19 **AAA Inspector Notes:** A variety of tasty Indian cuisine is served, including a good selection of appetizers, vegetarian, seafood, chicken, lamb and tandoori specialties. Belly dancing is presented on Friday and Saturday nights. **Bar:** full bar. **Address:** 1315 21st St 95811 **Location:** Jct 21st St and Capitol Ave; midtown. **Parking:** street only. [L] [D]

THE BROILER 916/444-3444 **19**

Steak. Casual Dining. $14-$39 **AAA Inspector Notes:** Since 1950, this traditional restaurant has been serving steak along with a varied menu which includes seafood. A pub menu is available on the patio and lunch is served Monday through Friday. Look for the sign on 12th Street to the alley for free parking after 5 p.m. in the basement of the garage. Day parking is validated at any city of Sacramento parking structure—the closest is on 10th St, between K and L Sts. **Bar:** full bar. **Address:** 1201 K St 95814 **Location:** Jct 12th St. [L] [D] CALL [icons]

CAFE BERNARDO MIDTOWN/MONKEY BAR
916/443-1180 **37**

Regional American. Quick Serve. $6-$15 **AAA Inspector Notes:** Close to hospitals and medical offices, this popular neighborhood café serves tasty California cuisine menu items with breads, pastries and desserts made fresh daily and served up by efficient servers. Local and seasonal ingredients are emphasized. This was the first restaurant in Sacramento County certified as a green business. Patio dining is available. **Bar:** beer & wine. **Address:** 2726 Capitol Ave 95816 **Location:** Business Rt I-80 (Capitol City Frwy) exit J St, just w, then just s; jct 28th Ave; midtown. **Parking:** street only. [B] [L] [D] CALL [icons]

CAFETERIA 15L 916/492-1960 **24**

American. Casual Dining. $11-$22 **AAA Inspector Notes:** Do not let the name deceive you, this restaurant (not a cafeteria) offers creative spins on familiar favorites. Daily blue plate specials and small and large plates are perfect for sharing. Lunch is served Monday through Friday. An eclectic, contemporary décor and an inviting patio area can be enjoyed here. **Bar:** full bar. **Address:** 1116 15th St 95814 **Location:** Jct 15th and L sts; just e of state capitol. **Parking:** valet and street only. [L] [D] [LATE] CALL [icons] [icon]

CHICAGO FIRE 916/443-0440 **30**

Pizza. Casual Dining. $9-$22 **AAA Inspector Notes:** Authentic Chicago-style pizza, including thin crust (sliced in squares), deep dish and stuffed, is offered at this upscale, casual spot. Salads and sandwiches round out the menu. On the weekend arrive early (before 4:30 p.m.) otherwise expect a long wait. **Bar:** full bar. **Address:** 2416 J St 95816 **Location:** Business Rt I-80 (Capital City Frwy) exit J St, just w on K St, just n on 24th St, then just e; between 24th and 25th sts; midtown. **Parking:** street only. [L] [D] [LATE] CALL [icons]

CRAWDAD'S RIVER CANTINA 916/929-2268 **2**

Cajun. Casual Dining. $9-$19 **AAA Inspector Notes:** For 23 years this floating restaurant on the Sacramento River has been offering Cajun cooking, covered deck seating and live music most nights in the summer. Drive your boat and park at the dock. Friendly servers dish up breakfast Saturday and Sunday from 10:30 a.m. to 1 p.m. **Bar:** full bar. **Address:** 13750 Garden Hwy 95833 **Location:** I-5 exit 521 (Garden Hwy), just w. [L] [D] CALL [icons]

DAWSON'S 916/321-3600 **21**

American. Fine Dining. $26-$37 **AAA Inspector Notes:** American bistro cuisine with flair is what diners can find at this upscale restaurant. Some menu options are offered in a smaller portion size. Privacy partitions are available at some booths. Parking is validated for three hours. **Bar:** full bar. **Reservations:** suggested. **Address:** 1209 L St 95814 **Location:** 1/2 blk from state capitol, at 12th and L sts; in Hyatt Regency Sacramento. **Parking:** on-site (fee) and valet. [D] CALL [icons]

ELLA DINING ROOM & BAR 916/443-3772 **18**

American. Casual Dining. $12-$32 **AAA Inspector Notes:** This lovely restaurant, located just a block from the state Capitol, features upscale, contemporary décor and the menu offers fresh and seasonal New American cuisine with French influences. It has an extensive wine list. The delightful patio overlooks the street scene. **Bar:** full bar. **Reservations:** suggested. **Address:** 1131 K St 95814 **Location:** Jct 12th St. **Parking:** valet and street only. [L] [D] CALL [icons]

ENOTRIA RESTAURANT & WINE BAR 916/922-6792 **4**

California. Casual Dining. $20-$30 **AAA Inspector Notes:** Not far from the Arden Fair Mall, this relaxing, recently remodeled restaurant focuses on wine dinners. Knowledgeable, first-class servers are acquainted with the wine and creative cuisine. The menu is frequently updated. The cozy décor is evocative of a wine cellar. The extensive wine list offers more than 700 labels. A popular, seasonal outdoor patio with a water feature and live music is offered on Friday and Saturday evenings. **Bar:** full bar. **Reservations:** suggested. **Address:** 1431 Del Paso Blvd 95815 **Location:** Business Rt I-80 exit Arden Way, 1.1 mi w, then just s; jct Arden Way. [D]

FAT CITY BAR & CAFE 916/446-6768 **6**

American
Casual Dining
$10-$27

AAA Inspector Notes: Housed in what was once a general merchandise store built in 1849, this historic bar and café features stained glass and Tiffany lamp shades. A varied menu, including sandwiches, pasta and entrées, is offered. Come for brunch on Saturday and Sunday. Validated parking is at nearby lots for two hours if you do not prepay. **Bar:** full bar. **Address:** 1001 Front St 95814 **Location:** Jct Front and J sts; in Old Sacramento historic area. **Parking:** street only. [L] [D] CALL [icons]

THE FIREHOUSE 916/442-4772 **9**

Continental. Fine Dining. $12-$45 **AAA Inspector Notes:** *Classic Historic.* For more than 45 years, thousands of customers, including governors past and present, have been attracted to this restaurant housed in a former 1853 firehouse. This spot is well-known for its splendid ambience and reputation for excellence in food, wine and hospitality. More than 20,000 bottles of wine are offered from the restaurant's wine cellar. Large Victorian works of art and elaborate mirrors decorate the elegant dining room. The delightful courtyard is open in season. **Bar:** full bar. **Reservations:** suggested. **Address:** 1112 2nd St 95814 **Location:** In Old Sacramento historic area. **Parking:** valet and street only. [L] [D]

(See map & index p. 311.)

FRANK FAT'S   916/442-7092 16

▼▼▼
Chinese
Casual Dining
$9-$26

AAA Inspector Notes: Since 1939, Sacramento's oldest landmark restaurant has been serving Chinese cuisine from the four provinces of Peking, Szechuan, Canton and Shanghai along with some American fare in attractive, contemporary surroundings. Located one block from the state capitol building. **Bar:** full bar. **Reservations:** suggested. **Address:** 806 L St 95814 **Location:** Between 8th and 9th sts. **Parking:** street only. L D CALL 🅼

GRANGE RESTAURANT & BAR   916/492-4450 14

▼▼▼ American. Fine Dining. $12-$38 **AAA Inspector Notes:** The menu changes daily at this restaurant offering sophisticated and interesting menu items from California farms. Large windows look out onto the street scene and the wine list is all Californian. **Bar:** full bar. **Reservations:** suggested. **Address:** 926 J St 95814 **Location:** I-5 exit J St (Old Sacramento), 0.6 mi e; jct 10th St; in The Citizen, a Joie de Vivre hotel. **Parking:** valet and street only.

B L CALL 🅼

HOT ITALIAN   916/444-3000 34

▼▼ Italian Pizza. Casual Dining. $9-$16 **AAA Inspector Notes:** In addition to the authentic, delicious pizza with interesting Italian ingredients, this eatery offers salads, calzones and panini sandwiches in an ultra contemporary décor. Seasonal changing pizza combinations and cocktails are a fusion of California and Italian ingredients . Recommended is the gelato for dessert and there are some distinctive flavors. Bike delivery is available as well as a weekend brunch. **Bar:** full bar. **Address:** 1627 16th St 95814 **Location:** Jct Q St; Midtown. **Parking:** street only. L D CALL 🅼

IL FORNAIO   916/446-4100 13

▼▼ Italian. Fine Dining. $10-$35 **AAA Inspector Notes:** Accomplished servers begin guests' experiences with crisp, crusty bread hot from the oven. Pasta and flavorful sauces enhance the roasted meats and vegetables. The spacious restaurant thoughtfully replicates the trattorias of Italy. **Bar:** full bar. **Reservations:** suggested. **Address:** 400 Capitol Mall 95814 **Location:** I-5 exit Q St, just e, just n on 5th St, then just w on N St; at 4th St; in Wells Fargo Center. **Parking:** on-site and street. D CALL 🅼

KRU   916/551-1559 33

▼▼ Japanese Sushi. Casual Dining. $7-$35 **AAA Inspector Notes:** Creative contemporary Japanese cuisine utilizing fresh fish is served at this hip, popular eatery offering big and small plates, salads, sushi, hand rolls, nigiri and sashimi. An extensive sake menu is offered. Expect long waits at busy times. Closed for lunch on Sunday. **Bar:** full bar. **Address:** 2516 J St 95816 **Location:** Business Rt I-80 (Capitol City Frwy) exit J St, just w; e of jct 25th St. **Parking:** street only. L D CALL 🅼

LA TRATTORIA BOHEMIA   916/455-7803 39

▼▼ Czechoslovakian. Casual Dining. $10-$18 **AAA Inspector Notes:** Czech and Italian cuisine co-exist harmoniously on the menu at this neighborhood restaurant. Homemade bread, pasta, pizza, Czech specialties and desserts pair well with imported Czech beer and wine. Also available are Bohemia's specialty dumplings, made from wheat flour. Guests have a choice of indoor or outdoor seating, when weather permits. **Bar:** beer & wine. **Address:** 3649 J St 95816 **Location:** I-80 business route exit J St, just e; I-5 exit Downtown/J St, 2.5 mi e; at Dolores Way. **Parking:** street only. L D

MA JONG'S ASIAN DINER   916/442-7555 26

▼ Asian. Quick Serve. $9-$11 **AAA Inspector Notes:** This eatery offers noodle dishes, rice bowls and a few signature dishes. Busy at lunch, the line forms early and out the door at times. Grab a menu near the entry and consider sharing one of the family-style tables. Delivery by rickshaw or curbside pick up is available. A patio is available in season. Open late on Friday and Saturday nights. **Bar:** beer & wine. **Address:** 1431 L St 95814 **Location:** Jct 15th St; across from Capitol building. L D CALL 🅼

MCCORMICK & SCHMICK'S   916/442-8200 15

▼▼ Seafood. Fine Dining. $10-$32 **AAA Inspector Notes:** This place is all about seafood, which is imported from all over the world. Among good choices are Washington state oysters, Maine clams, delicate Hawaiian escolar and tuna from Ecuador. The clublike decor is cozy and the staff is attentive. **Bar:** full bar. **Reservations:** suggested. **Address:** 1111 J St 95814 **Location:** I-5 exit J St, 0.7 mi e; jct 11th St; historic Elks Club building. **Parking:** valet only.

L D CALL 🅼

MIKUNI JAPANESE RESTAURANT & SUSHI BAR
                                   916/447-2111 22

▼▼ Japanese Sushi. Casual Dining. $10-$19 **AAA Inspector Notes:** This popular restaurant offers an extensive variety of sushi, interesting rolls, boxes, seafood plates and dinner entrées. A good selection of sakes are available. Sit at the sushi bar to watch the chefs prepare the sushi or upstairs overlooking the tables below. Valet parking is an option. **Bar:** full bar. **Address:** 1530 J St 95814 **Location:** Jct 16th St. **Parking:** valet and street only.

L D CALL 🅼

MONTEREY BAY CANNERS   916/441-3474 3

▼▼ Seafood. Casual Dining. $9-$30 **AAA Inspector Notes:** This restaurant, with a seaport-style cannery decor, offers a variety of seafood prepared several different ways, including charbroiled mesquite, macadamia and pecan-encrusted. At lunch, sandwiches, burgers, wraps, entrées and salads are offered. Or share one of the appetizer platters. **Bar:** full bar. **Address:** 400 Bercut Dr 95814 **Location:** I-5 exit Richards Blvd, just e, then just n.

L D CALL 🅼

MULVANEY'S BUILDING & LOAN   916/441-6022 28

▼▼ American. Fine Dining. $11-$34 **AAA Inspector Notes:** Do not let the name fool you. Housed in a firehouse dating from 1893, this restaurant offers new American cuisine and a lovely garden patio. The menu changes daily and lunch is served Tuesday through Friday. **Bar:** full bar. **Address:** 1215 19th St, Suite 100 95811 **Location:** Midtown; between L St and Capitol Ave. **Parking:** street only.

D CALL 🅼

PAESANOS PRONTO   916/444-5850 29

▼▼ Italian. Quick Serve. $7-$10 **AAA Inspector Notes:** Tasty menu items, including panini sandwiches, oversize salads, polenta bowls and pasta dishes are served at this busy eatery with an outdoor patio. Breakfast is served on Saturday and Sunday 9 a.m. to 2 p.m. **Bar:** beer & wine. **Address:** 1501 16th St 95814 **Location:** Jct 16th and O sts; midtown. **Parking:** street only.

L D CALL 🅼

PARAGARY'S BAR AND OVEN   916/457-5737 38

▼▼ Mediterranean. Casual Dining. $11-$24 **AAA Inspector Notes:** This neighborhood establishment near Sutter General Hospital serves wood-burning oven pizza and pasta from a frequently changing menu. An inviting outdoor patio features a stone fireplace in season. Parking is available in a lot across the street. **Bar:** full bar. **Reservations:** suggested. **Address:** 1401 28th St 95816 **Location:** Business Rt I-80 exit J St southbound, just s on 29th St, then just w; exit N St northbound, just w; jct N St; midtown. D CALL 🅼

PEARL ON THE RIVER   916/567-3275 1

▼▼▼ American. Casual Dining. $12-$35 **AAA Inspector Notes:** With sunset views of the river and downtown in the distance, this restaurant on the second floor serves well-prepared food with local ingredients and offers leisurely dining inside and on a heated deck. **Bar:** full bar. **Reservations:** suggested. **Address:** 1379 Garden Hwy 95833 **Location:** I-5 exit Garden Hwy, just w; at Riverbank Marina. L D CALL 🅼

PETE'S RESTAURANT & BREWHOUSE 916/442-6770 27

▼▼ Italian. Casual Dining. $7-$20 **AAA Inspector Notes:** This eatery features hand-tossed New York-style pizza, pasta, sandwiches and healthy wraps, along with a limited craft beer selection. Recommend are the pizza dough knots in garlic butter. Several TVs continuously play sports while a small patio is out front. Be sure to check out the lunch specials. **Bar:** beer & wine. **Address:** 2001 J St 95814 **Location:** Jct 20th St; midtown. **Parking:** street only.

L D CALL 🅼

(See map & index p. 311.)

P.F. CHANG'S CHINA BISTRO
916/288-0970 **23**

Chinese. Casual Dining. $10-$21 **AAA Inspector Notes:** Trendy, upscale decor provides a pleasant backdrop for New Age Chinese dining. Appetizers, soups and salads are a meal by themselves. Vegetarian plates and sides, noodles, meins, chicken and meat dishes are created from exotic, fresh ingredients. **Bar:** full bar. **Reservations:** suggested. **Address:** 1530 J St 95814 **Location:** Jct 16th St; midtown. **Parking:** street only. CALL

PILOTHOUSE RESTAURANT ABOARD THE DELTA KING
916/441-4440 **5**

Continental. Fine Dining. $9-$24 **AAA Inspector Notes:** This restaurant, located in an authentic 285-foot riverboat christened in 1927 and operated between San Francisco and Sacramento, offers nice views of the river. Daily fish special, steaks and an assortment of well-prepared entrées make up the menu. Professional servers add to the refined ambience. Parking is in two nearby Old Sacramento lots for a fee or valet parking is available. **Bar:** full bar. **Reservations:** suggested. **Address:** 1000 Front St 95814 **Location:** I-5 exit J St (Old Sacramento), just s on 3rd St, just w, then just n; in Delta King Hotel. **Parking:** valet and street only. D

PIZZA ROCK
916/737-5777 **17**

Pizza. Casual Dining. $11-$30 **AAA Inspector Notes:** Delicious, gourmet pizzas are served. You can enjoy them inside or on the patio. **Bar:** full bar. **Address:** 1020 K St 95814 **Location:** Between 10th and 11th sts. **Parking:** street only. L D LATE CALL

RIO CITY CAFE
916/442-8226 **8**

California. Casual Dining. $9-$23 **AAA Inspector Notes:** For more than 15 years this establishment has served California cuisine in a casual setting along the Sacramento River on a heated deck with a view of the nearby Tower Bridge. Seafood dishes, pasta, salads and sandwiches are offered. Saturday and Sunday brunch is available from 10-2:30. Validated parking is offered for the two nearby lots in Old Town. **Bar:** full bar. **Reservations:** suggested. **Address:** 1110 Front St 95814 **Location:** I-5 exit J St; in Old Sacramento historic area. **Parking:** valet and street only. L D

RIVER CITY BREWING COMPANY
916/447-2739 **11**

American. Casual Dining. $9-$18 **AAA Inspector Notes:** This downtown brewpub offers several microbrews, pizza, salads, California pub fare and Mexican dishes. Patio seating is great for people watching. Parking is validated for four hours at a nearby city parking garage. **Bar:** full bar. **Address:** 545 Downtown Plaza, Suite 1115 95814 **Location:** I-5 exit J St (Old Sacramento), just s on 3rd St (parking lot entry adjacent to Holiday Inn Capitol Plaza); in Sacramento Downtown Plaza. **Parking:** on-site (fee). L D CALL

SPATARO RESTAURANT AND BAR
916/440-8888 **25**

Italian. Fine Dining. $10-$23 **AAA Inspector Notes:** Modern Italian fare is offered at this attractive, contemporary restaurant not far from the capitol building. Fresh, local ingredients are used whenever possible. Valet parking is available Wednesday through Saturday. **Bar:** full bar. **Reservations:** suggested. **Address:** 1415 L St 95814 **Location:** I-5 exit J St, just w to 15th St, just s, then e; jct 14th and L sts; in Meridian Plaza Building. **Parking:** street only. L D CALL

SUSPECTS MYSTERY COMEDY DINNER THEATER
916/443-3600 **7**

American. Dinner Theatre. $40 **AAA Inspector Notes:** This long running comedy who-done-it mystery evolves around suspects that may be at your dinner table. Guests are given a choice of three entrées on the prix fixe menu. Children must be 11 years of age or older. Seatings take place every Friday and Saturday at 7:30 p.m. **Bar:** full bar. **Reservations:** required. **Address:** 1000 Front St 95814 **Location:** I-5 exit J St (Old Sacramento), just s on 3rd St, just w, then just n; in Delta King Hotel. **Parking:** valet and street only. D

TEMPLE COFFEE & TEA
916/443-4960 **12**

Coffee/Tea. Quick Serve. $2-$5 **AAA Inspector Notes:** A local favorite, the contemporary décor at this eatery enhances the fresh and delicious coffee and espresso beverages made from the top coffees of the world. Monthly coffee education courses are offered on coffee brewing, tasting and espresso preparation. A patio is open in season. Only cash is accepted. **Address:** 1010 9th St 95814 **Location:** From jct J St, just s. **Parking:** street only. B L D CALL

THAI BASIL
916/442-7690 **31**

Thai. Casual Dining. $8-$14 **AAA Inspector Notes:** Curries, noodles, rice plates and house specialties are served at this restaurant. Sidewalk seating is available in season. **Bar:** full bar. **Address:** 2431 J St 95816 **Location:** Business Rt I-80 (Capitol City Frwy) exit J St, just w on K St, just n on 24th St, then just e; between 24th and 25th sts; midtown. **Parking:** street only. L D CALL

TOWER BRIDGE BISTRO
916/326-5050 **10**

American. Casual Dining. $10-$38 **AAA Inspector Notes:** Situated with great views of the Tower Bridge and located along the Riverwalk Promenade, this restaurant offers a varied seasonally-changing menu with patio seating. **Bar:** full bar. **Address:** 100 Capitol Mall 95814 **Location:** I-5 exit J St (Old Sacramento), just s on 3rd St, then just w; in Embassy Suites Sacramento-Riverfront Promenade. **Parking:** valet and street only. L D CALL

TRES HERMANAS
916/443-6919 **35**

Mexican. Casual Dining. $10-$14 **AAA Inspector Notes:** This busy eatery offers Northern Mexican cuisine, including seafood, beef and vegetarian dishes. A variety of tequilas and margaritas are served as is Saturday and Sunday breakfast. Diners can expect a short wait at peak times. The patio overlooks the street scene. **Bar:** full bar. **Address:** 2416 K St 95816 **Location:** Jct 24th and K sts; midtown. **Parking:** street only. L D CALL

THE WATERBOY RESTAURANT
916/498-9891 **32**

French. Casual Dining. $17-$25 **AAA Inspector Notes:** Southern French and Northern Italian cuisines are the inspirations for the monthly changing menu at this restaurant. High-quality ingredients permeate the menu offerings. Lunch is served daily except Saturday and Sunday. Patio sidewalk seating is available in season. **Bar:** full bar. **Reservations:** required. **Address:** 2000 Capitol Ave 95811 **Location:** Jct 20th St; midtown. **Parking:** street only. D CALL

ZEN SUSHI
916/446-9628 **20**

Japanese Sushi. Casual Dining. $8-$19 **AAA Inspector Notes:** A popular sushi spot for lunch, a variety of chef's special rolls are prepared here, along with a lunch and dinner combination box. Sit at the bar and watch the chef prepare the sushi if the tables are full. **Bar:** full bar. **Address:** 900 15th St 95814 **Location:** Jct I and 15th sts. **Parking:** street only. L D

GOODIE TUCHEWS
916/444-6048

fyi Not evaluated. This local favorite has been around more than 25 years and serves an assortment of fresh made cookies and hand-made ice cream sandwiches. It is best to go early in the day as the owner closes when the cookies are sold out. The owner will hold cookies with a call ahead. Only cash is accepted. **Address:** 1015 L St 95814 **Location:** Between 10th and 11 sts; across from the Capitol.

SACRAMENTO (E-3)

• Restaurants p. 332
• Hotels & Restaurants map & index p. 314

BEST WESTERN JOHN JAY INN
(916)689-4425

Hotel
$70-$130

AAA Benefit: Members save up to 20%, plus 10% bonus points with Best Western Rewards®.

Address: 15 Massie Ct 95823 **Location:** SR 99 exit Stockton Blvd/Mack Rd northbound, 0.8 mi n, then just w; exit Mack Rd E southbound, just e, just n on Stockton Blvd, then just w. **Facility:** 58 units. 3 stories, interior corridors. **Terms:** 3 day cancellation notice. **Amenities:** high-speed Internet. **Pool(s):** outdoor. **Activities:** sauna, whirlpool, exercise room. **Guest Services:** coin laundry. **Free Special Amenities:** local telephone calls and high-speed Internet.

SAVE CALL BIZ
/ SOME UNITS FEE

(See map & index p. 314.)

COMFORT INN & SUITES
(916)379-0400 **27**

▼▼▼▼ Hotel $90-$250

Address: 21 Howe Ave 95826 **Location:** US 50 exit Howe Ave, just s. **Facility:** 68 units. 3 stories, interior corridors. **Terms:** cancellation fee imposed. **Amenities:** high-speed Internet. **Pool(s):** heated indoor. **Activities:** whirlpool, exercise room. **Guest Services:** valet and coin laundry. **Free Special Amenities: full breakfast and high-speed Internet.**

SAVE ![] CALL ![M] ![] BIZ ![] ![] ![] ![]

COURTYARD BY MARRIOTT MIDTOWN SACRAMENTO
(916)455-6800 **25**

▼▼▼▼ Hotel $169-$189 **Address:** 4422 Y St 95817 **Location:** US 50 exit 34th St eastbound, just n to T St, just e to Stockton Blvd, then just s; adjacent to University of California Medical Center. **Facility:** 139 units, some efficiencies and kitchens. 4 stories, interior corridors. **Amenities:** high-speed Internet. **Pool(s):** heated outdoor. **Activities:** whirlpool, exercise room. **Guest Services:** valet and coin laundry.

AAA Benefit: AAA hotel discounts of 5% or more.

![] ![] CALL ![M] ![] BIZ ![] ![] ![] / SOME UNITS ![] ![]

COURTYARD SACRAMENTO CAL EXPO
(916)929-7900 **21**

▼▼▼▼ Hotel $79-$144

AAA Benefit: AAA hotel discounts of 5% or more.

Address: 1782 Tribute Rd 95815 **Location:** Business Rt I-80 exit Cal Expo westbound, just w; exit Exposition Blvd eastbound, just w. **Facility:** 152 units. 3 stories, interior corridors. **Amenities:** high-speed Internet. **Pool(s):** outdoor. **Activities:** whirlpool, rental bicycles, exercise room. **Guest Services:** valet and coin laundry, area transportation-within 5 mi.

SAVE ECO ![] ![] ![] CALL ![M] ![] BIZ ![] ![] ![] ![] / SOME UNITS ![] ![]

CROWNE PLAZA SACRAMENTO
(916)338-5800 **9**

▼▼▼▼ Hotel $75-$95 **Address:** 5321 Date Ave 95841 **Location:** I-80 exit Madison Ave, just e, then just n. **Facility:** 230 units. 6 stories, interior corridors. **Amenities:** video games, high-speed Internet. **Pool(s):** outdoor. **Activities:** whirlpool, exercise room. **Guest Services:** valet laundry.

![] ![] CALL ![M] ![] BIZ ![] ![] ![] ![] / SOME UNITS ![] ![]

DOUBLETREE BY HILTON HOTEL SACRAMENTO
(916)929-8855 **18**

▼▼▼▼ Hotel $89-$229

DOUBLETREE

AAA Benefit: Members save 5% or more!

Address: 2001 Point West Way 95815 **Location:** Business Rt I-80 exit Arden Way, just e. Across from Arden Fair Mall. **Facility:** 448 units, some two bedrooms. 3-4 stories, interior corridors. **Parking:** on-site (fee) and valet. **Terms:** check-in 4 pm, 1-7 night minimum stay, cancellation fee imposed. **Amenities:** high-speed Internet (fee). **Pool(s):** outdoor. **Activities:** whirlpool, exercise room. **Guest Services:** valet and coin laundry, area transportation-within 3 mi.

SAVE ECO ![] ![] ![] CALL ![M] ![] BIZ ![] ![] / SOME UNITS FEE ![] ![]

EXTENDED STAYAMERICA-SACRAMENTO-ARDEN WAY
(916)921-9942 **16**

▼▼▼ Extended Stay Hotel $76-$91 **Address:** 2100 Harvard St 95815 **Location:** I-80 business route exit Arden Way, just w. **Facility:** 120 efficiencies. 3 stories, exterior corridors. **Guest Services:** coin laundry.

![] CALL ![M] ![] ![] ![] ![] / SOME UNITS FEE ![]

FAIRFIELD INN & SUITES SACRAMENTO AIRPORT NATOMAS
(916)923-7472 **11**

▼▼▼▼ Hotel $76-$160

FAIRFIELD INN & SUITES

AAA Benefit: AAA hotel discounts of 5% or more.

Address: 2730 El Centro Rd 95833 **Location:** I-80 exit W El Camino Ave, just w, just s on El Centro Rd, then just e on Tomato Patch Ln (before Burger King). **Facility:** 93 units. 3 stories, interior corridors. **Amenities:** high-speed Internet. **Pool(s):** heated outdoor. **Activities:** whirlpool, exercise room. **Guest Services:** valet and coin laundry, area transportation-Amtrak station. **Free Special Amenities: expanded continental breakfast and airport transportation.**

SAVE ![] ![] ![] BIZ ![] ![] ![] / SOME UNITS ![] ![]

FAIRFIELD INN BY MARRIOTT SACRAMENTO CAL EXPO
(916)920-5300 **19**

▼▼▼▼ Hotel $69-$134

FAIRFIELD INN

AAA Benefit: AAA hotel discounts of 5% or more.

Address: 1780 Tribute Rd 95815 **Location:** Business Rt I-80 exit Cal Expo westbound; exit Exposition Blvd eastbound, just w. **Facility:** 74 units. 3 stories, interior corridors. **Amenities:** high-speed Internet. **Pool(s):** outdoor. **Activities:** whirlpool, rental bicycles, exercise room. **Guest Services:** valet and coin laundry.

SAVE ECO ![] CALL ![M] ![] BIZ ![] ![] ![] / SOME UNITS ![]

FOUR POINTS BY SHERATON SACRAMENTO INTERNATIONAL AIRPORT
(916)263-9000 **1**

▼▼▼▼ Hotel $169-$369

FOUR POINTS BY SHERATON

AAA Benefit: Members get up to 20% off, plus Starwood Preferred Guest® bonuses.

Address: 4900 Duckhorn Dr 95834 **Location:** I-5 exit 525A (Del Paso Rd), just w. **Facility:** 100 units. 4 stories, interior corridors. **Terms:** cancellation fee imposed, resort fee. **Amenities:** high-speed Internet. **Pool(s):** heated outdoor. **Activities:** whirlpool, exercise room. **Guest Services:** valet and coin laundry. **Free Special Amenities: high-speed Internet and airport transportation.**

SAVE ![] ![] ![] CALL ![M] ![] BIZ ![] ![] ![] / SOME UNITS ![]

HAMPTON INN & SUITES
(916)927-2222 **13**

▼▼▼▼ Hotel $99-$149 **Address:** 2230 Auburn Blvd 95821 **Location:** Business Rt I-80 exit Howe Ave eastbound; exit 11 (Auburn Blvd/Marconi Ave) westbound, just s on Connie Dr, just e on Marconi Ave, then 0.5 mi ne. Across from Haggin Oaks Golf Course. **Facility:** 70 units. 3 stories, interior corridors. **Terms:** 1-7 night minimum stay, cancellation fee imposed. **Amenities:** video games (fee), high-speed Internet. **Pool(s):** heated outdoor. **Activities:** exercise room. **Guest Services:** valet and coin laundry, area transportation-within 3 mi.

AAA Benefit: Members save up to 10%!

![] CALL ![M] ![] BIZ ![] ![] ![] ![] ![] ![]

(See map & index p. 314.)

HAMPTON INN & SUITES SAC-AIRPORT/NATOMAS
(916)928-5700

 Hotel
$109-$199

 AAA Benefit: Members save up to 10%!

Address: 3021 Advantage Way 95834 **Location:** I-5 exit Del Paso Rd, just e, just s on East Commerce Way, then just w. **Facility:** 100 units. 3 stories, interior corridors. **Terms:** 1-7 night minimum stay, cancellation fee imposed. **Amenities:** video games (fee), high-speed Internet. **Pool(s):** heated outdoor. **Activities:** whirlpool, exercise room. **Guest Services:** valet and coin laundry. **Free Special Amenities: expanded continental breakfast and high-speed Internet.**

Get an insider view from
AAA/CAA travel experts
at AAATravelViews.com

HILTON SACRAMENTO ARDEN WEST
(916)922-4700

Hotel
$89-$239

Hilton

AAA Benefit: Members save 5% or more!

Address: 2200 Harvard St 95815 **Location:** Business Rt I-80 exit Arden Way, just w, then just n. Located near Arden Fair Mall. **Facility:** 332 units. 12 stories, interior corridors. **Terms:** 1-7 night minimum stay, cancellation fee imposed. **Amenities:** Fee: video games, high-speed Internet. **Pool(s):** outdoor. **Activities:** whirlpool, exercise room. **Guest Services:** valet laundry, area transportation-Arden Fair Mall.

HOLIDAY INN EXPRESS & SUITES-SACRAMENTO AIRPORT/NATOMAS
(916)928-9400

Hotel
$129-$199

Address: 2981 Advantage Way 95834 **Location:** I-5 exit Del Paso Rd, just e, just s on East Commerce Way, then just w. **Facility:** 100 units. 3 stories, interior corridors. **Amenities:** video games (fee), high-speed Internet. **Pool(s):** heated outdoor. **Activities:** whirlpool, exercise room. **Guest Services:** valet and coin laundry. **Free Special Amenities: expanded continental breakfast and high-speed Internet.**

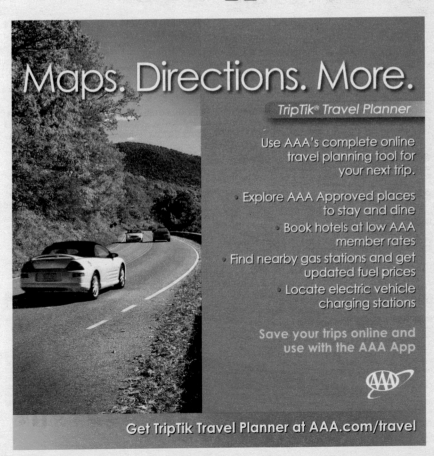

(See map & index p. 314.)

HOLIDAY INN EXPRESS & SUITES SACRAMENTO CAL EXPO
(916)923-1100 **14**

 Hotel $99-$139 Address: 2224 Auburn Blvd 95821 **Location:** Business Rt I-80 exit Howe Ave eastbound; exit Auburn Blvd/Marconi westbound, just s on Connie Dr, just e on Marconi Ave, then 0.5 mi ne. Across from Haggin Oaks Golf Course. **Facility:** 81 units. 4 stories, interior corridors. **Terms:** resort fee. **Amenities:** high-speed Internet. **Pool(s):** outdoor. **Activities:** exercise room. **Guest Services:** valet and coin laundry, area transportation-within 3 mi.

HOMEWOOD SUITES BY HILTON SACRAMENTO AIRPORT
(916)263-9510 **2**

Extended Stay Hotel
$109-$300

HOMEWOOD SUITES BY HILTON
AAA Benefit: Contemporary luxury at a special Member rate.

Address: 3001 Advantage Way 95834 **Location:** I-5 exit Del Paso Rd, just e, just s on East Commerce Way, then just w. **Facility:** 123 efficiencies, some two bedrooms. 3 stories, interior corridors. **Terms:** 1-7 night minimum stay, cancellation fee imposed. **Amenities:** high-speed Internet. **Pool(s):** heated outdoor. **Activities:** whirlpool, sports court, exercise room. **Guest Services:** valet and coin laundry. **Free Special Amenities: full breakfast and high-speed Internet.**

HOTEL MED PARK, SACRAMENTO (916)455-4000 **24**

Hotel
$129-$149

Address: 2356 Stockton Blvd 95817 **Location:** US 50 exit 34th St eastbound, just n to T St, just e to Stockton Blvd, then just s; just n of jct X St. **Facility:** 32 units. 4 stories, interior corridors. **Terms:** cancellation fee imposed. **Amenities:** high-speed Internet, safes. **Activities:** exercise room. **Guest Services:** valet laundry. **Free Special Amenities: continental breakfast and high-speed Internet.**

LA QUINTA INN SACRAMENTO NORTH (916)348-0900 **10**

Hotel $71-$133 Address: 4604 Madison Ave 95841 **Location:** I-80 exit Madison Ave, 0.3 mi e. **Facility:** 126 units. 3 stories, exterior corridors. **Amenities:** video games (fee). **Pool(s):** outdoor. **Activities:** whirlpool. **Guest Services:** coin laundry.

LARKSPUR LANDING SACRAMENTO (916)646-1212 **23**

Extended Stay Hotel $109-$189 Address: 555 Howe Ave 95825 **Location:** US 50 exit Howe Ave, 1.5 mi n. **Facility:** 124 efficiencies. 4 stories, interior corridors. **Terms:** 7 day cancellation notice, resort fee. **Amenities:** high-speed Internet. **Activities:** whirlpool, exercise room. **Guest Services:** complimentary and valet laundry.

LE RIVAGE HOTEL, A PREFERRED HOTEL
(916)443-8400 **26**

Boutique Hotel $129-$799 Address: 4800 Riverside Blvd 95822 **Location:** Waterfront. I-5 exit Fruitridge/Seamas, just w, then 0.7 mi n. Located along the Sacramento River. **Facility:** Set on a hill overlooking the Sacramento River, this upscale hotel features warm and inviting Italian décor throughout. Luxurious Italian bed linens and deep, soaking claw-foot tubs are featured. 100 units. 3 stories, interior corridors. **Parking:** on-site and valet. **Terms:** cancellation fee imposed, resort fee. **Amenities:** high-speed Internet, safes. **Dining:** Scott's Seafood Grill & Bar, see separate listing. **Pool(s):** heated outdoor. **Activities:** marina, rental bicycles, jogging, exercise room, spa. **Fee:** sauna, whirlpool. **Guest Services:** valet laundry, area transportation-within 5 mi.

LIONS GATE HOTEL & CONFERENCE CENTER
(916)643-6222 **5**

Hotel
$99-$109

Address: 3410 Westover St 95652 **Location:** I-80 exit Watt Ave, 1.3 mi n to Palm St, just w, then just s on Arnold Ave. Located in McClellan Business Park. **Facility:** 122 units, some two bedrooms, houses and cottages. 2 stories, interior/exterior corridors. **Terms:** cancellation fee imposed. **Amenities:** high-speed Internet. **Pool(s):** outdoor. **Guest Services:** valet and coin laundry, area transportation-within 5 mi. **Free Special Amenities: full breakfast and high-speed Internet.**

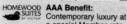

QUALITY INN & SUITES 916/922-9833 **22**

Hotel
Rates not provided

Address: 1413 Howe Ave 95825 **Location:** US 50 exit Howe Ave, 2.5 mi n; I-80 business route exit Howe Ave, 2 mi s; just n of jct Hurley and Howe aves. **Facility:** 125 units, some two bedrooms and kitchens. 2 stories (no elevator), interior corridors. **Amenities:** Some: high-speed Internet, safes (fee). **Pool(s):** outdoor. **Activities:** whirlpool, exercise room. **Guest Services:** valet and coin laundry, area transportation-within 5 mi, bus & train stations. **Free Special Amenities: full breakfast and early check-in/late check-out.**

QUALITY INN NATOMAS (916)927-7117 **8**

Hotel
$55-$90

Address: 3796 Northgate Blvd 95834 **Location:** I-80 exit Northgate Blvd, just s. **Facility:** 132 units, some two bedrooms. 3 stories, exterior corridors. **Pool(s):** outdoor. **Activities:** whirlpool.

RED LION HOTEL WOODLAKE CONFERENCE CENTER SACRAMENTO
(916)922-2020 **17**

Hotel
$89-$209

Address: 500 Leisure Ln 95815 **Location:** Business Rt I-80 exit Cal Expo/Exposition Blvd, 0.4 mi w on Exposition Blvd; SR 160 exit 47B (Exposition Blvd) eastbound, just sw; SR 160 exit 47A (Leisure Ln/Canterbury Rd) westbound, just e. **Facility:** 306 units. 1-2 stories (no elevator), exterior corridors. **Parking:** on-site and valet. **Terms:** check-in 4 pm, cancellation fee imposed. **Amenities:** high-speed Internet. Some: safes. **Pool(s):** heated outdoor. **Activities:** whirlpool, rental paddleboats, rental bicycles, exercise room. **Fee:** massage. **Guest Services:** valet laundry, area transportation-within 5 mi. **Free Special Amenities: high-speed Internet and local transportation.**

RESIDENCE INN BY MARRIOTT-SACRAMENTO AIRPORT NATOMAS
(916)649-1300 **12**

Extended Stay Hotel
$189-$199

AAA Benefit: AAA hotel discounts of 5% or more.

Address: 2410 W El Camino Ave 95833 **Location:** I-5 exit 521B (W El Camino Ave) northbound only, just w, then just s on Gateway Oaks Dr; I-80 exit W El Camino Ave, 1.5 mi e, then just s on Gateway Oaks Dr. **Facility:** 126 kitchen units, some two bedrooms. 2 stories (no elevator), exterior corridors. **Amenities:** Some: high-speed Internet. **Pool(s):** heated outdoor. **Activities:** whirlpool, sports court, exercise room. **Guest Services:** valet and coin laundry.

YOUR NEW LUCKY NUMBER

RESORT + WHITNEY OAKS
GOLF PACKAGES FROM

$149*

Welcome to Thunder Valley Casino Resort, one of Northern California's premier AAA rated Four Diamond resorts. Enjoy nonstop gaming action, including slots, blackjack, poker and other casino favorites. Plus, 14 unique restaurants & bars, live headline entertainment, 300 stunning hotel rooms starting at just $99* and our newest amenity, Whitney Oaks Golf Club, enhance the Thunder Valley Casino Resort, Four Diamond experience you've always wanted. Lucky You.

THUNDER
VALLEY
CASINO · RESORT
TM

AAA
Four Diamond
Award

I-80 TO HWY 65 • LEFT ON SUNSET • 877-468-8777
THUNDERVALLEYRESORT.COM

*Based on single/double occupancy. Rates are plus tax and vary by unit and season.

(See map & index p. 314.)

STAYBRIDGE SUITES SACRAMENTO AIRPORT/NATOMAS
(916)575-7907 **6**

WWW **Extended Stay Hotel** $99-$159 **Address:** 140 Promenade Cir 95834 **Location:** I-80 exit Truxel Rd, just nw, n on Gateway Park Blvd, e on N Freeway Blvd, then just s. **Facility:** 117 units, some two bedrooms and efficiencies. 4 stories, interior corridors. **Terms:** cancellation fee imposed. **Amenities:** high-speed Internet. **Pool(s):** heated outdoor. **Activities:** whirlpool, exercise room. **Guest Services:** complimentary and valet laundry.

SUPER 8 SACRAMENTO (916)331-1483 **7**

WW **Motel** $65-$79 **Address:** 4317 Madison Ave 95842 **Location:** I-80 exit Madison Ave, just w, then just n. **Facility:** 127 units. 2-3 stories (no elevator), interior corridors. **Amenities:** high-speed Internet. **Pool(s):** outdoor.

TOWNEPLACE SUITES BY MARRIOTT SACRAMENTO CAL EXPO (916)920-5400 **20**

WWW
Extended Stay Hotel
$79-$159

AAA Benefit: AAA hotel discounts of 5% or more.

Address: 1784 Tribute Rd 95815 **Location:** Business Rt I-80 exit Cal Expo westbound; exit Exposition Blvd eastbound, just w, then just s. **Facility:** 117 efficiencies, some two bedrooms. 4 stories, interior corridors. **Amenities:** video games (fee), high-speed Internet. **Pool(s):** heated outdoor. **Activities:** whirlpool, exercise room. **Guest Services:** valet and coin laundry, area transportation-within 5 mi.

VALUE PLACE 916/688-1330

[fyi] Not evaluated. **Address:** 7789 La Mancha Way 95823 **Location:** SR 99 exit 291B (Mack Rd), just w, then just n. Facilities, services, and décor characterize an economy property.

WHERE TO EAT

ANDY NGUYEN'S VEGETARIAN RESTAURANT
916/736-1157 **11**

WW **Vegetarian. Casual Dining.** $9-$15 **AAA Inspector Notes:** Since 1984, delightful and creative vegetarian cuisine has been served with vegan and gluten-free options available. Soy meats are utilized. Family-style plates and a variety of spring rolls, salads, soups and clay pot entrées are offered. **Address:** 2007 Broadway 95818 **Location:** Business Rt I-80 (Capital City Frwy) exit P St (which becomes W St), 1 mi sw, just s on 21 St, then just w; jct 20th St. **Parking:** on-site and street.

BLACK BEAR DINER 916/641-2327

WWW **American. Family Dining.** $7-$16 **AAA Inspector Notes:** A homey atmosphere characterizes this family-oriented restaurant. Familiar comfort foods, such as meatloaf with mashed potatoes, are at the heart of the menu and are served in generous portions. **Bar:** beer & wine. **Address:** 2700 El Centro Rd 95833 **Location:** I-80 exit W El Camino, just w, just s, then just e on Tomato Patch Ln (before Burger King).

BOUDIN SF 916/973-1849 **16**

WW **American. Family Dining.** $6-$10 **AAA Inspector Notes:** San Francisco sourdough bread is featured throughout the menu at this eatery which offers salads, sandwiches, burgers and bread bowls containing soup or a hearty stew. Counter and sidewalk seating both are available. **Bar:** beer & wine. **Address:** 2573 Fair Oaks Blvd 95825 **Location:** US 50 exit Howe Ave, 1.5 mi n, 0.7 mi e; jct Munroe St; in Loehmann's Plaza.

BROOKFIELDS RESTAURANT 916/332-0108 **3**

WW **American. Casual Dining.** $8-$16 **AAA Inspector Notes:** Breakfast served all day, daily soups and lunch and dinner specials, along with burgers and sandwiches and a few south-of-the-border favorites are offered at this family-friendly restaurant with easy access from I-80. Baked goods are made from scratch. A super value menu also is available. Expect efficient and polite service. **Bar:** beer & wine. **Address:** 4343 Madison Ave 95842 **Location:** I-80 exit 96 (Madison Ave), just n.

CAFE VINOTECA 916/487-1331 **18**

WW **Italian. Casual Dining.** $9-$28 **AAA Inspector Notes:** This neighborhood bistro serves panini at lunch and several pasta selections at dinner. Recommended is the grilled romaine salad served with Gorgonzola buttermilk dressing. The house specialty is homemade potato gnocchi. Patio seating in season. Nightly specials. Sunday through Tuesday is all-you-can-eat spaghetti or a three-course pasta dinner. **Bar:** full bar. **Address:** 3535 Fair Oaks Blvd 95864 **Location:** US 50 exit Watt Ave, just n, then just e; in Arden Town Center.

CHOW KING 916/393-7406

W **Philippine. Quick Serve.** $4-$8 **AAA Inspector Notes:** This Philippine-based chain is popular with the local Filipino crowd and serves a variety of fast food at budget prices, including lumpia and adobo. For dessert try the halo-halo. **Address:** 6051 Mack Rd, Suite C 95823 **Location:** SR 99 exit Mack Rd, just w; in Seafood City Supermarket.

EL TORITO 916/927-0071

WW **Mexican. Casual Dining.** $9-$17 **AAA Inspector Notes:** Homemade Mexican favorites span from classic preparations to specialties from the country's central regions. Spicy taqueria-style tacos and carnitas Michoacan (marinated pork) are tasty choices. **Bar:** full bar. **Reservations:** suggested. **Address:** 1598 Arden Way 95815 **Location:** I-80 business route (Capital City Frwy) exit Arden Way, 0.5 mi e; across from Arden Fair Mall.

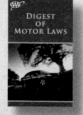

(See map & index p. 314.)

ETTORE'S EUROPEAN BAKERY & RESTAURANT
916/482-0708   (15)

♦♦ American. Casual Dining. $8-$18 **AAA Inspector Notes:** Order at the counter and select from daily quiche specials, salads, pizza made in a wood-burning brick oven, hand-crafted sandwiches and a display cases of tempting bakery goods. A few dinner entrées are available from 5 p.m. Arrive early or late for lunch to avoid the crowd. A heated patio is offered in season. **Bar:** wine only. **Address:** 2376 Fair Oaks Blvd 95825 **Location:** US 50 exit Howe Ave, 1.5 mi n, then just e; in Arden Arcade neighborhood.

L   D   CALL 🅂M

FREEPORT BAKERY   916/442-4256   (20)

♦ Breads/Pastries. Quick Serve. $2-$10 **AAA Inspector Notes:** Located in what was once a home, this charming neighborhood bakery is one of Sacramento's best. Beautifully decorated cakes and a good assortment of delicious pastries and breads are made fresh daily. Patio seating is available out front. **Address:** 2966 Freeport Blvd 95818 **Location:** Business Rt I-80 exit P St westbound, straight on 29th St (which becomes W St), then 0.6 mi s on 21st St; exit 15th St eastbound, just s to Broadway, just e to Freeport Blvd, then 0.5 mi s; jct Vallejo Way. **Parking:** on-site and street.   L   CALL 🅂M

FRESH CHOICE

♦ American. Cafeteria. $8-$10 **AAA Inspector Notes:** The salad bar of salad bars, the casual restaurant invites patrons to make their own or try one of the already prepared varieties. Other items include freshly baked breads, pizza and soup, as well as make-your-own sundaes for dessert. **Bar:** beer & wine.   L   D   CALL 🅂M

For additional information, visit AAA.com

LOCATIONS:
Address: 1689 Arden Way, Suite 1065 95815 **Location:** I-80 business route exit Arden Way, 0.5 mi sw; jct Heritage Ln; in Arden Fair Mall. **Phone:** 916/649-3839
Address: 535 Howe Ave 95825 **Location:** US 50 exit Howe Ave, 1.5 mi n; jct Cadillac Dr. **Phone:** 916/649-8046

THE HABIT BURGER GRILL   916/927-2604   (8)

♦ Burgers. Quick Serve. $4-$7 **AAA Inspector Notes:** The burgers at this eatery are 100 percent fresh lean beef. Fresh salads and grilled sandwiches also are offered. All of the products are cooked using 100 percent trans fat-free oil. Grab a seat on the patio out back if the weather permits. **Address:** 1431 Howe Ave 95825 **Location:** US 50 exit Howe Ave, 2.5 mi n; Business Rt I-80 exit Arden Way, 1 mi se to Howe Ave, then just n; jct Hallmark Dr; behind Panda Express.   L   D   CALL 🅂M

THE KITCHEN RESTAURANT   916/568-7171   (9)

♦♦♦♦ American Fine Dining $125   **AAA Inspector Notes:** The exhibition kitchen here is the center of an informative and entertaining display of the culinary arts where a host of local and international ingredients are prepared into distinctive and savory creations. Guests are encouraged to circulate through the kitchen and mingle with the chefs. Sit at the counter for an up close view. One seating only at 6:30 p.m. and a 20 percent gratuity is added to your bill. **Bar:** beer & wine. **Reservations:** required. **Address:** 2225 Hurley Way 95825 **Location:** US 50 exit Howe Ave, 2.5 mi n; I-80 business route exit Howe Ave, 2 mi s; jct Howe Ave.   D   CALL 🅂M

LEMON GRASS ASIAN GRILL & NOODLE BAR
916/929-9888   (10)

♦ Asian. Quick Serve. $7-$10 **AAA Inspector Notes:** This popular eatery serves Vietnamese and Thai cuisine such as curries, noodle bowls and soups. A few tables are located outside. The line forms early. **Address:** 945 Howe Ave 95825 **Location:** US 50 exit Howe Ave, 2.3 mi n; I-80 business route exit Howe Ave, 2.9 mi s; jct Enterprise Dr; in La Bou Bakery and Cafe.   L   D   CALL 🅂M

LOUIE'S RESTAURANT & CATERING   916/739-8646   (22)

♦♦ Chinese. Casual Dining. $8-$18 **AAA Inspector Notes:** Not far from the University of California Davis Medical Center, this restaurant serves fresh, traditional Chinese dishes. Recommended is the calamari house specialty for an appetizer. Family meals and lunch specials are available. **Bar:** beer only. **Address:** 4605 Broadway 95820 **Location:** US 50 exit 34th St eastbound, just n to T St, just e to Stockton Blvd, then just s; jct Stockton Blvd.   L   D   CALL 🅂M

MALABAR   916/574-9074   (1)

♦♦ American. Casual Dining. $10-$25 **AAA Inspector Notes:** Sleek, contemporary decor characterizes this spacious, lively restaurant, which serves American fare with some noticeable international influences. **Bar:** full bar. **Reservations:** suggested. **Address:** 2960 Del Paso Rd 95834 **Location:** I-5 exit 525A (Del Paso Rd), just e.   L   D   CALL 🅂M

(See map & index p. 314.)

ONESPEED 916/706-1748 (17)

♦♦ Pizza. Casual Dining. $9-$18 **AAA Inspector Notes:** Located in a residential neighborhood, this restaurant offers quality pizza, pasta and a few daily changing entrées. Plan to arrive early on Friday and Saturday nights to avoid long wait times. There is a small parking lot behind the restaurant. **Bar:** beer & wine. **Address:** 4818 Folsom Blvd 95819 **Location:** US 50 exit 65th St, just n, then 1.1 mi w; I-80 business route (Capitol City Frwy) exit J St, 1.4 mi e, then 0.4 mi s on 48th St; jct 48th St; in East Sacramento. **Parking:** on-site and street. [L] [D] CALL ⓈⓂ

PERKO'S CAFE & GRILL 916/362-3274 (23)

♦♦ American. Family Dining. $8-$16 **AAA Inspector Notes:** This cafe offers breakfast anytime (with early bird specials before 8 am), along with a varied menu of burgers, wraps, sandwiches, steak, chicken, salads and pasta dishes. A log cabin feel fills the dining room. **Bar:** beer & wine. **Address:** 9647 Micron Ave 95827 **Location:** On south side of US 50, at Bradshaw Rd. [B] [L] [D]

PIATTI RISTORANTE & BAR 916/649-8885 (12)

♦♦♦ Italian. Casual Dining. $12-$28 **AAA Inspector Notes:** Casually upscale, this restaurant features contemporary, rustic Italian cuisine prepared in an open exhibition kitchen. Highlights include stone hearth pizza, delicious pasta and an inviting patio. A few selections of barrel-to-tables wines are poured from a custom tap barrel. **Bar:** full bar. **Reservations:** suggested. **Address:** 571 Pavilions Ln 95825 **Location:** US 50 exit Howe Ave, 1.5 mi n, then just e; in Arden Arcade neighborhood; in Pavilions Shopping Center. [L] [D] CALL ⓈⓂ

RUTH'S CHRIS STEAK HOUSE 916/286-2702 (13)

♦♦♦♦ American Steak. Casual Dining. $21-$48 **AAA Inspector Notes:** The main fare is steak, which is prepared from several cuts of prime beef and cooked to perfection, but the menu also lists lamb, chicken and seafood dishes. Guests should come hungry because the side dishes, which are among the a la carte offerings, could make a meal in themselves. **Bar:** full bar. **Reservations:** suggested. **Address:** 501 Pavilions Ln 95825 **Location:** US 50 exit Howe Ave, 1.5 mi n, then just e; located in Arden Arcade neighborhood; in Pavilions Shopping Center. [L] [D] CALL ⓈⓂ

SAM'S HOF BRAU 916/482-2175 (5)

♦ Comfort Food Sandwiches. Cafeteria. $5-$12 **AAA Inspector Notes:** *Classic.* Since 1959, this landmark eatery and saloon has been serving the freshest quality, hand-carved prime rib, corned beef, pastrami, turkey and roast beef sandwiches and entrées. Meats are roasted daily. A line forms at lunch so it is best to arrive early or a bit late. **Bar:** full bar. **Address:** 2500 Watt Ave 95825 **Location:** Business Rt I-80 exit Watt Ave, 2.4 mi s; jct El Camino Ave. [L] [D] CALL ⓈⓂ

SCOTT'S SEAFOOD GRILL & BAR 916/379-5959 (21)

♦♦♦ Seafood. Casual Dining. $11-$41 **AAA Inspector Notes:** Dine overlooking the Sacramento River at this restaurant where seafood and steaks prevail. Light lunch combinations and casual, upscale fare is available including salads and sandwiches in addition to the delicious seafood and pasta entrées. Glass fire pits enhance an attractive outdoor patio. A Saturday and Sunday champagne brunch is offered. **Bar:** full bar. **Reservations:** suggested. **Address:** 4800 Riverside Blvd 95822 **Location:** I-5 exit Fruitridge/Seamas, just w, then 0.7 mi n; adjacent to Le Rivage Hotel, A Preferred Hotel. **Parking:** on-site and valet. [B] [L] [D] CALL ⓈⓂ

SELLAND'S MARKET - CAFE 916/736-3333 (14)

♦♦ American. Casual Dining. $5-$23 **AAA Inspector Notes:** Order at the tempting display cases, then either dine inside or on the patio out front. Take out also is available. Menu items are prepared from scratch using the freshest ingredients and most of the produce comes right from local farmer's markets. Pizza, hot and cold sandwiches, a few hot entrée items, salads and a variety of desserts are offered. Breakfast is served on Sunday. **Bar:** wine only. **Address:** 5340 H St 95819 **Location:** Business Rt I-80 (Capital City Frwy) exit J St, 1.7 mi e, then just n on El Dorado Way; jct El Dorado Way. [L] [D] CALL ⓈⓂ

TARO'S BY MIKUNI 916/564-2114 (6)

♦♦ Japanese Sushi. Casual Dining. $9-$19 **AAA Inspector Notes:** An excellent choice of nigiri, sashimi, donburi and fun-style maki rolls are available at this contemporary Japanese restaurant and sushi bar. Other highlights include lunch specials, bento combinations and a fine selection of sake. **Bar:** full bar. **Reservations:** suggested. **Address:** 1735 Arden Way, Suite 200 95815 **Location:** Business Rt I-80 exit E Arden Way; in Arden Fair Mall. [L] [D] CALL ⓈⓂ

TAYLORS MARKET 916/443-6881 (19)

♦ Sandwiches. Quick Serve. $6-$8 **AAA Inspector Notes:** Since 1962, this Sacramento landmark located in the Curtis Park neighborhood, offers a gourmet grocery and fresh, made-to-order deli sandwiches. **Address:** 2924 Freeport Blvd 95818 **Location:** Business Rt I-80 (Capitol City Freeway) exit P St westbound, straight on 29th St (which becomes W St), then 0.6 mi s on 21st St; exit 15th St eastbound, just s to Broadway, just e to Freeport Blvd, then 0.5 mi s. [L] CALL ⓈⓂ

TEX WASABI'S 916/927-8399 (7)

♦♦ Japanese. Casual Dining. $11-$29 **AAA Inspector Notes:** This restaurant combines two food cultures-creative California-style sushi and Southern barbecue-and then adds a California twist, all in a whimsical fashion. The sometimes noisy bar offers specialty cocktails, live music on the weekends and ottomans that provide seating around a fireplace. **Bar:** full bar. **Address:** 2243 Arden Way 95825 **Location:** Business Rt I-80 exit Arden Way, 1.3 mi se; US 50 exit Howe Ave, 3 mi n, then just e. [L] [D] CALL ⓈⓂ

THAI BASIL RESTAURANT 916/681-8424

♦♦ Thai. Casual Dining. $8-$16 **AAA Inspector Notes:** Tucked within an attractive shopping plaza, this restaurant offers tasty Thai food including salads, curries, wok-fried items and noodle dishes. The service is relaxed. **Bar:** beer & wine. **Address:** 8785 Center Pkwy, Suite B120 95823 **Location:** SR 99 exit 288 (Sheldon Rd), 1.2 mi w; in Laguna Village Shopping Center. [L] [D]

TUK TUK RESTAURANT 916/575-7957 (2)

♦♦ Thai. Casual Dining. $7-$16 **AAA Inspector Notes:** This restaurant with attractive contemporary Thai decor, offers several specialties, along with some traditional offerings. Tuk tuk's are vehicles used for urban transport in Bangkok. **Bar:** full bar. **Reservations:** suggested. **Address:** 4630 Natomas Blvd, Suite 150 95835 **Location:** I-5 exit Del Paso Rd, 1 mi e, then just n; in Park Place. [L] [D] CALL ⓈⓂ

THE VIRGIN STURGEON RESTAURANT-MARINA 916/921-2694 (4)

♦♦ American. Casual Dining. $8-$18 **AAA Inspector Notes:** Just a 10 minute drive from downtown Sacramento this restaurant is on the Sacramento River. Park at the top and walk the former Pan American Airlines jet way from the San Francisco International Airport down to this very casual, funky comfortable restaurant built on a barge. Serving patrons for more than 25 years, a few smoked specialties, such as sturgeon and salmon, as well as salads and sandwiches are offered. The restaurant dabbles in Cajun preparations, too. **Bar:** full bar. **Address:** 1577 Garden Hwy 95833 **Location:** I-5 exit 521 (Garden Hwy), 0.7 mi w. [L] [D] CALL ⓈⓂ

DELTA BAR & GRILL 916/444-5464

[fyi] Not evaluated. Take advantage of the wonderful river views at the outside tables on the deck of the Delta King. Appetizers and small plates are offered here. Entertainment is featured Wednesday through Saturday. **Address:** 1000 Front St 95814 **Location:** I-5 exit J St (Old Sacramento); in Delta King Hotel.

LALO'S RESTAURANT 916/736-2389

[fyi] Not evaluated. Expect a wait at this popular hole-in-the-wall serving authentic Mexican favorites such as huaraches, sopes, molcajetes and tortas. Breakfast is offered on the weekends. **Address:** 5063 24th St 95822 **Location:** SR 99 exit Fruitridge Rd, just w, then just n.

OPA! OPA! 916/451-4000

[fyi] Not evaluated. This budget eatery offers Greek fast food-gyros, pitas, pita pizza, souvlaki (kebabs) and such hearty entrées as traditional Greek moussaka and pastitso. On busy nights, grab a table first, then order at the counter. A patio is available in season. **Address:** 5644 J St 95825 **Location:** US 50 exit 59th St, just n, just w on Folsom Blvd to 57th St, then just ne; jct 57th St; just w of California State University.

ST. HELENA (B-8) pop. 5,814, elev. 255'
- **Restaurants p. 336**
- **Attractions map p. 568**
- **Hotels & Restaurants map & index p. 570**
- **Part of Wine Country area — see map p. 562**

In addition to those ever-present wineries, the Napa Valley community of St. Helena offers such locally handcrafted items as the candles produced at the Hurd Beeswax Candle Factory, at 345 Lafata St. Tours of the facility are available by appointment; phone (707) 963-7211. St. Helena is located along a scenic stretch of SR 29 running from Calistoga to Napa.

The Culinary Institute of America has a campus in St. Helena, housed in the imposing Greystone Cellars building at 2555 Main St. (accessible from SR 29). Cooking demonstrations are given regularly, and there are herb and organic gardens on the grounds. For more information phone (707) 967-1010.

St. Helena Chamber of Commerce: 657 Main St., St. Helena, CA 94574. **Phone:** (707) 963-4456 or (800) 799-6456.

BALE GRIST MILL STATE HISTORIC PARK is 3 mi. n. on SR 29. The 1849 mill has a 36-foot-diameter wheel that was once used to grind flour for local farmers. It has been restored and once again grinds flour and cornmeal. Hiking trails lead from the access road to the mill pond as well as to Bothe-Napa Valley State Park *(see Recreation Areas Chart)*.

Hours: Sat.-Sun. 10-5. Tours are offered as needed 10-4 when staff is available. Closed Jan. 1, Thanksgiving and Christmas. Phone ahead to confirm schedule. **Cost:** $5; $2 (ages 0-16). **Phone:** (707) 942-4575.

ROBERT LOUIS STEVENSON SILVERADO MUSEUM, 1490 Library Ln., off E. Adams St., contains more than 11,000 items related to Scottish author Robert Louis Stevenson, who spent a year in California, including a 9-week honeymoon in Napa Valley. **Hours:** Tues.-Sat. noon-4. Closed major holidays. **Cost:** Donations. **Phone:** (707) 963-3757.

WINERIES

- **Beringer Winery** is at 2000 Main St. **Hours:** Daily 10-6, late May-late Oct.; 10-5, rest of year. Various tours are conducted throughout the day; phone ahead for schedule. Closed Jan. 1, Thanksgiving and Christmas. **Phone:** (707) 967-4412.
- **Franciscan** is s. on St. Helena Hwy. (SR 29) at jct. Galleron Rd. **Hours:** Tastings daily 10-5. Guided tours are available by appointment. Closed major holidays. **Phone:** (707) 967-3830.
- **Louis M. Martini Winery** is at 254 S. St. Helena Hwy. **Hours:** Tastings daily 10-6. Tours are given daily by appointment. Closed major holidays. Phone ahead to confirm schedule. **Phone:** (707) 968-3362.

- **V. Sattui Winery** is 1.5 mi. s. at jct. White Ln. and US 29 at 1111 White Ln. **Hours:** Daily 9-6, Mar.-Oct.; 9-5, rest of year. Closed Christmas. **Phone:** (707) 963-7774.

AMBROSE BIERCE HOUSE (707)963-3003 **19**
Historic Bed & Breakfast $159-$299 **Address:** 1515 Main St 94574 **Location:** On SR 29, 0.3 mi n. **Facility:** This attractively restored 1872 Victorian home offers gracious hospitality and close proximity to the downtown area. 4 units. 2 stories, interior corridors. **Terms:** check-in 4 pm, 2-3 night minimum stay - seasonal and/or weekends, 15 day cancellation notice-fee imposed.

EL BONITA MOTEL 707/963-3216 **22**
Motel $80-$300 **Address:** 195 Main St 94574 **Location:** 1 mi s of center on SR 29; at El Bonita Ave and Main St (SR 29). **Facility:** 42 units, some efficiencies. 2 stories, exterior corridors. **Terms:** 2 night minimum stay - seasonal and/or weekends, 3 day cancellation notice. **Pool(s):** heated outdoor. **Activities:** sauna, whirlpool.

HARVEST INN (707)963-9463 **23**
Hotel $229-$899 **Address:** One Main St 94574 **Location:** 1.5 mi s of center on SR 29 (Main St). **Facility:** This Tudor-style country estate is surrounded by vineyards, spectacular gardens and landscaping. Beautifully appointed rooms are spacious and many feature a fireplace and a private deck or terrace. 74 units. 2 stories, exterior corridors. **Terms:** check-in 4 pm, 2-3 night minimum stay - seasonal and/or weekends, 14 day cancellation notice-fee imposed. **Amenities:** high-speed Internet. *Some:* safes. **Pool(s):** 2 heated outdoor. **Activities:** whirlpools, exercise room. *Fee:* bicycles, massage. **Guest Services:** valet laundry. **Free Special Amenities:** expanded continental breakfast and high-speed Internet.

HOTEL ST. HELENA 707/963-4388 **20**
Historic Hotel $145-$595 **Address:** 1309 Main St 94574 **Location:** On SR 29; center. **Facility:** Located downtown close to many shops and restaurants, the restored 1888 Victorian inn features rooms reflecting an era long gone. 18 units. 2 stories (no elevator), interior corridors. *Bath:* some shared. **Terms:** 3 day cancellation notice-fee imposed.

THE INK HOUSE BED & BREAKFAST (707)963-3890 **25**
Historic Bed & Breakfast $140-$275 **Address:** 1575 St. Helena Hwy S 94574 **Location:** On SR 29, 2 mi s. **Facility:** A casual Victorian elegance characterizes this landmark 1884 home. 7 units. 2 stories (no elevator), interior corridors. **Terms:** 2 night minimum stay - weekends, 14 day cancellation notice-fee imposed. **Activities:** bicycles, game room.

MEADOWOOD NAPA VALLEY (707)963-3646 **18**
Resort Hotel $475-$1875 **Address:** 900 Meadowood Ln 94574 **Location:** Jct SR 29 and 12 exit Pope St, 0.8 mi e to Silverado Tr, just n, then 1 blk e on Howell Mountain Rd. **Facility:** A 250-acre, private, wooded reserve wraps around these country-style lodges, many with a wood-burning fireplace. 85 units, some two and three bedrooms. 2 stories, exterior corridors. **Terms:** check-in 4 pm, 2 night minimum stay - weekends, 14 day cancellation notice-fee imposed. **Amenities:** video games (fee), high-speed Internet, safes. **Dining:** The Grill At Meadowood, see separate listing. **Pool(s):** 2 heated outdoor. **Activities:** whirlpools, recreation programs, hiking trails, exercise room, spa. *Fee:* golf-9 holes, 7 tennis courts. **Guest Services:** valet laundry.

(See map & index p. 570.)

SHADY OAKS COUNTRY INN (707)963-1190 **24**

▽▽▽ **Historic Bed & Breakfast** $149-$289 **Address:** 399 Zinfandel Ln 94574 **Location:** 0.5 mi e of SR 29. **Facility:** This secluded inn is surrounded by vineyards; guest rooms are appointed with antiques and some include a fireplace. 5 units. 1-2 stories (no elevator), interior/exterior corridors. **Terms:** check-in 4 pm, 2-3 night minimum stay - seasonal and/or weekends, 15 day cancellation notice-fee imposed.

CALL 🔊M 📶 ✕ 🅉 / SOME UNITS 💻

SPANISH VILLA INN (707)963-7483 **17**

▽▽▽ **Bed & Breakfast** $175-$275 **Address:** 474 Glass Mt. Rd 94574 **Location:** 1.4 mi n on SR 29 to Deer Park Rd, 1.6 mi e to Glass Mt. Rd, then just n. **Facility:** This Mediterranean-style property boasts a very European feel with its lovely gardens and lawn. Located one mile west of the Culinary Institute of America. 6 units. 2 stories (no elevator), interior/exterior corridors. **Terms:** 2 night minimum stay - seasonal and/or weekends, 14 day cancellation notice-fee imposed. 📶 ✕ 🎿 🅉

VINEYARD COUNTRY INN (707)963-1000 **21**

Country Inn
$175-$325

Address: 201 Main St 94574 **Location:** 0.8 mi s on SR 29. **Facility:** Wood-burning fireplaces are featured in all of the inn's rooms, some also have a patio or deck with views of the vineyard. 20 units. 2 stories (no elevator), exterior corridors. **Terms:** check-in 4 pm, 2-3 night minimum stay - seasonal and/or weekends, 14 day cancellation notice-fee imposed. **Amenities:** high-speed Internet. **Pool(s):** outdoor. **Activities:** whirlpool. *(See ad p. 241.)*

SAVE CALL 🔊M 🏊 📶 ✕
🔋 💻

WHERE TO EAT

GOTT'S ROADSIDE 707/963-3486 **9**

▽ American. Quick Serve. $8-$15 **AAA Inspector Notes:** Since 1949, this roadside stand has been known as Taylor's Refresher and the sign still has the original name-the town of St. Helena designated the sign a historic landmark. The fast food served here is top notch. Sushi-grade tuna is used in their fish burger. The mesclun comes from the garden behind the stand. And of course, there is wine and beer from local producers for accompaniment. **Bar:** beer & wine. **Address:** 933 Main St 94574 **Location:** On SR 29; between Mitchell Dr and McCorkle Ave. L D 🎿

THE GRILL AT MEADOWOOD 707/963-3646 **7**

▽▽▽
California
Casual Dining
$18-$34

AAA Inspector Notes: Views of the wooded hillsides are particularly scenic from the relaxed, seasonal deck. **Bar:** full bar. **Reservations:** suggested. **Address:** 900 Meadowood Ln 94574 **Location:** Jct SR 29 and 12 exit Pope St, 0.8 mi e to Silverado Tr, just n, then 1 blk e on Howell Mountain Rd; in Meadowood Napa Valley. B L D

MARKET 707/963-3799 **8**

▽▽▽ American. Casual Dining. $13-$25 **AAA Inspector Notes:** This cozy elegant eatery prepares American fare with a flair, with such selections as succulent lamb shank, organic fried chicken and macaroni and cheese with a gourmet twist. **Bar:** full bar. **Address:** 1347 Main St 94574 **Location:** On SR 29; center. **Parking:** street only. L D CALL 🔊M

Be a better driver.
Keep your mind on the road.

TRA VIGNE 707/963-4444 **10**

▽▽▽ Italian. Fine Dining. $18-$30 **AAA Inspector Notes:** This restaurant is set in an attractive location in the heart of Napa Valley. The menu offers a wide selection of pasta with homemade sauces, fresh fish and beef items. **Bar:** full bar. **Reservations:** suggested. **Address:** 1050 Charter Oak Ave 94574 **Location:** 0.5 mi s on SR 29. L D

WINE SPECTATOR GREYSTONE RESTAURANT
707/967-1010 **6**

▽▽▽ California. Fine Dining. $23-$32 **AAA Inspector Notes:** Located on the grounds of the old Christian Brothers Winery, this restaurant employs students from the Culinary Institute of America. Local seasonal ingredients are the inspiration for the cuisine. **Bar:** full bar. **Reservations:** suggested. **Address:** 2555 Main St 94574 **Location:** 1.5 mi n on SR 29. **Parking:** on-site and valet.

L D CALL 🔊M

SALIDA pop. 13,722

FAIRFIELD INN & SUITES BY MARRIOTT (209)543-7800

▽▽▽ Hotel $85-$99 **Address:** 4342 Salida Blvd 95368 **Location:** SR 99 exit Pelandale Ave W, just n. **Facility:** 69 units. 2 stories, interior corridors. **Amenities:** high-speed Internet. **Pool(s):** outdoor. **Activities:** sauna, whirlpool, exercise room. **Guest Services:** valet and coin laundry.

AAA Benefit:
AAA hotel discounts of 5% or more.

🍴 CALL 🔊M 🏊 BIZ 📶 ✕ 🔋 🖥 💻

HAMPTON INN & SUITES (209)543-3650

▽▽▽ Hotel $109-$139 **Address:** 4921 Sisk Rd 95368 **Location:** SR 99 exit SR 219, just e. **Facility:** 70 units. 3 stories, interior corridors. **Terms:** 1-7 night minimum stay, cancellation fee imposed. **Pool(s):** outdoor. **Activities:** exercise room. **Guest Services:** valet and coin laundry.

AAA Benefit:
Members save up to 10%!

🍴 CALL 🔊M 🏊 BIZ 📶 🔋 🖥 💻

LA QUINTA INN & SUITES MODESTO SALIDA
(209)579-8723

Hotel
$89-$161

Address: 4909 Sisk Rd 95368 **Location:** SR 99 exit SR 219, just e. **Facility:** 67 units. 3 stories, interior corridors. **Amenities:** video games (fee), high-speed Internet. **Pool(s):** outdoor. **Activities:** whirlpool, exercise room. **Guest Services:** coin laundry. **Free Special Amenities:** full breakfast and high-speed Internet.

SAVE 🍴 CALL 🔊M 🏊 BIZ 📶 🐾 🔋 🖥 💻
/ SOME UNITS FEE 🐕

SALINAS (G-3) pop. 150,441, elev. 55'
• Restaurants p. 338

Salinas was the birthplace of Nobel and Pulitzer prize-winning author John Steinbeck and the setting for many of his novels. A statue of the man who wrote such classics as "The Grapes of Wrath" and "East of Eden" stands on the lawn of the John Steinbeck Library, 350 Lincoln Ave.; phone (831) 758-7311. Steinbeck is buried in Garden of Memories Memorial Park, 768 Abbott St.; phone (831) 422-6417.

The vast quantities and varieties of vegetables and fruits grown in the Salinas Valley are responsible for the nickname "Salad Bowl of the World."

Salinas Valley Chamber of Commerce: 119 E. Alisal St., Salinas, CA 93901. **Phone:** (831) 751-7725.

Shopping areas: The anchor stores at Northridge Mall, US 101 at Boronda Road and N. Main Street, are JCPenney, Macy's and Sears.

JOSÉ EUSEBIO BORONDA ADOBE, 333 Boronda Rd., was built 1844-46 and is the city's oldest structure. The wood shingles used on the adobe are a departure from traditional red-clay tiles. The 1897 Old Lagunita School House also is at the site. **Time:** Allow 30 minutes minimum. **Hours:** Guided 30- to 60-minute tours are given Mon.-Fri. 10-2, Sat.-Sun. by appointment. Phone ahead to confirm schedule. **Cost:** Donations. **Phone:** (831) 757-8085.

 NATIONAL STEINBECK CENTER, One Main St., consists of the John Steinbeck Exhibition Hall; the Rabobank Agricultural Museum, which provides information and displays about the agricultural history of the fertile Salinas Valley; and the Gabilan Gallery, which offers changing art and cultural exhibits.

The Steinbeck Exhibition Hall features several themed galleries of interactive exhibits about Steinbeck's life and literature. Stage settings and film clips help bring this Nobel prize-winning author's works to life; other displays allow you to explore "Cannery Row" and "Of Mice and Men." Visitors also can see the camper that transported the author and his poodle Charley across America while Steinbeck wrote "Travels with Charley."

Time: Allow 2 hours minimum. **Hours:** Daily 10-5. Closed Jan. 1, Thanksgiving and Christmas. **Cost:** $10.95; $8.95 (ages 62+ and students, teachers and military with ID); $7.95 (ages 13-17); $5.95 (ages 6-12). **Phone:** (831) 775-4721.

SALINAS COMMUNITY CENTER, 940 N. Main St., displays varied artwork and stages musical and theatrical performances throughout the year. **Time:** Allow 30 minutes minimum. **Hours:** Office open Mon.-Fri. 8-5. **Cost:** Free. A fee may be charged for some displays or performances. **Phone:** (831) 758-7351.

"Hat In Three Stages of Landing" is on the lawn at the Salinas Community Center. Claes Oldenberg's giant sculpture depicts three hats at different levels, each painted a vivid yellow and weighing approximately 3,500 pounds. The sculpture is a tribute to farmers and ranchers and represents a Western hat tossed in the air from the nearby rodeo stands.

WILD THINGS is 4 mi. e. off SR 68 River Rd./Reservation Rd. exit, following signs to Vision Quest Ranch at 400 River Rd. The organization provides professionally trained wild, exotic and domestic animals for use in movies, television, music videos, print and education. Guided walking tours introduce some of the more than 100 residents, including lions, tigers, cheetahs, servals, elephants, porcupines, bears, kangaroos and baboons. Visitors learn about the animals' personalities, their appearances and how they are trained.

Time: Allow 1 hour minimum. **Hours:** Guided tours are given daily at 1 and 3, June-Aug.; at 1, rest

of year. Closed Thanksgiving and Christmas. **Cost:** $10; $8 (ages 0-14). **Phone:** (831) 455-1901.

AMERICAS BEST VALUE INN   (831)422-6486

Motel
$59-$299

Address: 1030 Fairview Ave 93905 **Location:** US 101 exit Sanborn Rd or Fairview Ave, just e. **Facility:** 44 units. 2 stories (no elevator), exterior corridors. **Terms:** cancellation fee imposed. **Guest Services:** coin laundry. **Free Special Amenities:** continental breakfast and high-speed Internet.

[SAVE] CALL [&M] [BIZ] [📶] [🛏] [🖥] [🖥]

BEST WESTERN PLUS SALINAS VALLEY INN & SUITES
(831)751-6411

Hotel
$89-$299

AAA Benefit: Members save up to 20%, plus 10% bonus points with Best Western Rewards®.

Address: 187 Kern St 93905 **Location:** US 101 exit Market St, just e. **Facility:** 62 units. 3 stories, interior corridors. **Terms:** cancellation fee imposed. **Pool(s):** heated outdoor. **Activities:** sauna, whirlpool, exercise room. **Guest Services:** coin laundry. **Free Special Amenities: full breakfast and high-speed Internet.**

[SAVE] [📶+] CALL [&M] [🛒] [📶] [✕] [🛏] [🖥] [🖥] / SOME UNITS FEE [🐾]

BEST WESTERN SALINAS MONTEREY HOTEL
(831)784-0176

Hotel
$90-$400

AAA Benefit: Members save up to 20%, plus 10% bonus points with Best Western Rewards®.

Address: 175 Kern St 93905 **Location:** US 101 exit Market St, just e., then just n. **Facility:** 58 units. 3 stories, interior corridors. **Terms:** 2-4 night minimum stay - seasonal and/or weekends, cancellation fee imposed. **Amenities:** high-speed Internet. **Pool(s):** outdoor. **Activities:** whirlpool, exercise room. **Guest Services:** coin laundry. **Free Special Amenities: local telephone calls and high-speed Internet.**

[SAVE] [📶+] [🛒] [BIZ] [📶] [🛏] [🖥] [🖥]

COMFORT INN & SUITES   (831)770-1400

[📶📶📶] Hotel $90-$300 **Address:** 181 Kern St 93905 **Location:** US 101 exit Market St, just e. **Facility:** 61 units. 3 stories, interior corridors. **Terms:** cancellation fee imposed. **Amenities:** high-speed Internet. **Pool(s):** heated indoor. **Activities:** exercise room. **Guest Services:** coin laundry.

[📶+] CALL [&M] [🛒] [📶] [🛏] [🖥] [🖥]

COURTYARD BY MARRIOTT-SALINAS   (831)775-0491

[📶📶📶] Hotel $109-$339 **Address:** 17225 El Rancho Way 93907 **Location:** US 101 exit Laurel Dr, just w. **Facility:** 90 units. 3 stories, interior corridors. **Pool(s):** heated indoor. **Activities:** whirlpool, exercise room. **Guest Services:** valet and coin laundry.

AAA Benefit: AAA hotel discounts of 5% or more.

[🍴] CALL [&M] [🛒] [BIZ] [📶] [✕] [🖥] / SOME UNITS [🛏]

HOLIDAY INN EXPRESS & SUITES-SALINAS
(831)737-1160

Hotel
$99-$399

Address: 195 Kern St 93905 **Location:** US 101 exit Market St, just e. **Facility:** 74 units. 3 stories, interior corridors. **Amenities:** high-speed Internet, safes. **Pool(s):** heated indoor. **Activities:** whirlpool, exercise room. **Guest Services:** valet and coin laundry. **Free Special Amenities: full breakfast and high-speed Internet.**

[SAVE] CALL [&M] [🛒] [BIZ] [📶] [✕] [🛏] [🖥] [🖥]

HOWARD JOHNSON (831)757-1020

Motel
$60-$400

Address: 131 John St 93901 **Location:** US 101 exit John St, 0.5 mi w. **Facility:** 38 units. 3 stories, exterior corridors. **Amenities:** high-speed Internet. **Free Special Amenities: continental breakfast and high-speed Internet.**

LAUREL INN (831)449-2474

Hotel
$71-$275

Address: 801 W Laurel Dr 93906 **Location:** US 101 exit Laurel Dr, just e. **Facility:** 142 units. 2 stories (no elevator), exterior corridors. **Terms:** 7 day cancellation notice. **Pool(s):** outdoor. **Activities:** sauna, whirlpool. **Free Special Amenities: continental breakfast and high-speed Internet.**

QUALITY INN (831)758-8850

Motel
$70-$330

Address: 144 Kern St 93905 **Location:** US 101 exit Market St, just e. **Facility:** 32 units. 3 stories, exterior corridors. **Amenities:** high-speed Internet. **Guest Services:** valet laundry. **Free Special Amenities: continental breakfast and high-speed Internet.**

RESIDENCE INN BY MARRIOTT-SALINAS (831)775-0410

Extended Stay Hotel
$119-$349 **Address:** 17215 El Rancho Way 93907 **Location:** US 101 exit Laurel Dr, just w. **Facility:** 107 units, some two bedrooms, efficiencies and kitchens. 3 stories, interior corridors. **Pool(s):** heated indoor. **Activities:** whirlpool, sports court, exercise room. **Guest Services:** valet and coin laundry.

AAA Benefit:
AAA hotel discounts of 5% or more.

TRAVELODGE (831)424-4801

Motel
$90-$290

Address: 109 John St 93901 **Location:** US 101 exit John St, 0.7 mi w. **Facility:** 38 units. 2 stories (no elevator), exterior corridors. **Terms:** 2 night minimum stay - seasonal and/or weekends, cancellation fee imposed. **Amenities:** high-speed Internet, safes. **Activities:** exercise room. **Free Special Amenities: continental breakfast and high-speed Internet.**

WHERE TO EAT

BLACK BEAR DINER 831/449-1545

American. Casual Dining. $7-$16 **AAA Inspector Notes:** A homey atmosphere characterizes this family-oriented restaurant. Familiar comfort foods, such as meatloaf with mashed potatoes, are at the heart of the menu and are served in generous portions. **Bar:** beer & wine. **Address:** 805 W Laurel Dr 93906 **Location:** US 101 exit Laurel Dr, just e.

GINO'S FINE ITALIAN FOOD 831/422-1814

Italian. Casual Dining. $9-$30 **AAA Inspector Notes:** In a small converted house, the locally-owned family restaurant builds its menu on Italian specialties. Guests can enjoy a relaxing dining experience in one of the inside dining rooms or outside on the patio. **Bar:** full bar. **Reservations:** suggested. **Address:** 1410 S Main St 93908 **Location:** On SR 68, just e of Reservation Rd/River Rd.

THE GOLDEN FISH 831/422-4946

Seafood. Casual Dining. $10-$17 **AAA Inspector Notes:** This local favorite offers several fresh fish and pasta items in a casual and relaxed atmosphere. It is within walking distance of the Steinbeck Center. **Bar:** beer & wine. **Address:** 221 Main St 93901 **Location:** Between E Gabian St and Midtown Ln; in historic downtown area. **Parking:** street only.

HABANERO COCINA MEXICANA 831/757-1975

Mexican. Casual Dining. $8-$12 **AAA Inspector Notes:** Fresh and flavorful items are prepared as ordered at this Mexican eatery. Homemade salsa and sauces are not heavy and complement a menu that includes a variety of taco specialties, including carne asada, fish, chicken and shrimp and taco salad as well as fajitas and burritos. **Bar:** beer & wine. **Address:** 152 N Main St 93901 **Location:** Just s of Market St; in historic downtown area. **Parking:** street only.

MARGIE'S DINER 831/783-1078

American. Casual Dining. $8-$20 **AAA Inspector Notes:** A fun atmosphere enlivens this family-friendly, 1950s-style diner. On the menu are traditional favorites including hearty breakfasts, specialty burgers and sandwiches, fried chicken and meatloaf. Be sure to come hungry because portions are hearty. **Bar:** beer & wine. **Address:** 155 Kern St 93905 **Location:** US 101 exit Market St, just e.

MONTEREY COAST BREWING 831/758-2337

American. Casual Dining. $9-$17 **AAA Inspector Notes:** A family, fun atmosphere is offered at this casual spot where traditional pub-style cuisine includes great burgers, pizza, pasta dishes, steaks and seafood. Brewed on site is beer made from premium ingredients. Portions are hearty, so come hungry. **Bar:** beer & wine. **Address:** 165 Main St 93901 **Location:** Just s of Market St; in historic downtown area. **Parking:** street only.

ROUND TABLE PIZZA

Pizza. Casual Dining. $7-$28 **AAA Inspector Notes:** This casual, family-oriented pizza place features high-quality ingredients and dough rolled fresh daily. Distinctive specialty pizzas are piled high with toppings. **Bar:** beer & wine.

For additional information, visit AAA.com

LOCATIONS:
Address: 1160 S Main St 93901 **Location:** Just n of Blanco Rd. **Phone:** 831/757-7400
Address: 1457 N Main St 93906 **Location:** US 101 exit Boronda Rd E, then s; between Alvin and E Navajo drs. **Phone:** 831/449-9121

SAMOA pop. 258

SAMOA COOKHOUSE 707/442-1659

American
Casual Dining
$12-$16

AAA Inspector Notes: *Historic.* Built in 1885, this eatery is a holdout among the West's lumber-camp cookhouses. Families are welcome to browse the relics of bygone days and sample hearty food. A typical dinner includes a beverage, soup (such as black bean and ham), green salad, meat loaf with brown gravy, pork ribs with barbecue sauce, corn, potatoes and a slice of apple pie topped with whipped cream. **Bar:** beer & wine. **Address:** 908 Vance Ave 95564 **Location:** 1.9 mi w on SR 255 from jct US 101, just s to Cookhouse Rd, then just e.

SAN ANDREAS (E-4) pop. 2,783, elev. 1,008'

About 16 miles west of San Andreas via SR 12, Paloma Road, Watertown Road and Campo Seco-Chile Camp Road are the remains of Campo Seco, a once-thriving mining settlement. Dubbed Campo Seco (dry camp) by prospectors, the site produced some gold, but the real treasure was copper. During the Civil War Penn Copper Co. supplied the Union

Army with the metal. Although officially a ghost town, Campo Seco has a post office and also claims to be the site of the largest cork oak tree in California.

CALAVERAS COUNTY MUSEUM, 30 N. Main St., served as the county jail and the county courthouse 1867-1962. Featured are a garden of native California plants and trees, Miwok Indian artifacts, mining relics, 1850-1900 period exhibits and an Italian stone oven. **Time:** Allow 30 minutes minimum. **Hours:** Daily 10-4. Closed major holidays. **Cost:** $3; $2 (ages 60+); $1 (ages 6-12). **Phone:** (209) 754-1058.

THE ROBINS NEST (209)754-1076

▼▼▼ **Historic Bed & Breakfast** $100-$175 **Address:** 247 W St. Charles St 95249 **Location:** SR 49; north end of town. This 1895 Queen Anne Victorian has been restored and improved upon to provide comfortable accommodations for guests. 9 units. 2 stories (no elevator), interior corridors. **Terms:** 7 day cancellation notice. **Amenities:** high-speed Internet. **Activities:** whirlpool. **Guest Services:** complimentary laundry.

SAN BRUNO pop. 41,114
• Hotels & Restaurants map & index p. 410
• Part of San Francisco area — see map p. 342

COMFORT INN & SUITES (650)589-5089 **28**

▼▼▼ **Hotel** $79-$199 **Address:** 611 San Bruno Ave E 94066 **Location:** US 101 exit San Bruno Ave, 0.4 mi w. San Bruno, 43. **Facility:** 29 units. 2 stories, interior corridors. **Terms:** cancellation fee imposed. **Free Special Amenities: full breakfast and airport transportation.**

COURTYARD BY MARRIOTT SAN FRANCISCO AIRPORT (650)952-3333 **27**

▼▼▼ **Hotel** $149-$309 **Address:** 1050 Bayhill Dr 94066 **Location:** I-380 exit El Camino Real S, 0.3 mi, then just w. San Bruno, 43. **Facility:** 147 units. 2-3 stories, interior corridors. **Amenities:** high-speed Internet. **Pool(s):** heated indoor. **Activities:** whirlpool, exercise room. **Guest Services:** valet and coin laundry.

AAA Benefit:
AAA hotel discounts of 5% or more.

DAYS INN-SFO INTERNATIONAL-WEST (650)616-9600 **32**

▼▼ **Hotel** $55-$175 **Address:** 1550 El Camino Real 94066 **Location:** US 101 exit 420 (Millbrae Ave), 1.2 mi n. San Francisco International Airport, 44. **Facility:** 48 units. 3 stories, interior corridors. **Amenities:** high-speed Internet. *Some:* safes.

GATEWAY INN & SUITES (650)583-4555 **29**

▼▼ **Hotel** $89-$159 **Address:** 516 El Camino Real 94066 **Location:** US 101 exit San Bruno Ave, 1 mi w, then 0.4 mi s. San Bruno, 43. **Facility:** 31 units. 3 stories, interior corridors. **Amenities:** high-speed Internet. **Guest Services:** valet laundry.

HOWARD JOHNSON EXPRESS INN (650)588-0800 **31**

▼▼▼ **Hotel** $65-$149 **Address:** 190 El Camino Real 94066 **Location:** US 101 exit San Bruno Ave, 1 mi w, then 0.8 mi s. San Francisco International Airport, 44. **Facility:** 49 units. 3 stories, interior corridors. **Terms:** cancellation fee imposed. **Amenities:** high-speed Internet, safes. **Free Special Amenities: continental breakfast and high-speed Internet.**

STAYBRIDGE SUITES (650)588-0770 **26**

▼▼▼ **Extended Stay Hotel** $129-$309 **Address:** 1350 Huntington Ave 94066 **Location:** I-380 exit El Camino Real N, e on Sneath Ln, then just n. San Bruno, 43. **Facility:** 92 kitchen units, some two bedrooms. 3 stories (no elevator), exterior corridors. **Terms:** cancellation fee imposed. **Amenities:** high-speed Internet. **Pool(s):** heated outdoor. **Activities:** whirlpool, sports court, exercise room. **Guest Services:** valet and coin laundry, area transportation-within 5 mi. **Free Special Amenities: full breakfast and airport transportation.**

SUPER 8 (650)624-0999 **30**

▼▼ **Hotel** $80-$159 **Address:** 421 El Camino Real 94066 **Location:** US 101 exit San Bruno Ave, 1 mi w, then 0.5 mi s. **Facility:** 52 units. 3 stories, interior corridors. **Terms:** cancellation fee imposed. **Amenities:** high-speed Internet. **Guest Services:** coin laundry. **Free Special Amenities: continental breakfast and high-speed Internet.**

WHERE TO EAT

DON PICO'S MEXICAN BISTRO 650/589-1163 **16**

▼▼ **Mexican. Casual Dining.** $14-$25 **AAA Inspector Notes:** Popular with the locals, this modest restaurant's focus is on food. Menu highlights include paella, jambalaya and lomo saltados. For a light appetizer, try the grilled asparagus in season, carnitas Yucatan (braised then pan fried to crispy perfection) and, if it is on the menu, mango flan. Try their coffee served in a mug that doubles as a French press. Live music nightly gives the restaurant a lively ambience. **Bar:** beer & wine. **Address:** 461 El Camino Real 94066 **Location:** US 101 exit San Bruno Ave, 1 mi w, then 0.5 mi s. **Parking:** on-site and street. L D

SAN CARLOS (E-8) pop. 28,406, elev. 76'
• Restaurants p. 340
• Hotels & Restaurants map & index p. 410
• Part of San Francisco area — see map p. 342

HILLER AVIATION MUSEUM is at 601 Skyway Rd. at the San Carlos Airport. The museum chronicles Northern California's contributions to aviation history. Hanging and ground displays of restored aircraft, full-size replicas and models range from an unmanned 1869 aeroplane to a 21st-century robotic flying wing. Youngsters can climb into the cockpit of a Navy jet and a Boeing 747. Other features include interactive displays, multimedia presentations and a glass-fronted restoration workshop. **Hours:** Daily 10-5. Closed Easter, Thanksgiving and Christmas. **Cost:** $12; $8 (ages 5-17 and 65+). **Phone:** (650) 654-0200.

AMERICAS BEST VALUE INN (650)591-6655 **84**

▼▼ **Motel** $75-$95 **Address:** 1562 El Camino Real 94070 **Location:** US 101 exit Holly St, 1 mi s on SR 82. **Facility:** 32 units, some efficiencies. 2 stories (no elevator), exterior corridors. **Terms:** cancellation fee imposed. **Amenities:** safes. **Activities:** sauna, whirlpool. **Free Special Amenities: continental breakfast and high-speed Internet.**

(See map & index p. 410.)

COUNTRY INN & SUITES BY CARLSON

(650)508-1800

Hotel
$79-S259

Address: 251 El Camino Real 94070 **Location:** N of US 101 exit Holly St, 0.3 mi n on SR 82. **Facility:** 50 units. 3 stories, interior corridors. **Terms:** cancellation fee imposed. **Amenities:** high-speed Internet. **Pool(s):** outdoor. **Activities:** exercise room. **Guest Services:** valet and coin laundry. **Free Special Amenities: expanded continental breakfast and high-speed Internet.**

FAIRFIELD INN & SUITES BY MARRIOTT (650)631-0777

Hotel $189-$249 **Address:** 555 Skyway Rd 94070 **Location:** US 101 exit Holly St/Redwood Shores Pkwy, e to Airport Blvd, then 0.3 mi s. **Facility:** 112 units. 3 stories, interior corridors.

AAA Benefit: AAA hotel discounts of 5% or more.

Amenities: Some: high-speed Internet. **Pool(s):** heated outdoor. **Activities:** exercise room. **Guest Services:** valet and coin laundry, area transportation-within 5 mi.

HOTEL SAN CARLOS

(650)591-5771

Motel
$89-S159

Address: 26 El Camino Real 94070 **Location:** US 101 exit Holly St, 0.5 mi n on SR 82 (El Camino Real). **Facility:** 29 units. 2 stories (no elevator), exterior corridors. **Terms:** 1-4 night minimum stay - seasonal and/or weekends, cancellation fee imposed. **Pool(s):** outdoor.

Keep seasonal vehicles
travel-ready with a
AAA/CAA Battery Tender®

JERSEY JOE'S HOAGIES & CHEESESTEAKS

650/592-7317

Sandwiches. Quick Serve. $5-$9 **AAA Inspector Notes:** An East Coast transplant, longing for good cheesesteaks and hoagies, decided to open his own sports bar to serve these beloved items. Also on the menu are burgers and tuna melts. If pizza is a love, then try the pizza steak—pizza sauce and provolone drenched beef on a soft roll. **Bar:** beer & wine. **Address:** 21 El Camino Real 94070 **Location:** US 101 exit Holly St, 0.4 mi n; in San Carlos Plaza.

KAYA TOFU & BBQ

650/595-9292

Korean Barbecue. Casual Dining. $10-$25 **AAA Inspector Notes:** High ceiling with a well-appointed décor gives this restaurant a spacious feel. Diners have a choice of grilling meats at the table or having the kitchen take care of it. **Bar:** beer & wine. **Address:** 39 El Camino Real 94070 **Location:** US 101 exit Holly St, 0.4 mi n; in San Carlos Plaza.

LOCANDA POSITANO

650/591-5700

Italian. Casual Dining. $13-$28 **AAA Inspector Notes:** Packed nightly since their opening, a vibrant atmosphere permeates this restaurant. There is bar seating in front of the imported pizza oven where guests can watch the master pizzaiolo work his magic. Fresh made pasta and crostini with various toppings also are on the menu. The staff is from Italy, adding even more to the lively atmosphere. For a more quiet dining experience, make sure to request the tables at the front of the restaurant. **Bar:** full bar. **Address:** 617 Laurel St 94070 **Location:** US 101 exit Holly St, 0.3 mi w, then just s. **Parking:** street only.

PIACERE RISTORANTE

650/592-3536

Italian. Casual Dining. $10-$39 **AAA Inspector Notes:** This contemporary restaurant offers a choice of dining experiences from casual al fresco and bar/lounge to a more formal dining area. The menu is an offering of Californian and Italian items ranging from burgers and pizza to grilled whole fish and buffalo tri-tip. **Bar:** full bar. **Address:** 727 Laurel St 94070 **Location:** SR 82, just w on San Carlos Ave, 0.3 mi s. **Parking:** street only.

SNEAKERS PUB & GRILL

650/802-0177

American. Casual Dining. $10-$19 **AAA Inspector Notes:** The laid-back spot presents a simple menu of sandwiches and hamburgers. Several large-screen TVs provide entertainment. **Bar:** full bar. **Address:** 1163 San Carlos Ave 94070 **Location:** Just w of SR 82 (El Camino Real). **Parking:** street only.

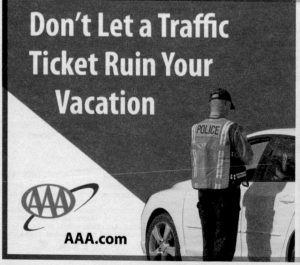

San Francisco

Then & Now

Fog rolls in off the Pacific, alternately obscuring and then revealing ferry boats as they scurry to and from Alcatraz, the fortress-like former prison ensconced on an island in a steel-blue bay. Intertwined dragons coil around ornate lampposts. Cable cars crest a death-defying hill, standing passengers clinging to their sides like matchsticks in a box. A row of sherbet-hued Victorians almost glows in the late afternoon sun.

San Francisco's many charms are undeniable, starting with that enviable setting at the top of a narrow peninsula rimmed by a bay and an ocean. The city is a swirl of diversity, a stronghold of tolerance. It's insanely photogenic—a Kodak moment waiting around every corner—and also a survivor, not only of the boom and bust gold rush days but of earthquakes that shook its very foundations.

The Spanish built a *presidio,* or military post, at the northern tip of the peninsula in 1776, the same year that Franciscan fathers established Mission San Francisco de Asis (better known as Mission Dolores). The presidio, an active military outpost for 218 years, is now part of Golden Gate National Recreation Area, where locals and visitors hike, bike, wind surf and gape at awesomely scenic views of the city and an iconic suspension bridge.

The Golden Gate Bridge's ruddy orange-red towers are San Francisco's most instantly identifiable landmark. This engineering marvel arches 8,981 feet over the entrance to San Francisco Bay, connecting the city's northern tip with Marin County. The bridge's 75th anniversary was officially commemorated with an explosion of fireworks on May 27, 2012.

An earlier defining but devastating historical moment occurred early on an April morning in 1906. A massive earthquake and the colossal fire that followed destroyed much of the central business district. But less than a decade later San Francisco celebrated its rebirth by hosting the 1915 Panama-Pacific International Exposition, which left behind the classically elegant facade of the Palace of Fine Arts.

The earth again shook violently in October 1989 at the start of the third World Series game between the San Francisco Giants and the Oakland A's. The Loma Prieta quake crumpled buildings in the Marina District and collapsed sections of the I-880 freeway and the Oakland Bay

San Francisco's famous "painted ladies"

(Continued on p. 343.)

Destination San Francisco

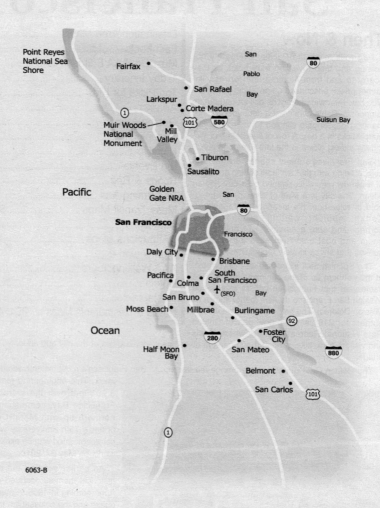

6063-B

This map shows cities in the San Francisco vicinity where you will find attractions, hotels and restaurants. Cities are listed alphabetically in this book on the following pages.

Fast Facts

ABOUT THE CITY

POP: 805,235 ▪ **ELEV:** 63 ft.

MONEY

SALES TAX: State and county sales taxes total 9.5 percent in San Francisco. In addition a hotel room tax of 15 to 15.5 percent is levied.

WHOM TO CALL

EMERGENCY: 911

POLICE (non-emergency): (415) 553-0123

HOSPITALS: California Pacific Medical Center, (415) 600-6000 ▪ Saint Francis Memorial Hospital, (415) 353-6000 ▪ St. Mary's Medical Center, (415) 668-1000 ▪ San Francisco General Hospital Medical Center, (415) 206-8000 ▪ University of California San Francisco Medical Center, (415) 476-1000.

WHERE TO LOOK AND LISTEN

NEWSPAPERS: The major daily newspaper is the morning *San Francisco Chronicle*. The free tabloid *The Examiner* is published Monday through Saturday.

RADIO: San Francisco radio station KCBS (740 AM) is an all-news/weather station ▪ KQED (88.5 FM) is a member of National Public Radio.

VISITOR INFORMATION

San Francisco Visitor Information Center: 900 Market St., San Francisco, CA 94102. **Phone:** (415) 391-2000 or TTY (415) 392-0328.

The San Francisco Visitor Information Center is on the lower level of Hallidie Plaza. The center is open Mon.-Fri. 9-5, Sat.-Sun. and holidays 9-3, May-Oct.; Mon.-Fri. 9-5, Sat. 9-3, rest of year. Closed Jan. 1, Thanksgiving and Christmas.

TRANSPORTATION

AIR TRAVEL: The San Francisco Bay Area is served by three major airports. One of the nation's five busiest, San Francisco International Airport (SFO) is about 13 miles south near San Bruno off US 101 (Bayshore Freeway); it's served by some 50 carriers as well as by private charters. Norman Y. Mineta San Jose International Airport (SJC) is about 3 miles northwest of downtown San Jose. If your destination is on the east side of San Francisco Bay, Oakland International Airport (OAK), off I-880 about 10 miles south of downtown Oakland, may be a better choice. *For additional information, see Arriving, Air Travel.*

RENTAL CARS: Hertz, with locations at the San Francisco, Oakland and San Jose airports, offers discounts to AAA members. Phone (650) 624-6600 for the San Francisco airport location, (415) 771-2200 for the outlet at 433 Mason St., (510) 639-0200 for the Oakland airport location, (408) 437-5700 for the San Jose airport location, or (800) 654-3080.

RAIL SERVICE: For schedule and fare information phone Amtrak at (800) 872-7245. *For additional information see Arriving, Rail Service.*

BUSES: Greyhound Lines Inc., (800) 231-2222, departs from the Transbay Terminal at 1st and Mission streets.

TAXIS: Taxis in San Francisco are metered, with fares averaging about $3.10 for the first mile and $2.25 for each additional mile. Either phone for a cab or wait at a hotel taxi stand (hailing one on the street is rarely successful). Limousine service ranges from $60-$80 per hour.

PUBLIC TRANSPORTATION: San Francisco Municipal Railway (Muni) provides public transportation consisting of buses, streetcars, light rail, trolley buses and cable cars. BART (Bay Area Rapid Transit) connects San Francisco with East Bay cities, and passenger ferries link the city with the northern Bay Area. *For additional information see Getting Around, Public Transportation.*

(Continued from p. 341.)

Bridge. Small wonder, then, that schools conduct regular earthquake drills.

Life goes on, however, and here it's definitely worth celebrating with food. Whether it's a rockin' carne asada burrito at a humble Mission *taquería* or the rarefied cuisine at a chichi SOMA hot spot, San Francisco is foodie nirvana. Sample the cornucopia of organic northern California fruits and veggies at the Ferry Plaza Farmers Market on The Embarcadero, *the* place to be on a Saturday morning.

Where else is so cutting edge while holding on to hazy memories? In an age of apps and smartphones, Jefferson Airplane's psychedelic anthem "White Rabbit" wafts out of a Haight Street head shop doorway and patchouli incense hangs in the air, fondly evoking 1967's Summer of Love.

San Francisco neighborhoods are true communities, not polished versions of reality designed for tourists, and that makes them particularly appealing. Chinatown has bustled since the 1850s. Vibrantly colorful murals cover buildings and alley walls in the predominantly Hispanic Mission. Open-minded acceptance, embodied by North Beach's nonconformist beat and Haight-Ashbury flower power, paved the way for San Francisco's prominent gay and lesbian community, centered in the Castro.

All told, it's easy to leave your heart in the City by the Bay. We ♥ San Francisco.

Must Do: AAA Editor's Picks

- Spend the day in ⚡Golden Gate Park. Observe multicolored tropical fish and other marine creatures at ⚡The California Academy of Sciences, contemplate great art at the ⚡de Young Museum and stroll through plantings from around the world at the San Francisco Botanical Garden at Strybing Arboretum. Or simply sit on a bench and watch the ducks at Lloyd Lake, a tranquil retreat in the middle of this expansive and beloved green space.

- Walk across the ⚡Golden Gate Bridge, an iconic city landmark and one of the engineering marvels of the world. Dress in layers and leave your car in the north or south-side parking lots for the 1.7-mile jaunt across Golden Gate Strait, the entrance to San Francisco Bay; just remember that you'll have to turn around and walk back.

- Journey to the city's far northwestern corner and explore the Sutro Baths, the ocean-side ruins (due to a fire) of what once was a lavish bathing spa complex with the world's largest indoor swimming pool. Then watch the sun set from the elevated vantage point of the nearby Cliff House.

- Yes, Fisherman's Wharf is touristy—but nibbling Dungeness crab or scarfing down clam chowder from a sourdough bread bowl while seagulls cry and sea lions bark is one of those things you just have to do. Stop by the flagship location of Boudin Bakery, watch the team of bakers from a 30-foot observation window and don't forget to pick up a fresh loaf or two to take home.

- While at Fisherman's Wharf, take a sightseeing ferry cruise from Pier 33 to ⚡Alcatraz Island, site of the infamous federal penitentiary where the likes of Al Capone and George "Machine Gun" Kelly did time.

- Definitely ride a cable car (just don't call it a trolley). The Powell-Hyde line begins at Powell and Market streets, runs past tony hotels and apartment buildings as it ascends up and over Nob Hill, and ends up at Beach and Hyde streets near Ghirardelli Square. If you're interested in learning more about the massive engines and wheels that power this manually operated system, visit the Cable Car Museum and Powerhouse Viewing Gallery.

- Climb the Filbert Steps ascending the east side of Telegraph Hill—passing luxuriant gardens along the way—and then take the elevator to the observation deck at the top of 210-foot Coit Tower for panoramic views of San Francisco Bay and the Golden Gate and Bay bridges.

- Lombard Street calls itself the "crookedest street in the world," but that only applies to the block between Hyde and Leavenworth streets. The serpentine brick street, with its sculpted hedges and blooming hydrangeas, is a prime photo op—and of course it's easier walking down than up.

- Wander up Grant Avenue through bustling, vibrant ⚡Chinatown, ducking into herbal remedy and souvenir shops, then wander back down Stockton Street past produce and meat markets overflowing with sidewalk shoppers.

- Sip a sidewalk cappuccino in North Beach, San Francisco's own Little Italy. Browse the tomes at City Lights bookstore, an iconic Beat generation hangout, and then have dinner at the North Beach Restaurant, an old-school Italian experience all the way.

- The smell of incense still wafts along Haight Street, which remains resolutely groovy more than 40 years after the Summer of Love. Indulge your inner hippie and pick up a Grateful Dead or tie-dye T-shirt at Positively Haight Street.

Stroll along the streets of Chinatown

San Francisco 1-day Itinerary

AAA editors suggest these activities for a great short vacation experience. Those staying in the area for a longer visit can access a 3-day itinerary at AAA.com/TravelGuide.

Morning

- Begin your San Francisco day with a brisk walk along The Embarcadero, the street that runs along the city's northeastern perimeter, as seagulls swoop and streams of passengers en route from Sausalito and Tiburon ferries disembark at the Ferry Building—all against the panoramic backdrop of the mighty Bay Bridge.

- Browse the gourmet food shops in **Ferry Building Marketplace**. Pick up a loaf of ciabatta or a baguette from the Acme Bread Company and sample cow's milk cheeses at Cowgirl Creamery. Have an espresso or café au lait at Blue Bottle Coffee; the cafe roasts organic, shade-grown, pesticide-free beans on vintage gear and brews every drip drink individually.

- On Saturday mornings there's a bustling farmers market in front of and behind the Ferry Building. Vendors sell organic fruits and veggies, boysenberry jam, bear's head mushrooms and fresh-cut bouquets of bright yellow sunflowers, among many other delights. A smaller version sets up on Tuesday and Thursday mornings.

- From the Ferry Building, walk up Market Street to Grant Avenue, turn right and continue to the arched gate marking the symbolic entryway into ☜**Chinatown**. You could take a guided walking tour, but it isn't really necessary to appreciate this densely packed neighborhood; just wander up and down Grant and parallel Stockton Street, and check out the narrow alleyways running in between both.

- In Portsmouth Square you'll see elderly men engaging in fervent *xiangqi* (Chinese chess) matches. Throngs of grocery-laden shoppers on Stockton Street shuffle by businesses displaying rows of skinned ducks, brightly packaged medicinal cures and overflowing bins of produce. Try an egg tart, flaky pastry surrounding a smooth custard filling, at the Golden Gate Bakery on Grant Avenue. And you'll catch a whiff of vanilla-scented fortune cookies wafting from the Golden Gate Fortune Cookie Factory on tiny Ross Alley.

Afternoon

- There's no way you can take on all of ☜**Golden Gate Park** in an afternoon, or even an entire day—the verdant 1,107-acre expanse is 174 acres larger than New York's Central Park. Just focus on your particular area of interest. There are orchids and other exotic plants at the **Conservatory of Flowers**, an impressive collection of art at the ☜**de Young Museum** and way-cool aquarium exhibits at ☜**The California Academy of Sciences**. Take a contemplative stroll through the precisely manicured **Japanese Tea Garden** or the National AIDS Memorial Grove. For exercise with a scenic

Vesuvio, Jack Kerouac's funky hangout

backdrop, walk the approximately 3-mile length of this rectangular green space from east to west; the park's western edge abuts the Pacific Ocean. (Just remember that you'll have to walk or take a bus back.)

- For lunch, **San Tung Chinese Restaurant** is a short detour away (a block south of Lincoln Way at 1031 Irving St., between 11th and 12th avenues). Regulars swear by the crispy dry-fried chicken wings, a featured lunch special, at this bustling Inner Sunset eatery.

Evening

- No San Francisco visit is complete without riding a cable car. Get on the Powell-Hyde Street line at Market Street and disembark at **Lombard Street** for a stroll *down* the famously steep and winding block landscaped with pink and blue hydrangeas; it's much easier than walking up.

- Columbus Avenue in **North Beach** (San Francisco's own Little Italy) is, of course, chockablock with Italian restaurants, and it's a delightful dilemma choosing one for dinner. **Calzone's** certainly fills the bill as far as atmosphere goes, and try to snag a sidewalk table for unparalleled people watching. You also can't go wrong with a simple but well-prepared pizza Margherita or a homey, filling dish of broccolini, red peppers, olive oil and thick garlic slices strewn over homemade fettucine.

- Order the house drink named after Beat Generation icon Jack Kerouac (rum, tequila, orange and cranberry juice served in a bucket glass with a lime) at Vesuvio (255 Columbus Ave.). Artists, poets and hipsters have frequented this funky bar since the "On the Road" author first made it his hangout.

Top Picks for Kids

Under 13

- Cutting-edge technology takes center stage at the **Children's Creativity Museum**, whether it's using an iMac computer to fashion a one-of-a-kind postcard or testing out cool new apps and high-tech games in the Innovation Lab.

- What kid wouldn't be mesmerized at the sight of a giant thorny phasmid (more commonly known as a walking stick), amused by the antics of black-tailed prairie dogs and saucer-eyed meerkats, or delight in feeding baby farm animals? The emphasis is on personal animal encounters at the San Francisco Zoo's **Fisher Family Children's Zoo**.

- The panoramic view from the top of the hill in **Grandview Park** is one of the city's best, offering not only visual "Wow!" but an opportunity for an impromptu geography lesson pointing out the various landmarks. Kids will love the colorful tile designs embedded in the **Mosaic Stairway** that ascends the hill.

Teens

- The roundup of sophisticated interactive exhibits at the ▽ **Exploratorium** (relocating from the Palace of Fine Arts to Pier 15 in 2013) will pique the curiosity of scientific and nonscientific minds alike. A peek at the inner workings of a tooth and decoding the science of skateboarding are two of the many intellectually stimulating offerings.

- **Haight Street** still channels 1967, the Summer of Love, and teens whose only connection to the '60s is via Youtube videos will want to check it out. Amoeba Music (1855 Haight St.) has a huge collection of CDs, albums and rock posters. Cheap Thrills (between Cole and Belvedere streets) stocks vintage punk rock clothing and gag gifts galore. Burning incense, exotic music and an array of silk scarves, paisley shirts and turquoise jewelry sets the groovy vibe at The Love of Ganesha (1310 Haight St.).

All Ages

- A San Francisco institution, **Fisherman's Wharf** is *the* place for families to spend a fun-filled day. The aroma of funnel cakes permeates the air, but the nosh of choice at the wharf is clam chowder in a sourdough bread bowl. And there are plenty of mimes, jugglers and sidewalk artists on hand to keep everyone entertained.

- How do you get kids interested in history? One way is to take a ferry to ▽ **Alcatraz Island**, the notorious former federal penitentiary that is one of the city's top tourist attractions, and with good reason: The views are spectacular, the crumbling buildings fascinating and a ferry cruise is *always* fun. Exploring the forbidding cellblocks on a night tour increases the spook factor considerably.

- There are lots of things to see and do in ▽ **Golden Gate Park**, but put ▽ **The California Academy of Sciences** at the top of the list. Huge tanks full of multicolored tropical fish and other sea creatures are majorly awesome, and the planetarium is spectacularly state of the art. The domed Rainforests of the World is a re-created environment right down to the steamy humidity. And the building's undulating living roof is a cool-looking lesson in green sustainability.

- **Stow Lake** is an idyllic refuge in the middle of Golden Gate Park. Rent a paddleboat and putt along in a lush green setting complete with quacking ducks and turtle sunning on logs. Or bring a picnic lunch, hike to the top of 430-foot Strawberry Hill and enjoy the views.

- The aptly named **Cliff House** has been around in one form or another since 1863. Have breakfast or lunch at Cliff House-The Bistro, and try to snag a window table for the terrific views of Ocean Beach and Seal Rocks. Afterward, explore the adjacent **Sutro Baths**, the ruins of a once-luxurious bathing resort.

- The **Southwest Airlines Chinese New Year Festival and Parade** in February is one eye-popping spectacle, complete with floats, costumes and the serpentine Gum Lung (Golden Dragon). But on any day San Francisco's Chinatown neighborhood is a fascinating, educational immersion in Asian culture.

Fisherman's Wharf

Arriving
By Car

Scenic north-south routes passing directly through San Francisco are US 101 and SR 1. They enter the city separately from the south, merge on the San Francisco approach to the Golden Gate Bridge and continue together through a few miles of southern Marin County. Because SR 1, the curvy coastal route, is subject to dense fog and the possibility of landslides, you should check weather and road conditions before driving it.

The fast north-south route, I-5, lies east of San Francisco; connections to the San Francisco-Oakland Bay Bridge are via I-505 and I-80 from the north and I-580 from the south. Another route, SR 99, closely parallels I-5 and also has connections into the city.

Most traffic from the east approaches via I-80 across the Sierras. I-80 is closely paralleled by US 50 to Sacramento; from Sacramento the interstate heads west, heading into the city via the San Francisco-Oakland Bay Bridge.

Air Travel

The San Francisco Bay Area is served by three major airports. One of the nation's five busiest, San Francisco International Airport (SFO) is about 13 miles south near San Bruno off US 101 (Bayshore Freeway); it's served by 50 carriers as well as by private charters. Norman Y. Mineta San Jose International Airport (SJC) is about 3 miles northwest of downtown San Jose. If your destination is on the east side of San Francisco Bay, Oakland International Airport (OAK), off I-880 about 10 miles south of downtown Oakland, may be a better choice.

To reach downtown from San Francisco International Airport, exit from the north terminal area and take US 101 north. At the US 101/I-80 junction, choose I-80 and then take the 4th Street exit. Follow 4th Street north past Moscone Center to Market Street; Union Square's hotels and the Financial District are just a few blocks to the north and east.

SuperShuttle, (650) 558-8500 or (650) 246-8942, travels from San Francisco International to major downtown hotels every 30 minutes, 5 a.m.-4 p.m. One-way fare for the 30-minute ride is $17. For reservations phone (800) 258-3826.

Door-to-door minivan shuttle service between the airport and hotels, businesses and residences is offered by several companies, including SuperShuttle San Francisco, (800) 258-3826, and Airport Express, (415) 775-5121. The vans make frequent pickups from the blue zones on pedestrian islands on the airport's upper level. One-way fare is $15-$17 per person.

Airport shuttle buses pick up passengers on the lower level pedestrian islands near the blue columns. Or take a taxi or limousine to downtown. Taxi fares between the Civic Center and San Francisco International Airport average $35-$50; limousine service costs $50-$75.

AirTrain, an automated light rail system with nine stops throughout the airport, links the International Terminal with other terminals, parking garages, the BART station and the rental car center.

BART, San Francisco's commuter line, provides a rail connection to the airport. The Pittsburg/Baypoint line provides direct service to the airport. Transfer at the San Bruno station to a Millbrae train to connect with Caltrain rail service down the peninsula to San Jose. Other BART lines can be accessed via the Balboa Park transfer station. The approximately 30-minute ride from the airport to Powell Street downtown costs $8.25. For schedule and fare information phone (415) 989-2278.

Norman Y. Mineta San Jose International Airport is conveniently located just off US 101. When leaving Terminal C (which receives most domestic flights) or Terminal A (which receives American Airlines and two regional carriers), follow signs to US 101 and head north. On the way to downtown San Francisco US 101 bypasses Palo Alto and San Mateo.

To reach downtown San Francisco from Oakland International Airport, exit the terminal building and take Airport Drive east toward downtown Oakland. Exit north onto I-880 (Nimitz Freeway), which connects with I-80. Take I-80 west over the San Francisco-Oakland Bay Bridge; the toll is $6 for automobiles. Once across, take exit 2A (5th Street) north to Market Street and the Union Square/Financial District area.

Hertz, with locations at the San Francisco, Oakland and San Jose airports, offers discounts to AAA members. Phone (650) 624-6600 for the San Francisco airport location, (415) 771-2200 for the outlet at 433 Mason St., (510) 639-0200 for the Oakland

BART provides a rail connection to the airport

On-street parking is strictly regulated

airport location, (408) 437-5700 for the San Jose airport location, or (800) 654-3080.

Rail Service

Most rail service terminates in Oakland at Jack London Square, Alice Street and the Embarcadero, or at Emeryville. From there, passengers are transported via shuttle bus to the following stops: the Ferry Building, downtown at the foot of Market Street; Fisherman's Wharf at Pier 39; the Westfield San Francisco Centre mall at 4th and Market streets; in front of Macy's at Union Square; outside the Hyatt Regency San Francisco at California and Drumm streets; and at the Caltrain depot, 4th and King streets. For schedule, fare and additional information phone Amtrak at (800) 872-7245.

Getting Around
Street System

Market Street, the main thoroughfare, runs diagonally from 17th and Castro streets to The Embarcadero. Major east-west arteries through downtown San Francisco are Bush and Pine, both one-way streets with synchronized traffic signals. Bush goes toward downtown, while Pine heads out. Numbered avenues run north-south in the residential neighborhoods north and south of Golden Gate Park, and the streets form a grid pattern. Streets also form a grid in much of the downtown area, although the city's hills frequently dictate where they lead.

Skyscrapers and office buildings are concentrated in the Financial District, centered around Montgomery and Sansome streets. Major stores and hotels surround Union Square, bordered north-south by Post and Geary streets and east-west by Stockton and Powell streets. Government buildings cluster around the Civic Center, between Van Ness Avenue and Leavenworth Street and Golden Gate Avenue and Market Street. All three of these areas are north of Market Street; south of Market north-south streets are numbered.

Van Ness Avenue is a principal north-south downtown artery and San Francisco's widest street. Many major thoroughfares are one way; a good street map will come in handy. Although the street layout looks straightforward on a map, keep the city's extremely variable topography in mind when traveling: The steep hills are difficult to negotiate. Depending upon your agenda, it may be more advantageous to use public transportation or walk rather than drive. If driving your own car, it is strongly recommended that you have your brakes checked before you visit.

San Francisco intersections are subject to strict enforcement of the Anti-Gridlock Act, which prohibits entering an intersection when traffic makes it questionable that you will get through before the light turns red. Motorists convicted of this violation are subject to a fine of $50-$103.

"The Boot" (also known as "The Denver Boot") is a metal clamp that immobilizes a car when attached to its wheel. This device is applied when five or more parking tickets have accumulated or if registration is not current; it is removed only when all outstanding fines and/or registration fees and a $215 de-booting fee have been paid. If the fines are not paid, the car may be towed within 72 hours.

Visitors should also be aware that municipal buses are equipped with a video camera used to ticket, at a fee of $100, drivers who stray into or park in designated bus-only lanes.

The downtown speed limit, unless otherwise posted, is 25 mph—15 mph at blind intersections. Right turns on red are legal unless otherwise posted. Traffic is heavy throughout the day in the downtown area and on major thoroughfares. Avoid the San Francisco-Oakland Bay Bridge during rush hours, about 7-9 a.m. and 4-6:30 p.m.

Pedestrians using designated crosswalks **always** have the right-of-way. Many major intersections downtown and throughout the Bay Area have visual countdown displays, indicating the number of seconds remaining before the light changes for pedestrians.

Parking

San Francisco is not a parking-friendly city. There is a shortage of on-street spaces and a plethora of parking regulations, which are strictly enforced. On-street meter parking is permitted in some areas, but much neighborhood parking is reserved for local residents and is by permit only.

Downtown does have some large garages and many convenient smaller garages and lots. There are garages at Fisherman's Wharf, 655 Beach St. at Hyde Street, (415) 673-1735 ; downtown at 833 Mission St. (at 5th Street), (415) 982-8522; at the Moscone Center, 255 3rd St., (415) 777-2782; and in Chinatown at 733 Kearny St., (415) 982-6353.

Fees range from $2.50-$6 per hour and $15-$33 per day. The only public parking available for recreational vehicles is at Candlestick RV Park, south of the city off US 101 on Gilman Avenue; phone (415) 822-2299.

On-street parking in hilly San Francisco is strictly regulated. In addition to posted tow-away zones, pay particular attention to curb colors, which determine parking availability. Red means no stopping, standing or parking whatsoever; yellow curbs indicate commercial loading and unloading (7 a.m.-6 p.m.). Passenger cars left unattended in downtown loading zones are subject to heavy fines and towing.

White curbs allow a 5-minute limit to pick up or discharge passengers during the hours the adjacent public building is open. White curbs marked with a taxi sign are within a taxi zone. Green curbs indicate 10-minute parking 9 a.m.-6 p.m. Blue marks spaces for use by the disabled; the fine for illegally parking in designated spaces for the disabled is a hefty $966, while the fine for parking in bus zone spaces is $267. In several areas of the city local residents have priority parking rights; be sure to read carefully all posted regulations wherever you park.

How you park also is subject to regulation. It is illegal to park a vehicle on any grade exceeding 3 percent without effectively setting the brakes and blocking the wheels by turning them against the curb or by other means. When parking uphill, the front wheels must be "heeled," or turned out, so that a tire is resting securely against the curb. When parking downhill, they must be "toed," or turned in. If there is no curb you must use a block. The emergency brake must always be firmly set.

If your car is towed, expect to pay dearly to get it back. Parking violations start at $45 for blocking a private entranceway, plus another $453.75 (or more for larger vehicles) for towing and additional daily storage fees. Fines for illegally parking in disabled-designated spaces, in bus zones or in an area blocking access to a wheelchair ramp are $267-$966. To settle your fees and release your car, go to the City Tow Office at 850 Bryant St., Room 145 in the Hall of Justice. For additional information phone the City of San Francisco Parking and Traffic Department, (415) 553-1200.

Public Transportation

San Francisco Municipal Railway (Muni) provides public transportation consisting of buses, streetcars, light rail, trolley buses and cable cars. The fare for buses, streetcars, light rail and trolley buses is $2; 75c (ages 65+, the physically impaired and ages 5-17). Exact change is required. The fare includes a free transfer good for use on any two other vehicles within a 90-minute period; ask for a transfer when you board. Transfers are not valid on cable cars.

Muni buses are numbered and destinations are marked on the front of the vehicle above the windshield. During the day most buses make stops every 10 to 15 minutes; stops are more frequent on heavily traveled routes. Routes that traverse major

thoroughfares like Van Ness Avenue provide 24-hour service, although stops are less frequent at night. Many of the covered bus stops have an automated timetable that displays the number of minutes until the next bus arrives.

Muni light rail cars run underground in the downtown area and above ground in outlying neighborhoods. There are eight lines: F (Market & Wharves), J (Church), K (Ingleside), L (Taraval), M (Ocean View), N (Judah), S (Castro-Embarcadero shuttle) and T (Third Street). Color-coded maps of the system are posted on the wall at each underground station.

The Muni's F Line (also called the Market Street Railway) carries passengers on vintage streetcars. Although some of the cars are San Francisco originals, others ran their routes in such diverse locales as Milan, Italy; Melbourne, Australia; and Osaka, Japan. The route begins at Market and Castro streets, runs down Market to The Embarcadero, then runs up The Embarcadero to Fisherman's Wharf, ending at Jones and Beach streets. Don't board a streetcar if you're in a hurry; they're much slower and make more stops than the light rail lines.

Preserved as national historic landmarks and purportedly the only ones on wheels, San Francisco's famous cable cars are painted in their original 1873 colors—maroon with cream and blue trim. They run daily approximately 6 a.m.-1 a.m. and travel three routes. The Powell-Hyde line begins at Powell and Market streets and runs to Victorian Park at Beach and Hyde streets. The Powell-Mason line also begins at Powell and Market streets but ends at Bay and Taylor streets near Fisherman's Wharf. The

Tour the city from a cable car

Transamerica Pyramid, just a block from Jackson Square

California Street line runs between Market Street and Van Ness Avenue.

Although there are frequent stops and the trip is slow (travel speed is 9.5 mph), taking a cable car ride is an essential San Francisco experience. One-way fare is $6; $3 (ages 65+ and the physically impaired from 6-7 a.m. and 9 p.m.-1 a.m. only; a valid ID is required). An all-day cable car pass costs $14. Clipper cards containing Muni monthly passes or cash value also are accepted. No transfers are issued or accepted. If you're just riding for fun, the California Street line is likely to be the least crowded.

The Muni Passport, valid on all Muni buses and cable cars, offers unlimited usage each day and is worth purchasing if you plan on using the system multiple times. A 1-day pass costs $14; a 3-day pass costs $21; a 7-day pass costs $27. The 3- and 7-day passports are valid for consecutive days only. A Fast Pass is valid for 1 month and costs $64; $22 (ages 5-17 and 65+). Passports can be purchased at San Francisco International Airport; at the San Francisco Visitor Information Center, Hallidie Plaza (lower level) at Market and Powell streets; and at TIX Bay Area, inside the Union Square Garage at the Geary Street entrance. For schedules, routing and other information phone (415) 673-6864.

Note: You must show proof of payment (Muni pass, Clipper card, single-ride ticket or transfer) for the duration of your travel on all forms of Muni transportation. Random checks of passengers exiting the turnstiles at Muni stations are frequently conducted, and a citation of up to $500 may be issued if you cannot show proof of payment.

AC Transit is a bus service that runs from the Transbay Terminal to various destinations in the East Bay area (Alameda and Contra Costa counties).

BART (Bay Area Rapid Transit) connects San Francisco with East Bay cities, terminating at Richmond (north), Pittsburg/Bay Point (east), Dublin/Pleasanton (southeast) and Fremont (south). On the San Francisco side of the bay the terminus is Millbrae, approximately 30 minutes south of downtown.

BART operates Mon.-Fri. 4 a.m.-midnight, Sat. 6 a.m.-midnight, Sun. and holidays 8 a.m.-midnight. Color-keyed wall maps at the stations list destinations and fares; tickets are dispensed from machines at each station. The one-way fare between downtown San Francisco stations is $1.40; all fares are posted at the ticket machines. Phone (415) 989-2278 for schedule and other information. *(For more information see the San Francisco Metrorail System map p. 364.)*

The Clipper card is an all-purpose electronic transit card that can be used on Muni, BART, Caltrain, and Golden Gate Transit and Ferry transportation. Clipper card readers on buses and at Muni and BART entrance stations tag the card and then display the remaining cash balance or pass expiration date. Transfers are automatically calculated, eliminating the need for a paper transfer. A variety of different passes and cash value options can be added to customize the card. Cards can be obtained at Walgreens stores and other locations; for more information phone (877) 878-8883.

Bus service connects San Francisco to Marin County and the cities of Sausalito, Mill Valley, Tiburon and Santa Rosa in Sonoma County via the Golden Gate Bridge; phone (415) 455-2000 for schedule, fare and other information.

Passenger ferries link San Francisco with northern Bay Area destinations and also criss-cross San Francisco Bay, providing both commuter service and sightseeing pleasure. The Blue and Gold Fleet, (415) 773-1188, operates daily commuter service to Tiburon and Sausalito. Golden Gate Ferry, (415) 455-2000, has daily service to Larkspur and Sausalito; no service is available Jan. 1, Thanksgiving or Christmas. One-way rates to Sausalito are $9.75; $4.75 (ages 6-18, ages 65+ and the physically impaired). Rates to Larkspur are $9; $4.50 (ages 6-18, ages 65+ and the physically impaired). The family rate for both routes allows two children under 12 free with a paid adult on weekends.

Harbor Bay Maritime, (510) 769-5500, operates ferries from Alameda to the San Francisco Ferry Building. One-way fares are $6.50; $5.25 (military with ID); $3.75 (ages 62+ and the physically impaired); $3.25 (ages 5-12). The Alameda/Oakland Ferry, (510) 522-3300, provides service to and from Alameda, Angel Island, Oakland and San Francisco. The Alameda/Oakland/San Francisco one-way fare is $6.25; $5 (military with ID); $3.50 (ages 5-12); $3.10 (ages 65+ and the physically impaired).

LUCKY YOU

THUNDER VALLEY
CASINO • RESORT

Shopping

"Shop 'til you drop" easily applies in San Francisco. Whether it's malls, farmers markets, retail complexes, souvenir shops, stylish boutiques, secondhand stores, designer showrooms or exotic emporiums, an amazing assortment of cosmopolitan, funky, kitschy and trendy choices are guaranteed to keep any browser, window shopper or committed shopaholic blissfully happy. And some shopping districts are so identified with the city that they're attractions in their own right.

Antiques

Just a block from a San Francisco icon—the 853-foot-tall Transamerica Pyramid building—is historic **Jackson Square**. The handsome brick and cast iron commercial buildings here are among the city's oldest, dating from the gold rush era, and most survived the 1906 earthquake. In the 1870s it was a rough-and-tumble part of town known as the Barbary Coast. Today this historic area—wedged between the Financial District, Chinatown and North Beach—is the best place in the city to browse for high-quality art and antiques.

Within a two-block radius along Jackson, Washington and Montgomery streets you can find dealers specializing in fine and decorative arts, 17th- and 18th-century English and European furniture, 19th-century French impressionist paintings, fine rugs, antique posters and maps, early California art and cutting-edge contemporary design. For furniture and decorative arts, try **Chappell & McCullar** (441 Jackson St.) or the **Lebreton Gallery** (412 Jackson St.). **Sarah Stocking Inc.** (368 Jackson St.) stocks antique posters; **Arader Galleries** (432-435 Jackson St.), paintings, watercolors and prints. **Carrots** (843 Montgomery St.) and the **Hedge Gallery** (48 Gold St.) carry modern home accessories.

Malls

Within easy walking distance of Jackson Square is **Embarcadero Center**, near The Embarcadero and the waterfront between Sacramento, Clay, Battery and Drumm streets (an area that also was part of the rowdy Barbary Coast in the 19th century). This mixed-use office and retail development consists of four separate buildings (conveniently called One, Two, Three and Four) that cover a five-block area, each with three levels of semi open-air shopping and landscaped plazas at the promenade level where you can relax in a green setting above busy downtown streets.

Here you'll find more than 70 upscale shops (think Coach, JoS. A. Bank and L'Occitane), service businesses, a wide assortment of casual eateries and sit-down restaurants, the Embarcadero Center Cinema and a Peet's Coffee (on Front Street at street level in Two Embarcadero Center). It's a boon for nearby office workers, and tourists can also peruse Embarcadero Center's collection of public art. Louise Nevelson's soaring steel sculpture "Sky Tree" at Three Embarcadero Center rises from a reflecting pool. Nicholas Schoffer's "Chronos XIV" at

Two Embarcadero Center is a steel sculpture incorporating light projectors and movable discs. And check out the Villancourt Fountain in Justin Herman Plaza (between Four Embarcadero Center and The Embarcadero); its assemblage of concrete boxes is arranged so you can walk over, under and through the cascades of water.

Max out your credit cards at **Westfield San Francisco Centre**, which covers an entire block of prime real estate on Market Street between 4th and 5th streets, two blocks from Union Square. The center's classic Beaux Arts exterior, which dates to 1896, contrasts with the contemporary glass-fronted entrance on Mission Street.

Inside is a sleek, nine-story vertical mall with dizzying spiral escalators and a glass-domed, colonnaded rotunda. Bloomingdale's (the largest outside the New York City flagship store) and Nordstrom (the second largest in the chain) anchor the center and set the upscale tone. More than 170 specialty retailers—including Herve Leger, Hugo Boss, Calvin Klein and Edition by Banana Republic—services, eateries, a plush nine-screen multiplex and a day spa add to the center's draw.

It's probably safe to say that San Francisco is the only city with a mall designed to resemble the Galleria Vittorio Emanuele II in Milan, Italy—or at least the dome of that galleria. Both **Crocker Galleria** and its Italian counterpart have an arching glass dome as their main architectural feature; this one is notable for a huge clock set in the center of its arch.

Crocker, three blocks from Union Square at Post and Montgomery streets (with entrances on both Sutter and Post streets), has two levels of boutiques

Shop for organic produce at the Ferry Plaza Farmers Market

Neiman Marcus, Union Square

specializing in apparel, jewelry and home accessories as well as a handful of specialty shops and businesses. The third level features about a dozen eateries.

Markets

If a visit to the Ferry Building Marketplace (see attraction listing at the end of this section) is on your agenda, make sure and schedule it for Saturday morning. That's when the **Ferry Plaza Farmers Market** sets up, and it's a must-visit. A fabulous assortment of fresh fruits and vegetables, artisanal cheeses, olive oils, flowers, herbs, preserves, breads and baked goods are temptingly displayed. Almost everything is organic, and you can graze your way through the vendor stalls—which crowd the front and back of the Ferry Building—nibbling on free samples and reveling in northern California's agricultural bounty. Most all of it comes from farms in nearby counties and is so fresh it was more than likely picked within the past 24 hours.

You can get your breakfast here too, courtesy of the food vendors (concentrated on the south side of the Ferry Building) who offer everything from mushroom omelets to fried oyster po'boys. And the view of the Bay Bridge simply can't be beat. The people watching is fun, the street musicians are cool and you'll mingle with locals carrying reusable cloth bags as well as chefs from local restaurants picking up what will appear on the evening menu.

The market, at the foot of (appropriately enough) Market Street, is open Saturday 8-2 and, in smaller versions, Tuesday and Thursday mornings. After making the rounds—if you aren't loaded down with purchases and especially if it's a sunny day—take a stroll along The Embarcadero.

Not as well known, but with its own devoted local following, is the **Alemany Farmers Market** at 100 Alemany Blvd. in Bernal Heights. This one's a little more ramshackle—some of the produce is sold out of the back of trucks—but it offers a similar bounty of fruits, vegetables, cheeses, herbs and bunches of freshly cut flowers. Alemany has lots of prepared ethnic foods, along with spices, nuts, olive oil, hummus and Thai chiles, and food trucks dish up yummy Mexican, Filipino and Afghan dishes. It's open Saturdays 8-3. Parking can be problematic, especially before noon, but the market is within walking distance of Muni's #67 bus, which you can board near BART's 24th Street station.

Specialty Districts

Union Square is a block-square plaza bordered by Powell, Geary, Post and Stockton streets and named for the pro-Union rallies held at this location during the Civil War. But that long-ago nugget of history is likely lost on present-day shoppers, who see this gathering place (complete with in-season ice skating rink and plenty of benches and tables for hanging out) as the hub of downtown's shopping scene. "Union Square" also incorporates the nearby blocks brimming with specialty retailers, restaurants, theaters and fancy lodgings like The Westin St. Francis and the Sir Francis Drake Hotel.

Serious shoppers can spend serious time and money at old standbys like Macy's, Neiman Marcus, Saks Fifth Avenue, Tiffany & Co., Louis Vuitton and Salvatore Ferragamo; in this heady company the likes of Williams-Sonoma, Levi's and Victoria's Secret are rather small potatoes. A cluster of designer boutiques can be found on fashionable **Maiden Lane**, including Chanel, Hermès, Prada, Gucci, Marc Jacobs and Yves St. Laurent. Burberry, Cartier and Giorgio Armani are on Post Street between Stockton and Grant Avenue. About a block farther at 135 Post St. is **Gump's**, a San Francisco institution known for its fine selection of giftware, home furnishings and Asian-inspired jewelry. Refuel at Lefty O'Doul's, on Geary Street just west of Powell, another San Francisco institution that packs 'em in with reasonably priced meals and a convivial, saloon-like atmosphere.

A perennial favorite with visitors, if not necessarily locals, is the area at the northern end of The Embarcadero, where souvenir shops vie for your attention with waterfront seafood restaurants, ferries to Alcatraz and Sausalito, the occasional gallery, wheeling sea gulls and barking sea lions. The crowd-pleasing marine mammals hung out at Pier 39 for more than 20 years, staged a mysterious mass exodus in late 2009, then returned—although in reduced numbers—the following year.

You can find that "I escaped from Alcatraz" T-shirt or your choice of tchotchke stamped with the city's name at **Anchorage Square**, a mix of shops, services and casual eateries, or at one of the myriad tourist-oriented businesses peppering **Fisherman's Wharf, Pier 39, The Cannery** and **Ghirardelli Square** (see attraction listings at the end of this section).

Although visitors tend to think of **Chinatown** as a place to go for dim sum and inexpensive trinkets, this neighborhood bordered by Broadway, Stockton, Bush and Kearny streets is actually a vibrant city within a city, its streets crowded with residents hurrying between shops and markets while conversing animatedly in various Chinese dialects. For shoppers and souvenir hunters an all-purpose stop is **Peking Bazaar**, 826-832 Grant Ave., which has everything from kimonos to porcelain smoking pipes to plush panda dolls. But in addition to the requisite tourist-oriented shops you can also find painstakingly crafted items made of jade and ivory, jewelry, silks, herbs, electronics, teas, kitchenware and bookmarks with your first name elegantly scribed in Chinese calligraphy. (*Also see attraction listing p. 371*).

Much lower key is **Japantown** (also known as Nihonmachi), where shopping is concentrated at the **Japan Center** complex bounded by Post, Geary, Laguna and Fillmore streets, and the Kintetsu and Kinokuniya buildings in particular (*also see attraction listing p. 377*). Check out a few of the sushi restaurants while you shop for colorful kimonos, wind chimes, bonsai trees, electronics, teapots and Oriental chests.

From Japantown it's a short walk up Fillmore Street to **Pacific Heights.** The blocks from California Street north to Jackson Street have a distinct neighborhood feel and are perfect for a leisurely stroll. Window-shop to your heart's content in charming clothing boutiques and shops featuring the latest in trendy interior decor. Pamper yourself at an emporium specializing in cosmetics and skin care products, then stop for coffee (there's a place on almost every block) or get a bite to eat at one of several sidewalk cafes.

Hop on a #22 Muni bus as it heads north on Fillmore toward the bay (visible once you're at the crest of Russian Hill). Once you reach **Union Street** you're in **Cow Hollow**, a reference to the days when this part of the city was better known for dairy farming. The six blocks of Union between Steiner and Gough streets also have a neighborhood feel; it's a favorite place for well-heeled residents occupying beautifully restored Victorians to congregate for a bite at a bistro or to browse hip, upscale boutiques and jewelry, gift and antique shops.

If you remember—and want to relive—the counterculture days of the Summer of Love, then a trip to **Haight Street** in **Haight-Ashbury** is a must. Parts of Haight still look like they're stuck in 1967, even though the neighborhood as a whole has been gentrifying for years and isn't nearly as gritty as it used to be. Head shops and funky boutiques offer the ubiquitous T-shirt (tie-dyed and otherwise), rock posters, "hippie" jewelry, incense, candles and used books, and vintage clothing stores abound.

At **Positively Haight Street**, at the corner of Haight and Masonic, you'll find all things Grateful Dead as well as clothes, rings, hemp necklaces, wall hangings and gifts. There's a similar array of merchandise at **The Love of Ganesha**, on Haight near Central Avenue, along with a great selection of incense. This welcoming shop is full of color and good vibes, and it even has a small meditation room where you can sip tea.

No Haight visit is complete without a stop at **Amoeba Music** (at the foot of Haight near Stanyan Street). The selection of albums and CDs in this cavernous space is encyclopedic, plenty of signs identify the different music genres and store staff will knowledgeably steer you in the right direction. The murals that practically cover the building are sterling examples of Haight Street wall art.

THE CANNERY is on the e. side of the block bordered by Jefferson, Leavenworth, Beach and Hyde sts. Formerly a Del Monte fruit cannery, it houses two levels of specialty shops, art galleries and restaurants, all linked by arcades, bridges and balconies. Street performers also frequent this spot. **Phone:** (415) 771-3112.

FERRY BUILDING MARKETPLACE is on the waterfront along The Embarcadero at the foot of Market St. It was built as a ferry terminal in 1898, and until the 1930s this was the transportation focal point for anyone arriving by ferry from points east and north. After the opening of the San Francisco Bay Bridge in 1936 and the Golden Gate Bridge a year later the terminal building declined in importance, and by the time the Embarcadero Freeway was built across its face in 1957 it was being used very little. The freeway was torn down after being heavily damaged by the 1989 Loma Prieta earthquake, providing an impetus to restore the building to its former grandeur.

Shop for a funky t-shirt at Positively Haight Street

Ride the carousel at Pier 39

Ferry Building Marketplace opened to the public in 2003. The terminal's clock tower remains a San Francisco landmark, and the building still serves ferry passengers (to and from Alameda, Oakland, Larkspur, Sausalito, Vallejo, Tiburon and Angel Island). There's also a collection of eateries and gourmet food shops. Visitors can pick up local specialties—a loaf of sourdough bread at the Acme Bread Company, artisanal cheeses at Cowgirl Creamery, organic mushrooms at Far West Fungi—and other establishments offer fresh seafood, organic meats and produce, olive oil, wine, flowers, chocolate and gelato.

Popular Blue Bottle Coffee brews every one of its caffeinated concoctions individually. Shop for Chinese teaware and indulge in a traditional tea service complete with organic dim sum at the Imperial Tea Court. The Ferry Plaza Farmers Market sets up in front of, behind and to the side of the Ferry Building on Saturday morning; smaller versions operate on Tuesday and Thursday mornings.

Hours: Marketplace open Mon.-Fri. 10-6, Sat. 9-6, Sun. 11-5. Hours for individual businesses may vary. Closed Jan. 1, Thanksgiving and Christmas. **Phone:** (415) 983-8030. 🚇 Embarcadero, 31

FISHERMAN'S WHARF is part of the northern waterfront. This is a working wharf that also has enough picturesque sights and pungent smells to attract millions of visitors annually. The area is packed with restaurants, hotels, souvenir shops and attractions. On sunny weekends and throughout the summer season it can be extremely busy. But there are several good reasons to spend some time here. First and foremost, the nearby piers are departure

points for scenic bay cruises and ferries to Sausalito, Angel and Alcatraz islands, and other destinations.

Sidewalk vendors sell fresh crab, one of the wharf's original attractions. You also have to try clam chowder in a sourdough bread bowl, which is offered at practically every restaurant. And all kinds of street performers—artists, musicians, mimes—are on hand to entertain the crowds.

Note: Street parking is very hard to come by, especially during the high season. There are public garages and parking lots along Beach and North Point streets. The Powell-Hyde cable car line beginning at Market Street lets off passengers in Victorian Park at Beach and Hyde streets, while the Powell-Mason cable car line lets passengers off at Taylor and Bay streets, both within easy walking distance. Muni's historic F Line streetcar, as well as the #30 and #47 Muni buses, also make stops near Fisherman's Wharf. **Phone:** (415) 674-7503.

GHIRARDELLI SQUARE, between Beach, Polk, North Point and Larkin sts., is within walking distance of Fisherman's Wharf and the cable car turnaround. This complex of brick buildings is the site of the former Ghirardelli Chocolate Factory. They now house a handful of specialty retailers, and yes—you can still get your chocolate fix at the Ghirardelli Ice Cream and Chocolate Shop. Take a look at original chocolate manufacturing equipment and then indulge in one of their signature chocolate squares or have a dish of ice cream in the cafe. **Phone:** (415) 775-5500.

SAVE **PIER 39** is at Beach St. at the northern end of The Embarcadero. This waterfront shopping and dining complex has a touristy vibe, with souvenir shops and eateries galore, an arcade and frequent live entertainment on the entrance plaza—magicians, jugglers, acrobats, comedians and other street performers. There's also a state welcome center on the second level.

One of the pier's chief attractions since 1989—when they began showing up just after the Loma Prieta earthquake—are sea lions. Lolling on the floating docks built especially for them, uttering their distinctive bark, engaging in mock shoving matches or lazily rolling over like a dog playing dead, the blubbery, whiskered marine mammals seem to bask in their reputation as local celebrities, almost seeming to pose for camera-toting tourists who position themselves for that one special shot.

In late 2009 almost all of the sea lions mysteriously disappeared. No one really knows what was behind the pinniped defection, although biologists suspect that changes in the food supply—specifically, a notable lack of herring in San Francisco Bay—drove them to seek sustenance elsewhere. Since then they've made something of a comeback; anywhere from around 50 to as many as 300 of the animals congregate, depending on the time of year. Learn more about these critters at the

Marine Mammal Center information kiosk located at the pier. **Phone:** (415) 705-5500.

Nightlife

Diversity is what this city is all about. The raucous forty-niners knew how to live it up way back when, and that good-time tradition continues. Cool blues, chill jazz, frenetic rock, classy cocktail lounges, bars with history, views with your booze (or some combination thereof)—San Francisco won't disappoint.

Bars

The perfect spot on a cool San Francisco night might just be the **Buena Vista Café,** near Ghirardelli Square and the cable car turnaround at 2765 Hyde St., where you can warm up with an Irish coffee. Legend has it the cafe is the birthplace of that whiskey-infused cup of joe, but in actuality it's the first place the drink was served in the U.S. (in 1952, to be exact). Regardless, grab a seat and warm the cockles of your heart after a busy day of sightseeing. Phone (415) 474-5044.

In addition to being known as San Francisco's "Little Italy," **North Beach** is also where you'll find some of the city's most popular late-night hangouts. This is where the beat generation poets caroused in the 1950s, and two bars still recall that era.

Lawrence Ferlinghetti (former owner of the famed City Lights Bookstore on Columbus Avenue), Allen Ginsberg and Jack Kerouac were regulars at **Vesuvio** (255 Columbus Ave., just off tiny Jack Kerouac Alley). From the paintings on the walls to the random San Francisco memorabilia on the second floor to absinthe on the drink menu, this place has retained every bit of its hipster cred.

In an alley just across Columbus at 12 Saroyan Pl. is **Spec's Twelve Adler Museum Café** (Spec's for short), where irreverent cartoons, buttons with avant-garde sayings and even an armadillo cover the walls, and the wood tables and chairs are well worn. Both bars are frequented by a mix of ages and income levels who come to enjoy a beer or three and relive a bit of the past. Phone (415) 362-3370 for Vesuvio or (415) 421-4112 for Spec's.

Another favorite North Beach watering hole is **Tosca Café** (242 Columbus Ave.), which has a definite Italian feel and a jukebox that leans toward operatic standards. Celebrities have been known to drop by when they're in town. Phone (415) 391-1244.

Climb to the top of ritzy Nob Hill to The Fairmont San Francisco, then take the elevator downstairs to **The Tonga Room & Hurricane Bar.** It's a kitschy Polynesian explosion, from the palm trees, thatched tiki huts and a lagoon with a ship (doubling as a bandstand) floating in the middle to the thunderstorm that arrives on cue every 20 minutes. They make a mean mai tai—and yes, your drink comes with a paper umbrella. There's an Asian-inspired buffet weekdays during happy hour, and dancing begins at 8 p.m. Phone (415) 772-5278.

If you're looking for a classic dive bar, try **Toronado** in the Lower Haight (547 Haight St., between Steiner and Fillmore streets). There's plenty of space for locals and tourists to congregate while watching playoff games or knocking back brews to a classic rock soundtrack. The craft beer selection is notable. Phone (415) 863-2276.

The **Castro** is full of casual, friendly hangouts. Although it's a restaurant, **Cafe Flore** also has a full-service bar. The location—at the high-visibility corner of Market and Noe streets—makes this a prime spot to see and be seen. Go for one of the happy hour drink specials and sit outside for the best view of the always entertaining street parade. The place is packed on warm evenings (or at least what passes for a warm evening in San Francisco), but even if the weather's chilly there are heat lamps and twinkling lights to keep the mood festive. Phone (415) 621-8579.

You won't encounter a lot of attitude at **Midnight Sun** (4067 18th St., between Castro and Hartford streets). Convivial crowds gather at this small, laid-back video bar for the 2-for-1 drink specials while watching "RuPaul's Drag Race," "Glee" and "American Idol" on big TV screens. **Twin Peaks Tavern** (401 Castro St. across from the Castro Muni station) is locally referred to as the "Glass Coffin" for its big windows and more mature clientele. It's not as loud as many other bars and therefore more amenable to actual conversation. The upstairs balcony is a prime spot for people watching. Next door is Hot Cookie, highly regarded for their fresh-baked treats. Phone (415) 861-4186 for Midnight Sun or (415) 864-9470 for Twin Peaks Tavern.

Cocktail Lounges

Indulge yourself with cocktails at **Top of the Mark,** the classy lounge at the top of the InterContinental Mark Hopkins San Francisco that has been a

Tosca Café is a local favorite

Listen to live music at Bimbo's 365 Club

Nob Hill landmark since 1939. The room isn't small but still feels intimate and cozy. Live music (mostly jazz) enhances the mood Tuesday through Saturday evenings. Request a seat along the wall of windows for breathtaking views of the bay and city. Arrive with someone special at twilight, then watch the sun set and the lights of "The City" come twinkling on for a truly magical experience. Phone (415) 616-6916.

Cool, sleek and fashionable defines the **Redwood Room** in the Clift Hotel at Union Square (495 Geary St.). This modern lounge exudes panache, from its redwood paneling to the changing display of digital artwork. Phone (415) 929-2372.

Harry Denton's Starlight Room is a throwback to when a night on the town meant dressing up for an evening at a swanky hotel's top-floor lounge—in this case Union Square's Sir Francis Drake Hotel (450 Powell St.). Cocktails and hors d'oeuvres are served in an opulent setting reminiscent of 1930s San Francisco—red velvet booths, silk draperies and imported chandeliers. Entertainment consists of both bands and DJs playing hits from the 1960s through the '80s. The dance floor can get crowded on weekend evenings. Sunday afternoon shifts gears with "Sunday's a Drag," a show featuring female impersonators hosted by local drag performer Donna Sachet, along with an all-you-can-eat buffet brunch. Phone (415) 395-8595.

The **Bubble Lounge** (714 Montgomery St. at Jackson Square) specializes in a beverage primarily associated with New Year's Eve celebrations. Two rooms with high ceilings, red velvet sofas, thick drapes and Oriental rugs provide an elegant atmosphere suitable for sampling a collection of more than 300 varieties of champagne and sparkling

wines—by the bottle or the glass—along with noshes like oysters and chocolate-dipped strawberries. You'll want to dress for the evening, which means no athletic gear, shorts, flip-flops or ball caps. Tables can be reserved ahead; phone (415) 434-4204.

Dance Clubs

The **SoMa** district south of Market Street is known for its hip clubs. Depending on the night, the **DNA Lounge** (375 11th St.) might feature DJ sets, live music, a burlesque show or a mashup dance event. Two levels of dance floors throb to hip-hop, rock and metal. The club provides internet kiosks as well as streaming audio and video webcasts of all events. Phone (415) 626-1409 to see what's going on any given night.

111 Minna Gallery has a split personality—art gallery by day, dance club at night. The club's name doubles as its address, which is also in SoMa between Second and New Montgomery streets. It has a loft-like warehouse feel, with DJs spinning a mix of styles. Phone (415) 974-1719.

Mezzanine (444 Jessie St. at Mint Street) is a cavernous, brick-walled space with a booming sound system that showcases live and electronic music—everything from salsa to hip-hop to electro-funk disco. When bands aren't playing, hot DJs like Alex Ridha, aka Boys Noize, take over. Mezzanine also hosts multimedia art and fashion shows. Purchasing advance tickets for some events is strongly recommended. Phone (415) 625-8880.

Temple Nightclub (540 Howard St.) has two dance floors. The floor on the main level is more spacious than at many other clubs; the music is mostly house. Downstairs it's crowded and sweaty, and the music is mostly hip-hop. Phone (415) 978-9942.

Housed in a vintage theater with a New York feel, **Ruby Skye** (420 Mason St., a block west of Union Square) has a state-of-the-art sound system taken over by a revolving roster of international DJs. Buzz bands like the Crystal Method also play at the club. If you don't feel like sweating it out on the dance floor, balcony boxes above the action can be reserved. Phone (415) 693-0777.

Rock and Blues Clubs

Swanky and retro describe the main room of **Bimbo's 365 Club** (1025 Columbus Ave.), which has been cranking out live rock and jazz in North Beach since 1951. With elegant red-accented surroundings, table service, a huge dance floor and a reliable schedule of name acts, this place packs 'em in. Phone (415) 474-0365.

Another San Francisco mainstay is the **Boom Boom Room** (1601 Fillmore St. at Geary). This was a blues spot in the 1930s, although nowadays you'll hear R&B, funk and soul as well. Check out the assemblage of old photos from past gigs on the club's walls. Legendary blues artist John Lee Hooker was affiliated with the Boom Boom Room in the late 1990s. Phone (415) 673-8000.

Bottom of the Hill (1233 17th St.) is at the bottom of Potrero Hills. Pop, punk and noise bands, many local, play to young, enthusiastic crowds seven nights a week. The back patio is good for taking a break and chilling with friends. Go with a group, since the neighborhood tends to get a little sketchy late at night. Phone (415) 621-4455.

The **Great American Music Hall** (859 O'Farrell St.) started out in 1907 as a bordello; Sally Rand entranced audiences with fan dances during the 1930s, and it was a Moose Lodge in the '50s. Classically decorated with marble columns, balconies and frescoed ceilings, the hall is a venue for an eclectic array of folk, indie rock and blues acts. You can even bring the kids (ages 6+, but check out who's playing first) and have dinner. Phone (415) 885-0750.

The Fillmore (1805 Geary Blvd. at Fillmore) was a big name in the '60s San Francisco music scene: Promoter Bill Graham brought local rock bands like the Grateful Dead, Jefferson Airplane and Quicksilver Messenger Service as well as visionaries like Jimi Hendrix to his ballroom for concert "happenings" complete with psychedelic light shows. It's still the city venue of choice for many performers today. Another longtime rock palace is **The Warfield,** a former vaudeville theater. The cozy ambiance—complete with a beautifully detailed gold-leaf ceiling—is perfect for watching musicians like PJ Harvey and Zappa Plays Zappa do their thing. Phone (415) 346-6000 for The Fillmore or (888) 929-7849 for The Warfield box office.

Yoshi's (1330 Fillmore St. at Eddy Street) is San Francisco's premier jazz club, drawing the genre's top talent (and more than a few funk and hip-hop artists as well). The lighting is dim, the decor swanky. If you feel like sushi, get there early and have dinner at the adjoining restaurant. There's also an upstairs lounge. Phone (415) 655-5600.

Big Events

San Francisco's calendar is packed with events ranging from gigantic exhibits of boats, cars, vacation equipment, furniture and antiques to small one-man sidewalk art shows.

The year begins with the **Sports and Boat Show,** a huge exhibition held in January at the Cow Palace. Also in January is **Sea Lions' Arrival at Pier 39,** the annual celebration welcoming the crowd-pleasing creatures back to Pier 39's K-Dock. Following is one of the most colorful of all celebrations—the ➤**Southwest Airlines Chinese New Year Festival and Parade.** Featuring the Golden Dragon Parade, it is held in January or February in Chinatown.

March's main event, the **St. Patrick's Day Parade and Festival,** is held the Sunday nearest the 17th and includes religious services at St. Patrick's Church. The parade starts at Second and Market streets and proceeds to Civic Center Plaza.

Mid-April brings the **Northern California Cherry Blossom Festival,** an elaborate display of Japanese culture and customs. The **San Francisco International Film Festival,** which spotlights

adventurous filmmakers, is presented in various locations. The festival has been held nearly every spring since 1956.

In May **Armed Forces Day** is observed; the festivities include a parade, entertainment, arts and crafts and an open house at several nearby military installations.

Also in May is the **Bay to Breakers** race. This venerable event celebrated its centennial in 2011. The name Bay to Breakers was adopted in 1965, and it also describes the course—from a starting point a block east of The Embarcadero (and San Francisco Bay) to the finish line at the Great Highway at the western end of Golden Gate Park (and the ocean's crashing waves). The east-west route across the city officially measures 7.46 miles. By the 1980s running boom the number of race participants had swelled to more than 100,000, and these days tens of thousands of people join in the trek along downtown streets and across the length of Golden Gate Park. Over the years different traditions also have emerged, from Batman and Wonder Woman costumes to occasional displays of public nudity. Today the party vibe is such that serious runners usually get an early start before the route becomes crowded with revelers.

In late May or early June, **Carnaval San Francisco,** a multicultural Mardi Gras-inspired street festival with a Latin American/Caribbean vibe, takes place in the Mission District; a parade is followed by a masquerade ball. On a different note, the San Francisco Symphony presents a series of **Beethoven concerts** in June and a series of pops concerts in July.

Carnaval San Francisco

Bicycling on the Golden Gate Bridge

In early June the **Union Street Spring Festival Arts & Crafts Fair** takes place. The mood is that of an elegant garden party, with gourmet food, California wines, musical entertainment and art and craft exhibits. In mid-June the Bay Area celebrates San Francisco's African-American heritage during the 2-day **Juneteenth Festival**.

A parade up Market Street is the highlight of **SF Pride** in late June. The 2-day parade, the musical performances on the Main Stage in Civic Center Plaza and the attendant festivities celebrating Gay Pride Month is the largest LGBT gathering in the nation, bringing visitors from around the world, and rivals Chinese New Year as the city's biggest event.

The **California Shakespeare Festival** is held in Orinda from late May to early October. Golden Gate Park provides a sylvan setting for the Bard's works. Also celebrated in September is **The Chinatown Autumn Moon Festival**.

North Beach's Italian community holds a week-long **Columbus Day Celebration** in early October. The event, which continues the centuries-old Sicilian custom of blessing the fishing fleet, features the Italian Heritage Parade beginning at Fisherman's Wharf and ending at Washington Square in front of the Church of Saints Peter and Paul.

In mid-October the Cow Palace is the scene of the **Grand National Rodeo, Horse and Livestock Show**, which includes rodeo events along with prize-winning horse and livestock exhibits. The **San Francisco International Auto Show** revs up in late November at Moscone Center, and in late December the ☗ **Kraft Fight Hunger Bowl** matches

top college football teams from the Pacific-10 and ACC conferences in competition at AT&T Park.

Sports & Rec

Bay Area fans vigorously support their hometown teams, and San Francisco's and Oakland's professional and college teams—the Giants, Oakland A's, 49ers, Golden State Warriors, Raiders and Sharks—offer plenty to cheer for. In addition to the spectator sports venues listed below, the **Cow Palace**, 2600 Geneva Ave. at Santos Street in nearby Daly City, is a venue for rodeos, ice shows and other events; phone (415) 404-4111.

The 76,500-acre **Golden Gate National Recreation Area** (see place listing p. 137) represents San Francisco's wilder natural side. Encompassing the northern and western city shoreline, it offers bracing scenery, miles of trails and several camping sites. It's a peaceful, exuberantly scenic getaway for birdwatchers, beachcombers, hikers, bicyclists, surfers, surf fishers, picnickers and naturalists.

Baseball The **San Francisco Giants**—the 2012 World Series champions—play at **AT&T Park**. The stadium is right off The Embarcadero at 24 Willie Mays Plaza, seven blocks south of Market Street and just south of Pier 40. Phone (877) 473-4849 for ticket information. The rival **Oakland A's** play at the **O.co Coliseum**, I-880 at the 66th Avenue exit in Oakland; phone (510) 568-5600.

Basketball The Bay Area's **Golden State Warriors** play at the **Oracle Arena** in Oakland, off I-880 at either the 66th Avenue or Hegenberger Road exits; phone (510) 986-2222 for ticket information.

Area universities whet hoop appetites as well. In San Jose, the **San Jose State University Spartans** play their home games at the **San Jose Event Center,** 7th and E. San Carlos streets; phone (408) 924-1000. The **University of California Golden Bears** play at **Haas Pavilion** in Berkeley; phone (510) 642-3277 or (800) 462-3277. And fans of the **University of San Francisco Dons** head to **War Memorial Gymnasium**, 2335 Golden Gate Ave.; phone (415) 422-2873.

Football Two NFL teams are represented in the Bay Area. The **San Francisco 49ers**, dubbed the "team of the '80s" for its four Super Bowl wins following the 1981, 1984, 1988 and 1989 seasons—not to mention its clinching the title following the 1994 season—play at **Candlestick Park**, at the southeast corner of the city off US 101 on Jamestown Avenue. For ticket information phone (415) 656-4900.

The 49ers' new $1.2 billion stadium in Santa Clara, now under construction, will be in the forefront of sustainable design concepts and technological innovations, featuring a green roof, stadiumwide WiFi capability and enormous HD video screens. It is tentatively scheduled to open in fall 2014.

The **Oakland Raiders** play at O.co Coliseum; phone (510) 569-2121 for Raiders ticket information.

Hockey South of San Francisco Bay, **San Jose Sharks** players circle their prey. The Bay Area's

NHL representatives take to the ice at the **HP Pavilion at San Jose,** 525 W. Santa Clara St. at Autumn Street; phone (408) 287-9200.

Bicycling A bike is a great way to get some exercise, get around the city and see the sights, but two key factors present challenges: numerous steep hills and constant vehicle traffic. Two of the best—and safest—areas to ride a bike are along the coast at the city's western edge and in **Golden Gate Park.**

Bay City Bike provides rentals, maps and recommended itineraries for those who want to pedal their way around the Bay Area. Two routes are especially popular: north across the Golden Gate Bridge to Sausalito, then returning by ferry; and through the Presidio into Golden Gate Park. Bikes can be rented at two locations, both at Fisherman's Wharf—2661 Taylor St. and 1325 Columbus Ave. For more information phone (415) 346-2453.

Bicycle rental outfits are located along Stanyan Street and Geary Boulevard near Golden Gate Park. Several area touring companies organize jaunts to the Sonoma wine country and other scenic spots around the Greater Bay Area. **Golden Gate Park Skate and Bike,** 3038 Fulton St. at 6th Avenue, is another convenient rental outlet for a ride through Golden Gate Park, the Presidio or across the Golden Gate Bridge. Roller blades and roller skates also can be rented; phone (415) 668-1117.

Bike and Roll offers bike rentals as well as tours, including a popular route along the San Francisco Bay Trail over the Golden Gate Bridge to Sausalito; the return trip is by ferry. This 9-mile-long route, which can be done as either a self-guiding or guided excursion, is quite scenic, stays close to the bay and covers mostly flat terrain, with the last 3 miles to Sausalito going downhill. Bikes can be rented at 5 Embarcadero Center (across from the Ferry Building) and at 899 Columbus Ave. (at the corner of Lombard Street); phone (415) 229-2000.

Fishing At **Lake Merced,** south of the San Francisco Zoo, anglers can fish for largemouth bass, trout and catfish. Fly-casting pools are south of the bison paddock in Golden Gate Park next to the Angler's Lodge; bring your own equipment. There are municipal fishing piers along the northern waterfront and at **Aquatic Park,** while fishing boats ply the waters of San Francisco Bay for striped bass and giant sturgeon.

Golf Rain may dampen fairways during winter, but otherwise year-round mild weather is nearly ideal for a game. With space at such a premium, however, there are only a few public golf courses within the city limits.

Municipal courses open to the public include **Harding Park Golf Course** on Lake Merced, Harding Road off Skyline Boulevard, (415) 664-4690; **Lincoln Park Municipal Golf Course,** 34th Avenue and Clement Street, (415) 221-9911; and the **Presidio Golf Course,** on Finley Road at Arguello Boulevard, (415) 561-4664. There also is a nine-hole course in **Golden Gate Park** at 47th Avenue and John F. Kennedy Drive; phone (415) 751-8987.

Hiking A 4-mile stretch of sandy coastline, **Ocean Beach** parallels the Great Highway that runs along San Francisco's Pacific back door. It offers few frills but maximum atmosphere and flat terrain for a brisk hike.

Miles of hiking trails run through the Presidio. One of the most delightful getaways in San Francisco is the **Coastal Trail,** which runs above the rocky shoreline at **Lands End** from 32nd Avenue west to the Sutro Baths site. At the signed detour to Mile Rock Beach, descend a set of steep steps down to a rock-strewn beach with crashing waves and a view of the Golden Gate Bridge. It's hard to believe this serene, spectacularly scenic trail is in a densely packed urban area.

The Golden Gate National Recreational Area's **Mount Tamalpais State Park** and the **Marin Headlands,** just across the Golden Gate Bridge in Marin County, offer hiking routes ranging from gentle to strenuous. Trails at higher elevations have the added bonus of sweeping San Francisco views. Hiking the paved walkways through a forest of towering redwoods at **Muir Woods National Monument** is also particularly scenic. Miles of hiking trails run through the Presidio as well.

Jogging and Walking Stroll the foot trails from Golden Gate Park's eastern boundary to the ocean, admiring the gardens and verdant parklands along the way; just remember that the distance is 3 miles and you'll have to walk back (or hop on a Muni bus). If you don't mind whipping winds, the pedestrian

War Memorial Opera House

Watch an independent film at Castro Theatre

walkway along the **Golden Gate Bridge** offers breathtaking views. It's 1.7 miles across, so unless you're up for the trek back, arrange to have someone pick you up at the north end.

One of the city's most popular jogging areas is the paved **Golden Gate Promenade**, which runs along the northern edge of Crissy Field. The flat route offers great views of the Golden Gate Bridge.

If it's plain old exercise you're looking for, simply step outside your hotel room door. The city's steep hills provide challenging climbs and scenic vistas galore, and many of the steeper sidewalks have built-in stairways. For a strenuous workout, puff your way up the block of **Lombard Street** dubbed "the crookedest street in the world"—then turn around and take the much easier way back down.

Tennis There are courts in Golden Gate Park off John F. Kennedy Drive opposite the Conservatory of Flowers. A fee is charged and reservations are required on weekends; phone (415) 753-7001. The **San Francisco Recreation and Parks Department** maintains some 150 public courts available on a first-come, first-served basis, as well as eight indoor swimming pools and an outdoor pool; for more information phone (415) 831-2700.

Water Sports Sailing the blue waters of **San Francisco Bay** offers year-round enjoyment and a close-up look at Alcatraz and Angel islands, the Golden Gate Bridge, the San Francisco-Oakland Bay Bridge and the picturesque waterfront communities of Sausalito and Tiburon. Currents are tricky, however, so it's best to leave the sailing to experienced hands.

Boat rentals and charters are available throughout the greater Bay Area. Row, paddle and electric boats can be rented at **Stow Lake** in Golden Gate Park—perfect for a lazy afternoon sojourn around Strawberry Hill, which rises from the middle of this man-made body of water. Phone (415) 752-0347 for rates and information.

Performing Arts

San Francisco's tempestuous 19th-century adolescence was more attuned to drinking and gambling than refined pleasures. Even so, 15 legitimate theaters operated amid the saloons of the Barbary Coast. But today residents and visitors take advantage of a world-class symphony, opera and ballet companies, and theatrical fare from touring Broadway blockbusters to a full house of offbeat experimental productions.

Two major performing arts facilities are just west of the Civic Center. A bronze Henry Moore sculpture squats in front of **Louise M. Davies Symphony Hall**. The building's wraparound design places seating around and even behind the orchestra. Opera, dance and performing arts troupes perform at the **War Memorial Opera House**, opposite the Davies. This venerable structure looks just like it did in 1931.

The *San Francisco Chronicle's* pink-page Datebook section, published in the newspaper's Sunday edition, carries complete listings of area theaters and nightspots as well as information about upcoming events. TIXBay Area offers cash-only, half-price tickets for selected theater, dance and music events on the day of the performance, and also serves as a Ticketmaster ticket outlet (for credit card purchases). It is located inside the Union Square Garage, accessible through the Geary Street entrance; phone (415) 433-7827.

Dance Innovative new productions as well as classics are performed by the **San Francisco Ballet** at the War Memorial Opera House. The company's repertory season lasts from February into early May, although the Nutcracker Suite is performed in December. For information phone (415) 865-2000.

Across the bay, the **Oakland Ballet** has been presenting its own revivals and contemporary productions since 1965. The season begins in September; performances take place at the **Paramount Theater of the Arts**, 2025 Broadway near the 19th Street BART station. Phone (510) 465-6400 for information.

Film The Bay Area is a mecca for film lovers. Independent film-making tradition thrives here: Documentaries and experimental features are produced on cut-rate budgets throughout the city. Many movie theaters in San Francisco show primarily art-house or foreign films, and film showings at several colleges and universities also ensure a wide variety of fare.

The following show a mix of foreign and independent films in addition to repertory programs and revivals of old classics: the **Castro Theatre**, 429

Castro St., (415) 621-6120; **Embarcadero Cinema**, promenade level 1 at Embarcadero Center, (415) 267-4893; the **Opera Plaza Cinema**, (601 Van Ness Ave.), (415) 267-4893; the **Roxie Theater**, 3117 16th St., (415) 863-1087; and **Yerba Buena Center for the Arts**, 701 Mission St. in the Yerba Buena Gardens complex, (415) 978-2787.

Music Under the direction of Michael Tilson Thomas, the **San Francisco Symphony** performs in Louise M. Davies Symphony Hall from September through June and also at the **Flint Center for the Performing Arts**, 21250 Stevens Creek Blvd. in Cupertino. Guest conductors and internationally known soloists round out the repertoire of standards. For ticket information phone (408) 864-8820.

As a free alternative to the often sold-out symphony productions, orchestral and band concerts take place summer Sundays in the natural amphitheater of **Sigmund Stern Memorial Park**, Sloat Boulevard and 19th Avenue; phone (415) 252-6252 for concert information. **Golden Gate Park** also plays host to concerts throughout the year; phone (415) 831-5500.

During the academic year both students and faculty perform at the San Francisco Conservatory of Music's **Hellman Hall**, 1201 Ortega St. in the Sunset District. Phone (415) 503-6277 for 24-hour schedule and price information, or (415) 864-7326 Mon.-Fri. 9-5 for tickets. Occasional classical music concerts take place at the **Nob Hill Masonic Center**, 1111 California St.; phone (415) 281-9217.

Opera The **San Francisco Opera**, founded in 1923, is the resident company at the War Memorial Opera House. International names frequently appear during the season, which begins in early September and lasts into December. Many performances are sold out long in advance, but standing-room tickets are always made available the day of performance; they go on sale (cash only and one per person) at the box office, 301 Van Ness Ave., beginning at 10 a.m. Phone (415) 864-3330 for performance and additional ticket information.

Theater Major touring plays and productions of Broadway shows are presented at the **Curran Theater** (445 Geary St.) and the **Orpheum Theater** (1192 Market St.). Musicals run at the **Golden Gate Theater**, at the intersection of Market and Taylor streets and Golden Gate Avenue, and at the Curran Theatre. Phone (415) 551-2000 for ticket information for all three venues.

The **American Conservatory Theater** (ACT) is San Francisco's major repertory group and presents plays at the 1910 Edwardian-style **Geary Theatre** (405 Geary St.); phone (415) 749-2228. **Lamplighters Music Theatre,** another repertory company, specializes in operettas and musical spoofs, with an emphasis on Gilbert & Sullivan musicals. Lamplighters performances are given Wednesday through Sunday at the **Yerba Buena Center for the Arts**, 700 Howard St. at Third Street; at the **University of San Francisco Presentation Theater**, 2350 Turk St.; and at the **Lesher Center for the Arts**,

1601 Civic Dr. at Locust Street in Walnut Creek. Phone (925) 943-7469 for Lesher Center ticket information.

A uniquely San Francisco theater experience is "**Beach Blanket Babylon**" at **Club Fugazi** (678 Green St.). Running since 1974, the show features cabaret-style entertainment paired with outlandish costumes; phone (415) 421-4222 for reservations. The **Lorraine Hansberry Theatre** (450 Post St.) showcases the works of African-American writers; phone (415) 474-8800.

The **Magic Theatre** in Building D at Fort Mason, Marina Boulevard and Buchanan Street in the Marina District, presents West Coast premieres and occasional solo shows; phone (415) 441-8822. And Fort Mason's **Cowell Theater**, Marina Boulevard at Buchanan Street, features one-man shows as well as smaller performances; phone (415) 345-7575.

INSIDER INFO:
CityPASS and Go San Francisco Card

San Francisco CityPASS offers savings to those planning to visit several San Francisco attractions. San Francisco CityPASS includes a Muni & Cable Car 7-Day Passport, covering a week of unlimited use of all Muni public transportation (cable cars, Muni light rail and the city's bus system) as well as admission to five attractions: the Aquarium of the Bay at Pier 39; Blue & Gold Fleet's Bay Cruise Adventure; The California Academy of Sciences in Golden Gate Park; San Francisco Museum of Modern Art; and an option ticket for either the de Young Museum and the Legion of Honor museum *or* the Exploratorium museum.

See a show at the Palace of Fine Arts

San Francisco CityPASS is valid for 9 consecutive days, starting with the first day of use (Muni passport valid for 7 days). The cost is $84; $54 (ages 5-12). These rates are valid Mar. 1, 2013, through Feb. 28, 2014. CityPASS is available from participating attractions. For information phone (208) 787-4300 or (888) 330-5008. *(See ad this page.)*

Go San Francisco Card is an all-access pass offering admission to more than 30 San Francisco attractions plus more than 20 additional attractions and wineries in Santa Cruz, the Monterey Peninsula and Wine Country. The card, which is purchased by the day (1, 2, 3, 5 or 7 consecutive calendar days), includes attractions such as the Aquarium of the Bay, Six Flags Discovery Kingdom (in Vallejo), The California Academy of Sciences, the Exploratorium, a Golden Gate Bridge bay cruise and a cable car ride. The card is priced as low as $21 per day (based on a 7-day card). Go San Francisco Card is available at the San Francisco Visitor Information Center at 900 Market St., the Wax Museum at Fisherman's Wharf or the Red and White Fleet's ticket booth; phone (866) 628-9028.

The Lincoln Highway

The horseless carriage rolled onto the American landscape in the 1890s. By 1910 there were more than 450,000 registered automobiles, yet the country still lacked a public road system.

Organized movements for better roads brought issues to the attention of the federal government, which had not participated in major road construction since it funded the National Road project in 1806.

But one particular initiative captured the public's support with a unique idea. In 1913 Carl Fisher—the man who built the Indianapolis Motor Speedway in 1909—and automobile industry leaders chartered the Lincoln Highway Association for the purpose of defining a direct coast-to-coast automobile route.

The LHA's first official act was to delineate a 3,389-mile, 12-state continuous route from New York to California—one that would be passable before the opening of the 1915 Panama-Pacific International Exposition in San Francisco. Although not perfect, the throughway was ready as promised, and a motion picture of America's transcontinental highway was shown at the exposition. Over time, the association improved surfaces by using better materials, shortened the driving distance with re-alignments and published guidebooks about the Lincoln Highway. Automobile touring had never been so good.

Through example, the LHA educated the public as well as state and federal governments about the value of good roads for almost 15 years. The 1919 moving of a military convoy over the "Lincolnway" foretold the utility of an integrated highway system for national defense and interstate commerce.

With the 1921 Federal Highway Act came the funds for states to construct and maintain connecting arteries. Four years later the United States adopted a highway numbering system, and most of the Lincoln route became US 30, 40 and 50. The association disbanded in 1928, but not before it engaged Boy Scout troops across the country to place some 3,000 concrete Lincoln Highway markers along the route in all 12 states: New York, New Jersey, Pennsylvania, Ohio, Indiana, Illinois, Iowa, Nebraska, Wyoming, Utah, Nevada and California. Many of these markers still exist.

San Francisco's Lincoln Park marked the western terminus of the Lincoln Highway. To get there from the Nevada border, motorists entered California through **Truckee** and negotiated the Sierra Nevada via historic Donner Pass; an optional route from Carson City took motorists along the southern shore of **Lake Tahoe,** followed the American River toward **Placerville,** then went through **Folsom.** The roads converged at **Sacramento** and the highway continued south through **Lodi** to **Stockton,** west through **Livermore** to **Hayward,** then north into **Oakland,** where a ferry served as the only connector to San Francisco until a bridge was completed in 1936. Another route from Sacramento approached Oakland from the north through **Davis** and **Vacaville.**

For descriptions of places in bold type, see individual listings.

For more information about the old Lincoln Highway contact the new Lincoln Highway Association, P.O. Box 308, Franklin Grove, IL 61031; phone (815) 456-3030.

ATTRACTIONS

ALCATRAZ ISLAND, in San Francisco Bay, can be reached via Alcatraz Cruises ferries that depart from Pier 33 on The Embarcadero. Known as "The Rock," Alcatraz was a maximum security federal penitentiary for almost 30 years before closing in 1963 due to high operating costs and deteriorating facilities. Among the notorious criminals who did time on The Rock were Al Capone, Machine Gun Kelly and Robert Stroud, the "Birdman of Alcatraz."

One of the city's biggest tourist attractions is a fascinating piece of history. The buildings, including a guard tower, water tower, power plant, warden's house and four cellblocks, are in various states of disrepair. The recreation yard is a dismal-looking, fenced-in concrete rectangle. The prison cells—each furnished with a toilet, tiny sink and single bunk—are depressingly small and grim. Alcatraz was never filled to capacity; the average number of inmates was around 260.

The gardens add splashes of color and a great deal of beauty to the stark surroundings. Because it has no natural predators, the island also is a bird sanctuary. In addition to a large population of Western gulls, visitors will see such species as cormorants, black-crowned night herons and snowy egrets.

The ferry cruise takes about 15 minutes and offers a view of the San Francisco skyline and the Golden Gate Bridge. A 45-minute, self-guiding audio tour of the main prison building, narrated by inmates, correctional officers and their families, provides insight into what life was like on The Rock. A 17-minute orientation video, "Alcatraz: Stories from the Rock," offers an informative overview.

Ranger- and volunteer-led outdoor interpretive walks focus on the island's military history, famous inmates, escape attempts, historic gardens and 2-year occupation by the Indians of All Tribes. Visitors also can explore on their own; self-guiding tour brochures are available at the dock for a small fee. Building 64 contains historical exhibits.

The Alcatraz Night Tour features a boat cruise around the island, a guided tour from the dock to the cell house, special programs and dramatic evening views of the city.

Note: Visitors are advised to buy tickets in advance year-round and especially from May through September, when they should be purchased at least 1 week ahead. Wear comfortable shoes and layered clothing to accommodate the unpredictable weather. **Hours:** Ferries depart daily beginning at 9 and run at 30- to 40-minute intervals throughout the day. The Alcatraz Night Tour departs Pier 33 Thurs.-Mon. at 4:20; phone ahead to confirm schedule. The island closes at 6:30 p.m. during the summer months; at 4:30, rest of year. Closed Jan. 1, Thanksgiving and Christmas.

Cost: $26 (includes audio tour and round-trip ferry transportation); $24.50 (ages 62+); $16 (ages 5-11). Alcatraz Night Tour $33; $32 (ages 12-17); $30.50 (ages 62+); $19.50 (ages 5-11). Rates may vary; phone ahead. **Phone:** (415) 981-7625.

The Gardens of Alcatraz are on Alcatraz Island. Created by the families of correctional officers and the inmates themselves, they made maximum use of limited space and added touches of beauty to the otherwise forbidding atmosphere of "The Rock."

The natural environment—rocky ground, poor soil, a scarcity of fresh water and chilly, salt-laden winds—was not conducive to horticulture, but Alcatraz's early gardeners chose hardy, sustainable plants from places like South Africa and the Mediterranean, where weather conditions are similar to those in the San Francisco Bay Area. When the prison closed in 1963 the cultivated landscape became overgrown and wild, but since 2003 a crew of volunteers has worked to restore and maintain these historic gardens.

Fuschias, geraniums and nasturtiums flourish in carefully tended flower beds. Creamy white calla lilies accent stone walls. Fig trees, fragrant roses and aeoniums, succulents with fleshy leaves in the shape of a rosette, provide a colorful contrast to the

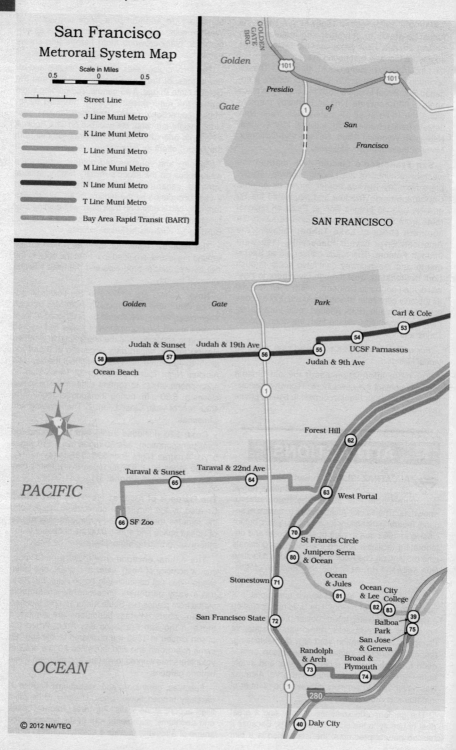

San Francisco
Metrorail System Map

Scale in Miles
0.5   0   0.5

——┼—— Street Line
━━━━━ J Line Muni Metro
━━━━━ K Line Muni Metro
━━━━━ L Line Muni Metro
━━━━━ M Line Muni Metro
━━━━━ N Line Muni Metro
━━━━━ T Line Muni Metro
━━━━━ Bay Area Rapid Transit (BART)

GOLDEN GATE BRG

Golden

Gate

Presidio

of

San

Francisco

SAN FRANCISCO

Golden   Gate   Park

Carl & Cole

53

54

Judah & Sunset   Judah & 19th Ave   55   UCSF Parnassus

58   57   56   Judah & 9th Ave

Ocean Beach

N

Forest Hill

62

Taraval & Sunset   Taraval & 22nd Ave

PACIFIC   65   64

63   West Portal

66 SF Zoo

70   St Francis Circle

80   Junipero Serra
     & Ocean

Ocean
& Jules

Stonestown 71   81   Ocean City
                              & Lee College

                         82   83

San Francisco State 72   Balboa
                             Park

                    San Jose   39
                    & Geneva   75

Randolph   Broad &
& Arch   Plymouth

OCEAN   73   74

1   280

40 Daly City

© 2012 NAVTEQ

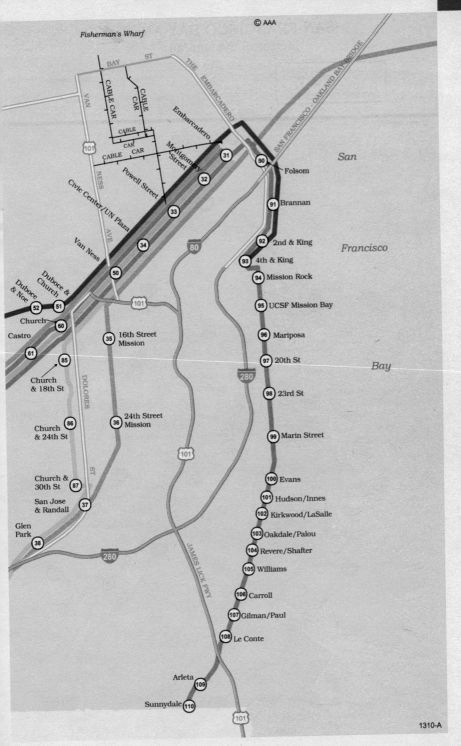

© AAA

Fisherman's Wharf

San

Francisco

Bay

Glen Park

Arleta

Sunnydale

31
32
33
34
50
51
52
60
61
85
86
87
37
38
35
36
90 Folsom
91 Brannan
92 2nd & King
93 4th & King
94 Mission Rock
95 UCSF Mission Bay
96 Mariposa
97 20th St
98 23rd St
99 Marin Street
100 Evans
101 Hudson/Innes
102 Kirkwood/LaSalle
103 Oakdale/Palou
104 Revere/Shafter
105 Williams
106 Carroll
107 Gilman/Paul
108 Le Conte
109
110

Duboce & Church
Duboce & Noe
Church
Castro
Church & 18th St
Church & 24th St
Church & 30th St
San Jose & Randall
16th Street Mission
24th Street Mission
Civic Center/UN Plaza
Van Ness
Powell Street
Montgomery Street
Embarcadero

1310-A

SAN FRANCISCO BAY AREA
Metrorail System Map

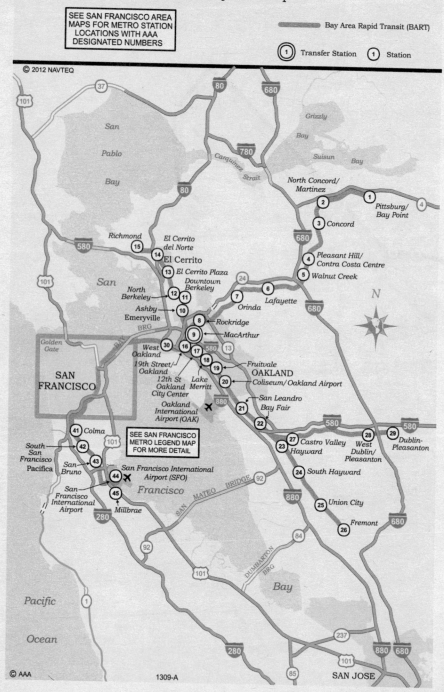

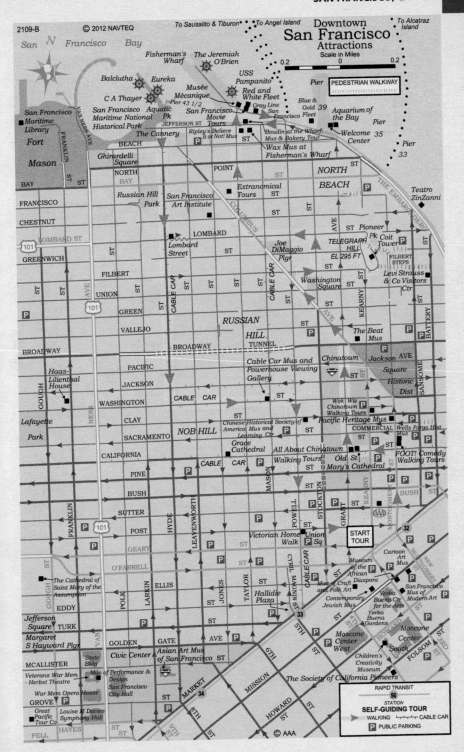

Downtown
San Francisco
Attractions

2109-B   © 2012 NAVTEQ   To Sausalito & Tiburon•   To Angel Island   To Alcatraz Island

San N Francisco Bay

Scale in Miles
0.2   0   0.2

Fisherman's Wharf   The Jeremiah O'Brien

Balclutha   Eureka   Musée Mécanique   USS Pampanito   Red and White Fleet   Pier   PEDESTRIAN WALKWAY

C A Thayer   Pier 43 1/2   Gray Line San Francisco Tours   Blue & Gold Fleet   39   Aquarium of the Bay   Pier 35

San Francisco Maritime Library   San Francisco Maritime National Historical Park   Aquatic Pk   San Francisco Movie Tours   Welcome Center   Pier 33

Fort Mason   JEFFERSON ST   Boudin at the Wharf Mus & Bakery Tour

The Cannery   Ripley's Believe It or Not! Mus   Wax Mus at Fisherman's Wharf

BEACH   ST   BAY

Ghirardelli Square

NORTH   POINT   ST   NORTH BEACH   Teatro ZinZanni

FRANCISCO   BAY   Russian Hill Park   San Francisco Art Institute   Extranomical Tours   ST   ST   AVE   ST Pioneer   Pk Coit Tower

CHESTNUT   LOMBARD ST   LOMBARD   Joe DiMaggio Plgr   TELEGRAPH HILL   EL 295 FT   FILBERT STEPS

101   GREENWICH   Lombard Street   ST   Washington Square   Levi Strauss & Co Visitors Ctr

FILBERT   CABLE CAR   CABLE CAR

UNION   The Beat Mus

101   GREEN   RUSSIAN   ST   KEARNY   BATTERY

VALLEJO   HILL   ST   Jackson   AVE   Square   SANSOME

BROADWAY   BROADWAY   TUNNEL   Cable Car Mus and Powerhouse Viewing Gallery   Chinatown   Historic Dist

PACIFIC   Wok Wiz Chinatown Tours   Pacific Heritage Mus   COMMERCIAL   Wells Fargo Hist Mus

Haas-Lilienthal House   JACKSON   CABLE   CAR

WASHINGTON   Chinese Historical Society of America Mus and Learning Ctr   FOOT! Comedy Walking Tours

Lafayette Park   CLAY   NOB HILL   Grace Cathedral   All About Chinatown Walking Tours   Old St Mary's Cathedral

SACRAMENTO

CALIFORNIA   CABLE   CAR

PINE   MASON   ST

BUSH   POWELL   STOCKTON   GRANT   KEARNY   BUSH   MONTGOMERY

SUTTER   HYDE   LEAVENWORTH   32

101   POST   Victorian Home Walk   Union Sq   START TOUR   AAA

GEARY   Cartoon Art Mus

O'FARRELL   Museum of the African Diaspora   San Francisco Mus of Modern Art

The Cathedral of Saint Mary of the Assumption   ELLIS   JONES   TAYLOR   Mus of Craft and Folk Art   Yerba Buena Ctr for the Arts

EDDY   Hallidie Plaza   Contemporary Jewish Mus   Yerba Buena Gardens   Moscone Center South

Jefferson Square   TURK   33   Moscone Center West   HOWARD   FOLSOM

Margaret S Hayward Plgr   GOLDEN   GATE   AVE   Children's Creativity Museum

MCALLISTER   State Bldg   Asian Art Mus of San Francisco   ST   The Society of California Pioneers

Veterans War Mem - Herbst Theatre   Mus of Performance & Design   San Francisco City Hall   MARKET   34   MISSION   HOWARD

War Mem Opera House   GROVE   Great Pacific Tour Co   Louise M Davies Symphony Hall   RAPID TRANSIT

HAYES   50   STATION

FELL   SELF-GUIDING TOUR   WALKING   CABLE CAR   P PUBLIC PARKING

© AAA

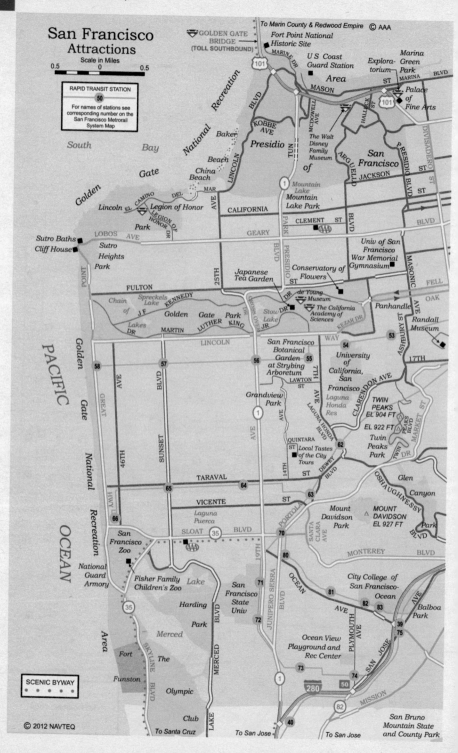

San Francisco
Attractions

Scale in Miles
0.5   0   0.5

RAPID TRANSIT STATION
50
For names of stations see
corresponding number on the
San Francisco Metrorail
System Map

© 2012 NAVTEQ

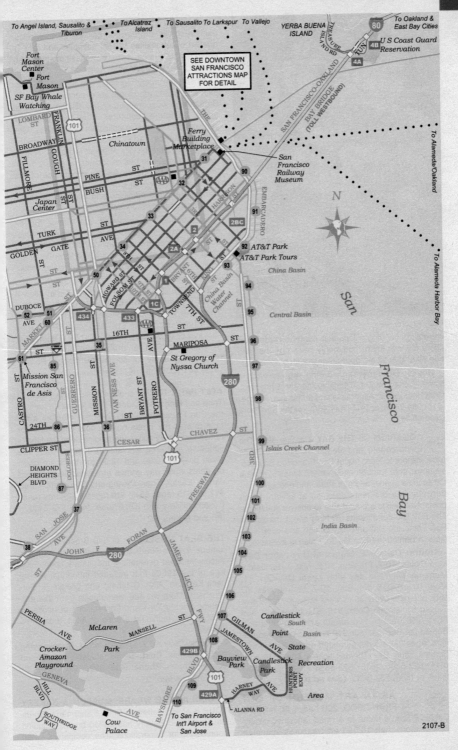

To Angel Island, Sausalito & Tiburon
To Alcatraz Island
To Sausalito To Larkspur To Vallejo
YERBA BUENA ISLAND
To Oakland & East Bay Cities
80
US Coast Guard Reservation
4B
4A

Fort Mason Center
Fort Mason
SF Bay Whale Watching

LOMBARD ST
FRANKLIN
101
BROADWAY
FILLMORE
GOUGH
Chinatown
PINE ST
BUSH ST
Japan Center
TURK AVE
GOLDEN GATE AVE
DUBOCE AVE
MARKET
HOWARD ST
FOLSOM ST
16TH
VAN NESS AVE
GUERRERO
MISSION ST
BRYANT ST
POTRERO
Mission San Francisco de Asis
24TH
CLIPPER ST
DIAMOND HEIGHTS BLVD
SAN JOSE AVE
JOHN F
280
FORAN
JAMES LICK FREEWAY
PERSIA AVE
McLaren Park
MANSELL
Crocker-Amazon Playground
GENEVA BLVD
HILL BLVD
SOUTHRIDGE WAY
Cow Palace

SEE DOWNTOWN SAN FRANCISCO ATTRACTIONS MAP FOR DETAIL

Ferry Building Marketplace
San Francisco Railway Museum
EMBARCADERO
31
90
32
33
2BC
2
2A
1
1C
434
433
35
MARIPOSA
St Gregory of Nyssa Church
280
CHAVEZ ST
101
37
38
85
61
86
36
CESAR
TOWNSEND
7TH ST
AT&T Park
AT&T Park Tours
China Basin
92
93
China Basin Water Channel
94
95
Central Basin
96
97
98
99
Islais Creek Channel
100
101
102
103
104
105
106
107
108
109
110

To Oakland
To Alameda/Oakland
To Alameda Harbor Bay

N

San Francisco Bay

India Basin

GILMAN
Candlestick South Basin
Point State
Candlestick Recreation
Bayview Park
Park Area
HUNTERS POINT EXPY
JAMESTOWN AVE
429B
HARNEY WAY
429A
ALANNA RD
BAYSHORE BLVD
BAYSHORE AVE
To San Francisco Int'l Airport & San Jose

2107-B

Aquarium of the Bay

crumbling buildings. Unusual plants include *Gordonia axillaris*, more commonly known as the fried egg plant due to the appearance of its blooms.

Hours: Gardens open during regular visiting hours. Closed Jan. 1, Thanksgiving and Christmas. **Cost:** Included in Alcatraz Island admission. **Phone:** (415) 981-7625, or (415) 441-4300 for the San Francisco office of The Garden Conservancy.

[SAVE] **AQUARIUM OF THE BAY** is at Pier 39 at The Embarcadero and Beach St. Three exhibits allow visitors to learn about San Francisco Bay ecosystems; see, through clear acrylic tunnels, marine life such as sharks and sea stars; and encounter underwater bay residents up-close at several touch pools. Naturalists are available to answer questions. The Bay Theater screens 3D films about sharks, the San Francisco-Oakland Bay Bridge and other subjects. A Behind-the-Scenes Tour also is available.

Hours: Daily 9-8, Memorial Day-Labor Day; Mon.-Thurs. 10-7, Fri.-Sun. 10-8, Mar. 1-day before Memorial Day and day after Labor Day-Oct. 31; Mon.-Thurs. 10-6, Fri.-Sun. 10-7, rest of year. 3D films alternate every 30 minutes throughout the day. Closed Christmas. **Cost:** $18; $10 (ages 3-11 and 65+); $50 (family, two adults and two children). Behind-the-Scenes Tour $10 plus aquarium admission. Ages 0-4 are not permitted on the Behind-the-Scenes Tour. Bay Theater tickets $6.50. **Phone:** (415) 623-5300, (415) 623-5333 for 3D film show times or (888) 732-3483. *(See ad p. 362.)*

[GEM] [SAVE] **ASIAN ART MUSEUM OF SAN FRANCISCO,** 200 Larkin St. on Civic Center Plaza, is home to a world-renowned collection of more than 18,000 art treasures spanning

some 6,000 years of history. From Japanese painted scrolls and bamboo baskets to Korean lacquerware and textiles to Thai paintings and rare Tibetan scrolls, the museum showcases the incredibly rich and varied spectrum of Asian art.

Among the many highlights are Indonesian puppets and *krises* (daggers), jewel-encrusted swords, Bronze Age weapons and chariot fittings, arms and armor, miniature sculptures, ritual food and wine vessels, and a notable collection of Buddhas. Chinese ceramics, jades, bronzes and porcelains survey the entire history of these art forms. A ritual vessel in the shape of a rhinoceros (in gallery 14 on the third floor) underscores the importance of this endangered animal in Chinese culture; their horns were ground into medicine and carved into elaborate cups used by the wealthy.

An extravagantly decorated, late 19th-century elephant throne, or howdah, from India once functioned as a ceremonial conveyance for kings and other members of royalty. In addition to works of antiquity, the museum also displays a growing collection of contemporary and 21st-century art.

Tours: Guided tours are available. **Time:** Allow 2 hours minimum. **Hours:** Tues.-Sun. 10-5 (also Thurs. 5-9, Feb.-Sept.). Closed Jan. 1, Thanksgiving and Christmas. **Cost:** $12; $8 (ages 13-17, ages 65+ and college students with ID); $5 (Thurs. after 5); free (first Sun. of the month). An additional charge may apply for special exhibitions. **Phone:** (415) 581-3500. [fl] [♿] Civic Center/UN Plaza, 34

AT&T PARK TOURS is at 24 Willie Mays Plaza, at Third and King sts. Guided 1.5-hour walking tours of the San Francisco Giants' baseball stadium allow fans to visit the press box, dugout, visitors' clubhouse and luxury suites (depending upon the team's schedule and area availability). **Hours:** Tours are given daily at 10:30 and 12:30 (no tours are given on dates when day games are scheduled). Closed Jan. 1, Easter, Thanksgiving and Christmas. **Cost:** $17.50; $15 (ages 55+); $10 (ages 3-12); free (ages 0-2 and military with ID). **Phone:** (415) 972-2400. [♿] 2nd & King, 92

THE BEAT MUSEUM is at 540 Broadway at Columbus Ave. in North Beach. This small museum traces the Beat generation, the literary counterculture of the 1950s that included influential writers Jack Kerouac, Allen Ginsberg and William S. Burroughs. Visitors will see memorabilia from that era, vintage photographs and first editions of books by Beat writers, including a copy of Allen Ginsburg's "Howl."

Hours: Daily 10-7. Closed Jan. 1, Thanksgiving and Christmas. **Cost:** $8; $5 (students with ID and senior citizens). **Phone:** (415) 399-9626. [♿] Embarcadero, 31

BOUDIN AT THE WHARF: MUSEUM & BAKERY TOUR is at 160 Jefferson St. at Fisherman's Wharf. Boudin French Bakery has baked bread, including sourdough, for generations. The company's wharf location offers a museum with photographs, artifacts and exhibits that trace the history of the bakery and the science behind the production of sourdough bread, one of this foodie city's signature culinary creations.

A demonstration bakery provides viewpoints, including a glass-walled catwalk directly over the production facility, from which visitors can watch the steps involved in the production of the company's products. **Time:** Allow 1 hour, 30 minutes minimum. **Hours:** Wed.-Mon. 11:30-6. **Cost:** $3; free (ages 0-12). **Phone:** (415) 928-1849. 🍴

CABLE CAR MUSEUM AND POWERHOUSE VIEWING GALLERY, 1201 Mason St. at Washington St., contains models, photographs and relics of San Francisco's early transit system, including the first cable car, built in 1873. A videotape presentation about cable cars describes how they work, and an underground viewing room enables visitors to observe the huge sheaves that guide the vehicles from under the street.

Time: Allow 1 hour minimum. **Hours:** Daily 10-6, Apr.-Sept.; 10-5, rest of year. Closed Jan. 1, Thanksgiving and Christmas. **Cost:** Donations. **Phone:** (415) 474-1887.

🚇 Montgomery Street, 32

THE CALIFORNIA ACADEMY OF SCIENCES—see Golden Gate Park p. 375.

THE CANNERY—see Shopping p. 353.

CARTOON ART MUSEUM is at 655 Mission St. Focusing on original cartoon and animation art, the museum presents rotating exhibits in addition to its permanent collection. Categories of cartoon art displayed include Underground, which emerged in the late 1960s San Francisco hippie scene; Editorial, typically found in newspapers; Magazine; and Animation, art used to produce animated films. Also shown are comic strip and comic book art.

Time: Allow 1 hour minimum. **Hours:** Tues.-Sun. 11-5. Closed Jan. 1, Easter, July 4, Thanksgiving and Christmas. **Cost:** $7; $5 (ages 61+ and students with ID); $3 (ages 6-12); donation (first Tues. of the month). **Phone:** (415) 227-8666.

🚇 Montgomery Street, 32

THE CATHEDRAL OF SAINT MARY OF THE ASSUMPTION, 1111 Gough St. on Cathedral Hill, is a modern structure of Italian marble. A baldachino (canopy) of aluminum and gold, a large mosaic and a Ruffati organ highlight the interior. **Hours:** Office open Mon.-Fri. 8:30-noon and 1-5, Sat. 9:30-3:30, Sun. 10-3:30. Docents lead tours Mon.-Sat. 9-noon and Sun. after 11 a.m. mass, Apr.-Oct. Phone ahead to confirm tour schedule. **Cost:** Donations. **Phone:** (415) 567-2020. 🚇 Civic Center/UN Plaza, 34

CHILDREN'S CREATIVITY MUSEUM is at 221 Fourth St. at jct. Howard St., in the Yerba Buena Gardens complex. This innovative arts and technology museum, geared to children and their families, offers hands-on opportunities to create movies, music and art. Kids can create a clay animation, produce and/or star in a music video and learn about digital art. Visitors also can take a spin on a restored 1906 Looff carousel that operated for more than 50 years at the city's Playland-at-the-Beach amusement park.

Time: Allow 2 hours minimum. **Hours:** Tues.-Sun. 10-4, in summer; Wed.-Sun. 10-4, during the school year. Carousel daily 10-5; last ride is at 4:55. Closed major holidays. **Cost:** $11; free (under 1). Two rides on the carousel $3. **Phone:** (415) 820-3320.

🍴 ⊗ 🚇 Powell Street, 33

CHINATOWN is bounded roughly n. and s. by Vallejo and Bush sts. and e. and w. by Kearny and Powell sts. Although there are other Chinese enclaves in San Francisco, notably in the Richmond and Inner Sunset areas of the city, Chinatown is the first and still the foremost. It leads a double life—part tourist mecca, part workaday neighborhood—and has an atmosphere all its own.

The first Chinese immigrants arrived in San Francisco in 1848. They came to work for companies seeking cheap labor, and many ended up toiling at back-breaking menial jobs. Anti-immigration sentiment during the 1870s targeted these industrious new arrivals and reached its peak with the passage of the Chinese Exclusion Act of 1882. Today's Chinatown began taking shape in the 1880s as a safe haven for Chinese workers and their families.

An ornamental gate, dedicated in 1970, arches over Grant Avenue at Bush Street, its green tiles

Browse the Grant Avenue shops, Chinatown

San Francisco City Hall

and twin stone lions forming a symbolic entryway to the neighborhood. You don't really need a planned itinerary to "do" Chinatown. Grant Avenue is tourist central, with a multitude of shops selling everything from cheap plastic Buddhas to fine jewelry and more restaurants than you can shake a chopstick at. Buildings have ornate tiled roofs, intertwined dragons coil around old-fashioned lampposts, red and yellow banners flutter in the breeze, and the numerous storefront signs are a mix of Chinese and English.

Stockton Street, a block west, isn't as touristy as Grant, but it's every bit as fascinating. For a full Chinatown immersion experience stroll along Stockton on Saturday, when locals do their grocery shopping. Muni buses lurch to a stop, disgorging streams of passengers. Boxes of produce are unloaded from double-parked trucks. Grocers hustle back and forth arranging the merchandise in wooden bins while matriarchs inspect it with a discerning eye. Rows of roasted ducks, their brown skins glistening, hang in the windows of meat markets, along with whole fish and sundry unidentifiable animal parts.

Tiered pagoda roofs stand in the shadow of ultramodern skyscrapers. The United Commercial Bank at the corner of Grant Avenue and Washington Street, formerly the Bank of Canton, was built in 1909 and originally housed the Chinatown telephone office. The buildings are especially intriguing along Waverly Place (parallel to Grant Avenue between Washington and Sacramento streets). There are several temples along this narrow little street. Every floor of the Tien Hau Temple (on Waverly at Clay Street) has a different look; it's a little jewel of a building. The temple itself is on the top floor (visitors must climb three flights of stairs) and has exhibits about Chinatown's history.

All About Chinatown Walking Tours spotlights the area's history, culture and traditions via 2- and 3-hour tours; the 3-hour tour includes a dim sum lunch. Wok Wiz Chinatown Walking Tours also offers a historical walking tour and lunch as well as a 3-hour tour called "I Can't Believe I Ate My Way Through Chinatown!" *See attraction listings beginning on p. 387.*

The Chinese Culture Center of San Francisco, on the third floor of the Hilton San Francisco Financial District at 750 Kearny St., provides information about Chinatown and features displays of Chinese art. The center also offers a 90-minute heritage walking tour that visits food markets, herbal and tea shops, and architectural and historical points of interest. Advance reservations are necessary; phone (415) 986-1822.

Hours: Chinese Culture Center open Tues.-Fri. 9:30-6, Sat. 10-4. Chinese Culture Center walking tours are given Tues.-Sat. at 10, noon and 2. Closed major holidays. **Cost:** Chinese Culture Center free. Heritage walking tour $30; $25 (ages 6-14 and students with ID). Reservations are required for all tours. **Phone:** (415) 986-1822 for the Chinese Culture Center. ▣ Montgomery Street, 32

CHINESE HISTORICAL SOCIETY OF AMERICA MUSEUM AND LEARNING CENTER, 965 Clay St., is in the historic Julia Morgan Chinese YWCA building, dating to 1932. The museum's permanent exhibit, The Chinese of America: Toward a More Perfect Union, recalls the important role of the Chinese in the settlement of the city and the West beginning with the 1800s. Changing exhibitions of contemporary culture and art also are available.

Tours: Guided tours are available. **Time:** Allow 30 minutes minimum. **Hours:** Tues.-Fri. noon-5, Sat. 11-4. Closed major holidays. **Cost:** $5; $3 (ages 62+ and college students with ID); $2 (ages 6-17); free (first Thurs. of each month). **Phone:** (415) 391-1188. ▣ Montgomery Street, 32

CIVIC CENTER, covering 8 blks. and bordered by Market, Hayes and Franklin sts. and Golden Gate Ave., groups federal, state and city structures and parklands. With a dome taller than the U.S. Capitol, San Francisco's city hall commands a view of the plaza, which is surrounded by the State and Federal buildings, Main Public Library, Auditorium and the Health Center, all reflecting French and Neo-Renaissance architectural styles. The United Nations Conference on International Organization, culminating in the signing of the Charter of the United Nations, was held at the Civic Center in 1945. ▣ Civic Center/UN Plaza, 34

Performing Arts Center is across Van Ness Ave. opposite City Hall. The center is comprised of the

San Francisco Performing Arts Library, Herbst Theatre in the Veterans Memorial Building, War Memorial Opera House, Davies Symphony Hall and the San Francisco Ballet Association. The San Francisco Symphony's electro-pneumatic Ruffatti organ has more than 10,000 pipes, five manuals and 163 ranks. Guided tours of the Herbst Theatre, the War Memorial Opera House and Davies Symphony Hall leave from the Grove Street entrance of the symphony hall.

Hours: Tours are given on the hour Mon. 10-2, except on holidays. **Cost:** Tours $7; $5 (ages 65+ and students with ID). **Phone:** (415) 552-8338 for reservations, or (415) 255-4800 for library information. 🚇 Van Ness, 50

San Francisco City Hall is at the Civic Center between Polk, Grove and McAllister sts. and Van Ness Ave. at 1 Dr. Carlton B. Goodlett Pl. Opened in 1915, the expansive building, which covers two full city blocks, is said to have one of the largest domes in the world.

Two "light courts" featuring skylights and marble walls are the sites of changing art exhibits; the building's original marble staircase separates the two courts. Docents provide 45-minute guided tours of the Beaux Arts building. **Time:** Allow 1 hour minimum. **Hours:** Guided tours are given Mon.-Fri. at 10, noon and 2. Closed major holidays. **Cost:** Donations. **Phone:** (415) 554-4933, or (415) 554-6139 for tour information. 🚇 Van Ness, 50

CONTEMPORARY JEWISH MUSEUM is at 736 Mission St. between Third and Fourth sts. in the Yerba Buena cultural district. Designed by noted architect Daniel Libeskind, the museum is in the 1907 former Jessie Street Power Station. The museum's contemporary design is reminiscent of the Hebrew letters that form the word *l'chaim*, which means "to life." Its traveling exhibits examine and celebrate Jewish culture, history, art and ideas.

Hours: Thurs.-Tues. 11-5 (also Thurs. 5-8). Guided tours are given Fri.-Tues. at 11:30, 1 and 2:30, Thurs. at 5 and 6. Closed Jan. 1, the first day of Passover, July 4, the first day of Rosh Hashanah, Yom Kippur and Thanksgiving. **Cost:** $12; $10 (ages 65+ and students with ID); $5 (Thurs. after 5); free (ages 0-18). **Phone:** (415) 655-7800. 🍴 🚇 Montgomery Street, 32

EXPLORATORIUM is at 3601 Lyon St. inside the Palace of Fine Arts. More than 650 interactive exhibits—with some 400 on view at any given time—encourage you to see, touch, hear and feel in ways you might not ordinarily be accustomed to. Everyday Science applies scientific principles to relatable subjects like hair, cooking and skateboarding. The marvel that is the Human Body explores things like the herculean lung power of opera singers and the inner workings of a tooth, while the hands-on displays in Material World explore the mysteries behind magnets, bubbles and molecules.

One of the Exploratorium's highlights is the Tactile Dome, a pitch-black geodesic dome containing 13 chambers and no right angles. You feel your way through the chambers by crawling and sliding, using only your sense of touch and most likely gaining a renewed appreciation of your sense of sight.

Note: The Exploratorium is slated to open at its new location at Pier 15 in spring 2013. The Palace of Fine Arts facility was scheduled to remain open through the end of 2012; phone ahead for updated information regarding the reopening. **Time:** Allow 2 hours minimum. **Hours:** Tues.-Sun. and some Mon. holidays 10-5. Tactile Dome sessions last 75 minutes and begin at 10:15, noon, 1:45, 3:30 and 5 (also Fri.-Sat. at 6:45 p.m.). Closed Thanksgiving and Christmas. Phone ahead to confirm schedule. **Cost:** Exploratorium admission $25; $19 (ages 13-17, ages 65+, college students with ID and the physically impaired); free (ages 0-5 and to all the first Wed. of the month). Separate Tactile Dome admission $12; children under 7 are not permitted. Advance reservations for the Tactile Dome are strongly recommended. **Phone:** (415) 561-0360, or (415) 561-0362 for Tactile Dome reservations. *(See ad p. 362.)* 🍴

DE YOUNG MUSEUM—see Golden Gate Park p. 375.

FISHERMAN'S WHARF—see Shopping p. 354.

FORT MASON CENTER, Buchanan St. and Marina Blvd., is a former military base and World War II point of embarkation turned art and culture center, with space devoted to theaters, galleries and various exhibits. Galleries such as the Museo Italo-Americano, the Mexican Museum, SFMOMA Artists Gallery and Long Now are free and open to the public. Traveling exhibits include the SF Antiques Fair, Arts of the Pacific and the American Crafts Council.

Theater and dance performances, wine tastings, classes and workshops are presented throughout the year. **Hours:** Office open daily 8:30-8. Phone ahead for performance and event schedule information. **Cost:** Free. Fees are charged for some events.

Dahlia Dell, Golden Gate Park

Parking: Free for the first 30 minutes; hourly rates range from $1-$8 weekdays, $1-$10 on weekends. A cashier is on duty daily 8 a.m.-midnight. **Phone:** (415) 345-7500 for general information, or (415) 345-7575 for the box office.

FORT POINT NATIONAL HISTORIC SITE—see Golden Gate National Recreation Area p. 138.

GHIRARDELLI SQUARE—see Shopping p. 354.

GLBT HISTORY MUSEUM is at 4127 18th St. (between Castro and Collingwood sts.). This small but very well curated museum presents the San Francisco Bay Area's gay, lesbian, bisexual and transgender history from the late 19th century to the present. Exhibits, artifacts and multimedia presentations explore such deeply human themes as the search for companionship, the value of individual expression and the struggle for respect and equality in an often-hostile society. **Note:** Some displays include sexually themed material. **Hours:** Mon.-Sat. 11-7, Sun. noon-5. **Cost:** $5; $3 (California students with ID); free (first Wed. of the month). An audio tour is included; visitors also can call in on their cellphones or smartphones. **Phone:** (415) 621-1107. 📺 Castro, 61

GOLDEN GATE BRIDGE spans Golden Gate Strait, the entrance to San Francisco Bay, via US 101. Is there a more iconic San Francisco sight than the Golden Gate Bridge? The mighty span that connects the city with neighboring Marin County and the Golden Gate National Recreation Area is not only a vital transportation link but a landmark recognized the world over thanks to its appearance in countless dramatic photographs.

With a total length of 8,981 feet and a main span of 4,200 feet, the Golden Gate is one of the longest single-span suspension bridges ever built. At 746 feet above the water, its two massive towers are the world's highest bridge towers. A crew of painters works full time to maintain the distinctive color (known as international orange) that protects the bridge's steel components from the high salt content in the air.

The bridge took 4 years to build and was considered an engineering marvel upon its completion. An estimated 1,900,000,000 vehicles (both northbound and southbound) have crossed since it opened to traffic on May 28, 1937. A clearance of 220 feet allows passage of the largest oceangoing vessels. Walking or cycling across the bridge (a 1.7-mile trek one way) is a popular activity for both residents and visitors, and with good reason—the views of the city, the bay and the Marin Headlands are amazing.

Note: There are visitor parking lots on the southeast and northeast sides of the bridge. Pedestrians are only allowed to use the east sidewalk; cyclists can access both the east and west sidewalks but must yield to pedestrians where the sidewalk is shared. Inline skates, roller skates and skateboards are not permitted on the east sidewalk. Both visitor parking areas have restrooms and viewing observation points, and the southeast side visitor lot also features landscaping that accentuates the bridge views.

Hours: Cars and bicycles have access daily 24 hours. Pedestrians may utilize the bridge's east sidewalk daily during daylight hours. **Cost:** Toll fee for cars $6 (southbound from Marin County to San Francisco); northbound free. Bicyclists and pedestrians free.

GOLDEN GATE NATIONAL RECREATION AREA—see place listing p. 137.

GOLDEN GATE PARK is bordered by the Great Hwy. on the w., Lincoln Way on the s., Stanyan St. on the e. and Fulton St. on the n., extending 3 mi. from Fell and Stanyan sts. to the ocean. You can thank Scottish landscape gardener John McLaren for one of San Francisco's great treasures. A park superintendent for 60 years, he was largely responsible for transforming a windswept site consisting mostly of sand dunes and scrub oaks—a tract of land once beyond the city's western outskirts—into a verdant oasis of trees and plants speckled with man-made lakes.

Golden Gate Park is a wonderfully serene haven in the middle of a bustling city, a place to relax, stroll and forget life's cares (if only for an hour). Miles of roads and walking paths wind through this almost perfectly rectangular, 1,017-acre green space.

Gardens are chief among the park's many attractions. Seasonal blooms enhance the Rose Garden, between John F. Kennedy and Park Presidio drives; the Dahlia Dell, next to the Conservatory of Flowers;

and the tulip gardens surrounding the Dutch Windmill in the park's northwest corner. The windmill (one of two in the park) once was part of an irrigation system, but today its function is purely scenic.

The Music Concourse, between the de Young Museum and The California Academy of Sciences, is a place to relax on a bench amid burbling fountains or enjoy Sunday band concerts. The children's playground at Bowling Green, in the southeast corner of the park, features a lovingly restored Herschel Spillman carousel. At the corner of Bowling Green Drive and Middle Drive East is the National AIDS Memorial Grove, a quiet, contemplative retreat planted with redwoods. Stowe Lake—actually a moat—encircles Strawberry Hill. Its summit is the park's highest point; climb to the breezy, tree-crowned top for views of the surrounding neighborhoods, and relax for a few minutes using a fallen log as a perch.

Numerous recreational facilities include archery, baseball, soccer and polo fields, basketball, tennis and handball courts, a nine-hole golf course, fly-casting pools, horseshoe pits and a boathouse at Stowe Lake. The park visitor center, in the Beach Chalet on Great Highway, has Works Progress Administration (WPA) murals depicting scenes of the city during the Great Depression. You can also get a bite to eat or sip a micro-brewed beer while watching Pacific breakers crash against the shore.

Hours: Park open to visitors on foot daily 5 a.m.-midnight. Visitor center open daily 9-6. John F. Kennedy Dr. between Stanyan St. and Park Presidio Dr. is closed to vehicle traffic Sun. Band concerts are given Sun. 1-3, mid-Apr. to mid-Oct. **Cost:** Park free. **Phone:** (415) 831-2700 for general information, (415) 750-5442 for walking tour information, or (415) 751-2766 for the visitor center.
Judah & 9th Ave, 55

The California Academy of Sciences is in Golden Gate Park at 55 Music Concourse Dr. The completely refurbished Academy is leading the way in the concept of sustainable architecture. Not only does the wall insulation make use of recycled blue jeans, but the building's "living roof" is just that: a 2.5-acre carpet of native plants (four species of perennials and five species of wildflowers). Seven green hillocks give the roof its distinctive undulating profile, which visitors can view up close from the rooftop observation deck.

Inside are former Academy mainstays the Morrison Planetarium, the Steinhart Aquarium and the Kimball Natural History Museum, now gathered together in one facility. The aquarium's twin highlights are the Philippine Coral Reef, a 212,000-gallon tank populated with a spectacular assemblage of tropical fish that gleam like multicolored jewels, and the 100,000-gallon Northern California Coast tank, inhabited by such indigenous marine life as sea anemones, sardines, rockfish and grouper.

The all-digital Morrison Planetarium incorporates state-of-the-art projector and software technologies to present programs onto a 75-foot screen tilted at a 30-degree angle, seemingly immersing the viewer in space. Traditional star shows are augmented by special programming such as live NASA feeds.

At Rainforests of the World, a four-story domed enclosure, visitors follow a spiraling path upward through an exhibit lush with orchids, bromeliads and mahogany trees and filled with free-flying birds and butterflies, reptiles and amphibians.

Tours: Guided tours are available. **Time:** Allow 4 hours minimum. **Hours:** Mon.-Sat. 9:30-5, Sun. 11-5. Last admission 1 hour before closing. The schedule for the planetarium varies; phone ahead. The planetarium show is not recommended for children under 7. Closed Thanksgiving and Christmas. Phone ahead to confirm schedule. **Cost:** $29.95; $24.95 (ages 12-17, ages 65+ and students with ID); $19.95 (ages 4-11). Phone ahead to confirm rates. **Phone:** (415) 379-8000.
(See ad p. 362.) Judah & 9th Ave, 55

Conservatory of Flowers is at 100 John F. Kennedy Dr. at the eastern end of Golden Gate Park. This Victorian-style white building, capped with an ornate dome, encapsulates the original intent of a plant conservatory: to transplant a bit of wonder and beauty from faraway jungles to a climate-controlled environment for the enjoyment of the masses.

The Lowland Tropics room, which sits beneath the conservatory's upper dome, contains a tangled assortment of exotic plants and trees, while the damp, humid environment in the Aquatic Plants room nurtures pitcher plants, bromeliads and Amazon water lilies. The name is actually a misnomer, since there aren't that many flowers aside from the lovely orchids in the Highland Tropics room. This is, however, the perfect place to try out your new high-tech camera. Special plant exhibits also are presented.

Time: Allow 30 minutes minimum. **Hours:** Tues.-Sun. 10-4:30. Last admission 30 minutes before closing. **Cost:** $7; $5 (ages 12-17, ages 65+ and college students with ID); $2 (ages 5-11); free (first Tues. of the month). **Phone:** (415) 831-2090.
UCSF Parnassus, 54

de Young Museum is in Golden Gate Park at 50 Hagiwara Tea Garden Dr. at jct. John F. Kennedy Dr., following signs. The museum has an outstanding collection of art from the Americas, Africa, New Guinea and Oceania. Art in America to the 20th Century, on the upper level, displays paintings, sculpture, furniture and decorative arts in spacious, high-ceilinged galleries. Among the masterpieces here are Albert Bierstadt's "California Spring," which portrays a peacefully bucolic scene of cows grazing in a field contrasted with the fury of an approaching thunderstorm, and George Caleb Bingham's idyllic "Boatmen on the Missouri."

The Art of New Guinea features beautifully displayed shields, ceremonial masks and carved wooden figures. Also among the de Young's more than 2,000 works are displays of 20th-century and contemporary art; Native American, Central American and South American art; Maori sculptures; textiles and costumes; photography; and murals. Major special exhibitions are presented regularly.

A highlight is the indoor observation deck at the top of the Hamon Tower. The floor-to-ceiling glass walls from this ninth-floor perspective offer great views, including a peek at San Francisco Bay and the Golden Gate Bridge. You can access the tower without paying the museum admission by following signs from the main entrance on the concourse level. Docent-led tours generally meet in Wilsey Court on the concourse level; rentals for self-paced audio tours are available near the main entrance.

Hours: Tues.-Sun. 9:30-5:15 (also Fri. 5:15-8:45, Mar.-Nov.). Last admission 1 hour before closing. Tower closes 45 minutes before museum. Closed Thanksgiving and Christmas. **Cost:** $10; $7 (ages 65+); $6 (ages 13-17 and college students with ID); free (first Tues. of the month, except during special exhibitions). An additional fee may be charged for special exhibitions. **Parking:** $3.50 per hour (Mon.-Fri.), $4 per hour (Sat.-Sun.) in the Music Concourse Garage. **Phone:** (415) 750-3600.
(See ad p. 362.) 🚇 Judah & 9th Ave, 55

Japanese Tea Garden, 8th Ave. and John F. Kennedy Dr. in Golden Gate Park, was originally built as a Japanese village for the 1894 California Midwinter International Exposition. Japanese immigrant Makoto Hagiwara designed the bulk of this elegantly landscaped 3.8-acre site and was its official caretaker for a number of years.

Mosaic Stairway, Grandview Park

The shaded stone walkways and footbridges are meant to be strolled at a leisurely pace. Among the sculpted trees and hedges are many plants native to Japan and China. Ponds, miniature waterfalls, a big bronze Buddha, stone lanterns, statuary and a couple of pagodas all contribute to the beauty of this tranquil little spot. Spring, when the cherry trees bloom, is a spectacular time to visit. Green teas and Japanese confections are served in the garden's tea house.

Hours: Daily 9-6, Mar.-Oct.; 9-4:45, rest of year. **Cost:** $7; $5 (ages 12-17 and 65+); $2 (ages 5-11); free (Mon., Wed. and Fri. if entering before 10 a.m.). **Phone:** (415) 752-1171.
🚇 Judah & 9th Ave, 55

San Francisco Botanical Garden at Strybing Arboretum, 9th Ave. and Lincoln Way in Golden Gate Park, has more than 7,000 varieties of plants from around the world. Within its 55 acres are a cloud forest, a fragrance garden, a redwood grove, a primitive plant garden and a Japanese moonviewing garden. A highlight is the garden's collection of plants native to California.

Hours: Daily 9-6, Apr.-Oct.; 10-5, rest of year. Last admission 1 hour before closing. Free guided 45-minute tours are given Mon.-Fri. at 1:30 (also Wed. and Fri. at 2), Sat.-Sun. at 10:30 and 1:30 (also Sun. at 2). **Cost:** $7; $5 (ages 12-17 and college students with ID); $2 (ages 5-11); $15 family (two adults and one or more children); free (San Francisco city and county residents with ID and to all Jan. 1, Thanksgiving, Christmas and second Tues. of the month). **Phone:** (415) 661-1316. 🚇 Judah & 9th Ave, 55

GRACE CATHEDRAL is atop Nob Hill at 1100 California St. at jct. Taylor St. The wealthy Crocker family offered property for a cathedral after the family's two homes on the site were destroyed by fire following the 1906 earthquake. Nearby Grace Church, located where The Ritz-Carlton, San Francisco stands today, was devastated the same day.

The French Gothic-style Episcopal cathedral, completed in 1964, has replicas of the bronze doors of the Baptistery in Florence, Italy ("The Gates of Paradise") by Lorenzo Ghiberti, "The Life of Christ" triptych altarpiece by Keith Haring, two labyrinths, stained glass, and medieval and contemporary furnishings. **Hours:** Mon.-Fri. 7-6, Sat. 8-6, Sun. 8-7. Guided tours are given Mon.-Fri. 1-3, Sat. 11:30-1:30, Sun. 12:30-2. **Cost:** Donations. **Phone:** (415) 749-6300. 🚇 Powell Street, 33

GRANDVIEW PARK is surrounded by Noriega St. and 14th and 15th aves. What this aptly named park lacks in size it more than makes up for in the spectacular 360-degree views that encompass downtown, Golden Gate Park, the Golden Gate Bridge, San Francisco Bay, the Marin Headlands and the Pacific. This hilltop in the Sunset neighborhood, crowned with several Monterey cypresses and one graceful eucalyptus tree, is not only one of the most delightfully secluded spots in San Francisco, but—to those in the know—also an unsurpassed vantage point for sunset watching.

Longtime residents call the 665-foot-tall outcrop of Franciscan chert rock Turtle Hill. Not all that many years ago the Sunset was nothing but shifting sand dunes, but residential development cut off the supply of ocean sand, and as a result the underlying rock is becoming more and more exposed. Native dune plants like beach strawberry, bush monkey flower and the endangered Franciscan wallflower and dune tansy grow on the hill; all must contend with a harsh, windswept environment and ground that retains little moisture.

Note: Reaching the summit involves climbing one of two steep sets of stairs that ascend the hill from 14th and 15th avenues. A wood fence surrounds the summit, part of an ongoing restoration program to help protect the fragile plant community; stay on marked paths to help minimize the effects of erosion. **Hours:** Daily 24 hours. **Cost:** Free. **Phone:** (415) 831-2700. 🚇 Judah & 19th Ave, 56

Mosaic Stairway begins at 16th Ave. and Moraga St., on the w. side of Grandview Park. This striking staircase is the most dramatic way to reach the top of the park's hill. You can't miss it—163 steps ascending straight as an arrow up to 15th Street, every step riser adorned with a mosaic panel featuring whimsical birds, fish, flowers and marine creatures. More than 300 residents in the surrounding Golden Gate Heights neighborhood helped create the panels. The stairway is further beautified by beds of succulents and other plants.
🚇 Judah & 19th Ave, 56

HAAS-LILIENTHAL HOUSE is at 2007 Franklin St., between Washington and Jackson in the Pacific Heights neighborhood. The Queen Anne Victorian, accented by a circular corner tower and wooden gables, was built in 1886 for William Haas, a prosperous merchant. Docents point out various furnishings and architectural features and explain how they reflect the lifestyle of a typical upper-middle-class family of the period. A collection of photographs depicts family members who lived in the home up to 1972.

Time: Allow 1 hour minimum. **Hours:** Guided tours are given Wed. and Sat. noon-3, Sun. 11-4. Phone ahead to confirm Sat. tours. Closed Jan. 1 and Christmas. **Cost:** $8; $5 (ages 5-12 and 60+). **Phone:** (415) 441-3000.

JAPAN CENTER (Nihonmachi), is bounded by Post, Geary, Laguna and Fillmore sts.; underground parking is available. The 5-acre complex has diverse cultural and commercial points of interest. The Peace Pagoda, a gift of the Japanese people, stands in the central plaza. Music, dance, tea ceremonies and martial arts presentations are given many weekends in summer. The area has restaurants, art galleries, movie theaters, gardens, Japanese baths and shops (see Specialty Districts in the Shopping section p. 353). 🚇 Van Ness, 50

JAPANESE TEA GARDEN—see Golden Gate Park p. 376.

THE JEREMIAH O'BRIEN is berthed at Pier 45 at Fisherman's Wharf. This restored World War II Liberty ship is one of only two in operating condition out of 2,710 built during that war.

During "steaming" weekends, usually the third weekend of the month, the ship's engine is in operation. Special cruises take place seasonally.

Tours: Guided tours are available. **Time:** Allow 1 hour minimum. **Hours:** Daily 9-6, mid-July through Sept. 30; 9-4, rest of year. Tours are not available when the ship is cruising on selected days in May, July-Aug. and Oct. Closed Thanksgiving and Christmas. Phone ahead to confirm schedule. **Cost:** $12; $8 (ages 62+ and students with ID); $6 (ages 6-12); $25 (family, two adults and two children); free (active military with ID). **Phone:** (415) 544-0100.

KIMBALL NATURAL HISTORY MUSEUM—see The California Academy of Sciences p. 375.

LANDS END is accessible from Point Lobos Ave. and Merrie Way. This little patch of wilderness at the outer western edge of urban San Francisco, overlooking the Pacific Ocean, is part of Golden Gate National Recreation Area (see place listing p. 137). It's a great place for a quiet, relaxing hike, taking in a plethora of scenic views and otherwise escaping the city's bustle for an afternoon.

The California Coastal Trail runs the length of Lands End. To the east the hard-packed dirt trail is narrow and winds through a forest of tall conifers before ending at El Camino del Mar, at the eastern end of Lincoln Park. To the west it's wider and runs along the edge of tall cliffs. From this vantage point there are stunning views of the Golden Gate Bridge, the Marin Headlands and offshore rocks (this is the geographic point where bay and ocean merge). From the trail you can access the Sutro Baths (about a 20-minute walk from the Legion of Honor parking lot to the signed turnoff).

Just before Point Lobos, on the way to the Sutro Baths, stands a memorial to the men who died on the USS San Francisco during the Battle of Guadalcanal on Nov. 12-13, 1942. The memorial is a piece of the ship's bridge.

Note: There are free parking lots off Point Lobos Avenue in Sutro Heights Park. The #1 and #38 Muni bus lines make a stop a block away from the entrance to Lincoln Park at 34th Avenue and Clement Street. From here walk up Legion of Honor Drive to the Legion of Honor parking lot, then follow the walking path that skirts the Lincoln Park Municipal Golf Course and runs into the coastal trail. **Cost:** Free. **Phone:** (415) 561-3000.

Lombard Street

Cliff House is at 1090 Point Lobos Ave. (at Great Hwy.). The first Cliff House opened in 1863, a modest building frequented by such prominent San Francisco families as the Hearsts and the Stanfords, who would arrive at Ocean Beach in horse-drawn carriages. Destroyed by a chimney fire in 1894, it reopened 2 years later as an elegant destination for dining, dancing and entertainment—only to burn to the ground again in 1907.

The third and present Cliff House opened in 1909. Renovations restored the original neoclassic architecture, and the recent addition of the Sutro Wing added a two-story dining room with a stunning view of the ocean. More than 200 autographed photos of various dignitaries and movie stars offer a glimpse back at the landmark's nearly 150-year history.

The building overlooks Seal Rocks; the guano-covered formations just offshore are the site of occasional sea lion sightings from May through October. The sidewalk approach along Great Highway and a walkway around the property are good vantage points to take in the coastline views. Window tables are popular at The Bistro, a casual walk-in restaurant; reservations are strongly recommended at the more upscale Sutro's at the Cliff House.

The Camera Obscura, on a lower terrace behind the Cliff House, was built in 1946. It produces 360-degree live images of the area around Seal Rocks through a series of mirrors and sunlight reflecting off a concave disk.

Hours: Lower observation deck open daily 24 hours. Camera Obscura daily 11-5 (weather permitting). **Cost:** Cliff House free. Camera Obscura $3; $2 (ages 2-12 and 65+). **Phone:** (415) 386-3330 for the Cliff House, or (415) 750-0415 for the Camera Obscura. 🍴

Lands End Lookout Visitor Center is at Merrie Way and Point Lobos Ave., just e. of the Cliff House. The new visitor center, part of an ongoing project to restore the habitat at Lands End and improve visitor amenities, has exhibits about the history and natural features of San Francisco's northwestern corner as well as information about Golden Gate National Recreation Area. This small building also incorporates a number of "green" features. **Hours:** Daily 9-5. **Cost:** Free. **Phone:** (415) 561-4323. 🍴

Sutro Baths are off Point Lobos Ave. in Sutro Heights Park. Tucked away in the city's far northwestern corner, these ruins have a fascinating history. A lavish playground developed by wealthy former mayor Adolph Sutro opened to the public in 1896. Standing literally at the ocean's edge, it boasted seven swimming pools (six saltwater and one freshwater), more than 500 private dressing rooms, an amphitheater, grand staircases and landscaped promenades, all looking out over the Pacific.

The extravagant structure was prohibitively expensive to operate, which led to its eventual closing. Fire destroyed the Sutro Baths in 1966 as it was in the process of being demolished. Nothing remains but a destroyed foundation, rusted pipes jutting out from vestiges of walls and long-abandoned stairways—and every inch of it can be explored. One interesting feature is a short tunnel that ends at a cavelike opening with a view of waves crashing against the rocks.

Among the tangle of vegetation carpeting the hillside above the ruins is the bright green, fleshy-leaved ice plant, a low-growing succulent that blankets the sand dunes at many northern California beaches. Ice plants produce pretty pink and yellow flowers at various times of the year. Adding to the scenic quotient are sweeping views of the ocean and the Marin Headlands. Stairways and paved walking paths lead down to the baths from Point Lobos Avenue and the Coastal Trail.

Note: There are no guards on duty, and no guardrails or other protective aids; poke around at your leisure but also at your own risk. Watch for slippery spots near the water, and heed all warning signs. **Hours:** Site accessible daily during daylight hours. **Cost:** Free.

LEVI STRAUSS & CO. is just off The Embarcadero at 1155 Battery St. Levi Strauss began his dry goods business in San Francisco in 1853. In the lobby a wall of photographs depicts the company's history, and there are displays of vintage jeans and jackets. You can get your Dockers straight from the source at a boutique. Benches dot the grounds of the campus-like corporate headquarters and burbling fountains help drown out the sound of Embarcadero traffic, making this a favored spot for brown-bag lunches or a place to relax for a few minutes. **Time:**

Allow 30 minutes minimum. **Hours:** Mon.-Fri. 9-6, Sat. noon-5. Closed major holidays. **Cost:** Free. **Phone:** (415) 501-6000. 📺 Embarcadero, 31

LINCOLN PARK, at 34th Ave. and Clement St., contains American artist George Segal's memorial to the victims of the World War II Holocaust. The park is an attractive starting point for hikes along El Camino del Mar and the Coastal Trail; both trails run the length of Lands End. **Cost:** Free.

▰▰ **Legion of Honor** is in Lincoln Park near 34th Ave. and Clement St., in a hilltop location with views of the Golden Gate Bridge and the ocean. This world-class art museum owes its existence to Alma Spreckels, wife of 20th-century sugar magnate Adolph B. Spreckels.

Mrs. Spreckels, an avid art collector, became enamored with France's neoclassical pavilion at the Panama-Pacific International Exposition held in San Francisco in 1915. The pavilion was a replica of the 18th-century Palais de la Légion d'Honneur in Paris, France. She convinced her husband to construct a permanent version of the pavilion to be used as a fine arts museum to honor California soldiers who died in France during World War I. The three-quarter-scale replica opened on Armistice Day in 1924.

The permanent collection spans more than 4,000 years of ancient and European art and include the Achenbach Foundation for Graphic Arts. Mrs. Spreckels' sculptures by Auguste Rodin were among the museum's earliest treasures. An original cast of "The Thinker," one of the museum's more than 70 Rodin sculptures, is a highlight of the outdoor Court of Honor. Other major gifts from Mrs. Spreckels include masterpieces of French furniture, ceramics, silver and antiquities.

Items of ancient art include relics from the Mediterranean and the Near East, and an extensive collection of European art features works by Fra Angelico, El Greco, Claude Monet, Pablo Picasso, Rembrandt and Pierre Auguste Renoir. Tapestries, porcelains, a group of illustrated books and an extensive collection of prints, drawings and photographs are other major components of the museum.

Time: Allow 2 hours minimum. **Hours:** Tues.-Sun. 9:30-5:15. Closed major holidays. **Cost:** $10; $7 (ages 65+); $6 (ages 13-17 and college students with ID); free (first Tues. of the month). An additional fee is charged for some special exhibitions. **Phone:** (415) 750-3600, (415) 750-7645 for sign language tour requests or TTY (415) 750-3509. *(See ad p. 362.)* 🎟

LOMBARD STREET, between Hyde and Leavenworth sts., is often referred to as "the crookedest street in the world." This brick-paved, one-block stretch of Lombard descends a 40-degree slope from Hyde to Leavenworth in a series of eight tight S-curves. The crookedest claim really should belong to an even more winding stretch of Vermont Street on Potrero Hill, but Lombard is decidedly more

scenic. Handsome homes and condos stand on either side, blooming bougainvillea covers walls and the block is landscaped with sculpted hedges and a profusion of pink and blue hydrangeas.

If you'd rather walk than take the one-way, 5-mile-per-hour drive down the curvy switchbacks, there are stairways on each side of the street. While Lombard attracts a constant stream of shutterbugs, it's actually difficult to get a photo that clearly shows the series of S-curves due to the steep grade. Campers, trailers and skateboarders are prohibited on this block.

▰▰ **MISSION SAN FRANCISCO DE ASIS** (Misión San Francisco de Asís, or Mission Dolores) is at 3321 16th St. at Dolores St.; street parking is limited. The oldest standing structure in San Francisco, the mission was founded by Father Francisco Palou under the direction of Father Junípero Serra on June 29, 1776, and dedicated on Oct. 9.

Daily mass still takes place in this venerable building, which has adobe walls 4 feet thick and retains the original redwood logs, still lashed together with rawhide, that support the roof. The *reredos* (altar screen), one of the most ornate examples of Baroque art among the California missions, was brought from San Blas, Mexico in 1797. The two side altars also came from Mexico in 1810 and feature wood columns that imitate marble.

While the mission withstood the 1906 earthquake, the adjacent brick parish church did not. The present concrete building was completed in 1918 and offers a striking contrast to the mission's simple appearance. The 1918 church was declared a basilica in 1952 by Pope Pius XII. It has an extravagantly decorative interior and beautiful stained-glass windows depicting St. Francis of Assisi, the mission's patron saint. A one-room museum displays religious artifacts and has exhibits about daily life at the mission, Father Serra and the Ohlone Indians who built the mission church.

More than 11,000 burials took place in the mission cemetery between 1782 and 1898; most of the markers designate individuals who died in the decades following the California gold rush, when San Francisco was a rapidly growing settlement that experienced a great deal of illness and many early deaths. A wooden grave marker acknowledges two Indians who were baptized, married and buried at the mission. The tall statue in the center of the garden is a likeness of Father Serra. Kim Novak and Jimmy Stewart walked through the cemetery in a scene from Alfred Hitchcock's "Vertigo." Cool, leafy and quiet, it's a lovely spot for quiet reflection.

Two blocks south of Mission Dolores at 18th Street (between Church and Dolores streets) is Dolores Park, a large swath of green that offers tennis courts, a basketball court, a children's playground, a dog play area and other recreational facilities. The park has been a neighborhood center for political rallies, Cinco de Mayo celebrations and all manner of festivals since the 1960s. On clear days there's an exceptional view of downtown San Francisco from the park's southwest corner at 20th and Church streets.

Hours: Daily 9-4:30, May-Oct.; 9-4, rest of year. Closed Jan. 1, Thanksgiving and Christmas. **Cost:** $5; $4 (ages 65+); $3 (students with ID). **Phone:** (415) 621-8203, ext. 15. 🚇 Church & 18th St, 85

MORRISON PLANETARIUM—see The California Academy of Sciences p. 375.

MUSÉE MÉCANIQUE is at Pier 45 at Fisherman's Wharf at the end of Taylor St. This "mechanical museum" is a treasure-trove of working antique mechanical games—bring plenty of quarters. The collection includes more than 200 coin-operated musical instruments and arcade machines such as player pianos, a boxing match, a 1930s Laffing Sal, pinball machines, an arm wrestling game and gypsy fortune tellers.

Time: Allow 30 minutes minimum. **Hours:** Mon.-Fri. 10-7, Sat.-Sun. and holidays 10-8. Phone ahead to confirm schedule. **Cost:** Free. **Phone:** (415) 346-2000.

MUSEUM OF THE AFRICAN DIASPORA, adjacent to Yerba Buena Gardens at 685 Mission St., is dedicated to the art, culture, history and literature that have come from people of African descent as they migrated to other nations. **Time:** Allow 1 hour, 30 minutes minimum. **Hours:** Wed.-Sat. 11-6, Sun. noon-5. Closed major holidays. **Cost:** $10; $5 (ages 65+ and students with ID); free (ages 0-12). **Phone:** (415) 358-7200. 🚇 Montgomery Street, 32

Try Molinari's house-cured salami

MUSEUM OF CRAFT AND FOLK ART is at 51 Yerba Buena Ln., across from Yerba Buena Gardens at Mission St. in a pedestrian walkway between 3rd and 4th sts. The museum features changing exhibits of crafts and folk art, both traditional and contemporary, created by master folk artists from around the world. **Time:** Allow 1 hour minimum. **Hours:** Wed.-Sat. 11-6. Closed major holidays. **Cost:** $5; $4 (age 62+); free (ages 0-17). **Phone:** (415) 227-4888. 🚇 Powell Street, 33

MUSEUM OF PERFORMANCE & DESIGN is in the Veterans Building at 401 Van Ness Ave., Suite 402, next to the San Francisco Opera House. Dedicated to the performing arts and theatrical design, the Main Gallery presents exhibitions such as The Extra Ordinary Life of Performance Objects: From the Stage to Our Stacks, which showcases rarely exhibited objects from the museum's collection. **Note:** The museum was scheduled to close Dec. 16, 2012, in preparation for a relocation. Phone ahead for updated information regarding the reopening. **Hours:** Mon.-Fri. 10-5. **Cost:** Donations. **Phone:** (415) 255-4800. 🚇 Van Ness, 50

NOB HILL, in the vicinity of California, Sacramento, Jones and Taylor sts., was the center of luxurious living in the last half of the 19th century, when men who had made fortunes in railroading and gold mining had built their mansions atop this windswept crag. Almost all of them were destroyed in the fire that resulted from the 1906 earthquake, but this elevated location has always signified prestige, and today Nob Hill bristles with elegant apartment buildings and swanky hotels.

Visitors who don't want to make the arduous trek on foot up Jones or Taylor streets can take advantage of the Powell/Mason or California Street cable car lines, a less physically demanding and more enjoyable way to see the sights. Grace Cathedral (see attraction listing p. 376) is a Nob Hill landmark. Another intriguing institution is Masonic Auditorium, 1111 California St. In addition to being one of the city's notable venues for live jazz, it features stained-glass windows that depict symbols associated with the Freemasons, a long-standing fraternal organization whose membership once included George Washington, Benjamin Franklin and Henry Ford. 🚇 Powell Street, 33

NORTH BEACH spreads w. and s. from Telegraph Hill to Columbus Ave. Located in one of the hilliest sections of a hilly city (stairways rather than sidewalks line some of the steeper streets), North Beach is compact, crowded and vibrant. The neighborhood's nickname, "Little Italy," is well earned; the delis, bakeries, cafes and restaurants lining Columbus Avenue and its side streets create an atmosphere that's more than a little reminiscent of Rome or Naples.

Here you've got history at the City Lights Bookstore on Columbus Avenue, founded by San Francisco poet laureate Lawrence Ferlinghetti and once a hangout for Beat Generation poets and literary figures like Jack Kerouac. Check out the murals and wall quotations from the author of "On the Road" on tiny Jack Kerouac Alley, between Grant and Columbus avenues. You've also got seedy appeal in a smattering of strip joints that include the Condor Club, where topless go-go dancer Carol Doda gyrated her way to 15 minutes of fame in the swinging '60s.

And of course you've got food. Just walking around North Beach tends to make most people start salivating. Molinari (373 Columbus Ave.) is a deli and market chock-full of specialty items like dried pastas, marinated artichokes and robust, house-cured salamis hanging above the counter. The Liguria Bakery (1700 Stockton St.) turns out freshly baked focaccia bread—rosemary, raisin and pizza are fave flavors—and invariably sells out before noon (get there early).

Tosca Cafe (242 Columbus Ave.) has red vinyl booths, worn linoleum floors and a classic dark wood bar. It's a great spot to sip an Irish coffee or hot chocolate laced with brandy while listening to big-band jazz or Italian opera on the vintage jukebox. Another North beach hangout is Vesuvio, across the alley from City Lights. It's a classic bar in every sense, from the ambience (all kinds of cool stuff on the walls) to the wide drink selection and the jovial crowd of regulars.

Washington Square, at Columbus Avenue and Union Street, is a tree-shaded patch of lawn sprinkled with park benches and frequented by pigeons, dog walkers, scrambling kids and early morning practitioners of tai chi.

OLD ST. MARY'S CATHEDRAL is in Chinatown at Grant Ave. and California St. The 1854 church's interior was patterned after the Spanish church of California's first bishop, Joseph Sadoc Alemany. **Hours:** Mon.-Fri. 7:30-4:30, Sat. 10:30-6, Sun. 8-3:30. **Cost:** Donations. **Phone:** (415) 288-3800. 🚇 Montgomery Street, 32

PACIFIC HERITAGE MUSEUM, 608 Commercial St., displays changing exhibits chronicling the history and culture of peoples from both sides of the Pacific Basin. Housed in the restored U.S. Subtreasury Building, the museum features an exhibit depicting the building's history. **Time:** Allow 30 minutes minimum. **Hours:** Thurs.-Sat. 10-4. Closed major holidays. **Cost:** Free. **Phone:** (415) 399-1124. 🚇 Embarcadero, 31

PALACE OF FINE ARTS is at Palace Dr. and Lyon St., at the w. end of the Marina District. It is the last remaining structure associated with the 1915 Panama-Pacific Exposition, and the only one located at its original site. The design of this classically elegant building took its inspiration from ancient Greek and Roman architecture. After the exposition ended the palace functioned as a World War II storage facility for trucks and jeeps, a city Parks Department warehouse and a temporary fire department headquarters. The crumbling structure was demolished in 1964 and reconstructed right down to the original sculptures, ornamental urns, friezes and carved decorations that collectively symbolize Greek culture.

Built around an artificial lagoon, the palace complex is made up of a domed, colonnaded pergola flanked by rows of Corinthian columns. Walkways wind beneath the dome and around the lagoon, which not only provides a mirrored surface to reflect the grand architecture but offers a home for ducks, swans and migrating waterfowl. Although the Exploratorium *(see attraction listing)* is relocating to Pier 15 in the spring of 2013, the palace still houses a 962-seat theater. **Time:** Allow 30 minutes minimum. **Hours:** Daily dawn-dusk. **Cost:** Free. **Phone:** (415) 567-6642 for theater events and information.

PIER 39—see Shopping p. 354.

PRESIDIO OF SAN FRANCISCO—see Golden Gate National Recreation Area p. 138.

RANDALL MUSEUM, off Roosevelt Way at 199 Museum Way, has exhibits about animals, arts and crafts, and science. The Golden Gate Model Railroad Club provides a train exhibit. **Hours:** Museum open Tues.-Sat. 10-5. Train exhibit Sat. 10-4. Closed major holidays. **Cost:** Donations. **Phone:** (415) 554-9600. 🚇 Castro, 61

RIPLEY'S BELIEVE IT OR NOT! ODDITORIUM is at 175 Jefferson St. at Fisherman's Wharf. Like other Ripley's museums, it displays bizarre, oddball and unusual artifacts from around the world that will appeal to just about everyone, including a couple of gross-out exhibits for kids and some historically interesting ones for adults. Among the interactive elements are a shooting gallery, a "mystery gate" and a human-sized kaleidoscope. The Mirror Maze is summed up by its name. **Hours:** Sun.-Thurs. 9 a.m.-11 p.m., Fri.-Sat. 9 a.m.-midnight, mid-June through Labor Day; Sun.-Thurs. 10-10, Fri.-Sat. 10 a.m.-midnight, rest of year. **Cost:** Museum $19.99; $15.99 (ages 65+); $9.99 (ages 5-12). Mirror Maze $9.99 without museum admission. Combination ticket with Mirror Maze $23.99; $15.99 (ages 5-12). **Phone:** (415) 202-9850.

ST. GREGORY OF NYSSA CHURCH is at 500 De Haro St. on Potrero Hill. In addition to an interesting wood exterior, the rotunda wall of this Episcopal church is encircled by a beautiful iconographic mural of 100 larger-than-life saints both secular and nonsecular, chosen by the congregation and depicted in dancing poses that reflect various facets of worship.

Representing many eras, cultures and faith traditions, they include such luminaries as King David, Thomas Aquinas, Emily Dickinson, Mohandas Gandhi, Pope John Paul XXIII and John Coltrane, along with bishop, theologian and church patron Gregory of Nyssa. **Hours:** Sun. morning services at 8:30 and 10:45, weekday services at 8 a.m. The public is welcome to visit Mon.-Fri. 8-4; phone

"Making a Fresco," Diego Rivera, San Francisco Art Institute

ahead for an appointment. **Cost:** Donations. **Phone:** (415) 255-8100 (church office). 🅿 Mariposa, 96

SAN FRANCISCO ART INSTITUTE is at 800 Chestnut St. between Leavenworth and Jones sts. Founded in 1871, SFAI is said to be the city's oldest fine arts institution. The small campus features a traditional Spanish courtyard and a bell tower. There are panoramic views of San Francisco Bay and North Beach from its elevated location on Russian Hill.

The institute promotes an environment that nurtures advanced and experimental forms of contemporary art. The Diego Rivera Gallery houses a Rivera fresco, and student works are displayed on the courtyard walls. The Walter and McBean galleries showcase global contemporary art. Rotating art exhibits, lectures and film showings are presented; phone for information. **Hours:** Campus daily 8 a.m.-10 p.m. Diego Rivera Gallery open daily 9-5. Walter and McBean galleries open Tues.-Sat. 11-6. **Cost:** Free. **Phone:** (415) 771-7020. 🍴

SAN FRANCISCO BOTANICAL GARDEN AT STRYBING ARBORETUM—see Golden Gate Park p. 376.

SAN FRANCISCO MARITIME NATIONAL HISTORICAL PARK is at the w. end of Fisherman's Wharf. In addition to a fleet of historic ships, a maritime museum and a library, the site also includes the bayside Aquatic Park's beach and cove.

The visitor center, in a restored 1907 warehouse, has interactive displays that relate the city's maritime history. Highlights include a first-order Fresnel lighthouse lens and an exhibit that allows visitors to walk through time along San Francisco's historic waterfront. **Hours:** Visitor center daily 9:30-5:30. Closed Jan. 1, Thanksgiving and Christmas. **Cost:** Visitor center free. **Phone:** (415) 447-5000.

Aquatic Park Bathhouse Building/Maritime Museum is at 900 Beach St. Built in 1939, its Art Deco-inspired exterior mimics an ocean liner. Displayed in the lobby are fanciful and colorful murals, several miniature model ships encased in glass and a large chunk of the vessel *Niantic*; the veranda also is open to the public. Changing exhibits are presented as well. **Hours:** Daily 10-4. Closed Jan. 1, Thanksgiving and Christmas. **Cost:** Free. **Phone:** (415) 447-5000.

Hyde Street Pier Historic Ships, at the foot of Hyde St., displays ships dating from the late 19th century. Visitors can board four ships: the *Balclutha*, a three-masted square-rigged sailing vessel containing ship relics and photographs; the *C.A. Thayer*, a coastal lumber schooner; the *Eureka*, the largest ferry operating on San Francisco Bay in its time; and the *Hercules*, a steam-powered tugboat. The scow schooner *Alma*, which offers sailing tours in summer, and the tugboat *Eppleton Hall* are anchored nearby. Programs and demonstrations are offered.

Hours: Daily 9:30-5:30. Last admission 30 minutes before closing. Closed Jan. 1, Thanksgiving and Christmas. **Cost:** $5; free (ages 0-15). **Phone:** (415) 447-5000.

San Francisco Maritime Library, at Fort Mason, Building E, houses more than 250,000 historic photographs, documents and maritime literature. **Hours:** Tues.-Thurs. 1-5; Mon., Fri. and third Sat. of the month by appointment. **Cost:** Free. **Phone:** (415) 561-7030.

SAN FRANCISCO MUSEUM OF MODERN ART (SFMOMA) is at 151 Third St. (between Mission and Howard sts.). It is housed in a modernistic, five-story brick, granite and glass building designed by Swiss architect Mario Botta. Spacious galleries illuminated by skylights exhibit a comprehensive collection of modern and contemporary art, including paintings and sculpture, architecture and design, media arts and photography. Rotating exhibitions are featured. Works also are displayed in the rooftop sculpture garden. Guided 45-minute tours are offered.

Note: SFMOMA is scheduled to close in June 2013 for a major expansion and renovation project that is slated for completion in early 2016. While the new building is being constructed the museum plans to present major exhibitions from its collection to partner museums. **Time:** Allow 2 hours minimum. **Hours:** Thurs.-Tues. 10-5:45 (also Thurs. 5:45-8:45), Memorial Day-Labor Day; Thurs.-Tues. 11-5:45 (also Thurs. 5:45-8:45), rest of year. Closed Jan. 1, Thanksgiving and Christmas. **Cost:** $18; $13 (ages 62+); $11 (students with ID); free (ages 0-12, military with ID and first Tues. of the month). Admission half-price Thurs. 6-8:45 p.m. Under 13 must be with an adult. An additional fee may be charged for special exhibitions. **Phone:** (415) 357-4000, (415) 357-4197 for guided tours or TTY (415) 357-4154 🚇 Montgomery Street, 32

SAN FRANCISCO-OAKLAND BAY BRIDGE spans San Francisco Bay and links San Francisco with the East Bay cities. Including approaches, it is 8.4 miles long, 4.5 miles of it over navigable water. The east and west spans are connected by a double-deck tunnel through Yerba Buena Island.

Note: The bridge is undergoing a seismic retrofit that is expected to be completed sometime in 2013; expect periodic delays. **Cost:** A $2.50-$6 toll is charged westbound only (toll varies depending on the time of day and number of people in vehicle). **Phone:** (510) 286-1148. 🚇 Folsom, 90

SAN FRANCISCO RAILWAY MUSEUM is just s. of Market St. near the Ferry Building at 77 Steuart St. The museum, at the actual stop for the Steuart Street F-line, is dedicated to telling the story of San Francisco's streetcars, cable cars and transportation history through artifacts, displays, audiovisual presentations, photographs and video touch screens. **Time:** Allow 30 minutes minimum. **Hours:** Tues.-Sun. 10-6. **Cost:** Free. **Phone:** (415) 974-1948. 🚇 Embarcadero, 31

SAN FRANCISCO ZOO, on Great Hwy. between Skyline and Sloat blvds. at 1 Zoo Rd., is home to a variety of exotic animals. Of interest are grizzly sisters Kachina and Kiona; the African Savanna, a multi-species landscape where giraffes gallop among other African wildlife; the leaping lemurs at Lemur Forest; Penguin Island; Gorilla World; the Children's Zoo; an antique Dentzel carousel; and a miniature steam train.

Hours: Daily 10-5, mid-Mar. to early Nov.; 10-4, rest of year. **Cost:** $15; $12 (ages 65+); $9 (ages 4-14). Train rides $4; carousel rides $2. **Parking:** $8-$10. **Phone:** (415) 753-7080. 🚇 SF Zoo, 66

Fisher Family Children's Zoo, within the San Francisco Zoo, includes nature trails, a barnyard, an insect zoo and animals that may be petted and fed. **Hours:** Daily 10-5, mid-Mar. to early Nov.; 10-4, rest of year. Phone ahead to confirm schedule. **Cost:** Included with fee for San Francisco Zoo. 🚇 SF Zoo, 66

THE SOCIETY OF CALIFORNIA PIONEERS is at 300 Fourth St. Changing annual exhibits highlight the early years of California's heritage and history. The museum's collections were gathered by pioneer families and their descendants and include 19th- and early 20th-century paintings, artifacts, photographs and manuscripts. **Time:** Allow 1 hour minimum. **Hours:** Wed.-Fri. and first Sat. of the month 10-4. Closed major holidays. **Cost:** $5; $2.50

(ages 62+ and students with ID). **Phone:** (415) 957-1849. 🚇 Powell Street, 33

STEINHART AQUARIUM—see The California Academy of Sciences p. 375.

TEATRO ZINZANNI is on The Embarcadero at the foot of Broadway. This theatrical troupe presents 3-hour productions that are a blend of European cabaret entertainment, Cirque du Soleil-style spectacle, diva antics, music and comedy, all woven into the indulgence of a five-course gourmet meal. **Note:** The production is currently on hiatus as Teatro Zinzanni moves from Pier 29 to its new location at the foot of Broadway. The new facility is scheduled to open in the first half of 2013; phone ahead for updated information. **Hours:** Phone ahead for performance times and prices. **Phone:** (415) 438-2668. 🚇 Embarcadero, 31

TELEGRAPH HILL rises near the e. end of Lombard St. Called Loma Alta by the Spanish and Goat Hill by early city residents, Telegraph Hill's current name was adopted in 1849 from a structure similar to a windmill on the top of the hill that used a semaphore-like system to signal merchants of the imminent arrival of ships. Telegraph Hill is now crowned by Coit Tower, the monument to San Francisco firefighters that is a distinctive North Beach landmark.

One of the most visually rewarding ways to ascend Telegraph Hill is via the Filbert Steps, which rise in three sections up the east side. The steps end at Telegraph Hill Boulevard, the road that encircles the base of Coit Tower. The tower grounds are lovely, and from this elevated perspective there are fine views of the bay. **Phone:** (415) 362-0808. 🚇 Embarcadero, 31

Coit Tower stands atop Telegraph Hill. Built in 1934, this 210-foot Art Deco tower was given to the city by eccentric philanthropist Lillie Hitchcock Coit; the tower's resemblance to a fire hose nozzle is said to be a respectful tip of the hat by Ms. Coit to the efforts of the city's firefighters. The lobby features Diego Rivera-inspired murals created by WPA artists that depict the lives of the state's Depression-era working class.

From the observation deck at the top of the tower there are panoramas of North Beach, Lombard Street, the Golden Gate and Bay bridges and Alcatraz Island. There may be a wait for the elevator during peak periods. **Time:** Allow 1 hour minimum. **Hours:** Daily 10-6:30, Mar.-Sept.; 10-4:30, rest of year. Closed Thanksgiving, Christmas and Dec. 31. Phone ahead to confirm schedule. **Cost:** Murals on first floor free. Elevator to top of tower $7; $5 (ages 12-17 and 65+); $2 (ages 5-11). Cash only. **Phone:** (415) 362-0808. 🚇 Embarcadero, 31

Filbert Steps ascend the e. side of Telegraph Hill. The stairs begin at the foot of Filbert Street (at Sansome Street); look for the sign that says "Steps to

Coit Tower." They rise in three sections and are wood as far up as Montgomery Street; the higher you climb, the better the views of San Francisco Bay, the Bay Bridge and Alcatraz Island, although the vista is always partially obscured by the luxuriant vegetation filling the backyard gardens of houses perched on either side of the steps. This lush, leafy enclave is a lovely retreat removed from the bustle of the city below.

The steps end at Telegraph Hill Boulevard, the road that encircles the base of Coit Tower. For a different perspective, take the parallel Greenwich Steps back down the hill (a sign in the Coit Tower parking area points the way to the head of the steps). There are more gardens and exotic flowering plants along these steps, and less huffing and puffing is involved. **Hours:** Daily during daylight hours. **Cost:** Free. 🚇 Embarcadero, 31

SAVE USS *PAMPANITO*, docked at Pier 45 on The Embarcadero near Taylor St., is a restored World War II submarine that saw action in the Pacific theater. A self-guiding audio tour features the voices of actual crew members telling their stories about life aboard the submarine during the war. Historic artifacts can be seen throughout the boat.

Note: The tours require climbing stairs and stooping through low bulkheads. **Hours:** Daily 9-8, June-Sept.; Sun.-Thurs. 9-6, Fri.-Sat., 9-8, rest of year. Phone ahead to confirm schedule. **Cost:** Guided tour $12; $8 (ages 62+); $6 (ages 6-12 and active military with ID); $25 (family, two adults and up to four children ages 0-17). Self-guiding tours $3. **Phone:** (415) 775-1943.

Yerba Buena Center for the Arts

SAVE **WAX MUSEUM AT FISHERMAN'S WHARF** is at 145 Jefferson St. between Taylor and Mason sts. More than 250 lifelike wax creations are displayed in such settings as the Chamber of Horrors, Hall of Religion, Library of U.S. Presidents, King Tut's Tomb and Palace of Living Art. Among the figures displayed are Leonardo DiCaprio, Angelina Jolie, Marilyn Monroe, President Barack Obama, Donny and Marie Osmond, Brad Pitt, Sylvester Stallone and John Wayne.

Time: Allow 1 hour minimum. **Hours:** Daily 10-9. Phone ahead to confirm schedule. **Cost:** $16; $12 (ages 12-17 and 55+); $8 (ages 6-11). **Phone:** (415) 202-0402 or (800) 439-4305.

WELLS FARGO HISTORY MUSEUM is in the Wells Fargo Bank Building at 420 Montgomery St. The museum contains a stagecoach, relics of the gold rush, nuggets, Western franks and stamps and other articles from 1848 to the present. **Hours:** Mon.-Fri. 9-5. Closed bank holidays. **Cost:** Free. **Phone:** (415) 396-2619.
🚇 Montgomery Street, 32

WOMEN'S BUILDING is at 3543 18th St. (at Lapidge St.). This community center in the Mission District, founded in 1971, is owned and operated by women, provides community social services and programs, and has event space for rent. Its multiethnic and multicultural purpose is embodied by MaestraPeace, the stunning mural that completely covers two of the four-story building's exterior walls. The work of seven female artists, this mural is as educational and inspirational as it is visually striking, embracing the historical contributions of women as well as their healing power and wisdom.

Among the well-known real-life figures depicted are painter Georgia O'Keeffe and Caribbean-American writer and poet Audre Lorde, along with feminine archetypes like East Asian devotional figure Guan Lin. Particularly noteworthy is the way the art is seamlessly integrated with structural elements like windows and doors. You can pick up an informational key inside and also support the building's mission by purchasing a T-shirt or some note cards. **Hours:** Mon.-Fri. 1-5 (also Wed. 5-7). **Cost:** Free. **Phone:** (415) 431-1180.
🚇 16th Street Mission, 35

YERBA BUENA CENTER FOR THE ARTS, on Third St. between Mission and Howard sts., is a venue for contemporary visual art, performances and film/video. Two buildings house contemporary art galleries, a screening room, two theaters and a sculpture court. Year-round performances, exhibitions and screenings feature artists from the Bay Area and around the world. Lectures and workshops are offered.

Hours: Galleries open Thurs.-Sat. and first Tues. of the month noon-8, Sun. noon-6. **Cost:** Galleries $10; $8 (ages 65+, students with ID and teachers). **Phone:** (415) 978-2787.
🚇 Montgomery Street, 32

Sightseeing

Sightseeing tours are available by land, sea and air; if your time is limited, the bus tours that touch briefly on city highlights are recommended.

Boat Tours

Tours of the harbor operate from Fisherman's Wharf. In addition to 1-hour bay cruises, The Red and White Fleet *(see attraction listing)* also schedules combination boat and bus tours and boat and musical show tours.

If you're interested in seeing what life on Alcatraz Island *(see attraction listing p. 363)* was like, be sure and buy your tickets ahead of time, as the tours frequently sell out. Ferries operated by Alcatraz Cruises depart for "The Rock" from Pier 33 on The Embarcadero. Reservations 2 weeks or more in advance are recommended during the summer months and around holidays; phone (415) 981-7625.

Cruises to Six Flags Discovery Kingdom in Vallejo *(see attraction listing p. 552)* are scheduled by Baylink Ferry and depart from the Ferry Building; phone (707) 643-3779.

The Angel Island-Tiburon Ferry runs daily. The schedule varies with the season; phone (415) 435-2131 for information. Angel Island State Park *(see attraction listing in Tiburon p. 542, and the Recreation Areas Chart)* offers picnic facilities, beaches and hiking trails. The park includes the Angel Island Immigration Station *(see attraction listing in Tiburon p. 542).*

Blue and Gold Fleet Bay Cruises and Motor Coach Tours conducts 60-minute bay cruises that depart Pier 39 daily at frequent intervals *(see attraction listing).* The company also offers San Francisco, Muir Woods, Sausalito, Tiburon and Angel Island tours by boat; phone (415) 773-1188 or (415) 705-8200.

Hornblower Cruises and Events, Pier 3 on The Embarcadero, offers daily dinner and lunch cruises and weekend brunch cruises aboard the motor yacht *California Hornblower.* Live music is provided with dinner and brunch, and there are dance floors on two decks. Reservations are required; phone (415) 788-8866.

BLUE & GOLD FLEET departs from Pier 39 on The Embarcadero at Beach St. The fleet's 1-hour Bay Cruise Adventure gives passengers a scenic waterfront view of San Francisco as it sails past Pier 39 and its resident sea lions, under the Golden Gate Bridge, past Sausalito and Angel Island and around Alcatraz. A historical narration is provided along the way. Other cruises also are offered, as are combination tours.

Time: Allow 1 hour minimum. **Hours:** Bay Cruise Adventure departs frequently daily 11-6:45, May-Oct.; 11-4:30, rest of year (weather permitting). Schedule varies; phone ahead. **Cost:** Bay Cruise Adventure $25; $21 (ages 12-18 and 65+); $17 (ages 5-11). **Phone:** (415) 773-1188. *(See ad p. 362.)*

RED AND WHITE FLEET departs from Pier 43 1/2 at the foot of Taylor St. at Fisherman's Wharf. The 1-hour Golden Gate Bay Cruise takes passengers sightseeing along the San Francisco waterfront, around Alcatraz and under the Golden Gate Bridge. Audio is available in a choice of 12 languages. Sunset cruises and combination tours also are available.

Time: Allow 1 hour minimum. **Hours:** Golden Gate Bay Cruise departs 8-14 times daily beginning at 10 a.m. (trips are generally 30-45 minutes apart). Phone ahead to confirm schedule. **Cost:** Golden Gate Bay Cruise $26; $18 (ages 5-17); $69 (family, two adults and four children). Reservations are recommended. **Phone:** (415) 673-2900.

RIDE THE DUCKS SAN FRANCISCO departs from Fisherman's Wharf at 2766 Taylor St. (at jct. Jefferson St.) year-round and from Union Square on Geary St. (across from Macy's) Mar.-Sept. Passengers ride vehicles that resemble a DUKWs, a World War II amphibious landing craft, on a sightseeing tour of such San Francisco landmarks as Chinatown, North Beach, the Ferry Building and the Transamerica Pyramid. The vessel then proceeds to splash into San Francisco Bay for views of the downtown skyline, the Bay Bridge and AT&T Ballpark. You'll get to enjoy spots like McCovey Cove, behind the ballpark, that are only visible if you're on the water.

Prepare to get a little wet when "driving" into the bay. **Time:** Allow 1 hour, 30 minutes minimum. **Hours:** Trips depart from Fisherman's Wharf approximately every 30 minutes daily 10-6. Phone for seasonal departure schedule from Union Square. Closed Jan. 1, Christmas Eve and Christmas. **Cost:** $34; $32 (ages 62+); $25 (ages 4-17). A photo ID is required. Reservations are required. **Phone:** (877) 887-8225.

ROCKETBOAT departs from Pier 39 at Fisherman's Wharf. This high-speed, twisting and turning, 30-minute sightseeing tour of San Francisco Bay is accompanied by a captain who provides entertaining narration, a soundtrack of classic rock tunes and a very good possibility of getting wet. Hint: If you actually *do* want to get wet, sit toward the back.

Riders should be in good health and free from high blood pressure; heart, back or neck problems; osteoporosis; motion sickness; or other similar conditions. Expectant mothers should not participate. **Hours:** Departures daily at 12:15, 1, 1:45, 2:30, 3:30, 4:15, 5 and 6, June-Aug.; Wed.-Sun. at 12:15, 1, 1:45, 2:30, 3:30, 4:15, 5 and 6, mid-May through May 31 and Sept. 1-late Oct. (weather permitting).

Cost: $24; $20 (ages 12-18 and 65+); $16 (ages 5-11); $65 (family, two adults and up to four children). Under 41 inches tall are not permitted. Under age 12 must be accompanied by an adult. **Phone:** (415) 773-1188.

SF BAY WHALE WATCHING trips meet at the picnic table in front of Building A at Fort Mason. Eight-hour excursions on the 46-passenger *Outer*

Take a guided segway tour in Golden Gate Park

Limits take passengers on whale-watching/natural history trips 27 miles outside the Golden Gate Bridge into the Gulf of the Farallones National Marine Sanctuary to the Farallon Islands, a major breeding ground for sea birds.

In addition to whales, possible sightings include sea lions, elephant seals, fur seals, white sharks and dolphins. An on-board naturalist as well as the captain and crew provide information about the sights and marine animals.

You might even be joined by additional companions; the company frequently transports rehabilitated animals from The Marine Mammal Center in Sausalito *(see attraction listing p. 511)* for release near the Farallon Islands.

Note: Phone after 7 p.m. the night before the trip to make sure that weather will not cause a cancellation. Dress warmly and in layers; a hat, gloves and rain gear are recommended. Bring food, water, thermoses of coffee and snacks; food and beverages are not available on board. **Hours:** Excursions depart Sat.-Sun. and some holidays at 8 a.m. and return between 3:30 and 4 p.m., Jan. 1-day after Thanksgiving. Passengers should arrive at 7:30 a.m. for check-in and a pre-boarding talk. **Cost:** $115-$125. Reservations are required. **Phone:** (415) 331-6267.

Bus and Van Tours

Numerous companies offer limousine tours of San Francisco, the Bay Area and Wine Country. The Blue and Gold Fleet offers motor coach tours to destinations like the Napa and Sonoma valleys, Monterey, Carmel-by-the-Sea and Yosemite National Park; phone (415) 773-1188.

EXTRANOMICAL TOURS provides pickup service from various hotels and places of interest in and around San Francisco. The company provides tours of San Francisco as well as trips to outlying areas. Two popular full-day trips are the Total Yosemite Experience and the Wine Country and Redwoods Escape. Other options include the City Insider's Tour (half-day), the Wine Lover's Tour (full-day), the Muir Woods Expedition (half-day) and the Monterey Explorer (full-day).

Hours: Tours are offered daily; times vary depending on the tour chosen. **Cost:** Total Yosemite Experience $149; $129 (ages 0-11). Wine Country and Redwoods Escape $95; $57 (ages 0-11). San Francisco City Insider's Tour $75; $55 (ages 0-11). Wine Lover's Wine Country Tour $139; $79 (ages 0-11). Muir Woods Expedition $75; $65 (ages 0-11). Monterey Explorer $149; $129 (ages 0-11). Reservations are required. **Phone:** (415) 357-0700 or (866) 231-3752.

[SAVE] **GRAY LINE SAN FRANCISCO** tours depart from the Pier 41 Marine Terminal at Fisherman's Wharf. Various full- and half-day excursions of the San Francisco Bay Area and beyond are offered; pick-up service is available at most San Francisco hotels. **Hours:** The 3.5-hour San Francisco City Tour departs daily at 9:15, 11:15 and 2:15. **Cost:** San Francisco City Tour $49; $47 (ages 60+); $25 (ages 5-11). Reservations are required. **Phone:** (415) 434-8687 or (888) 428-6937.

[SAVE] **GREAT PACIFIC TOUR CO.** offers pickup service at local hotels. The half-day City Tour gives passengers a comprehensive overview of San Francisco, including Fisherman's Wharf, Nob Hill and the city's famous Victorians. Stops are made at Twin Peaks and at the Marin Headlands across the Golden Gate Bridge (weather permitting). Tours are conducted in 13-passenger minivans. Other tours are available.

Time: Allow 3 hours, 30 minutes minimum. **Hours:** City Tour departs daily at 9, 11 and 2. **Cost:** City Tour $59; $57 (ages 62+); $49 (ages 5-11). Reservations are required. **Phone:** (415) 626-4499. Van Ness, 50

SAN FRANCISCO COMPREHENSIVE SHUTTLE TOURS depart from the front of the Ferry Building

on The Embarcadero (across from the end of Market St.). The 5-hour City Tour visits such landmarks as Chinatown, Lombard Street (both of these stops include a guided walk), the Palace of Fine Arts and the Golden Gate Bridge, plus an hour of shopping in Sausalito. The half-day Muir Woods Tour also schedules stops at the Marin Headlands and Muir Beach Overlook.   The two tours can be combined into one all-day experience. All-day Wine Country tours visit Napa Valley or Sonoma wineries. All itineraries include a ferry cruise across

San Francisco Bay. **Hours:** City Tour departs Mon.-Fri. at 9 and 11, Sat.-Sun. at 9 and 11:45. Muir Woods Tour departs daily at 8:45 and 12:45. Muir Woods/City Tour combination departs daily at 9. **Cost:** City Tour $69; $64 (ages 65+); $55 (ages 0-12). Muir Woods Tour $65; $62 (ages 65+); $57 (ages 0-12). Muir Woods/City Tour combination $120; $115 (ages 65+); $97 (ages 0-12). Reservations are required. **Phone:** (415) 513-5400. Embarcadero, 31

SAN FRANCISCO FIRE ENGINE TOURS depart from The Cannery, Beach St. and Columbus Ave. at Fisherman's Wharf. Instead of a bus or van, passengers board a large red Mack fire truck for this 75-minute sightseeing trip, which approaches the Golden Gate Bridge via Crissy Field, the Presidio and Fort Point, crosses the bridge to Sausalito and includes a photo stop at Fort Baker before crossing the bridge again and returning to Fisherman's Wharf via Union Street. You can even don real fire gear to help ward off the chill on the windswept bridge. **Time:** Allow 1 hour, 30 minutes minimum. **Hours:** Tours are given daily at 9, 11, 1 and 3. Closed major holidays. **Cost:** $50; $40 (ages 13-17); $30 (ages 2-12). Reservations are required. **Phone:** (415) 333-7077.

SAN FRANCISCO MOVIE TOURS depart from Pier 43 1/2 at Fisherman's Wharf; pickup service is available from central locations in the Union Square and Nob Hill areas. Three-hour tours take passengers to San Francisco sites made famous by Hollywood movies, including locations from "Mrs. Doubtfire," "Bullitt," "Dirty Harry" and "The Princess Diaries." Scenes from each movie are shown on a big-screen TV while the van passes by that location.

The guide provides information about San Francisco and movie history and trivia about films, actors and directors. Photo and rest stops are made along the way. **Time:** Allow 3 hours minimum. **Hours:** Tours depart daily at 10:30 and 2:30, July-Aug.; at 10:30, rest of year. **Cost:** $47; $37 (ages 5-17 and 65+). Reservations are required. **Phone:** (212) 209-3370 or (800) 979-3370.

Driving Tours

Skyline Boulevard (SR 35) follows the peninsula divide south of the city into the Santa Cruz Mountains, offering simultaneous scenic views of the bay and ocean.

Upon presentation of your AAA membership card, AAA Northern California, Nevada & Utah can furnish a map with a suggested tour covering much of San Francisco. The 49-Mile Scenic Drive map also is available from the San Francisco Convention & Visitors Bureau Visitor Information Center on the lower level of Hallidie Plaza at Market and Powell streets (near the cable cars turnaround).

Segway Tours

GOLDEN GATE PARK GUIDED SEGWAY TOUR departs from the paved area behind the bandshell in the Music Concourse. After a beginning 40-minute training session, visitors embark on a Segway for a narrated, 8-mile tour that explores the eastern half of the park. Stops include the Japanese Tea Garden, the Conservatory of Flowers, the National AIDS Memorial Grove, Stow Lake and Strawberry Hill, plus numerous stops for photos. It's a fun way to see park highlights without doing all that walking.

Guests must weigh between 100 and 250 pounds. The tour is not recommended for those over age 70 or who have mobility challenges. Under age 12 are not permitted. Tours are subject to a minimum of four participants. **Time:** Allow 2 hours minimum. **Hours:** Tours depart daily at 9, 12:30 and 4, Apr.-Oct.; at 10 and 1:30, rest of year. Guests should arrive at least 15 minutes before the scheduled departure time. Closed Jan. 1, Christmas and during major park events. **Cost:** Tour fee $70. Advance reservations are required. **Phone:** (415) 474-3130. Judah & 9th Ave, 55

Guided Walking Tours

City Guides Walking Tours, sponsored by the San Francisco Library, provides free 1.5- to 2-hour tours of historic Market Street, the Civic Center, North Beach, Chinatown, Golden Gate Bridge, the Mission murals, the Palace of Fine Arts, Victorian San Francisco, Pacific Heights mansions and other parts of the city; phone (415) 557-4266 for schedules and information.

San Francisco Architectural Heritage offers a 2-hour Pacific Heights walking tour that is conducted on Sunday and three different 2-hour walking tours that are given on a rotating basis on three Saturdays each month. The tours cost $8; $5 (ages 0-12 and 65+). For information phone (415) 441-3000.

Art Deco Walking Tours sponsored by the Art Deco Society of California cover various San Francisco neighborhoods—including downtown, the Marina District, Pacific Heights and SOMA—as well as downtown Berkeley, Uptown Oakland and Alameda. Most tours depart Saturday or Sunday at 11 a.m. (weather permitting). The Pacific Heights tour traverses hilly terrain. The tour fee is $10. Phone (415) 982-3326 for schedules and departure locations.

The murals along Balmy Alley in the Mission District can be viewed via walking tours. Tours offered by the Precita Eyes Mural Arts Center depart Sat.-Sun. at 11 and 1:30. Fee $12-$15; $8 (ages 65+ and college students with ID); $5 (ages 12-17); $2 (ages 0-11). Bicycle tours are available by appointment. Phone (415) 285-2287.

ALL ABOUT CHINATOWN WALKING TOURS meets on the steps of Old St. Mary's Cathedral at California St. and Grant Ave. The 2-hour, guided half-mile walking tour focuses on history, architecture, culture and traditions. Stops are made at an herbal pharmacy, a fortune cookie factory, food markets, a Buddhist temple and other representative sites. The 3-hour tour includes a dim sum lunch.

Time: Allow 2 hours minimum. **Hours:** Tours depart daily at 10 a.m. **Cost:** Two-hour tour $30; $20 (ages 6-17). Three-hour lunch tour $50; $40 (ages 6-17). Reservations are required and should be made at least 7 days in advance. **Phone:** (415) 982-8839. [image] Montgomery Street, 32

FOOT! COMEDY WALKING TOURS depart from different areas of San Francisco, depending on the tour chosen. Visitors can choose from nine 2- and 3-hour comedy/history walking tours through San Francisco neighborhoods. A sampling of the 2-hour tours, all led by professional comedians, includes Flashback: Summer of Love, Winter of Discontent (Haight-Ashbury); Go West, Young Woman: Daring Divas of the Past; and Hobnobbing with Gobs of Snobs: Nob Hill Tour.

Time: Allow 2 hours minimum. **Hours:** Tours depart daily, usually at 1. **Cost:** Two-hour tours $30; $25 (college students with ID); $20 (ages 5-18 and 60+). Three-hour tours $45; $40 (college students with ID); $35 (ages 5-18 and 60+). Reservations are required. **Phone:** (415) 793-5378. [image] Montgomery Street, 32

LOCAL TASTES OF THE CITY TOURS have various departure points. Guides share their gastronomic, historical and cultural knowledge of the city on 3-hour walking tours of either North Beach or Chinatown. A 2-hour evening tour covers both North Beach and Chinatown. Participants get to sample local delicacies such as dim sum, fortune cookies, tea, pizza, wine and cappuccino.

Time: Allow 2 hours minimum. **Hours:** Three-hour tours are given daily at 10 and 2. A 2-hour tour is given daily at 6. **Cost:** $59; $39 (ages 12-16); $25 (ages 8-11). Reservations are recommended.

Visit a fortune cookie factory on a walking tour in Chinatown

Phone: (415) 665-0480 or (888) 358-8687. [image] West Portal, 63

VICTORIAN HOME WALK departs from Union Square at jct. Powell and Post sts. After a brief trolley bus ride, participants explore the interior of a Queen Anne bed-and-breakfast, then embark on an easy (no hills) walk among the "painted ladies" of the Victorian neighborhoods of Pacific Heights and Cow Hollow.

The guide explains differences between Italianate, Queen Anne and Stick Style architecture while relating the history of the era and pointing out homes that have appeared in films. **Time:** Allow 2 hours, 30 minutes minimum. **Hours:** Tours depart daily at 11. Closed Jan. 1 and Christmas. **Cost:** $25; $10 (ages 0-12). **Phone:** (415) 252-9485. [image] Powell Street, 33

WOK WIZ CHINATOWN WALKING TOURS depart from the Financial District; the exact location is provided when reservations are confirmed. A 2-hour cultural and historical walking tour of Chinatown concludes with an optional multicourse, hosted dim sum luncheon; the tour lasts 3 hours if lunch is included. Participants visit neighborhood markets, a Chinese temple, a tea shop and have a chance to explore Chinatown's alleyways and side streets. All guides were either born in Chinatown or grew up there, and all are fluent in Chinese.

Time: Allow 2 hours minimum. **Hours:** Tours are given daily at 10. **Cost:** Two-hour walking tour $35; $25 (ages 0-10). Walking tour with lunch included $50; $35 (ages 0-10). Reservations are required. **Phone:** (650) 355-9657. [image] Montgomery Street, 32

Self-guiding Walking Tours

The well-known attraction at Alamo Square —captured in many a photograph and a classic San Francisco postcard image—is the row of elegant Victorians along Steiner Street, backed by the downtown skyline. This grassy hilltop park, bordered by Fulton, Hayes, Scott and Steiner streets, is a pleasant spot for an afternoon bench break or an early evening stroll.

AAA Walking Tours
Downtown San Francisco

Refer to the Downtown San Francisco map. The self-guiding tour takes 4-6 hours, depending on your pace and the number of stops you make along the way. *Those that appear in bold type have detailed listings in the Attractions or Shopping sections. Even if you decide not to visit a listed site, reading the listing when you reach that point should make the tour more interesting.*

Let's face it—San Francisco is known for its treacherous hills, which can tax even the fittest walkers. But walking also is the best way to explore areas like Union Square, the Financial District, Chinatown, North Beach, Telegraph Hill, Fisherman's

Wharf and Russian Hill. While this route takes advantage of flat stretches as often as possible, we still recommended wearing comfortable shoes for those unavoidable climbs. If you're unwilling or unable to navigate the steep sections of streets, you can hop on a bus or cable car at these points along the tour route.

Union Square, bordered by Geary, Powell, Post and Stockton streets, is an ideal place to start. To get there, take the Powell-Hyde cable car, which stops on the south side of the square. Garage parking is pricey, but if you must drive, there's the underground Union Square Garage, accessed from Geary Street (one-way westbound). Rates are cheaper at the garage at 330 Sutter St. (one-way westbound) near Stockton Street.

Built in 1850, this expansive paved plaza, framed by date palms and attractively landscaped, was named for the demonstrations held here in support of Union troops at the start of the Civil War. Its focal point is the 97-foot-tall Dewey Monument, erected in 1903 to honor Commodore George Dewey's 1898 Manila Bay victory over the Spanish. A Goddess of Victory with a fine patina tops the column.

Surrounded by luxury hotels, fancy stores and ultra-chic boutiques, Union Square is the heart of the downtown hangout scene. Sidewalk vendors sell flowers, streetcar bells clang (and car horns ceaselessly honk), and people relax on benches, nap on grassy areas and fill umbrella-shaded tables at the Emporio Rulli Café. The historic Westin St. Francis (335 Powell St.) survived the 1906 earthquake and purportedly served breakfast to the masses on the morning of the disaster. The hotel's spectacular lobby features an antique grandfather clock and served as a local meeting place for years, coining the well-known request "Meet me at the St. Francis" (a catchphrase also sported on the city's cable cars).

Here are some of San Francisco's fanciest retailers and department stores. A huge Macy's dominates the Geary block, and Saks Fifth Avenue rubs elbows with Tiffany. Neiman Marcus, at Geary and Stockton streets, boasts a six-story rotunda topped with an elaborate stained-glass dome. Originally the City of Paris department store and dating back to 1909, the building's arched ceiling features a mural of a sailing ship and crowns the store's restaurant, a perfect spot for afternoon tea.

After doing some window-shopping, head east on Maiden Lane. Part of San Francisco's raucous Barbary Coast district in the early 20th century, this small side street—then called Morton Street—was once lined with bordellos. The chic boutiques and bistros lining Maiden Lane now serve clients of a decidedly different sort. Look to the left; the brick gallery at 140 Maiden Ln. was designed by Frank Lloyd Wright and served as a prototype for the Guggenheim Museum in New York.

At Grant Avenue, turn left. Two blocks ahead at the corner of Bush Street is the symbolic entrance to Chinatown, marked by a green-tiled gate bedecked with golden dragons. The gate, dedicated in 1970, was a gift to the city from the Republic of China. It is traditional for Chinese villages to have ceremonial gates similar to this one; the carved stone guard dogs at either end are said to ward off evil.

But first, turn right at Post Street. There's more window-shopping to do along this block of Post that's lined with swanky retailers. The Crocker Galleria (50 Post St. at Kearny Street) is designed to mimic the Galleria Vittorio Emanuele II in Milan, Italy. Beneath its dome are large English ivy topiaries, elite shops and cafe-style eateries.

At Montgomery Street make a sharp left. You've entered the concrete canyons of "Wall Street West," the Financial District. Here, between Market and Sacramento streets and east toward The Embarcadero, deals have been made since the 1850s, when prospectors returned from the gold mines with treasure and created a demand for banks. This is one of the country's top financial centers. During the day the narrow sidewalks are crowded with expensively dressed businesspeople consulting their smartphones; except for restaurants, the district all but empties out after bankers' hours end around 6 p.m.

Not surprisingly, Montgomery Street is lined with skyscrapers. Lean and seemingly striped, the Wells Fargo Building (44 Montgomery St., just north of Post Street) was built to house the bank's world headquarters. The concrete and steel structure stands 561 feet tall. At Bush Street, look right for the Mills Building (220 Montgomery St.). Built in 1892 (the tower was added in 1907), the steel building nearly occupies the entire block; its large lobby displays varied artwork. The 1928 Russ Building (235 Montgomery St., just north of Bush) was the city's tallest building until the 1960s, when construction of the Transamerica Pyramid began; back then the 435-foot-tall building was referred to simply as "the skyscraper." Its Gothic design was modeled after the Chicago Tribune tower.

Speaking of "the pyramid," San Francisco's tallest building can be seen looking north. Located at 600 Montgomery St. where Columbus Avenue meets Washington Street, this 48-story skyscraper has nearly 6,000 windows and is topped by a 212-foot-tall spire.

In its shadow is the **Jackson Square Historical District,** which dates from the gold rush era. Brick buildings with iron shutters lining Gold and Balance streets now contain antique shops and restaurants, and Victorian-style lampposts accentuate the old-timey feel.

Turn left from Montgomery onto California, a street lined with more imposing buildings. Carved concrete, marble, brown stone and red brick decorate the facades of banks and title companies; inside, magnificent chandeliers hang from the ceiling in extravagant lobbies. The 52-story Bank of America Center (555 California St. on the left) is a modern structure with an accordion-like exterior that features carnelian marble; a top-floor restaurant, aptly named the Carnelian Room, provides stunning views of downtown. Bring some cash and your camera—you'll pay for the view with the price of one cocktail.

Continue up a relatively short but steep hill to Grant Avenue. **Old St. Mary's Cathedral** is on the right, sandwiched between sleek high-rises and contrasting Chinese architecture. Built in 1854, the Catholic church is said to be the first cathedral in California. It survived the 1906 earthquake and subsequent fires; following renovation, it was rededicated in 1909. Across the street in St. Mary's Square is a 12-foot-tall metal and granite statue of Dr. Sun Yat-sen, founder of the Republic of China.

Turn right onto Grant Avenue, **Chinatown's** main drag. Originally called Calle de Fundacion, this is the city's oldest street. In the blocks north to Broadway multicolored flag pennants flutter over the street, entwined dragons decorate lampposts, and store window and market signs are predominantly in Chinese. Apartment houses with filigreed balconies—some draped with laundry—stand in between more conventional-looking buildings.

Grant is the more touristy of Chinatown's two main streets. The narrow, crowded avenue is crammed with restaurants advertising dim sum; herb shops tempting passersby with ancient potions; stores selling fine antiques and jade sculpture; and souvenir shop bins filled with Chinese Barbie dolls, plastic Buddha statues, tea sets, embroidered slippers, postcards, ear-piercing cricket toys, bamboo

flutes, Chinese iron balls, three-for-$10 T-shirts and mah-jongg games—all identified with colorful laminated Chinese signs.

Stockton Street, a block west, is where you'll find mostly produce markets, bakeries and delicatessens, the latter usually featuring a row of skinned ducks (with the heads still attached) hanging upside-down in the window. Saturday morning is the time to get a true feel for the neighborhood. It's an explosion of activity as residents pack the sidewalks, running errands and socializing. Elderly women crowd the vegetable markets, picking over fresh water chestnuts and giant jackfruit; street vendors hawk Chinese newspapers. The scents of barbecued pork and simmering soup mingle in the air, and you may be one of the few people speaking English.

Browse the merchandise at the Canton Bazaar (616 Grant Ave.), a popular import shop. The Chinatown Kite Shop (717 Grant Ave.) is a great place to purchase fish kites or hand-painted paper kites. The Wok Shop (718 Grant Ave.) peddles all sorts of Chinese housewares. Check out the Bank of America branch at the northwest corner of Grant Avenue and Sacramento Street (701 Grant Ave.); dragons adorn the columns and guard the front doors.

Chinatown is known for its maze of tucked-away back alleys. Waverly Place, called "the street of the painted balconies," is just west of Grant between Sacramento and Washington streets. Turn left on

Clay, then right on Waverly Place. The smell of incense pervades this compact little alley, which is somewhat reminiscent of streets in New Orleans' French Quarter—with a Chinese emphasis, of course. Red and green, considered symbols of happiness and longevity, respectively, embellish three temples: Jeng Sen at #146, Tin How at #125 and Norras at #109.

At Washington Street, turn right and continue just past Grant to the three-tiered United Commercial Bank at 743 Washington St. (formerly the Bank of Canton). Awash in blue, gold and vibrant red, it was built in 1909 to house the Chinatown Telephone Exchange (known as "China-5")—which it did until 1945. Sandwiched between two brick buildings, this is the neighborhood's oldest pagoda-style edifice.

Backtrack to Grant Avenue and turn right. As you leave Chinatown behind you're heading to the 1950s stomping grounds of the Beat poets. Proceed about two blocks to tiny Jack Kerouac Alley (just past Pacific) and turn right. Vesuvio (255 Columbus Ave.) is one of the few remaining Beat landmarks. A faded sign over the bar's front door proclaims, "We are itching to get away from Portland, Oregon!" Established in 1948, Vesuvio was—and remains—a favorite hangout for Bohemian types; the signature drink is appropriately named the Jack Kerouac. Also check out the cool murals decorating the alley walls.

At the corner of Columbus and Broadway is City Lights, the first all-paperback bookstore in the country. Established in 1953 by poet Lawrence Ferlinghetti, it also attracted Beat writers, and a section of this three-level bookstore, packed with a maze of aisles and shelves, is devoted to their works.

Continue northwest along busy Columbus Avenue, the main artery of **North Beach,** San Francisco's Little Italy. Italians settled here first, and later the writers followed. The name dates to the city's early days, when the neighborhood overlooked the water; this part of the bay was filled in the mid-19th century.

If it's time for lunch, you're at the right place. Settle into a sidewalk chair at one of the restaurants or cafes lining this stretch of Columbus—or put together a picnic from the many delectable deli offerings at Molinari (373 Columbus Ave.) and take your little feast to nearby Washington Square (*see below*). For some of the best coffee in town—and that's saying something in a city where excellent coffee is basically taken for granted—stop by Caffe Trieste (609 Vallejo St., just east of Columbus), owned and operated by the singing Giotta family since 1956. You can pick up a sandwich there, too.

Backtracking to Columbus, you'll pass the National Shrine of St. Francis of Assisi (610 Vallejo St.). The imposing 1860 Norman Gothic church is dedicated to St. Francis, the city's namesake. Make a right on Columbus and continue north for two blocks to Union Street and Washington Square.

Just as North Beach isn't a beach, Washington Square is not a true square but a pentagon. On sunny days you'll find kids playing and people sunbathing on park benches, picnicking or practicing tai chi on the lawn. On the square stands a statue of Benjamin Franklin (not George Washington, as its name would suggest), donated to the city in 1879.

The white towers of the Romanesque Church of Saints Peter and Paul overlook the square's north side. Known as the "fisherman's church," it offers mass in English, Italian and Cantonese. The annual Blessing of the Fleet celebration, an old Sicilian tradition held in early October, begins at the church and proceeds to Fisherman's Wharf for a fishing boat parade and memorial ceremony at sea.

Take Filbert Street east to Stockton Street. At the corner of Filbert and Stockton look directly east. **Coit Tower,** which some say resembles a fire hose nozzle, is visible above the neat row houses. That's your next stop. To get there, you have two options. If you don't feel like walking you can catch the #39 Muni bus (Coit; fare $2) to the top of **Telegraph Hill.** The bus stop is at the corner of Stockton and Union streets.

Walkers can take Stockton north for two blocks (following signs to Coit Tower), then turn right on Lombard Street. From here it's approximately two more blocks to the base of Telegraph Hill, but keep in mind that in San Francisco, distance can be misleading—these two blocks are quite steep. Alternate walking routes are Filbert or Greenwich streets, both uphill (there's a sidewalk stairway built into Filbert Street).

If you get tired, stop to admire the neat, flat-topped row houses. At Grant Avenue there's a great view of San Francisco Bay to the left (dotted with sailboats in good weather), the **Golden Gate Bridge** and the headlands of **Golden Gate National Recreation Area** beyond. Also look west (behind you) for a good perspective of the zigzagging block of **Lombard Street,** the short stretch often referred to as "the crookedest street in the world."

Once at the base of Telegraph Hill, catch your breath (or get off the bus) and take a peek at the **San Francisco-Oakland Bay Bridge** (to the east), with the piers along The Embarcadero in the foreground. Follow shaded Telegraph Hill Boulevard as it circles to the top of the hill and the Coit Tower parking lot. A regal bronze statue of Christopher Columbus—donated by the Italian community and the focus of annual Columbus Day festivities—overlooks the bay. Behind the statue stands 210-foot-tall Coit Memorial Tower, built in 1933 through a financial donation from wealthy local eccentric Lillie Hitchcock Coit.

At the summit there are panoramic views of the northern part of the city and San Francisco Bay. The crooked block of Lombard Street is visible among the hilly streets crammed with row houses (directly west);

the Golden Gate Bridge and the **Presidio of San Francisco** are in the distance to the northwest; **Alcatraz Island** is directly north; and the towers of the Financial District are to the south. Take the elevator to the top of the tower for more spectacular views.

The Greenwich and **Filbert Steps** are staircases that hug the east side of Telegraph Hill. Look for the "Greenwich Steps" sign in the Coit Tower parking lot and follow the brick stairs down past flowering hillside gardens next to private residences. You could walk all the way down to Sansome Street, but to minimize the return hike we recommend turning right onto Montgomery (about halfway down) and climbing back up the wooden Filbert Steps. (Follow the lower—or eastern—side of Montgomery.) The luxuriant vegetation along the Filbert Steps is even prettier.

Where Montgomery meets the Filbert Steps, note the Malloch Apartment Building (1360 Montgomery St.). This 1937 Art Deco structure was featured in the movie "Dark Passage," starring Lauren Bacall and Humphrey Bogart. Take the Filbert Steps to the base of Telegraph Hill and head downhill on Telegraph Hill Boulevard, then continue down Lombard Street for about five blocks. At Lombard and Powell there's another glimpse of cars slowly winding their way down the serpentine block. To the right as you pass Stockton and Powell streets are splendid vistas of Victorians, with the bay as a backdrop.

At Columbus make a quick right, then another right onto Taylor Street, heading north. Walk three blocks to Bay Street, where you can see the cable cars being turned around (with a great deal of physical effort) at the end of the Powell-Mason line. Continue along Taylor, where postcard stands hint at the kitschy souvenirs to come.

Once you get to Taylor and Jefferson streets you've arrived at **Fisherman's Wharf,** marked by a nifty sign that ends up in many a vacation photo. The wharf, built during the gold rush, is home to the city's fishing fleet, which docks along the Jefferson Street promenade. Fishermen unload their catches in the early morning fog at Pier 45.

Head east along the waterfront to Pier 39, past tourist shops selling everything from fog in a can to T-shirts proclaiming "I escaped from Alcatraz." Fisherman's Wharf is known for its street performers, and here you'll see folks painted head to toe in silver or gold, mimes; stilt-walkers, palm readers; people dressed in goofy outfits posing for photos and others twirling hoops or juggling. Look out for the "Bushman"; he hides behind a tree branch and startles unsuspecting pedestrians.

More performers take the stage at **Pier 39,** but arguably the most crowd-pleasing entertainers are the barking sea lions that congregate on the floating docks just west of the pier, although there aren't as many of them as there were prior to late 2009, when the pinnipeds staged a mysterious mass exodus only to return in smaller numbers. After exploring the touristy shops and perhaps taking a whirl on the carousel, head back west along Jefferson; you'll pass more souvenir shops as well as the **Wax Museum at Fisherman's Wharf** and **Ripley's Believe It or Not! Odditorium.**

At Jefferson and Taylor the smell of fresh fish lingers in the air. Seagulls hover and squawk, on the lookout for treats. You've entered "Fish Alley," where you can nibble on "take-away" shrimp or a Dungeness crab cocktail—assembled on the spot by one of the sidewalk vendors. Or indulge in some clam chowder; at **Boudin at the Wharf: Museum and Bakery Tour** you can have it served a very popular way, in a sourdough bread bowl.

Continue along Jefferson for two blocks. At the corner of Leavenworth Street is **The Cannery,** a three-story brick building filled with shops and restaurants. Constructed in 1907, it was originally owned by Del Monte and used to can peaches before closing during the Great Depression. The courtyard, shaded by olive trees, is a great place to kick back and listen to the jazz bands that frequently perform.

At Hyde Street, turn right and stroll along the Hyde Street Pier, part of **San Francisco Maritime National Historical Park.** Four berthed boats here comprise the nation's only floating national park, where you can tour the vessels or participate in a boat-building class. From the end of the pier you'll see the giant Ghirardelli sign. That's your next stop. Backtrack to Hyde Street, continue on Hyde to Beach Street, then turn right and proceed two blocks to **Ghirardelli Square.** This collection of 19th-century brick factory buildings, now occupied by shops, is where the chocolatier whipped up sweet concoctions until the 1960s. Indulge in a sinfully delicious Ghirardelli hot fudge sundae at the soda fountain.

Backtrack along Beach to Hyde, the end of the Powell & Hyde cable car line. While walking back (uphill) to Union Square may appeal to the prodigiously fit, it's much less physically demanding—and more fun—to hop on a cable car (fare $6). Across from the cable car turnaround is the Buena Vista Cafe, where Irish coffee was introduced to America based on a recipe brought from Dublin in the 1950s.

Hold on tight while the car is pulled up Russian Hill (named for Russian sailors buried here), one of the city's steepest, and marvel at the mansions along the route. If you like, get off at Lombard Street to peer (or climb) down the stairs along either side—the view is best from the bottom, although the climb back up is a bit grueling. Neatly manicured hedges, seasonal hydrangea blooms and Art Deco-style houses frame the figure eight-curving brick street. Remember that if you disembark the cable car you'll have to pay another $6 fare if you reboard, unless you have a Muni passport offering unlimited usage of Muni buses and cable cars for the duration of its validity period.

Once en route again, look east at Greenwich Street for a great view of Coit Tower. The cable car makes a swift turn at Washington Street, passing the **Cable Car Museum and Powerhouse Viewing Gallery** at Washington and Mason streets. Get off at Geary Street and you're back at Union Square, where the tour began.

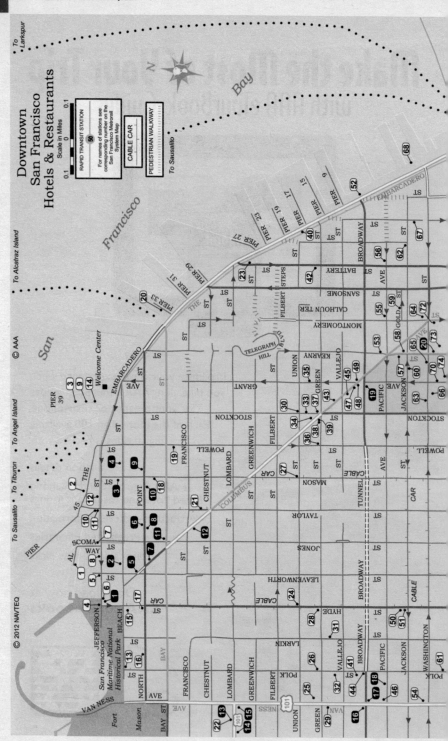

Downtown
San Francisco
Hotels & Restaurants

Scale in Miles

RAPID TRANSIT STATION 50
For names of stations see
corresponding number on the
San Francisco Metrorail
System Map

CABLE CAR

PEDESTRIAN WALKWAY

© 2012 NAVTEQ

© AAA

San Francisco Bay

To Larkspur
To Sausalito
To Alcatraz Island
To Angel Island
To Tiburon
To Sausalito
To Sausalito

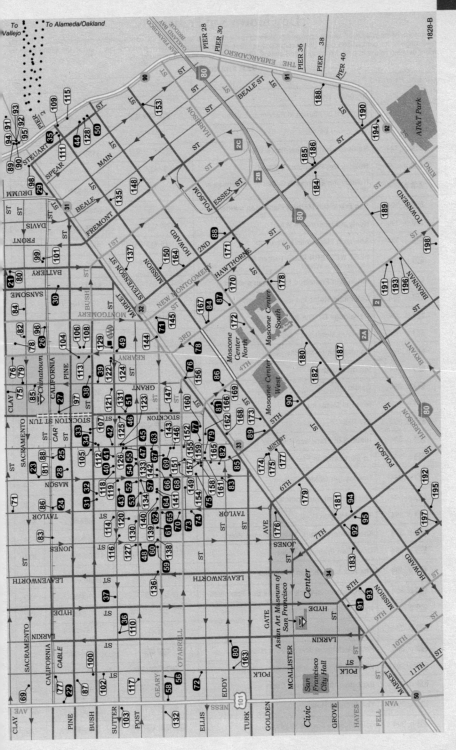

Downtown San Francisco

This index helps you "spot" where approved hotels and restaurants are located on the corresponding detailed maps. Hotel daily rate range is for comparison only. Restaurant price range is a combination of lunch and/or dinner. Turn to the listing page for more detailed rate and price information and consult display ads for special promotions.

SAN FRANCISCO

Map Page	Hotels	Diamond Rated	Rate Range	Page
① p. 394	Argonaut Hotel	◆◆◆◆	$209-$719 SAVE	418
② p. 394	Courtyard by Marriott at Fisherman's Wharf	◆◆◆	$159-$409	421
③ p. 394	The Wharf Inn (See ad p. 436.)	◆◆	$119-$225 SAVE	436
④ p. 394	Radisson Hotel Fisherman's Wharf	◆◆◆	$139-$559 SAVE	433
⑤ p. 394	Holiday Inn Fisherman's Wharf	◆◆◆	$125-$365 SAVE	425
⑥ p. 394	Holiday Inn Express & Suites at Fisherman's Wharf	◆◆◆	$139-$399 SAVE	425
⑦ p. 394	San Francisco Marriott Fisherman's Wharf	◆◆◆	$169-$589 SAVE	433
⑧ p. 394	Hyatt at Fisherman's Wharf	◆◆◆	$126-$387 SAVE	429
⑨ p. 394	Sheraton Fisherman's Wharf	◆◆◆	$139-$479 SAVE	434
⑩ p. 394	BEST WESTERN PLUS Tuscan Inn at Fisherman's Wharf	◆◆◆	$189-$389 SAVE	419
⑪ p. 394	Hilton San Francisco Fisherman's Wharf	◆◆◆	$159-$459 SAVE	424
⑫ p. 394	Columbus Motor Inn (See ad p. 421.)	◆◆◆	$90-$195 SAVE	419
⑬ p. 394	Travelodge By The Bay	◆◆	$69-$209 SAVE	434
⑭ p. 394	Lombard Motor Inn (See ad p. 420.)	◆◆	$86-$155 SAVE	430
⑮ p. 394	Comfort Inn by the Bay (See ad p. 422.)	◆◆	$79-$289 SAVE	421
⑯ p. 394	Inn on Broadway	◆◆	$64-$164 SAVE	429
⑰ p. 394	Castle Inn	◆◆	$69-$359 SAVE	419
⑱ p. 394	Nob Hill Motor Inn	◆◆	$74-$179 SAVE	431
⑲ p. 394	SW Hotel	◆◆	$139-$550	434
⑳ p. 394	Hilton San Francisco Financial District	◆◆◆	$189-$339 SAVE	424
㉑ p. 394	Le Meridien San Francisco	◆◆◆◆	$179-$699 SAVE	430
㉒ p. 394	Holiday Inn Golden Gateway	◆◆◆	Rates not provided SAVE	425
㉓ p. 394	The Fairmont San Francisco	◆◆◆◆	$199-$999 SAVE	422
㉔ p. 394	The Huntington Hotel	◆◆◆	$425-$595	429
㉕ p. 394	The Stanford Court, A Renaissance Hotel	◆◆◆	$179-$399 SAVE	434
㉖ p. 394	Omni San Francisco Hotel	◆◆◆	$189-$699 SAVE	431
㉗ p. 394	The Ritz-Carlton, San Francisco	◆◆◆◆◆	Rates not provided SAVE	433
㉘ p. 394	InterContinental Mark Hopkins San Francisco	◆◆◆◆	$159-$489 SAVE	430
㉙ p. 394	Hyatt Regency San Francisco	◆◆◆◆	$126-$423 SAVE	429
㉚ p. 394	Mandarin Oriental San Francisco	[fyi]	Rates not provided	430
㉛ p. 394	Petite Auberge, a Joie de Vivre hotel	◆◆	$109-$409	431
㉜ p. 394	White Swan Inn, a Joie de Vivre hotel	◆◆◆	$119-$419	436
㉝ p. 394	Executive Hotel Vintage Court	◆◆◆	$229-$459 SAVE	422
㉞ p. 394	The Orchard Hotel	◆◆◆	Rates not provided SAVE	431
㉟ p. 394	Hotel Vitale, a Joie de Vivre hotel	◆◆◆◆	$499-$3500	429

SAN FRANCISCO (cont'd)

Map Page	Hotels (cont'd)	Diamond Rated	Rate Range	Page
36 p. 394	Hotel Carlton, a Joie de Vivre hotel	◆◆◆	$109-$499	425
37 p. 394	**Hotel Vertigo**	◇◇◇	$119-$369 [SAVE]	429
38 p. 394	The Orchard Garden Hotel	◆◆◆	Rates not provided	431
39 p. 394	**Hotel Triton**	◇◇◇	$149-$489 [SAVE]	429
40 p. 394	Hotel Rex, a Joie de Vivre hotel	◆◆◆	$149-$409	429
41 p. 394	Larkspur Hotel Union Square	◆◆	Rates not provided	430
42 p. 394	San Francisco Marriott Union Square	◆◆◆	$199-$399	434
43 p. 394	**Beresford Hotel**	◇◇	$79-$169 [SAVE]	419
44 p. 394	**Hotel Griffon**	◇◇◇	$169-$499 [SAVE]	428
45 p. 394	**Sir Francis Drake Hotel**	◇◇◇	$129-$509 [SAVE]	434
46 p. 394	**Grand Hyatt San Francisco**	◇◇◇◇	$153-$423 [SAVE]	424
47 p. 394	Chancellor Hotel on Union Square	◆◆◆	Rates not provided	419
48 p. 394	**Beresford Arms Hotel & Suites**	◇◇◇	$89-$299 [SAVE]	418
49 p. 394	Galleria Park Hotel, a Joie de Vivre hotel	◆◆◆	Rates not provided	424
50 p. 394	**Harbor Court Hotel**	◇◇◇	$209-$359 [SAVE]	424
51 p. 394	Taj Campton Place San Francisco	◆◆◆◆	Rates not provided	434
52 p. 394	JW Marriott San Francisco	◇◇◇◇	$219-$489	430
53 p. 394	**The Prescott Hotel**	◇◇◇	Rates not provided [SAVE]	433
54 p. 394	Kensington Park Hotel	◆◆◆	$199-$399	430
55 p. 394	**Inn @Union Square**	◇◇◇	$209-$409 [SAVE]	430
56 p. 394	**The Monarch Hotel**	◇◇	$109-$189 [SAVE]	431
57 p. 394	**The Donatello**	◇◇◇	$129-$350 [SAVE]	422
58 p. 394	**The Opal San Francisco**	◇◇◇	Rates not provided [SAVE]	431
59 p. 394	**Adante Hotel**	◇◇	$79-$350 [SAVE]	418
60 p. 394	**BEST WESTERN The Hotel California**	◇◇◇	Rates not provided [SAVE]	419
61 p. 394	Hotel Adagio San Francisco	[fyi]	Rates not provided	425
62 p. 394	Warwick San Francisco Hotel (See ad p. 418.)	◆◆◆	$99-$349	436
63 p. 394	The Westin St. Francis San Francisco on Union Square	◇◇◇◇	$199-$629 [SAVE]	436
64 p. 394	Hotel Diva	◆◆◆	$199-$369	425
65 p. 394	**Hotel Monaco**	◇◇◇◇	$189-$459 [SAVE]	428
66 p. 394	Hotel Frank	◆◆◆	$109-$399	425
67 p. 394	**The Handley Union Square Hotel**	◇◇◇	$189-$499 [SAVE]	424
68 p. 394	**King George Hotel**	◇◇	$99-$309 [SAVE]	430
69 p. 394	Villa Florence	◆◆◆	$169-$449	434
70 p. 394	**Serrano Hotel**	◇◇◇	Rates not provided [SAVE]	434
71 p. 394	**Palace Hotel**	◇◇◇◇	$179-$619 [SAVE]	431
72 p. 394	**Alexis Park-San Francisco**	◇◇	$99-$499 [SAVE]	418

SAN FRANCISCO (cont'd)

Map Page	Hotels (cont'd)	Diamond Rated	Rate Range	Page
73 p. 394	Hilton San Francisco Union Square	◆◆◆◆	$109-$299	424
74 p. 394	**Hotel Mark Twain**	◆◆	$109-$399 SAVE	428
75 p. 394	**Hotel Nikko San Francisco**	◆◆◆	$169-$399 SAVE	428
76 p. 394	Four Seasons Hotel San Francisco	◆◆◆◆	$395-$795	424
77 p. 394	Hotel Union Square	◆◆	Rates not provided	429
78 p. 394	**Westin San Francisco Market Street**	◆◆◆	$159-$899 SAVE	436
79 p. 394	**Hotel Abri**	◆◆◆	$229-$389 SAVE	425
80 p. 394	Phoenix Hotel, a Joie de Vivre hotel	◆◆	$109-$359	431
81 p. 394	**Hotel Palomar**	◆◆◆	Rates not provided SAVE	428
82 p. 394	**Parc 55 Wyndham San Francisco Union Square** (See ad p. 432.)	◆◆◆◆	$159-$400 SAVE	431
83 p. 394	Hotel Bijou	◆◆	Rates not provided	425
84 p. 394	**St. Regis Hotel San Francisco**	◆◆◆◆	$329-$649 SAVE	433
85 p. 394	The Powell Hotel	◆◆	Rates not provided	433
86 p. 394	**San Francisco Marriott Marquis**	◆◆◆	$149-$589 SAVE	433
87 p. 394	**W San Francisco**	◆◆◆◆	$249-$669 SAVE	437
88 p. 394	Courtyard by Marriott San Francisco Downtown	◆◆◆	$189-$389	421
89 p. 394	The Pickwick Hotel	◆◆	$99-$309	433
90 p. 394	**InterContinental San Francisco**	◆◆◆◆	$159-$489 SAVE	430
91 p. 394	**Hotel Whitcomb**	◆◆	$129-$289 SAVE	429
92 p. 394	**The Good Hotel**	◆◆	$99-$289 SAVE	424
93 p. 394	**Holiday Inn Civic Center**	◆◆◆	$99-$339 SAVE	425
94 p. 394	**BEST WESTERN PLUS Americania**	◆◆◆	$119-$349 SAVE	419
95 p. 394	**BEST WESTERN PLUS Carriage Inn**	◆◆◆	$129-$369 SAVE	419

Map Page	Restaurants	Diamond Rated	Cuisine	Price Range	Page
1 p. 394	**Scoma's Restaurant**	◆◆◆	Seafood	$16-$46	456
2 p. 394	**Franciscan Crab Restaurant**	◆◆◆	Seafood	$15-$60	445
3 p. 394	Pier Market Seafood Restaurant	◆◆	Seafood	$12-$39	454
4 p. 394	Capurro's Restaurant & Bar	◆◆	Italian	$10-$28	442
5 p. 394	Cioppino's on the Wharf	◆◆	Italian	$10-$35	443
6 p. 394	**Blue Mermaid Chowder House & Bar**	◆◆◆	Seafood	$12-$28	440
7 p. 394	**Castagnola's**	◆◆	Seafood	$13-$46	442
8 p. 394	Pompei's Grotto	◆◆	Seafood	$11-$29	454
9 p. 394	**Crab House at Pier 39**	◆◆	Seafood	$15-$60	443
10 p. 394	Alioto's	◆◆◆	Seafood	$11-$62	437
11 p. 394	**Nick's Lighthouse**	◆◆	Seafood	$11-$30	452
12 p. 394	Bistro Boudin At The Wharf	◆◆◆	Seafood	$13-$29	440
13 p. 394	Ana Mandara	◆◆◆	Vietnamese	$14-$36	438
14 p. 394	Fog Harbor Fish House	◆◆	Seafood	$12-$50	445
15 p. 394	The Buena Vista Cafe	◆◆	American	$9-$18	441

Map Page	Restaurants (cont'd)	Diamond Rated	Cuisine	Price Range	Page
⑯ p. 394	McCormick & Kuleto's Seafood Restaurant	◆◆◆	Seafood	$15-$41	450
⑰ p. 394	**Gary Danko**	◆◆◆◆◆	Continental	$71-$104	445
⑱ p. 394	**Cafe Pescatore**	◆◆	Italian	$11-$25	441
⑲ p. 394	China House Jumbo Seafood Restaurant	◆◆	Chinese	$8-$24	442
⑳ p. 394	Butterfly	◆◆◆	Pacific Rim	$12-$39	441
㉑ p. 394	Pat's Cafe	◆◆	California	$7-$16	454
㉒ p. 394	**Boboquivaris**	◆◆◆	Continental	$19-$70	440
㉓ p. 394	Fog City Diner	◆◆	American	$10-$24	445
㉔ p. 394	Zarzuela	◆◆◆	Spanish	$14-$21	460
㉕ p. 394	The Helmand Palace	◆◆	Afghan	$12-$23	447
㉖ p. 394	La Folie	◆◆◆◆	French	$80-$100	448
㉗ p. 394	Trattoria Contadina	◆◆◆	Italian	$17-$28	459
㉘ p. 394	Frascati	◆◆◆	Continental	$22-$28	445
㉙ p. 394	The Matterhorn Swiss Restaurant	◆◆	Swiss	$20-$46	450
㉚ p. 394	**Cafe Divine**	◆◆	American	$8-$20	441
㉛ p. 394	Amarena	◆◆	Italian	$17-$30	437
㉜ p. 394	Pesce	◆◆	Italian	$7-$17	454
㉝ p. 394	Tony's Pizza Napoletana	◆◆	Pizza	$12-$38	459
㉞ p. 394	Rose Pistola	◆◆◆	Italian	$13-$37	456
㉟ p. 394	Cafe Jacqueline	◆◆◆	French	$28-$55	441
㊱ p. 394	Capp's Corner	◆◆	Italian	$10-$26	442
㊲ p. 394	**North Beach Restaurant**	◆◆◆	Italian	$19-$35	452
㊳ p. 394	O'Reilly's Irish Pub & Restaurant	◆◆	Irish	$14-$20	452
㊴ p. 394	Original U.S. Restaurant	◆◆	Italian	$9-$25	453
㊵ p. 394	Pier 23	◆◆	American	$13-$22	454
㊶ p. 394	Street Restaurant	◆◆	Northern California	$14-$24	458
㊷ p. 394	Piperade	◆◆◆	French	$13-$30	454
㊸ p. 394	**Calzone's**	◆◆	Italian	$9-$28	441
㊹ p. 394	Nick's Crispy Tacos	◆	Mexican	$4-$9	452
㊺ p. 394	Ristorante Mona Lisa	◆◆	Italian	$12-$34	455
㊻ p. 394	Harris'	◆◆◆	Steak	$26-$54	447
㊼ p. 394	**The Stinking Rose**	◆◆	Italian	$10-$60	457
㊽ p. 394	Giordano Bros	◆	American	$7-$8	446
㊾ p. 394	The House	◆◆◆	Asian	$12-$27	447
㊿ p. 394	Hyde Street Bistro	◆◆	French	$17-$25	447
(51) p. 394	Hyde Street Seafood House and Raw Bar	◆◆	Seafood	$14-$20	447
(52) p. 394	The Waterfront Restaurant	◆◆◆	California	$16-$35	459
(53) p. 394	Tommaso's Restaurant	◆◆	Italian	$15-$28	458
(54) p. 394	House of Prime Rib	◆◆◆	American	$28-$38	447
(55) p. 394	Cotogna	◆◆◆	Italian	$12-$30	443
(56) p. 394	Globe	◆◆◆	California	$11-$28	446
(57) p. 394	Tandoori Mahal	◆◆	Indian	$10-$22	458
(58) p. 394	Cafe Zoetrope	◆◆	Southern Italian	$8-$18	441

Map Page	Restaurants (cont'd)	Diamond Rated	Cuisine	Price Range	Page
59 p. 394	Bix	◆◆◆	Continental	$14-$40	440
60 p. 394	Great Eastern Restaurant	◆◆	Chinese	$9-$44	446
61 p. 394	**Thai Spice**	◇◆	Thai	$8-$15	458
62 p. 394	Kokkari Estiatorio	◆◆◆	Greek	$14-$40	448
63 p. 394	Lucky Creation Vegetarian Restaurant	◆◆	Chinese	$6-$18	450
64 p. 394	Bocadillos	◆◆	Spanish	$6-$16	440
65 p. 394	Penang Garden Restaurant	◆◆	Thai	$8-$21	454
66 p. 394	**Utopia Cafe**	◇◆	Cantonese	$6-$12	459
67 p. 394	L'Olivier Restaurant	◆◆◆	Regional French	$12-$28	449
68 p. 394	La Mar Cebicheria Peruana	◆◆◆	Peruvian	$11-$34	449
69 p. 394	Acquerello	◆◆◆◆	Italian	$70-$135	437
70 p. 394	Empress of China	◆◆	Chinese	$15-$45	444
71 p. 394	Nob Hill Cafe	◆◆	Italian	$10-$19	452
72 p. 394	Tommy Toy's Haute Cuisine	◆◆◆	New Chinese	$14-$29	459
73 p. 394	Alfred's Steakhouse	◆◆◆	Steak	$14-$59	437
74 p. 394	**Oriental Pearl Restaurant**	◇◆	Chinese	$11-$55	453
75 p. 394	New Chef Hung's Restaurant	◆◆	Chinese	$6-$19	452
76 p. 394	R & G Lounge	◆◆	Chinese	$9-$40	455
77 p. 394	Crustacean Restaurant	◆◆	Asian	$15-$39	444
78 p. 394	City View Restaurant	◆◆	Chinese	$4-$20	443
79 p. 394	Kan's	◆◆	Chinese	$10-$48	448
80 p. 394	Park Grill	◆◆◆	California	$15-$40	453
81 p. 394	The Laurel Court Restaurant & Bar	◆◆◆	California	$16-$36	449
82 p. 394	Palio D'Asti	◆◆◆	Italian	$13-$45	453
83 p. 394	Leopold's	◆◆◆	German	$12-$19	449
84 p. 394	Wayfare Tavern	◆◆◆	American	$19-$32	459
85 p. 394	Far East Cafe	◆◆	Cantonese	$9-$50	444
86 p. 394	Big 4 Restaurant	◆◆◆◆	California	$18-$44	440
87 p. 394	Grubstake	◆◆	American	$8-$19	446
88 p. 394	Aurea	◆◆◆	California	$13-$33	438
89 p. 394	Il Cane Rosso	◆◆	California	$6-$13	447
90 p. 394	The Slanted Door	◆◆◆	Vietnamese	$12-$38	457
91 p. 394	Hog Island Oyster Co	◆◆	Seafood	$12-$18	447
92 p. 394	Boulettes Larder	◆◆	Natural/Organic	$7-$25	440
93 p. 394	Mijita Cocina Mexicana	◆	Mexican	$5-$13	451
94 p. 394	Gott's Roadside	◆	American	$6-$15	446
95 p. 394	DELICA rf-1	◆	Japanese	$10-$13	444
96 p. 394	Bob's Steak & Chop House	◆◆◆	Steak	$15-$70	440
97 p. 394	Parallel 37	◆◆◆◆	New American	$24-$29	453
98 p. 394	One Market Restaurant	◆◆◆	American	$15-$36	452
99 p. 394	Michael Mina	◆◆◆◆	New American	$21-$49	451
100 p. 394	Aicha Moroccan Cuisine	◆◆	Moroccan	$11-$15	437
101 p. 394	Tadich Grill	◆◆	Seafood	$15-$45	458

Map Page	Restaurants (cont'd)	Diamond Rated	Cuisine	Price Range	Page
102 p. 394	Modern Thai	◆◆	Thai	$8-$14	451
103 p. 394	Alborz	◆◆	Middle Eastern	$10-$16	437
104 p. 394	Ramen Underground	◆◆	Japanese	$8	455
105 p. 394	Sons and Daughters	◆◆◆	California	$20-$25	457
106 p. 394	Plouf	◆◆	Seafood	$12-$34	454
107 p. 394	Masa's	◆◆◆◆	French	$98-$140	450
108 p. 394	Cafe Tiramisu	◆◆	Italian	$19-$40	441
109 p. 394	Boulevard	◆◆◆	American	$16-$42	440
110 p. 394	Saha	◆◆	Arabic	$17-$25	456
111 p. 394	Americano Restaurant & Bar	◆◆	Northern Italian	$12-$30	438
112 p. 394	Roxanne Cafe	◆◆	Italian	$11-$20	456
113 p. 394	Muracci's Japanese Curry & Grill	◆	Japanese	$8-$10	451
114 p. 394	Sanraku Restaurant	◆◆	Japanese	$10-$38	456
115 p. 394	Chaya Brasserie	◆◆◆	Asian	$15-$39	442
116 p. 394	Fleur de Lys	◆◆◆◆	French	$72-$95	445
117 p. 394	Maharani	◆◆	Indian	$9-$28	450
118 p. 394	Persimmon Cafe	◆◆	International	$8-$21	454
119 p. 394	Cesario's Fine Food	◆◆	Northern Italian	$11-$25	442
120 p. 394	Le Colonial	◆◆◆	Vietnamese	$22-$32	449
121 p. 394	E & O Trading Company	◆◆	Asian	$13-$24	444
122 p. 394	Cafe Claude	◆◆◆	French	$11-$29	441
123 p. 394	**Scala's Bistro**	◆◆◆	Italian	$12-$30	456
124 p. 394	Gitane Restaurant & Bar	◆◆◆	Spanish	$23-$28	446
125 p. 394	Grandviews	◆◆◆	American	$13-$38	446
126 p. 394	Sears Fine Foods	◆◆	American	$9-$30	457
127 p. 394	Borobudur Restaurant	◆◆	Indonesian	$8-$18	440
128 p. 394	Ozumo	◆◆◆	Japanese	$11-$46	453
129 p. 394	Cafe Metropol	◆◆	Continental	$13-$20	441
130 p. 394	Fino Bar & Ristorante	◆◆◆	Italian	$15-$29	444
131 p. 394	Campton Place Restaurant	◆◆◆◆	Regional French	$23-$41	442
132 p. 394	Tommy's Joynt	◆	American	$6-$9	459
133 p. 394	Farallon	◆◆◆	Seafood	$27-$42	444
134 p. 394	Zingari	◆◆◆	Italian	$12-$29	460
135 p. 394	RN74	◆◆◆	California	$16-$38	455
136 p. 394	Osha Thai Noodle Cafe	◆◆	Thai	$11-$17	453
137 p. 394	Yank Sing	◆◆	Chinese	$12-$25	460
138 p. 394	Millennium Restaurant	◆◆	Vegetarian	$23-$26	451
139 p. 394	La Scene Cafe (See ad p. 418.)	◆◆◆	California	$18-$35	449
140 p. 394	David's Deli	◆	Jewish	$9-$20	444
141 p. 394	colibri Mexican-Bistro	◆◆◆	Mexican	$12-$20	443
142 p. 394	Max's on the Square	◆◆	American	$10-$28	450
143 p. 394	Burger Bar San Francisco	◆◆	American	$9-$25	441
144 p. 394	Grain D' Or Bakery	◆	American	$5-$8	446
145 p. 394	The Garden Court	◆◆◆	American	$23-$36	445

Map Page	Restaurants (cont'd)	Diamond Rated	Cuisine	Price Range	Page
(146) p. 394	Kuleto's	◆◆◆	Italian	$18-$37	448
(147) p. 394	Neiman Marcus-The Rotunda Restaurant	◆◆◆	California	$17-$28	451
(148) p. 394	Town Hall	◆◆◆	American	$13-$30	459
(149) p. 394	Santorini's	◆◆	Mediterranean	$12-$23	456
(150) p. 394	Roy's	◆◆◆	Pacific Rim	$16-$40	456
(151) p. 394	Johnny Foley's	◆◆	Irish	$15-$28	448
(152) p. 394	Lori's Diner	◆◆	American	$8-$15	450
(153) p. 394	Prospect	◆◆◆	California	$25-$32	455
(154) p. 394	Anzu Restaurant	◆◆◆	Pacific Rim	$11-$42	438
(155) p. 394	Tian Sing Chinese Restaurant	◆◆	Chinese	$10-$36	458
(156) p. 394	Seasons Restaurant	◆◆◆◆	California	$17-$52	457
(157) p. 394	Hana Zen	◆◆	Japanese	$10-$47	446
(158) p. 394	New Delhi	◆◆	Indian	$11-$25	452
(159) p. 394	First Crush Restaurant Wine Bar & Lounge	◆◆◆	American	$15-$29	445
(160) p. 394	Les Joulins Jazz Bistro	◆◆	French	$8-$23	449
(161) p. 394	**Puccini & Pinetti**	◆◆	Italian	$13-$30	455
(162) p. 394	**John's Grill**	◆◆	American	$12-$38	448
(163) p. 394	Brenda's French Soul Food	◆◆	Creole	$7-$17	441
(164) p. 394	Osha Thai Restaurant	◆◆◆	Thai	$11-$20	453
(165) p. 394	cityhouse restaurant	◆◆◆	American	$12-$36	443
(166) p. 394	**Fifth Floor**	◆◆◆◆	New French	$28-$42	444
(167) p. 394	Ame restaurant	◆◆◆◆	Northern California	$35-$39	438
(168) p. 394	Straits Restaurant	◆◆◆	Philippine	$10-$39	457
(169) p. 394	annabelle's Bar & Bistro	◆◆◆	New California	$13-$32	438
(170) p. 394	Thirsty Bear Brewing Co.	◆◆	Spanish	$8-$23	458
(171) p. 394	Zare at Fly Trap	◆◆	Mediterranean	$12-$27	460
(172) p. 394	Samovar Tea Lounge	◆◆	International	$5-$24	456
(173) p. 394	'wichcraft	◆	Sandwiches	$7-$10	459
(174) p. 394	Chez Papa Resto	◆◆◆	French	$14-$30	442
(175) p. 394	54 Mint	◆◆◆	Italian	$15-$26	437
(176) p. 394	Showdogs	◆	American	$8-$15	457
(177) p. 394	Blue Bottle Cafe	◆	American	$5-$10	440
(178) p. 394	Cha-am Thai Restaurant Bar & Grill	◆◆	Thai	$9-$18	442
(179) p. 394	**Grand Cafe**	◆◆◆	French	$13-$34	446
(180) p. 394	Lu Lu	◆◆◆	American	$9-$32	450
(181) p. 394	AQ Restaurant & Bar	◆◆◆	California	$25	438
(182) p. 394	Oola	◆◆◆	American	$10-$32	452
(183) p. 394	Heaven's Dog	◆◆	Chinese	$10-$19	447
(184) p. 394	The American Grilled Cheese Kitchen	◆	American	$4-$9	438
(185) p. 394	Nova Bar & Restaurant	◆◆	American	$7-$19	452
(186) p. 394	21st Amendment	◆◆	American	$11-$25	437
(187) p. 394	Le Charm French Bistro	◆◆◆	French	$9-$30	449
(188) p. 394	Town's End Restaurant & Bakery	◆◆	California	$9-$18	459

Map Page	Restaurants (cont'd)	Diamond Rated	Cuisine	Price Range	Page
189 p. 394	Koh Samui and the Monkey	▽▽▽	Thai	$9-$23	448
190 p. 394	Paragon	▽▽	American	$9-$25	453
191 p. 394	Zuppa	▽▽▽	Italian	$11-$24	460
192 p. 394	Rocco's Cafe	▽▽	Italian	$10-$23	455
193 p. 394	Fringale	▽▽▽	French	$15-$26	445
194 p. 394	MoMo's Restaurant	▽▽▽	American	$13-$25	451
195 p. 394	Basil Thai Restaurant & Bar	▽▽	Thai	$9-$17	439
196 p. 394	Coco 500	▽▽▽	Mediterranean	$14-$25	443
197 p. 394	Citizen's Band	▽▽	American	$10-$24	443
198 p. 394	Marlowe	▽▽▽	American	$13-$25	450

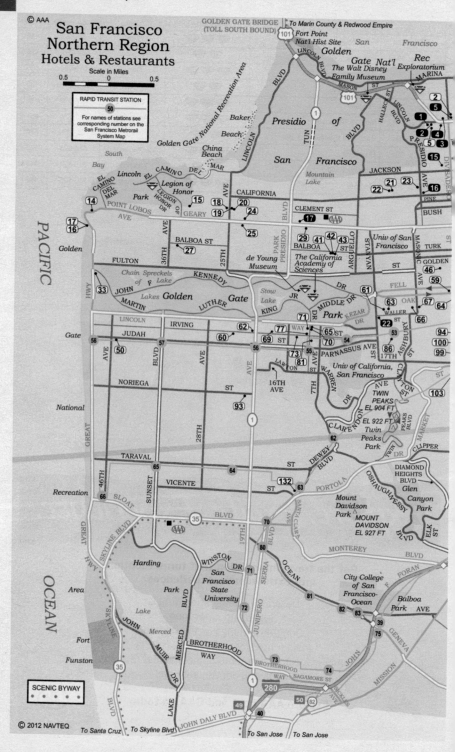

© AAA

San Francisco
Northern Region
Hotels & Restaurants

Scale in Miles
0.5   0   0.5

RAPID TRANSIT STATION

50

For names of stations see
corresponding number on the
San Francisco Metrorail
System Map

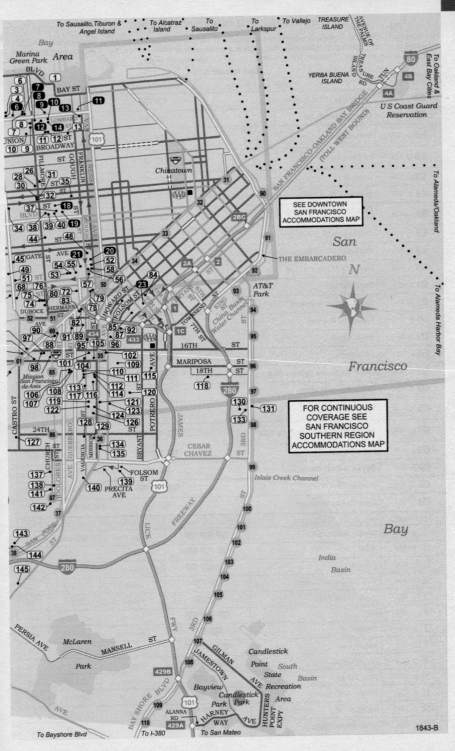

1843-B

San Francisco Northern Region

This index helps you "spot" where approved hotels and restaurants are located on the corresponding detailed maps. Hotel daily rate range is for comparison only. Restaurant price range is a combination of lunch and/or dinner. Turn to the listing page for more detailed rate and price information and consult display ads for special promotions.

SAN FRANCISCO

Map Page	Hotels	Diamond Rated	Rate Range	Page
1 p. 404	Travelodge at the Presidio	◆◆	$129-$259	434
2 p. 404	**Country Hearth Inn**	◆◆	$75-$135 SAVE	421
3 p. 404	**Marina Motel**	◆◆	Rates not provided SAVE	431
4 p. 404	**La Luna Inn**	◆◆	Rates not provided SAVE	430
5 p. 404	**Super 8**	◆◆	$79-$239 SAVE	434
6 p. 404	**Americas Best Value Inn & Suites Golden Gate**	◆◆	$58-$199 SAVE	418
7 p. 404	**Cow Hollow Motor Inn & Suites** *(See ad p. 420, p. 423.)*	◆◆	$86-$325 SAVE	422
8 p. 404	**Chelsea Motor Inn** *(See ad p. 420.)*	◆◆	$86-$155 SAVE	419
9 p. 404	**Ramada Limited-Golden Gate**	◆◆	$119-$259 SAVE	433
10 p. 404	**Coventry Motor Inn** *(See ad p. 420.)*	◆◆	$86-$155 SAVE	421
11 p. 404	**Redwood Inn**	◆◆	$69-$199 SAVE	433
12 p. 404	**Hotel Del Sol, a Joie de Vivre hotel**	◆◆	$129-$269 SAVE	425
13 p. 404	**Francisco Bay Inn**	◆◆	$69-$179 SAVE	424
14 p. 404	**Motel Capri**	◆	$80-$240 SAVE	431
15 p. 404	Hotel Drisco	◆◆◆	$225-$785	425
16 p. 404	Laurel Inn, a Joie de Vivre hotel	◆◆◆	$159-$329	430
17 p. 404	**Geary Parkway Motel**	◆◆	$80-$200 SAVE	424
18 p. 404	**Hotel Tomo**	◆◆	Rates not provided SAVE	429
19 p. 404	Hotel Kabuki, a Joie de Vivre hotel	◆◆◆	Rates not provided	428
20 p. 404	Inn at the Opera	◆◆◆	$139-$259	429
21 p. 404	**Days Inn-Civic Center**	◆◆	$75-$350 SAVE	422
22 p. 404	Stanyan Park Hotel	◆◆◆	$175-$450	434
23 p. 404	Civic Center Motor Inn	◆◆	$74-$179 SAVE	419

Map Page	Restaurants	Diamond Rated	Cuisine	Price Range	Page
1 p. 404	Greens Restaurant	◆◆◆	Vegetarian	$12-$24	446
2 p. 404	A 16	◆◆◆	Italian	$12-$26	437
3 p. 404	Ristobar	◆◆◆	Italian	$13-$29	455
4 p. 404	Viva Goa Indian Cuisine	◆◆	Indian	$9-$16	459
5 p. 404	Baker Street Bistro	◆◆	French	$9-$29	438
6 p. 404	Isa	◆◆◆	French	$12-$24	448
7 p. 404	Chotto	◆◆	Japanese	$5-$16	442
8 p. 404	Balboa Cafe	◆◆◆	American	$10-$30	439
9 p. 404	Atelier Crenn	◆◆◆	French	$75-$125	438
10 p. 404	Rose's Cafe	◆◆	Italian	$12-$27	456
11 p. 404	Nettie's Crab Shack	◆◆	Seafood	$11-$35	452
12 p. 404	Betelnut	◆◆◆	Asian	$12-$22	439
13 p. 404	Roam Artisan Burgers	◆	Burgers	$6-$8	455

Map Page	Restaurants (cont'd)	Diamond Rated	Cuisine	Price Range	Page
14 p. 404	Louis'	◆◆	American	$8-$18	450
15 p. 404	Oyaji Restaurant	◆◆	Japanese	$5-$45	453
16 p. 404	Cliff House-The Bistro	◆◆	American	$14-$30	443
17 p. 404	Cliff House - Sutro's	◆◆◆	American	$19-$39	443
18 p. 404	Hard Knox Cafe	◆◆	Soul Food	$6-$15	446
19 p. 404	PPQ Dungeness Island	◆◆	Vietnamese	$5-$17	455
20 p. 404	Bill's Place	◆◆	American	$6-$14	440
21 p. 404	Spruce	◆◆◆	California	$13-$39	457
22 p. 404	Sociale Caffe & Wine Bar	◆◆◆	Italian	$12-$32	457
23 p. 404	Garibaldi's on Presidio	◆◆◆	American	$12-$27	445
24 p. 404	Aziza	◆◆◆	Moroccan	$19-$29	438
25 p. 404	Ton Kiang Restaurant Dim Sum-Seafood	◆◆	Chinese	$9-$26	459
26 p. 404	La Mediterranee	◆◆	Mediterranean	$12-$15	449
27 p. 404	Shanghai Dumpling King	◆◆	Chinese	$6-$10	457
28 p. 404	Pizzeria Delfina	◆◆	Pizza	$10-$17	454
29 p. 404	My Tofu House	◆◆	Korean	$11-$22	451
30 p. 404	Boulangerie Bay Bread	◆	Breads/Pastries	$4-$9	440
31 p. 404	Florio Cafe and Bar	◆◆◆	Continental	$15-$29	445
32 p. 404	SPQR	◆◆◆	Italian	$18-$29	457
33 p. 404	Beach Chalet Brewery and Restaurant	◆◆	American	$12-$32	439
34 p. 404	Cheese Steak Shop	◆	American	$4-$9	442
35 p. 404	Baker & Banker	◆◆◆	American	$24-$31	438
37 p. 404	Shabusen Restaurant	◆◆	Japanese	$14-$45	457
38 p. 404	Suzu Noodle House	◆◆	Noodles	$8-$13	458
39 p. 404	Izumiya	◆◆	Japanese	$8-$20	448
40 p. 404	Isobune Sushi	◆◆	Sushi	$8-$25	448
41 p. 404	Namu	◆◆	Asian	$9-$26	451
42 p. 404	Mugu Boka Korean BBQ Restaurant	◆◆	Korean	$8-$36	451
43 p. 404	Katia's	◆◆	Russian	$13-$19	448
44 p. 404	1300 on Fillmore	◆◆◆	Soul Food	$15-$31	437
45 p. 404	Little Star Pizza	◆◆	Pizza	$12-$24	449
46 p. 404	Chili Pies & Ice Cream	◆	American	$7-$8	442
48 p. 404	Indigo Restaurant	◆◆◆	American	$11-$30	447
49 p. 404	Bar Crudo	◆◆◆	Seafood	$14-$26	439
50 p. 404	Outerlands	◆◆	California	$5-$25	453
51 p. 404	NOPA	◆◆◆	California	$13-$26	452
52 p. 404	Jardiniere	◆◆◆◆	French	$18-$44	448
53 p. 404	Bar Jules	◆◆	California	$13-$27	439
54 p. 404	Suppenkuche	◆◆	Traditional German	$15-$20	458
55 p. 404	Sebo	◆◆	Sushi	$6-$35	457
56 p. 404	Absinthe Brasserie and Bar	◆◆◆	Regional French	$14-$36	437
57 p. 404	Caffe Delle Stelle	◆◆	Italian	$10-$19	441
58 p. 404	Hayes Street Grill	◆◆◆	Seafood	$12-$28	447

Map Page	Restaurants (cont'd)	Diamond Rated	Cuisine	Price Range	Page
59 p. 404	Nopalito	◆◆	Mexican	$9-$16	452
60 p. 404	Marnee Thai	◆◆	Thai	$10-$19	450
61 p. 404	Parada 22	◆◆	Puerto Rican	$8-$13	453
62 p. 404	The Taco Shop at Underdogs	◆◆	Mexican	$4-$9	458
63 p. 404	The Alembic	◆◆	California	$9-$23	437
64 p. 404	Ragazza	◆◆	Italian	$13-$19	455
65 p. 404	Pacific Catch Fresh Fish Grill	◆◆	Pacific Rim	$11-$20	453
66 p. 404	Pork Store Cafe	◆◆	American	$6-$11	455
67 p. 404	Magnolia Pub & Brewery	◆	American	$10-$25	450
68 p. 404	The Little Chihuahua	◆	Mexican	$6-$11	449
69 p. 404	Izakaya Sozai	◆◆	Small Plates	$3-$19	448
70 p. 404	Park Chow	◆◆	American	$9-$14	453
71 p. 404	Marnee Thai	◆◆	Thai	$9-$17	450
72 p. 404	Straw	◆◆	American	$12-$16	458
73 p. 404	San Tung Chinese Restaurant	◆◆	Chinese	$6-$16	456
74 p. 404	Memphis Minnie's	◆	Barbecue	$9-$24	450
75 p. 404	Uva Enoteca	◆◆	Italian	$14-$20	459
76 p. 404	Rosamunde Sausage Grill	◆	Hot Dogs	$6-$7	455
77 p. 404	Patxi's Chicago Pizza	◆◆	Pizza	$12-$31	454
78 p. 404	Zuni Cafe	◆◆◆	California	$15-$28	460
79 p. 404	Espetus Churrascaria	◆◆◆	Brazilian	$50-$50	444
80 p. 404	Thep Phanom	◆◆	Thai	$10-$17	458
81 p. 404	Craw Station	◆◆	Seafood	$10-$12	443
82 p. 404	It's Tops Coffee Shop	◆◆	American	$8-$17	448
83 p. 404	Destino	◆◆	New Latin American	$6-$24	444
84 p. 404	India Garden	◆◆	Indian	$11-$18	447
85 p. 404	Una Pizza Napoletana	◆◆	Italian	$20-$20	459
86 p. 404	Zazie	◆◆	French	$10-$22	460
87 p. 404	Bar Agricole	◆◆◆	California	$18-$28	439
88 p. 404	Woodhouse Fish Company	◆◆	Seafood	$10-$20	460
89 p. 404	Pauline's Pizza	◆◆	Pizza	$14-$24	454
90 p. 404	Chow	◆◆	American	$8-$22	443
91 p. 404	Mission Beach Cafe	◆◆	California	$8-$28	451
92 p. 404	Chez Spencer	◆◆◆	French	$26-$32	442
93 p. 404	Cafe Bakery & Restaurant	◆◆	International	$9-$19	441
94 p. 404	Super Duper Burgers	◆	American	$5-$7	458
95 p. 404	Pica Pica Maize Kitchen	◆	Latin American	$8-$9	454
96 p. 404	Walzwerk	◆	Eastern German	$13-$18	459
97 p. 404	Ike's Place	◆	Sandwiches	$8-$20	447
98 p. 404	Restaurant Eiji	◆◆	Japanese	$5-$18	455
99 p. 404	Catch	◆◆◆	Mediterranean	$10-$24	442
100 p. 404	Frances	◆◆◆	California	$20-$28	445
101 p. 404	Pancho Villa Taqueria	◆	Mexican	$7-$16	453

Map Page	Restaurants (cont'd)	Diamond Rated	Cuisine	Price Range	Page
102 p. 404	Bar Bambino Cafe & Wine Bar	◆◆◆	Italian	$17-$30	439
103 p. 404	Firewood Cafe	◆	Italian	$9-$15	445
104 p. 404	El Toro Taqueria	◆	Mexican	$3-$15	444
105 p. 404	Maverick American Eatery & Wine Bar	◆◆◆	Regional American	$17-$26	450
106 p. 404	Delfina	◆◆◆	Italian	$9-$26	444
107 p. 404	Pizzeria Delfina	◆◆	Pizza	$10-$17	454
108 p. 404	Tartine Bakery & Cafe	◆	Breads/Pastries	$4-$13	458
109 p. 404	Saison	◆◆◆◆	French	$198-$248	456
110 p. 404	Luna Park Kitchen and Cocktails	◆◆	American	$13-$36	450
111 p. 404	Mission Cheese	◆	Specialty	$7-$10	451
112 p. 404	Commonwealth	◆◆◆	California	$13-$16	443
113 p. 404	Grub	◆◆	American	$9-$19	446
114 p. 404	Mission Chinese Food	◆◆	Chinese	$7-$13	451
115 p. 404	Slow Club	◆◆	California	$11-$28	457
116 p. 404	Hog & Rocks	◆◆	North American	$11-$18	447
117 p. 404	Range	◆◆◆	California	$19-$27	455
118 p. 404	Chez Maman	◆◆	French	$10-$21	442
119 p. 404	Dosa on Valencia	◆◆	Southern Indian	$13-$18	444
120 p. 404	Flour + Water	◆◆◆	Italian	$14-$27	445
121 p. 404	Nombe	◆◆	Japanese	$4-$16	452
122 p. 404	Aslam's Rasoi	◆◆	Indian	$10-$22	438
123 p. 404	Limon Rotisserie	◆◆	Peruvian	$6-$10	449
124 p. 404	Foreign Cinema	◆◆◆	California	$22-$28	445
126 p. 404	Lolo	◆◆	New Latin American	$6-$26	449
127 p. 404	Contigo Kitchen & Cava	◆◆◆	Small Plates	$9-$23	443
128 p. 404	Papalote Mexican Grill	◆	Mexican	$8-$16	453
129 p. 404	Rosamunde Sausage Grill	◆	Hot Dogs	$6-$7	456
130 p. 404	Piccino	◆◆	Italian	$9-$22	454
131 p. 404	Serpentine	◆◆	California	$11-$26	457
132 p. 404	Roti Indian Bistro	◆◆	Indian	$9-$22	456
133 p. 404	Hard Knox Cafe	◆◆	Soul Food	$6-$15	446
134 p. 404	La Taqueria	◆	Mexican	$5-$8	449
135 p. 404	Mission Pie	◆	American	$4-$9	451
137 p. 404	Incanto	◆◆◆	Italian	$16-$27	447
138 p. 404	Clay Oven Indian Cuisine	◆◆	Indian	$11-$18	443
139 p. 404	Caffe Cozzolino	◆◆	Italian	$10-$18	441
140 p. 404	Mi Lindo Peru	◆◆	Peruvian	$7-$18	451
141 p. 404	Tataki South	◆◆	Japanese	$11-$36	458
142 p. 404	La Ciccia	◆◆◆	Italian	$12-$26	448
143 p. 404	Chenery Park	◆◆◆	American	$15-$24	442
144 p. 404	Gialina	◆◆	Pizza	$14-$19	446
145 p. 404	Joe's Cable Car Restaurant	◆◆	American	$7-$20	448

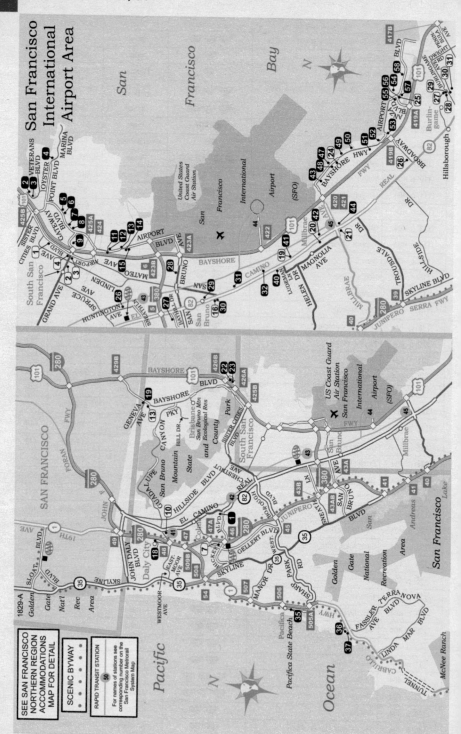

San Francisco International Airport Area

See San Francisco Northern Region Accommodations Map for Detail

SCENIC BYWAY

RAPID TRANSIT STATION

For names of stations see corresponding number on the San Francisco Metrorail System Map

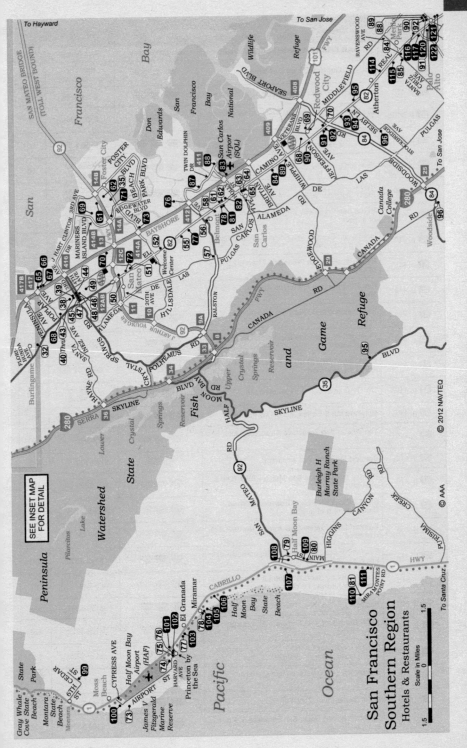

San Francisco Southern Region

Hotels & Restaurants

Scale in Miles

1.5   0   1.5

© 2012 NAVTEQ

© AAA

SEE INSET MAP FOR DETAIL

✈ Airport Accommodations

Map Page	SAN FRANCISCO INTERNATIONAL	Diamond Rated	Rate Range	Page
50 p. 410	Bay Landing Hotel, 1 mi s of airport	◆◆◆	Rates not provided (SAVE)	60
53 p. 410	Crowne Plaza, 2.5 mi s of airport	◆◆◆	$129-$229	60
55 p. 410	DoubleTree by Hilton Hotel San Francisco Airport, 1.3 mi s of airport	◆◆◆	$129-$309	60
54 p. 410	Embassy Suites-San Francisco Airport-Burlingame, 1.5 mi s of airport	◆◆◆	$150-$350	60
48 p. 410	Hampton Inn & Suites, 1 mi s of airport	◆◆◆	Rates not provided	60
57 p. 410	Hilton Garden Inn San Francisco Airport/Burlingame, 2 mi s of airport	◆◆◆	Rates not provided	60
58 p. 410	Hilton San Francisco Airport Bayfront, 1.5 mi s of airport	◆◆◆	Rates not provided (SAVE)	61
52 p. 410	Holiday Inn Express San Francisco Airport South, 2.5 mi s of airport	◆◆◆	Rates not provided	61
51 p. 410	Hyatt Regency San Francisco Airport, 2.5 mi s of airport	◆◆◆	$81-$360 (SAVE)	61
56 p. 410	Red Roof Inn San Francisco Airport, 1.5 mi s of airport	◆◆	$60-$140 (SAVE)	61
47 p. 410	San Francisco Airport Marriott Waterfront, 2 mi s of airport	◆◆◆	$169-$329	61
49 p. 410	Vagabond Inn Executive San Francisco Airport, 1 mi s of airport	◆◆	$69-$199	61
41 p. 410	BEST WESTERN PLUS El Rancho Inn & Suites, 2.5 mi sw of airport	◆◆◆	$109-$199 (SAVE)	194
44 p. 410	The Dylan at SFO, 1.5 mi sw of airport	◆◆	Rates not provided	194
40 p. 410	Millwood Inn & Suites, 2.5 mi sw of airport	◆◆◆	$97-$280 (SAVE)	194
43 p. 410	The Westin San Francisco Airport, 0.5 mi s of airport	◆◆◆	$129-$409 (SAVE)	194
66 p. 410	Comfort Inn, 5 mi s of airport	◆◆	$79-$199 (SAVE)	481
67 p. 410	Holiday Inn & Suites San Mateo - SFO, 5 mi s of airport	◆◆◆	$99-$209 (SAVE)	481
14 p. 410	BEST WESTERN PLUS Grosvenor Airport Hotel, 1.5 mi n of airport	◆◆◆	$119-$209 (SAVE)	531
9 p. 410	Comfort Inn & Suites SFO Airport North, 2.5 mi n of airport	◆◆◆	$100-$400 (SAVE)	531
8 p. 410	Embassy Suites San Francisco Airport-South San Francisco, 2.5 mi n of airport	◆◆◆	$140-$350	531
11 p. 410	Four Points by Sheraton Hotel & Suites San Francisco Airport, 1.5 mi n of airport	◆◆◆	$109-$349 (SAVE)	532
7 p. 410	Hampton Inn, 2.5 mi n of airport	◆◆◆	$199-$299	532
6 p. 410	Hilton Garden Inn San Francisco Airport North, 2.5 mi n of airport	◆◆◆	$129-$229	532
13 p. 410	Holiday Inn Express Hotel & Suites San Francisco Airport North, 1.5 mi n of airport	◆◆◆	$119-$259	532
12 p. 410	Holiday Inn San Francisco International Airport, 1.5 mi n of airport	◆◆◆	$99-$199	532
4 p. 410	Inn at Oyster Point, 2 mi n of airport	◆◆◆	$169-$239	532
5 p. 410	Larkspur Landing South San Francisco, 2.5 mi n of airport	◆◆◆	$109-$309	532

San Francisco Southern Region

This index helps you "spot" where approved hotels and restaurants are located on the corresponding detailed maps. Hotel daily rate range is for comparison only. Restaurant price range is a combination of lunch and/or dinner. Turn to the listing page for more detailed rate and price information and consult display ads for special promotions.

SOUTH SAN FRANCISCO

Map Page	Hotels	Diamond Rated	Rate Range	Page
① p. 410	**Travelers Inn**	◈◈	$69-$210 SAVE	532
② p. 410	Residence Inn by Marriott at Oyster Point	◈◈◈	$159-$285	532
③ p. 410	**Courtyard San Francisco Airport/Oyster Point Waterfront**	◈◈◈	$139-$152 SAVE	531
④ p. 410	Inn at Oyster Point	◈◈◈	$169-$239	532
⑤ p. 410	Larkspur Landing South San Francisco	◈◈◈	$109-$309	532
⑥ p. 410	Hilton Garden Inn San Francisco Airport North	◈◈◈	$129-$229	532
⑦ p. 410	Hampton Inn	◈◈◈	$199-$299	532
⑧ p. 410	Embassy Suites San Francisco Airport-South San Francisco	◈◈◈	$140-$350	531
⑨ p. 410	**Comfort Inn & Suites SFO Airport North**	◈◈◈	$100-$400 SAVE	531
⑪ p. 410	**Four Points by Sheraton Hotel & Suites San Francisco Airport**	◈◈◈	$109-$349 SAVE	532
⑫ p. 410	Holiday Inn San Francisco International Airport	◈◈◈	$99-$199	532
⑬ p. 410	Holiday Inn Express Hotel & Suites San Francisco Airport North	◈◈◈	$119-$259	532
⑭ p. 410	**BEST WESTERN PLUS Grosvenor Airport Hotel**	◈◈◈	$119-$209 SAVE	531
⑮ p. 410	**Quality Inn & Suites**	◈◈	$79-$389 SAVE	532

Map Page	Restaurants	Diamond Rated	Cuisine	Price Range	Page
① p. 410	Darby Dan's Sandwich Company	◈	Sandwiches	$6-$9	532
② p. 410	Grand Palace Seafood Restaurant	◈◈	Cantonese	$7-$38	533
③ p. 410	Ben Tre Restaurant	◈◈	Vietnamese	$7-$29	532
④ p. 410	Buon Gusto Ristorante	◈◈	Italian	$12-$23	532

DALY CITY

Map Page	Hotels	Diamond Rated	Rate Range	Page
⑱ p. 410	Hampton Inn	◈◈◈	$119-$169	92
⑲ p. 410	BridgePoint Inn	◈◈	Rates not provided	92

Map Page	Restaurant	Diamond Rated	Cuisine	Price Range	Page
⑦ p. 410	Koi Palace Restaurant	◈◈◈	Chinese	$9-$68	93

BRISBANE

Map Page	Hotels	Diamond Rated	Rate Range	Page
㉒ p. 410	Radisson Hotel San Francisco Airport at Sierra Point	◈◈◈	$109-$459	59
㉓ p. 410	Homewood Suites By Hilton	◈◈◈	$169-$189	59

Map Page	Restaurant	Diamond Rated	Cuisine	Price Range	Page
⑬ p. 410	7 Mile House	◈◈	American	$9-$17	59

SAN BRUNO

Map Page	Hotels	Diamond Rated	Rate Range	Page
㉖ p. 410	**Staybridge Suites**	◈◈◈	$129-$309 SAVE	339
㉗ p. 410	Courtyard by Marriott San Francisco Airport	◈◈◈	$149-$309	339
㉘ p. 410	**Comfort Inn & Suites**	◈◈◈	$79-$199 SAVE	339
㉙ p. 410	Gateway Inn & Suites	◈◈	$89-$159	339

SAN BRUNO (cont'd)

Map Page	Hotels (cont'd)	Diamond Rated	Rate Range	Page
30 p. 410	**Super 8**	◈◈	$80-$159 [SAVE]	339
31 p. 410	**Howard Johnson Express Inn**	◈◈	$65-$149 [SAVE]	339
32 p. 410	Days Inn-SFO International-West	◆◆	$55-$175	339

Map Page	Restaurant	Diamond Rated	Cuisine	Price Range	Page
16 p. 410	Don Pico's Mexican Bistro	◆◆	Mexican	$14-$25	339

PACIFICA

Map Page	Hotels	Diamond Rated	Rate Range	Page
35 p. 410	Americas Best Value Inn	◆◆	Rates not provided	266
36 p. 410	**BEST WESTERN PLUS Lighthouse Hotel**	◈◈◈	$139-$209 [SAVE]	266
37 p. 410	**Holiday Inn Express Hotel & Suites**	◈◈◈	$149-$399 [SAVE]	266

MILLBRAE

Map Page	Hotels	Diamond Rated	Rate Range	Page
40 p. 410	**Millwood Inn & Suites**	◈◈◈	$97-$280 [SAVE]	194
41 p. 410	**BEST WESTERN PLUS El Rancho Inn & Suites** *(See ad p. 195.)*	◈◈◈	$109-$199 [SAVE]	194
42 p. 410	Fairfield Inn & Suites San Francisco Airport/Millbrae	◆◆◆	$119-$269	194
43 p. 410	**The Westin San Francisco Airport**	◈◈◈◈	$129-$409 [SAVE]	194
44 p. 410	The Dylan at SFO	◆◆	Rates not provided	194

Map Page	Restaurants	Diamond Rated	Cuisine	Price Range	Page
19 p. 410	Terrace Cafe *(See ad p. 195.)*	◆◆	American	$9-$20	194
20 p. 410	La Collina Ristorante	◆◆	Italian	$14-$23	194
21 p. 410	Hong Kong Flower Lounge Restaurant	◆◆	Chinese	$10-$58	194

BURLINGAME

Map Page	Hotels	Diamond Rated	Rate Range	Page
47 p. 410	San Francisco Airport Marriott Waterfront	◆◆◆	$169-$329	61
48 p. 410	Hampton Inn & Suites	◆◆◆	Rates not provided	60
49 p. 410	Vagabond Inn Executive San Francisco Airport	◆◆	$69-$199	61
50 p. 410	**Bay Landing Hotel** *(See ad p. 60.)*	◈◈◈	Rates not provided [SAVE]	60
51 p. 410	**Hyatt Regency San Francisco Airport**	◈◈◈	$81-$360 [SAVE]	61
52 p. 410	Holiday Inn Express San Francisco Airport South	◆◆◆	Rates not provided	61
53 p. 410	Crowne Plaza	◆◆◆	$129-$229	60
54 p. 410	Embassy Suites-San Francisco Airport-Burlingame	◆◆◆	$150-$350	60
55 p. 410	DoubleTree by Hilton Hotel San Francisco Airport	◆◆◆	$129-$309	60
56 p. 410	**Red Roof Inn San Francisco Airport**	◈◈	$60-$140 [SAVE]	61
57 p. 410	Hilton Garden Inn San Francisco Airport/Burlingame	◆◆◆	Rates not provided	60
58 p. 410	**Hilton San Francisco Airport Bayfront**	◈◈◈	Rates not provided [SAVE]	61

Map Page	Restaurants	Diamond Rated	Cuisine	Price Range	Page
24 p. 410	Gulliver's	◆◆◆	American	$15-$29	61
25 p. 410	LeAnn's Cafe	◆	American	$7-$20	61
26 p. 410	Cafe Figaro	◆◆	Italian	$9-$24	61

Map Page	Restaurants (cont'd)	Diamond Rated	Cuisine	Price Range	Page
27 p. 410	Steelhead Brewing Co.	▽▽	American	$9-$24	62
28 p. 410	Ecco Restaurant	▽▽▽	American	$15-$30	61
29 p. 410	Straits	▽▽▽	Asian	$12-$40	62
30 p. 410	Mingalaba Restaurant	▽▽	Burmese	$10-$16	61
31 p. 410	Trapeze	▽▽▽	Continental	$12-$32	62
32 p. 410	Sapore Italiano	▽▽	Italian	$9-$24	62

FOSTER CITY

Map Page	Hotels	Diamond Rated	Rate Range	Page
61 p. 410	Crowne Plaza Hotel Foster City-San Mateo	▽▽▽	Rates not provided	121
62 p. 410	**Courtyard by Marriott**	▽▽▽	$116-$126 SAVE	121

Map Page	Restaurant	Diamond Rated	Cuisine	Price Range	Page
35 p. 410	ABC Seafood Restaurant	▽▽	Cantonese	$10-$35	121

SAN MATEO

Map Page	Hotels	Diamond Rated	Rate Range	Page
65 p. 410	**BEST WESTERN PLUS Coyote Point Inn**	▽▽▽	$89-$259 SAVE	480
66 p. 410	Comfort Inn	▽▽	$79-$199 SAVE	481
67 p. 410	**Holiday Inn & Suites San Mateo - SFO**	▽▽▽	$99-$209 SAVE	481
68 p. 410	Coxhead House Bed & Breakfast	▽▽▽	$169-$295	481
69 p. 410	Hilton Garden Inn San Mateo	▽▽▽	$89-$259	481
70 p. 410	**Marriott San Mateo/San Francisco Airport**	▽▽▽	$84-$104 SAVE	481
71 p. 410	Residence Inn by Marriott	▽▽▽	$229-$269	481
72 p. 410	**Stone Villa Inn**	▽▽	$65-$500 SAVE	481
73 p. 410	**BEST WESTERN San Mateo/Los Prados Inn**	▽▽	Rates not provided SAVE	481

Map Page	Restaurants	Diamond Rated	Cuisine	Price Range	Page
38 p. 410	Ristorante Capellini	▽▽▽	Italian	$13-$40	482
39 p. 410	Kingfish	▽▽▽	American	$11-$48	482
40 p. 410	Izakaya Mai	▽▽	Japanese	$10-$16	482
41 p. 410	Little Sheep Mongolian Hot Pot	▽▽	Mongolian	$3-$14	482
42 p. 410	231 Ellsworth	▽▽▽	California	$9-$79	481
43 p. 410	San Mateo Prime	▽▽	Steak	$20-$40	482
44 p. 410	Spiedo Ristorante	▽▽▽	Italian	$10-$25	482
45 p. 410	Clay Oven	▽▽	Indian	$10-$19	482
46 p. 410	Viognier	▽▽▽	French	$11-$39	482
47 p. 410	Astaria	▽▽▽	American	$11-$30	481
48 p. 410	Central Park Bistro	▽▽▽	American	$10-$34	481
49 p. 410	Ramen Dojo	▽▽	Japanese	$9-$9	482
50 p. 410	Santa Ramen	▽▽	Japanese	$8-$8	482
51 p. 410	Little Shanghai Restaurant	▽▽	Chinese	$7-$20	482
52 p. 410	Jack's Prime Burgers	▽▽	Burgers	$9-$12	482

BELMONT

Map Page	Hotels	Diamond Rated	Rate Range	Page
76 p. 410	**Hyatt house Belmont/Redwood Shores**	◆◆◆	$119-$219 SAVE	50
77 p. 410	**Hotel Belmont**	◆◆	$90-$120 SAVE	50
78 p. 410	**Holiday Inn Express Hotel & Suites**	◆◆◆	$99-$189 SAVE	50

Map Page	Restaurants	Diamond Rated	Cuisine	Price Range	Page
55 p. 410	The Van's Restaurant	◆◆	Continental	$10-$37	51
56 p. 410	Caprino's	◆◆◆	Italian	$9-$29	50
57 p. 410	Vivace Ristorante	◆◆◆	Italian	$11-$28	51
58 p. 410	Godfather's Burger Lounge	◆◆	Burgers	$9-$12	50

SAN CARLOS

Map Page	Hotels	Diamond Rated	Rate Range	Page
81 p. 410	**Hotel San Carlos**	◆◆	$89-$159 SAVE	340
82 p. 410	**Country Inn & Suites By Carlson**	◆◆◆	$79-$259 SAVE	340
83 p. 410	Fairfield Inn & Suites by Marriott	◆◆◆	$189-$249	340
84 p. 410	**Americas Best Value Inn**	◆◆	$75-$95 SAVE	339

Map Page	Restaurants	Diamond Rated	Cuisine	Price Range	Page
61 p. 410	Jersey Joe's Hoagies & Cheesesteaks	◆	Sandwiches	$5-$9	340
62 p. 410	Kaya Tofu & BBQ	◆◆	Korean	$10-$25	340
63 p. 410	Sneakers Pub & Grill	◆◆	American	$10-$19	340
64 p. 410	Locanda Positano	◆◆◆	Italian	$13-$28	340
65 p. 410	Piacere Ristorante	◆◆◆	Italian	$10-$39	340

REDWOOD CITY

Map Page	Hotels	Diamond Rated	Rate Range	Page
87 p. 410	**Sofitel San Francisco Bay**	◆◆◆◆	$110-$315 SAVE	295
88 p. 410	TownePlace Suites by Marriott	◆◆◆	$149-$249	296
89 p. 410	**BEST WESTERN PLUS Inn**	◆◆	$105-$165 SAVE	295
90 p. 410	**America's Best Inn & Suites**	◆◆	$79-$100 SAVE	295
91 p. 410	**Comfort Inn by Choice Hotels**	◆◆	$130-$160 SAVE	295
92 p. 410	Holiday Inn Express Redwood City Central	◆◆◆	$159-$209	295
93 p. 410	**Pacific Inn Redwood City**	◆◆	$79-$169 SAVE	295
94 p. 410	Holiday Inn Express Redwood City/Menlo Park	◆◆◆	Rates not provided	295
95 p. 410	**BEST WESTERN PLUS Executive Suites**	◆◆◆	$89-$179 SAVE	295
96 p. 410	Atherton Inn	◆◆◆	$139-$259	295

Map Page	Restaurants	Diamond Rated	Cuisine	Price Range	Page
68 p. 410	New Kapadokia	◆◆	Turkish	$8-$24	296
69 p. 410	Milagros Cantina Restaurant	◆◆	Mexican	$9-$20	296
70 p. 410	Harry's Hofbrau	◆	American	$5-$18	296

HALF MOON BAY

Map Page	Hotels	Diamond Rated	Rate Range	Page
101 p. 410	**Harbor View Inn**	◆◆	$79-$249 SAVE	143
102 p. 410	Oceano Hotel & Spa	◆◆◆	Rates not provided	144
103 p. 410	Beach House Hotel	◆◆◆	$195-$425	143
104 p. 410	Landis Shores Oceanfront Inn	◆◆◆	$225-$345	143

HALF MOON BAY (cont'd)

Map Page		Hotels (cont'd)	Diamond Rated	Rate Range	Page
105	p. 410	Cypress Inn on Miramar Beach	◆◆	$199-$399 SAVE	143
106	p. 410	Comfort Inn Half Moon Bay	◆◆◆	$100-$230 SAVE	143
107	p. 410	Coastside Inn Half Moon Bay	◆◆◆	$89-$239 SAVE	143
108	p. 410	Mill Rose Inn	◆◆◆	$175-$360	143
109	p. 410	Old Thyme Inn	◆◆◆	$159-$349	144
110	p. 410	The Ritz-Carlton, Half Moon Bay	◆◆◆◆	$355-$4050 SAVE	144
111	p. 410	BEST WESTERN PLUS Half Moon Bay Lodge	◆◆◆	$149-$239 SAVE	143

Map Page		Restaurants	Diamond Rated	Cuisine	Price Range	Page
74	p. 410	Mezzaluna Italian Restaurant	◆◆	Italian	$11-$26	144
75	p. 410	Half Moon Bay Brewing Company	◆◆	American	$13-$27	144
76	p. 410	Caffe Mezza Luna	◆	Italian	$5-$10	144
77	p. 410	Sam's Chowder House	◆◆	Seafood	$12-$35	144
78	p. 410	Miramar Beach Restaurant	◆◆	California	$11-$35	144
79	p. 410	Pasta Moon Ristorante	◆◆◆	Italian	$12-$26	144
80	p. 410	Cetrella	◆◆◆	Mediterranean	$17-$27	144
81	p. 410	Navio	◆◆◆◆	Northern California	$28-$38	144

MENLO PARK

Map Page		Hotels	Diamond Rated	Rate Range	Page
114	p. 410	Red Cottage Inn & Suites	◆◆◆	$129-$219 SAVE	192
115	p. 410	Menlo Park Inn (See ad p. 192.)	◆◆◆	$109-$249 SAVE	192
116	p. 410	Stanford Park Hotel	◆◆◆◆	$199-$705 SAVE	192
117	p. 410	BEST WESTERN PLUS Riviera	◆◆◆	$119-$269 SAVE	191

Map Page		Restaurants	Diamond Rated	Cuisine	Price Range	Page
84	p. 410	Left Bank	◆◆◆	French	$11-$27	192
85	p. 410	Carpaccio	◆◆◆	Italian	$12-$23	192

PALO ALTO

Map Page		Hotels	Diamond Rated	Rate Range	Page
120	p. 410	Hotel Keen	◆◆	$119-$309	271
121	p. 410	Sheraton Palo Alto Hotel	◆◆◆	$109-$509 SAVE	271
122	p. 410	The Westin Palo Alto	◆◆◆◆	$129-$559 SAVE	271

Map Page		Restaurants	Diamond Rated	Cuisine	Price Range	Page
88	p. 410	Mandarin Gourmet	◆◆◆	Chinese	$10-$33	272
89	p. 410	University Cafe	◆◆	American	$9-$21	272
90	p. 410	Evvia Estiatorio	◆◆◆	Greek	$15-$37	271
91	p. 410	P.F. Chang's China Bistro	◆◆◆	Chinese	$10-$21	272
92	p. 410	Lavanda Restaurant & Wine Bar	◆◆◆	Mediterranean	$12-$38	272

COLMA

Map Page		Restaurant	Diamond Rated	Cuisine	Price Range	Page
10	p. 410	Estrada's Mexican Restaurant	◆◆	Mexican	$6-$17	82

WOODSIDE

Map Page		Restaurants	Diamond Rated	Cuisine	Price Range	Page
95	p. 410	Bella Vista Restaurant	◆◆◆	Continental	$26-$35	577
96	p. 410	The Village Pub	◆◆◆◆	New American	$14-$39	577

SAN FRANCISCO (D-7)
- Restaurants p. 437
- Hotels & Restaurants map & index p. 394, 404

ADANTE HOTEL　(415)673-9221 ⑲

Hotel
$79-S350
Address: 610 Geary St 94102 **Location:** Between Jones and Leavenworth sts. 🅟 Powell Street, 33. **Facility:** 90 units. 7 stories, interior corridors. **Parking:** valet only. **Terms:** 3 night minimum stay - seasonal and/or weekends, cancellation fee imposed. **Amenities:** safes. **Guest Services:** valet laundry. **Free Special Amenities:** continental breakfast and high-speed Internet.

ALEXIS PARK-SAN FRANCISCO　(415)673-0411 ⑫

Motel
$99-S499
Address: 825 Polk St 94109 **Location:** At Ellis St. 🅟 Civic Center/UN Plaza, 34. **Facility:** 29 units. 2 stories (no elevator), exterior corridors. **Terms:** cancellation fee imposed. **Amenities:** high-speed Internet, safes. **Free Special Amenities:** expanded continental breakfast and high-speed Internet.

AMERICAS BEST VALUE INN & SUITES GOLDEN GATE
(415)921-4980 ⑥

Motel
$58-S199
Address: 2322 Lombard St 94123 **Location:** Between Pierce and Scott sts. **Facility:** 42 units. 2 stories, exterior corridors. **Free Special Amenities:** continental breakfast and high-speed Internet.

ARGONAUT HOTEL　(415)563-0800 ❶

Hotel
S209-S719
Address: 495 Jefferson St 94109 **Location:** Fisherman's Wharf; adjacent to The Cannery. **Facility:** Located in the renovated Cannery building at Fisherman's Wharf, the hotel sports a nautical design that gives the impression of a luxury ocean liner. 252 units. 4 stories, interior corridors. **Parking:** valet only. **Terms:** cancellation fee imposed. **Amenities:** video games (fee), high-speed Internet, safes. **Dining:** Blue Mermaid Chowder House & Bar, see separate listing. **Activities:** exercise room. **Guest Services:** valet laundry, area transportation-Financial District. **Free Special Amenities:** high-speed Internet and manager's reception.

BERESFORD ARMS HOTEL & SUITES
(415)673-2600 ㊽
Historic Hotel
$89-S299
Address: 701 Post St 94109 **Location:** 3 blks w of Union Square; at Jones St. 🅟 Powell Street, 33. **Facility:** Victorian styling brings an elegant ambiance to the lobby of this hotel. 95 units, some kitchens. 7 stories, interior corridors. **Parking:** valet only. **Terms:** cancellation fee imposed. **Guest Services:** valet laundry. **Free Special Amenities:** continental breakfast and high-speed Internet.

▼ See AAA listing p. 436 ▼

AAA/CAA travel information: Available in print, online and on the go!

(See maps & indexes p. 394, 404.)

BERESFORD HOTEL
(415)673-9900 **43**

Historic Hotel
$79-$169

Address: 635 Sutter St 94102 **Location:** 1 blk nw of Union Square at Mason St. Powell Street, 33. **Facility:** This service-oriented hotel offers comfortably furnished accommodations and the convenience of a Union Square location. 114 units. 7 stories, interior corridors. **Parking:** valet only. **Terms:** cancellation fee imposed. **Guest Services:** valet laundry. **Free Special Amenities:** expanded continental breakfast and early check-in/late check-out.

BEST WESTERN PLUS AMERICANIA
(415)626-0200 **94**

Contemporary Hotel
$119-$349

AAA Benefit: Members save up to 20%, plus 10% bonus points with Best Western Rewards®.

Address: 121 7th St 94103 **Location:** Just s of Market St; between Minna and Natoma sts. Civic Center/UN Plaza, 34. **Facility:** 143 units. 4 stories, exterior corridors. **Parking:** valet only. **Terms:** 2-4 night minimum stay - seasonal and/or weekends, cancellation fee imposed. **Amenities:** safes. **Pool(s):** heated outdoor. **Activities:** exercise room. *Fee:* game room. **Guest Services:** valet and coin laundry. **Free Special Amenities:** local telephone calls and high-speed Internet.

BEST WESTERN PLUS CARRIAGE INN
(415)552-8600 **95**

Boutique Hotel
$129-$369

AAA Benefit: Members save up to 20%, plus 10% bonus points with Best Western Rewards®.

Address: 140 7th St 94103 **Location:** Just s of Market St; between Minna and Natoma sts. Civic Center/UN Plaza, 34. **Facility:** Victorian meets modern San Francisco at this hotel, where each room is named after a famous San Franciscan, such as Emperor Norton and Danielle Steele. 48 units. 4 stories, interior corridors. **Parking:** on-site (fee). **Terms:** 2-4 night minimum stay - seasonal and/or weekends, cancellation fee imposed. **Amenities:** safes. *Some:* high-speed Internet. **Activities:** whirlpool. **Guest Services:** valet laundry. **Free Special Amenities:** local telephone calls and high-speed Internet.

BEST WESTERN PLUS TUSCAN INN AT FISHERMAN'S WHARF
(415)561-1100 **10**

Hotel
$189-$389

AAA Benefit: Members save up to 20%, plus 10% bonus points with Best Western Rewards®.

Address: 425 Northpoint St 94133 **Location:** Just s of Fisherman's Wharf at Mason St. **Facility:** 221 units. 4 stories, interior corridors. **Parking:** valet only. **Terms:** cancellation fee imposed. **Amenities:** video games (fee), safes. **Guest Services:** valet laundry. **Free Special Amenities:** high-speed Internet and manager's reception.

BEST WESTERN THE HOTEL CALIFORNIA
415/441-2700 **60**

Hotel
Rates not provided

AAA Benefit: Members save up to 20%, plus 10% bonus points with Best Western Rewards®.

Address: 580 Geary St 94102 **Location:** 0.3 mi w of Union Square at Jones St. Powell Street, 33. **Facility:** 82 units. 7 stories, interior corridors. **Parking:** valet only. **Amenities:** safes. **Dining:** Millennium Restaurant, see separate listing. **Activities:** exercise room. **Guest Services:** valet laundry. **Free Special Amenities:** continental breakfast and high-speed Internet.

CASTLE INN
(415)441-1155 **17**

Motel
$69-$359

Address: 1565 Broadway St 94109 **Location:** Just e of US 101. **Facility:** 26 units. 5 stories, exterior corridors. **Terms:** 3 day cancellation notice-fee imposed. **Free Special Amenities:** continental breakfast and high-speed Internet.

CHANCELLOR HOTEL ON UNION SQUARE
415/362-2004 **47**

Hotel. Rates not provided. **Address:** 433 Powell St 94102 **Location:** Just n of Union Square; between Sutter and Post sts. Powell Street, 33. **Facility:** 137 units. 15 stories, interior corridors. **Parking:** on-site (fee) and valet. **Amenities:** video games (fee), safes. **Guest Services:** valet laundry.

CHELSEA MOTOR INN
415/563-5600 **8**

Hotel
$86-$155

Address: 2095 Lombard St 94123 **Location:** Jct US 101 (Lombard St) and Fillmore St. **Facility:** 60 units. 3 stories, interior corridors. **Amenities:** high-speed Internet, safes. (See ad p. 420.)

CIVIC CENTER MOTOR INN
(415)621-2826 **23**

Motel
$74-$179

Address: 364 9th St 94103 **Location:** I-80 exit Civic Center, just n at Harrison St. Van Ness, 50. **Facility:** 57 units. 2 stories (no elevator), exterior corridors. **Terms:** cancellation fee imposed. **Pool(s):** heated outdoor. **Guest Services:** coin laundry. **Free Special Amenities:** expanded continental breakfast and early check-in/late check-out.

COLUMBUS MOTOR INN
415/885-1492 **12**

Hotel
$90-$195

Address: 1075 Columbus Ave 94133 **Location:** Just s of Fisherman's Wharf; between Francisco and Chestnut sts. **Facility:** 45 units, some two bedrooms. 3 stories, interior corridors. **Terms:** 2 night minimum stay - seasonal and/or weekends. **Amenities:** high-speed Internet, safes. (See ad p. 421.)

Give the gift of security, value and peace of mind: Gift Membership

(See maps & indexes p. 394, 404.)

COMFORT INN BY THE BAY   (415)928-5000

Hotel
$79-$289

Address: 2775 Van Ness Ave 94109 **Location:** On US 101 (Van Ness Ave) at Lombard St. **Facility:** 138 units. 11 stories, interior corridors. **Parking:** on-site (fee). **Terms:** check-in 4 pm, cancellation fee imposed. **Amenities:** high-speed Internet, safes (fee). **Guest Services:** valet laundry. **Free Special Amenities: full breakfast and high-speed Internet.** *(See ad p. 422.)*

Complimentary hot breakfast. Free Wi-Fi access. Within walking distance to many area attractions.

COUNTRY HEARTH INN   (415)567-2425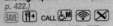

Motel
$75-$135

Address: 2707 Lombard St 94123 **Location:** Between Lyon and Baker sts. **Facility:** 23 units. 2 stories (no elevator), exterior corridors. **Parking:** no self-parking. **Terms:** cancellation fee imposed, resort fee. **Amenities:** high-speed Internet. *Some:* safes. **Free Special Amenities: continental breakfast and high-speed Internet.**

COURTYARD BY MARRIOTT AT FISHERMAN'S WHARF   (415)775-3800

Hotel $159-$409 **Address:** 580 Beach St 94133 **Location:** Between Jones and Leavenworth sts. Adjacent to The Cannery. **Facility:** 127 units. 4 stories, interior corridors. **Parking:** valet only. **Amenities:** high-speed Internet. **Guest Services:** valet and coin laundry.

AAA Benefit: AAA hotel discounts of 5% or more.

Activities: exercise room.

COURTYARD BY MARRIOTT SAN FRANCISCO DOWNTOWN   (415)947-0700   88

Hotel $189-$389 **Address:** 299 2nd St 94105 **Location:** Corner of 2nd and Folsom sts. Montgomery Street, 32. **Facility:** 405 units. 18 stories, interior corridors. **Parking:** valet only. **Amenities:** video games (fee). **Pool(s):** heated indoor. **Activities:** whirlpool, exercise room. **Guest Services:** valet and coin laundry.

AAA Benefit: AAA hotel discounts of 5% or more.

COVENTRY MOTOR INN   415/567-1200   10

Hotel
$86-$155

Address: 1901 Lombard St 94123 **Location:** US 101 (Lombard St) at Buchanan St. **Facility:** 69 units. 4 stories, interior corridors. **Amenities:** high-speed Internet, safes. *(See ad p. 420.)*

▼ See AAA listing p. 419 ▼

(See maps & indexes p. 394, 404.)

COW HOLLOW MOTOR INN & SUITES
415/921-5800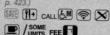

Hotel
$86-$325

Address: 2190 Lombard St 94123 **Location:** US 101 (Lombard St) at Steiner St. **Facility:** 129 units, some two bedrooms and kitchens. 3 stories, interior corridors. **Amenities:** high-speed Internet. *(See ad p. 420, p. 423.)*

DAYS INN-CIVIC CENTER
(415)864-4040 **21**

Motel
$75-$350

Address: 465 Grove St 94102 **Location:** Just w of US 101 (Van Ness Ave); between Octavia and Gough sts. Van Ness, 50. **Facility:** 40 units. 4 stories, exterior corridors. **Amenities:** high-speed Internet. **Free Special Amenities: continental breakfast and high-speed Internet.**

THE DONATELLO
(415)441-7100 **57**

Hotel
$129-$350

Address: 501 Post St 94102 **Location:** Just w of Union Square at Mason St. Powell Street, 33. **Facility:** 94 units. 15 stories, interior corridors. **Parking:** valet only. **Amenities:** safes. **Activities:** saunas, whirlpool, exercise room. *Fee:* massage. **Guest Services:** valet laundry. **Free Special Amenities: high-speed Internet.**

EXECUTIVE HOTEL VINTAGE COURT
(415)392-4666 **33**

Boutique Hotel
$229-$459

Address: 650 Bush St 94108 **Location:** Between Powell and Stockton sts; 2 blks n of Union Square. Montgomery Street, 32. **Facility:** This retreat-like property is within walking distance of Union Square and Chinatown, and it hosts daily wine tastings in the evenings. 106 units. 8 stories, interior corridors. **Parking:** on-site (fee) and valet. **Terms:** 2 night minimum stay - weekends, cancellation fee imposed, resort fee. **Amenities:** video games (fee), safes. *Some:* high-speed Internet. **Activities:** exercise room. **Guest Services:** valet laundry. **Free Special Amenities: high-speed Internet and manager's reception.**

THE FAIRMONT SAN FRANCISCO   (415)772-5000 **23**

Hotel
$199-$999

Address: 950 Mason St (atop Nob Hill) 94108 **Location:** Atop Nob Hill at California St. Montgomery Street, 32. **Facility:** This historic hotel, perched upon Nob Hill, features an impressive lobby and a selection of fine shops and restaurants. Not to be missed is The Tonga Room, beloved by locals for its tiki drinks and music. 591 units, some two bedrooms. 7-22 stories, interior corridors. **Parking:** valet only. **Terms:** cancellation fee imposed. **Amenities:** safes. *Fee:* video games, high-speed Internet. **Dining:** The Laurel Court Restaurant & Bar, see separate listing, entertainment. **Activities:** *Fee:* massage. **Guest Services:** valet laundry, area transportation-within 5 mi. **Free Special Amenities: local telephone calls and newspaper.**

Give the gift of security, value and peace of mind: Gift Membership

▼ See AAA listing p. 421 ▼

Safety tip: Keep a current AAA/CAA Road Atlas in every vehicle

▼ See AAA listing p. 422 ▼

❧ COW HOLLOW SUITES ☙

In the heart of the Marina District, affordable elegance awaits you.

Our spacious suites feature fireplaces, antique furnishings, hardwood floors, in-room safes, free in-room DSL and wireless internet access and full kitchens. Free indoor parking. All suites non-smoking.

1 bedroom, 1 bath $275.00, 1–2 persons
2 bedroom, 2 bath $325.00, 1–4 persons

2190 Lombard St., San Francisco, CA 94123
TEL (415) 921-5800
www.CowHollowSuites.com

Weekly and monthly rates available.

▼ See AAA listing p. 483 ▼

Get pet travel tips and enter the
photo contest at AAA.com/PetBook

(See maps & indexes p. 394, 404.)

FOUR SEASONS HOTEL SAN FRANCISCO
(415)633-3000 **76**

◈◈◈◈ **Hotel $395-$795 Address:** 757 Market St 94103 **Location:** Between 3rd and 4th sts. 🚇 Montgomery Street, 32. **Facility:** This is an elegant downtown hotel located between Union Square and the Yerba Buena cultural district. A Sports Club/LA health club and a Destination CitySpa Splash are located in the building. 277 units. 17 stories, interior corridors. **Parking:** valet only. **Terms:** 3 day cancellation notice-fee imposed. **Amenities:** high-speed Internet (fee), safes. **Dining:** Seasons Restaurant, see separate listing. **Pool(s):** heated indoor. **Activities:** saunas, whirlpools, steamrooms, spa. **Guest Services:** valet laundry, area transportation-within 2 mi.

🍴 ♿ 🍸 CALL 🛗 🏊 ⊞ BIZ 🛜 📹
/ SOME UNITS FEE 🐾 🛗 🖥 ⊞ 💻

FRANCISCO BAY INN
(415)474-3030 **13**

◈◈◈ Motel $69-$179 **Address:** 1501 Lombard St 94123 **Location:** US 101 (Lombard St) at Franklin St. **Facility:** 39 units. 4 stories, exterior corridors. **Terms:** 3 day cancellation notice-fee imposed. **Amenities:** continental breakfast and high-speed Internet.

SAVE 🍴 CALL 🛗 🛜 📹 ⊞ 💻

GALLERIA PARK HOTEL, A JOIE DE VIVRE HOTEL
415/781-3060 **49**

◈◈◈◈ Hotel. Rates not provided. **Address:** 191 Sutter St 94104 **Location:** 2 blks ne of Union Square; between Kearny and Trinity sts. 🚇 Montgomery Street, 32. **Facility:** 177 units. 8 stories, interior corridors. **Parking:** valet only. **Amenities:** high-speed Internet, safes. **Activities:** jogging, exercise room. **Guest Services:** valet laundry.

ECO 🍴 📶 CALL 🛗 BIZ 🛜 📹 💻
/ SOME UNITS 🐾 🖥

GEARY PARKWAY MOTEL
(415)752-4406 **17**

◈◈◈ Motel $80-$200 **Address:** 4750 Geary Blvd 94118 **Location:** Between 11th and 12th Aves. **Facility:** 20 units. 2 stories (no elevator), exterior corridors. **Bath:** shower only. **Amenities:** high-speed Internet. **Free Special Amenities:** continental breakfast and early check-in/late check-out.

SAVE 🍴 🛜 📹 ⊞ 🖥 💻

THE GOOD HOTEL
(415)621-7001 **92**

◈◈◈ Contemporary Hotel $99-$289 **Address:** 112 7th St 94103 **Location:** Just s of Market St; at Mission St. 🚇 Civic Center/UN Plaza, 34. **Facility:** 117 units. 5 stories, interior corridors. **Parking:** on-site (fee). **Terms:** 2-4 night minimum stay - seasonal and/or weekends, cancellation fee imposed. **Amenities:** safes. **Guest Services:** valet laundry. **Free Special Amenities:** high-speed Internet.

SAVE 🍴 CALL 🛗 🛜 📹 🎮 💻
/ UNITS FEE 🐾 🐕 ⊞ 🖥

GRAND HYATT SAN FRANCISCO
(415)398-1234 **46**

◈◈◈◈ Hotel $153-$423

 HYATT°

AAA Benefit: Members save 10% or more everyday.

Address: 345 Stockton St 94108 **Location:** On Union Square at Sutter St. 🚇 Montgomery Street, 32. **Facility:** This sophisticated hotel offers high-tech, stylish accommodations. This property is well suited for the business traveler, and it has a prime shopping location convenient to Union Square. 659 units. 3-34 stories, interior corridors. **Parking:** on-site (fee) and valet. **Terms:** cancellation fee imposed. **Amenities:** safes. **Fee:** video games, high-speed Internet. **Dining:** Grandviews, see separate listing. **Activities:** exercise room. **Guest Services:** valet laundry.

SAVE ECO 🍴 ♿ 🍸 CALL 🛗 BIZ 🛜 📹 ⊞
💻 / SOME UNITS FEE 🖥

THE HANDLERY UNION SQUARE HOTEL
(415)781-7800 **67**

◈◈◈ Hotel $189-$499 **Address:** 351 Geary St 94102 **Location:** Between Powell and Mason sts; just sw of Union Square. 🚇 Powell Street, 33. **Facility:** 377 units. 8 stories, interior/exterior corridors. **Parking:** valet only. **Terms:** cancellation fee imposed. **Amenities:** safes. **Pool(s):** heated outdoor. **Activities:** sauna. **Guest Services:** valet laundry.

SAVE ECO 🍴 📶 CALL 🛗 🏊 🛜 BIZ 🛜 📹
⊞ 💻 / SOME UNITS FEE 🐾 🖥 ⊞

HARBOR COURT HOTEL
(415)882-1300 **50**

◈◈◈ Hotel $209-$359 **Address:** 165 Steuart St 94105 **Location:** On Embarcadero; between Howard and Mission sts. 🚇 Folsom, 90. **Facility:** 131 units. 8 stories, interior corridors. **Parking:** valet only. **Terms:** cancellation fee imposed. **Amenities:** video games (fee). **Guest Services:** valet laundry. **Free Special Amenities:** high-speed Internet and manager's reception.

SAVE ECO 🍴 CALL 🛗 FEE 🛜 🛜 📹 🎮 💻
/ SOME UNITS 🐾 ⊞

HILTON SAN FRANCISCO FINANCIAL DISTRICT
(415)433-6600 **20**

◈◈◈ Hotel $189-$339

 Hilton

AAA Benefit: Members save 5% or more!

Address: 750 Kearny St 94108 **Location:** Between Clay and Washington sts. 🚇 Montgomery Street, 32. **Facility:** 544 units. 27 stories, interior corridors. **Parking:** on-site (fee) and valet. **Terms:** 1-7 night minimum stay, cancellation fee imposed. **Amenities:** high-speed Internet, safes. **Activities:** exercise room, spa. **Guest Services:** valet laundry. **Free Special Amenities:** local telephone calls and newspaper.

SAVE ⊟ 🍴 📶 🍸 CALL 🛗 BIZ 🛜 📹 💻
💻 / SOME UNITS FEE 🐾 ⊞ 🖥 ⊞

HILTON SAN FRANCISCO FISHERMAN'S WHARF
(415)885-4700 **11**

◈◈◈ Hotel $159-$459

Hilton

AAA Benefit: Members save 5% or more!

Address: 2620 Jones St 94133 **Location:** Just sw of Fisherman's Wharf; at Columbus Ave and Jones St. **Facility:** 234 units. 4 stories, interior corridors. **Parking:** on-site (fee) and valet. **Terms:** 1-7 night minimum stay, cancellation fee imposed. **Amenities:** high-speed Internet (fee), safes. **Activities:** exercise room. **Guest Services:** valet laundry. **Free Special Amenities:** newspaper.

SAVE ECO 🍴 📶 🍸 CALL 🛗 BIZ 🛜 📹 💻
💻 / SOME UNITS ⊞

HILTON SAN FRANCISCO UNION SQUARE
(415)771-1400 **73**

◈◈◈ ◈◈◈ Hotel $109-$299 **Address:** 333 O'Farrell St 94102 **Location:** Just w of Mason and O'Farrell sts. 🚇 Powell Street, 33. **Facility:** This high-rise hotel features a nice selection of well-appointed guest rooms. 1908 units. 19-46 stories, interior corridors. **Parking:** on-site (fee) and valet. **Terms:** 1-7 night minimum stay, cancellation fee imposed. **Amenities:** high-speed Internet (fee). *Some:* safes. **Pool(s):** heated outdoor. **Activities:** whirlpool, exercise room. **Guest Services:** valet laundry.

AAA Benefit: Members save 5% or more!

ECO 🍴 📶 🍸 CALL 🛗 🏊 BIZ 🛜 🎮 💻
/ SOME UNITS FEE 🐾 FEE ⊞ 🖥

(See maps & indexes p. 394, 404.)

HOLIDAY INN CIVIC CENTER (415)626-6103 [93]

Hotel
$99-$339

Address: 50 8th St 94103 **Location:** Between Market and Mission sts. Civic Center/UN Plaza, 34. **Facility:** 388 units. 14 stories, interior corridors. **Parking:** on-site (fee). **Terms:** cancellation fee imposed. **Amenities:** video games (fee), safes. **Pool(s):** heated outdoor. **Activities:** exercise room. **Guest Services:** valet and coin laundry. **Free Special Amenities:** high-speed Internet.

HOLIDAY INN EXPRESS & SUITES AT FISHERMAN'S WHARF (415)409-4600 [6]

Hotel
$139-$399

Address: 550 North Point St 94133 **Location:** Jct Columbus Ave. **Facility:** 252 units. 4 stories, interior corridors. **Parking:** valet only. **Terms:** cancellation fee imposed. **Amenities:** high-speed Internet, safes. **Activities:** exercise room. **Guest Services:** valet laundry. **Free Special Amenities:** full breakfast and high-speed Internet.

HOLIDAY INN FISHERMAN'S WHARF (415)771-9000 [5]

Hotel
$125-$365

Address: 1300 Columbus Ave 94133 **Location:** Jct North Point St. **Facility:** 585 units. 5 stories, interior corridors. **Parking:** on-site (fee). **Terms:** cancellation fee imposed. **Amenities:** video games, safes. **Dining:** 2 restaurants. **Pool(s):** heated outdoor. **Activities:** jogging, exercise room. **Guest Services:** valet and coin laundry. **Free Special Amenities:** newspaper and high-speed Internet.

HOLIDAY INN GOLDEN GATEWAY 415/441-4000 [22]

Hotel
Rates not provided

Address: 1500 Van Ness Ave 94109 **Location:** US 101 (Van Ness Ave) at Pine St. Civic Center/UN Plaza, 34. **Facility:** 499 units. 26 stories, interior corridors. **Parking:** on-site (fee). **Amenities:** video games (fee). **Pool(s):** heated outdoor. **Activities:** exercise room. **Guest Services:** valet and coin laundry. **Free Special Amenities:** high-speed Internet.

HOTEL ABRI (415)392-8800 [79]

Hotel
$229-$389

Address: 127 Ellis St 94102 **Location:** Just w of Union Square at Mason St. Powell Street, 33. **Facility:** 91 units. 5 stories, interior corridors. **Parking:** valet only. **Terms:** cancellation fee imposed. **Amenities:** high-speed Internet, safes. **Dining:** Puccini & Pinetti, see separate listing. **Guest Services:** valet laundry. **Free Special Amenities:** local telephone calls and high-speed Internet.

HOTEL ADAGIO SAN FRANCISCO 415/775-5000 [61]

fyi **Hotel.** Rates not provided. Under major renovation, scheduled to be completed September 2012. **Last Rated:** **Address:** 550 Geary St 94102 **Location:** 2 blks w of Union Square; between Jones and Taylor sts. Powell Street, 33. **Facility:** 171 units. 15 stories, interior corridors. **Parking:** valet only. **Amenities:** high-speed Internet, safes. **Activities:** exercise room. **Guest Services:** valet laundry, area transportation-within 2 mi.

HOTEL BIJOU 415/771-1200 [83]

Hotel. Rates not provided. **Address:** 111 Mason St 94102 **Location:** Just n of Market St; between Eddy and Ellis sts. Powell Street, 33. **Facility:** 65 units. 5 stories, interior corridors. **Parking:** valet only. **Amenities:** Some: high-speed Internet. **Guest Services:** valet laundry.

HOTEL CARLTON, A JOIE DE VIVRE HOTEL (415)673-0242 [36]

Boutique Hotel $109-$499 **Address:** 1075 Sutter St 94109 **Location:** 0.5 mi w of Union Square; between Hyde and Larkin sts. Powell Street, 33. **Facility:** The theme at this boutique hotel is travel. The lobby is decorated with paraphernalia from all over the world and the elevator is adorned with a world map. Even the headboards have a world globe on it. 161 units. 9 stories, interior corridors. **Parking:** valet only. **Terms:** cancellation fee imposed. **Amenities:** safes. **Dining:** Saha, see separate listing. **Guest Services:** valet laundry, area transportation-Financial District.

HOTEL DEL SOL, A JOIE DE VIVRE HOTEL (415)921-5520 [12]

Motel
$129-$269

Address: 3100 Webster St 94123 **Location:** Just s of Lombard St at Greenwich St. **Facility:** 57 units. 3 stories, exterior corridors. **Terms:** 2-3 night minimum stay - seasonal and/or weekends, cancellation fee imposed. **Amenities:** safes. **Pool(s):** heated outdoor. **Guest Services:** valet laundry. **Free Special Amenities:** continental breakfast and children's activities.

HOTEL DIVA (415)885-0200 [64]

Contemporary Hotel $199-$369 **Address:** 440 Geary St 94102 **Location:** Between Taylor and Mason sts; on Theater Row. Powell Street, 33. **Facility:** 116 units. 7 stories, interior corridors. **Parking:** valet only. **Terms:** cancellation fee imposed. **Amenities:** safes. **Dining:** colibri Mexican-Bistro, see separate listing. **Activities:** exercise room. **Guest Services:** valet laundry.

HOTEL DRISCO (415)346-2880 [15]

Historic Boutique Hotel $225-$785 **Address:** 2901 Pacific Ave 94115 **Location:** At Broderick St; in Pacific Heights. **Facility:** Situated in the prestigious Pacific Heights neighborhood, this hotel features wonderful bay and city views as well as charming guest rooms. 48 units. 5 stories, interior corridors. **Parking:** street only. **Terms:** 3 day cancellation notice-fee imposed. **Amenities:** high-speed Internet, safes. **Activities:** exercise room. **Guest Services:** valet laundry, area transportation-Union Square & Financial District.

HOTEL FRANK (415)986-2000 [66]

Contemporary Hotel $109-$399 **Address:** 386 Geary St 94102 **Location:** Just w of Union Square at Mason St. Powell Street, 33. **Facility:** 153 units. 12 stories, interior corridors. **Parking:** valet only. **Terms:** cancellation fee imposed. **Amenities:** safes. **Dining:** Max's on the Square, see separate listing. **Guest Services:** valet laundry.

THINK OF US AS A
Wishlist for your Soul.

Bask in our oceanfront settings and spectacular beaches.

Stretch out in your elegantly appointed amenity-filled room or suite.

Request 24-hour room service to your private terrace.

Limitless dining, snacks, premium wines and spirits.

Endless ways to play for every age and interest.

Exercise, spa time and napping — all encouraged!

Our family-friendly resorts include a supervised Explorer's Club for kids.

Nightly parties and gala shows.

Close to golf, shopping, exploring and adventures.

Vacations are very personal. That's why we give you so many choices.
With 30 locations, our oceanfront resorts give you *Endless Privileges,*
Unlimited-Luxury or *Unlimited-Fun.* There are sensuous settings for adults-
only, classic and contemporary masterpieces for families, couples and friends,
and elegant retreats focused on wellness and cultural enrichment.

You make the wish. We'll make it happen.
Call your AAA Travel Agent to save an additional 10% at **AMResorts.com/AAA**

©2012

(See maps & indexes p. 394, 404.)

HOTEL GRIFFON (415)495-2100

Hotel
$169-$499

Address: 155 Steuart St 94105 **Location:** On Embarcadero; between Howard and Mission sts. Folsom, 90. **Facility:** 62 units. 5 stories, interior corridors. **Parking:** valet only. **Terms:** cancellation fee imposed. **Amenities:** high-speed Internet, safes. **Guest Services:** valet laundry. **Free Special Amenities:** high-speed Internet.

[icons]

HOTEL KABUKI, A JOIE DE VIVRE HOTEL

415/922-3200

Hotel. Rates not provided. **Address:** 1625 Post St 94115 **Location:** Jct Laguna St; in Japan Center.  Van Ness, 50. **Facility:** 218 units. 5-16 stories, interior corridors. **Parking:** on-site (fee) and valet. **Amenities:** safes. **Activities:** exercise room. **Guest Services:** valet laundry.

[icons]

HOTEL MARK TWAIN (415)673-2332 74

Hotel
$109-$399

Address: 345 Taylor St 94102 **Location:** Just w of Union Square. Powell Street, 33. **Facility:** 118 units. 8 stories, interior corridors. **Parking:** valet only. **Amenities:** high-speed Internet, safes. **Activities:** exercise room. **Guest Services:** valet laundry. **Free Special Amenities:** high-speed Internet.

[icons]

HOTEL MONACO (415)292-0100 65

Hotel
$189-$459

Address: 501 Geary St 94102 **Location:** Just w of Union Square at Taylor St. Powell Street, 33. **Facility:** Distinctive architecture, eclectic decor and attention to service characterize this restored 1910 American beaux arts hotel. 201 units. 7 stories, interior corridors. **Parking:** valet only. **Terms:** cancellation fee imposed. **Amenities:** video games (fee), safes. *Some:* high-speed Internet. **Dining:** Grand Cafe, see separate listing. **Activities:** sauna, whirlpool, exercise room, spa. **Guest Services:** valet laundry, area transportation-Financial District. **Free Special Amenities:** high-speed Internet and manager's reception.

[icons]

HOTEL NIKKO SAN FRANCISCO (415)394-1111 75

Hotel
$169-$399

Address: 222 Mason St 94102 **Location:** At O'Farrell St. Powell Street, 33. **Facility:** Located in Union Square, the Hotel Nikko features an indoor pool and spa. Showcasing the simplicity of contemporary Japanese style, works of art line the walls throughout. 533 units. 25 stories, interior corridors. **Parking:** valet only. **Terms:** cancellation fee imposed. **Amenities:** safes. *Some:* high-speed Internet (fee). **Dining:** Anzu Restaurant, see separate listing, entertainment. **Pool(s):** heated indoor. **Activities:** saunas, whirlpool, steamrooms, spa. **Guest Services:** valet laundry, area transportation-Financial District.

[icons]

HOTEL PALOMAR 415/348-1111 81

Hotel
Rates not provided

Address: 12 4th St 94103 **Location:** At Market St. Powell Street, 33. **Facility:** Formerly an office building, this contemporary hotel reaps the benefit of noise tampering construction. 195 units. 5 stories, interior corridors. **Parking:** valet only. **Amenities:** safes. **Fee:** video games, high-speed Internet. **Dining:** Fifth Floor, see separate listing. **Activities:** exercise room. **Fee:** massage. **Guest Services:** valet laundry. **Free Special Amenities:** high-speed Internet and manager's reception.

[icons]

(See maps & indexes p. 394, 404.)

HOTEL REX, A JOIE DE VIVRE HOTEL (415)433-4434 40

◇◇◇◇ **Hotel** $149-$409 **Address:** 562 Sutter St 94102 **Location:** Just nw of Union Square; between Mason and Powell sts. Ⓟ Powell Street, 33. **Facility:** 94 units. 7 stories, interior corridors. **Parking:** valet only. **Terms:** cancellation fee imposed. **Guest Services:** valet laundry.

HOTEL TOMO 415/921-4000 18

Hotel
Rates not provided

Address: 1800 Sutter St 94115 **Location:** At Sutter and Buchanan sts; 1 blk from Japan Center. Ⓟ Van Ness, 50. **Facility:** 125 units. 8 stories, interior corridors. **Parking:** on-site (fee). **Amenities:** video games (fee), high-speed Internet, safes. **Activities:** exercise room. **Guest Services:** valet laundry. **Free Special Amenities:** local telephone calls and high-speed Internet.

HOTEL TRITON (415)394-0500 39

Boutique Hotel
$149-$489

Address: 342 Grant Ave 94108 **Location:** Near Union Square at Bush St. Ⓟ Montgomery Street, 32. **Facility:** A hip, vibrant, eco-friendly hotel located just steps from Chinatown, this newly renovated Kimpton property also is known for its suites that are designed by celebrities, such as Jerry Garcia and Kathy Griffin. 140 units. 7 stories, interior corridors. **Parking:** valet only. **Terms:** cancellation fee imposed, resort fee. **Amenities:** Some: safes. **Activities:** exercise room. **Guest Services:** valet laundry. **Free Special Amenities:** high-speed Internet and manager's reception.

HOTEL UNION SQUARE 415/397-3000 77

◇◇ **Hotel.** Rates not provided. **Address:** 114 Powell St 94102 **Location:** At Ellis St; just n of cable car turnaround. Ⓟ Powell Street, 33. **Facility:** 131 units. 5 stories, interior corridors. **Parking:** valet only. **Amenities:** Some: safes. **Guest Services:** valet laundry.

HOTEL VERTIGO (415)885-6800 37

Boutique Hotel
$119-$369

Address: 940 Sutter St 94109 **Location:** Between Leavenworth and Hyde sts. Ⓟ Powell Street, 33. **Facility:** Inspired by Alfred Hitchcock's masterpiece Vertigo, the hotel's rooms feature playful eclectic pieces with modern-day conveniences. 102 units. 7 stories, interior corridors. **Parking:** valet only. **Terms:** 2-4 night minimum stay - seasonal and/or weekends, cancellation fee imposed. **Amenities:** safes. **Guest Services:** valet laundry. **Free Special Amenities:** newspaper and high-speed Internet.

HOTEL VITALE, A JOIE DE VIVRE HOTEL (415)278-3700 35

◇◇◇◇ **Boutique Hotel** $499-$3500 **Address:** 8 Mission St 94105 **Location:** Waterfront. At The Embarcadero and Mission St. Ⓟ Embarcadero, 31. **Facility:** Prominently located across from the Ferry Building Marketplace, this hotel has a modern urban feel and features a complimentary morning yoga class and an array of beautifully appointed guest rooms. 200 units. 8 stories, interior corridors. **Parking:** valet only. **Terms:** cancellation fee imposed. **Amenities:** high-speed Internet (fee), safes. **Dining:** Americano Restaurant & Bar, see separate listing. **Activities:** exercise room, spa. **Guest Services:** valet laundry, area transportation-within 1 mi.

HOTEL WHITCOMB (415)626-8000 91

Historic Hotel
$129-$289

Address: 1231 Market St 94103 **Location:** Between 7th and 8th sts. Ⓟ Civic Center/UN Plaza, 34. **Facility:** A San Francisco landmark, the property served as City Hall from 1912-1915; the lobby is accentuated with Austrian crystal chandeliers and rich woods. 459 units. 8 stories, interior corridors. **Parking:** valet only. **Terms:** 3 day cancellation notice-fee imposed. **Activities:** exercise room. **Guest Services:** valet laundry. **Free Special Amenities:** local telephone calls and high-speed Internet.

THE HUNTINGTON HOTEL (415)474-5400 24

◇◇◇◇ **Hotel** $425-$595 **Address:** 1075 California St 94108 **Location:** Atop Nob Hill; corner of California and Taylor sts. Ⓟ Powell Street, 33. **Facility:** 135 units, some efficiencies. 12 stories, interior corridors. **Parking:** valet only. **Amenities:** safes. **Dining:** Big 4 Restaurant, see separate listing. **Activities:** whirlpool, exercise room, spa. **Guest Services:** valet laundry. Affiliated with A Preferred Hotel.

HYATT AT FISHERMAN'S WHARF (415)563-1234 8

Hotel
$126-$387

 HYATT® **AAA Benefit:** Members save 10% or more everyday.

Address: 555 North Point St 94133 **Location:** Just s of Fisherman's Wharf at Taylor St. **Facility:** 313 units. 5 stories, interior corridors. **Parking:** valet only. **Terms:** cancellation fee imposed. **Amenities:** safes. **Pool(s):** heated outdoor. **Activities:** whirlpool, exercise room. **Guest Services:** valet and coin laundry, area transportation-Financial District.

HYATT REGENCY SAN FRANCISCO (415)788-1234 29

Hotel
$126-$423

HYATT® **AAA Benefit:** Members save 10% or more everyday.

Address: 5 Embarcadero Center 94111 **Location:** Foot of California and Market sts; in Financial District. Ⓟ Embarcadero, 31. **Facility:** This hotel features an enormous and inviting lobby area and is located on the Embarcadero just across from the Ferry Building and close to Fisherman's Wharf. 802 units. 17 stories, interior corridors. **Parking:** valet only. **Terms:** cancellation fee imposed. **Amenities:** high-speed Internet (fee), safes. **Activities:** exercise room. **Fee:** massage. **Guest Services:** valet laundry. **Free Special Amenities:** newspaper.

INN AT THE OPERA (415)863-8400 20

◇◇◇◇ **Hotel** $139-$259 **Address:** 333 Fulton St 94102 **Location:** Just w of US 101 (Van Ness Ave); between Franklin and Gough sts. Ⓟ Van Ness, 50. **Facility:** 48 units. 7 stories, interior corridors. **Parking:** valet only. **Terms:** 2-3 night minimum stay - weekends, 3 day cancellation notice-fee imposed. **Guest Services:** valet laundry.

INN ON BROADWAY (415)776-7900 16

Motel
$64-$164

Address: 2201 Van Ness Ave 94109 **Location:** On US 101 (Van Ness Ave) at Broadway St. **Facility:** 56 units. 4 stories, exterior corridors. **Terms:** cancellation fee imposed. **Free Special Amenities:** early check-in/late check-out and high-speed Internet.

(See maps & indexes p. 394, 404.)

INN @UNION SQUARE (415)397-3510 55

Boutique Hotel
$209-$409

Address: 440 Post St 94102 **Location:** Between Powell and Mason sts; just w of Union Square. Powell Street, 33. **Facility:** This European-style hotel offers many personalized services, such as an early evening wine hour and a fresh-baked cookie hour. 30 units. 6 stories, interior corridors. **Parking:** on-site (fee) and valet. **Terms:** cancellation fee imposed. **Amenities:** safes. Some: high-speed Internet. **Free Special Amenities: expanded continental breakfast and high-speed Internet.**

INTERCONTINENTAL MARK HOPKINS SAN FRANCISCO (415)392-3434 28

Historic Hotel
$159-$489

Address: One Nob Hill 94108 **Location:** Corner of California and Mason sts. Montgomery Street, 32. **Facility:** The historic hotel on Nob Hill is notable for its panoramic views. 380 units. 17 stories, interior corridors. **Parking:** on-site (fee) and valet. **Terms:** cancellation fee imposed. **Amenities:** high-speed Internet (fee). **Dining:** entertainment. **Activities:** exercise room. Fee: massage. **Guest Services:** valet laundry, area transportation-Financial District & Union Square.

INTERCONTINENTAL SAN FRANCISCO (415)616-6500 90

Contemporary Hotel
$159-$489

Address: 888 Howard St 94103 **Location:** Between 4th and 5th sts; in SoMa District. Adjacent to Moscone West Convention Center. Powell Street, 33. **Facility:** Natural light showcases this contemporary hotel's upscale, residential-style décor. Floor-to-ceiling windows afford most guest rooms a beautiful view. 550 units. 32 stories, interior corridors. **Parking:** valet only. **Amenities:** high-speed Internet (fee), safes. **Pool(s):** heated indoor. **Activities:** whirlpool, exercise room, spa. **Guest Services:** valet laundry, area transportation-within 2 mi.

JW MARRIOTT SAN FRANCISCO (415)771-8600 52

Hotel $219-$489 **Address:** 500 Post St 94102 **Location:** Just w of Union Square at Mason St. Powell Street, 33. **Facility:** Designed by John Portman, this service-oriented landmark property strives for the highest

AAA Benefit:
A deluxe level of comfort and a Member rate.

levels of luxury. 337 units. 21 stories, interior corridors. **Parking:** valet only. **Amenities:** safes. Fee: video games, high-speed Internet. **Activities:** exercise room. Fee: massage. **Guest Services:** valet laundry, area transportation-within 2 mi.

KENSINGTON PARK HOTEL (415)788-6400 54

Hotel $199-$399 **Address:** 450 Post St 94102 **Location:** Just w of Union Square. Powell Street, 33. **Facility:** 93 units. 12 stories, interior corridors. **Parking:** valet only. **Terms:** cancellation fee imposed. **Dining:** Farallon, see separate listing. **Guest Services:** valet laundry.

KING GEORGE HOTEL (415)781-5050 68

Hotel
$99-$309

Address: 334 Mason St 94102 **Location:** Just w of Union Square. Powell Street, 33. **Facility:** 153 units. 9 stories, interior corridors. **Parking:** valet only. **Terms:** cancellation fee imposed. **Amenities:** safes. **Guest Services:** valet laundry. **Free Special Amenities: high-speed Internet.**

LA LUNA INN 415/346-4664 4

Motel
Rates not provided

Address: 2599 Lombard St 94123 **Location:** US 101 at Broderick St. **Facility:** 61 units. 3 stories, exterior corridors. **Free Special Amenities: continental breakfast and high-speed Internet.**

LARKSPUR HOTEL UNION SQUARE 415/421-2865 41

Hotel. Rates not provided. **Address:** 524 Sutter St 94102 **Location:** Union Square at Powell St. Powell Street, 33. **Facility:** 114 units. 8 stories, interior corridors. **Parking:** on-site (fee) and valet. **Guest Services:** valet laundry.

LAUREL INN, A JOIE DE VIVRE HOTEL (415)567-8467 16

Hotel $159-$329 **Address:** 444 Presidio Ave 94115 **Location:** 1 mi w of US 101 (Van Ness Ave); 1 mi e of Park Presidio Blvd (SR 1) at California St. **Facility:** 49 units, some efficiencies. 4 stories, interior corridors. **Parking:** on-site (fee). **Terms:** 2 night minimum stay - seasonal and/or weekends, cancellation fee imposed. **Guest Services:** valet laundry.

LE MERIDIEN SAN FRANCISCO (415)296-2900 21

Hotel
$179-$699

AAA Benefit: Members get up to 20% off, plus Starwood Preferred Guest® bonuses.

Address: 333 Battery St 94111 **Location:** Just s of Clay and Battery sts; in Financial District. Embarcadero, 31. **Facility:** The hotel offers a stylish lobby area and a nice selection of well-appointed guest rooms, some with a balcony and a few with views of San Francisco Bay. 360 units. 5-24 stories, interior corridors. **Parking:** valet only. **Terms:** cancellation fee imposed. **Amenities:** safes. Fee: video games, high-speed Internet. **Dining:** Park Grill, see separate listing. **Activities:** exercise room. **Guest Services:** valet laundry.

LOMBARD MOTOR INN (415)441-6000 14

Hotel
$86-$155

Address: 1475 Lombard St 94123 **Location:** US 101 (Lombard St), at Franklin St. **Facility:** 48 units. 4 stories, interior corridors. **Amenities:** high-speed Internet. (See ad p. 420.)

MANDARIN ORIENTAL SAN FRANCISCO 415/276-9888 30

fyi Hotel. Rates not provided. Under major renovation, scheduled to be completed July 2012. Last Rated: **Address:** 222 Sansome St 94104 **Location:** Between Pine and California sts; in Financial District. Embarcadero, 31. **Facility:** 158 units. 48 stories, interior corridors. **Parking:** on-site (fee) and valet. **Amenities:** high-speed Internet (fee), safes. **Activities:** exercise room. Fee: massage. **Guest Services:** valet laundry, area transportation-within 1 mi.

(See maps & indexes p. 394, 404.)

MARINA MOTEL 415/921-9406 [3]

Motel
Rates not provided
Address: 2576 Lombard St 94123 **Location:** Between Broderick and Divisadero sts. **Facility:** 39 units, some two bedrooms and kitchens. 1 story, interior/exterior corridors. **Free Special Amenities:** room upgrade (subject to availability with advance reservations) and high-speed Internet.

THE MONARCH HOTEL (415)673-5232 [56]

Hotel
$109-$189
Address: 1015 Geary St 94109 **Location:** Just e of US 101 (Van Ness Ave); between Polk St and Van Ness Ave. Civic Center/UN Plaza, 34. **Facility:** 101 units. 6 stories, interior corridors. **Parking:** valet only. **Terms:** cancellation fee imposed. **Amenities:** safes (fee). **Free Special Amenities:** early check-in/late check-out and high-speed Internet.

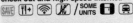

MOTEL CAPRI (415)346-4667 [14]

Motel
$80-$240
Address: 2015 Greenwich St 94123 **Location:** Just s of US 101 (Lombard St) at Buchanan St. **Facility:** 46 units, some efficiencies. 3 stories, exterior corridors. **Free Special Amenities:** continental breakfast and early check-in/late check-out.

NOB HILL MOTOR INN (415)775-8160 [18]
Motel
$74-$179
Address: 1630 Pacific Ave 94109 **Location:** Just e of US 101 (Van Ness Ave). **Facility:** 29 units. 2 stories, exterior corridors. **Terms:** 3 day cancellation notice-fee imposed. **Free Special Amenities:** continental breakfast and high-speed Internet.

OMNI SAN FRANCISCO HOTEL (415)677-9494 [26]
Hotel
$189-$699
Address: 500 California St 94104 **Location:** At Montgomery St; in Financial District. Montgomery Street, 32. **Facility:** The hotel offers spacious and elegantly appointed guest rooms and public areas. 362 units. 17 stories, interior corridors. **Parking:** valet only. **Terms:** cancellation fee imposed. **Amenities:** safes. **Fee:** video games, high-speed Internet. **Dining:** Bob's Steak & Chop House, see separate listing. **Activities:** exercise room. **Guest Services:** valet laundry, area transportation-within 2 mi. **Free Special Amenities:** newspaper and high-speed Internet.

THE OPAL SAN FRANCISCO 415/673-4711 [53]
Hotel
Rates not provided
Address: 1050 Van Ness Ave 94109 **Location:** On US 101 (Van Ness Ave); between Geary and Myrtle sts. Civic Center/UN Plaza, 34. **Facility:** 164 units. 5 stories, interior/exterior corridors. **Parking:** on-site (fee). **Amenities:** high-speed Internet. **Activities:** exercise room. **Guest Services:** valet and coin laundry.

THE ORCHARD GARDEN HOTEL 415/399-9807 [38]
Hotel. Rates not provided. **Address:** 466 Bush St 94108 **Location:** At Grant Ave. Montgomery Street, 32. **Facility:** 86 units. 10 stories, interior corridors. **Parking:** valet only. **Amenities:** high-speed Internet, safes. **Activities:** exercise room. **Guest Services:** valet laundry, area transportation-Financial District.

THE ORCHARD HOTEL 415/362-8878 [34]

Hotel
Rates not provided
Address: 665 Bush St 94108 **Location:** Between Powell and Stockton sts; just n of Union Square. Montgomery Street, 32. **Facility:** 104 units. 10 stories, interior corridors. **Parking:** valet only. **Amenities:** high-speed Internet, safes. **Activities:** exercise room. **Guest Services:** valet laundry, area transportation-Financial District. **Free Special Amenities:** newspaper and high-speed Internet.

PALACE HOTEL (415)512-1111 [71]

THE LUXURY COLLECTION
Hotels & Resorts
Historic Hotel
$179-$619
AAA Benefit: Inspiring travels with your AAA Preferred rates.

Address: 2 New Montgomery St 94105 **Location:** Just e of Union Square; at Market St. Montgomery Street, 32. **Facility:** A 1909 San Francisco landmark, the hotel has been restored and offers attractively furnished guest rooms and common areas. 553 units. 8 stories, interior corridors. **Parking:** valet only. **Terms:** cancellation fee imposed. **Amenities:** safes. **Fee:** video games, high-speed Internet. **Dining:** 3 restaurants, also, The Garden Court, see separate listing. **Pool(s):** heated indoor. **Activities:** sauna, whirlpool, exercise room. **Guest Services:** valet laundry, area transportation-within 3 mi.

PARC 55 WYNDHAM SAN FRANCISCO UNION SQUARE (415)392-8000 [82]

Hotel
$159-$400
Address: 55 Cyril Magnin St 94102 **Location:** Corner of Cyril Magnin and Eddy sts; just sw of Union Square. Powell Street, 33. **Facility:** Located steps from Union Square and Market Street, the hotel features a tiered building design affording great views of the city and skyline. 1015 units. 32 stories, interior corridors. **Parking:** valet only. **Terms:** 3 day cancellation notice-fee imposed. **Amenities:** safes. **Fee:** video games, high-speed Internet. **Dining:** city-house restaurant, see separate listing. **Activities:** exercise room. **Fee:** massage. **Guest Services:** valet laundry. (See ad p. 432.)

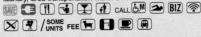

PETITE AUBERGE, A JOIE DE VIVRE HOTEL (415)928-6000 [31]
Hotel $109-$409 **Address:** 863 Bush St 94108 **Location:** Just nw of Union Square at Taylor St. Powell Street, 33. **Facility:** 26 units. 5 stories, interior corridors. **Parking:** valet only. **Terms:** 2-3 night minimum stay - seasonal and/or weekends. **Guest Services:** valet laundry.

PHOENIX HOTEL, A JOIE DE VIVRE HOTEL (415)776-1380 [80]
Boutique Hotel $109-$359 **Address:** 601 Eddy St 94109 **Location:** Just e of US 101 (Van Ness Ave) at Larkin St. Civic Center/UN Plaza, 34. **Facility:** This famed rock-n-roll hotel has lodged many famous rock bands, including Red Hot Chili Peppers and Joan Jett. 44 units. 2 stories (no elevator), exterior corridors. **Terms:** 2 night minimum stay - seasonal and/or weekends, cancellation fee imposed. **Pool(s):** heated outdoor. **Guest Services:** valet laundry.

▼ See AAA listing p. 431 ▼

Explore...

At the heart of San Francisco lies a playground.
Where shopping, dining and lush accommodations
swallow you up after a playful day. 800.595.0507

 **PARC 55 WYNDHAM**
San Francisco - Union Square

myparc55vacation.com

(See maps & indexes p. 394, 404.)

THE PICKWICK HOTEL
(415)421-7500   **89**

◆◆ **Hotel** $99-$309 **Address:** 85 5th St 94103 **Location:** 1 blk s of Market St at Mission St. Ⓡ Powell Street, 33. **Facility:** 189 units. 8 stories, interior corridors. **Parking:** on-site (fee). **Terms:** cancellation fee imposed. **Dining:** 3 restaurants. **Activities:** exercise room. **Guest Services:** valet laundry.

🍴 🍸 CALL 📶 BIZ 🛰 ✕ 🔋 🖥 📺

THE POWELL HOTEL
415/398-3200   **85**

◆◆ **Hotel.** Rates not provided. **Address:** 28 Cyril Magnin St 94102 **Location:** At Powell St cable car turnaround. Ⓡ Powell Street, 33. **Facility:** 137 units. 6 stories, interior corridors. **Parking:** valet only. **Guest Services:** valet laundry.

🍴 CALL 📶 FEE 🛰 ✕ 🔋 🖥
/SOME UNITS 🐕 🔋 📺

THE PRESCOTT HOTEL
415/563-0303   **53**

◆◆◆ **Hotel** Rates not provided **Address:** 545 Post St 94102 **Location:** Just w of Union Square. Ⓡ Powell Street, 33. **Facility:** 164 units. 7 stories, interior corridors. **Parking:** valet only. **Amenities:** video games (fee), safes. **Activities:** exercise room. **Fee:** massage. **Guest Services:** valet laundry, area transportation-within 5 mi. **Free Special Amenities:** high-speed Internet and manager's reception.

SAVE ECO 🍴 🍸 🛰 ✕ 🔋 /SOME UNITS 🐕 📺

RADISSON HOTEL FISHERMAN'S WHARF
(415)392-6700   **4**

◆◆◆ **Hotel** $139-$559 **Address:** 250 Beach St 94133 **Location:** At Powell St. **Facility:** 355 units. 4 stories, interior corridors. **Parking:** on-site (fee). **Terms:** check-in 4 pm, cancellation fee imposed. **Amenities:** high-speed Internet, safes. **Pool(s):** heated outdoor. **Activities:** exercise room. **Guest Services:** valet laundry.

SAVE 🍴 CALL 📶 🏊 BIZ 🛰 ✕ 🖥
/SOME UNITS FEE 🐕 🔋

RAMADA LIMITED-GOLDEN GATE
(415)775-8116   **9**

◆◆◆ **Motel** $119-$259 **Address:** 1940 Lombard St 94123 **Location:** 0.3 mi w of US 101; between Buchanan and Webster sts. **Facility:** 37 units. 3 stories (no elevator), interior/exterior corridors. **Terms:** cancellation fee imposed. **Free Special Amenities:** continental breakfast and high-speed Internet.

SAVE 🍴 🛰 🖥 /SOME UNITS 🔋 📺

REDWOOD INN
415/776-3800   **11**

◆◆ **Motel** $69-$199 **Address:** 1530 Lombard St 94123 **Location:** On US 101 (Lombard St); between Franklin and Gough sts. **Facility:** 33 units, some kitchens. 2-4 stories, exterior corridors. **Guest Services:** coin laundry. **Free Special Amenities:** continental breakfast and high-speed Internet.

SAVE 🍴 CALL 📶 🛰 🔋 🖥 /SOME UNITS 📺

THE RITZ-CARLTON, SAN FRANCISCO
415/296-7465   **27**

◆◆◆◆ **Hotel** Rates not provided

THE RITZ-CARLTON
AAA Benefit: Unequaled service at Special Member Savings.

Address: 600 Stockton St 94108 **Location:** Just n of Union Square at California St. Ⓡ Montgomery Street, 32. **Facility:** On the brow of Knob Hill, this impressive 1909 landmark property was remarkably renovated and restored to become a stately and elegant hotel. Sophisticated service provides for a memorable experience. 336 units. 9 stories, interior corridors. **Parking:** valet only. **Amenities:** safes. **Fee:** video games, high-speed Internet. **Dining:** 2 restaurants, also, Parallel 37, see separate listing. **Activities:** steamrooms, spa. **Guest Services:** valet laundry, area transportation-within 5 mi.

SAVE 🍴 🛁 🍸 CALL 📶 🏊 BIZ 🛰 ✕ 🔋 🖥 /SOME UNITS FEE 🐕 📺

ST. REGIS HOTEL SAN FRANCISCO
(415)284-4000   **84**

◆◆◆◆ **Hotel** $329-$649

ST REGIS
AAA Benefit: Legendary stays at a preferred rate.

Address: 125 3rd St 94103 **Location:** At Mission St. Ⓡ Montgomery Street, 32. **Facility:** This handsome, sophisticated hotel with a warm and inviting fireplace in the lobby offers rooms with 42-inch plasma TVs, superb bedding and outstanding marble baths with rain shower heads and deep soaking tubs. 260 units. 20 stories, interior corridors. **Parking:** valet only. **Terms:** cancellation fee imposed. **Amenities:** high-speed Internet (fee), safes. **Dining:** 2 restaurants, also, Ame restaurant, see separate listing. **Pool(s):** heated indoor. **Activities:** saunas, whirlpools, steamrooms, exercise room, spa. **Guest Services:** valet laundry, area transportation-within 2 mi.

SAVE 🍴 🛁 🍸 CALL 📶 🏊 🛰 ✕ 🎥 /SOME UNITS FEE 🐕 📺

SAN FRANCISCO MARRIOTT FISHERMAN'S WHARF
(415)775-7555   **7**

◆◆◆ **Hotel** $169-$589

Marriott HOTELS & RESORTS
AAA Benefit: AAA hotel discounts of 5% or more.

Address: 1250 Columbus Ave 94133 **Location:** Just s of Fisherman's Wharf at Bay St. **Facility:** 285 units. 5 stories, interior corridors. **Parking:** valet only. **Terms:** check-in 4 pm. **Amenities:** high-speed Internet (fee), safes. **Activities:** exercise room. **Guest Services:** valet and coin laundry.

SAVE 🍴 🛁 🍸 CALL 📶 BIZ 🛰 ✕ 🎥 🔋 🖥 /SOME UNITS FEE 🐕

SAN FRANCISCO MARRIOTT MARQUIS
(415)896-1600   **86**

◆◆◆ **Contemporary Hotel** $149-$589

Marriott HOTELS & RESORTS
AAA Benefit: AAA hotel discounts of 5% or more.

Address: 55 4th St 94103 **Location:** Corner of Mission and 4th sts. Ⓡ Powell Street, 33. **Facility:** 1498 units. 39 stories, interior corridors. **Parking:** valet only. **Terms:** check-in 4 pm. **Amenities:** video games (fee), safes. **Dining:** 4 restaurants. **Pool(s):** heated indoor. **Activities:** saunas, whirlpool, exercise room. **Fee:** massage. **Guest Services:** valet laundry. **Free Special Amenities:** newspaper and preferred room (subject to availability with advance reservations).

SAVE ECO 🍴 🛁 🍸 CALL 📶 🏊 🛁 BIZ 🛰 ✕ 🎥 🖥 📺

(See maps & indexes p. 394, 404.)

SAN FRANCISCO MARRIOTT UNION SQUARE
(415)398-8900 **42**

▼▼▼ **Hotel** $199-$399 **Address:** 480 Sutter St 94108 **Location:** Just n off Union Square; corner of Powell St. Powell Street, 33. **Facility:** 400 units. 30 stories, interior corridors. **Parking:** valet only. **Amenities:** high-speed Internet (fee). **Activities:** exercise room. **Guest Services:** valet and coin laundry.

AAA Benefit: AAA hotel discounts of 5% or more.

SERRANO HOTEL
415/885-2500 **70**

▼▼▼ Boutique Hotel Rates not provided

Address: 405 Taylor St 94102 **Location:** Just w of Union Square at O'Farrell St. Powell Street, 33. **Facility:** Housed in a 17th-century Spanish Revival building, rooms include animal-print bathrobes and such modern amenities as an iHome stereo and flat-panel TV. 236 units. 17 stories, interior corridors. **Parking:** valet only. **Amenities:** video games (fee), high-speed Internet, safes. **Activities:** sauna, exercise room. *Fee:* massage. **Guest Services:** valet laundry, area transportation-within 5 mi. **Free Special Amenities:** high-speed Internet and manager's reception.

SHERATON FISHERMAN'S WHARF
(415)362-5500 **9**

▼▼▼ Hotel $139-$479 Sheraton

AAA Benefit: Members get up to 20% off, plus Starwood Preferred Guest® bonuses.

Address: 2500 Mason St 94133 **Location:** Just se of Fisherman's Wharf at Beach St. **Facility:** 531 units. 4 stories, interior corridors. **Parking:** on-site (fee) and valet. **Terms:** cancellation fee imposed. **Amenities:** safes. **Pool(s):** heated outdoor. **Activities:** exercise room. **Guest Services:** valet laundry, area transportation-Financial District.

SIR FRANCIS DRAKE HOTEL
(415)392-7755 **45**

▼▼▼ Historic Hotel $129-$509

Address: 450 Powell St 94102 **Location:** Just n of Union Square at Sutter St. Powell Street, 33. **Facility:** A historic building offering the charm of a bygone era, the property is centrally located at Union Square. 416 units. 21 stories, interior corridors. **Parking:** valet only. **Amenities:** safes. **Dining:** Scala's Bistro, see separate listing, nightclub, entertainment. **Activities:** exercise room. *Fee:* massage. **Guest Services:** valet laundry.

THE STANFORD COURT, A RENAISSANCE HOTEL
(415)989-3500 **25**

▼▼▼▼ Hotel $179-$399 RENAISSANCE HOTELS & RESORTS

AAA Benefit: AAA hotel discounts of 5% or more.

Address: 905 California St 94108 **Location:** Atop Nob Hill; corner of California and Powell sts. Montgomery Street, 32. **Facility:** A long heritage distinguishes this service-oriented hotel, where some rooms offer sweeping views of the city's renowned skyline. 393 units. 8 stories, interior corridors. **Parking:** valet only. **Terms:** check-in 4 pm. **Amenities:** safes. *Fee:* video games, high-speed Internet. **Dining:** Aurea, see separate listing. **Activities:** exercise room. **Guest Services:** valet laundry, area transportation-within 3 mi. **Free Special Amenities:** local transportation.

STANYAN PARK HOTEL
(415)751-1000 **22**

▼▼▼ **Historic Hotel** $175-$450 **Address:** 750 Stanyan St 94117 **Location:** At Waller St. Carl & Cole, 53. **Facility:** Within walking distance of the Haight-Ashbury district, this restored Victorian hotel offers some rooms overlooking Golden Gate Park. 36 units, some two bedrooms and kitchens. 3 stories, interior corridors. **Parking:** on-site (fee). **Terms:** cancellation fee imposed. **Amenities:** *Some:* safes. **Guest Services:** valet laundry.

SUPER 8
(415)922-0244 **5**

▼▼ Motel $79-$239

Address: 2440 Lombard St 94123 **Location:** On US 101 (Lombard St); between Scott and Divisadero sts. **Facility:** 32 units. 3 stories (no elevator), exterior corridors. **Free Special Amenities:** continental breakfast and high-speed Internet.

SW HOTEL
(415)362-2999 **19**

▼▼▼ Hotel $139-$550 **Address:** 615 Broadway St 94133 **Location:** Corner of Grant Ave and Broadway St; in Chinatown. Embarcadero, 31. **Facility:** 81 units. 4 stories, interior corridors. **Parking:** on-site (fee). **Terms:** cancellation fee imposed, resort fee.

TAJ CAMPTON PLACE SAN FRANCISCO
415/781-5555 **51**

▼▼▼ ▼▼▼ **Hotel.** Rates not provided. **Address:** 340 Stockton St 94108 **Location:** Just n of Union Square; jct Sutter St. Montgomery Street, 32. **Facility:** For over a hundred years, this unassuming, upscale hotel has enticed travelers for return stays with their service and cozy ambiance. 110 units. 17 stories, interior corridors. **Parking:** valet only. **Amenities:** safes. *Fee:* video games, high-speed Internet. **Dining:** Campton Place Restaurant, see separate listing. **Activities:** exercise room. **Guest Services:** valet laundry, area transportation-within 2 mi.

TRAVELODGE AT THE PRESIDIO
(415)931-8581 **1**

▼▼ Motel $129-$259 **Address:** 2755 Lombard St 94123 **Location:** Between Lyon and Baker sts. **Facility:** 27 units. 3 stories (no elevator), exterior corridors. *Bath:* shower only. **Terms:** cancellation fee imposed. **Amenities:** safes.

TRAVELODGE BY THE BAY
(415)673-0691 **13**

▼▼ Motel $69-$209

Address: 1450 Lombard St 94123 **Location:** On US 101 (Lombard St); between Van Ness Ave and Franklin St. **Facility:** 70 units, some two bedrooms and efficiencies. 2-3 stories, interior/exterior corridors. **Parking:** on-site (fee). **Guest Services:** coin laundry. **Free Special Amenities:** expanded continental breakfast and high-speed Internet.

VILLA FLORENCE
(415)397-7700 **69**

▼▼▼ **Hotel** $169-$449 **Address:** 225 Powell St 94107 **Location:** Just s of Union Square; between O'Farrell and Geary sts. Powell Street, 33. **Facility:** 182 units. 7 stories, interior corridors. **Parking:** valet only. **Terms:** 3 day cancellation notice-fee imposed, resort fee. **Amenities:** video games (fee), safes. **Dining:** Kuleto's, see separate listing. **Activities:** exercise room. **Guest Services:** valet laundry.

YOUR NEW LUCKY NUMBER

RESORT + WHITNEY OAKS GOLF PACKAGES FROM

$149*

Welcome to Thunder Valley Casino Resort, one of Northern California's premier AAA rated Four Diamond resorts. Enjoy nonstop gaming action, including slots, blackjack, poker and other casino favorites. Plus, 14 unique restaurants & bars, live headline entertainment, 300 stunning hotel rooms starting at just $99* and our newest amenity, Whitney Oaks Golf Club, enhance the Thunder Valley Casino Resort, Four Diamond experience you've always wanted. Lucky You.

THUNDER VALLEY CASINO · RESORT

AAA
Four Diamond Award

I-80 TO HWY 65 • LEFT ON SUNSET • 877-468-8777
THUNDERVALLEYRESORT.COM

*Based on single/double occupancy. Rates are plus tax and vary by unit and season.

(See maps & indexes p. 394, 404.)

WARWICK SAN FRANCISCO HOTEL (415)928-7900 [62]

◆◆◆ **Hotel** $99-$349 **Address:** 490 Geary St 94102 **Location:** Between Taylor and Mason sts. Powell Street, 33. **Facility:** 74 units. 8 stories, interior corridors. **Parking:** valet only. **Terms:** cancellation fee imposed. **Amenities:** video games (fee), safes. *Some:* high-speed Internet (fee). **Dining:** La Scene Cafe, see separate listing. **Guest Services:** valet laundry. *(See ad p. 418.)*

[icons] FEE / SOME UNITS

THE WESTIN ST. FRANCIS SAN FRANCISCO ON UNION SQUARE (415)397-7000 [63]

◆◆◆ Hotel $199-$629 **WESTIN** HOTELS & RESORTS **AAA Benefit:** Enjoy up to 20% off your next stay, plus Starwood Preferred Guest® bonuses.

Address: 335 Powell St 94102 **Location:** On Union Square. Powell Street, 33. **Facility:** Across from Union Square, the hotel is noted for its comfortable beds and high-standard services. 1195 units. 32 stories, interior corridors. **Parking:** valet only. **Terms:** 3 day cancellation notice-fee imposed. **Amenities:** high-speed Internet (fee), safes. **Dining:** 2 restaurants. **Activities:** steamrooms, spa. **Guest Services:** valet laundry.

[icons] SAVE CALL BIZ / SOME UNITS

Tell Us How We're Doing

If your visit to a TourBook-listed property doesn't meet your expectations, tell us about it.

AAA.com/TourBookComments

WESTIN SAN FRANCISCO MARKET STREET
(415)974-6400 [78]

◆◆◆ Hotel $159-$899 **WESTIN** HOTELS & RESORTS **AAA Benefit:** Enjoy up to 20% off your next stay, plus Starwood Preferred Guest® bonuses.

Address: 50 3rd St 94103 **Location:** Just n of Moscone Convention Center; between Jessie and Stevenson sts. Montgomery Street, 32. **Facility:** With each of its guest rooms featuring a dramatic floor-to-ceiling window, the hotel offers sweeping views of scenic San Francisco. 676 units. 32 stories, interior corridors. **Parking:** valet only. **Terms:** 2-4 night minimum stay - seasonal and/or weekends, 3 day cancellation notice-fee imposed. **Amenities:** high-speed Internet (fee), safes. **Activities:** exercise room. *Fee:* massage. **Guest Services:** valet laundry. **Free Special Amenities:** newspaper.

[icons] SAVE CALL BIZ / SOME UNITS

THE WHARF INN (415)673-7411 [3]

◆◆ Motel $119-$225 **Address:** 2601 Mason St 94133 **Location:** At Beach St; adjacent to Fisherman's Wharf and San Francisco Bay. **Facility:** 51 units, some two bedrooms and kitchens. 3 stories, exterior corridors. **Free Special Amenities:** newspaper and high-speed Internet. *(See ad this page.)*

[icons] SAVE CALL FEE / SOME UNITS FEE

WHITE SWAN INN, A JOIE DE VIVRE HOTEL
(415)775-1755 [32]

◆◆◆ **Historic Hotel** $119-$419 **Address:** 845 Bush St 94108 **Location:** Just nw of Union Square at Taylor St. Powell Street, 33. **Facility:** Every room in this enchanting French countryside retreat has a fireplace, creating the ideal spot to end each memorable day. 26 units. 4 stories, interior corridors. **Parking:** valet only. **Terms:** 2-3 night minimum stay - seasonal and/or weekends. **Activities:** limited exercise equipment. **Guest Services:** valet laundry.

[icons]

▼ *See AAA listing this page* ▼

(See maps & indexes p. 394, 404.)

W SAN FRANCISCO
(415)777-5300 **87**

WWWW

Contemporary Hotel
$249-$669

W HOTELS

AAA Benefit: Special member room rates, plus Starwood Preferred Guest® bonuses.

Address: 181 3rd St 94103 **Location:** At Howard St. Montgomery Street, 32. **Facility:** This ultra-contemporary facility offers "cool" luxury in all respects. The 410 guest units are housed in a 31-story modern high-rise located across from the Museum of Modern Art and Moscone Convention Center. 404 units. 31 stories, interior corridors. **Parking:** valet only. **Terms:** cancellation fee imposed. **Amenities:** high-speed Internet (fee), safes. **Pool(s):** heated indoor. **Activities:** whirlpool, exercise room, spa. **Guest Services:** valet laundry, area transportation-within 4 mi.

SAVE ECO ⊞ ✦ ⊥ CALL &M ⚲ 📶 ✕ ⚑ / SOME UNITS FEE 🐾 ⬛ 🛏 🖥 ⊞

CLIFT HOTEL
415/775-4700

[fyi] Not evaluated. **Address:** 495 Geary St 94102. Powell Street, 33. Facilities, services, and décor characterize an upscale property.

WHERE TO EAT

1300 ON FILLMORE
415/771-7100 **44**

WWW Soul Food. Casual Dining. $15-$31 **AAA Inspector Notes:** Elegantly jazzy, snazzy decor can be found at this eatery where high ceilings and ceiling-to-floor windows dominate the dining area. Sophisticated soul food includes hush puppies (when available), fried green tomatoes and fried chicken. For dessert, try the apple cobbler or the banana cream pie. **Bar:** full bar. **Reservations:** suggested. **Address:** 1300 Fillmore St 94115 **Location:** Jct Eddy St. Van Ness, 50. **Parking:** street only. D 🅺 ⊞

21ST AMENDMENT
415/369-0900 **186**

WW American. Casual Dining. $11-$25 **AAA Inspector Notes:** This classic American grill is in a 1920s warehouse. It nurtures a lively atmosphere. Try their Cubano sandwich and a cold beer. **Bar:** full bar. **Address:** 563 2nd St 94107 **Location:** Between Brannan and Bryant sts; in Financial District. 2nd & King, 92. **Parking:** street only. L D ⊞

54 MINT
415/543-5100 **175**

WWW Italian. Casual Dining. $15-$26 **AAA Inspector Notes:** This sophisticated, rustic downtown eatery offers simple Italian dishes that are well-flavored. Start with arancino al nero (deep-fried squid-ink-infused rice ball stuffed with spicy shrimp), or parmigiano al balsamico (slivers of three-year-aged cheese drizzled with extra aged balsamic vinegar). For an entree, try the linguine alla pescatora or the classic carbonara. The restaurant also is an alimentari (seller of pasta, cheese, oil and salt) and a vineria (seller of wine). **Bar:** beer & wine. **Reservations:** suggested. **Address:** 16 Mint Plaza 94103 **Location:** On the Plaza; enter on 5th or Mission sts. Powell Street, 33. **Parking:** street only. L D 🅺 ⊞

A 16
415/771-2216 **2**

WWW Italian. Casual Dining. $12-$26 **AAA Inspector Notes:** This stylish and energetic restaurant offers a distinctive ambience featuring mermaid artwork and cork board-style walls. The menu changes regularly and is primarily Italian with many appetizers, wood-fired pizza, pasta, duck, wild boar, lamb, Alaskan cod and braised pork shoulder occasionally offered. The wine bar is popular and offers up to 40 wines by the glass and more than 500 wines by the bottle. Lunch is served Wednesday through Friday. **Bar:** beer & wine. **Reservations:** suggested. **Address:** 2355 Chestnut St 94123 **Location:** Between Scott and Divisadero sts. **Parking:** street only. D CALL &M

ABSINTHE BRASSERIE AND BAR
415/551-1590 **56**

WWWW Regional French. Fine Dining. $14-$36 **AAA Inspector Notes:** Patrons enjoy creative French cuisine at this eatery that focuses on fresh local seafood and quality meats. Several dining sections and a pleasant bar area offer space to unwind. **Bar:** full bar. **Address:** 398 Hayes St 94102 **Location:** Corner of Gough St. Van Ness, 50. **Parking:** valet and street only. L D LATE ⊞

ACQUERELLO
415/567-5432 **69**

WWWW Italian. Fine Dining. $70-$135 **AAA Inspector Notes:** This intimate, cozy restaurant serves elegant seasonally changing Northern Italian cuisine. An extensive list of Italian wines is there to enhance the dining experience. **Bar:** beer & wine. **Reservations:** suggested. **Address:** 1722 Sacramento St 94109 **Location:** Between Van Ness Ave and Polk St. Powell Street, 33. **Parking:** street only. D 🅺 ⊞

AICHA MOROCCAN CUISINE
415/345-9947 **100**

WW Moroccan. Casual Dining. $11-$15 **AAA Inspector Notes:** Modest with a neighborhood vibe, this restaurant serves halal Moroccan cuisine. Well-flavored tagines, kebabs and vegetarian starters are some of the dishes on the menu. Some prix fixe offerings are available, too. **Address:** 1303 Polk St 94109 **Location:** Between Bush and Austin sts. Civic Center/UN Plaza, 34. **Parking:** street only. L D 🅺 ⊞

ALBORZ
415/440-4321 **103**

WW Middle Eastern. Casual Dining. $10-$16 **AAA Inspector Notes:** Topping this Persian menu is a combination platter with kashk bademjan, eggplant topped with whey, mint, fried onions and chopped walnuts; joojeh, a Cornish hen with a side of basmati rice topped with almond slivers, orange peel and raisins; fesenjan with chicken, a stew with roasted ground walnut cooked in pomegranate sauce. The makhlut, a rose ice cream with frozen rose water and rice noodles, is a must-try dessert. **Bar:** beer & wine. **Address:** 1245 Van Ness Ave 94109 **Location:** US 101 (Van Ness Ave); at Sutter St. Civic Center/UN Plaza, 34. **Parking:** street only. L D 🅺 ⊞

THE ALEMBIC
415/666-0822 **63**

WWW California. Gastro Pub. $9-$23 **AAA Inspector Notes:** The nondescript exterior, along with a dim interior, houses an amazingly detailed décor (purposely distressed) with high tin ceilings and chemist's mixing bottles on the wall. Drinks are taken seriously here—dedicated to beer, hard liquor and crafted cocktails with no blended drinks served. Food is taken just as seriously. Menu items include pickled quail eggs, simple sliders, crispy pork belly, squid and a cheese plate. The best deal is the three-course meal that can be shared. **Bar:** full bar. **Address:** 1725 Haight St 94117 **Location:** Between Cole and Sharader sts. Carl & Cole, 53. **Parking:** street only. L D LATE 🅺 ⊞

ALFRED'S STEAKHOUSE
415/781-7058 **73**

WWW Steak. Fine Dining. $14-$59 **AAA Inspector Notes:** A San Francisco institution since 1928, this classic steakhouse serves massive cuts of beef in a Victorian bordello-style dining room. Also popular are the mesquite preparations and Caesar salads. **Bar:** full bar. **Reservations:** suggested. **Address:** 659 Merchant St 94111 **Location:** Between Kearny and Montgomery sts. Montgomery Street, 32. **Parking:** street only. D ⊞

ALIOTO'S
415/673-0183 **10**

WWW Seafood. Casual Dining. $11-$62 **AAA Inspector Notes:** Established in 1928, this third-floor restaurant overlooks the fishing fleet. Seafood specialties are at the heart of the menu. Try the oysters Rockefeller, grilled wild rockfish with mashed potatoes and mushroom sauce. Have the tasting plate for dessert, with gelato, cannoli and crème brûlée. Parking is validated for the lot across the street. **Bar:** full bar. **Reservations:** suggested. **Address:** 8 Fisherman's Wharf 94133 **Location:** In the "Heart" of Fisherman's Wharf. **Parking:** street only. L D

AMARENA
415/447-0441 **31**

WW Italian. Casual Dining. $17-$30 **AAA Inspector Notes:** In the downtown Russian Hill neighborhood, this cozy, stylish eatery serves tasty fine Italian cuisine. **Bar:** beer & wine. **Reservations:** suggested. **Address:** 2162 Larkin St 94109 **Location:** Corner of Green St. **Parking:** street only. D

(See maps & indexes p. 394, 404.)

AME RESTAURANT
415/284-4040 **167**

♦♦♦♦ ♦♦♦♦ Northern California. Fine Dining. $35-$39 **AAA Inspector Notes:** Tucked away off the lobby of a luxury hotel, this restaurant occupies an eclectic space with an exhibition kitchen, cloth-covered tables and spot lighting. The extensive menu changes regularly with the season. The food is a clever union between California and Asian cuisine. Fresh sashimi always is available along with Dungeness crab, grilled fish, pork chop, quail and Wagyu beef cheeks and sweetbread. Fine artisan cheese and decadent desserts are offered. **Bar:** full bar. **Reservations:** suggested. **Address:** 689 Mission St 94105 **Location:** At Mission St; in St. Regis Hotel San Francisco. ⊛ Montgomery Street, 32. **Parking:** valet only.

D CALL ⑤M ⊞

THE AMERICAN GRILLED CHEESE KITCHEN
415/243-0107 **184**

♦ American. Quick Serve. $4-$9 **AAA Inspector Notes:** The name says it all—comfort food made with the best ingredients. Get the piglet and the smoky tomato soup. Indulge and have it with a glass of wine. Extended hours until the first pitch for all San Francisco Giants home night games and other events at AT&T Park. **Bar:** beer & wine. **Address:** 1 S Park Ave 94107 **Location:** At 2nd St (entrance on 2nd St). ⊛ 2nd & King, 92. **Parking:** street only.

B L CALL ⑤M ⅃ ⊞

AMERICANO RESTAURANT & BAR
415/278-3777 **111**

♦♦♦ Northern Italian. Casual Dining. $12-$30 **AAA Inspector Notes:** Paintings on the ceiling lend to the appeal of the trendy and boisterous restaurant. A heavy California influence is evident in preparations of innovative Northern Italian food. **Bar:** full bar. **Reservations:** suggested. **Address:** 8 Mission St 94105 **Location:** At Embarcadero; in Hotel Vitale, a Joie de Vivre hotel. ⊛ Embarcadero, 31. **Parking:** valet and street only. B L D CALL ⑤M ⊞

ANA MANDARA
415/771-6800 **13**

♦♦♦ Vietnamese. Fine Dining. $14-$36 **AAA Inspector Notes:** Just west of the wharf, this restaurant nurtures a calm atmosphere and soothing, quiet elegance. Dishes reflect intriguing flavors, textures and ingredients. Mekong basa, a mild white fish, comes with snow pea sprouts and a blend of sauces that contain red pepper heat and sweet orange flavors. Homemade sorbets and ice creams are refreshing and tangy. The bar upstairs has a happy hour discount on appetizers and drinks. **Bar:** full bar. **Reservations:** required. **Address:** 891 Beach St 94109 **Location:** Just w of Larkin St; at Ghirardelli Square. **Parking:** valet and street only. L D

ANNABELLE'S BAR & BISTRO
415/777-1200 **169**

♦♦♦ New California. Casual Dining. $13-$32 **AAA Inspector Notes:** Since 1913, this classic San Francisco restaurant has been serving such bistro fare as cioppino, roasted mussels and lamb chops. Diners can park nearby at Fifth and Mission for a fee. **Bar:** full bar. **Reservations:** suggested. **Address:** 68 4th St 94103 **Location:** At Jessie St; across from San Francisco Marriott Marquis. ⊛ Powell Street, 33. **Parking:** valet and street only.

L D ⅃ ⊞

ANZU RESTAURANT
415/394-1100 **154**

♦♦♦ Pacific Rim. Fine Dining. $11-$42 **AAA Inspector Notes:** Combining fine aged beef and masterfully prepared sushi, this restaurant offers items from both sea and land. An elegant dining room sets the scene for equally refined service and special sake martinis. Seating is available in the dining room or at the sushi bar. **Bar:** full bar. **Reservations:** suggested. **Address:** 222 Mason St 94102 **Location:** At O'Farrell St; in Hotel Nikko San Francisco. ⊛ Powell Street, 33. **Parking:** valet only. B L D ⊞

AQ RESTAURANT & BAR
415/341-9000 **181**

♦♦♦ California. Casual Dining. $25 **AAA Inspector Notes:** Diners must come to this restaurant four times a year to experience seasonal changes in décor and food. For winter, this warehouse with exposed red bricks and soaring ceilings and windows is transformed with simple drapery and distinctive ceiling lights that cast a romantic glow throughout the restaurant. Food is just as creative. Who would have thought that the lowly cauliflower could look like snowflakes and miniature trees? **Bar:** full bar. **Reservations:** suggested. **Address:** 1085 Mission St 94103 **Location:** Between 6th and 7th sts. ⊛ Civic Center/UN Plaza, 34. **Parking:** street only. D ⅃ ⊞

ASLAM'S RASOI
415/695-0599 **122**

♦♦ Indian. Casual Dining. $10-$22 **AAA Inspector Notes:** Indian and Pakistani cuisine come together on this stylish restaurant's menu. Naan and curry dishes are favorites. **Bar:** beer & wine. **Address:** 1037 Valencia St 94110 **Location:** 1 mi s of Market St; at 21st St. ⊛ 24th Street Mission, 36. **Parking:** street only.

D

ASQEW GRILL

♦ Barbecue. Quick Serve. $9-$18 **AAA Inspector Notes:** This casual, neighborhood grill offers no fried items making this a great option for the health conscious. **Bar:** beer & wine.

L D ⅃

For additional information, visit AAA.com

LOCATIONS:
Address: 3348 Steiner St 94125 **Location:** Jct Chestnut and Steiner sts. **Phone:** 415/931-9200
Address: 1607 Haight St 94117 **Location:** At Clayton St; in Haight-Ashbury District. ⊛ Carl & Cole, 53. **Phone:** 415/701-9301

ATELIER CRENN
415/440-0460 **9**

♦♦ French. Casual Dining. $75-$125 **AAA Inspector Notes:** The restaurant decor is like a Japanese room - minimal and serene, with the ceiling serving the same purpose as a tokonoma. A woven straw mat diffuses the ceiling light with a twig nest encircling the hanging lights. Aptly named, "poetic culinaria" each dish is edible artwork. Presentation is also spectacular, like using a bonsai as a prop for a sweets plate. For a simpler presentation there's the "walk through the garden" complete with edible dirt. **Bar:** wine only. **Reservations:** suggested. **Address:** 3127 Filmore St 94123 **Location:** Between Filbert and Greenwich sts. **Parking:** valet and street only.

D ⅃

AUREA
415/989-3500 **88**

♦♦♦ California. Casual Dining. $13-$33 **AAA Inspector Notes:** This hotel restaurant features an open floorplan with lounge sofas interspersed with formal dining tables as well as communal tables. The seasonal menu is simple but entrées boast a sophisticated presentation and taste. For breakfast, try the airy lemon soufflé pancakes with raspberry sauce. At dinner, start with grilled crab cakes followed by sea scallops. **Bar:** full bar. **Reservations:** suggested. **Address:** 905 California St 94108 **Location:** Atop Nob Hill; corner of California and Powell sts; in The Stanford Court, A Renaissance Hotel. ⊛ Montgomery Street, 32. **Parking:** valet only.

B L D CALL ⑤M ⊞

AZIZA
415/752-2222 **24**

♦♦♦ Moroccan. Casual Dining. $19-$29 **AAA Inspector Notes:** Owner-chef Mourad Lahlou, a native of Marrakech, creates a sophisticated dining experience through the use of blue walls, low lit burgundy chandeliers and arched wall accents as well as a menu lined with delicious foods. The five-course tasting plate-which includes the famed basteeya and a fabulous dessert-is an excellent choice for groups. No meal is complete without a creative cocktail such as almond, tequila rimmed with smoked grey sea salt. **Bar:** full bar. **Reservations:** suggested. **Address:** 5800 Geary Blvd 94121 **Location:** Corner of 22nd Ave. **Parking:** valet and street only.

D CALL ⑤M

BAKER & BANKER
415/351-2500 **35**

♦♦♦ American. Casual Dining. $24-$31 **AAA Inspector Notes:** Blackboards list specials at this intimate and cozy dining spot. Masculine decor sets the ambience with the water closet displaying signed menus from various chefs including Mr. Keller of French Laundry, Gary Danko and David Chang of Momofuku. Try the four-course chef's tasting menu and wine pairing. Breads are made on site and they are delicious-get a loaf to bring home. **Bar:** beer & wine. **Address:** 1701 Octavia St 94109 **Location:** At Bush St. ⊛ Civic Center/UN Plaza, 34. **Parking:** valet and street only.

D ⊞

BAKER STREET BISTRO
415/931-1475 **5**

♦♦ French. Fine Dining. $9-$29 **AAA Inspector Notes:** American and Mediterranean influences punctuate this small and charming neighborhood restaurant's French cuisine. Seating is tight, but the interesting and varied menu makes up for the lack of space. Sidewalk seating beckons patrons during nice weather. **Bar:** beer & wine. **Reservations:** required. **Address:** 2953 Baker St 94123 **Location:** Between Green and Lombard sts. **Parking:** street only.

L D

(See maps & indexes p. 394, 404.)

BALBOA CAFE 415/921-3944 [8]

▼▼▼ American. Gastro Pub. $10-$30 **AAA Inspector Notes:** One of the oldest saloons in San Francisco, this popular neighborhood restaurant/pub has retained most of its original elegant decor. On the menu are quality classics from ahi tuna tartare to burgers. **Bar:** full bar. **Address:** 3199 Fillmore St 94123 **Location:** At Greenwich St; in Cow Hollow District. **Parking:** street only.

L D

BAR AGRICOLE 415/355-9400 [87]

▼▼▼ California. Gastro Pub. $18-$28 **AAA Inspector Notes:** This contemporary urban tavern, with sleek lines of wood and concrete, takes their drinks seriously with two bars—one for drinkers, another for making drinks for diners only. Liquor is sourced from small companies and organic mixes are made on site. Try a single glass offering of wine from Jura or Canary Islands. Equal attention and care are lavished on the food. Some menu items change daily. **Bar:** full bar. **Reservations:** suggested. **Address:** 355 11th St 94103 **Location:** Between Harrison and Folsom sts. Van Ness, 50. **Parking:** street only. D

BAR BAMBINO CAFE & WINE BAR 415/701-8466 [102]

▼▼▼ Italian. Casual Dining. $17-$30 **AAA Inspector Notes:** Contemporary casual ambience, this café and bar offers a simple, yet sophisticated, menu. Choose from a great selection of European wines. **Bar:** beer & wine. **Address:** 2931 16th St 94103 **Location:** Between Mission St and S Van Ness Ave. 16th Street Mission, 35. **Parking:** street only. D

BAR CRUDO 415/409-0679 [49]

▼▼▼ Seafood. Casual Dining. $14-$26 **AAA Inspector Notes:** Crudo is an Italian term meaning raw, and this chic and trendy spot appeals primarily to the hip, foodie-oriented guest. Service is casual, but there is nothing casual about what goes on in the kitchen. The spectacular food is the real reason to come here. Start with the crudo sampler, followed by uni avocado toast and Louisiana devil prawns. Check out happy hour with great-priced oysters. **Bar:** beer & wine. **Address:** 655 Divisadero St 94117 **Location:** Between Grove and Hayes sts. Duboce & Noe, 52. **Parking:** street only.

D

BAR JULES 415/621-5482 [53]

▼▼▼ California. Casual Dining. $13-$27 **AAA Inspector Notes:** This neighborhood bistro has been packing them in since it opened, so go early or later in the evening to avoid the crowd. The menu changes daily so check their website. Wild mushroom and eggplant gratin, oxtail stew with mashed potatoes and huckleberry tart with whipped cream are just a few of the items offered. Flavors are sophisticated with a touch of home cooking. **Bar:** beer & wine. **Address:** 609 Hayes St 94199 **Location:** Between Laguna and Buchanan sts. Van Ness, 50. **Parking:** street only. D

BASIL THAI RESTAURANT & BAR 415/552-8999 [195]

▼▼ Thai. Fine Dining. $9-$17 **AAA Inspector Notes:** Contemporary decor with concrete columns, glass bricks and ceiling lights fashioned from string can be found at this restaurant where excellent quality Thai cuisine with sophisticated flavors is served. An extensive variety of choices is available and some combinations are quite interesting. A special lunch menu offers a choice of two entrées with rice and a spring roll for a very reasonable rate. **Bar:** beer & wine. **Address:** 1175 Folsom St 94103 **Location:** Between 7th and 8th sts. Civic Center/UN Plaza, 34. **Parking:** street only. L D

BEACH CHALET BREWERY AND RESTAURANT 415/386-8439 [33]

▼▼ American. Casual Dining. $12-$32 **AAA Inspector Notes:** This eatery is popular with tourists, as it affords a great view of the ocean and easy access to the park. The menu lists American bistro fare, such as salads, sandwiches, burgers, ribs, fish and chips and several handcrafted ales. **Bar:** full bar. **Reservations:** suggested. **Address:** 1000 Great Hwy 94121 **Location:** Northwest corner of Golden Gate Park, below the Dutch Windmill facing the Pacific Ocean; near JFK Dr. Ocean Beach, 58.

B L D CALL

BETELNUT 415/929-8855 [12]

▼▼▼ Asian. Casual Dining. $12-$22 **AAA Inspector Notes:** A walk into this restaurant transports guests to the Far East. The sounds and smells emanating from the open kitchen sets the tone for this side street beer house while the ambient lighting sets the mood. From simple dumplings to more complex stir fried dishes, the food is vibrant. Check out the beggar's clay chicken—it takes 40 minutes so order early. Encased in clay and baked, the tableside presentation allows guests to weld the mallet to crack open the clay. **Bar:** full bar. **Reservations:** suggested. **Address:** 2030 Union St 94123 **Location:** Between Buchanan and Webster sts; in Cow Hollow District. **Parking:** street only. L D

(See maps & indexes p. 394, 404.)

BIG 4 RESTAURANT 415/771-1140 86
▼▼▼ California. Fine Dining. $18-$44 **AAA Inspector Notes:** This restaurant takes its name from four 19th century railroad tycoons. The decor hearkens back to a private gentleman's club with its rich leather banquettes, dark wood paneling, sparkling mirrors, soft sconce lighting and mellow relaxed mood as soothing live piano tunes float from the entry. The special is always a good choice, but if you're looking for something smaller, the bistro fare includes chicken pot pie and Dijon chicken breast sandwiches. **Bar:** full bar. **Reservations:** suggested. **Address:** 1075 California St 94108 **Location:** Atop Nob Hill; corner of California and Taylor sts; in The Huntington Hotel. 🚇 Powell Street, 33. **Parking:** street only.
B D 🚇

BILL'S PLACE 415/221-5262 20
▼ American. Casual Dining. $6-$14 **AAA Inspector Notes:** A neighborhood institution, located in the city's Richmond district, this eatery is a down-home diner. Friendly atmosphere, good burgers, fresh salads and hand-cut French fries are all offered. There also is outdoor patio seating in the back. **Bar:** beer & wine. **Address:** 2315 Clement St 94121 **Location:** Between 24th and 25th aves.
L D 🎦

BISTRO BOUDIN AT THE WHARF 415/928-1849 12
▼▼▼ Seafood. Casual Dining. $13-$29 **AAA Inspector Notes:** Enjoy the view of the San Francisco Bay and Alcatraz in this elegant restaurant located on the second floor. The menu includes pasta, seafood, pizza, salads and soups. In the mood for something a little more than soup in a bread bowl? Begin with the shrimp cocktail in salsa sauce, then move on to grilled sea bass with Brussels sprouts and mushroom cream sauce. Finish with a tasting of three desserts. **Bar:** full bar. **Address:** 160 Jefferson St 94133 **Location:** Just e of jct Taylor St.
B L D

BIX 415/433-6300 59
▼▼▼ Continental. Fine Dining. $14-$40 **AAA Inspector Notes:** This high-end supper club brings guests down an alley and back to the 1930s. Dishes are elegant and flavorful. **Bar:** full bar. **Reservations:** suggested. **Address:** 56 Gold St 94133 **Location:** Between Montgomery and Sansome sts. 🚇 Embarcadero, 31. **Parking:** valet and street only.
D 🚇

BLUE BOTTLE CAFE 415/495-3394 177
▼ American. Quick Serve. $5-$10 **AAA Inspector Notes:** Modern, minimalist décor is the perfect backdrop to showcase the fantastical coffee making apparatus—the sky-high Kyoto-style iced coffee drip and the five-light siphon bar. Perfect brew should be accompanied by perfect morsels of food and they do not disappoint. **Bar:** beer & wine. **Address:** 66 Mint St 94103 **Location:** At Jessie St. 🚇 Powell Street, 33. **Parking:** street only.
B L 🎦 🚇

BLUE MERMAID CHOWDER HOUSE & BAR
  415/771-2222 6
▼▼▼
Seafood
Casual Dining
$12-$28

AAA Inspector Notes: In the heart of Fisherman's wharf, this eatery sits in The Cannery, a renovated warehouse complex. Its wide selection of clam and crab chowders is a specialty. Service is friendly, and the atmosphere is casual and relaxed. **Bar:** full bar. **Address:** 471 Jefferson St 94109 **Location:** Fisherman's Wharf; adjacent to The Cannery; in Argonaut Hotel. **Parking:** valet and street only.
B L D CALL 🅜

BOBOQUIVARIS 415/441-8880 22
▼▼▼
Continental
Fine Dining
$19-$70

AAA Inspector Notes: A convenient location helps make this a favorite spot for both tourists and locals alike. The eclectic menu and decor lend to an enjoyable experience. Try the crab cake and make sure you get the bone-in filet mignon. **Bar:** full bar. **Address:** 1450 Lombard St 94123 **Location:** Just w of Van Ness Ave.
Menu on AAA.com D

BOB'S STEAK & CHOP HOUSE 415/273-3085 96
▼▼▼ Steak. Casual Dining. $15-$70 **AAA Inspector Notes:** On the menu at this restaurant is a 20-ounce bone-in rib-eye, rack of lamb and a variety of fresh seafood. All entrées are accompanied by a choice of potato and a large glazed carrot. **Bar:** full bar. **Reservations:** suggested. **Address:** 500 California St at Montgomery St; in Financial District; in Omni San Francisco Hotel. 🚇 Montgomery Street, 32. **Parking:** valet only.
B L D CALL 🅜 🚇

BOCADILLOS 415/982-2622 64
▼▼▼ Spanish. Casual Dining. $6-$16 **AAA Inspector Notes:** The name of this casual spot literally means little sandwiches. The tapas bar features both Spanish and Basque small plates which are big on flavor. Examples include the bocadillo of chorizo with walnut spread and parsley. This wildly popular spot can get crowded. **Bar:** beer & wine. **Address:** 710 Montgomery St 94111 **Location:** At Washington St. 🚇 Embarcadero, 31. **Parking:** street only.
B L D CALL 🅜 🚇

BOROBUDUR RESTAURANT 415/775-1512 127
▼▼ Indonesian. Casual Dining. $8-$18 **AAA Inspector Notes:** Rated by the local Indonesian transplants as the most authentic, this restaurant does not disappoint. Diners who think Thai food is a bit too sweet but love the spicy complex flavor, will enjoy the less sweet, yet still complex flavors of the Indonesian dishes served here. Service can be leisurely at times. **Bar:** beer & wine. **Address:** 700 Post St 94109 **Location:** At James St. 🚇 Powell Street, 33. **Parking:** street only.
L D 🎦 🚇

BOUDIN BAKERY & CAFE
▼ American. Cafeteria. $7-$12 **AAA Inspector Notes:** The original and still the master at baking sourdough bread, this institution dates back to 1849. Patrons can watch the bakers make the bread and then line up to buy it. B L D

For additional information, visit AAA.com
LOCATIONS:
Address: 160 Jefferson St 94133 **Location:** Between Taylor and Mason sts; at Fisherman's Wharf. **Bar:** beer & wine.
Phone: 415/928-1849
Address: Pier 39, Space 5-Q 94133 **Location:** At Fisherman's Wharf, near Pier 45. **Bar:** beer only. **Phone:** 415/421-0185

BOULANGERIE BAY BREAD 415/440-0356 30
▼ Breads/Pastries. Casual Dining. $4-$9 **AAA Inspector Notes:** Pastries at this casual spot are as good as those epicures might experience in Paris. Also mouthwatering are rustic, crusty French breads, delicate desserts and such sandwiches as the croque monsieur, which is covered with several kinds of cheese. Varied flavors of the signature macaroons, as well as the house specialty cannelles, are magnifique. **Address:** 2325 Pine St 94115 **Location:** Jct Fillmore St, just w. **Parking:** street only.
B L 🎦

BOULETTES LARDER 415/399-1155 92
▼▼ Natural/Organic. Casual Dining. $7-$25 **AAA Inspector Notes:** On the San Francisco Bay side of the Ferry Building Marketplace, this restaurant prepares dishes from fresh, organically grown food items, herbs and spices. The menu changes daily in accordance with availability at the farmers' market. Offerings might include seafood, quail, fish stew, fresh mixed-green salads and a variety of soups. Guests dine at one large table and should call ahead, as seating is limited. Their beignets are airy and divine and only available for Sunday brunch. **Address:** 1 Ferry Building Marketplace 94111 **Location:** In northeast corner of Ferry Building Marketplace. 🚇 Embarcadero, 31. **Parking:** on-site (fee).
B L 🚇

BOULEVARD 415/543-6084 109
▼▼▼▼ American. Fine Dining. $16-$42 **AAA Inspector Notes:** With exceptional food and spectacular views of the San Francisco Bay, the restaurant offers an elegant dining experience perfect for special occasions. **Bar:** full bar. **Reservations:** suggested. **Address:** 1 Mission St 94105 **Location:** Jct Steuart St; at Embarcadero. 🚇 Embarcadero, 31. **Parking:** valet and street only.
L D 🚇

(See maps & indexes p. 394, 404.)

BRENDA'S FRENCH SOUL FOOD   415/345-8100   163

▼▼ Creole. Casual Dining. $7-$17 **AAA Inspector Notes:** High ceilings give this compact restaurant breathing space. Well seasoned, hearty portions and reasonable prices keep this restaurant busy, especially during lunch. Shrimp and grits, gumbo, hangtown fry, beignets and watermelon ice tea are some of its offerings. **Bar:** beer & wine. **Address:** 652 Polk St 94102 **Location:** Between Eddy and Turk sts. 🚇 Civic Center/UN Plaza, 34.

[B] [L] [D] [K] [🚇]

THE BUENA VISTA CAFE   415/474-5044   15

▼▼ American. Casual Dining. $9-$18 **AAA Inspector Notes:** A decidedly retro feel punctuates this neighborhood cafe, which sports leaded stained-glass window accents, ceiling fans and an antique back bar. Photographs of early San Francisco complete the decor. Diners enjoy good home-cooking, as well as fresh Dungeness crabs in season. This place introduced Irish coffee to the city and estimates it has served some 34,845,000 of them since opening in 1952. **Bar:** full bar. **Address:** 2765 Hyde St 94109 **Location:** At Beach St. **Parking:** street only. [B] [L] [D] [LATE]

BURGER BAR SAN FRANCISCO   415/296-4272   143

▼▼ American. Casual Dining. $9-$25 **AAA Inspector Notes:** Visitors can experience a decadent Kobe beef, foie gras and truffle burger at this casual eatery. Order a custom-made milkshake or choose from the extensive wine list or the pages and pages of beer from all over the world. Get a window seat and enjoy the view of Union Square from the 6th floor. **Bar:** full bar. **Address:** 251 Geary St 94102 **Location:** Between Powell and Stockton sts; in Macy's. 🚇 Powell Street, 33. **Parking:** street only. [L] [D] [🚇]

BUTTERFLY   415/864-8999   20

▼▼▼ Pacific Rim. Casual Dining. $12-$39 **AAA Inspector Notes:** This stylish restaurant offers soaring ceilings with pin-points of lights emulating the night sky and huge hanging lights shaped like sea urchin shells. Get a seat at the dockside window and the view just might include some sea lions frolicking about. Menu items whet the appetite with fresh produce enhanced with exotic flavoring and artful presentation. **Bar:** full bar. **Address:** Pier 33 94111 **Location:** Jct The Embarcadero and Bay St. **Parking:** street only.

[L] [D]

CAFE BAKERY & RESTAURANT   415/661-6136   93

▼▼ International Comfort Food. Casual Dining. $9-$19 **AAA Inspector Notes:** This eatery, often packed with families, offers classic Hong Kong-style western food. Entrées comes with choice of salad or soup and warm dinner rolls, as well as a small dish of Jello for dessert. One of the more popular dishes is the pan-fried pork chop placed on top of fried rice or spaghetti noodles, covered with tomato sauce and baked. Wash it all down with a Hong Kong-style milk tea, Horlick (hot malted milk) or a glass of Ovaltine. **Address:** 1345-65 Noriega St 94122 **Location:** Between 20th and 21st aves. 🚇 Judah & 19th Ave, 56. **Parking:** street only. [L] [D] [K] [🚇]

CAFE CLAUDE   415/392-3505   122

▼▼▼ French. Casual Dining. $11-$29 **AAA Inspector Notes:** Wonderfully warm and intimate, this classic French bistro tucked away in an alley, highlights the cuisine of executive chef Philippe Chevalier. Try the classic escargot, coq au vin and the coconut flan. **Bar:** full bar. **Address:** 7 Claude Ln 94108 **Location:** Between Grant and Kearny sts. 🚇 Montgomery Street, 32. **Parking:** street only.

[L] [D] [🚇]

CAFE DIVINE   415/986-3414   30

American
Casual Dining
$8-$20

AAA Inspector Notes: Facing Washington Square, this restaurant offers a menu with café flavor combined with a bit of European flavor mixed with a bit of San Francisco spice. Arrive early for the three-course special, which features great lamb and lentil stews. Nightly entertainment ranges from blues to accordionist's solo. **Bar:** beer & wine. **Address:** 1600 Stockton St 94133 **Location:** At Union St. 🚇 Embarcadero, 31. **Parking:** street only.

[B] [L] [D] CALL [GM] [K] [🚇]

CAFE JACQUELINE   415/981-5565   35

▼▼▼ French. Fine Dining. $28-$55 **AAA Inspector Notes:** While guests can start with a soup or salad, everything else on the menu is soufflés, and the kitchen staff is talented at making them. Made one at a time, an appetizer is the perfect way to start the meal. Choose the chocolate souffle, not too sweet and perfect with a cup of coffee or a glass of dessert wine. **Bar:** beer & wine. **Reservations:** required. **Address:** 1454 Grant Ave 94133 **Location:** Between Green and Union sts. 🚇 Embarcadero, 31. **Parking:** street only.

[D] [K] [🚇]

CAFE METROPOL   415/732-7777   129

▼▼ Continental. Casual Dining. $13-$20 **AAA Inspector Notes:** Distinctive framed artwork adorn the walls of this soigné French-style bistro. High ceilings give this petite restaurant an airy feel. Menu items include salads, pizza and sandwiches as well as such entrées as seared-ahi tuna. Sweet endings are made fresh daily by the owner/pastry chef. **Bar:** full bar. **Address:** 168 Sutter St 94104 **Location:** Between Kearny and Montgomery sts. 🚇 Montgomery Street, 32. **Parking:** street only. [L] [D] CALL [GM] [K] [🚇]

CAFE PESCATORE   415/561-1111   18

Italian
Casual Dining
$11-$25

AAA Inspector Notes: This small Italian bistro has a casual, welcoming atmosphere. Guests can dine inside by the open-grill kitchen or out on the sidewalk. **Bar:** full bar. **Address:** 2455 Mason St 94133 **Location:** Just s of Fisherman's Wharf at North Point St. **Parking:** street only. [B] [L] [D] CALL [GM] [K]

CAFE TIRAMISU   415/421-7044   108

▼▼▼ Italian. Casual Dining. $19-$40 **AAA Inspector Notes:** A bustling atmosphere with a true European feel sets the tone at this cafe. Patrons can request seating in the Roman villa-themed dining room or on the quaint patio. Wonderfully presented fine Italian cuisine is the main draw. Starters include fresh crab cakes, mussels and a variety of salads, while the entree section of the menu lists home-made pasta, fresh fish, meat and poultry offerings. Save room for one of the decadent desserts. **Bar:** beer & wine. **Reservations:** suggested. **Address:** 28 Belden Pl 94104 **Location:** Between Pine and Bush sts. 🚇 Montgomery Street, 32. **Parking:** street only.

[L] [D] [🚇]

CAFE ZOETROPE   415/291-1700   58

▼ Southern Italian. Casual Dining. $8-$18 **AAA Inspector Notes:** With a distinctive location on the street level of the Sentinel Building, this cafe is named after its owner, American Zoetrope, which is Francis Ford Coppola's film production company. In keeping with the theme, it is decorated with some movie memorabilia. The menu lists classic Italian fare, and some recipes are Francis' own. Highlights include New York style pizza and fresh-made pasta. **Bar:** full bar. **Address:** 916 Kearny St 94133 **Location:** At Columbus Ave; in Sentinel Building. 🚇 Embarcadero, 31. **Parking:** street only.

[L] [D] [🚇]

CAFFE COZZOLINO   415/285-6005   139

▼▼ Italian. Casual Dining. $10-$18 **AAA Inspector Notes:** This modest restaurant offers cooked-to-order home-style food. **Bar:** beer & wine. **Address:** 300 Precita Ave 94110 **Location:** At Folsom St. 🚇 24th Street Mission, 36. **Parking:** street only.

[L] [D] [K] [🚇]

CAFFE DELLE STELLE   415/252-1110   57

▼▼ Italian. Casual Dining. $10-$19 **AAA Inspector Notes:** Fine Italian cuisine is served in this small informal restaurant, which is in a pleasant residential neighborhood near the opera and symphony halls. **Bar:** beer & wine. **Reservations:** suggested. **Address:** 395 Hayes St 94102 **Location:** Corner of Gough St. 🚇 Van Ness, 50. **Parking:** street only. [L] [D] [🚇]

CALZONE'S   415/397-3600   43

Italian
Casual Dining
$9-$28

AAA Inspector Notes: Located in the North Beach district, this popular local restaurant serves some of the best foods from Italy in a very relaxed, street-front bistro. **Bar:** full bar. **Address:** 430 Columbus Ave 94133 **Location:** Just n of Vallejo St. 🚇 Embarcadero, 31.

Parking: street only. [L] [D] [LATE] [🚇]

(See maps & indexes p. 394, 404.)

CAMPTON PLACE RESTAURANT   415/955-5555 (131)
▼▼▼▼ Regional French. Fine Dining. $23-$41 **AAA Inspector Notes:** Inventive, eclectic American dishes showcase a French influence with a whiff of Indian flavorings. Artful presentation distinguishes each selection. The atmosphere is intimate and elegant. **Bar:** full bar. **Reservations:** suggested. **Address:** 340 Stockton St 94108 **Location:** Just n of Union Square; jct Sutter St; in Taj Campton Place San Francisco. 🚇 Montgomery Street, 32. **Parking:** valet only. B L D 🚇

CAPP'S CORNER   415/989-2589 (36)
▼▼▼ Italian. Family Dining. $10-$26 **AAA Inspector Notes:** This Italian restaurant with Irish bartenders is almost an institution in North Beach. Joe DiMaggio and Marilyn Monroe used to dine here. Located next door to Club Fugazi, home to the long-running musical Beach Blanket Babylon, it is the restaurant people go to before shows. Food is served family style on classic red and white checkered tables. **Bar:** full bar. **Address:** 1600 Powell St 94133 **Location:** Corner of Powell and Green sts. 🚇 Montgomery Street, 32. **Parking:** street only. L D 🚇

CAPURRO'S RESTAURANT & BAR   415/771-9371 (4)
▼▼ Italian. Casual Dining. $10-$28 **AAA Inspector Notes:** High ceilings and well-placed tables give the main dining room a spacious feel. Shielded outdoor patio seating is available. Try the crab pasta with white wine cream sauce, tomato and pancetta. Finish with the classic tiramisu. Parking is limited. **Bar:** full bar. **Address:** 498 Jefferson St 94109 **Location:** Between Hyde and Leavenworth sts. L D 🎟

CASTAGNOLA'S   415/776-5015 (7)
◆◆◆
Seafood
Casual Dining
$13-$46
AAA Inspector Notes: Since 1916, this established eatery has prepared Italian specialties, along with many seafood selections. The view overlooks the boat marina. **Bar:** full bar. **Reservations:** suggested. **Address:** 286 Jefferson St 94133 **Location:** 1 blk w of Fisherman's Wharf; at Jones St. **Parking:** on-site (fee). L D

CATCH   415/431-5000 (99)
▼▼▼▼ Mediterranean. Casual Dining. $10-$24 **AAA Inspector Notes:** A blue awning covers the patio, with its warm fireplace and view of the sidewalk activities. Creative fresh seafood, steaks and pasta dishes are served in a relaxed, casual atmosphere. **Bar:** full bar. **Address:** 2362 Market St 94114 **Location:** Between Castro and 16th sts. 🚇 Castro, 61. **Parking:** street only. L D 🚇

CESARIO'S FINE FOOD   415/441-9898 (119)
▼▼▼ Northern Italian. Casual Dining. $11-$25 **AAA Inspector Notes:** On a busy downtown corner, this tiny eatery presents a limited menu of interesting Northern Italian food. Soothing jazz in the background helps give business professionals and travelers a respite from the city's hustle and bustle. **Bar:** beer & wine. **Address:** 601 Sutter St 94102 **Location:** Jct Sutter and Mason sts. 🚇 Powell Street, 33. **Parking:** street only. L D 🚇

CHA-AM THAI RESTAURANT BAR & GRILL
415/546-9711 (178)
▼▼▼ Thai. Casual Dining. $9-$18 **AAA Inspector Notes:** Downtown behind the Moscone Center South and near other major attractions, this restaurant serves well-prepared Thai dishes centered on chicken, beef, pork, fish and vegetarian ingredients. The atmosphere is smart, sophisticated and quieting. **Bar:** full bar. **Reservations:** suggested, weekends. **Address:** 701 Folsom St 94107 **Location:** Jct 3rd and Folsom sts. 🚇 Montgomery Street, 32. **Parking:** street only. L D CALL 🅼 🚇

CHAYA BRASSERIE   415/777-8688 (115)
▼▼▼ Asian. Casual Dining. $15-$39 **AAA Inspector Notes:** French-Asian cuisine tops the menu at this chic bistro, which faces the Bay Bridge. Sushi bar preparations are offered along with preparations of yellowfin tuna, king salmon, filet mignon, pan-roasted chicken and lamb chops. **Bar:** full bar. **Reservations:** suggested. **Address:** 132 The Embarcadero 94105 **Location:** Between Mission and Howard sts; at waterfront. 🚇 Embarcadero, 31. **Parking:** valet and street only. L D CALL 🅼 🚇

CHEESE STEAK SHOP   415/346-3712 (34)
▼ American. Quick Serve. $4-$9 **AAA Inspector Notes:** Caution: May be habit forming is this spot's catchphrase. The buns, sweet peppers and Tastykakes are flown in daily from Philadelphia. **Bar:** beer & wine. **Address:** 1716 Divisadero St 94115 **Location:** Between Sutter and Bush sts. L D 🎟

CHENERY PARK   415/337-8537 (143)
▼▼▼ American. Casual Dining. $15-$24 **AAA Inspector Notes:** This comfortable and quiet restaurant offers Southern-style food with a Californian twist. Pillowy cheese beignets and heavenly smoked pork chops are some of the offerings. **Bar:** full bar. **Reservations:** suggested. **Address:** 683 Chenery St 94131 **Location:** Just ne of jct Diamond St; in Glen Park area. 🚇 Glen Park, 38. **Parking:** street only. D 🎟 🚇

CHEZ MAMAN   415/824-7166 (118)
▼▼▼ French. Casual Dining. $10-$21 **AAA Inspector Notes:** Small and intimate with cafe-style seating, this eatery has a menu which is varied and includes panini, crepes and fresh seafood. **Bar:** beer & wine. **Address:** 1453 18th St 94107 **Location:** Just e of jct Connecticut St; in Potrero Hill. 🚇 Mariposa, 96. **Parking:** street only. L D 🚇

CHEZ PAPA RESTO   415/546-4134 (174)
▼▼▼ French. Casual Dining. $14-$30 **AAA Inspector Notes:** Opened in the newly renovated Mint Plaza area, this is the second Chez Papa in Portrero Hill and already is attracting the locals for its contemporary French cuisine. The dining room sports a modern take on Art Deco with dark walls, black chandeliers and smoky mirrored accents. The menu changes often but, if it is available, try the purple, white and green asparagus salad. **Bar:** full bar. **Address:** 4 Mint Plaza 94103 **Location:** Between 5th and Mint sts. 🚇 Powell Street, 33. **Parking:** street only. L CALL 🅼 🚇

CHEZ SPENCER   415/864-2191 (92)
▼▼▼ French. Casual Dining. $26-$32 **AAA Inspector Notes:** Ignore the street, and head inside to sample French-influenced culinary delights prepared by chef Yasu Ueno. Experienced service and tasteful offerings from foie gras to poached asparagus to olive-crusted ling cod with sauteed eggplant make for a delightful dining experience. Save room for a cheese course or mouthwatering crème brûlée. **Bar:** full bar. **Reservations:** suggested. **Address:** 82 14th St 94103 **Location:** Just e of Folsom St; in Mission District. 🚇 16th Street Mission, 35. **Parking:** street only. D CALL 🅼 🚇

CHILI PIES & ICE CREAM   415/614-9411 (46)
▼ American. Casual Dining. $7-$8 **AAA Inspector Notes:** Perfectly named, this homey bakery serves chili, pies and ice cream. Frito pie has finally made its way to San Francisco. It is just a small bag of goodness-Frito chips, chili, shredded cheese, a dollop of sour cream and a nod to health (a small leaf of lettuce). Pot pies come piping hot with fresh ingredients, nothing from a can. The ultimate dessert is the green chili apple pie a la mode. Check out the pie shake-a whole slice of pie blended with ice cream. **Bar:** beer & wine. **Address:** 601 Baker St 94117 **Location:** Between Fulton and McAllister sts. 🚇 Duboce & Noe, 52. **Parking:** street only. L D 🎟 🚇

CHINA HOUSE JUMBO SEAFOOD RESTAURANT
415/362-3838 (19)
▼▼ Chinese. Casual Dining. $8-$24 **AAA Inspector Notes:** For something different while in the Fisherman's Wharf area, try this casual eatery where flavorful Chinese food is served. Popular with the local lunch crowd, the menu offers tasty and reasonably priced entrées. Menu highlights include hot garlic sauce chicken wings, eggplant in Szechuan sauce and spicy salty fried pork chops. **Bar:** full bar. **Address:** 2237 Powell St 94133 **Location:** At Bay St. **Parking:** street only. L D

CHOTTO   415/441-2223 (7)
▼▼ Japanese Small Plates. Casual Dining. $5-$16 **AAA Inspector Notes:** With elegant trendy decor befitting the Marina neighborhood, this izakaya or Japanese tapas bar, offers well-executed menu items using top-shelf ingredients. Select a dish from each category and share. Pleasing to the eye, each dish whets the appetite. **Bar:** beer & wine. **Address:** 3317 Steiner St 94123 **Location:** Between Chestnut and Lombard sts. **Parking:** street only. D 🎟

(See maps & indexes p. 394, 404.)

CHOW 415/552-2469 **90**

▼▼▼ American. Casual Dining. $8-$22 **AAA Inspector** This casual neighborhood eatery serves American comfort food prepared with a twist of Chinese. Menu items at the popular spot include won ton, Thai noodles, Italian pasta, pizza and such classics as burgers and pot roasts. Offering good value for the dollar, many entrees and desserts have a choice of entreé size or small size. Make sure to try the pumpkin ice cream with ginger cake. **Bar:** beer & wine. **Address:** 215 Church St 94114 **Location:** Just s of Market St; between 14th and 15th sts. 🚇 Church, 60. **Parking:** street only.

B L D 🍴 🚇

CIOPPINO'S ON THE WHARF 415/775-9311 **5**

▼ Italian. Casual Dining. $10-$35 **AAA Inspector Notes:** This longstanding Italian seafood restaurant nurtures a warm and casual nautical feel. The cioppino name refers to a rich and flavorful seafood soup that is distinctly San Franciscan. The menu bursts with fresh fish, seafood and pasta choices, in addition to surf and turf, gourmet pizza, soups and salads. **Bar:** full bar. **Address:** 400 Jefferson St 94109 **Location:** Jct Leavenworth St; across from The Cannery. **Parking:** street only. L D

CITIZEN'S BAND 415/556-4901 **197**

▼▼ American. Casual Dining. $10-$24 **AAA Inspector Notes:** This modern diner serves updated comfort food. Start with corn soup or a hearty salad, followed by fried chicken with biscuits and finish with some tasty butterscotch pudding. **Bar:** beer & wine. **Address:** 1192 Folsom St 94103 **Location:** At 8th St. 🚇 Civic Center/UN Plaza, 34. **Parking:** street only. L D 🍴 🚇

CITYHOUSE RESTAURANT 415/392-8000 **165**

▼▼▼ American. Fine Dining. $12-$36 **AAA Inspector Notes:** You walk through the high ceilinged, spacious hotel check-in area to get to this restaurant with the decor and ambience of a posh members-only airport lounge. Sophisticated offerings of fresh seafood and top quality beef are complemented by an extensive wine list. **Bar:** full bar. **Address:** 55 Cyril Magnin St 94102 **Location:** Corner of Cyril Magnin and Eddy sts; 3 blks sw of Union Square; in Parc 55 Wyndham San Francisco Union Square. 🚇 Powell Street, 33. **Parking:** valet only. 🚌 B L D 🚇

CITY VIEW RESTAURANT 415/398-2838 **78**

▼▼ Chinese Dim Sum. Casual Dining. $4-$20 **AAA Inspector Notes:** On a small side street in the Financial District, this Chinese dim sum restaurant is particularly popular at lunchtime. **Bar:** beer & wine. **Address:** 662 Commercial St 94111 **Location:** Between Montgomery and Kearny sts. 🚇 Montgomery Street, 32. **Parking:** street only. L 🚇

CLAY OVEN INDIAN CUISINE 415/826-2400 **138**

▼▼ Indian. Casual Dining. $11-$18 **AAA Inspector Notes:** From the wall murals to the background music to the cuisine offerings, there is no denying this neighborhood restaurant is authentic Indian. Order the preset dinner menu if you cannot decide what to eat. Portions are served large so come prepared to eat. **Bar:** beer & wine. **Address:** 1689 Church St 94131 **Location:** At 29th St. 🚇 Church & 30th St, 87. **Parking:** street only. D CALL 🗺️🅜 🍴 🚇

CLIFF HOUSE - SUTRO'S 415/386-3330 **17**

▼▼ American. Fine Dining. $19-$39 **AAA Inspector Notes:** In the Sutro wing of the historic Cliff House, this restaurant is perched above Ocean Beach. Take the elevator down to the restaurant. As the door opens guests enter the waiting area showcasing the open kitchen. The contemporary dining room features ceiling-to-floor panoramic views of the Pacific. The most memorable dining experience is at sunset with the orange sun setting, the sky changing from blue to pink to purple, and finally, twinkling stars appearing in the sky. **Bar:** full bar. **Reservations:** suggested. **Address:** 1090 Point Lobos Ave 94121 **Location:** At Ocean Beach. **Parking:** valet and street only. L D

CLIFF HOUSE-THE BISTRO 415/386-3330 **16**

▼▼ American. Casual Dining. $14-$30 **AAA Inspector Notes:** On the upper level of the historic Cliff House, this casual restaurant overlooks Seal Rock and the ocean. A classic menu lists omelets, soups, sandwiches and full entrées. **Bar:** full bar. **Address:** 1090 Point Lobos Ave 94121 **Location:** At Ocean Beach. **Parking:** street only. B L D

COCO 500 415/543-2222 **196**

▼▼▼ Mediterranean. Casual Dining. $14-$25 **AAA Inspector Notes:** This high-energy, post-modern, Euro-style restaurant is a popular spot. Loud chattering shouldn't detract from the superbly prepared and presented food, including small plates and thin-crust pizzas from the wood-fired oven which are seen on nearly every table. **Bar:** full bar. **Reservations:** suggested. **Address:** 500 Brannan St 94107 **Location:** At 4th St; downtown. 🚇 4th & King, 93. **Parking:** street only. L D 🚇

COLIBRI MEXICAN-BISTRO 415/440-2737 **141**

▼▼▼ Mexican. Casual Dining. $12-$20 **AAA Inspector Notes:** Polished servers circulate through the upscale bistro, enticing guests with tableside preparation of guacamole. The convenient downtown spot features a large mirrored bar and Mexican tile work throughout. Try the made-to-order guacamole with salsa and mole poblano. For dessert, share the creme-filled churros and dulce de leche ice cream. **Bar:** full bar. **Reservations:** suggested. **Location:** Between Taylor and Mason sts; on Theater Row; in Hotel Diva. 🚇 Powell Street, 33. **Parking:** street only. L D 🚇

COMMONWEALTH 415/355-1500 **112**

▼▼▼ California. Casual Dining. $13-$16 **AAA Inspector Notes:** Featuring a contemporary decor, this eatery will donate $10 to a worthy cause should you choose from the chef's tasting menu. Must-try items include the watermelon salad, corn custard with uni and pork stuffed squid. **Bar:** beer & wine. **Reservations:** suggested. **Address:** 2224 Mission St 94110 **Location:** Between 18th and 19th sts. 🚇 16th Street Mission, 35. **Parking:** on-site and street.

D 🍴 🚇

CONTIGO KITCHEN & CAVA 415/285-0250 **127**

▼▼▼ Small Plates. Casual Dining. $9-$23 **AAA Inspector Notes:** This contemporary tapas bar, located in the Castro neighborhood, is popular with locals. Try the jamón iberico de bellota (ham aged for 36 months), the paella-stuffed calamari and oxtail-stuffed piquillo peppers. Be sure to end the meal on a sweet note with almond cake or a glass of sherry. **Bar:** beer & wine. **Address:** 1320 Castro St 94114 **Location:** Between 24th and Jersey sts. 🚇 Church & 24th St, 86. **Parking:** street only. D 🚇

COTOGNA 415/775-8508 **55**

▼▼▼ Italian. Casual Dining. $12-$30 **AAA Inspector Notes:** Packed since day one, this lively contemporary restaurant offers a sophisticated version of rustic Italian fare. Some items change daily. Pasta is made on-site, with pizza toppings ranging from the unusual such as nettles to the more familiar pork sausage. A French-influenced dish of lamb cassoulet warms the tummy on a foggy night. **Bar:** full bar. **Reservations:** suggested. **Address:** 490 Pacific Ave 94133 **Location:** Between Osgood Pl and Montgomery St. 🚇 Embarcadero, 31. **Parking:** street only.

L D CALL 🗺️🅜 🍴 🚇

CRAB HOUSE AT PIER 39 415/434-2722 **9**

▼▼▼
Seafood
Casual Dining
$15-$60

AAA Inspector Notes: Located upstairs on the pier, this restaurant affords guests a view of Fisherman's Wharf and the bay. Rotated seasonally, the whimsical decor features more than 400 distinctively decorated crabs displayed along the walls-a fruit crab and a computer crab are just two of the many. Start with the skillet mussels and move on to crabs cooked your way. **Bar:** full bar. **Address:** 203 C Pier 39 94133 **Location:** On Pier 39. **Parking:** on-site (fee).

Menu on AAA.com L D 🍴

CRAW STATION 415/682-9980 **81**

▼▼ Seafood. Casual Dining. $10-$12 **AAA Inspector Notes:** Messy, messy fun eating can be had at this spot where plastic bibs are the norm. The more the merrier or hog it all just for yourself. Choose such sides as sweet potato fries and gumbo to go along with the crustacean of choice seasoned with sauces and as much or as little spice as desired. The food comes in plastic bags—for convenient transport from kitchen to table. It goes without saying that the crayfish and shrimp are best with Cajun sauce and the clams with lemon black pepper. **Bar:** beer & wine. **Address:** 1336 9th Ave 94122 **Location:** Between Irving and Judah sts. 🚇 Judah & 9th Ave, 55. **Parking:** street only. D 🍴 🚇

(See maps & indexes p. 394, 404.)

CRUSTACEAN RESTAURANT   415/776-2722   **77**
▼▼▼ Asian. Fine Dining. $15-$39 **AAA Inspector Notes:** Euro-Asian fusion cuisine is served at this dimly lit restaurant decorated with Asian accents. The signature garlic-roasted Dungeness crab and garlic noodles are not to be missed. Outdoor patio dining is available—weather permitting. Lunch is available only on Sunday. **Bar:** full bar. **Reservations:** suggested. **Address:** 1475 Polk St 94109 **Location:** Corner of California St; top floor of Plaza. 🚇 Powell Street, 33. **Parking:** valet and street only.   **D**   🚇

DAILY GRILL   415/616-5000
▼▼ American. Casual Dining. $12-$33 **AAA Inspector Notes:** This eatery is an updated version of San Francisco's grills of the past, featuring good food, comfortable ambience and a friendly staff. **Bar:** full bar. **Address:** 347 Geary St 94102 **Location:** Jct Powell St; adjacent to Union Square. 🚇 Powell Street, 33. **Parking:** street only.
B   **L**   **D**   CALL 🔊M   🚇

DAVID'S DELI   415/276-5950   **140**
▼ Jewish. Casual Dining. $9-$20 **AAA Inspector Notes:** In the Theatre District, the New York-style Jewish delicatessen prepares mile-high sandwiches, huge bowls of soup brimming with noodles and chicken and the tempting baked goods that fill the case in the front. The dining room, with a take-out area to one side and a stool counter in the middle, evokes the 1950s. **Bar:** beer & wine. **Address:** 474 Geary St 94102 **Location:** Jct Taylor St. 🚇 Powell Street, 33. **Parking:** street only.   **B**   **L**   🚇

DELFINA   415/552-4055   **106**
▼▼▼ Italian. Casual Dining. $9-$26 **AAA Inspector Notes:** Pasta, chicken, seafood and beef dishes, as well as frequently changing specialty items and a wide variety of wines, await customers of the restaurant with a bistro atmosphere. **Bar:** beer & wine. **Reservations:** suggested. **Address:** 3621 18th St 94110 **Location:** Between Guerrero and Dolores sts. 🚇 Church & 18th St, 85. **Parking:** street only.   **D**   CALL 🔊M   🚇

DELICA RF-1   415/834-0344   **95**
▼ Japanese. Casual Dining. $10-$13 **AAA Inspector Notes:** Small dishes are boxed for take-out at this Japanese delicatessen-style eatery at the Ferry Building San Francisco. Small plates, sold by the pound or in bento boxes, include tofu steak, edamame salad, crab cream croquettes, lamb curry and miso soup. Communal seating is offered. **Address:** 1 Ferry Bldg, Suite 45 94111 **Location:** US 101, e on Market St to the end; in Ferry Building. 🚇 Embarcadero, 31. **Parking:** street only.   **L**   **D**   CALL 🔊M   🚇

DESTINO   415/552-4451   **83**
▼ New Latin American Small Plates. Casual Dining. $6-$24 **AAA Inspector Notes:** Peruvian influences punctuate this Nuevo Latino bistro. The innovative menu features mouthwatering tapas as well as such entrées as ceviche, mofongo and lomo saltado. Do not miss the famous alfajores cookies—a butter cookie filled with dulce de leche (caramel). **Bar:** full bar. **Address:** 1815 Market St 94103 **Location:** Between Guerrero and Octavia sts. 🚇 Duboce & Church, 51. **Parking:** street only.   **D**   🦆   🚇

DOSA ON VALENCIA   415/642-3672   **119**
▼▼ Southern Indian. Casual Dining. $13-$18 **AAA Inspector Notes:** Contemporary decor and ambience can be found at this restaurant specializing in South Indian street food. Start with dosa, an over-sized crepe which is dipped into various spicy condiments. Follow it with a fiery prawn curry from Goa. Cool the palate with rasmalai (round discs of cheese in creme) or with a mango lassi soju (yogurt milkshake). **Address:** 995 Valencia St 94110 **Location:** Between 20th and 21st sts. 🚇 24th Street Mission, 36. **Parking:** street only.   **D**   🦆   🚇

E & O TRADING COMPANY   415/693-0303   **121**
▼▼▼ Asian. Casual Dining. $13-$24 **AAA Inspector Notes:** Appointed in export warehouse decor, this brewpub prepares Malaysian, Balinese and Southeast Asian tapas-style dishes. Start with corn fritters, and then move to the short ribs or the hanger steak, add some dan dan noodles or fried rice and finish with a silk smooth chocolate dessert. A perfect accompaniment would be one of their signature cocktail drinks or a cool beer. **Bar:** full bar. **Address:** 314 Sutter St 94108 **Location:** Between Grant Ave and Stockton St. 🚇 Montgomery Street, 32. **Parking:** street only.
L   **D**   CALL 🔊M   🚇

EL TORO TAQUERIA   415/431-3351   **104**
▼ Mexican. Quick Serve. $3-$15 **AAA Inspector Notes:** Hearty portions are dished up as patrons move through the line at this popular eatery. **Bar:** beer only. **Address:** 598 Valencia St 94110 **Location:** Just s of 16th St. 🚇 16th Street Mission, 35. **Parking:** street only.   **L**   **D**   🚇

EMPRESS OF CHINA   415/434-1345   **70**
▼▼▼ Chinese. Casual Dining. $15-$45 **AAA Inspector Notes:** Featuring classic dishes from various regions of China, the eatery is popular for its fabulous views of the bay and the North Beach/Telegraph Hill area. Expect to find a variety of patrons, from tourists in jeans to businessmen in suits. **Bar:** full bar. **Reservations:** suggested. **Address:** 838 Grant Ave 94108 **Location:** In Chinatown; on top floor of China Trade Center Building. 🚇 Montgomery Street, 32.   **L**   **D**   CALL 🔊M   🚇

ESPETUS CHURRASCARIA   415/552-8792   **79**
▼▼▼ Brazilian Barbecue. Casual Dining. **AAA Inspector Notes:** This elegant restaurant is full of guests happily gorging themselves on perfectly grilled meats. Try the addictive cheese popovers but save room for the perfectly grilled meal. **Bar:** full bar. **Reservations:** suggested. **Address:** 1686 Market St 94102 **Location:** At Gough St. 🚇 Van Ness, 50. **Parking:** street only.
L   **D**   🦆   🚇

EXTREME PIZZA
▼ Pizza. Casual Dining. $8-$18 **AAA Inspector Notes:** The name of the restaurant says it all, and pizza named holy cow, green with envy, the screaming tomato and Pandora's box make even ordering fun. Pies come in 8-, 12-, 14-, 16- and 18-inch sizes. **Bar:** beer & wine.   **L**   **D**   **LATE**
For additional information, visit AAA.com

LOCATIONS:
Address: 1980 Union St 94123 **Location:** Between Buchanan and Laguna sts. **Phone:** 415/929-8234
Address: 1730 Fillmore St 94115 **Location:** Between Post and Sutter sts. **Phone:** 415/929-9900

FARALLON   415/956-6969   **133**
▼▼▼ Seafood. Casual Dining. $27-$42 **AAA Inspector Notes:** This sophisticated, softly illuminated seafood restaurant is near Union Square. Professional servers deliver dishes that show a flair for presentation. **Bar:** full bar. **Reservations:** suggested. **Address:** 450 Post St 94102 **Location:** Just w of Union Square; in Kensington Park Hotel. 🚇 Powell Street, 33. **Parking:** valet only.
D   🚇

FAR EAST CAFE   415/982-3245   **85**
▼▼ Cantonese. Casual Dining. $9-$50 **AAA Inspector Notes:** High ceilings and a Chinese decor of antique hanging imperial lanterns and private booths transport you back to the Chinatown of the 1920s. Go as a group and get seated in one of the private booths. Well-prepared Cantonese food includes beef with Chinese broccoli and Peking duck. **Bar:** beer & wine. **Address:** 631 Grant Ave 94108 **Location:** Between Sacramento and California sts; in Chinatown. 🚇 Montgomery Street, 32. **Parking:** street only.
L   **D**   🦆   🚇

FIFTH FLOOR   415/348-1555   **166**
▼▼▼▼
New
French
Fine Dining
$28-$42
AAA Inspector Notes: This contemporary restaurant is all about optimizing the best flavors from the finest of fresh local ingredients in California-inspired, French-style cuisine. The crowning achievement is the chef's tasting menu which is paired with expertly chosen wines. **Bar:** full bar. **Reservations:** suggested. **Address:** 12 4th St 94103 **Location:** At Market St; in Hotel Palomar. 🚇 Powell Street, 33. **Parking:** valet only.
D   🚇

FINO BAR & RISTORANTE   415/928-2080   **130**
▼▼ Italian. Fine Dining. $15-$29 **AAA Inspector Notes:** This classy and comfortable neighborhood restaurant serves well-executed dishes including fresh pasta made on-site. Start with clam and mussels in garlic wine sauce, calamari steak and finally their chocolate fino-a warm chocolate crème brûlée flavored with raspberry. **Bar:** full bar. **Address:** 624 Post St 94109 **Location:** Between Post and Sutter sts; on Taylor St; in Andrews Hotel. 🚇 Powell Street, 33. **Parking:** street only.   **D**   🚇

(See maps & indexes p. 394, 404.)

FIREWOOD CAFE   415/252-0999   103

Italian. Quick Serve. $9-$15 **AAA Inspector Notes:** Locals love this cafe's pizza, which cooks in a wood-fired oven. Also tempting are chicken and pasta dishes and creative sides. The service is basic, with guests ordering at the counter and waitstaff bringing out the food. **Bar:** beer & wine. **Address:** 4248 18th St 94114 **Location:** At Diamond St. Castro, 61. **Parking:** street only. L D

FIRST CRUSH RESTAURANT WINE BAR & LOUNGE
415/982-7874   159

American. Casual Dining. $15-$29 **AAA Inspector Notes:** Diners can enjoy entrées of beef, lamb, chicken and seafood, as well as salads, in this downtown location near Union Square. **Bar:** full bar. **Address:** 101 Cyril Magnin St 94102 **Location:** Corner of Cyril Magnin and Ellis sts. Powell Street, 33. **Parking:** street only. D

FLEUR DE LYS   415/673-7779   116

French. Fine Dining. $72-$95 **AAA Inspector Notes:** A Mediterranean touch influences contemporary French cuisine served in the elegant dining area. This restaurant presents two prix fixe menus, one of which is designed for vegetarians. Semi-formal attire. **Bar:** full bar. **Reservations:** required. **Address:** 777 Sutter St 94109 **Location:** Between Taylor and Jones sts. Powell Street, 33. **Parking:** valet and street only. D

FLORIO CAFE AND BAR   415/775-4300   31

Continental. Fine Dining. $15-$29 **AAA Inspector Notes:** Rustic French and Italian cuisine is prepared using local ingredients. The action of the city is just outside the door, and the decor is warm and inviting. **Bar:** full bar. **Address:** 1915 Fillmore St 94115 **Location:** At Pine St. **Parking:** street only. D

FLOUR + WATER   415/826-7000   120

Italian. Casual Dining. $14-$27 **AAA Inspector Notes:** Contemporary laid back decor can be found at this eatery. All menu items are made from scratch and menus change daily. Try some of their unusual pasta including chestnut maltagliati with braised pork and mustard greens. Good selections of Italian wines are available. Come early or make reservations as the lines are long; half of the restaurant is reserved for walk-ins. **Bar:** beer & wine. **Reservations:** suggested. **Address:** 2401 Harrison St 94110 **Location:** At 20th St. 16th Street Mission, 35. **Parking:** street only.
D

FOG CITY DINER   415/982-2000   23

American. Casual Dining. $10-$24 **AAA Inspector Notes:** This upscale Art Deco dining room is popular for lunch. On the refined menu are large portions of such classics as meatloaf with wild mushroom gravy, macaroni and Gouda cheese and chicken schnitzel with garlic mashed potatoes. **Bar:** full bar. **Reservations:** suggested. **Address:** 1300 Battery St 94111 **Location:** Jct The Embarcadero. Embarcadero, 31. **Parking:** street only.
L D CALL

FOG HARBOR FISH HOUSE   415/421-2442   14

Seafood. Casual Dining. $12-$50 **AAA Inspector Notes:** With large windows, guests can look out over the marina and bay while dining at this fish house. Dinner and lighter fare are served all day in the contemporary dining room. **Bar:** full bar. **Address:** Pier 39, Suite A202 94133 **Location:** On Pier 39 at Fisherman's Wharf. **Parking:** on-site (fee). L D

FOREIGN CINEMA   415/648-7600   124

California. Casual Dining. $22-$28 **AAA Inspector Notes:** After dark, popular international films are projected onto an outdoor wall at the lively and elegant eatery. Friendly waiters serve fine California cuisine. **Bar:** full bar. **Reservations:** suggested. **Address:** 2534 Mission St 94110 **Location:** Just s of 21st St. 24th Street Mission, 36. **Parking:** valet and street only. D

FRANCES   415/621-3870   100

California. Casual Dining. $20-$28 **AAA Inspector Notes:** This little gem of a restaurant does not disappoint. While the menu may be streamlined it still is hard to make a choice. A well-seasoned team offering genuine hospitality makes this one of the most popular dining destinations in the city. **Bar:** beer & wine. **Address:** 3870 17th St 94114 **Location:** Between Sanchez and Noe sts. Castro, 61. **Parking:** street only. D

FRANCISCAN CRAB RESTAURANT   415/362-7733   2

Seafood
Casual Dining
$15-$60

AAA Inspector Notes: Located behind the famous crab sign, this restaurant offers a panoramic view of San Francisco Bay. All seats have full or partial views. The roasted crab, prepared with a secret garlic sauce, is not to be missed. For snacking, there is a good selection of antipasti as well as homemade dolce to satisfy the sweet tooth. **Bar:** full bar. **Address:** Pier 43 1/2 Embarcadero 94133 **Location:** At Fisherman's Wharf. *Menu on AAA.com*
L D CALL

FRASCATI   415/928-1406   28

Continental. Fine Dining. $22-$28 **AAA Inspector Notes:** A cozy, bustling dining room awaits guests, who enjoy the casually elegant atmosphere of this restaurant. Dishes blend California, Mediterranean and French influences with fresh ingredients. Among starters are grilled bread salad, pea soup and freshly prepared gnocchi. Entrées center on pasta, seafood, pork and veal. The chef also creates an innovative mix of changing specials. **Bar:** beer & wine. **Reservations:** suggested. **Address:** 1901 Hyde St 94109 **Location:** Jct Green St. **Parking:** street only. D

FRINGALE   415/543-0573   193

French. Casual Dining. $15-$26 **AAA Inspector Notes:** In the SOMA district, this restaurant provides quality, reasonably priced French cuisine that is served in a casual, cozy, hometown atmosphere. Favorite entrées include signature crab meat and avocado Napoleon and a perfectly executed rack of lamb. Among must-have desserts is a slice of the hazelnut and almond mousse cake. **Bar:** full bar. **Reservations:** suggested. **Address:** 570 4th St 94107 **Location:** Between Bryant and Townsend sts. 4th & King, 93. **Parking:** street only. L D

THE GARDEN COURT   415/546-5089   145

American. Fine Dining. $23-$36 **AAA Inspector Notes:** An Old World atmosphere punctuates this elegantly restored 1909 landmark. Contributing to the style are a glass-domed atrium, lavish crystal chandeliers and marble and gold-leaf accents. **Bar:** full bar. **Reservations:** suggested. **Address:** 2 New Montgomery St 94105 **Location:** Just e of Union Square at Market St; in Palace Hotel. Montgomery Street, 32. **Parking:** on-site (fee) and valet.
B L CALL

GARIBALDI'S ON PRESIDIO   415/563-8841   23

American. Casual Dining. $12-$27 **AAA Inspector Notes:** This Presidio Heights restaurant is a favorite among the local clientele and provides a casual yet elegant atmosphere. For the entrée, try the melt-in-your-mouth lamb tenderloin spiced with Moroccan flavors. **Bar:** full bar. **Address:** 347 Presidio Ave 94115 **Location:** Jct Sacramento St; in Presidio Heights. **Parking:** valet and street only. L D

GARY DANKO   415/749-2060   17

Continental
Fine Dining
$71-$104

AAA Inspector Notes: The world-renowned restaurant will not disappoint. It takes diners on a pleasurable culinary adventure that incorporates the cosmopolitan atmosphere of the dining room, the sophistication of the service and the culinary prowess of the namesake chef. Semi-formal attire. **Bar:** full bar. **Reservations:** required. **Address:** 800 North Point St 94109 **Location:** Just e of Ghirardelli Square at Hyde St. **Parking:** valet only. D CALL

(See maps & indexes p. 394, 404.)

GIALINA 415/239-8500 (144)
▼▼▼ Pizza. Casual Dining. $14-$19 **AAA Inspector Notes:** Adding to the eatery's homey, family-friendly atmosphere are poster-size pictures of the owner's nonna proudly displayed on the walls. Boasting a contemporary decor with snug seating, this neighborhood restaurant serves Neapolitan-style pizza and a specialty roast of the day. A must-try is the pizza with nettles and truffle cheese. Make sure you leave room for dessert. **Bar:** beer & wine. **Address:** 2842 Diamond St 94131 **Location:** I-280 exit Monterey Blvd, just e, then 0.4 mi ne. Glen Park, 38. **Parking:** street only. D

GIORDANO BROS 415/397-2767 (48)
▼ American. Casual Dining. $7-$8 **AAA Inspector Notes:** For those that are Pittsburgh Steelers fans, this basic sports bar is the place to be. Flat-screen TVs blare games on the walls while the menu offers simple dishes—Pittsburgh-style sandwiches with a choice of meat that come with fries and coleslaw with special sauce. Complete the meal with a side of chili or some fried onion rings. **Bar:** beer & wine. **Address:** 303 Columbus Ave 94133 **Location:** Between Grant Ave and Broadway St. Embarcadero, 31. **Parking:** street only. L D LATE

GITANE RESTAURANT & BAR 415/788-6686 (124)
▼▼▼ Spanish. Casual Dining. $23-$28 **AAA Inspector Notes:** With a name meaning gypsy, this restaurant is located in an alley and down a flight of stairs. The décor is a mix of Euro-themed 1950s, hippie-driven 1960s and bling bling 1970s all combined into one eclectic package. Have a drink at the bar while awaiting a table. Make sure to visit the bathroom—listed as one of the most memorable in the city. **Bar:** full bar. **Address:** 6 Claude Ln 94108 **Location:** Between Grant and Kearny sts. Montgomery Street, 32. **Parking:** street only. D

GLOBE 415/391-4132 (56)
▼▼▼ California. Fine Dining. $11-$28 **AAA Inspector Notes:** This restaurant features an open kitchen that serves French, Italian and California cuisine. A 50-bottle wine selection is available with several available by the glass. **Bar:** full bar. **Reservations:** suggested. **Address:** 290 Pacific Ave 94111 **Location:** Between Battery and Front sts. Embarcadero, 31. **Parking:** street only. L D

GOTT'S ROADSIDE 415/318-3407 (94)
▼ American. Quick Serve. $6-$15 **AAA Inspector Notes:** The ahi burgers and thick shakes at this location are just as good as the ones offered at the original spot in Napa. Diners can wash down a decadent Western bacon blue ring burger with a Cabernet from Napa Valley. **Bar:** beer & wine. **Address:** 1 Ferry Bldg, Suite 6 94101 **Location:** US 101, e on Market St to the end; in Ferry Building. Embarcadero, 31. **Parking:** street only. L D CALL

GRAIN D' OR BAKERY 415/512-8160 (144)
▼ American. Quick Serve. $5-$8 **AAA Inspector Notes:** Geared for quick service, this contemporary-style restaurant invites guests to enjoy wholesome soups, salads and sandwiches. Breads and bakery items are delicious. **Address:** 665 Market St 94105 **Location:** Just s of New Montgomery St. Montgomery Street, 32. **Parking:** street only. B L D

GRAND CAFE 415/292-0101 (179)
▼▼▼▼
French
Casual Dining
$13-$34
AAA Inspector Notes: Featuring contemporary French-California cuisine, the menu takes advantage of fresh local ingredients. The setting is most impressive; the dining room is a restored ballroom with high ceilings and an abundance of artwork. **Bar:** full bar. **Address:** 501 Geary St (at Taylor St) 94102 **Location:** Just w of Union Square at Taylor St; next to Hotel Monaco. Powell Street, 33. **Parking:** valet and street only. B L D

GRANDVIEWS 415/848-6100 (125)
▼▼▼ American. Fine Dining. $13-$38 **AAA Inspector Notes:** Atop the Grand Hyatt San Francisco at Union Square, this restaurant affords panoramic views of the city and the bay. **Bar:** full bar. **Address:** 345 Stockton St 94108 **Location:** On Union Square at Sutter St; in Grand Hyatt San Francisco. Montgomery Street, 32. **Parking:** valet only. B L D

GREAT EASTERN RESTAURANT 415/986-2500 (60)
▼▼ Chinese. Casual Dining. $9-$44 **AAA Inspector Notes:** This restaurant is known for the fresh seafood dishes whose main ingredients were taken out of the display tanks just moments before being cooked. Dim sum also is served during lunch. A picture dim sum menu helps customers select their favorite dish. **Bar:** beer & wine. **Address:** 649 Jackson St 94133 **Location:** Between Grant and Kearny sts. Montgomery Street, 32. **Parking:** street only. L D LATE

GREENS RESTAURANT 415/771-6222 (1)
▼▼▼▼ Vegetarian. Casual Dining. $12-$24 **AAA Inspector Notes:** This local favorite presents a daily changing menu of innovative Northern Californian dishes made with the freshest produce from the owner's organic farm in Marin County. Examples include the grilled blossom bluff peach salad with watercress, red endive, mascarpone and Marshall Farms honey salad. The seats facing the window offer views of the marina and the Golden Gate Bridge. **Bar:** beer & wine. **Reservations:** suggested. **Address:** Fort Mason Center, Bldg A 94123 **Location:** US 101 (Van Ness Ave), 0.4 mi w on Bay St, just n on Buchanan St, then just e on Marina Blvd. L D CALL

GRUB 415/431-4782 (113)
▼▼ American. Casual Dining. $9-$19 **AAA Inspector Notes:** Trendy decor, a hip vibe and food to match, this spot offers a burger bar and a macaroni and cheese bar. Personalize the selection with choices of meat, toppings and sauces. For less personalization, but equally tasty, try the fisherman's stew or a hearty pork chop. **Bar:** beer & wine. **Address:** 758 Valencia St 94110 **Location:** Between 18th and 19th sts. 16th Street Mission, 35. **Parking:** street only. D LATE

GRUBSTAKE 415/673-8268 (87)
▼▼ American. Casual Dining. $8-$19 **AAA Inspector Notes:** A rail car from the Key Line route between San Francisco and Berkeley was made into a diner in 1927. A warm bowl of caldo verde soup is a must; try the hearty American breakfast served on weekends. Portuguese-American cuisine makes up the menu. **Bar:** beer & wine. **Address:** 1525 Pine St 94109 **Location:** Between Van Ness Ave and Polk St. Civic Center/UN Plaza, 34. **Parking:** street only. D LATE

HANA ZEN 415/421-2101 (157)
▼▼ Japanese. Casual Dining. $10-$47 **AAA Inspector Notes:** A few dollars go a long way at this affordable sushi bar and restaurant in the Financial District. Sushi and sashimi top a menu that also lists lamb chops, chicken with mushrooms, crispy pork and fresh fish. **Bar:** beer & wine. **Reservations:** suggested. **Address:** 115 Cyril Magnin St 94102 **Location:** Between Ellis and O'Farrell sts. Powell Street, 33. **Parking:** street only. L D LATE

HARD KNOX CAFE 415/648-3770 (133)
▼▼ Soul Food. Casual Dining. $6-$15 **AAA Inspector Notes:** The Vietnamese owners of this small cafe grew up in the South and learned to cook soul food from their African American godmother. Decorated like a shack with corrugated aluminum sheet walls, the eatery brews their own beer. Menu highlights include fall-from-the-bone oxtail, crispy fried chicken, collard greens, yams and lemonade served from mason jars. **Bar:** beer & wine. **Address:** 2526 3rd St 94107 **Location:** Between 22nd and 23rd sts. 23rd St, 98. **Parking:** street only. L D

HARD KNOX CAFE 415/752-3770 (18)
▼▼ Soul Food. Casual Dining. $6-$15 **AAA Inspector Notes:** The Vietnamese owners of this small cafe grew up in the South and learned to cook soul food from their African American godmother. Decorated like a shack with corrugated aluminum sheet walls, the eatery brews their own beer. Menu highlights include fall-from-the-bone oxtail, crispy fried chicken, collard greens, yams and lemonade served from mason jars. **Bar:** beer & wine. **Address:** 2448 Clement St 94121 **Location:** Between 25th and 26th aves. **Parking:** street only. L D

(See maps & indexes p. 394, 404.)

HARRIS' 415/673-1888 **46**
▼▼▼▼ Steak. Fine Dining. $26-$54 **AAA Inspector Notes:** An old San Francisco atmosphere prevails at this modestly sophisticated restaurant, where patrons linger over dry-aged, Midwestern beef and fresh seafood. Pair a California vintage wine with a juicy and well-flavored T-bone or porterhouse steak for a memorable meal. For an elegant sweet ending, finish with baked Alaska. **Bar:** full bar. **Reservations:** suggested. **Address:** 2100 Van Ness Ave 94109 **Location:** On US 101 (Van Ness Ave) at Pacific Ave. **Parking:** on-site and valet. D

HAYES STREET GRILL 415/863-5545 **58**
▼▼▼ Seafood. Casual Dining. $12-$28 **AAA Inspector Notes:** A popular spot with the theater and opera crowd, expect this eatery to be packed prior to performances. One section of the menu focuses on fish prepared in the California style with an array of fresh ingredients. A three-course menu is available after 7:30 pm. **Bar:** full bar. **Reservations:** suggested. **Address:** 320 Hayes St 94102 **Location:** Just w of US 101 (Van Ness Ave). Van Ness, 50. **Parking:** street only. L D

HEAVEN'S DOG 415/863-6008 **183**
▼▼ Chinese. Casual Dining. $10-$19 **AAA Inspector Notes:** Strong flavored Chinese dishes pair well with pre-Prohibition era cocktails. Cocktail drinks are taken seriously here-depending on the drink, the ice used may be hand-cut. As for the food, try the pork belly in clamshell buns. **Bar:** full bar. **Address:** 1148 Mission St 94103 **Location:** Between 7th and 8th sts. Civic Center/UN Plaza, 34. **Parking:** street only. D LATE

THE HELMAND PALACE 415/345-0072 **25**
▼▼ Afghan. Casual Dining. $12-$23 **AAA Inspector Notes:** Decor may be white tablecloth with cobalt blue water goblets but service is unassuming and the food is made with care. Start with aushak-ravioli pillows of goodness filled with leeks and scallions served on yogurt, garlic and mint. Entrées of lamb are a great choice. Finish with feereny-a cream pudding with fruit toppings. **Bar:** beer & wine. **Address:** 2424 Van Ness Ave 94109 **Location:** Between Union and Green sts. **Parking:** valet and street only.
D CALL

HOG & ROCKS 415/550-8627 **116**
▼▼ North American Seafood. Casual Dining. $11-$18 **AAA Inspector Notes:** Choices abound at this contemporary, casual pub which specializes in ham and oysters. Choose from three hams (domestic and European) and some eight different oyster varieties from both the east and west coasts. There also are some heartier dishes including fish pie and patty melts. **Bar:** full bar. **Address:** 3431 19th St 94110 **Location:** Between San Carlos & Mission sts. 16th Street Mission, 35. **Parking:** street only.
D LATE

HOG ISLAND OYSTER CO 415/391-7117 **91**
▼ Seafood. Casual Dining. $12-$18 **AAA Inspector Notes:** At this spot, exceptionally fresh oysters come in at least six varieties and share menu space with clam chowder, salads and a yummy grilled cheese sandwich that blends three Cowgirl Creamery cheeses. Beverages include local beers and a nice choice of wines. Happy hour is offered Monday and Thursday from 5 to 7 p.m. with half-priced oysters. Go early as it is packed by 5 p.m. Make sure to get a table facing the Bay—especially during sunset to watch the sky change colors. **Bar:** beer & wine. **Address:** One Ferry Bldg, Suite 11A 94111 **Location:** On The Embarcadero; in Ferry Building. Embarcadero, 31. **Parking:** street only.
L D

THE HOUSE 415/986-8612 **49**
▼▼▼ Asian. Casual Dining. $12-$27 **AAA Inspector Notes:** In the Little Italy section of the city, this small storefront eatery focuses on evolutionary Asian-American cuisine. Eclectic decor accents the interior. If it is on the menu, patrons should try the grilled calamari for starters, then for an entrée the grilled sea bass with ginger soy sauce is a good choice. Coconut brûlée is a great way to end the dining experience. **Bar:** beer & wine. **Reservations:** suggested. **Address:** 1230 Grant Ave 94133 **Location:** Between Vallejo St and Columbus Ave. Embarcadero, 31. **Parking:** street only.
L D

HOUSE OF PRIME RIB 415/885-4605 **54**
▼▼▼▼ American. Fine Dining. $28-$38 **AAA Inspector Notes:** A great prime rib dinner for a reasonable price keeps this restaurant packed. Salad is dressed tableside. Also on the menu are fresh fish and specialty items. **Bar:** full bar. **Reservations:** suggested. **Address:** 1906 Van Ness Ave 94109 **Location:** On US 101 (Van Ness Ave). **Parking:** valet and street only. D

HYDE STREET BISTRO 415/292-4415 **50**
▼▼ French. Casual Dining. $17-$25 **AAA Inspector Notes:** Diners can experience a sweet little neighborhood bistro, as well as well-prepared classic French fare. **Bar:** beer & wine. **Address:** 1521 Hyde St 94109 **Location:** Jct Jackson St, just n. Powell Street, 33. **Parking:** street only. D

HYDE STREET SEAFOOD HOUSE AND RAW BAR 415/931-3474 **51**
▼▼ Seafood. Casual Dining. $14-$20 **AAA Inspector Notes:** Nautical decor and friendly service, as well as fine seafood prepared in a variety of styles, are what patrons find at the neighborhood restaurant. Dungeness crab Mornay teases palates with its delicate taste. **Bar:** full bar. **Reservations:** suggested. **Address:** 1509 Hyde St 94109 **Location:** Jct Jackson St, just n. Powell Street, 33. **Parking:** street only. D

IKE'S PLACE 415/553-6888 **97**
◆ Sandwiches. Quick Serve. $8-$20 **AAA Inspector Notes:** Literally a hole in the wall, this spot has a cash register for orders and extremely limited tables. All sandwiches are made to order, and arrive hot, crunchy and soft. With more than 100 combinations it may be hard to decide what to eat. Just tell them what you want in the sandwich or just choose by such names as Super Mario or Name of Girl I'm Dating. Ingredients are fresh and breads are delivered the same day. Lines can be long and there is a wait as they toast sandwiches. **Address:** 3489 16th St 94114 **Location:** Between Sanchez and Church sts. Church & 18th St, 85. **Parking:** street only.
L D

IL CANE ROSSO 413/391-7599 **89**
▼▼ California. Casual Dining. $6-$13 **AAA Inspector Notes:** Patrons to this eatery can enjoy quick serve/take out dining during breakfast and lunch or bistro service with a limited menu for dinner. Menu highlights include padrone peppers and heirloom tomato with aioli sauce, braised melt-in-your-mouth short ribs and a panna cotta with huckleberries and fennel. A prix fixe ($25) selection of a well-executed appetizer, entrée and dessert is available. Happy hour offers a limited beer and wine selection. **Bar:** beer & wine. **Address:** One Ferry Building, Suite 41 94111 **Location:** On The Embarcadero. Embarcadero, 31. **Parking:** street only.
B L D CALL

INCANTO 415/641-4500 **137**
▼▼▼ Italian. Casual Dining. $16-$27 **AAA Inspector Notes:** In a residential area, this rustic yet upscale restaurant serves what can best be described as Californian-Italian cuisine. The ever-changing menu focuses on the freshest possible ingredients, including some herbs from the rooftop garden. **Bar:** beer & wine. **Reservations:** suggested. **Address:** 1550 Church St 94131 **Location:** 1.3 mi s of Market St; southwest corner of Duncan and Church sts. Church & 30th St, 87. **Parking:** street only. D

INDIA GARDEN 415/626-2798 **84**
▼▼ Indian. Casual Dining. $11-$18 **AAA Inspector Notes:** At this eatery, clay oven specialties are cooked over a charcoal fire in clay pots and served on a hot sizzling platter. All dishes are served mild, medium or spicy hot. The bread is crispy and fun to eat. **Bar:** beer & wine. **Address:** 1261 Folsom St 94103 **Location:** Between 8th and 9th sts. Civic Center/UN Plaza, 34. **Parking:** street only.
L D

INDIGO RESTAURANT 415/673-9353 **48**
▼▼▼ American. Casual Dining. $11-$30 **AAA Inspector Notes:** Popular with local guests and theatergoers, this restaurant nurtures a lively atmosphere. The prix fixe menu, which is available from 5 to 7 pm, might list pasta, grilled chicken breast, grilled sterling salmon or Australian lamb. The ultimate wine dinner comes with an ample supply of wine. **Bar:** full bar. **Address:** 687 McAllister St 94102 **Location:** Between Gough and Franklin sts; west side of downtown. Van Ness, 50. **Parking:** street only. D

(See maps & indexes p. 394, 404.)

ISA
◆◆ 415/567-9588 [6]

French. Casual Dining. $12-$24 **AAA Inspector Notes:** The intimate gray dining room sets the stage for a California-inspired French tapas-style menu. Among choices are truffle risotto, seared rare tuna and grilled Monterey Bay calamari. **Bar:** beer & wine. **Address:** 3324 Steiner St 94123 **Location:** Jct Lombard and Steiner sts. **Parking:** street only. [D]

ISOBUNE SUSHI
◆◆ 415/563-1030 [40]

Sushi. Casual Dining. $8-$25 **AAA Inspector Notes:** In Japan Town Japanese Center, this restaurant patented the sushi boat concept in 1982. The delivery system uses small boats that float around the bar seating area, giving diners the option of removing any of the traditional sushi and sashimi that appeal to them. There is no point looking for hot food because none is here. **Bar:** beer & wine. **Address:** 1737 Post St 94115 **Location:** Between Buchanan and Webster sts. Van Ness, 50. [L] [D] CALL [M]

IT'S TOPS COFFEE SHOP
◆◆ 415/431-6395 [82]

American. Casual Dining. $8-$17 **AAA Inspector Notes:** The decor of this tiny diner is straight from the 1930s with a 1950s upgrade of jukebox music. Go for the ambience and homey, made-from-scratch food. Hamburgers-soft buns, meat ground daily and fries cut and fried to order-are solid and classic, with none of those fancy breads and condiments. Waffles are made on an old classic waffle iron. There only is one server so bring patience and enjoy the ambience and music while awaiting the meal. **Bar:** beer & wine. **Address:** 1801 Market St 94103 **Location:** Between Octavia Blvd and Guerrero St. Duboce & Church, 51. **Parking:** street only. [B] [L] [D] LATE [K]

IZAKAYA SOZAI
◆◆ 415/742-5122 [69]

Small Plates. Casual Dining. $3-$19 **AAA Inspector Notes:** Packed since it opened, this casual, contemporary Japanese tapas bar is run by a young mom and pop. There is a good selection of everything from sashimi carpaccio to yakitori. Try the tonkotsu ramen and for a sweet treat, the green tea pancake (dorayaki) with ice cream is a good way to end the meal. **Bar:** beer & wine. **Address:** 1500 Irving St 94122 **Location:** Between 15th and 16th aves. Judah & 19th Ave, 56. **Parking:** street only. [D] [K]

IZUMIYA
◆ 415/441-6867 [39]

Japanese. Casual Dining. $8-$20 **AAA Inspector Notes:** This casual eatery offers an extensive izakaya menu as well as okonomiyaki and standard Japanese fare. **Bar:** beer & wine. **Address:** 1581 Webster St, Suite 290 94115 **Location:** Between Geary and Post sts; in Japantown Mall. Van Ness, 50. **Parking:** street only.

JARDINIERE
◆◆◆ 415/861-5555 [52]

French. Fine Dining. $18-$44 **AAA Inspector Notes:** Contributing to the sophisticated surroundings are a oval atrium and glowing, gold dome. Creme-colored railings swoop gracefully between softly lit lamp posts that double as champagne buckets. Menu offerings change daily. A temperature-controlled cave keeps a good selection of cheese fresh. **Bar:** full bar. **Reservations:** suggested. **Address:** 300 Grove St 94102 **Location:** US 101 (Van Ness Ave), just w at Franklin St. Van Ness, 50. **Parking:** valet only. [D]

JOE'S CABLE CAR RESTAURANT
◆ 415/334-6699 [145]

American. Family Dining. $7-$20 **AAA Inspector Notes:** Frequently recognized as serving some of the city's best burgers, this restaurant has been in the same location since 1965. Hearty burgers come in 4-, 6- or 8-ounce sizes. **Bar:** beer & wine. **Address:** 4320 Mission St 94112 **Location:** At Silver Ave. Glen Park, 38. [L] [D] [K]

JOHNNY FOLEY'S
◆◆ 415/954-0777 [151]

Irish. Casual Dining. $15-$28 **AAA Inspector Notes:** This authentic Irish Pub offers 12 beers on tap, traditional Irish dishes, cottage pie, fish and chips, and Irish stew. Try the mussels in Irish whiskey flavored with cream and bacon sauce (great for dipping bread into) and served with fries that are thick, light and crunchy. A former Prohibition speakeasy occupies the cellar. **Bar:** full bar. **Address:** 243 O'Farrell St 94102 **Location:** Between Mason and Powell sts. Powell Street, 33. **Parking:** street only. [L] [D] [K]

JOHN'S GRILL
◆◆ 415/986-3274 [162]

American Casual Dining $12-$38

AAA Inspector Notes: Established in 1908, this relaxed restaurant is furnished in turn-of-the-20th-century decor. This place was a setting in "The Maltese Falcon" by author Dashiell Hammett. **Bar:** full bar. **Reservations:** suggested. **Address:** 63 Ellis St 94102 **Location:** Between Powell and Stockton sts. Powell Street, 33. **Parking:** no self-parking. [L] [D]

KAN'S
◆◆ 415/362-5267 [79]

Chinese. Casual Dining. $10-$48 **AAA Inspector Notes:** Cantonese dishes make up most of the menu at this long-established Chinese restaurant. **Bar:** full bar. **Reservations:** suggested. **Address:** Upstairs at 708 Grant Ave 94108 **Location:** Between Commercial and Sacramento sts; in Chinatown. Montgomery Street, 32. **Parking:** street only. [L] [D]

KATIA'S
◆◆ 415/668-9292 [43]

Russian. Casual Dining. $13-$19 **AAA Inspector Notes:** This quaint, homey restaurant, located in a residential neighborhood, offers authentic Russian comfort food—just like Grandma used to make. Quite a few repeat customers frequent this eatery. **Bar:** beer & wine. **Address:** 600 5th Ave 94118 **Location:** Jct Balboa St; in Richmond District. UCSF Parnassus, 54. **Parking:** street only. [D]

KOH SAMUI AND THE MONKEY
◆◆ 415/369-0007 [189]

Thai. Casual Dining. $9-$23 **AAA Inspector Notes:** Sleekly elegant Thai artwork and statues gives this restaurant a sophisticated feel. Try the fish cakes, papaya salad and pumpkin curry served in its own shell. **Bar:** beer & wine. **Reservations:** suggested. **Address:** 415 Brannan St 94107 **Location:** Between 3rd and 4th sts. 4th & King, 93. **Parking:** street only. [L] [D]

KOKKARI ESTIATORIO
◆◆◆ 415/981-0983 [62]

Greek. Fine Dining. $14-$40 **AAA Inspector Notes:** Named after a small fishing village in Greece, the upscale, rustic restaurant with an oversize fireplace serves contemporary Hellenic cuisine prepared from the freshest ingredients. Recommended are persimmon salad and grilled lamb riblet appetizer. Greek and California wines dominate, and a cauldron heats the Greek coffees. Valet parking is offered after 5 pm. **Bar:** full bar. **Reservations:** suggested. **Address:** 200 Jackson St 94111 **Location:** At Front St; in Financial District. Embarcadero, 31. **Parking:** valet and street only. [L] [D]

KULETO'S
◆◆ 415/397-7720 [146]

Italian. Casual Dining. $18-$37 **AAA Inspector Notes:** In-house cured prosciutto and other flavorful foods are served in an upscale, lively atmosphere. **Bar:** full bar. **Reservations:** suggested. **Address:** 221 Powell St 94102 **Location:** Just s of Union Square; between O'Farrell and Geary sts; in Villa Florence. Powell Street, 33. **Parking:** valet only. [B] [L] [D]

LA CICCIA
◆◆ 415/550-8114 [142]

Italian. Casual Dining. $12-$26 **AAA Inspector Notes:** Ever wonder how the food of Sardinia tasted after watching Anthony Bourdain's show? Wonder no more. This unpretentious, yet elegant, restaurant specializes in Sardinian cuisine. Try the calamari salad with some addictive flatbread, followed by an entrée of spaghetti with bottarga, and finish with the saffron and ricotta cake drizzled with honey. Pair the food with Sardinian wines for a complete meal. **Bar:** beer & wine. **Reservations:** suggested. **Address:** 291 30th St 94131 **Location:** At Church St. Church & 30th St, 87. **Parking:** street only. [D] [K]

LA FOLIE
◆◆◆◆ 415/776-5577 [26]

French. Fine Dining. $80-$100 **AAA Inspector Notes:** High ceilings, tall mirror panels, soft lighting and rich russet-orange drapes add a contemporary warmth to the dining room. Creative amuse-bouche entertain the palette while waiting for such seasonal course offerings as roasted Arctic char, corn fondue, lobster-stuffed squash blossom and lobster bordelaise. **Bar:** full bar. **Reservations:** required. **Address:** 2316 Polk St 94109 **Location:** Just n of jct Green St; in Russian Hill District. **Parking:** valet and street only. [D] CALL [M]

(See maps & indexes p. 394, 404.)

LA MAR CEBICHERIA PERUANA 415/397-8880 (68)

▼▼▼ Peruvian. Casual Dining. $11-$34 **AAA Inspector Notes:** With branches in Lima, Mexico City, Santiago and Panama, this contemporary eatery offers sophisticated decor with views of the Bay. Classic Peruvian dishes are well-represented on the menu. Try the ceviche sampler, the hearty loma saltados and for dessert the bunuelos (Mexican pastry sprinkled with cinnamon and sugar) with chocolate sauce. **Bar:** full bar. **Reservations:** suggested. **Address:** Pier 1.5 94111 **Location:** Just n of Ferry Building; on The Embarcadero. ▣ Embarcadero, 31. **Parking:** street only.
L D ▣

LA MEDITERRANEE 415/921-2956 (26)

▼▼ Mediterranean. Casual Dining. $12-$15 **AAA Inspector Notes:** This eatery, offering a mix of Mediterranean and Middle Eastern flavors, is as close as one might get to a Parisian bistro in San Francisco. The menu emphasizes appetizers and salads, while the charmingly decorated interior encourages guests to linger over lunch. **Bar:** beer & wine. **Address:** 2210 Fillmore St 94115 **Location:** Between Sacramento and Clay sts. **Parking:** no self-parking.
L D ▣

LA SCENE CAFE 415/292-6430 (139)

▼▼ California. Casual Dining. $18-$35 **AAA Inspector Notes:** Elegant and intimate, this restaurant offers a comfortable ambience and is popular with the theater crowd. Go for a pre-show or after-show dessert and coffee. Start with an orange and ginger bisque followed by crab risotto, and finish with crème brûlée. For breakfast try their huevos rancheros. **Bar:** full bar. **Address:** 490 Geary St 94102 **Location:** Between Taylor and Mason sts; in Warwick San Francisco Hotel. ▣ Powell Street, 33. **Parking:** street only. *(See ad p. 418.)* B D CALL ▣M ▣ ▣

LA TAQUERIA 415/285-7117 (134)

▼ Mexican. Quick Serve. $5-$8 **AAA Inspector Notes:** Locals and visitors alike crowd into this popular and affordable taco shop. A server takes orders in line and hands guests a numbered slip so they can claim their tacos, burritos, quesadillas or fruit drinks when they are ready. **Bar:** beer only. **Address:** 2889 Mission St 94110 **Location:** Just n of 25th St. ▣ 24th Street Mission, 36. **Parking:** street only. L D ▣

THE LAUREL COURT RESTAURANT & BAR 415/772-5260 (81)

▼▼▼ California. Fine Dining. $16-$36 **AAA Inspector Notes:** Before or after a day in San Francisco, guests stop here for a meal in an elegant hotel setting. The menu of California cuisine has something for everyone. **Bar:** full bar. **Reservations:** suggested. **Address:** 950 Mason St 94108 **Location:** Atop Nob Hill at California St; in The Fairmont San Francisco. ▣ Montgomery Street, 32. **Parking:** on-site (fee). B L D CALL ▣M ▣

LE CHARM FRENCH BISTRO 415/546-6128 (187)

▼▼▼ French. Fine Dining. $9-$30 **AAA Inspector Notes:** This cozy bistro has a garden patio. The excellent three-course prix fixe menu is a good value for the money. The French onion soup, lamb stew and floating island are notable items. **Bar:** beer & wine. **Reservations:** suggested. **Address:** 315 5th St 94107 **Location:** Just s of Folsom St. ▣ Powell Street, 33. **Parking:** street only.
D ▣

LE COLONIAL 415/931-3600 (120)

▼▼▼ Vietnamese. Fine Dining. $22-$32 **AAA Inspector Notes:** The restaurant focuses on Vietnamese cuisine from the French Colonial Southeast Asia of the 1920s. The building sustains the tropical atmosphere of that period with large palm trees, ceiling fans, plantation-style shuttered windows and rattan furniture. **Bar:** full bar. **Reservations:** suggested. **Address:** 20 Cosmo Pl 94109 **Location:** Between Jones and Taylor sts. ▣ Powell Street, 33. **Parking:** valet and street only. D CALL ▣M ▣

LEOPOLD'S 415/474-2000 (83)

▼▼▼ German. Casual Dining. $12-$19 **AAA Inspector Notes:** This gasthaus is usually packed so go early if not making a reservation. The food's classic dishes are made with care and sophistication. Crispy pig trotters are crunchy, fatty and porky. Try the crunchy, flavorful wiener schnitzel with a dab of lingonberry sauce. For a sweet ending try the warm apfelstrudel, with a crunchy shell and vanilla sauce that adds another dimension to it. Finish with a shot of Underberg, an herbal disgestif. **Bar:** beer & wine. **Reservations:** suggested. **Address:** 2400 Polk St 94109 **Location:** At Union St. ▣ Powell Street, 33. **Parking:** street only. D ▣ ▣

LES JOULINS JAZZ BISTRO 415/397-5397 (160)

▼▼ French. Casual Dining. $8-$23 **AAA Inspector Notes:** French cuisine, including a nice selection of fresh seafood, is the main draw at this bistro. This place has two sides: a casual cafe in which breakfast and lunch are served and a more intimate bistro in which live jazz is played at dinner. Classic dishes such as escargots and frog legs are some of the offerings. **Bar:** full bar. **Address:** 44 Ellis St 94102 **Location:** Between Powell and Stockton sts; in Union Square area. ▣ Powell Street, 33. **Parking:** street only.
B L D LATE ▣

LIMON ROTISSERIE 415/821-2134 (123)

▼▼ Peruvian. Casual Dining. $6-$10 **AAA Inspector Notes:** The well-appointed yet casual atmosphere at this eatery is perfect to dine on rotisserie chicken with traditional Peruvian flavors and such small plates as ceviche, loma saltado and crunchy but melt in your mouth yucca fritas. Try their own blue-corn soda called chica morada under the brand Inca Blu-it is a refreshing accompaniment to the strongly flavored food. **Bar:** beer & wine. **Reservations:** suggested. **Address:** 1001 S Van Ness Ave 94110 **Location:** Between 20th and 21st sts. ▣ 24th Street Mission, 36. **Parking:** street only.
L D ▣ ▣

THE LITTLE CHIHUAHUA 415/255-8225 (68)

▼ Mexican. Quick Serve. $6-$11 **AAA Inspector Notes:** This tiny eatery, a taqueria which specializes in tacos and burritos, is in the Lower Haight area and offers a bit of a hipster vibe. Featured are a cozy interior with big wood tables and stained-glass windows. Everything is outstanding, including the chips and salsa bar, the burritos and the salmon tacos. Notable is the black bean vegetarian burrito. All of the tortillas for the burritos are toasted on the grill for an added crunch. Homemade horchata is enriched with milk for a milk shake texture. **Bar:** beer & wine. **Address:** 292 Divisadero St 94117 **Location:** At Page St. ▣ Duboce & Noe, 52. **Parking:** street only.
L D ▣ ▣

LITTLE STAR PIZZA 415/441-1118 (45)

▼▼▼ Pizza. Casual Dining. $12-$24 **AAA Inspector Notes:** This casually funky spot offers a great neighborhood vibe. The pizza crust is made of cornmeal, lighter than a typical deep dish but no less flavorful. You can have two slices instead of one and still be lucid. **Bar:** beer & wine. **Address:** 846 Divisadero St 94117 **Location:** Between Fulton and McAllister sts. ▣ Duboce & Noe, 52. **Parking:** street only. D ▣ ▣

L'OLIVIER RESTAURANT 415/981-7824 (67)

▼▼▼ Regional French. Fine Dining. $12-$28 **AAA Inspector Notes:** Country French decor with a touch of Continental elegance can be witnessed at this fine dining restaurant. Enjoy such classic French dishes as escargot, duck confit and crème brûlée. **Bar:** full bar. **Reservations:** suggested. **Address:** 465 Davis Ct 94111 **Location:** Off Jackson St; in Golden Gateway Center. ▣ Embarcadero, 31. **Parking:** valet and street only. L D CALL ▣M ▣

LOLO 415/244-9798 (126)

▼▼▼ New Latin American Small Plates. Casual Dining. $6-$26 **AAA Inspector Notes:** The decor at this eatery is eclectic Mission-where different ethnicities live side by side. The color scheme is either festive colorful or elegant colorful depending on which wall patrons are facing. Tapa dishes are drawn from Latin American countries and Turkey. Menu highlights include tuna tacon (tuna tacos), ceviche and hearty beef kofte (beef patties atop pureed eggplant and covered in morita sauce). **Bar:** beer & wine. **Address:** 3234 22nd St 94110 **Location:** Between Mission and Bartlett sts. ▣ 24th Street Mission, 36. **Parking:** street only. D ▣ ▣

(See maps & indexes p. 394, 404.)

LORI'S DINER
415/677-9999 (152)

American. Family Dining. $8-$15 **AAA Inspector Notes:** This 1950s diner prepares great burgers, shakes, fries and appetizers. Mexican dishes, as well as steamed vegetables and Chinese chicken salads, also are available. Lending to the decor are neon, red vinyl, chrome and buxom waitress pinup pictures. **Bar:** beer & wine. **Address:** 149 Powell St 94102 **Location:** Between O'Farrell and Ellis sts; near Union Square. Powell Street, 33. **Parking:** street only. B L D

LOUIS'
415/387-6330 (14)

American. Casual Dining. $8-$18 **AAA Inspector Notes:** Get a seat near the window at this spot to enjoy the panoramic view of the Pacific Ocean. **Bar:** beer & wine. **Address:** 902 Pt Lobos Ave 94121 **Location:** Between Merrie Way and Upper Great Hwy. **Parking:** street only. B L D CALL

LUCKY CREATION VEGETARIAN RESTAURANT
415/989-0818 (63)

Chinese Vegetarian. Casual Dining. $6-$18 **AAA Inspector Notes:** A long time fixture in Chinatown, this tiny unadorned, bustling restaurant does brisk business selling ready-made vegetarian items such as flavored gluten, barbecue pork buns and glutinous rice rolls. Dishes such as imitation sweet and sour pork, minced mushroom and taro cream soup are some of the menu items. **Address:** 854 Washington St 94108 **Location:** Between Stockton and Grant sts. Montgomery Street, 32. **Parking:** street only. L D

LU LU
415/495-5775 (180)

American. Casual Dining. $9-$32 **AAA Inspector Notes:** The lively restaurant's specialty is California French cuisine, with crusty bread, eclectic soups, pasta, pizza and nightly rotisserie specials. In combination with a light, bright, cheery look, patrons have everything necessary for a pleasant dining experience. Great choices are the leg of lamb sandwich and portobello mushroom soup. Diners enjoy good views of the wood-fired oven. **Bar:** full bar. **Reservations:** suggested. **Address:** 816 Folsom St 94107 **Location:** Just sw of jct 4th St. Powell Street, 33. **Parking:** valet and street only. L D

LUNA PARK KITCHEN AND COCKTAILS
415/553-8584 (110)

American. Casual Dining. $13-$36 **AAA Inspector Notes:** This casual restaurant is a local favorite for the hip crowd, who enjoy its bustling atmosphere and wild cocktail list. Menu offerings reflect a fusion of cuisine types: French, Italian, Asian and some American influences. **Bar:** full bar. **Address:** 694 Valencia St 94110 **Location:** At 18th St. 16th Street Mission, 35. **Parking:** street only. L D CALL

MAGNOLIA PUB & BREWERY
415/864-7468 (67)

American. Casual Dining. $10-$25 **AAA Inspector Notes:** This casual, high-energy place is where friends gather to chat or watch the four of Haight-Ashbury pass by the large glass windows. Its great pub menu offers a few surprises, like honey and lavender-glazed lamb spare ribs, and the in-house-brewed beer is another draw. **Bar:** beer & wine. **Address:** 1398 Haight St 94117 **Location:** In Haight-Ashbury District; corner of Masonic Ave. Carl & Cole, 53. **Parking:** street only. L D LATE

MAHARANI
415/775-1988 (117)

Indian. Casual Dining. $9-$28 **AAA Inspector Notes:** The menu here focuses on the cuisine of India with a sophisticated touch. Guests can opt to have dinner in the traditional, cushioned and curtained fantasy room rather than the main dining room. Maharani rack of lamb, okra curry, naan, biryani and raita is just right for two. Champagne sweetened with fruit-flavored syrup help add a touch of elegance to the meal. **Bar:** full bar. **Reservations:** suggested. **Address:** 1122 Post St 94109 **Location:** US 101 (Van Ness Ave), just e; between Van Ness Ave and Polk St. Civic Center/UN Plaza, 34. **Parking:** street only. D

MARLOWE
415/974-5599 (198)

American. Casual Dining. $13-$25 **AAA Inspector Notes:** Elegant, with ambient lighting and candlelight warming the room, locals linger over their dinner. Appetites will be satiated by the rich, bold flavors without supersized portion. Fried Brussels sprout chips and burgers are the claim to fame. **Bar:** beer & wine. **Address:** 330 Townsend St, Suite 101 94107 **Location:** Between 4th and 5th sts. 4th & King, 93. **Parking:** street only. L D

MARNEE THAI
415/731-9999 (71)

Thai. Casual Dining. $9-$17 **AAA Inspector Notes:** At this spot, authentic Siamese cuisine, served at reasonable prices, includes a wide variety of menu choices. Many spices are used and will please all palates. Vegetarian dishes are available. Conveniently located near one of the entrances to Golden Gate Park. **Bar:** beer & wine. **Address:** 1243 9th Ave 94122 **Location:** Jct Lincoln Way and 19th Ave (SR 1), 0.6 mi e on Lincoln Way, then just s. Judah & 9th Ave, 55. **Parking:** street only. L D CALL

MARNEE THAI
415/665-9500 (60)

Thai. Casual Dining. $10-$19 **AAA Inspector Notes:** Since opening more than 20 years ago, chef Chai has won numerous awards and accolades for delivering such delicious classics as spring rolls and pad thai. Consistent quality and lines out the door can be expected. Patrons with an adventurous appetite should try the whole fried fish. **Bar:** beer & wine. **Address:** 2225 Irving St 94122 **Location:** 0.4 mi w of 19th Ave (SR 1). Judah & 19th Ave, 56. **Parking:** street only. L D

MASA'S
415/989-7154 (107)

French. Fine Dining. $98-$140 **AAA Inspector Notes:** This elegant, sophisticated restaurant offers diners a choice of prix fixe menus. In the dining room, the atmosphere is quiet and intimate. Semi-formal attire. **Bar:** full bar. **Reservations:** required. **Address:** 648 Bush St 94108 **Location:** Just w of Stockton St. Montgomery Street, 32. **Parking:** valet and street only.

THE MATTERHORN SWISS RESTAURANT
415/885-6116 (29)

Swiss Fondue. Casual Dining. $20-$46 **AAA Inspector Notes:** Once guests enter this restaurant, they will feel like they've been transported to the Swiss Alps. On the menu is meat fondue—meat is cooked in a choice of vegetable broth, red wine broth or oil. Finish the meal with chocolate fondue. **Bar:** full bar. **Address:** 2323 Van Ness Ave 94109 **Location:** Between Green and Vallejo sts. **Parking:** valet and street only. D

MAVERICK AMERICAN EATERY & WINE BAR
415/863-3061 (105)

Regional American. Casual Dining. $17-$26 **AAA Inspector Notes:** This Mission District eatery is decorated Spartanly, with highly polished hardwood floors, wooden sconces and tables. Because seating is limited, reservations are all but a must. Offerings of regional American cuisine change seasonally, and all desserts are prepared in house. The wine list includes choices by glass, bottle and flight. **Bar:** beer & wine. **Address:** 3316 17th St 94110 **Location:** Just n of Mission St. 16th Street Mission, 35. **Parking:** street only. D

MAX'S ON THE SQUARE
415/646-8600 (142)

American. Casual Dining. $10-$28 **AAA Inspector Notes:** Near Union Square, this fine downtown restaurant located on the first floor of the Hotel Frank, serves large portions of American fare. Max's rules, which can be read on the menu, are valid and entertaining. In-house desserts are simple and tasty. **Bar:** full bar. **Address:** 398 Geary St 94102 **Location:** Just w of Union Square at Mason St; in Hotel Frank. Powell Street, 33. **Parking:** street only. B L D CALL

MCCORMICK & KULETO'S SEAFOOD RESTAURANT
415/929-1730 (16)

Seafood. Fine Dining. $15-$41 **AAA Inspector Notes:** This restaurant affords spectacular views of San Francisco Bay and its bridges. **Bar:** full bar. **Address:** 900 North Point St, Suite H301 94109 **Location:** At Ghirardelli Square. **Parking:** on-site (fee). L D

MEMPHIS MINNIE'S
415/864-7675 (74)

Barbecue. Quick Serve. $9-$24 **AAA Inspector Notes:** This popular barbecue joint's brightly colored interior incorporates walls covered with cartoonish pig faces, hats and T-shirts emblazoned with the restaurant's logo. Pulled pork, beef brisket and chicken slathered in barbecue sauce are staples here. On the tables are squirt bottles of mustard, classic barbecue and spicy vinegar sauces. A roll of paper towels mounted to each table allows for easy clean-up after the meal. **Bar:** beer & wine. **Address:** 576 Haight St 94117 **Location:** Between Fillmore and Steiner sts. Duboce & Noe, 52. **Parking:** street only. L D

(See maps & indexes p. 394, 404.)

MICHAEL MINA
415/397-9222 (99)

New American. Fine Dining. $21-$49 **AAA Inspector Notes:** The chef here leads guests through a dining experience of flavor and texture by preparing mini tastings within each course with the trios of the main ingredients prepared three ways with different sauces and accompaniments. Dessert service is a distinctive experience. Lunch in the dining room features three- or four-course menu options while the bar menu is a la carte. Semi-formal attire. **Bar:** full bar. **Reservations:** suggested. **Address:** 252 California St 94111 **Location:** Between Front and Battery sts; in Financial District. Embarcadero, 31. **Parking:** valet and street only.

L D

MIJITA COCINA MEXICANA
415/399-0814 (93)

Mexican. Quick Serve. $5-$13 **AAA Inspector Notes:** Shoppers needing a break after a few hours of wandering the shops of the Ferry Building can drop by this casual restaurant for a quick meal of Mexican food. Although the menu is limited, the food is made fresh. Patio seats give a great view of the boat traffic on the bay, but those in a hurry can get their food to go. **Bar:** beer & wine. **Address:** One Ferry Bldg, Number 44 94111 **Location:** On The Embarcadero; in Ferry Building. Embarcadero, 31. **Parking:** street only.

L D

MI LINDO PERU
415/642-4897 (140)

Peruvian. Casual Dining. $7-$18 **AAA Inspector Notes:** Warm browns and orange with wall mounted Inca figurines decorate the walls at this Peruvian restaurant. Distinctive lights are shaped like crepe bowls. Check out such classic dishes as ceviche, lomo saltados and alfajores or lucuma ice cream. **Bar:** beer & wine. **Address:** 3226 Mission St 94110 **Location:** Between Valencia and 29th sts. Church & 30th St, 87. **Parking:** street only.

L D

MILLENNIUM RESTAURANT
415/345-3900 (138)

Vegetarian. Casual Dining. $23-$26 **AAA Inspector Notes:** Located in a historic building, the décor here is an ambient blend of classic and contemporary touches. Healthy, environmentally friendly food with fresh produce (organic when available) are used to create a gourmet dining experience. **Bar:** full bar. **Reservations:** suggested. **Address:** 580 Geary St 94102 **Location:** 0.3 mi w of Union Square at Jones St; in BEST WESTERN The Hotel California. Powell Street, 33. **Parking:** valet and street only.

D

MISSION BEACH CAFE
415/861-0198 (91)

California. Casual Dining. $8-$28 **AAA Inspector Notes:** An airy, warm urban décor serves as a backdrop for a simple breakfast of pastry and coffee or a sophisticated dining experience of tea-smoked tuna and saffron risotto, followed by filet mignon with port jus. Desserts are homey and delicious with a rotating menu of such pies and cakes as banana cream pie or velvet cake. **Bar:** beer & wine. **Address:** 198 Guerrero St 94103 **Location:** At 14th St. Church, 60. **Parking:** street only. B L D

MISSION CHEESE
415/484-6553 (111)

Specialty. Quick Serve. $7-$10 **AAA Inspector Notes:** For those who love cheese, this is the place to go. This small, contemporary cheese bar also offers cheese for sale. Menu items include a cheese plate, grilled cheese sandwiches, raclette potatoes and, of course, macaroni and cheese. **Bar:** beer & wine. **Address:** 736 Valencia St 94110 **Location:** Between 18th and 19th sts. 16th Street Mission, 35. **Parking:** street only. L D

MISSION CHINESE FOOD
415/863-2800 (114)

Chinese. Casual Dining. $7-$13 **AAA Inspector Notes:** A permanent pop-up restaurant located inside Lung Shan Restaurant, the décor here is old school Chinese complete with a paper dragon hanging from the ceiling and silk flowers at each table. The chef/owner, a Korean raised in Oklahoma, claims not to know how to cook Chinese food. A sampling of dishes include kung pao pastrami with chili, celery, potatoes and roasted peanut as well as gai-lan (Chinese broccoli) with beef cheeks, poached oyster and smoked oyster sauce. **Bar:** beer & wine. **Address:** 2234 Mission St 94110 **Location:** Between 18th and 19th sts. 16th Street Mission, 35. **Parking:** street only. L D

MISSION PIE
415/282-1500 (135)

American. Quick Serve. $4-$9 **AAA Inspector Notes:** This comfy neighborhood bakery/café is run by a youth advocacy group. Training starts at Pie Ranch where trainees learn the basics of farming. Try their banana cream pie or the savory pot pies. **Address:** 2901 Mission St 94110 **Location:** At 25th St. 24th Street Mission, 36. **Parking:** street only. B L D

MODERN THAI
415/922-8424 (102)

Thai. Casual Dining. $8-$14 **AAA Inspector Notes:** Each wall and ceiling of this dining room is painted a vibrant sorbet color. Rattan chairs and a covered porch dining area adds a bit of a Southern Colonial plantation feel. Food is vibrant in presentation and taste while a gracious staff complete the ambience. **Bar:** beer & wine. **Address:** 1247 Polk St 94109 **Location:** Between Bush and Sutter sts. Civic Center/UN Plaza, 34. **Parking:** street only.

L D

MOMO'S RESTAURANT
415/227-8660 (194)

American. Fine Dining. $13-$25 **AAA Inspector Notes:** This restaurant, across from the ballpark, can be extremely busy on game day. American-style cuisine includes such favorites as crispy onion strings, wood-grilled pork chops with garlic mashed potatoes, baby back ribs in bourbon sauce and crisp, thin-crust pizza. Finish the meal with a tangy blackberry crisp. **Bar:** full bar. **Reservations:** suggested. **Address:** 760 2nd St 94107 **Location:** At King St. 2nd & King, 92. **Parking:** on-site and valet.

L D

MUGU BOKA KOREAN BBQ RESTAURANT
415/668-6007 (42)

Korean. Casual Dining. $8-$36 **AAA Inspector Notes:** This casual neighborhood restaurant serves well-made Korean comfort food. Start with a seafood pancake, followed by kalbi (short ribs). Complimentary dishes of banchan will fill diners up. **Bar:** beer only. **Address:** 401 Balboa St 94118 **Location:** At 5th Ave. UCSF Parnassus, 54. **Parking:** street only. L D

MURACCI'S JAPANESE CURRY & GRILL
415/773-1101 (113)

Japanese. Quick Serve. $8-$10 **AAA Inspector Notes:** A hole in wall catering to downtown workers, people come here for the tonkatsu curry. Choose the level of heat, followed by such main toppings as tonkatsu (pork cutlet), shrimp, salmon, chicken or vegetarian and other toppings including cheese, egg, choice of white or brown rice and udon. Lunch comes with a salad, mini-appetizers and miso soup. Japanese tea and Calpico water also are available to cool the heat. Seating is very limited. **Address:** 307 Kearny St 94108 **Location:** Between Bush and Pine sts. Montgomery Street, 32. **Parking:** street only. L

MY TOFU HOUSE
415/750-1818 (29)

Korean. Casual Dining. $11-$22 **AAA Inspector Notes:** This neighborhood favorite serves Korean comfort food with some added touches such as tofu made in-house and rice cooked in a stone pot and served tableside. Once all the rice is scooped out, the server pours hot tea into the pot to loosen the crispy rice—it is like eating sizzling rice soup and a perfect ending to the meal. **Address:** 4627 Geary Blvd 94118 **Location:** Between 10th and 11th aves. **Parking:** street only. L D

NAMU
415/386-8332 (41)

Asian Small Plates. Casual Dining. $9-$26 **AAA Inspector Notes:** Modern, minimalist décor is warmed by touches of wood in this contemporary Pan Asian tapas bar. Served are trendy, flavorful Korean and Japanese items on a rotating basis. Korean-style tacos, okonomiyaki and ramen are some of the choices. Open Saturday and Sunday for brunch only. **Bar:** beer & wine. **Address:** 439 Balboa St 94118 **Location:** At 6th Ave. UCSF Parnassus, 54. **Parking:** street only. D CALL

NEIMAN MARCUS-THE ROTUNDA RESTAURANT
415/362-4777 (147)

California. Casual Dining. $17-$28 **AAA Inspector Notes:** The dome of The Rotunda was the glass ship originally featured in the 1909 city of Paris department store. Patrons unwind in a casually upscale atmosphere for a respite from shopping for lunch or afternoon tea. **Bar:** full bar. **Address:** 150 Stockton St 94108 **Location:** In Neiman Marcus Department Store. Powell Street, 33. **Parking:** street only. L CALL

(See maps & indexes p. 394, 404.)

NETTIE'S CRAB SHACK
415/409-0300 (11)

Seafood. Casual Dining. $11-$35 **AAA Inspector Notes:** This eatery is an East Coast crab shack stuck in the middle of chic Union Street with an actual palm tree on the grounds. The food is casually sophisticated San Franciscan. There is a great selection of oysters and roast crab. For dessert, sample the candy apple or caramel apple made with petite crab apples. Monday Night Dinner with Nettie includes a prix fixe menu and is offered from 5 to 8 pm for the first 30 guests to make reservations. **Bar:** full bar. **Address:** 2032 Union St 94123 **Location:** Between Buchanan and Webster sts. **Parking:** street only. [L] [D] [X]

NEW CHEF HUNG'S RESTAURANT
415/398-6883 (75)

Chinese. Casual Dining. $6-$19 **AAA Inspector Notes:** Visitors to this casual spot will find Chinese American items along with some other no-nonsense, home-cooked items. Try the braised oxtail with yuba-it has a slightly chewy texture. Fresh vegetable-of-the-day selections are stir fried to the diner's request. The whole catfish steamed with black bean sauce is accompanied by egg whites and dried scallop stir fried rice. Dinner comes with soup. For lunch the daily specials include Hong Kong-style Western food such as beef stew and corned beef. **Bar:** beer only. **Address:** 823 Clay St 94108 **Location:** Between Grant Ave and Stockton St. Montgomery Street, 32. **Parking:** street only. [L] [D] [X] [🚋]

NEW DELHI
415/397-8470 (158)

Indian. Casual Dining. $11-$25 **AAA Inspector Notes:** Fresh spices and other ingredients flavor this downtown restaurant's food. In a former hotel ballroom, the convenient and beautiful spot has red-brick walls and antique floor tiles from Italy. **Bar:** full bar. **Address:** 160 Ellis St 94102 **Location:** Between Mason and Cyril Magnin sts. Powell Street, 33. **Parking:** street only. [L] [D] [🚋]

NICK'S CRISPY TACOS
415/409-8226 (44)

Mexican. Casual Dining. $4-$9 **AAA Inspector Notes:** This casual eatery is located in a nightclub called Rogue. Order at the counter, get a number and find a table. Try the tacos Nick's way with an addition of a crunchy taco shell, jack cheese and guacamole. This goes especially well with the pescado—Baja-style fried fish. They accept only cash. **Bar:** full bar. **Address:** 1500 Broadway St 94109 **Location:** At Polk St. **Parking:** street only. [L] [D] [X]

NICK'S LIGHTHOUSE
415/929-1300 (11)

Seafood
Casual Dining
$11-$30

AAA Inspector Notes: Patrons can stop at a take-out stand with steaming kettles of crustaceans out front or dine in the restaurant for fresh shellfish and fish. Dungeness crab and California lobster merit top billing at this busy spot. Views look out to the wharf's fishing boats. **Bar:** full bar. **Address:** 2815 Taylor St 94133 **Location:** At Jefferson St, on Fisherman's Wharf. **Parking:** street only.
Menu on AAA.com [L] [D] [X]

NOB HILL CAFE
415/776-6500 (71)

Italian. Casual Dining. $10-$19 **AAA Inspector Notes:** A regular meeting place for locals, this quaint bistro is perched out of the mainstream. The menu centers on homemade pasta, pizza and light antipasto and is perfect for a quick lunch or casual dinner. No reservations are accepted, and there is often a wait. **Bar:** beer & wine. **Address:** 1152 Taylor St 94108 **Location:** Atop Nob Hill; between Sacramento and Clay sts. Montgomery Street, 32. **Parking:** street only. [L] [D] [X] [🚋]

NOMBE
415/681-7150 (121)

Japanese Small Plates. Casual Dining. $4-$16 **AAA Inspector Notes:** This casual eatery offers a good introduction to Japanese izakaya-style small plates of food to accompany beer and sake. Yakitori, salads, croquettes, tempura and dessert are just some of the options. The beignets are little puffs of wonderful sweetness. **Bar:** beer & wine. **Address:** 2491 Mission St 94110 **Location:** Between 20th and 21st sts. 24th Street Mission, 36. **Parking:** street only. [D] [X] [🚋]

NOPA
415/864-8643 (51)

California. Casual Dining. $13-$26 **AAA Inspector Notes:** Casual and elegant, this restaurant has been packing them in since they opened. There is a vibrant vibe to the place, making it a magnet for people from all over San Francisco. Choose from bar seating, a communal table, group seating and an alcove set up mostly for couples seating. Cocktails are sophisticated and well made. Highlights include oven-roasted calamari, baked pasta with goat and lamb meat and for dessert, a Mexican coffee pot de creme is offered. **Bar:** full bar. **Reservations:** suggested. **Address:** 560 Divisadero St 94117 **Location:** At Hayes St. Duboce & Noe, 52. **Parking:** street only. [D] [LATE] [X] [🚋]

NOPALITO
415/437-0303 (59)

Mexican. Casual Dining. $9-$16 **AAA Inspector Notes:** This popular neighborhood restaurant offers authentic Mexican cuisine served in a casual, contemporary setting. Do not expect to find burritos on the menu. All of the menu items are made on the premises including the hearty taco chips. Start with the complimentary spicy garbanzo beans followed by a bowl of ceviche. Try the goat stew or chicken mole, both are great choices. Sip a glass of fruity sangria to cool the mouth. Call-ahead seating is available. **Bar:** beer & wine. **Address:** 306 Broderick St 94117 **Location:** At Oak St. Duboce & Noe, 52. **Parking:** street only. [L] [D] [X] [🚋]

NORTH BEACH RESTAURANT
415/392-1700 (37)

Italian
Fine Dining
$19-$35

AAA Inspector Notes: Servers in tuxedos circulate through this Old World Italian restaurant, where Tuscan entrées lead up to luscious New York cheesecake for dessert. Classic, well-prepared dishes such as veal cannelloni, imported fresh burrata and freshly made zabaglione with berries are some of the offerings. **Bar:** full bar. **Reservations:** suggested. **Address:** 1512 Stockton St 94133 **Location:** At Columbus Ave. Embarcadero, 31. **Parking:** valet and street only. [L] [D] [🚋]

NOVA BAR & RESTAURANT
415/543-2282 (185)

American. Casual Dining. $7-$19 **AAA Inspector Notes:** This chic restaurant and bar serves American comfort foods, small plate style. The bar features a host of infused vodkas and excellent wines. **Bar:** full bar. **Address:** 555 2nd St 94107 **Location:** Between Bryant and Brannan sts. 2nd & King, 92. **Parking:** street only. [L] [D] [X] [🚋]

ONE MARKET RESTAURANT
415/777-5577 (98)

American. Fine Dining. $15-$36 **AAA Inspector Notes:** At the end of Market Street within view of the Bay Bridge, this popular restaurant has received accolades from San Francisco magazines. A prime seating spot is the chef's table in the open exhibition kitchen. Although the main feature is seafood, the menu also lists selections of beef, lamb and chicken. **Bar:** full bar. **Reservations:** suggested. **Address:** 1 Market St 94105 **Location:** Southeast corner of Market and Steuart sts; near Embarcadero Station. Embarcadero, 31. **Parking:** valet and street only. [L] [D] CALL [&M] [🚋]

OOLA
415/995-2061 (182)

American. Casual Dining. $10-$32 **AAA Inspector Notes:** Menu offerings combine French, Italian and American influences. With exposed brick walls and comfortable seating, the dining room nurtures an intimate and comfortable feel. **Bar:** full bar. **Reservations:** suggested. **Address:** 860 Folsom St 94107 **Location:** Between 4th and 5th sts. Powell Street, 33. **Parking:** street only. [L] [D] [LATE] [🚋]

O'REILLY'S IRISH PUB & RESTAURANT
415/989-6222 (38)

Irish. Casual Dining. $14-$20 **AAA Inspector Notes:** This popular pub serves traditional Irish dishes, ranging from boxty to stews, hamburgers and hash. Irish soda bread accompanies each meal, and a pint of Guinness is always a nice addition. Guests seat themselves in the casual neighborhood spot. Do not be surprised if the server has an Irish brogue. **Bar:** full bar. **Address:** 622 Green St 94133 **Location:** Jct Green St and Columbus Ave. Embarcadero, 31. **Parking:** street only. [B] [L] [D] [🚋]

(See maps & indexes p. 394, 404.)

ORIENTAL PEARL RESTAURANT 415/433-1817 **74**

Chinese
Casual Dining
$11-$55

Menu on AAA.com L D 🚲

AAA Inspector Notes: An authentic dim sum menu, which centers on traditional choices, is offered at this locally popular Chinatown spot. **Bar:** full bar. **Address:** 778 Clay St 94108 **Location:** Jct Grant St; 2nd Floor; in Chinatown. 🚇 Montgomery Street, 32. **Parking:** street only.

ORIGINAL U.S. RESTAURANT 415/397-5200 **39**

Italian. Family Dining. $9-$25 **AAA Inspector Notes:** This quaint, historic eatery has been faithfully serving the North Beach area for more than 40 years. Friendly servers bring out well-prepared traditional Italian food. Limited exterior seating is available. **Bar:** beer & wine. **Address:** 515 Columbus Ave 94133 **Location:** Jct Columbus Ave and Green St. 🚇 Embarcadero, 31. **Parking:** street only. L D 🚲

OSHA THAI NOODLE CAFE 415/673-2368 **136**

Thai. Casual Dining. $11-$17 **AAA Inspector Notes:** The casual, trendy decor of monotone chocolate taupe gives a hip vibe to this cafe. Food is well-prepared and presented. Try the spicy calamari with green apple slices or the catfish and eggplant curry. Cool off with a glass of Thai iced tea. **Bar:** beer & wine. **Address:** 696 Geary St 94102 **Location:** Jct Leavenworth St. 🚇 Powell Street, 33. **Parking:** street only. L D LATE 🚲

OSHA THAI RESTAURANT 415/278-9991 **164**

Thai. Casual Dining. $11-$20 **AAA Inspector Notes:** The décor and food here are vibrant, exciting, fun and luscious. Servers in casual black are efficient and nimble. **Address:** 149 2nd St 94105 **Location:** Between Minna and Natoma sts. 🚇 Montgomery Street, 32. **Parking:** street only. L D 🚲

OUTERLANDS 415/661-6140 **50**

California. Casual Dining. $5-$25 **AAA Inspector Notes:** This is what happens when a bunch of surfer chefs get together and build a warm, comfortable diner shack. Lines are long but they have some hand-made blankets to keep you warm. During brunch and breakfast, service is limited—order and pay at the counter after getting a table. Sandwiches and soup are served for lunch, with an expanded menu and full service for dinner. For brunch, make sure to order the Dutch pancake. **Bar:** beer & wine. **Address:** 4001 Judah St 94122 **Location:** At 45th Ave. 🚇 Ocean Beach, 58. **Parking:** street only. B L D 🚲

OYAJI RESTAURANT 415/379-3604 **15**

Japanese Sushi Small Plates. Casual Dining. $5-$45 **AAA Inspector Notes:** This popular neighborhood spot offers fresh sashimi flown in daily from Tsukiji as well as such izakaya items as horumon yaki, sake steam clams and ramen. The atmosphere is just like an izakaya in the Shinjuku area of Tokyo. **Bar:** beer & wine. **Address:** 3123 Clement St 94121 **Location:** Between 32nd and 33rd aves. **Parking:** street only. L D 🍴

OZUMO 415/882-1333 **128**

Japanese. Casual Dining. $11-$46 **AAA Inspector Notes:** This restaurant caters to sushi lovers with a sleek European/Japanese granite and light oak decor and spacious sushi bar area. The innovative menu also includes grilled fresh fish, miso-marinated spare ribs and, for lunch, nagasaki chanpon. A wonderful selection of sake is offered. Panoramic views of the Bay Bridge can be enjoyed through large windows. **Bar:** full bar. **Reservations:** suggested. **Address:** 161 Steuart St 94105 **Location:** Between Howard and Mission sts; at waterfront. 🚇 Folsom, 90. **Parking:** street only. L D 🚲

PACIFIC CATCH FRESH FISH GRILL 415/504-6905 **65**

Pacific Rim. Casual Dining. $11-$20 **AAA Inspector Notes:** Comfortable, yet a bit laughable, this grill offers a contemporary décor with Asian accents of bamboo and rice paper covered lighting. Seafood is expertly prepared using spices and flavorings from Hawaii, Latin America and Asian countries. Check the board for daily specials. Share a fun dessert of mochi fondue. **Bar:** full bar. **Reservations:** suggested. **Address:** 1200 9th Ave 94122 **Location:** Corner of 9th Ave and Lincoln Way. 🚇 Judah & 9th Ave, 55. L D CALL ♿M 🚲

PALIO D'ASTI 415/395-9800 **82**

Italian. Casual Dining. $13-$45 **AAA Inspector Notes:** This eatery is elegant, spacious and features wall-mounted horse figurines accentuating one wall. The menu comprises traditional favorites as well as regional specialties. Start with an appetizer of grilled scallops, and follow it with osso buco. A Sicilian cannoli makes a nice meal-ender. **Bar:** full bar. **Reservations:** suggested. **Address:** 640 Sacramento St 94111 **Location:** In Financial District. 🚇 Montgomery Street, 32. **Parking:** street only. L D 🚲

PANCHO VILLA TAQUERIA 415/864-8840 **101**

Mexican. Casual Dining. $7-$16 **AAA Inspector Notes:** In the Mission District, this restaurant is extremely popular with locals desiring good Mexican cuisine. The dining room is basic but comfortable. Lines move quickly, so this place should not be passed up by those who are in the neighborhood. **Bar:** beer only. **Address:** 3071 16th St 94103 **Location:** Just w of Mission St. 🚇 16th Street Mission, 35. **Parking:** street only. L D LATE 🚲

PAPALOTE MEXICAN GRILL 415/970-8815 **128**

Mexican. Quick Serve. $8-$16 **AAA Inspector Notes:** The name means kite, and the festive decorations at this Noe Valley spot include two paper dragon kites suspended from the ceiling. It is filled with families and young couples scarfing down burritos, tacos and nacho plates. A must try is the sought-after adobo burrito. **Bar:** beer only. **Address:** 3409 24th St 94110 **Location:** Between Valencia and Poplar sts. 🚇 24th Street Mission, 36. **Parking:** street only. L D 🍴 🚲

PARADA 22 415/750-1111 **61**

Puerto Rican. Casual Dining. $8-$13 **AAA Inspector Notes:** This bright little eatery offers home-style cooking. Get the combination plate to try a little of everything, including the camarones a la criolla (sauteed shrimp in tomato, onion, pepper cream sauce), Spanish rice, red beans and ham, fried plantains and greens. Walk out and explore Haight-Ashbury or Golden Gate Park after the meal. **Bar:** beer & wine. **Address:** 1805 Haight St 94117 **Location:** Between Stanyan and Shrader sts. 🚇 Carl & Cole, 53. **Parking:** street only. L D 🍴 🚲

PARAGON 415/537-9020 **190**

American. Casual Dining. $9-$25 **AAA Inspector Notes:** Near PacBell Park, this American brasserie combines a sophisticated dining experience with a lively bar atmosphere. **Bar:** full bar. **Address:** 701 2nd St 94107 **Location:** Southeast corner of Townsend and 2nd sts; in Financial District. 🚇 2nd & King, 92. **Parking:** street only. L D 🚲

PARALLEL 37 415/773-6168 **97**

New American. Casual Dining. $24-$29 **AAA Inspector Notes:** This sleek eatery features small bites, appetizers, entrées and sides. The changing menu offers creative presentations on such items as poached salmon on ponzu, oysters in elderflower mignonette, English pea ravioli, duck breast in green garlic puree with pickled strawberries and Alaskan halibut in a bacon morel vinaigrette. Artistic desserts come with a wow factor. **Bar:** full bar. **Reservations:** suggested. **Address:** 600 Stockton St 94108 **Location:** Just n of Union Square at California St; in The Ritz-Carlton, San Francisco. 🚇 Montgomery Street, 32. **Parking:** valet only. B L D CALL ♿M 🚲

PARK CHOW 415/665-9912 **70**

American. Casual Dining. $9-$14 **AAA Inspector Notes:** This casual neighborhood eatery serves San Francisco's version of American comfort food with a bit of Chinese (won ton and Thai noodles), Italian (pasta and pizza) and such classics as burgers and pot roasts. The popular spot offers a good value for the dollar. Many dishes, including desserts, have a choice of entrée size or small size. Make sure to try the pumpkin ice cream with ginger cake. **Bar:** beer & wine. **Address:** 1240 9th Ave 94122 **Location:** Between Lincoln Way and Irving St. 🚇 Judah & 9th Ave, 55. **Parking:** street only. B L D 🍴 🚲

PARK GRILL 415/296-2933 **80**

California. Casual Dining. $15-$40 **AAA Inspector Notes:** Fine California cuisine stands out in this upscale hotel dining room. Well-spaced tables are ideal for private conversations. **Bar:** full bar. **Reservations:** suggested. **Address:** 333 Battery St 94111 **Location:** At Clay St; in Financial District; in Le Meridien San Francisco. 🚇 Embarcadero, 31. **Parking:** valet only. B L 🚲

(See maps & indexes p. 394, 404.)

PASTA POMODORO
415/920-9904

▼▼ Italian. Casual Dining. $10-$19 **AAA Inspector Notes:** Families are welcomed at this laid-back restaurant, which brings in plenty of loyal locals who enjoy its varied Italian favorites, including tempting pasta and chicken dishes. **Bar:** beer & wine. **Address:** 4000 24th St 94114 **Location:** At Noe St. Church & 24th St, 86. **Parking:** street only.

PAT'S CAFE
415/776-8735 [21]

▼▼ California. Casual Dining. $7-$16 **AAA Inspector Notes:** This modest cafe, off the beaten path on a quiet side street, features uplifting bright orange and lemon walls. Diners can enjoy a hearty home-style breakfast or lunch before exploring the city on foot. **Bar:** beer & wine. **Address:** 2330 Taylor St 94133 **Location:** Between Francisco and Chestnut sts. **Parking:** street only.

PATXI'S CHICAGO PIZZA
415/759-9000 [77]

▼▼ Pizza. Casual Dining. $12-$31 **AAA Inspector Notes:** This contemporary pizza restaurant features a family friendly, neighborhood vibe. Simple appetizers, salads and four styles of pizza (Chicago, pan, thin and extra-thin crust) are offered. **Bar:** beer & wine. **Address:** 822 Irving St 94122 **Location:** Between 9th and 10th aves. Judah & 9th Ave, 55. **Parking:** street only.

PAULINE'S PIZZA
415/552-2050 [89]

▼▼ Pizza. Casual Dining. $14-$24 **AAA Inspector Notes:** A Mission District staple since 1985, this restaurant features organically grown greens and many herbs and spices in the salads and adds unusual but tasty toppings to its well-made pizza. A good choice is the signature pesto pizza, but daily specials also are hard to resist. **Bar:** beer & wine. **Address:** 260 Valencia St 94103 **Location:** Between 14th St and Duboce Ave. 16th Street Mission, 35. **Parking:** street only.

PENANG GARDEN RESTAURANT
415/296-7878 [65]

▼▼ Thai. Casual Dining. $8-$21 **AAA Inspector Notes:** Cuisine from Thailand and Malaysia is central to the menu of this modern, energetic restaurant. Large plants divide the dining room, and colorful murals line the walls. While the atmosphere is laid back and family-oriented, the menu and food quality is not. Representative of the excellent fare are seafood, poultry, lamb, beef, rice, vegetarian and noodle dishes. **Bar:** beer & wine. **Address:** 728 Washington St 94108 **Location:** Jct Kearny St, just w. Montgomery Street, 32. **Parking:** street only.

PERSIMMON CAFE
415/433-5525 [118]

▼▼ International. Casual Dining. $8-$21 **AAA Inspector Notes:** This modest restaurant offers a variety of cuisines. Highlights include the American burger, Mediterranean fare, Greek moussaka, Middle Eastern chicken fesenjoon and Italian pasta dishes. **Bar:** beer only. **Address:** 582 Sutter St 94101 **Location:** Between Mason and Powell sts. Powell Street, 33. **Parking:** street only.

PESCE
415/928-8025 [32]

▼▼ Italian Seafood Small Plates. Casual Dining. $7-$17 **AAA Inspector Notes:** Great seafood is prepared in an intimate venue where reservations are highly recommended. More than 25 wines by the glass accompany such dishes as braised octopus salad with garlic lemon vinaigrette and drunken tuna braised in red wine and tomato. **Bar:** full bar. **Address:** 2227 Polk St 94109 **Location:** Just n of Vallejo St. **Parking:** street only.

PICA PICA MAIZE KITCHEN
415/400-5453 [95]

▼ Latin American. Quick Serve. $8-$9 **AAA Inspector Notes:** This vibrant, casual eatery serves Venezuelan sandwiches. The sandwich carriers are called arepa, or grilled corn meal patties, and come in wheat and gluten free. **Bar:** beer & wine. **Address:** 401 Valencia St 94103 **Location:** At 15th St. 16th Street Mission, 35. **Parking:** street only.

PICCINO
415/824-4224 [130]

▼▼ Italian. Casual Dining. $9-$22 **AAA Inspector Notes:** Located in the up and coming Dogpatch, this Italian restaurant is an unexpected find. California Italian fare is offered along with a limited, but good, selection of Italian and French wines. **Bar:** beer & wine. **Reservations:** suggested. **Address:** 1001 Minnesota St 94107 **Location:** At 22nd St. 23rd St, 98. **Parking:** street only.

PIER 23
415/362-8138 [40]

▼▼ American. Casual Dining. $13-$22 **AAA Inspector Notes:** Come during the day and enjoy the view of the bay; at night enjoy the live music. On some nights there is a cover charge. Food is simple, yet well flavored. Try the roasted crab with a helmet full of butter/sauce. Dip the crab meat in the bold sauce and finish off the sauce by sopping it up with sourdough bread. For a lighter meal, try the grilled fish tacos. **Bar:** full bar. **Address:** The Embarcadero 94111 **Location:** On The Embarcadero. Embarcadero, 31. **Parking:** street only.

PIER MARKET SEAFOOD RESTAURANT
415/989-7437 [3]

▼▼ Seafood. Casual Dining. $12-$39 **AAA Inspector Notes:** This seaside restaurant beckons to both tourists and locals alike. Seafood is featured and friendly service awaits. Super-sized cocktails can double as desserts-be sure to try their pina coladas. **Bar:** full bar. **Address:** Pier 39, Suite 103 94133 **Location:** At Fisherman's Wharf. **Parking:** on-site (fee).

PIPERADE
415/391-2555 [42]

▼▼ French. Fine Dining. $13-$30 **AAA Inspector Notes:** This French/Spanish restaurant has a distinct Basque style. Guests may dine inside or on the patio. While the service is professional and attentive, the atmosphere is relaxed. Savory dishes incorporate fresh local seafood, as well as lamb, chicken and steaks. Varied wines complement any meal. **Bar:** full bar. **Reservations:** suggested. **Address:** 1015 Battery St 94111 **Location:** At Green St. Embarcadero, 31. **Parking:** street only.

PIZZERIA DELFINA
415/437-6800 [107]

▼▼ Pizza. Casual Dining. $10-$17 **AAA Inspector Notes:** Californian and Italian meet the New York-style thin-crust pizza at this pizzeria. Blistered-crust pizza with toppings such as cherry stone clams, broccoli rabe and prosciutto di Parma are offered. Simple antipasti and dolce items round out the menu. Check the board for daily specials. **Bar:** beer & wine. **Address:** 3611 18th St 94110 **Location:** Between Guerrero and Dolores sts. Church & 18th St, 85. **Parking:** street only.

PIZZERIA DELFINA
415/440-1189 [28]

▼▼ Pizza. Casual Dining. $10-$17 **AAA Inspector Notes:** The first pizzeria was so popular that the owners opened a second one. Here at the second eatery, mozzarella balls and fennel sausage still are made on-site. Neapolitan-style pizza is crunchy and chewy with a blistered crust. One difference between the sister eateries is that this one makes their own gelato with rotating flavors such as Meyer lemon, Concord grape and peanut butter chocolate. **Bar:** beer & wine. **Address:** 2406 California St 94115 **Location:** Between Fillmore and Steiner sts. **Parking:** street only.

PLOUF
415/986-6491 [106]

▼▼ Seafood. Casual Dining. $12-$34 **AAA Inspector Notes:** This bustling seafood bistro in the Financial District presents a menu of fish and chips, halibut, tuna, oven-roasted chicken, ravioli, lamb chops, bouillabaisse, salads and sandwiches. **Bar:** full bar. **Reservations:** suggested. **Address:** 40 Belden Pl 94104 **Location:** Just n of Bush St; between Kearny and Montgomery sts. Montgomery Street, 32. **Parking:** street only.

POMPEI'S GROTTO
415/776-9265 [8]

▼▼▼ **AAA Inspector Notes:** Homemade pasta and Northern Italian dishes are what diners can expect at this cozy restaurant, which is in a popular tourist area. **Bar:** full bar. **Reservations:** suggested. **Address:** 340 Jefferson St 94133 **Location:** At Fisherman's Wharf. **Parking:** street only. *Menu on AAA.com*

Seafood
Casual Dining
$11-$29

(See maps & indexes p. 394, 404.)

PORK STORE CAFE   415/864-6981 `66`

▼▼ American. Casual Dining. $6-$11 **AAA Inspector Notes:** There may be a line out the door at this little cafe, but it moves quickly. Food here is a mixture of classic diner with just a pinch of San Francisco. Check out the eggs in a tasty nest-a nest of hash browns, two over-easy eggs, bacon, grilled green peppers, fresh tomatoes, onions and garlic, topped with cheddar cheese and served with a side of biscuits. Order one blueberry pancake to share with a friend-it is the size of a dinner plate. **Address:** 1451 Haight St 94117 **Location:** At Ashbury St. ⓡ Carl & Cole, 53. **Parking:** street only.

`B` `L` `ⓚ` `⇧`

PPQ DUNGENESS ISLAND   415/386-8266 `19`

▼ Vietnamese. Casual Dining. $5-$17 **AAA Inspector Notes:** If you do not want to dress up to go to Crustacean but want to eat roasted whole crab and garlic noodles, this is the place to go. Bring home the sauce/juices from the roasted crab and make a simple pasta dish for next day's dinner. Divine! **Bar:** beer & wine. **Address:** 2332 Clement St 94121 **Location:** Between 24th and 25th aves. **Parking:** street only. `L` `D` `ⓚ`

PROSPECT   415/247-7770 `153`

▼ California. Fine Dining. $25-$32 **AAA Inspector Notes:** This cavernous and energetic eatery offers a relaxed, fine dining experience. Brought to you by the Boulevard team, this contemporary restaurant is for the next generation who have grown up dining at Boulevard with their parents. **Bar:** full bar. **Reservations:** suggested. **Address:** 300 Spear St 94105 **Location:** At Folsom St. ⓡ Folsom, 90. **Parking:** valet and street only. `L` `D` `⇧`

PUCCINI & PINETTI   415/392-5500 `161`

▼▼▼
Italian
Casual Dining
$13-$30

AAA Inspector Notes: A classic tin-tile ceiling and dark wood booth seating are updated with contemporary accents at this popular hangout for locals and tourists. Well-executed classics such as frito misto and frutti de mare are offered. **Bar:** full bar. **Address:** 129 Ellis St 94102 **Location:** Just w of Union Square at Mason St; next to Hotel Max a Larkspur Collection Hotel. ⓡ Powell Street, 33. **Parking:** no self-parking. `B` `L` `D` `⇧`

RAGAZZA   415/255-1133 `64`

▼ Italian. Casual Dining. $13-$19 **AAA Inspector Notes:** Earthy tones, ambient lighting and poster-size blow ups of family pictures warm up the contemporary décor found here. Sister restaurant to Gialina, this spot offers the same style pizza that always is listed as being one of the best nationwide. Other menu items' quality are just as uncompromisingly good. **Bar:** beer & wine. **Address:** 311 Divisadero St 94117 **Location:** Between Page and Oak sts. ⓡ Duboce & Noe, 52. **Parking:** street only. `D` `ⓚ` `⇧`

RAMEN UNDERGROUND   415/765-9909 `104`

▼▼ Japanese Noodles. Casual Dining. $8 **AAA Inspector Notes:** This is the perfect hole-in-the-wall ramen shop, just like the ones in Tokyo or Osaka. Packed during lunch with office workers this is a great stop at night for a quick meal after work. The menu is a form that you check off for ordering. For the sedate, check out the classic salt, shoyu and miso flavor. Adventurers should try the soy milk—the depth of flavor will surprise diners. For the big eater, add a donburi (rice bowl) to the ramen. Appropriately this spot is cash only. **Address:** 355 Kearny St 94108 **Location:** Between Bush and Pine sts. ⓡ Montgomery Street, 32. **Parking:** street only. `L` `D` `ⓚ` `⇧`

R & G LOUNGE   415/982-7877 `76`

▼▼▼ Chinese. Casual Dining. $9-$40 **AAA Inspector Notes:** Seating options here range from the more private and upscale upstairs to the bustling downstairs that is popular with families. On the menu are excellent Cantonese entrées of fresh seafood, poultry, barbecued pork loin and some fine noodle and rice dishes. One section lists combinations of meats and vegetables prepared in a clay pot, including eggplant and salted fish, oxtail stew and oysters with black mushrooms. They are renowned for crab with ginger and green onion or garlic and black beans. **Bar:** full bar. **Reservations:** suggested. **Address:** 631 Kearny St 94108 **Location:** Between Commercial and Clay sts. ⓡ Montgomery Street, 32. **Parking:** street only. `L` `D` `⇧`

RANGE   415/282-8283 `117`

▼▼ California. Casual Dining. $19-$27 **AAA Inspector Notes:** A perennial favorite of local foodies, this eatery offers a laid back, contemporary ambience with professional, casual service. The well-executed ingredients shine through and the natural flavors can be tasted in every bite; vegetables are not an afterthought here. Some menu items change weekly. If it is on the menu, try the raw scallop appetizer followed by the steelhead trout. With the bill comes two heavenly miniature chocolate truffles. **Bar:** full bar. **Reservations:** suggested. **Address:** 842 Valencia St 94110 **Location:** Between 19th and 20th sts. ⓡ 16th Street Mission, 35. **Parking:** street only. `D`

RESTAURANT EIJI   415/558-8149 `98`

▼▼ Japanese. Casual Dining. $5-$18 **AAA Inspector Notes:** This tiny eatery offers up authentic Japanese tapas, sushi, sashimi and homemade tofu. For a heartier meal, try their nabemono, a pot of bite-sized delicacies. Make sure to reserve a piece of the strawberry mochi (strawberry covered with red bean paste and wrapped with mochi, or a rice cake). **Bar:** beer & wine. **Reservations:** suggested. **Address:** 317 Sanchez St 94114 **Location:** Between 16th and 17th sts. ⓡ Church & 18th St, 85. **Parking:** street only.

`L` `D` `ⓚ` `⇧`

RISTOBAR   415/923-6464 `3`

▼▼▼ Italian. Gastro Pub. $13-$29 **AAA Inspector Notes:** Feast on Italian pub food at this contemporary restaurant where murals adorn the tray ceilings and a chandelier offers an elegant palazzo feel. The bar has two flat-screen TVs making it a great neighborhood meeting place. Menu highlights include salami and cheese plates, pizza, risottos and osso buco. Make sure to save room for dessert. **Bar:** beer & wine. **Address:** 2300 Chestnut St 94123 **Location:** At Scott St. **Parking:** street only. `D`

RISTORANTE MONA LISA   415/989-4917 `45`

▼▼ Italian. Casual Dining. $12-$34 **AAA Inspector Notes:** The experience is enchanted at this crowded, tightly spaced and lively restaurant, where guests dig in to large portions of favorite Italian dishes. The staff is friendly. **Bar:** beer & wine. **Address:** 353 Columbus Ave 94133 **Location:** In North Beach area. ⓡ Embarcadero, 31. **Parking:** street only. `L` `D` `⇧`

RN74   415/543-7474 `135`

▼▼▼ California. Casual Dining. $16-$38 **AAA Inspector Notes:** This restaurant, especially the bar, is the place to see and be seen. As for the food it more than matches up with the décor. Food is appropriately sized and elegant in its presentation with great attention to detail. Check out the newspaper lining on the maitake tempura—it is a cutout from a Japanese newspaper. Also known for an extensive wine list, there are some 70 pages in a binder. When there is only one bottle left, it is announced on the board along with the price. **Bar:** full bar. **Address:** 301 Mission St 94199 **Location:** At Beale St. ⓡ Embarcadero, 31. **Parking:** street only. `L` `D` `ⓚ` `⇧`

ROAM ARTISAN BURGERS   415/440-7626 `13`

▼ Burgers Natural/Organic. Quick Serve. $6-$8 **AAA Inspector Notes:** This unpretentious, contemporary burger joint is family-friendly. All of the ingredients are natural, locally sourced, organic and eco friendly. Even the wines are on tap. To order the meat, say pink or not pink. Try the sunny side burger—carefully smash the yolk or it will burst when bitten. Try the fry-fecta - a combination of white and sweet potatoes and zucchini onion haystack fries. Finish off with a fabulous shakes such as salted caramel or a healthful drink such as the kombucha. **Bar:** beer & wine. **Address:** 1785 Union St 94123 **Location:** Between Gough and Octavia sts. **Parking:** street only.

`L` `D` `ⓚ`

ROCCO'S CAFE   415/554-0522 `192`

▼▼ Italian. Casual Dining. $10-$23 **AAA Inspector Notes:** Diners kick back in a lively setting to enjoy generous portions of Italian food at this cafe. Linguine vongole, chicken piccata or chicken Bolognese are some of the popular items on the menu. **Bar:** beer & wine. **Address:** 1131 Folsom St 94103 **Location:** Between 7th and 8th sts. ⓡ Civic Center/UN Plaza, 34. **Parking:** street only.

`B` `L` `D` `⇧`

ROSAMUNDE SAUSAGE GRILL   415/437-6851 `76`

▼ Hot Dogs. Quick Serve. $6-$7 **AAA Inspector Notes:** This tiny sausage joint serves gourmet sausage. Try the wild boar or the Hungarian and eat it at the Toronado Bar next door. They only accept cash. **Address:** 545 Haight St 94117 **Location:** Between Fillmore and Steiner sts. ⓡ Duboce & Church, 51. **Parking:** street only.

`L` `D` `ⓚ` `⇧`

(See maps & indexes p. 394, 404.)

ROSAMUNDE SAUSAGE GRILL 415/970-9015 `129`

Hot Dogs. Quick Serve. $6-$7 **AAA Inspector Notes:** This lively, contemporary sausage joint serves homemade sausage from the standard to such exotics as duck and figs. The beer selection is extensive with 30 beers on tap and many bottled ones. **Bar:** beer & wine. **Address:** 2832 Mission St 94110 **Location:** Between 24th and 25th sts. 24th Street Mission, 36. **Parking:** street only.

`L` `D`

ROSE PISTOLA 415/399-0499 `34`

Italian. Casual Dining. $13-$37 **AAA Inspector Notes:** A delightful decor, friendly, casual service and an excellent selection of freshly prepared dishes are found at the popular, busy restaurant. An excellent selection of wines complements the pasta, pizza and seasonal antipasto choices. **Bar:** full bar. **Reservations:** suggested. **Address:** 532 Columbus Ave 94133 **Location:** Between Green and Union sts. Embarcadero, 31. **Parking:** valet and street only.

`L` `D`

ROSE'S CAFE 415/775-2200 `10`

Italian. Casual Dining. $12-$27 **AAA Inspector Notes:** The light and breezy Cow Hollow neighborhood gathering place presents a menu with fresh salads and light entrées, as well as pizza. Guests come here to kick back and relax in the afternoon or enjoy a night out after dark. **Bar:** beer & wine. **Address:** 2298 Union St 94123 **Location:** At Steiner St. **Parking:** street only.

`B` `L` `D`

ROTI INDIAN BISTRO 415/665-7684 `132`

Indian. Casual Dining. $9-$22 **AAA Inspector Notes:** This contemporary neighborhood establishment is accented with gentle salmon hues giving a soft glow throughout and large, vibrant photographs depicting everyday life in India. Great starters include tandoori or mixed seafood biryani, which is loaded with various seafood. Mango lassi will cool the mouth as will the ice cream that is not too sweet and a bit exotic. Attentive friendly waiters are eager to assist. **Bar:** beer & wine. **Address:** 53 W Portal Ave 94127 **Location:** Between Vicente and Ulloa sts. West Portal, 63. **Parking:** street only. `L` `D` `CALL` `M`

ROUND TABLE PIZZA 415/387-5054

Pizza. Family Dining. $7-$28 **AAA Inspector Notes:** This casual, family-oriented pizza place features high-quality ingredients and dough rolled fresh daily. Distinctive specialty pizzas are piled high with toppings. **Bar:** beer & wine. **Address:** 3567 Geary Blvd 94118 **Location:** 2 mi w of US 101 (Van Ness Ave). **Parking:** street only.

`L` `D`

ROXANNE CAFE 415/989-5555 `112`

Italian. Casual Dining. $11-$20 **AAA Inspector Notes:** Close to Union Square and hotels, this casual, intimate cafe is a great place to meet for breakfast or lunch when working or staying downtown. **Bar:** beer & wine. **Address:** 570 Powell St 94108 **Location:** At Bush St. Montgomery Street, 32. **Parking:** street only.

`B` `L` `D` `CALL` `M`

ROY'S 415/777-0277 `150`

Pacific Rim. Fine Dining. $16-$40 **AAA Inspector Notes:** Enjoy fusion of fresh Pacific seafood, French sauces and Asian seasonings. The ever-changing menu has many entrées such as, grilled salmon and barbecue lamb rack, and the signature dessert, chocolate soufflé. **Bar:** full bar. **Reservations:** suggested. **Address:** 575 Mission St 94109 **Location:** Jct 2nd St; downtown. Montgomery Street, 32. **Parking:** street only.

`L` `D`

SAHA 415/345-9547 `110`

Arabic. Casual Dining. $17-$25 **AAA Inspector Notes:** Meaning toast to good health, this restaurant's menu features a distinctive fusion of Arabic, California and French cuisines. A great way to enjoy an evening here is to share a number of small plates. A lovely contemporary ambience with just a hint of exotic Arabian Nights is created. **Bar:** beer & wine. **Address:** 1075 Sutter St 94109 **Location:** 0.5 mi w of Union Square; between Hyde and Larkin sts; in Hotel Carlton, a Joie de Vivre hotel. Powell Street, 33. **Parking:** street only. `D`

SAISON 415/828-7990 `109`

French. Fine Dining. $198-$248 **AAA Inspector Notes:** Elegant upscale dining is made casual at this restaurant where guests walk through the kitchen to enter the dining room where an intimate ambience features some eclectic artwork on the walls. There only is one menu set up by courses which can change daily. Let the staff know of any dietary restrictions ahead of time. Wine pairing, with a pour known to be generous, is available and recommended for the full culinary experience. Be sure to make reservations as they are required. **Bar:** wine only. **Reservations:** required. **Address:** 2124 Folsom St 94110 **Location:** Between 17th and 18th sts. 16th Street Mission, 35. **Parking:** street only.

`D` `M`

SAMOVAR TEA LOUNGE 415/227-9400 `172`

International. Casual Dining. $5-$24 **AAA Inspector Notes:** The decor as inviting as is if someone traveled the world and blended East and West together into an exotic harmony of Zen tranquility. Take time out and enjoy a quiet ritual of taking tea and food. Everything from a traditional English tea service complete with strong black tea and scones with cream to a Moorish platter of kebabs and mint tea is featured as well as meals featuring Chinese duck and a Japanese rice bowl. **Address:** 730 Howard St 94103 **Location:** Between 3rd and 4th sts; at Yerba Buena Gardens. Montgomery Street, 32. **Parking:** street only.

`L` `D` `M`

SANRAKU RESTAURANT 415/771-0803 `114`

Japanese. Casual Dining. $10-$38 **AAA Inspector Notes:** Located just blocks from Union Square, this casual sushi bar/restaurant is popular with hotel staff from nearby hotels during lunch and bustling with locals during dinner. For lunch, check out the daily bento specials and do not miss the sesame chicken entrée and, of course, the sushi. **Bar:** beer & wine. **Address:** 704 Sutter St 94109 **Location:** Between Taylor and Jones sts; nw of Union Square. Powell Street, 33. **Parking:** street only.

`L` `D` `CALL` `M`

SANTORINI'S 415/402-0060 `149`

Mediterranean. Casual Dining. $12-$23 **AAA Inspector Notes:** This Union Square restaurant serves traditional Mediterranean dishes in a setting marked by colorful decor. **Bar:** full bar. **Address:** 242 O'Farrell St 94102 **Location:** Between Powell and Mason sts. Powell Street, 33. **Parking:** street only.

`B` `L` `D`

SAN TUNG CHINESE RESTAURANT 415/242-0828 `73`

Chinese. Casual Dining. $6-$16 **AAA Inspector Notes:** This very popular neighborhood restaurant specializes in Northern Chinese cuisine. Made-to-order dumplings, handmade noodles, sautéed string beans and desirable original dry-fried chicken are favorites. There usually is a line going out the door at night and on weekends. **Bar:** beer only. **Address:** 1031 Irving St 94122 **Location:** Between 11th and 12th aves. Judah & 9th Ave, 55. **Parking:** street only. `L` `D` `CALL` `M`

SCALA'S BISTRO 415/395-8555 `123`

Italian
Casual Dining
$12-$30

AAA Inspector Notes: The bustling Mediterranean-style bistro merges regional Italian and country French cooking on its creative menu. **Bar:** full bar. **Reservations:** suggested. **Address:** 432 Powell St 94102 **Location:** Just n of Union Square at Sutter St; in Sir Francis Drake Hotel. Powell Street, 33. **Parking:** valet and street only. `B` `L` `D`

SCOMA'S RESTAURANT 415/771-4383 `1`

Seafood
Casual Dining
$16-$46

AAA Inspector Notes: A casual mood pervades this landmark restaurant. Picturesque views of the harbor invite wistful daydreaming. **Address:** Fisherman's Wharf, Pier 47 94133 **Location:** On Fisherman's Wharf. **Parking:** on-site (fee).

`L` `D`

(See maps & indexes p. 394, 404.)

SEARS FINE FOODS
415/986-0700 **126**

▼▼ American. Family Dining. $9-$30 **AAA Inspector Notes:** Since 1938, customers have kept coming back for this bustling restaurant's great Swedish pancakes and other tasty fare. In addition to breakfast items served until 3 pm, patrons can get home-style dinners and local seafood. **Bar:** beer & wine. **Address:** 439 Powell St 94102 **Location:** Just s of Sutter St; off Union Square. Powell Street, 33. **Parking:** street only. B L D CALL M

SEASONS RESTAURANT
415/633-3838 **156**

▼▼▼ ▼▼ California. Fine Dining. $17-$52 **AAA Inspector Notes:** Patrons can unwind in the elegant yet informal room over California-style cuisine prepared with a French influence. Cityscape views are captivating from any seat. The décor incorporates rich wood paneling and granite floors. **Bar:** full bar. **Reservations:** suggested. **Address:** 757 Market St 94103 **Location:** Between 3rd and 4th sts; in Four Seasons Hotel San Francisco. Montgomery Street, 32. **Parking:** valet only. B L D

SEBO
415/864-2122 **55**

▼▼ Sushi. Casual Dining. $6-$35 **AAA Inspector Notes:** Since opening in 2008, Sebo has quickly become San Francisco's hottest sushi bar and izakaya. The establishment offers the freshest sashimi from Tsukiji and local areas. **Bar:** beer & wine. **Address:** 517 Hayes St 94102 **Location:** Between Laguna and Octavia sts. Van Ness, 50. **Parking:** street only. D CALL M

SERPENTINE
415/252-2000 **131**

▼▼ California. Casual Dining. $11-$26 **AAA Inspector Notes:** Off the beaten path but worth the trip to find, this restaurant, with a minimalist industrial decor, is housed in the corner of a converted warehouse. Hamburger and fries never disappoint, but if it is on the menu, start with chicken livers and brown gravy-sop up the gravy with the bread. The lemon curd buttermilk cake is a good way to end the meal. **Bar:** full bar. **Address:** 2495 3rd St 94107 **Location:** At 22nd St. 20th St, 97. **Parking:** street only. L D

SHABUSEN RESTAURANT
415/440-0466 **37**

▼▼ Japanese Specialty. Casual Dining. $14-$45 **AAA Inspector Notes:** High ceilings and a contemporary décor are offered at this restaurant, one of the few offering both shabu shabu and sukiyaki. Go with a group and enjoy both dishes. There is individual eating at the counter. On a cold, rainy day, warm up with a delectable hot pot. **Bar:** beer & wine. **Address:** 1726 Buchanan St 94115 **Location:** Between Post and Sutter sts. Van Ness, 50. **Parking:** street only. L D

SHANGHAI DUMPLING KING
415/387-2088 **27**

▼▼ Chinese. Casual Dining. $6-$10 **AAA Inspector Notes:** People come to this hole-in-the-wall for the food not the decor. Packed wall-to-wall, this rustic eatery features home-style Shanghai food. Service is so basic that soups are brought to the table in the pot in which they were cooked. Order the pork preserved vegetable-fried rice cakes (actually it is stir fried), the Shanghai noodles and braised string beans. For dessert try the sugar egg puff. **Address:** 3319 Balboa St 94121 **Location:** Between 34th and 35th aves. **Parking:** street only. L D

SHOWDOGS
415/558-9560 **176**

▼ American. Quick Serve. $8-$15 **AAA Inspector Notes:** Adjacent to the Golden Gate Theater, patrons can stop in to catch a quick bite before or after a show. Try the lamb/pork dog, a traditional chili dog or a made-in-house sausage. They also serve chicken, fish and beef sandwiches. **Bar:** beer & wine. **Address:** 1020 Market St 94102 **Location:** At Golden Gate Ave. Powell Street, 33. **Parking:** street only. L D

THE SLANTED DOOR
415/861-8032 **90**

▼▼▼ Vietnamese. Casual Dining. $12-$38 **AAA Inspector Notes:** This restaurant serves creative Vietnamese cuisine in an above-average atmosphere. Guests are treated to a fantastic view of the Bay Bridge. Start with spring rolls, then a refreshing and bracing papaya salad, pork chop and a side of eggplant stir fried in coconut milk. Finish with a refreshing dessert of cherry tomatoes and buttermilk gelato with basil flavored syrup. **Bar:** full bar. **Reservations:** suggested. **Address:** 1 Ferry Building, Suite 3 94111 **Location:** On The Embarcadero. Embarcadero, 31. **Parking:** street only. L D CALL M

SLOW CLUB
415/241-9390 **115**

▼▼ California. Casual Dining. $11-$28 **AAA Inspector Notes:** Off the beaten path but worth the trip to find, this restaurant is housed in a corner of a converted warehouse. Soft music and plenty of candles soften the setting and boost the intimacy factor. Hamburger and fries never disappoint but if it is on the menu, start with the chicken livers and finish with brown gravy. Sop up the gravy with bread and proceed to your choice of entrée and finish with the lemon curd buttermilk cake. **Bar:** full bar. **Address:** 2501 Mariposa St 94110 **Location:** Corner of Mariposa and Hampshire sts. 16th Street Mission, 35. **Parking:** street only. L D CALL M

SOCIALE CAFFE & WINE BAR
415/921-3200 **22**

▼▼▼ Italian. Casual Dining. $12-$32 **AAA Inspector Notes:** Laughter and Italian music is heard while guests enjoy irresistible warm pasta, herb-infused meats and eclectic wines. **Bar:** beer & wine. **Address:** 3665 Sacramento St 94118 **Location:** Just w of jct Locust St; in Laurel Heights. **Parking:** street only. L D CALL M

SONS AND DAUGHTERS
415/391-8311 **105**

▼▼▼ California. Casual Dining. $20-$25 **AAA Inspector Notes:** Upon entering this restaurant, guests encounter a tiny open kitchen and then an elegant dining room with all kinds of rock music playing in the background. The young chefs and servers (the term Young Turks comes to mind) try out their culinary skills and do it well here. The theme is fine dining with reasonable prices in a casual atmosphere. Portions are small so try the four-course meal with a wine pairing to get the full experience. **Bar:** wine only. **Reservations:** suggested. **Address:** 708 Bush St 94108 **Location:** Between Powell and Mason sts. Montgomery Street, 32. **Parking:** street only. D

SPQR
415/771-7779 **32**

▼▼ Italian. Casual Dining. $18-$29 **AAA Inspector Notes:** A rustic contemporary décor, packed with tables (making it almost claustrophobic at peak hours), is made bearable at this eatery by the sophisticated, flavorful food and carefully chosen wine offerings from Italy by owner/sommelier, Shelley Lindgren. There is wine by the ounce, by the glass, half carafes and full bottles. **Bar:** beer & wine. **Reservations:** suggested. **Address:** 1911 Fillmore St 94115 **Location:** Between Bush and Pine sts. **Parking:** street only. D

SPRUCE
415/931-5100 **21**

▼▼▼ California. Fine Dining. $13-$39 **AAA Inspector Notes:** An impressive elegant decor with a casual feel can be found at this typical restaurant in an upscale neighborhood. Patrons can enjoy a burger and fries fried in duck fat and follow it up with a cup of fresh coffee-the beans were roasted just days ago at their Emeryville roastery. Their burger and fries were highly regarded in a local poll. A take-out shop offers cookies and cheese to go. **Bar:** full bar. **Reservations:** suggested. **Address:** 3640 Sacramento St 94118 **Location:** Between Locust and Spruce sts. **Parking:** valet and street only. L D

THE STINKING ROSE
415/781-7673 **47**

▼▼ ▼ Italian Casual Dining $10-$60 **AAA Inspector Notes:** In the city's Little Italy, this restaurant is known for its abundant use of garlic, which it publicizes via its motto: We season our garlic with food. The menu features grilled, baked and roasted dishes all cooked with plenty of garlic. Those who prefer can get some selections without the pungent herb. A huge garlic braid winds through the establishment. **Bar:** full bar. **Reservations:** suggested. **Address:** 325 Columbus Ave 94133 **Location:** Between Vallejo and Broadway sts; in North Beach area. Embarcadero, 31. **Parking:** street only. L D

STRAITS RESTAURANT
415/668-1783 **168**

▼▼▼ Philippine. Casual Dining. $10-$39 **AAA Inspector Notes:** Contemporary, high-energy décor is the perfect backdrop to enjoy boldly flavored Southeast Asian dishes. **Bar:** full bar. **Address:** 845 Market St 94118 **Location:** On 4th Floor of Westlake San Francisco Centre. Powell Street, 33. **Parking:** street only. L D

(See maps & indexes p. 394, 404.)

STRAW 415/431-3663 72
▼▼▼ American. Casual Dining. $12-$16 **AAA Inspector Notes:** Shabby chic meets circus decor at this casual eatery where comfort food with a twist is served. Start with easy cheese revisited-some house-fried potato chip nachos with sharp cheddar and bechamel cheese, scallions and diced tomatoes. Sandwiches range from the simple peanut butter and jelly to the bearded lady consisting of pulled pork with blackberry coulis and chipotle barbecue. Entrées change monthly. One of the yummy desserts is peanut butter, chocolate crust pie sprinkled with bacon bits. **Address:** 203 Octavia Blvd 94102 **Location:** At Page St. 🚇 Van Ness, 50. **Parking:** street only.
D 🅺 🚇

STREET RESTAURANT 415/775-1055 41
▼▼ Northern California. Casual Dining. $14-$24 **AAA Inspector Notes:** In the Russian Hill neighborhood, this boisterous bistro whips up full entrées and small plates of California cuisine with French influences. **Bar:** full bar. **Address:** 2141 Polk St 94109 **Location:** Between Broadway and Vallejo sts. **Parking:** street only.
D

SUPER DUPER BURGERS 415/558-8123 94
▼ American. Quick Serve. $5-$7 **AAA Inspector Notes:** Families are welcomed at this laid-back restaurant, which brings in plenty of loyal locals who enjoy its varied Italian favorites, including tempting pasta and chicken dishes. **Bar:** beer & wine. **Address:** 2304 Market St 94114 **Location:** Between 16th & Noe sts. **Parking:** street only. L D 🅺 🚇

SUPPENKUCHE 415/252-9289 54
▼▼ Traditional German. Casual Dining. $15-$20 **AAA Inspector Notes:** Rustic decor sets the mood for this German kitchen. Intriguing selections include venison medallions, pork loin and some vegetarian dishes. **Bar:** full bar. **Address:** 525 Laguna St 94102 **Location:** Jct Hayes St. 🚇 Van Ness, 50. **Parking:** valet and street only. D

SUZU NOODLE HOUSE 415/346-5083 38
▼▼ Noodles. Casual Dining. $8-$13 **AAA Inspector Notes:** Known to all ramen noodle buffs in the Bay Area, this small restaurant is always packed. They also offer sashimi appetizers and rice bowls. Try the non-traditional mabo tofu ramen. **Bar:** beer & wine. **Address:** 1825 Post St 94115 **Location:** Between Webster and Fillmore sts; in Japantown Mall. 🚇 Van Ness, 50. **Parking:** street only.
L D 🅺 🚇

THE TACO SHOP AT UNDERDOGS 415/566-8700 62
▼ Mexican. Casual Dining. $4-$9 **AAA Inspector Notes:** After exploring Golden Gate Park, refuel at this sports bar and check the scores of your favorite team. Serving tacos, quesadillas and burritos, this eatery's fish tacos placed well in a local poll two years in a row. They do not offer dessert, but there is a donut shop, yogurt shop and a Chinese dessert cafe nearby. **Bar:** full bar. **Address:** 1824 Irving St 94122 **Location:** Between 19th and 20th aves. 🚇 Judah & 19th Ave, 56. **Parking:** street only. L D 🅺 🚇

TADICH GRILL 415/391-1849 101
▼▼ Seafood. Casual Dining. $15-$45 **AAA Inspector Notes:** *Classic Historic.* Established in 1849, the original restaurant began during the California Gold Rush and is listed with the California Historical Society. This popular spot usually bustles, so be prepared to wait for a table. Varied beef, chicken and pasta dishes are available, but the fish plates get the gold star. Waiters are somewhat rough around the edges, but this adds to the ambience. **Bar:** full bar. **Address:** 240 California St 94111 **Location:** Between Battery and Front sts. 🚇 Embarcadero, 31. **Parking:** street only.
L D 🚇

TANDOORI MAHAL 415/951-0505 57
▼▼ Indian. Casual Dining. $10-$22 **AAA Inspector Notes:** The popular buffet option at this casual spot is available daily from 11:30 am to 2:30 pm. On the dinner menu is a large variety of Indian classics. **Bar:** beer & wine. **Address:** 941 Kearny St 94133 **Location:** Just n of jct Jackson St. 🚇 Embarcadero, 31. **Parking:** street only. L D CALL 🚹M 🚇

TARTINE BAKERY & CAFE 415/487-2600 108
▼ Breads/Pastries. Casual Dining. $4-$13 **AAA Inspector Notes:** Bread baked in a brick oven at this bakery complements such savories as foie gras and croque monsieur, and pastries are full of the good stuff: cream, butter, cheese and high-grade chocolate. This place off the beaten track, stays extremely busy. True lunch is not served until after noon, when it gets even busier. The seating area is cramped, tables are closely spaced and servers must squeeze between tables, but the food is worth any minimal discomfort or wait. **Bar:** wine only. **Address:** 600 Guerrero St 94110 **Location:** Jct 18th St; in Mission District. 🚇 Church & 18th St, 85. **Parking:** street only. B L D 🚇

TATAKI SOUTH 415/282-1889 141
▼▼ Japanese Sushi. Casual Dining. $11-$36 **AAA Inspector Notes:** With concern over diminishing catches of fish, this casual spot's claim to fame is being the first all-sustainable sushi bar in North America. Diners will not see blue fin toro, hamachi, octopus or farmed salmon (try the arctic char, instead) on this menu. Small Japanese izakaya plates are also part of the menu. The char carpaccio is rich, buttery with just enough citrus flavor to cut the richness. **Bar:** beer & wine. **Address:** 1740 Church St 94131 **Location:** Between 29th and Day sts. 🚇 Church & 30th St, 87. **Parking:** street only.
D 🅺 🚇

THAI SPICE 415/775-4777 61
▼▼ Thai Family Dining $8-$15 **AAA Inspector Notes:** A contemporary decor of industrial ceilings, warm-hued walls and a muted hanging lamplight offers up a romantic casual atmosphere at this eatery. A wide assortment of Thai favorites are served up appealingly in elegant plates with cute decorative squiggles of green and red pepper coulis. Try one of their petite exotic lychee (Chinese fruit) cocktails served in stacked, double glasses with an orchid, frozen cherry and of course, lychee skewered on bamboo. **Bar:** beer & wine. **Address:** 1730 Polk St 94109 **Location:** Between Clay and Washington sts. 🚇 Powell Street, 33. **Parking:** street only.
Menu on AAA.com L D 🚇

Dine in service and free delivery every day.

THEP PHANOM 415/431-2526 80
▼▼ Thai. Casual Dining. $10-$17 **AAA Inspector Notes:** Often busy, this smallish dining room lets loyal patrons relax over plates of well-prepared Thai food. **Bar:** beer & wine. **Address:** 400 Waller St 94117 **Location:** Jct Fillmore St. 🚇 Duboce & Church, 51. **Parking:** street only. D 🚇

THIRSTY BEAR BREWING CO. 415/974-0905 170
▼▼ Spanish Small Plates. Casual Dining. $8-$23 **AAA Inspector Notes:** So many tapas, so little time. Guests can prepare their taste buds for a number of tempting appetizers and Spanish eats. **Bar:** full bar. **Address:** 661 Howard St 94105 **Location:** Between Montgomery and 3rd sts. 🚇 Montgomery Street, 32. **Parking:** street only. L D CALL 🚹M 🚇

TIAN SING CHINESE RESTAURANT 415/398-1338 155
▼▼ Chinese. Casual Dining. $10-$36 **AAA Inspector Notes:** Well-lit and spacious, this restaurant serves dim sum all day. Prices are a bit on the high side due to its location near Union Square. **Bar:** beer & wine. **Address:** 138 Cyril Magnin St 94102 **Location:** Between Ellis and O'Farrell sts. 🚇 Powell Street, 33. **Parking:** street only. L D 🚇

TOMMASO'S RESTAURANT 415/398-9696 53
▼▼ Italian. Casual Dining. $15-$28 **AAA Inspector Notes:** This old-time Italian restaurant is in the heart of North Beach. Charming, homey and always crowded, the food is outstanding and the chewy, wood-fired pizza is among the best in the city. **Bar:** beer & wine. **Address:** 1042 Kearny St 94133 **Location:** Between Broadway and Columbus sts. 🚇 Embarcadero, 31.
D 🅺 🚇

TOMMY'S JOYNT
415/775-4216 [132]

American. Quick Serve. $6-$9 **AAA Inspector Notes:** Established in 1947, this San Francisco institution draws a devoted crowd of regulars who hang out at the bar. The food is unpretentious and good, and the ambience is classic neighborhood hangout. It is one of those places that San Franciscans take visitors to see. Walls and ceiling are adorned with memorabilia. Rock band Metallica and former Mayor Feinstein are some of the glitterati that have graced the bar/eatery with their presence. **Bar:** full bar. **Address:** 1101 Geary Blvd 94109 **Location:** At Van Ness. Civic Center/UN Plaza, 34. **Parking:** street only. L D LATE

TOMMY TOY'S HAUTE CUISINE
415/397-4888 [72]

New Chinese. Fine Dining. $14-$29 **AAA Inspector Notes:** Reminiscent of an Imperial Palace, the fantastic dining room at this eatery is the setting for classic French service and artistic presentations. **Bar:** full bar. **Reservations:** suggested. **Address:** 655 Montgomery St 94111 **Location:** In Financial District. Embarcadero, 31. **Parking:** on-site (fee) and valet. L D

TON KIANG RESTAURANT DIM SUM-SEAFOOD
415/752-4440 [25]

Chinese. Casual Dining. $9-$26 **AAA Inspector Notes:** Noted for its fine dim sum, this restaurant also presents a complete menu of traditional dishes from various regions in China. The specialty is fine-quality Hakka cuisine. Portions are generous. **Bar:** beer & wine. **Address:** 5821 Geary Blvd 94121 **Location:** Between 22nd and 23rd aves. **Parking:** street only. L D CALL

TONY'S PIZZA NAPOLETANA
415/835-9888 [33]

Pizza. Casual Dining. $12-$38 **AAA Inspector Notes:** World pizza-making champ Tony Gemignani's restaurant offers four types of pizza: Italian, American, Sicilian and Napoletana. All are baked in four ovens with different temperatures. Other offerings include calamari and pasta dishes. **Bar:** beer & wine. **Address:** 1570 Stockton St 94133 **Location:** Between Green and Union sts. Embarcadero, 31. **Parking:** street only. L D

TOWN HALL
415/908-3900 [148]

American. Casual Dining. $13-$30 **AAA Inspector Notes:** An elegant, rustic ambience, polished service and creative and sophisticated cuisine please this restaurant's patrons. Among entrees are sauteed Alaskan halibut with crawfish, grilled Niman Ranch rib-eye steak and roasted whole trout. Many imports appear on the good wine list. Creativity marks the desserts. **Bar:** full bar. **Reservations:** suggested. **Address:** 342 Howard St 94105 **Location:** Between Fremont and Beale sts. Embarcadero, 31. **Parking:** street only. L D

TOWN'S END RESTAURANT & BAKERY
415/512-0749 [188]

California. Casual Dining. $9-$18 **AAA Inspector Notes:** The goal at this eatery is to use as much organic and locally-sourced produce as possible during preparation. Mini muffins and homemade fruit butter complement the great breakfast offerings. A nightly three-course early bird special is offered. **Bar:** beer & wine. **Address:** 2 Townsend St 94107 **Location:** Jct The Embarcadero. Brannan, 91. **Parking:** street only. B L D CALL

TRATTORIA CONTADINA
415/982-5728 [27]

Italian. Casual Dining. $17-$28 **AAA Inspector Notes:** The intimate white-linen dining room and vintage photographs on the wall lend to a feeling of being at home. A hearty selection of Northern Italian dishes, such as ravioli correnti, linguine vongole and rigatoni melanzana, keeps guests coming back for more. **Bar:** full bar. **Reservations:** suggested. **Address:** 1800 Mason St 94133 **Location:** Corner of Mason and Union sts. Montgomery Street, 32. **Parking:** street only. L D

UNA PIZZA NAPOLETANA
415/861-3444 [85]

Italian Pizza. Casual Dining. **AAA Inspector Notes:** Am I in a pizza joint? More like a temple dedicated to the napoletana pizza. Décor is minimal to the point of sterility. The focal point is the wood-fired oven elegantly tiled in vibrant sky blue and the master pizzaiolo (pizza chef) in action. The menu is limited to five different 12-inch pizzas and drinks. **Bar:** beer & wine. **Address:** 210 11th St 94103 **Location:** At Howard St. Van Ness, 50. **Parking:** street only. D

UTOPIA CAFE
415/956-2902 [66]

Cantonese
Casual Dining
$6-$12

AAA Inspector Notes: This modest restaurant is known for rice in clay pot dishes. Order it first as it takes 20 minutes to prepare. Ask to have it crisp, pour some hot water over the crisp rice and you have sizzling rice soup. The rice porridge has a clean taste. Minimum credit card use is $15. Two-hour free parking is available at Portsmouth Garage(minimum $20 charge). **Bar:** beer & wine. **Address:** 139 Waverly Pl 94108 **Location:** Between Washington and Clay sts. Montgomery Street, 32. **Parking:** street only. L D

UVA ENOTECA
415/829-2024 [75]

Italian. Casual Dining. $14-$20 **AAA Inspector Notes:** This elegant and contemporary Italian bistro serves simple yet sophisticated dishes to accompany well-chosen wines. **Bar:** beer & wine. **Address:** 568 Haight St 94117 **Location:** Between Steiner and Fillmore sts. Duboce & Noe, 52. **Parking:** street only. D

VIVA GOA INDIAN CUISINE
415/440-2600 [4]

Indian. Casual Dining. $9-$16 **AAA Inspector Notes:** This restaurant is one of the very few restaurants specializing in Goan cuisine from southern India. Goa, with its palm trees and white sand beaches, is to Indians what Hawaii is to Americans. This state was under Portuguese control for 450 years until it was annexed in 1961 by India. Flavorful dishes feature Indian foods with strong Portuguese influences as well as use of local ingredients including coconut. Representative dishes are ricardo pomfret fish, chicken cafreal, beef asado, xacutis and vindaloo. **Bar:** beer & wine. **Address:** 2420 Lombard St 94123 **Location:** Between Scott and Divisadero sts. **Parking:** street only. L D

WALZWERK
415/551-7181 [96]

Eastern German. Casual Dining. $13-$18 **AAA Inspector Notes:** This restaurant brings East German cuisine to the masses. Try schnitzel or apple-stuffed chicken breast. **Bar:** beer & wine. **Address:** 381 S Van Ness Ave 94103 **Location:** Between 14th and 15th sts. 16th Street Mission, 35. **Parking:** street only. D

THE WATERFRONT RESTAURANT
415/391-2696 [52]

California Seafood. Fine Dining. $16-$35 **AAA Inspector Notes:** Panoramic views of the Bay Bridge can be found at this restaurant. Patrons can sample fresh seafood and good California wines all served by a seasoned efficient staff. **Bar:** full bar. **Reservations:** suggested. **Address:** Pier 7 94111 **Location:** Just n of the Ferry Building; on the Embarcadero at Broadway St. Embarcadero, 31. **Parking:** valet and street only. L D CALL

WAYFARE TAVERN
415/772-9060 [84]

American. Gastro Pub. $19-$32 **AAA Inspector Notes:** Food at celebrity chef Tyler Florence's first restaurant is mostly hearty ranging from deviled eggs to such exotics as uni (roe) with cauliflower pudding for appetizers. Entrée offerings, a nod to San Francisco classics, include the hangtown fry and a flavorful roasted duck with parsnip puree, prunes, bacon lardoon. For heartier appetites, try the braised short ribs. Make room for dessert and a cup of French press coffee. The multi-level tavern offers numerous seating options. **Bar:** full bar. **Reservations:** suggested. **Address:** 558 Sacramento St 94111 **Location:** Between Montgomery and Sansome sts. Embarcadero, 31. **Parking:** valet and street only. L D CALL

'WICHCRAFT
415/593-3895 [173]

Sandwiches. Quick Serve. $7-$10 **AAA Inspector Notes:** This spot is a contemporary sandwich restaurant with a distinguished pedigree. The owner/chef Tom Colicchio is the head judge of Bravo station's Top Chef television show. **Bar:** beer & wine. **Address:** 868 Mission St 94103 **Location:** Between 4th and 5th sts. Powell Street, 33. **Parking:** street only. B L D

WOODHOUSE FISH COMPANY
415/437-2722 (88)

▼▼ ▼▼ Seafood. Casual Dining. $10-$20 **AAA Inspector Notes:** This small, casual seafood restaurant is in a busy area yet it retains a neighborhood ambience. The charming decor features fish posters and fishing artifacts. When available, try the fried whole-belly Ipswich clams and a lobster roll. Finish with strawberry shortcake for a classic East Coast seafood meal. **Bar:** beer & wine. **Address:** 2073 Market St 94114 **Location:** At 14th St. Church, 60. **Parking:** street only.

L D X ⚒

YANK SING
415/541-4949 (137)

▼▼ ▼▼ Chinese. Casual Dining. $12-$25 **AAA Inspector Notes:** No menus are needed here, as guests just point as dishes are rolled by. Among choices are more than 60 varieties of fresh dim sum, including such specialties as pot stickers, steamed dumplings and spring rolls. **Bar:** beer & wine. **Address:** 49 Stevenson St 94105 **Location:** Between 1st and 2nd sts; near Union Square. Montgomery Street, 32. **Parking:** street only. L ⚒

ZARE AT FLY TRAP
415/243-0580 (171)

▼▼ ▼▼ Mediterranean. Casual Dining. $12-$27 **AAA Inspector Notes:** This elegant restaurant offers a vibrant ambience with upscale contemporary Persian and Mediterranean cuisine. For starters, try the pistachio meatballs, followed by oxtail tagliatelle. For a sweet treat, finish with Greek yogurt panna cotta and honey. **Bar:** full bar. **Address:** 606 Folsom St 94107 **Location:** At Second St. Montgomery Street, 32. **Parking:** street only.

L D X ⚒

ZARZUELA
415/346-0800 (24)

▼▼ ▼▼ Spanish. Casual Dining. $14-$21 **AAA Inspector Notes:** This restaurant serves fine tapas in an authentic Madrid-style setting, complete with Spanish music. It also serves its namesake, seafood stew. Other popular entrées include poached octopus, spicy shrimp with aioli, paella and escalvada. A good selection of Spanish wines is available. **Bar:** beer & wine. **Address:** 2000 Hyde St 94109 **Location:** Jct Hyde and Union sts. **Parking:** street only.

D X

ZAZIE
415/564-5332 (86)

▼▼ ◆ French. Casual Dining. $10-$22 **AAA Inspector Notes:** A local favorite, this charming neighborhood bistro draws a crowd, especially for brunch with their scrumptious food. Monday night is dining on the patio with your beloved pet. Tuesday is free corkage night. **Bar:** beer & wine. **Address:** 941 Cole St 94117 **Location:** Between Carl St and Parnassus Ave. Carl & Cole, 53. **Parking:** street only. B L D X ⚒

ZINGARI
415/885-8850 (134)

▼▼ ▼▼ ▼▼ Italian. Casual Dining. $12-$29 **AAA Inspector Notes:** Located in prime town heaven, this restaurant features beautiful marble floors and Italian villa-style murals, a perfect setting in which to enjoy country-style Italian cooking. Order the crab cakes for an appetizer, wild boar osso buco with mushroom risotto for an entrée and finish with the classic tiramisu. **Bar:** full bar. **Reservations:** suggested. **Address:** 501 Post St 94102 **Location:** Just w of Union Square at Mason St. Powell Street, 32. **Parking:** on-site (fee).

L D ⚒

ZUNI CAFE
415/552-2522 (78)

▼▼ ▼▼ California. Fine Dining. $15-$28 **AAA Inspector Notes:** Popular with the local crowd since it opened more than 20 years ago, this restaurant offers Californian cuisine in a casual atmosphere. Patrons can sample freshly shucked oysters at the copper-topped bar downstairs. The whole roasted chicken, which is worth a taste, must be ordered in advance, as it takes about an hour to cook. Just as tasty and prepared in less time is the hamburger with shoestring fries. Menus can change up to four times daily, and reservations are recommended. **Bar:** full bar. **Reservations:** suggested. **Address:** 1658 Market St 94102 **Location:** At Gough St. Van Ness, 50. **Parking:** valet and street only. L D X ⚒

ZUPPA
415/777-5900 (191)

▼▼ ▼▼ ▼▼ Italian. Casual Dining. $11-$24 **AAA Inspector Notes:** Contemporary decor with high industrial ceiling and exposed concrete walls gives this intimate restaurant a feeling of airiness. The dining area includes a balcony area, a bar area that seats around 12 and a show kitchen area. Pasta is made from scratch, pizza is of the thin crusted variety. The best deals are during happy hour, so go early. **Bar:** full bar. **Address:** 564 4th St 94107 **Location:** Just s of jct Bryant St. 4th & King, 93. **Parking:** street only.

L D ⚒

BENU
415/685-4860

[fyi] Not evaluated. Upscale restaurant features a la carte or tasting menus. Food choices are derived from a plethora of fine, global ingredients. **Address:** 22 Hawthorne St 94105 Montgomery Street, 32.

EL BURRITO EXPRESS
415/566-8300

[fyi] Not evaluated. This small, take-out oriented restaurant features large, tasty and inexpensive burritos. **Address:** 1601 Taraval St 94116 Taraval & 22nd Ave, 64.

GORDO TAQUERIA
415/387-4484

[fyi] Not evaluated. Established in 1977, this eatery features tasty tacos and burritos. **Address:** 2252 Clement St 94121

GRILL HOUSE MEDITERRANEAN
415/440-7786

[fyi] Not evaluated. This homey little restaurant dishes up such Middle Eastern specialties as lamb, beef and chicken shawarma wraps, feta cheese pie and piyaz (white bean salad with tomatoes, hard-boiled eggs, lemon juice and parsley). **Address:** 533 Jones St 94102 Powell Street, 33.

LUCE
415/616-6566

[fyi] Not evaluated. Inspirational Tuscan flavors infuse with seasonal freshness of Napa and Sonoma at this upscale restaurant. **Address:** 888 Howard St 94163 **Location:** Between 4th and 5th sts; in SoMa District (South of Market); in InterContinental San Francisco. Powell Street, 33.

SUNFLOWER RESTAURANT
415/626-5022

[fyi] Not evaluated. The smaller, more casual sister of a restaurant just around the corner on 16th Street, this eatery serves up homestyle Vietnamese cooking. Pho, the classic Vietnamese soup, is done well here—for $1 extra diners can get a generous addition of such mixed veggies as broccoli, zucchini, yellow squash, snow peas and cabbage. **Address:** 506 Valencia St 94103 16th Street Mission, 35.

TAQUERIA SAN FRANCISCO
415/641-1770

[fyi] Not evaluated. This modest, but popular restaurant features very good tacos and burritos. **Address:** 2794 24th St 94110 24th Street Mission, 36.

SANGER pop. 24,270

BLOSSOM TRAIL BED & BREAKFAST
559/875-6036

▼▼ ▼▼ ▼▼ Bed & Breakfast. Rates not provided. **Address:** 3700 S Newmark Ave 93657 **Location:** SR 180, 3.5 mi s on Reed Ave, 5 mi w on Goodfellow Ave to Newmark Ave, then just n. **Facility:** A relaxed country setting with beautifully landscaped rose and flower gardens awaits. Rooms are attractively appointed and spacious, and some offers views of the gardens. 5 units. 1 story, interior/exterior corridors.

CALL M 🛜 X 📞 / SOME UNITS W 🍴 📷 📖

WONDER VALLEY RANCH RESORT
(559)787-2551

▼▼ ▼▼ Ranch $149-$278 **Address:** 6450 Elwood Rd 93657 **Location:** SR 180, 7.8 mi n on Piedra Rd, 5.4 mi e. **Facility:** 53 units. 1 story, exterior corridors. **Terms:** closed 6/8-8/17, cancellation fee imposed. **Amenities:** high-speed Internet. **Pool(s):** 3 outdoor. **Activities:** whirlpool, canoeing, sailboats, 2 tennis courts, jogging, playground, sports court, game room, horseshoes, volleyball. *Fee:* horseback riding. **Guest Services:** coin laundry.

CALL M 🛶 🛜 X 📖 / SOME UNITS FEE 🐾 🍴 📷

SAN JOSE (E-9) pop. 945,942, elev. 94'

San Jose anchors the southern end of the San Francisco Peninsula, lying in the Santa Clara Valley between the Mount Hamilton and Santa Cruz ranges. Founded as Pueblo de San José de Guadalupe in November 1777, the settlement was established to raise crops and cattle for the nearby presidios of San Francisco and Monterey. In 1849 San Jose became the state's first capital, a distinction that lasted only until 1851. Flash forward more than a century: California's third most populous city gained a nickname, "Capital of Silicon Valley," for its central role in the technological innovations contributing to the dot.com revolution that exploded in the last half of the 1990s.

The Japanese-American Internment Memorial, downtown in front of the Robert Peckham Federal Building at 280 S. First St., remembers those citizens confined in the U.S. during World War II. Narrative panels relate the experiences of those detained during this period.

The historic, Moorish-style California Theatre, downtown at 345 S. First St., opened in 1927 as an ornate movie palace. Opulently restored, it is home to both Opera San Jose and Symphony Silicon Valley. For schedule and ticket information phone the opera company at (408) 437-4450 or the symphony at (408) 286-2600.

At the junction of I-280, I-680 and US 101, just off King Road—in the middle of bustling, high-tech San Jose—is Emma Prusch Farm Park, a reminder of the city's agricultural past. A barn, vintage farm equipment and fruit orchards are still at the site of this former dairy farm, as well as resident sheep, pigs, cows, geese and rabbits. It's a reminder of what life was like before the Santa Clara Valley hopped on the technological bandwagon; phone (408) 794-6262.

HP Pavilion at San Jose, at W. Santa Clara and Autumn streets, is home to the city's NHL hockey team, the San Jose Sharks. Other college and professional sporting events, concerts and live performances take place at the arena; phone (408) 287-9200 for ticket information. The San Jose State University Spartans play basketball at the San Jose Event Center, 7th and E. San Carlos streets; phone (408) 924-7589 for ticket information.

A year-end highlight is the ▽ San Jose Holiday Parade, complete with colorful floats, marching bands, drill teams, helium balloons, clowns and an appearance by Santa. A variety of cultural festivals, among them Japanese, Italian, Spanish, German, Portuguese and Vietnamese, as well as a Mexican Day of the Dead celebration, take place throughout the year. For schedule and event information contact the convention and visitors bureau.

There are more than 50 wineries in the San Jose area, ranging from family-run establishments to large corporate ventures. Throughout the year festivals, concerts and other events celebrate viticulture. Santa Clara Valley Transportation Authority provides transportation to regional wineries; phone (408) 321-2300 for additional information.

San Jose Convention & Visitors Bureau: 408 Almaden Blvd., San Jose, CA 95110. **Phone:** (408) 295-9600 or (800) 726-5673.

Self-guiding tours: Walking tour maps are available from the convention and visitors bureau and from the San Jose Visitor Information and Business Center, located in the lobby of the San Jose McEnery Convention Center at 150 W. San Carlos St.

Shopping areas: JCPenney, Macy's and Sears are the anchor stores at Eastridge Mall, east of US 101 on Tully Road. Westfield Oakridge, Blossom Hill Road and Santa Teresa Boulevard, has Macy's and Sears.

Great Mall of the Bay Area, off I-880 in nearby Milpitas, features more than 180 outlet stores, including Calvin Klein, Last Call by Neiman Marcus and Saks Fifth Avenue OFF 5th.

Santana Row, off Stevens Creek Boulevard between I-880, I-280 and Winchester Boulevard, is an upscale area featuring retailers like Anthropologie, Chico's, Crate & Barrel, Gucci and Sur La Table, as well as more than 30 restaurants. The San Jose Flea Market, 1590 Berryessa Rd., offers more than 2,000 booths and 25 restaurants, drawing as many as 80,000 people on a sunny weekend.

ALUM ROCK PARK is e. of US 101 on Alum Rock Ave.; use Penitencia Creek Rd. for vehicle access to the park. A 730-acre site in the foothills, the park offers scenic views of the Santa Clara Valley, picnic facilities, mineral springs, marked trails and the Youth Science Institute. The institute's nature center features animal exhibits such as birds of prey that have been injured and cannot be released back into the wild.

Landslides sometimes close the road through the park. Dogs are not permitted. **Hours:** Park open Tues.-Sun. 8 a.m.-half-hour after dusk. Institute open Tues.-Fri. noon-4, Sat. noon-4:30. Because of brush fire danger, the park may be closed at times June-Oct.; phone ahead. **Cost:** Free. Institute $1; 50¢ (ages 0-17). **Parking:** $6 per private vehicle Sat.-Sun. and holidays. Parking free other times. **Phone:** (408) 259-5477, or (408) 258-4322 for the institute.

CHILDREN'S DISCOVERY MUSEUM OF SAN JOSE, jct. Woz Way and Auzerais St., offers changing interactive exhibits and programs that lead children to discoveries about themselves and the world around them. Discovery Meadow in Guadalupe River Park surrounds the museum.

Hours: Mon.-Sat. 10-5, Sun. noon-5, Memorial Day-Labor Day; Tues.-Sat. 10-5, Sun. noon-5, rest of year. Closed Thanksgiving and Christmas. **Cost:**

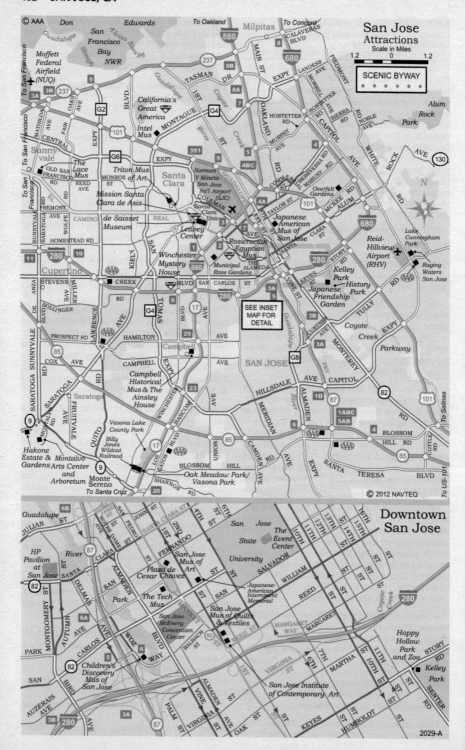

San Jose
Attractions
Scale in Miles
1.2   0   1.2

SCENIC BYWAY

© AAA

Don
Edwards
To Oakland
Milpitas
To Concord

Moffett
Federal
Airfield
(NUO)

Guadalupe

San
Francisco
Bay
NWR

Alviso
Slough

To San Francisco

To San Francisco

To San Francisco

Sunnyvale

The
Lace
Mus

Old San
Francisco
RD

REED
AVE

MONROE
ST

Triton Mus
of Art

Santa
Clara

Mission Santa
Clara de Asis

Santa
Clara
Univ

de Saisset
Museum

Leavey
Center

Winchester
Mystery
House

Municipal
Rose Gardens

CREEK

Campbell

Campbell
Historical
Mus & The
Ainsley
House

Vasona Lake
County Park

Billy
Jones
Wildcat
Railroad

Hakone
Estate & Montalvo
Gardens Arts Center
and
Arboretum

Monte
Sereno
To Santa Cruz

California's
Great
America

Intel
Mus

Normandy Mineta
San Jose
Int'l Airport
(SJC)

Coleman

Rosicrucian
Egyptian
Mus

THE
ALAMEDA

Japanese
American
Mus of
San Jose

Kelley
Park

Japanese
Friendship
Garden

History
Park

Coyote
Creek

SAN JOSE

Campbell

Oak Meadow Park/
Vasona Park

Blossom
Hill

Overfelt
Gardens

Reid-
Hillview
Airport
(RHV)

Lake
Cunningham
Park

Raging
Waters
San Jose

Alum
Rock
Park

Parkway

To Salinas

To US-101

© 2012 NAVTEQ

Downtown
San Jose

Guadalupe

HP
Pavilion
at
San Jose

San Jose
Mus of
Art

Plaza de
Cesar Chavez

The Tech
Mus

San Jose
McEnery
Convention
Center

Children's
Discovery
Mus of
San Jose

San
Jose
State
University

The
Event
Center

Japanese-
American
Internment
Memorial

San Jose
Mus of Quilts
& Textiles

San Jose Institute
of Contemporary Art

Happy
Hollow
Park
and Zoo

Kelley
Park

2029-A

(See maps & indexes p. 466, 468.)

$12; $11 (ages 60+); free (ages 0-1). Ages 0-12 must be with an adult. **Parking:** $5-$7. **Phone:** (408) 298-5437.

JAPANESE AMERICAN MUSEUM OF SAN JOSE is at 535 N. Fifth St., between Jackson and Empire sts. The museum focuses on Japanese American life in the Greater Bay Area from immigration during the early 1900s to the present. Exhibits include vintage vehicles and farm equipment as well as an authentic replica of a barracks room that served as living quarters for Japanese Americans incarcerated during World War II. Photographs and memorabilia chronicle the history of Japanese immigration to America in the 1890s and show how the people lived, worked and survived.

Knowledgeable docents are available to answer questions and provide background information. **Note:** The museum parking lot is very small, and street parking can be difficult. **Tours:** Guided tours are available. **Time:** Allow 1 hour, 30 minutes minimum. **Hours:** Thurs.-Sun. noon-4. Closed major holidays. Phone ahead to confirm schedule. **Cost:** $5; $3 (ages 12-17 and 65+). **Phone:** (408) 294-3138.

KELLEY PARK, at Senter and Story rds., is actually two parks—one geared toward children's activities, the other to area history and culture—as well as a Japanese-themed garden. **Hours:** Park open daily 8 a.m.-30 minutes after dusk. **Cost:** Free. **Parking:** $6-$10 per private vehicle. **Phone:** (408) 794-7275.

Happy Hollow Park and Zoo, 1300 Senter Rd., is a family park with a playground, riverboat replica, tree house, rides and a zoo. **Hours:** Mon.-Fri. 10-5, Sat.-Sun. 10-6, Memorial Day-Labor Day (weather permitting); Mon.-Fri. 10-4, Sat.-Sun. 10-5, rest of year. Closed Christmas. **Cost:** $12.95 (includes playground, rides and zoo); $9.95 (ages 70+); free (ages 0-1). **Parking:** $10. **Phone:** (408) 794-6400.

History Park, 1650 Senter Rd. at Phelan Ave., contains 27 structures that highlight the history and culture of San Jose and the Santa Clara Valley, depicting area life at the turn of the 20th century. Visitors can experience a Chinese temple and a Portuguese *império* (church), observe letterpress printing and hop aboard a historic trolley.

Time: Allow 2 hours minimum. **Hours:** Tues.-Sun. 11-5. Building exhibits and working print shop Sat.-Sun. 11-5. Closed major holidays. **Cost:** Sat.-Sun. admission (May-Oct.) $8; $5 (ages 65+ and students with ID); free (ages 0-5). Free to all Tues.-Fri. year-round and Sat.-Sun., Nov.-Apr. **Parking:** $6. **Phone:** (408) 287-2290.

Japanese Friendship Garden, jct. Senter and Story rds., features landscaping and lanterns representing Japanese culture. The garden is patterned after a park in Okayama, Japan—San Jose's sister city. **Hours:** Daily 10 a.m.-dusk. **Cost:** Free. **Parking:** $6. **Phone:** (408) 794-7275.

LICK OBSERVATORY is e. via Alum Rock Rd., then 19 mi. on narrow, winding Mount Hamilton Rd. (SR 130). The observatory, at the 4,209-foot summit of Mount Hamilton, was built in 1888 and is the center of observational astronomy for the University of California.

A visitor center in the Main Building contains exhibits, high-definition video displays and the original 36-inch refracting telescope. Guided tours, given in the dome of the 36-inch refractor, relate the history of the observatory and provide information about current research utilizing the nine telescopes at the mountaintop. A short walk leads to the Shane Dome, where the 120-inch reflector can be seen from a visitors gallery; the gallery also offers an audiovisual presentation and interpretive displays.

Note: Mount Hamilton Rd. is closed during heavy snowfalls and when there is snow at the observatory. Food and automotive services are not available. **Time:** Allow 2 hours minimum. **Hours:** Visitor center open daily noon-5, Memorial Day-Labor Day; Thurs.-Sun. noon-5, rest of year. Tours of the 36-inch Great Lick Refractor are given every half-hour. Visitor gallery at the 120-inch telescope open daily 10-5. Closed Thanksgiving, Christmas Eve and Christmas. Phone ahead to confirm schedule. **Cost:** Free. **Phone:** (408) 274-5061 for information and detailed directions.

MUNICIPAL ROSE GARDENS is on Naglee Ave. between Dana Ave. and Garden Dr. The gardens contain more than 5,000 plants and 189 varieties of roses. Peak bloom is in May and June, but the bushes bloom throughout the summer. **Time:** Allow 30 minutes minimum. **Hours:** Daily 8 a.m.-30 minutes after dusk. **Cost:** Free. **Phone:** (408) 794-7275.

OVERFELT GARDENS, Educational Park Dr. and McKee Rd., has a self-guiding arboreal trail, wildflower path, fragrance garden and three small lakes. The 5-acre Chinese Cultural Garden contains statues, memorials and displays devoted to ancient Chinese architecture and culture. **Time:** Allow 1 hour, 30 minutes minimum. **Hours:** Tues. 10 a.m.-dusk. **Cost:** Free. **Phone:** (408) 251-3323.

RAGING WATERS SAN JOSE is off Capitol Expwy. at Tully Rd., in Lake Cunningham Regional Park. This 23-acre water has a tropical look and offers more than 20 waterslides, an endless river and a wave pool. The popular Bombs Away drops thrillseekers through a trap door in a sealed capsule, sending them down an enclosed, looping flume.

Time: Allow 4 hours minimum. **Hours:** Opens daily at 10:30 a.m. mid-June to mid-Aug. (weather permitting); closing time varies. Schedule varies mid-May to mid-June and mid-Aug. to mid-Sept.; phone ahead to confirm. **Cost:** $33.99; $23.99 (under 48 inches tall); free (ages 0-2). **Parking:** $6-$10. **Phone:** (408) 238-9900.

(See maps & indexes p. 466, 468.)

ROSICRUCIAN EGYPTIAN MUSEUM [GEM] [SAVE] is at 1660 Park Ave. (between Naglee and Randol aves.). The museum building and its garden setting were designed to resemble the Temple of Amon at Karnak. The museum has a collection of Egyptian artifacts, including human and animal mummies, ancient ritual objects, textiles, musical instruments, toys, jewelry and other objects from daily and temple life; a replica of an Egyptian rock tomb; and Babylonian, Sumerian and Assyrian artifacts, including seals and tablets with examples of early writing.

Among the Egyptian artifacts visitors can see are a 5,000-year-old coffin, an ancient marriage contract, kohl mascara tubes and a fragment from "The Book of the Dead." The Rosicrucian Peace Garden is an educational garden authentic to the 18th dynasty of ancient Egypt, featuring an outdoor temple, arbor, plants and a reflection pond.

Time: Allow 2 hours minimum. **Hours:** Wed.-Fri. 9-5, Sat.-Sun. 10-6. Last admission 30 minutes before closing. Garden 8 a.m.-dusk. Closed major holidays. **Cost:** $9; $7 (ages 55+ and students with ID); $5 (ages 5-10). **Phone:** (408) 947-3636.

SAN JOSE INSTITUTE OF CONTEMPORARY ART, 560 S. First St., presents changing exhibits of contemporary art by Bay Area artists, including paintings, sculptures, photography and emerging media. **Time:** Allow 1 hour minimum. **Hours:** Tues.-Fri. 10-5, Sat. noon-5. **Cost:** Free. **Phone:** (408) 283-8155.

SAN JOSE MUSEUM OF ART, 110 S. Market St., was built in 1892 by local architect Willoughby Edbrooke. The museum contains changing exhibits of contemporary art. **Time:** Allow 2 hours minimum. **Hours:** Tues.-Sun. 11-5. Closed Jan. 1, Thanksgiving and Christmas. **Cost:** $8; $5 (ages 65+ and students with ID); free (ages 0-5). **Phone:** (408) 271-6840. [⑪]

SAN JOSE MUSEUM OF QUILTS & TEXTILES is at 520 S. First St. Exhibits at this museum explore the art, craft and history of quilts and textile-based art. Displays from the permanent collection, which rotate regularly, include historic quilts, quilts that are more contemporary art than traditional bed coverings, and costumes and garments from global cultures. There is a particular emphasis on Bay Area artists who are in the forefront of the quilting and textile arts revival that began in the last half of the 20th century and continues today.

Time: Allow 1 hour minimum. **Hours:** Tues.-Sun. 10-5 (also first Fri. of the month 7-11 p.m.). Closed major holidays. **Cost:** $8; $6.50 (ages 65+ and students with ID); free (ages 0-12 and to all first Fri. of the month). **Phone:** (408) 971-0323.

THE TECH MUSEUM is at jct. Park Ave. and [SAVE] Market St. You can't miss this mango-colored building, which has hundreds of hands-on interactive exhibits that show how technology affects everyday life. Subjects range from the human body to genetics research to Silicon Valley innovations.

Visitors can design virtual roller coasters, insert real DNA into bacteria, interact with exhibits using 3D computer vision and explore the basic technologies behind space exploration. Educational films are shown on an 8-story, 270-degree screen in the Hackworth IMAX Dome Theater. **Hours:** Opens daily at 10 a.m. Closing times vary; phone to confirm. Closed Christmas and in early Sept. **Cost:** Museum galleries only $12; $9 (ages 3-17 and 65+). Combination ticket with IMAX film $16; $13 (ages 3-17 and 65+). **Phone:** (408) 294-8324.

WINCHESTER MYSTERY HOUSE, 525 S. [GEM] Winchester Blvd. between I-280 and Stevens Creek Blvd., is a Victorian mansion that many believe was designed to baffle the spirits that haunted Sarah Winchester, heiress to the Winchester Arms fortune, and mistress of the house.

With 160 rooms, 2,000 doors, 13 bathrooms, 10,000 windows, 47 fireplaces, blind closets, secret passageways and 40 staircases, the house is so complex that even the owner and servants needed maps to find their way. The wooden home, bristling with a multitude of gables and cupolas, was under continuous construction for 38 years until the heiress passed away in 1922.

The Mansion Tour includes a 65-minute guided walk through the interior, a self-guiding tour of the Victorian gardens and access to two museums displaying collections of Winchester rifles and other products made by the arms manufacturing company. The 55-minute Behind-the-Scenes Tour shows how the estate operated while Mrs. Winchester lived in it. The Grand Estate Tour combines the Mansion and Behind-the-Scenes tours.

Time: Allow 2 hours minimum. **Hours:** Daily 8-7, Apr. 1-late Sept; daily 9-5, rest of year. Tour times vary; phone for schedule. Closed Christmas. **Cost:** Mansion Tour $30; $27 (ages 65+); $20 (ages 6-12); free (ages 0-5 with paying adult). Behind-the-Scenes Tour $27; $26 (ages 65+); $24 (ages 6-12). Grand Estate Tour $35; $32 (ages 65+); $30 (ages 6-12). Under 6 not permitted on Behind-the-Scenes or Grand Estate tours. **Phone:** (408) 247-2101

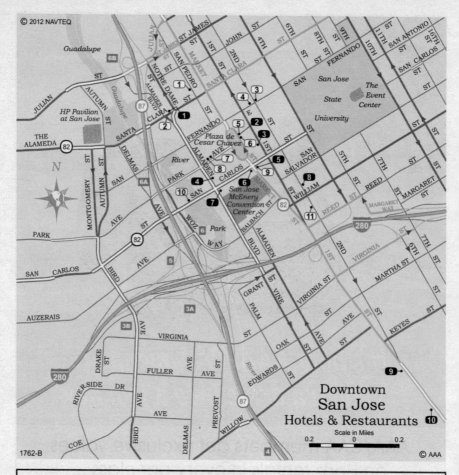

Downtown
San Jose
Hotels & Restaurants

Scale in Miles
0.2   0   0.2

© AAA

1762-B

Downtown San Jose

This index helps you "spot" where approved hotels and restaurants are located on the corresponding detailed maps. Hotel daily rate range is for comparison only. Restaurant price range is a combination of lunch and/or dinner. Turn to the listing page for more detailed rate and price information and consult display ads for special promotions.

DOWNTOWN SAN JOSE

Map Page	Hotels	Diamond Rated	Rate Range	Page
1 p. 466	**Hotel De Anza**	◇◇◇◇	$129-$399 SAVE	474
2 p. 466	**The Fairmont San Jose**	◇◇◇◇	$129-$429 SAVE	474
3 p. 466	**Four Points by Sheraton San Jose Downtown**	◇◇◇	$119-$299 SAVE	474
4 p. 466	**Hyatt Place San Jose/Downtown**	◇◇◇	$109-$285 SAVE	474
5 p. 466	The Sainte Claire Hotel	◇◇◇	Rates not provided	474
6 p. 466	**San Jose Marriott**	◇◇◇◇	$129-$319 SAVE	474
7 p. 466	**Hilton San Jose**	◇◇◇	$99-$319 SAVE	474
8 p. 466	**Ramada San Jose**	◇◇	$90-$120 SAVE	474
10 p. 466	**Americas Best Value Inn San Jose Convention Center**	◇◇	$79-$199 SAVE	474

Map Page	Restaurants	Diamond Rated	Cuisine	Price Range	Page
① p. 466	Peggy Sue's	◇	American	$5-$8	475
② p. 466	La Pastaia	◇◇◇	Italian	$13-$42	475
③ p. 466	P.F. Chang's China Bistro	◇◇◇	Chinese	$10-$20	475
④ p. 466	Gordon Biersch Brewery Restaurant	◇◇◇	American	$9-$25	474
⑤ p. 466	McCormick & Schmick's	◇◇◇	Seafood	$12-$35	475
⑥ p. 466	The Grill on the Alley	◇◇◇	American	$15-$52	475
⑦ p. 466	Morton's The Steakhouse	◇◇◇	Steak	$27-$52	475
⑧ p. 466	Peggy Sue's	◇	American	$5-$9	475
⑨ p. 466	Il Fornaio	◇◇◇	Italian	$9-$36	475
⑩ p. 466	Paolo's Restaurant	◇◇◇	Italian	$15-$37	475
⑪ p. 466	Emile's Restaurant	◇◇◇	French	$17-$39	474

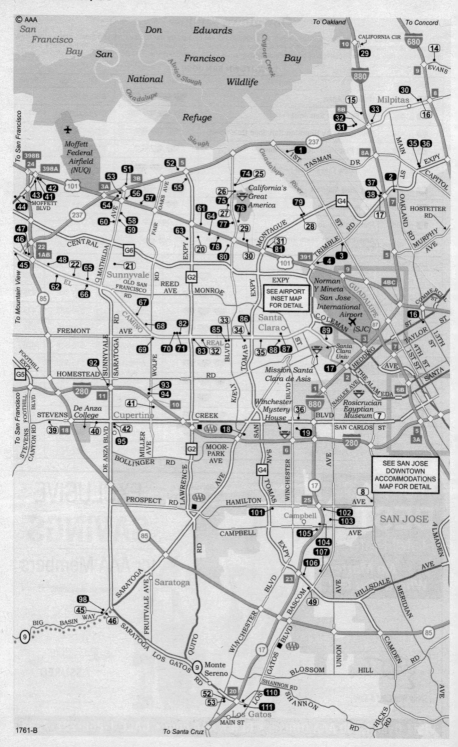

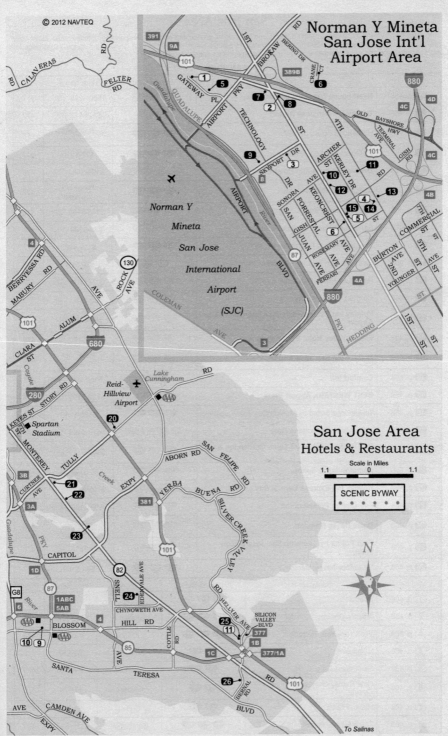

© 2012 NAVTEQ

Norman Y Mineta San Jose Int'l Airport Area

Norman Y Mineta San Jose International Airport (SJC)

San Jose Area
Hotels & Restaurants

Scale in Miles
1.1   0   1.1

SCENIC BYWAY

N

To Salinas

San Jose Area

This index helps you "spot" where approved hotels and restaurants are located on the corresponding detailed maps. Hotel daily rate range is for comparison only. Restaurant price range is a combination of lunch and/or dinner. Turn to the listing page for more detailed rate and price information and consult display ads for special promotions.

SAN JOSE

Map Page	Hotels	Diamond Rated	Rate Range	Page
❶ p. 468	Hyatt house San Jose/Silicon Valley	◆◆◆	$89-$249 SAVE	477
❷ p. 468	Quality Inn San Jose Airport	◆◆	$70-$141 SAVE	477
❸ p. 468	Homewood Suites by Hilton	◆◆◆	Rates not provided	476
❹ p. 468	La Quinta Inn San Jose Airport	◆◆◆	$77-$210	477
❺ p. 468	DoubleTree by Hilton Hotel San Jose	◆◆◆◆	$199-$459 SAVE	476
❻ p. 468	Staybridge Suites San Jose	◆◆◆	Rates not provided	478
❼ p. 468	Fairfield Inn & Suites	◆◆◆	$145-$160 SAVE	476
❽ p. 468	San Jose Airport Garden Hotel	◆◆◆	$89-$209 SAVE	477
❾ p. 468	San Jose Airport Courtyard	◆◆◆	$119-$269	477
❿ p. 468	Extended StayAmerica-San Jose-Downtown	◆◆	$89-$104	476
⓫ p. 468	Radisson Hotel, San Jose Airport	◆◆◆	$79-$209 SAVE	477
⓬ p. 468	Comfort Suites Airport	◆◆◆	$80-$150 SAVE	475
⓭ p. 468	Holiday Inn Express-San Jose International Airport	◆◆◆	$84-$189 SAVE	476
⓮ p. 468	Silicon Valley Hotel San Jose Airport	◆◆◆	$115-$170 SAVE	478
⓯ p. 468	Holiday Inn San Jose Airport	◆◆◆	Rates not provided SAVE	476
⓰ p. 468	Comfort Inn	◆◆	$85-$195 SAVE	475
⓱ p. 468	BEST WESTERN Airport Plaza	◆◆	$129-$199 SAVE	475
⓲ p. 468	TownePlace Suites by Marriott San Jose/Cupertino	◆◆◆	$129-$249	478
⓳ p. 468	Hotel Valencia Santana Row	◆◆◆◆	$419-$499 SAVE	477
⓴ p. 468	BEST WESTERN PLUS Lanai Garden Inn & Suites	◆◆◆	$109-$139 SAVE	475
21 p. 468	Hampton Inn & Suites	◆◆◆	$98-$142 SAVE	476
22 p. 468	Holiday Inn Express Central City	◆◆◆	$109-$189 SAVE	476
23 p. 468	The Clarion President Inn	◆◆◆	$99-$139 SAVE	475
24 p. 468	Dolce Hayes Mansion	◆◆◆	Rates not provided SAVE	476
25 p. 468	Four Points by Sheraton San Jose Silicon Valley	◆◆◆	$89-$204 SAVE	476
26 p. 468	Residence Inn by Marriott	◆◆◆	$94-$169	477

Map Page	Restaurants	Diamond Rated	Cuisine	Price Range	Page
① p. 468	Spencer's	◆◆◆	Steak	$15-$50	479
② p. 468	Amalfi's Grill	◆◆◆	Italian	$12-$24	478
③ p. 468	Vito's New York Trattoria	◆◆◆	Italian	$10-$29	479
④ p. 468	Island Grill	◆◆	American	$9-$30	478
⑤ p. 468	San Fresco Cafe	◆◆	American	$10-$20	479
⑥ p. 468	Jade Cathay Chinese Seafood Cuisine	◆◆	Chinese	$7-$24	478
⑦ p. 468	Habana Cuba	◆◆	Cuban	$9-$32	478
⑧ p. 468	Three Flames Restaurant	◆◆◆	Continental	$15-$30	479

Map Page	Restaurants (cont'd)	Diamond Rated	Cuisine	Price Range	Page
⑨ p. 468	P.F. Chang's China Bistro	▽▽▽	Chinese	$10-$20	478
⑩ p. 468	The Cheesecake Factory	▽▽▽	American	$8-$20	478
⑪ p. 468	The Summit Sports Bar & Grill	▽▽	American	$8-$25	479

MILPITAS

Map Page	Hotels	Diamond Rated	Rate Range	Page
㉙ p. 468	Residence Inn by Marriott	▽▽▽	$109-$249	197
㉚ p. 468	Embassy Suites Milpitas/Silicon Valley	▽▽▽	$109-$259	197
㉛ p. 468	Hilton Garden Inn-San Jose/Milpitas	▽▽▽	$94-$329	197
㉜ p. 468	Larkspur Landing Milpitas/San Jose	▽▽▽	$99-$269	197
㉝ p. 468	**BEST WESTERN PLUS Brookside Inn**	▽▽▽	$99-$169 SAVE	196
㉟ p. 468	TownePlace Suites by Marriott	▽▽▽	$109-$249	198
㊱ p. 468	Milpitas Courtyard by Marriott	▽▽▽	$109-$249	197
㊲ p. 468	**Sheraton San Jose Hotel**	▽▽▽	$99-$269 SAVE	198
㊳ p. 468	**Beverly Heritage Hotel** (See ad p. 197.)	▽▽▽	$69-$239 SAVE	197

Map Page	Restaurants	Diamond Rated	Cuisine	Price Range	Page
⑭ p. 468	Chez Christina	▽▽	Vietnamese	$8-$20	198
⑮ p. 468	On The Border Mexican Grill & Cantina	▽▽	Mexican	$10-$20	198
⑯ p. 468	Swan Court Cafe	▽▽	American	$10-$25	198
⑰ p. 468	**Brandon's** (See ad p. 197.)	▽▽▽	California	$10-$35	198

MOUNTAIN VIEW

Map Page	Hotels	Diamond Rated	Rate Range	Page
㊶ p. 468	**Quality Inn & Suites at NASA Ames**	▽▽▽	$100-$200 SAVE	231
㊷ p. 468	Ramada Limited	▽▽	$99-$159	231
㊸ p. 468	County Inn	▽▽	$79-$169	230
㊹ p. 468	Hampton Inn & Suites	▽▽▽	$169-$219	230
㊺ p. 468	Hotel Strata - Mountain View Town Center	▽▽▽	$130-$280	230
㊻ p. 468	Extended StayAmerica-San Jose, Mountain View	▽▽	$119-$134	230
㊼ p. 468	**Hotel Zico** (See ad p. 231.)	▽▽▽	Rates not provided SAVE	231
㊽ p. 468	Hotel Avante, a Joie de Vivre hotel	▽▽▽	$89-$499	230

SUNNYVALE

Map Page	Hotels	Diamond Rated	Rate Range	Page
㊿ p. 468	**Sheraton Sunnyvale**	▽▽▽	$89-$329 SAVE	537
㊾ p. 468	**Country Inn & Suites By Carlson, Sunnyvale**	▽▽▽	$89-$350 SAVE	536
㊾ p. 468	Days Inn & Suites, Sunnyvale Sundowner	▽▽▽	$69-$89	536
㊾ p. 468	**Staybridge Suites**	▽▽▽	$140-$269 SAVE	537
㊾ p. 468	Quality Inn Santa Clara Convention Center	▽▽▽	$79-$189	537
㊾ p. 468	**Quality Inn & Suites-Sunnyvale/Silicon Valley**	▽▽	$69-$139 SAVE	537
㊾ p. 468	**Americas Best Value Inn**	▽▽	Rates not provided SAVE	536
㊾ p. 468	Larkspur Landing Sunnyvale	▽▽▽	$99-$199	536
㊾ p. 468	**BEST WESTERN PLUS Silicon Valley Inn**	▽▽▽	$89-$139 SAVE	536
60 p. 468	**Comfort Inn**	▽▽▽	$69-$189 SAVE	536

SUNNYVALE (cont'd)

Map Page	Hotels (cont'd)	Diamond Rated	Rate Range	Page
61 p. 468	**Ramada Inn-Silicon Valley**	◆◆	$69-$104 SAVE	537
62 p. 468	TownePlace Suites by Marriott Sunnyvale/Mountain View	◆◆◆	$129-$249	537
63 p. 468	Residence Inn by Marriott Sunnyvale Silicon Valley II	◆◆◆	$129-$239	537
64 p. 468	Residence Inn by Marriott Silicon Valley I	◆◆◆	$169-$289	537
65 p. 468	Grand Hotel	◆◆◆	Rates not provided	536
66 p. 468	Quality Inn Sunnyvale Civic Center	◆◆	$89-$169	537
67 p. 468	**Maple Tree Inn**	◆◆◆	$109-$169 SAVE	536
68 p. 468	Corporate Inn // Sunnyvale	◆◆◆	$79-$269	536
69 p. 468	Wild Palms Hotel	◆◆◆	$99-$209	537
70 p. 468	Comfort Inn Sunnyvale	◆◆	$69-$249	536
71 p. 468	Domain Hotel, a Joie de Vivre hotel	◆◆◆	Rates not provided	536

Map Page	Restaurants	Diamond Rated	Cuisine	Price Range	Page
20 p. 468	Faultline Brewing Company	◆◆	American	$10-$30	537
21 p. 468	Tarragon Restaurant	◆◆◆	California	$8-$27	538
22 p. 468	Pezzella's Villa Napoli	◆◆◆	Italian	$8-$26	538

SANTA CLARA

Map Page	Hotels	Diamond Rated	Rate Range	Page
74 p. 468	**Hyatt Regency Santa Clara**	◆◆◆◆	$72-$288 SAVE	487
75 p. 468	**Hilton Santa Clara Hotel**	◆◆◆◆	$95-$389 SAVE	487
76 p. 468	Santa Clara Marriott Hotel	◆◆◆	$99-$319	487
77 p. 468	**Avatar Hotel Great America**	◆◆◆	$79-$249 SAVE	486
78 p. 468	**The Plaza Suites**	◆◆◆	$139-$272 SAVE	487
79 p. 468	**Hyatt house Santa Clara/San Jose Airport**	◆◆◆	$99-$269 SAVE	487
80 p. 468	Embassy Suites Hotel	◆◆◆	$109-$279	486
81 p. 468	**Biltmore Hotel & Suites/Silicon Valley**	◆◆◆	$129-$299 SAVE	486
82 p. 468	**BEST WESTERN Inn Santa Clara**	◆◆	$99-$199 SAVE	486
83 p. 468	**Vagabond Inn Santa Clara**	◆◆	$59-$199 SAVE	487
85 p. 468	**Quality Inn & Suites Silicon Valley**	◆◆	$94-$105 SAVE	487
86 p. 468	Holiday Inn Express & Suites Santa Clara-Silicon Valley	◆◆◆	Rates not provided	487
87 p. 468	Ramada	◆◆	$79-$129	487
88 p. 468	Holiday Inn Express & Suites	◆◆◆	$119-$209	487
89 p. 468	Candlewood Suites-Silicon Valley/San Jose	◆◆	$119-$159	486

Map Page	Restaurants	Diamond Rated	Cuisine	Price Range	Page
25 p. 468	TusCA	◆◆◆	Regional Italian	$10-$30	488
26 p. 468	**La Fontana**	◆◆◆	Mediterranean	$10-$24	488
27 p. 468	Old Ironsides Cafe	◆	Mediterranean	$6-$10	488
28 p. 468	Piatti Ristorante & Bar	◆◆◆	Italian	$12-$32	488
29 p. 468	Birk's Restaurant	◆◆◆	American	$13-$42	488
30 p. 468	Pedro's Restaurant & Cantina	◆◆	Mexican	$10-$20	488

Map Page	Restaurants (cont'd)	Diamond Rated	Cuisine	Price Range	Page
31 p. 468	Montague's Cafe	◆◆	American	$9-$20	488
32 p. 468	En Japanese Tapas Restaurant	◆◆	Japanese	$6-$22	488
33 p. 468	Cherry Sushi	◆◆◆	Japanese	$8-$29	488
34 p. 468	Mariani's	◆◆	Italian	$9-$26	488
35 p. 468	La Paloma Restaurante	◆◆	Mexican	$10-$20	488
36 p. 468	The Cheesecake Factory	◆◆◆	American	$9-$30	488

CUPERTINO

Map Page	Hotels	Diamond Rated	Rate Range	Page
92 p. 468	Cupertino Inn	◆◆◆	Rates not provided	92
93 p. 468	**Hilton Garden Inn**	◆◆◆	$94-$227 SAVE	92
94 p. 468	Courtyard by Marriott	◆◆◆	$119-$269	92
95 p. 468	**Cypress Hotel**	◆◆◆◆	$84-$319 SAVE	92

Map Page	Restaurants	Diamond Rated	Cuisine	Price Range	Page
39 p. 468	Blue Pheasant Restaurant	◆◆	American	$8-$32	92
40 p. 468	Fontana's Italian Restaurant	◆◆◆	Italian	$12-$34	92
41 p. 468	**Alexander's Steakhouse**	◆◆◆◆	Steak	$16-$155	92
42 p. 468	**Park Place**	◆◆◆	American	$10-$30	92

SARATOGA

Map Page	Hotel	Diamond Rated	Rate Range	Page
98 p. 468	The Inn at Saratoga	◆◆◆	$199-$299	510

Map Page	Restaurants	Diamond Rated	Cuisine	Price Range	Page
45 p. 468	The Plumed Horse	◆◆◆◆	California	$34-$85	510
46 p. 468	La Fondue	◆◆◆	Fondue	$31-$50	510

CAMPBELL

Map Page	Hotels	Diamond Rated	Rate Range	Page
101 p. 468	Larkspur Landing Campbell	◆◆◆	Rates not provided	66
102 p. 468	Courtyard by Marriott San Jose/Campbell	◆◆◆	$119-$229	66
103 p. 468	The PruneYard Plaza Hotel	◆◆◆	$209-$269	66
104 p. 468	**Campbell Inn**	◆◆◆	$99-$249 SAVE	66
105 p. 468	TownePlace Suites by Marriott-San Jose/Campbell	◆◆◆	$129-$249	66
106 p. 468	Carlyle Hotel	◆◆	Rates not provided	66
107 p. 468	Residence Inn by Marriott-San Jose	◆◆◆	$113-$199	66

Map Page	Restaurant	Diamond Rated	Cuisine	Price Range	Page
49 p. 468	Al Castello Ristorante	◆◆	Italian	$8-$14	66

LOS GATOS

Map Page	Hotels	Diamond Rated	Rate Range	Page
110 p. 468	**Los Gatos Motor Inn**	◆◆	$120-$200 SAVE	181
111 p. 468	**Los Gatos Lodge**	◆◆◆	$109-$229 SAVE	181

Map Page	Restaurants	Diamond Rated	Cuisine	Price Range	Page
52 p. 468	Pedro's Restaurant & Cantina	◆◆	Mexican	$10-$22	181
53 p. 468	Manresa	◆◆◆◆	French	$95-$160	181

DOWNTOWN SAN JOSE

• Hotels & Restaurants map & index p. 466

AMERICAS BEST VALUE INN SAN JOSE CONVENTION CENTER
(408)993-1711 **10**

Motel
$79-$199

Address: 1415 Monterey Rd 95110 **Location:** 1 mi s of I-280 and SR 82 via S 1st St. **Facility:** 26 units. 2 stories, exterior corridors. **Terms:** cancellation fee imposed. **Amenities:** high-speed Internet, safes. **Free Special Amenities:** early check-in/late check-out and high-speed Internet.

THE FAIRMONT SAN JOSE
(408)998-1900 **2**

Hotel
$129-$429

Address: 170 S Market St 95113 **Location:** At Fairmont Plaza. **Location:** Located walking distance of the convention center, this hotel features an elegant ambiance. Poolside lanais adjoin some rooms. 805 units. 20 stories, interior corridors. **Parking:** valet only. **Terms:** 3 day cancellation notice. **Amenities:** *Fee:* video games, high-speed Internet. *Some:* safes. **Dining:** 4 restaurants, also, The Grill on the Alley, see separate listing. **Pool(s):** heated outdoor. **Activities:** saunas, spa. **Guest Services:** valet laundry.

FOUR POINTS BY SHERATON SAN JOSE DOWNTOWN
(408)282-8800 **3**

Hotel
$119-$299

FOUR POINTS BY SHERATON **AAA Benefit:** Members get up to 20% off, plus Starwood Preferred Guest® bonuses.

Address: 211 S 1st St 95113 **Location:** Between E San Carlos and E San Fernando sts; center. **Facility:** 86 units. 4 stories, interior corridors. **Parking:** on-site (fee). **Terms:** 7 day cancellation notice-fee imposed. **Amenities:** high-speed Internet, safes. **Activities:** exercise room. **Guest Services:** valet laundry. **Free Special Amenities:** newspaper and high-speed Internet.

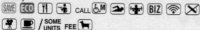

HILTON SAN JOSE
(408)287-2100 **7**

Hotel
$99-$319

Hilton **AAA Benefit:** Members save 5% or more!

Address: 300 Almaden Blvd 95110 **Location:** SR 87 exit Santa Clara St E, 0.4 mi s; at W San Carlos St. Adjacent to convention center. **Facility:** 353 units. 18 stories, interior corridors. **Parking:** on-site (fee). **Terms:** check-in 4 pm, 1-7 night minimum stay, cancellation fee imposed. **Amenities:** *Fee:* video games, high-speed Internet. **Pool(s):** heated outdoor. **Activities:** whirlpool, exercise room. **Guest Services:** valet and coin laundry. **Free Special Amenities:** local telephone calls and use of on-premises laundry facilities.

HOTEL DE ANZA
(408)286-1000 **1**

Hotel
$129-$399

Address: 233 W Santa Clara St 95113 **Location:** SR 87 exit Santa Clara St, just e. **Facility:** This attractively restored 1931 hotel has reintroduced elegance to the downtown scene; its public areas and guest units are well appointed. 101 units. 10 stories, interior corridors. **Parking:** valet only. **Terms:** cancellation fee imposed. **Amenities:** high-speed Internet (fee). **Dining:** La Pastaia, see separate listing, entertainment. **Activities:** exercise room. **Guest Services:** valet laundry. **Free Special Amenities:** newspaper and high-speed Internet.

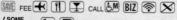

HYATT PLACE SAN JOSE/DOWNTOWN
(408)998-0400 **4**

Hotel
$109-$285

HYATT PLACE® **AAA Benefit:** Members save 10% or more everyday.

Address: 282 Almaden Blvd 95113 **Location:** I-280 exit Almaden-Vine, 6 blks n. Opposite convention center. **Facility:** 232 units. 9 stories, interior corridors. **Parking:** on-site (fee). **Terms:** cancellation fee imposed. **Amenities:** *Some:* high-speed Internet (fee). **Activities:** exercise room. **Guest Services:** valet laundry. **Free Special Amenities:** expanded continental breakfast and high-speed Internet.

RAMADA SAN JOSE
(408)298-3500 **8**

Hotel
$90-$120

Address: 455 S 2nd St 95113 **Location:** SR 82, just e. **Facility:** 72 units. 3 stories, exterior corridors. **Pool(s):** outdoor. **Activities:** exercise room. **Guest Services:** valet laundry. **Free Special Amenities:** continental breakfast and high-speed Internet.

THE SAINTE CLAIRE HOTEL
408/295-2000 **5**

Historic Hotel. Rates not provided. **Address:** 302 S Market St 95113 **Location:** SR 87 exit Santa Clara St E, s on Almaden Blvd, then just e on San Carlos St. Opposite convention center and Fairmont Square. **Facility:** This beautifully restored 1926 hotel features spacious and attractively appointed public spaces. 171 units. 6 stories, interior corridors. **Parking:** valet only. **Amenities:** safes. **Dining:** Il Fornaio, see separate listing. **Activities:** exercise room. **Guest Services:** valet laundry.

SAN JOSE MARRIOTT
(408)280-1300 **6**

Hotel
$129-$319

Marriott HOTELS & RESORTS **AAA Benefit:** AAA hotel discounts of 5% or more.

Address: 301 S Market St 95113 **Location:** SR 87 exit Santa Clara St E, s on Almaden Blvd, then just e on San Carlos St. Adjacent to Fairmont Square. **Facility:** Offering views of the surrounding mountains, this property is located in the downtown area adjacent to the San Jose Convention Center. 506 units. 26 stories, interior corridors. **Parking:** on-site (fee) and valet. **Amenities:** safes. *Fee:* video games, high-speed Internet. **Dining:** 2 restaurants. **Pool(s):** heated outdoor. **Activities:** whirlpool, exercise room. **Guest Services:** valet and coin laundry. **Free Special Amenities:** newspaper.

WHERE TO EAT

EMILE'S RESTAURANT
408/289-1960 **11**

French. Fine Dining. $17-$39 **AAA Inspector Notes:** Classic French specialties reflect an emphasis on healthy preparation. The atmosphere is warm and inviting. **Bar:** full bar. **Reservations:** suggested. **Address:** 545 S 2nd St 95112 **Location:** Between E William and E Reed sts. **Parking:** valet only. D

GORDON BIERSCH BREWERY RESTAURANT
408/294-6785 **4**

American. Casual Dining. $9-$25 **AAA Inspector Notes:** As the name implies this restaurant features fresh, brewed-on-site beer which is crafted in a German tradition. What may not be evident is the wide variety of foods like meal-sized salads, burgers and sandwiches, pizza, pastas, steaks and seafood that is also a huge draw for an upscale, casual dining experience. **Bar:** full bar. **Address:** 33 E San Fernando St 95113 **Location:** SR 87 exit Santa Clara St, 0.3 mi e, just s on Market St, then just e. **Parking:** on-site and street. L D CALL

(See map & index p. 466.)

THE GRILL ON THE ALLEY
408/294-2244

▼▼▼▼ American. Fine Dining. $15-$52 **AAA Inspector Notes:** This spot is well known among locals who visit for varied grilled meats and fish entrees, as well as traditional comfort foods, all of which are served in hearty portions. **Bar:** full bar. **Reservations:** suggested. **Address:** 172 S Market St 95113 **Location:** At Fairmont Plaza; in The Fairmont San Jose. **Parking:** on-site (fee).

L D CALL M

IL FORNAIO
408/271-3366 9

▼▼▼▼ Italian. Fine Dining. $9-$36 **AAA Inspector Notes:** Accomplished servers begin guests' experiences with crisp, crusty bread hot from the oven. Pasta and flavorful sauces enhance the roasted meats and vegetables. The spacious restaurant thoughtfully replicates the trattorias of Italy. **Bar:** full bar. **Reservations:** suggested. **Address:** 302 S Market St 95113 **Location:** SR 87 exit Santa Clara St, s on Almaden Blvd, then just e on San Carlos St; in The Sainte Claire. **Parking:** on-site (fee).

B L D CALL M

LA PASTAIA
408/286-8686 2

▼▼▼▼ Italian. Fine Dining. $13-$42 **AAA Inspector Notes:** In an historic 1931 hotel, this dining room is where guests savor tasty Italian dishes from both the lunch and dinner menus. In addition to the special pasta dishes, they also offer roasted chicken with soft polenta, osso buco and assorted cuts of beef. **Bar:** full bar. **Reservations:** suggested. **Address:** 233 W Santa Clara St 95113 **Location:** SR 87 exit Santa Clara St, just e; in Hotel De Anza. **Parking:** valet and street only. B L D CALL M

MCCORMICK & SCHMICK'S
408/283-7200 5

▼▼▼▼ Seafood. Fine Dining. $12-$35 **AAA Inspector Notes:** This place is all about seafood, which is imported from all over the world. Among good choices are Washington state oysters, Maine clams, delicate Hawaiian escolar and tuna from Ecuador. The club-like decor is cozy and the staff is attentive. **Bar:** full bar. **Reservations:** suggested. **Address:** 170 S Market St 95113 **Location:** At Fairmont Plaza. **Parking:** on-site (fee). L D CALL M

MORTON'S THE STEAKHOUSE
408/947-7000 7

▼▼▼▼ Steak. Fine Dining. $27-$52 **AAA Inspector Notes:** Patrons should make sure to reserve ahead for the popular, well-known steakhouse. Large portions, including huge cuts of fine beef and plentiful seafood, are the norm. Even the vegetables are oversized, with baked potatoes big enough for sharing. **Bar:** full bar. **Reservations:** suggested. **Address:** 177 Park Ave 95113 **Location:** SR 87 exit Santa Clara St E, s on Almaden Blvd, then just e; across from Tech Museum. **Parking:** on-site (fee). D CALL M

PAOLO'S RESTAURANT
408/294-2558 10

▼▼▼▼ Italian. Fine Dining. $15-$37 **AAA Inspector Notes:** The contemporary Italian menu lists pasta, veal and salmon preparations. Pasta is homemade daily. Guests can unwind in the attractive dining room overlooking a park-like setting. **Bar:** full bar. **Reservations:** suggested. **Address:** 333 W San Carlos St, Suite 150 95110 **Location:** Just e of SR 87. **Parking:** on-site (fee). L D

PEGGY SUE'S
408/294-0252 8

▼ American. Quick Serve. $5-$9 **AAA Inspector Notes:** This newer addition continues the tradition of serving breakfast dishes, great hamburgers, shakes and side orders in a '50s-type atmosphere. **Bar:** beer & wine. **Address:** 183 Park Ave 95113 **Location:** Opposite Tech Museum. **Parking:** street only.

B L D CALL M

PEGGY SUE'S
408/298-6750 1

▼ American. Quick Serve. $5-$8 **AAA Inspector Notes:** Serving the area since 1958, the diner serves breakfast items, great hamburgers, shakes and side orders in the atmosphere of the '50s era. **Bar:** beer & wine. **Address:** 29 N San Pedro St 95110 **Location:** In historic San Pedro Square. **Parking:** street only.

B L D

P.F. CHANG'S CHINA BISTRO
408/961-5250 3

▼▼▼▼ Chinese. Fine Dining. $10-$20 **AAA Inspector Notes:** Trendy, upscale decor provides a pleasant backdrop for New Age Chinese dining. Appetizers, soups and salads are a meal by themselves. Vegetarian plates and sides, noodles, meins, chicken and meat dishes are created from exotic, fresh ingredients. **Bar:** full bar. **Address:** 98 S 2nd St 95113 **Location:** SR 87 exit Santa Clara St, 0.5 mi e, then just s. **Parking:** street only. L D CALL M

SAN JOSE (E-9)

- **Restaurants p. 478**
- **Hotels & Restaurants map & index p. 468**

BEST WESTERN AIRPORT PLAZA
(408)243-2400 17

◆◆◆

Hotel

$129-$199

AAA Benefit: Members save up to 20%, plus 10% bonus points with Best Western Rewards®.

Address: 2118 The Alameda 95126 **Location:** I-880 exit The Alameda, just w. **Facility:** 40 units. 3 stories, interior corridors. **Amenities:** high-speed Internet, safes. **Pool(s):** outdoor. **Activities:** whirlpool. **Guest Services:** valet laundry. **Free Special Amenities: local telephone calls and high-speed Internet.**

SAVE CALL M

BEST WESTERN PLUS LANAI GARDEN INN & SUITES
(408)929-8100 20

◆◆◆

Hotel

$109-$139

AAA Benefit: Members save up to 20%, plus 10% bonus points with Best Western Rewards®.

Address: 1575 Tully Rd 95122 **Location:** US 101 exit Tully Rd, just e. **Facility:** 52 units. 2 stories, interior corridors. **Terms:** 2-4 night minimum stay - seasonal and/or weekends. **Pool(s):** outdoor. **Free Special Amenities: local telephone calls and high-speed Internet.**

SAVE CALL M

THE CLARION PRESIDENT INN
(408)972-2200 23

◆◆◆

Hotel

$99-$139

Address: 3200 Monterey Rd 95111 **Location:** US 101 exit Tully Rd, 1 mi e, then s. **Facility:** 47 units. 2-3 stories, interior corridors. **Terms:** cancellation fee imposed. **Amenities:** high-speed Internet. **Pool(s):** outdoor. **Activities:** whirlpool, exercise room. **Guest Services:** valet and coin laundry. **Free Special Amenities: expanded continental breakfast and high-speed Internet.**

SAVE CALL M

COMFORT INN
(408)287-9380 16

◆◆◆

Hotel

$85-$195

Address: 875 N 13th St 95112 **Location:** US 101 exit 13th St/Old Oakland Rd, just w. Located in an industrial area. **Facility:** 45 units. 3 stories, interior corridors. **Terms:** cancellation fee imposed. **Amenities:** high-speed Internet. **Activities:** limited exercise equipment. **Free Special Amenities: expanded continental breakfast and high-speed Internet.**

SAVE CALL M BIZ

COMFORT SUITES AIRPORT
(408)392-9009 12

◆◆◆

Hotel

$80-$150

Address: 1510 N 1st St 95112 **Location:** US 101 exit 1st St, just s. **Facility:** 51 units. 3 stories, interior corridors. **Terms:** cancellation fee imposed. **Amenities:** high-speed Internet. **Activities:** exercise room. **Guest Services:** valet and coin laundry. **Free Special Amenities: full breakfast and high-speed Internet.**

SAVE CALL M BIZ

(See map & index p. 468.)

DOLCE HAYES MANSION
408/226-3200 24

Hotel
Rates not provided

Address: 200 Edenvale Ave 95136 **Location:** US 101 exit Blossom Hill Rd W, 1 mi n on Lean Ave. **Facility:** 214 units. 2-3 stories, interior corridors. **Amenities:** video games (fee), high-speed Internet, safes. **Dining:** 2 restaurants. **Pool(s):** heated outdoor. **Activities:** whirlpool, exercise room, spa. **Guest Services:** area transportation-within 5 mi.

SAVE FEE [+] [†|] CALL [&M] [🚲] [BIZ] [🛜] [✕] [🎥]
[📶] [💻] / SOME UNITS [🖨]

DOUBLETREE BY HILTON HOTEL SAN JOSE
(408)453-4000 5

Hotel
$199-$459

 AAA Benefit: Members save 5% or more!

Address: 2050 Gateway Pl 95110 **Location:** 0.3 mi e of Norman Y. Mineta San Jose International Airport via Airport Blvd; w of US 101 exit N 1st St; US 101 exit Brokaw Rd northbound. **Facility:** The property features extensive conference facilities as well as spacious, well-appointed guest rooms and public areas. 505 units. 10 stories, interior corridors. **Parking:** on-site (fee). **Terms:** 1-7 night minimum stay, cancellation fee imposed. **Amenities:** Fee: video games, high-speed Internet. **Dining:** 2 restaurants, also, Spencer's, see separate listing. **Pool(s):** heated outdoor. **Activities:** whirlpool, exercise room. **Guest Services:** valet laundry. **Free Special Amenities: airport transportation.**

SAVE [ECO] [+] [†|] [🍽] [Y] CALL [&M] [🚲] [BIZ] [🛜]
[✕] [🎥] [💻] / SOME UNITS FEE [🐾] FEE [📶] FEE [🖨]

EXTENDED STAYAMERICA-SAN JOSE-DOWNTOWN
(408)573-0648 10

Extended Stay Hotel $89-$104 **Address:** 1560 N 1st St 95112 **Location:** 1 mi e of Norman Y. Mineta San Jose International Airport; US 101 exit N 1st St, then s. **Facility:** 152 efficiencies. 3 stories, interior corridors. **Guest Services:** coin laundry.

CALL [&M] [🛜] [📶] [🖨] [💻] / SOME UNITS FEE [🐾]

FAIRFIELD INN & SUITES
(408)453-3133 7

Hotel
$145-$160

 AAA Benefit: AAA hotel discounts of 5% or more.

Address: 1755 N 1st St 95112 **Location:** US 101 exit N 1st St, just w. **Facility:** 186 units. 3 stories, interior corridors. **Amenities:** video games (fee), high-speed Internet, safes. **Pool(s):** heated outdoor. **Activities:** whirlpool, exercise room. **Guest Services:** valet and coin laundry, area transportation-within 2 mi. **Free Special Amenities: expanded continental breakfast and high-speed Internet.**

SAVE [+] [†|] CALL [&M] [🚲] [BIZ] [🛜] [✕] [🎥] [📶]
[🖨] [💻] / SOME UNITS FEE [🐾]

FOUR POINTS BY SHERATON SAN JOSE SILICON VALLEY
(408)972-7800 25

Hotel
$89-$204

 AAA Benefit: Members get up to 20% off, plus Starwood Preferred Guest® bonuses.

Address: 399 Silicon Valley Blvd 95138 **Location:** US 101 exit Bernal Rd, just e. **Facility:** 210 units. 3 stories, interior corridors. **Terms:** cancellation fee imposed. **Amenities:** Some: high-speed Internet. **Pool(s):** heated outdoor. **Activities:** whirlpool, exercise room. **Guest Services:** valet laundry, area transportation-within 5 mi. **Free Special Amenities: preferred room (subject to availability with advance reservations) and high-speed Internet.**

SAVE [+] [†|] CALL [&M] [🚲] [BIZ] [🛜] [✕] [💻]
/ SOME UNITS FEE [🐾] [📶] [🖨]

HAMPTON INN & SUITES
(408)298-7373 21

Hotel
$98-$142

 AAA Benefit: Members save up to 10%!

Address: 55 Old Tully Rd 95111 **Location:** US 101 exit Tully Rd, 1 mi w, then just s. **Facility:** 80 units. 3 stories, interior corridors. **Terms:** 1-7 night minimum stay, cancellation fee imposed. **Amenities:** high-speed Internet. **Pool(s):** heated outdoor. **Activities:** exercise room. **Guest Services:** valet laundry. **Free Special Amenities: full breakfast and high-speed Internet.**

SAVE CALL [&M] [🚲] [🛜] [📶] [🖨] [💻]

HOLIDAY INN EXPRESS CENTRAL CITY
(408)279-6600 22

Hotel
$109-$189

Address: 2660 Monterey Hwy 95111 **Location:** US 101 exit Tully Rd 1 mi w, then 0.8 mi s. **Facility:** 57 units. 2 stories (no elevator), exterior corridors. **Terms:** cancellation fee imposed. **Amenities:** high-speed Internet. **Pool(s):** outdoor. **Activities:** sauna, whirlpool, exercise room. **Guest Services:** valet and coin laundry. **Free Special Amenities: full breakfast and high-speed Internet.**

SAVE [†|+] CALL [&M] [🚲] [🛜] [✕] [📶] [🖨] [💻]

HOLIDAY INN EXPRESS-SAN JOSE INTERNATIONAL AIRPORT
(408)467-1789 13

Hotel
$84-$189

Address: 1350 N 4th St 95112 **Location:** US 101 exit N 1st St, 0.5 mi s to Rosemary St E. **Facility:** 126 units, some efficiencies. 3 stories, interior corridors. **Amenities:** video games (fee). Some: high-speed Internet. **Pool(s):** outdoor. **Activities:** whirlpool, exercise room. **Guest Services:** valet and coin laundry. **Free Special Amenities: expanded continental breakfast and high-speed Internet.**

SAVE [+] [†|+] CALL [&M] [🚲] [🛜] [🎥] [📶] [🖨] [💻]

HOLIDAY INN SAN JOSE AIRPORT
408/453-6200 15

Hotel
Rates not provided

Address: 1350 N 1st St 95112 **Location:** I-880 exit N 1st St, just w. **Facility:** 354 units. 9 stories, interior corridors. **Bath:** shower only. Some: high-speed Internet. **Dining:** San Fresco Cafe, see separate listing. **Pool(s):** heated outdoor. **Activities:** exercise room. **Guest Services:** valet laundry. **Free Special Amenities: newspaper and high-speed Internet.**

SAVE [+] [†|] CALL [&M] [🚲] [BIZ] [🛜] [✕] [🎥] [💻]
/ SOME UNITS [📶] [🖨]

HOMEWOOD SUITES BY HILTON
408/428-9900 3

Extended Stay Hotel. Rates not provided. **Address:** 10 W Trimble Rd 95131 **Location:** US 101 exit Trimble Rd, 1.3 mi w; 2 mi ne of Norman Y. Mineta San Jose International Airport. **Facility:** 140 efficiencies, some two bedrooms. 2-3 stories, interior/exterior corridors. **Amenities:** video games (fee), high-speed Internet. **Pool(s):** heated outdoor. **Activities:** whirlpool, sports court, exercise room. **Guest Services:** valet and coin laundry, area transportation-within 3 mi.

AAA Benefit: Contemporary luxury at a special Member rate.

[+] [†|+] CALL [&M] [🚲] [BIZ] [🛜] [🎥] [📶] [🖨] [💻]
/ SOME UNITS [🐾]

Save on theme park tickets
at AAA.com/discounts

(See map & index p. 468.)

HOTEL VALENCIA SANTANA ROW (408)551-0010 [19]

Hotel
$419-$499

Address: 355 Santana Row 95128 **Location:** I-880 exit Stevens Creek Blvd, just w; in Santana Row Shopping area. **Facility:** In the heart of Santana Row, an upscale shopping center, this attractively appointed hotel is steps from shops and restaurants. 212 units. 7 stories, interior corridors. **Parking:** on-site and valet. **Terms:** cancellation fee imposed. **Amenities:** high-speed Internet. **Pool(s):** heated outdoor. **Activities:** whirlpool, exercise room, spa. **Guest Services:** valet laundry.

/ SOME UNITS

HYATT HOUSE SAN JOSE/SILICON VALLEY
(408)324-1155 [1]

Hotel
$89-$249

HYATT house™ **AAA Benefit:** Members save 10% or more everyday.

Address: 75 Headquarters Dr 95134 **Location:** SR 237 exit N 1st St, just s, then just e. **Facility:** 164 units, some two bedrooms and efficiencies. 7 stories, interior corridors. **Terms:** cancellation fee imposed. **Amenities:** high-speed Internet. *Some:* video games. **Pool(s):** heated outdoor. **Activities:** exercise room. **Guest Services:** valet and coin laundry. **Free Special Amenities: expanded continental breakfast and high-speed Internet.**

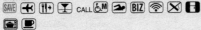

LA QUINTA INN SAN JOSE AIRPORT (408)435-8800 [4]

Hotel $77-$210 **Address:** 2585 Seaboard Ave 95131 **Location:** US 101 exit Trimble Rd E; 1 mi ne of Norman Y. Mineta San Jose International Airport. **Facility:** 148 units. 2 stories (no elevator), interior corridors. **Terms:** 7 day cancellation notice. **Pool(s):** outdoor. **Activities:** exercise room. **Guest Services:** valet and coin laundry.

/ SOME UNITS

QUALITY INN SAN JOSE AIRPORT (408)434-9330 [2]

Hotel
$70-$141

Address: 2390 Harris Way 95131 **Location:** I-880 exit Montague Expwy, just e. **Facility:** 47 units. 3 stories, interior corridors. **Terms:** cancellation fee imposed. **Amenities:** *Some:* high-speed Internet. **Activities:** exercise room. **Guest Services:** coin laundry. **Free Special Amenities: full breakfast and local telephone calls.**

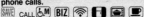

RADISSON HOTEL, SAN JOSE AIRPORT
(408)452-0200 [11]

Hotel
$79-$209

Address: 1471 N 4th St 95112 **Location:** US 101 exit N 1st St; 0.5 mi n of Norman Y. Mineta San Jose International Airport. **Facility:** 196 units. 5 stories, interior corridors. **Terms:** cancellation fee imposed. **Amenities:** high-speed Internet. **Pool(s):** outdoor. **Activities:** exercise room. **Guest Services:** valet laundry.

SAVE FEE FEE

/ SOME UNITS

RESIDENCE INN BY MARRIOTT (408)226-7676 [26]

Extended Stay Hotel $94-$169 **Address:** 6111 San Ignacio Ave 95119 **Location:** US 101 exit Bernal Rd w, then just n. **Facility:** 150 kitchen units, some two bedrooms. 3 stories, interior corridors. **Amenities:** video games (fee), high-speed Internet. **Pool(s):** outdoor, whirlpool, sports court, exercise room. **Guest Services:** valet and coin laundry.

AAA Benefit: AAA hotel discounts of 5% or more.

/ SOME UNITS FEE

SAN JOSE AIRPORT COURTYARD (408)441-6111 [9]

Hotel $119-$269 **Address:** 1727 Technology Dr 95110 **Location:** SR 87 exit Skyport Dr, just e. **Facility:** 151 units. 4 stories, interior corridors. **Amenities:** high-speed Internet. **Pool(s):** heated outdoor. **Activities:** whirlpool, exercise room. **Guest Services:** valet and coin laundry.

AAA Benefit: AAA hotel discounts of 5% or more.

ECO

/ SOME UNITS

SAN JOSE AIRPORT GARDEN HOTEL
(408)793-3300 [8]

Hotel
$89-$209

Address: 1740 N 1st St 95112 **Location:** W of US 101 exit N 1st St; 0.5 mi e of Norman Y. Mineta San Jose International Airport via Airport Pkwy. **Facility:** 512 units. 2-3 stories, interior corridors. **Terms:** cancellation fee imposed. **Dining:** Amalfi's Grill, see separate listing. **Pool(s):** outdoor. **Activities:** whirlpool, jogging, exercise room. **Guest Services:** valet laundry. **Free Special Amenities: high-speed Internet and airport transportation.**

SAVE

/ SOME UNITS FEE

(See map & index p. 468.)

SILICON VALLEY HOTEL SAN JOSE AIRPORT
(408)453-5340 **14**

Hotel
$115-$170

Address: 1355 N 4th St 95112 **Location:** Just s of jct US 101 and I-880; I-880 exit 1st St NW, n on Rosemary St, then just w; 1 mi e of airport. Located in a quiet area. **Facility:** 194 units. 2 stories, exterior corridors. **Terms:** cancellation fee imposed. **Amenities:** video games (fee), high-speed Internet, safes. **Dining:** Island Grill, see separate listing. **Pool(s):** outdoor. **Activities:** whirlpool, putting green, exercise room. **Guest Services:** valet and coin laundry. **Free Special Amenities: high-speed Internet and airport transportation.**

STAYBRIDGE SUITES SAN JOSE
408/436-1600 **6**

Extended Stay Hotel. Rates not provided. **Address:** 1602 Crane Ct 95112 **Location:** US 101 exit 1st St/Brokaw Rd, 0.4 mi e to Bering Dr, then 0.5 mi s. **Facility:** 114 kitchen units, some two bedrooms. 3 stories (no elevator), exterior corridors. **Amenities:** high-speed Internet. **Pool(s):** heated outdoor. **Activities:** whirlpool, exercise room. **Guest Services:** valet laundry, area transportation-within 5 mi.

TOWNEPLACE SUITES BY MARRIOTT SAN JOSE/CUPERTINO
(408)984-5903 **18**

Extended Stay Hotel
$129-$249 Address: 440 Saratoga Ave, just n. **Location:** I-280 exit Saratoga Ave, just n. **Facility:** 101 kitchen units, some two bedrooms. 3 stories, interior corridors. **Amenities:** high-speed Internet. **Pool(s):** heated outdoor. **Activities:** whirlpool, exercise room. **Guest Services:** valet and coin laundry.

AAA Benefit:
AAA hotel discounts of 5% or more.

WHERE TO EAT

AMALFI'S GRILL
408/793-3928 **2**

Italian. Casual Dining. $12-$24 **AAA Inspector Notes:** A nice selection of entrees awaits guests of the casually upscale restaurant. Tables offer views of the surrounding patio, grounds and gardens. **Bar:** full bar. **Reservations:** suggested. **Address:** 1740 N 1st St 95112 **Location:** W of US 101 exit N 1st St; 0.5 mi e of Norman Y. Mineta San Jose International Airport via Airport Pkwy; in San Jose Airport Garden Hotel.

ARMADILLO WILLY'S BARBECUE

Barbecue. Quick Service. $6-$18 **AAA Inspector Notes:** Menu offerings at this eatery include a wide selection of barbecue favorites including ribs, chicken, beef brisket, burgers and salad. The atmosphere here is fun and lively. **Bar:** beer & wine.

For additional information, visit AAA.com

LOCATIONS:
Address: 878 Blossom Hill Rd 95123 **Location:** SR 85 exit Santa Teresa Blvd, 0.5 mi s. **Phone:** 408/224-7427
Address: 2071 Camden Ave 95124 **Location:** SR 17 exit Camden Ave, 1 mi e. **Phone:** 408/371-9033

THE CHEESECAKE FACTORY
408/225-6948 **10**

American. Casual Dining. $8-$20 **AAA Inspector Notes:** A display case of mouthwatering cheesecakes is the first thing visitors see as they walk through the door. The extensive menu incorporates many types of cuisine, including Asian, Italian, Greek and Spanish. **Bar:** full bar. **Address:** 925 Blossom Hill Rd 95123 **Location:** SR 85 exit Santa Teresa Blvd, 0.3 mi s, then 0.4 mi w; in Westfield Oakridge Shopping Center.

FRESH CHOICE

American. Cafeteria. $8-$15 **AAA Inspector Notes:** The salad bar of salad bars, the casual restaurant invites patrons to make their own or try one of the already prepared varieties. Other items include freshly baked breads, pizza and soup, as well as make-your-own sundaes for dessert. **Bar:** beer & wine.

For additional information, visit AAA.com

LOCATIONS:
Address: 1600 Saratoga Ave 95129 **Location:** Just n of Campbell Ave. **Phone:** 408/866-1491
Address: 5353 Almaden Expwy, Suite 39A 95118 **Location:** At Blossom Hill Rd. **Phone:** 408/723-7991

HABANA CUBA
408/998-2822 **7**

Cuban. Casual Dining. $9-$32 **AAA Inspector Notes:** A favorite for many years in this area, this spot offers up a great selection of Cuban favorites. Patio dining is available when the weather is nice. **Bar:** beer & wine. **Address:** 238 Race St 95126 **Location:** I-280 exit Race St, just n, at San Carlos St.

ISLAND GRILL
408/392-2468 **4**

American. Casual Dining. $9-$30 **AAA Inspector Notes:** Diners experience the feel of the islands, as palm trees and water fountains surround the room. Great selections of specialty salads, sandwiches, burgers and grilled meats are offered as well as fresh fish dishes. **Bar:** full bar. **Address:** 1355 N 4th St 95112 **Location:** Just s of jct US 101 and I-880; I-880 exit 1st St NW, n on Rosemary St, then just w; 1 mi e of airport; in Clarion Hotel San Jose Airport.

JADE CATHAY CHINESE SEAFOOD CUISINE
408/392-9388 **6**

Chinese Seafood. Casual Dining. $7-$24 **AAA Inspector Notes:** The extensive menu at this Chinese restaurant will please everyone. In addition to traditional selections, they also offer dim sum, savory clay pots, chow fun and vegetable/tofu items. Guests can choose from an extensive seafood selection. **Bar:** beer & wine. **Address:** 1339 N First St 95112 **Location:** I-880 exit First St, just w.

PASTA POMODORO

Italian. Casual Dining. $9-$18 **AAA Inspector Notes:** Families are welcomed at this laid-back restaurant, which brings in plenty of loyal locals who enjoy its varied Italian favorites, including tempting pasta and chicken dishes. **Bar:** beer & wine.

For additional information, visit AAA.com

LOCATIONS:
Address: 378 Santana Row 95128 **Location:** I-880 exit Stevens Creek Blvd, just w; in Santana Row Shopping Center. **Phone:** 408/241-2200
Address: 4898 San Felipe Rd , Suite 150 95135 **Location:** US 101 exit Yerba Buena Rd, 2.3 mi e. **Phone:** 408/532-0271
Address: 2083 Camden Ave 95124 **Location:** Just e of S Bascom Ave. **Phone:** 408/371-2600
Address: 1205 The Alameda, Suite 30 95126 **Location:** On SR 82; at Race St. **Phone:** 408/292-9929

P.F. CHANG'S CHINA BISTRO
408/960-2940 **9**

Chinese. Fine Dining. $10-$20 **AAA Inspector Notes:** Trendy, upscale decor provides a pleasant backdrop for New Age Chinese dining. Appetizers, soups and salads are a meal by themselves. Vegetarian plates and sides, noodles, meins, chicken and meat dishes are created from exotic, fresh ingredients. **Bar:** full bar. **Address:** 925 Blossom Hill Rd, Suite 1515 95123 **Location:** SR 85 exit Santa Teresa Blvd, 0.3 mi s, then 0.4 mi w; in Westfield Oakridge Shopping Center.

(See map & index p. 468.)

ROUND TABLE PIZZA

Pizza. Casual Dining. $7-$28 **AAA Inspector Notes:** This casual, family-oriented pizza place features high-quality ingredients and dough rolled fresh daily. Distinctive specialty pizzas are piled high with toppings. **Bar:** beer & wine. L D

For additional information, visit AAA.com

LOCATIONS:
Address: 14940 Camden Ave 95124 **Location:** Between S Bascom and Union aves. **Phone:** 408/371-9550
Address: 5440-A Thornwood Dr 95123 **Location:** Just w of Santa Teresa Blvd. **Phone:** 408/578-5200
Address: 3253 Stevens Creek Blvd 95117 **Location:** Between San Tomas Expwy and Winchester. **Phone:** 408/296-3040
Address: 6217 Santa Teresa Blvd 95119 **Location:** SR 85 exit Cottle Rd S, just e. **Phone:** 408/226-0756
Address: 1125 S Bascom Ave 95128 **Location:** Just n of Downing Ave. **Phone:** 408/286-6222

SAN FRESCO CAFE   408/453-6200 5

American. Casual Dining. $10-$20 **AAA Inspector Notes:** Right off the main lobby, this relaxed cafe focuses on preparing a good selection of sandwiches, grilled meats, seafood, pasta dishes and salads. **Bar:** full bar. **Address:** 1350 N 1st St 95112 **Location:** US 101 exit N 1st St, 0.3 mi s; 1 mi e of Norman Y. Mineta San Jose International Airport via Airport Pkwy, just s; in Holiday Inn San Jose Airport. B L D CALL M

SPENCER'S   408/437-2170 1

Steak. Fine Dining. $15-$50 **AAA Inspector Notes:** A comfortable and relaxed atmosphere can be found at this restaurant. Expect warm and welcoming service as well as a great selection of grilled beef items, fresh seafood and specialty salads. **Bar:** full bar. **Reservations:** suggested. **Address:** 2050 Gateway Pl 95110 **Location:** 0.3 mi e of Norman Y. Mineta San Jose International Airport via Airport Blvd; w of US 101 exit N 1st St; US 101 exit Brokaw Rd northbound; in DoubleTree by Hilton Hotel San Jose. **Parking:** on-site (fee). L D CALL M

THE SUMMIT SPORTS BAR & GRILL   408/972-1961 11

American. Casual Dining. $8-$25 **AAA Inspector Notes:** This casual, family-style restaurant offers up such traditional favorites as sandwiches, burgers, pasta dishes, steaks and ribs. Service is warm and friendly. **Bar:** full bar. **Address:** 389 Silicon Valley Blvd 95138 **Location:** US 101 exit Bernal Rd, just e. B L D CALL M

THREE FLAMES RESTAURANT   408/269-3133 8

Continental. Fine Dining. $15-$30 **AAA Inspector Notes:** An area tradition for more than 25 years, this restaurant tempts with such specialties as pepper steak and rack of lamb. **Bar:** full bar. **Reservations:** suggested. **Address:** 1547 Meridian Ave 95125 **Location:** Just n of Hamilton Ave; in Carriage Square Shopping Center. L D CALL M

VITO'S NEW YORK TRATTORIA   408/453-1000 3

Italian. Casual Dining. $10-$29 **AAA Inspector Notes:** Italian entrees range from grilled meats, fish and chicken to pizza and pasta. Locals frequent this place. **Bar:** full bar. **Reservations:** suggested. **Address:** 90 Skyport Dr, Suite 170 95110 **Location:** SR 87 exit Skyport Dr, just e. L D CALL M

SAN JUAN BAUTISTA (G-3) pop. 1,862, elev. 200'

 MISSION SAN JUAN BAUTISTA is at 2nd and Mariposa sts. Founded June 24, 1797, the mission was named for St. John the Baptist. With a three-aisle entrance to the altar, it was the widest of the mission churches. In recognition of its importance, a set of nine bells once graced the chapel area; only three remain. The mission has period furnishings, and the convent wing contains relics.

Original artifacts include altar statues, wall decorations and a baptismal font as well as an 1816 altar screen. It is still an active Catholic church. **Hours:** Daily 9:30-4:30. Closed major holidays and Good Friday. **Cost:** $4; $3 (ages 60+); $2 (ages 3-16). **Phone:** (831) 623-4528.

SAN JUAN BAUTISTA STATE HISTORIC PARK, on the plaza, includes the Plaza Hotel, built in 1858 on the site of the old Spanish soldiers' barracks, and the 1840 Castro-Breen Adobe, headquarters of the Mexican government and later home of the Patrick Breen family, survivors of the ill-fated Donner party.

Other attractions are the 1868 Zanetta House, a blacksmith shop, a jail, gardens, a Spanish orchard, a livery stable with old carriages and a slide show about the history of San Juan Bautista. **Time:** Allow 30 minutes minimum. **Hours:** Tues.-Sun. 10-4:30. Closed Jan. 1, Thanksgiving and Christmas. **Cost:** $3; free (ages 0-16). **Phone:** (831) 623-4881.

DONA ESTHER MEXICAN RESTAURANT   831/623-2518

Mexican
Casual Dining
$7-$16

AAA Inspector Notes: Located in the historic downtown area, prepare for traditional Mexican favorites or savor one of the special recipes that has been handed down for generations. Sunday brunch is an area favorite. The staff is warm and friendly. **Bar:** full bar. **Address:** 25 Franklin St 95045 **Location:** Just n of SR 156, at 3rd St. **Parking:** street only. B L D

SAN LEANDRO (D-9) pop. 84,950, elev. 59'

- Restaurants p. 480
- Hotels & Restaurants map & index p. 254

CASA PERALTA is at 384 W. Estudillo. This 1901 casa has been restored to its 1920s appearance. Spanish tiles inside the fence relate the story of Don Quixote. **Time:** Allow 30 minutes minimum. **Hours:** Sat.-Sun. 11-3. Hours may vary; phone ahead. Closed major holidays. **Cost:** Donations. **Phone:** (510) 577-3474. San Leandro, 21

BUDGET INN   (510)276-6290 57

Hotel
$60-$95

Address: 16500 Foothill Blvd 94578 **Location:** I-580 exit 164th Ave, just se. **Facility:** 45 units. 3 stories, interior corridors. **Amenities:** high-speed Internet.

SAVE CALL M

HILTON GARDEN INN   (510)346-5533 58

Hotel $139-$169 **Address:** 510 Lewelling Blvd 94579 **Location:** I-880 exit Lewelling Blvd southbound; exit Hesperian Blvd northbound, just w. Bay Fair, 22. **Facility:** 119 units. 4 stories, interior corridors. **Terms:** 1-7 night minimum stay, cancellation fee imposed. **Amenities:** high-speed Internet. **Pool(s):** indoor. **Activities:** whirlpool, exercise room. **Guest Services:** valet and coin laundry.

AAA Benefit: Unparalleled hospitality at a special Member rate.

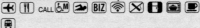

(See map & index p. 254.)

THE MARINA INN ON SAN FRANCISCO BAY
(510)895-1311 **56**

Hotel
$109-$149

Address: 68 Monarch Bay Dr 94577 **Location:** I-880 exit Marina Blvd, 1.3 mi w. **Facility:** 129 units. 3 stories, interior corridors. **Terms:** cancellation fee imposed. **Amenities:** video games (fee), high-speed Internet, safes. **Pool(s):** outdoor. **Activities:** whirlpool, bicycles, exercise room. **Guest Services:** valet laundry, area transportation-within 3 mi & BART. **Free Special Amenities:** expanded continental breakfast and early check-in/late check-out.

WHERE TO EAT

EL TORITO   510/351-8825

Mexican. Casual Dining. $8-$20 **AAA Inspector Notes:** Homemade Mexican favorites span from classic preparations to specialties from the country's central regions. Spicy taqueria-style tacos and carnitas Michoacan (marinated pork) are tasty choices. **Bar:** full bar. **Address:** 5 Monarch Bay Dr 94577 **Location:** I-880 exit Marina Blvd, 1.3 mi w.

FRESH CHOICE   510/278-5404

American. Cafeteria. $8-$15 **AAA Inspector Notes:** The salad bar of salad bars, the casual restaurant invites patrons to make their own or try one of the already prepared varieties. Other items include freshly baked breads, pizza and soup, as well as make-your-own sundaes for dessert. **Bar:** beer & wine. **Address:** 15555 E 14th St, Suite105 94578 **Location:** I-580 exit Fairmont Dr, w, then just s; in Bayfair Mall. Bay Fair, 22.

HORATIO'S   510/351-5556 **58**

American. Casual Dining. $8-$46 **AAA Inspector Notes:** Located at the San Leandro Marina, this nautically themed restaurant offers a great selection of entrées to please everyone. The menu features a wide selection of hot and cold appetizers which could make a meal on their own. Specialty items include cioppino, braised stuffed veal, Nova Scotia scallops and filet mignon Wellington. Service is friendly and attentive. **Bar:** full bar. **Address:** 60 Monarch Bay Dr 94577 **Location:** I-880 exit Marina Blvd, 1.3 mi w.

ROUND TABLE PIZZA

Pizza. Casual Dining. $7-$28 **AAA Inspector Notes:** This casual, family-oriented pizza place features high-quality ingredients and dough rolled fresh daily. Distinctive specialty pizzas are piled high with toppings. **Bar:** beer & wine.

For additional information, visit AAA.com

LOCATIONS:
Address: 1359 Washington Ave 94577 **Location:** At Joaquin Ave. Bay Fair, 22. **Phone:** 510/581-9994

Address: 15255 E 14th St 94578 **Location:** Between 152nd and 153rd aves. Bay Fair, 22. **Phone:** 510/278-3002

Address: 13700 Doolittle Dr 94577 **Location:** At Fairway Dr. **Phone:** 510/581-7777

SAN MARTIN (G-3) pop. 7,027, elev. 282'

WINGS OF HISTORY AIR MUSEUM is at 12777 Murphy Ave., adjacent to the South County Airport. The museum restores and displays antique aircraft and aviation artifacts in three hangars. Visitors can see collections of engines and aircraft in various stages of restoration, a propeller shop and craftsmen creating parts for the old planes. **Time:** Allow 1 hour minimum. **Hours:** Tues. and Thurs. 10-3, Sat.-Sun. 11-4. Closed major holidays. **Cost:** Donations. **Phone:** (408) 683-2290.

WINERIES

- **Clos LaChance Winery** is at 1 Hummingbird Ln. **Hours:** Tours and tastings daily 11-5. Closed Jan. 1, July 4, Thanksgiving, Christmas Eve and Christmas. Phone ahead to confirm schedule. **Phone:** (408) 686-1050 or (800) 487-9463.

SAN MATEO (D-8) pop. 97,207, elev. 29'
- **Hotels & Restaurants map & index p. 410**
- **Part of San Francisco area — see map p. 342**

This San Francisco residential suburb is connected to the East Bay via the 7-mile-long San Mateo-Hayward Bridge. Comprising five steel spans, it is one of the longest highway bridges in the country.

San Mateo Area Chamber of Commerce: 1700 S. El Camino Real, Suite 108, P.O. Box 936, San Mateo, CA 94402. **Phone:** (650) 401-2440.

CURIODYSSEY is on Coyote Point Dr. in Coyote Point Park. Children can explore hands-on science exhibitions and learn how nature's complex ecosystems work together to create our planet's environment. Wildlife habitats on the park grounds feature resident indigenous species, including mammals, reptiles, birds and invertebrates.

Hours: Tues.-Sat. 10-5, Sun. and holidays noon-5. Phone to confirm holiday schedule. **Cost:** (includes museum and wildlife habitats) $8; $6 (ages 13-17 and 62+); $4 (ages 2-12). Park admission $6 per private vehicle. **Phone:** (650) 342-7755.

JAPANESE TEA GARDEN is in Central Park, El Camino Real and 5th Ave. E. It was designed by Nagao Sakurai, chief landscape architect at Tokyo's Imperial Palace. The garden has labeled plants and evergreens, along with waterfalls and koi ponds. Other features include a granite pagoda, a teahouse and bamboo groves. Parking lots are under the tennis courts. **Hours:** Mon.-Fri. 10-4, Sat.-Sun. 11-4. Koi feeding Mon.-Fri. at 11 and 3, Mar.-Oct. **Cost:** Free. **Phone:** (650) 522-7440.

BEST WESTERN PLUS COYOTE POINT INN
(650)347-9990 **65**

Hotel
$89-$259

AAA Benefit: Members save up to 20%, plus 10% bonus points with Best Western Rewards®.

Address: 480 N Bayshore Blvd 94401 **Location:** US 101 exit Dore Ave northbound; exit 3rd Ave E southbound, re-enter US 101 exit Dore Ave. **Facility:** 98 units. 4 stories, interior corridors. **Terms:** cancellation fee imposed. **Amenities:** high-speed Internet, safes. **Activities:** sauna, whirlpool, exercise room. **Guest Services:** coin laundry. **Free Special Amenities:** expanded continental breakfast and airport transportation.

(See map & index p. 410.)

BEST WESTERN SAN MATEO/LOS PRADOS INN
650/341-3300 **73**

Hotel
Rates not provided

AAA Benefit: Members save up to 20%, plus 10% bonus points with Best Western Rewards®.

Address: 2940 S Norfolk St 94403 **Location:** Just e of and adjacent to US 101 exit E Hillsdale Blvd. **Facility:** 115 units. 2-3 stories, interior/exterior corridors. **Activities:** whirlpool, exercise room. **Free Special Amenities:** local telephone calls and high-speed Internet.

COMFORT INN
(650)344-6376 **66**

Hotel
$79-$199

Address: 350 N Bayshore Blvd 94401 **Location:** US 101 exit Dore Ave northbound; exit 3rd Ave E southbound, re-enter US 101 then, exit Dore Ave. **Facility:** 111 units. 4 stories, interior/exterior corridors. **Terms:** cancellation fee imposed. **Activities:** limited exercise equipment. **Guest Services:** coin laundry. **Free Special Amenities: expanded continental breakfast and high-speed Internet.**

COXHEAD HOUSE BED & BREAKFAST
(650)685-1600 **68**

Historic Bed & Breakfast $169-$295 **Address:** 37 E Santa Inez Ave 94401 **Location:** US 101 exit 416 (3rd Ave), w to SR 82 (S El Camino), 0.6 mi n, then just e. **Facility:** A quiet neighborhood is the setting for this Tudor Revival-style inn built in 1891. Some units have a fireplace. 4 units. 2 stories (no elevator), interior corridors. **Terms:** check-in 4 pm, 7 day cancellation notice. **Guest Services:** valet laundry.

HILTON GARDEN INN SAN MATEO
(650)522-9000 **69**

Hotel $89-$259 **Address:** 2000 Bridgepointe Cir 94404 **Location:** US 101 exit 414B (SR 92/E Hayward/San Mateo Bridge), 1.5 m e to exit 14B (Foster City Blvd), then 0.5 mi w on Chess Dr. Located in Bridgepointe Shopping Center.

AAA Benefit: Unparalleled hospitality at a special Member rate.

Facility: 156 units. 7 stories, interior corridors. **Terms:** 1-7 night minimum stay, cancellation fee imposed. **Amenities:** high-speed Internet. **Pool(s):** heated outdoor. **Activities:** whirlpool, exercise room. **Guest Services:** valet and coin laundry.

HOLIDAY INN & SUITES SAN MATEO - SFO
(650)344-3219 **67**

Hotel
$99-$209

Address: 330 N Bayshore Blvd 94401 **Location:** US 101 exit Dore Ave E northbound; exit 3rd Ave E southbound, re-enter US 101, then exit Dore Ave. **Facility:** 110 units. 4 stories, interior corridors. **Terms:** 3 day cancellation notice-fee imposed. **Amenities:** high-speed Internet. **Activities:** sauna, whirlpool, exercise room. **Guest Services:** valet and coin laundry. **Free Special Amenities: high-speed Internet and airport transportation.**

Learn the local driving laws
at DrivingLaws.AAA.com

MARRIOTT SAN MATEO/SAN FRANCISCO AIRPORT
(650)653-6000 **70**

Hotel
$84-$104

Marriott
HOTELS & RESORTS

AAA Benefit: AAA hotel discounts of 5% or more.

Address: 1770 S Amphlett Blvd 94402 **Location:** Nw of jct US 101 and SR 92; SR 92 exit Delaware St, e on Concar Dr. **Facility:** 476 units. 3-6 stories, interior corridors. **Parking:** on-site (fee) and valet. **Amenities:** Fee: video games, high-speed Internet. Some: safes. **Pool(s):** heated outdoor. **Activities:** whirlpool, exercise room. Fee: massage. **Guest Services:** valet laundry. **Free Special Amenities: continental breakfast.**

RESIDENCE INN BY MARRIOTT
(650)574-4700 **71**

Extended Stay Hotel $229-$269 **Address:** 2000 Winward Way 94404 **Location:** US 101 exit 414B (SR 92/E Hayward/Fashion Island) to Mariners Island exit, then just e. **Facility:**

AAA Benefit: AAA hotel discounts of 5% or more.

160 kitchen units, some two bedrooms. 2 stories, exterior corridors. **Pool(s):** heated outdoor. **Activities:** whirlpools, sports court, exercise room. **Guest Services:** valet and coin laundry, area transportation-within 5 mi.

STONE VILLA INN
(650)458-6556 **72**

Motel
$65-$500

Address: 2175 S El Camino Real 94403 **Location:** US 101 exit 414B (SR 92 W) to exit 12A (El Camino Real), 0.5 mi s. **Facility:** 45 units. 2 stories (no elevator), exterior corridors. Bath: shower only. **Terms:** cancellation fee imposed. **Free Special Amenities: continental breakfast and high-speed Internet.**

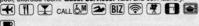

WHERE TO EAT

231 ELLSWORTH
650/347-7231 **42**

California. Fine Dining. $9-$79 **AAA Inspector Notes:** This elegant, upscale dining room features a distinctive sky-blue curved ceiling. Lunch is served a la carte and dinner is a choice of three to five courses as well as a chef's tasting menu with wine pairing available. **Bar:** wine only. **Reservations:** suggested. **Address:** 231 S Ellsworth Ave 94401 **Location:** Between 2nd and E 3rd aves. **Parking:** valet and street only.

ARMADILLO WILLY'S BARBECUE
650/571-7427

Barbecue. Quick Serve. $6-$18 **AAA Inspector Notes:** Menu offerings at this eatery include a wide selection of barbecue favorites including ribs, chicken, beef brisket, burgers and salad. The atmosphere here is fun and lively. **Bar:** beer & wine. **Address:** 2260 Bridgepointe Pkwy 94404 **Location:** N of SR 92 exit Mariners Island eastbound, n to Fashion Island (which becomes Bridgepointe Pkwy); in Bridgepointe Shopping Center.

ASTARIA
650/344-9444 **47**

American. Casual Dining. $11-$30 **AAA Inspector Notes:** Somewhere between casual and elegant, this restaurant prepares contemporary American cuisine. Small plates allow for sampling and sharing. Homemade flat-bread pizza also is a good choice. **Bar:** full bar. **Address:** 50 E 3rd Ave 94402 **Location:** US 101 exit E 3rd Ave, 0.7 mi w. **Parking:** street only.

CENTRAL PARK BISTRO
650/558-8401 **48**

American. Casual Dining. $10-$34 **AAA Inspector Notes:** This well-appointed, elegant bistro offers well-executed menu items ranging from panini and wood-fired oven pizza to sophisticated entrées. Make room for the signature dessert of warm toffee bread pudding sweetened with a secret ingredient. **Bar:** full bar. **Address:** 181 E 4th Ave 94401 **Location:** Between S Ellsworth Ave and S San Mateo Dr; downtown.

(See map & index p. 410.)

CLAY OVEN   650/342-9194   (45)
▼▼ ▼▼ Indian. Casual Dining. $10-$19 **AAA Inspector Notes:** Elegant hand-painted murals adorn the walls at this restaurant, which serves flavorful dishes. Lunch goers gravitate to the great buffet, which includes several different dishes and two authentic desserts, while dinner patrons can select from a course menu. **Bar:** beer & wine. **Address:** 78 E 3rd Ave 94401 **Location:** US 101 exit 3rd Ave, 0.5 mi w. **Parking:** street only. (L) (D)

IZAKAYA MAI   650/347-2511   (40)
▼▼ ▼▼ Japanese. Casual Dining. $10-$16 **AAA Inspector Notes:** Popular with the locals, this homey restaurant's walls are full of pictures and drawings courtesy of their repeat customers. An extensive menu features okonomiyakis, takoyaki appetizers and such California-style rolls as caterpillar and hamachi dragon. **Bar:** beer & wine. **Address:** 212 2nd Ave 94401 **Location:** Between S Ellsworth Ave and S B St; downtown. **Parking:** street only.

(L) (D) (LATE) (AC)

JACK'S PRIME BURGERS   650/638-1479   (52)
▼▼ ▼▼ Burgers. Casual Dining. $9-$12 **AAA Inspector Notes:** A comfortable ambience with an open kitchen and spacious, bright dining area with a communal table for single diners can be found at this eatery. A one-third-pound burger is the standard and comes with a choice of fries or salad. Long slices of fried pickles are accompanied by smoky Russian dressing and sweet potato fries come with tiger ranch sauce. Burgers are juicy and the sides are enhanced by the distinctive sauces. **Bar:** beer & wine. **Address:** 3723 S El Camino Real 94403 **Location:** US 101 exit 414A (Hillsdale Blvd W/San Mateo), 0.8 mi w on E Hillsdale Blvd, then just s. (L) (D)

KINGFISH   650/343-1226   (39)
▼▼ ▼▼ ▼▼ American. Casual Dining. $11-$48 **AAA Inspector Notes:** The casually elegant and festive restaurant offers an extensive menu and wine list. **Bar:** full bar. **Reservations:** suggested. **Address:** 201 S B St 94401 **Location:** US 101 exit 3rd Ave, 0.6 mi w, then just n. **Parking:** on-site (fee) and valet. (L) (D) CALL (M)

LITTLE SHANGHAI RESTAURANT   650/573-7161   (51)
▼▼ ▼▼ Chinese. Casual Dining. $7-$20 **AAA Inspector Notes:** Plain but comfortable, this restaurant offers no frills, authentic Shanghai cuisine. Start with a cold appetizer, followed by xial lung bao (Shanghai dumplings) noodles, stir fried rice stick noodles or onion pancakes. For dessert try the eight treasure sweet rice pudding. The eatery tends to be busy, so plan accordingly. **Bar:** beer & wine. **Address:** 17 E 25th Ave 94403 **Location:** Between S El Camino Real and Palm Place. (L) (D) (AC)

LITTLE SHEEP MONGOLIAN HOT POT   650/343-2566   (41)
▼▼ ▼▼ Mongolian. Casual Dining. $3-$14 **AAA Inspector Notes:** A visit to this contemporarily decorated eatery reveals a water wall with a built-in aquarium which serves as a background for the bar. Packed nightly with families and couples sharing a fun meal together, patrons check off from the menu the type of soup and ingredients they want. For a different type of dessert sample the hard-to-find Phoenix yolk bun-a steamed bun with a liquid sweetened yolk center. **Bar:** full bar. **Reservations:** suggested. **Address:** 215 S Ellsworth Ave 94401 **Location:** Between 2nd and E 3rd aves. **Parking:** street only. (L) (D)

RAMEN DOJO   650/401-6568   (49)
▼▼ ▼▼ Japanese Noodles. Casual Dining. **AAA Inspector Notes:** This tiny noodle house may only have 24 seats, but it has plenty of options when it comes to ramen noodles. Choose the basic flavor-soy sauce, pork or soybean. Then pick the level of spiciness. The following toppings are included: two thin pieces of chashu, fried whole garlic, kikurage mushroom, fresh green chives, quail egg, sesame chili oil, shredded red pepper and chicken gravy consisting of ground chicken meat, mushroom, ginger and dried shrimp. Looking for other toppings, for an additional charge there are more than 10 to choose from. **Bar:** beer only. **Address:** 805 S B St 94401 **Location:** Between 8th and 9th aves. **Parking:** street only.

(L) (D) (AC)

RISTORANTE CAPELLINI   650/348-2296   (38)
▼▼ ▼▼ ▼▼ Italian. Casual Dining. $13-$40 **AAA Inspector Notes:** Housed in a registered landmark Spanish Californian building, the interior of this eatery is just as cozy. Designed by Pat Kuleto, gorgeous wood paneling and unique lighting fixtures cast a warm glow to the dining room. The menu offers Northern Italian cuisine featuring pasta, fresh seafood, veal and other meat dishes. **Bar:** full bar. **Address:** 310 Baldwin Ave 94401 **Location:** US 101 exit 3rd Ave, 0.5 mi w to B St, then 0.3 mi n. **Parking:** valet and street only. (L) (D)

SAN MATEO PRIME   650/558-8918   (43)
▼▼ ▼▼ Steak. Casual Dining. $20-$40 **AAA Inspector Notes:** High ceilings accentuated by burgundy tiles gives this restaurant an airy feel. Prime rib is slow roasted in rock salt, tenderizing the meat. Dinner comes with salad, two sides and a popover. There is a junior cut for children under 12. **Bar:** beer & wine. **Address:** 174 3rd Ave 94401 **Location:** Between S San Mateo Dr and S Ellsworth Ave. **Parking:** street only. (D) (AC)

SANTA RAMEN   650/344-5918   (50)
▼▼ ▼▼ Japanese Noodles. Casual Dining. **AAA Inspector Notes:** When ramen aficionados get together and debate the best of the best in the Bay Area, this is one of the top 10. If the hearty bowl is not enough, try their sides of chicken karaage (fried chicken pieces) or buta no kakuni (braised pork). **Bar:** beer & wine. **Address:** 1944 S El Camino Real 94403 **Location:** US 101 exit 414B, 1.1 mi w on SR 92, then exit 12A, just s. (L) (D)

SPIEDO RISTORANTE   650/375-0818   (44)
▼▼ ▼▼ Italian. Casual Dining. $10-$25 **AAA Inspector Notes:** Guests have a choice of seating at this ristorante—al fresco, semi-enclosed and the main dining area with high ceilings and skylights. Menu offerings range from rotisserie and pizza to homemade pasta and such specials as roasted sea bass or osso buco. **Bar:** full bar. **Address:** 223 E 4th Ave 94401 **Location:** US 101 exit E 3rd Ave, 0.5 mi w. **Parking:** street only. (L) (D) CALL (M)

VIOGNIER   650/685-3727   (46)
▼▼ ▼▼ ▼▼ French. Fine Dining. $11-$39 **AAA Inspector Notes:** Menu items at this fine dining establishment creatively combine classic French technique with California cuisine. For a start-to-finish example of this cooking style, diners might order the grand tasting menu. **Bar:** full bar. **Reservations:** suggested. **Address:** 222 E 4th Ave 94401 **Location:** US 101 exit 3rd Ave, w to B St, then just s; in Draeger's Market. (D)

SAN PABLO pop. 29,139

HOLIDAY INN EXPRESS HOTEL & SUITES   (510)965-1900
▼▼ ▼▼ ▼▼ Hotel $104-$149 **Address:** 2525 San Pablo Dam Rd 94806 **Location:** I-80 exit San Pablo Dam Rd, just w, then just n. **Facility:** 85 units. 3 stories, interior corridors. **Amenities:** high-speed Internet. **Activities:** sauna, exercise room. **Guest Services:** valet and coin laundry.

(⊩) CALL (M) (BIZ) (📶) (✕) (▼) (🛏) (🖼) (▭)

SAN RAFAEL (C-8) pop. 57,713, elev. 34'
- **Restaurants p. 484**
- **Part of San Francisco area — see map p. 342**

This bustling residential city grew up in the early 19th century around Mission San Rafael. Marin County's history and culture are preserved at the Marin History Museum, 1125 B St. The museum, located in the 1879 Boyd Gate House, has articles dating from the Spanish mission period through the 20th century. Collections include decorative and fine arts, clothing and textiles, domestic and household goods, and photographs; other exhibits pertain to local business, industry and transportation. Phone (415) 454-8538.

The Marin Shakespeare Company presents plays by the bard at Forest Meadows Amphitheatre, on the campus of the Dominican University of California; take the US 101 Central San Rafael exit and follow signs to the university. Visitor parking is available in the lot on Belle Avenue (across from the Marin Tennis Club). The July through September season features performances on Friday, Saturday and Sunday evenings, plus a Sunday matinee; phone (415) 499-4488 for the box office.

The Downtown San Rafael Farmers Market sets up along Fourth Street (between Lincoln Avenue and B Street) Thursday evenings from 6 to 9 p.m., early April to late September. In addition to seasonal produce from area farmers, the market offers healthy, yummy prepared foods from vendors and local businesses. Street musicians, art and craft booths and activities for kids add to the family-friendly atmosphere.

Marin Convention & Visitors Bureau: 1 Mitchell Blvd., Suite B, San Rafael, CA 94903. **Phone:** (415) 925-2060 or (866) 925-2060.

GUIDE DOGS FOR THE BLIND is w. off US 101 Freitas Pkwy. exit (southbound) or N. San Pedro Rd. exit (northbound), then w. to 350 Los Ranchitos Rd. The organization, which provides guide dogs and training for the visually impaired, offers guided walking tours of its facility.

Visitors see Labrador and Golden Retriever pups and learn about the guide dog training process. The tour also includes a veterinary clinic, puppy socialization area and the area where the graduation ceremony is held. A video presentation provides a look at the organization's living and dining facilities.

Time: Allow 1 hour minimum. **Hours:** Guided tours are given Mon.-Sat. at 10:30 and 2. Phone to confirm holiday schedule. **Cost:** Free. Tours are not recommended for under age 5. **Phone:** (415) 499-4000 or (800) 295-4050.

MARIN COUNTY CIVIC CENTER, just n. off US 101, was the last major project of renowned architect Frank Lloyd Wright. The 140 landscaped acres include fairgrounds, theaters, exhibit halls and a lagoon. The civic center itself is divided into two wings—the administrative offices and the Hall of Justice—joined by an 80-foot dome. Both are included on a 1.5-hour, docent-led guided tour.

Time: Allow 1 hour, 30 minutes minimum. **Hours:** Self-guiding tours Mon.-Fri. 9-4. Guided tour offered Wed. at 10:30. Closed major holidays. **Cost:** Building free. Self-guiding tour booklet available for a small fee. Guided tour $5; free (ages 0-12). **Phone:** (415) 499-7009.

MISSION SAN RAFAEL ARCANGEL, 1104 5th Ave. at A St., is a replica built in 1949 on the approximate site of the original 1817 mission. In the museum are three bells that hung outside the chapel and a painting of the archangel Raphael. Religious relics and old pictures also can be seen. **Time:** Allow 30 minutes minimum. **Hours:** Mission open daily 6:30-5:30. Museum open Wed.-Mon. 11-4. Phone ahead for mass schedule. **Cost:** Free. **Phone:** (415) 454-8141.

WILDCARE, 76 Albert Park Ln. off B St., is a nature education and wildlife rehabilitation center that treats injured, orphaned and sick wild animals until they can be released back to their natural habitats. An exhibit hall contains California wildlife displays and offers hands-on exhibits for children. "Wildlife ambassadors"—animals that recovered but are unreleasable—include a spotted owl, raptors, and brown and white pelicans.

Time: Allow 30 minutes minimum. **Hours:** Daily 9-5. Pool birds are fed daily at 12:30 and 4:30. Phone ahead to confirm times for special presentations. **Cost:** Donations. **Phone:** (415) 453-1000.

EMBASSY SUITES HOTEL   (415)499-9222

Hotel
$159-$209

AAA Benefit: Members save 5% or more!

Address: 101 McInnis Pkwy 94903 **Location:** US 101 exit E San Pedro Dr northbound; exit Freitas Pkwy southbound. Adjacent to Marin County Civic Center. **Facility:** 235 units. 5 stories, interior corridors. **Terms:** 1-7 night minimum stay, cancellation fee imposed. **Amenities:** Fee: video games, high-speed Internet. **Pool(s):** heated indoor. **Activities:** whirlpool, exercise room. **Guest Services:** valet and coin laundry, area transportation-within 5 mi. **Free Special Amenities: full breakfast and manager's reception.**

EXTENDED STAY AMERICA-SANRAFAEL-FRANCISCO BLVD
(415)451-1887

Extended Stay Hotel $119-$154 **Address:** 1775 Francisco Blvd E 94901 **Location:** US 101 exit 451 (I-580/Richmond Br/Oakland) northbound; exit 451B (I-580/Richmond/Oakland) southbound, just e on Bellam Blvd, then 1 mi s. **Facility:** 112 units, some efficiencies and kitchens. 4 stories, interior corridors. **Amenities:** high-speed Internet (fee). **Pool(s):** heated indoor. **Activities:** whirlpool. **Guest Services:** coin laundry.

FOUR POINTS BY SHERATON SAN RAFAEL
(415)479-8800

Hotel
$99-$260

FOUR POINTS BY SHERATON

AAA Benefit: Members get up to 20% off, plus Starwood Preferred Guest® bonuses.

Address: 1010 Northgate Dr 94903 **Location:** US 101 exit Terra Linda, 3 mi n, just e. Located in Terra Linda. **Facility:** 235 units. 4 stories, interior corridors. **Terms:** 3 day cancellation notice-fee imposed. **Amenities:** safes. **Pool(s):** heated outdoor. **Activities:** whirlpool, exercise room. **Guest Services:** valet and coin laundry. **Free Special Amenities: room upgrade (subject to availability with advance reservations) and high-speed Internet.** (See ad p. 423.)

GERSTLE PARK INN
(415)721-7611

▼▼▼ **Historic Bed & Breakfast** $189-$275 **Address:** 34 Grove St 94901 **Location:** US 101 exit Central San Rafael, 0.5 mi w on 4th St, 0.5 mi s on D St, then just w on San Rafael Ave. **Facility:** Nestled in the foothills in a residential area, the one-and-a-half-acre grounds overlook the city and contain oak, cedar, redwood and fruit trees. 11 units, some kitchens. 2 stories (no elevator); interior/exterior corridors. **Terms:** 3 day cancellation notice. **Guest Services:** complimentary laundry.

CALL ⚬M 📶 ✕ / SOME UNITS FEE 🐾 🦮

TRAVELODGE SAN RAFAEL
(415)454-9470

▼▼
Motel
$79-$134

Address: 865 Francisco Blvd E 94901 **Location:** US 101 exit Francisco Blvd E, 0.3 mi n. **Facility:** 32 units. 2 stories (no elevator); exterior corridors. **Terms:** cancellation fee imposed. **Amenities:** safes.

Pool(s): heated outdoor.

SAVE CALL ⚬M 🛌 📶 🖥 💻 / SOME UNITS

COLONIAL INN
415/453-9188

[fyi] Not evaluated. **Address:** 1735 Lincoln Ave 94901. Facilities, services, and décor characterize a mid-scale property.

WHERE TO EAT

CHALET BASQUE RESTAURANT
415/479-1070

▼▼▼ Basque. Casual Dining. $9-$29 **AAA Inspector Notes:** Nestled in a residential area, this casual restaurant offers patio dining, weather permitting. The friendly owner makes the rounds to greet each customer. Try the tomato-based lamb stew and gâteau Basque for dessert. For a full Basque cuisine experience, go for dinner. **Bar:** full bar. **Address:** 405 N San Pedro Rd 94903 **Location:** US 101 exit N San Pedro Rd, 1.5 mi ne. L D

IL DAVIDE RESTAURANT
415/454-8080

▼▼▼ Italian. Casual Dining. $11-$24 **AAA Inspector Notes:** This place appeals to those in search of an upscale experience. Italian cuisine includes a fine array of pasta, with orecchiette being a favorite. **Bar:** full bar. **Address:** 901 A St 94901 **Location:** Between 3rd and 4th sts; downtown. **Parking:** street only. L D

LOTUS INDIAN CUISINE
415/456-5808

▼▼ Indian. Casual Dining. $11-$23 **AAA Inspector Notes:** This popular Indian restaurant serves solid North Indian cuisine. A buffet lunch served everyday is a good way to sample some of the traditional dishes of India. **Bar:** beer & wine. **Address:** 704 4th St 94901 **Location:** At Tamalpais Ave; downtown. **Parking:** street only. L D

SOL FOOD PUERTO RICAN CUISINE
415/256-8900

▼ Puerto Rican. Quick Serve. $8-$18 **AAA Inspector Notes:** Not hard to find, this restaurant is housed in a lime-colored building. Brightly colored tables, live plants, background music and family pictures adorning brightly colored walls transport patrons to Puerto Rico. Food portions are good so any appetite is sure to be satisfied. Try the combination plate of pan-fried pork chops, beans and tostones or maduros, the refreshing limonada fresca, and the rich flan. **Address:** 901 Lincoln Ave 94901 **Location:** At 3rd St. **Parking:** street only. B L D 🦮

WEST BROOKLYN PIZZA
415/453-7914

▼▼ Pizza. Family Dining. $3-$31 **AAA Inspector Notes:** This pizzeria pays homage to the Big Apple not only in its name but also in its choices of traditional New York-style thin-crust pizza and in its displays of New York memorabilia. Sicilian-style pizza also appears on the menu. **Bar:** beer & wine. **Address:** 900 B Anderson Dr 94901 **Location:** US 101 exit W Francisco Blvd. L D

YET WAH
415/460-9883

▼▼ Chinese. Casual Dining. $8-$16 **AAA Inspector Notes:** Meaning the moon's brightness, this restaurant offers dim sum and a host of Chinese favorites in a cozy, warm atmosphere. **Bar:** full bar. **Address:** 1238 4th St 94901 **Location:** US 101 exit 4th St, 0.5 mi w; between B and C sts. **Parking:** street only. L D CALL ⚬M

SAN RAMON pop. 72,148
• Hotels & Restaurants map & index p. 254

COURTYARD BY MARRIOTT
(925)866-2900 **53**

▼▼▼ **Hotel** $99-$209 **Address:** 18090 San Ramon Valley Blvd 94583 **Location:** I-680 exit Bollinger Canyon Rd W, then s. **Facility:** 136 units. 4 stories, interior corridors. **Amenities:** high-speed Internet. **Pool(s):** outdoor. **Activities:** exercise room. **Guest Services:** valet and coin laundry.

AAA Benefit: AAA hotel discounts of 5% or more.

ECO 🍴 CALL ⚬M 🛌 BIZ 📶 ✕ 💻 / SOME UNITS 🖥 🖼

EXTENDED STAYAMERICA-SAN RAMON-BISHOP RANCH-WEST
(925)277-0833 **51**

▼▼ **Extended Stay Hotel** $94-$109 **Address:** 18000 San Ramon Valley Blvd 94583 **Location:** I-680 exit Bollinger Canyon Rd E, just n. **Facility:** 148 efficiencies. 3 stories, exterior corridors. **Guest Services:** coin laundry.

🍴➕ 📶 🖥 🖼 💻 / SOME UNITS FEE 🐾

HYATT HOUSE SAN RAMON
(925)743-1882 **49**

▼▼▼
Hotel
$79-$249

H HYATT house™ **AAA Benefit:** Members save 10% or more everyday.

Address: 2323 San Ramon Valley Blvd 94583 **Location:** I-680 exit Crow Canyon Rd W, just n. **Facility:** 142 units, some efficiencies. 4 stories, interior corridors. **Terms:** cancellation fee imposed. **Amenities:** high-speed Internet. **Pool(s):** heated outdoor. **Activities:** whirlpool, exercise room. **Guest Services:** valet and coin laundry. **Free Special Amenities:** expanded continental breakfast and high-speed Internet.

SAVE 🍴➕ CALL ⚬M 🛌 BIZ 📶 ✕ 🖥 💻

RESIDENCE INN BY MARRIOTT
(925)277-9292 **52**

▼▼▼ **Extended Stay Hotel** $123-$224 **Address:** 1071 Market Pl 94583 **Location:** I-680 exit Bollinger Canyon Rd E, 0.5 mi e. **Facility:** 106 kitchen units, some two bedrooms. 2 stories, exterior corridors. **Amenities:** high-speed Internet. **Pool(s):** heated outdoor. **Activities:** whirlpool, sports court, exercise room. **Guest Services:** valet and coin laundry.

AAA Benefit: AAA hotel discounts of 5% or more.

ECO 🍴➕ CALL ⚬M 🛌 BIZ 📶 ✕ 🖥 💻 / SOME UNITS FEE 🐾

SAN RAMON MARRIOTT AT BISHOP RANCH
(925)867-9200 **50**

▼▼▼ **Hotel** $109-$299 **Address:** 2600 Bishop Dr 94583 **Location:** I-680 exit Bollinger Canyon Rd E, n on Sunset, then just w. **Facility:** 368 units. 6 stories, interior corridors. **Amenities:** Fee: video games, high-speed Internet. **Dining:** Stixx & Steaks, see separate listing. **Pool(s):** outdoor. **Activities:** saunas, exercise room. **Guest Services:** valet and coin laundry.

AAA Benefit: AAA hotel discounts of 5% or more.

ECO 🍴 🍷 CALL ⚬M 🛌 BIZ 📶 ✕ 📷 💻 / SOME UNITS FEE 🐾 🖥

WHERE TO EAT

THE HOPYARD AMERICAN ALEHOUSE & GRILL
925/277-9600 **55**

▼▼ American. Casual Dining. $8-$18 **AAA Inspector Notes:** The sports bar is a favorite among locals for its friendly service and traditional grilled favorites. Assorted beers and ales are on tap. **Bar:** full bar. **Address:** 470 Market Pl 94583 **Location:** I-680 exit Bollinger Canyon, 0.6 mi e, then 0.3 mi s; in Market Place Shopping Center. L D CALL ⚬M

(See map & index p. 254.)

KILOHANA GRILL 925/830-1144 (54)

▼ Hawaiian. Quick Serve. $5-$12 **AAA Inspector Notes:** A taste of the islands has come to the East Bay area with sounds of Hawaiian music playing in the background at this small restaurant. Barbecue beef and chicken, with an incredible homemade teriyaki glaze is a favorite of the local crowd. Other selections include Kahlua pork, kalbi ribs, Hawaiian-style chili and even a burger topped with pineapple. Be sure to save room for pineapple upside down cake for dessert. **Address:** 1061-A Market Pl 94583 **Location:** I-680 exit Bollinger Canyon, 0.5 mi e, then just s. L D

LEVY'S BAGELS & CO 925/838-8508 (51)

▼ Deli. Quick Serve. $4-$8 **AAA Inspector Notes:** The casual and relaxed eatery is a great place to stop for a bagel or quick sandwich. **Address:** 2435 San Ramon Valley Blvd, Suite 7 94583 **Location:** Just s of Crow Canyon Rd. B L

MAX'S RESTAURANT & BAR 925/277-9300 (48)

▼▼ American. Casual Dining. $8-$24 **AAA Inspector Notes:** A menu that will please everyone is offered here where hearty appetizers, entrée salads, burgers, pasta dishes and grilled meats are featured. A favorite on the menu is the Reuben sandwich. While portions are very hearty, saving room for dessert is a must as they offer cakes, sundaes and a chocolate éclair or macaroon that has to be seen to believe the slice–big enough for the entire family to share. **Bar:** full bar. **Address:** 2015 Crow Canyon Pl 94583 **Location:** I-680 exit Crow Canyon Rd, just e. L D CALL 🚼M

NEW YORK PIZZA 925/838-7655 (52)

▼ Pizza. Casual Dining. $12-$28 **AAA Inspector Notes:** A fun place for families, this pizzeria prepares hot wings, salad and, of course, pizza. Video games provide entertainment while parties wait for their food. **Bar:** beer & wine. **Address:** 2468 San Ramon Valley Blvd 94583 **Location:** Just s of Crow Canyon Rd. L D

PASTA POMODORO 925/867-1407

▼▼ Italian. Casual Dining. $8-$18 **AAA Inspector Notes:** Families are welcomed at this laid-back restaurant, which brings in plenty of loyal locals who enjoy its varied Italian favorites, including tempting pasta and chicken dishes. **Bar:** beer & wine. **Address:** 146 Sunset Dr 94583 **Location:** I-680 exit Bollinger Canyon Rd, just e; in The Shops at Bishop Ranch Shopping Center.

L D CALL 🚼M

ROUND TABLE PIZZA

▼ Pizza. Casual Dining. $7-$28 **AAA Inspector Notes:** This casual, family-oriented pizza place features high-quality ingredients and dough rolled fresh daily. Distinctive specialty pizzas are piled high with toppings. **Bar:** beer & wine. L D CALL 🚼M

For additional information, visit AAA.com

LOCATIONS:
Address: 3203 Crow Canyon Pl 94583 **Location:** I-680 exit Crow Canyon Rd, just e; in Crow Canyon Commons Shopping Center. **Phone:** 925/866-1331
Address: 450 Market Pl 94583 **Location:** I-680 exit Bollinger Canyon Rd E; in Market Place Shopping Center. **Phone:** 925/867-1606

STIXX & STEAKS 925/244-6114 (53)

▼▼▼ Pacific Rim. Fine Dining. $10-$36 **AAA Inspector Notes:** Among the diverse offerings on the extensive menu are grilled steaks, freshly made sushi and some Asian and Pacific Rim specialties. Some tables overlook the patio. **Bar:** full bar. **Reservations:** suggested. **Address:** 2600 Bishop Dr 94583 **Location:** I-680 exit Bollinger Canyon Rd E, n on Sunset Dr, then just w; in San Ramon Marriott at Bishop Ranch. **Parking:** on-site and valet.

L D CALL 🚼M

UNCLE YU'S 925/275-1818 (49)

▼▼▼ Szechuan. Casual Dining. $8-$30 **AAA Inspector Notes:** A tradition in this area for more than 20 years, the menu at this spot serves up traditional favorites and some specialties of their own. The spicy crispy chef's prawns is a favorite. Diners can expect the service to be warm and welcoming. **Address:** 2005 Crow Canyon Pl, Suite 160 94583 **Location:** I-680 exit Crow Canyon Rd, just e, just n; in Magnolia Square Shopping Center.

L D CALL 🚼M

ZACHARY'S CHICAGO PIZZA 925/244-1222 (50)

▼▼▼ Pizza. Casual Dining. $15-$30 **AAA Inspector Notes:** The East Bay's favorite place for pizza offers traditional deep-dish, Chicago-style pies that are two inches deep and feature homemade crust, sauce, cheese and a variety of toppings. Create your own pizza or select from one of their specialty pizzas: Zachary's special offers sausage, green peppers, onions and mushrooms. A variety of salads, from Caesar to spinach to traditional garden-style, rounds out the menu. **Bar:** beer & wine. **Address:** 3110 Crow Canyon Pl 94583 **Location:** I-680 exit Crow Canyon Rd, just e. L D CALL 🚼M

SANTA CLARA (E-9) pop. 116,468, elev. 88'
• Hotels p. 486 • Restaurants p. 487
• Hotels & Restaurants map & index p. 468

An agricultural community once renowned for its orchards, Santa Clara is better known these days as an integral component of Silicon Valley. Intel Corporation is among the high-tech giants headquartered in the city.

Guided and self-guiding campus tours are available at Santa Clara University, founded in 1851. From US 101, take the De La Cruz Boulevard/Santa Clara exit to El Camino Real and follow signs to the university. Visitors are welcome at the free Music at Noon series, which takes place every Wednesday during the academic year at Music Recital Hall and frequently features high-profile Bay Area performers. Pick up a campus map at the Admission & Enrollment Services Building (#406); for additional campus information phone (408) 554-4000.

Santa Clara Chamber of Commerce & Convention-Visitors Bureau: 1850 Warburton Ave., Santa Clara, CA 95050. **Phone:** (408) 244-9660 or (408) 244-8244.

Shopping areas: Westfield Valley Fair, off I-880 at Stevens Creek Boulevard, features Macy's, Nordstrom and more than 250 upscale specialty stores.

CALIFORNIA'S GREAT AMERICA, on Great America Pkwy. between US 101 and SR 237, is a 100-acre family theme park combining movie magic with theme park thrills and excitement. Among more than 50 rides and attractions are the Great Barrier Reef wave pool; a double-decker carousel; Drop Tower Scream Zone, a 22-story free-fall ride; Delirium, a spinning pendulum-like ride; FireFall, a 60-foot spinning free-fall ride; and eight roller coasters.

Other highlights include the Australian-themed Boomerang Bay Beach Club water park; Rip Roaring Rapids, a white-water raft ride; an aerial gondola; and an antique auto turnpike ride.

Planet Snoopy has rides, shows and opportunities to meet the Peanuts gang. Theaters present stage shows, and concerts are held in an outdoor amphitheater. Laser tag, games galleries and video game arcades also are featured.

Hours: Open daily at 10, June 1-Labor Day; schedule varies, Apr.-May and day after Labor Day-late Oct. Water park open daily at 11, early June to mid-Aug.; schedule varies, mid-May to early June and mid-Aug. through Labor Day. Closing times vary for both parks. Phone ahead to confirm schedules.

(See map & index p. 468.)

Closed Easter. **Cost:** $57.99 (includes water park); $37.99 (ages 62+ and under 48 inches tall). **Parking:** $12. **Phone:** (408) 988-1776.

DE SAISSET MUSEUM, on the Santa Clara University campus, is both an art and history museum. The permanent collection includes paintings by Renaissance, baroque and rococo artists; 19th-century, modernist and contemporary prints; and photographs. California historical items range from Native American jewelry, baskets and hand tools to such Mission period artifacts as devotional and decorative arts.

Time: Allow 1 hour minimum. **Hours:** Tues.-Sun. 11-4, mid-Aug. through June 30. Closed major holidays and between exhibitions. Phone ahead to confirm schedule. **Cost:** Free. **Phone:** (408) 554-4528.

INTEL MUSEUM is .5 mi. n. off US 101 Montague Expwy. exit, then .4 mi. w. to 2200 Mission College Blvd., in the Intel Corp.'s Robert Noyce Building. Exhibits focus on the manufacture and use of computer chips. Visitors can communicate in binary code and learn how a computer performs simple calculations using a giant talking microprocessor. A section about clean rooms ("fabs") details 47 steps workers perform before entering a chip-making factory. A "bunny suit" also is on display.

A time line details the progress of computers and Intel history. **Time:** Allow 1 hour minimum. **Hours:** Mon.-Fri. 9-6, Sat. 10-5. Closed major holidays. **Cost:** Free. **Phone:** (408) 765-0503.

 MISSION SANTA CLARA DE ASIS is on the Santa Clara University campus, off the US 101 De La Cruz exit to 500 El Camino Real. It was founded in 1777, the eighth of 21 missions built in California in the 1700s. It has the distinction of being the first mission named for a woman, Saint Clare of Assisi, the founder of the Poor Clares order. Established to help protect early settlers in the San Francisco Bay Area, it is the only mission associated with a university.

The building is a replica of the third mission, which was built in 1825. Artifacts on display include three bells given to the mission by the king of Spain. The original mission garden is intact; the months of peak bloom are April and May. Guided tours are available by appointment. **Time:** Allow 30 minutes minimum. **Hours:** Mission church open daily 6 a.m.-8 p.m. Office open Mon.-Fri. 1-5. **Cost:** Free. **Phone:** (408) 554-4023, or (408) 554-4528 for guided tours.

TRITON MUSEUM OF ART, across from the Santa Clara Civic Center at jct. Lincoln St. and Warburton Ave., features rotating exhibits of Bay Area and California artists. Exhibits are changed every 2 to 3 months. **Time:** Allow 30 minutes minimum. **Hours:** Tues.-Sat. 11-5, Sun. noon-4. Closed major holidays. **Cost:** Donations. **Phone:** (408) 247-3754.

AVATAR HOTEL GREAT AMERICA (408)235-8900 **77**

 Hotel $79-$249

Address: 4200 Great America Pkwy 95054 **Location:** 0.5 mi e off US 101 exit Great America Pkwy; 0.8 mi s of California's Great America theme park. **Facility:** 168 units. 4 stories, exterior corridors. **Terms:** cancellation fee imposed. **Amenities:** high-speed Internet. **Pool(s):** outdoor. **Activities:** whirlpool, exercise room. **Guest Services:** valet laundry, area transportation-within 5 mi.

SAVE ECO ⤋ ¶¶ CALL ⤷M ⤰ BIZ 🛜 ▤ ⬛ / SOME UNITS 🐾

BEST WESTERN INN SANTA CLARA

(408)244-3366 **82**

Motel $99-$199

Best Western

AAA Benefit: Members save up to 20%, plus 10% bonus points with Best Western Rewards®.

Address: 4341 El Camino Real 95051 **Location:** SR 82, 2 blks w of Lawrence Expwy. **Facility:** 52 units. 2 stories (no elevator), exterior corridors. **Terms:** cancellation fee imposed. **Amenities:** *Some:* high-speed Internet. **Pool(s):** outdoor. **Guest Services:** valet and coin laundry. **Free Special Amenities:** expanded continental breakfast and high-speed Internet.

SAVE ¶¶ ⤰ ⤷M 🛜 ▤ ⬛ ⬛

BILTMORE HOTEL & SUITES/SILICON VALLEY

(408)988-8411 **81**

 Hotel $129-$299

Address: 2151 Laurelwood Rd 95054 **Location:** US 101 exit Montague Expwy, just e; 1 mi s of Great America Pkwy. **Facility:** 263 units. 2-9 stories, interior/exterior corridors. **Terms:** cancellation fee imposed. **Amenities:** video games (fee). **Dining:** Montague's Cafe, see separate listing. **Pool(s):** outdoor. **Activities:** whirlpool, exercise room. **Guest Services:** valet laundry, area transportation-within 5 mi. **Free Special Amenities:** high-speed Internet and airport transportation.

SAVE ⤋ ⤓ CALL ⤷M ⤰ BIZ 🛜 ✕ 🎥 ⬛ / SOME UNITS FEE 🐾 FEE ▤ FEE ⬛

CANDLEWOOD SUITES-SILICON VALLEY/SAN JOSE

(408)241-9305 **89**

⬧⬧ Extended Stay Hotel $119-$159 **Address:** 481 El Camino Real 95050 **Location:** I-880 exit The Alameda, 1.5 mi w. **Facility:** 122 efficiencies. 3 stories, interior corridors. **Amenities:** high-speed Internet. **Activities:** exercise room. **Guest Services:** valet and coin laundry.

CALL ⤷M 🛜 ▤ ⬛ ⬛ / SOME UNITS FEE 🐾

EMBASSY SUITES HOTEL (408)496-6400 **80**

⬧⬧⬧ Hotel $109-$279 **Address:** 2885 Lakeside Dr 95054 **Location:** US 101 exit Great America Pkwy, then w. **Facility:** 257 units. 10 stories, interior corridors. **Terms:** check-in 4 pm, 1-7 night minimum stay, cancellation fee imposed. **Pool(s):** heated indoor. **Activities:** whirlpool, exercise room. **Guest Services:** valet and coin laundry.

AAA Benefit: Members save 5% or more!

ECO ¶¶ ⥿ CALL ⤷M ⤰ BIZ 🛜 ▤ ⬛ ⬛

(See map & index p. 468.)

HILTON SANTA CLARA HOTEL   (408)330-0001 75

Hotel
$95-$389

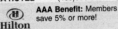

AAA Benefit: Members save 5% or more!

Address: 4949 Great America Pkwy 95054 **Location:** US 101 exit Great America Pkwy, 0.5 mi n. **Facility:** Silicon Valley is the setting for this centrally located hotel offering manicured grounds and attractively appointed accommodations. It's convenient to California's Great America theme park. 280 units. 8 stories, interior corridors. **Terms:** 1-7 night minimum stay, cancellation fee imposed. **Amenities:** safes. *Fee:* video games, high-speed Internet. **Dining:** La Fontana, see separate listing. **Pool(s):** heated outdoor. **Activities:** whirlpool, exercise room. **Guest Services:** valet laundry.

HOLIDAY INN EXPRESS & SUITES   (408)554-9200 88

Hotel $119-$209 **Address:** 1700 El Camino Real 95050 **Location:** I-880 exit The Alameda (SR 82), 2.1 mi w. **Facility:** 47 units. 2 stories, interior corridors. **Terms:** cancellation fee imposed. **Amenities:** high-speed Internet. **Guest Services:** complimentary laundry.

HOLIDAY INN EXPRESS & SUITES SANTA CLARA-SILICON VALLEY   408/241-0100 86

Hotel. Rates not provided. **Address:** 2455 El Camino Real 95051 **Location:** Just w of San Tomas Expwy. **Facility:** 97 units. 3 stories, interior corridors. **Amenities:** high-speed Internet. **Pool(s):** heated outdoor. **Activities:** whirlpool, exercise room. **Guest Services:** complimentary laundry.

HYATT HOUSE SANTA CLARA/SAN JOSE AIRPORT   (408)486-0800 79

Hotel
$99-$269

HYATT house™ AAA Benefit: Members save 10% or more everyday.

Address: 3915 Rivermark Plaza 95054 **Location:** US 101 exit Montague Expwy, 1 mi e. **Facility:** 150 efficiencies. 7 stories, interior corridors. **Terms:** cancellation fee imposed. **Amenities:** high-speed Internet. **Pool(s):** heated outdoor. **Activities:** whirlpool, exercise room. **Guest Services:** valet and coin laundry, area transportation-within 5 mi. **Free Special Amenities:** expanded continental breakfast and high-speed Internet.

HYATT REGENCY SANTA CLARA   (408)200-1234 74

Hotel
$72-$288

HYATT® AAA Benefit: Members save 10% or more everyday.

Address: 5101 Great America Pkwy 95054 **Location:** US 101 exit Great America Pkwy, 0.8 mi e. **Facility:** Manicured lawns and gardens with fountains surround this high-rise hotel, which sits adjacent to Santa Clara Convention Center. The property's public areas are spacious and the guest rooms inviting. 501 units. 14 stories, interior corridors. **Terms:** cancellation fee imposed. **Amenities:** high-speed Internet (fee), safes. **Dining:** TusCA, see separate listing. **Pool(s):** heated outdoor. **Activities:** whirlpool, exercise room. *Fee:* golf-18 holes, 4 lighted tennis courts. **Guest Services:** valet laundry.

THE PLAZA SUITES   (408)748-9800 78

Hotel
$139-$272

Address: 3100 Lakeside Dr 95054 **Location:** W of US 101 exit Lawrence Expwy, s on Oakmead Pkwy at Peterson Way. **Facility:** 219 units. 7 stories, interior corridors. **Terms:** cancellation fee imposed. **Amenities:** high-speed Internet (fee), safes. **Pool(s):** outdoor. **Activities:** whirlpool, exercise room. **Guest Services:** valet and coin laundry, area transportation-within 5 mi. **Free Special Amenities:** full breakfast and manager's reception.

QUALITY INN & SUITES SILICON VALLEY   (408)241-3010 85

Motel
$94-$105

Address: 2930 El Camino Real 95051 **Location:** SR 82, 0.5 mi w of San Tomas Expwy; US 101 exit S Bowers Ave. **Facility:** 69 units, some two bedrooms and kitchens. 2 stories (no elevator), exterior corridors. **Terms:** cancellation fee imposed. **Pool(s):** heated outdoor. **Guest Services:** valet laundry.

RAMADA   (408)244-8313 87

Hotel $79-$129 **Address:** 1655 El Camino Real 95050 **Location:** I-880 exit The Alameda, 2 mi w. **Facility:** 68 units. 2 stories (no elevator), exterior corridors. **Terms:** cancellation fee imposed. **Amenities:** high-speed Internet. **Pool(s):** outdoor. **Guest Services:** valet laundry.

SANTA CLARA MARRIOTT HOTEL   (408)988-1500 76

Hotel $99-$319 **Address:** 2700 Mission College Blvd 95054 **Location:** 0.5 mi e off US 101 exit Great America Pkwy; 0.8 mi s of California's Great America theme park. **Facility:** 759 units. 2-15 stories, interior corridors. **Parking:** on-site (fee). **Amenities:** *Fee:* video games, high-speed Internet. **Dining:** 2 restaurants. **Pool(s):** heated outdoor. **Activities:** whirlpool, 4 lighted tennis courts, sports court, exercise room. **Guest Services:** valet laundry.

AAA Benefit: AAA hotel discounts of 5% or more.

VAGABOND INN SANTA CLARA   (408)241-0771 83

Motel
$59-$199

Address: 3580 El Camino Real 95051 **Location:** On SR 82, southeast corner of Lawrence Expwy cloverleaf. **Facility:** 70 units. 2 stories (no elevator), exterior corridors. **Terms:** cancellation fee imposed. **Amenities:** safes (fee). **Pool(s):** outdoor. **Guest Services:** coin laundry. **Free Special Amenities:** expanded continental breakfast and high-speed Internet.

WHERE TO EAT

ARMADILLO WILLY'S BARBECUE   408/247-1100

Barbecue. Quick Serve. $7-$22 **AAA Inspector Notes:** Menu offerings at this eatery include a wide selection of barbecue favorites including ribs, chicken, beef brisket, burgers and salad. The atmosphere here is fun and lively. **Bar:** beer & wine. **Address:** 2624 Homestead Rd 95051 **Location:** Just w of San Tomas Expwy.

Learn about inspections and Diamond Ratings at AAA.com/Diamonds

(See map & index p. 468.)

BIRK'S RESTAURANT
408/980-6400 (29)

American. Fine Dining. $13-$42 **AAA Inspector Notes:** In a small, upscale business park in the Santa Clara Valley, this restaurant is appointed in an attractive décor. The atmosphere is friendly and the menu varied. Frequent patrons include local business clientèle and visitors. A great selections of steaks, chops and seafood are available. **Bar:** full bar. **Reservations:** suggested. **Address:** 3955 Freedom Cir 95054 **Location:** US 101 exit Great America Pkwy, 0.5 mi e, then just s on Mission College Blvd.

L D

THE CHEESECAKE FACTORY
408/246-0092 (36)

American. Casual Dining. $9-$30 **AAA Inspector Notes:** A display case of mouthwatering cheesecakes is the first thing visitors see as they walk through the door. The extensive menu incorporates many types of cuisine, including Asian, Italian, Greek and Spanish. **Bar:** full bar. **Address:** 3041 Stevens Creek Blvd, Space L1 95050 **Location:** I-880 exit Stevens Creek Blvd, just w; in Westfield Shopping Center/Valley Fair Mall. L D CALL M

CHERRY SUSHI
408/557-0770 (33)

Japanese Sushi. Casual Dining. $8-$29 **AAA Inspector Notes:** This is a favorite spot of the locals so get here early. An extensive selection of sushi and sashimi rolls are featured. Tempura and teriyaki dishes also are offered. Expect warm and friendly service. **Bar:** beer & wine. **Address:** 2910 El Camino Real 95051 **Location:** On SR 82, just w of San Tomas Expwy.

L D CALL M

EL TORITO
408/727-4426

Mexican. Casual Dining. $8-$20 **AAA Inspector Notes:** Homemade Mexican favorites span from classic preparations to specialties from the country's central regions. Spicy taqueria-style tacos and carnitas Michoacan (marinated pork) are tasty choices. **Bar:** full bar. **Address:** 2950 Lakeside Dr 95054 **Location:** US 101 exit Great America Pkwy/Bowers Ave, just w. L D CALL M

EN JAPANESE TAPAS RESTAURANT
408/246-0011 (32)

Japanese Small Plates. Casual Dining. $6-$22 **AAA Inspector Notes:** Enjoy the authentic ambience and food at this Japanese izakaya. An extensive menu ranges from tako yaki and akashi yaki to uni fried rice and classic oden. **Bar:** beer & wine. **Address:** 3450 El Camino Real 95051 **Location:** US 101 exit Lawrence Expwy, 2.6 mi s, 0.3 mi e. L D

LA FONTANA
408/330-0001 (26)

Mediterranean
Fine Dining
$10-$24

AAA Inspector Notes: Mediterranean influences are evident in fresh and innovative preparations of grilled chicken, meat and fish and pasta specialties, which are made in an open grill kitchen. Floor-to-ceiling windows enable guests to view the patio area. **Bar:** full bar. **Reservations:** suggested. **Address:** 4949 Great America Pkwy 95054 **Location:** US 101 exit Great America Pkwy, 0.5 mi n; in Hilton Santa Clara Hotel.

L D CALL M

American restaurant with fresh fish, pasta & Angus beef

LA PALOMA RESTAURANTE
408/247-0990 (35)

Mexican. Casual Dining. $10-$20 **AAA Inspector Notes:** Now in its third generation, customers have made this a favorite stop since 1977. A great selection of Mexican specialties include traditional favorites and some specialties of their own. A few seafood selections include enchiladas filled with crab, grilled salmon with a tomatillo avocado salsa and shrimp fajitas. The midweek lunch buffet is a favorite so be sure to arrive early as the crowds line up quickly. **Bar:** full bar. **Address:** 2280 El Camino Real 95050 **Location:** I-880 exit The Alameda, 2.5 mi e, at San Tomas Expwy. L D CALL M

MARIANI'S
408/243-1431 (34)

Italian. Casual Dining. $9-$26 **AAA Inspector Notes:** Guests can relax amid comfortable décor to sample foods from a menu featuring pasta, seafood, chops and poultry. This spot is a long-time tradition in the area. **Bar:** full bar. **Reservations:** suggested. **Address:** 2500 El Camino Real 95051 **Location:** US 101 exit San Tomas Expwy, 3 mi s, then just w. B L D

MONTAGUE'S CAFE
408/988-8411 (31)

American. Casual Dining. $9-$20 **AAA Inspector Notes:** Freshly prepared, home-style cooking has made this restaurant a favorite with the local clientèle. In addition to the regular menu, a buffet is offered during the lunch hour. **Bar:** full bar. **Address:** 2151 Laurelwood Rd 95054 **Location:** US 101 exit Montague Expwy, just e; 1 mi s of Great America Pkwy; in Biltmore Hotel & Suites/Silicon Valley. B L D CALL M

OLD IRONSIDES CAFE
408/727-5147 (27)

Mediterranean Deli. Quick Serve. $6-$10 **AAA Inspector Notes:** This small café is incorporated into an upscale business park and is a favorite of the locals. Family owned and operated, they offer a variety of hot and cold sandwiches including burgers; beef, chicken or lamb gyros along with some vegetarian items. They also offer Mediterranean specialties including kebabs, falafel, mujadarra and tabbouleh, Items are very tasty and plentiful so bring your appetite. **Bar:** beer & wine. **Address:** 4655 Old Ironsides Dr, Suite 150 95054 **Location:** US 101 exit Great America Pkwy/Bowers Ave, 1 mi n, just w on Patrick Henry, then just n; in Marriott Business Park. B L CALL M

PEDRO'S RESTAURANT & CANTINA
408/496-6777 (30)

Mexican. Casual Dining. $10-$20 **AAA Inspector Notes:** With its distinctive dining rooms and wall murals, the restaurant makes guests feel as though they're dining in Mexico. Traditional homemade specialties make up the menu. **Bar:** full bar. **Address:** 3935 Freedom Cir 95054 **Location:** US 101 exit Great America Pkwy E, right on Mission College Blvd, then right. L D CALL M

PIATTI RISTORANTE & BAR
408/330-9212 (28)

Italian. Casual Dining. $12-$32 **AAA Inspector Notes:** This casual eatery resembles dining in an Italian bistro with its open-grill kitchen and distinctive décor. The extensive menu consists of authentic pasta dishes with homemade sauces, sautéed seafood and poultry items, specialty salads, panini and pizza. Traditional desserts include tiramisu, panna cotta and an incredible bitter sweet chocolate cake with raspberry gelato and freshly whipped cream. Service is warm and friendly. **Bar:** full bar. **Address:** 2905 Rivermark Plaza 95054 **Location:** US 101 exit San Tomas Expwy/Montague Expwy, 1.2 mi e. L D CALL M

ROUND TABLE PIZZA

Pizza. Casual Dining. $7-$28 **AAA Inspector Notes:** This casual, family-oriented pizza place features high-quality ingredients and dough rolled fresh daily. Distinctive specialty pizzas are piled high with toppings. **Bar:** beer & wine. L D

For additional information, visit AAA.com

LOCATIONS:

Address: 2615 The Alameda 95050 **Location:** I-880 exit The Alameda, just w. **Phone:** 408/248-9123

Address: 4300 Great America Pkwy 95050 **Location:** US 101 exit Great America Pkwy E; at Mission College Blvd. **Phone:** 408/970-9000

TUSCA
408/510-6480 (25)

Regional Italian. Casual Dining. $10-$30 **AAA Inspector Notes:** A casual atmosphere prevails at this spot where a variety of salads, panini and homemade pizza serve up the lunch menu. The more extensive dinner menu offers hearty pasta dishes, beef and seafood items. Everything is fresh and most items are prepared from locally-grown produce. **Bar:** full bar. **Reservations:** suggested. **Address:** 5101 Great America Pkwy 95054 **Location:** US 101 exit Great America Pkwy, 0.8 mi e; in Hyatt Regency Santa Clara. B L D CALL M

Learn about inspections and Diamond Ratings at AAA.com/Diamonds

SANTA CRUZ (G-2) pop. 59,946, elev. 20'
• Hotels p. 495 • Restaurants p. 501
• Hotels & Restaurants map & index p. 492

The northern end of Monterey Bay was first explored in 1769 by Spaniard Gaspar de Portolá, who gave the area its name, which means "holy cross." It also was the site of one of Father Junípero Serra's 21 California missions.

This beautiful city on the Pacific coast off scenic SR 1 has long been a quintessential beach town. Surfing became popular in the 1930s, and Steamer Lane is an internationally renowned surfing site. The Santa Cruz Surfing Museum, inside the Mark Abbott Memorial Lighthouse on West Cliff Drive, displays a collection of surfboards and surfing photographs from the 1930s to the present; phone (831) 420-6289.

A half-scale replica of the original Santa Cruz mission is on the grounds of Holy Cross Church, at 126 High St. facing the downtown plaza. All that remains of the original mission, built in 1791 and destroyed by an earthquake in 1857, are the ruins of soldiers' barracks and part of a stone foundation. The chapel is open to visitors; phone (831) 423-1043.

A summer highlight is the ⧫ Shakespeare Santa Cruz Summer Festival. The University of California Santa Cruz's resident repertory company presents four of Shakespeare's works from mid-July through August at two venues: outdoors at the Sinsheimer-Stanley Festival Glen, with a backdrop of majestic redwood trees; and inside at the UCSC Mainstage Theater, which has a traditional "thrust" stage and seating on three sides for a more intimate theater-going experience. For schedule and ticket information phone (831) 459-2157.

Santa Cruz County Conference and Visitors Council: 303 Water St. #100, Santa Cruz, CA 95060. **Phone:** (831) 425-1234 or (800) 833-3494. *(See ad p. 496.)*

CHARDONNAY SAILING CHARTERS departs from Santa Cruz Yacht Harbor. Two-hour themed cruises through Monterey Bay National Marine Sanctuary aboard a 70-foot sailing yacht include winemakers, brewmasters, a champagne brunch, Hawaiian and sunset sails and a Wednesday night race. During the summer months a Thursday night beach party features a 1-hour bay cruise.

Hours: Excursions depart year-round; phone for schedule. **Cost:** Two-hour themed cruises and whale-watching cruises $49.50; $29.50 (ages 4-14). One-hour beach party cruise $23.81; $19.05 (ages 4-14). Reservations are recommended. **Phone:** (831) 423-1213 for schedules and reservations.

THE MUSEUM OF ART AND HISTORY is at 705 Front St. at jct. Cooper St. (in the McPherson Center). It promotes interest in contemporary art and Santa Cruz County history through traveling exhibits and a collection of artifacts and memorabilia.

(See map & index p. 492.)

Historical exhibits trace area history from early inhabitants the Ohlone Indians and the mission period to the lumber industry and the 1989 Loma Prieta earthquake. Installed in the outdoor sculpture garden are works from the museum's permanent collection.

Time: Allow 1 hour minimum. **Hours:** Tues.-Sun. 11-5 (also first and third Fri. of the month 5-9). Closed major holidays. **Cost:** $5; $3 (ages 62+ and students with ID); free (ages 0-12 and to all first Fri. of the month). **Phone:** (831) 429-1964.

MYSTERY SPOT is 2.5 mi. n. on Market St., which becomes Branciforte Dr. Sir Isaac Newton's law of universal gravitation seemingly does not apply to this circular area of redwood forest approximately 150 feet in diameter, where visitors will experience puzzling variations in perspective. Theories run the gamut from a hole in the ozone layer to an underground guidance system for alien spacecraft, but the reason remains a mystery. There's nothing mysterious, however, about the scenic hiking trail that winds through the redwoods. **Hours:** Guided 45-minute tours are given daily every 15 minutes Mon.-Fri. 10-6, Sat.-Sun. 9-7, Memorial Day-Labor Day; daily 9-5, rest of year. Last tour begins at closing. Advance ticket purchase recommended Sat.-Sun. and holidays. **Cost:** $6 (if purchased in advance); $5 (at the entrance); free (ages 0-3 and military with ID). **Parking:** $5. **Phone:** (831) 423-8897 for information and to purchase tickets.

NATURAL BRIDGES STATE BEACH is off West Cliff Dr. It offers many tide pools for exploring. From about mid-October through February it's possible to observe monarch butterflies, which pass through on their annual migration; a boardwalk leads to the grove of trees where they can be spotted. A visitor center offers exhibits about area ecology and wildlife. *See Recreation Areas Chart.*

Time: Allow 2 hours minimum. **Hours:** Beach open daily 8 a.m.-dusk. Visitor center open Fri.-Mon. 10-4; Tues.-Thurs. when staff is available. Phone ahead to confirm visitor center hours. **Cost:** Day use $10 per private vehicle. **Phone:** (831) 423-4609. ⊠ 🏞

SANTA CRUZ ART LEAGUE, 526 Broadway, presents changing art exhibits in all forms of media and has space for theater, dance and music performances. **Time:** Allow 30 minutes minimum. **Hours:** Wed.-Sat. noon-5, Sun. noon-4. Closed major holidays. **Cost:** Donations. **Phone:** (831) 426-5787.

🔻GEM SAVE **SANTA CRUZ BEACH BOARDWALK** is off SR 1 following signs to the beach area and municipal wharf. Established in 1907, the half-mile-long boardwalk still retains the atmosphere of a turn-of-the-20th-century beachside amusement park. A highlight is the hand-carved Looff carousel, with a rare brass ring machine and an original 342-pipe organ; it dates from 1911. Both the carousel

and the Giant Dipper wooden roller coaster, built in 1924, are National Historic Landmarks.

In addition to more than 35 rides and attractions, there are game arcades, miniature golf, laser tag, a bowling alley, shops, eateries and special event facilities. A park highlight is the Double Shot thrill ride, which propels riders 125 feet skyward for a spectacular bird's-eye view of the coast before shooting them back down to Earth.

The beach and ocean provide a classically scenic backdrop to the boardwalk and amusement park rides. During the summer months free band concerts take place at the beach bandstand on Friday nights.

Time: Allow 1 hour minimum. **Hours:** Amusement park facilities open daily; hours vary. Rides operate daily, April 1-Labor Day; weekends only, rest of year. Phone ahead to confirm schedule. **Cost:** Boardwalk admission free. Individual rides $3-$5; unlimited ride package $29.95. **Parking:** $12. **Phone:** (831) 426-7433 or (831) 423-5590. 🍴

SANTA CRUZ MISSION STATE HISTORIC PARK is at 144 School St. Built by Ohlone and Yokut Indians 1822-24, the adobe structure originally served as housing for Native Americans who worked at the mission. The exterior is restored to its 1840s appearance; inside are exhibits about Native American life and re-creations of living quarters and cooking rooms.

Time: Allow 1 hour minimum. **Hours:** Thurs.-Sat. 10-4. **Cost:** Free. **Phone:** (831) 425-5849.

SANTA CRUZ MUSEUM OF NATURAL HISTORY, 1305 E. Cliff Dr., contains displays of Native American artifacts, rocks, fossils, a touch tide pool exhibit and examples of local fauna. The museum sponsors programs, field trips and special events. **Time:** Allow 1 hour minimum. **Hours:** Wed.-Sun. 10-5, early June-Labor Day; Tues.-Sat. 10-5, rest of year. **Cost:** $4; $2 (ages 60+); free (ages 0-17). **Phone:** (831) 420-6115.

SAVE **SEYMOUR MARINE DISCOVERY CENTER AT LONG MARINE LABORATORY** is w. off SR 1 (Mission St.) on Swift St., then n. on Delaware Ave. to the end of the road. The center, part of the Joseph M. Long Marine Laboratory, is a research and educational facility of the University of California, Santa Cruz. The lab serves as a base for field research in Monterey Bay and the ocean beyond. Visitors can see an aquarium and a blue whale skeleton, check out the interactive displays in the exhibit hall, and touch sea stars and other marine animals.

Hours: Mon.-Sat. 10-5, Sun. noon-5, July-Aug.; Tues.-Sat. 10-5, Sun. noon-5, rest of year. Guided 45-minute lab tours are given on a first-come, first-served basis at 1, 2 and 3. Family tours are given Tues.-Sat. at 11, Sun. at 12:30. Closed Jan. 1, July 4, Thanksgiving, Christmas Eve, Christmas and Dec. 31. **Cost:** $6; $4 (ages 4-16, ages 64+ and students with ID). **Phone:** (831) 459-3800.

(See map & index p. 492.)

UNIVERSITY OF CALIFORNIA SANTA CRUZ

(UCSC), corner of Bay and High sts., was founded in 1965 on a 2,000-acre portion of the Cowell Ranch overlooking Monterey Bay and Santa Cruz. Roads and walkways situated amid redwoods and meadows connect nine residential colleges. Barn Theater, just inside the main entrance, is a former horse barn turned 158-seat theater. Self-guiding tour maps are available at the main entrance information booth.

Hours: Student-led walking/shuttle tours lasting 1.75 hours are given Mon.-Fri. at 1. Additional tours are sometimes offered; phone ahead for information. **Cost:** Tours free. Reservations must be made at least 2 to 4 weeks in advance. **Parking:** Permits $6; metered spaces are limited. Free lot parking is available during tour times; phone for instructions. **Phone:** (831) 459-4008.

Arboretum at UCSC is near 1490 High St. at Arboretum Rd., .5 mi. w. of the main campus entrance. Many of the rare plant specimens displayed here are not otherwise available for study in American botanical gardens. Sections of the arboretum are devoted to plants from Australia, South Africa and New Zealand in addition to California—all regions that share a similar Mediterranean climate. The flowering plants attract many hummingbirds and butterflies. **Hours:** Daily 9-5. Closed Thanksgiving and Christmas. **Cost:** $5; $2 (ages 6-17); free (first Tues. of the month). **Phone:** (831) 427-2998.

Center for Agroecology & Sustainable Food Systems, reached by footpath from Coolidge Dr., is a 25-acre teaching and research facility. Vegetables, flowers, herbs and fruit trees are grown on this organic farm. **Hours:** Daily 8-6. **Cost:** Free. **Phone:** (831) 459-4140.

Cook House, 1156 High St., is now the college's admissions office. Built in 1860, the building is the former Cowell Ranch cookhouse. The well-preserved structure also has served as the chancellor's office and headquarters for the campus police. **Phone:** (831) 459-4008.

Theater Arts Center, 1156 High St., is a complex that contains the 535-seat UCSC MainstageTheater as well as dance, drama and sound recording studios; a 231-seat second stage; a 400-seat music and recital hall; and specialized visual arts facilities. Shakespeare Santa Cruz Festival performances take place at both the Mainstage Theater and the outdoor Sinsheimer-Stanley Festival Glen, with a seating capacity of 700. **Phone:** (831) 459-2159.

WILDER RANCH STATE PARK

1401 Old Coast Rd., is a 6,000-acre site with some 33 miles of trails open to mountain bikers, horseback riders and hikers. An interpretive center includes exhibits about plant and animal life on the ranch. The main house and outbuildings once utilized by ranchers and workers can be explored and include a barn, stables, a water-powered machine shop and a blacksmith shop. **Time:** Allow 1 hour minimum. **Hours:** Park open daily 8 a.m.-dusk. Interpretive center open daily 10-4, Memorial Day-Labor Day; Thurs.-Sun. 10-4, rest of year. Phone ahead to confirm interpretive center schedule. **Cost:** $10 per private vehicle; $9 (ages 62+ per private vehicle). **Phone:** (831) 423-9703, or (831) 426-0505 for the interpretive center.

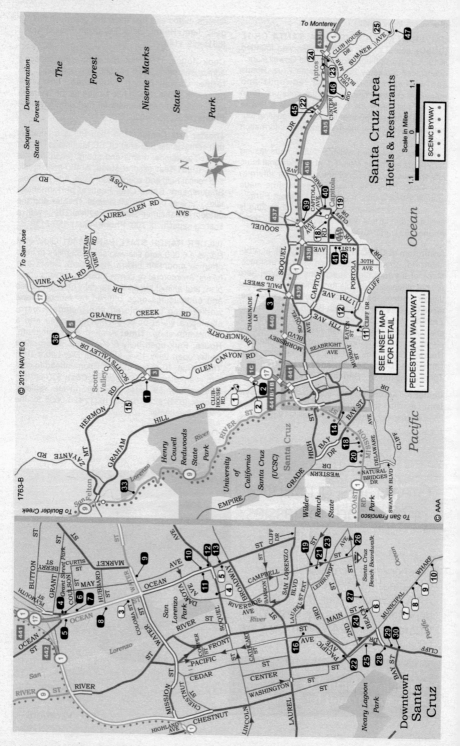

Santa Cruz Area
Hotels & Restaurants

Santa Cruz

This index helps you "spot" where approved hotels and restaurants are located on the corresponding detailed maps. Hotel daily rate range is for comparison only. Restaurant price range is a combination of lunch and/or dinner. Turn to the listing page for more detailed rate and price information and consult display ads for special promotions.

SANTA CRUZ

Map Page	Hotels	Diamond Rated	Rate Range	Page
1 p. 492	Hilton Santa Cruz/Scotts Valley *(See ad p. 498.)*	◆◆◆	$99-$399 SAVE	498
2 p. 492	The Inn at Pasatiempo	◆◆◆	$75-$305 SAVE	499
3 p. 492	Chaminade Resort & Spa	◆◆◆◆	$199-$439 SAVE	495
4 p. 492	BEST WESTERN Inn	◆◆	$99-$169 SAVE	495
5 p. 492	Hampton Inn	◆◆◆	$99-$349 SAVE	498
6 p. 492	Comfort Inn-Santa Cruz	◆◆	$69-$150	497
7 p. 492	Holiday Inn Express & Suites Santa Cruz	◆◆◆	$105-$365	498
8 p. 492	Quality Inn	◆◆	$69-$299 SAVE	500
9 p. 492	Ramada Limited	◆◆	$75-$400 SAVE	500
10 p. 492	The Islander Motel	◆	$70-$260 SAVE	499
11 p. 492	Oceana Inn	◆	$50-$299 SAVE	499
12 p. 492	BEST WESTERN PLUS All Suites Inn	◆◆◆	$85-$220 SAVE	495
13 p. 492	Continental Inn	◆◆◆	$75-$260 SAVE	497
14 p. 492	Babbling Brook Bed & Breakfast Inn	◆◆◆	$219-$299 SAVE	495
16 p. 492	Pacific Blue Inn	◆◆◆	$149-$269	500
18 p. 492	Mission Inn *(See ad p. 499.)*	◆◆	$95-$195 SAVE	499
19 p. 492	Super 8-Beach Boardwalk	◆◆	$79-$399 SAVE	500
20 p. 492	Sunset Inn	◆◆	$69-$279 SAVE	500
21 p. 492	Super 8-Boardwalk	◆◆	$65-$269	500
22 p. 492	Ocean Pacific Lodge *(See ad p. 500, p. 496.)*	◆◆	$69-$399 SAVE	499
23 p. 492	Comfort Inn Beach Boardwalk	◆◆	$80-$300 SAVE	497
24 p. 492	Edgewater Beach Inn & Suites *(See ad p. 496.)*	◆◆	$129-$319 SAVE	497
25 p. 492	Howard Johnson Inn, Fisherman's Wharf Santa Cruz *(See ad p. 496.)*	◆◆	$110-$337 SAVE	499
26 p. 492	Carousel Motel *(See ad p. 496.)*	◆◆	$89-$229 SAVE	495
27 p. 492	Coastview Inn	◆◆	Rates not provided SAVE	495
28 p. 492	West Cliff Inn	◆◆◆	$195-$410	500
29 p. 492	Dream Inn, a Joie de Vivre hotel	◆◆◆	$169-$399	497
30 p. 492	Sea & Sand Inn *(See ad p. 496.)*	◆◆◆	$129-$459	500

Map Page	Restaurants	Diamond Rated	Cuisine	Price Range	Page
1 p. 492	Hollins House Restaurant	◆◆◆	Continental	$10-$30	501
2 p. 492	Peachwood's Steakhouse	◆◆◆	Steak	$12-$36	501
3 p. 492	Santa Cruz Diner	◆◆	American	$6-$15	501

Map Page	Restaurants (cont'd)	Diamond Rated	Cuisine	Price Range	Page
④ p. 492	**Hindquarter Bar & Grille**	◆◆◆	Steak	$10-$36	501
⑤ p. 492	Golden Palace	◆◆	Chinese	$7-$15	501
⑥ p. 492	Casablanca Restaurant	◆◆	American	$8-$26	501
⑦ p. 492	Woodies Cafe	◆	Seafood	$8-$13	501
⑧ p. 492	Gilbert's Firefish Grill	◆◆	Seafood	$10-$20	501
⑨ p. 492	Gilda's Family Restaurant	◆◆	American	$8-$20	501
⑩ p. 492	Olitas Cantina & Grille	◆◆	Mexican	$10-$25	501
⑪ p. 492	**Crow's Nest**	◆◆◆	Seafood	$8-$37	501
⑫ p. 492	Star Bene Ristorante Italiano	◆◆	Italian	$12-$20	501

FELTON

Map Page	Hotel	Diamond Rated	Rate Range	Page
㉝ p. 492	**Fern River Resort**	◆◆	$69-$198 [SAVE]	109

SCOTTS VALLEY

Map Page	Hotel	Diamond Rated	Rate Range	Page
㊱ p. 492	**BEST WESTERN PLUS Inn Scotts Valley**	◆◆◆	$89-$199 [SAVE]	512

Map Page	Restaurant	Diamond Rated	Cuisine	Price Range	Page
⑮ p. 492	Bruno's Barbeque Restaurant and Catering	◆◆	Barbecue	$8-$22	512

CAPITOLA

Map Page	Hotels	Diamond Rated	Rate Range	Page
㊴ p. 492	**Quality Inn & Suites**	◆◆	$79-$350 [SAVE]	67
㊵ p. 492	**The Inn at Depot Hill**	◆◆◆◆	$279-$389 [SAVE]	66
㊶ p. 492	**BEST WESTERN PLUS Capitola By-the-Sea Inn & Suites**	◆◆◆	$100-$230 [SAVE]	66
㊷ p. 492	Fairfield Inn & Suites Santa Cruz-Capitola	◆◆◆	$109-$339	66

Map Page	Restaurants	Diamond Rated	Cuisine	Price Range	Page
⑱ p. 492	Shadowbrook Restaurant	◆◆◆	Regional American	$20-$32	67
⑲ p. 492	Paradise Beach Grille	◆◆◆	Island	$10-$34	67

APTOS

Map Page	Hotels	Diamond Rated	Rate Range	Page
㊺ p. 492	**BEST WESTERN PLUS Seacliff Inn** (See ad p. 495.)	◆◆◆	$90-$200 [SAVE]	46
㊻ p. 492	Rio Sands Motel	◆◆	$59-$219	46
㊼ p. 492	**Seascape Beach Resort** (See ad p. 496.)	◆◆◆	$350-$790 [SAVE]	46

Map Page	Restaurants	Diamond Rated	Cuisine	Price Range	Page
㉒ p. 492	Severino's Grill (See ad p. 495.)	◆◆◆	American	$10-$32	46
㉓ p. 492	Ma Maison	◆◆◆	French	$11-$34	46
㉔ p. 492	Bittersweet Cafe	◆◆	American	$6-$14	46
㉕ p. 492	Palapas Restaurant & Cantina	◆◆◆	Mexican	$10-$25	46

Visit AAA.com/Travel or CAA.ca/Travel for
complete trip planning and reservations

(See map & index p. 492.)

BABBLING BROOK BED & BREAKFAST INN
(831)427-2437

Bed & Breakfast
$219-$299

Address: 1025 Laurel St 95060 **Location:** Just s of SR 1 (Mission Blvd). **Facility:** In a shaded setting along a brook with a water wheel, this B&B features extensively landscaped grounds and many units with fireplaces. 13 units. 2 stories (no elevator), exterior corridors. **Terms:** 2 night minimum stay - weekends, 3 day cancellation notice. **Free Special Amenities: full breakfast and high-speed Internet.**

BEST WESTERN INN
(831)425-4717

Hotel
$99-$169

AAA Benefit: Members save up to 20%, plus 10% bonus points with Best Western Rewards®.

Address: 126 Plymouth St 95060 **Location:** Jct SR 1 and 17 exit Ocean St; east side of Ocean St. **Facility:** 28 units. 2 stories, exterior corridors. **Terms:** 20 day cancellation notice-fee imposed, resort fee. **Amenities:** high-speed Internet. **Activities:** sauna, whirlpool, limited exercise equipment. **Guest Services:** valet laundry. **Free Special Amenities: expanded continental breakfast and high-speed Internet.**

  CALL

BEST WESTERN PLUS ALL SUITES INN
(831)458-9898

Hotel
$85-$220

AAA Benefit: Members save up to 20%, plus 10% bonus points with Best Western Rewards®.

Address: 500 Ocean St 95060 **Location:** Jct SR 1 and 17 exit Ocean St; at Soquel Ave. **Facility:** 77 units, some two bedrooms. 3 stories, interior corridors. **Terms:** 2 night minimum stay - seasonal. **Amenities:** high-speed Internet. **Activities:** sauna, whirlpool, exercise room. **Guest Services:** valet laundry. **Free Special Amenities: local telephone calls and high-speed Internet.**

 CALL

CAROUSEL MOTEL
(831)425-7090

Motel
$89-$229

Address: 110 Riverside Ave 95060 **Location:** Across from boardwalk and beach. **Facility:** 34 units. 3 stories, interior corridors. **Terms:** 2-3 night minimum stay - seasonal and/or weekends. **Free Special Amenities: continental breakfast and high-speed Internet.** (See ad p. 496.)

CHAMINADE RESORT & SPA
(831)475-5600

Hotel
$199-$439

Address: 1 Chaminade Ln 95065 **Location:** 1.5 mi e of SR 1 and 17; SR 1 exit Soquel Ave, just w to Paul Sweet Rd, then 0.5 mi n. Located in a quiet area. **Facility:** A hillside setting gives this property good views of Santa Cruz and the ocean; grounds are well-tended and recreational facilities are extensive. 156 units. 2 stories (no elevator), interior corridors. **Terms:** check-in 4 pm, 2-3 night minimum stay - seasonal and/or weekends, 3 day cancellation notice-fee imposed, resort fee. **Amenities:** video games (fee), high-speed Internet, safes. **Dining:** 2 restaurants. **Pool(s):** heated outdoor. **Activities:** sauna, whirlpools, 4 lighted tennis courts, hiking trails, exercise room, spa. **Guest Services:** valet laundry.

  CALL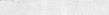

/ SOME UNITS FEE FEE FEE

COASTVIEW INN
831/426-0420

Motel
Rates not provided

Address: 301 Beach St 95060 **Location:** Oceanfront. At Westbrook St; between Municipal Wharf and boardwalk. **Facility:** 32 units. 2 stories (no elevator), exterior corridors. **Amenities:** high-speed Internet. **Pool(s):** outdoor. **Free Special Amenities: continental breakfast and high-speed Internet.**

▼ See AAA listing p. 46 ▼

(See map & index p. 492.)

COMFORT INN BEACH BOARDWALK

(831)471-9999 **23**

Hotel
$80-S300

Address: 314 Riverside Ave 95060 **Location:** 1 blk from boardwalk. **Facility:** 30 units. 2 stories (no elevator), exterior corridors. **Terms:** cancellation fee imposed. **Amenities:** high-speed Internet.
Pool(s): outdoor. **Free Special Amenities:** expanded continental breakfast and high-speed Internet.

COMFORT INN-SANTA CRUZ

(831)426-2664 **6**

Hotel $69-$150 **Address:** 110 Plymouth St 95060 **Location:** Jct SR 1 and 17 exit Ocean St; south side of Ocean St. **Facility:** 62 units. 2 stories (no elevator), exterior corridors. **Terms:** cancellation fee imposed. **Amenities:** high-speed Internet. **Pool(s):** heated outdoor. **Activities:** whirlpool. **Guest Services:** coin laundry.

CONTINENTAL INN

(831)429-1221 **13**

Hotel
$75-S260

Address: 414 Ocean St 95060 **Location:** 5 blks from beach; between Broadway and Soquel aves. **Facility:** 49 units. 2 stories, exterior corridors. **Terms:** cancellation fee imposed. **Pool(s):** outdoor. **Activities:** whirlpool. **Free Special Amenities:** continental breakfast and high-speed Internet.

DREAM INN, A JOIE DE VIVRE HOTEL

(831)426-4330 **29**

Hotel $169-$399 **Address:** 175 W Cliff Dr 95060 **Location:** Oceanfront. At the wharf. **Facility:** 165 units. 3-10 stories, interior corridors. **Parking:** on-site (fee). **Terms:** check-in 4 pm, 2 night minimum stay - seasonal and/or weekends, cancellation fee imposed. **Amenities:** high-speed Internet, safes. **Pool(s):** heated outdoor. **Activities:** whirlpool, limited beach access. **Guest Services:** valet laundry.

EDGEWATER BEACH INN & SUITES

(831)423-0440 **24**

Motel
$129-S319

Address: 525 Second St 95060 **Location:** Across from beach and Boardwalk. **Facility:** 17 units, some kitchens. 1 story, exterior corridors. **Terms:** 2-3 night minimum stay - seasonal and/or weekends, 3 day cancellation notice-fee imposed. **Pool(s):** outdoor. **Guest Services:** coin laundry. **Free Special Amenities:** expanded continental breakfast and high-speed Internet.
(See ad p. 496.)

/ SOME
/ UNITS FEE

Get an insider view from AAA/CAA travel experts at AAATravelViews.com

Get Involved and Keep Teens Safe

TeenDriving.AAA.com

Exploring the countryside or visiting a nearby city can be perfect opportunities for your teen to gain important driving experience. Visit TeenDriving.AAA.com for valuable learning-to-drive resources including teaching tools, safety tips, licensing information and a parent-teen driving agreement.

Plus, check out the free StartSmart teen driving program, developed by AAA and the National Institutes of Health.

Visit **TeenDriving.AAA.com** today. Get involved. Keep teens safe.

Be a better driver. Keep your mind on the road.

(See map & index p. 492.)

HAMPTON INN

(831)457-8000 **5**

Hotel
$99-$349

 AAA Benefit: Members save up to 10%!

Address: 1505 Ocean St 95060 **Location:** Just w of jct SR 1 and 17 exit Ocean St. **Facility:** 46 units. 3 stories, interior corridors. **Terms:** 1-7 night minimum stay, cancellation fee imposed. **Amenities:** high-speed Internet. **Pool(s):** heated indoor. **Guest Services:** valet laundry. **Free Special Amenities: expanded continental breakfast and high-speed Internet.**

HILTON SANTA CRUZ/SCOTTS VALLEY

(831)440-1000 **1**

Hotel
$99-$389

AAA Benefit: Members save 5% or more!

Address: 6001 La Madrona Dr 95060 **Location:** SR 17 exit Mt Hermon Rd. **Facility:** 174 units. 4 stories, interior corridors. **Terms:** check-in 4 pm, 1-7 night minimum stay, cancellation fee imposed. **Amenities:** video games (fee), high-speed Internet. **Pool(s):** heated outdoor. **Activities:** whirlpool, exercise room. **Guest Services:** valet and coin laundry. **Free Special Amenities:** newspaper and high-speed Internet. *(See ad this page.)*

HOLIDAY INN EXPRESS & SUITES SANTA CRUZ

(831)466-9100 **7**

Hotel $105-$365 **Address:** 1410 Ocean St 95060 **Location:** Just w of jct SR 1 and 17. **Facility:** 100 units. 3 stories, interior corridors. **Terms:** cancellation fee imposed. **Amenities:** high-speed Internet. **Pool(s):** heated outdoor. **Activities:** sauna, steamroom, exercise room. **Guest Services:** valet laundry.

Ratings
Members
Trust

Learn more at **AAA.com/Diamonds**

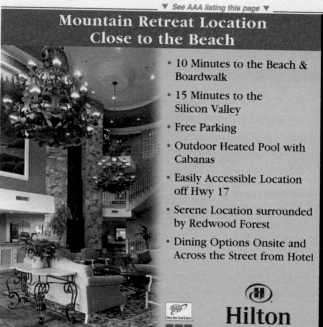

(See map & index p. 492.)

HOWARD JOHNSON INN, FISHERMAN'S WHARF SANTA CRUZ

Hotel
$110-$337

(831)423-7737 **25**

Address: 130 W Cliff Dr 95060 **Location:** 2 blks from beach. **Facility:** 30 units, some efficiencies. 2 stories (no elevator), exterior corridors. **Terms:** cancellation fee imposed. **Amenities:** high-speed Internet. **Activities:** whirlpool. **Guest Services:** coin laundry. **Free Special Amenities:** continental breakfast and high-speed Internet. *(See ad p. 496.)*

THE INN AT PASATIEMPO

Hotel
$75-$305

(831)423-5000 **2**

Address: 555 Hwy 17 95060 **Location:** 0.8 mi n of jct SR 1 and 17; SR 17 exit Pasatiempo Dr. **Facility:** 54 units. 1 story, exterior corridors. **Terms:** cancellation fee imposed. **Dining:** Peachwood's Steakhouse, see separate listing. **Pool(s):** outdoor. **Guest Services:** valet laundry. **Free Special Amenities:** high-speed Internet.

THE ISLANDER MOTEL

Motel
$70-$260

(831)426-7766 **10**

Address: 522 Ocean St 95060 **Location:** Jct SR 1 and 17 exit Ocean St, just w. **Facility:** 22 units. 2 stories (no elevator), exterior corridors. **Terms:** cancellation fee imposed. **Amenities:** high-speed Internet. **Pool(s):** outdoor. **Free Special Amenities:** continental breakfast and high-speed Internet.

MISSION INN

Hotel
$95-$195

(831)425-5455 **18**

Address: 2250 Mission St 95060 **Location:** Jct SR 1 and 17, 2.5 mi sw on SR 1 northbound. **Facility:** 53 units. 2 stories (no elevator), exterior corridors. **Activities:** sauna, whirlpool. **Free Special Amenities:** expanded continental breakfast and high-speed Internet. *(See ad this page.)*

OCEANA INN

Motel
$50-$299

(831)426-2300 **11**

Address: 525 Ocean St 95060 **Location:** Jct SR 1 and 17 exit Ocean St. **Facility:** 55 units. 2 stories (no elevator), interior/exterior corridors. **Terms:** 3 day cancellation notice-fee imposed, resort fee. **Amenities:** safes (fee). **Pool(s):** outdoor. **Free Special Amenities:** continental breakfast and early check-in/late check-out.

OCEAN PACIFIC LODGE

Hotel
$69-$399

(831)457-1234 **22**

Address: 301 Pacific Ave 95060 **Location:** SR 1 and 17 exit w via Ocean St, 1 mi w to Broadway, turn right, left on Front St to Pacific Ave, then just right. **Facility:** 56 units. 3 stories, exterior corridors. **Pool(s):** outdoor. **Activities:** whirlpools. **Guest Services:** coin laundry. **Free Special Amenities:** continental breakfast and high-speed Internet. *(See ad p. 500, p. 496.)*

▼ See AAA listing this page ▼

Keep seasonal vehicles travel-ready with a AAA/CAA Battery Tender®

(See map & index p. 492.)

PACIFIC BLUE INN (831)600-8880
♦♦♦ Bed & Breakfast $149-$269 **Address:** 636 Pacific Ave 95060 **Location:** Between Laurel and Front sts. **Facility:** Artwork by local artists decorate the guest rooms at this attractively appointed inn. 9 units. 3 stories, exterior corridors. *Bath:* shower only. **Terms:** 2 night minimum stay - seasonal and/or weekends, age restrictions may apply, 7 day cancellation notice-fee imposed. **Amenities:** high-speed Internet.

QUALITY INN (831)427-1616 8
♦♦♦ Motel $69-$299 **Address:** 1101 Ocean St 95060 **Location:** 3 blks w off SR 1 and 17 exit Ocean St. **Facility:** 42 units. 2-3 stories (no elevator), exterior corridors. **Terms:** cancellation fee imposed. **Amenities:** high-speed Internet, safes. **Pool(s):** outdoor. **Free Special Amenities: expanded continental breakfast and high-speed Internet.**

RAMADA LIMITED (831)426-6111 9
♦♦♦ Hotel $75-$400 **Address:** 516 Water St 95060 **Location:** 0.4 mi w of jct SR 1 and 17, just s. **Facility:** 50 units. 1-2 stories (no elevator), exterior corridors. **Terms:** cancellation fee imposed. **Pool(s):** outdoor.
Free Special Amenities: expanded continental breakfast and high-speed Internet.

SEA & SAND INN (831)427-3400 30
♦♦♦♦ Hotel $129-$459 **Address:** 201 W Cliff Dr 95060 **Location:** Overlooking the wharf. **Facility:** 22 units. 2 stories (no elevator), exterior corridors. **Terms:** 2-3 night minimum stay - weekends. **Guest Services:** valet laundry. *(See ad p. 496.)*

SUNSET INN 831/423-7500 20
♦♦♦ Motel $69-$279 **Address:** 2424 Mission St 95060 **Location:** SR 1 exit Mission St, 2.5 mi w. **Facility:** 32 units, some two bedrooms. 2 stories (no elevator), exterior corridors. **Terms:** cancellation fee imposed. **Amenities:** high-speed Internet. **Activities:** sauna, whirlpool. **Free Special Amenities: continental breakfast and high-speed Internet.**

SUPER 8-BEACH BOARDWALK (831)426-3707 19
♦♦ Hotel $79-$399 **Address:** 338 Riverside Ave 95060 **Location:** 2 blks from beach and boardwalk. **Facility:** 24 units. 2 stories, exterior corridors. **Terms:** cancellation fee imposed. **Pool(s):** outdoor. **Free Special Amenities: expanded continental breakfast and high-speed Internet.**

SUPER 8-BOARDWALK (831)423-9449 21
♦♦ Hotel $65-$269 **Address:** 321 Riverside Ave 95060 **Location:** 2 blks from beach and boardwalk. **Facility:** 23 units. 2 stories, exterior corridors. **Terms:** cancellation fee imposed. **Pool(s):** outdoor.

WEST CLIFF INN (831)457-2200 28
♦♦♦♦ Bed & Breakfast $195-$410 **Address:** 174 W Cliff Dr 95060 **Location:** Just n of boardwalk and adjacent to Fisherman's Wharf. **Facility:** The Italianate Victorian offers nicely appointed guests rooms, many with ocean views and baths boasting white Italian marble. 9 units. 3 stories (no elevator), interior corridors. **Terms:** 7 day cancellation notice-fee imposed. **Amenities:** high-speed Internet.

HOTEL PARADOX 831/425-7100
[fyi] Not evaluated. **Address:** 611 Ocean St 95060 **Location:** Jct SR 1 and 17 exit Ocean St, 0.5 mi w. Facilities, services, and décor characterize a mid-scale property.

▼ See AAA listing p. 499 ▼

(See map & index p. 492.)

WHERE TO EAT

CASABLANCA RESTAURANT   831/426-9063   6
American. Casual Dining. $8-$26 **AAA Inspector Notes:** Located right across the street from the beach and boardwalk, this restaurant offers spectacular ocean views. The menu serves up a wide selection of seafood items, rack of lamb, duck and beef selections. Open for lunch in the summer months. **Bar:** full bar. **Address:** 101 Main St 95060 **Location:** Across from beach and boardwalk. **Parking:** street only. L D

CROW'S NEST   831/476-4560   11

Seafood
Casual Dining
$8-$37

AAA Inspector Notes: Diners are treated to picturesque views of the bay and Pacific Ocean, as well as well-prepared selections of fresh local seafood. The lively atmosphere makes this place popular with locals. **Bar:** full bar. **Reservations:** suggested. **Address:** 2218 E Cliff Dr 95062 **Location:** 1.3 mi e; at South Shore Santa Cruz Small Crafts Harbor via Murray St Bridge. **Parking:** on-site (fee). *Menu on AAA.com* B L D CALL

GILBERT'S FIREFISH GRILL   831/423-5200   8
Seafood. Casual Dining. $10-$20 **AAA Inspector Notes:** The restaurant's location on the pier allows for ocean-view dining from all tables. The friendly staff serves preparations of fresh local seafood. **Bar:** full bar. **Address:** 25 Municipal Wharf 95060 **Location:** On Santa Cruz Municipal Wharf. **Parking:** on-site (fee). L D CALL

GILDA'S FAMILY RESTAURANT   831/423-2010   9
American. Casual Dining. $8-$20 **AAA Inspector Notes:** On the pier, the family-owned restaurant presents a menu of traditional home cooking. Friendly service and ocean views are other highlights. **Bar:** full bar. **Address:** 37 Municipal Wharf 95060 **Location:** On Santa Cruz Municipal Wharf. **Parking:** on-site (fee). B L D

GOLDEN PALACE   831/427-9275   5
Chinese. Casual Dining. $7-$15 **AAA Inspector Notes:** This dining room is distinctively designed with red lamps, high booths and Chinese memorabilia. The extensive menu offers traditional favorites. **Bar:** beer & wine. **Address:** 415 Ocean St 95060 **Location:** Between Broadway and Soquel aves. L D

HINDQUARTER BAR & GRILLE   831/426-7770   4

Steak
Casual Dining
$10-$36

AAA Inspector Notes: Freshly grilled meat and fish have made this restaurant a local favorite. Service is friendly and inviting. **Bar:** full bar. **Reservations:** suggested. **Address:** 303 Soquel Ave 95060 **Location:** Between Ocean and Pacific sts. L D CALL

HOLLINS HOUSE RESTAURANT   831/459-9177   1
Continental. Fine Dining. $10-$30 **AAA Inspector Notes:** From its perch atop a hill, this restaurant overlooks the city, bay and Pacific Ocean. The feel is casual yet elegant. The menu offers several fresh fish selections, stuffed filet mignon and a variety of pasta dishes. **Bar:** full bar. **Reservations:** suggested. **Address:** 20 Club House Rd 95060 **Location:** 0.5 mi n of jct SR 1 and 17; w of SR 17 exit Pasatiempo Dr; at golf course. D

OLITAS CANTINA & GRILLE   831/458-9393   10
Mexican. Casual Dining. $10-$25 **AAA Inspector Notes:** Upstairs on the pier, this cantina affords guests a view of the Pacific Ocean and boardwalk. The menu lists a variety of Mexican specialties including locally caught seafood. Try the favorite specialty-a lobster quesadilla. **Bar:** full bar. **Reservations:** suggested. **Address:** Municipal Wharf, #49B 95060 **Location:** On Santa Cruz Municipal Wharf. **Parking:** on-site (fee). L D CALL

PEACHWOOD'S STEAKHOUSE   831/426-6333   2

Steak
Casual Dining
$12-$36

AAA Inspector Notes: A favorite area stop for many years, the grill presents a menu of locally caught seafood and grilled meat dishes. When the weather permits, the patio opens for al fresco dining. **Bar:** full bar. **Address:** 555 Hwy 17 95060 **Location:** 0.8 mi n of jct SR 1 and 17; SR 17 exit Pasatiempo Dr; in The Inn at Pasatiempo. L D CALL

SANTA CRUZ DINER   831/426-7151   3
American. Casual Dining. $6-$15 **AAA Inspector Notes:** The friendly staff serves good food day and night. Locals consider this place a favorite. **Bar:** beer & wine. **Address:** 909 Ocean St 95060 **Location:** Just w of jct SR 1 and 17 exit Ocean St. B L D 24 CALL

STAR BENE RISTORANTE ITALIANO   831/479-4307   12
Italian. Casual Dining. $12-$20 **AAA Inspector Notes:** Family owned and operated, this quaint local favorite Italian ristorante offers patrons a wide selection of pasta specialties with homemade sauces and pasta. **Bar:** beer & wine. **Address:** 2-1245 E Cliff Dr 95062 **Location:** SR 1 exit 41st Ave, 1.5 mi w, then 1.6 mi n on Portola Dr (which becomes E Cliff Dr); between 12th and 13th aves. D

WOODIES CAFE   831/421-9410   7
Seafood. Quick Serve. $8-$13 **AAA Inspector Notes:** A great spot for families who want to enjoy a quick meal while enjoying the memorabilia of the Woody cars that decorates the restaurant. Traditional clam chowder is served in a sour dough bowl. Sandwiches, burgers and fish and chips also are featured. Located on the wharf, this spot overlooks the boardwalk and beach. **Bar:** full bar. **Address:** 25 Municipal Wharf 95060 **Location:** On Santa Cruz Municipal Wharf. **Parking:** on-site (fee). L D CALL

SANTA NELLA (G-3) pop. 1,380, elev. 78'
• Restaurants p. 502

REMEMBRANCE MEMORIAL FOR CALIFORNIA KOREAN WAR VETERANS is in San Joaquin Valley National Cemetery on W. McCabe Rd. Dedicated to the 2,496 Californians missing or killed in action during the Korean War, the memorial consists of 16 white granite panels engraved with the soldiers' names. Services are conducted on Memorial Day and Veterans Day. **Time:** Allow 1 hour minimum. **Hours:** Daily 8-5. **Cost:** Free. **Phone:** (209) 854-1040.

BEST WESTERN ANDERSEN'S INN   209/826-5534

Hotel
Rates not provided

AAA Benefit: Members save up to 20%, plus 10% bonus points with Best Western Rewards®.

Address: 12367 Hwy 33 S 95322 **Location:** I-5 exit 407 (SR 33), just e. **Facility:** 94 units. 2 stories (no elevator), exterior corridors. **Amenities:** Some: high-speed Internet. **Pool(s):** heated outdoor. **Guest Services:** coin laundry. **Free Special Amenities:** local telephone calls and high-speed Internet.
SAVE CALL BIZ / SOME UNITS FEE

HOLIDAY INN EXPRESS   (209)826-8282

Hotel
$79-$99

Address: 28976 Plaza Dr 95322 **Location:** I-5 exit 407 (SR 33), just e. **Facility:** 100 units. 2 stories, exterior corridors. **Pool(s):** outdoor. **Activities:** whirlpool, exercise room. **Guest Services:** coin laundry.
SAVE CALL BIZ / SOME UNITS FEE

WHERE TO EAT

PEA SOUP ANDERSEN'S RESTAURANT 209/826-1685
▼▼ Soup. Casual Dining. $8-$20 **AAA Inspector Notes:** More than just great soup, the menu lists a wide selection of traditional home favorites, including pasta dishes, fried chicken, burgers and sandwiches. **Bar:** full bar. **Address:** 12411 S State Hwy 33 95322 **Location:** I-5 exit SR 33, just e. B L D CALL &M

SANTA ROSA (B-7) pop. 167,815, elev. 164'
- **Restaurants p. 509**
- **Attractions map p. 567**
- **Part of Wine Country area — see map p. 562**

Three entrepreneurial businessmen joined forces in the early 1850s, plotted the town of Santa Rosa and sold lots for $25 apiece. After they promised to donate land for a courthouse, the county seat was moved to the fledgling town from Sonoma. The railroad arrived in 1870, and within 7 years the population of Santa Rosa grew tenfold.

The largest city in Sonoma County is closely associated with two of its most famous citizens. Horticulturist Luther Burbank, a resident for 50 years, called the town "the chosen spot of all the earth"; his home and gardens can be seen on guided tours. And cartoonist Charles Schulz, creator of the beloved "Peanuts" cartoon gang, lived and worked here for 3 decades.

Those interested in post-World War II aviation will enjoy a visit to the Pacific Coast Air Museum at Charles M. Schulz-Sonoma County Airport. In addition to aviation-related displays indoors, visitors also can see an outdoor collection of vintage aircraft; phone (707) 575-7900.

Santa Rosa Convention & Visitors Bureau: 9 Fourth St., Santa Rosa, CA 95401. **Phone:** (707) 577-8674 or (800) 404-7673. *(See ad p. 507.)*

CHARLES M. SCHULZ MUSEUM is at 2301 Hardies Ln. (at W. Steele Ln.). It relates the life of the creator of the "Peanuts" comic strip and the development of its iconic characters—the lovable Charlie Brown, his sister Sally, his faithful dog Snoopy, Lucy and Linus Van Pelt, Peppermint Patty and the rest. A replica of Schulz's studio, a collection of his pencil sketches and doodles, a Snoopy labyrinth in an outdoor garden and a morphing Snoopy sculpture are highlights. Original "Peanuts" strips and other art by Schulz can be viewed.

Time: Allow 1 hour, 30 minutes minimum. **Hours:** Mon.-Fri. 11-5, Sat.-Sun. 10-5, Memorial Day-Labor Day; Mon. and Wed.-Fri. 11-5, Sat.-Sun. 10-5, rest of year. Closed Jan. 1, Easter, July 4, Thanksgiving, Christmas Eve and Christmas. **Cost:** $10; $5 (ages 4-18, ages 62+ and college students with ID). **Phone:** (707) 579-4452.

LUTHER BURBANK HOME & GARDENS is at the corner of Santa Rosa and Sonoma aves. Docent-led tours describe the life and work of the horticulturist who introduced more than 800 varieties of fruits, vegetables, nuts, grains and ornamental flowers, including the Santa Rosa plum and the Shasta daisy.

Examples of roses, fruit trees and other plants developed by Burbank are featured on the grounds. The 19th-century house, greenhouse and carriage house museum contain original furnishings and changing exhibits.

One star-studded photograph shows Burbank with Henry Ford, Thomas Alva Edison and other famous visitors following appearances at the 1915 Panama-Pacific International Exposition in San Francisco.

Hours: Gardens open daily 8-dusk. Guided house tours available Tues.-Sun. every half-hour 10-3:30, Apr.-Oct. Cell phone tours are offered. **Cost:** Gardens free. Guided tours $7; free (ages 0-12). **Phone:** (707) 524-5445.

▽ **SAFARI WEST** is at 3115 Porter Creek Rd.
GEM Narrated tours of the 400-acre wildlife preserve, home to more than 800 exotic animals and birds, are conducted by a naturalist in open-air safari vehicles. The sanctuary's residents include zebras, ostriches, antelopes, cape buffalo, gazelles and elands. You'll also visit an open-air aviary and walk through an animal compound for up-close meetings with giraffes and primates.

Time: Allow 3 hours minimum. **Hours:** Tours given daily (weather permitting) at 9, 10, 1, 2 and 4, early Apr.-late Oct.; at 10 and 2, rest of year. Closed Christmas. Phone ahead to confirm schedule. **Cost:** $78; $32 (ages 3-12); $15 (ages 1-2). Reservations are required. **Phone:** (707) 579-2551 or (800) 616-2695. ⊺⊺

SANTA ROSA JUNIOR COLLEGE MUSEUM is in Bussman Hall, 1501 Mendocino Ave. on the Santa Rosa Junior College campus. The museum exhibits works from cultures throughout the Americas as well as Africa, Asia and the Pacific. Native American art forms the bulk of the collection and includes a model of a Pomo roundhouse, baskets, jewelry, kachina dolls and pottery. Many of the items were created by noted 20th-century Native American artists.

Time: Allow 30 minutes minimum. **Hours:** Mon.-Thurs. 9-4:30, Fri. 9-noon. Closed school holidays and breaks. **Cost:** Free. **Phone:** (707) 527-4479.

SONOMA COUNTY MUSEUM, in the restored post office building at 425 Seventh St., features Northern California history exhibits and rotating exhibitions of contemporary art. Programs and lectures are offered periodically. **Time:** Allow 30 minutes minimum. **Hours:** Tues.-Sun. 11-5. Closed major holidays. **Cost:** $7; $5 (ages 12-17, ages 65+, the physically impaired and students with ID). **Phone:** (707) 579-1500.

RECREATIONAL ACTIVITIES
Hot Air Ballooning
- **Above the Wine Country Ballooning** departs from Kaffe Mocha & Grill, 5.5 mi. n. on US 101, then 1 mi. e. off Airport Blvd. exit to 397 Aviation Blvd. **Hours:** Trips depart daily at dawn. Closed

Christmas. **Phone:** (707) 538-7359 or (800) 759-5638.

- **Up & Away Ballooning** departs from the Charles M. Schulz-Sonoma County Airport at 2200 Airport Blvd. **Hours:** Trips depart daily at dawn (weather permitting). Closed Christmas. **Phone:** (707) 836-0171 or (800) 711-2998.

WINERIES

- **DeLoach Vineyards** is 5 mi. w. off US 101 (River Road exit), then w. to 1791 Olivet Rd. **Hours:** Daily 10-5. Guided tours are given daily by appointment. Closed Jan. 1, Christmas Eve, Christmas and Dec. 31. Phone ahead to confirm schedule. **Phone:** (707) 526-9111.
- **Matanzas Creek Winery** is 6 mi. s.e. at 6097 Bennett Valley Rd. **Hours:** Daily 10-4:30. Tours are given daily by appointment. **Phone:** (800) 590-6464.

AMERICAS BEST VALUE INN (707)523-3480

Motel
$70-$179

Address: 1800 Santa Rosa Ave 95407 **Location:** US 101 exit Baker Ave northbound; exit Corby Ave southbound. **Facility:** 42 units. 2 stories (no elevator), exterior corridors. **Terms:** cancellation fee imposed. **Free Special Amenities:** continental breakfast and high-speed Internet.

AMERICAS BEST VALUE INN & SUITES (707)575-4600

Motel $69-$220 **Address:** 866 Hopper Ave 95403 **Location:** US 101 exit Mendocino Ave/Old Redwood Hwy northbound; exit Hopper Ave southbound, just w. **Facility:** 34 units. 2 stories (no elevator), exterior corridors. **Amenities:** high-speed Internet. **Pool(s):** outdoor.

BEST WESTERN PLUS GARDEN INN (707)546-4031

Hotel
$99-$224

AAA Benefit: Members save up to 20%, plus 10% bonus points with Best Western Rewards®.

Address: 1500 Santa Rosa Ave 95404 **Location:** US 101 exit Baker Ave northbound, just n; exit Corby Ave southbound. **Facility:** 79 units. 2 stories, exterior corridors. **Terms:** 2 night minimum stay - seasonal and/or weekends. **Pool(s):** outdoor, heated outdoor. **Guest Services:** coin laundry. **Free Special Amenities:** local telephone calls and high-speed Internet. *(See ad this page.)*

BEST WESTERN PLUS WINE COUNTRY INN & SUITES (707)545-9000

Hotel
$119-$169

AAA Benefit: Members save up to 20%, plus 10% bonus points with Best Western Rewards®.

Address: 870 Hopper Ave 95403 **Location:** US 101 exit Mendocino Ave/Old Redwood Hwy northbound, just w; exit Hopper Ave southbound. **Facility:** 85 units. 2 stories (no elevator), exterior corridors. **Amenities:** *Some:* high-speed Internet. **Pool(s):** heated outdoor. **Activities:** exercise room. **Guest Services:** valet laundry. **Free Special Amenities:** full breakfast and high-speed Internet.

▼ See AAA listing this page ▼

AAA/CAA travel information: Available in print, online and on the go!

COURTYARD BY MARRIOTT   (707)573-9000

Hotel
$119-$299

AAA Benefit: AAA hotel discounts of 5% or more.

Address: 175 Railroad St 95401 **Location:** US 101 exit downtown Santa Rosa, just w; jct 3rd and Railroad sts. Adjacent to Railroad Square, Old Town. **Facility:** 138 units. 5 stories, interior corridors. **Pool(s):** heated outdoor. **Activities:** whirlpool, exercise room. **Guest Services:** valet and coin laundry. *(See ad this page.)*

EXTENDED STAYAMERICA-SANTA ROSA-NORTH
                                            (707)541-0959

Extended Stay Hotel $89-$104 **Address:** 100 Fountain Grove Pkwy 95403 **Location:** US 101 exit Mendocino Ave/Old Redwood Hwy northbound, 0.3 mi e; exit Hopper Ave southbound, 0.6 mi e. **Facility:** 94 efficiencies. 3 stories, interior corridors. **Guest Services:** coin laundry.

EXTENDED STAYAMERICA-SANTA ROSA-SOUTH
                                            (707)546-4808

Extended Stay Hotel $79-$94 **Address:** 2600 Corby Ave 95407 **Location:** US 101 exit Hearn Ave/Yolanda Ave northbound; exit Hearn Ave southbound. **Facility:** 114 efficiencies. 3 stories, exterior corridors. **Amenities:** high-speed Internet (fee). **Guest Services:** coin laundry.

FLAMINGO CONFERENCE RESORT AND SPA
                                            (707)545-8530

Hotel
$109-$299

Address: 2777 4th St 95405 **Location:** Off SR 12; at Farmers Ln. **Facility:** 170 units. 2 stories, interior corridors. **Terms:** 2 night minimum stay - seasonal and/or weekends, cancellation fee imposed. **Amenities:** high-speed Internet (fee). **Pool(s):** 2 heated outdoor. **Activities:** saunas, whirlpool, steamrooms, 5 tennis courts, spa. **Guest Services:** valet and coin laundry. **Free Special Amenities: newspaper and early check-in/late check-out.**

FOUNTAINGROVE INN, HOTEL & CONFERENCE CENTER
                                            (707)578-6101

Hotel $99-$299 **Address:** 101 Fountaingrove Pkwy 95403 **Location:** 2.5 mi n on US 101 exit Mendocino Ave/Old Redwood Hwy, just e. **Facility:** 124 units. 2 stories (no elevator), interior corridors. **Terms:** 2-3 night minimum stay - seasonal and/or weekends, cancellation fee imposed. **Amenities:** high-speed Internet. **Dining:** Equus Restaurant, see separate listing. **Pool(s):** heated outdoor. **Activities:** whirlpool, exercise room. **Guest Services:** valet laundry. *(See ad p. 505.)*

THE GABLES WINE COUNTRY INN   707/585-7777

Historic Bed & Breakfast $195-$260 **Address:** 4257 Petaluma Hill Rd 95404 **Location:** US 101 exit Yolanda Ave/Hearn Ave, 0.4 mi e on Yolanda Ave, then 1.6 mi s. **Facility:** This 1877 Victorian mansion is in a tranquil country setting. 8 units, some cottages. 2 stories (no elevator), interior corridors. **Terms:** 2 night minimum stay - seasonal and/or weekends, age restrictions may apply, 10 day cancellation notice-fee imposed.

▼ See AAA listing this page ▼

Learn about inspections and Diamond
Ratings at AAA.com/Diamonds

▼ See AAA listing p. 504 ▼

▼ See AAA listing p. 561 ▼

HILLSIDE INN MOTEL (707)546-9353

Motel
S84-S99

Address: 2901 4th St 95409 **Location:** US 101, 2.5 mi e on SR 12; at Farmers Ln and 4th St. **Facility:** 36 units, some kitchens. 2 stories, exterior corridors. **Terms:** 3 day cancellation notice. **Amenities:** high-speed Internet (fee). **Pool(s):** outdoor. **Guest Services:** coin laundry. **Free Special Amenities:** high-speed Internet and use of on-premises laundry facilities. *(See ad this page.)*

 / SOME UNITS

HILTON GARDEN INN SONOMA COUNTY AIRPORT
(707)545-0444

Hotel $119-$201 Address: 417 Aviation Blvd 95403 **Location:** US 101 exit Airport Blvd, just w, then just n. **Facility:** 90 units. 3 stories, interior corridors. **Terms:** 1-7 night minimum stay, cancellation fee imposed. **Amenities:** high-speed Internet. **Pool(s):** heated outdoor. **Activities:** whirlpool, exercise room. **Guest Services:** valet and coin laundry, area transportation-within 5 mi.

AAA Benefit:
Unparalleled hospitality at a special Member rate.

 / SOME UNITS

HILTON SONOMA WINE COUNTRY
(707)523-7555

Hotel $109-$349 Address: 3555 Round Barn Blvd 95403 **Location:** US 101 exit Mendocino Ave/Old Redwood Hwy; just ne at top of hill. **Facility:** 250 units. 3 stories, interior corridors. **Terms:** 1-7 night minimum stay, cancellation fee imposed. **Amenities:** Fee: video games, high-speed Internet. **Pool(s):** heated outdoor. **Activities:** whirlpool, exercise room. **Guest Services:** valet laundry.

AAA Benefit:
Members save 5% or more!

 / SOME UNITS FEE

HOTEL LA ROSE
707/579-3200

Historic Hotel
Rates not provided

Address: 308 Wilson St 95401 **Location:** 2 blks w off US 101 exit downtown Santa Rosa; on Railroad Square. **Facility:** Cobblestones were used in the construction of this historic hotel, which was built in 1907. 49 units. 2-4 stories, interior/exterior corridors. **Guest Services:** valet laundry. **Free Special Amenities:** continental breakfast and high-speed Internet.

 / SOME UNITS FEE FEE

HYATT VINEYARD CREEK HOTEL AND SPA IN SONOMA COUNTY
(707)284-1234

Hotel
S90-S540

HYATT

AAA Benefit:
Members save 10% or more everyday.

Address: 170 Railroad St 95401 **Location:** US 101 exit downtown Santa Rosa, just w; jct 3rd St. Adjacent to Railroad Square and Old Town. **Facility:** Richly detailed Mediterranean architecture conveys a sense of privacy, romance and charm at the hotel located at historic Railroad Square. 155 units. 3 stories, interior corridors. **Terms:** cancellation fee imposed. **Amenities:** safes. Fee: video games, high-speed Internet. **Dining:** Brasserie Restaurant, see separate listing. **Pool(s):** heated outdoor. **Activities:** saunas, whirlpool, exercise room, spa. **Guest Services:** valet laundry. **Free Special Amenities:** continental breakfast and newspaper.

/ SOME UNITS FEE

QUALITY INN & SUITES SANTA ROSA
(707)521-2100

Hotel $80-$300 Address: 3000 Santa Rosa Ave 95407 **Location:** US 101 exit Todd Rd, 1.2 mi n. **Facility:** 64 units. 2 stories (no elevator), interior corridors. **Terms:** cancellation fee imposed. **Amenities:** safes (fee). **Activities:** exercise room. **Guest Services:** valet laundry.

CALL / SOME UNITS FEE

Safety tip: Keep a current AAA/CAA
Road Atlas in every vehicle

▼ See AAA listing this page ▼

SANDMAN INN
(707)544-8570

Hotel
S89-S125

Address: 3421 Cleveland Ave 95403 **Location:** US 101 exit W Mendocino Ave/Old Redwood Hwy. **Facility:** 136 units. 2 stories (no elevator), exterior corridors. **Terms:** check-in 4 pm. **Pool(s):** heated outdoor. **Activities:** whirlpool, exercise room. **Guest Services:** valet and coin laundry. **Free Special Amenities:** expanded continental breakfast and room upgrade (subject to availability with advance reservations). *(See ad this page.)*

SAVE ⛽↕ CALL ⚙M 🏊 📶
📺 🔌 🖥 📠 / SOME UNITS FEE 🐾

SANTA ROSA DOWNTOWN TRAVELODGE
(707)544-4141

💎💎 **Motel** $100-$179 **Address:** 635 Healdsburg Ave 95401 **Location:** US 101 exit College Ave, 0.3 mi e, then just s; at Mendocino Ave. **Facility:** 43 units. 3 stories, exterior corridors. **Terms:** cancellation fee imposed. **Amenities:** high-speed Internet, safes (fee). **Pool(s):** heated outdoor.

↕ 🏊 📶 🔌 🖥 📠 / SOME UNITS FEE 🐾

Get pet travel tips and enter the photo contest at AAA.com/PetBook

---

TRAVELODGE
(707)542-3472

Motel
$70-$170

Address: 1815 Santa Rosa Ave 95407 **Location:** US 101 exit Baker Ave northbound; exit Corby Ave southbound. **Facility:** 31 units. 1 story, exterior corridors. **Terms:** cancellation fee imposed. **Amenities:** safes. **Pool(s):** outdoor. **Free Special Amenities:** continental breakfast and high-speed Internet.

SAVE ↕ CALL ⚙M 🏊 📶 🔌 🖥 📠 / SOME UNITS FEE 🐾

VAGABOND INN SANTA ROSA
(707)542-5544

Hotel
$59-$119

Address: 2632 Cleveland Ave 95403 **Location:** US 101 exit Steele Ln, 1 mi n. **Facility:** 100 units. 3 stories, interior corridors. **Pool(s):** outdoor. **Free Special Amenities:** continental breakfast and high-speed Internet.

SAVE ↕ CALL ⚙M 🏊 📶 ❌ 🖥 / SOME UNITS FEE 🐾 🔌 🖥

VINTNERS INN
(707)575-7350

Hotel
$185-$575

Address: 4350 Barnes Rd 95403 **Location:** US 101 exit River Rd/Mark West Springs Rd, just sw. **Facility:** Several buildings around a shaded courtyard with manicured grass and paths are set amid scenic vineyards; some rooms feature a fireplace. 44 units. 2 stories (no elevator), interior corridors. **Terms:** check-in 4 pm, 2 night minimum stay - weekends, 7 day cancellation notice-fee imposed. **Amenities:** high-speed Internet, safes. **Dining:** John Ash & Co, see separate listing. **Activities:** whirlpool, exercise room. *Fee:* massage. **Guest Services:** valet laundry. **Free Special Amenities:** newspaper and high-speed Internet.

SAVE ECO ↕ 🐾 CALL ⚙M 📶 ❌

▼ *See AAA listing this page* ▼

MELITTA STATION INN 707/538-7712

fyi Not evaluated. **Address:** 5850 Melita Rd 95409 **Location:** SR 12 exit Los Alamos Rd, 0.4 mi w. Facilities, services, and décor characterize a mid-scale property.

WHERE TO EAT

BRASSERIE RESTAURANT 707/636-7388

▼▼▼ California. Casual Dining. $11-$28 **AAA Inspector Notes:** Boasting a warm contemporary sepia-toned setting, this restaurant features a simple Continental menu focusing on regional products. The roasted beets with a goat cheese sauce or pork tenderloin with potato risotto are excellent choices. Using finely diced Yukon potatoes, the mashed potatoes offers a nice texture. **Bar:** full bar. **Address:** 170 Railroad St 95401 **Location:** US 101 exit downtown Santa Rosa, just w; jct 3rd St; in Hyatt Vineyard Creek Hotel and Spa in Sonoma County. B L D CALL ⊜M

EQUUS RESTAURANT 707/578-0149

▼▼▼ American. Casual Dining. $10-$30 **AAA Inspector Notes:** The Gallery of Sonoma County Wines displays approximately 300 premium wines chosen by each local winery's winemaker. An upscale modern decor, which is somewhat masculine, is softened by ambient lighting. **Bar:** full bar. **Address:** 101 Fountaingrove Pkwy 95403 **Location:** 2.5 mi n on US 101 exit Mendocino Ave/Old Redwood Hwy, just e; in Fountaingrove Inn, Hotel & Conference Center. L D

FLAVOR BISTRO 707/573-9600

▼▼ California. Casual Dining. $9-$27 **AAA Inspector Notes:** Conveniently located downtown, this casual bistro is known for its hummus and sweet potato gnocchi appetizers. Meal portions are American size so no one leaves hungry. A kids' menu is available; crayons and paper keep the little ones busy before the meal arrives. An extensive wine list and good selection of beer is offered. **Bar:** full bar. **Address:** 96 Old Courthouse Square 95404 **Location:** US 101 exit downtown Santa Rosa/3rd St, 0.3 mi e on 3rd St, then just n. **Parking:** street only. L D CALL ⊜M

JOHN ASH & CO 707/527-7687

California Fine Dining $21-$39

AAA Inspector Notes: Sun-drenched outdoor patios are enclosed without sacrificing the sun-drenched feel at this fine dining spot. The lounge nurtures a relaxed, library-like mood. Menu items might include wild salmon grilled in grape leaves, risotto with rock shrimp, cider-brined pork tenderloin and shrimp Waldorf salad. **Bar:** full bar. **Reservations:** suggested. **Address:** 4330 Barnes Rd 95403 **Location:** US 101 exit River Rd/Mark West Springs Rd, just sw; in Vintners Inn. D

LA GARE FRENCH RESTAURANT 707/528-4355

▼▼▼▼

French Fine Dining $22-$30

AAA Inspector Notes: A popular dining spot since 1979, this restaurant transports guests to the French Swiss alps with its cozy alpine décor and Old World ambience. Dine on a variety of traditional country-style French dishes. Soup and salad is included with every entrée. **Bar:** beer & wine. **Reservations:** suggested. **Address:** 208 Wilson St 95401 **Location:** US 101 exit downtown Santa Rosa, just w; just s of Railroad Square. D

LA ROSA TEQUILERIA AND GRILLE 707/523-3663

▼▼ Mexican. Casual Dining. $8-$18 **AAA Inspector Notes:** Each area of this restaurant has a different theme. Upon entering, guests are greeted with a wall of crucifixes. In the bar is a grinning skull, while the main dining room is a contemporary cantina. The menu is a good representation of traditional Mexican dishes as well as some Latin ceviche. **Bar:** full bar. **Address:** 500 4th St 95401 **Location:** Downtown. **Parking:** street only. L D

LA VERA PIZZA 707/575-1113

▼▼ Pizza. Casual Dining. $9-$19 **AAA Inspector Notes:** Since 1983, the local favorite has served tasty pizzas with a wide selection of toppings. Pastas and calzones are other good choices. **Bar:** beer & wine. **Address:** 629 4th St 95404 **Location:** Downtown. **Parking:** street only. L D

RUSSIAN RIVER BREWING COMPANY 707/545-2337

▼▼▼ Pizza. Casual Dining. $8-$19 **AAA Inspector Notes:** Diners can request seating at sidewalk tables or in the high-energy warehouse-like room, where live bands are common and pizza is the top choice to accompany the crafted brews. **Bar:** beer & wine. **Address:** 725 4th St 95404 **Location:** Between D and E sts. **Parking:** street only. L D LATE

STAR RESTAURANT 707/544-8117

▼▼ American. Casual Dining. $7-$16 **AAA Inspector Notes:** This neighborhood diner serves well prepared meals of generous portions. **Bar:** beer & wine. **Address:** 1350 Farmers Ln 95405 **Location:** US 101 exit SR 12 (Sonoma), 1.5 mi e, then just n. B L D

THIRD STREET ALEWORKS 707/523-3060

▼▼ American. Casual Dining. $9-$18 **AAA Inspector Notes:** A bit more laid back, this restaurant crafts its own beers to wash down burgers, sandwiches, pizza, brats, tacos and meatloaf. The sunny patio is a seasonal seating option. **Bar:** beer & wine. **Address:** 610 3rd St 95404 **Location:** Between D St and Mendocino Ave. **Parking:** street only. L D LATE CALL ⊜M

TORCH OF INDIA 707/569-7500

▼▼ Indian. Casual Dining. $9-$19 **AAA Inspector Notes:** An elegant Indian motif and high ceilings give this restaurant a bit of a formal atmosphere. It is family run so the owner/chef pops out of the kitchen to visit with guests. Lunch is buffet style. Guests can cool their palate with a scoop of homemade mango-saffron-almond ice cream. **Bar:** beer & wine. **Address:** 507 4th St 95401 **Location:** Between B St and Santa Rosa Ave; downtown. **Parking:** street only. L D 🍴

WILLIE BIRD'S RESTAURANT 707/542-0861

American Casual Dining $8-$16

AAA Inspector Notes: This family-friendly roadside diner celebrates Thanksgiving every day with breakfast, lunch and dinner menus featuring its own free-range turkeys. In addition to turkey dishes, sandwiches, entrée salads, seafood and steaks are available. **Bar:** full bar. **Address:** 1150 Santa Rosa Ave 95404 **Location:** US 101 exit Baker Ave/Santa Rosa Ave northbound, 0.3 mi n; exit Santa Rosa Ave/Corby Ave southbound, just n. B L D CALL ⊜M

SARATOGA (E-9) pop. 29,926, elev. 480'

• Hotels p. 510 • Restaurants p. 510
• Hotels & Restaurants map & index p. 468

Saratoga is at the northern end of a scenic 38-mile stretch of SR 9.

Saratoga Chamber of Commerce: 14460 Big Basin Way, Saratoga, CA 95070. **Phone:** (408) 867-0753.

HAKONE ESTATE & GARDENS, 21000 Big Basin Way, is an 18-acre estate garden containing four gardens—Hill and Pond Garden; Tea Garden; Zen Garden; and Kizuna En, a bamboo garden. A tea ceremony is performed the third Sunday of the month, March through November. Private guided tours and tea ceremonies also are offered.

Time: Allow 1 hour minimum. **Hours:** Mon.-Fri. 10-5, Sat.-Sun. and holidays 11-5. Closed Jan. 1 and Christmas. **Cost:** $7; $5 (ages 5-17 and 65+). **Phone:** (408) 741-4994.

MONTALVO ARTS CENTER AND ARBORETUM is .5 mi. s.e. on SR 9, then 1 mi. s.w. on Montalvo Rd. Formerly the summer home of U.S. senator and San Francisco mayor James D. Phelan, the estate now serves as a center for fine arts. The 1912

(See map & index p. 468.)

Mediterranean-style villa has a formal garden and trails to lookout points on the surrounding hills. A 10-studio artist residency complex, two performing arts venues and a gallery are on the grounds. Two-hour walking tours are offered.

Time: Allow 1 hour minimum. **Hours:** Mon.-Thurs. 8-7, Fri.-Sun. and holidays 9-5, Apr.-Sept.; Mon.-Thurs. 8-5, Fri.-Sun. and holidays 9-5, rest of year. Studio gallery open Thurs.-Sun. 11-3. The garden is occasionally closed for private events. Closed Jan. 1 and Christmas. Phone ahead to confirm schedule. **Cost:** Free. Walking tour fee $10. **Phone:** (408) 961-5800 for recorded information, or (408) 961-5858 for the ticket office.

RECREATIONAL ACTIVITIES
Horseback Riding

• **Garrod Farms Riding Stables** is at 22647 Garrod Rd. **Hours:** One-hour guided trail rides Mon.-Fri. at 4, Sat.-Sun. 8:30-4:30, mid-June through Labor Day; Mon.-Fri. at 10, 1:30 and 4, Sat.-Sun. 8:30-4:30, rest of year. Under 8 are not permitted; pony walks available for younger children. Closed Thanksgiving and Christmas. Phone ahead to confirm schedule. **Phone:** (408) 867-9527.

WINERIES

• **Cooper-Garrod Estate Vineyards** is at 22645 Garrod Rd. **Hours:** Tastings Mon.-Fri. noon-5, Sat.-Sun. 11-5. Tours are given Mon.-Fri. noon-5 (also first Sat. of the month at 11). Reservations are required for tours. Closed Jan. 1, Thanksgiving and Christmas. **Phone:** (408) 867-7116.

THE INN AT SARATOGA   (408)867-5020   98

▼▼▼▼ **Hotel** $199-$299 **Address:** 20645 4th St 95070 **Location:** Just n of SR 9; center. **Facility:** 47 units. 5 stories, interior corridors. **Activities:** exercise room. **Guest Services:** valet laundry.
🍴 CALL 🄼 BIZ 🛜 ✕

WHERE TO EAT

LA FONDUE   408/867-3332   46

▼▼▼ Fondue. Casual Dining. $31-$50 **AAA Inspector Notes:** Prepare for a wonderful dining experience as the fondues are prepared tableside. The menu includes over 50 varieties such as fresh fruits and vegetables, shrimp, scallops, lobster, chicken and steak. For a more exotic experience, diners can choose alligator, crocodile, kangaroo, ostrich and buffalo. The chocolate fondue is the perfect ending. **Bar:** full bar. **Reservations:** suggested. **Address:** 14550 Big Basin Way 95070 **Location:** At 4th St; downtown. D

THE PLUMED HORSE   408/867-4711   45

▼▼▼ ▼▼▼ California. Fine Dining. $34-$85 **AAA Inspector Notes:** For a relaxed meal, dine at the bar or lounge warmed by a fireplace. For a more formal experience, take a seat in the contemporary, elegant dining room where three fiber optic chandeliers with ever-changing colors and a Lucite wine cellar along one wall are the highlights. The often-changing menu occasionally includes a prix fixe dinner, and dishes are prepared from fresh seasonal products. The wine list is on an iPad. **Bar:** full bar. **Reservations:** suggested. **Address:** 14555 Big Basin Way 95070 **Location:** 0.3 mi sw on SR 9. **Parking:** valet and street only. D CALL 🄼

ROUND TABLE PIZZA   408/252-0277

▼▼ Pizza. Casual Dining. $7-$28 **AAA Inspector Notes:** This casual, family-oriented pizza place features high-quality ingredients and dough rolled fresh daily. Distinctive specialty pizzas are piled high with toppings. **Bar:** beer & wine. **Address:** 18482 Prospect Rd 95070 **Location:** Just e of Lawrence Expwy. L D

SAUSALITO (C-8) pop. 7,061, elev. 14'
• Part of San Francisco area — see map p. 342

Sausalito, Spanish for "little willow," is an impossibly charming Marin County town, just across the Golden Gate Bridge from San Francisco. Upscale boutiques, art galleries, gift shops and open-air cafes line Bridgeway, the main street, encouraging visitors to linger, shop and stop for lunch or a glass of wine. All the necessary scenic ingredients are present and accounted for: lovely, boat-dotted views of San Francisco Bay, houses picturesquely perched on the hillsides that rise behind Bridgeway, and Mount Tamalpais as a backdrop.

Sausalito's nautical history dates back to the early 1800s, when the area was settled by shipbuilders and sailors. The arrival of the railroad in the 1870s boosted development; ferries soon began plying the waters of the bay, transporting train passengers to San Francisco.

The opening of the Golden Gate Bridge in 1937 brought a decline in ferry service, but Sausalito's population took a leap when a huge shipyard that produced cargo vessels called Liberty ships for the U.S. Navy was established during the World War II years. After the war, the waterfront became home to a flotilla of houseboats occupied primarily by a bohemian crew of painters, writers and hippies—the beginning of Sausalito's artist colony. Today the houseboat community is concentrated north of the city, and you can take a guided walking tour of these funky floating residences.

The Sausalito Art Festival, held Labor Day weekend in Marinship Park, is not only one of the Bay Area's most popular outdoor art gatherings but is considered to be one of the finest juried art festivals in the nation. Many regional artists have been exhibiting at the festival for decades. This isn't a craft fair; the art for sale ranges from classic to modern to very quirky, and from affordable to seriously expensive. A convenient—and scenic—way to attend is by ferry; the Blue & Gold Fleet, based at San Francisco's Pier 41, offers a package deal that includes round-trip transportation to the festival site as well as the entrance fee. Phone (415) 332-3555 for festival information, or (415) 773-1188 for the Blue & Gold Fleet.

Passenger ferries link Sausalito with San Francisco. Regularly scheduled service by the Blue and Gold Fleet connects the two cities. Golden Gate Ferry also provides service; phone (415) 455-2000. See *Public Transportation in San Francisco p. 349.*

Sausalito is famous for those hillside-hugging houses and the panoramic views of San Francisco's skyline; the view is particularly impressive from aptly named Vista Point, at the north end of the Golden

Gate Bridge, and from the downtown marina. Sausalito is at the southern end of a scenic 212-mile stretch of SR 1 that proceeds north along the Pacific coast to Leggett *(see place listing p. 173)*.

Sausalito Chamber of Commerce: 1913 Bridgeway, Sausalito, CA 94965. **Phone:** (415) 331-7262.

BAY MODEL VISITOR CENTER is at 2100 Bridgeway at the foot of Spring St.; use the Marinship Way access road. This environmental education facility, operated by the U.S. Army Corps of Engineers, shows a 9-minute introductory video and has a 1.5-acre hydraulic model simulating the tidal action and currents of San Francisco Bay and the Sacramento-San Joaquin Delta region.

Interactive exhibits provide an interesting view of the estuary. Visitors also can see an exhibit about Marinship, the World War II shipyard previously at this site. Audio tours are available in several languages.

Hours: Tues.-Fri. 9-4, Sat.-Sun. and holidays 10-5, Memorial Day-Labor Day; Tues.-Sat. 9-4, rest of year. Phone ahead to confirm model operation. Closed Jan. 1, July 4, Thanksgiving and Christmas. **Cost:** Free. **Phone:** (415) 332-3871 or (415) 289-3007.

THE MARINE MAMMAL CENTER is in the Marin Headlands at 2000 Bunker Rd., within Fort Cronkhite. The center is an animal hospital that rescues and rehabilitates sick, injured and distressed marine animals from the California coast. Said to be the largest marine mammal facility in the world to combine rehabilitation with an on-site research lab, the center treats 600 to 800 animals a year.

Seals, sea lions, dolphins, porpoises and sea otters are frequent residents; visitors can see the animals in different "pens" being cared for by staff members. Exhibits provide information about marine mammals, ocean conservation and the center's work. **Time:** Allow 30 minutes minimum. **Hours:** Daily 10-5. Closed Jan. 1, Thanksgiving and Christmas. **Cost:** Donations. **Phone:** (415) 289-7325.

SAUSALITO WOODEN BOAT TOUR departs from in front of Mike's Bikes on Gate 6 Rd. at the n. end of Sausalito. This 3-hour walking tour of Sausalito's wooden boat community visits both well-maintained and scruffy houseboat enclaves, takes a look at a couple of famous houseboats and also makes a stop at a working shipyard. The tour guide, a knowledgeable local, provides background commentary that comes from an insider's perspective.

The tour also stops at the world-famous Heath Ceramics store and finishes with refreshments at the tour guide's art studio. This in-depth excursion will be most interesting to those with a specific interest in houseboat history, Sausalito or both.

Wear comfortable shoes and clothes and bring a bottle of water. There are no bathroom breaks until almost the end of the tour. **Time:** Allow 3 hours minimum. **Hours:** Tours depart Sat.-Sun. at 12:30. Closed major holidays. **Cost:** Tour fee $50. Reservations are required. **Phone:** (415) 332-6608.

CASA MADRONA HOTEL & SPA   (415)332-0502

(fyi)
Hotel
$199-$499

Under major renovation, scheduled to be completed May 2013. **Last Rated:** ▼▼▼ **Address:** 801 Bridgeway Blvd 94965 **Location:** US 101 exit Alexander Ave, 1.5 mi e. **Facility:** 63 units, some kitchens. 3 stories, interior/exterior corridors. **Parking:** on-site (fee) and valet. **Terms:** 3 day cancellation notice. **Dining:** Poggio, see separate listing. **Activities:** spa. **Guest Services:** valet laundry. **Free Special Amenities:** local telephone calls and high-speed Internet.

[SAVE] [ICONS]

THE GABLES INN-SAUSALITO   (415)289-1100

▼▼▼
Bed & Breakfast
$199-$600

Address: 62 Princess St 94965 **Location:** US 101 N exit Alexander Ave, 1.5 mi to Bridgeway Blvd; US 101 S exit Marin City/Sausalito, 2.5 mi se on Bridgeway Blvd, then just n. **Facility:** Picturesque views of San Francisco Bay are featured from this inn set on a hillside just above the historic downtown area. 15 units. 2 stories (no elevator), interior/exterior corridors. **Parking:** on-site (fee). **Terms:** 3 day cancellation notice. **Guest Services:** valet laundry. **Free Special Amenities:** continental breakfast and newspaper.

[SAVE] [ICONS]

THE INN ABOVE TIDE   (415)332-9535

▼▼▼▼ **Hotel** $330-$1275 **Address:** 30 El Portal 94965 **Location:** US 101 N exit Alexander Ave, 1.5 mi to Bridgeway Blvd; US 101 S exit Marin City/Sausalito, 2 mi s on Bridgeway Blvd; downtown. **Facility:** 29 units. 3 stories, interior/exterior corridors. **Parking:** valet only. **Terms:** 2 night minimum stay - seasonal and/or weekends, cancellation fee imposed. **Amenities:** safes. **Activities:** bicycles. **Guest Services:** valet laundry.

[ICONS]

CAVALLO POINT-THE LODGE AT THE GOLDEN GATE
415/339-4700

(fyi) Not evaluated. **Address:** 601 Murray Cir 94965 **Location:** US 101 exit Alexander Ave, just e on Sausalito Lateral Rd, 1 mi s on Bunker Rd, then 0.3 mi n. Facilities, services, and décor characterize an upscale property.

WHERE TO EAT

FISH.   415/331-3474

▼▼ American. Casual Dining. $13-$25 **AAA Inspector Notes:** This casual, laid-back contemporary fish shack dedicated to serving sustainable seafood and organic produce. Their claim to fame is the crab roll. Only bring cash as plastic is not accepted. **Bar:** beer & wine. **Address:** 350 Harbor Dr 94965 **Location:** US 101 exit Sausalito/Marin City, s on Bridgeway, then just e.

[L] [D] [ICON]

HAMBURGERS   415/332-9471

▼ American. Quick Serve. $5-$7 **AAA Inspector Notes:** This small burger joint usually is on the top 10 list of best burgers in the area. Other than burgers, they offer hot dogs and burritos on the limited menu. Diners can grab a table inside or head over to the small plaza to eat their meal. **Address:** 737 Bridgeway Blvd 94965 **Location:** US 101 exit Alexander Ave, 1.5 mi e. **Parking:** street only.

[L] [D]

MURRAY CIRCLE
415/339-4750

California
Fine Dining
$13-$30

AAA Inspector Notes: Bronze tin-tiled ceilings adds a touch of historic ambience to this elegant dining room. For the perfect dining experience, request a table with a stunning view of the Golden Gate Bridge. **Bar:** full bar. **Reservations:** suggested. **Address:** 601 Murray Cir 94965 **Location:** US 101 exit Alexander Ave, just e on Sausalito Lateral Rd, 1 mi s on Bunker Rd, then 0.3 mi n; in Cavallo Point- The Lodge at the Golden Gate. **Parking:** on-site and valet. B L D CALL ⑤M ⬚

POGGIO
415/332-7771

▼▼▼▼ Italian. Casual Dining. $14-$28 **AAA Inspector Notes:** Casually elegant, this restaurant is set up to accommodate day trippers with al fresco seating as well as a more formal dining experience in the evening. Food is Italian with a touch of California—an example would be the grilled octopus and pork belly appetizer. **Bar:** full bar. **Address:** 801 Bridgeway 94965 **Location:** US 101 exit Alexander Ave, 1.5 mi e; in Casa Madrona Hotel & Spa. **Parking:** street only.

B L D ⬚

THE SPINNAKER
415/332-1500

▼▼ Seafood Casual Dining $11-$34

AAA Inspector Notes: This dining room over water offers panoramic views of the San Francisco Bay, nearby Tiburon and Sausalito and the tips of the Golden Gate Bridge. The menu offers guests diverse selections. **Bar:** full bar. **Address:** 100 Spinnaker Dr 94965 **Location:** Center; adjacent to yacht harbor. *Menu on AAA.com*

L D

SCOTIA (C-1) pop. 850, elev. 164'

FISHERIES EXHIBIT is s. on Main St. from the Scotia Museum, at jct. 6th St. (watch for the sign with a fish on it). Aquariums display salamanders and various fish species, including salmon and trout. One long tank mimics a stream environment. A picture "show" shows the staff at work and the various stages in fish life cycles. **Hours:** Mon.-Fri. 8-4:30. **Cost:** Free. **Phone:** (707) 764-4492.

SCOTIA MUSEUM, 125 Main St., has exhibits about local history, redwoods and the town's logging days. Logging equipment, artifacts and old photographs also are displayed. Visitors can watch "California Redwoods," a 1935 movie produced by the California Redwood Association.

Time: Allow 1 hour minimum. **Hours:** Mon.-Fri. 8:30-5, Memorial Day-Labor Day. Closed major holidays. Phone ahead to confirm schedule. **Cost:** Free. **Phone:** (707) 764-5063, or (707) 764-4492 for the Fisheries Center.

SCOTTS VALLEY pop. 11,580
• Hotels & Restaurants map & index p. 492

BEST WESTERN PLUS INN SCOTTS VALLEY
(831)438-6666 ㊱

Hotel
$89-$199

Best Western PLUS

AAA Benefit: Members save up to 20%, plus 10% bonus points with Best Western Rewards®.

Address: 6020 Scotts Valley Dr 95066 **Location:** SR 17 exit Granite Creek, just w. **Facility:** 58 units. 2 stories, exterior corridors. **Terms:** cancellation fee imposed. **Amenities:** high-speed Internet. **Pool(s):** outdoor. **Activities:** whirlpool. **Guest Services:** coin laundry. **Free Special Amenities:** expanded continental breakfast and high-speed Internet.

SAVE ⬚ CALL ⑤M ⬚ BIZ ⬚ ✕ ⬚ ⬚
/SOME UNITS FEE ⬚

WHERE TO EAT

BRUNO'S BARBEQUE RESTAURANT AND CATERING
831/438-2227 ⑮

▼▼ Barbecue. Casual Dining. $8-$22 **AAA Inspector Notes:** This place serves up incredible barbecue. In addition to the traditional favorites of baby back ribs and chicken, steak also is available as well as a wide selection of specialty salads, sandwiches and burgers. A favorite among the local crowd, service at this joint is warm and friendly. **Bar:** beer & wine. **Address:** 230-G Mt. Herman Rd 95066 **Location:** SR 17 exit Mt. Herman Rd, 0.5 mi e; in Kings Village Shopping Center. L D CALL ⑤M

ROUND TABLE PIZZA
831/438-5446

▼ Pizza. Casual Dining. $7-$28 **AAA Inspector Notes:** This casual, family-oriented pizza place features high-quality ingredients and dough rolled fresh daily. Distinctive specialty pizzas are piled high with toppings. **Bar:** beer & wine. **Address:** 245-A Mt. Herman Rd 95066 **Location:** SR 17 exit Mt Herman Rd N, just n of Scotts Valley Dr. L D CALL ⑤M

SEASIDE pop. 33,025
• Hotels & Restaurants map & index p. 206
• Part of Monterey Peninsula area — see map p. 202

EMBASSY SUITES HOTEL & CONFERENCE CENTER
(831)393-1115 ㊲

▼▼▼ Hotel $159-$459 **Address:** 1441 Canyon Del Rey 93955 **Location:** SR 1 exit Seaside/Del Rey Oaks, just e. **Facility:** 234 units. 12 stories, interior corridors. **Terms:** check-in 4 pm, 1-7 night minimum stay, cancellation fee imposed. **Dining:** Pacifica Cafe, see separate listing. **Pool(s):** heated indoor. **Activities:** sauna, whirlpool, exercise room. **Guest Services:** valet and coin laundry.

AAA Benefit: Members save 5% or more!

⬚ ⬚ ⬚ CALL ⑤M ⬚ BIZ ⬚ ✕ ⬚ ⬚ ⬚

HOLIDAY INN EXPRESS AT MONTEREY BAY
(831)394-5335 �477

▼▼▼ Hotel $119-$299

Address: 1400 Del Monte Blvd 93955 **Location:** SR 1 exit Seaside/Del Rey Oaks, just e. **Facility:** 143 units. 3 stories, exterior corridors. **Terms:** cancellation fee imposed. **Amenities:** video games (fee). **Pool(s):** heated outdoor. **Activities:** whirlpool, exercise room. **Guest Services:** valet laundry. **Free Special Amenities:** expanded continental breakfast and high-speed Internet.

SAVE ⬚ CALL ⑤M ⬚ BIZ ⬚ ✕ ⬚ ⬚
/SOME UNITS ⬚

MAGIC CARPET LODGE
(831)899-4221 ㊗

▼▼▼ Motel $50-$199

Address: 1875 Fremont Blvd 93955 **Location:** SR 1 exit Seaside/Del Rey Oaks, 1.5 mi e. **Facility:** 40 units. 3 stories, interior/exterior corridors. **Terms:** 2-3 night minimum stay - seasonal and/or weekends, cancellation fee imposed. **Pool(s):** heated outdoor. **Free Special Amenities:** continental breakfast and local telephone calls.

SAVE ⬚ ⬚ ✕ ⬚ ⬚ /SOME UNITS FEE ⬚ FEE ⬚

SANDCASTLE INN
(831)394-6556 ㊴

▼▼▼ Hotel $59-$299

Address: 1011 La Salle Ave 93955 **Location:** SR 1 exit Sand City/Seaside, just e. **Facility:** 34 units. 2 stories (no elevator), exterior corridors. **Terms:** 3 day cancellation notice-fee imposed. **Amenities:** high-speed Internet. **Guest Services:** coin laundry. **Free Special Amenities:** continental breakfast and high-speed Internet.

SAVE ⬚ BIZ ⬚ ✕ ⬚ ⬚

(See map & index p. 206.)

SEASIDE INN
(831)394-4041

Motel
$59-$249

Address: 1986 Del Monte Blvd 93955 **Location:** SR 1 exit Sand City/Seaside, just e. **Facility:** 17 units, some two bedrooms. 1-2 stories (no elevator), exterior corridors. **Terms:** 3 day cancellation notice-fee imposed. **Free Special Amenities: continental breakfast and room upgrade (subject to availability with advance reservations).**

THUNDERBIRD MOTEL
831/394-6797

Motel
$39-$249

Address: 1933 Fremont Blvd 93955 **Location:** SR 1 business route, 0.3 mi n. **Facility:** 33 units, some two bedrooms. 2 stories (no elevator), exterior corridors. **Terms:** 3 day cancellation notice-fee imposed. **Guest Services:** coin laundry. **Free Special Amenities: early check-in/late check-out and use of on-premises laundry facilities.**

WHERE TO EAT

PACIFICA CAFE
831/393-1115

American. Casual Dining. $10-$30 **AAA Inspector Notes:** Diners can enjoy a salad, sandwich or freshly grilled meat or fish entree in a casual, friendly atmosphere. The menu changes seasonally. **Bar:** full bar. **Address:** 1441 Canyon Del Rey 93955 **Location:** SR 1 exit Seaside/Del Rey Oaks, just e; in Embassy Suites Hotel & Conference Center.

ROUND TABLE PIZZA
831/394-6869

Pizza. Casual Dining. $7-$28 **AAA Inspector Notes:** This casual, family-oriented pizza place features high-quality ingredients and dough rolled fresh daily. Distinctive specialty pizzas are piled high with toppings. **Bar:** beer & wine. **Address:** 1717 Fremont Blvd 93955 **Location:** SR 1 exit Fremont Blvd E, just n of Broadway Ave.

SEBASTOPOL (B-7) pop. 7,379, elev. 78'
• **Part of Wine Country area — see map p. 562**

Named after Sevastopol, the Russian seaport on the Crimean peninsula, Sebastopol became a center of canned applesauce production in the late 19th century. That industry is still economically important today, as are the Gravenstein apple orchards and vineyards that blanket the rolling hills surrounding this Sonoma Valley community.

The Sebastopol Farm Market is the perfect place to sample the region's agricultural bounty. Local farmers sell seasonal organic produce—including hard-to-find specialties like stone fruit and Amagaki persimmons—locally produced cheese and honey, flowers and baked goods. Food vendors dish up treats like Yucatán-style *tamales* steamed in banana leaves, and you can grab the requisite to-go coffee at the My Friend Joe wagon. A separate crafts section is always interesting to browse for items like handwoven baskets. And there's usually a strumming folk musician or two. The market sets up on the downtown plaza (across from Whole Foods) Sundays from 10-1:30, year-round.

Sebastopol Area Chamber of Commerce and Visitors Center: 265 S. Main St., Sebastopol, CA 95472. **Phone:** (707) 823-3032 or (877) 828-4748.

FAIRFIELD INN & SUITES BY MARRIOTT SANTA ROSA SEBASTOPOL
(707)829-6677

Hotel
$144-$229

 AAA Benefit: AAA hotel discounts of 5% or more.

Address: 1101 Gravenstein Hwy S 95472 **Location:** US 101 exit SR 116 W northbound, 8 mi w; exit SR 12 W southbound, 7 mi w to Main St. **Facility:** 82 units. 3 stories, interior corridors. **Amenities:** safes. *Some:* high-speed Internet. **Pool(s):** heated outdoor. **Activities:** whirlpool, exercise room. **Guest Services:** valet and coin laundry. **Free Special Amenities: expanded continental breakfast and high-speed Internet.**

SEBASTOPOL INN
707/829-2500

Hotel
$99-$299

Address: 6751 Sebastopol Ave 95472 **Location:** US 101 exit SR 12, 7 mi w. **Facility:** 31 units. 2 stories (no elevator), exterior corridors. **Terms:** 2 night minimum stay - seasonal and/or weekends, 3 day cancellation notice-fee imposed. **Pool(s):** heated outdoor. **Activities:** whirlpool.

WHERE TO EAT

K & L BISTRO
707/823-6614

French. Casual Dining. $14-$36 **AAA Inspector Notes:** High ceilings and exposed brick walls add character to this elegant, cozy bistro. If available, start off with a silky smooth pate followed by salmon with grilled gnocchi and crème brûlée. **Bar:** beer & wine. **Address:** 119 S Main St 95472 **Location:** Just s of SR 12. **Parking:** street only.

SELMA pop. 23,219
• **Restaurants p. 514**

BEST WESTERN COLONIAL INN
(559)891-0300

Hotel
$80-$130

 AAA Benefit: Members save up to 20%, plus 10% bonus points with Best Western Rewards®.

Address: 2799 Floral Ave 93662 **Location:** SR 99 exit Floral Ave, just e. **Facility:** 56 units. 3 stories, interior corridors. **Terms:** cancellation fee imposed. **Amenities:** high-speed Internet. **Pool(s):** outdoor. **Activities:** exercise room. **Guest Services:** coin laundry. **Free Special Amenities: local telephone calls and high-speed Internet.**

HOLIDAY INN-SWAN COURT
(559)891-8000

Hotel
$82-$104

Address: 2950 Pea Soup Anderson Blvd 93662 **Location:** SR 99 exit Floral Ave, just w. **Facility:** 115 units, some kitchens. 3 stories, interior corridors. **Pool(s):** outdoor. **Activities:** whirlpool, exercise room. **Guest Services:** valet and coin laundry. **Free Special Amenities: continental breakfast and room upgrade (subject to availability with advance reservations).**

SUPER 8 SELMA/FRESNO AREA
(559)896-2800

Hotel
$65-$125

Address: 3142 S Highland Ave 93662 **Location:** SR 99 exit Floral Ave, just e. **Facility:** 39 units. 2 stories (no elevator), interior corridors. **Terms:** 2 night minimum stay - seasonal and/or weekends, cancellation fee imposed. **Pool(s):** outdoor. **Free Special Amenities: continental breakfast and high-speed Internet.**

WHERE TO EAT

CHINA GARDEN RESTAURANT   559/896-3633

♦♦ Chinese. Casual Dining. $6-$11 **AAA Inspector Notes:** Diners can order off the menu or sample from the extensive, award-winning buffet, which lines up everything from appetizers to desserts. The established area tradition has been a favorite of locals and tourists alike for more than 20 years. **Bar:** beer & wine. **Address:** 2719 Whitson St 93662 **Location:** SR 99 exit Floral Ave E; in Selma Plaza Shopping Center. [L] [D]

SAL'S MEXICAN RESTAURANT   559/896-7257

♦♦ Mexican. Casual Dining. $6-$14 **AAA Inspector Notes:** Locals and visitors alike frequent this established central valley favorite for traditional Mexican fare, all prepared using fresh, locally-grown ingredients. It is a good idea to come early because this casual spot fills quickly. **Bar:** beer & wine. **Address:** 2163 Park St 93662 **Location:** SR 99 exit 2nd St W, s on Bauder St, just w on Nebraska Ave, s on Skelton St, then just e. [L] [D] CALL [&M]

SPIKE 'N RAIL STEAK HOUSE   559/891-7000

♦♦ American. Casual Dining. $6-$30 **AAA Inspector Notes:** Traditional steak-house favorites are served in a family-friendly atmosphere. Some tables afford views of a pond with swans. **Bar:** full bar. **Address:** 2910 Pea Soup Anderson Blvd 93662 **Location:** SR 99 exit Floral Ave, just w. [B] [L] [D] CALL [&M]

SEQUOIA AND KINGS CANYON NATIONAL PARKS (G-5)

• Hotels p. 516 • Restaurants p. 517

Elevations in the parks range from 1,500 ft. near the headquarters at Ash Mountain to 14,505 ft. at the summit of Mount Whitney. Refer to AAA maps for additional elevation information.

In central California, stretching northward from 35 miles east of Visalia to 55 miles east of Fresno, and from the foothills of the San Joaquin Valley to the crest of the High Sierras, these two parks abut one another and are managed together. Sequoia is the second-oldest national park, behind Yellowstone National Park.

One way to turn back the clock 3,000 years is to take a trip through Sequoia and Kings Canyon National Parks. The landscape is studded with the largest of trees, the giant sequoia (Sequoiadendron giganteum). Many of the trees are more than 200 feet high and some have trunks more than 30 feet in diameter. Mount Whitney, at 14,505 feet the highest point in the contiguous United States, is on the eastern edge of Sequoia National Park.

Although the sequoias sparked the formation of these parks, magnificent forests of sugar and ponderosa pine, white and red fir and incense-cedar also exist here. Sugar pines have been known to grow to a base diameter of 11 feet.

Its variable climate has endowed this region with a significant variety of plants. About 1,530 species of trees, shrubs, plants and flowers have been identified, including 22 deciduous tree and 26 evergreen tree species.

Mule deer, marmots, chipmunks and squirrels are common. Because American black bears frequently are seen in campgrounds, proper food storage is strictly enforced. Raccoons, gray foxes and bobcats can be seen occasionally at night. Rarely seen, however, are Sierra bighorns, mountain lions, pine martens and fishers. About 207 species of birds, including the golden eagle, have been spotted, and the streams along with some high-country lakes support rainbow, brook, brown and golden trout.

Only trails penetrate the alpine wilderness of both parks; therefore, the beauties of the High Sierra and backcountry are available only to hikers and horseback riders. Park trails are off-limits to bicyclists. *See Recreation Areas Chart.*

General Information and Activities

Sequoia and Kings Canyon National Parks are open all year, although the more remote areas are inaccessible in winter. High mountain passes are seldom open to travel before July 1. The roads to Giant Forest, Lodgepole and the Big Stump entrance are open all year; however, the Generals Highway between Lodgepole in Sequoia National Park and Grant Grove in Kings Canyon may be closed by heavy snow for periods during winter. Tire chains may be required at any time.

Connecting the two national parks is the Generals Highway, a 46-mile-long scenic road that extends from SR 198 at Ash Mountain in Sequoia National Park through Giant Sequoia National Monument to SR 180. The highway reaches 7,600 feet at Big Baldy Saddle. **Note:** From Ash Mountain to Giant Forest, the road is particularly difficult for motor homes and large trailers. The road is not recommended for vehicles longer than 22 feet. An alternate route for longer vehicles is SR 180 from Fresno through Kings Canyon National Park, a straighter, less steep and wider road. Vehicle combinations over 40 feet are prohibited between Hospital Rock and Giant Forest.

Sequoia Shuttle offers transportation to the Giant Forest Museum within Sequoia National Park from Visalia and Three Rivers. The shuttle operates Memorial Day weekend through Labor Day; reservations are required. Phone (877) 287-4453.

Accommodations generally are open all year. While most campgrounds usually operate from late May through October, some campgrounds are open all year.

Lodgepole and Grant Grove/Kings Canyon visitor centers, in Sequoia and Kings Canyon National Parks, respectively, are hubs for activities. Naturalists give illustrated talks or campfire programs several nights a week in summer at Cedar Grove, Dorst, Grant Grove/Kings Canyon, Lodgepole, Mineral King and Potwisha amphitheaters. Schedules of programs and daily guided walks are posted on bulletin boards and in prominent public places. The parks' free newspaper contains seasonal information. It is available at park entrance stations and visitor centers.

A state fishing license is required for all persons 16 years and over. The $44.85 fee is good for a year for residents but only 10 days for non-residents. A 2-day resident or non-resident license costs $22.42.

A second-pole license is $13.78. Hunting and weapons of any kind are prohibited.

Horseback trips over the hundreds of miles of backpacking trails are popular. Current information is available at the park visitor centers and in the park newspaper. Guided trail rides and pack trips or rental saddle stock are available from Grant Grove, Cedar Grove and Horse Corral in the national forest land between the parks. Pack trips also can be arranged from the Owens Valley area on the east side of the Sierras. Cross-country ski rentals and lessons are available at Grant Grove and Wuksachi Lodge.

Headquarters for both parks, which are administered jointly, is at Ash Mountain, on the Generals Hwy. 7 mi. above Three Rivers via SR 198. The Foothills Visitor Center includes a photographic exhibit depicting life in the foothills.

ADMISSION to the parks is $20 per private vehicle, good for 7 days, or $10 per person arriving by other means.

PETS are permitted only if they are on a leash, crated or otherwise restricted at all times. They are prohibited on all trails and in buildings and may not be left unattended at any time.

ADDRESS inquiries to the Superintendent, 47050 Generals Hwy., Sequoia and Kings Canyon National Parks, Three Rivers, CA 93271-9700; phone (559) 565-3341.

ALTA PEAK (Sequoia), about 7 mi. from the Wolverton parking area, is 11,204 feet high; it can be reached on foot by a strenuous hike. **Phone:** (559) 565-3341.

CEDAR GROVE (Kings Canyon) is within the canyon of the South Fork of the Kings River. Peaks rise nearly a mile above the stream, and spectacular views are available from road and trail. The level valley floor is especially well suited to leisurely bicycling. Cedar Grove also is a popular base point for longer trips into the high country. The area is inaccessible during winter. **Phone:** (559) 565-3341.

CRYSTAL CAVE (Sequoia) is 14 mi. from Lodgepole Visitor Center and accessible via a narrow, winding road that descends 2,000 feet to Marble Fork Kaweah River Bridge, and then from the parking area down a steep half-mile trail to the cave entrance. **Note:** Vehicles longer than 22 feet are prohibited on the road.

This is the only one of the more than 200 caves within these national parks that is open to the public. The temperature inside the cave is a constant 48 degrees Fahrenheit, so visitors should bring warm clothing. Tickets must be bought at least 90 minutes in advance at Lodgepole Visitor Center or at Foothills Visitor Center.

Strollers, baby backpacks and tripods are prohibited. **Hours:** Forty-five-minute guided tours are given every half hour Mon.-Fri. 10:30-4:30, Sat.-Sun. 10-5, mid-June through Labor Day; daily 11-4, mid-May to mid-June and day after Labor Day-late Oct. (weather permitting). Phone ahead to confirm schedule. **Cost:** Tours $13; $12 (ages 62+); $7 (ages 5-12); $2 (ages 0-4). **Phone:** (559) 565-3759 or (559) 565-4251.

GENERAL GRANT AND REDWOOD MOUNTAIN GROVES are in Kings Canyon. The General Grant Tree, one of the largest of known sequoias, stands in Grant Grove. It is 267 feet high and has a base circumference of approximately 107.6 feet. Big Stump Basin, the result of early logging operations, is nearby. Hart Tree, another large sequoia, stands in Redwood Mountain Grove. **Phone:** (559) 565-3341.

Kings Canyon Visitor Center (Kings Canyon) is 3 mi. e. of Big Stump entrance station on SR 180. Visitor center exhibits highlight the three major features of the park: the canyon, the giant sequoias, and the High Sierra. **Hours:** Daily 8-6, Memorial Day-Labor Day; otherwise varies, rest of year. Phone ahead to confirm schedule. **Cost:** Free. **Phone:** (559) 565-4307.

GIANT FOREST (Sequoia) is 18 mi. from the park entrance station via the steep and winding Generals Hwy. It was named in 1875 by conservationist John Muir. The General Sherman Tree is thought to be the largest living tree in the world; standing about 275 feet tall, its trunk has a diameter of 25 feet near the base and is about 103 feet in circumference. The Giant Forest Museum has exhibits focused on giant sequoia ecology and the and the forest's natural and human history. From the museum several hiking trails lead to the Round Meadow and Hazelwood areas. **Phone:** (559) 565-3341.

HEATHER LAKE (Sequoia), 5 mi. by trail from Wolverton, is the first of a chain of alpine lakes accessible by the Lakes Trail. Two miles beyond is Pear Lake, in a barren granite basin. **Note:** The Lakes Trail is a very steep and difficult hike.

THE HIGH COUNTRY extends from Coyote Peaks at the s. border of Sequoia to the n. boundary of Kings Canyon at Pavilion Dome. Trail trips are the only way to become acquainted with this rugged country. Mount Whitney is 72 miles from Giant Forest along the High Sierra Trail. A wilderness permit is required for overnight visitors. **Phone:** (559) 565-3341, or (559) 565-3766 for wilderness permits.

HOSPITAL ROCK (Sequoia) is 5 mi. beyond Ash Mountain entrance station on the road to Giant Forest. Native American pictographs on the boulder mark an old village site once occupied by the Potwisha tribe of the Western Mono Indians. Also at the site are 71 mortar-and-pestle holes used by the women to grind acorns into flour. Exhibits are on the site of an ancient village. **Phone:** (559) 565-3341.

LODGEPOLE VISITOR CENTER (Sequoia) is 4 mi. n.e. of Giant Forest on the Generals Hwy. The center has displays about the sequoias, geologic history and plant life. **Hours:** Daily 7-6, mid-May to late Oct.; Fri.-Mon. 9-4:30, rest of year. Phone to confirm schedule for ranger programs. **Cost:** Free. **Phone:** (559) 565-4436 June-Sept., (559) 565-3341 rest of year, or (877) 444-6777 for camping reservations for Lodgepole and Dorst (in summer only).

MINERAL KING (Sequoia) is 25 mi. e. of Three Rivers via Mineral King Rd. and a steep, narrow, winding and partially paved road. Once a silver-mining area, this remote and peaceful valley retreat is at an altitude of 7,500 feet, lying in the shadow of the Great Western Divide's towering peaks. Rangers lead walks and campfire programs in summer. **Note:** The area is unsuitable for RVs (trailers and vehicles longer than 22 feet are not permitted) and is inaccessible in winter. **Hours:** Road open late May-Oct. 31. **Phone:** (559) 565-3341.

MORO ROCK (Sequoia), 2 mi. by narrow road or hiking trail from Giant Forest, is 6,725 feet above sea level and more than 6,000 feet above the San Joaquin Valley floor. Scenic views of the Great Western Divide, especially at sunset, are the reward for reaching the top. A steep stairway, inaccessible in winter, leads to the summit. **Note:** Lightning storms may be a hazard in summer months. **Phone:** (559) 565-3341.

PANORAMIC POINT (Kings Canyon) at the e. boundary of General Grant Grove is accessible via a 2.3-mi. road and then a quarter-mile walk from the parking lot. **Note:** The road is narrow and winding and not recommended for trailers or motor homes.

The point offers views of the High Sierra to the east and the San Joaquin Valley and Coast Range to the west. Within walking distance is another observation point at Park Ridge. **Hours:** Road closed to vehicular traffic in the winter, when it becomes a cross-country ski trail. **Phone:** (559) 565-3341.

THARP'S LOG (Sequoia) is at the end of Log Meadow, 1 mi. by trail from Crescent Meadow; or reached from the Circle Meadow and Congress trails. An old pioneer cabin was built within this fire-hollowed sequoia log. **Phone:** (559) 565-3341.

JOHN MUIR LODGE AT GRANT GROVE VILLAGE
(559)335-5500

▼▼▼ **Hotel** $69-$186 **Address:** 86728 Hwy 180 93633 **Location:** On SR 180; in Grant Grove Village. **Facility:** 36 units. 2 stories (no elevator), interior corridors. **Terms:** check-in 4 pm, cancellation fee imposed, resort fee. **Activities:** hiking trails.

WUKSACHI VILLAGE & LODGE   559/565-4070

▼▼▼
Hotel
Rates not provided

Address: 64740 Wuksachi Way 93262 **Location:** 6 mi n of Giant Forest on General's Hwy. **Facility:** 102 units. 3 stories (no elevator), interior corridors. **Terms:** check-in 4 pm. **Amenities:** high-speed Internet. **Dining:** restaurant, see separate listing. **Activities:** fishing, cross country skiing, hiking trails.

CEDAR GROVE LODGE   559/565-0100

[fyi] Not evaluated. **Address:** Kings Canyon National Park 93633 **Location:** On SR 180, 31 mi ne of Grant Grove via winding mountain road. Facilities, services, and décor characterize an economy property.

MONTECITO-SEQUOIA LODGE   559/565-3388

[fyi] Not evaluated. **Address:** 8000 General's Hwy 93633 **Location:** 8 mi s of SR 180 off General's Hwy; between King's Canyon and Sequoia National Parks. Facilities, services, and décor characterize an economy property.

STONY CREEK LODGE   559/565-3909

[fyi] Not evaluated. **Address:** 65569 General's Hwy 93262 **Location:** Between Grant Grove and Giant Forest, 13 mi s of jct SR 180. Facilities, services, and décor characterize an economy property.

WHERE TO EAT

WUKSACHI VILLAGE & LODGE DINING ROOM   559/565-4070

▼▼ ▼▼ American. Casual Dining. $9-$36 **AAA Inspector Notes:** Picture windows in the large dining room look toward the forest and mountains. Lunch items features sandwiches, soups and salads, while the dinner menu lists a limited selection of beef, seafood, chicken and pasta dishes. Patrons can order boxed lunches to go. **Bar:** full bar. **Address:** 64740 Wuksachi Way 93262 **Location:** 6 mi n of Giant Forest on General's Hwy.   B   L   D

SEQUOIA NATIONAL FOREST (H-5)

Elevations in the forest range from 1,000 ft. at the Kings and Kern rivers along the forest's western edge to 12,432 ft. at Florence Peak in the Golden Trout Wilderness. Refer to AAA maps for additional elevation information.

Sequoia National Forest lies in Central California at the southern end of the Sierra Nevadas, extending from Kings River southward to the Kern River and Piute Mountains, and westward from the Sierra Nevada summit to the brush-covered foothills of the San Joaquin Valley.

Groves of giant sequoias, the Kern Plateau and the Golden Trout, Monarch, Jennie Lakes, South Sierra, Dome Land and Kiavah wildernesses are among the more popular attractions. The South Fork Kings Wild and Scenic River, Kings River Special Management Area, North Fork Kern Wild and Scenic River and South Fork Kern Wild and Scenic River also draw outdoor recreation enthusiasts to this spectacularly scenic wilderness area, which covers approximately 1,193,500 acres.

To permanently protect most of the nation's remaining giant sequoia trees, the Giant Sequoia National Monument was created in 2000. The monument's 353,000 acres, all within Sequoia National Forest, encompass 33 groves of these soaring specimens. The largest trees on Earth by volume, they can grow to nearly 300 feet in height and live more than 3,000 years. The monument is separated into two sections, divided by Sequoia National Park; the northern portion is in Fresno and Tulare counties, the southern entirely within Tulare County. Hiking and horseback riding are permitted, and motorcycles, all-terrain vehicles and snowmobiles may be used, although restrictions apply. For additional information phone the national forest office.

More than 50 campgrounds and picnic areas provide bases for activities that include fishing, swimming, boating, hiking, horseback riding, rock climbing and hunting. White-water rafting is popular on the Kern and Kings rivers. Swimming along the shoreline is permitted on 87-acre Hume Lake. Fall foliage color is particularly spectacular at Quaking Aspen, Indian Basin and the Kern Plateau. Winter activities include snowmobiling and cross-country and downhill skiing. Fire lookout towers and ranger cabins can be rented.

For information contact the Information Receptionist, Sequoia National Forest, 1839 S. Newcomb St., Porterville, CA 93257-2035; phone (559) 784-1500. *See Recreation Areas Chart.*

BALCH PARK is within Mountain Home State Forest and the general boundary of the Sequoia National Forest, 32 mi. n.e. of Porterville. At an elevation of 6,325 feet stands a beautiful sequoia grove. Two small stocked ponds are in the park. **Cost:** Day-use fee $5 per vehicle. Pets $3. Camping $16 per night. **Phone:** (559) 539-3896.   🏕 🏕

BOYDEN CAVERN is 22 mi. n.e. of Grant Grove, off SR 180 at 74101 E. Kings Canyon Rd. within Sequoia National Forest. Guided 45-minute tours wind through underground chambers filled with a variety of sparkling, crystalline formations. Other tours also are available; phone for details. The temperature inside is a cool 55 F; a sweater or light jacket is advised.

Time: Allow 1 hour minimum. **Hours:** Tours depart daily on the hour 10-5, mid-May to mid-Sept.; 11-4, last week in Apr. to mid-May and mid-Sept. to mid-Nov. **Cost:** Tour $13; $8 (ages 4-12). **Phone:** (888) 965-8243, ext. 550, for recorded information. 🅰

LAKE ISABELLA, off SR 178, is one of Southern California's largest reservoirs, covering more than 11,000 surface acres. The lake, within a few hours' drive of Los Angeles, offers fishing, boating, kayaking, wind surfing and water skiing; camping and picnicking also are available. Rentals are available at three marinas. **Note:** Sudden wind gusts up to 60 mph winds may occur, making crossing open water unsafe. **Phone:** (760) 379-5236.

SEQUOIA NATIONAL PARK—
See Sequoia and Kings Canyon NP p. 514.

SHASTA (C-2) pop. 1,771, elev. 1,026'

▽ GEM **SHASTA STATE HISTORIC PARK** is on SR 299. Formerly a robust mining town with a population of 2,500, Shasta was the gateway to a large area of riches and a rendezvous for gamblers; it is now an interesting gold rush relic. The old courthouse has been converted to a museum that contains historical exhibits as well as the Boggs Collection—100 Years of California Art. A restored barn and stagecoach can be seen. Also in the park are unrestored buildings that stand as reminders of Shasta's mining heyday.

Hours: Park and museum open Fri.-Sun. 10-5. Closed Jan. 1, Thanksgiving and Christmas. Phone ahead to confirm schedule. **Cost:** Historic park free. Museum $3; $2 (ages 6-17). **Phone:** (530) 225-2065 for park information, or (530) 243-8194 for the museum. 🅰

Get pet travel tips and enter the photo contest at AAA.com/PetBook

SHASTA LAKE (C-2) pop. 10,164, elev. 790'

SHASTA DAM is 6 mi. w. on SR 151 (Shasta Dam Blvd.), following signs. Shasta Dam is reputedly the world's highest center-overflow spillway. A 30-minute videotape depicting water usage in California is shown at the visitor center upon request. Guided walking tours provide information about visitor center displays and the dam.

Hours: Visitor center open daily 8-6, Memorial Day-Labor Day; hours vary rest of year. A 1-hour tour of the dam departs daily at 9, 10:15, 11:30, 1, 2:15 and 3:30, Memorial Day-Labor Day; at 9, 11, 1 and 3, rest of year. Visitors are advised to arrive 1 hour before tour time. Closed winter federal holidays. Phone ahead to confirm schedule. **Cost:** Free. **Phone:** (530) 275-4463. ⛱

THE TAIL O'THE WHALE RESTAURANT   530/275-3021

fyi Not evaluated. Friendly service and views of Lake Shasta from high among the pines is what guests can find at this restaurant offering salads, sandwiches and a variety of dinner entrées. An outdoor patio is available in season. **Address:** 10300 Bridge Bay Rd 96003 **Location:** I-5 exit 690, just w; in Bridge Bay Resort.

SHASTA-TRINITY NATIONAL FORESTS (B-3)

Elevations in the forests range from 620 ft. at Lake Shasta to 14,162 ft. at Mount Shasta. Refer to AAA maps for additional elevation information.

In northern California, the Shasta-Trinity National Forests cover more than 2,100,000 acres and include portions of the Yolla Bolly-Middle Eel Wilderness Area and the Trinity Alps Wilderness. Mount Shasta, a dormant volcano capped with five glaciers, is 14,162 feet tall.

Three impounded lakes—Whiskeytown, Shasta and Clair Engle—are within the Whiskeytown-Shasta-Trinity National Recreation Area *(see place listing p. 557)*. Almost 1,200 miles of hiking trails wind through this vast wilderness area, including 154 miles of the Pacific Crest Trail. There are numerous opportunities for lake and stream fishing as well as hunting for waterfowl, upland birds, deer, bear and small game. Phone (877) 444-6777 or TTY (877) 833-6777 for reservations made through the National Recreation Reservation System.

For more information contact the Forest Supervisor, Shasta-Trinity National Forests, 3644 Avtech Pkwy., Redding, CA 96002; phone (530) 226-2500 or TTY (530) 226-2490. *See Recreation Areas Chart.*

SHAVER LAKE pop. 634

ELLIOTT HOUSE BED & BREAKFAST   (559)841-8601

▼▼▼ **Bed & Breakfast** $169-$229 **Address:** 42062 Tollhouse Rd 93664 **Location:** Center. **Facility:** This attractively appointed inn offers the feel of a mountain setting with the comfort of casual elegance. Guest units are tastefully appointed, some with a fireplace; a few units are small. 7 units. 2 stories (no elevator), interior/exterior corridors. **Terms:** 2 night minimum stay - weekends, 3 day cancellation notice.

⓫ CALL ✆M 🛜 ✕ 💢 ✒ 🔲 🖵 🖵

SHAVER LAKE VILLAGE HOTEL   559/841-8289

▼▼▼ Hotel ◈   **Address:** 42135 Tollhouse Rd 93664 **Location:** Center. **Facility:** 13 units, some two bedrooms and cabins. 1 story, interior/exterior corridors. **Guest Services:** coin laundry. **Free Special Amenities:** continental breakfast and preferred room (subject to availability with advance reservations).

Rates not provided

SAVE ⓫ BIZ 🛜 ✕ 💢 ✒ 🔲 🖵 🖵

DINKEY CREEK INN & CHALETS   559/841-3435

fyi Not evaluated. **Address:** 53861 Dinkey Creek Rd 93664 **Location:** SR 168, 13.5 mi e. Facilities, services, and décor characterize an economy property.

WHERE TO EAT

WAHTOKE GRILL   559/841-4411

▼ American. Casual Dining. $8-$20 **AAA Inspector Notes:** The menu at this casual mountain eatery features many homemade specialties including chili, soups and pasta. A good selection of sandwiches and entrées also are offered. It is best to call ahead in the winter months to verify the hours of operation. **Bar:** full bar. **Address:** 41782 Dorabella Rd 93664 **Location:** Center.

L D 💢

SHELTER COVE pop. 693, elev. 138'

Rising just offshore from the mountainous headland of Cape Mendocino—the westernmost point in California—is Sugar Loaf, a 326-foot-tall sea stack. Several other large rocks protrude from the shallow waters just off this stretch of northern California coast, and they posed hidden dangers for 19th-century sailing ships.

The Cape Mendocino Lighthouse began operations in 1868. The first tower had 16 sides and a double balcony, and was bolted to a concrete foundation 422 feet above the ocean. The lighthouse remained active until the 1940s, when it was automated and the Fresnel lens removed. By the 1960s it had not only been abandoned but was inching down a hillside and succumbing to the debilitating effects of rust; in the late 1990s a grassroots movement was organized to save the lighthouse and relocate it 35 miles south to Shelter Cove.

The reassembled and refurbished structure stands at the tip of Point Delgada in Mal Coombs Park, 23 miles west of US 101 exit 642 (Redwood Drive). It is open to the public daily 11-3, Memorial Day-Labor Day; phone (707) 986-7646.

SHELTER COVE INN   (707)986-4030

▼▼▼ Hotel $275-$315 **Address:** 118 Dolphin Dr 95589 **Location:** Oceanfront. US 101 exit Shelter Cove, 1.7 mi s on Redwood Dr, 20.2 mi w on Briceland Rd/Shelter Cove Rd, 0.4 mi n on Upper Pacific Dr, just w on Lower Pacific Dr, then just n. **Facility:** 4 kitchen units. 2 stories (no elevator), exterior corridors. **Terms:** 2-3 night minimum stay - seasonal and/or weekends, 14 day cancellation notice-fee imposed.

🛜 ✕ 💢 ✒ 🔲 🖵 🖵

THE TIDES INN   707/986-7900

Motel
$165-$215

Address: 59 Surf Point 95589 **Location:** Oceanfront. US 101 exit Shelter Cove, 1.7 mi s on Redwood Dr, 20.2 mi w on Briceland Rd/Shelter Cove Rd, then 0.6 mi sw on Machi Rd/Lower Pacific Dr. **Facility:** 8 units, some kitchens. 3 stories (no elevator), exterior corridors. **Terms:** 3 day cancellation notice-fee imposed.

SIERRA CITY (D-4) pop. 221, elev. 4,187'

KENTUCKY MINE PARK AND MUSEUM, .5 mi. e. via SR 49 in Sierra County Historical Park, is on the site of a hard-rock gold mine. Guided 1-hour walking tours go from the mine portal through an operable ten stamp mill. Tools, photographs, documents and mineral samples displayed in the museum depict mining-camp life during California's gold rush era. Other exhibits include Native American and Chinese artifacts. Concerts take place Saturday evenings early July through August in an outdoor amphitheater; phone for concert information.

Hours: Open Wed.-Sun. 10-4, Memorial Day weekend-Labor Day weekend. Guided stamp mill and mine tours are given at 11 and 2. **Cost:** $7 (includes museum and tours); $3.50 (ages 7-17); $1 (museum only). Cash only. **Phone:** (530) 862-1310.

HERRINGTON'S SIERRA PINES RESORT   530/862-1151

Motel
$79-$140

Address: 104 Main St 96125 **Location:** 0.5 mi w of center on SR 49; 12 mi n of Downieville. **Facility:** 19 units, some kitchens and cabins. 1 story, exterior corridors. *Bath:* shower only. **Terms:** closed 11/2-4/30, 2 night minimum stay - weekends, 10 day cancellation notice. **Dining:** restaurant, see separate listing. **Activities:** hiking trails, jogging, game room, horseshoes. *Fee:* fishing. **Free Special Amenities:** local telephone calls and high-speed Internet.

/SOME UNITS

WHERE TO EAT

HERRINGTON'S SIERRA PINES RESTAURANT   530/862-1151

American. Casual Dining. $18-$29 **AAA Inspector Notes:** Cozy, knotty pine decor and a fireplace set the stage for such entrées as rainbow trout caught fresh from the property's pond, certified Angus beef and seafood. Views of the Sierra Buttes can be enjoyed from the large picture windows. **Bar:** full bar. **Address:** 104 Main St 96125 **Location:** 0.5 mi w of center on SR 49; 12 mi n of Downieville; in Herrington's Sierra Pines Resort.

SIERRA NATIONAL FOREST (F-5)

Elevations in the forest range from 990 ft. at the Merced River to 13,157 ft. at the summit of Mount Ritter. Refer to AAA maps for additional elevation information.

Located between two of California's scenic crown jewels, Kings Canyon and Yosemite national parks *(see place listings p. 514 and 578),* Sierra National Forest is a gem in its own right. This 1,300,000-acre wilderness area embraces almost all the land between these national parks—from the gently rolling

foothills bordering the San Joaquin Valley to the jagged Sierra crest. Within the forest's boundaries lies much of what naturalist and Sierra Club founder John Muir described as the "Range of Light." More commonly called the High Sierra, it's a spectacular landscape dominated by craggy peaks, giant glacial stairways and mountainside natural amphitheaters filled with lakes and open meadows.

How this rugged landscape came to be was debated by many 19th-century scientists. Yet it was Muir's remark that "tender snow-flowers noiselessly falling through unnumbered centuries" came closest to the truth. Glacial ice gave these peaks their distinctive shape, further refined by the many swift streams and rivers fed by melting of the yearly snowpack. Such major rivers as the San Joaquin, the Merced, the Kings and their tributaries all carved deep canyons and gorges within the forest.

Hidden deep within these watersheds are clusters of sequoias. One stand of these majestic trees is the Nelder Grove, south of Yosemite National Park near Bass Lake; the McKinley Grove is farther south near Dinkey Creek.

Two highways offering access to the forest are SRs 41 and 168; the most accessible recreation areas are along or just off these routes. Shaver Lake and Bass Lake are two popular destinations, offering camping, fishing and boating. Other recreation areas, such as Florence Lake, Edison Lake, Redinger Lake and Pine Flat Reservoir, are accessible from forest roads branching off SR 168. During the winter months the focus switches to downhill skiing.

The John Muir and Ansel Adams wilderness areas straddle the forest's eastern border and the Sierra crest. The former, with its snowcapped peaks, dense forests and numerous lakes, is one of California's largest wilderness areas. Highlights of this untamed area include the John Muir Trail—a segment of the Pacific Crest Trail—and Humphreys Basin, with its countless lakes and views of Mount Humphreys, a favorite challenge for experienced climbers.

Within the Ansel Adams Wilderness Area are the jagged peaks of Ritter Range. Smaller in size are the Monarch, Dinkey Lakes and Kaiser wilderness areas. The John Muir and Kaiser wilderness areas, as well as portions of the Ansel Adams, are so popular that there is a quota system for visitors; making reservations at least 3 weeks in advance is recommended. More than a thousand miles of hiking trails and over 400 lakes are waiting to be explored in these areas.

Indigenous wildlife includes deer, bears, quail, bobcats, foxes, beavers and coyotes. Lakes and streams teem with rainbow, golden, brown and eastern brook trout, along with large and small mouth bass, crappie and bluegill.

There is no central visitor center, but information about campgrounds and recreational opportunities is available at district ranger stations and the forest headquarters in Clovis. Campground reservations, usually required for the months of June through August at Shaver Lake, Huntington Lake, Dinkey Creek and Bass Lake, can be made through the National Recreation Reservation System; phone (877) 444-6777 or TTY (877) 833-6777.

For more information contact the Forest Headquarters, Sierra National Forest, 1600 Tollhouse Rd., Clovis, CA 93611-0532; phone (559) 297-0706. *See Recreation Areas Chart.*

SIX RIVERS NATIONAL FOREST (B-1)

Elevations in the forest range from 350 ft. at Adams Station to 6,957 ft. at the summit of Salmon Mountain. Refer to AAA maps for additional elevation information.

Extending 135 miles south from the Oregon border along the west slope of the Coast Range, Six Rivers National Forest covers almost 990,000 acres; it is named for the Smith, Klamath, Trinity, Mad, Van Duzen and Eel rivers.

Various roads access the forest, including SR 96 along the Trinity and Klamath rivers northward from Willow Creek through the Hoopa Valley Indian Reservation. Much of this region, however, is accessible only on foot or by horseback.

Many recreational opportunities center around water. Rafting and kayaking are especially popular on the Klamath, Trinity and Smith rivers. Trout, steelhead and salmon fishing and deer hunting are other activities.

Within the national forest is Smith River National Recreation Area. More than 65 miles of trails are used by horseback riders, mountain bikers and hikers, and wildlife observers can spot such rare and endangered species as bald eagles and peregrine falcons. For information contact the Forest Supervisor, Six Rivers National Forest, 1330 Bayshore Way, Eureka, CA 95501; phone (707) 442-1721. *See Recreation Areas Chart.*

SODA SPRINGS (D-4) pop. 81, elev. 6,768'

WESTERN SKISPORT MUSEUM, s. of I-80 at the Boreal Ski Area, has displays depicting the development of snow skiing as a sport. Exhibits date from 1850 to the present. Videos are shown by request. **Time:** Allow 30 minutes minimum. **Hours:** Fri.-Sun. 10-4, Dec.-Apr.; by appointment rest of year. Phone ahead to confirm schedule. **Cost:** Free. **Phone:** (530) 426-3313.

ICE LAKES LODGE   530/426-7660
[fyi] Not evaluated. **Address:** 1111 Soda Springs Rd 95728 **Location:** I-80 exit 174 (Soda Springs Rd), 0.6 mi e on Donner Pass Rd, then 2.5 mi s. Facilities, services, and décor characterize an economy property.

SOLEDAD (G-3) pop. 25,738, elev. 190'

MISSION NUESTRA SEÑORA DE LA SOLEDAD, 1.3 mi. w. off US 101 at 36641 Fort Romie Rd., was founded in 1791. It consists of adobe ruins, a museum and a restored chapel. **Time:** Allow 30 minutes minimum. **Hours:** Daily 10-4. Closed major holidays. **Cost:** Donations. **Phone:** (831) 678-2586.

SOLEDAD MOTEL 8   831/678-3814
 Motel $66-$99 **Address:** 1013 S Front St 93960 **Location:** US 101 exit Soledad, just e. **Facility:** 60 units. 2 stories (no elevator), exterior corridors. 📶 🛜 / SOME UNITS 🛏 🍴 ▢

VALLEY HARVEST INN   (831)678-3833
Hotel
$89-$149
Address: 1155 Front St 93960 **Location:** US 101 exit Soledad, just e. **Facility:** 57 units. 2 stories, interior/exterior corridors. **Terms:** cancellation fee imposed. **Amenities:** *Some:* high-speed Internet. **Pool(s):** outdoor. **Activities:** whirlpool, exercise room. **Guest Services:** coin laundry. **Free Special Amenities:** continental breakfast and high-speed Internet.
[SAVE] 🍴 🛜 BIZ 🛜 🛏 🖥 ▢

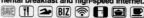
WHERE TO EAT

WINDMILL RESTAURANT   831/678-1775
🍷🍷 American. Casual Dining. $5-$18 **AAA Inspector Notes:** A great stop for travelers, the restaurant fills its menu with traditional favorites, including yummy freshly baked pies. The friendly staff is eager to please. **Bar:** beer & wine. **Address:** 1167 Front St 93960 **Location:** US 101 exit Soledad, just e.
B L D CALL 👤M

SONOMA (B-8) pop. 10,648, elev. 84'

• Hotels p. 522 • Restaurants p. 522
• Attractions map p. 568
• Hotels & Restaurants map & index p. 570
• Part of Wine Country area — see map p. 562

This Wine Country town is a big tourist destination, but it also left a prominent footprint on early California history. After overthrowing the Spanish government in 1823, the Mexican government issued a decree that all church properties be secularized. This included the Mission San Francisco Solano de Sonoma, recently established by Spanish priest Jose Altimira. Gen. Mariano Guadalupe Vallejo was sent from Monterey to confiscate the property, which he did; during his post he also founded the town of Sonoma around a central plaza, the Spanish model for cities in Mexico.

Settlers, lured to the area by the promise of free land, later were denied the opportunity to own property. Faced with the threat of deportation, their dissatisfaction came to a climax on June 14, 1846, when the group, calling themselves Osos (bears), arrested Vallejo at his home. They proclaimed California a republic and Sonoma its capital.

The Bear Flag—fashioned from unbleached muslin, a red petticoat and a crude berry-stained picture of a bear—was raised in Sonoma Plaza. The revolt was short-lived, however; on July 9 the flag was replaced by the Stars and Stripes. In 1911 the State Legislature adopted the Bear Flag as the state flag.

Depot Park Museum, in the original town depot on 1st Street W., preserves the history of the California Republic through displays of 19th-century clothing, railroad artifacts and furniture; phone (707) 938-1762.

(See map & index p. 570.)

Sonoma Valley Visitors Bureau: 453 1st St. E., Sonoma, CA 95476. **Phone:** (707) 996-1090 or (866) 996-1090.

CORNERSTONE SONOMA is 3 mi. s. at 23570 Arnold Dr. (SR 121). More than 20 different gardens are featured at this 9-acre property. Each garden is created by a landscape architect in approximately 1,800 square feet. The innovative designs are meant to serve as an inspiration for all gardeners. Plaques describe each garden and provide information about its creator. Wine tasting rooms, shops, an art gallery and a visitor center also are on the premises. **Time:** Allow 45 minutes minimum. **Hours:** Gardens daily 10-4. Wine tasting daily 10-5. **Cost:** Free. **Phone:** (707) 933-3010.

SONOMA STATE HISTORIC PARK is centered around Sonoma Plaza. More than a dozen buildings important to early California history can be explored. The Toscano Hotel and Sonoma Barracks are on the plaza. The hotel, built during the 1850s, resembles its turn-of-the-20th-century appearance. The two-story, partially restored adobe barracks once housed Mexican general Mariano Vallejo's troops. Following the raising of the Bear Flag in 1846, the building was used by U.S. troops.

The 1823 Mission San Francisco Solano de Sonoma was the last of the California missions, which were located a day's journey apart along the coast. Destroyed and rebuilt several times, it contains exhibits about mission life as well as the Jorgensen watercolors of the Missions of California. Gen. Vallejo's former home, Lachryma Montis, contains family furnishings, and there are gardens on the grounds. Near the house is the Chalet, a building originally used to store wine and produce; it is now the park's visitor center. The mission can be seen on a self-guiding tour.

Several guided tours are available. **Time:** Allow 1 hour minimum. **Hours:** Tues.-Sun. 10-5. Tours of several historic buildings, including the mission, hotel and Vallejo home, are offered; phone ahead for schedule. Closed Jan. 1, Thanksgiving and Christmas. **Cost:** $3 (includes mission, barracks and house); $2 (ages 0-16). **Phone:** (707) 938-9560.

SONOMA TRAINTOWN, 1 mi. s. on SR 12, offers a 20-minute miniature train ride through a forested railroad park past scaled-down reproductions of buildings and waterfalls. A diesel engine makes the trip Monday through Friday; a steam engine is used Saturday, Sunday and holidays. A petting zoo, Ferris wheel, merry-go-round and other rides are on the grounds.

Time: Allow 30 minutes minimum. **Hours:** Trips daily 10-5, June-Aug.; Fri.-Sun. and some holidays 10-5, rest of year. Closed Christmas. **Cost:** Park admission free. Train rides $5.75. Merry-go-round, Ferris wheel and other rides $2.75 each, or six rides for $12. **Phone:** (707) 938-3912.

SONOMA VALLEY MUSEUM OF ART is at 551 Broadway, just s. of Sonoma Plaza. Changing exhibits feature paintings, drawings, sculpture, photography, ceramics, film, crafts, architecture, printmaking and video by local, national and international artists. **Time:** Allow 1 hour, 30 minutes minimum. **Hours:** Wed.-Sun. 11-5. **Cost:** $5; free (ages 0-12 and to all on Wed.). **Phone:** (707) 939-7862.

RECREATIONAL ACTIVITIES

Bicycling

- **Goodtime Touring Company** offers bicycle and van tours and delivers bicycles for rent to local hotels and vacation rentals. **Hours:** Daily 9-6. **Phone:** (707) 938-0453 or (888) 525-0453.

WINERIES

- **Bartholomew Park Winery** is e. off SR 12 onto Napa St., n. onto 7th St. E., then n.e. on Castle Rd. **Hours:** Tastings daily 11-4:30. Tours are given Fri.- Sat. at 11:30 or by appointment. Closed Jan. 1, Easter, Thanksgiving and Christmas. **Phone:** (707) 935-9511, ext. 206.

- **Buena Vista Winery** is 2 mi. n.e. at 18000 Old Winery Rd. **Hours:** Daily 10-5. Closed major holidays. **Phone:** (800) 926-1266.

- **Cline Cellars** is at 24737 Arnold Dr. **Hours:** Daily 10-6. Guided tours are given daily at 11, 1 and 3. Closed Christmas. **Phone:** (707) 940-4030 or (800) 546-2070.

- **Gloria Ferrer Caves & Vineyards** is at 23555 Carneros Hwy. (SR 121). **Hours:** Daily 10-5. Guided tours are given daily at 11, 1 and 3; phone ahead after 9:45 on day of visit to confirm tour schedule. **Phone:** (707) 996-7256, or (707) 933-1917 to confirm the day's tour schedule.

- **Gundlach Bundschu Winery** is e. off SR 12 onto E. Napa St., s. onto 8th St. E., then e. to 2000 Denmark St. **Hours:** Daily 11-5:30, mid-June to mid-Oct.; 11-4:30, rest of year. Two different guided tours are available by appointment; phone ahead for tour schedule. Closed Jan. 1, Easter, Thanksgiving, Christmas Eve and Christmas. **Phone:** (707) 938-5277 or (707) 939-3015.

- **Ravenswood Winery** is at 18701 Gehricke Rd. **Hours:** Tastings daily 10-4:30. A guided tour is given daily at 10:30 by appointment. Closed Jan. 1, Easter, Thanksgiving and Christmas. Phone ahead to confirm schedule. **Phone:** (707) 933-2332 or (888) 669-4679.

- **Sebastiani Vineyards** is at 389 4th St. E. **Hours:** Tasting room open daily 11-5. Tours are given daily at 11, 1 and 3. Closed major holidays. **Phone:** (707) 933-3230.

- **Viansa Winery** is at 25200 Arnold Dr. (SR 121). **Hours:** Daily 10-5. **Phone:** (707) 935-4700 or (800) 995-4740.

(See map & index p. 570.)

BEST WESTERN PLUS SONOMA VALLEY INN & KRUG EVENT CENTER
(707)938-9200

Hotel
$109-$295

AAA Benefit: Members save up to 20%, plus 10% bonus points with Best Western Rewards®.

Address: 550 2nd St W 95476 **Location:** 1 blk w of town plaza. **Facility:** 80 units. 2 stories (no elevator), exterior corridors. **Terms:** check-in 4 pm, 2 night minimum stay - seasonal, 3 day cancellation notice-fee imposed. **Amenities:** Fee: video games, safes. **Pool(s):** heated outdoor. **Activities:** whirlpool, steamroom, exercise room. Fee: massage. **Guest Services:** valet and coin laundry. **Free Special Amenities:** local telephone calls and high-speed Internet.

EL PUEBLO INN
(707)996-3651

Motel
$90-$340

Address: 896 W Napa St 95476 **Location:** SR 12, 1 mi w of town plaza. **Facility:** 53 units. 2 stories (no elevator), exterior corridors. **Amenities:** high-speed Internet, safes. **Pool(s):** outdoor. **Activities:** whirlpool, exercise room. Fee: bicycles, massage. **Guest Services:** valet laundry. **Free Special Amenities:** expanded continental breakfast and high-speed Internet.

THE FAIRMONT SONOMA MISSION INN & SPA
(707)938-9000

Resort Hotel
$199-$649

Address: 100 Boyes Blvd 95476 **Location:** 2.5 mi n on SR 12. **Facility:** A mixture of Mediterranean and Spanish-Californian architecture distinguishes this inn set on spacious, landscaped grounds; a spa is featured. 226 units. 3 stories, interior/exterior corridors. **Parking:** on-site and valet. **Terms:** check-in 4 pm, 5 day cancellation notice-fee imposed. **Amenities:** high-speed Internet (fee), safes. **Dining:** 2 restaurants, also, Sante, see separate listing. **Pool(s):** heated outdoor. **Activities:** sauna, whirlpools, hiking trails, spa. Fee: golf-18 holes, 2 lighted tennis courts, bicycles. **Guest Services:** valet laundry.

INN AT SONOMA
(707)939-1340

Bed & Breakfast $225-$325 **Address:** 630 Broadway 95476 **Location:** On SR 12, just s of Sonoma Plaza. **Facility:** This lovely, well-appointed inn is just two blocks from Sonoma Plaza. Some rooms come with a balcony, and all rooms have a fireplace that's perfect for a chilly night. 19 units. 2 stories, interior corridors. **Terms:** 7 day cancellation notice-fee imposed. **Activities:** whirlpool, bicycles.

THE LODGE AT SONOMA, A RENAISSANCE RESORT & SPA
(707)935-6600

Hotel
$289-$599

RENAISSANCE
HOTELS & RESORTS

AAA Benefit: AAA hotel discounts of 5% or more.

Address: 1325 Broadway 95476 **Location:** On SR 12, 1 mi s of Sonoma Plaza. **Facility:** The spacious and extensive spa facilities and pool area are just a few of the amenities available to guests at this unique resort. 182 units. 2 stories, interior/exterior corridors. **Terms:** check-in 4 pm, 3 day cancellation notice. **Amenities:** high-speed Internet (fee), safes. **Dining:** Carneros Bistro & Wine Bar, see separate listing. **Pool(s):** heated outdoor. **Activities:** sauna, whirlpool, exercise room, spa. Fee: bicycles. **Guest Services:** valet laundry, area transportation-within 2 mi.

MACARTHUR PLACE
(707)938-2929

Country Inn $299-$725 **Address:** 29 E MacArthur St 95476 **Location:** Just e of SR 12 (Broadway). **Facility:** The property includes a Victorian manor house built in the 1860s as well as several cottages designed to replicate its vintage style. 64 units. 2 stories (no elevator), interior/exterior corridors. **Terms:** check-in 4 pm, 2 night minimum stay - seasonal and/or weekends, 7 day cancellation notice-fee imposed. **Dining:** Saddles Steakhouse, see separate listing. **Pool(s):** heated outdoor. **Activities:** whirlpool, exercise room, spa. Fee: bicycles. **Guest Services:** valet laundry.

MAGLIULO'S ROSE GARDEN INN
707/996-1031

Historic Bed & Breakfast. Rates not provided. **Address:** 681 Broadway 95476 **Location:** SR 12, just s. **Facility:** Located two blocks south of the historic Sonoma Plaza and near world famous wineries, this Victorian inn offers inviting accommodations but no breakfast. 4 units. 1 story, interior corridors. Bath: some shared.

SONOMA CREEK INN
(707)939-9463

Motel $89-$199 **Address:** 239 Boyes Blvd 95476 **Location:** SR 12, 0.5 mi w. **Facility:** 16 units. 2 stories (no elevator), exterior corridors. **Terms:** 7 day cancellation notice-fee imposed.

SONOMA HOTEL
707/996-2996

Historic Country Inn $140-$255 **Address:** 110 W Spain St 95476 **Location:** In historic Sonoma Plaza. **Facility:** This historic building's hallways are adorned with antiques from the past. Guest room décor is rustic country while the bathrooms are contemporary classic. 16 units. 3 stories (no elevator), interior corridors. **Parking:** street only. **Terms:** 2 night minimum stay - seasonal and/or weekends, 7 day cancellation notice-fee imposed. **Dining:** the girl & the fig, see separate listing.

WHERE TO EAT

CAFE LA HAYE
707/935-5994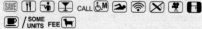

California. Casual Dining. $19-$30 **AAA Inspector Notes:** The tiny, artful restaurant serves creative California cuisine. Plenty of locally grown, organic produce is used to prepare the menu offerings. Wonderful original artwork adorns the walls. **Bar:** beer & wine. **Address:** 140 E Napa St 95476 **Location:** Just e of Sonoma Plaza. **Parking:** street only.

CARNEROS BISTRO & WINE BAR
707/931-2042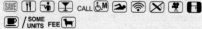

California
Casual Dining
$13-$33

AAA Inspector Notes: Wine country cuisine makes up the menu in this relaxed and casually elegant bistro, where service is crisp and attentive. This place brings in many foods from local artisan farms and the salad ingredients are freshly picked from gardens on the premises. Many items are cooked in the rotisserie and wood-burning ovens. Outdoor seating is an option when the weather permits. **Bar:** full bar. **Reservations:** suggested. **Address:** 1325 Broadway 95476 **Location:** On SR 12, 1 mi s of Sonoma Plaza; in The Lodge at Sonoma, A Renaissance Resort & Spa.

DELLA SANTINA'S
707/935-0576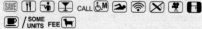

Italian. Casual Dining. $12-$33 **AAA Inspector Notes:** This Tuscan trattoria presents a menu of homemade pasta and rotisserie meats. The wine list features Sonoma and Tuscan wines. **Bar:** beer & wine. **Address:** 133 E Napa St 95476 **Location:** Just e of Sonoma Plaza. **Parking:** street only.

EL DORADO KITCHEN
707/996-3030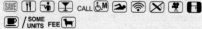

California. Casual Dining. $15-$32 **AAA Inspector Notes:** The décor at this kitchen is contemporary rustic. Well-executed dishes have an additional touch that may be textural such as popped rice sprinkled atop the Wagyu carpaccio or visual with a piece of salmon seemly floating on sea foam. Finish with a sweet ending that is both texturally and visually entertaining. **Bar:** full bar. **Address:** 405 1st St W 95476 **Location:** West side of Sonoma Plaza. **Parking:** street only.

(See map & index p. 570.)

THE FREMONT DINER 707/938-7370 (46)

▼▼ ▼▼ American. Casual Dining. $8-$12 **AAA Inspector Notes:** This casual spot features deliberately divey roadhouse decor with an old pickup truck prop parked in the front. Mostly self service with a friendly, attentive staff. Food consists of comfort food done in the NorCal way-organic, farm-to-table, seasonal and well executed. Try the pulled pork sandwich, salted caramel milk shake and any of their baked goods. **Bar:** beer & wine. **Address:** 2698 Fremont Dr 95476 **Location:** Between Burndale Rd and S Central Ave; on SR 121 N.

[B] [L] [K]

THE GIRL & THE FIG 707/938-3634 (37)

▼▼▼▼ French. Casual Dining. $12-$29 **AAA Inspector Notes:** This brasserie offers both indoor and outdoor seating. Available is a good selection of cheese made locally, in house and from around the world. Arrive early to take advantage of the reasonably priced three-course dinner. **Bar:** full bar. **Address:** 110 W Spain St 95476 **Location:** In historic Sonoma Plaza; in Sonoma Hotel. **Parking:** street only. [L] [D]

LA CASA RESTAURANT & BAR 707/996-3406 (40)

▼▼ ▼▼ Mexican. Casual Dining. $10-$18 **AAA Inspector Notes:** Open for 41 years, this restaurant is practically an institution. Known for their fajitas, this spot has served classic Mexican dishes to generations of Sonoma residents. **Bar:** full bar. **Address:** 121 E Spain St 95476 **Location:** Opposite San Francisco Solano Mission. **Parking:** street only. [L] [D]

LASALETTE RESTAURANT 707/938-1927 (41)

▼▼▼▼ Portuguese. Casual Dining. $11-$26 **AAA Inspector Notes:** Chef Manuel Azevedo combines Portuguese culture and classic cuisines to deliver an authentic culinary experience referred to as cozinha nova Portuguesa. Madeira glazed pork belly is a good choice as is such classics as bacalhau a Alexandre. Arroz doce makes a nice dessert. **Bar:** wine only. **Address:** 452-H 1st St E 95476 **Location:** In Sonoma Plaza. **Parking:** street only.

[L] [D] CALL [M]

SADDLES STEAKHOUSE 707/933-3191 (44)

▼▼▼▼ Steak. Casual Dining. $9-$48 **AAA Inspector Notes:** Although menu choices abound, the real reason to visit this spot is for the Prime steak. In a historic barn, the restaurant also deserves kudos for its wine list and signature martinis. **Bar:** full bar. **Address:** 29 E MacArthur St 95476 **Location:** Just e of SR 12 (Broadway); in MacArthur Place. [B] [L] [D]

SANTE 707/939-2415 (36)

▼▼ ▼▼ ▼▼

California
Fine Dining
$75-$129

AAA Inspector Notes: Located in a Mission-style room with wood beamed ceilings and iron chandeliers, this spot serves wine country cuisine using the freshest local ingredients with many organically grown. Three-, four- or chef's-tasting prix fixe menu are offered. **Bar:** full bar. **Reservations:** suggested. **Address:** 100 Boyes Blvd 95476 **Location:** 2.5 mi n on SR 12; in The Fairmont Sonoma Mission Inn & Spa. **Parking:** on-site and valet. [D]

SWISS HOTEL RESTAURANT 707/938-2884 (38)

▼▼ ▼▼ Swiss. Casual Dining. $8-$29 **AAA Inspector Notes:** Among top choices are pizza from the wood-burning oven and some excellent pasta dishes. The garden patio allows for great al fresco dining. **Bar:** full bar. **Address:** 18 W Spain St 95476 **Location:** In Sonoma Plaza. **Parking:** street only. [L] [D]

SONORA (F-4) pop. 4,903, elev. 1,796'
• Restaurants p. 524

Sonora was initially settled by miners from Sonora, Mexico, in 1848 and became one of the largest and wealthiest towns in the Mother Lode country. Tourism, lumbering and agriculture provide the income today. Handsome Victorian houses are a legacy of the town's gold rush days.

Tuolumne County Visitors Bureau: 542 Stockton St., P.O. Box 4020, Sonora, CA 95370. **Phone:** (209) 533-4420 or (800) 446-1333.

BRADFORD STREET PARK, Bradford St. at SR 49, has exhibits about mining equipment used in Sonora during the gold rush era. Among the artifacts on display are an arrastra, a drag-stone mill used for pulverizing ore, a stamp mill and a pelton wheel. **Hours:** Daily 24 hours. **Cost:** Free. [symbol]

TUOLUMNE COUNTY MUSEUM AND HISTORY CENTER, 158 W. Bradford Ave., is housed in the 1857 county jail. Displays depicting the gold rush era include photographs, guns, antiques, artifacts, gold samples and a Pioneer Trails exhibit. **Hours:** Sun.-Fri. 10-4, Sat. 10-3:30. Closed Jan. 1, Christmas Eve, Christmas and Dec. 31. **Cost:** Donations. **Phone:** (209) 532-1317. [symbol]

ALADDIN MOTOR INN 209/533-4971

Hotel
$81-$145

Address: 14260 Mono Way (Hwy 108) 95370 **Location:** On SR 108, 3.5 mi e. **Facility:** 61 units. 2 stories (no elevator), interior/exterior corridors. **Terms:** cancellation fee imposed. **Pool(s):** outdoor. **Activities:** whirlpool. **Guest Services:** coin laundry. **Free Special Amenities:** expanded continental breakfast and high-speed Internet.

[SAVE] [symbols] [BIZ] [symbols] / SOME UNITS FEE [symbol]

BARRETTA GARDENS INN (209)532-6039

▼▼▼▼ Bed & Breakfast $149-$250 **Address:** 700 S Barretta St 95370 **Location:** Downtown. **Facility:** Within the historic district, this turn-of-the-20th-century Victorian home offers shady porches, fragrant gardens and a cozy living room fireplace. 7 units. 2 stories (no elevator), interior corridors. **Terms:** check-in 4 pm, 2 night minimum stay - seasonal and/or weekends, 14 day cancellation notice. [symbols] / SOME UNITS [symbol]

BEST WESTERN PLUS SONORA OAKS HOTEL & CONFERENCE CENTER (209)533-4400

Hotel
$99-$149

AAA Benefit: Members save up to 20%, plus 10% bonus points with Best Western Rewards®.

Address: 19551 Hess Ave 95370 **Location:** 3.5 mi e on SR 108. **Facility:** 101 units, some two bedrooms. 2 stories (no elevator), interior/exterior corridors. **Terms:** 2 night minimum stay - seasonal and/or weekends. **Amenities:** video games (fee). Some: high-speed Internet. **Pool(s):** outdoor. **Activities:** whirlpool. **Guest Services:** valet laundry. **Free Special Amenities:** local telephone calls and high-speed Internet.

[SAVE] [symbols] CALL [M] [symbols] FEE [symbols] [BIZ] [symbols] [symbol] [symbols] / SOME UNITS FEE [symbol]

BRADFORD PLACE INN AND GARDENS (209)536-6075

▼▼▼▼ Bed & Breakfast $140-$265

Address: 56 W Bradford St 95370 **Location:** Just w of SR 49; downtown. **Facility:** Known as the Keil-Bergson House, this 1889 Victorian offers guests a peaceful setting reminiscent of a bygone era. The owner has dogs on the premises. 4 units. 2 stories (no elevator), interior corridors. **Terms:** 5 day cancellation notice. **Free Special Amenities:** full breakfast and high-speed Internet. [SAVE] [symbols] / SOME UNITS [symbols]

Plan complete trip routings with the TripTik® Travel Planner on AAA.com/CAA.ca

INNS OF CALIFORNIA-SONORA   (209)532-3633

Hotel
$70-$180

Address: 350 S Washington St 95370 **Location:** 3 blks e of jct SR 49 and 108; downtown. **Facility:** 111 units. 3 stories (no elevator), exterior corridors. **Terms:** cancellation fee imposed, resort fee. **Pool(s):** outdoor. **Activities:** whirlpool. **Guest Services:** coin laundry.

[SAVE] [TI+] [≈] [BIZ] [🖧] [🛏] [🖨] [💻] /SOME UNITS FEE [🐾]

SONORA INN   (209)532-2400

Historic Hotel
$59-$189

Address: 160 S Washington St 95370 **Location:** Jct SR 49 and 108; in historic downtown. **Facility:** This downtown hotel, 60 miles north of Yosemite, includes an annex and a restored 1849 Victorian house; the rooftop pool is nice. 30 units. 3 stories, interior corridors. **Pool(s):** outdoor. **Free Special Amenities:** continental breakfast and high-speed Internet.

(See ad p. 592.)

[SAVE] [TI] [≈] [🖧] [✕] [💻] /SOME UNITS [🛏] [🖨]

UNION HILL INN   (209)533-1494

▼▼▼ **Bed & Breakfast** $150-$195 **Address:** 21645 Parrotts Ferry Rd 95370 **Location:** Jct SR 49 and Parrotts Ferry Rd; 3 mi n of downtown. **Facility:** Along the rolling Sierra Foothills and close to Columbia State Historic Park, the 1849 inn features mature trees, a gazebo, pool, ponds and fountains. 7 units. 2 stories (no elevator), exterior corridors. **Terms:** 3 day cancellation notice-fee imposed. **Pool(s):** outdoor. **Activities:** whirlpool. **Guest Services:** complimentary laundry.

[≈] [BIZ] [🖧] [✕] [🔌] [🛏] [💻] /SOME UNITS [🐾] [🖨]

WHERE TO EAT

BE WOK & SUSHI   209/532-2638

▼▼▼ Chinese. Casual Dining. $6-$55 **AAA Inspector Notes:** This local favorite offers both Chinese and Japanese selections. Lunch specials are offered daily by a warm and friendly staff. **Bar:** beer & wine. **Address:** 764 E Mono Way 95370 **Location:** SR 108 exit S Washington St, 0.4 mi n, just e on Restano Way, then 0.7 mi e; in Sonora Plaza Shopping Center. [L] [D] CALL [♿M]

THE DIAMONDBACK GRILL   209/532-6661

▼▼ American. Casual Dining. $8-$12 **AAA Inspector Notes:** Especially noted for their half-pound burgers that range from the basic all-the-way burger to a Kobe or buffalo burger-my personal favorite being the Gorgonzola and bacon burger served with sweet potato fries. The menu also offers homemade soup, a special black bean chili, assorted specialty salads and sandwiches. Be sure arrive early as this is a favorite spot for locals. Come hungry as portions are hearty. **Bar:** beer & wine. **Address:** 93 S Washington St 95370 **Location:** Between Linoberg and Theall sts; in historic downtown. **Parking:** street only. [L] [D] CALL [♿M]

JEB'S HILL COUNTRY COOKIN'   209/588-9633

▼▼ Comfort Food. Family Dining. $6-$12 **AAA Inspector Notes:** This great family restaurant with friendly service offers breakfasts featuring Belgian waffles with fresh strawberries and special skillets with eggs, meat and potatoes. Lunch and dinner serve up great soups, salads and sandwiches as well as the traditional, home-style comfort foods. Portions are hearty so bring an appetite. **Bar:** beer & wine. **Address:** 729 Mono Way 95370 **Location:** 1.2 mi e of jct SR 49 and 108. [B] [L] [D] CALL [♿M]

PEPPERY GAR AND BRILL   209/533-9033

▼▼ American. Casual Dining. $9-$20 **AAA Inspector Notes:** A flavorful menu offers a wide variety of salads, pastas, sandwiches, fish and BBQ items. This fun and bustling atmosphere welcomes locals and visitors alike. **Bar:** full bar. **Address:** 13494 Mono Way 95370 **Location:** On SR 108, just w of jct Tuolumne Rd.

[L] [D]

ROUND TABLE PIZZA

▼ Pizza. Casual Dining. $7-$28 **AAA Inspector Notes:** This casual, family-oriented pizza place features high-quality ingredients and dough rolled fresh daily. Distinctive specialty pizzas are piled high with toppings. **Bar:** beer & wine. [L] [D]

For additional information, visit AAA.com

LOCATIONS:
Address: 154 W Stockton St 95370 **Location:** Just w of Washington St; downtown. **Phone:** 209/532-3443
Address: 13761 Mono Way, Suite B 95370 **Location:** Just w of Hess Ave; in East Sonora; in Junction Shopping Center. **Phone:** 209/532-1018

SOQUEL (G-2) pop. 9,644, elev. 40'

WINERIES

- **Bargetto's Santa Cruz Winery** is at 3535 N. Main St. **Hours:** Tastings daily noon-5. Reservations are required for tours; phone ahead. Closed Jan. 1, Easter, Thanksgiving and Christmas. **Phone:** (831) 475-2258, ext. 14.

SOUTH LAKE TAHOE (E-4) pop. 21,403, elev. 6,254'

This popular tourist mecca dominates the southern tip of Lake Tahoe. The lake and nearby mountains offer a wealth of recreational activities, making South Lake Tahoe a year-round destination.

ACTION WATERSPORTS is at 3411 Lake Tahoe Blvd. at Timber Cove Marina. The speedboat *Tahoe Thunder* zips passengers across Lake Tahoe to Emerald Bay, Meeks Bay and Camp Richardson on 1-hour tours. The captain provides historical information about the scenic bays, their settlement and the Lake Tahoe area. Sightseeing cruises on a sailing yacht and a catamaran also are available.

Time: Allow 1 hour minimum. **Hours:** Daily 9-5, May-Sept.; departures require a minimum of four adults. **Cost:** *Tahoe Thunder* $59; $30 (ages 0-12). Reservations are recommended. **Phone:** (530) 544-5387.

D.L. BLISS STATE PARK, on the west shore of Lake Tahoe between Meeks and Emerald bays, occupies 1,830 acres of forested mountain terrain. A sandy beach is at Rubicon Point, 2 miles north of Emerald Bay. Naturalist programs are available in the summer (staff permitting). **Time:** Allow 3 hours minimum. **Hours:** Daily dawn-dusk, mid-June to mid-Sept. **Cost:** Day use fee $8 (per private vehicle); $7 (ages 62+ per private vehicle). **Phone:** (530) 525-7277. [🅰] [✕] [🐾] [🏕]

GONDOLA SIGHTSEEING & ADVENTURE PEAK is at 4080 Lake Tahoe Blvd. Eight-passenger gondola cabins transport riders on a 15-minute ride 2.4 miles up Heavenly Mountain, offering spectacular views of Lake Tahoe and the Sierras. The first stop is the observation deck (the gondola doesn't stop here on the way back down, so be sure to disembark on the way up). Wrapped around a granite outcropping at an elevation of 9,123 feet, the deck has

(See maps & indexes p. 161, 164.)

Adirondack chairs for taking in the amazing vistas, and you also can look through binoculars. On the ride down passengers experience a dizzying 3,500-foot vertical drop.

At the top there are hiking trails of varying lengths and difficulty levels as well as a restaurant offering cafeteria-style dining. Other activities include tubing via a specially designed gliding mat, a 25-foot-tall climbing wall and an inflatable climbing structure for kids.

Wear sunscreen; water is provided at gondola stations to aid in acclimating to the high-altitude environment. The ascent and descent is very steep in places; the ride is not recommended for the faint of heart. The gondola may stop temporarily en route due to high winds.

Note: Parking in the lot behind Heavenly Village is expensive and there is no validation; those who park in the shopping center lot across the street will be towed. The least expensive option is to walk from your hotel. **Time:** Allow 2 hours minimum. **Hours:** Gondola operates daily 10-5, mid-June through Labor Day; Fri.-Sun. 10-4, day after Labor Day-Sept. 30; daily 9-3:30, mid-Nov. to mid-Apr. Phone ahead to confirm schedule. **Cost:** Gondola ride $34; $26 (ages 13-18 and 65+); $20 (ages 5-12); free (ages 0-3). **Phone:** (775) 586-7000 or (800) 432-8365. 🍴 🛆

LAKE TAHOE ADVENTURES departs from various locations, depending on the tour chosen. Guided tours of the Rubicon Trail and Pine Nut Mountains are available by ATVs and dune buggies. Guests, led by guides, drive themselves. Snowmobile and other tours also are available.

Hours: Daily 8-5:30. **Cost:** Two-hour ATV tour $120. Fee for 2-hour ride on a dune buggy $120 (single); $190 (double). Longer tours also are available. Reservations are required. **Phone:** (530) 577-2940 or (800) 865-4679.

LAKE TAHOE HISTORICAL SOCIETY MUSEUM, 3058 Lake Tahoe Blvd. (US 50), traces the history of the Lake Tahoe basin from the days when it was occupied by Native Americans to the present. Displays feature westward expansion, the gold and silver rushes, Pony Express stations, the logging and railroad eras and the development of the ski industry.

Behind the museum is a 1931 log cabin and the area's oldest building, the 1859 Osgood's Toll House. **Hours:** Wed.-Sun. 11-3, Memorial Day weekend-Aug. 31; schedule varies rest of year. Closed July 4. **Cost:** Free. **Phone:** (530) 541-5458.

TAHOE BOAT CRUISES departs from the Tahoe Keys Marina, 1 mi. n. off US 50 on Tahoe Keys Blvd., then e. on Venice Dr. A complimentary shuttle is available from South Shore area hotels and campgrounds.

The 4-hour narrated West Shore Cruise on the 80-foot motor yacht *Safari Rose* takes passengers along that part of Lake Tahoe offering views of Emerald Bay; Fleur-du-Lac, the estate where scenes from "The Godfather: Part II" were filmed; Sugar Pine Point, site of the Hellman-Ehrman Mansion *(see attraction listing p. 542)*; Fannette Island; and Eagle Falls. Lunch is included with the West Shore Cruise. Special summer evening cocktail cruises also are available.

Time: Allow 4 hours minimum. **Hours:** West Shore Cruise departs daily at 11, June-Sept.; schedule varies Apr.-May and in Oct. Boarding is 15 minutes before departure. **Cost:** West Shore Cruise $105; $55 (ages 0-12). Reservations are required. **Phone:** (775) 588-1881 or (888) 867-6394.

TAHOE DUCK TOURS departs from the ticket booth at the Shops at Heavenly Village, 1001 Heavenly Village Way, #31 (near the casino area). One-hour sightseeing tours are conducted in vintage World War II amphibious vehicles known as DUKWs (ducks). The truck takes about 15-20 minutes to reach the Tahoe Keys Marina, where it drives down the boat ramp and turns into a boat for a cruise offering beautiful lake and mountain views.

Due to Coast Guard regulations total time on the water is limited to 30 minutes. This is, however, a good opportunity to experience a scenic taste of Lake Tahoe for a cost much less than most boat rentals.

Note: There is an hourly rate to park in the Shops at Heavenly Village lot. Food and beverages are not permitted on the vehicle. The tour time may be longer on weekends due to heavy traffic getting to and from the marina. **Time:** Allow 1 hour, 30 minutes minimum. **Hours:** Tours depart daily at 11, 1 and 3, Memorial Day weekend-Labor Day; phone ahead for tour times rest of year. Tours are not given on winter days when roads are affected during inclement weather. **Cost:** $32; $29 (ages 65+ and military with ID); $19 (ages 3-17); $9 (ages 0-2). Reservations are required. **Phone:** (530) 525-7825.

TAHOE QUEEN CRUISES depart from Ski Run Marina, just off US 50 at 900 Ski Run Blvd. Several trips are available on the triple-deck paddlewheeler *Tahoe Queen.* The Scenic Emerald Bay Cruise, a 2.5-hour narrated sightseeing excursion, provides information about the lake's formation and its fascinating history. Dinner and dinner dance cruises also are available.

Time: Allow 2 hours, 30 minutes minimum. **Hours:** Emerald Bay cruise departs daily at 10 and 1:30, July-Sept.; schedule varies rest of year. **Cost:** Emerald Bay cruise $47; $10 (ages 3-11). Reservations are required. **Parking:** $8. **Phone:** (775) 589-4906 or (800) 238-2463.

TALLAC HISTORIC SITE is on SR 89 n. of Camp Richardson. These elaborate summer estates were built along the shore of Lake Tahoe by three socially prominent San Francisco families during the late 19th and early 20th centuries.

(See maps & indexes p. 161, 164.)

The 1921 Baldwin Estate serves as both a house museum and as the site's visitor center. The 1894 Pope Estate, one of the most elaborate homes, can be seen on tours led by costumed docents. The 1924 Heller Estate, also known as Valhalla, functions as an events center. Highlights include an art gallery where resident artists work and a schedule of concerts, plays and classic films presented during the summer.

Hours: Grounds daily dawn-dusk. Museum and visitor center daily 10-4:30, mid-June to mid-Sept.; daily 11-4, mid- to late Sept.; Sat.-Sun. 11-4, Memorial Day weekend to mid-June. **Cost:** House museum and visitor center free. **Phone:** (530) 541-5227 from 10-4 for historic site information, or TTY (530) 543-0956 year-round to verify schedule.

The Pope Estate is part of Tallac Historic Site, on SR 89 n. of Camp Richardson. Guided 60-minute tours are given of the historic 1894 Pope House, the oldest and largest of the three mansions at Tallac Historic Site. The house also serves as the site's interpretive center. Participants get a chance to see how the Popes and their servants lived as they tour the two-story house and various outbuildings, including the laundry, dairy, barn, gardener's quarters and boat house. An arboretum has a waterfall, a pond and a gazebo.

Tickets can be purchased at the Baldwin Estate. **Time:** Allow 2 hours minimum. **Hours:** Grounds daily dawn-dusk. Pope House guided tours are given Thurs.-Tues. at 11, 1 and 2:30, early June to mid-Sept.; at 1 and 2:30, Memorial Day weekend-early June and mid-Sept. to late Sept. Phone ahead to confirm schedule. **Cost:** Historic site free. Pope House guided tour $5; $3 (ages 0-16). **Phone:** (530) 541-5227.

TAYLOR CREEK VISITOR CENTER is 3 mi. n. on SR 89. The visitor center, operated by the U.S. Forest Service, offers naturalist-led interpretive programs; the Stream Profile Chamber, a diverted section of Taylor Creek and its stream environment that can be seen through floor-to-ceiling windows; and four short nature trails with educational signs.

Time: Allow 2 hours minimum. **Hours:** Visitor center daily 8-5:30, Memorial Day weekend-Sept. 30; 8-4:30, in Oct. The Stream Profile Chamber closes 30 minutes before the visitor center. Phone ahead to confirm schedule. **Cost:** Free. **Phone:** (530) 543-2674.

VIKINGSHOLM, at the southwest end of Emerald Bay, is a 38-room reproduction of a ninth-century Norse fortress. The castlelike building, built as a summer home in 1929, is in a setting of pines and cedars.

Note: Limited parking is available in the parking lot off SR 89 at Emerald Bay for $8; from the parking lot the home can be reached by a steep 1-mile hiking trail. Parking also is available for $8 (July through August only) at nearby Eagle Point State Park; a 1.7-mile, less steep, trail leads from the park's day-use area to Vikingsholm. Bus service to the parking lot is available from the North and South shores. **Time:** Allow 1 hour minimum. **Hours:** Thirty-minute guided tours depart daily every half-hour 10:30-4, Memorial Day-late Sept. **Cost:** $8; $5 (ages 6-12). **Phone:** (530) 541-3030.

RECREATIONAL ACTIVITIES

Hot Air Ballooning
- **Lake Tahoe Balloons** departs from the Tahoe Keys Marina, 2435 Venice Dr. E. **Hours:** Trips depart daily at dawn (weather permitting), May-Oct. **Phone:** (530) 544-1221 or (800) 872-9294.

Skiing
- **Heavenly Mountain Resort** is at jct. Saddle Rd. and Wildwood St. **Hours:** Mon.-Fri. 9-4, Sat.-Sun. 8:30-4, late Nov.-late Apr. **Phone:** (775) 586-7000.

ALPENROSE INN   (530)544-2985   **5**
▼▼▼ ◆◆ **Motel** $69-$199 **Address:** 4074 Pine Blvd 96150 **Location:** Just s of casino area to Stateline Ave, 0.3 mi w to Pine Blvd, then just s. **Facility:** 18 units. 2 stories (no elevator), exterior corridors. **Terms:** 2 night minimum stay - seasonal and/or weekends, 7 day cancellation notice. **Activities:** whirlpool.

AMERICANA VILLAGE   (530)541-8022   **15**
▼▼▼
Extended Stay Motel
$89-$200
Address: 3845 Pioneer Tr 96150 **Location:** 0.7 mi sw of casino area to Pioneer Tr, then just s. **Facility:** 70 units, some efficiencies. 2 stories (no elevator), exterior corridors. **Terms:** check-in 4 pm, 3 day cancellation notice-fee imposed, resort fee. **Pool(s):** heated outdoor. **Activities:** sauna, whirlpool, recreation programs, rental bicycles, playground, basketball, game room, horseshoes, volleyball, exercise room. **Guest Services:** complimentary laundry. **Free Special Amenities:** expanded continental breakfast and high-speed Internet.

AMERICAS BEST VALUE INN   (530)544-6455   **4**
▼▼▼
Motel
$49-$159
Address: 4107 Pine Blvd 96150 **Location:** Just s of casino area to Stateline Ave, 0.3 mi w to Pine Blvd, then just s. **Facility:** 63 units, some efficiencies. 2-3 stories (no elevator), exterior corridors. **Terms:** 2 night minimum stay - seasonal, cancellation fee imposed. **Pool(s):** heated outdoor. **Activities:** sauna, whirlpool, limited beach access, limited exercise equipment. **Guest Services:** complimentary laundry.

BEST WESTERN PLUS STATION HOUSE INN
                                (530)542-1101   **7**
▼▼▼
Hotel
$129-$169

AAA Benefit: Members save up to 20%, plus 10% bonus points with Best Western Rewards®.

Address: 901 Park Ave 96150 **Location:** 0.5 mi s of casino area to Park Ave, 0.3 mi w. **Facility:** 98 units, some cabins. 2 stories (no elevator), exterior corridors. **Terms:** 2-3 night minimum stay - seasonal and/or weekends, cancellation fee imposed, resort fee. **Amenities:** high-speed Internet. **Dining:** LewMarNel's Steaks & Spirits, see separate listing. **Pool(s):** heated outdoor. **Activities:** whirlpool, beach access. **Guest Services:** valet laundry. **Free Special Amenities:** local telephone calls and high-speed Internet.

(See maps & indexes p. 161, 164.)

BEST WESTERN PLUS TIMBER COVE LODGE
(530)541-6722

Hotel
$139-$269

AAA Benefit: Members save up to 20%, plus 10% bonus points with Best Western Rewards®.

Address: 3411 Lake Tahoe Blvd 96150 **Location:** Waterfront. 1.8 mi s of casino area on US 50. Located on the lake. **Facility:** 262 units. 3 stories, exterior corridors. **Amenities:** video games (fee). **Pool(s):** heated outdoor. **Activities:** whirlpool, beach access, rental boats, rental canoes, rental sailboats, marina, waterskiing, fishing, exercise room. **Guest Services:** valet and coin laundry, area transportation-Heavenly Village. **Free Special Amenities:** local telephone calls and high-speed Internet.

BIG PINES MOUNTAIN HOUSE OF TAHOE
(530)541-5155 **6**

Motel $55-$65 **Address:** 4083 Cedar Ave 96150 **Location:** Just s of casino area to Stateline Ave, just w, then just s. **Facility:** 73 units, some efficiencies. 2 stories (no elevator), exterior corridors. **Terms:** cancellation fee imposed. **Amenities:** Some: safes. **Pool(s):** heated outdoor. **Guest Services:** coin laundry.

CAPRI MOTEL
(530)544-3665 **2**

Motel
$40-$300

Address: 932 Stateline Ave 96150 **Location:** Just s of casino area to Stateline Ave, then just w. **Facility:** 25 units, some two bedrooms. 2 stories (no elevator), exterior corridors. **Terms:** 3 day cancellation notice. **Pool(s):** heated outdoor. **Free Special Amenities:** continental breakfast and high-speed Internet.

DAYS INN SOUTH LAKE TAHOE
(530)544-3445 **19**

Motel $39-$300 **Address:** 3530 Lake Tahoe Blvd 96150 **Location:** 1.5 mi sw of casino area. **Facility:** 42 units. 1 story, exterior corridors. **Terms:** cancellation fee imposed. **Pool(s):** heated outdoor. **Activities:** whirlpool.

ECONO LODGE
(530)544-3959 **26**

Motel $55-$65 **Address:** 2659 Lake Tahoe Blvd 96150 **Location:** 0.8 mi e of jct US 50 and SR 89. **Facility:** 60 units, some two bedrooms. 2 stories (no elevator), exterior corridors.

EMBASSY SUITES LAKE TAHOE-HOTEL & SKI RESORT
530/544-5400 **8**

Hotel. Rates not provided. **Address:** 4130 Lake Tahoe Blvd 96150 **Location:** At casino area. **Facility:** 398 units, some two bedrooms. 9 stories, interior corridors. **Parking:** on-site (fee) and valet. **Terms:** check-in 4 pm. **Amenities:** Fee: video games, high-speed Internet. **Dining:** Echo Restaurant & Lounge, see separate listing. **Pool(s):** heated indoor. **Activities:** whirlpool, exercise room. Fee: massage. **Guest Services:** valet and coin laundry.

AAA Benefit: Members save 5% or more!

Contact us about AAA/CAA Approved properties at AAA.com/TourBookComments

FIRESIDE LODGE - AN ALL INCLUSIVE PREMIER BED & BREAKFAST
530/544-5515 **24**

Bed & Breakfast
$119-$325

Address: 515 Emerald Bay Rd 96150 **Location:** 1.3 mi n of jct US 50 and SR 89. **Facility:** These themed cabin-style accommodations, each with knotty pine décor and a gas river rock fireplace, offer well-appointed and cozy furnishings with mountain views. 9 units. 1 story, exterior corridors. Bath: shower only. **Terms:** 2 night minimum stay - seasonal and/or weekends, 7 day cancellation notice. **Activities:** sauna, bicycles, massage. Fee: game room. **Free Special Amenities:** expanded continental breakfast and high-speed Internet.

HEAVENLY VALLEY LODGE
(530)564-1500 **23**

Bed & Breakfast $125-$290 **Address:** 1261 Ski Run Blvd 96150 **Location:** US 50 exit Ski Run Blvd, then 0.5 mi se; jct Pioneer Tr. **Facility:** 12 units. 1 story, exterior corridors. Bath: shower only. **Terms:** 2 night minimum stay - weekends. **Guest Services:** area transportation-Heavenly Ski Area and The Shops at Heavenly Village.

HIGHLAND INN
(530)544-3862 **11**

Motel $69-$299 **Address:** 3979 Lake Tahoe Blvd 96150 **Location:** 0.4 mi of casino area; near Heavenly Village. **Facility:** 26 units. 2 stories (no elevator), exterior corridors. Bath: shower only. **Terms:** 3 day cancellation notice-fee imposed.

HOLIDAY INN EXPRESS
(530)544-5900 **12**

Motel
$125-$185

Address: 3961 Lake Tahoe Blvd 96150 **Location:** 0.5 mi s of casino area; at US 50 and Pioneer Tr. **Facility:** 89 units, some kitchens. 2-3 stories, exterior corridors. **Amenities:** high-speed Internet. **Pool(s):** heated outdoor. **Activities:** sauna, whirlpools. **Guest Services:** valet and coin laundry. **Free Special Amenities:** full breakfast and high-speed Internet.

HOWARD JOHNSON INN
(530)541-4000 **20**

Motel $49-$229 **Address:** 3489 Lake Tahoe Blvd 96150 **Location:** 1.5 mi s of casino area. **Facility:** 59 units. 2 stories (no elevator), exterior corridors. **Amenities:** safes (fee). **Pool(s):** heated outdoor. **Activities:** whirlpool. **Guest Services:** coin laundry.

INN BY THE LAKE
(530)542-0330 **18**

Hotel
$130-$680

Address: 3300 Lake Tahoe Blvd 96150 **Location:** 2.2 mi sw of casino area on US 50. Across from Lake Tahoe. **Facility:** 99 units, some two bedrooms and kitchens. 3 stories, interior corridors. **Terms:** 1-2 night minimum stay - seasonal and/or weekends, 3 day cancellation notice-fee imposed. **Dining:** 2 restaurants. **Pool(s):** heated outdoor. **Activities:** sauna, whirlpool, limited beach access, bicycles, hiking trails, jogging, horseshoes, volleyball, exercise room. Fee: game room. **Guest Services:** valet and coin laundry. **Free Special Amenities:** local telephone calls and high-speed Internet.

LAKE TAHOE AMBASSADOR LODGE
(530)544-6461 **1**

Motel $95-$145 **Address:** 4130 Manzanita Ave 96150 **Location:** Just s of casino area, just w on Stateline Ave to Manzanita Ave, then just s. **Facility:** 56 units, some kitchens. 2 stories (no elevator), exterior corridors. **Terms:** 3 day cancellation notice-fee imposed, resort fee. **Pool(s):** heated outdoor. **Activities:** limited beach access.

(See maps & indexes p. 161, 164.)

LAKE TAHOE VACATION RESORT - A DIAMOND RESORT
530/541-6122 14

 Condominium. Rates not provided. **Address:** 901 Ski Run Blvd 96150 **Location:** 1 mi s of casino area; at US 50 and Ski Run Blvd. Next to Ski Run Marina. **Facility:** Near a ski resort, this property provides easy access to recreation. Offered is studio units and one- to two-bedroom condos with a fireplace and private patio or balcony. A few units offer a jetted tub. 356 condominiums. 6 stories, interior corridors. **Parking:** valet only. **Terms:** check-in 4 pm. **Amenities:** high-speed Internet (fee). *Some:* safes. **Pool(s):** heated indoor/outdoor. **Activities:** sauna, whirlpools, recreation programs, jogging, exercise room. *Fee:* game room, massage. **Guest Services:** complimentary laundry, area transportation-local ski resorts.

ECO ｜↑｜ ⊥ CALL ⎙M ⊅ BIZ 🛜 ✕ 🖥 🖨
🖥

THE LODGE AT LAKE TAHOE   (530)541-6226 17

 Motel
$120-$170

Address: 3840 Pioneer Tr 96150 **Location:** 0.7 mi sw of casino area to Pioneer Tr, just s. **Facility:** 45 units, some two bedrooms and kitchens. 2 stories (no elevator), exterior corridors. **Terms:** check-in 4 pm, 2 night minimum stay - weekends, 3 day cancellation notice-fee imposed. **Pool(s):** heated outdoor. **Activities:** whirlpool, playground, horseshoes, volleyball. **Guest Services:** coin laundry.

SAVE ｜↑｜ CALL ⎙M ⊅ 🛜 ✕ 𝒜 🖥 🖨 🖥

PARK TAHOE INN   530/544-6000 10

 **Motel.** Rates not provided. **Address:** 4011 Lake Tahoe Blvd 96150 **Location:** 0.4 mi sw of casino area; at Park Ave and Lake Tahoe Blvd (US 50); across from Heavenly Village. **Facility:** 116 units, 2 stories (no elevator), exterior corridors. **Amenities:** safes. **Pool(s):** heated outdoor. **Activities:** whirlpool.

｜↑｜ ⊅ 🛜 ✕ 🖥 / SOME UNITS FEE 🐾 🕅 🖥

RODEWAY INN CASINO CENTER   (530)541-7150 3

 Motel
$49-$249

Address: 4127 Pine Blvd 96150 **Location:** 0.3 mi w on Stateline Ave, just s on Pine Blvd. **Facility:** 114 units, some kitchens. 2-3 stories, interior/exterior corridors. **Terms:** 3 day cancellation notice-fee imposed. **Amenities:** high-speed Internet. **Pool(s):** heated outdoor. **Activities:** whirlpool, limited beach access. **Guest Services:** coin laundry. **Free Special Amenities:** full breakfast and high-speed Internet.

SAVE ｜↑｜ 🛜 ✕ 🖥 / SOME UNITS FEE 🐾 🖥 🖨

STARDUST LODGE   (530)544-5211 9

Extended Stay Motel
$100-$370

Address: 4061 Lake Tahoe Blvd 96150 **Location:** Just sw of casino area; at US 50 and LaSalle Ave. **Facility:** 86 units, some two bedrooms, efficiencies, kitchens and condominiums. 2 stories (no elevator), exterior corridors. **Terms:** check-in 4 pm, 3 day cancellation notice-fee imposed, resort fee. **Pool(s):** 2 heated outdoor. **Activities:** whirlpools, recreation programs, bicycles, exercise room. **Guest Services:** complimentary laundry. **Free Special Amenities: expanded continental breakfast and high-speed Internet.**

SAVE ｜↑｜ CALL ⎙M ⊅ BIZ 🛜 ✕ 🖥 🖨 🖥
/ SOME UNITS 🕅

TAHOE BEACH & SKI CLUB   (530)541-6220 16

Vacation Rental Condominium
$144-$309

Address: 3601 Lake Tahoe Blvd 96150 **Location:** 1.4 mi w of casino area on US 50; just w of Ski Run Blvd. **Facility:** Buffered by extensive grounds, this club offers some units with lake views and many with a whirlpool bath. 140 condominiums. 2-3 stories, interior corridors. **Terms:** check-in 4 pm, 2 night minimum stay, 3 day cancellation notice-fee imposed. **Activities:** saunas, whirlpools, beach access, tennis court, recreation programs in summer, playground, horseshoes, volleyball, exercise room. *Fee:* game room. **Guest Services:** valet and coin laundry.

SAVE ｜↑｜ CALL ⎙M ⊅ BIZ 🛜 ✕ 𝒜 🖥 🖨
🖥

TAHOE CHALET INN-THE THEME INN
530/544-3311 13

 Motel
Rates not provided

Address: 3860 Lake Tahoe Blvd 96150 **Location:** 0.7 mi s of casino area on US 50. **Facility:** 66 units, some kitchens. 1-2 stories (no elevator), exterior corridors. **Pool(s):** heated outdoor. **Guest Services:** coin laundry. **Free Special Amenities: local telephone calls and high-speed Internet.**

SAVE ｜↑｜ CALL ⎙M ⊅ 🛜 ✕
/ SOME UNITS FEE 🐾 🕅 🖥 🖨

Save on theme park tickets
at AAA.com/discounts

▼ *See AAA listing p. 530* ▼

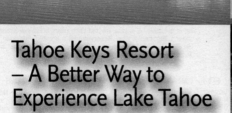

(See maps & indexes p. 161, 164.)

TAHOE KEYS RESORT
(530)544-5397 **22**

Vacation Rental Condominium
$112-$1700

Address: 599 Tahoe Keys Blvd 96150 **Location:** 0.5 mi e of jct US 50 and SR 89, 1 mi n. **Facility:** This property features some waterfront condos and vacation homes in a residential neighborhood adjacent to shops and restaurants. Many units have a private dock and hot tub, some with a fireplace. 250 kitchen units, some houses, cabins and condominiums. 3 stories (no elevator), exterior corridors. **Terms:** off-site registration, 2-7 night minimum stay - seasonal, cancellation fee imposed, resort fee. **Pool(s):** outdoor, heated indoor. **Activities:** whirlpool, rental boats, fishing, bicycles, jogging, playground, volleyball. *Fee:* marina, 6 lighted tennis courts, basketball. **Guest Services:** complimentary laundry. **Free Special Amenities:** local telephone calls and early check-in/late check-out. *(See ad p. 529.)*

TAHOE SEASONS RESORT
(530)541-6700 **25**

Hotel
$122-$180

Address: 3901 Saddle Rd 96150 **Location:** 1.2 mi sw of casino area to Ski Run Blvd, 1.2 mi se to Saddle Rd, then 0.5 mi e to Keller Rd. Across from Heavenly Ski Resort. **Facility:** 183 units, some two bedrooms. 8 stories, interior corridors. **Parking:** valet only. **Terms:** check-in 4 pm, cancellation fee imposed. **Pool(s):** heated outdoor. **Activities:** whirlpool, tennis court, shuffleboard. *Fee:* game room. **Guest Services:** valet laundry.

TAHOE VALLEY LODGE
(530)541-0353 **27**

Motel
$125-$495

Address: 2241 Lake Tahoe Blvd 96150 **Location:** 0.5 mi e of jct US 50 and SR 89. **Facility:** 17 units. 2 stories, exterior corridors. **Terms:** 7 day cancellation notice-fee imposed. **Pool(s):** heated outdoor. **Activities:** whirlpool. **Free Special Amenities:** local telephone calls and early check-in/late check-out.

MARRIOTT'S TIMBER LODGE
530/542-6600

[fyi] Not evaluated. **Address:** 4100 Lake Tahoe Blvd 96150 **Location:** Just s of casino area on US 50. Facilities, services, and décor characterize an upscale property.

AAA Benefit: AAA hotel discounts of 5% or more.

PARADICE MOTEL
530/544-6800

[fyi] Not evaluated. **Address:** 953 Park Ave 96150 **Location:** 0.5 mi s of casino area to Park Ave, just w; near Heavenly Village. Facilities, services, and décor characterize a mid-scale property.

SECRETS INN
530/544-6767

[fyi] Not evaluated. **Address:** 924 Park Ave 96150 **Location:** 0.3 mi s of casino area via US 50, just w. Facilities, services, and décor characterize a mid-scale property.

ARTEMIS MEDITERRANEAN GRILL
530/542-2500 **14**

Mediterranean. Casual Dining. $7-$19 **AAA Inspector Notes:** The warm and comfortable atmosphere in this eatery makes it a popular stop. Menu items are prepared from scratch daily using locally produced, organic and free-range products when possible. Many items such as tabbouleh, dolmas, savory saffron rice, a la carte kebabs and the highly addictive, house-seasoned Greek fries are available in single portions. Sampler plates are an easy way to enjoy a variety of selections. **Bar:** beer & wine. **Address:** 2229 Lake Tahoe Blvd, Suite A 96150 **Location:** 0.5 mi ne of jct US 50 and SR 89; 4.5 mi sw of casino area. [L] [D]

CAFE FIORE RISTORANTE ITALIANO
530/541-2908 **9**

Italian. Fine Dining. $16-$35 **AAA Inspector Notes:** Offering seven tables in an intimate dining room, this restaurant is housed in what was once a private residence. The menu features well-prepared pasta, seafood, chicken and veal selections. For dessert, try the homemade white chocolate ice cream. An extensive wine list is available. A private, heated patio offers additional seating in season. **Bar:** beer & wine. **Reservations:** suggested. **Address:** 1169 Ski Run Blvd 96151 **Location:** US 50 exit Ski Run Blvd, just sw; jct Tamarack Ave. [D] [X]

CANTINA BAR & GRILL
530/544-1233 **13**

Mexican. Casual Dining. $8-$17 **AAA Inspector Notes:** This locally popular restaurant dates back to 1977 and offers some cozy seating nooks in the dining room and a sports bar. The menu is comprised of Mexican favorites such as burritos, tacos and enchiladas. Vegetarian selections are available. **Bar:** full bar. **Address:** 765 Emerald Bay Rd (SR 89) 96150 **Location:** Jct US 50 and SR 89, 0.6 mi nw on SR 89. [L] [D]

ECHO RESTAURANT & LOUNGE
530/543-2140 **2**

American. Casual Dining. $9-$27 **AAA Inspector Notes:** This casual restaurant and lounge offers hot and cold small plates, salads and a wide selection of sandwiches. Seasonal dinner entrées include blackened Pacific ahi tuna, grilled salmon, filet mignon, boneless short ribs and pasta items, all served with a tasty side dish. The outdoor dining areas are quite popular. **Bar:** full bar. **Reservations:** suggested. **Address:** 4130 Lake Tahoe Blvd 96150 **Location:** At casino area; in Embassy Suites Lake Tahoe-Hotel & Ski Resort. **Parking:** on-site and valet. [B] [L] [D] CALL [&M]

EVANS AMERICAN GOURMET CAFE
530/542-1990 **11**

American. Fine Dining. $24-$35 **AAA Inspector Notes:** The atmosphere in this vintage Tahoe cabin is quiet and elegant, with large windows for taking in the view. Creative and well-prepared cuisine emphasizes fresh ingredients. **Bar:** full bar. **Reservations:** suggested. **Address:** 536 Emerald Bay Rd 96150 **Location:** 1.2 mi n of jct US 50 and SR 89. [D]

FRESHIES RESTAURANT & BAR
530/542-3630 **5**

Hawaiian. Casual Dining. $10-$28 **AAA Inspector Notes:** Diners will find a taste of the islands, as well as fresh salads and sandwiches, at this local favorite. An upstairs deck affords views of the lake. **Bar:** beer & wine. **Address:** 3330 Lake Tahoe Blvd, Suite 3 96150 **Location:** On US 50; 2 mi sw of casino area; in Lake View Plaza. [L] [D] [X]

THE FRESH KETCH
530/541-5683 **8**

Seafood. Casual Dining. $15-$39 **AAA Inspector Notes:** An excellent view of the marina adds to the dining enjoyment. Fresh seafood is a specialty at this great lunch and dinner spot. **Bar:** full bar. **Address:** 2435 Venice Dr 96150 **Location:** US 50, 1 mi w; in Tahoe Keys Marina. [L] [D] [X]

HEIDI'S PANCAKE HOUSE
530/544-8113 **6**

American. Family Dining. $8-$13 **AAA Inspector Notes:** An area tradition for more than 40 years, this Bavarian eatery appeals to tourists and locals alike. Tried-and-true breakfast favorites include huge, four-egg omelets, waffles and crepes. The lunch menu has a good selection. **Address:** 3485 Lake Tahoe Blvd 96150 **Location:** 1.5 mi w of casino area; adjacent to Howard Johnson Inn. [B] [L]

LEWMARNEL'S STEAKS & SPIRITS   530/542-1072

Steak
Casual Dining
$17-$40

AAA Inspector Notes: A rustic, Western atmosphere invites diners to relax. On the varied menu are plenty of Choice steak and seafood choices. Complimentary fondue is served and the wine list has many offerings. Lunch is served only during the summer. Guests can dine on the seasonal deck. **Bar:** full bar. **Reservations:** suggested. **Address:** 901 Park Ave 96157 **Location:** 0.5 mi s of casino area to Park Ave, 0.3 mi w; in BEST WESTERN PLUS Station House Inn. B D

MCP'S PUB TAHOE   530/542-4435   3

American. Casual Dining. $9-$18 **AAA Inspector Notes:** This place is nothing fancy, but the food is good. Burgers, sandwiches, pitas, wraps, salads, bread bowls and a few Mexican items round out the menu. The service is friendly. Guests can choose to sit upstairs or down, inside or out. A large tree goes through the upstairs deck which overlooks the street scene. Two hours free parking at a lot just down the street. Live music is offered on most nights. **Bar:** full bar. **Address:** 4093 Lake Tahoe Blvd 96150 **Location:** US 50, just w of casino area. L D

NEPHELES   530/544-8130   10

California. Casual Dining. $23-$34 **AAA Inspector Notes:** California cuisine is offered in this intimate dining room. The chef utilizes the freshest ingredients wherever possible. **Bar:** full bar. **Reservations:** suggested. **Address:** 1169 Ski Run Blvd 96150 **Location:** 1.1 mi s of casino area to Ski Run Blvd, then 0.3 mi w. D

PASSARETTI'S ITALIAN RESTAURANT   530/541-3433   15

Italian. Casual Dining. $9-$24 **AAA Inspector Notes:** Patrons can dine inside or out on the patio at this family restaurant. Offerings include hand-tossed pasta, traditional Italian specialties, seafood, chicken and veal dishes. Reservations are highly recommended during busy summer periods. **Bar:** beer & wine. **Reservations:** suggested. **Address:** 1181 Emerald Bay Rd 96150 **Location:** US 50, 0.5 mi n of airport. L D

RIVA GRILL   530/542-2600   4

Seafood. Casual Dining. $14-$39 **AAA Inspector Notes:** Right on the marina, this grill affords diners panoramic views of Lake Tahoe. Innovative California cuisine makes up the menu. A spacious, heated delightful deck is open in season. Happy hour is offered in winter. Valet parking and live music on Friday and Saturday nights is available during the summer. **Bar:** full bar. **Reservations:** suggested. **Address:** 900 Ski Run Blvd, Suite 3 96150 **Location:** US 50; center. **Parking:** on-site (fee) and valet. L D

SWISS CHALET RESTAURANT   530/544-3304   12

Continental
Casual Dining
$19-$32

AAA Inspector Notes: *Classic.* Chalet décor lends a warm, cozy feel to this casual restaurant that has been in operation for more than 55 years. European, German and Swiss selections line a menu that also includes steak and seafood. Fondue, of course, and a good selection of German, Swiss and California wines are available. **Bar:** full bar. **Reservations:** suggested. **Address:** 2544 Lake Tahoe Blvd 96150 **Location:** 4 mi w of casino area; on US 50 at Sierra Blvd. *Menu on AAA.com* D

TEP'S VILLA ROMA   530/541-8227   7

Italian
Family Dining
$10-$20

AAA Inspector Notes: Serving the area since 1975, patrons of this laid-back restaurant can order from an array of fresh seafood specialties as well as pasta, chicken and veal dishes. The antipasto salad bar lines up a nice variety. **Bar:** full bar. **Address:** 3450 Lake Tahoe Blvd 96150 **Location:** 1.5 mi w of casino area. *Menu on AAA.com* D

SOUTH SAN FRANCISCO   pop. 63,632
- **Restaurants p. 532**
- **Hotels & Restaurants map & index p. 410**
- **Part of San Francisco area — see map p. 342**

BEST WESTERN PLUS GROSVENOR AIRPORT HOTEL
(650)873-3200   14

Hotel
$119-$209

AAA Benefit: Members save up to 20%, plus 10% bonus points with Best Western Rewards®.

Address: 380 S Airport Blvd 94080 **Location:** US 101 exit S Airport Blvd, 0.5 mi s. San Bruno, 43. **Facility:** 206 units. 8 stories, interior corridors. **Parking:** on-site (fee). **Terms:** cancellation fee imposed. **Amenities:** high-speed Internet. **Pool(s):** heated outdoor. **Activities:** exercise room. **Guest Services:** valet laundry. **Free Special Amenities:** local telephone calls and high-speed Internet.

COMFORT INN & SUITES SFO AIRPORT NORTH
(650)589-7100   9

Hotel
$100-$400

Address: 121 E Grand Ave 94080 **Location:** US 101 exit 425A (Grand Ave), just e. Adjacent to railroad tracks. **Facility:** 167 units. 3 stories, exterior corridors. **Parking:** on-site (fee). **Terms:** cancellation fee imposed. **Activities:** whirlpool, exercise room. **Guest Services:** valet and coin laundry. **Free Special Amenities:** expanded continental breakfast and airport transportation.

COURTYARD SAN FRANCISCO AIRPORT/OYSTER POINT WATERFRONT
(650)871-4100   3

Hotel
$139-$152

AAA Benefit: AAA hotel discounts of 5% or more.

Address: 1300 Veterans Blvd 94080 **Location:** US 101 exit 425B Oyster Point Blvd E, 0.3 mi n. **Facility:** 198 units. 4 stories, interior corridors. **Amenities:** high-speed Internet. **Pool(s):** heated indoor. **Activities:** whirlpool, exercise room. **Guest Services:** valet and coin laundry, area transportation-within 2 mi. **Free Special Amenities:** high-speed Internet and airport transportation.

EMBASSY SUITES SAN FRANCISCO AIRPORT-SOUTH SAN FRANCISCO
(650)589-3400   8

Hotel $140-$350 **Address:** 250 Gateway Blvd 94080 **Location:** US 101 exit 425A (Grand Ave), just e. **Facility:** 312 units. 10 stories, interior corridors. **Parking:** on-site (fee). **Terms:** check-in 4 pm, 1-7 night minimum stay, cancellation fee imposed. **Amenities:** *Fee:* video games, high-speed Internet. **Pool(s):** heated indoor. **Activities:** whirlpool, exercise room. **Guest Services:** valet and coin laundry.

AAA Benefit: Members save 5% or more!

(See map & index p. 410.)

FOUR POINTS BY SHERATON HOTEL & SUITES SAN FRANCISCO AIRPORT   (650)624-3700 **11**

FOUR POINTS BY SHERATON
Hotel
$109-$349

AAA Benefit: Members get up to 20% off, plus Starwood Preferred Guest® bonuses.

Address: 264 S Airport Blvd 94080 **Location:** US 101 exit S Airport Blvd, just e. San Bruno, 43. **Facility:** 100 units. 4 stories, interior corridors. **Parking:** on-site (fee). **Terms:** cancellation fee imposed. **Amenities:** video games (fee), high-speed Internet, safes. **Activities:** exercise room. **Guest Services:** valet and coin laundry. **Free Special Amenities: high-speed Internet and airport transportation.**

SAVE ⊁ ¶┤ ⊥ CALL ⑤M ⤢ ⌧ ⌨ ⊟ ☒ ☒ / SOME UNITS ⊡ ⊞

HAMPTON INN   (650)876-0200 **7**

Hotel $199-$299 **Address:** 300 Watson Blvd 94080 **Location:** US 101 exit 425A (Grand Ave), 0.4 mi e, then just n. **Facility:** 99 units. 4 stories, interior corridors. **Terms:** 1-7 night

AAA Benefit: Members save up to 10%!

minimum stay, cancellation fee imposed. **Amenities:** video games (fee), high-speed Internet, safes. **Pool(s):** heated indoor. **Activities:** exercise room. **Guest Services:** valet and coin laundry.

ECO ⊁ ¶┤ CALL ⑤M ⤢ BIZ ⌨ ⌧ ⊟ ☒ ☒

HILTON GARDEN INN SAN FRANCISCO AIRPORT NORTH   (650)872-1515 **6**

Hotel $129-$229 **Address:** 670 Gateway Blvd 94080 **Location:** US 101 exit 425A (Grand Ave), 0.4 mi e, then 0.4 mi n. **Facility:** 169 units. 7 stories, interior corridors. **Terms:** 1-7 night

AAA Benefit: Unparalleled hospitality at a special Member rate.

minimum stay, cancellation fee imposed. **Amenities:** high-speed Internet. **Pool(s):** heated indoor. **Activities:** whirlpool, exercise room. **Guest Services:** valet and coin laundry, area transportation-within 3 mi.

⊁ ¶┤ ⊥ CALL ⑤M ⤢ BIZ ⌨ ⊟ ☒ ☒

HOLIDAY INN EXPRESS HOTEL & SUITES SAN FRANCISCO AIRPORT NORTH   (650)589-0600 **13**

Hotel $119-$259 **Address:** 373 S Airport Blvd 94080 **Location:** US 101 exit S Airport Blvd, 0.5 mi s. San Bruno, 43. **Facility:** 89 units. 4 stories, interior corridors. **Parking:** on-site (fee). **Terms:** resort fee. **Amenities:** video games (fee), high-speed Internet, safes. **Activities:** whirlpool, exercise room. **Guest Services:** valet and coin laundry.

⊁ ¶┤ CALL ⑤M BIZ ⌨ ⌧ ⊟ ☒ ☒ ⊞

HOLIDAY INN SAN FRANCISCO INTERNATIONAL AIRPORT   (650)873-3550 **12**

Hotel $99-$199 **Address:** 275 S Airport Blvd 94080 **Location:** US 101 exit S Airport Blvd, just e. Adjacent to convention center. San Bruno, 43. **Facility:** 224 units. 5 stories, interior corridors. **Parking:** on-site (fee). **Amenities:** video games (fee). **Activities:** exercise room. **Guest Services:** valet and coin laundry.

⊁ ¶┤ ⊥ CALL ⑤M ⌨ ⊟ ☒ / SOME UNITS FEE ⊡ ⊞

INN AT OYSTER POINT   (650)737-7633 **4**

Hotel $169-$239 **Address:** 425 Marina Blvd 94080 **Location:** US 101 exit 425B (Oyster Point Blvd E), 0.8 mi e, then just s. **Facility:** 30 units. 3 stories, interior corridors. **Terms:** cancellation fee imposed. **Activities:** jogging. **Guest Services:** valet laundry, area transportation-within 3 mi.

⊁ ⊥ ⌨ ☒ / SOME UNITS ⊡

LARKSPUR LANDING SOUTH SAN FRANCISCO   (650)827-1515 **5**

Extended Stay Contemporary Hotel $109-$309 **Address:** 690 Gateway Blvd 94080 **Location:** US 101 exit 425A (Grand Ave), 0.4 mi e, then 0.4 mi n. **Facility:** 111 efficiencies. 4 stories, interior corridors. **Terms:** cancellation fee imposed. **Amenities:** high-speed Internet. **Activities:** whirlpool, exercise room. **Guest Services:** complimentary laundry, area transportation-within 3 mi.

ECO ⊁ ¶┤ CALL ⑤M BIZ ⌨ ⌧ ⊟ ☒ ☒ ⊞ / SOME UNITS FEE ⊡

QUALITY INN & SUITES   (650)875-7878 **15**

Hotel $79-$389

Address: 410 S Airport Blvd 94080 **Location:** US 101 exit S Airport Blvd, 0.5 mi se. San Bruno, 43. **Facility:** 45 units. 3 stories, interior corridors. **Terms:** cancellation fee imposed. **Amenities:** high-speed Internet, safes. **Activities:** exercise room. **Guest Services:** valet laundry. **Free Special Amenities: full breakfast and airport transportation.**

SAVE ⊁ ¶┤ CALL ⑤M ⌨ ⌧ ⊟ ☒ ☒ ⊞

RESIDENCE INN BY MARRIOTT AT OYSTER POINT   (650)837-9000 **2**

Extended Stay Hotel $159-$285 **Location:** 1350 Veterans Blvd 94080 **Location:** US 101 exit 425B (Oyster Point Blvd), just ne. **Facility:** 152 units, some two bedrooms, efficiencies

AAA Benefit: AAA hotel discounts of 5% or more.

and kitchens. 4 stories, interior corridors. **Amenities:** high-speed Internet. **Pool(s):** heated outdoor. **Activities:** whirlpool, sports court, exercise room. **Guest Services:** valet and coin laundry, area transportation-within 2 mi.

ECO ⊁ ¶┤ CALL ⑤M ⤢ ⌨ ⌧ ⊟ ☒ ☒ ⊞ / SOME UNITS FEE ⊡

TRAVELERS INN   (650)755-9556 **1**

Motel
$69-$210

Address: 100 Hickey Blvd 94080 **Location:** I-280 exit Hickey Blvd E, just e; behind Chevron station. South San Francisco, 42. **Facility:** 20 units. 1 story, exterior corridors. **Bath:** shower only. **Free Special Amenities: early check-in/late check-out and high-speed Internet.**

SAVE ¶┤ CALL ⑤M ⌨ ⊟ ☒ ☒ ⊞

WHERE TO EAT

BEN TRE RESTAURANT   650/952-2243 **3**

Vietnamese. Casual Dining. $7-$29 **AAA Inspector Notes:** Modest surroundings, quick friendly service and delicious, fresh entrées make this restaurant a great place for a quick lunch or dinner stop. For a heartier dish, try their clay pot entrees. **Bar:** beer & wine. **Address:** 219 Grand Ave 94080 **Location:** US 101 exit 425A (Grand Ave), just w. **Parking:** street only. L D

BUON GUSTO RISTORANTE   650/742-9776 **4**

Italian. Casual Dining. $12-$23 **AAA Inspector Notes:** Diners sit down to fresh Italian dishes in a convenient and comfortable downtown setting. **Bar:** beer & wine. **Address:** 224 Grand Ave 94080 **Location:** US 101 exit 425A (Grand Ave), just w; downtown. L D

DARBY DAN'S SANDWICH COMPANY   650/876-0122 **1**

Sandwiches. Casual Dining. $6-$9 **AAA Inspector Notes:** People have been known to drive for miles just to get the crab sandwich and the appropriately named sleeper (consisting of ham, turkey, bacon and cheese on a Dutch crunch bread) at this sandwich shop. Do not forget to order it with everything, especially the garlic mayo. There is a hot grill menu where diners can order double dogs on Dutch crunch. A good selection of chips is available. **Bar:** beer & wine. **Address:** 733 N Airport Blvd 94080 **Location:** US 101 exit 425B (Oyster Point Blvd) northbound; US 101 exit 425C (S San Francisco Blvd) southbound, 0.5 mi w. B L

(See map & index p. 410.)

GRAND PALACE SEAFOOD RESTAURANT
650/872-1000 ②

▼▼ ▼▼ Cantonese. Casual Dining. $7-$38 **AAA Inspector Notes:** Built to accommodate large Chinese wedding parties, this restaurant features high ceilings with crystal chandeliers and uniformed waiters that add a touch of class. A good variety of dim sum is available for lunch. Try the four flavor stuffed rolled rice noodles, deep fried glutinous rice stuffed chicken wings and deep fried black sesame balls flavored with green tea. **Bar:** beer & wine. **Address:** 359 Grand Ave 94080 **Location:** US 101 exit 425A (Grand Ave), just w; between Maple and Linden aves; downtown. **Parking:** street only.

Ⓛ Ⓓ

STANISLAUS NATIONAL FOREST (E-4)

Elevations in the forest range from 1,200 ft. in the Lumsden area to 11,462 ft. at Sonora Peak. Refer to AAA maps for additional elevation information.

On the western slope of the Sierra Nevada Range, Stanislaus National Forest covers nearly 900,000 acres, forming the northwestern boundary of Yosemite National Park (see place listing p. 578). The Merced, Mokelumne, Clavey, Stanislaus and Tuolumne rivers cut deep canyons through this wilderness region.

Popular summer activities include swimming, camping, picnicking, boating, rafting, canoeing and hunting. More than 800 miles of rivers and streams offer myriad opportunities for fishing. Numerous trails are suitable for hiking, horseback riding, backpacking, off-roading and mountain biking. There are skiing facilities at Dodge Ridge off SR 108 and at Mount Reba off SR 4. Snowmobiling and cross-country skiing also are popular during the winter.

Reservations for Pinecrest campground can be made through the National Recreation Reservation System; phone (877) 444-6777 or TTY (877) 833-6777.

Visitor tours and programs are offered June through August at Pinecrest. The Emigrant and Carson-Iceberg wildernesses are at the eastern end of the forest. Permits can be obtained at any Stanislaus National Forest office. For general forest information contact the Supervisor's Office, Stanislaus National Forest, 19777 Greenley Rd., Sonora, CA 95370; phone (209) 532-3671. See Recreation Areas Chart.

STEVINSON pop. 313

STEVINSON RANCH GOLF CLUB
209/668-8200

▼▼▼▼ Cottage. Rates not provided. **Address:** 2700 N Van Clief Rd 95374 **Location:** 1 mi n of SR 140; at 3rd Ave. **Facility:** Surrounded by a golf course and wetlands, these attractively appointed cottages feature a separate living area and bedroom. 24 cottages. 1 story, exterior corridors. **Dining:** Stevinson Ranch Grill, see separate listing. **Pool(s):** outdoor. **Activities:** whirlpool. **Fee:** golf-18 holes.

Save on theme park tickets
at AAA.com/discounts

STEVINSON RANCH GRILL
209/664-6460

▼▼ ▼▼ American. Casual Dining. $8-$20 **AAA Inspector Notes:** A fun and lively crowd meets after a round of golf to relax at this popular grill where beautiful views of the golf course can be had. The menu features a nice selection of sandwiches, grilled steak, chicken and homemade chili. An outside patio is available for dining. **Bar:** full bar. **Address:** 2700 N Van Clief Rd 95374 **Location:** 1 mi n of SR 140; at 3rd Ave; in Stevinson Ranch Golf Club. Ⓛ Ⓓ

STINSON BEACH (C-8) pop. 632, elev. 18'

AUDUBON CANYON RANCH, 3.5 mi. n. on SR 1, is a wildlife preserve and educational center. The Martin Griffin Preserve (formerly known as Bolinas Lagoon Preserve) is a protected area frequented by great blue herons and great egrets. **Time:** Allow 2 hours minimum. **Hours:** Sat.-Sun. and holidays 10-4, during the mid-Mar. to mid-July nesting period (also Tues.-Fri. by appointment). **Cost:** Donations. **Phone:** (415) 868-9244.

STOCKTON (F-3) pop. 291,707, elev. 14'

• Hotels p. 534 • Restaurants p. 534

Like other northern California cities, Stockton—named after a distinguished Naval officer in the Mexican War—experienced a population boom during the gold rush. The city later became an agricultural center, and this heritage is celebrated in April during the 3-day ▼▼ Stockton Asparagus Festival, held downtown on the waterfront. San Joaquin county's main crop is featured in cooking demonstrations, exhibits, food tastings in Asparagus Alley and the Deep-Fried Asparagus-Eating Championship.

The first of California's two inland seaports, Stockton is connected with San Francisco Bay by a channel 60 miles long and 37 feet deep. The San Joaquin waterways, 1,000 miles of navigable inland waters, offer plenty of boating and fishing opportunities. The city also is the home of the University of the Pacific, which in 1852 became the first chartered university in California.

Stockton Convention and Visitors Bureau: 525 N. Center St., Stockton, CA 95202. **Phone:** (209) 938-1555 or (877) 778-6258.

THE CHILDREN'S MUSEUM OF STOCKTON is downtown across from the deep water channel at 402 W. Weber Ave. This hands-on museum has a fire truck, police car and an ambulance for youngsters to explore as well as a child-sized grocery store, emergency room and TV studio where pretending is the order of the day.

Time: Allow 30 minutes minimum. **Hours:** Mon.-Fri. 9-4, Sat. 9-5, Sun. noon-5, early July to mid-Aug.; Wed.-Fri. 9-4, Sat. 9-5, Sun. noon-5, rest of year. Closed major holidays. **Cost:** $5; free (ages 0-1). **Phone:** (209) 465-4386.

THE HAGGIN MUSEUM is .3 mi. n. of I-5 exit 473 (Pershing Ave.) to 1201 N. Pershing Ave. at Rose St., following signs. It contains 19th-century

American and European paintings as well as local historical artifacts. Works by Albert Bierstadt, Paul Gauguin, George Inness, "Golden Age" illustrator J.C. Leyendecker and Pierre Auguste Renoir are exhibited. Native American baskets; a Holt tractor and combine harvester, both developed locally; and reconstructed interiors of several turn-of-the-20th-century businesses are highlights. Touring exhibitions also are presented.

Tours are available by appointment. **Time:** Allow 1 hour, 30 minutes minimum. **Hours:** Wed.-Fri. 1:30-5, Sat.-Sun noon-5 (also first and third Thurs. of the month 5-9). Closed major holidays. **Cost:** $8; $7 (ages 65+); $5 (ages 10-17 and students with ID). **Phone:** (209) 940-6300.

PIXIE WOODS WONDERLAND, jct. Occidental Ave. and Monte Diablo Blvd. in Louis Park, is a children's playland featuring sets from popular stories and legends. Theater programs are held during the afternoon. The park also has amusement rides.

Hours: Fri.-Sun. noon-5, June-July; Sat.-Sun. noon-5, Aug.-Sept. **Cost:** $4; free (ages 0-1). Rides $2 each or three for $5. Unlimited ride pass $8. **Phone:** (209) 937-7366 or (209) 937-8206.

BEST WESTERN PLUS HERITAGE INN   (209)474-3301

 Hotel $70-$130

 AAA Benefit: Members save up to 20%, plus 10% bonus points with Best Western Rewards®.

Address: 111 E March Ln 95207 **Location:** I-5 exit March Ln, 2.5 mi e; corner of El Dorado St. **Facility:** 203 units. 3 stories, interior corridors. **Terms:** resort fee. **Pool(s):** outdoor. **Activities:** whirlpool, exercise room. **Guest Services:** valet and coin laundry. **Free Special Amenities: full breakfast and high-speed Internet.**

COURTYARD BY MARRIOTT   (209)472-9700

 Hotel $116-$159

 AAA Benefit: AAA hotel discounts of 5% or more.

Address: 3252 W March Ln 95219 **Location:** I-5 exit March Ln, 0.5 mi w. **Facility:** 89 units. 3 stories, interior corridors. **Pool(s):** heated outdoor. **Activities:** whirlpool, exercise room. **Guest Services:** valet and coin laundry.

HAMPTON INN & SUITES   (209)946-1234

Hotel $99-$114 **Address:** 5045 S Kingsley Rd 95215 **Location:** SR 99 exit Arch Rd, just e. **Facility:** 73 units. 3 stories, interior corridors. **Terms:** 1-7 night minimum stay, cancellation fee imposed.

AAA Benefit: Members save up to 10%!

Amenities: video games (fee), high-speed Internet. **Pool(s):** heated indoor. **Activities:** whirlpool, exercise room. **Guest Services:** valet and coin laundry.

Trust your vehicle to AAA/CAA Approved Auto Repair facilities

---

HILTON STOCKTON   (209)957-9090

 Hotel $109-$189

AAA Benefit: Members save 5% or more!

Address: 2323 Grand Canal Blvd 95207 **Location:** I-5 exit March Ln, 0.4 mi e. **Facility:** 198 units. 5 stories, interior corridors. **Terms:** 1-7 night minimum stay, cancellation fee imposed. **Pool(s):** outdoor. **Activities:** whirlpool, exercise room. **Guest Services:** valet laundry. **Free Special Amenities: newspaper and high-speed Internet.**

LA QUINTA INN STOCKTON   (209)952-7800

Hotel $59-$122 **Address:** 2710 W March Ln 95219 **Location:** I-5 exit March Ln, just w. **Facility:** 151 units. 3 stories, exterior corridors. **Pool(s):** outdoor. **Guest Services:** valet and coin laundry.

RESIDENCE INN BY MARRIOTT   (209)472-9800

 Extended Stay Hotel $107-$149 **Address:** 3240 W March Ln 95219 **Location:** I-5 exit March Ln, 0.5 mi w. **Facility:** 104 units, some two bedrooms and kitchens. 3 stories, interior corridors.

AAA Benefit: AAA hotel discounts of 5% or more.

Amenities: video games (fee). **Pool(s):** heated outdoor. **Activities:** whirlpool, sports court, exercise room. **Guest Services:** valet and coin laundry.

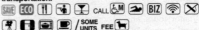

UNIVERSITY PLAZA WATERFRONT HOTEL   (209)944-1140

Hotel $99-$149

Address: 110 W Fremont St 95202 **Location:** SR 4 exit Downtown Stockton, 0.5 mi n on El Dorado St, then just w. **Facility:** 179 units. 4 stories, interior corridors. **Amenities:** video games (fee), high-speed Internet. **Pool(s):** heated outdoor. **Activities:** whirlpool, exercise room. **Guest Services:** valet laundry. **Free Special Amenities: high-speed Internet and local transportation.**

WHERE TO EAT

BUD'S SEAFOOD GRILLE   209/956-0270

Seafood. Casual Dining. $7-$25 **AAA Inspector Notes:** This family-owned restaurant turns out a nice selection of fresh seafood items. Whether it is in one of the specialty salads, pasta dishes or entrées it is sure to please everyone. Service is friendly and relaxed. **Bar:** full bar. **Address:** 314 Lincoln Center 95207 **Location:** I-5 exit Benjamin Holt Dr, 1.5 mi e, then just n on Gettysburg Pl; in Lincoln Center Shopping Center.

CASA FLORES   209/462-2272

Mexican. Casual Dining. $5-$12 **AAA Inspector Notes:** Located downtown adjacent to the court house and marina, this busy little restaurant is a favorite of the local crowd. Menu highlights features traditional Mexican favorites for breakfast, lunch and dinner. **Bar:** beer & wine. **Address:** 201 E Weber Ave 95202 **Location:** SR 4 exit Downtown Stockton/El Dorado St, just n, then just e. **Parking:** street only.

DAVE WONG'S CHINESE CUISINE   209/951-4152

Chinese. Casual Dining. $7-$20 **AAA Inspector Notes:** A favorite in the area for many years, the restaurant presents a menu of traditional Chinese favorites. The staff is warm and friendly. **Bar:** full bar. **Address:** 2828 W March Ln 95219 **Location:** I-5 exit March Ln, just w.

DE VEGA BROTHERS ITALIAN CUISINE   209/957-3839

▼▼ ▼ Italian. Casual Dining. $8-$27 **AAA Inspector Notes:** This family-run restaurant has become a favorite offering up some traditional Italian favorites as well as some specialties of their own. The service is warm and welcoming and the menu offers pasta, poultry, veal and seafood, including cioppino. **Bar:** beer & wine. **Address:** 2819 W March Ln, Suite A1 95219 **Location:** I-5 exit March Ln, just w. L D CALL ⑤M

EL TORITO   209/957-6891

▼▼ ▼ Mexican. Casual Dining. $8-$20 **AAA Inspector Notes:** Homemade Mexican favorites span from classic preparations to specialties from the country's central regions. Spicy taqueria-style tacos and carnitas Michoacan (marinated pork) are tasty choices. **Bar:** full bar. **Address:** 2593 March Ln 95209 **Location:** I-5 exit March Ln, just e. L D CALL ⑤M

LA IGUANA WANNA BAR & GRILL   209/474-1293

▼▼ ▼ Mexican. Casual Dining. $7-$14 **AAA Inspector Notes:** This small, quaint restaurant offers a variety of Mexican favorites, as well as a few Caribbean selections. Friendly servers dish up burgers and specialty sandwiches including pulled-pork. Be sure to save room for the delicious desserts. **Bar:** full bar. **Address:** 7555 Pacific Ave, Suite 101B 95207 **Location:** Just s of Hammer Ln. B L D CALL ⑤M

LE BISTRO   209/951-0885

▼▼▼▼ Continental. Fine Dining. $19-$29 **AAA Inspector Notes:** The menu at this bistro offers French Continental cuisine and includes seared duck breast, braised short ribs, grilled pork loin and a daily fresh fish selection. Be sure to save room for one of the special dessert soufflés. Semi-formal attire. **Bar:** full bar. **Reservations:** suggested. **Address:** 3121 W Benjamin Holt Dr 95219 **Location:** I-5 exit W Benjamin Holt Dr; in Village Square Center. D CALL ⑤M

LOVE CAFE SEAFOOD & BARBEQUE   209/477-4484

▼ Cajun. Quick Serve. $4-$20 **AAA Inspector Notes:** Tucked away in the corner of the Pavillion Shopping Center, this small restaurant boasts a lot of specialties from Louisiana. The owner, Mama Love, as she is now known, has brought a lot of her favorite specialties including barbecue chicken, ribs, beef and pork and seafood (catfish, red snapper, shrimp and oysters). Be sure to save room for dessert including such favorites as sweet potato or pecan pie, red velvet cake or rum bread pudding. Come hungry as the portions are hearty. **Address:** 3008 E Hammer Ln, Suite 104 95212 **Location:** SR 99 exit Hammer Ln, 1 mi w. L D

ROUND TABLE PIZZA

▼ Pizza. Casual Dining. $7-$28 **AAA Inspector Notes:** This casual, family-oriented pizza place features high-quality ingredients and dough rolled fresh daily. Distinctive specialty pizzas are piled high with toppings. **Bar:** beer & wine. L D

For additional information, visit AAA.com

LOCATIONS:
Address: 2405 Pacific Ave 95204 **Location:** At Central Ct. **Phone:** 209/466-7988
Address: 2819 W March Ln, Suite A-5 95219 **Location:** I-5 exit March Ln, just w. **Phone:** 209/477-8277

SUISUN CITY (B-9) pop. 28,111

WESTERN RAILWAY MUSEUM, e. on SR 12 to 5848 SR 12, preserves the area's heritage of electric railways, operating vintage streetcars, including Key System trains, California's last 5-cent street car and other equipment. Railway exhibits and more than 50 historic cars can be seen. Fifteen-minute streetcar rides around the grounds and 50-minute interurban car rides are available.

Hours: Wed.-Sun. 10:30-5, Memorial Day-Labor Day; Sat.-Sun. 10:30-5, rest of year. Streetcar rides operate Sat.-Sun.; interurban cars operate daily. Last train departs at 3:30. Closed major holidays.

Cost: $10 (includes rides on streetcars and interurban cars); $9 (ages 65+); $7 (ages 2-14). **Phone:** (707) 374-2978. ⌂

HAMPTON INN & SUITES SUISUN CITY WATERFRONT
(707)429-0900

Hotel
$109-$159

AAA Benefit: Members save up to 10%!

Address: 2 Harbor Center Dr 94585 **Location:** I-80 exit SR 12, 2.6 mi e to Suisun City exit, then just s. **Facility:** 102 units. 4 stories, interior corridors. **Terms:** 1-7 night minimum stay, cancellation fee imposed. **Amenities:** high-speed Internet. **Pool(s):** heated outdoor. **Activities:** whirlpool, exercise room. **Guest Services:** valet and coin laundry. **Free Special Amenities:** full breakfast and high-speed Internet.

SAVE ECO CALL ⑤M 🛏 🛜 ✕ 🛗 🖨 🖥 / SOME UNITS 🐕

WHERE TO EAT

BLACK BEAR DINER   707/422-4386

▼▼ ▼ American. Casual Dining. $8-$18 **AAA Inspector Notes:** A homey atmosphere characterizes this family-oriented restaurant. Familiar comfort foods, such as meatloaf with mashed potatoes, are at the heart of the menu and are served in generous portions. **Bar:** beer & wine. **Address:** 111 Sunset Center 94585 **Location:** Just n of Rio Vista Rd. B L D CALL ⑤M

SUNNYVALE (E-9) pop. 140,081, elev. 105'
• Hotels p. 536 • Restaurants p. 537
• Hotels & Restaurants map & index p. 468

Although Silicon Valley doesn't appear on any map, people the world over know that the nickname refers to the area around Sunnyvale. The city is the headquarters of more than 650 computer-related manufacturers whose products, whether software or hardware, are based on silicon chip technology.

Local inventors and entrepreneurs make good use of the Sunnyvale Public Library at 665 W. Olive Ave. The library, designated as a U.S. Patent and Trademark Depository Library (PTDL), has facilities for patent and trademark research as well as online access to the full patent database used by the Patent and Trademark Office in Washington, D.C. A research library features patents from 1790 to the present as well as trademark/logo information. Phone (408) 730-7300.

Sunnyvale Chamber of Commerce: 260 S. Sunnyvale Ave., Suite 4, Sunnyvale, CA 94086. **Phone:** (408) 736-4971.

THE LACE MUSEUM is at 552 S. Murphy Ave. The museum displays a comprehensive collection of lace, lace tools, books and other lace-related items. Changing exhibits feature many fine, detailed handmade lace pieces. **Hours:** Tues.-Sat. 11-4 and by appointment. Phone for holiday season schedule. **Cost:** Free. **Phone:** (408) 730-4695.

SUNNYVALE HERITAGE PARK MUSEUM is at 570 E. Remington Dr. The museum is housed in a replica of the home of the Martin Murphy family, who played an important role in early California history.

(See map & index p. 468.)

Murphy, the founder of Sunnyvale, came to California in 1844, reportedly the first person to cross the Sierra Mountains in a covered wagon. A 6-minute film depicts the harsh conditions early settlers endured.

Members of the family lived in the home until 1950; the original house was damaged by a fire in 1961 and demolished. Exhibits relate local history, including information about Del Monte, Libby's and other companies that started up in the Sunnyvale area. **Time:** Allow 30 minutes minimum. **Hours:** Tues., Thurs. and Sun. noon-4. Special events are scheduled periodically. **Cost:** Donations. **Phone:** (408) 749-0220.

AMERICAS BEST VALUE INN   408/734-0555 [57]

Hotel
Rates not provided

Address: 331 E Weddell Dr 94089 **Location:** US 101 exit Mathilda Ave, just e on Ross Dr; n of US 101. **Facility:** 14 units. 2 stories (no elevator), interior corridors. **Amenities:** high-speed Internet. **Free Special Amenities: continental breakfast and high-speed Internet.**

BEST WESTERN PLUS SILICON VALLEY INN   (408)735-7800 [59]

Hotel
$89-$139

AAA Benefit: Members save up to 20%, plus 10% bonus points with Best Western Rewards®.

Address: 600 N Mathilda Ave 94085 **Location:** US 101 exit Mathilda Ave, just s. **Facility:** 100 units, some efficiencies. 2 stories (no elevator), interior corridors. **Terms:** cancellation fee imposed. **Amenities:** high-speed Internet. **Activities:** exercise room. **Guest Services:** valet and coin laundry. **Free Special Amenities: full breakfast and high-speed Internet.**

COMFORT INN   (408)749-8000 [60]

Hotel
$69-$189

Address: 595 N Mathilda Ave 94085 **Location:** US 101 exit Mathilda Ave. **Facility:** 52 units. 2 stories (no elevator), interior corridors. **Terms:** cancellation fee imposed. **Amenities:** high-speed Internet. **Activities:** whirlpool. **Guest Services:** valet and coin laundry. **Free Special Amenities: full breakfast and high-speed Internet.**

COMFORT INN SUNNYVALE   (408)244-9000 [70]

Hotel $69-$249 **Address:** 1071 E El Camino Real 94087 **Location:** SR 82 (El Camino Real), between Sycamore Terrace and Henderson Ave, 0.3 mi w of Lawrence Expwy. **Facility:** 63 units. 3 stories, interior corridors. **Pool(s):** heated outdoor. **Activities:** whirlpool. **Guest Services:** valet and coin laundry.

CORPORATE INN // SUNNYVALE   (408)220-1000 [68]

Hotel $79-$269 **Address:** 805 E El Camino Real 94087 **Location:** US 101 exit Fair Oaks Ave, 2.4 mi w, then 0.6 mi s. **Facility:** 73 efficiencies. 3 stories, interior/exterior corridors. **Terms:** cancellation fee imposed, resort fee. **Amenities:** high-speed Internet, safes. **Pool(s):** heated outdoor. **Activities:** whirlpool, steamroom, exercise room. **Guest Services:** valet and coin laundry, area transportation-within 5 mi.

COUNTRY INN & SUITES BY CARLSON, SUNNYVALE   (408)747-0999 [52]

Hotel
$89-$350

Address: 1300 Chesapeake Terr 94089 **Location:** US 101 exit Lawrence Expwy N; northwest quadrant of SR 237 and Lawrence Expwy. **Facility:** 180 units. 5 stories, interior corridors. **Terms:** cancellation fee imposed. **Amenities:** high-speed Internet. **Pool(s):** heated outdoor. **Activities:** exercise room. **Guest Services:** valet and coin laundry, area transportation-within 5 mi. **Free Special Amenities: expanded continental breakfast and high-speed Internet.**

DAYS INN & SUITES, SUNNYVALE SUNDOWNER   (408)734-9900 [53]

Motel $69-$89 **Address:** 504 Ross Dr 94089 **Location:** Southwest corner of SR 237 and N Mathilda Ave; e off US 101. **Facility:** 105 units. 2 stories (no elevator), exterior corridors. **Terms:** 3 day cancellation notice-fee imposed. **Amenities:** high-speed Internet. *Some:* safes. **Pool(s):** heated outdoor. **Activities:** sauna, exercise room. **Guest Services:** valet and coin laundry, area transportation-within 5 mi.

DOMAIN HOTEL, A JOIE DE VIVRE HOTEL   408/247-0800 [71]

Hotel. Rates not provided. **Address:** 1085 E El Camino Real 94087 **Location:** On SR 82, 0.3 mi w of Lawrence Expwy. **Facility:** 136 units. 3 stories, interior corridors. **Amenities:** high-speed Internet. **Pool(s):** heated outdoor. **Activities:** whirlpool, exercise room. **Guest Services:** valet laundry.

GRAND HOTEL   408/720-8500 [65]

Hotel. Rates not provided. **Address:** 865 W El Camino Real 94087 **Location:** SR 82 (El Camino Real); between S Mary and S Pastoria aves. **Facility:** 104 units, some two bedrooms, efficiencies and condominiums. 2-3 stories, interior/exterior corridors. **Amenities:** high-speed Internet. **Pool(s):** heated outdoor. **Activities:** whirlpool. **Guest Services:** valet laundry, area transportation-within 10 mi.

LARKSPUR LANDING SUNNYVALE   (408)733-1212 [58]

Extended Stay Contemporary Hotel $99-$199 **Address:** 748 N Mathilda Ave 94085 **Location:** US 101 exit Mathilda Ave, just s. **Facility:** 126 efficiencies. 4 stories, interior corridors. **Terms:** cancellation fee imposed. **Amenities:** high-speed Internet. **Activities:** whirlpool, exercise room. **Guest Services:** valet and coin laundry, area transportation-within 5 mi.

MAPLE TREE INN   (408)720-9700 [67]

Hotel
$109-$169

Address: 711 E El Camino Real 94087 **Location:** US 101 exit 394 (Lawrence Expwy), 2.9 mi w to El Camino Real exit, then 1.8 mi n. **Facility:** 177 units. 3 stories, interior corridors. **Terms:** cancellation fee imposed, resort fee. **Amenities:** video games (fee), high-speed Internet. **Pool(s):** heated outdoor. **Activities:** whirlpool, exercise room. **Guest Services:** valet and coin laundry.

(See map & index p. 468.)

QUALITY INN & SUITES-SUNNYVALE/SILICON VALLEY
(408)734-3742 **56**

Hotel
$69-$139

Address: 940 W Weddell Dr 94089 **Location:** N of and adjacent to US 101 exit Mathilda Ave, just e on Ross Dr. **Facility:** 92 units, some efficiencies and kitchens. 3 stories, interior corridors. **Terms:** cancellation fee imposed. **Amenities:** high-speed Internet, safes. **Pool(s):** heated outdoor. **Activities:** exercise room. **Guest Services:** valet and coin laundry. **Free Special Amenities: full breakfast and use of on-premises laundry facilities.**

QUALITY INN SANTA CLARA CONVENTION CENTER
(408)744-1100 **55**

Hotel $79-$189 **Address:** 1280 Persian Dr 94089 **Location:** US 101 exit Lawrence Expwy N, 1 mi n to Persian Dr, then 0.3 mi w. **Facility:** 72 units. 2 stories (no elevator), interior corridors. **Terms:** cancellation fee imposed. **Amenities:** high-speed Internet. **Pool(s):** heated outdoor. **Activities:** exercise room. **Guest Services:** valet and coin laundry.

QUALITY INN SUNNYVALE CIVIC CENTER
(408)773-1234 **66**

Hotel $89-$169 **Address:** 852 W El Camino Real 94087 **Location:** On SR 82 (El Camino Real); between S Mary and Hollenbeck aves. **Facility:** 59 units. 3 stories, interior corridors. **Terms:** cancellation fee imposed. **Amenities:** high-speed Internet. **Activities:** exercise room. **Guest Services:** valet laundry.

RAMADA INN-SILICON VALLEY
(408)245-5330 **61**

Hotel
$69-$104

Address: 1217 Wildwood Ave 94089 **Location:** US 101 exit Lawrence Expwy N, just n. **Facility:** 176 units. 2 stories (no elevator), exterior corridors. **Amenities:** safes. **Pool(s):** heated outdoor. **Activities:** whirlpool. **Guest Services:** valet and coin laundry. **Free Special Amenities: continental breakfast and high-speed Internet.**

RESIDENCE INN BY MARRIOTT SILICON VALLEY I
(408)720-1000 **64**

Extended Stay Hotel $169-$289 **Address:** 750 Lakeway Dr 94085 **Location:** US 101 exit Lawrence Expwy, e on Oakmead Pkwy. **Facility:** 231 kitchen units, some two bedrooms. 2 stories, exterior corridors. **Amenities:** high-speed Internet. **Pool(s):** heated outdoor. **Activities:** whirlpools, sports court, exercise room. **Guest Services:** valet and coin laundry, area transportation-within 5 mi.

AAA Benefit: AAA hotel discounts of 5% or more.

RESIDENCE INN BY MARRIOTT SUNNYVALE SILICON VALLEY II
(408)720-8893 **63**

Extended Stay Hotel $129-$239 **Address:** 1080 Stewart Dr 94086 **Location:** US 101 exit Lawrence Expwy S, n on Duane Ave, just w. **Facility:** 247 kitchen units, some two bedrooms. 2 stories (no elevator), exterior corridors. **Amenities:** high-speed Internet. **Pool(s):** heated outdoor. **Activities:** whirlpools, sports court, exercise room. **Guest Services:** valet and coin laundry, area transportation-within 5 mi.

AAA Benefit: AAA hotel discounts of 5% or more.

SHERATON SUNNYVALE
(408)745-6000 **51**

Hotel
$89-$329

Sheraton
STARWOOD PREFERRED GUEST

AAA Benefit: Members get up to 20% off, plus Starwood Preferred Guest® bonuses.

Address: 1100 N Mathilda Ave 94089 **Location:** US 101 exit Mathilda Ave. **Facility:** 173 units. 2 stories (no elevator), interior corridors. **Terms:** cancellation fee imposed. **Amenities:** Fee: video games, high-speed Internet. **Pool(s):** heated outdoor. **Activities:** whirlpool, exercise room. **Guest Services:** valet laundry, area transportation-within 5 mi. **Free Special Amenities: newspaper.**

STAYBRIDGE SUITES
(408)745-1515 **54**

Extended Stay Hotel
$140-$269

Address: 900 Hamlin Ct 94089 **Location:** SR 237 exit Mathilda Ave S, w on Ross Dr. **Facility:** 138 kitchen units, some two bedrooms. 3 stories (no elevator), exterior corridors. **Terms:** cancellation fee imposed. **Amenities:** high-speed Internet. **Pool(s):** heated outdoor. **Activities:** whirlpool, sports court, exercise room. **Guest Services:** valet and coin laundry, area transportation-within 5 mi. **Free Special Amenities: manager's reception and children's activities.**

TOWNEPLACE SUITES BY MARRIOTT SUNNYVALE/MOUNTAIN VIEW
(408)733-4200 **62**

Extended Stay Hotel $129-$249 **Address:** 606 S Bernardo Ave 94087 **Location:** SR 85 exit SR 82, 0.5 mi s. **Facility:** 95 units, some two bedrooms, efficiencies and kitchens. 4 stories, interior corridors. **Amenities:** high-speed Internet. **Activities:** whirlpool, exercise room. **Guest Services:** valet and coin laundry.

AAA Benefit: AAA hotel discounts of 5% or more.

WILD PALMS HOTEL
(408)738-0500 **69**

Boutique Hotel $99-$209 **Address:** 910 E Fremont Ave 94087 **Location:** US 101 exit Lawrence Expwy S, 1.5 mi s, 0.9 mi n on E El Camino Real, just w on S Wolfe Rd, then just s. **Facility:** Bright, bold colors and plants create a tropical feel in the public spaces; vibrant, sunny décor in the rooms transport you to Mexico or Miami. 203 units. 2 stories (no elevator), interior/exterior corridors. **Terms:** cancellation fee imposed. **Amenities:** high-speed Internet, safes. **Pool(s):** heated outdoor. **Activities:** whirlpool, exercise room. **Guest Services:** valet laundry.

WHERE TO EAT

FAULTLINE BREWING COMPANY
408/736-2739 **20**

American. Casual Dining. $10-$30 **AAA Inspector Notes:** Several good fish choices are among offerings on the diverse menu, which touches on many cuisine styles. Diners can sip a beer brewed on the premises while looking out over the lake. **Bar:** beer & wine. **Address:** 1235 Oakmead Pkwy 94085 **Location:** US 101 exit Lawrence Expwy S, just e.

PASTA POMODORO
408/789-0037

Italian. Casual Dining. $10-$19 **AAA Inspector Notes:** Families are welcomed at this laid-back restaurant, which brings in plenty of loyal locals who enjoy its varied Italian favorites, including tempting pasta and chicken dishes. **Bar:** beer & wine. **Address:** 300 W El Camino Real 94087 **Location:** At Mathilda Ave.

(See map & index p. 468.)

PEZZELLA'S VILLA NAPOLI   408/738-2400 (22)

▼▼▼▼ Italian. Casual Dining. $8-$26 **AAA Inspector Notes:** Guests can sample seafood, steak, veal and pasta dishes in a comfortable, attractive dining room. The restaurant has been family-owned for three generations. **Bar:** full bar. **Reservations:** suggested. **Address:** 1025 W El Camino Real 94087 **Location:** W of Mary Ave. [L] [D]

TARRAGON RESTAURANT   408/737-8003 (21)

▼▼▼▼ California. Casual Dining. $8-$27 **AAA Inspector Notes:** This is a stylish, yet comfortable, restaurant. Using organic produce from local farms, the chef creates a seasonal menu. **Bar:** full bar. **Address:** 140 S Murphy Ave 94086 **Location:** Downtown. **Parking:** street only. [L] [D] CALL[&M]

SUSANVILLE (C-4) pop. 17,947, elev. 4,258'

Founded by pioneer Isaac Roop in 1854 and named for his daughter, the town of Susanville lies at the head of the Honey Lake Valley and is flanked by the cliffs of the Susan River Canyon. In the 19th century Susanville served as a stopping point on the Nobles Emigrant Trail, a popular alternate route to the Donner Pass Overland Trail.

The Bizz Johnson Trail follows an old branch line of the Southern Pacific Railroad for approximately 26 miles between Susanville and Westwood. Administered by the Bureau of Land Management and Lassen National Forest, the trail is popular with hikers, railroad history buffs and cross-country skiers. The Susanville Depot & Museum, 601 Richmond Rd. at the beginning of the trail, houses historic photographs and railroad memorabilia in a restored 1920s train station.

The Susanville murals, eight on outdoor walls and one indoors, are all are within a five-block area downtown. Begin a mural tour at the corner of Main and Union streets. Continue west on Main to Roop Street and then turn south; when you reach Cottage Street turn east. The last mural is at the corner of Cottage and Gay streets. The indoor mural is at the corner of Main and S. Lassen streets.

Lassen County Chamber of Commerce: 75 N. Weatherlow St., P.O. Box 338, Susanville, CA 96130. **Phone:** (530) 257-4323.

EAGLE LAKE, 16 mi. n.w. on Eagle Lake Rd., is the second largest natural lake in California. In summer campfire programs and slide presentations are held; phone ahead for schedule. *See Recreation Areas Chart.* **Hours:** Ranger office Mon.-Fri. 8-4:30. **Cost:** Free. **Phone:** (530) 257-4188 or (530) 825-3454.

APPLE INN MOTEL   530/257-4726

▼ Motel $45-$63 **Address:** 2720 Main St 96130 **Location:** Jct SR 36 and 139, 0.7 mi se on SR 36. **Facility:** 10 units, some two bedrooms. 1 story, exterior corridors. **Terms:** cancellation fee imposed. **Activities:** horseshoes.

[📶]⊕ 🛜 ✕ 🛎 🖼 / SOME UNITS 💻

Visit your AAA/CAA Travel office to book
a AAA Vacations® Disney package

BEST WESTERN PLUS TRAILSIDE INN   (530)257-4123

Motel
$80-$85

AAA Benefit: Members save up to 20%, plus 10% bonus points with Best Western Rewards®.

Address: 2785 Main St 96130 **Location:** 0.7 mi se of jct SR 36 (Main St) and 139. **Facility:** 82 units. 2 stories (no elevator), exterior corridors. **Pool(s):** heated outdoor. **Activities:** recreation programs. **Free Special Amenities: expanded continental breakfast and early check-in/late check-out.**

SAVE [11] CALL[&M] [2⊙] [BIZ] 🛜 ✕ 🛎 🖼 💻 / SOME UNITS FEE 🐾

DIAMOND MOUNTAIN CASINO & HOTEL   (530)252-1100

Hotel
$86-$189

Address: 900 Skyline Dr 96130 **Location:** Jct SR 36 and 139, 1 mi n on Ash St (SR 139), then 1 mi w, follow signs to rancheria. **Facility:** The property offers a water feature in the lobby and attractive guest rooms with modern amenities as well as a 24-hour casino. 70 units. 4 stories, interior corridors. **Amenities:** high-speed Internet, safes. **Pool(s):** heated indoor. **Activities:** whirlpool, exercise room. **Guest Services:** coin laundry. **Free Special Amenities: local telephone calls and high-speed Internet.**

SAVE [ECO] 🏍 [11] [⅄] CALL[&M] [2⊙] [BIZ] 🛜 ✕
💻 / SOME UNITS FEE 🛎 FEE 🖼

HIGH COUNTRY INN   (530)257-3450

Hotel
$90-$140

Address: 3015 E Riverside Dr 96130 **Location:** Jct SR 36 and 139, 1.3 mi se, then just ne. **Facility:** 66 units, some two bedrooms. 2 stories (no elevator), interior corridors. **Amenities:** *Some:* high-speed Internet. **Pool(s):** heated outdoor. **Activities:** whirlpool, exercise room. **Guest Services:** coin laundry. **Free Special Amenities: full breakfast and high-speed Internet.**

SAVE [11]⊕ CALL[&M] [2⊙] [BIZ] 🛜 ✕ 🛎 🖼 💻

RIVER INN MOTEL   (530)257-6051

Motel
$60-$90

Address: 1710 Main St 96130 **Location:** Jct SR 36 and 139, just e on SR 36. **Facility:** 49 units. 2 stories (no elevator), exterior corridors. **Dining:** El Tepeyac Grille, see separate listing. **Pool(s):** heated outdoor. **Free Special Amenities: continental breakfast and high-speed Internet.**

SAVE [11] CALL[&M] [2⊙] [BIZ] 🛜 🛎 🖼 / SOME UNITS FEE 🐾

THE ROSEBERRY HOUSE BED & BREAKFAST   530/257-5675

▼▼▼▼ Bed & Breakfast $110-$135 **Address:** 609 North St 96130 **Location:** Jct SR 36 and 139, 0.7 mi nw to N Lassen St, then just ne. **Facility:** Built at the turn-of-the-last-century, the home is located in historic uptown Susanville and features comfortable public areas and large plush rooms decorated in period antiques. 4 units. 2 stories (no elevator), interior corridors. **Guest Services:** area transportation-Bizz Johnson Trailhead.

🛜 ✕ [2⊘] / SOME UNITS FEE 🐾 [🕊] [🐾]

SUPER 8   (530)257-2782

Motel
$72-$82

Address: 2975 Johnstonville Rd 96130 **Location:** Jct SR 36 and 139, 1 mi se on SR 139. Located at entrance to fairgrounds. **Facility:** 69 units. 2 stories (no elevator), exterior corridors. **Pool(s):** heated outdoor. **Free Special Amenities: expanded continental breakfast and high-speed Internet.**

SAVE [11]⊕ CALL[&M] [2⊙] 🛜 🛎 🖼 💻 / SOME UNITS FEE 🐾

WHERE TO EAT

EL TEPEYAC GRILLE   530/257-7220

♦♦ Regional American. Casual Dining. $6-$20 **AAA Inspector Notes:** Set in the center of town, this simple, diner-style restaurant features an extensive menu of Mexican and American grill favorites. **Bar:** full bar. **Address:** 1700 Main St 96130 **Location:** Jct SR 36 and 139, just e on SR 36; in River Inn Motel.

L D

MAZATLAN GRILL   530/257-1800

♦♦ Mexican. Casual Dining. $7-$15 **AAA Inspector Notes:** Located in the center of town, this restaurant features an extensive menu of traditional Mexican fare as well as California-influenced dishes. Portions are hearty, and the beer is ice cold. **Bar:** full bar. **Address:** 1535 Main St 96130 **Location:** Jct SR 36 and 139, just nw on SR 36. L D

ROSE'S RESTAURANT   530/257-7673

♦♦ Italian. Casual Dining. $10-$27 **AAA Inspector Notes:** This cozy café is a nice stop to enjoy a menu offering an array of appetizers, salads, soups, burgers, chicken, steak, pasta and seafood. Features include all-you-can-eat pasta on Wednesday and Thursday and all-you-can-eat tri-tip on Friday and Saturday. Desserts are made in house by the family pastry chef. Vegetarian items also are available. Lunch is served Tuesday through Friday. **Bar:** beer & wine. **Address:** 2102 Main St 96130 **Location:** 0.3 mi e of center. **Parking:** on-site and street. L D

SUTTER CREEK (E-3) pop. 2,501, elev. 1,198'

Sutter Creek, in the Sierra foothills, has a restored Main Street with stone, brick and weathered wood frame buildings serving as reminders of the town's 19th-century gold rush heritage. The antique shops and bed and breakfasts that line SR 49 attract lots of weekend visitors.

The Monteverde Store Museum at 11 Randolph St., at one time an old-fashioned country store, was owned and operated by the same family for more than 70 years. It was closed for more than 20 years before reopening as a museum. Such items as miner's supplies, dry goods, groceries, hardware, long underwear, penny candy and the store's original ledgers all recall its turn-of-the-20th-century heyday. Guided tours can be arranged with advance notice; phone the visitor center for information.

Sutter Creek Visitor Center: 71A Main St., P.O. Box 1234, Sutter Creek, CA 95685. **Phone:** (209) 267-1344, or (800) 400-0305 in Calif.

Self-guiding tours: A brochure describing a walking tour past Sutter Creek's historic buildings is available from the visitor center.

GOLD COUNTRY WINE TOURS provides pickup service at area lodgings for tours of wineries and vineyards within Amador County's Shenandoah Valley, in the Sierra foothills. Grapes have been harvested here since gold rush days, and there are more than 40 wineries in this area known for its Zinfandel wines. Knowledgeable guides provide historical narration as the 14-passenger shuttle bus visits four to five wineries, including the Sobon Estate Winery, California's oldest. A picnic lunch at one of the stops and a complimentary souvenir wine glass are included. Tours last approximately 5 hours.

Hours: Tours operate daily 11-4, except if the wineries are closed. **Cost:** Tour fees depend on the departure city. Departures from Plymouth are $75 per person; from Sutter Creek, $81; from Jackson, $87. A cancellation fee applies if a tour is cancelled within 72 hours of a reservation; refunds are not given for tours cancelled more than 72 hours prior to a reservation. Reservations are required. **Phone:** (209) 267-8030 or (877) 534-4949.

**THE FOXES INN OF SUTTER CREEK BED &
BREAKFAST**   (209)267-5882

♦♦♦ **Bed & Breakfast** **Address:** 77 Main St 95685 **Location:** Center. **Facility:** This upscale, elegant inn features silver service and menu selections at breakfast, or you can dine in your room or in the attractive gardens. $160-$325 Some guest rooms offer a gas fireplace. 7 units. 2 stories (no elevator), interior/exterior corridors. **Terms:** 2 night minimum stay - weekends, 10 day cancellation notice-fee imposed. **Amenities:** *Some:* safes. **Guest Services:** valet laundry. **Free Special Amenities:** full breakfast and early check-in/late check-out.

SAVE ♦♦ FEE ♦♦ ⊛ ⊘ ▭ / SOME UNITS ⬛

GREY GABLES BED & BREAKFAST INN   (209)267-1039

♦♦♦ Bed & Breakfast $135-$236 **Address:** 161 Hanford St 95685 **Location:** 0.3 mi n on SR 49. **Facility:** Several shops and restaurants are walking distance from this English Country-style manor offering lovely garden views and a central downtown location. 8 units. 3 stories (no elevator), interior corridors. **Terms:** 2 night minimum stay - weekends, 10 day cancellation notice-fee imposed.

♦♦ CALL ⬛M ⊛ ✕ W ⊘

AMERICAN EXCHANGE HOTEL   209/267-0242

fyi Not evaluated. **Address:** 53 Main St 95685 **Location:** Center. Facilities, services, and décor characterize a mid-scale property.

WHERE TO EAT

TWISTED FORK RESTAURANT & BAR   209/267-5211

♦♦ Italian. Casual Dining. $13-$27 **AAA Inspector Notes:** Pasta specialties are offered at this popular, centrally located restaurant. **Bar:** full bar. **Reservations:** suggested. **Address:** 53 Main St 95685 **Location:** Center; in American Exchange Hotel. **Parking:** street only. L D CALL ⬛M

TAHOE CITY (D-4) elev. 6,302'

- **Hotels p. 540 • Restaurants p. 540**
- **Hotels & Restaurants map & index p. 161**
- **Part of Lake Tahoe Area — see map p. 158**

All the glory of winter at Lake Tahoe is celebrated in early March during ♦♦ SnowFest! of North Lake Tahoe and Truckee. Events take place both on and off the mountain during the 10 days of festivities held each year at nearby resorts and towns throughout the North Lake Tahoe area. The cold weather season is celebrated with parades, fireworks, concerts, ski races, ice carving demonstrations and a polar bear swim.

The North Lake Tahoe Water Shuttle is a convenient—not to mention gloriously scenic—way to travel between communities along Lake Tahoe's northern shore. The boat accommodates up to 12 passengers and eight bikes and makes stops at four docks: the Tahoe City Marina, 700 North Lake Blvd.; Captain John's Restaurant, 7220 North Lake Blvd. in Tahoe Vista; 5000 North Lake Blvd. in Carnelian Bay; and the West Shore Cafe, 5160 West Lake Blvd. in Homewood. One-way fares are $10-$20 (depending on the destination); $7-$14 (ages 0-12).

(See map & index p. 161.)

For schedule and reservations information phone (530) 581-8707.

GATEKEEPER'S MUSEUM & MARION STEIN-BACH INDIAN BASKET MUSEUM is just s. on SR 89 from jct. SR 28. The museum is a reconstruction of the original gatekeeper's cabin, which served as the residence for the dam attendant. Included are historic photographs and displays about Lake Tahoe, natural history and pioneers. The handiwork of more than 85 tribes is represented in the 800 baskets featured in the museum's collection. The exhibit Ursus Among Us: The American Black Bear in the Tahoe Basin includes a taxidermy display as well as information about the animals and their interactions with humans through history.

Time: Allow 30 minutes minimum. **Hours:** Wed.-Mon. 10-5, May-Sept.; by appointment rest of year. **Cost:** $5; $4 (ages 65+); free (ages 0-12 and military with ID). **Phone:** (530) 583-1762.

WATSON CABIN MUSEUM is at 560 N. Lake Blvd. (SR 28), just e. of jct. SR 89. Situated on a small bluff above the Commons Beach area of Lake Tahoe, the Watson Cabin stands on the original site where Tahoe pioneer Robert Watson built it in 1909 as a wedding gift for his son. It also was the first log cabin in Tahoe City to have indoor plumbing. The museum features artifacts from the early 20th century as well as displays about the history of Lake Tahoe and the Watson family.

The second floor is not open to visitors. **Time:** Allow 30 minutes minimum. **Hours:** Wed.-Sun. noon-4, June-Sept. Closed Labor Day. **Cost:** Donations. **Phone:** (530) 583-8717.

RECREATIONAL ACTIVITIES

Skiing

- **Alpine Meadows** is 3 mi. n. on SR 89, then 3 mi. w. on Alpine Meadows Rd. **Hours:** Open daily, mid-Nov. to late May. Hours vary; phone ahead. **Phone:** (530) 583-4232 or (800) 403-0206.

AMERICAS BEST VALUE INN LAKE TAHOE/TAHOE CITY (530)583-3766 **11**

Motel $70-$215

Address: 455 N Lake Blvd 96145 **Location:** SR 28 (N Lake Blvd), 0.3 mi e of jct SR 89. **Facility:** 46 units. 2 stories (no elevator), interior/exterior corridors. **Terms:** 2 night minimum stay - seasonal and/or weekends, 3 day cancellation notice-fee imposed. **Pool(s):** heated outdoor. **Activities:** whirlpool. **Free Special Amenities:** continental breakfast and high-speed Internet.

CHANEY HOUSE (530)525-7333 **15**

Bed & Breakfast $180-$275 **Address:** 4725 W Lake Blvd 96145 **Location:** Waterfront. SR 89, 5 mi s. **Facility:** Situated across from Lake Tahoe, this historic 1920s stone home offers picturesque views of the surrounding mountains. 4 units. 2 stories (no elevator), interior corridors. **Terms:** 2 night minimum stay - seasonal and/or weekends, 14 day cancellation notice-fee imposed. **Activities:** boat dock, horseshoes.

COTTAGE INN AT LAKE TAHOE (530)581-4073 **13**

Bed & Breakfast $160-$340 **Address:** 1690 W Lake Blvd 96145 **Location:** SR 89, 2 mi s. **Facility:** In a wooded area within walking distance of Lake Tahoe, the inn offers attractively appointed guest units with a fireplace. 22 units, some efficiencies. 1-2 stories (no elevator), exterior corridors. **Terms:** 2 night minimum stay - seasonal and/or weekends, 14 day cancellation notice-fee imposed. **Activities:** beach access.

GRANLIBAKKEN LODGE & CONFERENCE CENTER (530)583-4242 **12**

Resort Condominium $143-$236

Address: 725 Granlibakken Rd 96145 **Location:** 0.8 mi s of jct SR 89 and 28 (N Lake Blvd), 0.6 mi w. **Facility:** The resort, on 74 scenic wooded acres, is located in a quiet forest setting, yet it's convenient to Tahoe City and Lake Tahoe. There are a few compact rooms and a few units with a wood-burning stove. 196 condominiums. 3 stories (no elevator), interior/exterior corridors. **Terms:** check-in 4 pm, 2 night minimum stay - weekends, 30 day cancellation notice-fee imposed. **Amenities:** Some: high-speed Internet. **Dining:** 2 restaurants. **Pool(s):** heated outdoor. **Activities:** sauna, whirlpool, 5 tennis courts (2 lighted), hiking trails, jogging, volleyball, limited exercise equipment, spa. **Fee:** downhill skiing. **Guest Services:** coin laundry. **Free Special Amenities:** full breakfast and high-speed Internet.

MOTHER NATURE'S INN 530/581-4278 **10**

Motel $65-$149 **Address:** 551 N Lake Blvd 96145 **Location:** SR 28 (N Lake Blvd), 0.5 mi e of jct SR 89; behind Mother Nature's Store. **Facility:** 8 units. 2 stories (no elevator), interior corridors. **Bath:** shower only. **Terms:** 7 day cancellation notice-fee imposed.

PEPPER TREE INN (530)583-3711 **9**

Motel $75-$225

Address: 645 N Lake Blvd 96145 **Location:** SR 28 (N Lake Blvd), 0.5 mi e of SR 89. **Facility:** 44 units. 1-7 stories, exterior corridors. **Pool(s):** heated outdoor. **Guest Services:** coin laundry. **Free Special Amenities:** expanded continental breakfast and high-speed Internet.

RIVER RANCH LODGE 530/583-4264 **8**

Motel. Rates not provided. **Address:** 2285 River Rd 96145 **Location:** I-80 exit SR 89, 11 mi s; 3.5 mi n from city center. Adjacent to Alpine Meadows Ski Resort. **Facility:** 19 units. 2 stories (no elevator), interior/exterior corridors. **Dining:** River Ranch Lodge Restaurant, see separate listing. **Activities:** hiking trails, jogging.

SUNNYSIDE STEAKHOUSE & LODGE (530)583-7200 **14**

Resort Country Inn $135-$380 **Address:** 1850 W Lake Blvd 96145 **Location:** SR 89, 2 mi s. **Facility:** Located on the west shore of Lake Tahoe, this refurbished 1908 residence offers comfortably furnished lodgings, most facing the lake, some with a fireplace and some with a private patio or deck. 23 units. 2 stories (no elevator), interior/exterior corridors. **Terms:** 2-3 night minimum stay - seasonal and/or weekends, 30 day cancellation notice-fee imposed. **Activities:** rental boats, rental canoes, fishing. **Fee:** waterskiing.

WHERE TO EAT

THE BLUE AGAVE MEXICAN RESTAURANT & CANTINA 530/583-8113 **14**

Mexican. Casual Dining. $8-$26 **AAA Inspector Notes:** Affording good views of Lake Tahoe, this delightful Mexican/American restaurant enables guests to sit indoors or out, weather permitting. Large and small plates as well as several house specialties find space on the menu. **Bar:** full bar. **Address:** 425 N Lake Blvd 96145 **Location:** SR 28 (N Lake Blvd), 0.3 mi e of jct SR 89.

(See map & index p. 161.)

BRIDGE TENDER TAVERN & GRILL 530/583-3342 [15]
▼▼ American. Casual Dining. $5-$13 **AAA Inspector Notes:** Great hamburgers are just the beginning at this favorite spot of visitors and locals alike. Located on the Truckee River, this spot offers wonderful water views while the menu offers great salads, sandwiches, barbecue ribs and fish and chips. Service is friendly. Dine on the patio if the weather permits. **Bar:** full bar. **Address:** 65 W Lake Blvd 96145 **Location:** Just s of jct SR 89. [L] [D] CALL [&M]

CHRISTY HILL RESTAURANT 530/583-8551 [12]
▼▼ American. Casual Dining. $12-$30 **AAA Inspector Notes:** A small plates menu and varied entrées make up the menu at this eatery. Furnished in attractive decor, the tiered dining room affords views of the lake. Patio seating is available in season. **Bar:** beer & wine. **Reservations:** suggested. **Address:** 115 Grove St 96145 **Location:** E off SR 28 (N Lake Blvd), toward lake. [D] [&]

DOCKSIDE 700 WINE BAR & GRILL 530/581-0303 [13]
▼▼ American. Casual Dining. $5-$30 **AAA Inspector Notes:** Offering diners a picturesque view of the lake, this restaurant is known locally for serving up great pizza with homemade dough. **Bar:** full bar. **Address:** 700 N Lake Tahoe 96145 **Location:** Jct SR 89 and 28 (N Lake Blvd), just ne; at Tahoe City Marina. [L] [D] CALL [&M]

JAKE'S ON THE LAKE 530/583-0188 [9]
▼▼ Seafood. Casual Dining. $9-$32 **AAA Inspector Notes:** Located on the Northwestern shore of Lake Tahoe, this spot combines good food with breathtaking views of the lake and mountains. This place is known to be one of Tahoe's favorite local restaurants. They do offer some outdoor patio seating when the weather permits. **Bar:** full bar. **Address:** 780 N Lake Blvd 96145 **Location:** Jct SR 89 and 28 (N Lake Blvd), just ne; in Boatworks Mall. [D] CALL [&M]

RIVER RANCH LODGE RESTAURANT 530/583-4264 [8]
▼▼ American. Casual Dining. $20-$32 **AAA Inspector Notes:** This inviting spot is located along the banks of the Truckee River and features a spacious outdoor patio for summer dining enjoyment. After dinner, diners can relax in the fireplace lounge. Lunch is offered on the patio daily in summer. **Bar:** full bar. **Reservations:** suggested. **Address:** Hwy 89 & Alpine Meadows Rd 96145 **Location:** I-80 exit SR 89, 11 mi s; 3.5 mi n from city center; in River Ranch Lodge. [D] CALL [&M] [&]

ROSIE'S CAFE 530/583-8504 [11]
▼▼ American. Casual Dining. $10-$20 **AAA Inspector Notes:** For more than 20 years this Tahoe tradition has served a varied menu, including hot and cold sandwiches, burgers, pizza and salads. Set in an old Tahoe ambience, this café offers breakfast until 2:30 p.m. as well as a children's play area upstairs. **Bar:** full bar. **Address:** 571 N Lake Blvd 96145 **Location:** SR 28 (N Lake Blvd), 0.5 mi e of jct SR 89. **Parking:** street only. [B] [L] [D] [&]

WOLFDALE'S 530/583-5700 [10]
▼▼▼ Fusion. Fine Dining. $8-$40 **AAA Inspector Notes:** A fine dining experience can be had here for any special occasion. The menu changes periodically to reflect the seasons. An extensive wine selection is offered. **Bar:** full bar. **Reservations:** suggested. **Address:** 640 N Lake Blvd 96145 **Location:** Jct SR 89 and 28 (N Lake Blvd), just ne. [D] CALL [&M]

TAHOE NATIONAL FOREST (D-4)

Elevations in the forest range from 1,300 ft. on the Middle Fork of the American River to 9,143 ft. at the summit of Mount Lola. Refer to AAA maps for additional elevation information.

Covering land north and west of Lake Tahoe, Tahoe National Forest—despite its name—has little to do with the lake. Much of this 797,205-acre national forest lies in the Yuba River drainage. Here miners employed the placer pan, pick and hydraulic cannon, which utilized tons of pressurized water to blast away the hillsides, in their frantic pursuit of gold. The lake and its immediate environs are part of the Lake Tahoe Basin Management Unit.

Today, where pack trains and stagecoaches once traveled, automobiles now follow SR 49 past the remnants of mining camps since reclaimed by forest. Along the twisting course of the North Yuba River are steep-walled canyons and the dramatic Sierra Buttes, riddled with old quartz mines.

The 170-mile-long Yuba Donner Scenic Byway is a loop drive through the rugged mountains and valleys once traversed by the unlucky Donner party and also those in search of fortune during the gold rush. The byway covers portions of I-80 and SRs 20, 49 and 89 as it winds its way through the national forest and the Sierra Nevada mountains.

Miners weren't the only ones to leave their mark on the landscape. Touring the region as an entertainer in 1853, famed *femme-fatale* Lola Montez christened Independence Lake during a Fourth of July picnic. Just north of the site of her picnic, Mount Lola honors the adventuress.

Independence Lake is but one of many lakes within the forest boundaries. Some of the most popular areas are the French Meadows Reservoir, cradled in the upper reaches of the American River watershed; a cluster of glacial lakes north of Sierra City; and Bullards Bar Reservoir, on the edge of the Sacramento Valley.

Recreational opportunities abound in the forest. Alpine and Nordic skiing and snowmobiling are popular winter diversions, while hiking, camping, boating, horseback riding and fishing take over the rest of the year. Hikers can explore 400 miles of trails, and water recreation includes sailing, water skiing, swimming, rafting, kayaking and canoeing. Reservations for Logger Campground can be made through the National Recreation Reservation System; phone (877) 444-6777 or TTY (877) 833-6777.

Publications about recreational opportunities and maps are available at most forest service stations and the forest headquarters in Nevada City. For more information contact the Forest Supervisor, Tahoe National Forest, 631 Coyote St., Nevada City, CA 95959; phone (530) 265-4531 or TTY (530) 478-6118. *See Recreation Areas Chart.*

TAHOE VISTA pop. 1,433
- **Restaurants p. 542**
- **Hotels & Restaurants map & index p. 161**
- **Part of Lake Tahoe Area — see map p. 158**

CEDAR GLEN LODGE (530)546-4281 [25]
▼▼ Motel $99-$216 **Address:** 6589 N Lake Blvd 96148 **Location:** SR 28, 1.5 mi w of SR 267. **Facility:** 31 units, some efficiencies, kitchens and cottages. 1-2 stories, exterior corridors. **Terms:** check-in 4 pm, 2-3 night minimum stay - seasonal and/or weekends, 10 day cancellation notice-fee imposed. **Pool(s):** outdoor. **Activities:** sauna, whirlpool, game room, horseshoes, volleyball.
[†▶] CALL [&M] [⊕] [BIZ] [🛜] [✕] [&] [▭]
/ SOME UNITS FEE [🐾] [◧] [▤]

(See map & index p. 161.)

FRANCISCAN LAKESIDE LODGE   530/546-6300 **27**
WV WV **Motel.** Rates not provided. **Address:** 6944 N Lake Blvd 96148 **Location:** SR 28, 1 mi w of SR 267. **Facility:** 63 kitchen units, some two bedrooms and cottages. 1-2 stories, exterior corridors. **Pool(s):** heated outdoor. **Activities:** beach access, boat dock, fishing, playground, game room, horseshoes, volleyball.

🛗 CALL 📶Ⓜ 🛥 📶 ✕ 🅺 🗄 🖥 ▦

HOLIDAY HOUSE   (530)546-2369 **29**
WV WV **Motel** $125-$225 **Address:** 7276 N Lake Blvd 96148 **Location:** SR 28, 1 mi w of SR 267. Located on lake. **Facility:** 7 units, some two bedrooms and kitchens. 2 stories (no elevator), exterior corridors. **Terms:** 2 night minimum stay - weekends. **Activities:** limited beach access, windsurfing. **Guest Services:** coin laundry.

🛗 CALL 📶Ⓜ 📶 ✕ 🅺 🗄 🖥 ▦
/ SOME UNITS FEE 🐕

MOURELATOS LAKESHORE RESORT
                                   (530)546-9500 **26**

Motel
$130-$375
Address: 6834 N Lake Blvd 96148 **Location:** SR 28, 1.2 mi w of SR 267. **Facility:** 32 units, some kitchens. 2 stories (no elevator), exterior corridors. **Terms:** 2-3 night minimum stay - seasonal and/or weekends, 30 day cancellation notice-fee imposed. **Activities:** whirlpools, beach access, rental sailboats, rental bicycles, volleyball. **Guest Services:** coin laundry.

SAVE 🛗 CALL 📶Ⓜ BIZ 📶 ✕ 🅺 🗄 🖥 ▦

THE SHORE HOUSE AT LAKE TAHOE   (530)546-7270 **28**
WV WV WV **Bed & Breakfast** $149-$325 **Address:** 7170 N Lake Blvd 96148 **Location:** SR 28, 1 mi w of jct SR 28 and 267. **Facility:** The property is on the northern shore of Lake Tahoe and offers lake access, a private dock and an attractive lawn. All guest units have a gas fireplace, knotty pine lodge décor and down comforters. 9 units, some cottages. 2 stories (no elevator), exterior corridors. **Terms:** check-in 4 pm, 2 night minimum stay - seasonal and/or weekends, 14 day cancellation notice-fee imposed. **Activities:** whirlpool, limited beach access, boat dock. **Fee:** massage.

🛗 CALL 📶Ⓜ 📶 ✕ 🆉 🗄 🖥 ▦ / SOME UNITS 🅺

WHERE TO EAT

SPINDLESHANKS AMERICAN BISTRO   530/546-2191 **24**
WV WV **American.** Casual Dining. $13-$36 **AAA Inspector Notes:** This cozy, knotty pine-paneled dining room and bar is a welcoming spot for good food and a superb wine selection. A seasonal patio is available. **Bar:** full bar. **Address:** 6873 N Lake Blvd 96148 **Location:** SR 28, 1.5 mi w of SR 267. Ⓓ

TAHOMA (D-4) pop. 1,191, elev. 6,270'
• Part of Lake Tahoe Area — see map p. 158

HELLMAN-EHRMAN MANSION is on SR 89 in Ed Z'berg-Sugar Pine Point State Park. The two-story Queen Anne-style mansion known as Pine Lodge was built in 1902 for San Francisco banker Isaias W. Hellman and is a fine example of a Tahoe summer house. Exhibits pertaining to the Hellman-Ehrman family can be seen on the second floor. On the grounds are an 1870 cabin, a nature center and nature trails.

Hours: Park interpretive specialists conduct guided 45-minute tours of the mansion daily on the hour 10-3, Memorial Day-Labor Day. **Cost:** Park entrance $8 (per private vehicle); $7 (ages 62+ per private vehicle). Mansion tour $8; $5 (ages 6-17). **Phone:** (530) 525-7982 or (530) 525-7232.

THE SEA RANCH
• Part of Wine Country area — see map p. 562
BLACK POINT GRILL AT SEA RANCH LODGE
                                   707/785-2371

Regional
California
Casual Dining
$12-$29
AAA Inspector Notes: This oceanview restaurant entices diners with a menu of California cuisine prepared with local produce. **Bar:** full bar. **Reservations:** suggested. **Address:** 60 Sea Walk Dr 95497 **Location:** Just w of SR 1; in Sea Ranch Lodge. *Menu on AAA.com*

Ⓑ Ⓛ Ⓓ 🅺

TIBURON (C-8) pop. 8,962, elev. 577'
• Part of San Francisco area — see map p. 342

Tiburon Peninsula Chamber of Commerce: 96B Main St., Tiburon, CA 94920. **Phone:** (415) 435-5633.

ANGEL ISLAND STATE PARK is on Angel Island; access to the island is by public ferry from Tiburon or by private boat. Angel Island, scenically situated in the middle of San Francisco Bay, is famous for being a vantage point that offers splendid views of the San Francisco skyline, Mount Tamalpais, the Marin Headlands, Sausalito and the Golden Gate Bridge.

Initially inhabited by Coastal Miwok Indians, the hilly island also served as a U.S. Army post, and was a processing point for immigrants from 1910-40. POWs were detained on the island during World War II; it later functioned as a missile base and currently is home to two Coast Guard stations.

A 1-hour, open-air audio tram tour provides information about the island's history. Tours of many historic sites, including the Angel Island Immigration Station, are conducted seasonally. Segway tours are offered twice daily. Outdoor activities include biking, hiking, fishing, beachcombing, boating, picnicking and camping. Food and bike rentals are available seasonally. *See Recreation Areas Chart.*

Note: Ferry service also is available from San Francisco and, seasonally, from Oakland and Alameda. **Hours:** Park open daily 8 a.m.-dusk. Tram tours available several times daily, Apr.-Sept.; Sat.-Sun. in Mar. and Oct.-Nov. Phone ahead to confirm tour schedules. **Cost:** Park admission included in ferry fare. Round-trip ferry from Tiburon $13.50; $11.50 (ages 6-12); $3.50 (ages 3-5); $1 (bicycles); free (one child ages 0-2 per paying adult). Tram tour $15; $13.50 (ages 62+); $10 (children); free (ages 0-5 on lap). Segway tours $68. **Phone:** (415) 435-5390 for the state park, (415) 435-2131 for ferry information from Tiburon, or (415) 435-3392 for tram and Segway tour information. 🅰 🍴 ✕ 🛉

▼ GEM **Angel Island Immigration Station** is within Angel Island State Park; access to the island is by public ferry from Tiburon or by private boat. Angel Island Immigration Station was a processing center often called "the Ellis Island of the West." But unlike at Ellis Island, the immigrants—mostly from

China—who sought entrance into the United States at this point of entry were frequently detained in overcrowded, wooden barracks, endured embarrassing medical exams and lengthy interrogations, and were made to wait weeks (and sometimes months) to learn the outcome of their application.

Many of these immigrants carved poetry into the walls of the barracks to convey their plight. The carvings were considered graffiti and were covered over with coats of paint. Visitors can see photographs, artifacts, a re-creation of one of the living quarters and hundreds of poems that were etched into the walls.

From the ferry dock the immigration station is a 1-mile walk (including a climb of 140 stairs) that takes 30 to 45 minutes. A 1-hour guided tour provides a first-hand look at those who were incarcerated here and relates their strength and resiliency. Tour tickets can be purchased at the cafe at Ayala Cove.

Note: The hike and steep stair climb to the immigration station will be strenuous to those not in reasonably good physical shape. Shuttle service is available on a limited basis from the ferry landing to the immigration station; phone ahead for schedule and rates. Ferry service to Angel Island also is available from San Francisco and, seasonally, from Oakland and Alameda.

Hours: Guided tours are given Wed.-Sun. at 11, 12:30 and 1:45, May-Sept.; schedule varies rest of year. Phone ahead to confirm schedule and tour availability. **Cost:** Guided tour fee $7; $5 (ages 5-11). Tours are not recommended for under age 10. **Phone:** (415) 435-5537 for the immigration station, (415) 435-2131 for ferry information from Tiburon, or (415) 435-3392 for shuttle and tour ticket information.

THE LODGE AT TIBURON (415)435-3133
▼▼▼ Hotel $149-$469 **Address:** 1651 Tiburon Blvd 94920 **Location:** US 101 exit Tiburon-Belvedere, 4 mi e; in village; 1 blk from bay. **Facility:** 102 units. 2-3 stories, exterior corridors. **Terms:** 3 day cancellation notice-fee imposed. **Amenities:** safes. Some: high-speed Internet. **Pool(s):** heated outdoor. **Activities:** whirlpool, exercise room. **Guest Services:** valet laundry.

WATERS EDGE HOTEL (415)789-5999
▼▼▼ Hotel $159-$509 **Address:** 25 Main St 94920 **Location:** US 101 exit Tiburon-Belvedere, 4 mi e; downtown. **Facility:** 23 units. 2 stories, interior corridors. **Parking:** on-site (fee). **Terms:** 2 night minimum stay - seasonal and/or weekends, 7 day cancellation notice-fee imposed. **Amenities:** high-speed Internet. **Guest Services:** valet laundry.

TOMALES pop. 204

THE CONTINENTAL INN (707)878-2396
▼▼ Hotel $140-$220 **Address:** 26985 Hwy One 94971 **Location:** On SR 1; at Dillon Beach Rd. **Facility:** 9 units. 2 stories (no elevator), interior corridors. **Terms:** check-in 4 pm, 7 day cancellation notice-fee imposed. **Free Special Amenities:** room upgrade (subject to availability with advance reservations) and high-speed Internet.

TRACY pop. 82,922

BEST WESTERN LUXURY INN (209)832-0271

Hotel $70-$80 **AAA Benefit:** Members save up to 20%, plus 10% bonus points with Best Western Rewards®. **Address:** 811 W Clover Rd 95376 **Location:** I-205 exit Central Tracy/Tracy Blvd, just s, then just w. **Facility:** 57 units. 3 stories, interior corridors. **Amenities:** high-speed Internet. **Pool(s):** outdoor. **Activities:** whirlpool, exercise room. **Guest Services:** coin laundry. **Free Special Amenities:** expanded continental breakfast and high-speed Internet.

FAIRFIELD INN BY MARRIOTT (209)833-0135
▼▼▼ Hotel $94-$114 **Address:** 2410 Naglee Rd 95376 **Location:** I-205 exit Grant Line Rd/Naglee Rd, just n. **AAA Benefit:** AAA hotel discounts of 5% or more. **Facility:** 64 units. 3 stories, interior corridors. **Amenities:** Some: high-speed Internet. **Pool(s):** heated indoor. **Activities:** whirlpool. **Guest Services:** valet laundry.

HAMPTON INN BY HILTON (209)833-0483
▼▼▼ Hotel $94-$159 **Address:** 2400 Naglee Rd 95376 **Location:** I-205 exit Grant Line Rd/Naglee Rd, just n. **AAA Benefit:** Members save up to 10%! **Facility:** 62 units. 3 stories, interior corridors. **Terms:** 1-7 night minimum stay, cancellation fee imposed. **Amenities:** Some: high-speed Internet. **Pool(s):** heated indoor. **Activities:** whirlpool, exercise room. **Guest Services:** valet laundry.

HOLIDAY INN EXPRESS & SUITES (209)830-8500
▼▼▼ Hotel $99-$159 **Address:** 3751 N Tracy Blvd 95304 **Location:** I-205 exit Central Tracy/Tracy Blvd, just n. **Facility:** 102 units. 3 stories, interior corridors. **Terms:** cancellation fee imposed. **Amenities:** video games (fee), high-speed Internet. **Pool(s):** outdoor. **Activities:** sauna, whirlpool, exercise room. **Guest Services:** valet and coin laundry. **Free Special Amenities:** expanded continental breakfast and high-speed Internet.

WHERE TO EAT

BLACK BEAR DINER 209/835-5600
▼▼ American. Casual Dining. $8-$16 **AAA Inspector Notes:** A homey atmosphere characterizes this family-oriented restaurant. Familiar comfort foods, such as meatloaf with mashed potatoes, are at the heart of the menu and are served in generous portions. **Bar:** beer & wine. **Address:** 2351 Toste Rd 95377 **Location:** I-205 exit Grant Line Rd/Naglee Rd, just s. B L D CALL

THE GREAT PLATE BAR & GRILL 209/833-0862
▼▼ American. Casual Dining. $8-$20 **AAA Inspector Notes:** Located in the historic downtown, this is a great place to please everyone. Guests can choose from hearty appetizers, salads, steak, fish and chips, pizza, calzones and stromboli all homemade. Service is exceptionally friendly and relaxed. **Bar:** full bar. **Address:** 714 Central Ave 95376 **Location:** I-205 exit Tracy Blvd, 1.5 mi s, 0.5 mi e on 11th St, then just s. L D CALL

Download eTourBook guides
for top destinations at
AAA.com/ebooks

M & J BISTRO A TASTE OF SAN FRANCISCO   209/832-2727

▼▼▼ California. Casual Dining. $11-$29 **AAA Inspector Notes:** The chef calls his cuisine a French Basque California cuisine fusion which makes for a wonderful combination of flavors from meal-sized salads with grilled halibut and prawns to lamb chops, pork tenderloin and a wide selection of fresh fish items. Be sure to save room for one of the many crepe desserts including chocolate decadence. Service is friendly and welcoming. **Bar:** beer & wine. **Address:** 2515 N Tracy Blvd 95376 **Location:** I-205 exit Central Tracy/Tracy Blvd, 0.5 mi s. [L] [D] CALL [M]

TRINIDAD (B-1) pop. 367, elev. 175'

Spanish explorers, who came ashore near the site of present-day Trinidad on Trinity Sunday in 1775, named the area *La Santisima Trinidad,* "the most holy Trinity." Capt. George Vancouver arrived in 1793, and was followed in the early 19th century by a succession of fur traders.

Trinidad became a boomtown during gold rush days, as prospectors in search of instant wealth along nearby rivers loaded up with supplies before heading to the mines. Later a mill town and whaling port, this Pacific coast village today welcomes visitors in search of secluded beaches, hiking, fishing and opportunities for whale watching. A working lighthouse is near the edge of the promontory.

Greater Trinidad Chamber of Commerce: P.O. Box 356, Trinidad, CA 95570. **Phone:** (707) 677-1610.

PATRICK'S POINT STATE PARK is 5 mi. n. via US 101. Noted for its stunning coastal scenery, the heavily wooded state park features 6 miles of trails that thread through lush vegetation, along the tops of tall bluffs and down to sandy beaches. One path leads to Wedding Rock, a dramatic vantage point jutting out into the Pacific's pounding surf. A Yurok Indian village has been reconstructed in the park, and in spring a profusion of wildflowers bloom. *See Recreation Areas Chart.*

Note: Except for service animals, dogs are restricted from the beach and trails. Camping is permitted. **Hours:** Daily dawn-dusk. **Cost:** Day use $8 per private vehicle. **Phone:** (707) 677-3570, or (800) 444-7275 for camping reservations through ReserveAmerica. [icons]

EMERALD FOREST OF TRINIDAD   707/677-3554

▼▼ Cabin. Rates not provided. **Address:** 753 Patrick's Point Dr 95570 **Location:** US 101 exit Trinidad, just w on Main St, then 0.7 mi n. **Facility:** 20 cabins. 1 story, exterior corridors. **Activities:** playground, game room, horseshoes, volleyball. **Guest Services:** coin laundry.
[icons] / SOME UNITS FEE [icon]

LOST WHALE BED & BREAKFAST INN   707/677-3425

▼▼▼ Bed & Breakfast $199-$315 **Address:** 3452 Patrick's Point Dr 95570 **Location:** US 101 exit Patrick's Point Dr, 1.1 mi w. **Facility:** Gourmet breakfasts and the chance to get a glimpse of sea lions draw guests to this secluded property overlooking the Pacific Ocean. Afternoon wine and accompaniments start at 4 pm. 8 units. 2 stories (no elevator), interior corridors. **Terms:** 2 night minimum stay - seasonal and/or weekends, 7 day cancellation notice. **Activities:** whirlpool. [icons] / SOME UNITS [icon]

TRINIDAD BAY BED & BREAKFAST   (707)677-0840

▼▼▼ Bed & Breakfast $200-$350 **Address:** 560 Edwards St 95570 **Location:** US 101 exit Trinidad, 0.3 mi w on Main St, just s on Ocean Ave, then just w. **Facility:** Sweeping ocean views are a key feature of this traditional B&B situated opposite the Trinidad lighthouse. 4 units. 2 stories (no elevator), interior/exterior corridors. **Terms:** 5 day cancellation notice-fee imposed, resort fee.

 / SOME UNITS [icons]

TRINIDAD INN   707/677-3349

▼▼▼ Motel $110-$200 **Address:** 1170 Patrick's Point Dr 95570 **Location:** US 101 exit Trinidad, just w on Main St, then 1.3 mi n. **Facility:** 10 units, some two bedrooms and kitchens. 1 story, exterior corridors. **Terms:** cancellation fee imposed. **Activities:** basketball, horseshoes. **Free Special Amenities:** early check-in/late check-out and preferred room (subject to availability with advance reservations).

[SAVE] [icons] / SOME UNITS FEE [icons]

TURTLE ROCKS OCEANFRONT INN   707/677-3707

▼▼▼ Bed & Breakfast $180-$315 **Address:** 3392 Patrick's Point Dr 95570 **Location:** US 101 exit Patrick's Point Dr, 1.1 mi w. **Facility:** Sea lions, river otters and salt spray from the Pacific Ocean are among the enticements at this B&B, where all rooms have a view of nature. 6 units. 2 stories (no elevator), interior corridors. **Terms:** 2 night minimum stay - seasonal and/or weekends, 7 day cancellation notice-fee imposed. CALL [M] [icons]

VIEW CREST LODGE   707/677-3393

▼▼▼ Cottage $105-$240 **Address:** 3415 Patrick's Point Dr 95570 **Location:** US 101 exit Patrick's Point Dr, 1 mi s. **Facility:** The lodge features well-groomed gardens and modern, individual cottages with private decks offering vistas of the Pacific Ocean. 11 cottages. 1 story, exterior corridors. **Terms:** 14 day cancellation notice-fee imposed. **Guest Services:** coin laundry. **Free Special Amenities:** local telephone calls and high-speed Internet.

[SAVE]

BISHOP PINE LODGE   707/677-3314

[fyi] Not evaluated. **Address:** 1481 Patrick's Point Dr 95570 **Location:** US 101 exit Seawood Dr, just w, then 0.8 mi s. Facilities, services, and décor characterize a mid-scale property.

WHERE TO EAT

CATCH CAFE   707/677-0390

▼ Natural/Organic. Casual Dining. $7-$18 **AAA Inspector Notes:** Serving healthy fast food, the owner uses organic and fresh ingredients. Guests order at a window, then find a seat inside (which might be hard to find) or on the large patio. **Bar:** beer & wine. **Address:** 355 Main St 95570 **Location:** US 101 exit Trinidad, just w; at Trinidad Shopping Center. **Parking:** on-site and street.
[L] [D] [icon]

MOONSTONE GRILL   707/677-1616

▼▼▼ Regional American. Casual Dining. $18-$65 **AAA Inspector Notes:** Overlooking Moonstone Beach, this place boasts great water views. The owner, who runs two other restaurants in Arcata, offers an upscale dining experience featuring creative California cuisine, fresh seafood and regional delicacies. **Bar:** full bar. **Reservations:** required. **Address:** 100 Moonstone Beach Rd 95570 **Location:** US 101 S exit 6th Ave, just s on Kay Rd, just e on 6th Ave, just s on Westhaven Dr, just s on Scenic Dr, then just w. [D]

SEASCAPE RESTAURANT   707/677-3762

▼▼ Seafood. Casual Dining. $7-$30 **AAA Inspector Notes:** On the beach at Trinidad Harbor, this rustic restaurant affords views of the pier and bay. Fresh seafood specials-as well as omelets and beef, chicken and pasta selections-make up the menu. **Bar:** beer & wine. **Address:** Bay St 95570 **Location:** US 101 exit Trinidad, 0.3 mi w on Main St, then 0.3 mi n on Edwards St; at pier.
[B] [L] [D] [icon]

SUNSET RESTAURANT AT CHER-AE HEIGHTS CASINO
707/825-2760

American. Casual Dining. $19-$33 **AAA Inspector Notes:** High ceilings create a sense of spaciousness and large windows offer a panoramic view of Trinidad Bay at this inviting restaurant. Deliciously flavored dishes keep diners satisfied. Try the oven-roasted quail stuffed with pancetta and wild and basmatic rice. The quail is perfectly cooked with bits of toasty rice giving it a crunchy texture. Crème brûlée is the perfect sweet ending to a lovely meal. **Bar:** full bar. **Address:** 27 Scenic Dr 95570 **Location:** US 101 exit Trinidad, just w on Main St, then 1 mi s. ⓓ CALL 🄶M 🄰🄲

TRINIDAD BAY EATERY
707/677-3777

American. Casual Dining. $9-$23 **AAA Inspector Notes:** This small, family-owned restaurant specializes in preparing a fresh fish of the day and homemade desserts. **Bar:** beer & wine. **Address:** 607 Parker St 95570 **Location:** US 101 exit Trinidad, 0.3 mi w on Main St. **Parking:** street only. Ⓑ Ⓛ ⓓ 🄰🄲

TRINITY CENTER (B-2) pop. 267, elev. 2,311'

SCOTT MUSEUM OF TRINITY CENTER is 1 mi. e. off SR 3 on Airport Rd. Among the exhibits are horse-drawn vehicles, a barbed-wire collection, Native American artifacts and old utensils. **Tours:** Guided tours are available. **Hours:** Tues.-Sat. noon-4, June-Aug. **Cost:** Donations. **Phone:** (530) 266-3378.

TRUCKEE (D-4) pop. 16,180, elev. 5,820'

- **Hotels p. 546 • Restaurants p. 546**
- **Hotels & Restaurants map & index p. 161**
- **Part of Lake Tahoe Area — see map p. 158**

Truckee, named for Washoe Indian Chief Trokay, was at one time a lawless lumber and railroad town, and some of that Old West charm still survives in restored 19th-century buildings and a train that runs through the middle of town. Winter sports enthusiasts take advantage of nearby skiing and snowboarding as well as the cross-country ski and snowshoe trails at Donner Memorial State Park *(see attraction listing).*

Truckee Donner Chamber of Commerce: 10065 Donner Pass Rd., Truckee, CA 96161. **Phone:** (530) 587-8808.

Self-guiding tours: Maps outlining a self-guiding walking tour of the historic downtown district are available from the California Welcome Center, in the train depot at 10065 Donner Pass Rd.

DONNER MEMORIAL STATE PARK, 2 mi. w. on Donner Pass Rd., is near the site where the ill-fated Donner party was stranded trying to cross the Sierra Nevada Mountains during the severe winter of 1846-47. As members of the 89-person party died, some of those remaining resorted to cannibalism; only 47 were rescued.

The Emigrant Trail Museum has exhibits about railroad and natural history, logging and immigrants. The Pioneer Monument is near the museum. One- to 2-hour guided hikes are offered in summer; phone ahead to confirm availability.

Hours: Park open daily dawn-dusk. Museum open daily 10-5. Video presented daily at 10:15 and then on the hour until 1 hour before closing. Closed Jan. 1, Thanksgiving and Christmas. **Cost:** Fee for day use $8 (per private vehicle); $7 (ages 62+ per private vehicle). **Phone:** (530) 582-7892.
🄰 🄲 🄷 🄷 🄰

RECREATIONAL ACTIVITIES
Skiing

- **Northstar-at-Tahoe** is off I-80 exit 188B, then 6 mi. s. on SR 267. **Hours:** Open daily, week before Thanksgiving to mid-Apr. (weather permitting). Hours vary; phone ahead. **Phone:** (800) 466-6784.

(See map & index p. 161.)

THE CEDAR HOUSE SPORT HOTEL   (530)582-5655

▼▼▼ **Hotel** $170-$390 **Address:** 10918 Brockway Rd 96161 **Location:** I-80 exit 188 (SR 267) westbound; exit 188B (SR 267) eastbound, 1.5 mi s, then 0.8 mi nw. **Facility:** 40 units. 2 stories (no elevator), interior corridors. **Terms:** check-in 4 pm, 2-3 night minimum stay - seasonal and/or weekends, 3 day cancellation notice-fee imposed. **Amenities:** high-speed Internet, safes. **Activities:** whirlpool. **Guest Services:** valet laundry.

🍴 🍸 ⚕ 📶 ✕ 🛄 📠 🖥 / SOME UNITS FEE 🐾 📷

DONNER LAKE VILLAGE RESORT   (530)587-6081

▼▼ **Vacation Rental Condominium** $90-$412 **Address:** 15695 Donner Pass Rd 96161 **Location:** Waterfront. I-80 exit Donner Lake, 1.2 mi s on Donner Lake Rd; on Old Hwy 40 at west end of lake. **Facility:** Accommodations include studio, one- and two-bedroom units, some lakefront. 34 condominiums. 2 stories (no elevator), interior/exterior corridors. **Terms:** 2 night minimum stay - weekends, 7 day cancellation notice. **Activities:** saunas, rental boats, rental canoes, rental paddleboats, marina, fishing, hiking trails, jogging. **Guest Services:** coin laundry.

CALL 🛄M BIZ 📶 ✕ 🎿 🛄 🖥 📠

HAMPTON INN & SUITES TAHOE-TRUCKEE
          (530)587-1197

▼▼▼ **Hotel** $149-$399 **Address:** 11951 SR 267 96161 **Location:** I-80 exit 188 (SR 267) westbound; exit 188B (SR 267) eastbound, 1.5 mi s. **Facility:** 109 units. 3 stories, interior corridors. **Terms:** | **AAA Benefit:** Members save up to 10%!

Terms: 1-7 night minimum stay, cancellation fee imposed. **Amenities:** high-speed Internet. **Pool(s):** outdoor. **Activities:** whirlpool, exercise room. **Guest Services:** coin laundry.

CALL 🛄M 🏊 BIZ 📶 ✕ 🖥 / SOME UNITS 🛄 📷

LARKSPUR HOTEL TRUCKEE-TAHOE
          (530)587-4525

▼▼▼ Hotel $136-$212

Address: 11331 Brockway Rd 96161 **Location:** I-80 exit 188 (SR 267) westbound; exit 188B (SR 267) eastbound, 1.5 mi se, then just w. **Facility:** 100 units. 2 stories, interior corridors. **Amenities:** video games (fee). **Pool(s):** outdoor. **Activities:** sauna, whirlpool, exercise room. **Guest Services:** coin laundry. Free **Special Amenities:** full breakfast and high-speed Internet.

SAVE 🍴 CALL 🛄M 🏊 BIZ 📶 ✕ 🖥 / SOME UNITS FEE 🐾

THE RITZ-CARLTON, LAKE TAHOE (530)562-3000

▼▼▼▼ Contemporary Resort Hotel $249-$899

AAA Benefit: Unequaled service at Special Member Savings.

Address: 13031 Ritz-Carlton Highlands Ct 96161 **Location:** I-80 exit 188 (SR 267) westbound; exit 188B (SR 267) eastbound, 6.5 mi se, then 2.8 mi w. **Facility:** The luxurious hotel features a five-story fireplace as the centerpiece in the grand octagonal lobby; a gondola connects guests to Northstar Village. 170 units. 2-5 stories, interior corridors. **Parking:** on-site (fee) and valet. **Terms:** check-in 4 pm, 7 day cancellation notice-fee imposed, resort fee. **Amenities:** video games (fee), high-speed Internet, safes. **Dining:** 3 restaurants, also, Manzanita, see separate listing. **Pool(s):** 2 heated outdoor. **Activities:** saunas, whirlpools, steamrooms, recreation programs, rental bicycles, hiking trails, game room, spa. **Fee:** downhill & cross country skiing. **Guest Services:** valet laundry.

SAVE ECO 🍴 ⚕ 🍸 CALL 🛄M 🏊 ⚕ BIZ 📶 ✕ 🎿 🖥 / SOME UNITS FEE 🐾 📷

THE TRUCKEE DONNER LODGE   (530)582-9999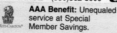

▼▼▼ Hotel $109-$219

Address: 10527 Cold Stream Rd 96161 **Location:** I-80 exit 184 (Donner Pass Rd), just s. Adjacent to Donner Memorial State Park. **Facility:** 64 units. 3 stories, interior corridors. **Terms:** cancellation fee imposed. **Amenities:** high-speed Internet. **Pool(s):** outdoor. **Activities:** whirlpool, exercise room. **Guest Services:** coin laundry, area transportation-historic downtown.

SAVE CALL 🛄M 🏊 BIZ 📶 ✕ 🛄 🖥 🖥

WHERE TO EAT

COTTONWOOD RESTAURANT & BAR   530/587-5711 ②

▼▼▼ American. Casual Dining. $12-$35 **AAA Inspector Notes:** In what was once the rustic Hilltop Lodge, this restaurant offers wonderful views overlooking the town below and vistas of the forested hillsides. A Sierra Mountain décor gives way to an expansive, seasonal deck—reserve a table for the sunset view. Nightly specials are offered and live music is played most Thursdays and Fridays. **Bar:** full bar. **Reservations:** suggested. **Address:** 10142 Rue Hilltop 96161 **Location:** I-80 exit 186 eastbound, just ne on Donner Pass Rd, just se on Bridge St/Brockway Rd, then just sw; exit 188 westbound, 1 mi sw on Donner Pass Rd, just se on Bridge St/Brockway Rd, then just sw; jct Brockway and Old Brockway Rd.

D CALL 🛄M

FIFTY FIFTY BREWING CO.   530/587-2337 ③

▼▼ American. Casual Dining. $9-$29 **AAA Inspector Notes:** A variety of pub food is served here, including burgers, sandwiches, salads, pizza, calzones, pasta and a few entrée selections. Choose from a selection of hand-crafted beers. **Bar:** full bar. **Address:** 11197 Brockway Rd 96161 **Location:** I-80 exit 188 (SR 267) westbound; exit 188B (SR 267) eastbound, 1.5 mi se, then just nw.

L D CALL 🛄M 🎿

MANZANITA   530/562-3050 ⑤

▼▼▼ California. Fine Dining. $12-$40 **AAA Inspector Notes:** The warm and inviting contemporary décor of this restaurant features delicious California cuisine with French and mountain influences utilizing organic, locally-grown meat and produce whenever possible. The restaurant is closed April 15 through May 15. **Reservations:** suggested. **Address:** 13031 Ritz-Carlton Highlands Ct 96161 **Location:** I-80 exit 188 (SR 267) westbound; exit 188B (SR 267) eastbound, 6.5 mi se, then 2.8 mi w; in The Ritz-Carlton, Lake Tahoe. **Parking:** valet only. B L D CALL 🛄M

MIKUNI JAPANESE RESTAURANT & SUSHI BAR
          530/562-2188

▼▼ Japanese Sushi. Casual Dining. $9-$24 **AAA Inspector Notes:** Located near the skating rink, this popular local chain features large windows overlooking the street scene. An extensive variety of creative sushi rolls and sakes is offered. Lunch is served on the weekends. **Bar:** full bar. **Address:** 5001 Northstar , Suite 5101 Dr 96161 **Location:** I-80 exit 188 westbound; exit 188B (SR 267) eastbound, 5 mi se on SR 267, then 2.1 mi sw to the Village-at-Northstar. D CALL 🛄M

PACIFIC CREST GRILL AT BAR OF AMERICA
          530/587-2626 ①

▼▼▼ American. Casual Dining. $13-$29 **AAA Inspector Notes:** Wood-fired pizza and a varied selection of entrées are available at this grill. Organic and local produce are used whenever possible. **Bar:** full bar. **Address:** 10042 Donner Pass Rd 96160 **Location:** Jct Brockway Rd; center. **Parking:** street only. L D

RUBICON PIZZA COMPANY   530/562-2199 ④

▼▼ Italian Pizza. Casual Dining. $13-$25 **AAA Inspector Notes:** A variety of Italian fare, from hand-tossed pizza to pasta, are served at this family-style cafe. Located by the skating rink, there is outdoor seating to watch the skaters go by. **Bar:** full bar. **Address:** 6001 Northstar Dr 96161 **Location:** I-80 exit 188 westbound; exit 188B (SR 267) eastbound, 5 mi se to Northstar Dr, then 2.1 mi sw to the Village-at-Northstar. L D CALL 🛄M

Learn about inspections and Diamond Ratings at AAA.com/Diamonds

TULELAKE (A-3) pop. 1,010, elev. 4,035'

About 10 miles south of Tulelake, past Newell on SR 139, a steel cross and a basalt rock and concrete monument commemorate the Tule Lake Segregation Center, a World War II internment camp for Japanese-Americans. The Tule Lake Unit is part of the WWII Valor in the Pacific National Monument.

The center operated 1942-46 and at its height housed more than 18,000 detainees. Tule Lake became known for residents' resistance to their internment and the protests and demonstrations that resulted from overcrowded living conditions. Over time much of the camp's acreage was sold, and buildings were demolished or removed from the site. A visitor center and memorial to the detainees are planned. For tour information phone (530) 260-0537.

A temporary visitor center is located at the Tulelake-Butte Valley Fair Museum of Local History, 800 S. Main St. in the Tulelake-Butte Valley Fairgrounds complex. On site is an exhibit about the internment camp, an original guard tower, part of a barracks, camp artifacts and a mural. The museum also covers other facets of area history; phone (530) 667-5312.

KLAMATH BASIN NATIONAL WILDLIFE REFUGES are near Tulelake; the visitor center is 5 mi. w. on East West Rd., then .5 mi. s. on Hill Rd. The refuges, which include the Lower Klamath and Tule Lake refuges, offer some 30 miles of auto tour routes for wildlife observation. An estimated 60 to 70 percent of Pacific Flyway waterfowl stop here in the fall, with peak migration from late October to mid-November. As many as 500 bald eagles can be seen during January and February, many from vantage points along the tour routes.

A self-guiding canoe trail at Tule Lake Refuge is open July through September. **Hours:** Visitor center open Mon.-Fri. 8-4:30, Sat.-Sun. and holidays 10-4. Closed Jan. 1, Thanksgiving and Christmas. **Cost:** Free. **Phone:** (530) 667-2231.

TURLOCK pop. 68,549

BEST WESTERN PLUS ORCHARD INN (209)667-2827

Hotel
$79-$84

AAA Benefit: Members save up to 20%, plus 10% bonus points with Best Western Rewards®.

Address: 5025 N Golden State Blvd 95382 **Location:** SR 99 exit Taylor Rd, just e. **Facility:** 72 units. 2 stories, exterior corridors. **Terms:** 3 day cancellation notice. **Amenities:** Some: high-speed Internet. **Pool(s):** outdoor. **Activities:** whirlpool. **Free Special Amenities: expanded continental breakfast and high-speed Internet.**

Visit AAA.com/Travel or CAA.ca/Travel for complete trip planning and reservations

CANDLEWOOD SUITES (209)250-1501

Extended Stay Hotel
$89-$249

Address: 1000 Powers Ct 95380 **Location:** SR 99 exit Monte Vista Ave, just w. **Facility:** 89 efficiencies. 3 stories, interior corridors. **Terms:** cancellation fee imposed. **Amenities:** high-speed Internet. **Activities:** exercise room. **Guest Services:** valet and coin laundry.

COMFORT SUITES (209)667-7777

Hotel
$79-$149

Address: 191 N Tully Rd 95380 **Location:** SR 99 exit West Main St E, just n. **Facility:** 71 units. 3 stories, interior corridors. **Terms:** cancellation fee imposed. **Amenities:** high-speed Internet. **Pool(s):** heated outdoor. **Activities:** whirlpool, exercise room. **Guest Services:** coin laundry. **Free Special Amenities: expanded continental breakfast and high-speed Internet.**

FAIRFIELD INN & SUITES BY MARRIOTT (209)668-3800

Hotel
$99-$179

AAA Benefit: AAA hotel discounts of 5% or more.

Address: 3301 Countryside Dr 95380 **Location:** SR 99 exit Monte Vista Ave, just e, then just n. **Facility:** 81 units. 3 stories, interior corridors. **Amenities:** high-speed Internet. **Pool(s):** outdoor. **Activities:** whirlpool, exercise room. **Guest Services:** valet and coin laundry. **Free Special Amenities: continental breakfast and high-speed Internet.**

HOLIDAY INN EXPRESS TURLOCK (209)664-9999

Hotel
$99-$109

Address: 3001 Hotel Dr 95380 **Location:** SR 99 exit Monte Vista Ave, just e. **Facility:** 78 units. 3 stories, interior corridors. **Pool(s):** outdoor. **Activities:** whirlpool, exercise room. **Guest Services:** valet and coin laundry. **Free Special Amenities: full breakfast and high-speed Internet.**

WHERE TO EAT

ANGELINI'S ITALIAN RESTAURANT 209/667-6644

Italian. Casual Dining. $7-$21 **AAA Inspector Notes:** Since 1985, this family-owned and -operated restaurant has taken pride in serving traditional favorites. Whether it is one of their pasta dishes, seafood, poultry, veal or specialty pizzas, there is something that will please everyone. Service is warm and friendly. **Bar:** beer & wine. **Address:** 2251 Geer Rd 95382 **Location:** SR 99 exit Monte Vista, 2 mi e, then 0.5 mi s at W Tuolumne Rd.

EL ROSAL AUTHENTIC MEXICAN CUISINE 209/669-6070

Mexican. Casual Dining. $6-$15 **AAA Inspector Notes:** Authentic preparations surround the menu at this local favorite with traditional favorites and a few specialties of their own made with homemade salsa and sauces. The super burrito is a great choice, be sure to try it with their special homemade green sauce. Portions are hearty so bring an appetite. **Bar:** full bar. **Address:** 3401 W Monte Vista Ave 95380 **Location:** SR 99 exit Monte Vista Ave, just w.

ROUND TABLE PIZZA 209/632-1083

Pizza. Casual Dining. $7-$28 **AAA Inspector Notes:** This casual, family-oriented pizza place features high-quality ingredients and dough rolled fresh daily. Distinctive specialty pizzas are piled high with toppings. **Bar:** beer & wine. **Address:** 2650 Geer Rd 95382 **Location:** Just s of E Monte Vista Ave.

TWAIN HARTE pop. 2,226

MCCAFFREY HOUSE BED & BREAKFAST INN
209/586-0757

Bed & Breakfast
$149-$199

Address: 23251 Hwy 108 95383 **Location:** On SR 108, 0.5 mi e; just beyond 4000' elevation marker. Located in a quiet area. **Facility:** Inviting paths wind through the forest surrounding this small country-style inn, which features guest rooms with traditional décor. 8 units, some two bedrooms. 3 stories (no elevator), interior corridors. **Terms:** 2 night minimum stay - weekends, 8 day cancellation notice-fee imposed. **Free Special Amenities: full breakfast and high-speed Internet.**

TWIN BRIDGES (E-4) elev. 6,115'

RECREATIONAL ACTIVITIES
Skiing

• **Sierra-at-Tahoe** is 4 mi. e. on US 50, then 2.4 mi. s. to 1111 Sierra-at-Tahoe Rd. **Hours:** Mon.-Fri. 9-4, Sat.-Sun. 8:30-4, mid-Nov. to mid-Apr. **Phone:** (530) 659-7453.

UKIAH (D-1) pop. 16,075, elev. 635'
• **Attractions map p. 566**
• **Part of Wine Country area — see map p. 562**

The center of a flourishing wine region, Ukiah's name derives from a Pomo Indian word meaning "deep valley." Two popular annual events take place at the Redwood Empire Fairgrounds, 1055 N. State St. The Redwood Empire Spring Fair in early June offers craft, gardening and home improvement vendors, carnival rides and a barbecue grilling competition. It's followed in early August by the 4-day Redwood Empire Fair, a summer celebration with a circus, jugglers, nightly concerts, food booths, farm animals, tractor races and other activities. For information about either event phone (707) 462-3884.

Greater Ukiah Chamber of Commerce: 309 E. Perkins St., Ukiah, CA 95482. **Phone:** (707) 462-4705.

GRACE HUDSON MUSEUM AND SUN HOUSE, 431 S. Main St., is a complex that includes a historic house, a park and a museum of art, history and anthropology. The museum displays works by noted painter Grace Carpenter Hudson, who chose Pomo Indians as her subjects; a collection of Pomo Indian basketry; family artifacts and historical photographs; and varied rotating exhibitions. Sun House was the home of the artist, who lived there for 25 years before her death in 1937.

Time: Allow 1 hour minimum. **Hours:** Museum open Wed.-Sat. 10-4:30 (also first Fri. of the month 4:30-8), Sun. noon-4:30. Free guided 30-minute tours of Sun House are available Wed.-Sun. noon-3. Closed major holidays. **Cost:** $4; $3 (ages 60+ and students with ID); $10 (family); free (first Fri. of the month). **Phone:** (707) 467-2836.

LAKE MENDOCINO VISITOR CENTER is .2 mi. s. of SR 20 at Marina Dr. The center has exhibits about the lake, Pomo Indian culture and the Coyote Valley.

The Pomo Cultural Center features displays of Pomo Indian crafts and decorative arts. Guided tours are available by appointment.

Note: The Pomo Cultural Center is currently closed for renovations; phone ahead for reopening information. **Hours:** Wed.-Sun. 9-5, mid-Apr. through Sept. 30; Sat.-Sun. 1-5, Oct. 1 to mid-Nov. Phone ahead to confirm schedule. **Cost:** Free. **Phone:** (707) 467-4200.

BEST WESTERN PLUS ORCHARD INN   (707)462-1514

Hotel
$99-$170

AAA Benefit: Members save up to 20%, plus 10% bonus points with Best Western Rewards®.

Address: 555 S Orchard Ave 95482 **Location:** US 101 exit Gobbi St, 0.5 mi w. **Facility:** 54 units. 2 stories (no elevator), interior corridors. **Amenities:** high-speed Internet. **Pool(s):** outdoor. **Activities:** whirlpool, exercise room. **Guest Services:** coin laundry. **Free Special Amenities: local telephone calls and high-speed Internet.**

COMFORT INN & SUITES   (707)462-3442

Hotel $89-$149 **Address:** 1220 Airport Park Blvd 95482 **Location:** US 101 exit Talmage Rd, just w, then just s. **Facility:** 63 units. 2 stories, interior corridors. **Terms:** cancellation fee imposed. **Amenities:** high-speed Internet. **Pool(s):** heated outdoor. **Guest Services:** valet and coin laundry.

DAYS INN   (707)462-7584

Motel
$52-$109

Address: 950 N State St 95482 **Location:** US 101 exit N State St, 0.5 mi s. Located in Old Town. **Facility:** 54 units, some two bedrooms. 2 stories (no elevator), exterior corridors. **Terms:** cancellation fee imposed. **Amenities:** high-speed Internet. **Pool(s):** outdoor. **Free Special Amenities: expanded continental breakfast and high-speed Internet.**

DISCOVERY INN   (707)462-8873

Hotel
$79-$129

Address: 1340 N State St 95482 **Location:** US 101 exit N State St, just sw. **Facility:** 177 units, some two bedrooms and kitchens. 2 stories (no elevator), exterior corridors. **Pool(s):** outdoor. **Activities:** whirlpools, exercise room. **Guest Services:** coin laundry. **Free Special Amenities: expanded continental breakfast and manager's reception.**

FAIRFIELD INN & SUITES UKIAH/MENDOCINO
(707)463-3600

Hotel
$89-$169

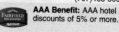

AAA Benefit: AAA hotel discounts of 5% or more.

Address: 1140 Airport Park Blvd 95482 **Location:** US 101 exit Talmage Rd, just w, then just s. **Facility:** 56 units. 3 stories, interior corridors. **Amenities:** high-speed Internet. **Pool(s):** heated indoor. **Activities:** whirlpool, exercise room. **Guest Services:** valet and coin laundry.

HAMPTON INN UKIAH 707/462-6555

Hotel
Rates not provided

AAA Benefit: Members save up to 10%!

Address: 1160 Airport Park Blvd 95482 **Location:** US 101 exit Talmage Rd, just w, then just s. **Facility:** 76 units. 3 stories, interior corridors. **Amenities:** video games (fee), high-speed Internet. **Pool(s):** heated outdoor. **Guest Services:** valet and coin laundry. **Free Special Amenities:** full breakfast and high-speed Internet.

QUALITY INN (707)462-2906

Motel
$75-$95

Address: 1050 S State St 95482 **Location:** US 101 exit Talmage Rd, 0.4 mi w, then just n. **Facility:** 40 units. 2 stories (no elevator), exterior corridors. **Pool(s):** outdoor. **Free Special Amenities:** full breakfast and high-speed Internet.

SUPER 8 UKIAH (707)468-8181

Motel
$59-$89

Address: 693 S Orchard Ave 95482 **Location:** US 101 exit Gobbi St W, just nw. Located in a commercial area. **Facility:** 54 units, some two bedrooms. 2 stories (no elevator), exterior corridors. **Amenities:** high-speed Internet. **Pool(s):** outdoor. **Activities:** whirlpool. **Guest Services:** coin laundry. **Free Special Amenities:** expanded continental breakfast and high-speed Internet.

/ SOME UNITS FEE

TRAVELODGE UKIAH (707)462-5745

Hotel
$70-$90

Address: 1720 N State St 95482 **Location:** US 101 exit N State St. **Facility:** 55 units. 2 stories, exterior corridors. **Terms:** cancellation fee imposed. **Amenities:** high-speed Internet. **Pool(s):** heated outdoor. **Activities:** whirlpool. **Guest Services:** coin laundry. **Free Special Amenities:** full breakfast and high-speed Internet.

/ SOME UNITS FEE

VAGABOND INN 707/462-8868

Motel
Rates not provided

Address: 601 Talmage Rd E 95482 **Location:** E off US 101 Bypass exit Talmage Rd. **Facility:** 39 units. 2 stories (no elevator), exterior corridors. **Pool(s):** outdoor. **Activities:** whirlpool. **Free Special Amenities:** continental breakfast and high-speed Internet.

VICHY HOT SPRINGS RESORT AND INN (707)462-9515

Historic Bed & Breakfast $195-$345 **Address:** 2605 Vichy Springs Rd 95482 **Location:** US 101 exit E Perkins St/Vichy Springs Rd, 3 mi e. **Facility:** On the property's 700-acre grounds is the only warm, carbonated mineral bath in North America as well as hiking and mountain biking trails. **Terms:** 7 day cancellation notice-fee imposed. **Pool(s):** outdoor. **Activities:** whirlpool, hiking trails. *Fee:* massage.

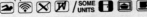

BE-BOPS DINER 707/462-1750

American. Casual Dining. $5-$10 **AAA Inspector Notes:** This spot is a complete replica of a 1950s diner from the neon sign to the music playing on the jukebox all the way to the menu items. **Address:** 1200 S State St 95482 **Location:** At Airport Rd.

ELLIE'S MUTT HUT & VEGETARIAN CAFE 707/468-5376

American. Quick Serve. $3-$9 **AAA Inspector Notes:** This eatery offers well-made comfort food ranging from hot dogs to Mexican nachos to vegetarian lasagna. **Bar:** beer & wine. **Address:** 732 S State St 95482 **Location:** US 101 exit Gobbi St, 0.5 mi w to S State St, then just s.

RUEN TONG 707/462-0238

Thai. Casual Dining. $10-$19 **AAA Inspector Notes:** Housed in a Victorian building, this gracious restaurant offers an extensive menu of Thai and some Indonesian items. Select from a variety of curries, classics such as Thai fried rice served in a half pineapple, and stuffed squid stir-fried with eggplant, bell peppers and Thai basil. **Bar:** beer & wine. **Reservations:** suggested. **Address:** 801 N State St 95482 **Location:** US 101 exit N State St, 0.7 mi s. **Parking:** on-site and street.

STARS RESTAURANT 707/462-1622

American. Casual Dining. $8-$19 **AAA Inspector Notes:** Ambience and decor may say diner but the little touches in the presentation set this restaurant apart. For the iced tea, there is a little paper umbrella, a skewered lemon, maraschino cherry and a sprig of mint. For the spaghetti and meatballs, parsley confetti scattered at the edge of the plate brightens up the classic dish. The garlic bread is hot, toasty and tasty. **Bar:** beer & wine. **Address:** 115 S Orchard Plaza 95482 **Location:** At E Perkins St; in Orchard Plaza Shopping Center.

WALTER'S CAFE 707/462-2080

International. Casual Dining. $9-$30 **AAA Inspector Notes:** The nondescript exterior of this café houses a sushi bar and main dining room with Thai accents. International cuisine offerings include sushi rolls, udon, mochi ice cream and appetizers ranging from coconut shrimp and entrées of pasta to hearty steak and lobster. **Bar:** full bar. **Reservations:** suggested. **Address:** 920 N State St 95482 **Location:** US 101 exit N State St, 0.5 mi s. **Parking:** on-site and street.

UNION CITY (D-9) pop. 69,516, elev. 92'
• Hotels p. 550 • Restaurants p. 550

FLIGHT 93 MEMORIAL is at jct. Alvarado-Niles Rd. and Dyer St. in Sugar Mill Landing Park. It was built for the 40 passengers and crew of the fourth plane hijacked on Sept. 11, 2001, which crashed in a Shanksville, Pa. field. The flight was bound for San Francisco International Airport, and the memorial honors and remembers its passengers and crew, many of whom were from the San Francisco Bay Area.

A flowing line of 40 individual granite stones represents each person aboard the flight; each stone is engraved with the hero's name, age and hometown. At the memorial entrance is the Circle of Remembrance; in the middle of the circle stands the Tree of Remembrance, surrounded by three granite stones depicting the flight, the story of the memorial and the names of donors/sponsors.

At the memorial's opposite end is the Circle of Hope, where a U.S. flagpole is encircled by handmade tiles created by local children that show images of their vision for the future. Six benches at the site allow visitors to pause for reflection. **Hours:** Daily 24 hours. The memorial is illuminated from dusk until dawn. **Cost:** Free.

CROWNE PLAZA OAKLAND SOUTH/UNION CITY
(510)489-2200

Hotel
$99-$159

Address: 32083 Alvarado-Niles Rd 94587 **Location:** I-880 exit Alvarado-Niles Rd, just e. **Facility:** 268 units. 6 stories, interior corridors. **Amenities:** high-speed Internet. **Pool(s):** outdoor. **Activities:** whirlpool, exercise room. **Guest Services:** valet and coin laundry. **Free Special Amenities: local telephone calls and high-speed Internet.**

HOLIDAY INN EXPRESS UNION CITY
(510)475-0600

Hotel $99-$169 **Address:** 31140 Alvarado-Niles Rd 94587 **Location:** I-880 exit Alvarado-Niles Rd, just w. **Facility:** 77 units. 4 stories, interior corridors. *Some:* high-speed Internet. **Pool(s):** outdoor. **Activities:** whirlpool, exercise room. **Guest Services:** valet and coin laundry.

WHERE TO EAT

FRESH CHOICE
510/675-0471

American. Cafeteria. $8-$15 **AAA Inspector Notes:** The salad bar of salad bars, the casual restaurant invites patrons to make their own or try one of the already prepared varieties. Other items include freshly baked breads, pizza and soup, as well as make-your-own sundaes for dessert. **Bar:** beer & wine. **Address:** 32155 Union Landing Blvd 94587 **Location:** I-880 exit Alvarado-Niles Rd, just w, then just n. L D

PASTA POMODORO
510/429-1991

Italian. Casual Dining. $8-$18 **AAA Inspector Notes:** Families are welcomed at this laid-back restaurant, which brings in plenty of loyal locals who enjoy its varied Italian favorites, including tempting pasta and chicken dishes. **Bar:** beer & wine. **Address:** 32216 Dyer St 94587 **Location:** I-880 exit Alvarado-Niles Rd, just w; in Union Landing Shopping Center. L D CALL &M

UPPER LAKE pop. 1,052
• Part of Wine Country area — see map p. 562

SUPER 8
(707)275-0888

Motel
$70-$229

Address: 450 E Hwy 20 95485 **Location:** Jct SR 29, 0.5 mi e. **Facility:** 34 units. 2 stories (no elevator), exterior corridors. **Terms:** 3 day cancellation notice. **Pool(s):** outdoor. **Activities:** whirlpool. **Guest Services:** coin laundry. **Free Special Amenities: expanded continental breakfast and high-speed Internet.**

TALLMAN HOTEL
(707)275-2244

Country Inn $149-$269 **Address:** 9550 Main St 95485 **Location:** Just n of SR 20; downtown. **Facility:** Rooms are located in the historic 1890s hotel and in newer outbuildings, all having been fully refurbished and furnished with Eastlake-style furniture to give the boutique-style hotel a modern feel. 17 units. 2 stories (no elevator), interior/exterior corridors. **Terms:** 2 night minimum stay - seasonal and/or weekends, 30 day cancellation notice-fee imposed. **Pool(s):** heated outdoor. **Activities:** whirlpool.

WHERE TO EAT

BLUE WING SALOON RESTAURANT
707/275-2233

American. Gastro Pub. $11-$26 **AAA Inspector Notes:** The restaurant is a beautiful replica of the town's original 1880's saloon. Menu items range from burgers to salmon with risotto and a decadent pot de crème for a sweet ending. Service as with the food is just right - not too casual and not too white cloth. There's a good selection of local wines and beer to accompany your meal. **Bar:** full bar. **Address:** 9520 Main St 95485 **Location:** Just n of SR 20; downtown. **Parking:** street only. L D

VACAVILLE (B-9) pop. 92,428, elev. 179'

VACAVILLE MUSEUM, A CENTER FOR SOLANO COUNTY HISTORY, 213 Buck Ave., displays photographs, documents, artwork and memorabilia pertaining to the history and culture of Solano County. The museum also contains changing exhibits and an interpretive garden of native plants. **Time:** Allow 30 minutes minimum. **Hours:** Wed.-Sun. 1-4:30. **Cost:** $3; $2 (ages 0-12 and 62+). **Phone:** (707) 447-4513.

BEST WESTERN HERITAGE INN
(707)448-8453

Motel
$60-$85

AAA Benefit: Members save up to 20%, plus 10% bonus points with Best Western Rewards®.

Address: 1420 E Monte Vista Ave 95688 **Location:** I-80 exit Monte Vista Ave, just nw. **Facility:** 41 units. 2 stories (no elevator), exterior corridors. **Pool(s):** outdoor. **Free Special Amenities: continental breakfast and high-speed Internet.**

COMFORT SUITES
(707)446-3000

Hotel $79-$119 **Address:** 191 Lawrence Dr 95687 **Location:** I-80 exit Orange Dr eastbound, 0.5 mi ne; exit Monte Vista Ave westbound to freeway overpass to E Nut Tree Pkwy, then just ne. **Facility:** 72 units. 3 stories, interior corridors. **Terms:** cancellation fee imposed. **Amenities:** high-speed Internet. **Pool(s):** heated indoor. **Activities:** whirlpool, exercise room. **Guest Services:** valet and coin laundry.

EXTENDED STAYAMERICA-SACRAMENTO-VACAVILLE
(707)469-1371

Extended Stay Hotel $74-$89 **Address:** 799 Orange Dr 95687 **Location:** I-80 exit Leisure Town Rd, just s; just e of I-505 interchange. **Facility:** 92 efficiencies. 3 stories, interior corridors. **Guest Services:** coin laundry.

FAIRFIELD INN BY MARRIOTT
(707)469-0800

Hotel $84-$139 **Address:** 370 Orange Dr 95687 **Location:** I-80 exit Orange Dr eastbound, 0.5 mi ne; exit Monte Vista Ave westbound to freeway overpass to E Nut Tree Pkwy. **Facility:** 81 units. 3 stories, interior corridors. **Pool(s):** heated indoor. **Activities:** whirlpool. **Guest Services:** valet laundry.

AAA Benefit: AAA hotel discounts of 5% or more.

HAMPTON INN & SUITES VACAVILLE/NAPA VALLEY
(707)469-6200

Hotel
$99-$129

AAA Benefit: Members save up to 10%!

Address: 800 Mason St 95688 **Location:** I-80 exit Davis St eastbound, just n, then ne on Porter Way; exit Mason St westbound, just w; jct Porter Way. **Facility:** 83 units. 3 stories, interior corridors. **Terms:** 1-7 night minimum stay, cancellation fee imposed. **Amenities:** high-speed Internet. **Pool(s):** heated outdoor. **Activities:** whirlpool, exercise room. **Guest Services:** valet and coin laundry. **Free Special Amenities: full breakfast and high-speed Internet.**

HOLIDAY INN EXPRESS HOTEL & SUITES VACAVILLE
(707)451-3500

▼▼▼ Hotel $89-$129 Address: 151 Lawrence Dr 95687 Location: I-80 exit Orange Dr eastbound, 0.5 mi ne; exit Monte Vista Ave westbound to freeway overpass to E Nut Tree Pkwy, then just ne. Facility: 91 units. 3 stories, interior corridors. Amenities: high-speed Internet, safes. Pool(s): heated indoor. Activities: whirlpool, exercise room. Guest Services: valet and coin laundry.

📶 CALL 🅶M 🛏 BIZ 📶 ✕ 🅱 🅱 🖥

QUALITY INN & SUITES VACAVILLE
(707)446-8888

▼▼ Motel $55-$109 Address: 1050 Orange Dr 95687 Location: I-80 exit Leisure Town Rd, just s, then just e. Facility: 114 units. 2 stories (no elevator), exterior corridors. Terms: cancellation fee imposed. Amenities: high-speed Internet. Pool(s): outdoor. Activities: whirlpool, exercise room. Guest Services: valet and coin laundry.

📶 CALL 🅶M 🛏 📶 🅱 🅱 🖥 /SOME UNITS FEE 🐾

RESIDENCE INN BY MARRIOTT
(707)469-0300

▼▼▼ Extended Stay Hotel $109-$179 Address: 360 Orange Dr 95687 Location: I-80 exit Orange Dr eastbound, 0.5 mi ne; exit Monte Vista Ave westbound to freeway overpass to E Nut Tree Pkwy, then just ne. **AAA Benefit:** AAA hotel discounts of 5% or more.

Facility: 78 units, some two bedrooms, efficiencies and kitchens. 3 stories, interior corridors. Pool(s): heated indoor. Activities: whirlpool, sports court, exercise room. Guest Services: valet and coin laundry.

📶 CALL 🅶M 🛏 📶 ✕ 🅱 🅱 🖥 /SOME UNITS FEE 🐾

VACAVILLE COURTYARD BY MARRIOTT
(707)451-9000

▼▼▼ Hotel $99-$159 **COURTYARD** Marriott **AAA Benefit:** AAA hotel discounts of 5% or more.

Address: 120 Nut Tree Pkwy 95687 Location: I-80 exit Orange Dr eastbound, just w; exit Monte Vista Ave westbound, just ne to freeway overpass to E Nut Tree Pkwy, then just w. Facility: 127 units. 2 stories (no elevator), interior corridors. Amenities: video games (fee). Pool(s): heated outdoor. Activities: whirlpool, exercise room. Guest Services: valet and coin laundry. **Free Special Amenities:** local telephone calls and high-speed Internet.

SAVE ECO 🍴 🍸 CALL 🅶M 🛏 📶 ✕ 📹 🅱 🖥 /SOME UNITS FEE 🐾 🅱 🅱

WHERE TO EAT

BLACK OAK RESTAURANT
707/448-1311

▼▼ 💎 American. Family Dining. $8-$14 AAA Inspector Notes: Extensive menu offerings include seafood and pasta dishes, sandwiches, burgers and Mexican specialties. A senior menu is available with select items. Booth seating lends to this roadside restaurant's casual appeal. Bar: beer & wine. Address: 320 Orange Dr 95687 Location: South side of I-80 at I-505. B L

MURILLO'S
707/447-3704

▼▼ Mexican. Casual Dining. $7-$15 AAA Inspector Notes: A long-established favorite among locals and sports teams, this Mexican restaurant presents a menu of traditional dishes, including fajitas, daily lunch specials and varied house specialties. A dining patio is out back. Bar: full bar. Address: 1591 E Monte Vista Ave 95687 Location: I-80 exit E Monte Vista Ave, just ne, then just w. L D

PURE GRAIN BAKERY & CAFE
707/447-4121

▼ Breads/Pastries. Quick Serve. $5-$8 AAA Inspector Notes: Overlooking the town square, this cafe serves breakfast and lunch. Cold and grilled sandwiches, seasonal salads, pastries, desserts and some German specialty items are served. Outside patio seating is available. Address: 11 Town Square, Suite A 95687 Location: I-80 exit Mason St westbound, just w, just n on Davis St, then just w on Main St; exit Davis St eastbound, just n, then just w on Main St. Parking: street only. B L

VALLECITO (F-4) pop. 442, elev. 1,745'

MOANING CAVERN, 2 mi. s.w. on Parrots Ferry Rd., was explored in 1851 by gold miners. Native Americans had been aware of the cave for centuries, however, due to the haunting, moaning sounds emanating from the cavern's entrance. Guided 45-minute walking tours descend 165 feet, 100 feet of which are via a steel spiral staircase that leads into a space big enough to hold the Statue of Liberty.

Visitors also can descend into the cavern on a 165-foot rappel (no experience necessary) or take a 3-hour Adventure Trip into its farthest depths. Gemstone mining, zip lines and a nature trail also are on site.

Hours: Daily 9-6, early Apr. to mid-Sept.; Mon.-Fri. 10-4, Sat.-Sun. and holidays 9-4, rest of year. Phone ahead to confirm schedule. **Cost:** Walking tour $14.95; $7.95 (ages 3-12). **Phone:** (209) 736-2708 or (866) 762-2837. 🅰

VALLEJO (C-8) pop. 115,942, elev. 40'
• Hotels p. 552 • Restaurants p. 552
• Attractions map p. 568

In 1851 Gen. Mariano Guadalupe Vallejo (val-LEH-hoh) founded the town that bears his name at the junction of the Carquinez Straits and the Napa River. The new town rose in prominence, serving as the state capital on two occasions between 1851 and 1853. Today Vallejo is home to the California Maritime Academy and Touro University.

From 1854 until 1996 Mare Island Naval Shipyard was a vital defense installation; during World War I the destroyer USS *Ward* was built here in less than 18 days. After it closed in the 1990s, the Mare Island Historic Park Foundation purchased some of the facilities in order to preserve them. Of particular interest is St. Peter's Chapel, which dates from 1901 and is believed to be the oldest military chapel in the country. Phone (707) 557-1538 to make a tour reservation and view the chapel's 29 Tiffany windows.

Vallejo Transit/Baylink Ferry Service provides transportation from both Pier 41 and the Ferry Building in San Francisco to the Vallejo Ferry Terminal at 289 Mare Island Way. From the terminal you can catch a shuttle bus to Six Flags Discovery Kingdom theme park as well as destinations in the Napa Valley. For schedule and fare information phone (707) 643-3779 or (877) 643-3779.

Vallejo Convention & Visitors Bureau: Vallejo Ferry Terminal, 289 Mare Island Way, Vallejo, CA 94590. **Phone:** (707) 642-3653 or (800) 482-5535.

MARE ISLAND HISTORIC PARK FOUNDATION ARTIFACTS MUSEUM is on Mare Island, at Railroad Ave. and 8th St. in Building 46. The museum, in a building that served as a pipe shop from 1855 to 1984, is easy to find—a 35-foot patrol boat with shark's teeth is parked in front. On display are artifacts from the Mare Island Naval Shipyard, based in Vallejo for the entirety of its 142-year history. Tools, historic radios, uniforms and photographs underscore the shipyard's significance during World War II. **Time:** Allow 1 hour minimum. **Hours:** Mon.-Fri. 10-2 (also first and third full weekends of the month 10-4). **Cost:** $4; free (ages 0-12). **Phone:** (707) 557-1538.

SIX FLAGS DISCOVERY KINGDOM is at 1001 Fairgrounds Dr. This 135-acre wildlife park, oceanarium and theme park features rides, shows, play areas and educational encounters with wildlife for the entire family. A killer whale, dolphins, sea lions, birds, tigers and elephants are featured in daily shows.

Highlights include Odin's Temple of the Tiger, a tiger show and exhibit; Ocean Discovery, a 2-acre Caribbean-themed destination where families can touch and feed dolphins and stingrays and, for an additional fee, swim with dolphins; Elephant Encounter, where pachyderms are featured in demonstration shows and rides; Lorikeet Aviary, where visitors can feed colorful Australian birds; Shark Experience, where the predators can be seen through an underwater tunnel; and Tava's Jungleland, a children's adventure area with family rides, interactive zones and up-close animal attractions.

Roller coasters include Medusa, a floorless, seven-loop mega coaster; Vertical Velocity, a spiraling coaster that propels riders up and down two 150-foot towers; ROAR, a classic wooden coaster; Kong; Boomerang; and Superman Ultimate Flight. The SkyScreamer swing ride spins visitors around a tower at speeds up to 43 mph.

Allow a full day. **Hours:** Opens daily at 10:30, Memorial Day weekend to mid-Aug.; Fri.-Sun. at 10:30, May 1-day before Memorial Day weekend and in Oct.; Sat.-Sun. at 10:30, Mar.-Apr., mid-Aug. through Sept. 30 and Nov.-Dec. Closing times vary. Phone ahead to confirm schedule. **Cost:** $54.99; $37.99 (under 48 inches tall); free (ages 0-2). AAA members save on select services and merchandise. See guest relations for details. **Parking:** $15. **Phone:** (707) 644-4000 to verify schedule and prices.

VALLEJO NAVAL AND HISTORICAL MUSEUM, in the old Vallejo City Hall building at 734 Marin St., offers exhibits about naval history, including artifacts and papers from Mare Island Naval Shipyard. Ship models, murals and an operating periscope are displayed. The museum also has exhibits about local and regional history.

Hours: Tues.-Sat. noon-4. Guided 40-minute tours are given; reservations are required. Closed major holidays. **Cost:** $5; $3 (ages 12-17 and 60+). **Phone:** (707) 643-0077.

BEST WESTERN PLUS INN & SUITES AT DISCOVERY KINGDOM   707/554-9655

Hotel
Rates not provided

AAA Benefit: Members save up to 20%, plus 10% bonus points with Best Western Rewards®.

Address: 1596 Fairgrounds Dr 94589 **Location:** I-80 exit SR 37 N (Marine World Pkwy), 0.3 mi w. **Facility:** 117 units. 3 stories, interior corridors. **Amenities:** high-speed Internet. **Pool(s):** heated outdoor. **Activities:** whirlpool. **Guest Services:** coin laundry, area transportation-Six Flags Discovery Kingdom. **Free Special Amenities:** local telephone calls and high-speed Internet.

COMFORT INN   707/648-1400

Hotel. Rates not provided. **Address:** 1185 Admiral Callaghan Ln 94591 **Location:** I-80 exit Columbus Pkwy, 0.5 mi n, then 0.3 mi s. **Facility:** 80 units. 2 stories (no elevator), interior corridors. **Pool(s):** outdoor. **Activities:** sauna, whirlpool, exercise room. **Guest Services:** coin laundry.

COURTYARD BY MARRIOTT   (707)644-1200

Hotel $79-$299 **Address:** 1000 Fairgrounds Dr 94589 **Location:** I-80 exit SR 37 (Marine World Pkwy), 0.3 mi n. Opposite Six Flags Discovery Kingdom Theme Park. **Facility:** 172 units. 5 stories, interior corridors. **Amenities:** *Some:* high-speed Internet. **Pool(s):** heated outdoor. **Activities:** whirlpool, exercise room. **Guest Services:** valet and coin laundry, area transportation-within 5 mi.

AAA Benefit: AAA hotel discounts of 5% or more.

WHERE TO EAT

BUTTERCUP GRILL & BAR   707/643-9030

American. Casual Dining. $8-$17 **AAA Inspector Notes:** Extensive choices of traditional comfort foods--including great sandwiches, hamburgers, soups and desserts--are served in hearty portions. The staff is warm and welcoming. **Bar:** full bar. **Address:** 3288 Sonoma Blvd 94590 **Location:** At Valle Vista Ave.

B   L   D   CALL

PASTA POMODORO   707/557-6100

Italian. Casual Dining. $8-$18 **AAA Inspector Notes:** Families are welcomed at this laid-back restaurant, which brings in plenty of loyal locals who enjoy its varied Italian favorites, including tempting pasta and chicken dishes. **Bar:** beer & wine. **Address:** 163 Plaza Dr 94591 **Location:** I-80 exit Redwood St, just w to Admiral Callaghan Ln, then just s.   L   D   CALL

ROUND TABLE PIZZA

Pizza. Casual Dining. $7-$28 **AAA Inspector Notes:** This casual, family-oriented pizza place features high-quality ingredients and dough rolled fresh daily. Distinctive specialty pizzas are piled high with toppings. **Bar:** beer & wine.   L   D

For additional information, visit AAA.com

LOCATIONS:

Address: 4300 Sonoma Blvd, Suite 100 94589 **Location:** At Yolano Dr. **Phone:** 707/552-9747

Address: 2633 Springs Rd 94591 **Location:** Just w of Columbus Pkwy. **Phone:** 707/649-1234

VOLCANO (E-4) pop. 115, elev. 2,053'

Volcano, in a deep depression resembling a crater, was aptly named. During the gold rush the city was famous for its dance halls and saloons. Daffodil Hill, 3 miles north, is covered with daffodils originally planted during the 1850s. Blooming season is late March to mid-April.

BLACK CHASM CAVERN is at 15701 Pioneer-Volcano Rd. The cavern has foot-long crystal formations, large rooms and deep turquoise lakes. Visitors descend 60 feet (152 steps) on a 45-minute tour to view stalactites, draperies and flowstones. The Landmark Room is known for its array of white helictite crystals. The temperature within the cave is a constant 57 degrees F. Visitors can take an above-ground labyrinth tour, search for gemstones and hike a nature trail.

Time: Allow 1 hour minimum. **Hours:** Daily 9-5. **Cost:** $14.95; $7.95 (ages 3-12). An additional fee is charged for gemstone mining. **Phone:** (209) 736-2708 or (866) 762-2837.

WALNUT CREEK (C-9) pop. 64,173, elev. 135'

- Restaurants p. 554
- Hotels & Restaurants map & index p. 254

THE GARDENS AT HEATHER FARM is at 1540 Marchbanks Dr. Paths wind among 6 acres, which feature 23 demonstration gardens. The Cowden Rose Garden contains more than 150 varieties of roses, with thousands of blooming flowers in the summer and fall. Water conservation, sensory, butterfly, native plant, waterfall and rock gardens also can be seen. **Hours:** Daily dawn-dusk. **Cost:** Free. **Phone:** (925) 947-1678.

Pleasant Hill/Contra Costa Centre, 4

LINDSAY WILDLIFE MUSEUM, 1931 First Ave., wears three hats: natural history museum, environmental education center and wildlife rehabilitation hospital. Visitors can, however, see more than 50 species of non-releasable native California animals, along with changing natural history and art exhibits. Other facilities include a pet education center and a hands-on discovery room for children. The exhibit Raptors: Hunters in the Sky features several interactive displays and a model raptor. At Wildlife Hospital: Behind the Scenes, visitors can observe the work of veterinary staff and volunteers behind one-way glass; more than 5,000 injured and orphaned wild animals are cared for each year.

Kids can participate in a rock-climbing activity. Also on site are a functioning beehive and a burrowing animals exhibit with a crawl-through tunnel. A life-size model of the Balancing Rock formation atop nearby Mount Diablo, complete with representations of native plants and animals, rises two stories through an opening in the ceiling.

Hours: Wed.-Sun. 10-5, mid-June through Aug. 31; Wed.-Fri. noon-5, Sat.-Sun. 10-5, rest of year. Holiday hours vary. **Cost:** $7; $6 (ages 65+ and students with ID); $5 (ages 2-17). **Phone:** (925) 935-1978.

MOUNT DIABLO STATE PARK—see Danville p. 93.

THE RUTH BANCROFT GARDEN is at 1552 Bancroft Rd., with a second entrance half a block north. Planted by Ruth Bancroft in 1972, the garden is a model of the use of xerophytes (plants that require little water). Among the more than 2,000 types of water-hoarding succulents and other drought-tolerant plants that can be seen are aloes, agaves, yuccas and echeverias; the plantings showcase their unusual forms and colors.

Time: Allow 1 hour minimum. **Hours:** Self-guiding tours daily 10-4. Docent-led tours are given Fri.-Sat. at 10, Sun. at 11, Apr.-Oct.; Sat. at 10, rest of year. The garden is closed for brief periods in spring and fall; phone ahead to confirm dates. **Cost:** $10; $7 (ages 65+ and students with ID); free (ages 0-11). **Phone:** (925) 944-9352.

EMBASSY SUITES HOTEL   (925)934-2500

Hotel $109-$219

AAA Benefit: Members save 5% or more!

Address: 1345 Treat Blvd 94597 **Location:** I-680 exit Geary Rd/Treat Blvd northbound; exit Oak Park Blvd southbound, then e. Pleasant Hill/Contra Costa Centre, 4. **Facility:** 249 units. 8 stories, interior corridors. **Parking:** valet only. **Terms:** 1-7 night minimum stay, cancellation fee imposed. **Dining:** Embassy Grill, see separate listing. **Pool(s):** heated indoor. **Activities:** whirlpool, exercise room. **Guest Services:** valet and coin laundry. **Free Special Amenities:** full breakfast and manager's reception.

HOLIDAY INN EXPRESS WALNUT CREEK   (925)932-3332

Hotel $89-$199 **Address:** 2730 N Main St 94597 **Location:** I-680 exit N Main St, just n. Pleasant Hill/Contra Costa Centre, 4. **Facility:** 161 units. 2 stories, interior corridors. **Terms:** cancellation fee imposed, resort fee. **Pool(s):** heated outdoor. **Activities:** whirlpool, exercise room. **Guest Services:** valet laundry.

RENAISSANCE CLUB SPORT   (925)938-8700

Hotel $139-$309

RENAISSANCE HOTELS & RESORTS

AAA Benefit: AAA hotel discounts of 5% or more.

Address: 2805 Jones Rd 94597 **Location:** I-680 exit Geary Rd/Treat Blvd, just e. Pleasant Hill/Contra Costa Centre, 4. **Facility:** This attractively appointed hotel doubles as a fitness resort offering guests access to various sport activities, including a full-service spa. 175 units. 6 stories, interior corridors. **Parking:** valet only. **Amenities:** high-speed Internet. *Some:* safes. **Dining:** C Blue, see separate listing. **Pool(s):** 3 heated outdoor. **Activities:** saunas, whirlpools, sports court, basketball, volleyball, spa. **Guest Services:** valet laundry. **Free Special Amenities:** local telephone calls and high-speed Internet.

(See map & index p. 254.)

WALNUT CREEK MARRIOTT (925)934-2000 [37]

▼▼▼ **Hotel** $132-$256 **Address:** 2355 N Main St 94596 **Location:** I-680 exit N Main St, 0.3 mi e, then s at Parkside Dr. [⊞] Walnut Creek, 5. **Facility:** 338 units. 6 stories, interior corridors. **Parking:** on-site and valet. **Amenities:** *Some:* high-speed Internet (fee). **Dining:** Atriu, see separate listing. **Pool(s):** heated outdoor. **Activities:** whirlpool, exercise room. **Guest Services:** valet laundry, area transportation-within 3 mi.

AAA Benefit: AAA hotel discounts of 5% or more.

[ECO] [🍴] [🛗] [👤] CALL [&M] [🏊] [BIZ] [📶] [✕] [▭] / SOME UNITS FEE [🐾] [🔒] [🖥] [📶]

WHERE TO EAT

ATRIU 925/934-2000 [34]

▼▼▼ American. Casual Dining. $10-$24 **AAA Inspector Notes:** Just off the main lobby and under a glass atrium ceiling, the eatery presents a menu of hearty sandwiches, wraps and specialty salads, in addition to grilled steaks, seafood and pasta. **Bar:** full bar. **Address:** 2355 N Main St 94596 **Location:** I-680 exit N Main St, 0.3 mi e, then s at Parkside Dr; in Walnut Creek Marriott. [⊞] Walnut Creek, 5. **Parking:** on-site and valet.

[B] [L] [D] CALL [&M] [📶]

BLACK BEAR DINER 925/941-0000

▼▼ American. Casual Dining. $7-$18 **AAA Inspector Notes:** A homey atmosphere characterizes this family-oriented restaurant. Familiar comfort foods, such as meatloaf with mashed potatoes, are at the heart of the menu and are served in generous portions. **Bar:** beer & wine. **Address:** 700 Bancroft Rd 94598 **Location:** I-680 exit Treat Blvd, 1 mi e, then just s; in Countrywood Shopping Center. [⊞] Pleasant Hill/Contra Costa Centre, 4.

[B] [L] [D] CALL [&M] [📶]

BUTTERCUP GRILL & BAR 925/932-2763

▼▼ American. Casual Dining. $7-$20 **AAA Inspector Notes:** Families are welcome at this casual restaurant, where choices range from burgers and sandwiches to entrées and breakfast items. Be sure to save room for one of the special desserts that are homemade pies and cakes. **Bar:** full bar. **Address:** 660 Ygnacio Valley Rd 94596 **Location:** I-680 exit Ygnacio Valley Rd, 0.5 mi e; between N Broadway and Civic Dr. [⊞] Walnut Creek, 5.

[B] [L] [D] [📶]

C BLUE 925/942-6360

▼▼ American. Casual Dining. $12-$26 **AAA Inspector Notes:** This kitchen's open grill prepares a variety of menu selections, including fresh fish, beef and chicken dishes. **Bar:** full bar. **Reservations:** suggested. **Address:** 2805 Jones Rd 94597 **Location:** I-680 exit Geary Rd/Treat Blvd, just e; in Renaissance Club Sport. [⊞] Pleasant Hill/Contra Costa Centre, 4. **Parking:** on-site (fee) and valet. [L] [D] CALL [&M] [📶]

THE CHEESECAKE FACTORY 925/952-8450 [39]

▼▼▼ American. Casual Dining. $6-$28 **AAA Inspector Notes:** A display case of mouthwatering cheesecakes is the first thing visitors see as they walk through the door. The extensive menu incorporates many types of cuisine, including Asian, Italian, Greek and Spanish. **Bar:** full bar. **Address:** 1181 Locust St 94596 **Location:** I-680 exit Olympic Blvd, 0.3 mi e, then just s; in Plaza Escuela. [⊞] Walnut Creek, 5. [L] [D] CALL [&M] [📶]

EMBASSY GRILL 925/934-2500

▼▼▼ American. Casual Dining. $10-$22 **AAA Inspector Notes:** Diners unwind in a relaxed setting to sample any of a variety of steak, seafood and pasta dishes, which are prepared in an open grill kitchen. The dining room looks out on the patio and garden area. **Bar:** full bar. **Reservations:** suggested. **Address:** 1345 Treat Blvd 94597 **Location:** I-680 exit Geary Rd/Treat Blvd northbound; exit Oak Park Blvd southbound, then e; in Embassy Suites Hotel. [⊞] Pleasant Hill/Contra Costa Centre, 4. **Parking:** valet only.

[L] [D] CALL [&M] [📶]

FRESH CHOICE 925/938-1529

▼▼ American. Cafeteria. $8-$15 **AAA Inspector Notes:** The salad bar of salad bars, the casual restaurant invites patrons to make their own or try one of the already prepared varieties. Other items include freshly baked breads, pizza and soup, as well as make-your-own sundaes for dessert. **Bar:** beer & wine. **Address:** 1275 S Main St 94596 **Location:** I-680 exit S Main St, just n; between Newell Ave and Botelho Dr. [⊞] Walnut Creek, 5. **Parking:** street only.

[L] [D] [📶]

IL FORNAIO 925/296-0100 [36]

▼▼▼ Italian. Fine Dining. $9-$36 **AAA Inspector Notes:** Accomplished servers begin guests' experiences with crisp, crusty bread hot from the oven. Pasta and flavorful sauces enhance the roasted meats and vegetables. The spacious restaurant thoughtfully replicates the trattorias of Italy. **Bar:** full bar. **Address:** 1430 Mt. Diablo Blvd 94596 **Location:** I-680 exit Main St, 1 mi n, then just e. [⊞] Walnut Creek, 5. **Parking:** street only.

[B] [L] [D] CALL [&M] [📶]

MASSIMO RISTORANTE 925/932-1474 [35]

▼▼▼ Northern Italian. Fine Dining. $10-$35 **AAA Inspector Notes:** An attractive, contemporary décor punctuates this downtown restaurant. Diners can relax in the casual and friendly atmosphere while enjoying a variety of fresh pasta, veal and seafood. **Bar:** full bar. **Reservations:** suggested. **Address:** 1604 Locust St 94596 **Location:** I-680 exit Ygnacio Valley Rd, s on California Blvd, then e on La Cassie Ave. [⊞] Walnut Creek, 5. **Parking:** street only.

[L] [D] [📶]

P.F. CHANG'S CHINA BISTRO 925/979-9070 [37]

▼▼▼ Chinese. Fine Dining. $10-$20 **AAA Inspector Notes:** Trendy, upscale decor provides a pleasant backdrop for New Age Chinese dining. Appetizers, soups and salads are a meal by themselves. Vegetarian plates and sides, noodles, meins, chicken and meat dishes are created from exotic, fresh ingredients. **Bar:** full bar. **Address:** 1205 Broadway Plaza 94596 **Location:** I-680 exit Main St E, 0.5 mi n, then just e. [⊞] Walnut Creek, 5. **Parking:** street only.

[L] [D] CALL [&M] [📶]

ROUND TABLE PIZZA 925/945-7878

▼ Pizza. Casual Dining. $7-$28 **AAA Inspector Notes:** This casual, family-oriented pizza place features high-quality ingredients and dough rolled fresh daily. Distinctive specialty pizzas are piled high with toppings. **Bar:** beer & wine. **Address:** 1776 N Broadway 94596 **Location:** Just n of Civic Dr. [L] [D]

RUTH'S CHRIS STEAK HOUSE 925/977-3477 [38]

▼▼▼ Steak. Fine Dining. $23-$70 **AAA Inspector Notes:** The main fare is steak, which is prepared from several cuts of prime beef and cooked to perfection, but the menu also lists lamb, chicken and seafood dishes. Guests should come hungry because the side dishes, which are among the a la carte offerings, could make a meal in themselves. **Bar:** full bar. **Reservations:** suggested. **Address:** 1553 Olympic Blvd, Bldg E 94596 **Location:** I-680 exit Olympic Blvd, 0.3 mi e. [⊞] Walnut Creek, 5. **Parking:** street only.

[D] CALL [&M] [📶]

WATSONVILLE (G-3) pop. 51,199, elev. 23'

Watsonville is in the lush Pajaro Valley. Its economy relies heavily on the growing of apples, strawberries and flowers. The main harvest time is celebrated in late September and early October.

Pajaro Valley Chamber of Commerce: 44 Brennan St., P.O. Box 1748, Watsonville, CA 95077. **Phone:** (831) 724-3900.

Self-guiding tours: Maps for walking and driving tours of Watsonville and the Pajaro Valley are available from the chamber of commerce.

AGRICULTURAL HISTORY PROJECT is on SR 152 (E. Lake Ave.) at the Santa Cruz County Fairgrounds. The agricultural history of California's central coast is depicted at this museum, which displays collections of antique farming implements such as tools, tractors and plows. An area devoted to the dairy industry has milking machines and bottles as well as an area where children can learn how to milk a cow. **Time:** Allow 1 hour minimum. **Hours:** Thurs.-Sun. noon-4. **Cost:** Donations. **Phone:** (831) 724-5898.

ELKHORN SLOUGH NATIONAL ESTUARINE RESEARCH RESERVE is 3.5 mi. e. of SR 1 on Dolan Rd., then 1.9 mi. n. to 1700 Elkhorn Rd. This 1,700-acre coastal area protects the habitat of hundreds of species of birds, fish and invertebrates. It is an important feeding and nesting ground for many waterfowl and migratory shorebirds. Walking trails wind beneath a canopy of coastal live oak trees and along fingers of salt marsh. The reserve's visitor center has educational displays.

Picnicking is permitted near the visitor center; smoking is prohibited. Dogs and bicycles are not permitted. **Hours:** Wed.-Sun. 9-5. Guided nature walks, originating at the visitor center, are offered Sat.-Sun. at 10 and 1. **Cost:** $4; free (ages 0-15). **Phone:** (831) 728-2822.

BEST WESTERN PLUS ROSE GARDEN INN
(831)724-3367

Hotel
$100-$300

AAA Benefit: Members save up to 20%, plus 10% bonus points with Best Western Rewards®.

Address: 740 Freedom Blvd 95076 **Location:** On SR 152 at the jct of Main St. **Facility:** 46 units, some two bedrooms and efficiencies. 2 stories (no elevator), exterior corridors. **Terms:** 2 night minimum stay - seasonal. **Amenities:** Some: high-speed Internet. **Pool(s):** heated outdoor. **Activities:** whirlpool, exercise room. **Guest Services:** valet and coin laundry. **Free Special Amenities:** expanded continental breakfast and high-speed Internet.

COMFORT INN
(831)728-2300

Hotel
$89-$159

Address: 112 Airport Blvd 95019 **Location:** SR 1 exit Airport Blvd, 1 mi e. **Facility:** 41 units. 3 stories, interior corridors. **Free Special Amenities:** expanded continental breakfast and high-speed Internet.

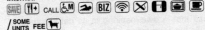

HOLIDAY INN EXPRESS HOTEL & SUITES
(831)728-3600

Hotel
$99-$199

Address: 1855 Main St 95076 **Location:** SR 1 exit SR 152 southbound; exit S Green Valley Rd northbound. **Facility:** 65 units. 3 stories, interior corridors. **Terms:** cancellation fee imposed. **Amenities:** high-speed Internet. **Pool(s):** heated indoor. **Activities:** whirlpool, exercise room. **Guest Services:** coin laundry. **Free Special Amenities:** expanded continental breakfast and high-speed Internet.

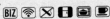

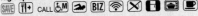
Keep seasonal vehicles travel-ready with a AAA/CAA Battery Tender®

WHERE TO EAT

GREEN VALLEY GRILL
831/728-0644

American. Casual Dining. $8-$33 **AAA Inspector Notes:** This local favorite offers a great selection of entrée salads, sandwiches, pasta, grilled meats and fresh seafood. **Bar:** full bar. **Address:** 972 Main St 95076 **Location:** Just n of jct SR 152, at Auto Center Dr. **Parking:** street only. L D CALL M

ROUND TABLE PIZZA
831/722-2492

Pizza. Casual Dining. $7-$28 **AAA Inspector Notes:** This casual, family-oriented pizza place features high-quality ingredients and dough rolled fresh daily. Distinctive specialty pizzas are piled high with toppings. **Bar:** beer & wine. **Address:** 1975 Main St 95076 **Location:** Just e of S Green Valley Rd. L D

WEAVERVILLE (C-2) pop. 3,600, elev. 2,045'
• Restaurants p. 556

This former mining town conjures up a bit of the colorful atmosphere depicted by author Bret Harte, best remembered for his stories about 19th-century California pioneer life. Weaverville is a starting point for trips into the Shasta-Trinity National Forests (*see place listing p. 518*) and Whiskeytown-Shasta-Trinity National Recreation Area (*see place listing p. 557*).

Trinity County Chamber of Commerce: 509 Main St., P.O. Box 517, Weaverville, CA 96093. **Phone:** (530) 623-6101 or (800) 487-4648.

J.J. "JAKE" JACKSON MEMORIAL MUSEUM, 780 Main St. (SR 299), explores Trinity County's Native American, gold rush and pioneer past. Highlights include an extensive textile collection, a working blacksmith shop, a steam-operated stamp mill, restored stagecoaches and buggies, and a miner's cabin. The History Research Center is a repository for photographs, maps and books detailing Trinity County history from the early 1800s to the present.

Hours: Museum daily 10-5, May-Oct.; daily noon-4, in Apr.; Wed. and Sat. noon-4, rest of year. History Research Center Tues.-Sat. noon-4, Apr.-Dec.; Wed. and Sat. noon-4, rest of year. Closed Christmas. **Cost:** Donations. **Phone:** (530) 623-5211.

WEAVERVILLE JOSS HOUSE STATE HISTORIC PARK, at the corner of Main and Oregon sts., contains the oldest wooden Chinese temple still in use in California. Exhibits depict Chinese life, early history and contributions to the state's development.

Hours: Thurs. and Sat.-Sun. 10-5. Guided 30-minute tours are given every hour 10-4. Closed Jan. 1, Thanksgiving and Christmas. Phone ahead to confirm schedule. **Cost:** $4; $2 (ages 6-17). **Phone:** (530) 623-5284.

49ER GOLD COUNTRY INN
(530)623-4937

Motel
$60-$120

Address: 880 Main St (Hwy 299) 96093 **Location:** Jct SR 3 and 299, just se on SR 299 (Main St). **Facility:** 25 units. 1 story, exterior corridors. **Terms:** 3 day cancellation notice-fee imposed. **Pool(s):** heated outdoor. **Free Special Amenities:** continental breakfast and early check-in/late check-out.

WEAVERVILLE VICTORIAN INN (530)623-4432

▽▽ **Motel** $79-$169 **Address:** 2051 Main St 96093 **Location:** Jct SR 3 and 299, 1.5 mi se on SR 299. **Facility:** 65 units. 2 stories (no elevator), exterior corridors. **Pool(s):** outdoor.

WHERE TO EAT

LA GRANGE CAFE 530/623-5325

▽▽ Steak Seafood. Casual Dining. $7-$28 **AAA Inspector Notes:** This rustic restaurant occupies a former drugstore in the town's historic section. Soft lights, brick walls and hardwood floors add to the ambience, while popular musical standards playing in the background set the mood. The seasonally-changing menu features light luncheon fare and skillfully prepared evening entrées including grilled local beef, buffalo, venison bratwurst, fresh seafood, pasta and burgers. Local produce is used when available. **Bar:** full bar. **Address:** 520 Main St 96093 **Location:** Just nw of jct SR 3 and 299 (Main St). L D

WEED (B-2) pop. 2,967, elev. 3,466'

LIVING MEMORIAL SCULPTURE GARDEN is 13 mi. n.e. on US 97 near jct. CR A12. This 132-acre memorial features metal sculptures grouped into 11 themed areas. In addition to American veterans in general, those specifically memorialized include army nurses, prisoners of war, World War II and Korean War veterans, and helicopter pilots from the Vietnam War. A marble memorial wall is engraved with the names of more than 1,000 veterans from Weed and the surrounding area. **Hours:** Daily dawn-dusk. **Cost:** Free. **Phone:** (530) 938-2218 or (530) 842-2477.

WEED HISTORIC LUMBER TOWN MUSEUM is at 303 Gilman Ave. It chronicles Weed's history through exhibits and artifacts dating to the time of the lumber town's founding. Three rooms depict a typical 1900s kitchen, sewing room and bedroom, and visitors also can see two jail cells and the booking room. Items displayed include logging tools, a 1923 LaFrance fire truck, a homemade still and articles from a lumber company store and hospital. **Time:** Allow 30 minutes minimum. **Hours:** Daily 10-5, Memorial Day weekend-Sept. 30. **Cost:** Donations. **Phone:** (530) 938-0550.

COMFORT INN (530)938-1982

Hotel
$95-$105

Address: 1844 Shastina Dr 96094 **Location:** I-5 exit 745 (S Weed Blvd), just e, then just n. **Facility:** 56 units. 3 stories, interior corridors. **Terms:** cancellation fee imposed. **Amenities:** high-speed Internet. **Pool(s):** outdoor. **Activities:** whirlpool, exercise room. **Guest Services:** coin laundry. **Free Special Amenities:** full breakfast and use of on-premises laundry facilities.

WEOTT (C-1) pop. 288, elev. 338'

HUMBOLDT REDWOODS STATE PARK, along the Redwood Hwy. (US 101) between Miranda and Redcrest, covers more than 53,000 acres, including some 17,000 acres of old-growth coast redwoods. Created in 1921 to protect these magnificent trees, the park is part of a diverse coast redwood ecosystem that includes the Rockefeller Forest, the largest remaining old-growth redwood forest in the world, and the Bull Creek watershed.

Within the park are more than 250 campsites and 100 miles of hiking, biking and horseback riding trails. Among the many breathtaking specimens in the park's memorial redwood groves is the famous Dyerville Giant Tree, a 362-foot redwood considered to be the world's tallest tree until it was felled by another tree in 1991. Popular day use areas are Dyerville Overlook, which offers expansive views of the south fork of the Eel River, and Williams Grove.

The Humboldt Redwoods Visitor Center, on SR 254 (Avenue of the Giants) between Weott and Myers Flat, has a theater, educational and wildlife displays and a brochure outlining the Avenue of the Giants driving tour route. Naturalist-led interpretive activities during the summer months include nature walks and Junior Ranger programs. *See Recreation Areas Chart.*

Note: Except for service animals, dogs are restricted from trails. **Hours:** Park open daily 8 a.m.-11:30 p.m. Visitor center open daily 9-5, Apr.-Oct.; 10-4, rest of year. Visitor center closed Thanksgiving and Christmas. **Cost:** Day use fee (Apr.-Oct.) $8 per private vehicle; $7 (ages 62+ per private vehicle). Visitor center free. **Phone:** (707) 946-2409 for the park, (707) 946-2263 for the visitor center, or (800) 444-7275 for camping reservations through ReserveAmerica.

Avenue of the Giants parallels US 101 between Phillipsville and Pepperwood. Winding along the course of the Eel River, this 31-mile section of pre-freeway US 101 passes through a wilderness that is awe-inspiring in its natural majesty. While the surrounding hills are lush with oak, maple and madrone trees, it is the magnificent redwoods along this route that tower above everything.

The two-lane highway has plenty of turnouts where you can park, get out, take photos and in general be awed by the sheer enormity of these trees. A shadowed solitude prevails in the redwood groves. Exuberant growths of ferns (one of the few plants that thrives in the damp, low-light conditions) carpet the ground beneath them. Signed trailheads for hikes (most of them short and level) are at the parking areas.

Numerous hiking trails traverse the Rockefeller Forest Redwood Grove. At Founders Grove is the Founders Tree, a redwood 346 feet tall and almost 13 feet in diameter at its base. There are a number of large redwoods in this grove, including a few fallen trees—you'll really get a sense of just how big they are when you encounter one lying on the ground. An oddity is the Eternal Tree, which survives despite being hit by lightning, flooded and cut by an axe; a fifth-generation redwood grows next to it. **Note:** Bring food and water if you plan on spending the day hiking.

WESTLEY pop. 603

DAYS INN WESTLEY   (209)894-5500

▼▼ Motel $54-$89 **Address:** 7144 McCracken Rd 95387 **Location:** I-5 exit Westley, just e. **Facility:** 33 units. 2 stories, exterior corridors. **Pool(s):** outdoor. **Activities:** whirlpool. **Guest Services:** coin laundry.

HOLIDAY INN EXPRESS   209/894-8940

▼▼▼ **Hotel.** Rates not provided. **Address:** 4525 Howard Rd 95387 **Location:** I-5 exit Westley, just e. **Facility:** 65 units. 3 stories, interior corridors. **Amenities:** high-speed Internet. **Pool(s):** outdoor. **Activities:** whirlpool, exercise room. **Guest Services:** coin laundry.

WEST SACRAMENTO pop. 48,744
• **Hotels & Restaurants map & index p. 314**

**EXTENDED STAYAMERICA-SACRAMENTO-WEST
SACRAMENTO**   (916)371-1270 64

▼▼ **Extended Stay Hotel** $84-$99 **Address:** 795 Stillwater Rd 95605 **Location:** I-80 exit Reed Ave, just n, then just w, then just s. **Facility:** 104 efficiencies. 3 stories, interior corridors. **Guest Services:** coin laundry.

HAMPTON INN & SUITES-WEST SACRAMENTO
                                 (916)374-1909 65

▼▼▼ **Hotel** $99-$179 **Address:** 800 Stillwater Rd 95605 **Location:** I-80 exit Reed Ave, just w, then just sw. **Facility:** 110 units. 4 stories, interior corridors. **Terms:** 1-7 night minimum stay, cancellation fee imposed. **Amenities:** high-speed Internet. **Pool(s):** heated outdoor. **Activities:** exercise room. **Guest Services:** valet and coin laundry.

> **AAA Benefit:**
> Members save up to 10%!

HOLIDAY INN EXPRESS - WEST SACRAMENTO
                                 916/372-6900 66

▼▼▼ **Hotel**
Rates not provided
Address: 2761 Evergreen Ave 95691 **Location:** Business Rt I-80 (Capital City Frwy) exit Harbor Blvd, just n. Located in an industrial area. **Facility:** 55 units. 4 stories, interior corridors. **Amenities:** high-speed Internet. **Activities:** whirlpool, exercise room. **Guest Services:** valet and coin laundry. **Free Special Amenities:** full breakfast and high-speed Internet.

RAMADA INN & PLAZA HARBOR CONFERENCE CENTER
                                 (916)371-2100 68

▼▼▼ **Hotel** $69-$104 **Address:** 1250 Halyard Dr 95691 **Location:** Business Rt I-80 (Capital City Frwy) exit 1 (Harbour Blvd S), just s to Beacon Blvd, just w, then just n. **Facility:** 137 units. 2-4 stories, interior/exterior corridors. **Pool(s):** outdoor. **Activities:** whirlpools, exercise room. **Guest Services:** valet and coin laundry.

Get more from your

membership with an

upgrade to Plus or Premier

RODEWAY INN CAPITOL   (916)371-6983 67

Motel
$50-$70
Address: 817 W Capitol Ave 95691 **Location:** Business Rt I-80 (Capital City Frwy) exit Jefferson Blvd westbound, 0.3 mi n, then just e; exit Jefferson Blvd eastbound, just s (make U-turn), 0.3 mi n on Jefferson Blvd, then just e. **Facility:** 39 units, some two bedrooms and efficiencies. 2 stories (no elevator), exterior corridors. **Amenities:** high-speed Internet. **Guest Services:** coin laundry. **Free Special Amenities:** continental breakfast and high-speed Internet.

WHERE TO EAT

IKEA RESTAURANT   916/371-4532 100

▼ Swedish. Cafeteria. $3-$7 **AAA Inspector Notes:** Swedish meatballs, of course, along with wraps and salads are offered at this family-friendly contemporary cafeteria located on the second floor of the IKEA store. **Address:** 700 IKEA Ct 95605 **Location:** I-80 exit Reed Ave, just e, then just s; in IKEA. **B** **L** **D** CALL

WHISKEYTOWN-SHASTA-TRINITY
NATIONAL RECREATION AREA (C-1)

At the head of the Sacramento Valley and Upper Trinity River country, north and west of Redding, Whiskeytown-Shasta-Trinity National Recreation Area's three components embrace 246,087 acres and four major dam-created lakes: Whiskeytown, about 8 miles west of Redding via SR 299; Trinity and Lewiston, northeast of Weaverville; and Shasta, north of Redding. Shasta, California's largest man-made lake, has 370 miles of shoreline.

The recreation area's three units are managed by two different federal agencies: Whiskeytown is part of the National Park Service, while the Shasta and Trinity units are under the jurisdiction of the Forest Service.

The visitor center for the Whiskeytown recreation area is at SR 299 and Kennedy Memorial Drive in Whiskeytown; phone (530) 246-1225. It is open daily 9-5, Memorial Day-Labor Day; 10-4, rest of year. Closed Jan. 1, Thanksgiving and Christmas. The Shasta Lake Visitor Information Center is at 14250 Holiday Rd. in Mountain Lake, outside Redding; phone (530) 275-1589. It is open daily 8-4:30, mid-May through Labor Day weekend; Tues.-Sat. 8-4:30, day after Labor Day weekend-Dec. 31. Information is available at the ranger station across the street the rest of the year. The Trinity unit's visitor center, 360 Main St. in Weaverville, is open Mon.-Sat. 8-4:30, Memorial Day-Labor Day; Mon.-Fri. 8-4:30, rest of year. Phone (530) 623-2121.

Recreational activities include hiking, swimming, boating, sailing, water skiing, camping, fishing, backpacking, horseback riding, wildlife viewing and mountain biking. Ranger-guided activities such as kayaking and hiking to waterfalls are available in summer. One hike includes a 1.7-mile trail that leads to recently discovered Whiskeytown Falls, a 220-foot cascade.

Recreational gold panning using a metal or plastic gold pan is permitted in the Whiskeytown unit only;

day permits are required and are available at the park for $1. Day use fee $5 (per private vehicle). An additional fee is charged for camping. Phone (530) 242-3400 for park information, or (877) 444-6777 for camping reservations through the National Recreation Reservation System. *See Recreation Areas Chart.*

WILLIAMS (D-2) pop. 5,123, elev. 80'

SACRAMENTO VALLEY MUSEUM is 1 mi. w. of I-5 at 1491 E St. Located In the former Williams High School building, the museum's 27 rooms depict life in the Sacramento Valley area from the mid-1800s to the 1930s. Exhibits include an apothecary, a kitchen, a children's room with dolls in vintage apparel, a dry goods store, an old-fashioned general store and a documents room with deeds signed by U. S. presidents.

Guided tours are available by appointment. **Hours:** Thurs.-Sat. 10-4, mid-Mar. to mid-Nov. Closed major holidays. **Cost:** $5; $3 (ages 5-12). There may be an additional charge for selected events. **Phone:** (530) 473-2978.

GRANZELLA'S INN (530)473-3310

Hotel
$89-$139

Address: 391 6th St 95987 **Location:** I-5 exit 577 (Williams), 0.5 mi w, then just n. **Facility:** 43 units. 2 stories (no elevator), interior corridors. **Terms:** check-in 4 pm. **Amenities:** high-speed Internet. **Dining:** Granzella's Restaurant, Deli, Bakery & Lounge, see separate listing. **Pool(s):** outdoor. **Activities:** whirlpool, limited exercise equipment. **Guest Services:** coin laundry. **Free Special Amenities:** continental breakfast and high-speed Internet. *(See ad this page.)*

QUALITY INN (530)473-2381

Motel
$65-$125

Address: 400 C St 95987 **Location:** I-5 exit 577 (Williams), just w on E St (SR 20 business route), just n on 4th St (at 76 gas station), then just e. **Facility:** 60 units. 2 stories (no elevator), exterior corridors. **Terms:** cancellation fee imposed. **Amenities:** high-speed Internet. **Pool(s):** outdoor. **Activities:** whirlpool. **Free Special Amenities: expanded continental breakfast and high-speed Internet.**

RAMADA (530)473-5120

Hotel
$79-$84

Address: 374 Ruggeri Way 95987 **Location:** I-5 exit 577 (Williams), just e. **Facility:** 51 units. 2 stories (no elevator), interior corridors. **Activities:** exercise room. **Guest Services:** coin laundry. **Free Special Amenities: expanded continental breakfast and high-speed Internet.**

TRAVELER'S INN (530)473-5387

Motel
$38-$60

Address: 215 N 7th St 95987 **Location:** I-5 exit 577 (Williams), just w on E St (SR 20 business route), then 0.3 mi n. **Facility:** 20 units. 1 story, exterior corridors. **Terms:** cancellation fee imposed. **Pool(s):** outdoor. **Free Special Amenities: expanded continental breakfast and high-speed Internet.**

Learn about inspections
and Diamond Ratings at
AAA.com/Diamonds

GRANZELLA'S RESTAURANT, DELI, BAKERY & LOUNGE 530/473-5496

American Casual Dining
$9-$19

AAA Inspector Notes: Sandwiches, pizza, charbroiled burgers, sausage sandwiches, a salad bar, pasta and prime rib (available on Saturday nights) is served in a comfortable décor. A senior menu is available as well as an on-site deli. **Bar:** full bar. **Address:** 451 6th St 95987 **Location:** I-5 exit 577 (Williams), 0.5 mi w, then just n; adjacent to Granzella's Inn. *(See ad p. 558.)*

B L D CALL &M

LOUIS CAIRO'S RESTAURANT 530/473-5927

Steak. Casual Dining. $9-$28 **AAA Inspector Notes:** Since 1945, this establishment has been serving salads, sandwiches, pasta dishes and USDA Choice hand-cut steaks. Be sure to try the garlic or Louie breads. Prime rib is served Friday through Sunday. Lunch is served Monday through Friday. **Bar:** full bar. **Address:** 558 7th St 95987 **Location:** Just w, then just s. **Parking:** street only.

L D CALL &M

AAA/CAA travel information: Available in print, online and on the go!

WILLITS (D-1) pop. 4,888, elev. 1,364'
• Attractions map p. 566
• Part of Wine Country area — see map p. 562

Settled by a group of pioneer ranchers in the 1850s and originally called Willitsville, this serene Mendocino County community benefits from a location that offers varied outdoor recreation, from hiking and bicycling to lake, river and ocean fishing. Willits also is the eastern terminus of the Skunk Train, based in Fort Bragg *(see place listing p. 113).*

Willits Chamber of Commerce: 299 E. Commercial St., Willits, CA 95490-3105. **Phone:** (707) 459-7910.

MENDOCINO COUNTY MUSEUM, 400 E. Commercial St., displays collections of Pomo and Yuki Indian baskets, Mendocino County artifacts, steampowered equipment and locomotives, and contemporary and traditional art. **Time:** Allow 30 minutes minimum. **Hours:** Wed.-Sun. 10-4:30. Closed major holidays except July 4. **Cost:** $4; $1 (students with ID); free (ages 0-6). **Phone:** (707) 459-2736.

SKUNK TRAIN-WILLITS departs from the Willits Depot, 3 blks. e. off Main St. (US 101) at 299 E. Commercial St. The scenic Northspur 3.5-hour round-trip

by diesel travels into the coastal mountain range, through Tunnel #2 to the California redwoods. Passengers can enjoy the scenery aboard historic motorcars. Another Skunk Train operates out of Fort Bragg *(see attraction listing in Fort Bragg p. 114).*

Hours: Northspur trip departs Wed.-Sun. at 9:45, Memorial Day-Labor Day. **Cost:** Northspur fare $40; $24 (ages 2-12). Reservations are recommended. **Phone:** (866) 457-5865 for reservations.

BAECHTEL CREEK INN & SPA, AN ASCEND COLLECTION HOTEL (707)459-9063

Hotel
$109-$189

Address: 101 Gregory Ln 95490 **Location:** US 101, just w. **Facility:** 43 units. 2 stories (no elevator), exterior corridors. **Pool(s):** heated outdoor. **Activities:** whirlpool, spa. **Free Special Amenities:** full breakfast and high-speed Internet.

BEST WESTERN WILLITS INN (707)459-5800

Hotel
$79-$125

AAA Benefit: Members save up to 20%, plus 10% bonus points with Best Western Rewards®.

Address: 1777 S Main St 95490 **Location:** US 101, 1.3 mi s of jct SR 20. **Facility:** 44 units. 3 stories (no elevator), exterior corridors. **Amenities:** high-speed Internet. **Pool(s):** heated outdoor. **Activities:** whirlpool. **Guest Services:** coin laundry. **Free Special Amenities: continental breakfast and early check-in/late check-out.**

HOLIDAY LODGE 707/459-5361

Motel. Rates not provided. **Address:** 1540 S Main St 95490 **Location:** US 101, 1 mi s of jct SR 20. **Facility:** 16 units. 1 story, exterior corridors. **Pool(s):** outdoor.

OLD WEST INN (707)459-4201

Motel
$55-$95

Address: 1221 S Main St 95490 **Location:** US 101, 0.5 mi s of jct SR 20. **Facility:** 19 units. 2 stories (no elevator), exterior corridors. **Free Special Amenities: continental breakfast and high-speed Internet.**

SUPER 8 WILLITS (707)459-3388

Hotel
$79-$139

Address: 1119 S Main St 95490 **Location:** SR 20, just n. **Facility:** 44 units. 2 stories (no elevator), exterior corridors. **Terms:** cancellation fee imposed. **Amenities:** high-speed Internet. **Pool(s):** outdoor. **Activities:** whirlpool. **Guest Services:** coin laundry. **Free Special Amenities: expanded continental breakfast and high-speed Internet.**

WHERE TO EAT

PURPLE THISTLE RESTAURANT 707/459-4750

California. Casual Dining. $15-$30 **AAA Inspector Notes:** This casually intimate restaurant serves sophisticated dishes using organic ingredients. Try the tuna and avocado tartare and, if it is on the menu, fish and vegetables in parchment paper. For dessert, order the crème brûlée. **Bar:** beer & wine. **Reservations:** suggested. **Address:** 50 S Main St 95490 **Location:** Between Van Ln and Mendocino Ave. **Parking:** street only. D

WILLOW CREEK pop. 1,710

BIGFOOT MOTEL 530/629-2142

Motel $70-$140 **Address:** 39039 Hwy 299 95573 **Location:** On SR 299; just e of SR 96; center. **Facility:** 27 units, some efficiencies and kitchens. 2 stories (no elevator), exterior corridors.

WILLOWS (D-2) pop. 6,166, elev. 135'

SACRAMENTO NATIONAL WILDLIFE REFUGE, 7 mi. s. on CR 99W, provides a nearly 11,000-acre wintering area for migratory birds, especially ducks and geese. More than 265 bird species frequent the area. The best season to view waterfowl is November through January. A 6-mile auto tour route and a 2-mile self-guiding walking trail meander through part of the refuge. Other refuges in the Sacramento Valley National Wildlife Refuge Complex are Colusa *(see place listing p. 84),* Delevan, Sacramento River and Sutter.

Hours: Refuge open daily 1 hour before dawn-1 hour after dusk. Visitor center open daily 7:30-4, Oct.-Mar.; Mon.-Fri. 7:30-4, rest of year. **Cost:** $3 per private vehicle. **Phone:** (530) 934-2801, (530) 934-7774 for recorded information or TTY (530) 934-7135.

BAYMONT INN & SUITES WILLOWS (530)934-9700

Hotel
$70-$190

Address: 199 N Humboldt Ave 95988 **Location:** I-5 exit 603 (SR 162/Willows/Oroville), just e, then s. **Facility:** 71 units. 2 stories (no elevator), interior corridors. **Terms:** cancellation fee imposed. **Amenities:** high-speed Internet. **Pool(s):** heated indoor. **Activities:** whirlpool, limited exercise equipment. **Guest Services:** coin laundry.

DAYS INN (530)934-4444

Motel
$55-$195

Address: 475 N Humboldt Ave 95988 **Location:** I-5 exit 603 (SR 162/Willows/Oroville), just e, then just n. **Facility:** 50 units. 2 stories (no elevator), exterior corridors. **Pool(s):** outdoor. **Free Special Amenities: continental breakfast and high-speed Internet.**

ECONOMY INN (530)934-4224

Motel
$60-$90

Address: 435 N Tehama St 95988 **Location:** I-5 exit 603 (SR 162/Willows/Oroville), 1 mi e, then just n. **Facility:** 20 units, some efficiencies. 1 story, exterior corridors. **Bath:** shower only. **Terms:** 3 day cancellation notice-fee imposed. **Free Special Amenities: local telephone calls and high-speed Internet.**

HOLIDAY INN EXPRESS WILLOWS (530)934-8900

Hotel
$119-$139

Address: 545 N Humboldt Ave 95988 **Location:** I-5 exit 603 (SR 162/Willows/Oroville), just e, then just n. **Facility:** 62 units. 3 stories, interior corridors. **Amenities:** high-speed Internet. **Pool(s):** outdoor. **Activities:** whirlpool, exercise room. **Guest Services:** coin laundry.

MOTEL 6 #4273

Motel
$49-$99

(530)934-7026
Address: 452 N Humboldt Ave 95988 **Location:** I-5 exit 603 (SR 162/Willows/Oroville), just e, then just n. **Facility:** 41 units. 2 stories (no elevator), exterior corridors. **Terms:** cancellation fee imposed. **Pool(s):** outdoor. **Guest Services:** coin laundry. **Free Special Amenities:** high-speed Internet and use of on-premises laundry facilities.

 / SOME UNITS

WHERE TO EAT

BLACK BEAR DINER 530/934-3797
American. Casual Dining. $7-$15 **AAA Inspector Notes:** A homey atmosphere characterizes this family-oriented restaurant. Familiar comfort foods, such as meatloaf with mashed potatoes, are at the heart of the menu and are served in generous portions. **Bar:** beer & wine. **Address:** 246 N Humboldt Ave 95988 **Location:** I-5 exit 603 (SR 162/Willows/Oroville) just e, then just s.

B L D CALL

CASA RAMOS 530/934-0600
Mexican. Casual Dining. $7-$16 **AAA Inspector Notes:** A varied Mexican menu is featured in a colorful atmosphere. Mexican favorites include fajitas, enchiladas, burritos and specialty steak and seafood entrees. **Bar:** full bar. **Address:** 247 N Humboldt Ave 95988 **Location:** I-5 exit 603 (SR 162/Willows/Oroville), just e, then just s.

L D CALL

THE LAST STAND 530/934-7246
American. Quick Serve. $5-$8 **AAA Inspector Notes:** Located on old, historic Highway 99, this is California's only remaining stand-up restaurant (it does sport a few tables). Burgers, sandwiches and fish and chips are the main bill of fare, and the menu lists a variety of beers. **Bar:** beer only. **Address:** 414 N Tehama St 95988 **Location:** I-5 exit 603 (SR 162/Willows/Oroville), 1 mi e, then just n.

L D

WONG'S CHINESE RESTAURANT 530/934-4344
fyi Not evaluated. This typical Chinese eatery offers a variety of pork, chicken, beef and seafood entrées as well as family dinner combinations and lunch specials. **Address:** 456 N Humboldt Ave 95988 **Location:** I-5 exit 603 (SR 162/Willows/Oroville), just e, then just n.

WINDSOR pop. 26,801

- **Attractions map p. 567**
- **Part of Wine Country area — see map p. 562**

HAMPTON INN & SUITES-WINDSOR-SONOMA WINE COUNTRY 707/837-9355

AAA Benefit:
Members save up to 10%!

Hotel. Rates not provided. **Address:** 8937 Brooks Rd S 95492 **Location:** US 101 exit Central Windsor, just n. **Facility:** 116 units. 3 stories, interior corridors. **Amenities:** high-speed Internet. **Pool(s):** heated outdoor. **Activities:** whirlpool, exercise room. **Guest Services:** valet and coin laundry. *(See ad p. 505.)*

/ SOME UNITS FEE

HOLIDAY INN EXPRESS WINDSOR-SONOMA COUNTY (707)837-0808
Hotel $89-$250 **Address:** 8865 Conde Ln 95492 **Location:** US 101 exit Central Windsor, just w. **Facility:** 75 units. 3 stories, interior corridors. **Terms:** 4 night minimum stay - seasonal, 4 day cancellation notice-fee imposed. **Amenities:** high-speed Internet. **Pool(s):** heated outdoor. **Activities:** sauna, whirlpool, exercise room. **Guest Services:** valet and coin laundry.

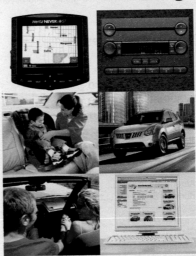

WINE COUNTRY

You're in a basket beneath a hot air balloon, soaring over a two-lane country road cradled in a lush valley. Acre upon acre is planted with neat rows of leafy grapevines, forming pale green pinstripes against the fertile soil. Rose bushes awash in red blooms mark the beginnings of some rows, which extend from the road and seem to disappear into rolling, forested hills. Beyond these hills are dark stands of redwoods, their feathery branches sheltering a damp, fern-carpeted ground, and beyond them rocky cliffs bordering the Pacific. The ride is quiet and seemingly still, following the whim of the wind with only the roar of the burners to break the silence.

"Heaven?" you ask. Close. You're in Wine Country. And while the views in Napa, Sonoma, Lake and Mendocino counties are enough to make you dizzy with delight, the extravagantly verdant countryside isn't for shutterbugs alone.

There's a business growing here, and a fruitful one at that. Every year some 300 wineries produce

This map shows cities in the Wine Country where you will find attractions, hotels and restaurants. Cities are listed alphabetically in this book on the following pages.

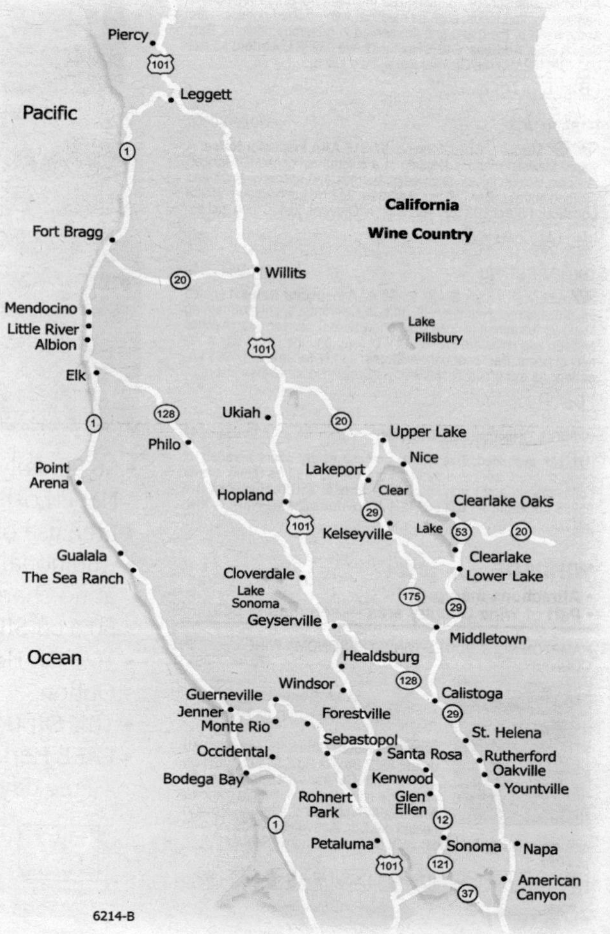

California
Wine Country

Pacific

Piercy
101
Leggett

Fort Bragg

Willits
20

Mendocino
Little River
Albion

Elk

Lake
Pillsbury

101

128
Ukiah
20
Philo
Upper Lake
Nice

Point
Arena

Lakeport
Clear

Hopland
29
Lake
Clearlake Oaks

101
Kelseyville
53
20
Clearlake

Gualala
The Sea Ranch
Cloverdale
Lake
Sonoma
Geyserville
175
Lower Lake
29

Middletown

Ocean

Healdsburg
Windsor
128
Calistoga
Guerneville
Jenner
Forestville
29
Monte Rio
Sebastopol
St. Helena
Occidental
Santa Rosa
Rutherford
Bodega Bay
Kenwood
Oakville
Rohnert
Glen
Yountville
Park
Ellen
12
1
Petaluma
Sonoma
Napa
101
121
American
37
Canyon

6214-B

nearly 2 billion bottles of wine thanks to an ideal, varied climate—balmy days with cool mornings and evenings interspersed with floating blankets of Pacific fog. Add relatively cheap labor and mineral-rich soil, and the bottled result has caught the eyes, noses and palates of connoisseurs around the globe.

With all its options for fun—hot air ballooning, shopping in elite boutiques, hiking, bicycling, touring historical sites, kayaking, gorging on sinfully delicious gourmet food, horseback riding, relaxing with a massage or sinking into a mud or mineral bath—it still comes as no surprise that most visitors are here for one thing: fermented grape juice. Yes, the sweet nectar of the gods.

It's All About the Wine

Napa Valley's main drag, SR 29—as well as its parallel counterpart, the Silverado Trail—is a north-south valley bisector with stunning mountain views to the east and west. The rural route leads from the town of Napa north through St. Helena's picturesque Main Street to the hot springs and mud bath mecca of Calistoga. Farmers in pickup trucks along with locals in Land Rovers pack the lanes, making way for bicyclists. Small wooden signs facing the road denote grapes grown here: Cabernet Sauvignon, Chardonnay, Chenin Blanc, Merlot, Pinot Noir, Riesling, Sauvignon Blanc or the precious, California-grown Zinfandel.

Large signs proclaim grape owners, names no doubt you've seen adorning labels on wine bottles in your local grocery store—Beringer, Robert Mondavi, Sutter Home and hundreds of others sharing the soil in this world-famous viticultural region.

Peppering the valley floor are magnificent winery estates: orange-hued, postmodern Clos Pegase; Sterling Vineyards' white, Greek island-style stucco building; Oscar-winning director Francis Ford Coppola's giant, gray stone chateau; the gabled Victorian Rhine House (complete with Art Nouveau-style stained-glass windows) at Beringer Winery; and the simple, California mission-style Robert Mondavi Winery.

Choose a winery—perhaps St. Supéry, Domaine Chandon, Rubicon Estate or Beaulieu—and follow the driveway to a majestic mansion. You'll pass workers tending expansive rows of vines. Take a tour to learn about the delicate art of winemaking, from the plucking of sweet, plump grapes to the long-awaited popping of the cork.

You may be surprised to find how scientific the process is; long gone are the days when ladies tied up their skirts, removed their shoes and stomped on juicy grapes until their toes turned purple. Wine-making is a complicated, subjective blend of technology, nature and experience. Biologists, chemists and winemakers each have a hand in the steps from grape to glass.

After you've walked through a vineyard, felt the cold steel of a giant, shiny fermentation tank, smelled the scent of grapes fermenting, watched bottles clattering along an assembly line and glimpsed the winery's high-tech presses, filters and computers, you might be convinced that paying $75 for a bottle of Cabernet Sauvignon is reasonable. But how does it *taste?*

First-time tasters might be intimidated by the overwhelming and confusing terminology used to evaluate wines. Don't fret! When sampling, just remember four little words: Look. Swirl. Smell. Taste.

Wine Tasting 101

First, take a good look at the wine. Hold the glass (by the stem, please) up to the light, or place a white napkin behind it. Note the *color* of the wine, a clue to its age. White wines, ranging from pale yellow (straw) to amber, darken with age. Red wines, which appear light purple to deep ruby, lighten with age. Also notice the *clarity* of the wine. Is it clear or cloudy? Next look at the *brightness*—brilliant or opaque?

Second, swirl the wine. Not only is this quite fun, but it oxygenates the wine, releasing its aromas. Observe its *legs*, little drops running down inside the glass after it's swirled.

Now hold the glass under your nose and sniff sharply. (Don't worry, everyone's doing it.) Remark about its *nose*—the scent determined by smelling alone. A good nose reveals a strong *bouquet*—the fragrance acquired as a result of the wine's aging process. Usually, the more prominent the bouquet, the older the wine. But here's the best part: determining the wine's *aroma*. Scents recall the grape used to make the wine, and there are numerous aromas associated with each varietal. They range from grapefruit to cream to butterscotch for a Chardonnay, mint to grass to apricot for a Sauvignon Blanc, and blackberry to cloves to olives for a Zinfandel.

Take a big drink of the wine. Let it flow over your tongue and chew it like pasta, allowing it to reach all the taste buds. Identify its *taste*—a Chenin Blanc may suggest red apple, while a Cabernet Sauvignon might hint of cedar. Determine the *balance* (how the flavors combine): A good wine evenly blends its sugar, tannins (astringents found in red wines) and fruit. Observe the *body*, the way the liquid feels on your tongue. This may range from thin and light to full and heavy. Finally, swallow and note the *length* or *finish*, the aftertaste: How long does it last, and how does the taste differ from the initial flavor?

Sound confusing? It just takes time, as it took time for this region to become famous for its wine. Missionary Padre José Altimira brought vine cuttings to the Sonoma Valley in 1823 to make wine for Catholic mass, but it was Hungarian nobleman "Count" Agoston Haraszthy who created the California wine industry as we know it. In 1857 he planted European varieties and established Buena Vista, the state's oldest winery. You'll find the original, ivy-clad stone buildings tucked away near the town of Sonoma, where this winery shares a quiet, rustic road alongside homes, farms and vineyards.

Take a relaxed bike ride along Sonoma's streets and you may catch a glimpse of one of the resident peacocks, often seen parading along Lovall Valley Road. Pedal to Sebastiani Vineyards for a sample. Then tour Sonoma State Historic Park, a group of historic sites near Sonoma Plaza. Together they tell the story of early "Alta" California and the establishment of a brief, 26-day California Republic.

Drive along SR 12, Sonoma Valley's main drag, for more tastings at Benziger Family Winery or Kunde Family Estate. The vintners at these two establishments are especially friendly and easygoing. West of SR 12, the Russian River Wine Road traverses the Russian River Valley, where vineyards and Gravenstein apple orchards cover hillsides, redwoods form magnificent groves and a lazy river flows.

Take a break from wine and head to Petaluma, where there are enough brightly-colored Victorians to make your jaw drop; to Santa Rosa for gorgeous gardens; or to Healdsburg for scads of antique shops and art galleries. Or pack your fishing pole and stake out a spot at giant Clear Lake.

And by all means do not pass up the chance to explore the spectacular Pacific coast. Mendocino, an artsy, laid-back hamlet with adorable New England-style architecture, rests on bluffs overlooking the steel blue ocean. Rainbow-colored wildflowers dot the grassy headlands in spring, and eruptive white water crashes against jagged ocean rocks. Day-trippers have the option of hiking, kayaking or horseback riding, and a coastal drive along winding SR 1 is sure to elicit gasps and awestruck grins on the faces of photographers, artists and nature buffs.

To end the day, stop by a deli, bakery or roadside produce stand and fill a picnic basket with homegrown and homemade delicacies. Find a quiet spot to relax on the coast and watch the sunset. Pull the cork on a bottle of the area's claim to fame, make a toast and drink it all up.

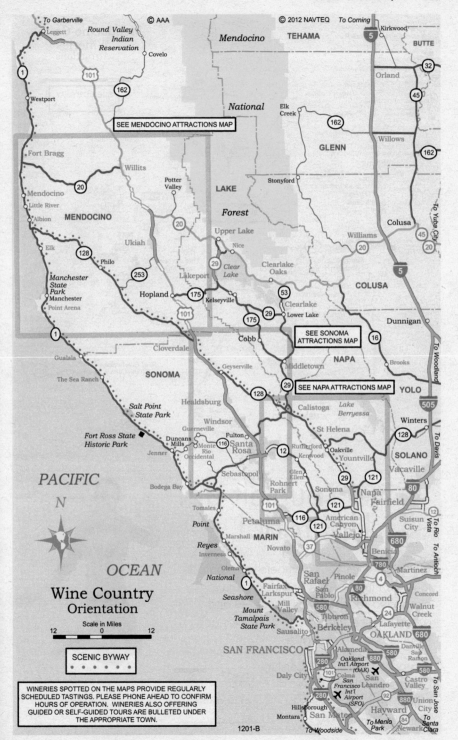

To Garberville
Leggett
© AAA
© 2012 NAVTEQ
To Corning
Kirkwood
Round Valley
Indian
Reservation
Covelo
Mendocino
TEHAMA
BUTTE
1
101
162
Orland
32
Westport
National
Elk
Creek
162
45
SEE MENDOCINO ATTRACTIONS MAP
GLENN
Willows
162
Fort Bragg
Willits
Potter
Valley
LAKE
Stonyford
Colusa
20
Mendocino
Little River
Albion
MENDOCINO
Ukiah
20
Upper Lake
Nice
Forest
Williams
20
45
20
Elk
128
Philo
253
Lakeport
Clear
Lake
Clearlake
Oaks
COLUSA
5
Manchester
State
Park
Manchester
Point Arena
Hopland
175
Kelseyville
29
53
Clearlake
Lower Lake
Dunnigan
101
175
Cobb
16
SEE SONOMA
ATTRACTIONS MAP
Cloverdale
Geyserville
Middletown
NAPA
Brooks
YOLO
Gualala
SONOMA
128
29
SEE NAPA ATTRACTIONS MAP
505
The Sea Ranch
Healdsburg
Calistoga
Lake
Berryessa
Winters
Salt Point
State Park
Windsor
Guerneville
Fulton
St Helena
128
Fort Ross State
Historic Park
Duncans
Mills
Monte
Rio
Occidental
116
Santa
Rosa
12
Rutherford
Kenwood
Oakville
Yountville
SOLANO
Vacaville
Jenner
Sebastopol
Glen
Ellen
29
121
Napa
Fairfield
Bodega Bay
Rohnert
Park
Sonoma
121
80
Tomales
101
116
121
American
Canyon
Vallejo
Suisun
City
Point
Petaluma
MARIN
Novato
37
Benicia
680
780
Martinez
4
Reyes
Inverness
Marshall
Olema
National
1
Fairfax
Larkspur
San
Rafael
San
Pablo
Pinole
80
Richmond
Concord
Walnut
Creek
PACIFIC
N
Seashore
Mill
Valley
Tiburon
580
Berkeley
24
Lafayette
OAKLAND
680
OCEAN
Mount
Tamalpais
State Park
Sausalito
SAN FRANCISCO
Alameda
Oakland
Int'l Airport
(OAK)
880
580
Danville
San
Ramon
Castro
Valley
Wine Country
Orientation
Daly City
Colma
280
San
Francisco
Int'l
Airport
(SFO)
San
Leandro
92
880
Union
City
Hayward
Scale in Miles
12   0   12
Hillsborough
Montara
San Mateo
84
Newark
Santa
Clara

SCENIC BYWAY
• • • • •

WINERIES SPOTTED ON THE MAPS PROVIDE REGULARLY
SCHEDULED TASTINGS. PLEASE PHONE AHEAD TO CONFIRM
HOURS OF OPERATION. WINERIES ALSO OFFERING
GUIDED OR SELF-GUIDED TOURS ARE BULLETED UNDER
THE APPROPRIATE TOWN.

1201-B

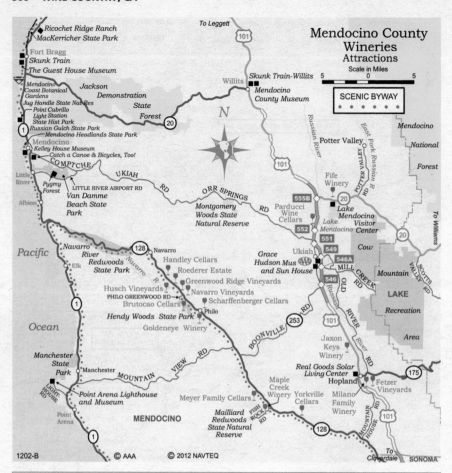

Mendocino County
Wineries
Attractions

Scale in Miles

SCENIC BYWAY

1202-B © AAA © 2012 NAVTEQ SONOMA

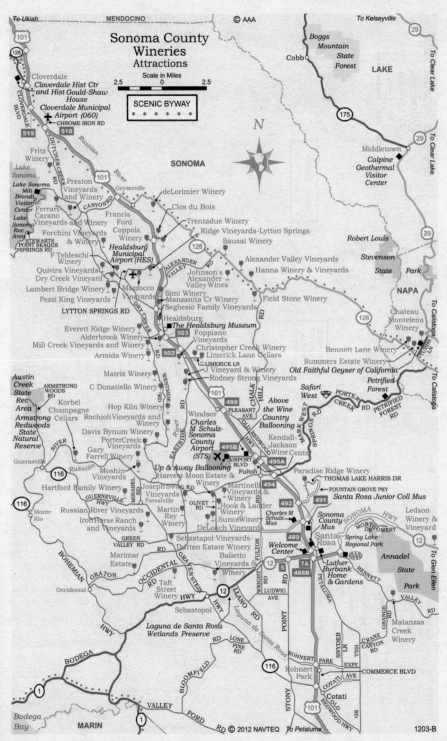

Sonoma County
Wineries
Attractions

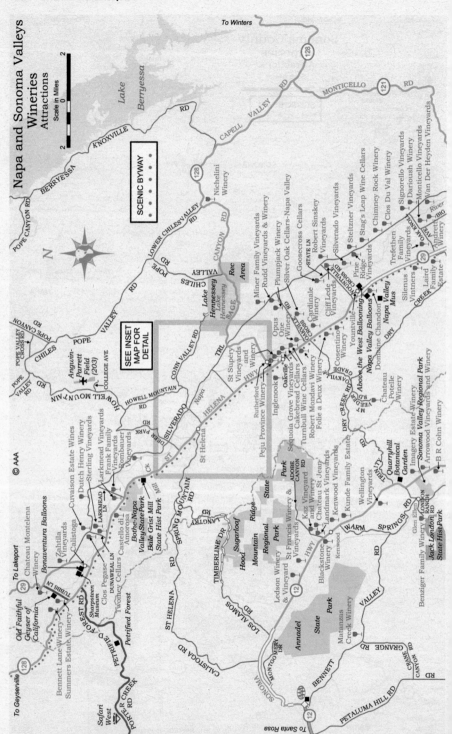

Napa and Sonoma Valleys
Wineries
Attractions

SCENIC BYWAY

SEE INSET
MAP FOR
DETAIL

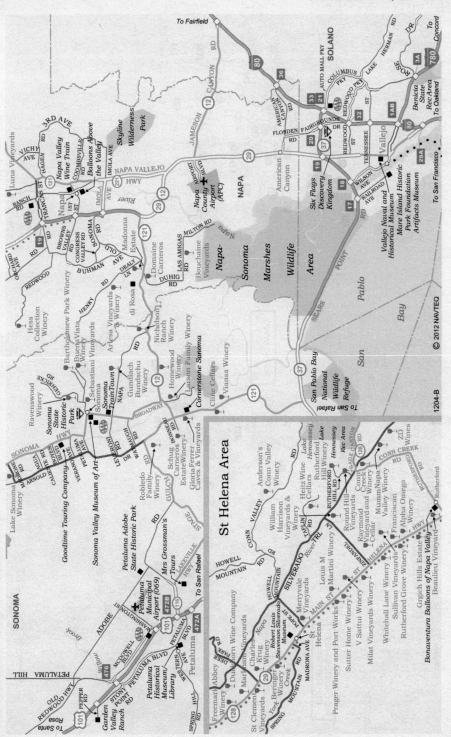

1204-B

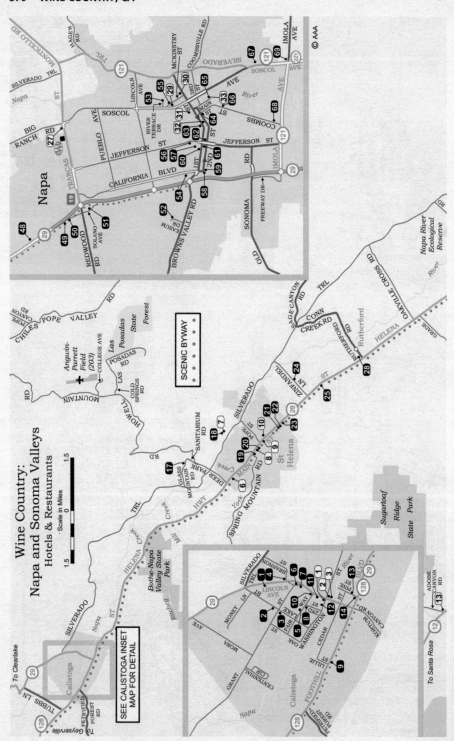

Wine Country:
Napa and Sonoma Valleys
Hotels & Restaurants

Scale in Miles

© AAA

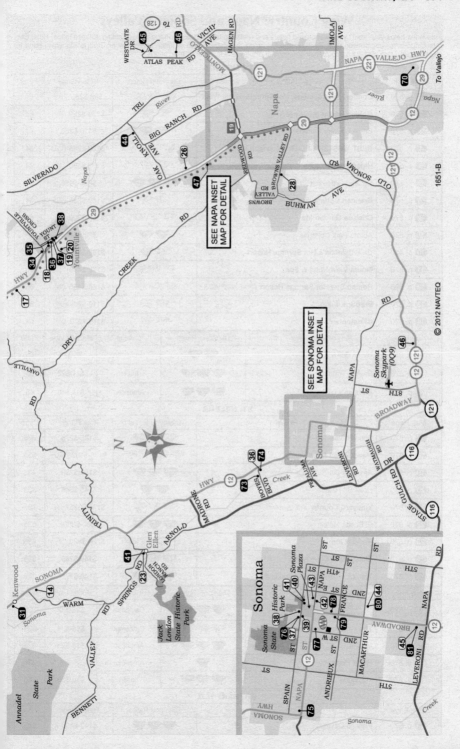

Wine Country: Napa and Sonoma Valleys

This index helps you "spot" where approved hotels and restaurants are located on the corresponding detailed maps. Hotel daily rate range is for comparison only. Restaurant price range is a combination of lunch and/or dinner. Turn to the listing page for more detailed rate and price information and consult display ads for special promotions.

CALISTOGA

Map Page	Hotels	Diamond Rated	Rate Range	Page
1 p. 570	**Comfort Inn Calistoga, Hot Springs of the West**	◆◆◆	$99-$289 SAVE	64
2 p. 570	**Golden Haven Spa Resort**	◆◆	$159-$229 SAVE	64
3 p. 570	Carlin Country Cottages	◆◆	$110-$260	64
4 p. 570	**BEST WESTERN PLUS Stevenson Manor**	◆◆◆	$129-$285 SAVE	64
5 p. 570	**Hideaway Cottages**	◆◆	$169-$650 SAVE	64
6 p. 570	Cottage Grove Inn	◆◆◆	$250-$450	64
7 p. 570	**Brannan Cottage Inn**	◆◆	$160-$285 SAVE	64
8 p. 570	**Chelsea Garden Inn**	◆◆◆	$155-$300 SAVE	64
9 p. 570	Aurora Park Cottages	◆◆	$229-$289	64
10 p. 570	**Dr. Wilkinson's Hot Springs Resort**	◆◆	$139-$329 SAVE	64
11 p. 570	**Mount View Hotel & Spa**	◆◆◆	$179-$449 SAVE	65
12 p. 570	**Roman Spa Hot Springs Resort** (See ad p. 65.)	◆◆◆	$160-$450 SAVE	65
13 p. 570	**EuroSpa & Inn**	◆◆	$119-$289 SAVE	64
14 p. 570	**Christopher's Inn**	◆◆	$119-$279 SAVE	64

Map Page	Restaurants	Diamond Rated	Cuisine	Price Range	Page
1 p. 570	Hydro Bar & Grill	◆◆	American	$8-$20	65
2 p. 570	Boskos Trattoria	◆◆◆	Italian	$11-$22	65
3 p. 570	Brannan's Grill	◆◆◆	American	$11-$40	65

ST. HELENA

Map Page	Hotels	Diamond Rated	Rate Range	Page
17 p. 570	Spanish Villa Inn	◆◆◆	$175-$275	336
18 p. 570	**Meadowood Napa Valley**	◆◆◆◆	$475-$1875 SAVE	335
19 p. 570	Ambrose Bierce House	◆◆◆	$159-$299	335
20 p. 570	Hotel St. Helena	◆◆	$145-$595	335
21 p. 570	**Vineyard Country Inn** (See ad p. 241.)	◆◆◆	$175-$325 SAVE	336
22 p. 570	El Bonita Motel	◆◆◆	$80-$300	335
23 p. 570	**Harvest Inn**	◆◆◆◆	$229-$899 SAVE	335
24 p. 570	Shady Oaks Country Inn	◆◆◆	$149-$289	336
25 p. 570	The Ink House Bed & Breakfast	◆◆◆	$140-$275	335

Map Page	Restaurants	Diamond Rated	Cuisine	Price Range	Page
6 p. 570	Wine Spectator Greystone Restaurant	◆◆◆	California	$23-$32	336
7 p. 570	**The Grill At Meadowood**	◆◆◆	California	$18-$34	336
8 p. 570	Market	◆◆◆	American	$13-$25	336
9 p. 570	Gott's Roadside	◆	American	$8-$15	336
10 p. 570	Tra Vigne	◆◆◆	Italian	$18-$30	336

RUTHERFORD

Map Page	Hotel	Diamond Rated	Rate Range	Page
28 p. 570	Rancho Caymus	◆◆◆	$149-$499	305

KENWOOD

Map Page	Hotel	Diamond Rated	Rate Range	Page
31 p. 570	Birmingham Bed & Breakfast	◈◈	Rates not provided	153

Map Page	Restaurants	Diamond Rated	Cuisine	Price Range	Page
13 p. 570	The Vineyards Inn Bar & Grill	◈◈	Spanish	$10-$29	153
14 p. 570	Kenwood Restaurant	◈◈◈	Continental	$13-$27	153

YOUNTVILLE

Map Page	Hotels	Diamond Rated	Rate Range	Page
34 p. 570	**Napa Valley Lodge**	◈◈◈◈	$295-$665 (SAVE)	593
35 p. 570	Lavender	◈◈◈	$235-$350	593
36 p. 570	**Vintage Inn**	◈◈◈◈	$225-$700 (SAVE)	593
37 p. 570	Maison Fleurie	◈◈◈	$155-$325	593
38 p. 570	**Villagio Inn & Spa**	◈◈◈◈	Rates not provided (SAVE)	593

Map Page	Restaurants	Diamond Rated	Cuisine	Price Range	Page
17 p. 570	Mustard's Grill	◈◈◈	American	$12-$38	594
18 p. 570	**The French Laundry**	◈◈◈◈◈	American	$270	594
19 p. 570	Bottega Ristorante	◈◈◈	Italian	$16-$34	593
20 p. 570	**Etoile at Domaine Chandon**	◈◈◈◈	French	$24-$36	594

GLEN ELLEN

Map Page	Hotel	Diamond Rated	Rate Range	Page
41 p. 570	Jack London Lodge	◈◈	Rates not provided	137

Map Page	Restaurant	Diamond Rated	Cuisine	Price Range	Page
23 p. 570	Wolf House	◈◈	American	$11-$27	137

NAPA

Map Page	Hotels	Diamond Rated	Rate Range	Page
44 p. 570	Oak Knoll Inn	◈◈◈	$350-$750	240
45 p. 570	Napa Valley Resorts at Silverado	◈◈◈	Rates not provided	240
46 p. 570	**Silverado Resort and Spa**	◈◈◈◈	$179-$559 (SAVE)	240
47 p. 570	**BEST WESTERN PREMIER Ivy Hotel Napa**	◈◈◈	$159-$299 (SAVE)	238
48 p. 570	**Quality Inn Napa Winery Inn**	◈◈◈	$149-$399 (SAVE)	240
49 p. 570	Hilton Garden Inn-NAPA	◈◈◈	$129-$349	238
50 p. 570	Napa Valley Marriott Hotel & Spa	◈◈◈	$155-$379	240
51 p. 570	The Chablis Inn	◈◈	$79-$179	238
52 p. 570	Stahlecker House	◈◈◈	$112-$339	240
53 p. 570	River Terrace Inn	◈◈◈	$149-$699	240
54 p. 570	Embassy Suites Napa Valley	◈◈◈	$179-$399	238
55 p. 570	**The Westin Verasa, Napa** (See ad p. 242.)	◈◈◈◈	$159-$699 (SAVE)	242
56 p. 570	Napa Old World Inn	◈◈◈	Rates not provided	240
57 p. 570	**The Napa Inn**	◈◈◈	$149-$295 (SAVE)	238
58 p. 570	**Bel Abri**	◈◈◈	$129-$310 (SAVE)	237
59 p. 570	**BEST WESTERN PLUS Elm House Inn**	◈◈◈	$109-$329 (SAVE)	237
60 p. 570	**The Inn on First**	◈◈◈	$199-$425 (SAVE)	238
61 p. 570	The 1801 Inn	◈◈◈	$225-$495	236
62 p. 570	Blackbird Inn	◈◈◈	$195-$310	238

NAPA (cont'd)

Map Page	Hotels (cont'd)	Diamond Rated	Rate Range	Page
63 p. 570	**Andaz Napa**	♦♦♦♦	$169-$799 SAVE	237
64 p. 570	**Napa Valley Hotel & Suites/A 3 Palms Hotel & Resort at the Napa River**	♦♦	$129-$249	240
65 p. 570	Napa River Inn	♦♦♦	$209-$599	240
66 p. 570	Cedar Gables Inn	♦♦♦	$199-$359	238
67 p. 570	**Hawthorn Suites by Wyndham** (See ad p. 239.)	♦♦♦	$105-$249 SAVE	238
68 p. 570	**Wine Valley Lodge**	♦♦	$79-$225 SAVE	242
69 p. 570	**BEST WESTERN PLUS Inn at the Vines** (See ad p. 237.)	♦♦♦	$110-$260 SAVE	238
70 p. 570	**The Meritage Resort and Spa**	♦♦♦♦	Rates not provided SAVE	238

Map Page	Restaurants	Diamond Rated	Cuisine	Price Range	Page
26 p. 570	Bistro Don Giovanni	♦♦♦	Italian	$13-$38	243
27 p. 570	The Food Mill	♦	American	$6-$23	243
28 p. 570	Zinsvalley Restaurant	♦♦♦	New American	$13-$28	243
29 p. 570	**Napa Valley Wine Train** (See ad p. 236.)	♦♦♦	Continental	$99-$139	243
30 p. 570	Hog Island Oyster Bar Napa	♦♦	Seafood	$12-$24	243
31 p. 570	Cole's Chop House	♦♦♦	Steak	$15-$69	243
32 p. 570	Oenotri	♦♦♦	Italian	$10-$29	243
33 p. 570	Celadon	♦♦♦	American	$13-$35	243

SONOMA

Map Page	Hotels	Diamond Rated	Rate Range	Page
73 p. 570	Sonoma Creek Inn	♦♦	$89-$199	522
74 p. 570	**The Fairmont Sonoma Mission Inn & Spa**	♦♦♦♦	$199-$649 SAVE	522
75 p. 570	**El Pueblo Inn**	♦♦♦	$90-$340 SAVE	522
76 p. 570	Sonoma Hotel	♦♦♦	$140-$255	522
77 p. 570	**BEST WESTERN PLUS Sonoma Valley Inn & Krug Event Center**	♦♦♦	$109-$295 SAVE	522
78 p. 570	Inn at Sonoma	♦♦♦	$225-$325	522
79 p. 570	Magliulo's Rose Garden Inn	♦♦	Rates not provided	522
80 p. 570	MacArthur Place	♦♦♦♦	$299-$725	522
81 p. 570	**The Lodge at Sonoma, A Renaissance Resort & Spa**	♦♦♦♦	$209-$599 SAVE	522

Map Page	Restaurants	Diamond Rated	Cuisine	Price Range	Page
36 p. 570	**Sante**	♦♦♦♦	California	$75-$129	523
37 p. 570	the girl & the fig	♦♦♦	French	$12-$29	523
38 p. 570	Swiss Hotel Restaurant	♦♦	Swiss	$8-$29	523
39 p. 570	El Dorado Kitchen	♦♦♦	California	$15-$32	522
40 p. 570	La Casa Restaurant & Bar	♦♦	Mexican	$10-$18	523
41 p. 570	LaSalette Restaurant	♦♦♦	Portuguese	$11-$26	523
42 p. 570	Della Santina's	♦♦♦	Italian	$12-$33	522
43 p. 570	Cafe La Haye	♦♦♦	California	$19-$30	522
44 p. 570	Saddles Steakhouse	♦♦♦	Steak	$9-$48	523
45 p. 570	**Carneros Bistro & Wine Bar**	♦♦♦	California	$13-$33	522
46 p. 570	The Fremont Diner	♦♦	American	$8-$12	523

For over 100 years members have counted on AAA for their emergency road service, maps, TripTik® routings, travel information and services.

Did you know that AAA offers Insurance?

Most AAA clubs provide a variety of insurance products with competitive rates for all phases of your life. Policies most often available include coverage for your:

- Automobile
- Home
- Life
- Health and Medicare Supplement
- Long Term Care
- Home and Vehicle Warranties
- Boat and RV
- Travel Insurance

Visit us at AAA.com or call your local AAA office today. One of our knowledgeable insurance representatives will be glad to help you with your insurance needs.

Some insurance products may not be available through all AAA clubs.

AAA.com/Insurance

WOODLAND (E-3) pop. 55,468, elev. 65'

First known as Yolo City, Woodland was a gold rush town established in 1861. Downtown at Main and Second streets is the Woodland Opera House. The original building, built in 1885, burned down in 1892 when a major fire destroyed much of the downtown area. The opera house was rebuilt and was the site of theatrical productions until 1913, after which the building remained boarded up for almost 60 years. Saved from the wrecking ball by the county historical society, the restored brick opera house presents live entertainment throughout the year; phone (530) 666-9617 for event information.

Gibson House Yolo County Historical Museum, 512 Gibson Rd., occupies a Classical Revival-style mansion. Three outbuildings and a barn with historical exhibits also are on the grounds; phone (530) 666-1045. At the Woodland Museum of Biblical Archaeology, 240 N. West St., guided tours provide information about more than 200 excavated artifacts and antiquities dating from 4000 B.C. to 200 A.D. and how the items relate to stories in the Bible; phone (530) 662-2773.

The Woodland Farmer's Market offers a summer bonanza of locally grown fruits and vegetables, fresh eggs and artisan breads. There are two locations: at Woodland Healthcare, 1325 Cottonwood St. (Tues. 4:30-7 p.m., June through September), and at Freeman Park, on Main Street between 4th and 6th streets (Sat. 9-noon, May through September). The Freeman Park location has plenty of nearby street parking and also a gazebo for live music performances.

Woodland Chamber of Commerce: 307 First St., Woodland, CA 95695. **Phone:** (530) 662-7327.

SAVE **HEIDRICK AG HISTORY CENTER,** 1962 Hays Ln., houses collections of antique agricultural equipment, trucks and tractors. The center chronicles the history of agricultural machinery and commercial trucking through displays and interactive exhibits. Trucks dating from 1901 through the 1950s represent various manufacturers, and there are vehicles like an 1890 horse-drawn Deering Reaper and gasoline- and diesel-operated farm machinery dating from the early 20th century. Also on display is a section of the Old Plank Road, which once negotiated the sand dunes between Yuma, Ariz., and El Centro, Calif.

Tours: Guided tours are available. **Hours:** Wed.-Sun. 10-5. Last admission 1 hour before closing. Closed major holidays. **Cost:** $8; $7 (ages 62+); $5 (ages 5-12). Docent-led guided tour $5. **Phone:** (530) 666-9700.

REIFF'S RETRO AUTOMOBILE GAS STATION MUSEUM is e. of West St. at 52 Jefferson St. (at McKinley Ave.). This suburban house has been turned into an automotive museum of sorts. It's rather hard to miss, courtesy of the car crashed into the garage and a Cessna that appears to have landed on the roof. Guided tours conducted by Mr.

Reiff take you past the gas station memorabilia in his house to the back yard (with more memorabilia) and to a garage with an antique tow truck.

In another garage are approximately 40 antique gas pumps, some restored (the oldest is from 1906). More than 200 vintage gas station signs are displayed indoors as well as outdoors. Also on the premises are re-creations of a gas station, a general store, a diner and a vintage movie theater.

Time: Allow 1 hour minimum. **Hours:** Guided tours are given daily 9-5. **Cost:** $7. Reservations for guided tours should be made 2 days in advance. Cash only. Reservations are required. **Phone:** (530) 666-1758.

WINERIES

• **Satiety Winery** is at SR 113 and CR 25-A. **Hours:** Daily 11-6. **Phone:** (530) 661-0680.

AMERICAS BEST VALUE INN (530)662-1091

◆◆◆ **Motel** $54-$84 **Address:** 99 W Main St 95695 **Location:** I-5 exit 537 (Main St) northbound, 2 mi w; exit West St southbound, 1.5 mi s to Main St, then just w; jct California St. **Facility:** 29 units. 2 stories (no elevator), exterior corridors. **Terms:** cancellation fee imposed. **Pool(s):** outdoor.

BEST WESTERN SHADOW INN (530)666-1251

◆◆◆ Hotel $89-$103

AAA Benefit: Members save up to 20%, plus 10% bonus points with Best Western Rewards®.

Address: 584 N East St 95776 **Location:** I-5 exit 538 (Yuba City/SR 113 N), 0.3 mi w. **Facility:** 119 units. 2 stories, exterior corridors. **Pool(s):** heated outdoor. **Activities:** whirlpools. **Guest Services:** coin laundry. **Free Special Amenities:** local telephone calls and high-speed Internet.

DAYS INN (530)666-3800

◆◆◆ Hotel $55

Address: 1524 E Main St 95776 **Location:** I-5 exit 537 (Main St) northbound; exit SR 113 (Davis) southbound, just w; behind McDonalds. **Facility:** 50 units. 3 stories (no elevator), interior corridors. **Pool(s):** outdoor. **Guest Services:** coin laundry. **Free Special Amenities:** expanded continental breakfast and high-speed Internet.

 /SOME UNITS FEE

ECONO LODGE (530)662-9335

◆◆ **Motel** $45-$85 **Address:** 53 W Main St 95695 **Location:** I-5 exit 537 (Main St) northbound, 2 mi w; exit West St southbound, 1.5 mi s to Main St, then just w. **Facility:** 39 units. 2 stories (no elevator), exterior corridors. **Terms:** cancellation fee imposed. **Pool(s):** outdoor.

HAMPTON INN & SUITES WOODLAND/SACRAMENTO AREA (530)662-9100

◆◆◆ Hotel $119-$169

AAA Benefit: Members save up to 10%!

Address: 2060 Freeway Dr 95776 **Location:** I-5 exit 536 (CR 102), just n, just e on E Main St, then just s. **Facility:** 71 units. 3 stories, interior corridors. **Terms:** 1-7 night minimum stay, cancellation fee imposed. **Amenities:** high-speed Internet. **Pool(s):** outdoor. **Activities:** whirlpool, exercise room. **Guest Services:** valet and coin laundry. **Free Special Amenities:** full breakfast and airport transportation.

HOLIDAY INN EXPRESS HOTEL & SUITES

(530)662-7750

Hotel
$109-$179

Address: 2070 Freeway Dr 95776 **Location:** I-5 exit 536 (CR 102), just n, just e on E Main St, then just s. **Facility:** 70 units. 3 stories, interior corridors. **Amenities:** high-speed Internet. **Pool(s):** heated indoor. **Activities:** whirlpool, exercise room. **Guest Services:** complimentary and valet laundry, area transportation-within 2 mi.

QUALITY INN & SUITES

(530)666-3050

Motel
$80-$150

Address: 1562 E Main St 95776 **Location:** I-5 exit 537 (Main St) northbound; exit SR 113 (Davis) southbound, just w; behind Denny's. **Facility:** 49 units, some two bedrooms. 2 stories (no elevator), exterior corridors. **Pool(s):** outdoor. **Activities:** whirlpool. **Guest Services:** coin laundry. **Free Special Amenities: expanded continental breakfast and high-speed Internet.**

VALLEY OAKS INN

530/666-5511

Motel
Rates not provided

Address: 600 N East St 95776 **Location:** I-5 exit 538 (Yuba City/East St), northbound just s; southbound just n. **Facility:** 62 units. 2 stories (no elevator), exterior corridors. **Pool(s):** outdoor. **Activities:** whirlpool. **Guest Services:** coin laundry. **Free Special Amenities: continental breakfast and high-speed Internet.**

WHERE TO EAT

EL CHARRO MEXICAN RESTAURANT

530/661-3166

Mexican. Casual Dining. $6-$19 **AAA Inspector Notes:** This basic restaurant offers traditional renditions of Mexican food. **Bar:** full bar. **Address:** 415-417 Main St 95695 **Location:** I-5 exit Main St, 1.9 mi w. **Parking:** on-site and street.

LUDY'S MAIN ST BBQ & CATERING

530/666-4400

Barbecue. Casual Dining. $6-$25 **AAA Inspector Notes:** A corral-style decor lends character to this Western-style barbecue where burgers, sandwiches and smokehouse platters are offered. Select from the indoor dining room or an outdoor area, complete with heat lamps during the winter and fans during the summer, along with several water features including a brook, paddlewheel and fountains. **Bar:** beer & wine. **Address:** 667 Main St 95695 **Location:** I-5 exit 537 (Main St) northbound; exit SR 113 (Davis) southbound, 2 mi w.

PACO'S MEXICAN RESTAURANT

530/669-7946

Mexican. Casual Dining. $7-$15 **AAA Inspector Notes:** In what once was a bank, this renovated spot offers Mexican favorites, including a variety of shrimp dishes, burritos and enchiladas. Other offerings include selections for lighter eaters. **Bar:** beer & wine. **Reservations:** suggested. **Address:** 435 Main St 95695 **Location:** I-5 exit 537 (Main St), 1.9 mi w; jct College St. **Parking:** street only.

WOODSIDE (E-8) pop. 5,287, elev. 382'
• Hotels & Restaurants map & index p. 410

Woodside was founded in 1849, when the gold rush drastically increased the size and population of San Francisco. The wood needed for wharves, houses and commercial buildings was harvested from virgin redwood forests in this part of San Mateo County, and at one time there were 14 lumber mills in the vicinity.

FILOLI is off I-280 via Edgewood Rd. to Cañada Rd. This country estate was built over a 2-year period beginning in 1915 for prominent San Franciscans Mr. and Mrs. William B. Bourn II. The property includes a beautiful, 16-acre formal English Renaissance garden. The elegant, Georgian-style house is decorated with a large collection of 17th- and 18th-century English antiques. Docent-led nature hikes and orchard tours are offered.

Time: Allow 2 hours minimum. **Hours:** Grounds open Tues.-Sat. 10-3:30, Sun. 11-3:30, mid-Feb. to late Oct. Guided, 2-hour house and garden tours are given Tues.-Sat. at 10 and 1. Last admission 1 hour before closing. Nature hikes depart Sat. at 10, Feb.-July and Sept.-Oct. Orchard tours depart Wed. and Sat. at 10:30, June-Oct. Closed major holidays. **Cost:** $15; $12 (ages 65+); $5 (ages 5-17 and students with ID). Guided tours free. Reservations are required for guided tours. **Phone:** (650) 364-8300, ext. 507.

THE WOODSIDE STORE, 3300 Tripp Rd. at King's Mountain Rd., was built in 1854 and operated as a country store and post office until 1909. Restored to reflect its late 19th-century appearance, this living museum contains many examples of clothing, hardware and fixtures from that era. **Hours:** Tues. and Thurs. 10-4, Sat.-Sun. noon-4. Closed major holidays. **Cost:** Free. **Phone:** (650) 851-7615.

BELLA VISTA RESTAURANT

650/851-1229 **(95)**

Continental. Fine Dining. $26-$35 **AAA Inspector Notes:** Located up in the hills of Woodside, this restaurant offers panoramic views of the planes arriving and departing from the San Francisco Airport. Dark wood paneling and a cozy fireplace at the bar invite guests to linger with a glass of wine from the extensive wine collection. The souffle is a must-have for dessert. **Bar:** full bar. **Reservations:** suggested. **Address:** 13451 Skyline Blvd 94062 **Location:** On SR 35, between SR 92 and 84; n of SR 84; 5 mi s of SR 92.

THE VILLAGE PUB

650/851-9888 **(96)**

New American. Fine Dining. $14-$39 **AAA Inspector Notes:** This elegant, fine dining neighborhood pub offers two menus: one for dinner and one for the pub. High-quality ingredients, that are predominately organic, are used in the preparation of the dishes. The produce is grown on the restaurant's own organic farm nearby. **Bar:** full bar. **Reservations:** suggested. **Address:** 2967 Woodside Rd 94062 **Location:** I-280 exit SR 84 (Woodside Rd), 0.7 mi sw.

YOSEMITE NATIONAL PARK (F-4)

• Hotels p. 587 • Restaurants p. 587
• Attractions map p. 581
• Hotels & Restaurants map & index p. 584

Elevations in the park range from 2,000 ft. at
the park boundary at El Portal on SR 140 to
13,014 ft. at the summit of Mount Lyell. Refer
to AAA maps for additional
elevation information.

Reached by SR 140 (El Portal Road) from
Merced, SR 41 (Wawona Road) from Fresno, and
SR 120 (Big Oak Flat Road) from Stockton,
Yosemite National Park lies in central California on
the western slope of the Sierra Nevada in a region
of unusual beauty.

Glaciers transformed the rolling hills and meandering streams of pre-Pleistocene Yosemite into the
colossal landscape of the present. And although Indian tribes lived in the Yosemite area for thousands
of years, the first non-Indian visit was probably

made by the Joseph Walker expedition in 1833.

It was not until 1851, however, before the existence of the magnificent valley became well-known.
The Mariposa Battalion was sent to the area that
year to extinguish an ongoing conflict between gold
miners seeking their fortune and the resident
American Indians. The battalion entered Yosemite
Valley at Inspiration Point, and word of the land's
beauty quickly spread.

To preserve it for posterity, Abraham Lincoln set
aside the Mariposa grove of giant sequoias in the
Yosemite Valley as the nation's first state park on
June 30, 1864. John Muir, one of America's earliest
and foremost naturalists and conservationists, tire-
lessly advocated federal park status for Yosemite
Valley and its surroundings, and 26 years later, in
1890, Yosemite became a national park.

The park is much greater both in area and beauty
than most people generally realize; Yosemite Valley
actually comprises only a very small portion of park

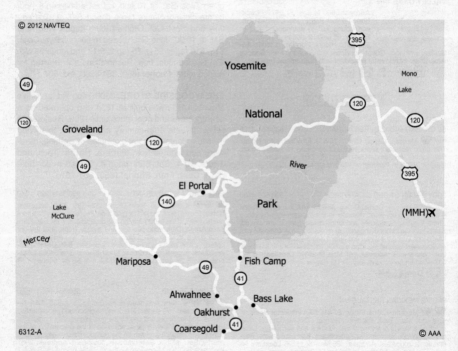

This map shows cities in Yosemite National Park where you will find attractions,
hotels and restaurants. Cities are listed alphabetically in this book on the following
pages.

(See map & index p. 584.)

land. The territory above the rim of the valley is less celebrated principally because it is less well-known. However, 196 miles of primary roads and more than 800 miles of trails now make much of this mountain region easily accessible to both motorist and hiker.

The crest of the Sierra Nevada is the park's eastern boundary, and the two rivers that flow through the park—the Merced and Tuolumne—originate among the snowy peaks. The Merced River flows through Yosemite Valley, and the Tuolumne River carves a magnificent gorge through the northern half of the park. Though spectacular through most of the year, many of the park's famous waterfalls are often dry during the late summer months.

With the exception of the Tioga Pass Road portion of SR 120, the Glacier Point Road and the Mariposa Grove Road, all of which are closed late fall through early summer, all roads are open year round; chains may be required at any time during winter months.

The road to Mirror Lake and Happy Isles, at the eastern end of Yosemite Valley, is closed to most cars but is served by a free shuttle bus. Southside Drive is one-way eastbound from Bridalveil Fall to Curry Village; Northside Drive is one-way westbound from Yosemite Lodge; and the road between Curry Village and Yosemite Village also is one-way westbound.

General Information and Activities

Yosemite National Park is open daily all year. Many roads in Yosemite Valley are one-way, and traffic can be heavy, especially in summer. Maps and information are available at the park's four visitor centers, and schedules of events are provided at park entrances and posted throughout the valley. A free shuttle bus operates in the east end of the valley daily 7 a.m.-10 p.m., in summer; hours vary rest of year. In the winter a shuttle runs from Yosemite Lodge to the Badger Pass Ski Area.

Wilderness permits, required of all overnight backpackers, are free at the Yosemite Valley Visitor Center or at any other wilderness permit station.

Some stations are open seasonally; phone ahead to confirm locations and hours. Reservations also are available for a fee of $5 per reservation plus $5 per person if obtained by phone or mail; phone (209) 372-0740. To make reservations by mail write Wilderness Association, P.O. Box 545, Yosemite, CA 95389. For information about wilderness permits phone (209) 372-0200.

A California fishing license is required for all park waters; an annual permit costs $44.85 for residents. A 10-day non-resident pass also is $44.85. A 2-day resident or non-resident license costs $22.42. Information about bicycle rentals is available at Curry Village and Yosemite Lodge; tour bus information also is given at these spots as well as at all lodging facilities.

Ranger-naturalists conduct year-round nature walks that last from a half-hour to 2 hours; snowshoe walks are available in the winter. Evening programs are presented all year at the Yosemite Lodge, and in summer at Curry Village, Lower Pines, Glacier Point, Tuolumne Meadows, Crane Flat, Wawona and White Wolf campgrounds.

An open-air tram offers frequent 2-hour tours of the valley during summer and occasional trips after Labor Day; reservations can be made at The Ahwahnee Hotel, Curry Village and Yosemite Lodge. Other tours depart daily in summer to Glacier Point and Mariposa Grove. Guided horseback tours of Wawona, Tuolumne Meadows and the valley also are available, as are multiday saddle and pack trips. A hiker shuttle goes to Glacier Point and Tuolumne Meadows.

Self-guiding tours of a re-created Ahwahneechee Indian village as well as a historic cemetery are available at Yosemite Village in Yosemite Valley. A museum houses photographs and historic books, while the artifacts in the Indian Cultural Exhibit depict the history of the Miwok and Paiute. A visitor center, a theater and an art center also are found in the village.

Skiing and skating can be enjoyed in winter. Curry Village has an outdoor skating rink; Badger Pass Ski Area has downhill and cross-country skiing. Cross-country ski trails lead from the Badger Pass and Crane Flat areas. Snowshoe tours are offered.

(See map & index p. 584.)

Child care is available in winter for a fee at Ski Tots Playhouse at Badger Pass. During summer the Junior Ranger Program of nature walks and classes welcomes students in grades 3 through 6; phone (209) 372-0200.

Campground reservations are available through the National Recreation Reservation System; phone (877) 444-6777, or TTY (877) 833-6777. *See Recreation Areas Chart.*

The main visitor center in Yosemite Valley is open year-round. Additional visitor information can be obtained at Big Oak Flat, Tuolumne Meadows and Wawona centers that usually are open June through September; for recorded information about camping, roads, weather conditions and recreation, phone (209) 372-0200.

ADMISSION to the park is by $20 private vehicle fee or $10 per person arriving by other means, and is good for 7 days.

PETS are not allowed on the trails or in public buildings and accommodations and must be leashed at all times. Pets are permitted in Upper Pines in Yosemite Valley, the west end of the campground at Tuolumne Meadows, and at White Wolf (Section C), Bridalveil (Section A), Crane Flat (Section A), Wawona, Hodgdon Meadows and Yosemite Creek campgrounds. Dogs can be boarded in Yosemite Valley from late May to mid-October.

ADDRESS inquiries concerning the park to the Superintendent, Yosemite National Park, P.O. Box 577, Yosemite National Park, CA 95389. Phone (209) 372-0200.

INSIDER INFO:
High-Altitude Health

Temples throbbing, gasping for breath and nauseated, you barely notice the scudding clouds or the spectacular view.

You might be suffering from Acute Mountain Sickness (AMS). Usually striking at around 8,000 feet (2,450 m) in altitude, AMS is your body's way of coping with the reduced oxygen and humidity of high altitudes. Among the symptoms are headaches, shortness of breath, loss of appetite, insomnia and lethargy. Some people complain of temporary weight gain or swelling in the face, hands and feet.

You can reduce the effect of high altitude by being in top condition. If you smoke or suffer from heart or lung ailments, consult your physician before your trip. Certain drugs will intensify the symptoms. To avoid Acute Mountain Sickness, adjust to elevations slowly; a gradual ascent with a couple days of acclimatization is best if you have time. For example, if you are planning a trip to the Rocky Mountains of Colorado, you might want to spend the first night in a lower altitude city such as Denver as opposed to heading directly to an environment with extreme elevations.

On the way up, eat light, nutritious meals and stay hydrated by drinking a large amount of water, taking care to avoid caffeine, alcohol and salt. In addition, your doctor may be able to prescribe medication that can offset the effects of high-altitude.

If you develop AMS, you should stop ascending; you will recover in a few days. If the AMS is mild, a quick descent will end the suffering immediately.

Other high-altitude health problems include sunburn and hypothermia. Dress in layers to protect yourself from the intense sun and wide fluctuations in temperature.

Finally, after you lounge in the sauna or whirlpool bath at your lodgings, remember to stand up carefully, for the heat has relaxed your blood vessels and lowered your blood pressure.

GLACIER POINT, 30 mi. from Yosemite Valley via Wawona Rd. to Chinquapin, then Glacier Point Rd., offers a panorama of domes, pinnacles, waterfalls and—dominating all—Half Dome *(see attraction listing p. 583).* From the stone lookout you can study the detail of the distant High Sierra and its flanking ranges. On the valley floor 3,214 feet below, automobiles appear as moving specks, and the Merced River resembles a silver thread.

The paved road to the point winds through pine and fir forests. In summer, bus tours and hiker shuttles to the point are available and ranger-naturalists are on duty. A 1.5-mile walk from the parking area leads to 8,122-foot Sentinel Dome. **Hours:** The road to Glacier Point normally is open late May through October; it is closed in winter past Badger Pass.

THE GRAND CANYON OF THE TUOLUMNE can be traversed only on foot; Waterwheel Falls is accessible by a trail 6 mi. from Tioga Rd. along the Tuolumne River Gorge to Glen Aulin High Sierra Camp, then 3 mi. down the river. At Waterwheel Falls the rushing river hits shelves of projecting rock with terrific force, throwing enormous arcs of water into the air; this spectacle is best viewed mid-June to mid-July.

Below the falls the river descends abruptly, plunging through a mile-deep gorge. Trails lead to Pate Valley, where only ancient mortar holes remain as a reminder of the Native Americans who once lived in this region. North of the Tuolumne River is a vast area of lakes and valleys. Though it is threaded with numerous trails, it remains lightly visited and offers a true wilderness experience. Hikers should inquire in advance about trail conditions.

HETCH HETCHY RESERVOIR is accessed from SR 120, just w. of the Big Oak Flat entrance; visitors can follow Evergreen Rd. to re-enter the park at Hetch Hetchy. The 38-mile drive from the valley can be covered easily in 2 hours. A paved road leads 7 miles from Mather to the 312-foot dam, which impounds San Francisco's water supply.

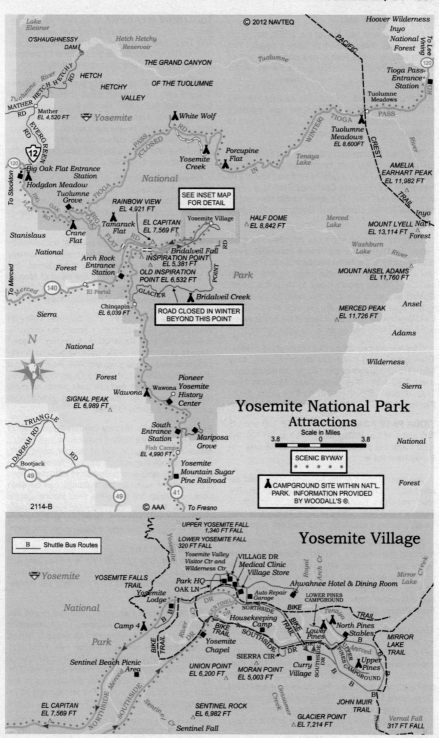

© 2012 NAVTEQ

Lake Eleanor

O'SHAUGHNESSY DAM

Hetch Hetchy Reservoir

Hoover Wilderness
Inyo National Forest

To Lee Vining

THE GRAND CANYON

OF THE TUOLUMNE

HETCH HETCHY VALLEY

Tuolumne River

HETCH HETCHY RD

MATHER RD

Mather EL 4,520 FT

Yosemite

White Wolf

Yosemite Creek

Porcupine Flat

Tuolumne Meadows EL 8,600 FT

Tioga Pass Entrance Station

120

TIOGA PASS

PACIFIC

AMELIA EARHART PEAK EL 11,982 FT

EVERGREEN RD

12

Big Oak Flat Entrance Station

To Stockton
120

Hodgdon Meadow
Tuolumne Grove

RAINBOW VIEW EL 4,921 FT

Tamarack Flat

EL CAPITAN EL 7,569 FT

Yosemite Village

SEE INSET MAP FOR DETAIL

HALF DOME △ EL 8,842 FT

Merced Lake

MOUNT LYELL Nat'l EL 13,114 FT Forest

National

TIOGA PASS RD (CLOSED IN WINTER)

BIG OAK FLAT RD

Crane Flat

Stanislaus

National

Forest

Arch Rock Entrance Station

To Merced
140

El Portal

Bridalveil Fall

INSPIRATION POINT EL 5,381 FT △

OLD INSPIRATION POINT EL 6,532 FT △

GLACIER POINT RD

Bridalveil Creek

Washburn Lake

Merced River

MOUNT ANSEL ADAMS EL 11,760 FT

Park

Chinquapin EL 6,039 FT

ROAD CLOSED IN WINTER BEYOND THIS POINT

MERCED PEAK EL 11,726 FT

Ansel

Sierra

National

Forest

N

Wilderness

Adams

TRIANGLE RD

Wawona

Wawona

Pioneer Yosemite History Center

SIGNAL PEAK EL 6,989 FT

Sierra

Yosemite National Park
Attractions

Scale in Miles

3.8   0   3.8

National

DARRAH RD

Bootjack

49

South Entrance Station

Fish Camp EL 4,990 FT

Mariposa Grove

Yosemite Mountain Sugar Pine Railroad

SCENIC BYWAY

CAMPGROUND SITE WITHIN NAT'L. PARK. INFORMATION PROVIDED BY WOODALL'S ®.

Forest

2114-B

© AAA

49

41

To Fresno

B — Shuttle Bus Routes

UPPER YOSEMITE FALL 1,340 FT FALL

LOWER YOSEMITE FALL 320 FT FALL

Yosemite Village

Yosemite

Yosemite Valley Visitor Ctr and Wilderness Ctr

VILLAGE DR

Medical Clinic Village Store

Royal Arch Cr

Mirror Lake

YOSEMITE FALLS TRAIL

Yosemite Lodge

National

Camp 4

Park

Sentinel Beach Picnic Area

EL CAPITAN EL 7,569 FT

Park HQ

OAK LN

Auto Repair Garage

NORTHSIDE DR

Housekeeping Camp

BIKE TRAIL

Yosemite Chapel

UNION POINT EL 6,200 FT

SENTINEL DR

SIERRA CIR

MORAN POINT EL 5,003 FT

SOUTHSIDE DR

Ahwahnee Hotel & Dining Room

LOWER PINES CAMPGROUND

BIKE TRAIL

Lower Pines

North Pines Stables

UPPER PINES CAMPGROUND

Upper Pines

TRAIL

Tenaya Cr

MIRROR LAKE TRAIL

Curry Village

SENTINEL ROCK △ EL 6,982 FT

Sentinel Fall

Merced River

GLACIER POINT △ EL 7,214 FT

JOHN MUIR TRAIL

Vernal Fall 317 FT FALL

(See map & index p. 584.)

Before the dam was built in the 1920s, the Hetch Hetchy Valley rivaled Yosemite Valley in beauty. The Hetch Hetchy Valley floor is now under 300 feet of water. You should carry tire chains in the fall, winter and spring.

MARIPOSA GROVE, reached via Wawona Rd. (SR 41), is in the extreme s. end of the park; the easy 36-mi. paved drive from Yosemite Valley is closed to vehicles during winter and spring.

This giant sequoia grove is one of the finest in the Sierras. The oldest tree, Grizzly Giant, has a base diameter of 30.7 feet, a girth of 96.5 feet and is 210 feet high; the 232-foot California Tree is a walk-through tunnel tree. The other tunnel tree in the park, the 40-foot stump Dead Giant, is in Tuolumne Grove.

Mariposa Grove Museum has exhibits about giant sequoias. During the summer a naturalist gives talks. Nearby is the fallen Massachusetts Tree, 280 feet long and 28 feet in diameter; several broken sections provide opportunities to study the wood. Guided bus tours run from the valley to the grove, with a stop in Wawona. An overlook at the 4,233-foot Wawona tunnel offers a view of the entire valley. A 2.5-mile hiking trail leads to the upper grove.

Cars are not permitted in the upper grove. **Hours:** Tram tours lasting 1.25 hours depart regularly, early May-Oct. 31 (weather permitting). Museum open daily 9:30-4:30, May-Sept. **Cost:** Museum free. Tram $26.50; $25 (ages 62+); $19 (ages 5-12). **Phone:** (209) 372-4386.

TIOGA PASS ROAD begins at jct. SR 120 and US 395 just s. of Lee Vining; also known as SR 120, the road traverses the park and provides the only entrance from the e.

The first 12 miles of the two-lane paved road ascend nearly a mile and overlook a vast canyon. The road traverses Tuolumne Meadows, descends to Tenaya Lake and continues west to Big Oak Flat Road, offering a scenic trip with frequent overlooks.

Although portions of the drive are more demanding than relaxing, the magnificent scenery attracts many motorists. Motorists should carry tire chains, since weather and road conditions can change quickly. **Hours:** The road is usually open late May-early Nov. (weather permitting). **Cost:** Free. **Phone:** (209) 372-0200 for road conditions.

TUOLUMNE GROVE, on old Big Oak Flat Rd., 17 mi. from Yosemite Valley, contains 20 giant sequoia trees, including the Dead Giant stump. Automobiles are no longer permitted on the section of Big Oak Flat Road adjacent to the grove. Visitors may park their cars near the Crane Flat Junction at a lot off of Tioga Road and walk to Tuolumne Grove; however, the mile-long route descends approximately 700 feet and the return ascent to the parking lot is a moderately strenuous climb.

TUOLUMNE MEADOWS is in the High Sierra, about 56 mi. from Yosemite Valley over Big Oak Flat and Tioga rds. At 8,600 feet in elevation and surrounded by lofty peaks, the area is ideal for camping and fishing, hiking and mountain-climbing.

Trips can be taken on foot or horseback to Waterwheel Falls, Mount Lyell, Lyell Glacier, Lembert Dome, Glen Aulin, Muir Gorge, Soda Springs and Tenaya Lake. Nature walks, hikes and evening campfire programs are conducted seasonally. Saddle horses, gas station, store and post office services and a mountaineering school and guide service also are available.

Hours: The meadows is accessible by car from about early June-Oct. 31. Daily bus service from Yosemite Valley is available early June to mid-Sept. (weather permitting), as are walks, hikes and campfire programs.

WASHBURN AND MERCED LAKES, accessible by trail only from Yosemite Valley, are typical of the many lakes bordering the western slopes of the Sierras. One of six High Sierra camps is at the head of Merced Lake and can be reached by trail from Yosemite Valley, Tenaya Lake or Tuolumne Meadows.

WAWONA is about 27 mi. s. of Yosemite Valley off Wawona Rd. (SR 41). Native Americans originally dubbed the area *Pallahchun,* meaning "a good place to stop." In the 1800s Wawona became an important pioneer stage stop and later evolved into a popular mountain resort. Its meadows, nearby river, and surrounding pine and oak trees create an idyllic recreation area that offers camping, riding, golf, swimming and tennis facilities.

Pioneer Yosemite History Center, 10 mi. n.w. of the South Entrance Station in Wawona, has historic cabins and buildings as well as outdoor, self-guiding exhibits about stagecoach days in Yosemite. The buildings are open and living-history demonstrations are offered in summer; the buildings can be seen from the outside the rest of the year. **Hours:** Center open daily. Buildings open and living-history demonstrations July 1-Labor Day; check at the visitor center to confirm schedule. **Phone:** (209) 375-9531.

YOSEMITE VALLEY, 27 mi. n. on SR 41 or also accessible from SRs 120 and 140, is 7 miles long and averages .7 mile wide; its walls rise to 3,200 feet. Immense precipices and lofty waterfalls are impressive natural features.

Upper Yosemite Fall drops 1,430 feet in one fall, a height equal to nine Niagaras. Lower Yosemite Fall drops 320 feet. Illilouette Fall drops 370 feet; Nevada Fall, 594 feet; and Ribbon Fall, 1,612 feet. The falls are at their fullest in May and June while winter snows melt. Fairly abundant up to mid-July, many practically disappear for the balance of the summer, then reappear with the first autumn storm and run lightly during winter.

The valley's domes and pinnacles—Three Brothers, El Capitan, Cathedral Spires, North Dome

(See map & index p. 584.)
and Half Dome—are as celebrated as the falls. **Hours:** Open all year.

Bridalveil Fall is accessed via the Bridalveil Fall parking area, .5 mi. e. of the start of Wawona Rd. (SR 41) in Yosemite Valley. Flowing all year, the 620-foot-tall waterfall is often the first seen by entering park visitors. Because the fall doesn't always reach the ground due to its light, swaying flow summer through winter, the Ahwahneechee Indians named it *Pohono,* meaning "spirit of the puffing wind." A .25-mile paved trail leads to a viewing area. **Note:** Visitors without full mobility are advised the last 50 feet of the trail are very steep.

El Capitan is about 4 mi. s.w. of Yosemite Village, reached via Yosemite Valley hiking trails. Rising nearly 3,000 feet above the valley floor, the world's largest monolith of granite is popular with experienced rock climbers. El Capitan was first conquered in 1958 over a period of 17 months; in 1975, a trio of climbers ascended it in 1 day. One of the best views of El Capitan is found just opposite the rock formation at Bridalveil Fall. El Capitan Meadow off Northside Drive is another good viewpoint.

Half Dome is about 3.3 mi. e. of Yosemite Village, reached via Yosemite Valley hiking trails. The granite dome, a familiar landmark, rises more than 4,000 feet above the valley floor; it can be seen throughout eastern Yosemite Valley and Glacier Point.

A very strenuous 8.5-mile hike to the top typically takes 5-6 hours one way, with metal cables assisting hikers up the last 900 feet. Permits are required above the subdome and can be reserved up to 4 months in advance. **Note:** Visitors are advised not to ascend Half Dome when cables are not erected or if thunderclouds are visible. **Hours:** Daily 24 hours (weather permitting); cables available late May-early Oct.

Vernal Fall is accessible via the 1.5-mi. Mist Trail from Happy Isles in Yosemite Valley. Visitors climb the uphill trail through the mist of the fall, which flows year-round. By mid- to late summer, the 317-foot-tall waterfall often splits into separate falls as water flows decrease. A footbridge along Mist Trail offers great views of Vernal Fall, as does Glacier Point. The top of Vernal Fall is accessible via the Mist Trail, May through October; access is via the John Muir Trail the rest of the year.

Note: The steep hike to the top of the fall requires climbing 600 granite steps. In spring and early summer, hikers should expect to get wet. **Hours:** Daily 24 hours (weather permitting).

Yosemite Falls is .5 mi. e. of Yosemite Village, accessed via Yosemite Valley hiking trails. Towering at 2,425 feet, the highest North American waterfall is actually made up of three separate falls: Upper Yosemite Fall, the middle cascades and Lower Yosemite Fall. Starting at the Lower Yosemite Fall shuttle bus stop, a .25-mile paved trail leads to the bottom of the lower fall. A strenuous 3.6-mile hike to the top of the upper fall typically takes about 3-4 hours one way. **Note:** Hiking to the top of the upper fall requires full mobility.

YOSEMITE VALLEY VISITOR CENTER AND WILDERNESS CENTER is in Yosemite Village; take El Portal Rd. (SR 140) e. 3.3 mi. to Southside Dr./Tecoya Rd., then .3 mi. to Village Dr. The center provides detailed trip-planning information about the park, offering maps, books, exhibits and audiovisual programs. An orientation film called "Spirit of Yosemite" is shown in the Valley Visitor Center Theater.

Also featuring information about the park's back country and wilderness areas, it contains a variety of displays for hikers and climbers. Interactive exhibits for children include a bear cave and a simulated sequoia tree and glacier. **Hours:** Visitor center daily 9-6, year-round. Wilderness center daily 8-5, in summer. Film is presented Mon.-Sat. every 30 minutes 9:30-5:30, Sun. noon-5:30. **Cost:** Free. **Phone:** (209) 372-0200.

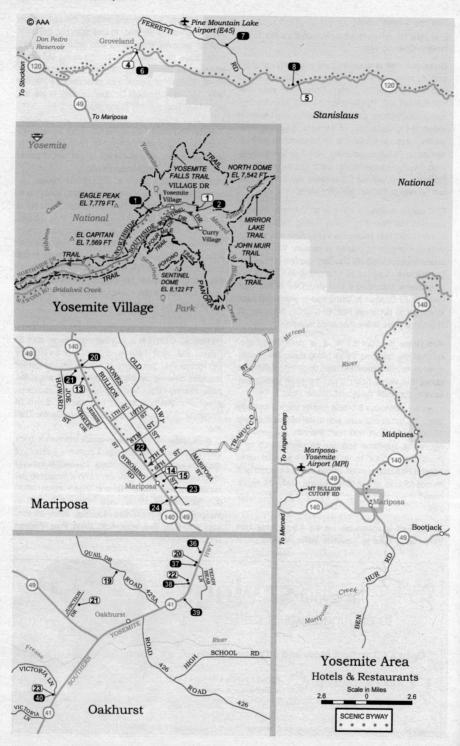

© AAA

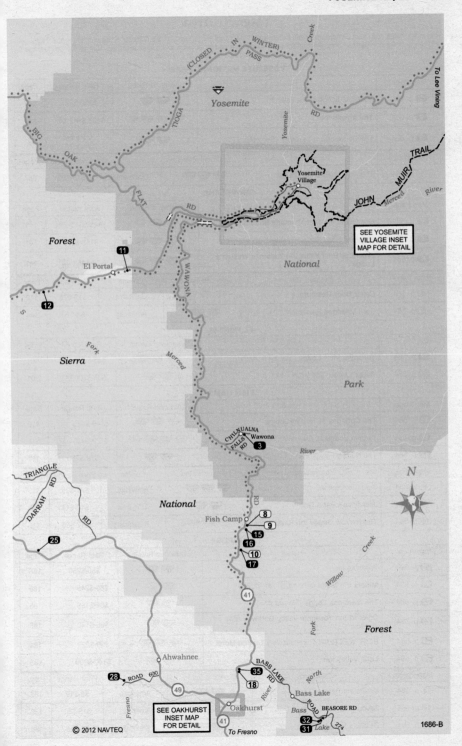

1686-B

Yosemite Area

This index helps you "spot" where approved hotels and restaurants are located on the corresponding detailed maps. Hotel daily rate range is for comparison only. Restaurant price range is a combination of lunch and/or dinner. Turn to the listing page for more detailed rate and price information and consult display ads for special promotions.

YOSEMITE NATIONAL PARK

Map Page	Hotels	Diamond Rated	Rate Range	Page
1 p. 584	Yosemite Lodge at the Falls	◆◆	$150-$227	587
2 p. 584	**The Ahwahnee**	◆◆◆◆	$433-$542 (SAVE)	587
3 p. 584	The Redwoods In Yosemite *(See ad p. 591.)*	◆◆	Rates not provided	587

Map Page	Restaurant	Diamond Rated	Cuisine	Price Range	Page
(1) p. 584	The Ahwahnee Dining Room	◆◆◆	Continental	$15-$50	587

GROVELAND

Map Page	Hotels	Diamond Rated	Rate Range	Page
6 p. 584	**Groveland Hotel at Yosemite National Park**	◆◆◆	$145-$345 (SAVE)	141
7 p. 584	Yosemite Rose Bed & Breakfast	◆◆◆	$155-$275	141
8 p. 584	**Americas Best Value Inn-Yosemite Westgate Lodge**	◆◆◆	$79-$459 (SAVE)	141

Map Page	Restaurants	Diamond Rated	Cuisine	Price Range	Page
(4) p. 584	**Cellar Door Restaurant**	◆◆◆	California	$12-$25	142
(5) p. 584	Buck Meadows Restaurant	◆◆	American	$8-$23	141

EL PORTAL

Map Page	Hotels	Diamond Rated	Rate Range	Page
11 p. 584	**Yosemite View Lodge** *(See ad p. 589.)*	◆◆◆	$95-$499 (SAVE)	101
12 p. 584	**Cedar Lodge** *(See ad p. 589.)*	◆◆	$95-$700 (SAVE)	101

FISH CAMP

Map Page	Hotels	Diamond Rated	Rate Range	Page
15 p. 584	**The Cottages at Tenaya Lodge**	◆◆◆	$149-$425 (SAVE)	110
16 p. 584	**Tenaya Lodge at Yosemite** *(See ad p. 588.)*	◆◆◆◆	$129-$425 (SAVE)	111
17 p. 584	The Narrow Gauge Inn	◆◆	$79-$250	111

Map Page	Restaurants	Diamond Rated	Cuisine	Price Range	Page
(8) p. 584	Sierra Restaurant	◆◆◆	American	$21-$35	111
(9) p. 584	Jackalope's Bar & Grill	◆◆	American	$10-$14	111
(10) p. 584	**The Narrow Gauge Inn Restaurant**	◆◆◆	American	$17-$36	111

MARIPOSA

Map Page	Hotels	Diamond Rated	Rate Range	Page
20 p. 584	Yosemite Inn	◆◆	$50-$250	186
21 p. 584	**Miners Inn Motel** *(See ad p. 186, p. 588.)*	◆◆	$69-$249 (SAVE)	186
22 p. 584	**The Mariposa Lodge** *(See ad p. 590.)*	◆◆	$69-$159 (SAVE)	185
23 p. 584	**Comfort Inn Yosemite Valley Gateway** *(See ad p. 185.)*	◆◆	$90-$170 (SAVE)	185
24 p. 584	**BEST WESTERN Yosemite Way Station Motel**	◆◆◆	$59-$229 (SAVE)	184
25 p. 584	**Little Valley Inn**	◆◆	$140-$200 (SAVE)	185

Map Page	Restaurants	Diamond Rated	Cuisine	Price Range	Page
(13) p. 584	Miners Inn Restaurant	◆◆	American	$8-$19	186
(14) p. 584	Savoury's	◆◆◆	American	$15-$30	186
(15) p. 584	Castillo's Mexican Restaurant	◆◆	Mexican	$8-$16	186

AHWAHNEE

Map Page	Hotel	Diamond Rated	Rate Range	Page
28 p. 584	The Homestead	◈◈◈	$149-$399	42

BASS LAKE

Map Page	Hotels	Diamond Rated	Rate Range	Page
31 p. 584	**The Pines Resort Chalets**	◈◈	Rates not provided [SAVE]	50
32 p. 584	**The Pines Resort Suites**	◈◈◈	Rates not provided [SAVE]	50

OAKHURST

Map Page	Hotels	Diamond Rated	Rate Range	Page
35 p. 584	Hounds Tooth Inn	◈◈◈	$95-$235	248
36 p. 584	**Days Inn**	◈◈	$80-$259 [SAVE]	248
37 p. 584	Yosemite Southgate Hotel & Suites	◈◈◈	$79-$300	248
38 p. 584	**BEST WESTERN PLUS Yosemite Gateway Inn**	◈◈◈	$85-$199 [SAVE]	248
39 p. 584	**Comfort Inn Yosemite Area**	◈◈	$70-$200 [SAVE]	248
40 p. 584	**Château du Sureau**	◈◈◈◈	$385-$585 [SAVE]	248

Map Page	Restaurants	Diamond Rated	Cuisine	Price Range	Page
18 p. 584	El Cid	◈◈	Mexican	$8-$20	248
19 p. 584	**Crab Cakes**	◈◈	Seafood	$7-$40	248
20 p. 584	Ol'Kettle Restaurant	◈◈	American	$8-$18	249
21 p. 584	Woody's New Orleans West	◈◈	Cajun	$13-$26	249
22 p. 584	Yosemite Gateway Restaurant	◈◈	American	$8-$27	249
23 p. 584	**Erna's Elderberry House Restaurant**	◈◈◈◈	French	$45-$95	248

YOSEMITE NATIONAL PARK
- Attractions map p. 581
- Hotels & Restaurants map & index p. 584

THE AHWAHNEE   (209)372-1407 **2**
◈◈◈◈
Historic Hotel
$433-$542

Address: 1 Ahwahnee Rd 95389 **Location:** 0.8 mi e; beyond park headquarters. **Facility:** On spacious, shady grounds with park views, the property has impressive common areas. Guest rooms are tight with a love seat and chair. Reservations should be made far in advance. 123 units. 1-7 stories, interior/exterior corridors. **Parking:** on-site and valet. **Terms:** check-in 4 pm, 7 day cancellation notice-fee imposed. **Amenities:** safes. **Dining:** restaurant, see separate listing. **Pool(s):** heated outdoor. **Activities:** fishing, hiking trails, jogging. **Fee:** downhill & cross country skiing, ice skating, bicycles, horseback riding. **Guest Services:** valet laundry, area transportation-valley floor. **Free Special Amenities:** local telephone calls and high-speed Internet.

THE REDWOODS IN YOSEMITE   209/375-6666 **3**

◈◈ **Vacation Rental House.** Rates not provided. **Location:** 6 mi inside southern entrance via SR 41 and Chilnualna Falls Rd. Located in Wawona. **Facility:** Choose between several types of homes, each set in a mature wooded setting and some near flowing creeks. The units allow you to experience all of the park's natural wonders. 132 houses. 1-2 stories (no elevator), exterior corridors. **Terms:** check-in 4 pm. **Amenities:** Some: high-speed Internet. **Guest Services:** coin laundry. (See ad p. 591.)

YOSEMITE LODGE AT THE FALLS   (209)372-1274 **1**
◈◈ **Hotel** $150-$227 **Address:** 9006 Yosemite Lodge Dr 95389 **Location:** In Yosemite Valley; 0.8 mi w of park headquarters. Located near Yosemite Falls. **Facility:** 245 units. 1-2 stories (no elevator), interior/exterior corridors. **Terms:** check-in 5 pm, 7 day cancellation notice-fee imposed. **Dining:** 2 restaurants. **Pool(s):** outdoor. **Activities:** fishing, recreation programs in summer, rental bicycles, hiking trails, jogging. **Fee:** downhill & cross country skiing, ice skating, horseback riding. **Guest Services:** area transportation.

WHERE TO EAT

THE AHWAHNEE DINING ROOM   209/372-1489 **1**
◈◈◈ Continental. Fine Dining. $15-$50 **AAA Inspector Notes:** Everyone makes a grand entrance into this cavernous yet breathtaking dining room. Large windows bring nature's beauty inside-breakfast and lunch are best to experience this. Experienced staffers provide service in an elegant setting where Yosemite National Park serves as the backdrop. Be prepared to dress for dinner, and call ahead for reservations. **Bar:** full bar. **Reservations:** suggested. **Address:** 1 Ahwahnee Rd 95389 **Location:** 0.8 mi e; beyond park headquarters; in The Ahwahnee. **Parking:** on-site and valet.

Give the gift of security, value and peace of mind:

Gift Membership

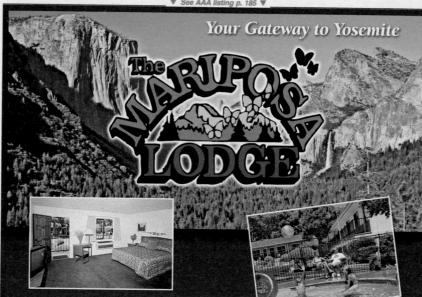

▼ See AAA listing p. 587 ▼

YOUNTVILLE (B-8) pop. 2,933, elev. 100'
- **Attractions map p. 568**
- **Hotels & Restaurants map & index p. 570**
- **Part of Wine Country area — see map p. 562**

Yountville, on a scenic stretch of SR 29 extending from Calistoga to Napa, was founded by George Yount, a fur trader from North Carolina, in 1835. Yount is said to have planted the first grapevines in the Napa Valley.

Yountville Chamber of Commerce: 6484 Washington St., Suite F, P.O. Box 2064, Yountville, CA 94599. **Phone:** (707) 944-0904.

Shopping areas: V Marketplace 1870, 6525 Washington St., offers specialty shops, art galleries and upscale dining choices in a restored 19th-century winery.

NAPA VALLEY MUSEUM is at 55 Presidents Cir., on the grounds of the Veterans Home. Two permanent exhibits explore the culture of the Napa Valley, the process of winemaking—from growing the grapes to bottling the final product—and the region's natural environment and human history. Changing art exhibits also are on display.

Time: Allow 1 hour minimum. **Hours:** Tues.-Sun. 10-4. Closed major holidays. **Cost:** $5; $3.50 (ages 60+ and students with ID); $2.50 (ages 7-17). **Phone:** (707) 944-0500.

RECREATIONAL ACTIVITIES
Hot Air Ballooning
- **Napa Valley Aloft** departs from the V Marketplace 1870 shopping complex, 6525 Washington St. **Hours:** Trips depart daily at dawn (weather permitting). Closed Christmas. **Phone:** (707) 944-4400 or (855) 944-4408.

WINERIES
- **Cliff Lede Vineyards** is n. on SR 29, e. on Madison St., n. onto Yount St., then 1.5 mi. e. to 1473 Yountville Cross Rd. **Hours:** Daily 10-4. Tours are given Tues.-Sat. by appointment. Closed Jan. 1, Easter, Thanksgiving and Christmas. **Phone:** (707) 944-8642 or (800) 428-2259.
- **Domaine Chandon** is at 1 California Dr. **Hours:** Daily 10-5. Tours are given at 10:30, 11 and 3. Closed Jan. 1, Thanksgiving, Christmas Eve and Christmas. **Phone:** (707) 944-2280.
- **Goosecross Cellars** is 1.4 mi. n.e. on Yountville Cross Rd., then .3 mi. w. to 1119 State Ln. **Hours:** Tastings daily 10-4:30. Reservations are required for the Top Flight tasting room. Closed Jan. 1, Easter, Thanksgiving and Christmas. **Phone:** (707) 944-1986 or (800) 276-9210.

LAVENDER (707)944-1388 **35**
▼▼▼ Bed & Breakfast $235-$350 **Address:** 2020 Webber Ave 94599 **Location:** SR 29 exit Yountville, just w of Yount St at Webber Ave and Jefferson St; center. **Facility:** This charming inn offers accommodations in the main house or at the courtyard. Some units include a fireplace, private patio or jetted tub. The swing on the wrap-around veranda is a popular spot for relaxation. 8 units. 3 stories, interior/exterior corridors. **Terms:** 7 day cancellation notice-fee imposed. **Guest Services:** valet laundry.
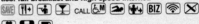

MAISON FLEURIE (707)944-2056 **37**
▼▼▼ Bed & Breakfast $155-$325 **Address:** 6529 Yount St 94599 **Location:** SR 29 exit Yountville; just s of Finnell Rd and Yount St; center. **Facility:** 13 units. 3 stories (no elevator), interior/exterior corridors. **Terms:** 7 day cancellation notice-fee imposed. **Pool(s):** heated outdoor. **Activities:** whirlpool, bicycles.

NAPA VALLEY LODGE (707)944-2468 **34**
▼▼▼ ▼▼▼
Hotel
$295-$665
Address: 2230 Madison St 94599 **Location:** SR 29 exit Madison St, just e. **Facility:** Many of the lodge's guest rooms, some of which overlook vineyards and the surrounding hills, feature a fireplace. Some rooms are close to SR 29. 55 units. 2 stories (no elevator), exterior corridors. **Terms:** check-in 4 pm, 2 night minimum stay - seasonal and/or weekends, 7 day cancellation notice-fee imposed. **Amenities:** video games (fee), high-speed Internet, safes. **Pool(s):** heated outdoor. **Activities:** whirlpool, exercise room, spa. **Guest Services:** valet laundry. **Free Special Amenities: expanded continental breakfast and high-speed Internet.**

VILLAGIO INN & SPA 707/944-8877 **38**
▼▼▼ ▼▼▼
Hotel
Rates not provided
Address: 6481 Washington St 94599 **Location:** SR 29 exit Yountville; at Humboldt and Washington sts; center. **Facility:** This beautiful property offers well-appointed guest rooms, some with a fireplace and private balcony or patio. Decorative waterways cascade along the walkways to create a peaceful setting. 112 units. 2 stories, exterior corridors. **Terms:** check-in 4 pm. **Amenities:** high-speed Internet, safes. **Pool(s):** heated outdoor. **Activities:** sauna, whirlpool, 2 lighted tennis courts, spa. **Fee:** bicycles. **Guest Services:** valet laundry. **Free Special Amenities: full breakfast and high-speed Internet.**

VINTAGE INN (707)944-1112 **36**
▼▼▼ ▼▼▼
Boutique Hotel
$225-$700
Address: 6541 Washington St 94599 **Location:** SR 29 exit Yountville; at Humboldt and Washington sts; center. **Facility:** Picturesque vineyard, mountain and town views can be seen from the inn's many balconies and patios; all rooms have a wood-burning fireplace and whirlpool tub. 80 units. 2 stories (no elevator), exterior corridors. **Terms:** check-in 4 pm, 2 night minimum stay - weekends, 7 day cancellation notice-fee imposed. **Amenities:** high-speed Internet, safes. **Pool(s):** heated outdoor. **Activities:** whirlpool, 2 tennis courts, spa. **Fee:** bicycles. **Guest Services:** valet laundry. **Free Special Amenities: full breakfast and high-speed Internet.**

BARDESSONO HOTEL 707/204-6000
[fyi] Not evaluated. **Address:** 6526 Yount St 94599 **Location:** Just s at Finnell Rd and Yount St; center. Facilities, services, and décor characterize an upscale property.

WHERE TO EAT

BOTTEGA RISTORANTE 707/945-1050 **19**
▼▼▼ Italian. Fine Dining. $16-$34 **AAA Inspector Notes:** Celebrity chef Michael Chiarello's creations-including such standouts as braised short ribs, polenta under glass and homemade pasta-are complemented by a contemporary dining space accented by exposed beams, leather and copper. **Bar:** full bar. **Address:** 6525 Washington St, Suite A-9 94599 **Location:** SR 29 exit Yountville; center. [L] [D]

(See map & index p. 570.)

ETOILE AT DOMAINE CHANDON　707/944-2892　⑳

French
Fine Dining
$24-$36

AAA Inspector Notes: This upscale restaurant's lunch menu focuses on California cuisine, while dinner offerings are more French in scope. The restaurant is surrounded by beautifully landscaped gardens and fountains. A visitors center displays the history of the winery. **Bar:** wine only. **Reservations:** suggested. **Address:** 1 California Dr 94599 **Location:** W off SR 29; adjacent to Veteran's Home. ⓛ ⓓ

THE FRENCH LAUNDRY　707/944-2380　⑱

American
Fine Dining
$270

AAA Inspector Notes: Chef Thomas Keller has created a distinctive dining experience in the midst of Napa Valley wine country. The old stone farm house has been delightfully outfitted for an intimate outing with just a few more than a dozen tables. The meal might include delectable morsels such as sesame cornets with smoked salmon, Elysian Fields Farm lamb chops with Belgian endive gratin and Hen-of-the-Woods mushrooms. Semi-formal attire. **Bar:** beer & wine. **Reservations:** required. **Address:** 6640 Washington St 94599 **Location:** Jct SR 29 exit Madison St, just e, then just s; center. **Parking:** street only. ⓓ

MUSTARD'S GRILL　707/944-2424　⑰
American. Fine Dining. $12-$38 **AAA Inspector Notes:** A popular spot with locals and tourists alike, this casual establishment has been defining fine dining for two decades. Herbs used in the preparation of the food are grown just outside the door. **Bar:** full bar. **Reservations:** suggested. **Address:** 7399 St. Helena Hwy 94558 **Location:** On SR 29, 1.5 mi n. ⓛ ⓓ

YREKA (A-2) pop. 7,765, elev. 2,625'

Yreka (pronounced Why-REEK-uh), 22 miles south of the Oregon border, was incorporated in 1857, 6 years after Abraham Thompson discovered gold flecks on the roots of the grass his mules were eating. Miners soon swarmed into this lush valley, which had long been home to the Karuk and Shasta Indians. The boom fizzled out about 1885, after more than $60 million worth of valuable ore had been extracted from the earth. I-5 is a scenic route to and through Yreka.

The historic downtown district—including the appropriately named main thoroughfare, Miner Street—contains a number of beautifully restored, late 19th- and early 20th-century buildings housing shops and restaurants. Information markers throughout the district describe the original purpose of many of the structures. Such residential areas as Third Street are rich with Gothic Revival and Victorian houses that date back to the 1800s.

The headquarters office of Klamath National Forest (see place listing p. 156), 1711 S. Main St., has information about recreational activities, which include hiking, white-water rafting, fishing, snowmobiling and biking; phone (530) 842-6131. See Recreation Areas Chart.

Yreka Chamber of Commerce: 117 W. Miner St., Yreka, CA 96097. **Phone:** (530) 842-1649.

Self-guiding tours: Stop by the chamber of commerce office for walking and driving tour maps of the historic district and historic homes area.

GREENHORN PARK, w. off Greenhorn Rd. at Greenhorn Reservoir, features a restored miner's cabin and mining equipment. Nature trails, a playground and picnic facilities are available. Fishing and non-motorized boating are permitted. **Hours:** Daily 7:30-dusk. **Cost:** Free. **Phone:** (530) 841-2386.

LIBERTY ARTS GALLERY is at 108 W. Miner St. This contemporary art gallery features rotating exhibits by local and regional artists and also serves as a community exhibition space and education center. **Time:** Allow 30 minutes minimum. **Hours:** Wed.-Sat. 10-5. Closed major holidays. **Cost:** Free. **Phone:** (530) 842-0222.

SISKIYOU COUNTY COURTHOUSE, 311 Fourth St., exhibits various forms of gold. **Hours:** Mon.-Fri. 8-5. Closed major holidays. **Cost:** Free. **Phone:** (530) 842-8005.

SISKIYOU COUNTY MUSEUM, 910 S. Main St., contains exhibits of the region dating from the 19th and 20th centuries. Featured are displays about Native Americans, fur trappers, gold mining, logging and lumbering, and the military. The outdoor museum displays equipment and restored buildings in a mid-1800s mining and pioneer settlement. **Time:** Allow 2 hours minimum. **Hours:** Tues.-Fri. 9-3, Sat. 10-4, Memorial Day-Sept. 30; Tues.-Thurs. 9-3, Sat. 10-4, rest of year. Closed major holidays. **Cost:** $3; 75c (ages 7-12). **Phone:** (530) 842-3836.

RECREATIONAL ACTIVITIES

White-water Rafting

• **Orange Torpedo Trips** travels the Klamath River. **Hours:** Daily Apr.-Oct. **Phone:** (541) 479-5061 or (866) 479-5061.

BAYMONT INN & SUITES　(530)841-1300

Hotel
$59-$90

Address: 148 Moonlit Oaks Ave 96097 **Location:** I-5 exit 773, just w. **Facility:** 60 units. 2 stories (no elevator), interior corridors. **Amenities:** safes (fee). *Some:* high-speed Internet. **Pool(s):** heated indoor. **Activities:** whirlpool, limited exercise equipment. *Fee:* game room. **Guest Services:** coin laundry.

SAVE ⅱ↾ 🛀 BIZ 🛜 ☕ / SOME UNITS FEE 🐾 🛏 🖼

BEST WESTERN MINER'S INN & CONVENTION CENTER　(530)842-4355

Motel
$106-$124

AAA Benefit: Members save up to 20%, plus 10% bonus points with Best Western Rewards®.

Address: 122 E Miner St 96097 **Location:** I-5 exit 776, just w to N Main St, then just s; exit 775, just w to N Main St, then just n; center. **Facility:** 134 units, some two bedrooms and efficiencies. 2 stories (no elevator), exterior corridors. **Amenities:** *Some:* high-speed Internet. **Pool(s):** 2 heated outdoor. **Activities:** playground, horseshoes, volleyball. **Free Special Amenities:** expanded continental breakfast and local telephone calls.

SAVE ⅱ↾ 🛁 FEE ↾┼ 🛜 🛏 🖼 🖼

 / SOME UNITS FEE 🐾

COMFORT INN
(530)842-1612

Hotel
$70-$150

Address: 1804-B Fort Jones Rd 96097 **Location:** I-5 exit 773, just w. **Facility:** 50 units. 3 stories (no elevator), interior corridors. **Terms:** cancellation fee imposed. **Pool(s):** outdoor. **Free Special Amenities: full breakfast and high-speed Internet.**

ECONO LODGE INN & SUITES
(530)842-4404

Motel
$46-$130

Address: 526 S Main St 96097 **Location:** I-5 exit 775, just w to Main St, then just s. **Facility:** 43 units, some kitchens. 2 stories (no elevator), exterior corridors. **Bath:** shower only. **Terms:** cancellation fee imposed. **Pool(s):** outdoor. **Free Special Amenities: continental breakfast and high-speed Internet.**

     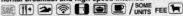

HOLIDAY INN EXPRESS & SUITES YREKA-SHASTA
(530)842-1600

Contemporary Hotel
$99-$159

Address: 707 Montague Rd 96097 **Location:** I-5 exit 776, just e. **Facility:** 68 units. 3 stories, interior corridors. **Terms:** 3 day cancellation notice. **Amenities:** high-speed Internet. **Pool(s):** heated indoor. **Activities:** exercise room. **Guest Services:** coin laundry. **Free Special Amenities: full breakfast and high-speed Internet.**

KLAMATH MOTOR LODGE
(530)842-2751

Motel
$50-$65

Address: 1111 S Main St 96097 **Location:** I-5 exit 775 southbound, just w to Main St, then 0.9 mi s; exit 773 northbound, just w to Main St, then 1.1 mi n; center. **Facility:** 28 units. 2 stories (no elevator), exterior corridors. **Pool(s):** heated outdoor. **Free Special Amenities: continental breakfast and high-speed Internet.**

RODEWAY INN
(530)842-4412
Motel
$46-$70

Address: 1235 S Main St 96097 **Location:** I-5 exit 775 southbound, just w to Main St, then 0.9 mi s; exit 773 northbound, just w to Main St, then 1.1 mi n. **Facility:** 23 units. 1 story, exterior corridors. **Terms:** cancellation fee imposed. **Pool(s):** outdoor. **Guest Services:** coin laundry. **Free Special Amenities: continental breakfast and high-speed Internet.**

SUPER 8
(530)842-5781
Motel
$55-$75

Address: 136 Montague Rd 96097 **Location:** I-5 exit 776, just w. **Facility:** 61 units. 2 stories (no elevator), exterior corridors. **Amenities:** safes. **Pool(s):** outdoor. **Activities:** exercise room. **Guest Services:** coin laundry. **Free Special Amenities: continental breakfast and high-speed Internet.**

BLACK BEAR DINER
530/842-9324
American. Casual Dining. $7-$18 **AAA Inspector Notes:** A homey atmosphere characterizes this family-oriented restaurant. Familiar comfort foods, such as meatloaf with mashed potatoes, are at the heart of the menu and are served in generous portions. **Bar:** beer & wine. **Address:** 1747 S Main St 96097 **Location:** On SR 3, just s. [B] [L] [D]

BRICKHOUSE BAKERY & PIZZERIA
530/841-0553
American. Quick Serve. $6-$25 **AAA Inspector Notes:** Popular local hangout serving made-to-order piping hot pizza with generous toppings. Get one of their pastries for a sweet ending. **Bar:** beer & wine. **Address:** 313 W Miner St 96097 **Location:** I-5 exit 775, just w; center. **Parking:** street only. [L] [D]

CASA RAMOS
530/842-7172
Mexican. Casual Dining. $7-$17 **AAA Inspector Notes:** A varied Mexican menu is featured in a colorful atmosphere. Mexican favorites include fajitas, enchiladas, burritos and specialty steak and seafood entrees. **Bar:** full bar. **Address:** 145 Montague Rd 96097 **Location:** I-5 exit 776, just w. [L] [D]

NATURE'S KITCHEN CAFE 530/842-1136

◆◆◆ ◆◆◆ Sandwiches Natural/Organic. Casual Dining. $8-$11 **AAA Inspector Notes:** Located in a popular natural foods store and gift shop, this eatery features simple, well-prepared food such as cold and hot vegetarian sandwiches and a nice selection of chicken, egg and tuna salads, as well as a salad sampler. **Address:** 412 S Main St 96097 **Location:** I-5 exit 775, just w to SR 3, then just s. **Parking:** street only. L

PURPLE PLUM 530/842-0640

◆◆◆ ◆◆◆ American. Casual Dining. $8-$18 **AAA Inspector Notes:** In the center of town, the gray building with blue awnings is hard to miss. This family-friendly spot serves food that is cooked from scratch including chicken, seafood, steak and pasta dishes as well as salads. **Bar:** beer & wine. **Address:** 105 E Miner St 96097 **Location:** I-5 exit 775, just w. B L D

YUBA CITY (D-3) pop. 64,925, elev. 60'

Yuba City was founded in 1849 as a gold rush development; it is now a marketing center for the surrounding agricultural area. The 1899 county courthouse and the 1891 county hall of records are both part of the Second Street historic district. Surrounding blocks contain a collection of Victorian residences that reflect Italianate, Classical and East-lake characteristics.

Yuba-Sutter Chamber of Commerce 1300 Franklin Rd., Yuba City, CA 95993. **Phone:** (530) 743-6501.

COMMUNITY MEMORIAL MUSEUM, 1333 Butte House Rd., contains Native American and pioneer artifacts, furniture, clothing, agricultural equipment, photographs and historical documents from Sutter County. **Hours:** Wed.-Fri. 9-5, Sat. noon-4. **Cost:** Donations. **Phone:** (530) 822-7141.

SUTTER BUTTES are 10 mi. w. on Butte House Rd. Sometimes referred to as the world's smallest mountain range, this brooding cluster of dark rocks rises some 2,000 feet and covers about 75 square miles. The buttes are a volcanic upthrust formation, something of a geologic anomaly for this area, and are popular with nature lovers, who enjoy the abundant bird life and wildflowers. Although much of the region is private property, visitors can join nature study groups and guided hikes. **Phone:** (530) 671-6116.

BEST WESTERN YUBA CITY INN (530)674-1650

◆◆◆ ◆◆◆ ◆◆◆
Motel
$80-$120

AAA Benefit: Members save up to 20%, plus 10% bonus points with Best Western Rewards®.

Address: 894 W Onstott Rd 95991 **Location:** Just s of jct SR 99 and 20. **Facility:** 91 units. 2 stories (no elevator), exterior corridors. **Amenities:** video games (fee), high-speed Internet. **Pool(s):** outdoor. **Activities:** whirlpool, exercise room. **Guest Services:** valet and coin laundry. **Free Special Amenities:** local telephone calls and high-speed Internet.

SAVE ⑪ CALL ⓈⓂ ⌲ BIZ 🛜 ✕ 🎦 🎱 🛗 📺 / SOME UNITS FEE 🐾

HAMPTON INN & SUITES (530)751-1714

◆◆◆ ◆◆◆ ◆◆◆
Hotel
$109-$179

AAA Benefit: Members save up to 10%!

Address: 1375 Sunsweet Blvd 95991 **Location:** Just s of jct SR 99 and 20, just w. **Facility:** 88 units. 3 stories, interior corridors. **Terms:** 1-7 night minimum stay, cancellation fee imposed. **Amenities:** video games (fee), high-speed Internet. **Pool(s):** outdoor. **Activities:** whirlpool, exercise room. **Guest Services:** valet and coin laundry. **Free Special Amenities:** expanded continental breakfast and high-speed Internet.

SAVE ⑪ CALL ⓈⓂ ⌲ BIZ 🛜 ✕ 🛗 📺 📺

THE HARKEY HOUSE (530)674-1942

◆◆◆ ◆◆◆ ◆◆◆ Historic Bed & Breakfast $120-$235 **Address:** 212 C St 95991 **Location:** At C and 2nd sts; downtown. Adjacent to Sutter County Offices. **Facility:** Once owned by Sheriff William Harkey, this 1874 home features attractively landscaped gardens and a large, inviting patio area. 4 units, some cottages. 2 stories, interior corridors. **Terms:** 7 day cancellation notice-fee imposed. **Pool(s):** outdoor. **Activities:** whirlpool.

⑪ ⌲ 🛜 🈲 📺 / SOME UNITS FEE 🐾 🛗 📺

WHERE TO EAT

THE CITY CAFE 530/671-1501

◆◆◆ ◆◆◆ ◆◆◆ American. Casual Dining. $9-$32 **AAA Inspector Notes:** Tucked in between shops, this restaurant serves tasty cuisine in a warm and inviting décor that also features lovely summer dining in the romantic courtyard. A lighter fare menu also is available. Parking is offered behind the building. **Bar:** full bar. **Address:** 667 Plumas St 95991 **Location:** Jct SR 99/20, 0.9 mi e on SR 20, just s; just n of jct Center St. **Parking:** on-site and street. L D CALL ⓈⓂ

COSTA VIDA FRESH MEXICAN GRILL 530/673-9283

◆◆◆ Mexican. Quick Serve. $6-$10 **AAA Inspector Notes:** This eatery serves traditional Mexican food such as burritos, enchiladas, nachos, quesadillas and tacos for those in a hurry. Gluten-free options are available. Save room for the tres leches dessert. **Address:** 1074 Harter Rd, Suite 101B 95993 **Location:** On SR 99, 1.2 mi w of jct SR 99 and 20; near Walmart. L D CALL ⓈⓂ

DANCING TOMATO CAFFE 530/790-0300

◆◆◆ ◆◆◆ Italian. Casual Dining. $6-$22 **AAA Inspector Notes:** Breakfast here includes a variety of omelets including a pizza omelet. Gourmet pizza made with fresh homemade dough, hot and cold deli sandwiches, traditional pasta and steak are served at this family friendly café. Be sure to save room for the chocolate lasagna. **Bar:** full bar. **Address:** 990 N Walton Ave 95993 **Location:** Just w of jct SR 99 and 20. B L D CALL ⓈⓂ

MARCELLO'S ITALIAN RESTAURANT 530/674-2171

◆◆◆ ◆◆◆ Italian. Casual Dining. $10-$24 **AAA Inspector Notes:** This family-friendly restaurant prepares classic Italian fare, including pizza, seafood, steak and chicken dishes. Family-style meals are available and a lunch buffet is offered. Most items are made from scratch. Service is polite and efficient. **Bar:** beer & wine. **Address:** 1235 Bridge St 95991 **Location:** 0.5 mi s of jct SR 99 and 20, just e. L D CALL ⓈⓂ

THE REFUGE RESTAURANT & LOUNGE 530/673-7620

◆◆◆ ◆◆◆ American. Casual Dining. $9-$25 **AAA Inspector Notes:** Steaks, pasta, salads, burgers, sandwiches and tasty Indian cuisine (including curries and entrées) are offered at this restaurant with large windows and a modern décor. On Sunday only dinner is served. **Bar:** full bar. **Address:** 1501 Butte House Rd 95991 **Location:** Jct SR 99/20, just w on SR 20, just n on Stabler Ln, then just e. L D

New **Fantasyland**

Artist Rendering

©Disney/Pixar

Cars Land

WITH ENCHANTING AAA BENEFITS!

LET AAA BE YOUR GUIDE...

With a *AAA Vacations*® package, you can create the Disney vacation that fits your family, your taste and your budget. And not only will your AAA Travel professional help put everything (like accommodations, tickets and flights) together, you'll also get to enjoy great Disney benefits on top of the exclusive AAA benefits and savings once you get there! Then all you need to do is relax and have fun.

 ### READY TO START MAKING MAGIC?
Then contact your **AAA Travel professional** today!

DISNEY PARKS

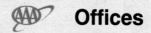 **Offices**

Cities with main offices are listed in **BOLD TYPE** and toll-free member service numbers in *ITALIC TYPE*.
All are closed Saturdays, Sundays and holidays unless otherwise indicated.
The addresses, phone numbers and hours for any AAA/CAA office are subject to change.
The type of service provided is designated below the name of the city where the office is located:

✛ Auto travel services, including books and maps, and on-demand TripTik® routings.
● Auto travel services, including selected books and maps, and on-demand TripTik® routings.
■ Books/maps only, no marked maps or on-demand TripTik® routings.
▲ Travel Agency Services, cruise, tour, air, car and rail reservations; domestic and international hotel reservations; passport photo services; international and domestic travel guides and maps; travel money products; and International Driving Permits. In addition, assistance with travel related insurance products including trip cancellation, travel accident, lost luggage, trip delay and assistance products.
❂ Insurance services provided. If only this icon appears, only insurance services are provided at that office.
◖ Car Care Plus Facility provides car care services.
▣ Electric vehicle charging station on premises.

AAA NATIONAL OFFICE: 1000 AAA DRIVE, HEATHROW, FLORIDA 32746-5063, (407) 444-7000

NORTHERN CALIFORNIA

ANGELS CAMP—AAA NORTHERN CALIFORNIA NEVADA & UTAH, 465 S MAIN ST HWY 49, 95222. WEEKDAYS (M-F) 8:30-5:30 (CLOSED FOR LUNCH MON-FRI 1-2. SAT BY APPOINTMENT ONLY). (209) 736-3560 ✛ ●

ANTIOCH—AAA NORTHERN CALIFORNIA NEVADA & UTAH, 1700 AUTO CENTER DR, 94509. WEEKDAYS (M-F) 8:30-5:30 (SAT BY APPOINTMENT ONLY). (925) 522-7920 ✛ ▲ ❂

AUBURN—AAA NORTHERN CALIFORNIA NEVADA & UTAH, 2495 BELL RD, 95603. WEEKDAYS (M-F) 8:30-5:30 (SAT BY APPOINTMENT ONLY). (530) 886-2500 ✛ ▲ ❂

BERKELEY—AAA NORTHERN CALIFORNIA NEVADA & UTAH, 1775 UNIVERSITY AVE, 94703. WEEKDAYS (M-F) 8:30-6:00, SAT 10:00-4:00. (510) 898-7600 ✛ ❂

CAPITOLA—AAA NORTHERN CALIFORNIA NEVADA & UTAH, 4400 CAPITOLA RD STE 100, 95010. WEEKDAYS (M-F) 9:00-5:30 (SAT BY APPOINTMENT ONLY). (831) 824-9128 ✛ ▲ ❂

CHICO—AAA NORTHERN CALIFORNIA NEVADA & UTAH, 2221 FOREST AVE, 95928. WEEKDAYS (M-F) 8:30-5:30 (SALES: SAT BY APPOINTMENT ONLY). (530) 332-2600 ✛ ▲ ❂

CITRUS HEIGHTS—AAA NORTHERN CALIFORNIA NEVADA & UTAH, 6109 SUNRISE BLVD, 95610. WEEKDAYS (M-F) 8:30-5:30 (SAT BY APPOINTMENT ONLY). (916) 560-0501 ✛ ▲ ❂

CLOVIS—AAA NORTHERN CALIFORNIA NEVADA & UTAH, 1595 SHAW AVE, 93611. WEEKDAYS (M-F) 8:30-5:30 (SAT BY APPOINTMENT ONLY). (559) 323-3000 ✛ ▲ ❂

CONCORD—AAA NORTHERN CALIFORNIA NEVADA & UTAH, 2055 MERIDIAN PARK BLVD, 94520. WEEKDAYS (M-F) 8:30-5:30 (SAT BY APPOINTMENT ONLY). (925) 808-6201 ✛ ▲ ❂

DALY CITY—AAA NORTHERN CALIFORNIA NEVADA & UTAH, 455 HICKEY BLVD 3RD FL, 94015. WEEKDAYS (M-F) 8:30-5:30 (SAT BY APPOINTMENT ONLY). (650) 301-1400 ✛ ▲ ❂

DUBLIN—AAA NORTHERN CALIFORNIA NEVADA & UTAH, 4460 TASSAJARA RD STE B, 94568. WEEKDAYS (M-F) 9:00-6:00, SAT 10:00-2:00. (925) 479-7840 ✛ ▲ ❂

EL CERRITO—AAA NORTHERN CALIFORNIA NEVADA & UTAH, 1000 EL CERRITO PLZ, 94530. WEEKDAYS (M-F) 9:00-7:00, SAT 9:00-6:00. (510) 898-2076 ■ ❂

ELK GROVE—AAA NORTHERN CALIFORNIA NEVADA & UTAH, 8225 LAGUNA BLVD STE 120, 95758. WEEKDAYS (M-F) 8:30-5:30 (SAT BY APPOINTMENT ONLY). (916) 478-7500 ✛ ▲ ❂

EUREKA—AAA NORTHERN CALIFORNIA NEVADA & UTAH, 707 L ST, 95501. WEEKDAYS (M-F) 8:30-5:30 (SAT BY APPOINTMENT ONLY). (707) 444-1000 ✛ ❂

FOLSOM—AAA NORTHERN CALIFORNIA NEVADA & UTAH, 2405 IRON POINT RD #130, 95630. WEEKDAYS (M-F) 8:30-5:30. (916) 351-2600 ✛ ▲ ❂

FRESNO—AAA NORTHERN CALIFORNIA NEVADA & UTAH, 5040 N FORKNER AVE, 93711. WEEKDAYS (M-F) 8:30-5:30 (SAT BY APPOINTMENT ONLY). (559) 440-7200 ✛ ▲ ❂

GILROY—AAA NORTHERN CALIFORNIA NEVADA & UTAH, 1395 FIRST ST, 95020. WEEKDAYS (M-F) 9:00-5:00 (SAT BY APPOINTMENT ONLY). (408) 847-9220 ✛ ❂

GRASS VALLEY—AAA NORTHERN CALIFORNIA NEVADA & UTAH, 113 DORSEY DR, 95945. WEEKDAYS (M-F) 8:30-5:30 (SAT BY APPOINTMENT ONLY). (530) 271-2600 ✛ ❂

HANFORD—AAA NORTHERN CALIFORNIA NEVADA & UTAH, 780 N IRWIN ST, 93230. WEEKDAYS (M-F) 8:30-5:30 (SAT BY APPOINTMENT ONLY). (559) 587-4600 ✛ ❂

HAYWARD—AAA NORTHERN CALIFORNIA NEVADA & UTAH, 1580 CHABOT CT, 94545. WEEKDAYS (M-F) 9:00-6:00 (SAT BY APPOINTMENT ONLY). (510) 670-4380 ✛ ▲ ❂

HOLLISTER—AAA NORTHERN CALIFORNIA NEVADA & UTAH, 351 TRES PINOS RD STE D, 95023. WEEKDAYS (M-F) 9:00-5:00 (SAT BY APPOINTMENT ONLY). (831) 635-3900 ✛ ❂

JACKSON—AAA NORTHERN CALIFORNIA NEVADA & UTAH, 11992 ST HWY 88 STE 2048, 95642. WEEKDAYS (M-F) 8:30-5:30 (SAT BY APPOINTMENT ONLY). (209) 223-6900 ✛ ❂

LAKEPORT—AAA NORTHERN CALIFORNIA NEVADA & UTAH, 1464 PARALLEL DR, 95453. WEEKDAYS (M-F) 8:30-5:30 (SAT BY APPOINTMENT ONLY). (707) 262-5900 ✛ ❂

LODI—AAA NORTHERN CALIFORNIA NEVADA & UTAH, 2715 W KETTLEMAN LN #201, 95242. WEEKDAYS (M-F) 8:30-5:30 (SAT BY APPOINTMENT ONLY). (209) 366-6900 ✛ ❂

LOS BANOS—AAA NORTHERN CALIFORNIA NEVADA & UTAH, 919 W PACHECO BLVD, 93635. WEEKDAYS (M-F) 9:00-5:00 (CLOSED FOR LUNCH MON-FRI 1-2. SAT BY APPOINTMENT ONLY). (209) 827-5000 ✛ ❂

LOS GATOS—AAA NORTHERN CALIFORNIA NEVADA & UTAH, 15450 LOS GATOS BLVD #300, 95032. WEEKDAYS (M-F) 8:30-5:30 (SAT BY APPOINTMENT ONLY). (408) 399-8400 ✛ ❂

MADERA—AAA NORTHERN CALIFORNIA NEVADA & UTAH, 221 N G ST, 93637. WEEKDAYS (M-F) 8:30-5:30 (SAT BY APPOINTMENT ONLY). (559) 662-4700 ✛ ❂

MANTECA—AAA NORTHERN CALIFORNIA NEVADA & UTAH, 145 TREVINO AVE, 95337. WEEKDAYS (M-F) 8:30-5:30 (SAT BY APPOINTMENT ONLY). (209) 824-6100 ✛ ❂

MARYSVILLE—AAA NORTHERN CALIFORNIA NEVADA & UTAH, 1205 D ST, 95901. WEEKDAYS (M-F) 8:30-5:30 (SAT BY APPOINTMENT ONLY). (530) 634-7800 ✛ ❂

MERCED—AAA NORTHERN CALIFORNIA NEVADA & UTAH, 3065 M ST, 95348. WEEKDAYS (M-F) 8:30-5:30 (SAT BY APPOINTMENT ONLY). (209) 726-7440 ✚ ▲ ✺

MILL VALLEY—AAA NORTHERN CALIFORNIA NEVADA & UTAH, 60 BELEVEDERE DR, 94941. WEEKDAYS (M-F) 8:30-5:30 (SAT BY APPOINTMENT ONLY). (415) 380-6000 ✚ ▲ ✺

MODESTO—AAA NORTHERN CALIFORNIA NEVADA & UTAH, 3525 COFFEE RD, 95355. WEEKDAYS (M-F) 8:30-5:30 (SAT BY APPOINTMENT ONLY). (209) 530-2600 ✚ ▲ ✺

MONTEREY—AAA NORTHERN CALIFORNIA NEVADA & UTAH, 53 SOLEDAD DR, 93940. WEEKDAYS (M-F) 9:00-5:00 (SAT BY APPOINTMENT ONLY). (831) 645-1900 ✚ ▲ ✺

MOUNTAIN VIEW—AAA NORTHERN CALIFORNIA NEVADA & UTAH, 900 MIRAMONTE AVE, 94040. WEEKDAYS (M-F) 8:30-5:30 (SAT BY APPOINTMENT ONLY). (650) 623-3200 ✚ ▲ ✺

NAPA—AAA NORTHERN CALIFORNIA NEVADA & UTAH, 800 TRANCAS ST STE C, 94558. WEEKDAYS (M-F) 8:30-5:30 (SAT BY APPOINTMENT ONLY). (707) 252-5600 ✚ ▲ ✺

NEWARK—AAA NORTHERN CALIFORNIA NEVADA & UTAH, 39600 BALENTINE DR, 94560. WEEKDAYS (M-F) 8:30-5:30 (SAT BY APPOINTMENT ONLY). (510) 360-3300 ✚ ▲ ✺

OAKLAND—AAA NORTHERN CALIFORNIA NEVADA & UTAH, 1982 PLEASANT VALLEY AV A, 94611. WEEKDAYS (M-F) 8:00-6:00 (SAT BY APPOINTMENT ONLY). (510) 350-2042 ✚ ▲ ✺

OAKLAND—AAA NORTHERN CALIFORNIA NEVADA & UTAH, 2220 MOUNTAIN BLVD #120, 94611. WEEKDAYS (M-F) 9:00-6:00 (SAT BY APPOINTMENT ONLY). (510) 531-6298 ✚ ▲ ✺

OROVILLE—AAA NORTHERN CALIFORNIA NEVADA & UTAH, 1430 FEATHER RIVER BLVD, 95965. WEEKDAYS (M-F) 8:30-5:30 (SAT BY APPOINTMENT ONLY). (530) 538-8900 ✚ ✺

PALO ALTO—AAA NORTHERN CALIFORNIA NEVADA & UTAH, 430 FOREST AVE, 94301. WEEKDAYS (M-F) 8:30-5:30 (SAT BY APPOINTMENT ONLY). (650) 798-3200 ✚ ▲ ✺

PETALUMA—AAA NORTHERN CALIFORNIA NEVADA & UTAH, 111 LYNCH CREEK WAY, 94954. WEEKDAYS (M-F) 8:30-5:30 (SAT BY APPOINTMENT ONLY). (707) 781-6700 ✚ ▲ ✺

PLACERVILLE—AAA NORTHERN CALIFORNIA NEVADA & UTAH, 3979 MISSOURI FLAT RD 120, 95667. WEEKDAYS (M-F) 8:30-5:30 (SAT BY APPOINTMENT ONLY). (530) 295-6600 ✚ ✺

RED BLUFF—AAA NORTHERN CALIFORNIA NEVADA & UTAH, 151 SALE LN, 96080. WEEKDAYS (M-F) 8:30-5:00 (SAT BY APPOINTMENT ONLY). (530) 529-9000 ✚ ✺

REDDING—AAA NORTHERN CALIFORNIA NEVADA & UTAH, 943 MISSION DE ORO DR, 96003. WEEKDAYS (M-F) 8:30-5:30 (SAT BY APPOINTMENT ONLY). (530) 722-1600 ✚ ▲ ✺

REDWOOD CITY—AAA NORTHERN CALIFORNIA NEVADA & UTAH, 510 VETERANS BLVD STE A, 94063. WEEKDAYS (M-F) 8:30-5:30 (SAT BY APPOINTMENT ONLY). (650) 216-3100 ✚ ▲ ✺

RICHMOND—AAA NORTHERN CALIFORNIA NEVADA & UTAH, 3060 HILLTOP MALL RD, 94806. WEEKDAYS (M-F) 8:30-5:30 (SAT BY APPOINTMENT ONLY). (510) 262-4900 ✚ ▲ ✺

ROSEVILLE—AAA NORTHERN CALIFORNIA NEVADA & UTAH, 1850 DOUGLAS BLVD STE 406, 95661. WEEKDAYS (M-F) 8:30-5:30 (SAT BY APPOINTMENT ONLY). (916) 782-2898 ✚ ▲ ✺

ROSEVILLE—AAA NORTHERN CALIFORNIA NEVADA & UTAH, 908 PLEASANT GROVE BLVD, 95678. WEEKDAYS (M-F) 8:30-5:30 (SAT BY APPOINTMENT ONLY). (916) 724-0200

SACRAMENTO—AAA NORTHERN CALIFORNIA NEVADA & UTAH, 1056 FLORIN RD, 95831. WEEKDAYS (M-F) 8:30-5:30 (SAT BY APPOINTMENT ONLY). (916) 288-2000 ✚ ▲ ✺

SACRAMENTO—AAA NORTHERN CALIFORNIA NEVADA & UTAH, 15 BICENTENNIAL CIR, 95826. WEEKDAYS (M-F) 8:30-5:30 (SAT BY APPOINTMENT ONLY). (916) 379-1300 ✚ ✺

SACRAMENTO—AAA NORTHERN CALIFORNIA NEVADA & UTAH, 4740 NATOMAS BLVD STE 140, 95835. WEEKDAYS (M-F) 8:30-5:30 (SAT BY APPOINTMENT ONLY). (916) 574-8700 ✚ ✺

SALINAS—AAA NORTHERN CALIFORNIA NEVADA & UTAH, 1019 POST DR, 93907. WEEKDAYS (M-F) 9:00-5:30 (SAT BY APPOINTMENT ONLY). (831) 771-4000 ✚ ✺

SAN BRUNO—AAA NORTHERN CALIFORNIA NEVADA & UTAH, 1322 EL CAMINO REAL, 94066. WEEKDAYS (M-F) 9:00-7:00, SAT 9:00-6:00. (650) 301-8500 ■ ✺

SAN FRANCISCO—AAA NORTHERN CALIFORNIA NEVADA & UTAH, 1585 SLOAT BLVD, 94132. WEEKDAYS (M-F) 8:30-5:30, SAT 10:00-2:00. (415) 682-3400 ✚ ▲ ✺

SAN FRANCISCO—AAA NORTHERN CALIFORNIA NEVADA & UTAH, 160 SUTTER ST, 94104. WEEKDAYS (M-F) 8:30-5:30 (SAT BY APPOINTMENT ONLY). (415) 773-1900 ✚ ✺

SAN FRANCISCO—AAA NORTHERN CALIFORNIA NEVADA & UTAH, 2300 16TH ST STE 280, 94103. WEEKDAYS (M-F) 8:30-5:30, SAT 10:00-2:00. (415) 553-7200 ✚ ▲ ✺

SAN FRANCISCO—AAA NORTHERN CALIFORNIA NEVADA & UTAH, 599 CLEMENT ST, 94118. WEEKDAYS (M-F) 8:30-5:30 (SAT BY APPOINTMENT ONLY). (415) 750-7800 ✚ ▲ ✺

SAN JOSE—AAA NORTHERN CALIFORNIA NEVADA & UTAH, 2980 E CAPITOL EXPY, 95148. WEEKDAYS (M-F) 9:00-7:00, SAT 9:00-6:00. (408) 574-3420 ■ ✺

SAN JOSE—AAA NORTHERN CALIFORNIA NEVADA & UTAH, 5120 STEVENS CREEK BLVD, 95129. WEEKDAYS (M-F) 8:30-5:30 (SAT BY APPOINTMENT ONLY). (408) 551-4900 ✚ ▲ ✺

SAN JOSE—AAA NORTHERN CALIFORNIA NEVADA & UTAH, 5291 PROSPECT RD, 95129. WEEKDAYS (M-F) 8:30-5:30 (SAT BY APPOINTMENT ONLY). (408) 725-4300 ✚ ▲ ✺

SAN JOSE—AAA NORTHERN CALIFORNIA NEVADA & UTAH, 5340 THORNWOOD DR, 95123. WEEKDAYS (M-F) 8:30-5:30 (SAT BY APPOINTMENT ONLY). (408) 574-2300 ✚ ▲ ✺

SAN JOSE—AAA NORTHERN CALIFORNIA NEVADA & UTAH, 844 BLOSSOM HILL RD, 95123. WEEKDAYS (M-F) 9:00-7:00, SAT 9:00-6:00. (408) 574-3400 ■ ✺

SAN LEANDRO—AAA NORTHERN CALIFORNIA NEVADA & UTAH, 1300 FAIRMONT DR, 94578. WEEKDAYS (M-F) 9:00-7:00, SAT 9:00-6:00. (510) 670-2200 ■ ✺

SAN MATEO—AAA NORTHERN CALIFORNIA NEVADA & UTAH, 1650 S DELAWARE ST, 94402. WEEKDAYS (M-F) 8:30-5:30 (SAT BY APPOINTMENT ONLY). (650) 572-5600 ✚ ▲ ✺

SAN RAFAEL—AAA NORTHERN CALIFORNIA NEVADA & UTAH, 99 SMITH RANCH RD, 94903. WEEKDAYS (M-F) 8:30-5:30 (SAT BY APPOINTMENT ONLY). (415) 488-2900 ✚ ▲ ✺

SAN RAMON—AAA NORTHERN CALIFORNIA NEVADA & UTAH, 2435 SAN RAMON VLY BLVD 5, 94583. WEEKDAYS (M-F) 9:00-6:00 (SAT BY APPOINTMENT ONLY). (925) 314-2600 ✚ ▲ ✺

SANTA CLARA—AAA NORTHERN CALIFORNIA NEVADA & UTAH, 2615 KEYSTONE AVE, 95051. WEEKDAYS (M-F) 7:30-5:30, SAT 8:00-5:00. (408) 247-5405 ◖

SANTA ROSA—AAA NORTHERN CALIFORNIA NEVADA & UTAH, 1500 FARMERS LN, 95405. WEEKDAYS (M-F) 8:30-5:30 (SAT BY APPOINTMENT ONLY). (707) 566-4000 ✚ ▲ ✺

SONOMA—AAA NORTHERN CALIFORNIA NEVADA & UTAH, 650 2ND ST W, 95476. WEEKDAYS (M-F) 8:30-5:30 (SAT BY APPOINTMENT ONLY). (707) 528-5900 ✚ ▲ ✺

SONORA—AAA NORTHERN CALIFORNIA NEVADA & UTAH, 1071 SANGUINETTI RD, 95370. WEEKDAYS (M-F) 8:30-5:30 (SAT BY APPOINTMENT ONLY). (209) 532-3134 ✚ ▲ ✺

602

STOCKTON—AAA NORTHERN CALIFORNIA NEVADA & UTAH, 10916 TRINITY PKWY STE A, 95219. WEEKDAYS (M-F) 8:30-5:30 (SAT BY APPOINTMENT ONLY). (209) 952-4100

SUSANVILLE—AAA NORTHERN CALIFORNIA NEVADA & UTAH, 2920 D MAIN ST, 96130. WEEKDAYS (M-F) 8:30-5:30 (SAT BY APPOINTMENT ONLY). (530) 252-5000

TRACY—AAA NORTHERN CALIFORNIA NEVADA & UTAH, 2102 W GRANT LINE RD, 95377. WEEKDAYS (M-F) 8:30-5:30 (SAT BY APPOINTMENT ONLY). (209) 832-9401

TRUCKEE—AAA NORTHERN CALIFORNIA NEVADA & UTAH, 11200 DONNER PASS RD #E3, 96161. WEEKDAYS (M-F) 9:00-5:00 (SAT BY APPOINTMENT ONLY). (530) 550-2060

TURLOCK—AAA NORTHERN CALIFORNIA NEVADA & UTAH, 3180 HOTEL DR, 95380. WEEKDAYS (M-F) 8:30-5:30 (SAT BY APPOINTMENT ONLY). (209) 656-3060

UKIAH—AAA NORTHERN CALIFORNIA NEVADA & UTAH, 601 KINGS CT, 95482. WEEKDAYS (M-F) 8:30-5:30 (SAT BY APPOINTMENT ONLY). (707) 463-3000

UNION CITY—AAA NORTHERN CALIFORNIA NEVADA & UTAH, 32300 DYER ST, 94587. WEEKDAYS (M-F) 9:00-7:00, SAT 9:00-6:00. (510) 360-3500

VACAVILLE—AAA NORTHERN CALIFORNIA NEVADA & UTAH, 555 MASON ST STE 150, 95688. WEEKDAYS (M-F) 8:30-5:30 (SAT BY APPOINTMENT ONLY). (707) 451-7150

VALLEJO—AAA NORTHERN CALIFORNIA NEVADA & UTAH, 1183 ADMIRAL CALLAGHAN LN, 94591. WEEKDAYS (M-F) 8:30-5:30 (SAT BY APPOINTMENT ONLY). (707) 551-3500

WALNUT CREEK—AAA NORTHERN CALIFORNIA NEVADA & UTAH, 1276 S CALIFORNIA BLVD, 94596. WEEKDAYS (M-F) 9:00-6:00 (SAT BY APPOINTMENT ONLY). (925) 287-7600

WATSONVILLE—AAA NORTHERN CALIFORNIA NEVADA & UTAH, 1195 S GREEN VALLEY RD, 95076. WEEKDAYS (M-F) 9:00-5:30 (SAT BY APPOINTMENT ONLY). (831) 768-4540

WILLOWS—AAA NORTHERN CALIFORNIA NEVADA & UTAH, 505 N HUMBOLDT AVE STE D, 95988. WEEKDAYS (M-F) 8:30-5:30 (CLOSED FOR LUNCH MON-FRI 1-2. SAT BY APPOINTMENT ONLY). (530) 566-9900

WOODLAND—AAA NORTHERN CALIFORNIA NEVADA & UTAH, 95 W LINCOLN AVE, 95695. WEEKDAYS (M-F) 8:30-5:30 (SAT BY APPOINTMENT ONLY). (530) 406-3500

YREKA—AAA NORTHERN CALIFORNIA NEVADA & UTAH, 1876 FORT JONES RD, 96097. WEEKDAYS (M-F) 9:00-5:30 (SAT BY APPOINTMENT ONLY). (530) 841-6340

Metric Equivalents Chart

TEMPERATURE

To convert Fahrenheit to Celsius, subtract 32 from the Fahrenheit temperature, multiply by 5 and divide by 9.
To convert Celsius to Fahrenheit, multiply by 9, divide by 5 and add 32.

ACRES

1 acre = 0.4 hectare (ha)   1 hectare = 2.47 acres

MILES AND KILOMETERS

Note: A kilometer is approximately 5/8 or 0.6 of a mile.
To convert kilometers to miles multiply by 0.6.

Miles/Kilometers		Kilometers/Miles	
15	24.1	30	18.6
20	32.2	35	21.7
25	40.2	40	24.8
30	48.3	45	27.9
35	56.3	50	31.0
40	64.4	55	34.1
45	72.4	60	37.2
50	80.5	65	40.3
55	88.5	70	43.4
60	96.6	75	46.6
65	104.6	80	49.7
70	112.7	85	52.8
75	120.7	90	55.9
80	128.7	95	59.0
85	136.8	100	62.1
90	144.8	105	65.2
95	152.9	110	68.3
100	160.9	115	71.4

Celsius°		Fahrenheit°
100	BOILING	212
37		100
35		95
32		90
29		85
27		80
24		75
21		70
18		65
16		60
13		55
10		50
7		45
4		40
2		35
0	FREEZING	32
-4		25
-7		20
-9		15
-12		10
-15		5
-18		0
-21		-5
-24		-10
-27		-15

LINEAR MEASURE

Customary	Metric
1 inch = 2.54 centimeters	1 centimeter = 0.4 inches
1 foot = 30 centimeters	1 meter = 3.3 feet
1 yard = 0.91 meters	1 meter = 1.09 yards
1 mile = 1.6 kilometers	1 kilometer = .62 miles

WEIGHT

If You Know:	Multiply By:	To Find:
Ounces	28	Grams
Pounds	0.45	Kilograms
Grams	0.035	Ounces
Kilograms	2.2	Pounds

LIQUID MEASURE

Customary	Metric
1 fluid ounce = 30 milliliters	1 milliliter = .03 fluid ounces
1 cup = .24 liters	1 liter = 2.1 pints
1 pint = .47 liters	1 liter = 1.06 quarts
1 quart = .95 liters	1 liter = .26 gallons
1 gallon = 3.8 liters	

PRESSURE

Air pressure in automobile tires is expressed
in kilopascals. Multiply pound-force per
square inch (psi) by 6.89 to find kilopascals
(kPa).

24 psi = 165 kPa   28 psi = 193 kPa
26 psi = 179 kPa   30 psi = 207 kPa

GALLONS AND LITERS

Gallons/Liters				Liters/Gallons			
5	19.0	12	45.6	10	2.6	40	10.4
6	22.8	14	53.2	15	3.9	50	13.0
7	26.6	16	60.8	20	5.2	60	15.6
8	30.4	18	68.4	25	6.5	70	18.2
9	34.2	20	76.0	30	7.8	80	20.8
10	38.0	25	95.0	35	9.1	90	23.4

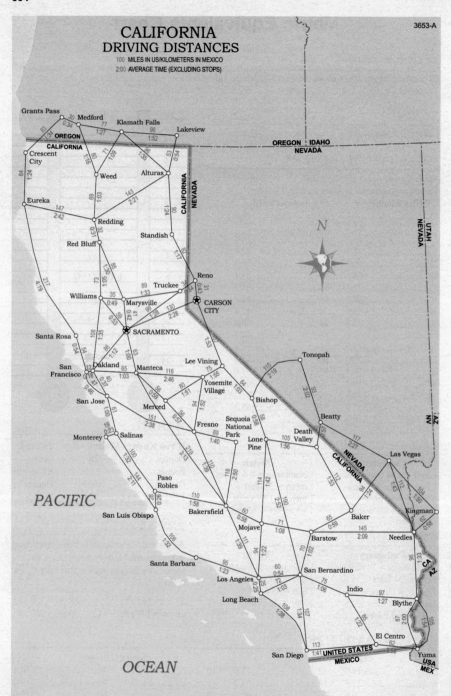

CALIFORNIA
DRIVING DISTANCES
100 MILES IN US/KILOMETERS IN MEXICO
2:00 AVERAGE TIME (EXCLUDING STOPS)

3653-A

© AAA

© 2012 NAVTEQ

Points of Interest Index

 Attractions appear at the top of each category
and offer a Great Experience for Members®.

Index Legend

NB.	national battlefield
NBP.	national battlefield park
NC.	national cemetery
NF.	national forest
NHM.	national historic(al) monument
NHP.	national historic(al) park
NHS.	national historic(al) site
NL.	national lakeshore
NME.	national memorial
NMO.	national monument
NMP.	national military park
NP.	national park
NRA.	national recreation area
NR.	national river
NS.	national seashore
NWR.	national wildlife refuge
PHP.	provincial historic(al) park
PHS.	provincial historic(al) site
PP.	provincial park
SF.	state forest
SHM.	state historic(al) monument
SHP.	state historic(al) park
SHS.	state historic(al) site
SME.	state memorial
SP.	state park
SRA.	state recreation area

CHILDREN'S ACTIVITIES

EVENTS & FESTIVALS

HISTORIC SITES & EXHIBITS

612   OUTDOORS & SCIENCE

SHOPPING

SPORTS & RECREATION

TOURS & SIGHTSEEING

Photo Credits

Page numbers are in bold type. Picture credit abbreviations are as follows:
- (i) numeric sequence from top to bottom, left to right ▪ (AAA) AAA Travel library.

▪ **(Cover)** "MaestraPeace" (1994-2000) by Juana Alicia Miranda Bergman, Edythe Boone, Susan Kelke Cervantes, Meera Desai, Yvonne Littleton, and Irene Pereze All Rights Reserved, Women's Building, San Francisco / Printed with permission from AAA travel editor Greg Weekes

▪ **2** (i) © Nikhilesh Haval / age fotostock

▪ **2** (ii) Printed with permission from AAA associate Thuyvi Gates

▪ **2** (iii) Printed with permission from AAA travel editor Greg Weekes

▪ **2** (iv) © Sam Bloomberg-Rissman / Alamy

▪ **7** © Monashee Frantz / age fotostock

▪ **13** © Adivin / iStockphoto

▪ **18** (i) © FOOD AND DRINK PHOTOS / age fotostock

▪ **18** (ii) © William Helsel / age fotostock

▪ **19** © Walter Bibikow / eStock Photo

▪ **20** (i) © North Wind Picture Archives / Alamy

▪ **20** (ii) © Lauren Zeid / eStock Photo

▪ **23** (i) © Rachael Nusbaum

▪ **23** (ii) © Carlos S. Pereyra / age fotostock

▪ **23** (iii) © AAA. Photo by AAA travel editor Greg Weekes for AAA

▪ **23** (iv) © John Warburton-Lee Photography / Alamy

▪ **23** (v) © John Meyer / Alamy

▪ **24** (i) © Allstar Picture Library / Alamy

▪ **24** (ii) © Kanwarjit Singh Boparai / Alamy

▪ **24** (iii) © Eric Nathan / Alamy

▪ **24** (iv) © Ian Shaw / Alamy

▪ **341** © Nikhilesh Haval / age fotostock

▪ **344** © Claudia Uripos / eStock Photo

▪ **345** © Rachael Nusbaum

▪ **346** © Kord.com / age fotostock

▪ **347** © Joseph Sohm / age fotostock

▪ **348** © Rachael Nusbaum

▪ **349** © Rachael Nusbaum

▪ **350** © Gavin Hellier / Alamy

▪ **351** Printed with permission from AAA travel editor Greg Weekes

▪ **352** © Sam Bloomberg-Rissman / Alamy

▪ **353** Printed with permission from AAA travel editor Greg Weekes

▪ **354** © Rachael Nusbaum

▪ **355** © Rachael Nusbaum

▪ **356** © Rachael Nusbaum

▪ **357** © Rachael Nusbaum

▪ **358** © Ty Milford / Aurora O / age fotostock

▪ **359** © Rachael Nusbaum

▪ **360** Printed with permission from AAA travel editor Greg Weekes

▪ **361** Printed with permission from AAA travel editor Greg Weekes

▪ **370** © Blaine Harrington / age fotostock

▪ **371** Printed with permission from AAA associate Thuyvi Gates

▪ **372** © Travel Pictures / Alamy

▪ **374** Printed with permission from AAA travel editor Greg Weekes

▪ **376** Printed with permission from AAA travel editor Greg Weekes

▪ **378** © MARKA / Alamy

▪ **380** © Rachael Nusbaum

▪ **382** © Bjanka Kadic / Alamy

▪ **384** Printed with permission from AAA travel editor Greg Weekes

▪ **386** © Huntstock / age fotostock

▪ **388** © Walter Bibikow / age fotostock